Library of
VOID
Davidson College

TABULAE

ORDINIS THEUTONICI

EX TABULARII REGII BEROLINENSIS CODICE POTISSIMUM

EDIDIT

ERNESTUS STREHLKE

Praefationem huius editionis addidit

HANS E. MAYER

BEROLINI
APUD WEIDMANNOS
MDCCCLXIX

Prelum Academicum Universitatis Torontonensis
MCMLXXV

940.1
T352t

Published in Canada
and the United States of America by
University of Toronto Press
Toronto and Buffalo

ISBN 0-8020-1966-8

© 1975 Massada Press Ltd., Jerusalem
PRINTED IN ISRAEL
by Peli Printing Works Ltd.

81-1484

INDEX

PREFACE

The photographic reprint of Strehlke's *Tabulae Ordinis Theutonici* will be warmly welcomed by mediaevalists in general and historians of the Crusader establishments in the East in particular. This collection of documents dealing with the Teutonic Knights belongs to the basic sources of Mediaeval History. Published more than a hundred years ago, its scarcity is such that it cannot be found even in some of the most important university libraries.

The reissue of the *Tabulae* was a long standing *desideratum*, but the new publication is far more than an excellent photographic reproduction. The detailed introduction, written by Hans E. Mayer, makes the collection not only more useful but furnishes a scholarly basis for further diplomatic and historical study. His emphatic biography of Ernst Strehlke is in itself an illuminating chapter in nineteenth-century German historiography, when the study of the antiquities of the Teutonic Order, or the quest for the remains of Emperor Frederick I Barbarossa, became an interesting issue in the national Prussian propaganda for hegemony in an Imperial united Germany.

The major importance of the introduction is that it describes for the first time the manuscript at the disposal of Strehlke and the way in which it was used. The Tables of Concordance are invaluable and show clearly the lights and the *lacunae* of Strehlke's monumental work, and thus lay a solid basis for future research.

Only a historian of the rank of Hans E. Mayer, as much at home in the histories of Germany and the Crusades, in the *minutiae* of mediaeval diplomatic usage and the history of Crusader and German archives in the Middle Ages, could have written the last part of the introduction, the hypothetical but extremely plausible reconstruction of the fate of the archives of the Teutonic Knights in the Holy Land. This is not only an important chapter in the history of the Crusader archives, but in itself an insightful contribution to the history of the Teutonic Order.

JOSHUA PRAWER

Jerusalem, 1974

INTRODUCTION

by

HANS EBERHARD MAYER

A. Life and Works of Ernst Strehlke

It is now a little over a hundred years since the *Tabulae Ordinis Theutonici*, edited by Ernst Strehlke, were published posthumously by the well-known publishers Weidmann of Berlin. The edition, one of the most important editions of source material on the history of the Order of the Teutonic Knights, remains the basic tool for those wishing to deal with the early history of the Teutonic Knights.

The Order began as a field hospital which was presumably founded by citizens of Lübeck and Bremen during the 1190 siege of Acre. It became a permanent hospital in that city after it fell to the Third Crusade in 1191, and was transformed gradually into the military-religious Order later recognized by the Church. Thus, an original *bourgeois* foundation became feudalized and monopolized by the knightly class; moreover, its membership was restricted to Germans, although it has been shown that this limitation was not always strictly adhered to in the Order's possessions outside the frontiers of the Holy Roman Empire and Prussia[1]. The documents, presented by Strehlke, permit us to follow these early stages in the development of the Order, as well as to go into the controversial problem whether the field hospital in the army camp near Acre was in any way, legally or *de facto*, linked with the old German hospital in Jerusalem[2]. His *Tabulae* also provide invaluable material on the

1. Kurt Forstreuter, 'Der Deutsche Orden am Mittelmeer', *Quellen und Studien zur Geschichte des Deutschen Ordens*, 2, (1967), pp. 214 *sqq*.
2. This problem was investigated mainly by Marian Tumler, *Der Deutsche Orden im Werden, Wachsen und Wirken bis 1400* (1954), pp. 583 *sqq*; Walther Hubatsch, 'Montfort und die Bildung des Deutschordensstaates im Heiligen Lande', *Nachrichten der Akademie der Wissenschaften in Göttingen*, I, *Philologisch-Historische Klasse* (1966), pp. 162 *sqq*; K. Forstreuter, *op. cit.* pp. 12 *sqq*; 29 *sqq*; J. Prawer, *Latin Kingdom of Jerusalem*, 1972, p. 269 *sqq*; and lately by Marie-Luise Favreau, *Studien zur Frühgeschichte des Deutschen Ordens*, Ph. D. thesis submitted to the University of Kiel. The latter is the most detailed investigation of the problem. It will be published in the *Kieler Historische Studien* in 1974.

Order's possessions and its development in the whole Mediterranean area, Palestine, Armenia, Cyprus, Frankish Greece, Apulia and the rest of Italy, and southern France, notwithstanding the fact that the sources now available are even wider in scope and quantity[3]. It need also be stressed with emphasis that Strehlke's *Tabulae* are still the largest and best collection of documents pertaining to the history of the Teutonic Knights in Palestine and, indeed, one of the basic collections of charters for the history of the Crusader states. In this field in particular, historical research will never be able to do without Strehlke's edition.

His collection on the short-lived attempt of the Order to create a more or less sovereign territory in the *Burzenland* in Hungary (a prelude to its gigantic Prussian state), and on the Order's possessions in Germany, Bohemia and, of course, in Prussia and Livonia, has been superseded by more detailed regional

3. On the history of the Teutonic Knights in the Mediterranean, see Forstreuter, *op. cit., passim.* To Strehlke's *Tabulae* the following publications should be added: (a) General: *Die Berichte der Generalprokuratoren des Deutschen Ordens an der Kurie*, Volumes 1–3 in 4 vols. (*Veröffentlichungen der Niedersächsischen Archivverwaltung*, Heft 12.13.21.29, 1960–1971) to be continued. *Regesta historico-diplomatica Ordinis S. Mariae Theutonicorum*, bearb. v. Erich Joachim, herausgegeben von Walther Hubatsch, Pars I. vol 1.2. Pars II and *Indices* (1948–1965). Pettenegg's abstracts of the Order's Central Archives in Vienna see below n. 7. Riccardo Predelli, 'Le reliquie dell'archivio dell'Ordine Teutonico in Venezia', *Atti del Reale Istituto Veneto di Science, Lettere ed Arti*, 64 (1905/06), pp. 1379–1463 (general, but also important for the Holy Land). (b) Cyprus: Walther Hubatsch, 'Der Deutsche Orden und die Reichslehnschaft über Cypern', *Nachrichten der Akademie der Wissenschaften in Göttingen. Philologisch-historische Klasse*, Jahrgang 1955, pp. 245–306. (c) Frankish Greece: Karl Hopf, 'Der Deutsche Orden in Griechenland', *Veneto-Byzantinische Analekten, Sitzungsberichte der Kaiserlichen Academie der Wissenschaften zu Wien. Phil.-hist. Klasse*, 32 (1859), pp. 367–378. F. Rühl, 'Der Deutsche Orden in Griechenland', *Nord und Süd* 89 (1899), p. 327 ff. (d) Spain: Duque de Alba, 'Documentos sobre propriedades de la Orden de los Caballeros Teutonicos en España', *Boletin de la Real Academia de la Historia*, 122 (1948), pp. 7–11. (e) Southern France: D'Arbois de Jubainville, 'L'ordre teutonique en France', *Bibliothèque de l'École des Chartes*, 32 (1871), pp. 63–83. (f) Sicily: Antonino Mongitore, *Monumenta historica domus Mansionis S. Trinitatis militaris ordinis Teutonici et magni preceptoris urbis Panormi* (1721); Giorgio Battaglia, 'Tabulario della Chiesa della Magione', *I diplomi inediti relativi all'ordinamento della proprietà fondiaria in Sicilia sotto i Normanni e gli Svevi*, in: *Documenti per servire alla storia di Sicilia.* Ser. I. Vol. 16, (1895); second pagination pp. 29–109. (g) Apulia: F. Camobreco, *Regesto di S. Leonardo di Siponto*, in: *Regesta chartarum Italiae*, vol. 10(1913); Primaldo Coco, *I cavalieri Teutonici nel Salento* (*Appunti e documenti*) (1925). For the whole Mediterranean region the appendix to Forstreuter, *Der Deutsche Orden am Mittelmeer* (note 1) is very valuable.

publications[4]. However, the *Tabulae* remain the most important collection of the Order's *generalia*, i.e., of the general privileges issued by the two universal powers of the Middle Ages: The Roman Emperors and the Popes. This is especially true with respect to the papal *generalia*, i.e., those papal charters which granted specific rights that could be claimed wherever the Order had establishments or possessions throughout the Christian world. These papal *generalia* form the largest subsection of Strehlke's edition, comprising about two-fifths of its contents.

Strehlke's comprehensive *Tabulae* immediately supplanted the earlier collections of Hennes[5], and Duellius[6], who drew the bulk of their material from the provincial archives of the Order. Strehlke, on the other hand, had access to a venerable source, the Cartulary of the Order of the Teutonic Knights. This treasured possession of the Order's archives represents the earliest attempt to assemble the archive material into one *codex*, into which the original charters deposited in the Order's archives were entered as copies. This project was initiated in the early forties of the thirteenth century, when almost all the charters copied concerned the Holy Land, and was continued in the sixties of that century, with the addition of new materials. At an unknown time, but surely still during the thirteenth century, the collection of papal charters was formed, either as a separate volume or immediately added to the one already existing. It is likely that the Cartulary was complete, and very similar to its present form, by the late sixties of the thirteenth century. Later additions dating from the late Middle Ages were bound with the original collection for reasons of convenience, although they did not form part of the original Cartulary.

Strehlke was restricted in his work by the nature of the manuscript. One must keep Strehlke's aim in mind in order to know what to expect from his edition. Being a Prussian himself, he did not attempt to provide an edition of all the charters pertaining to the Teutonic Knights, as he knew that this would amount to editing large parts of the material deposited in the Prussian State Archives at Königsberg up to the year 1525. It was then that the last Grand Master of the Order became a Protestant and transformed the anachronistic Prussian State of the Order into a secular Duchy under the Hohen-

4. For these editions, which do not concern us here, see Rudolf ten Haaf, *Kurze Bibliographie zur Geschichte des Deutschen Ordens* (1949), *passim*. Germany, Prussia, Livonia and Bohemia are printed in Strehlke's edition only inasmuch as contained in the manuscript he edited.
5. J. H. Hennes, *Codex diplomaticus Ordinis S. Mariae Theutonicorum*, Vols. I–II (1845–1861).
6. R. Duellius, *Historia Ordinis Equitum Teutonicorum Hospitalis S. Mariae Virginis Hierosolymitani* (1727).

zollern, to whom he happened to belong. The foundations were thus set for the further rise of this already illustrious family and, in fact, for the state of Brandenburg-Prussia which was destined (if at the expense of excluding Austria and its dependent territories from an all-German state) to unify Germany in the late nineteenth century.

Strehlke did not aim for the scope of Johannes Voigt's *Codex diplomaticus Prussicus* (6 vols., 1836–61) or of the *Preussisches Urkundenbuch* (since 1882), which will eventually provide a general comprehensive edition dealing with the Prussian state of the Order. He merely undertook to execute meticulously an enterprise which had been decided upon at a higher level, undoubtedly by the Director of the *Preussisches Geheimes Staatsarchiv* in Berlin. Philipp Jaffé, in his introduction to Strehlke's edition, hints at the Berlin authorities' concern regarding the Cartulary, which was known to the scholarly world to contain much more material on the history of the Teutonic Knights than was available in print. The *Preussisches Urkundenbuch* had not yet been started, and the remains of the Order's Palestinian archives were still scattered, and therefore almost unknown, in the vast series of the *Patti sciolti* and the *Atti Diplomatici Misti* of the *Archivio di Stato* in Venice. There was no proper repertory for the charters and letters in the Prussian State Archives in Königsberg and the *Deutschordenszentralarchiv* in Vienna had only recently been begun to be formed. Count Pettenegg had not even begun his very poor, but still indispensable guide[7] to the charters of this body of source material, which had not grown historically but had been assembled by administrative decisions from a variety of provincial archives of the Order (most noticeably from the *Deutschmeister's* archives at Mergentheim). All that existed was a hand-written catalogue of 400 charters preserved in Vienna.

The Berlin manuscript finally edited by Strehlke was bound to attract attention from scholars interested in the history of the Order who were familiar with the paucity of printed material available in the 1860's. Those knowledgeable in the field were aware that the Berlin manuscript comprised more material on the Order's history than was available elsewhere, indispensable material which was, furthermore, conveniently assembled in one manuscript of manageable proportions. The authorities were not only bothered by the many inquiries

7. E. G. Graf von Pettenegg, *Die Urkunden des Deutschordenscentralarchivs zu Wien*, Vol. I (the only one published, 1887). The book is relatively rare, because it was so poorly done that the Grand Master intervened and prohibited its further sale. On the history of the Vienna archives of the Teutonic Order, see K. H. Lampe, 'Die Auflösung des Deutschordenshauptarchives zu Mergentheim, *Archivalische Zeitschrift*, 57 (1961) pp. 66–130; K. Wieser, 'Das Zentralarchiv des Deutschen Ordens in Wien', *Archivalische Zeitschrift*, 60 (1964), pp. 131–152.

in writing from people from outside of Berlin some of whom, according to Philipp Jaffé, went so far as to demand handwritten copies of the whole volume (*descripta totius voluminis exempla requirerent.*) The chief archivist's most pressing concern were requests to have the manuscript sent to other places for perusal. As such requests could not always be refused, he, as the principal guardian of Prussian public records, must have worried about the manuscript in transit, especially as the Berlin repertory records that in the late eighteenth century a part of the manuscript had once been estranged from the Berlin archives. From the archivist's point of view, publication of the manuscript would greatly increase the source material for the history of the Teutonic Knights as well as relieve the Berlin archives of decisions and responsibilities which they apparently felt they could no longer incur.

It is not known whether public funds were used to subsidize the printing of the book. But Jaffé states explicitly that the project was submitted to and approved by Count Otto von Bismarck, then Prime Minister of Prussia and already well on his way to unifying Germany under Prussian leadership in 1871. It is evident that this was a political decision on Bismarck's part and not, as had been the case with the Berlin archivists, one based on the need to preserve public records. Bismarck was not insensitive to the fact that for the leading strata of German society his was an historically-minded age. He was Chancellor of the *Deutsches Reich* for less than a decade when he used public funds to finance a doubtful expedition to excavate the tomb and remnants of Emperor Frederick Barbarossa in Tyre in Ottoman Palestine, entrusting the expedition to the incompetent Johann Nepomuk Sepp, who looked for the tomb and bones where no capable mediaevalist would ever have searched[8]. The undertaking drew acid sarcasm from the pen of Paul Scheffer-Boichorst, a leading mediaevalist at the University of Berlin[9]. Scheffer-Boichorst was correct in his estimate that no remains could reasonably be expected to have survived and that the matter could have been more efficiently investigated from a desk in Berlin.

But Bismarck chose Sepp and embarked on the project in the hope that if the bones were found it would have contributed to give a cohesive political identity to the nation. Since the late Middle Ages Germany had been broken up into territorial fragments which were loosely held together by the shadowy framework of the Holy Roman Empire and a sense of a common cultural and

8. See Johann Nepomuk Sepp, *Meerfahrt nach Tyrus* (1879). Hans Prutz, also a member of the expedition, wrote a report that is considerably better: *Kaiser Friedrichs I. Grabstätte. Eine kritische Studie* (1879).
9. P. Scheffer-Boichorst, 'Das Grab Barbarossas', *Im neuen Reich*, Jahrgang 9, Vol. 2 (1879), pp. 693–701.

historical heritage. At the beginning of the century the Romanticists, disillusioned politicians and politically-minded historians, had devoted themselves to the study of the Middle Ages. They found in the greatness of the Ottonian, Salian and Swabian Roman Empire consolation from the defeats suffered from Napoleon, and they dreamt of a revival of the splendour of the old mediaeval *Reich*, which would mould the German principalities into one politically uniform entity that would restore Germany to its destined place in the sun. As the century drew to an end, these sentiments became one of many tools to round off psychologically, what had been achieved politically in 1871. The opposition to Prussian hegemony in Germany had not yet subsided in either South Germany or among the annexed Hanoverian subjects, although opinions here and there were divided. Bismarck therefore played on the historical sentiments of the age. Frederick Barbarossa was then considered the greatest of all German Emperors apart from Charlemagne, who was also claimed by France and was strictly speaking a Frankish Emperor rather than a German one. The Kyffhäuser legend originally linked to Barbarossa's grandson Frederick II, had been shifted to Frederick I, and romantic poems described him as sitting in the depth of the Kyffhäuser mountain, where his beard had grown through the stone table over the centuries, but where he was waiting to emerge at a suitable time to restore the Empire to its former brilliance. Such traditional sentiments were hammered into the people's minds by a battery of other historians. If Bismarck could have had the remains of Barbarossa, there is no doubt that he would have turned them into a national shrine of the first magnitude, a kind of German nineteenth century *Oriflamme*.

The political background of these events is underlined by the fact that Scheffer-Boichorst published his diatribe against the expedition to Tyre in a political periodical, *Im neuen Reich* (1879), rather than in a historical journal. He realized that he as an historian was dealing with a current political event. The ill-fated expedition to Tyre is symptomatic of the way in which history was used to influence the politics of the day, and we need not doubt that Bismarck also recognized the potential advantage which an edition of the Berlin Cartulary might be to his political aims. It was of paramount importance that the greatness of Prussia be demonstrated to the German public, because unification under Prussia was Bismarck's solution of the German problem.

In a simplified view of history that would easily appeal to the general public, Prussia had been built by the Teutonic Knights and by the Hohenzollern. It was the Knights and the German settlers they attracted, who christianized wide Slavonic areas and brought economic stimulants and prosperity to the Prussians and the Germans living in Prussia. They spread the superior Lübeck city law and let cities of considerable size spring up in Prussia and the Baltic countries, which were predominantly German in ethnic composition and cultural outlook. In general, they brought western culture in its German form to the underdeveloped peripheral areas of the Latin west. It was an enormous achievement exemplified by brick Gothic, to which the Marienburg and cities like Danzig, Königsberg, Riga and Reval bore ample testimony, although the toll of blood that goes with every conquest may not have pleased the Slavs.

The Knights had transformed Prussia, which took its name from the Slavonic *Pruteni*, into a German country with a lower stratum of Slavs that was becoming increasingly Germanized. In so doing they had pushed the German frontier greatly towards the east. Although the Cartulary did not really contain much material on Prussian and Baltic affairs — and one may be justified in asking the degree to which Bismarck was informed of this — its publication could be relied upon to stimulate studies on the Order of the Teutonic Knights. These were inevitably bound to lead to Prussian studies, as well as to studies on the Teutonic Knights proper, and serve to demonstrate Prussian greatness. Strehlke's edition, a politically as well as a scholarly motivated undertaking, is a product of, and a monument to, the patriotic and national spirit of nineteenth century Prussia and Germany.

Ernst Gottfried Wilhelm Strehlke[10] was born in Berlin on 27 September 1834, the second son of Friedrich Strehlke, a teacher at the *Kölnisches Gymnasium*. In 1838 the father became Director of the *Petrischule* in Danzig, where Ernst attended school until he moved to the Danzig Gymnasium in 1845. It was in Danzig that Ernst met Theodor Hirsch, the man who was to awaken in him an almost monomaniacal passion for history. Hirsch, who was then a teacher of history at the Danzig Gymnasium, is today considered one of the main figures in nineteenth century Prussian historical research and a leading contributor to the monumental *Scriptores Rerum Prussicarum* series. He turned Ernst Strehlke's attention to the history of Prussia, and Strehlke proved to be a rewarding student. While Strehlke was still in his secondary school, Hirsch

---

10. On Strehlke, see A. v. M(ülverstedt), 'Necrolog Ernst Strehlke', *Preussischer Staatsanzeiger* 1869, No. 84, 10 April 1869, Appendix (not included in the pagination); Theodor Hirsch, Preface to *Scriptores rerum Prussicarum. Die Geschichtsquellen der preussischen Vorzeit*, herausgegeben von Theodor Hirsch, Max Töppen, Ernst Strehlke, Vol. 4 (1870), pp. V–VIII; Max Perlbach's article on Strehlke in *Allgemeine Deutsche Biographie*, Vol. 54 (1908), p. 616 ff. Walther Hubatsch's article on Strehlke in *Altpreussische Biographie herausgegeben im Auftrage der Historischen Kommission für ost — und westpreussische Landesforschung*, Vol. 2 (1967), p. 709. For a bibliography of Strehlke's publications, see Max Perlbach, 'Verzeichnis der Schriften Ernst Strehlke's', *Altpreussische Monatsschrift*, New Series, Vol. 39 (1902), p. 307 ff.

enlisted him to help sort and catalogue the records of the Danzig city archives, a task which had been entrusted to him by the magistrates. Hirsch, who survived Strehlke by twelve years, although he was thirty years older, reports in the obituary he composed that even as a boy Strehlke had strolled among the antique shops to see that historical records were not being unnecessarily destroyed. Upon hearing that the peasants in Pommerellen were not being prevented by the civil servants in charge from destroying the monuments and muniments of the dissolved monasteries of Zuckau and Karthus, Strehlke walked the 20 miles from Danzig repeatedly until he had catalogued what was still there, making drawings of tombstones and their inscriptions before they were destroyed, but, above all, to save the written records and bring them into suitable repositories. Strehlke thus had the antiquarian respect for the past so typical of his generation, which enabled it to such an outstanding performance and achievement in the edition of sources.

From 1852 to 1856 Ernst Strehlke studied at the University of Berlin. While he did study history, it seems that Hirsch encouraged him to keep a broad perspective and not limit his horizons and personality with a narrow view of his studies. In his obituary, Hirsch clearly recognized the potential danger of the boy's passion for history, which might have led him to spend his time on its bypaths and details rather than arrive at a wider view of the field. Consequently, and surely because this was in keeping with the spirit of the time, Strehlke also did philological, philosophical, legal and geographical studies in the University. Philosophy was required of anyone matriculated in the Faculty of Philosophy, and the combination of history and philology was frequent in an age still wise enough to base the access to history on a sound philological basis. Geography was an obvious aid to the historian, and in the days of Savigny, indeed well into the twentieth century, it was very much *en vogue* for young historians to read law at the University, because law, particularly public law, was then being taught on a historical basis. Strehlke's main interests, however, remained in history. He won a prize with an unpublished essay on Wipo's *Gesta Henrici III Imperatoris* in 1854, thus deviating for the first time from Prussian and Pomeranian studies. But in his doctoral dissertation accepted by the Faculty in 1856, he moved east again, treating *De Henrici III Imperatoris Bellis Ungaricis.*

In addition to his studies, he worked as amanuensis in the library of the Royal Prussian War College. It was probably at this stage of his life that he developed the beginnings of a tubercular condition in his lungs, which restricted his life in many ways and undoubtedly changed its direction. It was now out of the question for him to become a secondary school teacher, as he would have been a potential threat to the children. He therefore accepted an offer by Privy Councellor von Quast to help him finish and publish a monumental work of four volumes *in quarto* plus 96 copper etchings *in folio* on *Denkmäler der Kunst des Mittelalters in Unteritalien.* The enterprise was begun by the Royal Saxon Privy Councellor Heinrich Wilhelm Schulz, who did not live to finish it. This will not surprise those who know that not less than seventeen different rough drafts of a preface were found among the papers of Schulz. Of the actual text only four or five quires were ready when Schulz died. The rest had to be done by von Quast and Strehlke, while the brother of the late Heinrich Wilhelm Schulz put up the money that was needed, which does not seem to have been a trifling amount. Even so, the four volumes and the atlas sold for 120 *Thaler* when the work was published in 1860. Strehlke devoted four years of his life to this description and depiction of mediaeval art monuments in Southern Italy, the last volume of which comprised 480 documents pertaining to the history of the monuments described. Strehlke even widened the scope of the original project, using as raw material the 160 diaries which Schulz had kept during his travels in Italy and into which he had entered descriptions and copies of documents. As the task of completing a project begun by someone else requires a great amount of sacrifice, it is understandable that Strehlke was deeply wounded that the four volumes and the atlas were published in 1860 bearing only the names of Schulz as author and von Quast as editor. Not only had young Strehlke been overridden, but he must have been particularly resentful as four years of what he knew was a short life span had gone into the preparation of the work. Although Hirsch, to whom he must have complained bitterly about this gross injustice, hinted at the matter in his obituary in words of noble restraint, the human drama is plainly to be seen between the lines.

By the time the four volumes on Italian mediaeval art monuments appeared, Strehlke's bibliography had already reached number 25. When still in secondary school he found a group of documents of some importance but had been too young and inexperienced to handle them; Hirsch published them in his *Pommerellische Studien* in the *Neue Preussische Provinzialblätter* in 1851. But when his illness transpired, Strehlke began to publish on his own, at first almost exclusively in the periodical just mentioned, to which Hirsch provided the access. His articles dealt mostly with Pommerellen, Prussia and Livland, as was to be expected, although he did once revert to the topic of his dissertation with a paper on the letter of Abbot Berno of Reichenau to King Henry III, which appeared in the *Archiv für Kunde österreichischer Geschichtsquellen.*

In 1860 Strehlke entered the Prussian civil service as an archivist at the *Königlich Preussisches Geheimes Staatsarchiv* (Royal Prussian Secret Archives) in Berlin. In the autumn of 1861 he was promoted to the vacant position of the

Privy Secretary to the Archives. Here he had to do general archive work, to which he submitted willingly. At first he was entrusted with abstracting charters concerning the Mark Brandenburg in the 13th century. He was one of those engaged in the reclassification of the oldest parchments of the Berlin archives, and he compiled an exemplary repertory of the documents of the *Oberpräsidium* in Posen (today Poznan in Poland), which led to the establishment of Prussian state archives in Posen. But he had embarked on another venture before he joined the archive service. For quite some time it had been felt that not only the charters, but also the chronicles and annals pertaining to Prussian mediaeval history should be made available to the general public in scholarly editions. They were not on the agenda of the *Monumenta Germaniae* because they dealt with provincial matters rather than imperial or national ones. When Theodor Hirsch, Max Töppen and Ernst Strehlke met accidentally at the centenary of the Danzig Gymnasium on 13 June 1858, they decided to meet this demand by jointly editing the *Scriptores Rerum Prussicarum.* From that time much of Strehlke's energies were devoted to this undertaking. He contributed the 'Chronicle of Prussia by Nicolaus von Jeroschin' to the first volume in 1861, the 'Livland Chronicle of Herman von Wartberge' to the second volume in 1863, as well as other minor texts. It was therefore a little out of place that he reviewed this second volume in the *Historische Zeitschrift*, 11 (1864), pp. 523–526. In the same year he published a German translation of this 'Livland Chronicle', which he had discovered in its original Latin form in the city archives of Danzig. Still in the same year he published in a private edition a volume of his poems. Although Max Perlbach, in his fine article on Strehlke in the *Allgemeine Deutsche Biographie*, is of the opinion that the poems showed more than the formal rhyming capacity of a dilettante, they should probably not be counted among the achievements of German literature or among the better works of Ernst Strehlke. They prove, however, that his was a sensitive soul, all the more open to the beauties of nature because he could not hope to enjoy them for very long. His illness prevented any thought of his getting married. Writing poems may have been an attempt to overcome the bitter frustrations which the limitations dictated by his poor health imposed on him. In any event, both his illness and his bachelorhood were a powerful incentive for him to go on working while he had time and opportunity to do it.

He contributed heavily to the third volume of the *Scriptores*, which appeared in 1866. The 'Annals of Thorn', portions of 'Detmar's Chronicle of Lübeck' and the 'Chronicle of the Land Prussia by Johann von Posilge' filled more than half of the bulky volume. Again he reviewed the volume himself in the *Historische Zeitschrift*, 17(1867), pp. 197–203. During these years he also published minor papers on Prussian history, continuing his work on the

Scriptores, but not at the old pace. This was probably because he was now busy transcribing and editing the Cartulary of the Order of the Teutonic Knights for the Berlin archives. He did not live to see the following volumes of the *Scriptores* or his edition of the Cartulary appear in print. He had tried repeatedly to improve his condition by residing in a milder climate on Lake Geneva, but to no avail. On 23 March 1869 he died from his lung ailment.

Ernst Strehlke left at his death some more or less worked out contributions to the *Scriptores Rerum Prussicarum*, which were published in Volumes Four and Five in 1870 and 1874, respectively. He also left four papers which appeared posthumously from 1870 to 1874 in the *Altpreussische Monatsschrift*. Most important, he did very nearly complete his edition of the Cartulary of the Teutonic Knights. He had composed a detailed Table of Contents, now preserved as Ms. Rep. 94.V.E.b2 in the *Deutsches Zentralarchiv* in Merseburg, where one can also still see his manuscript of the edition under the shelf-number Ms. Rep. 94.V.E.b4. It is a bulky parcel of about 800 loose leaves, very much in the fashion in which manuscripts were sent to print shops at that time. The basic part is formed of texts copied from the actual Cartulary (Ms. Rep. 94.V.E.b1 of the *Deutsches Zentralarchiv* in Merseburg). These copies are in a neat handwriting and seem to have been executed without any apparent difficulty in deciphering the original manuscript. To a trained Prussian archivist, the manuscript would not have presented palaeographical difficulties. The fair number of collations I had to do from the actual manuscript for my edition of the 'Charters of the Latin Kings of Jerusalem' now in preparation reveal that Strehlke's transcriptions are of a high degree of exactness and contain very few misreadings or other slips. They are in marked contrast to some of the French editions I had to collate for the same purpose, and give evidence of Strehlke's professional abilities as an editor as well as the highly selective and successful recruiting policy of the Prussian archive service, which remained on the highest scholarly level until Prussia came to its end in 1945. The same regard for Strehlke's professional proficiency is generally accorded to his contributions to the *Scriptores Rerum Prussicarum*. When he finished copying the manuscript he wrote the notes to individual charters on separate sheets, or smaller slips to be exact, which he inserted after each copy. At first glance these sheets look poorly. They have been much worked over and corrected time and again, surely not only by Strehlke, but also by Philipp Jaffé who put the edition through the printing process. It was not an easy job for the printer, and printers today would reject a manuscript in that condition. But in days when the printers themselves were scholars and when the printing budgets allowed for a much larger amount of corrections during the proofreading stage, such manuscripts were quite common.

The Cartulary as Strehlke found it consisted of seven clearly different parts which had not always been together. They ranged from a general cartulary or bullary of the Order to transcriptions of charters which happened to be in the archives of individual houses of the Order. Most parts surely were not chronologically arranged. This was especially true of most of the bullaries contained in the manuscript, because the papal charters contained therein had been copied mainly without the dates. Among the papal charters — except where they were dated and did form a chronological sequel — there was no recognizable classification according to subject matter. Among the non-papal charters in the Cartulary proper, Strehlke must have recognized that those for the Mediterranean region were roughly classified by countries: Holy Land, Lesser Armenia, Cyprus, Italy, Hungary and Frankish Greece, with a few other things interspersed. That there was a very definite attempt to classify the various subsections according to subject matter did not become obvious to Strehlke, because he was not familiar enough with the history of the Holy Land under the Crusaders; apart from the papal charters the Holy Land charters were precisely the largest subsection of the manuscript. Strehlke could not have been expected to know that the group of charters at the very beginning of the Cartulary formed what might be called the archives of the *Seigneurie de Joscelin*, the most important possession of the Teutonic Knights in the Holy Land. These charters were not issued for the Knights themselves but for Joscelin III, titular Count of Edessa who settled in the kingdom of Jerusalem and was accorded fiefs and possessions therein. Joscelin also bought the possessions of other people, along with their original titles, which were passed on to the Knights by Joscelin's heirs when they sold the inheritance to the Order. The subject-matter classification becomes less recognizable after this first group. However, Joscelin's charters being the second to twenty-eighth charters in the manuscript definitely belong to a historically grown body of archive material, thus making it evident that at least this part of the manuscript is not without a system of classification.

Since Strehlke did not realize this, he made two decisions, which could have been remedied by a Table of Concordance showing the original sequence of charters in the manuscript. He decided to break up the original order and to print the charters in groups according to certain geographical areas, regardless of where they were found in the actual manuscript. He added two series of general privileges pertaining to the Order as a whole that were issued by the Roman Kings and Emperors and by the Popes. Within each of these groups he arranged the charters chronologically, correctly placing those which could not be dated under the latest possible date. He also decided to expand the sections on the Holy Land and on the papal *generalia* to the best of his knowledge, using the bullaries of the Order in the archives at Königsberg and all other available information. In keeping with the spirit of his day, when quantity counted, he endeavoured to provide the public with as much material as was available. While Strehlke did not sacrifice quality for quantity, the contents of the charters were more important to him than any insight which might have been gained from a careful study of how the manuscript had been put together. Many editors of the period felt that as long as a text was edited in a philologically satisfactory manner the form and history of the manuscript transmitting the text were not too important. This was an unfortunate heritage from the classical philology of Lachmann, who tried to reconstruct archetypes by a rather mechanical selection of variant readings. While Lachmann's philological abilities and instincts were outstanding, he undervalued the worth of extant manuscripts in his attempts to reconstruct archetypes. However, this is an old controversy between Lachmann and his surely more advanced adherents, on the one side, and Joseph Bédier as the champion of the *codex unicus* method, on the other. What becomes clear is that Strehlke's decisions enabled him to make more texts available, and in a convenient order, while this hampered the scholar from gaining historical insights from the Cartulary itself, since manuscripts are rarely inspected once they have been printed.

Strehlke's edition included a considerable number of charters which were not in the manuscript and it did not include three which were (see Table of Concordance below, pp. 36, 40). Occasionally he slipped in identifying charters, giving a reference to a certain leaf in the manuscript in the notes to another charter which he had received from other sources and had chosen to include, rather than in the footnotes to the correct charter. His references to the manuscript leaves, which in the main do apply to the correct charters, contain uncorrected printer's errors. Whether this was Strehlke's responsibility or should be ascribed to Jaffé, one cannot say today.

Strehlke decided on another step which was to totally obscure any correct impression or evaluation of the manuscript to the scholarly world: he did not print in full all of the charters he included, whether they were derived from the Berlin manuscript or from other sources. He reprinted such charters only if his text, regardless of where it came from, seemed better than the one printed before, e.g. by Duellius, Hennes, Huillard-Bréholles or in the *Livländisches Urkundenbuch*. However, his transcriptions of imperial *diplomata* by Emperor Frederick II would probably have been better in most cases than those of Huillard-Bréholles, who gave us something very comprehensive, almost complete, but short of perfect.

In most cases, Strehlke did not reprint re-issues of former charters, an extremely frequent occurrence in papal diplomatics. The popes re-issued their own charters as well as those of their predecessors for various reasons. The numerous re-issues present one of the most tedious chores to those editing papal charters. It has only recently been realized that it does not suffice to merely state that a successor re-issued a predecessor's grant, and then to give the superscription, the opening words and the date, but omit the text. Today it is felt that the variant readings of all re-issues must be given in the footnotes to the original grant, because only in this way will the gradual development of the formulas become apparent. In fact, the development of the formulas may be seen much more clearly in those cases where popes consciously (and with recourse to the original grant presented by the recipient or looked up in the predecessor's register) re-issued the former charters than in the cases where the chancery used an accepted standard formulary to deal with similar legal transactions for various recipients. It is obvious that the temptation to deviate from the formulas was considerably less in the former case than in the latter; consequently, such deviations in re-issues point to a genuine change in the formulas.

If Strehlke had known how much more material from the archives in Königsberg, Vienna, Venice and the Vatican, to mention only the most important ones, could have been included, he probably would have confined himself to an edition of the Berlin manuscript proper. As it stands, his edition is neither complete in its collection of charters for the Teutonic Knights in the Holy Land, nor in its collection of papal *generalia.* It must again be stressed, however, that it is still the largest source collection for the Teutonic Knights in both fields. Whatever he did know about the material in Venice, for example, came to him through the medium of copies in a Königsberg manuscript, from which Friedrich Adolf Meckelburg, Director of the Königsberg archives, made copies for him. This is true, for example, of his Nos. 106 and 107, which Meckelburg copied out of the Königsberg Ms. A 16 (today OF 69 of the *Staatliches Archivlager* in Göttingen), where they were described as resting in Venice, if Meckelburg's references in this case are correct (at times they are not).

We must bear the fact that Strehlke did not print re-issues, but merely abstracted them and gave only the barest essentials of their text, with a high degree of tolerance. He did make an attempt to do what a modern editor would have done, i.e. to give variant readings of re-issues in the footnotes to the first issue. But he did not give all variant readings, and he did not always use all the texts of papal charters available more than once in the Berlin manuscript. One should reproach neither Strehlke nor Jaffé for not having given all variant readings of re-issues of papal charters, because this would have been out of step with the practice of the time. Strehlke seemed to work in the right direction when he gave the few variant readings he chose to give, as variants to the first issue. This was clearly intended only as a space-saving device, not as a scholarly way of showing the development of the *formulae* used by the papal chancery, because Strehlke applied his principle only to re-issues within the same pontificate. From a scholarly point of view, the preferential treatment given to the first pontificate, in which a frequently repeated *generale* appears, is a curious principle, because all re-issues, whether from the same pontificate or a later one, have an equally smaller value as a source than the very first issue. This is, indeed, the basic document. As for re-issues, one would expect variant readings for all of them (in one place alone or at least in one place for each pontificate) or none of them. There seems to be no justification for selecting variant readings from re-issues in the first pontificate to the total exclusion of later pontificates. Being of the opinion that there was nothing to be gained from printing a text which did not materially add to the rights of the Teutonic Knights but merely reasserted them, Strehlke felt that it was enough to mention the mere fact and date of the re-issue and even, with the imperfections mentioned, give the reference to his source, thus establishing a historical fact of no great significance. Neither Strehlke nor Jaffé realized the importance of the gradual development of the texts. One would expect that all the copies of a charter contained in the manuscript edited by him would have at least been mentioned. Why they are mentioned in some cases, and not in others is inexplicable. There is an erratic element here which is probably evidence that Strehlke's work was not quite completed.

Another source of confusion is presented by the many undated papal charters in the Berlin manuscript. In most cases Strehlke was able to supply the dates from other sources. But if such charters had been re-issued within the same pontificate (up to four times within one pontificate), as is the case for a not insignificant number of them, only the most exacting and accurate comparison of the undated copy in the Berlin manuscript with the other copies from outside sources would have allowed proper identification of the one contained in the manuscript. As there is no evidence in his printed edition or in his print shop manuscript that Strehlke carried out such a close comparison, he had no way of telling whether an undated copy in the manuscript was a first issue or a later one by the same pope. In the case of such undated copies Strehlke nevertheless invariably decided that they were the first issue and consequently used them for establishing his text. If there was more than one undated copy from the same pontificate in the manuscript, for which we have shown examples from the eighteen charters investigated in Bullary I[11], he disregarded the others completely.

While Strehlke's transcriptions are very good, his references to the manuscript are, in this section, poor. This is true only of the series of papal *generalia*, because in his other divisions he printed practically exclusively from the Berlin manuscript (the expanding of the Holy Land section is not very substantial) and did not have to deal with re-issues or more than one text of a given charter within the manuscript.

As we are concerned with the fine points of editing, we have therefore, evaluated Strehlke's work on this basis. It must, however, be stressed that the weaknesses pointed out above are not such that they would, on the whole, merit a new edition of Strehlke rather than a reprint of the book. A modern edition would not improve the usefulness of Strehlke's work for the historian. The fact that his edition does not meet all modern standards does not mean that his texts are unreliable, although it is unfortunate that from Strehlke's edition one cannot fully reconstruct or learn anything of the composition of the manuscript formerly in Berlin and now in Merseburg. (When I tried this

11. It may suffice to show this from the first eighteen charters of the first collection of papal *generalia* in the Berlin manuscript (see below Table of Concordance p. 35). The references to the manuscript in the footnotes Nos. 295, 296, 301, 47, 144 are correct. In the Bullary there follows Strehlke No. 302 on fol. 62^v. Although this charter occurs only here, we find no reference to the manuscript in Strehlke's footnotes but only to an *inspeximus* in the Königsberg Archives. His references to the manuscript in the footnotes to Nos. 54, 309 are again correct. In No. 309 he even correctly reports all three transmissions of the text contained in the Berlin manuscript and also lists not less than nine other transmissions of this charter and the two re-issues, but he gives only one variant reading. In the footnotes to No. 405 we find no reference to the dated copy on fol. 63^v, No. 3. The following charter, which is undated and cannot therefore be properly identified, may be either Strehlke No. 305, 313 or 397; he does not give a reference to the undated copy on fol. 63^v, No. 4. In the following No. 323 (or 371, 382, 386, respectively) the undated copy on fol. 64^r, No. 5 is not mentioned. Likewise, in the next charter, No. 404, the reference to the undated copy on fol. 64^r, No 6 is omitted. Following this we find in No. 328 a reference to an undated copy on fol. 76 which is wrong, whereas the manuscript contains an unmentioned dated copy on fol. 64^v, No. 7. In No. 310, which follows in the manuscript, the undated copy of fol. 65^r, No. 8 is not referred to, and the same is true of the next two charters, Nos. 341, 336, where the dated copies on fol. 65^r, No. 9 and fol. 66^r, No. 10 should have been mentioned in the footnotes. The references to the manuscript given in Nos. 342, 409, now following in the manuscript, are again correct. Thus, in eighteen successive charters picked at random, we have found in not less than half faulty or incomplete references to the manuscript.

before I had seen the manuscript, I arrived at quite false conclusions[12], which I now take the opportunity to rectify). This need is now met by our Table of Concordance and the description of the manuscript. The other deficiencies described are probably explained by Strehlke's anxiety that whatever life he had left would not suffice to complete the edition with the high degree of exactness with which he is normally credited. Such fears were justified because he did not quite finish his work. Its completion must have been the absorbing interest of his last years, because after his disappointment over having been omitted from the title page of the *Denkmäler der Kunst des Mittelalters in Unteritalien* by Schulz and von Quast and after his personal sacrifice in collaborating on the *Scriptores rerum Prussicarum*, where again he would not

12. H. E. Mayer, 'Marseilles Levantehandel und ein akkonensisches Fälscheratelier des 13. Jahrhunderts', *Bibliothek des Deutschen Historischen Instituts in Rom* 38, (1972), p. 168 f. We assumed there that the four forgeries (Strehlke Nos. 6, 8, 20, 34) were procured by the Teutonic Order around 1253/54 to serve two purposes: (a) to safeguard certain possessions which the Order acquired from the lord of Beirut and (b) to defend the Order against attempts by the Knights Hospitallers to incorporate the Teutonic Knights as successors to the old twelfth century German hospital in Jerusalem, which had formed a branch of the Knights Hospitallers. Marie-Luise Favreau (see above n. 2) further clarified the latter aspect. The attacks by the Knights Hospitallers against the Teutonic Knights were launched in 1190, 1229 and 1240–1, but the Teutonic Knights were still afraid that the question might be raised again as late as 1258. While we may retain the second reason for procuring the forgeries, we must discard the first, because we did not realize at the time, that the Cartulary of the Teutonic Knights must be divided into two sections, which were compiled at different times. Strehlke Nos. 6, 8, 34 are contained in the first portion of the Cartulary put together in 1243. While they could be used to fight off the Knights Hospitallers, they could not have been procured to safeguard possessions which were not within the Order's sphere of interest before 1253 at the earliest, and possibly not even before 1256. (Although they could, indeed, have been used to safeguard these possessions, if there was a quarrel over them, this could not have been foreseen in 1243). It is different for Strehlke No. 20, which was added to the first portion of the Cartulary about the middle of the century before the Cartulary was continued in about 1263 (see below p. 28). However, it is impossible to conclude that this particular forgery could have been used for safeguarding possessions at stake in the fifties. This rectification also has certain advantages; it brings Strehlke Nos. 6, 8, 34 closer to the time during which we know this forger to have worked for other clients, and it confirms my doubts (p. 174) whether Strehlke No. 20 should be grouped with Strehlke Nos. 6, 8, 34. While it seems that they should be attributed to the same workshop, certain inconsistencies between Strehlke No. 20 on the one hand, and Strehlke Nos. 6, 8, 34 on the other, can be better explained by the assumption that the latter three were produced considerably earlier than the last one.

appear on the title page except as co-editor, this edition was finally to be published under his name, and his alone. Philipp Jaffé, who himself suffered from ill treatment from the autocratic Georg Heinrich Pertz to the point where the latter's antisemitism drove Jaffé into suicide[13], nobly and tactfully omitted his own name from the title page of Strehlke's edition and merely signed the preface, which, indeed, he wrote.

Following the detailed description of the manuscript we compiled a Table of Concordance, which lists the charters printed by Strehlke in the order in which they appear in the manuscript and their correspondence with the printed order. This is supplemented by a list of charters in the order printed by Strehlke with the indication in which of the seven parts of the manuscript they are to be found. Additionally there is a table showing the charters printed by Strehlke but lacking in the manuscript. Finally an attempt will be made to reconstruct the history of the various parts of the manuscript.

---

13. Harry Bresslau, 'Geschichte der Monumenta Germaniae Historica', *Neues Archiv der Gesellschaft für ältere deutsche Geschichtskunde*, 42 (1921), p. 468. It must be said in fairness to Pertz that he had originally helped Jaffé's career by persuading a publisher to maintain him for three years so that he could complete his monumental *Regesta pontificum Romanorum* and by having him on the research staff of the *MGH*. Jaffé did not only come up against the anti-Semitism of Pertz; the same attitude prevented him from obtaining a higher position in a German university, for which he was eminently qualified. Pertz also tried to convince the Roman Curia to give Jaffé a position that would allow him to continue his papal *Regesta*, however Rome would not consider a Jew, and the honour was reserved for Potthast. Jaffé's relations with Pertz became increasingly strained when he began his *Bibliotheca rerum Germanicarum* in which Pertz saw nothing but competition for the *MGH*. Pertz fought with petty means, trying, among other things, to suppress the name of Jaffé from the introductions of *MGH* editions and to bar Jaffé from the Berlin library. He also circulated absurd rumours that Jaffé had once been a spy for foreign nations. Jaffé's honour was expressly rehabilitated by the Prussian government, but as a solitary person, he became increasingly bitter. He was deeply wounded when he received a salary raise in 1868, attributing it to his having become converted to the Christian faith, although it was the result of his having declined an appointment to the University of Florence. He went to the extreme of unsuccessfully trying to have his salary cut again. At the same time his bitterness was increased by the orthodox Jews of Berlin turning against him and circulating the rumour that his neurotic depressions were due to regrets over his conversion, which was not the case. His suicide was more than the mere result of Pertz's anti-Semitism. It was ironical that at that time Jaffé should have had no idea of Pertz's imminent downfall.

B. Description of the Manuscript

Merseburg (German Democratic Republic), *Deutsches Zentralarchiv, Historische Abteilung II* (formerly: Berlin, *Preussisches Geheimes Staatsarchiv*), Ms. Rep. 94.V.E.b1. On the back of the front paper as well as on the back cover, the older shelf number, still valid in Strehlke's days, is recorded: h.I.C.12.fol. (in full only on the back cover; on the back of the front paper it has been shortened to: I.C.12). Brown leather binding (size 310 × 220 millimeters) of the first half, maybe even the beginning of the nineteenth century, lightly embossed. Back title: *Cod. saec. XIII u. XIV. Deutsch-Orden. 1. u. 2. Besitzungen, bes. im Morgenlande, 12. u. 13. Jh., 3. Privilegia (Abschrift v. Transs. Sammlgg. des 15. Jahrhunderts). 4. Transsumpta vber die newe margk etc., 15. Jahrhunderts. 5. Privilegia (Transsumpt von 1445).* Three unnumbered paper front leaves, 19 unnumbered paper end leaves, (I) and 370 parchment or paper leaves, numbered consecutively by a nineteenth-century hand, plus the paper leaf 169a.

The repertory of the Berlin archives compiled by von Mörner recognizes only five parts into which the manuscript should be divided, whereas Strehlke, both in his handwritten Table of Contents (Merseburg, *Deutsches Zentralarchiv*, Rep. 94.V.E.b2, *passim*) and in his edition, distinguished seven parts. This is correct, although it must be admitted that at least Parts V and VI of Strehlke's division already formed a unit before they were bound together with the rest of the manuscript. To this must be added that the repertory erroneously draws Parts II and III of Strehlke's division together. The various parts are best described individually.

Part I

One unnumbered parchment front leaf (on recto in a script of the thirteenth century: §*XXXVI.* §*XXXIX.* §*IXII.* §*IXVII.* §*LXII.* §*LXXIX.* §*LXXXI.* §*CXII.* §*CXXIII.*) followed by leaves 1^r–89^v. Cartulary and Bullary I of the Order of the Teutonic Knights of the thirteenth century. "Southern" parchment, calcinated only on the flesh side. Written in a bookhand of the middle of the thirteenth century in brown ink. All in one hand except for some later additions. Red rubrics heading the individual charters. Some of the rubrics suffered from cutting on the upper and the outer margins when the manuscript was bound into its present form. Initials in red and blue, as indicated on the margin by corresponding very small letters. Unnumbered quires, partly with catchwords at the middle lower margin of the last page, some of which have been cut in the binding process. This part consists of the following quires: 1 *binio* (fol. 1^r–4^v), 1 *quaternio* (fol. 5^r–12^v), 1 *quaternio* (fol. 13^r–20^v), 1 *quaternio* (fol. 21^r–28^v), 1 *quaternio* (fol. 29^r–36^v), 1 *quaternio* (fol. 37^r–44^v), 1 *binio* with two added leaves (fol. 45^r–50^v), 1 *quaternio* (fol. 51^r–58^v), 1 *quaternio* (fol. 59^r–66^v), 1 *quaternio* (fol. 67^r–74^v), 1 *quaternio* (fol. 75^r–82^v), 1 *ternio* with one additional leaf added (fol. 83^r–89^v). Size of page 295 × 215 millimeters, size of written area 255 × 170 millimeters. Two columns of 37 lines each. Scored ruling with single vertical bounding lines. No pricking holes visible.

Contents: fol. 1^r–3^v a list of possessions of the Teutonic Knights headed by the rubric: *Hee sunt elemosine, emptiones, confirmationes, commutationes atque privilegia domus sancte Marie Theutonicorum in Ierusalem* (Strehlke No. 128). At some points there are marginal rubrics as indicated by Strehlke. The enumeration breaks off a first time on fol. 3ra in the middle of the column. The rest has been left vacant to add further possessions in the Latin Kingdom of Jerusalem. It resumes at the top of fol. 3rb. Here the sideheads read: *De Sydone. De Tripoli. De Anthiochia. De Armenia. De Herrenia* (= a town in Lesser Armenia). *De Cypro*. Then, still on fol. 3rb, there are two vacant lines, after which the possessions and donations in Europe are listed, beginning with the sidehead *De Ungaria*, which is followed by donations, possessions and sideheads pertaining to Frankish Greece, Italy, and as last item: *Confirmatio Livonie*. Ends on fol. 3vb, the lower half of which is vacant, as is fol. 4^r and 4va. On fol. 4vb there is a long rubric to the first actual charter, carrying over to fol. 5^r. The charters beginning on fol. 5^r are consecutively numbered from *I* to *XCVI* (Strehlke No. 158, beginning on fol. 44^r). The charters on fol. 45^r–49ra, upper half, are unnumbered. Fol. 49ra, lower half, and 49rb were originally vacant until a hand of the second half of the thirteenth century copied onto fol. 49^r the forgery Strehlke No. 20. The remainder of fol. 49^r and the rest of the quire up to fol. 50^v remain vacant. The numbering of the charters resumes on fol. 51^r with No. *XCVII* (Strehlke No. 159) and continues to No. *CXIIII* on fol. 58^v (Strehlke No. 137). On fol. 59^r Bullary I of papal charters for the Teutonic Knights begins, and continues up to fol. 85^r, roughly classified according to successive pontificates. It breaks off temporarily on fol. 60^v with the beginning of a *littera* by Pope Honorius III: *(H)onorius episcopus servus servorum dei dilectis filiis Hermanno magistro et fratribus hospitalis sancte Marie Theutonicorum Ierosolimitan salutem et apostolicam benedictionem.* Rest is missing. The remainder of fol. 60^v and fols. 61^r–62^r are vacant. The gap was most likely intended to insert more papal charters by Pope Innocent III, in whose pontificate the gap occurs. Either it was known that he had issued more charters than were available for copying or it was suspected, because of the length of his pontificate and the fact that at the very beginning of his pontificate the German field hospital had officially been elevated to a knightly religious-military order. From the pontificate of Honorius III on (fol. 63^r) up to the original end of Part I on fol. 84^v the papal charters are consecutively numbered by a hand of the fifteenth century 1–67, omitting only on fol. 68^r Strehlke No. 339, which was missed in counting. These numbers are on the upper margins and have partly been cut away by the binder. In all likelihood they served to distinguish the large number of charters by only two popes, Honorius III and Gregory IX (68 charters altogether). On fol. 63 there is a rather big hole without any loss of text. On fol. 84^v–85^v there are additions by three different hands of the middle of the thirteenth century: (1) fol. 84^v a charter by Gregory IX (Strehlke No. 481), which had been copied once before on fol. 81^r; (2) fol. 85^r two charters by Innocent IV (Strehlke Nos. 523, 497). Towards the end of fol. 85^r another charter by Innocent IV (Strehlke No. 531 footnote) was erased. It carries over to fol. 85^v, but breaks off incomplete at the end, and in the text there are erasures of one and three lines, respectively; (3) fol. 85^v, following the incomplete papal charter, a charter by King Baldwin IV of Jerusalem for Archbishop William II of Tyre (Strehlke No. 15) was copied, with a final note: *Hoc privilegium habet ecclesia Tyrensis.* Fol. 86^r–89^r are vacant. On fol. 89^v a hand of the middle of the thirteenth century copied Strehlke No. 1 as an obvious addition.

Part II

Leaves 90^r–153^v. Bullary II of the Order of the Teutonic Knights of the thirteenth century. Partly "southern" and partly "northern" parchment, i.e. partly calcinated only on the flesh side and partly on both sides. Written in a book hand of the second half of the thirteenth century, which is different from the hand of Part I, in brown ink. All in one hand. Red rubrics up to fol. 122^v. From fol. 123^v on there is empty space left for rubrics, which were never inserted, but partly replaced by sideheads written by a hand of the fourteenth century. Initials in red and blue up to fol. 123^r. Some pages have holes which have been patched up with strips of parchment. Part II consists of eight *quaterniones*, some of which are irregular, so that they are best described individually:

(1) fol. 90^{r}–97^{v} 90 91 92 93 94 95 96 97

(2) fol. 98^{r}–105^{v} (regular *quaternio*)

(3) fol. 106^{r}–113^{v} (regular *quaternio*)

(4) fol. 114^{r}–121^{v} 114 115 116 117 118 119 120 121

(5) fol. 122^{r}–129^{v} (regular *quaternio*)

(6) fol. 130^{r}–137^{v} (regular *quaternio*)

(7) fol. 138^{r}–145^{v} (regular *quaternio*)

(8) fol. 146^{r}–153^{v} 146 147 148 149 150 151 152 153

The quires are unnumbered, but there is a catchword at the end of the second quire. The charters have been numbered on the upper margin, by a hand of the fifteenth century, consecutively from *I* to *XC* on fol. 123^{r}. There is a counting mistake by ten on fol. 112^{v} (see Table of Concordance), which continues to the end and increases to 11 on fol. 120^{v} by one charter having been missed in counting, so that on fol. 90^{r}–123^{r} we have not 90 charters, as the numbering suggests, but 101. Size of page 29·5 × 215 millimeters, size of written area 210 × 120 millimeters. Two columns of 33 lines each. Lead pencil ruling with double vertical bounding lines. Pricking holes still visible.

Contents: Fol. 90^{r} we find the following rubric: *In hoc libro continentur rescripta libertatum et indulgentiarum, que hospitali sancte Marie Theutonicorum Ierosolimitano ab apostolica sede sunt concessa, que admodum in provinciali et in registro domini pape continentur.* In his Table of Contents (Merseburg, *Deutsches Zentralarchiv*, Ms. Rep. 94.V.E.b2, fol. 3^{r}), Strehlke reported the following as pertaining to this page: *Membranae inscripta* (!) *est: Versus finem et Ungaricam terram Borzae spectantiam* (!) *et Livoniam.* This notice is not found in the manuscript today. From fol. 90^{r}–123^{r} we have a pure bullary of only papal charters, which is roughly classified according to successive pontificates. The remainder of Part II (fol. 123^{v}–153^{v}) is practically a bullary, containing mostly papal charters. But towards the end it also contains charters by dignitaries other than the pope, so that it cannot be called a pure bullary. This part is clearly distinct from the first section of Part II in that both the numbering and the rubrics stop where the second section begins, as do the initials. Also, in many cases in the second section, the papal registers are indicated as the primary source from which the copy was taken, and the copyist, a certain Martin, is named. The classification of this section, however, is clearly not according to successive pontificates, but to geographical areas: Bohemia (Strehlke No. 176), Hungary (Strehlke Nos. 164, 167, 165, 166, 168 with Strehlke No. 177 concerning Mergentheim in Germany interspersed after No. 166). The rest indiscriminately pertains to Prussia and Livonia. This classification gives reason to suppose that, while the papal registers were the primary source for the papal charters, the copies in the manuscript were not taken directly from the registers but rather through the medium of a *provinciale*, as indicated in the rubric on fol. 90ʳ, which certainly comprised Prussia and Livonia as the countries taking up the bulk of the second section, but may also have included Bohemia and Hungary, whereas the one piece for Mergentheim seems to have gone astray.

Part III

Leaves 154ʳ–169ᵛ. Continuation of the Cartulary of the Order of the Teutonic Knights, but pertaining to the Holy Land exclusively. "Northern" parchment. Written by various hands of the late thirteenth century in cursive business hands in brown ink. Neither rubrics nor initials. Two unnumbered quires of the following composition:

(1) irregular *quinternio* with one additional leaf (fol. 154ʳ–164ᵛ)

(2) regular *binio* with one additional leaf (fol. 165ʳ–169ᵛ). Fol. 169a and 170 are paper end leaves to Part III. Size of page 295 × 215 millimeters. Size of written area varying between 240 × 160 millimeters (for pages with one column) and 230 × 130 millimeters (for pages with two columns). Fol. 154ʳ two columns of 39 lines each. Fol. 154ʳ–157ʳ one column of 43 lines. Fol. 157ᵛ is vacant. Fol. 158ʳ–161ᵛ two columns of 33 lines each. Fol. 162ʳ–169ᵛ one column of 45–46 lines, varying from page to page. Scored ruling with single vertical bounding lines. No pricking holes visible.

Part IV

Leaves 171ʳ–318ᵛ. Copy, executed in Konstanz in 1445 by Ulrich Mollitor, notary public, of two *inspeximus* of papal and imperial or royal charters. Paper quires, each covered on both ends by a parchment leaf, which was also used for the text of the copy. Written in one cursive business hand of the fifteenth century in black ink. No rubrics. Black initials as indicated on the margin by corresponding very small letters. Unnumbered quires, no catch words are visible. Three quires of 26 leaves each (fol. 171 parchment, fol. 172–195 paper, fol. 196 parchment; fol. 197 parchment, fol. 198–221 paper, fol. 222 parchment; fol. 223 parchment, fol. 224–247 paper, fol. 248 parchment) and one quire of 14 leaves (fol. 249 parchment, fol. 250–261 paper, fol. 262 parchment) in the first section of papal charters and two quires of 24 leaves (fol. 263 parchment, fol. 264–285 paper, fol. 286 parchment; fol. 287 parchment, fol. 288–309 paper, fol. 310 parchment) and one *quaternio* (fol. 311 parchment, fol. 312–317 paper, fol. 318 parchment) in the second section of royal charters. Size of page 295 × 215 millimeters, size of written area 235 × 145 millimeters. One column of mostly 27 lines. Unruled with single vertical bounding lines. No pricking holes visible.

Contents: Fol. 171^{r}–262^{v}, Mollitor's copy of *inspeximus* of papal charters for the Teutonic Knights executed by Cardinal Julian of the title of S. Angelo at the Council of Basle on 9 September 1434. Fol. 263^{r}–317^{r} Mollitor's copy of *inspeximus* of imperial and German royal charters for the Teutonic Knights executed by Louis, Count Palatine of the Rhine and Duke of Bavaria, on 21 March 1428. Fol. 317^{v}–318^{v} authentication of both subsections by Ulrich Mollitor, notary public.

Part V

Leaves 319^{r}–352^{v}. Series of charters concerning the Neumark. "Northern" parchment. Written in one cursive business hand of the fifteenth century in brown ink. Neither rubrics nor initials. Unnumbered quires without catchwords. Part V consists of the following quires: one *sexternio* (fol. 319^{r}–330^{v}, 319^{v} and 330^{r} and^{v} being vacant), one *quinternio* (fol. 331^{r}–340^{v}), one *sexternio* (fol. 341^{r}–352^{v}). Size of page 295 × 215 millimeters, size of written area 230 × 160 millimeters. One column of 39 lines. Scored ruling with single vertical bounding lines. No pricking holes visible.

Contents: Fol. 319^{r} only the superscription: *Transsumpta vber die newe margk vnd privilegia, die do liegen im hawss Friessach.* The second part of the superscription actually refers to Part VI. As the superscription is written in a hand of the seventeenth century, it must be assumed that Parts V and VI were together at least since then. Fol. 319^{v} is vacant. Fol. 320^{r}–352^{v}: Undated copy of *inspeximus* of several charters concerning the acquisition of the Neumark by the Order of the Teutonic Knights, executed by Francis, Bishop of Ermland

Part VI

Leaves 353^{r}–366^{v}. Series of papal *generalia* and charters concerning the possessions of the Teutonic Knights in the *Ballei* Austria. "Northern" parchment. Written in one bookhand of the fifteenth century in brown ink. Neither rubrics nor initials. Only one quire, a *sexternio* with two additional leaves. Size of page 295 × 215 millimeters, size of written area 210 × 160 millimeters. One column of mostly 30 lines. Lead pencil ruling with single vertical bounding lines. No pricking holes visible.

Contents: Fol. 353^{r} only the superscription by a sixteenth century hand: *Die privilegia hy inn verschrieben vindt man in dem haws ze Fryesach vnd zu Laybach* (*cf.* above Part V, superscription on fol. 319^{r}). Fol. 353^{v}–361^{v}: undated *inspeximus* executed by Lawrence, Patriarch of Aquileia, of various papal *generalia* and charters concerning the possessions of the Teutonic Knights in Carinthia and Krain from the archives of the houses of the Order in Friesach in Carinthia and Laibach in Krain. Fol. 362^{r}–366^{v} are vacant.

Part VII

Leaves 367^{r}–370^{v}. Series of papal *generalia* and charters concerning the Teutonic Order's house in Graz. "Northern" parchment. Written in one cursive business hand of the fifteenth century in black ink. Neither rubrics nor initials. Only one quire, a *binio* (fol. 367^{r}–370^{v}). Size of page 290 × 240 millimeters, i.e. wider than the rest of the manuscript, which is 295 × 215 millimeters. The leaves were folded in on the outer margins to make the size correspond to that of the *codex*. Size of written area 250×220 millimeters. One column varying between 43 and 54 lines. No ruling at all.

Contents: Fol. 367^{r}–369^{v} series of charters as indicated above, from the archives of the Order's house in Graz in Styria. Fol. 370^{r} is vacant. Fol. 370^{v} the following superscription by the same hand as above on fol. 353^{r} (see Part VI): *Dise privilegia sind in dem haws zu Grecz alls hy inn verschrieben sein.*

C. Table of Concordance

The following Table of Concordance shows all charters contained in the manuscript Rep. 94.V.E.b1 of the *Deutsches Zentralarchiv* in Merseburg, in the order in which they appear there. It also shows the page and number of Strehlke's edition, on and under which these charters were printed or mentioned by Strehlke. Among the papal charters it is indicated if the copy in manuscript is undated. In many instances this makes it impossible to clearly identify the charter in Strehlke's edition, because there could be various issues of a given charter within the same pontificate, distinguishable only by the date. In such cases, the various possibilities are shown in the Strehlke column.

Part I

Ms.	*Strehlke*	*Ms.*	*Strehlke*
fol. 1^r	p. 120 no. 128	fol. 18^v no. 29	p. 150 no. 153
4^v no. 1	p. 4 no. 3	19^r no. 30	p. 60 no. 76
6^r no. 2	p. 2 no. 2	19^r no. 31	p. 55 no. 69
6^v no. 3	p. 12 no. 12	19^v no. 32	p. 33 no. 41
6^v no. 4	p. 13 no. 14	20^r no. 33	p. 55 no. 70
7^r no. 5	p. 11 no. 11	20^v no. 34	p. 8 no. 7
7^v no. 6	p. 6 no. 5	21^r no. 35	p. 61 no. 77
8^r no. 7	p. 10 no. 10	21^r no. 36	p. 64 no. 81
8^r no. 8	p. 13 no. 13	21^v no. 37	p. 62 no. 78
8^v no. 9	p. 15 no. 16	21^v no. 38	p. 63 no. 79
8^v no. 10	p. 16 no. 17	22^v no. 39	p. 64 no. 82
9^r no. 11	p. 17 no. 18	22^v no. 40	p. 23 no. 26
9^v no. 12	p. 17 no. 19	23^r no. 41	p. 7 no. 6
9^v no. 13	p. 19 no. 21	23^r no. 42	p. 9 no. 8
10^r no. 14	p. 10 no. 9	23^v no. 43	p. 22 no. 25
10^v no. 15	p. 20 no. 22	24^r no. 44	p. 23 no. 27
10^v no. 16	p. 21 no. 23	24^r no. 45	p. 27 no. 34
11^r no. 17	p. 30 no. 37	24^v no. 46	p. 28 no. 35
11^v no. 18	p. 5 no. 4	25^r no. 47	p. 29 no. 36
11^v no. 19	p. 42 no. 52	25^r no. 48	p. 26 no. 31
12^r no. 20	p. 43 no. 53	25^v no. 49	p. 41 no. 50
12^v no. 21	p. 48 no. 59	25^v no. 50	p. 24 no. 28
13^r no. 22	p. 47 no. 58	25^v no. 51	p. 45 no. 55
15^r no. 23	p. 49 no. 60	26^r no. 52	p. 41 no. 49
15^r no. 24	p. 51 no. 63	26^r no. 53	p. 45 no. 56
16^r no. 25	p. 53 no. 65	26^v no. 54	p. 46 no. 57
17^r no. 26	p. 54 no. 66	26^v no. 55	p. 25 no. 29
17^v no. 27	p. 54 no. 67	27^r no. 56	p. 26 no. 30
18^r no. 28	p. 55 no. 68	27^r no. 57	p. 27 no. 32

Ms.	*Strehlke*
fol. 27^{r} no. 58	p. 21 no. 24
27^{v} no. 59	p. 36 no. 45
28^{r} no. 60	p. 67 no. 85
28^{r} no. 61	p. 50 no. 62
28^{v} no. 62	p. 32 no. 40
29^{r} no. 63	p. 34 no. 43
29^{r} no. 64	p. 60 no. 75
29^{v} no. 65	p. 66 no. 84
30^{r} no. 66	p. 40 no. 48
30^{r} no. 67	p. 53 no. 64
30^{v} no. 68	p. 63 no. 80
31^{r} no. 69	p. 70 no. 88
31^{r} no. 70	p. 68 no. 86
31^{v} no. 71	p. 70 no. 89
32^{r} no. 72	p. 69 no. 87
32^{v} no. 73	p. 31 no. 39
32^{v} no. 74	p. 73 no. 92
32^{v} no. 75	p. 34 no. 42
33^{r} no. 76	p. 57 no. 73
33^{v} no. 77	p. 72 no. 91
fol. 34^{r} no. 78	p. 58 no. 74
34^{v} no. 79	p. 72 no. 90
34^{v} no. 80	p. 35 no. 44
35^{r} no. 81	p. 50 no. 61
35^{v} no. 82	p. 37 no. 46
36^{v} no. 83	p. 65 no. 83
37^{r} no. 84	p. 56 no. 71
37^{v} no. 85	p. 141 no. 141
37^{v} no. 86	p. 141 no. 142
38^{r} no. 87	p. 148 no. 152
38^{v} no. 88	p. 142 no. 143
39^{r} no. 89	p. 143 no. 145
40^{r} no. 90	p. 143 no. 146
40^{r} no. 91	p. 147 no. 150
41^{r} no. 92	p. 241 no. 260
42^{r} no. 93	p. 143 no. 147
42^{v} no. 94	p. 145 no. 149 and p. 150 no. 154
43^{v} no. 95	p. 229 no. 235
44^{r} no. 96	p. 155 no. 158
45^{r}	p. 74 no. 95; inserted p. 63 no. 79
46^{r}	p. 74 no. 97; inserted p. 48 no. 59
46^{v}	p. 74 no. 96; inserted p. 60 no. 76
47^{v}	p. 74 no. 94; inserted p. 55 no. 70
48^{r}	p. 74 no. 93; inserted p. 55 no. 69
49^{r}	p. 18 no. 20
51^{r} no. 97	p. 155 no. 159
51^{r} no. 98	p. 157 no. 163
52^{r} no. 99	p. 137 no. 139
53^{r} no. 100	p. 132 no. 131
53^{r} no. 101	p. 134 no. 134
53^{v} no. 102	p. 135 no. 135
54^{r} no. 103	p. 136 no. 136
54^{r} no. 104	p. 137 no. 138; inserted p. 136 no. 136
55^{r} no. 105	p. 139 no. 140; inserted p. 133 no. 132 and the following six charters
55^{v} no. 106	p. 132 no. 131
55^{v} no. 107	p. 134 no. 134
56^{r} no. 108	p. 135 no. 135
56^{v} no. 109	p. 136 no. 136
56^{v} no. 110	p. 129 no. 129
57^{v} no. 111	p. 137 no. 138; inserted p. 136 no. 136
58^{r} no. 112	p. 131 no. 130
58^{v} no. 113	p. 134 no. 133
58^{v} no. 114	p. 136 no. 137
59^{r}	p. 263 no. 295

Ms.	*Strehlke*
fol. 59^r	p. 264 no. 296
60^r	p. 270 no. 301
60^r	p. 39 no. 47
60^r	p. 142 no. 144
60^v	Beginning of a letter by Pope Honorius III to Master Hermann and the Brethren of the Teutonic Order; address only up to *apostolicam benedictionem*. Unidentified and not printed by Strehlke.
62^v	p. 270 no. 302
63^r no. 1	p. 44 no. 54
63^v no. 2	p. 281 no. 309
63^v no. 3	p. 334 no. 405 (Potthast 7696) with date: 1221 March 1
63^v no. 4	p. 275 no. 305 or p. 284 no. 313 or p. 331 no. 397 (undated)
64^r no. 5	p. 292 no. 323 or p. 324 no. 371 or p. 326 no. 382 or p. 382 no. 386 (undated)
64^r no. 6	p. 334 no. 404 (undated)
64^v no. 7	p. 296 no. 328
65^r no. 8	p. 282 no. 310 (undated)
65^r no. 9	p. 305 no. 341
66^r no. 10	p. 302 no. 336
66^r no. 11	p. 306 no. 342
66^v no. 12	p. 332 no. 401 (undated)
66^v no. 13	p. 295 no. 327 (undated)
67^r no. 14	p. 301 no. 335 (undated)
67^r no. 15	p. 228 no. 317 (undated)
67^v no. 16	p. 290 no. 320 or p. 325 no. 377 (undated)
67^v no. 17	p. 294 no. 325 (undated)
68^r no. 18	p. 294 no. 326 (undated)
68^r	p. 304 no. 339 (undated)
68^r no. 19	p. 300 no. 332 (undated)
68^v no. 20	p. 335 no. 406 (undated)
68^v no. 21	p. 332 no. 400 (undated)
69^r no. 22	p. 304 no. 340 (undated)
69^r no. 23	p. 293 no. 324 (undated)
69^r no. 24	p. 340 no. 415 (undated)
69^v no. 25	p. 301 no. 334 (undated)
69^v no. 26	p. 303 no. 338 (undated)
69^v no. 27	p. 303 no. 337 or p. 326 no. 380 (undated)
70^r no. 28	p. 299 no. 331 (undated)
70^r no. 29	p. 337 no. 410 (undated)
70^r no. 30	p. 333 no. 403 (undated)
70^v no. 31	p. 280 no. 307 or p. 307 no. 343 (undated)
70^v no. 32	p. 280 no. 308 (undated)
71^r no. 33	p. 329 no. 390
71^r no. 34	p. 291 no. 322 or p. 331 no. 396 (undated)
71^v no. 35	p. 287 no. 316 or p. 327 no. 384 (undated)
71^v no. 36	p. 297 no. 329 (undated)

Ms.	*Strehlke*
fol. 72^{r} no. 37	p. 288 no. 318 or p. 326 no. 381 (undated)
72^{v} no. 38	p. 338 no. 413 (undated)
72^{v} no. 39	p. 320 no. 367 or p. 325 no. 378 (undated)
73^{r} no. 40	p. 286 no. 315 (undated)
73^{r} no. 41	p. 289 no. 319 (undated)
73^{v} no. 42	p. 323 no. 369 or p. 324 no. 372 (undated)
73^{v} no. 43	p. 336 no. 408 (undated)
73^{v} no. 44	p. 333 no. 402 (undated)
74^{r} no. 45	p. 337 no. 411 (undated)
74^{r} no. 46	p. 283 no. 312 (undated)
74^{r} no. 47	p. 283 no. 311 or p. 331 no. 395 (undated)
74^{v} no. 48	p. 325 no. 379 or p. 329 nos. 391.392 (undated)
74^{v} no. 49	p. 290 no. 321 (undated)
75^{r} no. 50	p. 298 no. 330 (undated)
75^{r} no. 51	p. 326 no. 383 (undated)
75^{v} no. 52	p. 294 no. 326 (undated)
75^{v} no. 53	p. 300 no. 333 (undated)
76^{r} no. 54	p. 330 no. 393
76^{v} no. 55	p. 148 no. 151
76^{v} no. 56	p. 327 no. 385
76^{v} no. 57	p. 322 no. 368
77^{r} no. 58	p. 272 no. 303
78^{r} no. 59	p. 275 no. 306
80^{r} no. 60	p. 284 no. 314 or p. 325 no. 375 or p. 332 no. 399 (undated)
80^{v} no. 61	p. 340 no. 416
81^{r} no. 62	p. 341 no. 418
81^{r} no. 63	p. 345 no. 428
81^{v} no. 64	p. 342 no. 422
81^{v} no. 65	p. 346 no. 435
82^{r} no. 66	p. 349 no. 449
82^{v} no. 67	p. 343 no. 424
84^{v}	p. 341 no. 418
85^{r}	p. 371 no. 523
85^{r}	p. 365 no. 497
85^{r}	p. 375 no. 531 footnote
85^{v}	p. 14 no. 15
89^{v}	p. 1 no. 1

Part II

Ms.	*Strehlke*
90^{r} no. 1	p. 281 no. 309
90^{r} no. 2	p. 334 no. 405 (undated)
90^{v} no. 3	p. 275 no. 305 or p. 284 no. 313 or p. 331 no. 397(undated)
90^{v} no. 4	p. 336 no. 408 (undated)
91^{r} no. 5	p. 295 no. 327 (undated)
91^{v} no. 6	p. 293 no. 324 (undated)

Ms.	*Strehlke*
fol. 91^{v} no. 7	p. 323 no. 369 or p. 324 no. 372 (undated)
92^{r} no. 8	p. 280 no. 308 (undated)
92^{r} no. 9	p. 148 no. 151
92^{v} no. 10	p. 332 no. 401 (undated)
92^{v} no. 11	p. 334 no. 404 (undated)
92^{v} no. 12	p. 300 no. 332 (undated)
93^{r} no. 13	p. 300 no. 333 (undated)
93^{r} no. 14	p. 299 no. 331 (undated)
93^{r} no. 15	p. 314 no. 356 (undated)
93^{v} no. 16	p. 317 no. 360 (undated)
94^{v} no. 17	p. 307 no. 345 (undated)
94^{v} no. 18	p. 284 no. 314 or p. 325 no. 375 or p. 332 no. 399 (undated)
95^{v} no. 19	p. 292 no. 323 or p. 324 no. 371 or p. 326 no. 382 or p. 328 no. 386 (undated)
96^{v} no. 20	p. 333 no. 402 (undated)
96^{r} no. 21	p. 283 no. 311 or p. 331 no. 395 (undated)
96^{r} no. 22	p. 309 no. 348 (undated)
96^{v} no. 23	p. 306 no. 342 or p. 320 no. 365 (undated)
97^{r} no. 24	p. 304 no. 339 (undated)
97^{r} no. 25	p. 335 no. 406 (undated)
97^{v} no. 26	p. 301 no. 334 (undated)
97^{v} no. 27	p. 303 no. 338 (undated)
97^{v} no. 28	p. 287 no. 316 or p. 327 no. 348 (undated)
98^{r} no. 29	p. 286 no. 315 (undated)
98^{r} no. 30	p. 333 no. 403 (undated)
98^{v} no. 31	p. 332 no. 400 (undated)
98^{v} no. 32	p. 323 no. 370 or p. 325 no. 374 or p. 329 no. 390 or p. 331 no. 394 (undated)
99^{r} no. 33	p. 282 no. 310 (undated)
99^{v} no. 34	p. 313 no. 355 (undated)
100^{r} no. 35	p. 308 no. 346 (undated)
100^{v} no. 36	p. 309 no. 347 (undated)
100^{v} no. 37	p. 301 no. 335 (undated)
101^{r} no. 38	p. 288 no. 317 (undated)
101^{r} no. 39	p. 294 no. 326 (undated)
101^{v} no. 40	p. 310 no. 350 or p. 320 no. 366 or p. 325 no. 376 (undated)
101^{v} no. 41	p. 318 no. 361 or p. 328 no. 387 (undated)
101^{v} no. 42	p. 310 no. 349 (undated)
102^{r} no. 43	p. 288 no. 318 or p. 326 no. 381 (undated)
102^{v} no. 44	p. 289 no. 319 (undated)
102^{v} no. 45	p. 335 no. 407 (undated)
102^{v} no. 46	p. 314 no. 357 (undated)
103^{v} no. 47	p. 328 no. 389 (undated)
103^{v} no. 48	p. 290 no. 320 or p. 325 no. 377 (undated)
103^{v} no. 49	p. 311 no. 351 (undated)
103^{v} no. 50	p. 302 no. 336 (undated)
104^{r} no. 51	p. 304 no. 340 (undated)

Ms.	*Strehlke*
fol. 104v no. 52	p. 290 no. 321 (undated)
105r no. 53	p. 291 no. 322 or p. 331 no. 396 (undated)
105v no. 54	p. 305 no. 341 or p. 307 no. 344 (undated)
106r no. 55	p. 327 no. 385 or p. 328 no. 388 (undated)
106v no. 56	p. 280 no. 307 or p. 307 no. 343 (undated)
106v no. 57	p. 311 no. 352 (undated)
106v no. 58	p. 325 no. 379 or p. 329 nos. 391. 392 (undated)
107r no. 59	p. 297 no. 329 (undated)
107v no. 60	p. 320 no. 367 or p. 325 no. 378 (undated)
108r no. 61	p. 337 no. 411 (undated)
108v no. 62	p. 283 no. 312 (undated)
108v no. 63	p. 319 no. 363 (undated)
109r no. 64	p. 318 no. 362 (undated)
109v no. 65	p. 296 no. 328 or p. 320 no. 364 (undated)
110v no. 66	p. 294 no. 325 (undated)
110v no. 67	p. 303 no. 337 or p. 326 no. 380 (undated)
110v no. 68	p. 337 no. 410 (undated)
111r no. 69	p. 311 no. 353 (undated)
111r no. 70	p. 315 no. 358 (undated)
112r no. 71	p. 298 no. 330 (undated)
112r no. 72	p. 338 no. 412 (undated)
112v no. 63	p. 338 no. 413 (undated) (*LXIII* instead of *LXXIII*; thus the numbering continues too low by ten)
113r no. 64	p. 326 no. 383 (undated)
113v no. 65	p. 316 no. 359 (undated)
113v no. 66	p. 339 no. 414 (undated)
113v no. 67	p. 313 no. 354 (undated)
114r no. 68	p. 340 no. 415 (undated)
114r no. 69	p. 336 no. 409 (undated)
114r no. 70	p. 322 no. 368
115r no. 71	p. 343 no. 424
117v no. 72	p. 394 no. 575
117v no. 73	p. 391 no. 567 (undated)
118r no. 74	p. 376 no. 534 (undated)
118v no. 75	p. 397 no. 581 (undated)
118v no. 76	p. 380 no. 539 (undated)
119r no. 77	p. 394 no. 577 (undated)
119r no. 78	p. 405 no. 604 (undated)
119v no. 79	p. 379 no. 537 (undated)
120r no. 80	p. 381 no. 540 or p. 389 no. 563a (undated)
120r no. 81	p. 397 no. 583 or p. 398 no. 584 (undated)
120v no. 82	p. 401 no. 594 (undated)
120v	p. 382 no. 541 or p. 583 no. 543 or p. 398 no. 586 or p. 399 no. 588 (undated)
121r no. 83	p. 410 no. 617 (undated)
121v no. 84	p. 411 no. 618 (undated)

Library of
Davidson College

Ms.	*Strehlke*
fol. 121^{v} no. 85	p. 395 no. 578 (undated)
121^{v} no. 86	p. 404 no. 603 (undated)
122^{r} no. 87	p. 389 no. 563 (undated)
122^{v} no. 88	p. 392 no. 568 or no. 570 (undated)
122^{v} no. 89	p. 393 no. 574 (undated)
123^{r} no. 90	p. 387 no. 560 or p. 388 no. 561 or p. 390 no. 565 (undated)
123^{v}	p. 161 no. 176 (undated); inserted p. 160 no. 175 (dated)
124^{v}	p. 157 no. 164 (undated)
125^{v}	p. 158 no. 167 (undated); inserted p. 156 nos. 158. 159 p. 157 no. 160 (all dated)
126^{v}	p. 158 no. 165 (undated)
127^{v}	p. 158 no. 166 (undated)
128^{r}	p. 161 no. 177 (undated)
128^{v}	p. 158 no. 168 (undated)
129^{r}	p. 229 no. 238 (undated); inserted p. 228 no. 230 (dated)
129^{v}	p. 230 no. 240 (undated)
130^{r}	p. 229 no. 236 (undated); inserted p. 228 no. 231 (dated)
130^{v}	p. 229 no. 237 (undated); inserted p. 226 no. 226 (dated)
131^{v}	p. 194 no. 200 (undated)
131^{v}	p. 194 no. 201 (undated)
132^{r}	p. 194 no. 202
133^{v}	p. 378 no. 536 (undated)
134^{r}	Erased charter by Pope Gregory IX, not to be identified
134^{v}	p. 200 no. 207 (undated); inserted p. 197 no. 205 (dated)
135^{v}	p. 233 no. 248 (undated); inserted p. 231 no. 246 (dated)
137^{r}	p. 233 no. 247; inserted p. 231 no. 245
137^{v}	p. 200 no. 208 (undated)
138^{r}	p. 197 no. 206
139^{v}	p. 200 no. 209 (undated and incomplete)
140^{r}	p. 231 no. 244
141^{r}	p. 230 no. 239 (undated); inserted p. 228 no. 230 (undated)
141^{v}	p. 235 no. 250 (undated)
142^{r}	p. 230 no. 241
142^{v}	p. 226 no. 226
143^{r}	Potthast no. 7628; not printed in Strehlke
143^{r}	p. 231 no. 243
143^{v}	p. 231 no. 245
144^{r}	p. 228 no. 229; inserted p. 226 nos. 226. 227
145^{v}	p. 228 no. 230
146^{r}	p. 228 no. 232
146^{v}	p. 229 no. 233
147^{r}	p. 229 no. 234
147^{v}	p. 226 no. 225 (undated)
148^{r}	p. 226 no. 227
148^{v}	p. 230 no. 242; inserted p. 226 no. 226
149^{r}	p. 229 no. 237 (undated); inserted p. 226 no. 226
150^{r}	p. 226 no. 228; inserted p. 226 nos. 226. 227

Part III

Ms.	*Strehlke*	*Ms.*	*Strehlke*
fol. 154^{r}	p. 84 no. 105	fol. 163^{r}	p. 103 no. 117
154^{r}	p. 106 no. 119	163^{v}	p. 96 no. 114
155^{v}	p. 111 no. 121	164^{r}	p. 90 no. 111
156^{v}	p. 109 no. 120	165^{r}	p. 41 no. 51
157^{r}	p. 114 no. 122	165^{r}	p. 30 no. 38
158^{r}	p. 78 no. 100	165^{r}	p. 25 no. 29
160^{r}	p. 88 no. 108	165^{r}	p. 91 no. 112
160^{v}	p. 89 no. 109	166^{v}	p. 75 no. 98
161^{r}	p. 89 no. 110	167^{r}	p. 77 no. 99
161^{v}	p. 82 no. 103	167^{v}	p. 95 no. 113
162^{r}	p. 97 no. 115	167^{v}	p. 115 no. 125
162^{r}	p. 104 no. 118	168^{r}	p. 98 no. 116

Part IV

171^{r}	p. 182 no. 196; inserted are the following 88 charters
172^{r}	p. 174 no. 193
174^{r} no. 1	p. 274 no. 304
174^{v} no. 2	p. 160 no. 174
174^{v} no. 3	p. 275 no. 306
178^{r} no. 4	p. 281 no. 309
178^{v} no. 5	p. 291 no. 322
179^{v} no. 6	p. 284 no. 314
181^{r} no. 7	p. 290 no. 321
182^{r} no. 8	p. 290 no. 320
182^{v} no. 9	p. 287 no. 316
183^{r} no. 10	p. 284 no. 313
183^{v} no. 11	p. 295 no. 327
184^{v} no. 12	p. 296 no. 328
185^{v} no. 13	p. 303 no. 338
185^{v} no. 14	p. 304 no. 339
186^{v} no. 15	p. 304 no. 340
186^{v} no. 16	p. 307 no. 343
187^{r} no. 17	p. 306 no. 342
187^{v} no. 18	p. 309 no. 347
187^{v} no. 19	p. 312 no. 353
188^{v} no. 20	p. 310 no. 350
188^{v} no. 21	p. 313 no. 354

189^{r} no. 22	p. 316 no. 359
189^{v} no. 23	p. 314 no. 356
190^{r} no. 24	p. 318 no. 362
191^{r} no. 25	p. 326 no. 380
191^{v} no. 26	p. 327 no. 385
192^{r} no. 1	p. 348 no. 442
192^{v} no. 2	p. 349 no. 443
193^{r} no. 3	p. 349 no. 444
193^{v} no. 4	p. 349 no. 446
194^{r} no. 5	p. 343 no. 424
197^{v} no. 6	p. 346 no. 431
198^{r} no. 6	p. 346 no. 435
198^{v} no. 10	p. 352 no. 454
199^{r} no. 11	p. 347 no. 439
199^{r} no. 12	p. 351 no. 451 (*cf.* p. 342 no. 420 footnotes)
200^{r} no. 13	p. 353 no. 458
202^{v} no. 14	p. 353 no. 465
202^{v} no. 15	p. 354 no. 466
203^{r} no. 1	p. 366 no. 499
203^{v} no. 2	p. 364 no. 493
205^{v} no. 3	p. 369 no. 513
205^{v} no. 4	p. 369 no. 514
206^{r} no. 5	p. 372 no. 526
206^{v} no. 6	p. 373 no. 528

Ms.	*Strehlke*	*Ms.*	*Strehlke*
fol. 207^{r} no. 1	p. 380 no. 538	fol. 218^{r}	p. 415 no. 633
207^{r} no. 2	p. 384 no. 545	218^{v}	p. 414 no. 630
207^{v} no. 3	p. 385 no. 552	219^{r}	p. 414 no. 631
208^{r} no. 4	p. 387 no. 560	219^{v}	p. 424 no. 663
209^{r} no. 5	p. 388 no. 562	219^{v}	p. 424 no. 664
209^{r} no. 6	p. 389 no. 563	221^{r}	p. 437 no. 692
209^{v} no. 7	p. 390 no. 564	222^{v}	p. 438 no. 693
210^{r} no. 8	p. 392 no. 570	223^{v}	p. 441 no. 695
210^{v} no. 9	p. 393 no. 572	224^{r}	p. 442 no. 696
212^{v} no. 10	p. 393 no. 574	225^{v}	p. 444 no. 699
213^{r} no. 11	p. 397 no. 583	229^{r}	p. 448 no. 701
213^{v} no. 12	p. 399 no. 588	231^{v}	p. 451 no. 703; inserted p. 275 no. 306
214^{v} no. 13	p. 399 no. 590	235^{v}	p. 452 no. 704
214^{v} no. 14	p. 400 no. 592	240^{r}	p. 457 no. 707
215^{r} no. 15	p. 400 no. 593	241^{v}	p. 460 no. 709
215^{v}	p. 419 no. 646	243^{v}	p. 459 no. 708
217^{v}	p. 411 no. 619		

Ms.	*Strehlke*
244^{v}	p. 465 no. 713; inserted p. 459 no. 708
246^{v}	p. 236 no. 251
248^{r}	p. 462 no. 710
249^{r}	p. 464 no. 711
249^{v}	p. 464 no. 712
250^{r}	p. 466 no. 715; inserted p. 260 no. 293
252^{v}	p. 179 no. 195
255^{v}	p. 469 no. 719; inserted p. 464 no. 712
257^{r}	p. 468 no. 718; inserted p. 466 no. 715
263^{r}	p. 176 no. 194; inserted are the following 39 charters
263^{r}	p. 261 no. 294
264^{r}	p. 239 no. 254
265^{r}	p. 239 no. 253
266^{r}	p. 240 no. 257
267^{v}	p. 241 no. 258
268^{v}	p. 241 no. 259
270^{r}	p. 241 no. 260
272^{r}	p. 242 no. 261
273^{v}	p. 242 no. 262
274^{v}	p. 242 no. 263; inserted p. 241 no. 259
276^{v}	p. 243 no. 264
277^{r}	p. 243 no. 266
277^{v}	p. 243 no. 265
278^{v}	p. 244 no. 267
279^{v}	p. 244 no. 268
280^{r}	p. 244 no. 269
281^{v}	p. 244 no. 271; inserted p. 239 no. 252
283^{r}	p. 245 no. 272; inserted p. 240 no. 255
284^{r}	p. 244 no. 270; inserted p. 244 no. 268

Ms.	*Strehlke*
fol. 285^{v}	p. 246 no. 273; inserted p. 240 no. 257
288^{r}	p. 246 no. 274; inserted p. 240 no. 257
290^{r}	p. 246 no. 275
290^{r}	p. 248 no. 278; inserted p. 240 no. 257
293^{r}	p. 247 no. 277
294^{v}	p. 246 no. 276
295^{v}	p. 248 no. 280
296^{r}	p. 249 no. 281; inserted p. 246 no. 275
297^{r}	p. 168 no. 188
298^{r}	p. 248 no. 279
299^{r}	p. 249 no. 283; inserted p. 248 no. 278, in which is, in turn, inserted p. 240 no. 257
302^{v}	p. 249 no. 282; inserted p. 246 no. 276
305^{r}	p. 249 no. 284
306^{r}	p. 250 no. 285
307^{v}	p. 252 no. 286
308^{v}	p. 252 no. 287
310^{r}	p. 252 no. 288; inserted German translation of p. 240 no. 257
312^{v}	p. 257 no. 290
314^{r}	p. 257 no. 291
315^{r}	p. 258 no. 292
317^{v}	p. 190 no. 198

Part V

320^{r}	p. 214 no. 223; inserted are the following ten charters
320^{r}	p. 208 no. 215
321^{v}	p. 204 no. 213
323^{v}	p. 208 no. 214
325^{r}	p. 209 no. 216
328^{r}	p. 209 no. 217; inserted p. 209 no. 216
332^{v}	p. 212 no. 218; inserted p. 209 no. 217, in which is, in turn, inserted p. 209 no. 216
336^{v}	p. 213 no. 221; inserted p. 209 no. 217, in which is, turn, inserted p. 209 no. 216.
340^{r}	p. 213 no. 219; inserted p. 209 no. 217, in which is, in turn, inserted p. 209 no. 216
344^{v}	p. 214 no. 222; inserted p. 209 no. 217, in which is, in turn, inserted p. 209 no. 216
348^{v}	p. 213 no. 220; inserted p. 209 no. 217, in which is, in turn, inserted p. 209 no. 216

Part VI

Ms.	*Strehlke*
353^r	p. 187 no. 197; inserted are the following ten charters
353^v	p. 413 no. 628
354^r	p. 344 no. 427
354^v	p. 424 no. 662
355^r	p. 386 no. 555
355^v	p. 389 no. 563
356^r	p. 165 no. 184; inserted p. 165 no. 183, in which is, in turn, inserted p. 163 no. 179
357^v	p. 164 no. 182
357^v	p. 166 no. 185
358^r	p. 171 no. 190; inserted p. 166 no. 186, in which is, in turn, inserted p. 163 no. 180, and p. 167 no. 187, in which is, in turn, inserted p. 163 no. 181
360^v	p. 173 no. 192

Part VII

367^r	p. 192 no. 199; inserted are the following seven charters
367^r	p. 305 no. 341
367^r	p. 325 no. 375
367^v	p. 364 no. 492
367^v	p. 346 no. 433
367^v	p. 410 no. 614
367^v	p. 169 no. 189; inserted p. 162 no. 178
369^r	p. 172 no. 191

The following is a table of charters printed in Strehlke's *Tabulae ordinis Theutonici* and contained in the Merseburg manuscript. As opposed to the preceding table, it does not start from the manuscript, but lists the charters contained therein in the sequence in which they were printed in Strehlke's edition. Their exact place in the manuscript can then be determined from the preceding list. The main purpose of the list is to show which material appears in which part of the manuscript, and which charters appear more than once. Due to the fact that undated re-issues of papal charters from the same pontificate cannot be identified properly, we have given in these instances a combination of Strehlke numbers with which the charter may be identified. These combinations appear in as many places as the number of elements of which they are composed. One must bear this in mind, particularly where a combination appears in several parts of the manuscript. There is a marked difference between an individual charter and a combination listed as appearing in more than one part of the manuscript: The individual charter actually appears more than once; the combination *may* appear more than once. To cite an example: The combination Strehlke No. 307/343 appears in Parts I and II both under No. 307 and under No. 343. We could conceivably have No. 307 in both parts in the first place, and No. 343 in the second place. The case would then not differ from an individual charter. But we could equally have No. 307 in Part I and No. 343 in Part II, or vice versa, and both in the first instance as well as in the second. We could also have No. 307 in both parts, in the first instance, and a combination of Nos. 307 and 343, in the second instance, or the reverse case.

Part I	1	2	3	4	5	6	7	8	9	10	11	12	13	14	15	16
Part II																
Part III																
Part IV																
Part V																
Part VI																
Part VII																
Part I	17	18	19	20	21	22	23	24	25	26	27	28	29	30	31	32
Part II																
Part III													29			
Part IV																
Part V																
Part VI																
Part VII																
Part I	34	35	36	37		39	40	41	42	43	44	45	46	47	48	49
Part II																
Part III					38											
Part IV																
Part V																
Part VI																
Part VII																
Part I	50		52	53	54	55	56	57	58	59	59	60	61	62	63	64
Part II																
Part III		51														
Part IV																
Part V																
Part VI																
Part VII																

Part I	65	66	67	68	69	69	70	70	71	73	74	75	76	76	77	78
Part II																
Part III																
Part IV																
Part V																
Part VI																
Part VII																
Part I	79	79	80	81	82	83	84	85	86	87	88	89	90	91	92	93
Part II																
Part III																
Part IV																
Part V																
Part VI																
Part VII																
Part I	94	95	96	97												
Part II																
Part III					98	99	100	103	105	108	109	110	111	112	113	114
Part IV																
Plat V																
Part VI																
Part VII																
Part I										128	129	130	131	131	132	133
Part II																
Part IiI	115	116	117	118	119	120	121	122	125							
Part III																
Part V																
Part VI																
Part VII																

Part I	134	134	135	135	136	136	136	136	137	138	138	139	140	141	142	143
Part II																
Part III																
Part IV																
Part V																
Part VI																
Part VII																

Part I	144	145	146	147	149	150	151	152	153	154	158	159		163		
Part II							151				158	159	160		164	165
Part III																
Part IV																
Part V																
Part VI																
Part VII																

Part I																
Part II	166	167	168		175	176	177									
Part III																
Part IV				174												
Part V																
Part VI									179	180	181	182	183	184	185	186
Part VII								178								

Part I																
Part II														200	201	202
Part III																
Part IV		188					193	194	195	196		198				
Part V																
Part VI	187			190		192					197					
Part VII			189		191								199			

Part I																
Part II	205	206	207	208	209											
Part III																
Part IV																
Part V						213	214	215	216	216	216	216	216	216	216	217
Part VI																
Part VII																

Part I																
Part II												225	226	226	226	226
Part III																
Part IV																
Part V	217	217	217	217	217	218	219	220	221	222	223					
Part VI																
Part VII																

Part I															235	
Part II	226	226	227	227	227	228	229	230	230	230	231	232	233	234		236
Part III																
Part IV																
Part V																
Part VI																
Part VII																

Part I																
Part II	237	237	238	239	240	241	242	243	244	245	245	246	247	248	250	
Part III																
Part IV																251
Part V																
Part VI																
Part VII																

Part I														260		
Part II																
Part III																
Part IV	252	253	254	255	257	257	257	257	257	257	258	259	259	260	261	262
Part V																
Part VI																
Part VII																
Part I																
Part II																
Part III																
Part IV	263	264	265	266	267	268	268	269	270	271	272	273	274	275	275	276
Part V																
Part VI																
Part VII																
Part I																
Part II																
Part III																
Part VI	276	277	278	278	279	280	281	282	283	284	285	286	287	288	290	291
Part V																
Part VI																
Part VII																
Part I									295			296		301		
Part II																
Part III																
Part IV	292			293		294										
Part V																
Part VI																
Part VII																

Part I	302	303		305/313/397	306	
Part II				305/313/397		
Part III						
Part IV			304		306	306
Part V						
Part VI						
Part VII						

Part I	307/343	308	309	310	311/395	312
Part II	307/343	308	309	310	311/395	312
Part III						
Part IV			309			
Part V						
Part VI						
Part VII						

Part I	305/313/397	314/375/399	315	316/384	317	318/381
Part II	305/313/397	314/375/399	315	316/384	317	318/381
Part III						
Part IV	313	314		316		
Part V						
Part VI						
Part VII						

Part I	319	320/377	321	322/396	323/371/382/386	324
Part II	319	320/377	321	322/396	323/371/382/386	324
Part III						
Part IV		320	321	322		
Part V						
Part VI						
Part VII						

Part I	325	326	326	327	328	329
Part II	325	326		327	328/364	329
Part III						
Part IV				327	328	
Part V						
Part VI						
Part VII						
Part I	330	331	332	333	334	335
Part II	330	331	332	333	334	335
Part III						
Part IV						
Part V						
Part VI						
Part VII						
Part I	336	337/380	338	339	340	341
Part II	336	337/380	338	339	340	341/344
Part III						
Part IV			338	339	340	
Part V						
Part VI						
Part VII						341
Part I	342	307/343				
Part II	342/365	307/343	341/344	345	346	347
Part III						
Part IV	342	343				347
Part V						
Part VI						
Part VII						

Part I						
Part II	348	349	350/366/376	351	352	353
Part III						
Part IV			350			353
Part V						
Part VI						
Part VII						

Part I						
Part II	354	355	356	357	358	359
Part III						
Part IV	354		356			359
Part V						
Part VI						
Part VII						

Part I						
Part II	360	361/387	362	363	328/364	342/365
Part III						
Part IV			362			
Part V						
Part VI						
Part VII						

Part I		367/378	368	369/372		323/371/382/386
Part II	350/366/376	367/378	368	369/372	370/374/390/394	323/371/382/386
Part III						
Part IV						
Part V						
Part VI						
Part VII						

Part I	369/372		314/375/399		320/377	367/378
Part II	369/372	370/374/382/386	314/375/399	350/366/376	320/377	367/378
Part III						
Part IV						
Part V						
Part VI						
Part VII			375			
Part I	379/391/392	337/380	318/381	323/371/382/386	383	316/384
Part II	379/391/392	337/380	318/381	323/371/382/386	383	316/384
Part III						
Part IV		380				
Part V						
Part VI						
Part VII						
Part I	385	323/371/382/386				390
Part II	385/388	323/371/382/386	361/387	385/388	389	370/374/390/394
Part III						
Part IV	385					
Part V						
Part VI						
Part VII						
Part I	379/391/392	379/391/392	393		311/395	322/396
Part II	379/391/392	379/391/392		370/374/390/394	311/395	322/396
Part III						
Part IV						
Part V						
Part VI						
Part VII						

Part I	305/313/397	314/375/399	400	401	402	403
Part II	305/313/397	314/375/399	400	401	402	403
Part III						
Part IV						
Part V						
Part VI						
Part VII						

Part I	404	405	406		408	
Part II	404	405	406	407	408	409
Part III						
Part IV						
Part V						
Part VI						
Part VII						

Part I	410	411		413		415
Part II	410	411	412	413	414	415
Part III						
Part IV						
Part V						
Part VI						
Part VII						

Part I	416	417	418	422	424	
Part II					424	
Part III						
Part IV					424	
Part V						
Part VI						427
Part VII						

Part I	428			435		
Part II						
Part III						
Part IV		431		435	439	442
Part V						
Part VI						
Part VII			433			
Part I				449		
Part II						
Part III						
Part IV	443	444	446		451	454
Part V						
Part VI						
Part VII						
Part I						497
Part II						
Part III						
Part IV	458	465	466		493	
Part V						
Part VI						
Part VII				492		
Part I					523	
Part II						
Part III						
Part IV	499		513	514		526
Part V						
Part VI						
Part VII						

Part I		531 footnote				
Part II			534	536	537	
Part III						
Part IV	528					538
Part V						
Part VI						
Part VII						

Part I						
Part II	539	540/563a	541/543/586/588	541/543/586/588		
Part III						
Part IV					545	552
Part V						
Part VI						
Part VII						

Part I						
Part II		560/561/565	560/561/565		563	540/563a
Part III						
Part IV		560		562	563	
Part V						
Part VI	555				563	
Part VII						

Part I						
Part II		560/561/565	567	568/570	568/570	
Part III						
Part IV	564				570	572
Part V						
Part VI						
Part VII						

Part I						
Part II	574	575	577	578	581	583/584
Part III						
Part IV	574					583
Part V						
Part VI						
Part VII						
Part I						
Part II	583/584	541/543/586/588	541/543/586/588			
Part III						
Part IV			588	590	592	593
Part V						
Part VI						
Part VII						
Part I						
Part II	594	603	604		617	618
Part III						
Part IV						
Part V						
Part VI						
Part VII				614		
Part I						
Part II						
Part III						
Part IV	619		630	631	633	646
Part V						
Part VI		628				
Part VII						

Part I						
Part II						
Part III						
Part IV		663	664	692	693	695
Part V						
Part VI	662					
Part VII						
Part I						
Part II						
Part III						
Part IV	696	699	701	703	704	707
Part V						
Part VI						
Part VII						
Part I						
Part II						
Part III						
Part IV	708	708	709	710	711	712
Part V						
Part VI						
Part VII						
Part I						
Part II						
Part III						
Part IV	712	713	715	715	718	719
Part V						
Part VI						
Part VII						

List of Charters Lacking in the Manuscript

The following is a list of charters published in Strehlke's *Tabulae ordinis Theutonici*, which do not appear in the Merseburg manuscript (formerly the Berlin manuscript). This list comprises both the charters which are totally lacking from the manuscript, and — with a question mark in brackets following Strehlke's number — the charters which *may* be lacking from it. That it is not always possible to determine whether a charter does appear in the manuscript or not, is due to the fact that not all charters of the manuscript, for reasons explained above in the introductory remarks to the Table of Concordance, can be properly identified in Strehlke's edition. Where, for one charter in the manuscript, we must give a combination of up to four numbers of Strehlke, of which only one actually corresponds to the charter in the manuscript, it is obvious that, by way of contrast, up to three numbers of Strehlke will not be represented in the manuscript at all, but only one number of the combination will be found there. We have no way of telling which one. We cannot, therefore, discard the possibility that any one Strehlke number of a combination of between two and four numbers may actually not be represented in the manuscript, because we only do know that any one number of a given combination is to be found there. We can only exclude from a given combination of Strehlke numbers those charters for which there is a second or third appearance in another part of the manuscript as well as a way to properly identify this second or third place. On fol. 98^{v} No. 32 of the manuscript we find an undated charter which may be identified with any of the following numbers of Strehlke: 370, 374, 390, 394. The fact that Strehlke gave the manuscript reference in the footnotes to No. 370 means nothing. Since he normally printed only the superscription, the opening words and the date of the re-issue of a charter, and since he did not normally footnote his short mentions of re-issues, he was bound to give the manuscript reference in the footnotes to the first issue of a given charter. In the case of an undated charter, it might be the second re-issue or any other re-issue of the same pontificate that actually appears in the manuscript. Only if he had made a very careful word-for-word comparison of all four issues, might he have arrived at a safe conclusion as to which issue should be identified with his undated charter on fol. 98^{v} No. 32, for occasionally re-issues even within the same pontificate show some slight variation. But this is not an absolute necessity, and in the absence of both a date and any ever-so-slight divergences in text, there would be absolutely no way to safely identify the charter on fol. 98^{v} No. 32. We have, however, no reason to assume that Strehlke did carry out such a careful investigation of the text. Had he done so, we certainly would not always get his manuscript references in the footnotes to the first issue only, but would find other cases where the reference would be to one of the re-issues only. It cannot be assumed that the compilators of the various parts of the manuscript consciously excluded all re-issues within the same pontificate from their collection, as they did not exclude all re-issues from later pontificates. They might not even have known that an earlier issue from the same pontificate existed, because, while a re-issue from a later pontificate would normally refer to the predecessor's grant, a re-issue within the same pontificate would not normally mention the fact that the same pope had granted the same charter before. In the case quoted, we must therefore list the combination of four Strehlke numbers in four different places in our preceding list of Strehlke numbers contained in the various parts of the manuscript. (In the Table of Concordance, which does not start from Strehlke's edition, but from the Merseburg manuscript, it suffices to list the combination in one place, which corresponds to fol. 98^{v} No. 32.) Under the same criteria, we must also list the combination in four places in the following list of charters missing from the manuscript, but contained in Strehlke, because we cannot tell which of the four possibilities is in the manuscript and which is not. It is evident that in such a case we include in the preceding list three possibilities which are actually false, while, due to the same lack of knowledge, there will be one false listing in the following list. One charter in the manuscript, which can theoretically correspond to four numbers in Strehlke's edition, should yet theoretically be listed only once in the preceding list, but three times in the following one. As it is, we must list it four times in both tables. The reader will have to bear this unavoidable confusion in mind. The preceding is an example of a combination of Strehlke numbers occurring in only one part and at only one place of the manuscript. Another case is more complicated, with the two undated charters appearing on fol. 72^{r} No. 37 and 102^{r} No. 43, because each of them must be identified with the combination of Strehlke Nos. 318 or 381. We could have No. 318 on fol. 72^{r} and no. 381 on fol. 102^{r}, but we could equally have Nos. 318 or 381 in both places. Or we could have No. 381 on fol. 72^{r} and No. 318 on fol. 102^{r}. There is no way of telling, and again we must include possibilities both in the preceding and the following list, of which we know that they cannot all be true, because we have only two charters, but four possibilities of identification. Again we must ask the reader to bear in mind that in every instance in which we offer a combination of Strehlke numbers in the preceding list, it will occur in the list as many times as it has elements, but that only one occurrence can be correct. Two occurrences may, but do not necessarily have to, be correct in those instances in which the same combination of Strehlke numbers occurs in two parts of the manuscript, thus corresponding to two actual charters in the manuscript which might still be the same issue, thus not really increasing the number of absolutely correct listings. Against these uncertainties we have only a small comfort to offer. In a number of cases one or several of the numbers in a given combination will reoccur elsewhere in the manuscript as a dated charter, which can then be properly identified. While this does not help us with the preceding list, it does reduce the number of questionable entries in the following list. A case in point are the two undated charters fol. 70^{v} No. 31 and fol. 106^{v} No. 56, and the dated charter on fol. 186^{v} No. 16. The latter is unquestionably Strehlke No. 343, whereas the two former may be either Strehlke No. 307 or No. 343. While we still have to list the combination Strehlke No. 307/343 in two places in the preceding list in Parts I and II, adding No. 343 in Part IV, we may, for the purpose of the following table, safely drop No. 343 altogether, because there is one properly identified copy of Strehlke No. 343 on fol. 186^{v}, and, thus, No. 343 is definitely not lacking in the manuscript. The following then is the list of charters contained in Strehlke's edition, but demonstrably or possibly missing in the manuscript:

Strehlke number:

33*	155	210	307(?)	370(?)	386(?)
72	156	211	311(?)	371(?)	387(?)
101	157	212	318(?)	372(?)	388(?)
102	161	224	323(?)	373	391(?)
104	162	249	337(?)	374(?)	392(?)
106	169	256	344(?)	376(?)	394(?)
107	170	289	361(?)	377(?)	395(?)
123	171	297	364(?)	378(?)	396(?)
124	172	298	365(?)	379(?)	397(?)
126	173	299	366(?)	381(?)	398
127	203	300	367(?)	382(?)	399(?)
148	204	305(?)	369(?)	384(?)	417

* (only cross-reference)

419
420
421
423
425
426
429
430
432
434
436
437
438
440
441
445
447
448
450
452
453
455
456
457
459
460
461
462
463
464
467
468
469
470
471
472
473
474
475
476
477
478
479
480
481
482
483
484
485
486
487
488
489
491
494
495
496
498
500
501
502
503
504
505
506
507
508
509
510
511
512
515
516
517
518
519
520
521
522
524
525
527
529
530
531
532
533
535
540(?)
541(?)
542
543(?)
544
546
547
548
549
550
551
553
554
556
557
558
561(?)
563a(?)
565(?)
566
568(?)
569
571
573
576
579
580
582
584(?)
585
586(?)
587
589
591
595
596
597
598
599
600
601
602
605
606
607
608
609
610
611
612
613
615
616
620
621
622
623
624
625
626
627
629
632
634
635
636
637
638
639
640
641
642
643
644
645
647
648
649
650
651
652
653
654
655
656
657
658
659
660
661
665
666
667
668
669
670
671
672
673
674
675
676
677
678
679
680
681
682
683
684
685
686
687
688
689
690
691
694
697
698
700
702
705
706
714
716
717
720
721
722
723
724
725

D. Reconstruction and Transmission of the Manuscript

The following remarks on the history of the manuscript, it must be stressed at the outset, are no more than a working hypothesis based on a detailed inspection of the manuscript in Merseburg itself and on the study of a microfilm supplied by the *Deutsches Zentralarchiv*. The problems connected with the history of the manuscript call for a far more penetrating study, for which the Table of Concordance, the first printed reconstruction of the sequence of documents in the manuscript, will, it is hoped, provide some material.

The manuscript as it appears today was put together (according to the handwritten repertory of the series of the Berlin Archives [Deutsches Zentralarchiv Merseburg, Rep. 94. V.E. b], drawn up between 1869 and 1874) from several individual parts by a Mr. Höfer in the early nineteenth century. The repertory assumes that the various parts of the manuscript once belonged to the Grandmaster's Archives at Marienburg, preserved after 1457 in Tapiau and later in Königsberg; however, this is only certain for Parts V and VI which were transferred from Königsberg to the *Kammer* (the public fisc), and later to the government of Marienwerder in West Prussia in 1772. It was at that time that separate archives were created for West Prussia as a result of the first division of Poland. This part was requested to be sent to Berlin in 1773.[14] It was later separated from the archives, and only returned in 1795 from the estate of Ewald Friedrich Graf von Hertzberg, a long-time Berlin archivist and foreign policy adviser of Frederick the Great of Prussia. This section of the manuscript was then still separately bound, and the old title, as recorded by the repertory, was *Privilegia teutschen Ordens. Transsumbt über die Neumark*. Thus, it is almost certain that Part IV, which contains two very comprehensive series of papal and imperial *generalia* produced in the fifteenth century (see description above p. 32), also came from the Grandmaster's archives, and was bound up with Parts V–VII. If this were not the case, the

14. *Cf.* K. Forstreuter, *Das Preussische Staatsarchiv in Königsberg. Ein geschichtlicher Rückblick mit einer Übersicht über seine Bestände* (*Veröffentlichungen der Niedersächsischen Archivverwaltung* 3, 1955), p. 37 f.

old title would reverse the present order, as Part V contains important documents concerning the acquisition of the Neumark by the Order[15], whereas Parts VI and VII contain only a few *generalia*, which were found and transcribed in the houses of Friesach, Laibach and Graz in the commanderies of Austria and Styria. Furthermore, the whole manuscript is essentially of parchment, except for the curious money-saving device of introducing paper in Part IV (see description p. 32). There are also two paper leaves (Fol. 169a and 170) which serve as end papers to Part III and do not belong to its last quire. However, the paper used for these two leaves is modern and was in all likelihood inserted by Mr. Höfer to indicate the spot where he had joined two formerly separate manuscripts. One section consisted of Parts IV–VII. Of these, Parts V–VII were together in 1795, when this part of the manuscript was returned to the Berlin Archives. But there is nothing to prevent the assumption that Part IV was also a part of the returning manuscript. If Parts V–VII formed one manuscript, they did so since the sixteenth century, for Parts VI and VII were surely together then, as the superscriptions in Parts VI and VII are in the same sixteenth-century hand. We know that Part IV was written in 1445. That Part V was also written in the fifteenth century, can be deduced from the handwriting as well as from the fact that the Neumark problem with which it is concerned was politically virulent until the fifties of that century. Part V cannot have been written before the settlement of this politically thorny question by the Diet of Nuremberg in September 1444. Part VI may have come into existence at about the same time. It cannot be later than 1446, and it was written at the request of an official of the Order who, if I am not mistaken, can first be found in this office in 1442. Part VII was written in 1445. Thus Parts IV–VII were written at about the same time, proof of efforts within the Order to have its records transcribed in the middle forties of the fifteenth century. At least Part V concerning the Neumark was made at the express demand of the Grandmaster; since it seems that Parts IV–VII were made at the same time and that they have been together since the sixteenth century, the initiative for collecting the Order's records may have come from the Grandmaster. This may probably be explained by the difficulties befalling the Order after it had suffered bad defeats from Poland and in facing the Prussian cities and nobility united in the Prussian League since 1440.

Among the remains of the Grandmaster's archives at Königsberg, now preserved in the *Staatliches Archivlager* in Göttingen, there is a "fragment" of

15. Johannes Voigt, *Die Erwerbung der Neumark. Ziel und Erfolg der brandenburgischen Politik unter den Kurfürsten Friedrich I. und Friedrich II. 1402–1457* (1863); K. Heidenreich, *Der Deutsche Ritterorden in der Neumark* (*1402–55*). (Einzelschriften der Historischen Kommission für die Provinz Brandenburg 5, 1932)

Part IV[16], which is really a series of three fragments from the first portion (papal *generalia*) of Part IV (in the form of the *inspeximus* of 1434; see above description p. 32). Another copy is listed by Strehlke in his footnotes to No. 196 as being preserved among the records of the Knights of St. John in Berlin. If we assume that the Grandmaster had the fragment as well as Part IV (because we maintain that Part IV formed part of his archives being bound up with Parts V–VII), this would leave the *Deutschmeister*, at whose request the *inspeximus* of 1434 was made, without a copy. But this does not prevent the assumption that Part IV was at one time in the Grandmaster's archives. The archives of the *Deutschmeister* were almost completely destroyed in 1525 by the revolt of the German peasants,[17] so that there may have been another copy of Part IV among the records that were burned.

Because it can be shown that this section of the manuscript had been in the Grandmaster's archives, the compiler of the Berlin repertory jumped to the conclusion that this was true also for Parts I–III. But while this is partly certain and partly at least probable for Parts IV–VII, there is neither evidence nor probability for the same having been true of Parts I–III. They are not listed in the oldest repertory of the records and manuscripts, when they were preserved at Tapiau (*Staatliches Archivlager* Göttingen, *Ostpreussischer Foliant* 14241a). The Grandmaster had almost no interest in these sections, inasmuch as they dealt with the Holy Land, having left the original records pertaining to the Holy Land in Venice when he moved his residence to Marienburg in 1309. The two bullaries containing *generalia* in Parts I and II, could have been of interest to him, but these were very difficult to use, as they were not in chronological order except by pontificates, consisted of mostly undated copies and show almost no attempt at a classification by subject matter. In any event the Grandmaster had a well stocked series of papal *generalia* in the original or in individual copies as well as in Part IV, so that he did not necessarily need the two bullaries. A fair number of these *generalia* may have been transferred from Venice in 1309, because the material now extant in Venice (which was heavily damaged by a corrupt prior of the Order's house there in 1365[18]) contains only nine papal *generalia* issued or transcribed before 1309. The Grandmaster demonstrably had four of these in his archives, and among the remaining five there is only one piece of the first importance (Strehlke No. 373, re-issuing No. 309) which he should (and may) have had because it equalled the Teutonic Knights to the Knights Templars and the

16. Joachim-Hubatsch (note 3), Part II, No. 4655.
17. K. H. Lampe, 'Die Auflösung des Deutschordenshauptarchives zu Mergentheim', *Archivalische Zeitschrift* 57 (1961), p. 66 f.
18. Predelli (note 3) p. 1404 ff.

Knights Hospitallers. As it may be said that Parts I–III of Strehlke's manuscript represent what the Grandmaster had no interest in or what he already had, there is no plausible support for the assumption of the Berlin repertory that Parts I–III were ever in his archives.

Parts I–III are difficult in composition. Part I consists of the Cartulary proper of the Teutonic Order from the Holy Land and some parts of the Mediterranean area. Annexed to it is a collection of papal *generalia* which we call Bullary I. Part II contains Bullary II, which comprises two distinct series: (see rubric on fol. 90r; description above p. 30). Part III is a later appendix to the Cartulary of Part I, to bring it up to date.

The two bullaries are the sections of the manuscript we know least about. Neither bullary has an obvious classification, except that the documents are very roughly grouped chronologically, i.e. according to successive pontificates. While this is a classification, it is not a very helpful one, least so for Pope Honorius III, who according to Strehlke's collection showered the Order with 113 *generalia* (many issued on the same day), of which Part I contains fifty-eight and Part II, seventy-six. The arrangement within the pontificates is definitely not chronological, as most of the charters lack dates. There is also no clearly recognizable attempt at a subject classification either in Bullary I or in the first part of Bullary II. The possible attempt at a subject classification at the beginning of Bullary I quickly came to an end due to the obvious difficulty that a *generale* might touch on two or more problems. The chronological classification by pontificates almost forces a systematic order into Bullary I for Clement III to Innocent III. The real test comes with Honorius III, where one may interpret the opening as having been classified according to subject matter, but if so, this attempt collapsed fairly early. In any case, the argument for a classification by subject matter remains very shady. The last conceivable classification system would be that the charters were transcribed from the papal registers in the order in which they appear there, but this test is totally unsuccessful in Bullary I, for both Honorius III and Gregory IX. This is not very surprising because the Order did not maintain a procurator general in Rome prior to 1257, whereas we have evidence that there was no procurator of the Order in Rome in 1241. And only a procurator general (as opposed to a professional procurator *pro tempore*) would have possessed archives for compiling a bullary of the Order or have gone to the trouble of reading through the papal registers to copy the charters for the Teutonic Knights.

If Bullary I was not compiled in Rome, it could only have been compiled in the main convent at Acre or at the seat of the Master in Italy. We think that the latter is the more probable solution. The same is true, we think, of the first sub-section of Part I, the first part of the Cartulary. It is difficult to see, however, why Bullary I should stop in 1230 while the Cartulary in Part I reaches 1242. There are, however, indications that the compilation of both Cartulary I and Bullary I were hastily done. It seems that the rubrics to the Cartulary were not supplied in the vacant spaces left for them (which were often so small that the rubric spilled over to the margin) until after this portion of the Cartulary had been brought to the Holy Land in 1244, although the numbering had been done before. If both Cartulary and Bullary were to be brought to the Holy Land and the work had to be finished by the time that an envoy started on his trip, and if the Cartulary was considered to be the more important part, then it can easily be seen why Bullary I stopped at 1230. The Bullary scribe (who worked independently from that of the Cartulary, since Bullary I opens a new quire and the Cartulary ends on the preceding page with the last charter spilling over at the end onto the lower margin by two lines) would have progressed only up to 1230 when the scribe of the Cartulary, who did not have to contend with the massive series of papal *generalia* extending from 15 December 1220 to 9 February 1221, had reached the end of his work with a charter dated August 1242. This is a more likely assumption than that Bullary I was annexed to the Cartulary at Acre and that the material available for transcription at Acre in the year 1244 did not reach beyond 1230.

Both sections of Bullary II were written by the same scribe, and the second sub-section opens in the middle of a quire. There is therefore no doubt as to the common origin of both sub-sections of Bullary II, even if numbering, rubrics and initials are only found in the first. This bullary contains two series of papal charters, transcribed from different sources at the same time and place. The first sub-section reaches 1259, but contains an undated piece which may be as late as May 1261. In the second sub-section the last dated *generale* is of February 1257, but this sub-section also contains *Livonica* and *Prussica* up to January 1261, *the terminus post quem* for Part II. This makes it roughly contemporary with Part III, the second portion of the Cartulary reaching up to June 1263. We cannot say why Bullary II was compiled, but it was definitely not done to bring Bullary I (which it duplicates to a large extent) up to date. While Bullary I does not go beyond 1230, it is puzzling, even if Bullary II was not intended to bring Bullary I up to date, to find in Bullary II (sub-section one) only one piece by Gregory IX and none by Innocent IV, when Strehlke lists fifty-four and sixty-two *generalia*, respectively, by these two popes. There is no recognizable classification in the first sub-section of Bullary II except by pontificates, and in contrast to the rubric on fol. 90^r, it is demonstrably not taken from the papal registers. This rubric seems to refer to the second sub-section of Bullary II, which consists at first mostly of (direct or indirect) copies from the papal registers, taken by a certain Martin, a person unidentified but perhaps linked with the office of the procurator general of the Order in Rome. Martin signed each copy and carefully indicated the place in the register where he had found it. The classification is by geographical area: Bohemia, Burzenland in Hungary (possibly classified according to importance or subject matter within the Hungarian charters), with one piece for Mergentheim in Germany interspersed, followed by charters pertaining to Livonia and Prussia (without strict distinction between the two) and mostly dealing with the ecclesiastical organization and the division of power between the Order and the bishops. The lack of distinction between Prussia and Livonia may be due to the fact that both belonged to the same archbishopric. Even Strehlke found it difficult to separate them correctly. He put No. 247 with Livonia and No. 208 with Prussia, although they obviously belong together by subject matter and are found together in both the manuscript and in the papal registers. There is no chronological classification in either of these geographical sub-sections. Among the Prussian charters it is possible to detect an attempt at a classification according to subject matter, less distinguishable than among the Hungarian charters, but again, as in Bullary I, the evidence for this is very tenuous. Among the *Livonica* there is not even a recognizable attempt. With regard to Bullary II we can only say that it was compiled after 1261, that it probably was added to the Merseburg manuscript before Part III was added after 1263, that the second sub-section lastly came from the papal registers and that the bulk of the material there concerns Prussia and Livonia (thirty-one charters against one for Bohemia, five for Hungary and one for Germany). A possible reason for the collection of the charters pertaining to the christianization and ecclesiastical organization of Livonia and Prussia after 1261 may be found in the great Prussian uprising of 1260, which made things look bad for the Order up to at least 1265. The material copied from the papal registers may have been supplemented by charters found in a provincial register, as indicated in fol. 90^r, and exclusively concerning Livonia and Prussia (because the rest comes from the papal registers). It is also possible that the whole sub-section was copied from a *provinciale* in which the registered charters had already been mixed with unregistered *Prussica* and *Livonica* and in which the sources for the register copies were indicated through the signatures of Martin. We cannot say which is the more likely possibility.

The historically most important part of Strehlke's manuscript are Parts I and III, which constitute the Cartulary of the Teutonic Knights for the Holy Land and certain parts of the Mediterranean and Hungary. Part I has an obvious classification, by country: Holy Land, Armenia, Cyprus, Southern Italy and Sicily (with one piece for Montpellier inserted and also one piece strictly belonging to *Reichsitalien* rather than to Southern Italy), followed by one for Livonia and sections for Hungary and Frankish Greece. For the Christian East the material goes up to August 1242; for Italy to 1239; for Hungary to 1222 (the only charters concerning Hungary after this date and before 1243 are papal and they are found in the Bullaries). The Livonia piece dates from 1226 (although there were non-papal charters concerning Livonia from between 1226 and 1243 which could have been included), and its inclusion is puzzling because it does not concern the Teutonic Knights, but the Brethren of the Sword which became united to the Teutonic Order in 1237. This does not necessarily mean that the piece could have been in the possession of the Teutonic Knights only after 1237, because they could have procured a copy when it was issued, since it is witnessed by the Master of the Teutonic Knights. The last charter concerning Frankish Greece is from 1241. This makes August 1242 the *terminus post quem* for Part I.

When the Cartulary in Part I was finished and numbered, but before the rubrics were supplied, an additional quire (fols. 45–50) was inserted. It interrupted the Hungarian series at the point where the end of Strehlke No. 158 (originally carrying over from fol. 44^{v} to 51^{r}) was erased on fol. 51^{r} and recopied on fol. 45^{r} as the eight opening words of the inserted quire. This is a clear sign that this quire was inserted *post festum*. The remainder of the quire contains Strehlke Nos. 95, 97, 96, 94, 93, 20. The first are five *diplomata* issued at Nuremberg in December 1243 by Conrad IV, King of Germany and heir to the Kingdom of Jerusalem. They reconfirmed grants concerning the Holy Land that Conrad's father had made earlier, which were re-issued because the *Haute Cour*, the highest political body in the Kingdom of Jerusalem, had declared the grants of Emperor Frederick II legally invalid. Conrad's five *diplomata* fill fols. 45^{r}–48^{v} of the inserted quire. On fol. 49^{r} another, younger hand from the second half of the thirteenth century inserted the forged document Strehlke No. 20. Fols. 49^{v}–50^{v} are blank. The quire originally contained only Conrad's five grants of December 1243. This means that Part I, containing material up to August 1242, was finished before the charters issued by Conrad were available for transcription. When they arrived, they were inserted at the last minute, almost immediately after Frederick's charters, being separated from them only by Strehlke Nos. 147 and 158. It would have been more appropriate to insert them after fol. 20 (where another quire ends), because then Conrad's confirmations would have immediately followed the grants of 1229, which he confirmed, rather than all of his father's charters. This would have posed a technical problem as the scribe would then have had to erase on fol. 21^{r} twelve lines (and recopy them as opening words of the new quire), instead of eight words covering a line and a half, as he had done on fols. $51^{r}/45^{r}$.

There can be no reasonable doubt that Part I was transcribed after the summer of 1242 and before the charters of December 1243 were available. Where was this done? The problem has never been investigated, since it seems to have been the general assumption that the Cartulary was put together in the main convent of the Order at Acre. But material reaching up to August 1242 could still have been copied in Acre in the same year. Conrad's charters of December 1243 would not, however, have been available in the East before April or May 1244, as there was no shipping from Europe to the Holy Land between early October and early March. By then almost a year and a half would have elapsed since the issue of the last Holy Land charter still copied. If the binding had been opened at that time to insert the new quire, there is no reason why Holy Land material which had accumulated since August 1242 should not have been included (especially since there are vacant pages even today at the end of the additional quire). Things look different if we reverse the assumption. The material dating up to August 1242 could have been brought back to Europe by one of the last summer sailings. The decision to assemble this material into a Cartulary could have been made in the winter of 1242/43, before new material arrived after shipping had been resumed in the Spring of 1243. In this case, Conrad's charters could have been inserted immediately after they were granted, because even in winter-time they could have reached the tip of Southern Italy, for example, in a few weeks. The theory that the Cartulary was compiled in Europe rather than in the Holy Land is confirmed by the fact that five charters by Frederick II concerning the Holy Land could be presented to Conrad IV in December 1243 for *verbatim* transcription and that two of the originals of these five imperial *diplomata* are still kept in the *Archivio di Stato* in Venice (Predelli Nos. 28, 34). The originals of two of the five *diplomata* by Conrad IV are still extant in Europe, at the *Deutschordens-zentralarchiv* in Vienna, where they were probably acquired from the *Deutsch-meister's* Archives in Mergentheim. This provenance is at least true for Böhmer-Ficker, *Regesta imperii* V/2 No. 4542, another charter by Conrad IV of which two originals are kept in Vienna. One of these can be demonstrated to have come from Mergentheim, where it was copied in 1797. Another original of Conrad's charters of 1243 was preserved in Barletta in 1336[19]. All this seems to indicate that the originals of Conrad's grants of December 1243 remained in Europe and never came to the East. In this case, they were in all likelihood copied into the Cartulary in Europe.

Something must be said about Strehlke No. 128, opening Part I. It was written on a quire of its own, in a hand of its own, and consisted of a list of

19. Joachim-Hubatsch (note 3), Part II, No. 85.

possessions of the Order mainly in the Holy Land, but also around the Mediterranean and in Hungary and Livonia. For the County of Tripoli, the Principality of Antioch, the Kingdoms of Lesser Armenia and Cyprus, Italy, Livonia and Hungary, Strehlke No. 128, is only a table of contents for Part I. But for the Holy Land and Frankish Greece things are different. Strehlke No. 128 omits twenty-six Holy Land charters transcribed in Part I and eight charters concerning Frankish Greece. On the other hand, it mentions thirty-six possessions or revenues of the Order in the Holy Land not copied in the Cartulary or in its later appendix (Part III). There seem to be in Strehlke No. 128 two mentionings of charters appearing only or also in Part III, Strehlke Nos. 29 and 98. No. 29 is contained in both Parts I and III and occurs twice (but not for this reason) in Strehlke No. 128, because the compiler of the list split it into two component parts so it could be conveniently grouped according to subject matter. A similar case is Strehlke No. 34, which is split and is mentioned three times in Strehlke No. 128. That Strehlke No. 29 appears twice in Strehlke No. 128 is, therefore, not evidence that Part III was already available when No. 128 was compiled. Neither is this the case for No. 98, for it can be demonstrated that the entry in No. 128, which Strehlke identified with No. 98, really refers to No. 66, which only appears in Part I. Thus, there is no charter in Strehlke No. 128 later than Part I, but there are quite a few which are missing in Part I (and, for that matter, in Part III). The charters by Conrad IV are mentioned. This means that Strehlke No. 128 was written after Part I had been finished and after Conrad's charters had been inserted, but earlier than Part III. Strehlke No. 128, which forms a quire of its own, is a second addition to Part I, added at the beginning. Whoever compiled it worked from different material than the man who wrote the Cartulary proper in 1243. He had only part of the same material available (unless he arbitrarily suppressed some which would not have been very logical in a list of possessions). The same considerations prevent the assumption that he worked directly from the Cartulary. That Strehlke No. 128 contains not only less, but also considerably more than the Cartulary, strongly suggests a different place of origin. We have assumed above that the Cartulary was compiled somewhere in Europe. Under this theory, we should now have to assume that Strehlke No. 128 was compiled somewhere else in Europe, or in the Holy Land. We may rule out Tripoli, Antioch, Lesser Armenia, Cyprus, Italy, France, Livonia and Hungary, since both the Cartulary and Strehlke No. 128 are identical for these areas. This leaves us with the Holy Land and Frankish Greece. We must also rule out the latter, because No. 128 contains for Frankish Greece less and not more than the Cartulary. Also no house in Greece would have had such extensive material on the Holy Land, which was available only at the headquarters of the Order at Acre or at the

Italian residence of the Master, most likely in Barletta.[20] If Italy is to be excluded (see above), we are left with Acre as the place of origin of Strehlke No. 128.

It may be pointed out that the Cartulary transcribes in Part I twenty-six charters not listed in Strehlke No. 128. According to our theory, they would have been available for copying in Europe, but noι at Acre. But we have also the reverse case of thirty-six possessions or revenues known only to the compiler of Strehlke No. 128 (in Acre) and not available to the compiler of Part I (in Europe). Moreover, of the twenty-six charters omitted from No. 128 eighteen belong to what is known as the archives of the *Seigneurie de Joscelin*. Whoever compiled the Cartulary had the complete archives of this most important complex of possessions of the Order in the Holy Land before him, including the charters to Joscelin's predecessors in certain parts of the lordship. The first charter of this group mentioned in Strehlke No. 128 is Strehlke No. 52 dated 1220, in which Joscelin's heirs sold the *Seigneurie de Joscelin* to the Order. Whoever compiled Strehlke No. 128 had the basic charter of sale to the Knights and succeeding charters dealing with the development of this lordship under the Knights. One must ask whether the archives of the *Seigneurie de Joscelin* were more urgently needed in Europe or in Acre around 1243/1244. Did it suffice for the main convent to have only the basic documents concerning this possession or did the Master in Europe need them all? As far as we can see the Knights settled out of court concerning the *Seigneurie* in the Holy Land (Strehlke Nos. 98, 99 of 1244). It was a bad time for the Order. The imperial administration in Palestine had collapsed after a long and bitter civil war in which the Knights had supported the Imperialists. Before their collapse the Emperor's court was the last court of appeal, and after 1243 it was the only one in which the Knights could reasonably expect a favourable verdict for matters concerning the Holy Land. In the East they had to settle by negotiation rather than litigation. There is much to be said, therefore, for the Master in Europe having the more pressing need for the complete records of the *Seigneurie de Joscelin*.

There is a clearly recognizable attempt at classification in Part I. The

20. Italy was the country where the Masters of the Order had their longest periods of residence during the first half of the thirteenth century. There they would be half way between the East and the German and Prussian possessions of the Order, they would be in touch with the Imperial court and would have at their disposal a sound economic basis in the southern-Italian possessions of the Order. On Barletta as one of the richest archives of the Order outside of Prussia, see the very illuminating remarks by Forstreuter, *Die Berichte der Generalprokuratoren* (note 3) Vol. 1, p. 38, Cf. also *ibid.*, 1, p. 247, n. 8.

first twenty-eight charters after Strehlke No. 128 concern the *Seigneurie de Joscelin*, although the inclusion of the last one (Strehlke No. 68) is doubtful. The other groups are smaller; they concern the *casalia* Arabia and Zechanin, the Order's tradition regarding its origins, houses in Tyre, *casale* Saphet and transactions with other ecclesiastical institutions. There is, however, no guiding principle to the arrangement of the material pertaining to the Order's possessions in Acre or its immediate vicinity. In three cases there might even be doubt as to whether the possessions were located in Acre (although, in fact, they were; Strehlke Nos. 42, 48, 92). This disorderly arrangement of the Acre charters (which are separated from one another by charters pertaining to Jerusalem, Tyre, the right of booty, exemption from customs and lands near Sidon and Caesarea) would be easily explained under the assumption that the Cartulary was put together in Europe.

That the Cartulary is incomplete can be demonstrated by carefully comparing it with the rests of the Order's archives in Venice, a fascinating and detailed investigation, which cannot be reproduced here. But it is quite obvious that Part I is incomplete because there is more in Strehlke No. 128, and that Part III is incomplete because there is more in Venice. Evidence from a comparison with the Venice material shows that there was a tendency for charters to be issued twice in the sixties of the thirteenth century. One copy was intended for the central administration of the Order, and the other for the local archive of an individual house. The Venetian material is the remainder of a "central" archive that is central in the sense that it was the only archive to the exclusion of local ones. Charters of general and of local interest would be thrown together indiscriminately in such a "central" archive, not a very practical arrangement for an increasingly international organization such as the Teutonic Knights. If the fragmentary nature of the Venetian material leads us to conclude that such a "system" was practised in the fifties and sixties of the thirteenth century, then we must also conclude that there must have been another division of the records, not reflected any more in the Venetian material. Otherwise the double issues, especially where they are made out to various officials of the Order such as the Master (central) and the *Grosskomtur* (local for Palestine) would make no sense. We are probably well advised to assume that the first of the two systems was never practised. The concentration of both "central" and "local" documentary evidence for the possessions in the Holy Land in the single body of the Venetian material was most likely due to the Order's expulsion from Palestine in 1291. After that, and as long as there was still hope for recovering the Holy Land, it was practical to assemble the former central archives and the material that had been saved from the various local archives in Palestine into a single repository. This would make it easier to reclaim all possessions after a reconquest and would not prevent a new division of the material in the event that new houses were set up in the Holy Land. In spite of the variant nature of the material now in Venice, we suggest that in the fifties and sixties of the thirteenth century when Part III was compiled the documentary evidence of the Order was divided into those documents important enough to merit the attention of the central administration and to be kept in its archives for transcription into Part III after 1263, and other documents which were in the archives of individual houses of the Order in the Holy Land and which did not become united with the central archives until after 1291. These last documents (as are found in Venice) were therefore not transcribed in the Cartulary at all.

If we have indications of a division of material in the fifties and sixties and of the central administration having its own archives as opposed to local ones, may this not also be true for the forties, when Part I was compiled? This seems to be the case. Both Predelli No. 6 and Strehlke No. 51 of 1200 and 1219, respectively, concern the same subject, but Strehlke No. 51 is considerably more liberal towards the Knights. Apparently both charters were still in Antioch in 1243, when Part I was written. Strehlke No. 51 had been deposited in the central archives before 1263, because it was copied in the second portion of the Cartulary after that time. It had been issued in 1219 and could have been copied in Part I in 1243, had it been available. Predelli No. 6 was also probably in the central archives by that time, but was only preserved there and not copied, because Strehlke No. 51 covered everything in Predelli No. 6, and even more. As the Antioch possessions concerned became increasingly endangered from 1260 on, it was probably felt that the Antioch charters would be safer in another place. This is not conclusive evidence that there were central archives in 1243; it merely proves that the individual houses had their own archives. Cases of double issues, which would allow us to conclude that there was a division between central and local archives, do not exist before 1243. Double issues, however, are conclusive only if they are addressed to various officials, as is the case, e.g., with Predelli No. 48 and Strehlke No. 111 of 1256 and 1257, respectively. We know nothing of this before 1243. Yet, demands of orderly business administration would suggest that archives of the central administration existed in some way at that time; a corporation operating from Palestine to Prussia could not do without them.

The crucial question is how we define a central archive. The normal location would have been the main convent at Acre, where, legally speaking, the Master with the brethren of the convent formed the corporation and where, under the statutes, the high officials were obliged to reside. It was also the place where, according to the statutes, chapters were to be held. However, it was probably the officials of the first rank rather than the simple brethren at Acre, who governed the Order together with the Master. They put checks on him in that he could act without the support of the convent at Acre, as long as he had their support. This dependence of the Master on the high officials has been shown clearly by Forstreuter,[21] who proved that the Master could only move his residence to Prussia by breaking up the common life of Master and high officials. This he could only accomplish by making all the officials, except for two, who he kept at his side, lords in their own right, assigning huge commanderies in Prussia to be attached to their offices. Thus, as long as they remained in office, the officials had access to enormous revenues. The *Grosskomtur* and the Treasurer were the officials retained; the *Grosskomtur* acted as Master in the latter's absence and also shared in the administration of the Marienburg, while the Treasurer was able to best employ his office and its powers at the Master's residence. This reduced the role of the main convent to one of nominal leadership. The antagonism between Master and main convent inherent in all knightly Orders turned into antagonism between Master and high officials. The Master's natural tendency must have been to sever the ties between himself and the high officials. The high officials, on the other hand, had every reason to preserve and strengthen these ties. The crucial problem then was the Master's absence. While the constitution of the Order required the Masters to reside in the main convent at Acre, the increasing internationalization of the Order and the growing employment of the Masters in the diplomatic service of the Emperor required their almost permanent absence from Acre. An excellent example is provided by the itinerary of Hermann von Salza, the great architect of the Order and Master from 1210 to 1239. Nevertheless, the Master had the interests of the Order at heart at all times, and Hermann's services to the Emperor were as costly as they were good. The Masters solicited large grants from the universal powers as payment for their services, and also petitioned any other potentates they happened to meet. Although this was to the advantage of the Order, it was to the disadvantage of the high officials. They could act as they pleased in the Holy Land during the Master's absence (as Forstreuter correctly pointed out[22]), but this became less and less attractive as they could keep less of a check on an absentee Master in the areas which were becoming more important to the Order than the Holy Land. The high officials tried, time and again, but quite unsuccessfully to tie the Master to the main convent, at Acre and then at Venice.

Under the constitution, the central archives should have been kept at

21. Forstreuter, *Deutscher Orden am Mittelmeer* (note 1) pp. 190 *sqq.*
22. *Ibid.*, p. 192.

Acre or Montfort, the Order's strongest castle in Palestine. With the central administration being divided between the main convent at Acre and the Master abroad, it is doubtful that the main convent did keep central archives. These were more probably kept by the Master, which would not have been any more unconstitutional than his almost permanent absence. If the Master wanted to further the interests of the Order effectively, it was indispensable that he keep archives. We concern ourselves with Hermann von Salza because a man of his organizational capacities would have recognized the need to have at least the more important of his Order's documents at his disposal. As we have no evidence for the high officials ever exercising effective checks on Hermann von Salza, there is little probability that the main convent would have voiced any protests if he had not sent the charters he received to Acre. Nor would it have been difficult for him to get any charters that he wanted from the main convent there.

Where Hermann kept these documents is another question. He traveled constantly, mostly in Italy, to the point where the Order tried to prevent him from further intervening in Italian affairs at the Marburg chapter of 1237. He died in Salerno and was buried in Barletta at the Order's main Apulian house. Since Apulia was also the favourite residence of the Emperor, it is likely that he kept the magisterial archives there.

This evidence leads us to assume that the archive material was divided up in several houses. We suggest the following reconstruction: When the German hospital was founded in Acre and developed slowly into a knightly Order from 1190 to 1198, the only archive was at Acre. As the Order spread and other houses were founded, the division of records began to develop. Individual houses started to have their own archives, of which we think Predelli No. 6 is an example. Still, the young Order's main convent at Acre had a legitimate interest in knowing about all the property it owned, and we presume that the bulk of the material was still there. The almost permanent absence of Hermann von Salza from Acre increased the number of records kept outside the main convent. The division was made in an arbitrary fashion, determined by the Master's interests and actions. Thus, while the archives at Acre were "central" in early times, they became increasingly "localized," while the Master created his own magisterial archives in Italy, as opposed to the conventual ones. It would, however, be more important to know how he treated the material of "central" interest that was at Acre at the time of his accession (today we would duplicate the entire "central" part of the conventual archives). Whether Hermann forced transfers of certain parts of the conventual archives or not, we cannot say. It would not unduly have harmed the Order which flourished under his administration. If we assume that he did ask for transfers, then this practice must have continued under his two successors, because the Holy Land material transcribed in Part I reaches up to 1242.

We have yet to explain why the decision was taken in 1243 to copy the material resting in the magisterial archive into a Cartulary. It seems that this was done to restore the "central" records in some manner to the conventual archives at Acre. There are indications that the Cartulary was at one time in the Holy Land, although we believe that it was compiled in Europe. We feel that Strehlke No. 128 was compiled in Acre and prefixed to the Cartulary there. It contains considerably more local Acre material than Part I. Also, we find on fol. 86^{v}, i.e. at the end of Part I (after Bullary I), a copy of Strehlke No. 15 as a later addition. This charter was never in any archives of the Order, as it was a royal grant of 1182 to the Archbishop of Tyre. It was precisely there, where the Knights copied it, because it has a final note to the effect: *Hoc privilegium habet ecclesia Tyrensis.* The charter concerns Toron, where the Knights only had interests either before 1229, when they lost Toron, or after 1244, when in a complicated transaction they had to repurchase half of Maron, which they had received in 1229 as reimbursement for Toron. It can be demonstrated from the manuscript that Strehlke No. 15 was added after 6 March 1252. As the chances of recovering Toron were then very slim, the charter in the Tyre archives could not have been of interest to the Master, but only to the central administration, as represented by the high officials and the main convent at Acre. Even if a copy had been taken in Tyre and sent to Europe, it would merely have been filed away in the magisterial archives, rather than copied into the Cartulary. It would have been quite different if the Cartulary had made its way East and the charter was copied into it there to serve the interests of the main convent. As Strehlke No. 15 was added to Part I, it follows that Part I, written in Europe, was in the Holy Land after 1252 but before Part III was written after 1263.

Since Part I was written in 1243, we must look for a suitable occasion for the Cartulary to have been commissioned at this time, and to have been brought to the East. One such occasion can be found in the mission of Heinrich von Hohenlohe to the Holy Land in 1244. The Order in Palestine had not only suffered from the collapse of the Imperialists, but a major crisis had developed within. This was solved in 1244 by Heinrich von Hohenlohe, who had been *Deutschmeister* from 1232 to 1242, and who now came with the Commander of Apulia, representing the European opposition to the rule of the Master Gerhard von Malberg who had been elected in 1240. The latter's grave deficiencies of character led to the assumption that he was elected only because he was willing to reside in the Holy Land. This must have provoked the opposition of the great commanders of Europe who represented the richer branch of the Order and wished to have the Master under their influence. They could not advise him at Acre, and the statutes gave only the commanders of Armenia and Cyprus the right to participate in chapter. The interests of the main convent and the *Landkomture* were mutually exclusive. Heinrich von Hohenlohe forced the resignation of Gerhard and was himself elected Master prior to 7 July 1244. On 9 February, and perhaps as late as 17 May 1244, he had still been at the Roman Curia. Surely he could have taken with him the Cartulary written in 1243, in which the charters by Conrad IV of December 1243 had been hastily inserted in early 1244. Under the weak Gerhard von Malberg the division of the central archives between magisterial and conventual ones in Europe and Acre became either painful and was remedied by the Cartulary, or Heinrich von Hohenlohe may have had the Cartulary written to ingratiate himself with the Acre convent. As he had no intention of remaining permanently in the Holy Land, he would not have contemplated the dissolution of the magisterial archive and the physical return of the records to Acre. A Cartulary seemed to be a good solution in every way. It gave the main convent the bulk of the Holy Land charters, and some, although not all, of the information on Italy. It gave it access to the charters pertaining to the Hungarian adventure, which was over, as well as to a dossier concerning unsuccessful litigation over possessions in Greece, which would not harm the master if it were known by the main convent. But the total absence of Prussian and German material from the Cartulary is conspicuous. We must doubt that there was not in the magisterial archives, at least a copy of the Golden Bull of Rimini of 1226, the great Prussian political program of Hermann von Salza. Even if the *Deutschmeister* and the Prussian *Landmeister* kept the bulk of the German and Prussian material, it is inconceivable that the Master should have had no German or Prussian records in his possession. We must assume that he deliberately chose to withhold such information from the main convent at Acre. The one piece for Livonia (Strehlke No. 235) is for the Brethren of the Sword, and the most basic charter for Livonia uniting the Brethren of the Sword to the Teutonic Knights (Strehlke No. 244 of 1237) was copied not in the first portion of the Cartulary or in Bullary I, but only in Bullary II which was put together much later than the 1243 Cartulary. This charter must have been in the hands of the Master; if it was not copied we can only infer, that this was intentional, and that the Acre convent was to stay out of German, Prussian and Livonian affairs. But the Cartulary was not even complete for the Holy Land in 1243; it did not contain the local Acre material when it was transcribed in the magisterial archives. We believe that this deficiency, which must have been felt at Acre, was the reason why Strehlke No. 128 was compiled containing an index to the Cartulary as well as abstracts of the additional originals which were available at Acre. If this is so, the rubrics were supplied at Acre. because the rubric to Strehlke No. 3 was begun on the last empty page of the quire containing only Strehlke No. 128, i. e. it was written after Strehlke No. 128 had been prefixed.

Part III of the Merseburg manuscript was put together after 1263, because the material contained in it reaches up to this point. Its exact purpose escapes us, except that it must have served to bring the 1243 Cartulary up to date. Yet one would like to know more about it, e.g. why the charters included were chosen to the exclusion of others, for Part III is so small that it cannot constitute all the additions to the Acre archives since 1242. One would also like to know why the decision to compile it was made in 1263. The guiding principle for Part III seems to have been to show only the more important developments in the Order's possessions in the Holy Land. We are aware that this is a dangerous argument since we do not know exactly what was left out. But it is a fact that Part III concerns the acquisition of the important lordship of Casel Imbert near Acre and the acquisition of A'hmid, which rounded off the Order's possession in the Schuf region, extending it to the coast, the lifeline of the Kingdom of Jerusalem. Next we find the sale of the small lordship of Mergecolon, and a whole series which may be called the archives of Julian of Sidon; the latter concern possessions sold to the Order by Julian or his vassals, mostly in the Schuf, the region west of the Lebanon mountains and north of the sharp bend of the Litani River. This is followed by some Antioch material and an agreement with the bishop of Acre over ecclesiastical tithes, and the more important developments in the *Seigneurie de Joscelin*, which confirms our view that only the more important affairs were shown in Part III. Finally, there is an important treaty with the Knights Templars and the Hospitallers, although this is preceded by two rather minor transactions.

At this point the Cartulary of the Teutonic Knights breaks off. What was added later to the magisterial archives was no longer copied into it, but is preserved in part in Venice (Predelli Nos. 59–66, 68, 70). We have no way of telling when the Cartulary of the Order was returned to Europe, except that it must have been after 1263. The conventual archives were still at Acre in 1277, when a fair number of papal *generalia* was transcribed there.[23] A

23. On the copying of 1277 see Comte Paul Riant, 'Charte de la grande-commanderie de l'Ordre Teutonique', *Bulletin de la Societé nationale des Antiquaires de France* 1877, pp. 63 *sqq.* Pettenegg (note 7), Nos. 535–555 lists papal charters then transcribed at Acre and now in the *Deutschordenszentralarchiv* in Vienna. Others have ended up in Göttingen, having passed through the Grandmaster's Archives in Marienburg and the Prussian State Archives in Königsberg (Joachim-Hubatsch, *op. cit.*, Part II, Nos. 4207, 4208, 4216, 4219, 4292, 4295, 4340, 4353).

single piece was copied and authenticated there as late as 1281,[24] and the records in Venice reach up to 1286 (Predelli No. 70). We may assume that the Cartulary remained in Acre as long as the records.

We have not been able to break all the secrets of the Merseburg manuscript, and we had to rely to a certain extent on probabilities more than on hard facts. But the careful inspection of the manuscript, of its quires and its composition, does reveal some of its secrets, It has produced a working hypothesis for further research, for which we hope the present reprint will provide the necessary stimulation.

We cannot conclude without thanking those who have made it possible for us to do this study: Joshua Prawer of the Hebrew University and the Israel Academy of Sciences and Humanities, who patiently endured, read and edited what we wrote; the authorities of the *Deutsches Zentralarchiv* in Merseburg, who kindly accomodated all our wishes with regard to microfilms and physical inspection of the manuscript; the Institute for Advanced Study in Princeton, New Jersey, where we enjoyed the matchless hospitality of a membership for the academic year 1972–1973, partly facilitated by funds given to the Institute by the National Endowment for the Humanities of the United States of America under Grant H5426, and were given time in peace and tranquillity to think about the problems of Strehlke's manuscript — which, given the deficiency in facts about its history, was what we needed most.

HANS EBERHARD MAYER

Princeton, N.J., December 1972

24. Forstreuter, *Berichte der Generalprokuratoren* (note 3) Vol. 1, p. 190, No. 32.

PRAEFATIO.

In tabulario regio Berolinensi cum codicem manu scriptum asservari cognitum esset, permultas easque aestimabiles et magnam partem ineditas ordinis Theutonici tabulas complexum, ac saepe viri docti propter singularia monumenta eundem aut ipsi adirent aut ab officialibus adiri vellent, quin etiam exteri modo eundem codicem peregre mittendum modo descripta totius voluminis exempla requirerent, consentiente comite de Bismarck statutum est, ut liber in publicum proderetur.

Ernestus itaque Strehlke, tabularii regii secretarius, quem constat et de cognoscendis monumentis Italiae inferioris medio aevo factis[1]) et de edendis rerum Prussicarum scriptoribus optime meruisse, huius quoque operis procurandi negotium libentissimo animo subiit. Qui cum non universum ordinis Theutonici tabularum corpus sed nonnullos tantum et eos diversos litterarum acervos in codice inesse perspexisset, totius materiae secundum annorum cursum digestionem minus idoneam esse ratus, novem in partes omnem

[1]) in eo libro, qui inscribitur: „Denkmäler der Kunst des Mittelalters in Unteritalien von Heinrich Wilhelm Schulz. Nach dem Tode des Verfassers herausgegeben von Ferdinand von Quast. Dresden 1860“.

librum distribuit; quarum partes septem ad singulas terras spectant, duabus partibus comprehenduntur tabulae imperatorum paparumque omni ordini communiter tributae. Et multarum quidem tabularum, quae melius, quam in codice illo leguntur, ab aliis foras datae sunt, argumenta tantum praebere satis habuit; at contra eas libri partes, quae tabulas ad terram sanctam spectantes paparumque bullas exhibent, quantumcumque aliis quoque usus auxiliis posset, supplendas esse duxit.

Habuit autem totius laboris sui consortem utilissimum v. d. Adolfum Meckelburg, tabulario regio Regimontano praefectum, qui ex iis, quas administrat, tabulis codicibusque manu scriptis gratissima assiduitate largitus est.

Cepit etiam magnum fructum ex quadringentorum in Vindobonensi ordinis Theutonici tabulario asservatorum archetyporum catalogo, insigni benignitate a Guilelmo, serenissimo archiduce Austriae, generali ordinis magistro, huc mitti iusso.

Uberrimus vero codicum adhibitorum est

(B) Codex tabularii regii Berolinensis, signatus: „h. I. C. 12 fol.“, a bibliopego ex septem diversis libris manuscriptis constitutus; quarum partium

(I) prima pars, membranacea saec. XIII, folia 1—89 continet. Fol. 1 hoc lemma habetur; „Hec sunt elemosine, empciones, confirmationes, commutationes atque privilegia domus sancte Marie Theutonicorum in Ierusalem“. Sequitur enumeratio possessionum et emptarum et dono acceptarum (fol. 1—3 v.). Deinde leguntur tabulae 214 (fol. 5—85 v. et fol. 89 v.).

(II) Secunda pars, membranacea saec. XIII, foliis 90—153 comprehenditur, in cuius exordio legimus hanc inscriptionem: „In hoc libro continentur rescripta libertatum et indulgentiarum, quae hospitali sancte Marie Theutonicorum Ierosolimitano ab apostolica sede sunt concessa, quemadmodum in provinciali et in registro domni papae continentur". Ibi habentur tabulae 157, maximam partem papales (fol. 90—151).

(III) Tertia pars, membranacea saec. XIII, foliis 154—169 constituta, exhibet variarum manuum tabulas 23, ex quibus quindecim tabulae Francogallico sermone scriptae sunt.

(IV) Quarta pars, partim chartacea partim membranacea, saeculo XV scripta, a fol. 171 usque ad fol. 318 pertinens, tabulas 135 complectitur.

(V) Quinta pars, membranacea saec. XV, folia 319—352 comprehendit, cum hoc titulo: „Transsumpta uber die newe margk und privilegia, die do liegen im haws Friessach". In hac parte inveniuntur tabulae 11.

(VI) Sexta pars, membranacea saec. XV; exstat in fol. 353—366, sic inscripta: „Die privilegia hy inn verschriben vindt man in dem haws ze Fryesach und zu Laybach"; servat tabulas 17.

(VII) Septima pars, membranacea saec. XV, folia 367—370 continens, tabulas 8 praebet, ad quas spectant in folio 370v. posita verba haec: „Dise privilegia sind in dem haws ze Grecz, alls hy inn verschriben sein".

Praeterea consulti sunt tres tabularii regii Regimontani codices, in quibus complures ordinis tabulae descriptae sunt:

A. 16 codex chartaceus saec. XIV, forma maxima,

A. 20 codex membranaceus saec. XV, forma quadrata,

(R) codex chartaceus saec. XIV et XV, forma quadrata, signatus A. 21.

Hoc igitur opus postquam summa cura et diligentia adhibita Ernestus Strehlke paene ad exitum adduxit, de vita migravit. Cuius viri, ingenio probitate doctrina praestantis multosque annos mecum grata necessitudine coniuncti, mortem praematuram cum lugeremus, ne declinarem ab officii religione, quem librum propemodum absolutum reliquerat, ad eum afferendam conclusionem facile suscepi.

Berolini 6 Kal. Iulias 1869.

PHILIPPUS JAFFÉ.

TERRA SANCTA. ARMENIA. CYPRUS.

---

1. *1153 febr. 26 Acchon. Balduinus III Hierosolymitanus rex confirmat conventiones Girardi de Valentia et Latinorum in casali Huberti de Paci ab eo positorum.*

In nomine sancte et individue trinitatis, patris et filii et spiritus sancti. Amen. Notum sit omnibus tam presentibus quam futuris, quod ego Balduwinus per graciam dei in sancta civitate[1] Ierusalem Latinorum rex quartus dona sive conventiones, quas Girardus de Valentia Latinis in casali Huberti de Paci ab eodem locatis iussu meo habuit, laudo et concedo. Que dona sive conventiones hee sunt: predictus namque Girardus memorati casalis incolis, quos[2] ibidem posuit, domos dedit, ipsis etiam et eorum heredibus quiete, libere et sine omni calumpnia vel impedimento habendas et iure perpetuo possidendas. Terram insuper, quam prephatis Latinis laborandam assignavit, hoc tenore habebunt, ut sex partes fructus terre sibi retineant, mihi septimam reservantes. Et de furno, qui Latinis ibidem constitutus est, quintum decimum panem manentes tantum in casali mihi reddent; si quis autem aliunde pro coquendo pane suo ad pretaxatum furnum venerit, decimum panem mihi reddet. Et quotquot in balneo eiusdem se laverint, dimidium denarium singuli dabunt, non amplius. Et quisquis in hoc, de quo agitur, casali annonam emerit, de una quaque bisantiata pro mensuratione denarium dabit. Ibidem etiam quislibet panem, vinum, carnes et omnia, que mandi possunt, sine omni exactione ut Ackon vendere poterit. Et molendinum de Ferge in pretaxato casali Latini habitatione commorantes tres dies et totidem noctes in singulis ebdomadibus sine omni impedimento habebunt salvo tamen iure regio. Et laboratores de vineis et iardinis, que vel nunc sunt vel in posterum inter terminos, quos Giraldus de Valentia mihi retinuit, fient, tres sibi partes habebunt, quartam mihi reddentes, et olivas, ubicunque sint in huius casalis territorio sive inter duo flumina vel extra, prout memoratus Giraldus cuique partem suam assignavit, de communi colligi facient, duas inde partes mihi reddentes et sibi terciam retinentes. Et si quis domum vel terram in casali predicto vel in eiusdem pertinentia emerit, hoc tenore, quo venditor prius habuerit, illam sine dubio possidebit. Et de domo, quam quis emerit, de singulis bisantiis carruplam solam regio iuri dabit, non amplius. Has itaque conventiones, quas, ut predictum est, Giraldus de Valentia Latinis in casali Huberti de Paci noviter locatis habuit, illis concedo et universis insuper, quotquot in sepe dictum casale in posterum gracia habitandi venerint. Et ut huius concessionis mee pagina rata et incorrupta permaneat, testibus eam subscriptis corroborari et sigilli mei suppressione muniri precepi. Factum est autem hoc anno ab incarnatione domini m° c° l° iii° indictione prima. Huius quidem rei testes sunt Humfredinus de Torono constabularius, Symon Tyberiadensis, Guido de Scandalione, Clarembaldus vicecomes Acchonensis, Petrus Aurifex vicecomes Tyrensis. Data Acchon per manum Radulfi[3] cancellarii iiii° kal. martii[4].

I, 89 v. post vacuas septem paginas in ultima I^ae^ partis. 1. supplevi. 2. quas B. 3. Ladulfi B. 4. martis B.

---

2. *1160 ianuar. 28 Sydonie. Balduinus III Hierosolymitanus rex donat Iohanni de Caypha custodiam et drogomanagium castri Mhalia et procurationem pro ipso et pro equitatura.*

Notum sit omnibus tam futuris quam presentibus, quod ego Balduinus per graciam dei in sancta civitate Ierusalem Latinorum rex quartus dono Iohanni de Caypha, filio Gambre, et heredibus suis in perpetuum custodiam et drogomanachgium omnium pertinenciarum cuiusdam castelli mei, quod[1] Mhalia nuncupatur, tam earum videlicet, que nunc habitantur, quam earum, que per dei graciam in futurum habitabuntur. Nomina vero earum, que nunc habitantur, pertinenciarum sunt hec: Capharsenie, Benna, Carcara, Ialin, Balaton, Torsia, Aithire, Tabaria, Iazon; et illarum similiter pertinenciarum, que nondum habitantur, drogomanachgium et custodiam, si que sunt et quotquot sunt, eidem Iohanni et suis heredibus perhenniter habenda dono et concedo, tali siquidem pacto, quod, si harum, que predicte sunt, pertinenciarum per donationem, vendicionem, commutationem sive quemlibet alium modum de manu ac de proprietate mea aliquam emisero, concambium eque valitudinis ei dabo. Dono preterea memorato Iohanni et heredibus suis in perpetuum habere concedo procurationem, sibi videlicet et equitature sue, quamdiu mecum in expeditione et in exercitu fuerit. Ut igitur huius donationis et concessionis mee pagina rata et stabilis permaneat, testibus eam subscriptis corroborari et sigilli mei suppressione muniri precepi. Predictorum omnium scribaniam cum omni iure suo eidem dono. Factum est autem hoc anno ab incarnatione domini m° c° lx° indictione viii[2]. Huius quidem rei testes sunt Odo de Sancto Amando, vicecomes et castellanus Ierosolimitanus; Poncius de Caypha, Rabellus de Monte Regali, Marsilius miles, Bernardus Bamqueth, Giraldus de Cunillis, Iohannes filius domine Osanne, Bonetus filius Garini Parvi, Rainaldus socius Andree,

Bernardus de Anegnia, Michael scriba. Datum Sydonie per manum Stephani, domini Radulfi Bethleemite episcopi regisque cancellarii in hoc officio vice fungentis, v° kal. februarii.

I, 6 n. 2. 1. in margine alia manu B „castrum regis". 2. sic correxi pro iii B.

---

3. *1161 iulii 31 Nazareth. Balduinus III Hierosolymitanus rex cambium facit cum Philippo Neapolitano de Monte Regali aliisque feudis.*

Notum sit omnibus tam futuris quam presentibus, quod ego Balduinus per gratiam dei in sancta civitate[1] Hirusalem Latinorum rex quartus concessione domine Theodore, illustris Hirosolimorum regine, uxoris siquidem mee, necnon et assensu Amalrici fratris mei, comitis videlicet Ascalonitani, et domini Raimundi Tripolitani comitis atque eciam concessu domine Milisendis, sororis eiusdem comitis, future Constantinopolitane sedis imperatricis, et consilio insuper domine Hodierne, inclite matris ipsius, Tripolitane scilicet comitisse atque matertere mee, omniumque mihi attinencium assensu dono Philippo Neapolitano et eiusdem heredibus in perpetuum Montem Regalem cum omnibus pertinenciis suis et cum omni terra et honore ipsius et Crach castellum similiter cum omnibus attinenciis suis et Ahamanth simili modo cum omnibus appendiciis suis et castellum eciam Vallis Moysis cum tota terra Balduini, Hulrici, vicecomitis Neapolitani, filii, ea scilicet integritate, qua ipse iam dictus Hulricus trans fluvium Iordanem eam in vita sua tenuit et filius ipsius Balduinus post ipsum. Dono insuper eidem Philippo et ipsius heredibus servicium Iohannis Gomanni, quod videlicet pro terra illa, quam ultra Iordanem ipse Iohannes possidet, michi facere debebat, ita duntaxat, quod prefatus Iohannes pro terra, quam ultra Iordanem tenet, michi, predicto regi, faciat hominium et domino Philippo servicium. Hec igitur omnia, que superius memorata sunt, Montem Regalem scilicet et Crach et Ahamant cum omnibus eorundem pertinenciis, ubicunque in longum sive in latum protenduntur, a Zerca usque ad Mare Rubrum et eo eciam amplius, si quid alicubi seu in aliqua parte de pertinenciis Montis Regalis fuisse deprehendi in futurum poterit vel in presenti fore cognoscitur, ea quidem integritate, qua Paganus pincerna regius in vita sua hec omnia, que pretaxata sunt, tenuit et habuit, et castellum[2] eciam Vallis Moysis et cum tota terra Balduini, quam trans Iordanem habebat, quam ego rex prefatus per concambium a Balduino optinui, necnon et cum omnibus villanis Surianis sive Sarracenis, ubicunque sint cis Iordanem vel citra[3], exceptis tamen illis villanis, quos Balduinus, Hulrici vicecomitis filius, in terra sua ad ignem et ad focum[4] hospitatos, locatos et manentes in die illa, qua inter me Balduinum memoratum regem et dominum Philippum Neapolitanum concambium istud mutuum factum fuit, habebat, sibi in perpetuum retinuit, et cum Iohannis Gomanni iam dicti servicio et cum reliquis aliis omnibus, si qua sunt, que dicenda restant, domino Philippo iam tociens dicto et eiusdem heredibus in sempiternum dono, tali quidem tenore, quod totum illud videlicet, quod in prefata terra Montis Regalis sive in toto honore eiusdem aut in ipsius pertinenciis in dominio habebam vel in spe sive expectatione future conquisitionis me habiturum sperabam, habeat et ipse Philippus in dominio suo, et, quicquid ibidem aliquis de me tenebat, ab ipso Philippo et eiusdem heredibus deinceps teneat. Predicta igitur omnia dominus Philippus, de quo hic agitur, et ipsius heredes libere, quiete et sine omni calumpnia vel impedimento in posterum habeant et iure hereditario in eternum possideant, salvo tamen regie maiestati servicio, quod ex honore et pro honore Montis Regalis fieri condecet, et salvis eciam Beduinis meis omnibus, qui de terra Montis Regalis nati non sunt, salvisque mihi omnibus caravanis, quotquot vel quecunque de partibus Alexandrie et tocius Egypti transeunt in Baldach et e converso, que duo mihi retineo. Hoc eciam fuit in pactis, quod, si unquam in futurum aliqua calumpnia pro sepe dicto Montis Regalis honore ex parte aliqua emerserit, ego et successores mei domino Philippo et ipsius heredibus nunc et usque in sempiternum calumpniam illam, quecunque fuerit, adquietare, sedare omnino prorsusque tollere ex ipsa conventione debemus. Ipse vero dominus Philippus concessu domine Helizabet uxoris sue et Rainerii filii sui et filiarum suarum omnium necnon et concessione fratrum suorum, Guidonis Francigene videlicet et Henrici Bubali, omniumque suorum parentum donat mihi in concambio Montis Regalis totum feodum illud, quod ei quondam a domino Rohardo et a domina Gisla uxore illius obvenerat, ea videlicet integritate, qua ipse Rohardus et iam dicta eiusdem uxor Gisla feodum illud annum et diem tenuerunt et habuerunt, excepto tamen casali quodam Adelemia[5] nomine cum omnibus pertinenciis suis et excepto quicquid habebat in Montanis Bassis, que sibi scilicet et heredibus suis in perpetuum retinuit. Dedit insuper et mihi feodum patris sui Guidonis scilicet de Mile ea quidem integritate, qua ipse Guido de Mile et dominus Philippus filius ipsius illud feodum diem et annum tenuerunt et habuerunt. Dedit et ipse predictus Philippus mihi feodum Guidonis Francigene, quod videlicet in montanis Neapolitanis tenuit prius de domino Rohardo et postmodum de domino Philippo Neapolitano fratre suo, ita quod amodo Guido Francigena illud ex me teneat michique servicium faciat. Dedit eciam mihi Philippus iam tociens dictus feodum Henrici Bubali, fratris siquidem sui, eo quidem tenore, quo ipse Henricus de domino Philippo illud tenebat et servicium illi faciebat. Dedit mihi preterea feodum Gaufridi Torti, ita videlicet quod, sicut Gaufridus Tortus illud prius a domino Philippo tenebat, sic deinceps illud ex me teneat mihique servicium faciat. Dedit quoque et Maronem mihi et totum eciam illud, quod in montanis Tyri et Toroni in dominio habebat et quicquid alius ibidem ex ipso tenebat, tali utique modo, quod dominium ipsius Philippi in meo dominio habeam et, quicquid alius ex ipso tenebat, deinceps ex me teneat et michi servicium faciat. Ut igitur hoc concambium eo modo, quo in superioribus seriatim enarratum et expressum est, necnon convenciones utrimque consilio et assensu omnium nobis attinencium gratanter contracte utrique parti firme, stabiles et inconvulse persistant, presenti pagina subscriptis testibus sigillique mei plumbei subpressione denotata muniri et confirmari precipio. Factum est autem hoc anno ab incarnatione domini m° c° lx° i° indictione viiii. Horum quidem omnium testes sunt Petrus archiepiscopus Tyrensis, Fredericus episcopus Aconensis, Girardus episcopus Laodicensis, Humfredus de Torono, constabularius et filius eius Humfredus; Gualterius de Sancto Audemaro, castellanus et Tyberiadis dominus; Gormundus Tyberiadensis, qui dominus est de Bezans; Hugo Cesariensis dominus; Gualterius Berithi dominus; Arnaldus de Crest; Hugo sine censu, constabularius Tripolitanus; Guillelmus Porcelet; Vivianus de Caypha et filius eius Paganus; Guillelmus marescalcus; Odo de Sancto Amando, castellanus et vicecomes Hierosolimitanus; Clarembaldus, vicecomes Aconensis; Paganus de Voch; Girardus de Pogi; Gaufridus Tortus; Gocellinus Pessellus; Rohardus Neapolitanus; Balduinus de Gebal; Iohannes de Valentinis; Gomerius de Neapoli; Hibertus. Data Nazareth per manum domini Radulfi Bethleemite episcopi regisque cancellarii ii kal. augusti.

I, 5 n. 1. cf. Guil. Tyr. 21, 4. 1. supplevi. 2. in margine alia manu: Petrocii comitis B. 3. sic etiam in rubro; lege: ultra. 4. locum B. 5. in margine: reg(is) B.

---

4. *1168 aprili. Gualterius, Galileae princeps, confirmat cambium inter Fulconem Tabariae constabularium et Paganum de Caypha confectum.*

Ego Galterus princeps Galilee notum facio tam presentibus quam futuris, quod Fulco conestabilis Thabarie et Paganus de Caypha venerunt in curia mea et meo assensu ac voluntate fecerunt cambium, quod predictus Paganus dedit predicto Fulconi Gybesovart et duas Gobias et Mogar et Gatregalee et Galafiee et Romane et Sellem et totam terram aliam, quam ipse tenebat a me. Et supradictus Fulco dedit iam dicto Pagano octingentos quinquaginta bisancios sarracenatos annuatim tali modo, quod dominus Almaricus rex Ierusalem reddet ei annuatim quingentos bisancios sarracenatos super macellum Acconense, quos ipse dedit iam dicto Fulconi pro castro suo Saphet, quod castrum iam dictus dominus Almaricus rex dedit deo et milicie Templi, et iam dictum Templum reddet ei annuatim bisancios sarracenatos cccl^a^ de bisanciis septingentis, quos ipsi dederunt predicto Fulconi annuatim propter sartum, quod ipse eis dedit. Et Paganus de Caypha faciet mihi de prenominatis octingentis quinquaginta bisanciis sarracenatis tale servicium, quale ipse mihi debebat facere de prenominatis casalibus, videlicet unum militum, quod ipse debebat mittere ad meum servicium omnes vices, quas habuero guerram cum Sarracenis in mea marcha et si ego ipsum requisiero. Hec conveniencia fuit facta in presencia domini mei Amalrici regis Ierusalem et de eius voluntate et assensu et de assensu mei G(alteri) principis Galilee et E(schive)[1] uxoris mee, et tenemur nos et nostri heredes supradicto Pagano de Caypha et heredibus eius facere habere iam dictos octingentos quinquaginta bisancios sarracenatos de locis supranominatis, quod si defecerit in ipsis, supra Legione[2] et pertinenciis suis. Et ut hec omnia supradicta firma sint et rata, ego Galterius princeps Galilee facio hanc presentem cartam sigillare meo sigillo. Hec conventio facta fuit in presencia domini mei regis Almarici, et vidente et concedente, et assensu et consilio G(alteri) principis Galilee et E(schive)[1] uxoris sue. Huius rei testes sunt Amalricus rex Ierusalem et G(alterius) Galilee princeps; et frater G. Fulco; frater R. de Tabaria; Iocelinus[3] de Samesac; G. de Tabaria; Guillelmus marescalcus; Ivo Ursus; G. de Belzy; Vivianus de Cayphas; Iohannes de Monte; Ludovicus; Iaquelinus; Guillelmus de Chivilli; Guillelmus Patrie. Anno ab incarnatione domini m° c° lx° viii° luna xx° mense aprilis regnante rege Almarico.

I, 11 v. n. 18. 1. cf. Pauli I, 42. 47. Guil. Tyr. 21, 5. 2. legionem B. 3. Iocelino B.

---

5. *1169 aug. 13 Neapoli. Amalricus I Hierosolymitanus rex confirmat Pagano de Caypha, Iozelini Peselli genero, reditus 1200 bisantiorum de catena Acconensi sive feudum 20 militum, et Pagano 600 bisantios de funda et 500 de macello Acconensibus.*

Notum sit omnibus tam futuris quam presentibus, quod ego Amalricus per gratiam dei in sancta civitate Ierusalem Latinorum rex quintus dono et confirmo tibi Pagano de Caypha et heredibus, quos de filia Iozelini Peselli habebis[1], quecunque dominus ac frater meus, inclitus Ierosolimorum rex Baldoinus, olim dedit ei et eiusdem heredibus. Que vero sint illa, sequencia demonstrant, scilicet mcc bisantii sarracenati in cathena Acconensi annuatim recipiendi[2] pro servitio duorum militum et primum feodum xx[ti] militum sive eciam minorem feodum ad voluntatem Iozellini et heredum suorum, quod in tota terra sua sibi acciderit vel heredibus suis; et quando predictus Iocelinus vel sui heredes predictum feodum tenebunt et habebunt in possessione, predicti[3] mcc bisantii ad regem debent reverti. Insuper eidem Iozelino et heredibus suis donavit et concessit feodum c militum in Babilonia[4], cum deus eam christianis dederit, et dc bisantios, quos predictus rex Balduinus, frater meus, donavit Iocelino Pesello, ego rex Amalricus dono et confirmo tibi Pagano de Caypha et heredibus tuis, predictos dc bisantios annuatim in funda Acconensi per iiii[or] terminos recipiendos[2] in augmento feodi tui pro servicio unius militis. Item dono et confirmo tibi Pagano de Caypha et heredibus tuis illos quingentos bisantios, quos ego dedi Fulconi Tiberiadensi pro castro de Saphet, quod castrum ego dedi deo et milicie Templi, quibus bisantios predictus Fulco dedit in cambio pro Gibosevart. Et istos predictos quingentos bisantios debet annuatim recipere in macello Acconensi per iiii[or] terminos. Ut igitur hec omnia, que superius memorata sunt, sepedicto Pagano de Caypha suisque heredibus fiima, fixa et incommutabilia persistant, presenti pagina subscriptis testibus sigilli mei subpressione denotata[5] confirmo. Factum est autem hoc ab incarnatione domini m° c° lx° ix° indictione xi[a 6]. Huius quidem rei testes sunt Humfredus de Torono, constabularius; Galterius de Sancto Audemaro, castellanus et dominus Tyberiadensis; Philippus Neapolitanus; Baldoinus de Insula; Guillelmus marescalcus; Clarambaldus vicecomes Acconensis; Gaufridus Tortus; Paganus de Voh; Odo de Sancto Amando. Datum Neapoli[7] per manum Stephani, domini Radulfi Bethleemite episcopi regisque cancellarii in hoc officio vice fungentis, idus augusti.

I, 7 v. n. 6. 1. habebit B. 2. recepturos B. 3. predictos B. 4. babiloniā. 5. denotatā B. 6. l. ii. 7. Neapolim B.

---

6. *1173 martii 26 Acchon. Amalricus I Hierosolymitanus rex donat b. Mariae s. domus hospitalis Theutonicorum 400 bisantios de funda Neapolitana, quatuor casalia in partibus S. Abrahae et Bethan, certos proventus frumenti et hordei de omnibus suis bonis in terris Ierusalem et Neapolis.*

Notum sit omnibus tam presentibus quam futuris, quod ego Amalricus per dei graciam in sancta civitate Ierusalem Latinorum rex quintus dono et concedo et confirmo pro pannis infirmorum beate Marie sancte domus hospitalis Theutonicorum pro anima mea et antecessorum meorum quadringentos bisantios sarracenatos in assisiam in funda Neapolitana per iiii[or] anni terminos, de tribus videlicet in tres menses ad unumquemque terminum c bisancios; et do vobis pro infirmis beate Marie Theutonicorum duo casalia in partibus sancti Abrahe, que vocantur Deldol et Seriie, cum omnibus pertinenciis suis et villanis et iardinis et vineis, et duo alia casalia in partibus Bethan, que vocantur Rehap et Ardelle, cum omnibus pertinenciis suis et villanis et canamellis. Et do vobis pro infirmis beate Marie sancte domus hospitalis Theutonicorum de tota terra mea Ierusalem et Neapoli et de omnibus casalibus, que sunt in partibus Ierusalem et Neapolis concedo de unaquaque carruca unam robbam frumenti, et unam ordei habebitis annuatim de parte rustici. Et si contigerit, quod de dictis rebus vos iam dictos hospitalis beate Marie Theutonicorum, ut supradictum est, non posset esse pagatum[1], volo, quod de omnibus rebus meis, ubicunque sunt intus vel extra Neapolim, et funda Acchon posset pagari. Ut huius donationis et concessionis mee[2] pagina rata tibi teneatur et indissoluta, presentem cartam testibus subscriptis et sigillo meo plumbeo muniri precepi. Factum est hoc anno ab incarnatione domini m° c° lxx° iii° indictione xi[a 3]. Huius rei testes sunt Guido Ioppensis et Ascalonis comes[4]; Rainaldus Sydonis, Milo dominus Montis Regalis[5]; Ainfridus constabularius regni; Iozcelinus de Samosac; dominus Balianus Neapolis[6] de Ybelino; Balianus frater eius; Milo de Planci[5]; Bertrandus de Ioppen; Henricus de Gerino; Galterius de Berito; Guillelmus de Tyro; Gualterius de Mirabel; Nicholaus de Huderic; Guilibertus de Sancto Dionisio. Datum Acchon per manum Radulfi episcopi Bethleemite regnique Ierusalem cancellarii vii kal. aprilis.

I, 23 n. 41; spurium. 1. B cf. n. 8. 2. mea B. 3. lege vi. 4. Guido demum 1180 aprili per nuptias cum Sibylla contractas Ioppes et Ascalonis comes evasit. 5. Ipse Milo de Planci octobri 1173 defunctus Montis Regalis dominus fuit: Guil. Tyr. 21, 4. 6. videtur supplendum: Balduinus.

---

7. *1174 iulii 3 Ierusalem. Amalricus I Hierosolymitanus rex confirmat Philippo Rufo castella Arabiam et Zakanin cum pertinentiis.*

Notum sit cunctis tam presentibus quam futuris, quod ego Amalricus per dei graciam in sancta civitate Ierusalem Latinorum rex quintus dono, concedo et confirmo tibi, Phillippe Ruffe[1], et heredibus tuis, quos de uxore tua legitime desponsata genueris, hec duo casalia Arabiam et Zakanin cum omnibus eorum pertinenciis et cum hiis gastinis: Derhenne, Mezera, Misklin, et cum omnibus illorum casalium gastinis et cum hiis villanis: Manket, Helel, Bulmali, Buchalet fratribus, et Zelzel, Nabe, Chazeraz fratribus, et Tharet, Bufares, Zacran, Aili, Raphaha, Ebisserur, Buder, Tarcan, Phaheit, Nazer, Meget?, Bulmene, Phet, Zieia, Zabaa, Sep, Numeir, Haus et cum eorum dumtaxat uxoribus et filiis et filiabus, qui ab eis descenderunt, et cum omnibus villanis, qui hodie in illis casalibus manent. Hec itaque omnia dono tibi et iam dictis heredibus tuis quieta et absoluta ab omni calumnia habenda in concambium mille bisanciorum, quos de me Accon tenuisti, sed mihi pro hiis omnibus liberos reliquisti. Pro hiis autem omnibus tu et heredes tui facietis mihi servicium unius militis. Octingentos vero bisancios, quos in funda Accon recipiendos tibi dedi, tantummodo quamdiu vixeris, habebis et pro eis duorum militum servicium mihi facies. Ut igitur hec omnia rata et inconvulsa permaneant, cartam presentem testibus subscriptis et sigillo meo corroboro. Factum est hoc anno ab incarnatione domini m° c° lxx° iiii° indictione vii°. Huius rei testes sunt: frater Berengarius senescalcus Templi[2]; frater Garinus[3] preceptor hospitalis; Hemfridus constabularius; Milo Montis Regalis dominus; Rainaldus Sydonis dominus; Guido dominus Cesaree; Gualterus frater eius; Gormundus de Tyberiade; Atto filius eius; Rohardus de Ioppe; Iohannes de Arsur[4]; Amalricus de Cesarea; Arnulfus de Blancagarda; Amalricus filius eius; Tirricus de Asper; Iordanus de Ripelmunde. Datum in Ierusalem per manum Petri vicecancellarii regis v° nonas iulii.

I, 20 v. n. 34. Quum Amalricus I rex 1173 iulii 11 iam obierit, aut notae chronologicae depravatae aut diploma totum falsum est. Incarnationis annus 1174 et indictio vii inter se concinunt. 1. Inter barones regni Amalrici regis testes nominatur 1170. indict. i (pro iii) ap. Pauli I, 52. 2. 1169 aug. 30 senescallus Templi fuit Gualterius (Pauli I, 50); Berengerius 1176 (Pauli I, 61). 3. 1174 martio, 1175 praeceptor Hospitalis Garinus (Pauli I, 56. 60); Guarnerius 1176 (p. 61), 1181 (p. 69). 4. Arsur B.

---

8. *1177 oct. 17 Ierusalem. Amalricus I Hierosolymitanus rex concedit b. Mariae sanctae domus Theutonicorum annuatim de porta David recipiendos 300 bisantios, casalia Saffir et Kafarhone in terra Neapolis, tres vineas in montania de Abel, reditus quosdam frumentarios de porta David et zucari de Neapoli.*

Notum sit omnibus tam futuris quam presentibus, quod ego Amalricus per dei graciam in sancta civitate Ierusalem Latinorum rex quintus dono et concedo et confirmo beate Marie sancte domus hospitalis Theutonicorum pro anima mea et antecessorum meorum ccc bisancios sarracenatos in feudum recipiendos annuatim ad portam David per iiii^{or} anni terminos, scilicet in festo sancti Iohannis Babtiste et in festo sancti Remigii et in natali domini et in pascha, recipiendos tali siquidem tenore, et[1] duos casalios Neapolis, quod dicitur Saffir, cum suis pertinenciis et villanis et Kafarhone cum suis pertinenciis et villanis et tres vineas in montania, que vocatur de Abel; in prima vinea est cisterna una sine aqua; in altera vinea est cava una de terra candida, et tertia[2] vinea est ibi iuxta; et xx^{ti} iiii^{or} modios frumenti et xx^{ti} iiii^{or} modios ordei et sex modios leguminum, scilicet ad portam David in tempore messium annuatim recipiendos. Et de omnibus canamellis Neapolis pro infirmis Zaribel habebitis duas roddas zucari de mazara et de unaquaque pertica, que laborabitur canamellis, unaquaque ebdomada habebitis unam cudariam zucari de mazera. Et dono insuper istam helemosinam: franchisiam scilicet intrandi et exeundi, vendendi et emendi per totum regnum Ierosolimitanum de omnibus iurisdictionibus, quas ullus[3] homo debeat reddere vel pagare, vos sitis liberi et quieti. Et si contingeret, quod de dictis rebus vos iam dictos[4] hospitalis beate Marie Theutonicorum, ut supra dictum est, non posset esse pagatum, volo, quod super omnibus rebus meis ubicunque sunt intus vel extra Ierusalem et Accon posset pagari. Ut huius donationis et concessionis mee pagina rata vobis teneatur et indissoluta, presentem cartam testibus subscriptis et sigillo meo plumbeo muniri precepi. Factum est anno ab incarnacione domini m° c° lxx° vii° indictione xiiii^{a}. Huius rei sunt testes dominus Eraclius sancte resurrectionis electus, Guido Ioppensis et Ascalonis comes, Anfridus constabularius regni, Rainaldus Sydonis dominus, Balianus Neapolis, Balduinus de Ybelin, Balianus frater eius, Milo de Plance, Galterus de Berito, Anselmus de Brie, Galterius de Mirabel vicecomes. Datum Ierusalem per manum Radulfi episcopi Bethleemite regnique Ierusalem vicecancellarii xvi° kal. novembris.

I, 23 n. 42. Quum Amalricus I rex 1173 iulii 11 iam obierit, quem paulo praecessit morte Radulfus Bethlehemitanus episcopus cancellarius, Milo de Planci 1173 octobri, Heraclius vero Hierosolymitanus patriarcha 1180 demum electus sit et Guido Ioppes et Ascalonis comes factus, pro falso diploma habendum est. Caeterum 1177 anno respondet indictio x. Toppen Des Deutschen Ordens Anfänge. Neue Preufsische Provinzialblätter 1849. VII, 234 ad annum 1166 reiiciendum esse coniecerat ob indictionem. In margine manu s. XIII B: respondeatur ut in prece(denti). 1. deesse aliquid videtur. 2. cetera B. 3. quod nullus B. 4. cf. p. 7.

9. *1178 febr. 5. Boamundus, Raimundi filius, Antiochiae princeps, donat Ioscelino caveam et abbatiam Granacherie cum ceteris.*

Notum sit omnibus tam futuris quam presentibus, quod ego Boamundus Raimundi principis filius, dei gracia princeps Anthiochie, dono et concedo Ioscelino, filio Ioscelini Edessani comitis, homini meo ligio, et heredibus suis, quos habuerit de legitima sponsa, in feodo et iure hereditario caveam et abbaciam, que dicitur Granacherie, et casale cavee Livonie, Baqfala et Gaigum et quantumcumque terre Guillelmi de Croisi tenebam et habebam, scilicet Sefferie, Bequoqua, Vaquer, Cofra. Insuper dono ei tres mille bisantios in assisia in tribus villarum mearum ad voluntatem singulis annis habendos et unum gripum liberum in laccu et tres mille listras vini ad sanctum Symeonem, tali scilicet pacto, quod ipse se quintus militum mihi debet servire; sed si ipse invenerit tres milites feodatos in terra mea, qui ei servire velint, salva mea fidelitate libenter concedo. Sed si aliquo modo contigerit, ut ipse vel heredes sui terram suam recuperare poterint, hec omnia supradicta mihi vel heredibus meis redeant. Hec omnia prescripta habeat Ioscelinus, tam ipse quam heredes sui, teneat et possideat libere, quiete, in pace et sine calumpnia in perpetuum. Ut autem hoc donum firmum sit et stabile, imminenti scripto et testibus subnotatis meoque principali sigillo munio et corroboro. Huius rei testes sunt Rainaldus de Margat; Bartolomeus filius comitis[1]; Guillelmus, marescalcus Antiochie; Petrus de Asart; Richerius de Lerminat; Philippus de Logis; Garinus Guengnart; Guido Falsart; Rogerius Corbel; Symon Burgevin. Datum hoc privilegium per manum Iohannis cancellarii anno domini m° c° lxx° viii° indictione xii^{a} mense februarii v die[2], infra principatus vero mei xv° anno.

I, 10 n. 14. 1. 1179 febr. ind. xi inter testes Boamundi principis Antiocheni offenduntur: „Rainaldus de ... connestabulus Antiochie, Bartolomeus filius comitis Gislaberti et Willelmus Cavee manescalcus, Rig. de Lerminato, Simon Buriavis, dux Antiochie"; Pauli I, 68. Simon dux Antiochiae 1175 martio; Pauli I, 59. Richerius de Herminat 1186 febr., p. 77. Richerus de Erminato et Symon Burgevin 1193 sept., p. 86. 2. dies B.

---

10. *1179 april. 2 apud Vadum Iacob. Balduinus IV Hierosolymitanus rex confirmat Ioscelino senescalco a Iohanne camerario regio emta domos Accone et casalia quinque in Acconensi territorio sita.*

Notum sit omnibus tam presentibus quam futuris, quod ego Balduinus per dei graciam in sancta civitate Ierusalem Latinorum rex sextus concedo et confirmo tibi Ioscelino, Ioscelini Edessani comitis filio, dilecto avunculo et senescalco meo, domos, quas Iohannes camerarius meus in Accon habebat, et casalia subscripta, que in Acconensi territorio de feodo camerarie mee possidebat, videlicet Lanahie, Casale Album, Ancre, Clie et Ambelie, que omnia cum pertinenciis eorum Iohannes predictus camerarius tibi pro solvendis debitis suis concedente uxore sua Isabella et Rohardo de Cabor et fratribus suis vendidit et pro quibus omnibus septem milia bisanciorum et quingentos eidem

Iohanni dedisti. Pro quibus eciam servicium duorum militum mihi et heredibus meis tu et heredes tui perpetuo facietis. Et ut huius concessionis a confirmationis mee pagina tibi et heredibus tuis rata teneatur in eternum et indissoluta, presentem cartam testibus subscriptis et sigillo meo muniri et corroborari precepi. Factum est hoc anno ab incarnatione domini m° c° lxx° ix° indictione xii. Huius rei sunt testes Humfridus, regius constabularius[1]; Balduinus Ramatensis dominus; Radulphus de Gerino; Amalricus de Franco loco; Abraham de Nazareth[2]; Gerardus de Pogi; Gazelus Tyrensis; Petrus de Cresera[3]; Gosihuinus Boccus; Symon de Bethleem; Iohannes de Herenc; Robertus de Pinqeigni; Laurencius de Franco loco; Guillelmus Patron; Guillelmus Raimundi; Radulfus Iterii; Rannulfus vicecomes; magister Bernardus. Datum apud Vadum Iacob per manum Willelmi Tyrensis archiepiscopi regisque cancellarii iiii° nonas aprilis.

I, 8 n. 7. Exhibet Pauli I, 65 num. lxv. eiusdem regis diploma de a. 1178 ind. xii. ap. vadum Iacob per manum Willelmi Tyrensis archiepiscopi regisque cancellarii nov. 17. Sed 1178 octobri, quo mense rex castrum apud Vadum Iacob construere coepit, Wilhelmus (hist. 21, 26) relicta terra sancta Romam profectus est ad concilium Lateranense, unde redux 1180 april. 24 Constantinopoli fuit. Concilium ipsum, cuius actis subscripsit, Romae 1179 martii 5, 7, 19 diebus habitum est. Neque igitur diploma caret suspicione. 1. Hunfridus constabularius † 1179 april. 23. 2. † 1179. 3. Ap. Pauli I, 53: 1173 P. de Creseto castellanus de Ierusalem; p. 61. 1176 Petrus de Creset; p. 66. 1178 nov. 17: Petrus de Creseca castellanus Iherusalem.

---

11. *1179 oct. 22 Accon. Balduinus IV Hierosolymitanus rex confirmat Ioscelino comiti, senescalco, a Petronilla Acconensi vicecomitissa emta duo casalia Samueth et Sophie.*

Notum sit omnibus tam futuris quam presentibus, quod ego Balduinus per dei graciam in sancta civitate Ierusalem Latinorum rex sextus concessione et assensu Sibille sororis mee, Ioppensis et Ascalonensis commitisse, concedo et confirmo tibi comiti Iocelino, avunculo et senescalco meo, et heredibus tuis omnia, quecunque a Petronilla Acconensi[1] vicecomitissa concessione et assensu filiorum suorum Bauduini et Clarenbaudi, concedente eciam Hodierna predicti Balduini uxore, pro quatuor milibus bisantiorum et quingentis emisti, duo scilicet casalia nomine Samueth et Sophie cum omnibus pertinenciis et divisionibus suis et cum omnibus villanis, domos eciam, quas in castello meo, quod Castellum Novum nominatur, possidebat, et omnes vineas et iardina et omnem possessionem, quam in prenominato castello et in eiusdem territorio tam in terra quam in domibus et vineis et iardinis iure hereditario possidere videbatur[2]. Hec autem omnia tali conditione tibi et heredibus tuis iure perpetuo possidenda concessi, quatinus ea optinere ex integro vel per partes dare, vendere vel invadiare cuilibet et omnimodam inde voluntatem tuam facere possis omni penitus contrarietatis obstaculo remoto et omni calumpnia. Ut igitur tu et heredes tui pretaxatam empcionem, sicut prediximus, libere et quiete et sine servicio possideatis in perpetuum et huius concessionis et confirmationis mee pagina rata permaneat in eternum et indissoluta, presentem cartam testibus subscriptis et sigillo meo muniri et corroborari precepi. Factum est hoc anno ab incarnacione domini m° c° lxx° ix° indictione xii[a]. Huius rei testes sunt princeps Renaldus Montis Regalis et Ebronis dominus; dominus Balianus de Ybelino, Renaldus Sydonis dominus; Gauterius de Berito; Guido frater eius; Paganus de Caypha; Balianus Ioppensis; Soherius de Memmedeo; Gosohuinus Boccus; Willelmus de Molembec; Giraldus de Ridefort, regius marescalcus; Giselbertus de Floriaco, Acconensis vicecomes; Poncius Marriani; Antelmus de Luca; Willelmus de Furcis; Raimundus Melangen; Rad(u)l(phus) de Nigella. Data Accon per manum Willelmi Tyrensis archiepiscopi regisque cancellarii undecimo kal. novembris.

I, 7 n. 5. 1. Acconensis B. 2. videatur B.

---

12. *1179 nov. 24 Accon. Balduinus IV Hierosolymitanus rex confirmat Ioscelino, Edessani comitis filio, senescalco, septennem terrae S. Georgii et baiulationis puerorum Adae Bethsamitis possessionem.*

Notum sit omnibus tam futuris quam presentibus, quod ego Balduinus per dei graciam in sancta civitate Ierusalem Latinorum rex sextus concedo et confirmo tibi Ioscelino, Edessani comitis filio, avunculo et senescalco meo, terram que dicitur de Sancto Georgio et baiulationem puerorum Ade Bethsamitis, que Hugo iuvenis, filius Hugonis Bibliensis domini, concessione uxoris sue Stephanie tibi usque ad septem annos plene completos possidenda pro sexcentis bisanciis singulis annis mense augusto censualiter reddendis et sine servicio possidendis vendidit et concessit, tali siquidem concessione, quod septem fruges et omnes alios terre redditus per septem prescriptos annos ex eadem terra recipies plenarie et servicium, quod pro prenominata terra fieri debet, mihi facies ac de omnibus, que de terre forisfacturis infra prefixum terminum habueris, pretaxato Hugoni medietatem reddes; quod, si predictus Hugo in partibus istis cum uxore sua mansionem suam facere voluerit, tu terram, de qua hic agitur, eidem reddere tenearis, et, si rusticis terre iam dicte de tuo aliquid commodaveris, ipse tibi integre reddi faciet. Prescriptorum etenim bisanciorum precepto iam dicti Hugonis in presenti mille et trecentos reddidisti. Ut autem huius concessionis mee pagina rata teneatur et indissoluta, presentem cartam testibus subscriptis et sigillo meo muniri precepi. Factum est hoc anno ab incarnatione domini m° c° lxx° ix° indictione xii[a] [1]. Huius rei sunt testes Reinaldus Sydonis dominus, Balianus de Ybelino, Balianus Ioppensis, Gerardus de Ridefort, regius marescalcus; Gozvinus Boccus; Giselbertus de Floriaco, vicecomes Acconensis; Raimundus de Montolivo. Data Accon per manum Willelmi Tyrensis archiepiscopi regisque cancellarii viii° kal. decembris.

I, 6v. n. 3. 1. pro xiii[a].

---

13. *1181 novbr. 13 Accon.*[1] *Balduinus IV Hierosolymitanus rex confert Ioscelino senescalco assisiam mille bisantiorum e funda Acconensi tam diu percipiendam, donec Philippus Rufus eam redemerit.*

Notum sit omnibus tam futuris quam presentibus, quod ego Balduinus per dei gratiam in sancta civitate Ierusalem Latinorum rex sextus concedo et confirmo tibi Ioscelino, avunculo et senescalco meo, assisiam mille bisanciorum, quam Philippus Rufus, consanguineus meus, ad fondam Accon annuatim in vita sua possidet, tam diu tenendam et habendam, donec ipse Philippus duo milia bisanciorum, quos ei super eandem assisiam commodasti, tibi plenarie persolvat. Hanc igitur assisiam tali conditione tibi concessi, quatinus servicium duorum militum mihi pro ea facias et predictus Philippus pro ea a te redimenda eandem alicui pignori obligare non possit. Verumtamen si terram suam invadiare voluerit vel alio aliquo modo predicta duo milia bisanciorum habuerit, unde predictam mille bisanciorum assisiam a te redimere possit, tu eam eidem reddere liberam et quietam de iure tenearis, tali siquidem tenore, quod, si iam dictus Philippus, antequam prescripta mille bisanciorum assisia redempta fuerit, decesserit, ego vel mei heredes, quia tociens dictus Philippus iam dictam assisiam post decessum suum non est possessurus, a te, quamdiu vixeris, vel a mandato tuo post tuum decessum, quia duorum militum servicium facis pro ea, non extorqueamus, donec prius tibi vel mandato tuo duo milia bisanciorum persolvamus. Ut igitur huius concessionis et confirmationis mee pagina tuta permaneat et indissoluta, presentem cartam testibus subscriptis et sigillo meo muniri precepi. Factum est hoc anno ab incarnatione domini m° c° lxxx° i° indictione xv^a^. Huius rei testes sunt Rainaldus Sydonis dominus, Milo de Colovardino, Symon de Vercenni, Tyri castellanus; Iohannes Lombardus, Fulco de Falesia, Laurencius de Franco loco. Datum Accon per manum Willelmi Tyrensis archiepiscopi regisque cancellarii idus novembris.

I, 8 n. 8. 1. De illis diebus diploma Balduini regis, in quo testis etiam Rainaldus Sydonis dominus invenitur, reperi in schedis Heinrici Guilielmi Schulz Dresdensis e Cavensis prope Salernum siti monasterii archivo descriptum: 1181 ind. xv (novembr. 8) 6 idus novembris apud Tyrum, Balduinus rex Cavensis monasterii navibus liberum a teloneo introitum in portus regni et exitum concedit; „per manum Wilhelmi Tyrensis archiepiscopi regisque cancellarii".

---

14. *1182 febr. 24 Acon. Balduinus IV Hierosolymitanus rex Ioscelino senescalco confert Castellum Novum in montanis Acconensibus, reditus quosdam de fundis Acconensi et Tyrensi, feudum Iohannis Banerii, Maronum.*

Notum sit omnibus tam futuris quam presentibus, quod ego Balduinus per dei graciam in sancta civitate Ierusalem Latinorum rex sextus dono et concedo regieque maiestatis auctoritate confirmo tibi comiti Ioscelino, avunculo et senescalco meo mihi dilectissimo, castellum novum, quod in montanis Achonensibus situm est, cum vineis et olivetis et iardinis, cum omnibus terris suis cultis et incultis, cum omnibus villanis terre et cum omnibus pertinenciis et divisionibus suis, sicut libere et quiete illud possedi et ea die, qua tibi illud et heredibus tuis iure hereditario possidendum donavi, possidebam, excepto casali, quod dicitur Iazun, quod cum omnibus pertinenciis suis mihi retineo. Dono preterea tibi et heredibus tuis quingentos bisancios ad fundam Achon et quingentos ad fundam Tyri annuatim per consuetos funde Achon et funde Tyri terminos recipiendos et iure hereditario possidendos. Dono nichilominus tibi et heredibus tuis feodum, qui fuit Iohannis Banerii, centum scilicet bisancios ad fundam Acon et quatuor carrucatas terre in territorio de Caimont; quem feodum tu donasti Garnerio homini tuo Parisiensi, qui predicti Iohannis Banerii filiam duxit uxorem, sub unius servientis servicio cum duabus equitaturis. Hec autem omnia tibi et heredibus tuis iure hereditario possidenda donavi pro commutatione castri sancti Helye, quod cum omnibus pertinenciis suis tibi perpetuo possidendum antea donaveram, et pro commutatione Lubani et Carrubie, que cum omnibus pertinenciis suis et cum hominio, quod fuit Iohannis de Lumbres, post mortem domine Marie, Ierosolimorum quondam regine, ad te reverti debebant. Dono eciam tibi et heredibus tuis Maronum cum omnibus pertinenciis suis tam in dominiis quam in feodis et hominium Gaufredi Torti, hominium eciam sancti Georgii et tocius terre pertinentis ad sanctum Georgium. Tali siquidem conditione hec omnia, sicut prescripta sunt, tibi concessi, quod pro dictis omnibus mihi et heredibus meis tu et heredes tui servicium sex militum exceptis feodatis perpetuo faciatis. Ut igitur hec omnia, sicut superius enarrata sunt, tu et heredes tui libere et quiete teneatis et habeatis in perpetuum et ut huius donationis et concessionis mee pagina rata tibi et heredibus tuis teneatur in eternum et indissoluta, presentem cartam testibus subscriptis et sigillo meo muniri et corroborari precepi. Factum est hoc anno ab incarnatione domini m° c° lxxx° ii°[1] indictione xv[a] concessione et assensu Guidonis Ioppes et Ascalonis comitis et Sibille sororis mee eorundem[2] comitisse. Huius rei testes sunt princeps Reinaldus Montis Regalis et Ebronis dominus; Renaldus Sydonis dominus; Balduinus Ramatensis dominus, Balianus frater eius; Aimericus constabularius; Gaufridus Tortus, Milo de Colovardino. Data Acon per manum Willelmi Tyrensis archiepiscopi regisque cancellarii viii kal. marcii.

I, 6v. n. 4. 1. m° c° lxx° ii° B; cf. p. 9. Nec Aimericus ante 1179 constabularius fuit. 2. B.

---

15. *1182 april. 27 Ierusalem. Balduinus IV Hierosolymitanis rex donat Guilielmo Tyrensi archiepiscopis decimam omnium xeniorum de terra Toroni.*

In nomine sancte et individue trinitatis, patris et filii et spiritus sancti. Amen. Notum sit omnibus tam futuris quam presentibus, quod ego Balduinus per dei graciam in sancta civitate Ierusalem Latinorum rex sextus dono et concedo tibi, Guilielme, venerabilis Tyrensis ecclesie archiepiscope, et successoribus tuis et per te ecclesie tue in perpetuum decimam exeniorum, id est presentium omnium, que fiunt ex tota terra Toroni in nativitate domini, in carnelevare et in pasca, in gallinis scilicet, ovis, caseis, ectulis[1] et lignis; decimam quoque bisantiorum, quos de liberis carrucis accipio vel accepturus sum. Dono nihilominus et concedo, quod villani universas decimas, quas de tota terra Toroni do et dare consueverunt predecessores mei, in domum tuam, que est apud Toronum, deportent, ut sicut nobis novem partes ita tibi decimam sine contradictione deferant. Et ut huius donationis et concessionis mee pagina rata tibi successoribusque tuis et ecclesie tue teneatur in eternum et indissoluta, presentem cartam testibus subscriptis et sigillo meo muniri precepi. Factum est hoc anno ab incarnatione domini m° c° lxxxii° indictione xv^a. Huius rei testes sunt Odo Beritensis episcopus; Reimundus comes Tripolitanus; Ioscelinus regis senescalcus; princeps Rainaldus; Rainaldus Sydonis dominus; Laurentius de Franco loco; Balduinus de Duaco. Datum Ierusalem per manus Guillielmi Tyrensis archiepiscopi regisque cancellarii v kal. maii.

I, 85 v. Annotatur in fine: „Hoc privilegium habet ecclesia Tyrensis". 1. ?

---

16. *1183 martii 19 Accon. Balduinus IV Hierosolymitanus rex confirmat Ioscelino senescalco a Gaufrido Torto comparata quatuordecim casalia.*

Notum sit omnibus tam futuris quam presentibus, quod ego Balduinus per dei graciam in sancta civitate Ierusalem Latinorum rex sextus concedo et confirmo tibi Ioscelino, avunculo et senescalco meo, et heredibus tuis hec subscripta casalia cum eorum pertinenciis et divisionibus, terris cultis et incultis, planis, montanis, aquis et nemoribus, rusticis quoque, qui de eisdem casalibus sunt nati, ubicumque sint. Que casalia cum prescriptis omnibus tu a Gaufrido Torto voluntate et assensu Flandrine uxoris sue et Gaufridi filii sui sex milibus bisanticrum comparasti; tali tenore, quod feodos, quos Seit et Guillelmus iam dicti Gaufridi servientes in eisdem casalibus habebant, scribaniam scilicet et drugumanagium, in presencia mea quietos clamaverunt et idem Gaufridus Tortus alibi eis alios assignavit feodos, tali quoque modo, quod tu pro eisdem casalibus servicium duorum militum tibi ipsi facias et ipse Gaufridus Tortus tale servicium, quale pro residuo terre sue debet, facere teneatur. Sunt autem hec casalia: Elgabcie[1], Hourfex, Carsilia, Cassie, Dere, Feenix, Bellum-videre, quod dicitur Sarracenice Fassove, Camsara, Terretrame, Accabara, Sorove, Sauroefoca, Tarrebresca, Deirbasta. Facta est autem hec venditio precatu ipsius Gaufridi, ut et debita sua persolveret et residuum feodi sui retineret; alioquin retinere non poterat occupatus mole debitorum. Ut igitur huius concessionis et confirmationis mee pagina rata tibi et heredibus tuis teneatur in eternum et indissoluta, presentem cartam testibus subscriptis et sigillo meo muniri precepi. Factum est hoc anno ab incarnatione domini m° c° lxxx° iii° indictione xv^{a}. Huius rei sunt testes M(onacus) Cesariensis archiepiscopus; Bernardus Lidensis episcopus; Remundus comes Tripolitanus; Guido Ioppensis et Ascalonensis comes; princeps Rainaldus; Aimericus constabularius; Balduinus de Ybelin et Balianus frater eius; Gosohvinus Boccus; Guillelmus de Molembecca; Milo de Colovardino; Gislebertus Acconensis vicecomes; Guilelmus de Furcis; Antelmus de Luca; Odo de Conchis; Raimundus de Tolosa. Datum Accon per manum Guillelmi Tyrensis archiepiscopi regisque cancellarii xiiii° kal. aprilis.

I, 8 v. n. 9. 1. Elgabacie B.

---

17. *1183 martii 19 Accon. Balduinus IV Hierosolymitanus rex concedit Ioscelino senescalco annuos 1000 bisantios de catena Acconensi, et casale Iesce pro commutatione Maron, praeterea domum apud Castellum Novum et Iohannem drugemannum cum familia.*

Notum sit omnibus tam futuris quam presentibus, quod ego Balduinus per dei graciam in civitate Ierusalem sancta Latinorum rex sextus dono et concedo tibi Ioscelino avunculo et senescalco meo et heredibus tuis concessu et voluntate Guidonis Ioppes et Ascalonis comitis et Sibille sororis mee, uxoris sue, earundem comitisse, mille bisancios ad cathenam Accon per consuetos cathene terminos annuatim recipiendos et quoddam casale, quod dicitur Iesce, in montanis Accon situm cum omnibus suis pertinenciis iure hereditario possidendum, excepto quod Alemandina eiusdem Iesse et pertinenciarum suarum medietatem tenet in dotem, sed totum post eius decessum ad te et heredes tuos revertetur. Hec autem omnia tibi donavi pro commutatione Maron, quam tibi cum omnibus suis pertinenciis et casalibus antea donaveram tali tenore, quod pro hiis omnibus idem mihi et heredibus meis tu et heredes tui faciatis servicium, quod pro Maron antea facere debueratis, exceptis assisis, qui sunt in terra Maroni. Concedo tibi preterea et heredibus tuis quandam domum apud Castellum Novum, quam[1] a Iohanne Bogalet scriba emisti cl bisantiis, cui ipsam domum antea donaveram. Dono eciam et concedo tibi et heredibus tuis Iohannem drugemannum Castelli Novi cum omnibus suis heredibus, rebus et possessionibus singulis, quas de me possidebat. Ut igitur huius donationis et concessionis mee pagina rata tibi et heredibus tuis teneatur in eternum et indissoluta, presentem cartam testibus subscriptis et sigillo meo muniri precepi. Factum est hoc anno ab incarnatione domini m° c° lxxx° iii° indictione xv^{a}. Huius rei sunt testes Guido Ioppes et Ascalonis comes; Aimericus constabularius; Balduinus de Ybelin; Balianus frater eius; Gaufridus Tortus; Gotsvinus Boccus; Guillelmus de Molembecca. Datum Accon per manum Guillelmi Tyrensis archiepiscopi regisque cancellarii xiiii kal. aprilis.

I, 9 n. 10. 1. qua B.

---

18. *1185 iunii 1 Accon. Balduinus V Hierosolymitanus rex confirmat Ioscelino senescalco libertatem de toto zucaro et de melle e casali Lanahia.*

Notum sit omnibus tam futuris quam presentibus, quod ego Balduinus per dei graciam in sancta civitate Ierusalem Latinorum rex septimus dono, concedo et confirmo assensu et voluntate Raimundi, comitis Tripolitani et tocius regni mei procuratoris, tibi Ioscelino, avunculo et senescalco meo, et heredibus tuis in perpetuum libertatem de toto zucaro tuo, quod habes seu habere debes de duobus pressoriis apud casale tuum Lanahiam et libertatem de toto melle eiusdem zucari, ita quod de ipso zucaro et de eiusdem zucari melle tu et heredes tui nichil penitus iuris de cetero dare teneamini intra Accon nec eciam extra Accon, nec eciam in Accon adducendo vel ab Accon educendo, sed cum omni libertate tu et heredes tui ipsum zucarum et eiusdem zucari mel in Accon habere et vendere possitis et eciam in Accon adducere, et ab Accon educere sine aliqua penitus iuris exhibitione ita eciam, quod, quandocunque tu et heredes tui volueritis, zucarum ipsum, ipsum quoque mel ab Accon possitis educere et in Accon, cuicunque volueritis, vendere, et ille, cui vendideritis, ab Accon, quandocunque voluerit, possit educere sine omni contradictione et sine omni iuris exhibitione. Et ut hanc libertatem tu et heredes tui iure hereditario teneatis in perpetuum et hec presens pagina rata tibi et heredibus tuis teneatur in eternum et indissoluta, presentem cartam testibus subscriptis et sigillo meo muniri feci. Factum est hoc anno ab incarnatione domini m° c° lxxx° v° indictione iii^a^. Huius rei testes sunt Milo, regius pincerna; Balianus, camerarius; Paganus, Cayphe dominus; Gualterius Durus, mariscalcus; Gilebertus de Flori, Acconensis[1] vicecomes; Gotsuinus Yrcus; Willelmus de Molembecca. Data Accon per manum Petri Lyddensis archidiachoni regisque cancellarii kal. iunii.

I, 9 n. 11. 1. Accon B.

19. *1185 nov. 1 Accon. Balduinus V[1] Hierosolymitanus rex assignat Ioscelino senescalco 1600 bisantios de funda Acconensi.*

Notum sit omnibus tam futuris quam presentibus, quod ego Balduinus per dei graciam in sancta civitate Ierusalem Latinorum rex septimus assigno voluntate et assensu Raimundi, comitis Tripolitani et tocius regni mei procuratoris, tibi Ioscelino, avunculo et senescalco meo, et mandato tuo cccc bisantios capiendos ad fundam Accon annuatim ab instanti omnium sanctorum festo usque ad iiii^or^ annos completos per consuetos ipsius funde terminos, donec scilicet plene receperis mille et sexcentos bisantios, quos comodasti super eandem cccc bisantiorum assisiam — primus autem terminus, quo incipies recipere, erit purificatio beate Marie proxima[2] futura — tali condicione, quod, si infra horum iiii^or^ annorum terminum decime vel alterius modi exactio de ipsis bisanciis capta fuerit, tam diu ipsam cccc bisantiorum assisiam tenebis, quod plene recuperaveris, quod captum fuerit. Et ut huius assignationis mee pagina rata

2

tibi et mandato tuo teneatur et indissoluta, presentem cartam testibus subscriptis et sigillo meo muniri feci. Factum est hoc anno ab incarnatione domini m° c° lxxx° vi°[3]. Huius rei sunt testes Milo, regius pincerna; Gualterius Durus, mariscalcus; Guillelmus de Molembecca; Gaufridus Heremita; Gerardus de Luco plantato; Gilebertus de Flori, Acconensis vicecomes. Datum Accon per manum Petri Lydensis archidiaconi regisque cancellarii kal. novembris.

I, 9v. n. 12. 1. † 1186. 2. l. proximo? 3. legendum m° c° lxxx° v°. Balduinus V rex obiit 1186; Guido rex coronatus est 1186 augusto.

---

20. *1186 martii 7 in civitate Ierosolimis. Guido Hierosolymitanus rex domui hospitalis b. Mariae Theotonicorum oppignerat casellum quoddam.*

In nomine sancte et individue trinitatis patris et filii et spiritus sancti. Amen. Ego Gwido de Lysanan rex nobilis Ierosolimis et Sibilla nobilis regina, uxor mea legittima, notum facimus omnibus[1], qui hoc presens privilegium videbunt, quod nos recepimus de accommodo centum et xi marcas argenti de domo hospitalis beate Marie Theotonicorum per manum fratris Severini, qui in illo tempore predicte domus hospitalarius erat. Pro quibus centum et xi marcis argenti prenominate domui dedimus in pignore unum casellum nostrum, qui est in partibus Ierosolimis prope viam regalem[2], qua vaditur[3] Ramelie, tali vero condictione, quod, si nos casellum nostrum predictum[4] non redimeremus infra annum et diem, casellum nostrum prenominatum predicte domui in honorem domini nostri Iesu Christi et beate Marie virginis et pro salute animarum nostrarum et predecessorum nostrorum ad sustentationem infirmorum et pauperum libere et absolute sine omni[5] occasione acquitamus, videlicet cum omnibus iuribus[6] suis et rusticis. Preterea, quia ego et uxor mea benigne volumus, ut hoc firmum sit et stabile et perpetuum et quod nulla post discessum nostrum super hoc discordia moveatur[7], hoc presens fecimus fieri privilegium et sigilli nostri plumbei muniri robore[8]. Istud accomodum et ista quitatio facta fuit in civitate Ierosolimis in presencia domini Euraclii, patriarche Ierosolimis, et[9] domini Renaldi principis Anthiochie, et domini G. de Arsuro, et[9] domini Gerhardi de Hatefert, et[9] domini Iohannis Poleni, et[9] domini Guidonis de Gibelet, et[9] domini Pluviani, domini de Boteron, et[9] Helie de Nasareth et[9] Heinmardi de Mongisardo et[9] Iozelin[10] de Samosac; et[9] Galtherus[10] Ardel et plures alii[11]. Factum est anno ab incarnatione domini mclxxxvi indictione v[a]. Hoc autem factum fuit et scriptum per manum domini Iocii sacerdotis regis vii die[12] marcii.

I, 49 speciali manu insertum post finem diplomatis de 1243 decbr. Guido rex coronatus est demum 1186 augusto mense; Radulf. de Diceto ap. Twysden p. 634. Caeterum totum hoc diploma spurium videtur etiam ob inusitatos initium et exitum, et ob verba: „in illo tempore ... erat". 1. supplevi. 2. regalis B. 3. qui vacatur B. 4. predicte B. 5. omnium B. 6. iuris B. 7. movetur B. 8. roborare B. 9. ubique „de" inserit B. 10. B. 11. B. 12. dies B.

---

21. *1186 oct. 21 Accon. Guido Hierosolymitanus rex donat Ioscelino senescalco Toronum et Castrum Novum et Belinas in eventum recuperationis aut pro illis iudicialiter forsan omittendis Marum, denique domum Tyri.*

Notum sit omnibus presentibus atque futuris, quod ego Guido per dei graciam in sancta civitate Ierusalem Latinorum rex octavus assensu et voluntate domine Sibille uxoris mee, eiusdem regni venerabilis regine, dono, concedo et confirmo tibi comiti Ioscelino, senescalco meo, et heredibus tuis in perpetuum Toronum et Castrum Novum cum omnibus eorum pertinenciis, cum villanis, gastinis, terris quoque cultis et incultis, montanis, planis et aquis, et Belinas cum universo iure suo, cum dominus sua miseratione christianitati reddiderit, sub tali tamen servitio mihi et meis heredibus faciendo, quale dominus Henfredus constabularius meis predecessoribus, dum eandem terram possideret, facere tenebatur. Concedo eciam tibi et confirmo et heredibus tuis in perpetuum Marum cum omnibus pertinentiis suis, Quabriquembelide, Cades, Lahare, Mees, duo Megeras, cum villanis, gastinis, terris quoque cultis et incultis, planis et montanis et aquis sub servitio quatuor militum mihi et meis heredibus[1] post me faciendo. Tali quidem condicione omnia predicta tibi et heredibus tuis dono, concedo et confirmo, quod, si Toronum et Castrum Novum iudicio mee curie te amittere aut pactiones, que inter dominum Baldoinum regem Ierusalem Latinorum sextum[2] et dominum Henfredum iuvenem facte fuerunt, solvi[3] contigerit, Maronum cum omnibus pertinenciis suis prenominatis et illud concambium, quod dominus Henfredus iuvenis pro Torono et Castro Novo tenet et possidet, tu et heredes tui habebitis et possidebitis in eternum. Ille vero, qui Toronum et Castrum Novum habuerit, missiones, quas tu vel heredes in eorum castrorum hedificatione testimonio proborum hominum ipsorum castrorum effeceritis, vobis reddere tenebitur. Dono eciam tibi et heredibus tuis quandam domum apud Tyrum, que fuit domine Vive, iure hereditario[4] habendam et possidendam in perpetuum. Et ut hec donatio, concessio et confirmatio mea tibi et heredibus tuis rata permaneat in eternum et indissoluta, presentem paginam testibus subscriptis et sigillo meo muniri feci. Huius rei testes sunt dominus Eraclius, Ierusalem venerabilis patriarcha; dominus Ioscius, Tyrensis archiepiscopus; dominus Monacus, Cesariensis archiepiscopus; dominus Letardus, de Nazareth archiepiscopus; dominus Bernardus, Liddensis episcopus; dominus Radulfus[5], Bethleemita episcopus; dominus Odo Beritensis episcopus, dominus Girardus, milicie domus Templi magister; dominus Rogerius, domus hospitalis Ierusalem magister; dominus princeps Rainaldus; Haymericus, constabularius domini regis; Milo, regis pincerna; Petrus de Creseca; Goscelinus Hyrcus; Anselinus Babini; Gaufridus Tortus; Willelmus de Molembec. Factum est hoc anno ab incarnatione domini m° c° lxxx° vi° indictione iiii^a. Datum Accon per manum Petri domini regis cancellarii Lyddensisque archidiaconi xii kal. nov.

I, 9v. n. 13. 1. supplevi. 2. sextus B. 3. solvere B. 4. hereditaria B. 5. Pandulfus B; forsan recte.

22. *1186 oct. 21 Accon. Guido Hierosolymitanus rex confirmat Ioscelino senescalco a Balduino IV rege collata bona, insuper casale Cabor cum domo Accone sita et libertatem zucari et mellis de casali Lanahiam.*

Notum sit omnibus presentibus atque futuris, quod ego Guido per dei graciam in sancta civitate Ierusalem Latinorum rex octavus assensu et voluntate domine Sybille, uxoris mee, eiusdem regni venerabilis regine, concedo et confirmo tibi comiti Ioscelino, senescalco meo, et heredibus tuis in perpetuum omnes hereditates et redditus universos a domino Balduino Ierusalem Latinorum rege sexto tibi datos et concessos et privilegio suo confirmatos, omnes eciam impignorationes, empciones, adquisitiones, quas idem dominus Balduinus privilegiorum suorum auctoritate tibi confirmavit. Concedo eciam et confirmo tibi[1] et heredibus tuis in perpetuum quoddam casale Cabor nuncupatum cum omnibus pertinenciis suis, villanis, gastinis, terris quoque cultis et incultis, planis, montanis, quod a nobis quinque milibus bisantiorum comparasti, pro quo servicium unius militis mihi et meis heredibus facere teneris, et quandam domum in Accon, que ad feudum de Chabor pertinet. Insuper te ipsum, comitem Ioscelinum, et heredes tuos penitus absolvo a testamento, quod domina Agnes comitissa, mater domine Sybille, uxoris mee, Ierosolimorum venerabilis regine, tue fidelitati comisit, quod secundum iussionem ipsius domine Agnetis comitisse te scimus fideliter complesse, ea tamen posita conditione, quod nec[2] tu nec heredes tui mihi aut meis heredibus de cetero iam dicti testamenti rationem reddere teneamini. Adhuc eciam concedo tibi, comiti Ioscelino, et heredibus tuis in perpetuum libertatem de toto zucaro tuo, quod habes seu habere debes apud casale tuum Lanahiam, ita quod de ipso zucaro et de eiusdem zucari melle tu et heredes tui ipsum zucarum et eiusdem zucari mel in Accon habere et vendere, cum vobis placuerit, possitis sine aliqua penitus iuris exhibitione et etiam in Accon adducere, cum volueritis, et ab Accon educere. Preterea concedo tibi, comiti Ioscelino, quod, si decesseris, antequam filie tue ad annos nubiles perveniant, in decessu tuo filias tuas et universam terram tuam, sub qualicunque manu et custodia volueris, salvo meo servitio ponas atque constituas. Et ut hec concessio et confirmatio mea tibi et heredibus tuis rata permaneat in eternum, et indissoluta, presentem paginam testibus subscriptis et sigillo meo muniri feci. Huius rei testes sunt: dominus Eraclius, Ierusalem venerabilis patriarcha; dominus Ioscius, Tyrensis archiepiscopus; dominus Monacus, Cesariensis archiepiscopus; dominus Letardus, de Nazareth archiepiscopus; dominus Bernardus, Lyddensis episcopus; dominus Radulfus, Bethleemita episcopus; dominus Odo Beritensis episcopus; dominus Girardus, milicie domus Templi magister; dominus princeps Rainaldus; Haymericus, constabularius regis; Milo, regis pincerna; Petrus de Creseca; Goscelinus Yrcus; Anselinus Babini; Gaufridus Tortus; Guillelmus de Molembec. Factum est hoc anno ab incarnatione domini m° c° lxxx° vi° indictione iiii^a. Data Accon per manum Petri domini regis cancellarii Liddensisque archidiachoni xii kal. novembris.

I, 10v. n. 15. 1. tibi et confirmo B. 2. supplevi.

23. *1186 oct. 21 Accon. Guido Hierosolymitanus rex paciscitur cum Ioscelino senescalco de maritandis eius filiabus.*

Ego Guido per dei graciam in sancta civitate Ierusalem Latinorum rex octavus notum fieri volo tam presentibus quam futuris, quod comes Ioscelinus, senescalcus meus, Guillelmo de Valence, fratri meo, primogenitam filiam suam donat et concedit in uxorem cum Torono et Castro Novo et pertinenciis eorum universis et cum omni terra, quam a Iohanne camerario comparavit, et cum Cabor et eius pertinenciis universis ita tamen, quod, si infra annos nubiles eam mori contigerit, idem Gwillelmus[1] frater meus reliquam nichilominus ducere teneatur. Si vero ipse Guillelmus frater meus filiam primogenitam duxerit, idem comes Ioscelinus alteram filiam suam uni nepoti meo cum reliqua terra sua et universa terra matris sue donat et concedit in uxorem. Preterea, si idem Guillelmus nec venerit nec aliquam ipsius comitis Ioscelini filiarum duxerit, iam dictus comes Ioscelinus nichilominus easdem filias suas duobus meis nepotibus donat et concedit in uxores. Et, si predictus Guillelmus frater meus venerit, ipse comes Ioscelinus eidem Guillelmo fratri meo quatuor milia bisantiorum annuatim donabit, donec idem Guillelmus frater meus filiam ipsius comitis Ioscelini ducat in uxorem. Qua in uxorem accepta in voluntate et beneplacito erit ipsius comitis Ioscelini terram universam, quam Guillelmo fratri meo cum filia sua donat, eidem Guillelmo dimittere aut iiii^{or} milia bisantiorum, quamdiu ipse comes Ioscelinus vixerit, annuatim Guillelmo fratri meo donare. Et ut hee conventiones, ut prescriptum est, rate teneantur et indissolute, presentem paginam testibus subscriptis et sigillo meo muniri feci. Huius rei testes sunt dominus Eraclius, Ierusalem venerabilis patriarcha; dominus Ioscius, Tyrensis archiepiscopus; dominus Monacus, Cesariensis archiepiscopus; dominus Letardus, de Nazareth archiepiscopus; dominus Bernardus, Liddensis episcopus; dominus Randulfus, Bethleemita episcopus; dominus Odo, Biritensis episcopus; dominus Girardus, milicie Templi magister; dominus Rogerius, domus hospitalis magister; dominus princeps Rainaldus; Aimericus, constabularius regis; Milo, regis pincerna; Petrus de Creseca; Goscelinus Yrcus; Gaufridus Tortus. Factum est hoc anno ab incarnatione domini m^{o} c^{o} lxxx^{o} vi^{o} indictione iiii^{a}. Data Accon per manum Petri domini regis cancellarii Liddensisque archidiachoni xii kal. novembris.

I, 10 v. n. 16. 1. Wigl̄ls B.

---

24. *1189 septembri Tyri. Conradus, marchionis Montis Ferrati filius, donat Martino Rociae Ianuensi domum Theodori Suriani Tyri sitam.*

Ut omnibus in posterum clareat et nulla ambiguitatis questio inde emergat, manifestum facio ego Conradus, marchionis[1] Montis Ferrati filius, quod pro bono servicio et maxima fidelitate, quam mihi in Tyro Martinus Rocia nobilis Ianuensis civis exibuit, donavi atque concessi et tradidi ei domum Theodori

Suriani cum omnibus pertinenciis suis superius et inferius, interius exteriusque positis in eadem Tyro, ita videlicet, ut ipse Martinus et sui heredes ac cui dederint prelibatam domum perpetuo habeant et iure hereditario possideant et ex ea quicquid voluerint faciant absque contradiecione, et calumpnia mei vel cuiuslibet alterius Tyrensis potestatis. Ut autem hoc factum signum firmitatis et robur stabilitatis optineat, hanc paginam scribi precepi et sigillo meo plumbeo muniri. Huius quoque rei sunt testes Ansaldus Bonivicini; Obertus Malus; Osellus; Franciscus de Portu Veneris; Oreicus Graucius; Guillelmus de Valga. Anno dominice incarnationis m° c° lxxx° ix° indictione vii. Actum est hoc in civitate Tyri mense septembris.

I, 27 n. 58. Conradus marchio Tyro relicta 1189 sept. 23 (vii die in fine sept.) ante Accon advenit; Radulfus de Diceto ap. Twysden Hist. Angl. scr. 648. — Idem initium praebent Conradi diplomata de 1188 maio ap. Borgo Raccolta di scelti diplomi Pisani. Pisa 1765. p. 105. 106. 1. marchonis B.

---

25. *1190 medio septembri in obsidione Accon. Guido Hierosolymitanus rex donat hospitali S. Mariae Alemannorum, a Sibrando in obsidione Acconis incepto, domum in hac urbe aut in eventum plateam iuxta illam.*

Notum sit omnibus tam presentibus quam futuris, quod ego Guido per dei gratiam in sancta civitate Ierusalem Latinorum rex octavus et domina Sybilla, uxor mea, per eandem venerabilis regina, donamus et concedimus domino deo et hospitali Alamannorum, quod est hedificatum in honore. . . .[1] et gloriose semperque virginis Marie, domum unam in Accon ad faciendum hospitale, illam videlicet, in qua Armeni et patrones[2] solebant hospitari. Si vero dictam domum dare non poterimus, donamus eis plateam iuxta dictam domum, ubi possint facere hospitale ad voluntatem suam. Hoc autem donamus et concedimus per manum magistri Sibrandi, qui hoc hospitale incepit et edificavit in obsidione Accon. Donamus eciam et concedimus prescripto hospitali[3] iiii^{or} carrucatas terre in territorio Accon. Ut autem huius nostre donacionis et concessionis auctoritas sepe nominato hospitali rata in eternum et indissoluta permaneat, presentem paginam testibus subscriptis muniri et sigillo nostro fecimus roborari. Huius rei testes sunt comes Ioscelinus, regis senescalcus; Anzellinus[4], regis constabularius; Henfridus Montis regalis; Hugo Tyberiadis; Rainaldus Sydonis; Gaufridus Tortus. Factum est anno incarnationis domini m° c° xc° indiccione viii^{a}[5]; datum in obsidione Accon per manum Petri, regii cancellarii, Tripolitane ecclesie archidiachoni, medio septembris.

I, 23v. n. 43. In titulo legitur: „dat nobis plateam“. 1. deest verbum (dei? eius?) non notata lacuna. 2. eadem manu correctum; antea „patroni“ ut videtur. 3. correctum ex „preceptori hospitalis“. 4. l. Amalricus? 5. antea vii ut videtur.

---

26. *1192 febr. 2. Garnerius de Neapoli, magister domus Hospitalis S. Iohannis, cedit Gerardo magistro hospitalis Alamannorum in Accon de terra et hereditate Galopini.*

Notum sit omnibus tam futuris quam presentibus, quod ego frater Garnerius de Neapoli, dei permissione sancte domus hospitalis Ierusalem humilis minister, similiter et fratres nostri, concedimus et quietam clamamus ac in pace dimittimus tibi, fratri Gerardo, magistro hospitalis Alamannorum, quod est in Accon, et omnibus fratribus eiusdem hospitalis futuris et presentibus illam calumpniam et controversiam, quam erga vos habuimus de terra et hereditate Galopini, quam nobis post decessum suum dederat, ut eam habeatis, teneatis libere et quiete in pace omni tempore possideatis, ita ut nullus successorum nostrorum nec ipse Galopinus vel aliquis heredum suorum prenominatam terram deinceps valeat calumpniare. Ut autem ista concessio rata semper maneat et inconcussa, sigilli nostri impressione testiumque subscriptione presentem corroboravimus cartam. Huius rei sunt testes: frater Guillelmus de Meleriis, domus Acconensis baiulus; frater Robertus, eiusdem domus ecclesie prior; frater Robertus, thesaurarius; Petrus Falcon[1]; Selet; Pipinus, filius Frederici; Hubertus Vulpis; Cornele Maial; Iacobus de la Clare, Pisanus; Bauduinus et multi alii. Factum est hoc anno dominice incarnationis[2] m°c°lxxxx°i°[3] mense februario, secundo die ipsius mensis.

I, 22 v. n. 40. Titulus: „De concordia inter domum nostram et domum hospitalis s. Ioh. de t. et h. G." Edidit Dudik Des hohen Deutschen Ritterordens Münzsammlung in Wien. Wien 1858. 4°. p. 49; unde repetivit R. liber baro a Toll in Mittheilungen aus dem Gebiete der Geschichte Liv-, Est- und Kurlands. Riga 1865. XI, 119 n. II. 1. Falcō; quod vel Falcero, vel Falcon potest esse. 2. d. i. a. B sed „anno" signo transpositum. 3. prius mclxxxvi B. Accon 1191 iulii 12 tradita erat christianis; statuendum ergo, quod annus 1192 autori in festivitate paschali initium habuerit seu in annunciatione B. M. V.

---

27. *1192 febr. 10 Accon. Guido Hierosolymitanus rex donat hospitali Alamannorum terram in urbe Acconensi, in qua domus eius sunt et hospitalis (titulus: „in qua sunt domus nostre") iuxta portam s. Nicolai intra terminos enarratos.*

Notum sit omnibus tam futuris quam presentibus, quod ego Guido per dei gratiam in sancta civitate Ierusalem Latinorum rex octavus pro redempcione et salute anime mee et pro salute anime sponse mee, bone recordationis domine Sibille venerabilis regine, dono, trado, concedo et in perpetuum confirmo tibi, fratri Curaudo, hospitalis Alamannorum preceptori, fratribusque et infirmis eiusdem domus terram apud Accon, in qua domus vestre sunt et hospitale, secundum continentias et divisas inferius subnotatas, ut ipsam terram vos vestrique successores habeatis, teneatis quiete et libere in posterum possideatis, ita siquidem, quod si aliquis hanc donationem meam contenderit vel calumpniaverit, eam ad opus vestrum successorumque vestrorum ab omnibus controversiis, querelis et calumpniis liberare, absolvere teneor et faciam pacificare. Unde Femianus et Dulcis, uxor eius, cum filio eorundem nomine Iohanne et heredibus suis aliis, qui predictam terram calumpniabant, eam in presencia mei et curie mee liberam et quietam vobis concesserunt, et quicquid iuris ibi habebant, pretermiserunt. Ideoque ego cambium in alio loco eis fieri feci et alternacionem; vos autem de domus vestre elemosinis quingentos bisantios et equum[1] unum mihi prebuistis. Divise vero prefate terre tales sunt et taliter consistunt: a duobus gradibus turris[2] perforate, ita quod gradus remaneant extra clausuram vestram a parte turris, prout divisa est inter vos et fratres sancti Thome, usque in stratam publicam, que extenditur ad portam sancti Nicholai; abinde siquidem ad plateam et curiam, sicut strata est hospitalis Armeniorum; a platea equidem illa usque ad murum civitatis, et exinde, prout murus adiacet terre, usque ad predictos gradus, hoc tamen retento, quod hedificium vel aliquid aliud in muro vel iuxta murum non faciatis, quod pretaxatos gradus ad muros gentes ad defensionem civitatis ascendere impedire valeat vel descendere. Ut igitur huius donationis, concessionis et confirmationis mee auctoritas vobis et successoribus vestris stabilis permaneat et inconcussa et in eternum indissoluta, presentem paginam sigilli mei impressione muniri et subscriptorum testium appositione corroborari precepi, quorum nomina sunt hec: Theobaldus, episcopus Acconensis; frater Robertus de Sablolio, magister Templi militum; frater Garnerius de Neapoli, magister hospitalis Ierusalem; Gaufridus de Lezigniaco, comes Ioppensis[3]; Aymericus conestabilis; frater Adam Brion[4], Templi militum senescalcus; frater Guillelmus de Viliers, preceptor hospitalis Acconis; Ugo de Tyberiade; Guillelmus Fortis; Ugo Martini, mariscalcus; Galvegnus de Cheniche; Galterius Bellus, vicecomes[5]; Reinerius de Gibeleto; consules Pisani: videlicet Bartholomeus de Tegrin, Selletus, Petrus de Falconio, et de aliis Pisanis[6] filius Frederici, Robertus[7] Vulp, Iacobus de Clar, Aselmus Bellus, Baldoinus de Cipro. Datum est apud Acchon per manus Petri, cancellarii nostri et ecclesie Tripolitane venerabilis episcopi, anno incarnati verbi m° c° xc° i° indictione x^a, quarto ydus februarii.

I, 24 n. 44. Diploma et ob supra ad n. 26 notata et ob indictionem et ob tenorem ipsum ad annum 1192 reiiciendum; sicut etiam Guidonis diploma de 1191 ind. x 2 kal. febr. apud Accon per manum Petri cancellarii nostri et ecclesie Tripolitane venerabilis episcopi, ap. Pauli I, 85 sq. — Ed. Dudik l. c. p. 50, unde repetivit R. l. b. a Toll l. c. n. III. Partem ediderat M. Töppen Des Deutschen Ordens Anfänge in Neue Preufsische Provinzialblätter. VII. Königsberg 1849, p. 246. 1. equm B. 2. duab^9 gradib^9 turis B. 3. Gaufridus haereditarius Ioppes comes declaratus est 1191 iulii 28; cf. Wilken Gesch. der Kreuzzüge IV, 373. 4. bon B. 5. scilicet Acconensis; cf. Pauli I, 86. 6. deest Pipinus? cf. p. 23. 7. Hubertus p. 23.

---

28. *1193 Accon. Henricus Trecensis comes palatinus donat fratribus domus hospitalis Theutonicorum barbacanam, turres, muros, fossatum Accone prope portam S. Nicolai.*

Notum sit omnibus presentibus et futuris, quod ego Henricus Trecensis comes palatinus assensu et voluntate domine Ysabellis, quondam regis Amalrici filie, pro salute animarum nostrarum et antecessorum nostrorum dono et in perpetuam helemosinam concedo domui hospitalis Theutonicorum et eiusdem domus fratribus totam barbacanam, turres quoque et muros et fossatum a meta proprisie, quam in ipsa barbacana domui hospitalis sancti Iohannis et fratribus dedi, usque portam sancti Nicholay. Ea tamen conditione predictam barbacanam cum turribus et muris et fossatis iam dicto hospitali Theutonicorum et fratribus dono et trado, ut ea repparent et meliorent, prout municioni civitatis necesse fuerit. Quod ut ratum permaneat, sigillo meo et testibus subscriptis confirmavi. Huius rei testes sunt Balianus de Ybelyno; Renaudus Sydonis; Hugo Tyberiadis; Nicholaus de Mally; Terricus de Terremunde[1]; Milo Brebanz; Antelmus de Lucha; Iohannes Burgundus; Nicholaus de Chonchis; Guido Antelmi. Actum Accon anno ab incarnatione domini m° c° xc° iii°. Datum per manus domini Ioscii Tyrensis archiepiscopi, regni cancellarii. Nota Radulfi.

I, 25 v. n. 50. 1. T'rremunde B.

---

29. *1193 februario Accon. Henricus Trecensis comes palatinus donat hospitali Alamannorum Acconensi casale Cafresi in Acconensi territorio et voltam in ipsa urbe Accone prope portam s. Nicolai.*

In nomine patris et filii et spiritus sancti[1]. Amen. Notum sit omnibus presentibus et futuris, quod ego Henricus Trecensis comes palatinus assensu et voluntate domine Ysabelle, uxoris mee, illustris quondam regis Almirici[2] filie, pro salute anime mee et antecessorum meorum dono et in liberam et perpetuam elemosinam concedo tibi Henrico, hospitalis Alemannorum[3] in Accon priori, et omnibus fratribus ibidem deo servientibus et servituris et universis eiusdem hospitalis infirmis quoddam casale in territorio Acconensi[4] situm, quod vocatur Cafresi[5], cum omni iure suo et cum[6] universis pertinenciis suis. Dono quoque vobis in elemosinam quandam vautam[7] in Ackon[8] iuxta portam, que dicitur porta sancti Nicolai[9], sitam, que videlicet vauta[10] est continua muris civitatis Acconensis[11]. Ut autem huius mee elemosine donatio et concessio vobis, predicto priori hospitalis Alemannorum[12] in Accon et universis eiusdem fratribus atque infirmis rata in eternum et stabilis permaneat, presentem cartam sigillo meo et testibus subscriptis precepi muniri et roborari. Huius rei testes sunt Balianus de Ybelino; Raginaldus[13] Sydonis; Hugo[14] Tyberiadis; Raymundus[15] de Scandelion[16]; Balduinus de Bethan; Nicolaus[17] de Malli; Milo Breibanz[18]; Bernardus de Templo, Acconensis[19] vicecomes; Silet[20], consul Pisanorum Accon; Symon Pisanus; Raymuldus Antelme; Wido[21] Antelme. Actum anno dominice incarnationis m° c° xc° iii° mense februario[22]. Datum Accon per manum domini Ioscii[23] Tyrensis archiepiscopi regnique cancellarii. Nota Radulfi[24].

1: III, 165; 2: I, 26 v. n. 55. Edidit Dudik l. c. 51, unde repetiit l. b. a Toll l. c. p. 122 n. IV forsan recte ad 1194 annum reiciens. Legit 2: 1. I. n. p. e. f. e. s. s. deest. 2. Amalrici. 3. alamannorum. 4. accon. 5. Caffresy. 6. deest. 7. vvoltam. 8. accon. 9. Nicholay. 10. uuolta. 11. accon. 12. alamannorum. 13. Rainaldus. 14. Ugo. 15. Raimundus. 16. scandaleon. 17. Nicholaus. 18. brebanz. 19. accon. 20. Scil'et. 21. Raimundus antelme Guido. 22. februarii. 23. Iozcii. 24. Rodulfi.

30. *1194 octobri. Henricus Trecensis palatinus comes donat fratribus ecclesiae Alamannorum in Accon immunitatem per regnum Hierosolymitanum de indumentis et victualibus ad usus proprios emtis.*

Notum sit omnibus presentibus et futuris, quod ego Henricus Trecensis comes palatinus assensu et voluntate domine Ysabelle, uxoris mee, illustris quondam regis Amalrici filie, dono pro salute anime mee et in liberam et in perpetuam elemosinam concedo tibi Henrico, ecclesie Alamannorum, que est in Accon, priori, cum omnibus eiusdem fratribus et infirmis, ut, sicut Templarii et Hospitalarii de indumentis et victualibus, que sibi ad proprios usus emunt, nullum ius nullamque consuetudinem in terra mea dant, ita et vos de universis indumentis ac victualibus, que ad vestros proprios usus emeritis, in tota terra mea nullum ius nullamque consuetudinem detis. Quod ut ratum habeatur, presentem cartam sigillo meo et testibus subscriptis confirmavi. Huius rei testes sunt: Hugo Tyberiadis; Rainaldus Sydonis; Radulfus Tyberiadis, regni senescalcus; Azmarus[1] Cesariensis; Balduinus de Bethan; Galtherus de Bethan; Dietericus de Orca; Milo Brebanz; Thomas camerarius, Acconensis vicecomes. Factum est hoc anno dominice incarnationis m° c° xciiii° mense octobris. Datum per manum domini Ioscii Tyrensis archiepiscopi regnique cancellarii.

I, 27 n. 56 in lemmate legitur: domui. Edidit Dudik l. c. 51, unde repetivit l. b. a Toll l. c. n. V. 1. prius: Aymarus B.

---

31. *1195 aprili Acchon. Henricus Trecensis comes palatinus donat hospitali Alamannorum in Accon domum Tyri sitam, quondam Theodori de Sarepta, et duas carrucatas terrae apud Sedinum.*

Notum sit omnibus presentibus et futuris, quod ego Henricus Trecensis comes palatinus assensu et voluntate domine Ysabellis uxoris mee, illustris quondam regis Amalrici filie, dono et in liberam et perpetuam elemosinam concedo infirmis hospitalis Alamannorum, quod est in Accon, et universis eiusdem fratribus hospitalis domum unam in Tyro, que fuit Theodori de Sarepta, cum iardino et universis ad eandem domum pertinentibus. Dono quoque eisdem duas carrucatas terre apud Sedinum francesias libere in perpetuum sibi possidendas. Ut autem hec mea donatio eisdem in helemosinam concessa rata et stabilis permaneat, presentem cartam sigillo meo et testibus subscriptis precepi communiri. Huius rei testes sunt Hugo Tyberiadis; Reinaldus Sydonis; Radulfus Tyberiadis, regni senescalcus; Terricus de Tenero monte; Terricus de Orca; Galterius de Bethan; Amalricus de Bethan; Girardus de Franlo; Radulfus de Balesme. Factum est hoc anno dominice incarnationis m° c° xc° v°

mense aprili. Datum Acchon per manum domini Ioscii Tyrensis archiepiscopi regnique cancellarii.

I, 25 n. 48. Ad vocem lemmatis „carucatis terre" rubricator in margine inferiori annotat: „Chascun charue dot havoir xxiiii cordes du longe et xvi du large; et la corde dot havoir xviii toise du home mezaine, et insi le t°ut (?) en la secrete du reame de Ierusalem par l'asise du reame duvant dit. — Quelibet carrucata habebit xxiiii funes in longitudine et xvi in latitudine. Item funis habebit xviii passus quantum potest mediocris homo capere expansis brachiis; et sic habet consuetudo regni Ierosolimitani".

---

32. *1196 marcio Accon. Henricus Trecensis comes palatinus donat domui hospitalis Alamanorum in Accon gastinam terrae ad faciendas domos in castello Ioppensi et quasdam vineas extra Ioppen.*

Notum sit omnibus presentibus et futuris, quod ego Herricus, Trecensis comes palatinus et regni Ierusalem dominus, assensu et voluntate domine Ysabellis, uxoris mee, illustris quondam regis Amalrici filie, dono et in perpetuam elemosinam concedo tibi, fratri Herrico, domus hospitalis Alamanorum in Accon preceptori, et eiusdem domus fratribus et infirmis quandam gastinam terre ad domos faciendas in castello Ioppen sitam et quasdam vineas extra Ioppen sitas. Ut autem hec mea donatio et helemosina rata et inconcussa permaneat, presentem cartam sigillo meo et testibus subscriptis precepi communiri. Huius rei testus sunt: Hugo Tyberiadis, Rainaldus Sydonis, Radulfus senescalcus, Iohannes marescalcus. Actum anno dominice incarnationis m° c° xc° vi° mense marcio. Datum Acchon per manum domini Ioscii Tyrensis archiepiscopi regnique cancellarii.

I, 27 n. 57. Edidit Dudik l. c. 52, unde repetiit l. b. a Toll l. c. p. 123 n. VI. Forsan rectius ad 1197 reiiciendum est.

---

33. *1196 dec. 21. Coelestini III confirmationem inter alia loci hospitalis s. M. Alamannorum Ieros., domus Scalone sitae, Zanzi, domorum apud Ramas, domus, vinearum, possessionum apud Iaffaz, domus apud Accon civitatem, casalis de Capharsim, voltae prope portam s. Nicolai, domus Tyri sitae vide infra inter bullas, ubi etiam Innocentii III de 1209, 1215, 1216.*

---

34. *1198 febr. 8 Acchon. Amalricus II Hierosolymitanus et Cypri rex beatae Mariae sanctae domus hospitalis Theutonicorum vendit casale Aguille in partibus Accon, et donat reditus quosdam de casalibus Fiergio, Umberto, caeteris, confirmat libertates in regno Cypri concessas.*

Notum sit omnibus presentibus et futuris, quod ego Aymericus per dei graciam rex Ierusalem nonus et rex Cipri assensu et voluntate domine Ysabellis uxoris mee, illustris quondam regis Amalrici filie[1], dono et concedo in perpetuum beate Marie sancte domus hospitalis Theutonicorum unum casale cum suis villanis et gastinis, quod vocatur Aguille, in partibus Accon pro tribus milibus bisanciis sarracenatis, quos ego recepi in manibus meis, et dono insupra hoc casali supradicto de alio casali meo, quod vocatur Fiergio, de quolibet laborando[2] in masario rotulam unam zucari quolibet die ad opus infirmorum beate Marie sancte domus hospitalis Theutonicorum. Et de tota terra mea de casali Umberto et de aliis casalibus meis in partibus illis concedo de unaquaque carruca laborante unam clicham frumenti, et unam ordei habebitis annuatim de parte rustici. Et de singulis centum capris, que hyemabunt in terra mea, habebitis v^{e} carrublas de rustico. Et de singulis decem capris, de quibus debeo habere decem carrublas, habebitis annuatim de rustico ii^{as} carrublas. Et de unaquaque carruca, que debet dare mihi ii bisancios, habebitis iii karrublas de rustico. Et dono insupra ista: elemosinam[3] et veterem[4] francisiam per totum regnum Cipri, quomodo rex Almaricus dedit in privilegio vestro. Ut autem hoc meum donum in perpetuum stabile sit et ratum, presentem cartam sigillo meo plumbeo et subscriptione testium feci communiri. Huius rei testes sunt: Rainaldus Sydonis; Radulfus Tiberyadensis, senescalcus regni; Iohannes de Ybelino, conestabilis regni; Terricus de Orca; Iohannes, marescalcus regni; Terricus de Terremonde; Rohardus de Cayphas; Raimundus de Gibeleto; Balduinus de Bethan; Nicholaus de Nazareth. Actum Acchon anno ab incarnatione domini m^{o} c^{o} xc^{o} vii^{o}. Datum per manum Iocii archiepiscopi regnique Ierusalem cancellarii vi^{o} idus februarii.

I, 24 n. 45. Spurium videtur diploma. Non fuit ante ipsum Amalricum autorem diplomatis huius Cypri rex Latinus; frater eius Guido tantum dominus Cypri vocatus est velut ipse Amalricus usque ad annum 1196; cf. Töche Heinrich VI, 392. Rex coronatus est 1197 septembri per Conradum Hildeshemensem episcopum, imperii cancellarium; sed iam inde a maio 1196 videtur Cypri regio titulo usus esse. Heinrici palatini comitis Trecensis 1197 septembri mortui viduam Isabellam ipso etiam 1197 anno Amalricus uxorem duxit; 1198 coronatus est Hierosolymitanus rex; cf. Sanudo Liber secret. ap. Bongars Gesta dei per Francos p. 201; Mas Latrie Histoire de l'île de Chypre sous le règne des princes de la maison de Lusignan. Paris 1861. I, 146. 1. filia B. 2. l. laborante? 3. elemosina B. 4. antea: uetus B.

---

35. *1198 aug. Accon. Amalricus II Hierosolymitanus et Cypri rex donat b. Mariae et hospitali Alamannorum turrim super portam S. Nicolai Accone.*

Notum sit omnibus presentibus et futuris, quod ego Aymericus dei gracia rex Ierusalem nonus et rex Cipri voluntate et assensu domine Ysabellis, uxoris mee, illustris regine et illustris quondam regis Amalrici filie, dono et in perpetuum concedo, domino deo et sancte Marie et hospitali Alamannorum fratribusque eiusdem hospitalis presentibus et futuris turrem, que est super portam Acconis, que porta appellatur porta sancti Nicholay, tali modo, quod ipsi fratres nichil habeant in porta, que est sub turre, per quam intratur et exitur de villa, nec in circumstanciis turris aliquid de novo possint erigere[1], ipsamque turrem nec dare poterunt alicui nec vendere nec invadiare; ut si forte religio eorum ad aliam transmutaretur religionem[2], predictam turrem mihi sive meis successoribus dominis regni resignarent. Preterea si pro guerra inimicorum vel pro aliquo casu accidente[3] dicta turris mihi meisque successoribus dominis regni fuerit necessaria, si voluerimus, turrem nobis debent reddere, nulla obstante occasione; nos vero post nostrum de turre peractum negocium predictis fratribus turrem debemus reddere, et ipsam nullis aliis quam ipsis vel dare vel concedere aut vendere poterimus vel invadiare. Ut autem hec nostra donatio prenominato hospitali et fratribus rata permaneat et immutata, presentem cartam sigillo nostro et[4] subscriptione testium fecimus communiri. Huius rei testes sunt: Rainaldus Sydonis; Radulfus Tyberiadis, senescalcus regni; Iohannes, constabularius regni; Iohannes, marescalcus regni; Rohardus, dominus Cayphe; Terricus de Orca; Terricus de Terrimonde; Raimundus de Gibelet. Actum Accon anno ab incarnatione domini m° c° xc° viii° mense augusto. Datum per manum domini Ioscii Tyrensis archiepiscopi regnique cancellarii.

I, 24v. n. 46. 1. exigere B. 2. Ante paucos menses 1198 martio hospitalis Theutonicorum Acconensi susceptis Templariorum militaribus statutis regeneratus et dilatatus erat; cf. Narrationem de primordiis ordinis Theutonici ed. Töppen in Scriptoribus rerum Prussicarum I, 220. Pro Aimerici regis nomine manuscriptum ibi p. 221 male habet Heinrici, qui nunquam rex tantum abusive ab aliquibus (Arnoldo Lubecensi) sic nominatus est. 3. accidenti B. 4. supplevi.

---

36. *1200 augusto Accon. Amalricus II Hierosolymitanus et Cypri rex confirmat hospitali s. Mariae Theutonicorum domum Tyri a Paulo et fratre, filiis Theodoria de Sarepta, emtam.*

Ego Aymericus dei gracia rex Ierusalem nonus et rex Cipri notum facio omnibus presentibus et futuris, quod Paulus et frater suus[1], filii Theodorici de Sarepta, in presencia nostra et in curia nostra et eciam curia iuratorum nostrorum existentes quandam domum cum iardino et universis suis pertinenciis, quam fratres hospitalis sancte Marie Theotonicorum ex dono bone memorie comitis Henrici et domine Isabelle tunc uxoris sue, illustris regis Amalrici filie[2], tenebant in Tyro et exinde privilegium habebant, eidem hospitali et fratribus et infirmis in perpetuum concesserunt, quitaverunt et quietam clamaverunt omni iure, quod in eadem domo expetebant, eisdem fratribus renunciato, unde ob hoc fratres eiusdem hospitalis predicto Paulo et fratri suo cc bisantios sarracenatos dederunt, nos rogantes, ut exinde eis privilegium faceremus. Nos autem eorum precibus acquiescentes voluntate et peticione predicti Pauli et fratris sui prenominatam domum cum iardino et universis suis pertinenciis predicto hospitali, fratribus et infirmis, voluntate et assensu predicte domine Ysabellis uxoris mee, venerabilis regine, concedimus et confirmamus in perpetuum, ita quod nos et successores nostri ipsam domum cum iardino et universis suis pertinenciis ab omni calumpnia dicti Pauli et fratris sui et universe eorum progeniei debemus garantizare prescriptis fratribus et infirmis. Et si forte ipsi vel aliquis ex eorum progenie de dicta domo deinceps querimoniam fecerint, prorsus non audiantur. Quod ut ratum habeatur, presentem cartam sigillo nostro et testibus subscriptis precepimus communiri. Huius rei testes sunt Raynaldus Sydonis; Iohannes de Ybelino, regni conestabilis; Balduinus de Betsan; Vilanus de Alneto; Terricus de Tenero monte; Iohannes, regius marescalcus; Adam Coste; Willelmus de Petra; Aimon Daus. Factum est hoc anno dominice incarnationis m° cc° mense augusti. Datum Accon per manum domini Ioscii Tyrensis archiepiscopi regnique cancellarii.

I, 25 n. 47. 1. suūs B. 2. cf. supra n. 1195 aprili.

---

37. *1200 augusto. Monachus Hierosolymitanus patriarcha et Guillelmus de Amigdalea paciscuntur de casali Ieth.*

Notum sit omnibus tam futuris quam presentibus inter nos Monacum Ierosolimitanum patriarcham et dominum Willelmum de Amigdalea pro se et uxore sua domina Agnete, filia comitis Ioscelini, de casali, quod dicitur Ieth, concordiam talem factam fuisse, quod nos casale Ieth cum omni iure suo et pertinenciis cultis et incultis et omnibus[1] villanis debemus in vita nostra libere et quiete tenere et pacifice et sine omni contradictione et calumpnia per nos vel submissam personam possidere; nobis vero decedentibus predictum casale Ieth cum omnibus pertinenciis et omni iure suo ad dominum W(illelmum) et uxorem suam et eorum heredes libere revertatur, nulla super hoc a nostris successoribus vel ab aliis inquietatione movenda. Facta fuit hec concordia per curiam domini Aimerici illustris regis Ierusalem, ipso presente et consensum prebente et rogante nos, ut domino G(uillelmo) et uxori sue et eorum heredibus privilegium iure perpetuo faceremus; presente eciam domino Rainaldo Sydonis, predicte domine avunculo, et consenciente. Ut autem hec concordia firma semper et illibata permaneat, nostro sigillo et sigillo domini regis presentem paginam fecimus communiri. Huius rei testes sunt ipse dominus rex Aimericus; Rainaldus Sydonis; Iohannes conestabilis; Iohannes marescalcus; Terricus de Orca; Villanus de Alneto; Balduinus de Bethsan; Adam Coste; Willelmus de Petra et multi alii. Anno dominice incarnationis m° cc° mense augusti indictione iii^a.

I, 11 n. 17. 1. omibus B.

---

38. *1200 octobri. Amalricus II Hierosolymitanus et Cypri rex vendit fratribus hospitalis ecclesiae s. Mariae Alemannorum casale Lebassa et gastinam Missop.*

In nomine sancte et individue trinitatis, patris, filii et spiritus sancti. Amen. Notum sit omnibus presentibus atque futuris, quod ego Aymericus dei gracia rex Ierusalem Latinorum nonus et rex Cypri, concessione et voluntate domine Ysabellis uxoris mee, venerabilis regine, quondam illustris regis Amalrici filie, vendidi et dedi pro duobus milibus et trecentis bisanciis sarracenatis vobis, fratribus hospitalis ecclesie sancte Marie Alemannorum et infirmis quoddam casale in territorio Ackon situm, quod vocatur Lebassa, cum omnibus suis pertinenciis et unam gastinam cum omni territorio suo, que vocatur Missop, que illa die erat gastina. Quod casale predictum cum omnibus suis pertinenciis et gastinam prenominatam, sicut superius divisum est, libere et imperpetuum habeatis et teneatis, sicut Iohannes marescalcus meus et homines mei precepto meo eiusdem predicti casalis et dicte gastine terram diviserunt et terminos posuerunt. Ut autem hec mea venditio et donatio rata in eternum et inconcussa permaneat, presentem cartam sigillo meo et testibus subscriptis precepi communiri. Huius rei testes sunt comes Bertodus; Bertodus eius filius; Rainaldus Sydonie; Azemarus[1] Cesariensis, Iohannes de Ybellino, regis conestabilis; Terricus de Orca; Balduinus de Bethsan; Iohannes, regius marescalcus; Vilanus de Alnetho; Terricus de Tenero monte; Garterius de Eissem; Willelmus de Petra; Muissardus; Adam Coste. Factum est hoc anno ab incarnatione domini m° cc° mense octobri. Datum per manuum domini Iocii Tyrensis archiepiscopi regnique cancellarii.

III, 165. 1. cf. supra 26.

---

39. *1200 octobr. Guillelmus de Amigdala donat fratribus hospitalis s. Mariae Alamannorum terram inter casale Album et Capharsine.*

Notum sit omnibus presentibus et futuris, quod ego Guillelmus de la Mandelie concessione et voluntate domine Agnetis uxoris mee, illustris quondam comitis Iozcelini filie, dono libere et quiete in perpetuum concedo vobis, fratribus hospitalis sancte Marie Alamannorum, et infirmis quandam peciam terre, que a meridie coheret terre hospitalis sancti Iohannis et a parte septentrionis coheret rivulo, qui coniungitur terre casalis Albi, ubi mete sunt, qui eciam rivulus descendit usque ad divisionem vestri casalis de Cafersie, ubi iungitur mea terra casalis Albi terre Cafersye. Ut autem hec mea donatio et concessio rata in eternum et inconcussa permaneat, presentem cartam sigillo meo et testibus subscriptis communivi. Huius rei testes sunt Iohannes Tortus; Willelmus Ruffus; Philippus de Castello; Gichardus de Kaber; Iohannes de Borc. Factum est hoc Accon anno dominice incarnationis m° cc° mense octobris.

I, 32 v. n. 73.

---

40. *1206 februario. Iuliana domina Caesareae donat hospitali s. Mariae Alamannorum quasdam turres et alias possessiones et confirmat a Iohanne Charles donatas.*

Ego Iuliana domina Cesaree notum facio tam presentibus quam futuris, quod ego assensu et voluntate mariti mei, domini Aymari de Lairon, et filii mei Galteri dono in helemosinam hospitali sancte Marie Alamannorum in Acchon domos, que fuerunt Georgii Lormine, cum omnibus pertinenciis suis et voltam Bernardi Falcille cum omnibus pertinenciis suis et gastinam, que est inter ipsas domos et inter domum Petri de Beugrant a via publica usque ad aliam viam publicam versus mare; et eciam dono eidem hospitali turrem Mallart cum platea, que est ante ipsam turrem, que protenditur usque ad divisionem gastine, que est de Templo domini; et aliam parvam turrem dono similiter, que est opposita huic, in cantone murorum civitatis a parte orientali, que predicte turres domino Cesaree debent tradi, si eidem essent necessarie contra inimicos suos; quibus inter se pacificatis predicti fratres predictas turres debent rehabere. Dono eidem hospitali campum, qui fuit domine Brime, qui habet ab occidente iardinum Hospitalis et a meridie campum domini Aymari; ab oriente habet viam, que dividit campum ipsum et campum domini Symonis; a septentrione vero habet viam, que dividit ipsum campum domine Grosse. Preterea notum facio omnibus, quod Iohannes Charles assensu matris sue et fratris sui Helye et sororis sue domine Orgoillose et assensu meo et mariti mei domini A(ymari) et filii mei G(alteri) dedit in elemosinam eidem hospitali duos campos et iardinum unum et aream, que est in capite unius campi; unus istorum camporum habet campum, in quo est agullia sancti Petri, a parte occidentali, a parte vero orientali continuatur campo, qui fuit Rainerii de Gibeleth, in quo fuit quondam vinea, a meridie autem adheret vie, que separat iardinum archiepiscopi ab ipso campo, a septemtrione habet viam, que ducit a Hadaydon, et area dicta superius est in capite huius campi. Alius campus est super ipsis ab oriente et parvus paries dividit ipsos; a parte meridiana adheret campo, qui fuit Rainerii de Gibeleth, in quo fuit olim vinea; a septemtrione continuatur campo Iohannis Charle, in quo sunt morvellarii; in capite istius campi a parte orientali est unus karoblers, qui est infra ipsum campum iusta[1] campum domini Galterii de Cesarea[2], in quo fuit quondam vinea. Iardinus autem adheret muris civitatis a parte occidentali, ab oriente habens viam, que dividit iardinum P. Gasta ab isto; a meridie adheret campo, qui fuit quondam iardinus Iohannis Lermine; et ab eadem parte continuatur campo Iohannis Charle; a septentrione habet iardinum archiepiscopi. Ut autem hec mea donatio et donatio Iohannis Charle firme forent et stabiles, maritus meus dominus Aymarus sigilli sui testimonium huic privilegio apposuit et munimen. Hiis interfuerunt donationibus plures, quorum nomina subscribuntur: dominus P(etrus)[3] archiepiscopus; Philippus decanus; dominus Symon et duo filii eius; Iohannes Gervasius vicecomes; Iohannes Charles et Helyas frater eius; P. de Beugrant; Michael; Salomon; Fulco; Robertus Perrer; G. Passereus;

Rainerius de Cassia, Iohannes Lermines; Stephanus Turquie; Guillelmus Britto. Actum anno incarnationis dominice m° cc° vi° mense februario.

I, 28 v. n. 62. 1. i. e. iuxta. 2. cesājz B sc. Caesareae. 3. cf. Iulianae eiusdem diploma de 1207 febr. ap. Pauli I, 95. XC. Decidere firme non ausim, nonne utrumque diploma posteriori anno, quam quem prae se fert, sit adnumerandum.

---

41. *1206 maii 1 Accon. Iohannes de Ybelino, dominus Beriti et regni Hierosolymitani baiulus, confirmat domui hospitalis Alamannorum Acconensi a Iohanne Torto emtam domum Accone sitam.*

In nomine patris et filii et spiritus sancti. Amen. Notum facio presentibus et futuris ego Iohannes de Ybelino, dominus Beriti et regni Ierosolimitani baiulus, quod Iohannes Tortus in presenciam meam et regalem curiam veniens a me et ab hominibus domine Marie, regni honorabilis domine, poposcit licenciam vendendi domum suam Accon pro debitis suis solvendis, super quo habito consilio cum hominibus domine mee predicte venditionem predicte domus eorum consilio tunc non concessi; verumptamen, cum ipse Iohannes Tortus vidisset, quod non potuisset habere licentiam vendendi domum suam, dixit, quod eum oportebat vendere feodum suum vel domum pro debitis suis solvendis, super quo habui consilium ab hominibus prenominate domine mee, qui, cum vidissent, quod oportebat predictum Iohannem Tortum ex necessitate vendere feudum suum vel domum pro debitis suis solvendis, mihi dederunt in consilium, ut ei darem licenciam vendendi domum suam ob feudum retinendum. Unde ipse Iohannes Tortus concessione predicte domine mee et voluntate mea et[1] assensu pro debitis suis solvendis et feudo sibi retinendo in presencia mea et regali curia concessione Marie uxoris sue et Beatricis sororis sue et Willelmi de Monliart, eius mariti, vendidit domui hospitali Alamannorum Accon et fratribus eiusdem hospitalis prenominatam domum suam cum omnibus pertinenciis suis pro duobus milibus et septingentis bisantiis sarracenatis. Que videlicet domus ab oriente adheret domibus Montis Thabor et domibus Beloais et vie regie et domibus, que fuerunt Petri Bordin; ab occidente domui Bonefrage filii Sahit et rue Iudeorum et domui Iudeorum et stabulo Renerii scriptoris; et a septentrione domui Marie, uxoris quondam sacerdotis ecclesie sancte Marie Magdalene; et a meridie vie regie et domui, quam domina Hauhis tenebat. Pro cuius domus empcione, quam ipsa tenebat, predicti fratres hospitalis dederunt eidem Hauhis[2] ccc bisancios sarracenatos et duas marchas argenti. Cuius eciam domus, quam ipsa Hauhis tenebat, omne ius, quod predictus Iohannes Tortus habebat et expectabat in ea habere, dicte domui hospitalis et fratribus vendidit et quietum clamavit. Sciendum est autem, quod prenominata domina mea pro concessione vendicionis dicte domus Iohannis Torti a fratribus dicti hospitalis cc bisancios habuit. Ut autem ista venditio et venditionis confirmatio rata in perpetuum et stabilis permaneat, presentem cartam sigillo meo et testibus subscriptis feci corroborari. Huius rei testes sunt Aymarus Cesariensis, regni mariscalcus; comes Bertholdus[3]; Vilanus de Alneto; Philippus de Ibelino; Garnerus Alamannus; Galterius Cesariensis; Gormundus de Bethan; Aymo Dais; Adam Coste; Thomas, vicecomes Acconensis. Factum est hoc anno dominice incarnationis m° cc° vi° prima die mensis maii. Datum Accon per manum domini Radulfi Acconensis dechani regnique cancellarii.

I, 19 v. n. 32. 1. e B. 2. haulis B. 3. Comes Bertot testis Iulianae in supra laudato diplomate de 1207 febr. Pauli I, 95.

---

42. *1207 iulii 27 in palatio Acconensis episcopi. Albertus, Hierosolymitanus patriarcha, testatur Heliam, Pagani Pictaviensis filium, hospitali Theutonicorum domo quadam (ut videtur, Accone) cessisse.*

Albertus dei gracia sancte resurrectionis vocatus patriarcha, apostolice sedis legatus, omnibus, ad quos littere iste pervenerint. Ea, que vel sentencia diffinita sunt vel amicabili compositione decisa, scriptorum dignum est munimine roborari, ut, quod per lapsum temporis in oblivionem deduci potest, semper quasi recens per stabilitatem pagine teneatur. Cum igitur inter Helyam quondam filium Pagani Pictaviensis et Girardum preceptorem hospitalis Theutonicorum ipsius nomine hospitalis super quadam domo, que sita est intra septa domorum eiusdem, quam predictus Helyas petens ad se pertinere dicebat, sub examine nostro controversia verteretur, placuit tandem utrique parti causam ipsam sub compositione amicabili terminare. Memoratus itaque Helyas viginti quinque bisanciis a prefato scriptore receptis renunciavit in perpetuum omni iuri, quod in iam dicta domo iure aliquo ad se pertinebat, ita videlicet, ut nec ipse nec aliquis successorum eius domum ipsam vel ex ea aliquid petere ab ipso hospitali vel ab eo, cui ab eodem hospitali fuisset data, de cetero posset, sed in iure ipsius hospitalis quantum ad ipsum et heredes eius libera et sine omni inquietudine remaneret. Interfuerunt Iohannes de Ybelino, baiulus regni Ierosolimitani; Radulfus de Tyberiade, eiusdem regni senescalcus; comes Bertoldus Theutonicus; Andreas de Vituli, vicecomes venatorum; Henricus Alamannus; Michael de Ierusalem. Datum in palatio Acconensis episcopi anno dominice incarnationis m° cc° vii° sexto kal. augusti indictione x[a].

I, 32 v. n. 75.

---

43. *1208 septembri Accon. Otto, comes de Henneberg, donat domui hospitalis Alamannorum Acconensi tres carrucatas terrae et unam domum in casali Saphet Acconensis territorii.*

Notum sit omnibus presentibus et futuris, quod ego comes Otto assensu et voluntate uxoris mee domine Beatricis, illustris quondam comitis Ioscelini filie[1], dono et in perpetuam elemosinam concedo domui hospitalis Alamannorum

Acchon tres carrucatas terre francesias aput casale, quod vocatur Saphet, in territorio Accon situm et unam domum in eodem casali. Ut autem huius mee elemosine donatio rata in perpetuum et stabilis permaneat, presentem cartam sigillo meo et testibus subscriptis communivi. Huius rei testes sunt: Iohannes Tortus; Henricus Alamannus; Gotsuinus; Eustachius de Cayphas; Thomas camerarius; Andreas de Vinea; Iohannes de Bort; Girardus de Cabur. De fratribus interfuerunt: frater Otto, eius domus magister; frater Gerardus, preceptor; frater Henricus, marescalcus; frater Henricus, custos infirmorum; frater Hugo; frater Bertoudus. Actum Accon anno dominice incarnacionis m° cc° viii° mense septembris, domino Iohanne de Ybelino regnum Ierosolimitanum procurante.

I, 29 n. 63. Ed. Ioh. Voigt Graf Otto von Henneberg und die Botenlaube bei Kissingen in Neue Beiträge zur Geschichte deutschen Alterthums. Herausgegeben von dem Hennebergischen alterthumsforschenden Verein durch Georg Brückner. Meiningen 1858. 8. I, 68 sq. 1. Eorundem diploma de 1208 intrante mense octobri pro Hospitalariis exhibet Pauli I, 96. XCII, ubi inter testes etiam Henricus Alemannus, Iohannes Tortus, Girardus de Cabor, Eustacius de Caiphas.

---

44. *1209 septbr. 4. Boamundus IV, Antiochiae princeps, donat domui hospitalis s. Mariae Theutonicorum quandam petiam terrae et tres turres infra burgum Tripolis.*

Notum sit omnibus hominibus tam presentibus quam futuris, quod ego Boamundus dei gracia princeps Anthiochie et comes Tripolis dono, laudo, concedo domui hospitalis sancte Marie Theutonicorum quandam peciam terre, que est mea et est infra burgum Tripolis prope magistrum murum burgi exceptis domibus, que sunt in ipsa terra hedificate, ubi mei homines manent et eas de me tenent. Ista terra sic terminatur, videlicet a gradu magne turris magistri muri burgi Tripolis, que est adversus orientem usque ad territorium episcopi Tripolitani et de territorio episcopi usque ad murum Templi, qui est adversus occidentem et adheret magistro muro[1] burgi, sicut terra debet partiri inter terram meam et terram Berengeri de Sura prope divisionem terre Templi. Dono eciam predicte domui hospitalis sancte Marie Theutonicorum tres turres, que sunt a gradu predicto usque ad terram domus Templi tali modo, quod nichil aliud possint facere in ipsa terra preter domos ad eorum mansionem. Si vero contingeret, quod ipsi murum burgi peiorarent pro aliquo, quod in predicta terra facerent, ipsi debent murum emendare. Hec omnia sicut in hoc continetur[2] privilegio dono, laudo et in perpetuum tenenda et possidenda concedo domui hospitalis sancte Marie Theutonicorum salvis posternis, que sunt in muro, ita quod ego et heredes mei et homines nostri possimus per posternas intrare et exire, cum nobis opus fuerit. Ut autem hoc donum firmum et ratum permaneat, presens privilegium scribi precepi et sigilli mei principalis impressione testibus subscriptis muniri atque confirmari. Testes sunt Guido, dominus Biblii; Plivanus, dominus Botroni; Girardus de Ham[3], conestabulus

Tripolis; Raimundus de Biblio; Wuillelmus de Biblio; Raimundus de Scandaleone. Factum est anno incarnati verbi m° cc° ix° quarta die mensis septembris[4].

I, 34 v. n. 80. 1. muri B. 2. B. 3. Guido de Ham comestabularius Tripolis, „Pieban dominus de Bot(ro)ne 1204 dec." ap. Pauli I, 103 ubi etiam Raimundus et Willelmus de Biblio, Raimundus de Scandelione. 4. setēbr.

---

45. *1211 febr. 14 Accon. Alberti Hierosolymitani patriarchae arbitrium de domo quadam Tyri sita inter Martinum Roziam Ianuensem et hospitale Alamannorum de Accon.*

Notum sit omnibus tam presentibus quam futuris, quod de querela, que vertebatur inter Martinum Roziam civem Ianuensem ex una parte et fratrem Hermannum magistrum hospitalis Alamanorum de Acon ex altera parte de quadam domo, que est in Tyro, que fuit quondam Theodori Suriani, ambe partes arbitrio domini Al(berti) venerabilis patriarche Ierosolimitani se comiserunt, quicquid ipse inde dictaret, ratum et illibatum habituri. Quo in casu idem dominus patriarcha visis, discussis et cognitis utriusque partis rationibus dixit et precepit, quod supradictus Martinus Rozia faceret finem et refutationem et pactum de non petendo per transactionem de predicta domo supradicto fratri Hermanno et per eum supradicto hospitali Alamannorum, ita quod de cetero predictus Martinus Rozia vel alius pro eo dicto fratri Harmanno vel dicto hospitali vel alteri pro ipsis pro predicta domo vel occasione predicte domus nullam posset movere vel facere questionem. Dixit eciam idem dominus patriarcha, quod predictus frater Harmannus daret iam dicto Martino Rozie pro predicto fine et refutatione de predicta domo bisancios lx[a] sarracenatos de Syria bonos et iusti ponderis. Quare dictus Martinus Rozia civis Ianuensis fecit finem et refutacionem et pactum de non petendo per transactionem de sepedicta domo prefato fratri Armanno et per eum sepedicto hospitali et eius successoribus in perpetuum in eodem hospitali, ita quod de cetero ipse Martinus Rozia vel alius pro eo prefato fratri Armanno vel dicto hospitali vel alteri pro ipsis de predicta domo vel occasione predicte domus nullam posset movere vel facere questionem, abrenuncians omni iuri et legum et consuetudinum terre auxilio et instrumentis, quibus iuvari posset in hoc casu, et specialiter illi privilegio, quod habet, in quo continetur confirmatio donationis de predicta domo ipsi Martino facte[1]. Et ad maius robur et firmitatem habendam ipse Martinus dedit fratri Armanno quoddam aliud privilegium, quod habebat de eadem domo. Insuper ipse Martinus vocavit se solutum et quietum de supradictis bisantiis lx[a] sarracenatis de Syria, abrenuncians excepcioni non numerate pecunie vel non ponderati auri vel non accepte rei. Alioquin, si contra faceret, penam dupli ipsi fratri Armanno promisit et per eum suis successoribus, in eodem hospitali supradicto et pro sorte et pena omnia bona sua habita et habenda illi pignori obligavit. Testes: dominus Galterius Acconensis episcopus, et frater Lodoicus et Aldo, ecclesie sancte crucis de Accon canonicus, et Obertus Aurie, et Nicholaus Spinola. Actum Accon in palatio ipsius domini patriarche anno nativitatis dominice m° cc° xi° indictione xii°[2] die quinta decima exeuntis februarii[3] post vesperas. Postea vero scilicet die vicesima eiusdem mensis Iacobus de Marino et Lanfrancus de Mari tunc consules Ianuenses in Syria in presencia Guillelmi de Nigro et Ingonis Spinole et Corradi de Mari testium ad hoc vocatorum predictam concordiam approbaverunt et confirmaverunt et auctoritate sua corroboraverunt. Stephanus de Valencia, Ianuensis notarius in Syria, rogatus scripsit.

I, 27 v. n. 59. Indictio xv in annum 1212 quadraret; ita ut hic liceat statuere computatum annum „secundum morem patriarchatus Hierosolimitani", secundum quem diploma ap. Pauli I, 192 editum est anno 1270 ind. xiv martii 11, secundum cursum Pisanum, anno usque ad martii 25 eodem atque solito, 1271. 1. cf. supra n. 24 1189 septembr. 2. B pro xv^a ut videtur. 3. febrorii B.

---

46. *1212 aprili. Leo, Armeniae rex de genere Rupinorum, donat domui hospitalis Theutonicorum castellum Amudain, casalia Sespin, Buquequia, Cumbethfor, Ayun, libertatem emendi et vendendi pro domus necessitate.*

In nomine patris et filii et spiritus sancti. Amen. Sicut apostolica testatur auctoritas: „Qui parce seminat, parce et metet, et qui seminat in benedictionibus, de benedictionibus et metet vitam eternam"[1]; proinde ego Leo, dei et Romani imperii gracia rex Armenie, filius Stephani de potenti et magnifico genere Rupinorum, notum facio omnibus hominibus presentibus et futuris, quod de bonis mihi desuper concessis et collatis pro amore dei et imperii Romani, sub cuius potestatis gracia rex sum constitutus, et pro salute anime mee et progenitorum meorum omnium venerabilibus et religiosis fratribus sancte domus hospitalis Teutonicorum vicem Machabeorum pro defensione domus Israel gerentibus, de quorum sum confraternitate et in quorum beneficiis ac oracionibus particeps effici cupio, atque bonorum meritorum suorum exigencia ad captandam illorum sinceram dilectionem et mutuam benivolenciam regali ex munificencia mea claro corde, bono et puro animo dono et concedo amodo in perpetuum peroptima et amplissima casalium et terrarum tenimenta, eo quod arbitror tam preclaram elemosinam inibi bene fore collocatam; inprimis famosum castellum Amudain nomine et casale inferius sibi adherens[2] nominatum cum pertinenciis et divisionibus ipsius signatis in hunc modum: a parte Simonaglam tendit usque ad antiquum adaquarium, ubi due sunt arbores salices et modo factus est laccus, dehinc usque rostrum de rocha media iusta gastinam, que est de territorio Adidy, a gastina illa superius ascenditur usque ad Quilli, quod dicitur Latine: Meta de Gammassa. Alia divisio inter Gammassa et Amudayn tendit ad cavam, ubi est arbor dicta chaisne spinosa et abbacia Chalot et agger vinee de Mechale, et extenditur meta usque viam. Alia divisio inter pastores et Amidain tendit usque ad collem, ante quem collem sunt duo rubi salvatici et arbor morarius; dehinc tendit usque ad gastinam dictam Dagie et extenditur usque ad Zamga, dehinc usque ad lacum Helia et Ioh, et inter Ioh et Ramam est quedam cava divisa. Item aliud casale nomine Sespin cum pertinenciis et divisionibus ipsius signatis a parte Baari extenditur usque ad crucem; dehinc usque ad cavam et usque ad turonum de Sabuhc et usque ad aggerem[3] de Bezequi. Inter Sespin et Baari et Abedi et Raselain est divisio quedam petra scilicet nigra et pertusum vulpis, et extenditur usque ad curbam Iohannis Turci; dehinc usque ad curbam de Moqun et usque ad Indapus. Hec infra situm est ipsum casale Sespin. Ex parte Alasines extenditur usque ad arborem morarium furcatam et usque ad flumen Iohan et ad vingum Dendieu et ad ecclesiam de Indapus et ad turonum platum et petram nigram et fractum arvoltum et usque ad laccum, ubi fuit domus Iohannis Cordin, et viam cruciatam, ubi est crux de petra. Hinc est recta via de Amudain ad Tractic et postea ad flumen. Item aliud casale nomine Buquequia cum pertinenciis et divisionibus suis signatis, sicut dominus Michael ipsum tenuit; eiusdem et Sespin territorium iungitur. Item in territorio Meloni aliud casale nomine Cumbethfor cum pertinenciis et divisionibus ipsius signatis a parte orientis extenditur, sicut vadit via usque ad petram inter Cumbethfor et Tetimec, et sunt infra petre pro metis fixe et subter carbones. Dehinc extenditur usque ad metas petrarum fixas ex parte Vancun et carbones subter. A parte occidentis inter Cumbethfor et casale dictum Beleguinos, quod habitant villani de Arench et est sancte Marie de turri, sunt mete petrarum fixe et subter carbones. Dehinc extenditur usque ad columpnam marmoream. A parte septemtrionis versus Casseriam sunt mete fixe et subter carbones et vadit usque ad turonum. A meridie extenditur usque ad metas de Bagnigun, ubi crux est posita, et usque ad rocham, et infra sunt petre fixe et carbones subter. A parte Abraainain et Casserie sunt petre fixe et carbones subter. Et in medio petrarum fixarum est crux de petra. Item aliud casale nomine Ayun cum pertinenciis et divisionibus ipsius signatis: a parte Calasie est crux de petra et carbones subter supra viam, que ducit ad Vancun. A parte orientis extenditur ad pertusum vulpis et est ibi crux de petra. Dehinc extenditur usque ad ovile et in medio sunt mete de petra quinque et carbones subter. A parte Vangun[4] usque ad aliam crucem de petra, que fixa est iusta gastinam supra viam, et in capite vie est alia petra et via ibi dividitur. Hiis ita assignatis item dono et concedo amodo in perpetuum eisdem fratribus plenam libertatem per terram, per mare, per totum regnum meum et per totam terram omnium mihi subiacencium et obediencium in civitatibus, in castellis, in villis, in casalibus, in montibus, in planis, in portibus vendendi et emendi ad opus domus sue omnia victualia et queque sibi necessaria, et eciam equitaturas libere, quiete, pacifice, sine contradictione, sine omni drictura, sine contrarietate et sine exactione aliqua. Predicta vero omnia castellum et casalia cum terris et pertinenciis et divisionibus signatis, cum aquis et molendinis et cum omni iure eisdem pertinenti dono predictis fratribus sancte domus hospitalis Theutonicorum libere, quiete, pacifice amodo in perpetuum sine calumpnia et sine contradictione aliqua omnium hominum mortalium, qui sunt et erunt sub potestate et dominio meo. Insuper precipio omnibus hominibus meis, qui sunt et qui erunt, ne de cetero habeant potestatem vel ausum super hec omnia, que caritative ac hereditario iure ad possidendum dono predictis fratribus, sicut continetur in presenti pagina, nec possunt aliquod servicium seu tributum seu angariam seu exactioem aliquam ab ipsis fratribus modo quolibet extorquere, immo teneantur eos amare, honorare et venerari per omnia et in omnibus, sicut decet religiosos viros persone mee ac heredum meorum et tocius regni mei amatores. Quicquid continetur in presenti pagina, dono predictis fratribus amodo in perpetuum, ut dictum est, libere, quiete, pacifice secundum legem et consuetudinem Francorum. Pro quibus confirmandis presens scribi iussi privilegium propria manu mea litteris rubeis signatum et regali sigillo meo aureo corroboratum et sigillatum. Factum est autem hoc privilegium incarnationis dominice anno m° cc° xii° mense aprilis.

I, 35 v. n. 82. Iam de fine 1211 anni loquens Wilbrandus de Oldenburg in Peregrinatione ed. Laurent. Hamburg. 1859. I, 19 p. 17 dicit: „Abhinc transeuntes Cumbetefort, ubi domus est et mansio bona hospitalis Alemannorum, venimus Tursolt". I, 22 p. 19: 1212 6. ianuar. Sisiae in urbe capitali Armeniae regni vidit cum Leone rege magistrum domus hospitalis S. Mariae Theutonicorum; deinde pergit I, 24 p. 20: „Inde venimus Adamodanam, quod est castrum hospitalis sive domus Alemannorum. Quod dominus rex, qui semper Alemannos dilexit, eis pro remedio anime sue cum villis attinentibus donavit". 1. 2 Cor. 9, 6. 2. non est lacuna in B. 3. agger B. 4. nangū B.

---

47. *1213 febr. 24. Romae ap. s. Petrum. Innocentius papa III confirmat fratribus hospitali Theotonicorum de Accon a Leone Armeniae rege donata castallum et casale Amudain, casalia Sespin, Bucona, Ayn.*

Innocentius episcopus servus servorum dei dilectis filiis magistro et fratribus hospitalis Theotonicorum de Accon salutem et apostolicam benedictionem. Iustis petencium desideriis dignum est nos facilem prebere consensum et vota, que a rationis tramite non discordant, effectu prosequente complere. Ea propter, dilecti in domino filii, vestris iustis precibus inclinati castellum Amudain[1] et casale sibi adherens, de Sespin quoque, de Buchecia[2] et de Ayn casalia, cum terris, aquis, divisionibus, molendinis, iuribus et pertinenciis eorundem domui vestre a karissimo in Christo[3] filio nostro L(eone)[4] illustri rege Armenie pia liberalitate[5] collata necnon libertates vobis concessas ab ipso, sicut ea omnia iuste ac pacifice possidetis et in[6] ipsius regis auctentico[4] plenius continetur, vobis et per vos eidem domui vestre auctoritate apostolica confirmamus et presentis scripti patrocinio communimus. Nulli ergo omnino hominum liceat hanc paginam nostre confirmationis infringere vel ei ausu temerario contraire. Si quis autem hoc attemptare presumpserit, indignationem omnipotentis dei et beatorum Petri et Pauli apostolorum eius se noverit incursu-

Davidson College Library

rum. Datum Rome apud Sanctum Petrum vi° kal. marcii pontificatus nostri anno xvi°.

I, 60. — In copiario Regimontano A. 16 p. 17 inter Veneta; contulit v. cl. Meckelburg. Cf. Voigt G. Pr. II, 63. 1. videtur: Amudaim A. 16. 2. Bucona B. 3. f. n. i. Ch. B. 4. deest A. 16. 5. libertate B. 6. deest B. — Hic annotandum, quod male Lünig Teutsches Reichsarchiv Spicilegici ecclesiastici Continuatio II. Leipzig 1721. fol. p. 318. Innocentii III confirmationem de (1210 aug. 3) p. n. a. 13. iii nonas augusti Laterani super Leonis Armeniae regis inserta donatione (s. a. Tharsi med. april.) civitatis Saleph, Castelli novi et Camard domui Hospitalis facta tanquam ordini Theutonico praestitam repetit.

---

48. *1215 aprilis 9. Mathildis, vidua Conradi advocati de Swarzenberg, concedit hospitali S. Mariae Theutonicorum in Accon a filia quondam Ioscelini comitis emtam domum.*

Universis sancte matris ecclesie filiis tam clericis quam laicis innotescat, quod ego domina Maccildis, uxor quondam domini Conradi advocati de Swarcenberch, dono et concedo pro anime dicti mariti mei[1] et mee antecessorumque meorum medela hospitali sancte Marie Theutonicorum in Accon domum meam cum omnibus pertinenciis suis, quam predictus maritus meus et ego emimus a filia quondam comitis Ioscelini, ut, sicut dictus maritus meus et ego eam pacifice possidebamus, ita et predictum hospitale pacifice possideat in perpetuum. Pro qua vero donatione frater Hermannus, dicti hospitalis magister, et eius fratres promiserunt mihi et concesserunt bona fide donare ad xv dies post pentecosten proximo post annum venturum apud Straceburch quadringentas marcas argenti albi et puri ad emendum terram, cuius redditus et fructus ego debeo percipere, dum vixero, et de illis pro voluntate mea disponere. Post mortem vero meam domui hospitalis dicta terra libera remanebit ita tamen, quod hospitale pretaxatum illius terre semper habebit saisinam. Et, si forte supranominati hospitalis fratres subscriptum argentum ad terminum nominatum mihi non assignaverint, eodem termino annuatim xl marcas mihi persolvent, quousque supranominatas cccc^as marcas mihi integre, ut suprascriptum est, persolverint. Huius autem rei sunt testes frater Ludovicus[2] de Horflegowe, tunc marescalcus; frater Drabodo de Utinge, tunc preceptor; frater Haymo de Falconeis; frater Hartungus de Sulmesse; frater Hunricus Gyr; frater Rodengerus de Fulcolfsem; frater Otto de Losenheum; frater Gunterus de Winrikesleve; dominus Vencardus de Carlesberch. Ut autem hec nostra donatio firma sit et a nullo valeat violari, hanc cartam scribi precepi et sigilli mei munimine roborari. Actum est anno ab incarnatione domini m° cc° xv° quinto ydus aprilis. Ego Guillelmus dominici sepulcri prior ex utraque parte rogatus testis subscribo[3] et bulla capituli confirmo.

I, 30 n. 66. 1. advocatus de Swarcenberch 1208 octobri Accone Ottonis Hennebergensis comitis et Beatricis uxoris eius testis occurrit; Pauli I, 97. 2. udoui supra rasuram; in margine: louudei B. 3. supplevi.

---

49. *1217 augusto. Iohannes Hierosolymitanus rex confirmat domui hospitalis Alamannorum Acconensi terram et hortum a Garnero Alamanno data.*

Ego Iohannes dei gratia Latinorum Ierusalem rex decimus et comes Brenensis notum facio universis tam presentibus quam futuris, quod Garnerus Alamannus dilectus et fidelis meus laude[1] et assensu meo dedit domui hospitalis Alamannorum Acchon terram, que fuit Iuliani de Faloisse, quam idem G(arnerus) emit, in qua calidus[2] furnus solet esse, et divisio ipsius terre versus sinistram[3] est via, versus meridiem est collis. Preterea dictus Garnerus dedit predicte domui iardinum, qui coheret areis de tarsia ex toto versus meridiem; et in eodem iardino est angulus terre deserte, et versus occidentalem plagam est quedam morus et campus quidam, qui dicitur Migramme, et superius est frustrum terre, que dividit terram domus sepulcri; et versus collem, qui est ex parte orientali, est modicum terre et quedam vouta, cuius medietas cecidit, et in eadem vouta est quedam cisterna et quidam vrequinnus[4] ad racemos decalcandos. In cuius rei testimonio presentem cartam feci fieri et sigillo meo et testibus subscriptis roborari. Huius autem rei sunt testes Radulfus, regni senescalcus; Iacobus, marescalcus; Oddo de Monte Beliardo; Gauffridus de Caffran. Actum anno incarnati verbi m° cc° xvii° mense augusti.

I, 26 n. 52. 1. leude B. 2. callidus B. 3. sinistrē B. 4. B.

---

50. *1217 augusto. Iohannes Hierosolymitanus rex donat domui hospitalis Alamannorum Acconensi barbacanam Accone.*

Notum sit omnibus tam presentibus quam futuris, quod ego Iohannes dei gratia Latinorum Ierusalem rex decimus et comes Brenensis, dono et concedo in elemosinam deo et domui hospitalis Alamannorum Acchon meam barbacanam a muro prope domum senescalci, que tendit ex adverso et dividit barbacanam senescalci ab eadem barbacana usque ad portam Gaufridi Torti. Totam scilicet barbacanam infra duos muros civitatis, sicut per metas predictas superius dictum est, dono predicte domui possidendam in perpetuum et habendam. Ut autem hec mea donatio rata maneat et firma, presentem cartam precepi fieri et sigillo meo et testibus subscriptis roborari. Huius rei sunt testes Radulfus, regni senescalcus; Iacobus marescalcus; Oddo de Monte Beliardo; Gaufridus de Caffran; Rohardus de Cayphas. Actum anno ab incarnatione domini m° cc° xvii° mense augusti.

I, 25 v. n. 49.

---

51. *1219 martio. Raimundus Rupini, Antiochiae princeps, fratribus hospitalis s. Mariae Theutonicorum concedit liberum commeatum per principatum suum.*

In nomine sancte et individue trinitatis, patris et filii et spiritus sancti. Amen. Notum sit omnibus hominibus tam presentibus quam futuris, quod ego

Raymundus Rupini, dei gracia princeps Antiochenus, Raymundi principis filius, dono et concedo magistro et fratribus hospitalis sancte Marie Theutonicorum, ut libertatem plenariam habeant emendi, vendendi, intrandi et exeundi cum rebus propriis per totam terram meam tam infra[1] Antiochiam quam extra, et per mare ac per omnia loca mei principatus et per universa passagia ipsi et res, que eorum erunt proprie, libere transire possint et redire, nullam penitus mihi vel balivis meis nec pactonariis nec hominibus meis dreituram neque consuetudinem exsolventes. Ut autem hoc donum firmum et stabile in eternum permaneat, presens privilegium feci scribi et sygilli mei principalis impressione muniri atque subscriptorum virorum testimonio corrobari, quorum hec sunt nomina: Mansellus, constabularius et maior Antiochie; Aymarus de Leron; Guillelmus de Assardo; Amalricus de Crusi; Anfredus de Margato; Willelmus de Flechia, dux Antiochie. Factum est anno ab incarnatione domini millesimo cc° nono decimo, principatus mei anno iiii° indictione vii^{a} mense marcio. Datum per manum Iordani, cancellarii aule principalis Antiochie.

III, 165. 1. B.

---

52. *1220 30 maii apud Accon civitatem. Otto, comes de Henneberg, cum Beatrice uxore et Ottone filio hospitali s. Mariae domus Theutonicorum in Ierusalem vendunt omnem a Beatrice in Hierosolymitano regno possessam hereditatem.*

Otto dei gracia comes de Hennemberc universis Christi fidelibus, ad quos presens scriptum pervenerit, salutem in auctore salutis. Suboriri solet de gestis hominum multa calumpnia, nisi robur lingua bonorum testium adhibeat aut scriptura. Eapropter ad noticiam presencium ac futurorum Ihesu Christi fidelium pervenire volumus, quod nos et uxor nostra, Beatrix nomine, Ioscelini comitis quondam filia, ac filius noster Otto unito penes nos consilio hospitali sancte Marie domus Theutonicorum in Ierusalem omnem hereditatem, quam ex progenitorum suorum successione uxor nostra predicta in regno Ierosolimitano possedit vel possidere debuit, diminutione qualibet remota pro septem milibus marcharum argenti et pro duobus milibus bisantiorum libere vendidimus. Insuper tria milia bisantiorum et cc et l^{a} bisancios, quos pro domino Guillelmo de Mandelia persolvere tenebamur, dicte domus fratres loco nostri persolverunt. Hunc autem vendicionis nostre contractum in presencia domini Iohannis regis Ierosolimitani et suorum baronum ac fidelium Hermanno de Salza, magistro domus Theutonicorum, suisque fratribus legitime stabilivimus, quingentis eciam marchis argenti proinde regi supradicto collatis ab eisdem fratribus. Ne igitur in posterum hec rationabilis expiret actio, sed rata et inconvulsa semper permaneat, presentem paginam plumbea bulla nostra communitam sepedicto[1] H(ermanno), magistro domus Theutonicorum, et suis fratribus pro confirmationis titulo tradidimus. Huius rei testes sunt dominus

Radulfus de Tyberiade, senescalcus regni Ierosolimitani; dominus Wernerus de Egisheim, cognatus eius; dominus Haymo; dominus Guillelmus de Beryto; dominus Rohardus de Caypha, camerarius, frater eius; dominus Ioffridus de Caffra; dominus Henricus de Brenne; dominus Albertus, frater eius; dominus Henricus de Gebwylre[2]; dominus Henricus de Ruwach et alii quam plures. Actum publice aput Accon civitatem anno ab incarnacione domini m° cc° xx° indiccione viii[a] iii° kal. iunii.

I, 11 v. n. 19. Edidit Iohannes Voigt, Graf Otto von Henneberg und die Botenlaube bei Kissingen in: Neue Beiträge zur Geschichte deutschen Alterthums. Herausgegeben von dem Hennebergischen alterthumsforschenden Verein durch Georg Brückner. Meiningen 1858. 1. Lieferung. 70 sq. 1. legendum videtur: supradicto. 2. ante y o expunctum.

---

53. *1220 maio (sc. 30 aut 31). Iohannes Hierosolymitanus rex confirmat Hermanno magistro et fratribus domus hospitalis s. Mariae Theutonicorum Hierosolymitani ab Ottone comite de Hennenberg, Beatrice uxore, Ottone filio eorum vendita Castellum Regis cum pertinentiis et domum quandam Accone sitam.*

Ego Iohannes dei gratia Latinorum Ierosolimitanus rex decimus notum facio tam presentibus quam futuris, quod vir nobilis Otto comes de Henneberk[1] et domina Beatrix, uxor sua, filia pie memorie comitis Ioscelini, et Otto, eorum filius, coram me et curia mea voluntate et assensu meo vendiderunt fratri Hermanno, magistro domus hospitalis sancte Marie Teutonicorum Ierosolimitani, et fratribus eiusdem domus presentibus et futuris Castellum Regis cum omnibus pertinenciis suis, excepto casali, quod vocatur Ihazon, pro septem milibus marchis argenti boni et legitimi et duobus milibus bisanciorum sarracenatorum, et preterea pro tribus milibus et ducentis quinquaginta bisanciis, quos ad mandatum dictorum comitis et uxoris sue dicti magister et fratres persolverunt de debito domini Guilermi de Amigdala, qui sororem dicte Beatricis, filiam dicti comitis Ioscelini, habuit in uxorem. Vendiderunt siquidem prefatis magistro H(ermanno) et fratribus quicquid habebant vel habere debebant in dicto Castello Regis, tenendum et possidendum, sicut prefati comes et uxor sua et eorum antecessores tenuerunt et possederunt pacifice et libere. Hee sunt pertinencie et casalia dicti Castelli Regis videlicet: Tersyha, Carphasonie, Samohete, Geelin, Zoenite, Beletim, Tarphile, Rasabde, Supheye, Capharra, Noseoquie, Danehyle, Lebeyne, Iubie, Bechera, Habelye, Amca, Gez, Clil et medietas Noie. Similiter sunt de pertinenciis predictis Fasoce, Achara, Tayeretrane, Tayerebika, Fennes, Carsilie, Serouh, Gabatye, Horfeis, Roeis, Camsara, Cassie, Deleha, Derbasta, Raheb, Ezefer, Berzei; similiter et tercium feodi de sancto Georgio, cuius pertinencie et casalia sunt hec: Arket, Yanot, Cabra, Meblie, Saphet, Lemezera, Kemelye et tercium casalis dou Bokehel cum pertinenciis eiusdem et tercium de assisia, que est de hoc eodem feodo, scilicet tercium octingentorum bisanciorum assignatorum ad cathenam Accon, cuius tercii summa est ducenti sexaginta vii bisancii minus tercia, quos prefati magister et fratres mihi et successoribus meis in perpetuum quitaverunt. Vendiderunt similiter prefati comes et uxor sua et eorum filius prefatis magistro et fratribus assisiam duorum milium bisanciorum ad cathenam Accon assignatorum, quos similiter predicti magister et fratres mihi et successoribus meis in perpetuum quitaverunt. Quitaverunt eciam predicti magister et fratres mihi et successoribus meis quicquid ad presens est in manibus Sarracenorum, quod pertinet ad ea, que vendiderunt prefati comes et uxor sua et eorum filius, cum a fidelibus fuerit acquisitum. Vendiderunt preterea prefati comes et uxor sua et eorum filius predictis magistro et fratribus quandam domum in Accon, que fuit comitis Ioscelini, cuius situs talis est: ab oriente habet quandam ruellam, ab occidente quandam clausuram domuum, que sunt abbatis Montis Thabor; a meridie est via publica; a septemtrione coheret domui Rohardi domini Cayphe. Si vero in civitatibus Tyri vel Accon alique domus fuerint, que ad supradictam vendicionem pertineant, cum a magistro vel fratribus dicti hospitalis fuerimus requisiti, in curia nostra plenum ius secundum consuetudines terre faciemus exhiberi. Pro hac autem venditione, cui consensi et acquievi, recepi ego quingentas marchas argenti a prefatis H(ermanno) magistro et fratribus. Ut hoc autem ratum sit et firmum in perpetuum, ego ad utriusque partis peticionem presens scriptum precepi fieri et sigillo meo testibus subscriptis confirmari. Huius autem rei sunt testes Otto de Monte Beliardo, regni constabilis; Radulfus Tyberiadis, regni senescalcus; Balianus, dominus Sydonis; Garnerus Alemannus; Gilo de Beritho; Rohardus de Cayphas; Gaufridus de Cafran; Haimo[2] Alamannus; Danyel de Malenbech. Actum anno domini m° cc° xx° mense mayo.

I, 12 n. 20. Ed. I. Voigt l. c. 71. 1. hennebeck B. 2. haimo B.

---

54. *1220 oct. 27 Laterani. Honorius papa III confirmat magistro et fratribus domus s. Mariae Theutonicorum Hierosolymitanae ab Ottone, comite de Henneberg, Beatrice uxore, Ottone filio eorum venditum Castellum Regis.*

Honorius episcopus servus servorum dei dilectis filiis magistro et fratribus domus sancte Marie Theutonicorum Iherosolimis[1] salutem et apostolicam benedictionem. Iustis petencium desideriis dignum est nos facilem prebere consensum et vota, que a[2] rationis tramite non discordant, effectu prosequente complere. Cum igitur Castellum Regis cum omnibus pertinenciis suis, excepto casali, quod vocatur Ihazon[3], a nobili viro comite de Hennenberch et nobili muliere Beatrice, uxore sua, et Ottone filio eorum, e meritis karissimo in Christo filio nostro Iohanne, illustri rege Ierosolimitano, presente ac prestante consensum, sicut in eius patentibus[4] litteris plumbea bulla munitis perspeximus contineri, nos precibus vestris benignum impercientes assensum, castellum ipsum cum omnibus pertinenciis eius, excepto casali predicto, sicut ea iuste ac[5] pacifice possidetis et in prefati regis litteris plenius continetur, vobis et per vos domui vestre auctoritate apostolica confirmamus et presentis scripti patrocinio communimus. Nulli ergo omnino hominum liceat hanc paginam nostre confirmacionis infringere vel ei ausu temerario contraire. Si quis autem hoc attemptare presumserit, indignationem omnipotentis dei et beatorum Petri et Pauli apostolorum eius se noverit incursurum. Datum Laterani vi° kal. novembris pontificatus nostri anno quinto.

I, 63 n. 1. In copiario Regimontano A. 16 p. 7 inter Veneta; contulit v. cl. Meckelburg. Ed. Voigt l. c. 73. 1. Thetonicorum Ierosolimis B. 2. ex A. 16. 3. Iaharon A. 16. 4. presentibus B. 5. et A. 16.

---

55. *1221 martio. Iohannes Hierosolymitanus rex concedit domui hospitalis S. Mariae Theutonicorum partem lucri sibi debitam, quotiescunque ipso absente homines sui cum fratribus expeditionem facturi sint.*

Notum sit omnibus tam presentibus quam futuris, quod ego Iohannes dei gracia Latinorum Ierusalem rex decimus, laude et concessu Ysabellis filie mee, dono et concedo et in perpetuum quitto in helemosinam fratri Hermanno magistro domus hospitalis sancte Marie Theutonicorum Ierusalem et fratribus eiusdem domus presentibus et futuris propter religionem et bonam famam eorum partem, quam habeo in lucro, quod faciunt in armis predicti fratres, cum homines mei cum signo regali cum eis sunt me absente; mihi vero et successoribus meis in regno Ierosolimitano retineo partem, quam habeo in lucro, quod faciunt predicti fratres in armis me presente, videlicet medietatem tocius lucri sui in villis sive in castris sive in campis sive in expeditionibus sive in quibuscunque aliis locis. Hoc autem, quod superius dictum est de quitatione et retentione, bona fide et absque omni malo ingenio intelligatur. Ut autem[1] donatio et quitatio predicta in perpetuum observetur, presentem cartam sigilli mei munimine et testibus subscriptis feci muniri. Huius rei testes sunt Balianus dominus Sydonis; Oddo de Montebeliardo, regni constabularius; Garnerus Alamannus; Rohardus, dominus Cayphe, Gaufridus de Caffran; Haymo Alamannus; Daniel de Malenbech. Actum anno dominice incarnationis m° cc° xxi° mense marcii.

I, 25 v. n. 51. 1. eciam B.

---

56. *1222 aprili. Iniorannus dominus Bovae vendit domui s. Mariae Theutonicorum domum quandam Tyri sitam.*

Notum sit omnibus tam presentibus quam futuris, quod ego Iniorannus dominus Bove in presencia domini mei Iohannis regis Ierusalem illustris et[1] in curia sua vendidi fratri Hermanno, magistro domus sancte Marie Theutonicorum Ierusalem, et fratribus eiusdem domus tam presentibus quam futuris domum unam in Tyro cum omnibus introitibus et exitibus, terraciis, appendiciis et aliis iuribus suis inferius et superius ad vendendum, donandum, inpignorandum[2] vel quocunque modo alienandum, quibus voluerint, personis ecclesiasticis et domibus religionum exceptis. Dictam equidem domum vendidi pro mille bisanciis sarracenatis ad pondus Acconense[3] ponderatis, de quibus me bene esse pagatum[4] confiteor. Ipsius domus situs talis est: a parte orientali habet mare, quod verberat ad pedem muri domus; a parte occidentali extenditur usque ad vicum, qui ducit a la tanerie; a parte meridionali propinqua est cuidam domui hospitalis sancti Iohannis, que domus fuit de Sanche Martin; a parte septentrionali extenditur usque ad domum Eustacii Busekae[5] et fratrum eius. Ad maiorem autem huius vendicionis securitatem et perpetuam firmitatem presentem cartam sigilli mei munimine et testibus subscriptis feci roborari. Huius rei testes sunt Balianus dominus Sydonis; Oddo de Montebliard[6], regni constabularius; Garnerus Alemannus[7]; Roardus[8] dominus Cayphe; Gauffridus de Cafran[9]; Haymo Alemannus[10]; Danyel de Malenbec[11]. Actum anno dominice incarnationis m° cc° xx° ii° mense aprilis.

I, 26 n. 53. Ex originali, cui deest sigillum, hausisse Sicklerum Monumenta graphica II, 3 monet v. cl. Meckelburg. 1. deest B. 2. impignorandum B. 3. acchonense B. 4. pagatum esse B. 5. Eustachii Busekie B. 6. Montebeliardo B. 7. Alamannus B. 8. Rohardus B. 9. Caffran B. 10. Aymo Alamannus B. 11. Daniel de Malenbech B.

---

57. *1222 aprili. Iohannes Hierosolymitanus rex confirmat domui s. Mariae Theutonicorum ab Inioranno domino Bovae emtam domum Tyri.*

Ego Iohannes dei gracia Latinorum Ierusalem rex decimus notum facio omnibus tam presentibus quam futuris, quod Iniorannus dominus Bove coram me et curia mea vendidit fratri Hermanno magistro domus sancte Marie Theutonicorum Ierusalem et fratribus eiusdem domus presentibus et futuris domum unam in Tyro cum omnibus introitibus et exitibus, terraciis, appendiciis et aliis iuribus suis inferius et superius. Fuit equidem domus dicta vendita pro m bisantiis sarracenatis ad pondus Accon ponderatis, de quibus dictus Innorannus se bene pagatum confessus est. Dicte domus situs talis est: a parte orientali habet mare, quod verberat ad pedem muri ipsius domus; a parte occidentali extenditur usque ad vicum, qui ducit a la tenerie[1]; a parte meridionali propinqua est cuidam domui hospitalis sancti Iohannis, que fuit de Sanche Martin; a parte septentrionali extenditur usque ad domum Eustachii Buseke et fratrum eius. Ego vero hanc vendicionem et empcionem laudavi et concessi et ad utriusque partis peticionem presentem cartam sigilli mei munimine et testibus subscriptis feci roborari. Huius rei testes sunt Balianus, dominus Sydonis; Oddo de Montebeliardo, regni constabularius; Garnerus Alamannus; Rohardus, dominus Cayphe; Gaufridus de Caffran; Aymo Alamannus; Daniel de Malenbech; Iohannes Coste; Gaufridus Tortus. Actum anno dominice incarnationis m° cc° xx° ii° mense aprilis.

I, 26 v. n. 54. 1. sic etiam in n. 56 antea legebatur.

---

58. *1226 ian. s. l. ind. xiv. i. 6 v. I. l. G. 28. Fridericus II imperator (Si religiosa loca), attendens domum s. M. Th. i. I. a Romanis principibus, progenitoribus suis, inchoatam et immensis beneficiis ampliatam, Isabellae imperatricis praedecessoribus devotam inventam esse, devotionemque revolvens Hermanni magistri et fratrum, domum ipsam et derivatas ab ea, fratres et confratres cum omnibus bonis, quae per dotale suum regnum Ierosolimitanum possident, etiam cum subditis et legatis eorum et negotia eorum exercentibus sub speciali protectione recipit; assentiente uxore confirmat omnia privilegia et possessiones, quorum quaedam sunt: Castellum Regis cum pertinentiis excepto casali Iharon*[1], *ab Ottone comite de Ennenberch*[2], *et Beatrice uxore, Iozcelini*[3] *comitis filia, et Ottone filio emtum, cuius casalia sunt: Tersiha*[4], *Carphasome, Samohete*[5], *Geelim*[6], *Zoenite*[7], *Beletini*[8], *Tarphile*[9], *Rasapde, Supheye*[10], *Caphara, Neiecchie*[11], *Danehile*[12], *Labeyne*[13], *Iubie*[14], *Bechera, Abelie*[15], *Amca*[16], *Geze*[17], *Clil*[18], *medietas Noie; Phasoce*[19], *Achara*[20], *Tayretrane*[21], *Tayrebica*[22], *Phennes*[23], *Carsylie*[24], *Serohu*[25], *Gabatie*[26], *Orpheis*[27], *Roeis, Campsera*[28], *Capsie*[29], *Deleha*[30], *Derbasta*[31], *Rapho, Rabeb*[32], *Ezefer, Berzey*[33]; *tertium feodi de S. Georgio, cuius pertinentiae sunt Archet*[34], *Yanot, Cabra*[35], *Meblie, Saphet*[36], *Lemezera, Kemelie et tertium casalis de Boukel*[37] *et tertium de assisia, quae est de eodem feodo, scilicet tercium 800 bisantiorum assignatorum ad catenam Acconensem, i. e. 266 2/3 bisancios, quos magister et fratres Iohanni regi remiserunt, una cum assisia 2000 bisanciorum similiter ad catenam Acconensem assignatorum, quam assisiam comes et uxor cum filio vendiderunt eisdem. Confirmat domui domum quondam Iozcelini*[38] *comitis Accone ab eisdem emtam, quae ab oriente habent ruellam, ab occidente clausuram domorum abbatis montis Tabor; a meridie viam publicam; a septentrione domum Rohardi domini Cayphas*[39]. *Relaxat domui remissionem Iohanni regi factam de partibus venditionis illius nunc per Saracenos occupatis. Confirmat igitur domui omnem Iozcelini*[40] *hereditatem, quo statu ante amissam terram sanctam habuerit, a Beatrice cum coniuge et filio domui venditam, exceptis praedictis assisiis bisanciorum ad catenam Acconensem assignatis, caeterum omnia ab omni servicio libera et exemta. Confirmat domui barbacanam, turres, muros, fossatum a meta porprisiae, quam Henricus Trecensis comes palatinus assentiente Isabella uxore, Almerici regis filia, domui concessit, usque ad portam s. Nicolai; insuper partem a Iohanne rege concessam lucri, quod faciunt fratres in armis, praesentibus regis hominibus absente tamen ipso rege, reservata vero medietate lucri praesente rege facti in villis, castris, caeteris. Concedit domui libertatem aquarum, herbarum, lignorum ubique per domanium suum ad domus usum; eximit a plateatico aliisque consuetudinibus per regnum Ierosolimitanum terra marique solvi solitis. Statuit, ne quis domum et fratres de possessionibus domus sine iudicio et iusticia praesumat aliquatenus dissasire. Confirmat, ne quid de proventibus et bonis suis, quae ad partes cisma-*

rinas pro domus et sua utilitate dirigant, pro portatico, falangatico, ripatico, teloneo, alia exactione exigatur; sed domus exemta sit ab omni collecta, angaria, onere servitutis. Testes: de imperio: Rainaldus, dux Spoleti; Brutoldus[41] frater eius; Gottifridus de Hunloch[42]; Albertus et Conradus de Stouphe[43] et Gavianus[44] de Cipro. De regno Ierosolimitano: Iacobus, Acconensis episcopus; Balianus dominus Sydonis; Daniel de Terramunde; Nicolaus Antelmi[45]; Gvido de Infante; Guido de Romau[46]; Rao cognatus patriarchae; Gervasius de Malgastel[47]; Philippus Cynardi[48]; Ioannes Pisanus; Raimundus Grimaldus; Gofridus[49] de Villiers; Guido de Nubie. De regno Siciliae: Landus[50], Reginus archiepiscopus; Bartolomeus, Syracusanus episcopus; Thomasius[51], comes Acerrarum; Symon, comes Teatinus[52]; comes Raynaldus de Lavareta[53]; Henricus de Morra, magister iusticiarius; Ricardus camerarius[54]. Per manus Symonis Tyrensis archiepiscopi, regni Ierosolimitani cancellarii.

E codice nostro I, 13 n. 22 ed. Huillard-Bréholles II, 531. Archivum Regimontanum referente v. cl. Meckelburg duo possidet transsumta: A. de 1336 per Tranensis archiepiscopi vicarium Rogerium de Barulo archidiaconum et Nicolaum Bertonum regalis terrae Baruli iudicem petente provinciali Apuliae O. S. M. Th.; et K. de 1393 febr. 5 Vindobonae per officialem curiae Pataviensis; cf. Napiersky Index I, 6 et 8. Variant in nominibus A et K: 1. Iharon A, Iaron K. 2. Hennenberc A, K. 3. Iotholini A, Iozcolini K. 4. Tersyha A, Tharssia K. 5. Samothete K. 6. Gerlin A, Geelin K. 7. Zoemte A. 8. Belethini K. 9. Tarfile A, Carfile K. 10. Supheie K. 11. Nesecchie macula tectum in A, Hesetchie K. 12. Danehyle A, Danehile K. 13. Lebeyne A, Labeine K. 14. Iubie, Inbie? A, Inbye K. 15. Habelie A. 16. Anica, Anita A, Amea K. 17. Gez A. 18. Olil A. 19. Phasote A. 20. Atbara A. 21. Tayretrane A, K. 22. Tayrebicca A, K. 23. Fennes A. 24. Carfilie A, Carsilie K. 25. Serchu K. 26. Gabacie A, Gabasye K. 27. Orfeis A. 28. Campsara A, K. 29. Capsie A, K. 30. Delhea K. 31. Derbasta A, K. 32. Rabeb A, K. 33. Berzey A, Bersei K. 34. het. Arclyet A. 35. Oabra A. 36. Sapher A, K. 37. Boubeeel A, Bukeel K. 38. Iozolini A, Iozcolini B. 39. Cayphis A, Caypha K. 40. Iozolini A, Iozcolini K et sic semper. 41. Bruttoldus A, Berchtoldus K. 42. Gottifridus de Honboth A, Gottfridus de Hohenloch K. 43. Stouphe A, Stüphen K. 44. Gaynanus A, K. 45. Antelin aut Aucelin A. 46. Gvido de Roman A, K. 47. Geruasius de Mangnastel A, Geruasius de Mangastel K. 48. Philippus Cuiard A, Philippus Chinardi K. 49. Goffridus A, Gotfridus K. 50. Sandus A, Lando K. 51. Thomas A, K. 52. Simon, comes Theatinus A, K. 53. lauar̄et (?) A, banareth K. 54. et Riccardus Imperialis aule camerarius A, K.

---

59. *1226 ianuario. Isabella, Romanorum imperatrix, Ierusalem et Siciliae regina, notum facit, quod Fridericus II imperator coniux assensu suo confirmavit domui S. M. Th. i. I. omnia privilegia et bona a praedecessoribus et parentibus suis concessa, specialiter Castellum Regis cum pertinentiis excepto casali Iaroth[1], quondam ab Ottone comite de Hennenberc et Beatrice uxore, filia Iozcelini[2] comitis, et ab Ottone filio domui venditum, praeter assisias bisanciorum ad catenam Accon assignatorum a magistro et fratribus regi patri suo remissas; praeterea, quod imperator re-*

laxavit domui remissionem a domo patri suo regi factam super eo toto, quod nunc est in manibus Sarracenorum, cum fuerit acquisitum per fideles, quodque domus a comite et uxore emerat. Item, quod confirmavit domui domum quondam Iozcelini[2] *comitis apud Acchon*[3]*; totam barbacanam, turres et muros et fossatum a meta proprisiae, quam Henricus Trecensis comes palatinus assentiente Isabella uxore, Almerici regis filia, domui pro eleemosyna concessit, usque ad portam b. Nicolai; deinde quod imperator quasdam immunitates domui concessit. Sub bulla cerea. Testes: Symon, Tyrensis archiepiscopus, regni Ierosolimitani cancellarius; Balianus, dominus Sydonis, Daniel de Terramunda, Nicolaus, Capuanus (Gainanus*[4]*) de Cipro, Guido Infans, Guido de Roman*[5]*, Raho de Patriarcha*[6]*, Gervasius de Emau*[7] *castello, Iohannes Pisanus, Raimont Grimaut*[8]*, Goffridus*[9] *de Villers, Guido de Nubie, et magister Petrus, medicus noster, fideles nostri regni Ierosolimitani. Per manus Symonis Tyrensis archiepiscopi, regni Ierosolomitani cancellarii, Isabellae imperatricis anno imperii et Ierosolimitani et Siciliae regnorum a. 1.*

E codice nostro I, 12v. n. 21 et in confirmatione 46 edidit Huillard-Bréholles II, 536. In archivo Regimontano asservatur transsumtum officialis Pataviensis curiae d. d. 1393 febr. Vindobonae, ubi legitur: 1. Iaroth. 2. Iozcolini. 3. Accon. 4. Gaynanus. 5. Romañ B 1, Gvido de Romav. 6. Rao de Patriarcha. 7. Geruasius de Emav. 8. Grimant. 9. Gotfridus.

---

60. *1226 iulio ap. S. Miniatum. Fridericus II imperator notum facit fidelibus suis per Ierosolimitanum regnum constitutis, quod, quum Hermannus magister domus h. s. M. Th. in I. possederit bona quondam Iozcelini comitis, emta a Otto comite de Ennenberch et Beatrice uxore et Ottone filio, et Iacobinum de Amigdala, filium quondam G.*[1] *iunioris filiae Iozcelini, secundum consuetudinem regni Ierosolimitani de portione, quae contigerit eum in eisdem bonis pro parte matris, investiverit; Iacobus de Amigdala magistrum et domum assecuravit, sicut pro parte matris suae Beatricem primogenitam comitis debuerit assecurare, de cuius venditione domus eadem bona possidebat; et praedictus Iacobinus convenit eidem domui restituere illam pecuniae quantitatem, quam pro redimenda eadem parte ipsum contingente, dudum per quondam Guilelmum de Amigdala patrem eius obligata, creditoribus suis exsolvit. Testes: G(eroldus) venerabilis („Wernerus") patriarcha Ierosolimitanus; Iacobus, Acconensis episcopus; Balianus, dominus Sydonis*[2]*; Daniel de Tenderemunde; Iohannes Pisanus; Goffridus de Williers; Guido de Nubie. Per manus Symonis Tyrensis archiepiscopi, regni Ierosolimitani cancellarii.*

I, 15 n. 23. E codice nostro ed. Huillard-Bréholles Historia diplomatica Friderici II imp. Parisiis 1852 sq. 4. II, 671. 1. p. 30 et 32 Agnes audit. 2. Sydonie B.

---

61. *1228 („1227") ianuario. Boemundus IV, Antiochiae princeps, donat domui s. Mariae hospitalis Theutonicorum molendinum prope Antiochiam cum vinea adiacente.*

Je Boemund per la grace de deu prince d'Anthioche et coms de Triple fais a saver a ceuas, qui sunt e qui avenir sunt, que je doing[1] et otrei e conferm en aumoine perdurablement por l'arme de mon pere et de ma mere e per l'arme de moi et de m'espose e de mes enfanz e de mes ancesors e de mes successors et[2] a tei frere Hermant, honorable maistre de la sancta maison de nostre dame de l'hospitau des Alamans et au convent et as freres, qui sont et qui seront de la dita maison, mon molin, que je achetai e fiz faire fors des murs de la cite d'Antioche, le[3] quel molin a iii peires et vos i poes metre la quarta, e si siet sur le fer desoz le molin del patriarche; et vos doing[4] totes les apartenences dou davant dit molin en aygues, en rentes, en pescherie et en totes autres drotures et vos doing tel franchise, que tuit cil, qui voudrunt modre a vostre molin par la dreiture payant a vos ou a celui, que vos i mettres, que il faire le poissent sens contradit et sens defense, que je ni heir, que je aye, metre y poissont. Et vos doing la vigne, que je fis planter pres de celui meesmes molin, et le pressoir et la terre en que la vigne est; lo quel molin et la quel vingne et le quel pressoir et la quel terre o tote lur apartenences en[2] aygues, en rentes et en pescherie tu, frere Hermant maistre de la maison de l'ospital[5] des Alamans et lo convent e li frere, qui sont et seront de cela meisme maison ayes et teingnes pardurablement franchement et quitement en haumoyne sens dreiture e sens acostumance, que je ni heir que je aye requerre i pouissons ni deons. Et por ce que je vueil, que ceste chose seit firme et estable, je ai fait seeler cest present privilege de mon seau de plom et confermer de garens desoz escriz, des quels ces sunt les noms: Boemont, li sires del Botron; Guiscart de l'Isle; Bertran Porcelet; Amauri Saleman[6]; Pierre de Scandalion; Raimund Arra; Manssel de Gibel; Auberi de Ranquerole. Cest privilege est fait l'an del incarnation de nostre seignor m° et cc° xxvii en mois de janveir.

I, 35 n. 81. 1. dong̃ B. 2. ⁊ B et sic saepe. 3. en B. 4. vox obscura correctis aliquibus literis: doni(ẽ)g B. 5. desospital B. 6. l'Aleman?

---

62. *(1228) febr. 11. Balianus dominus Sydonis donat hospitali s. Mariae domus Theutonicorum hortum et terram coci et mahumeriam magnam inter duas portas Sydonis.*

Balianus dei gracia dominus Sydonis universis Christi fidelibus presentem paginam inspecturis. Humana facta ne temporis prolixitate a memoria hominum avellantur[1], litterarum testimonio decet eternare. Hinc est, quod notum facio universis tam futuris quam presentibus scriptum presens inspecturis, quod ego Balianus dei gracia dominus Sydonis ob reverenciam dei et sancte genitricis sue virginis Marie et in remedium anime mee necnon progenitorum meorum iardinum quendam, qui dicitur iardinus comitisse, et vineam quandam et partem quandam terre, que dicitur terra coci, ad aratrum unum ante civitatem Sydonis hospitali sancte Marie domus Theutonicorum[2] contuli de bona voluntate libere et quiete in perpetuum possidenda. Divisiones vero iardini predicti tales sunt: contra orientem habet viam, que ducit Gasiam; ab occidente habens viam rectam, que transit inter iardinos et inter terram domini Rauli Ianuensis; contra meridiem tangens magnum campum, ubi fit canimel; contra aquilonem habens partem vie et olivas domini Guillelmi de Lye. Divisiones autem supradicte vinee tales sunt: ab oriente habet communem stratam et publicam; ab occidente viam rectam, que vadit inter iardinos contra flumen de ipsa civitate Sydonis; contra meridiem habens olivas domus Templi; contra aquilonem habens olivas domini Brixi. Divisiones vero terre supradicte tales sunt: ab oriente habet viam, que de Sydone ducit directe contra Sareptam; ab occidente habens viam maritimam; contra aquilonem habet campum, qui tangit iardinum domini Egidii; contra austrum nullam habet divisionem aliam, nisi quantum ipsa extenditur terra. Preterea mahumeriam magnam, que est infra[3] duas portas civitatis Sydonis, qua exitur versus Tyrum, predicte domui hospitalis sancte Marie Theutonicorum contuli libere habendam et in perpetuam elemosinam. Ut autem hec mea donatio tam libere et integre sepe dicto hospitali donata firma sit et rata, nec a meis successoribus et heredibus unquam possit aut debeat de cetero immutari, minui aut retractari, presens privilegium plumbeo sigillo mei typarii roboratum hospitali eidem scilicet sancte Marie domus Theutonicorum contuli in robur et testimonium sepedicte donationis perpetuo valiturum. Testes huius facti: dominus Daniel de Terremunde; dominus Hugo de Mazelria; dominus Baldovinus, marescalcus; dominus Ioffridus de Scimle; dominus Ioffridus de Vilier; dominus Michael Egidius et alij quam plures. Acta sunt anno gracie m° cc° xx° viii° undecimo die mensis februarii, tempore fratris Hermanni de Salza eiusdem sacre domus magistri.

I, 28 n. 61. 1. avellatur B. 2. thetonicorum B. 3. prius: intra.

---

63. *1228 apr. 20. Iacobus de Amigdala cambium facit cum domo Theutonicorum de tota terra ab ista sibi in feodum collata.*

Ego Iacobus de Amigdala notum facio omnibus tam presentibus quam futuris presentis scripti testimonio, quod de bona voluntate mea et ex altera parte de consensu et voluntate magistri et tocius conventus domus Theutonicorum accepi in excambium ab eodem magistro et fratribus predictis sex milia quadringentos bisantios sarracenatos, quos dominus Fridericus imperator Romanorum Ierusalem et Sicilie rex dicte domui donavit et concessit pro feudo meo, quod legitima successione matris mee, filie[1] comitis Iozcelini, me contingebat. Huius feudi casalia sunt hec: scilicet Mobilir, quod datum est in excambium mihi et heredibus meis pro Trefile et castro novo, quod dicitur Montfort, quod eciam eadem domus firmavit, ita ut illud castrum debeat domui perpetuo remanere, et pro orto et molendino, que sunt in pertinenciis de Trefile, et pro aliis casalibus, que nominatim exprimimus, scilicet Ialim et Tharbucha et Tarbosta et Suru et Beauer et Camesru et Tetramme et Fennes et Tersias et Ianot et Getz et Cabbara et una gastina, que dicitur Camesie, et Iunite et Blutun et una alia gastina, que dicitur Hemelie, que est in pertinenciis de Ianoth et Castrum Regis, salvis tamen omnibus, que magister et domus predicta Theutonicorum tenebant in domibus sive terris sive vineis in tenimentis eiusdem Castri Regis, priusquam illius terre dominium habuerint, et salvis omnibus, que pro eorum peccunia comparaverant et que domui predicte in helemosinam data fuerant in domibus, terris et vineis. Predictos vero bisancios debeo et heredes mei recipere in reditibus cathene et funde Ackonensium annuatim de tribus in tres menses, videlicet in utroque termino mille et dc bisancios. Etsi contigerit vel per dominum regni Ierosolimitani aut quocunque modo me hos bisancios non recipere, magister Hermannus vel successor eius et domus predicta Theutonicorum tenetur infra sex menses mihi vel meis heredibus integre persolvere tria milia et cc bisancios sarracenatos. Et si transactis sex mensibus infra dies xx[ti] bisancios antedictos mihi non solverint, dictus magister Hermannus et domus Theutonicorum tenentur mihi vel meis heredibus restituere integre et sine contradictione totum feudum superius nominatum excepto castro Montfort, quod domui dicte debet remanere, quia illud pro casali, quod dicitur Mobilie, datum est in excambium, et ad hoc curia regis eos per iusticiam coartabit, si contradicere vellent, et debent me vel heredes meos mittere in assisiam feudi antedicti, cambio, quod inter me et ipsos factum fuerat, penitus adnichilato, ita quod bisancii predicti, scilicet sex milia et quadraginta, ad domus dicte usum remanebunt. Pro tribus vero milibus et ducentis bisanciis mihi non solutis infra dies xx[ti] proximo subsequentes tenetur magister Hermanus vel successor eius et dicta domus Theutonicorum mihi et meis heredibus tria dicte domus casalia in pignore obligare, scilicet Erchat, Saphet et Ancre, tali conditione, quod si infra dimidium annum mihi vel meis heredibus non solverint bisancios nominatos, licitum sit mihi vel meis heredibus predicta tria casalia in vadimonio ponere aut vendere, ita ut meos bisancios inde rehabeam absque contradictione alicuius tanquam meum vadimonium salvo per omnia servicio, quod ego vel mei heredes tenemur domui inde facere prenominate, sive bisanciis sive terra perfruantur. Ut autem hec omnia, que supradicta sunt, firma et inconvulsa permaneant, presens privilegium meo sigillo roboratum eis tradidi. Testes vero sunt: frater Ludolfus, tunc temporis comendator magnus; frater Guntherus, tunc temporis marescalcus; frater Counradus, trapparius; frater Henricus, hospitalarius; frater

Henricus de Aneboz; frater Heinricus de Confluencia; frater Counradus de Nassowe; frater Andreas de Honlo; frater Uolricus de Durne; frater Eberardus; barones vero sancte terre: dominus Odo, conestabulus regni Ierusalem; dominus Balianus de Sydone; dominus Iohannes de Ybelino; dominus Garnerus de Egensheim, Alemannus; dominus Aimo de Ostehim; comes Thomas de Acerris; dominus Ricardus Filangerius[2], marescalcus regni[3] Sicilie; dominus Ricardus, camerarius domini imperatoris, et alii quam plures. Acta sunt anno domini m° cc° xx° viiii° indictione secunda[4] xx° die mensis aprilis.

I, 15 n. 24. 1. filia B. 2. Filag' B. 3. regis B. 4. scdō B.

---

64. *1228 iunio ineunte. Boemundus Antiochiae princeps donat domui hospitalis s. Mariae Theutonicorum c bisantios annuatim de assisia et funda et catena Acconensibus recipiendos.*

Coneua chose sia a toz ceus, qui sunt et qui avenir sunt, que je Boemunz, per la grace de deus prince de Anthioche et conte de Triple, en bona fei per bona volente doins et otrei et conferm en aumosne pardurablement por dei, por l'arme de moi et de mon pere et de ma mere et de toz mez antecessors a tei, freire Hermant, maestre de la chavalerie de la sainte maison de Nostre dame de l'hospital des Alamans, et a freires de la meismes maison et en aide deu labor deu chastel, que vos fermes per doner force a la cristiante encontre les Sarrazins, c bisances en assisa chascun an pardurablement, los qels c bisances vos recevrez et aurez et cil, qui serunt apres vos en la mesmes santa maison de Nostre dame de l'ospital des Alamans, en pais, senz calonge, franchemenz, quitement[1] de m'asize, que je ai en la fonde e en la chaene d'Acre, chascun an pardurablement en la manere, que je teins ceste moie acize en Acre, c'est a saver de iii mois en iii mois. Et por ce que c'est mien don, que je ai fait a tei, frere Herman, maistre de la chavaleria de la sancta maison de Nostre dame de l'ospital des Alamans, et a meesmes la maison et a freires seit ferm et estable perdurablement a toz jors, je ai fait escrivre ce present privilege et garnir et confermer de mon seel de plom et des garens dessos nomes, c'est a saver Boemon, sire deu Botron; Mansel de Gibel; Ugue Dalmas; Bonacors; Raimont de Mareclee; Raimunt Arra; Perre de Scandalion; Guiscart de l'Isle; Renaut Faisant. Ceste chose es faite et donee les l'entrant deu mois de juing en l'an de la encarnation nostre seignor m° et cc° et xxviii°.

I, 30 n. 67. 1. q̊ remt B.

---

65. *1229 aprili ap. Accon. Fridericus II imperator confirmat in palatio suo Acconensi commutationem ab Hermanno magistro domus s. Mariae Theutonicorum et domo ipsa cum Iacobo de Amigdala factam, ex qua*

his pro 6400 bisanciis sarracenatis, quondam domui ab imperatore in reditibus catenae sive etiam fundae Acconensium assignatis, totam terram suam in pertinentiis civitatis Acconensis a domo ipsi quondam ex successione matris, Iozcelini comitis filia, pro feudo concessam resignavit, scilicet Mebelie, „que data fuit in excambio dicto Iacobo a prefato magistro et domo sua pro Trefila et castro novo, quod dicitur Montfort, quod castrum domus ipsa firmavit in territorio Trefile, et pro iardino et molendino de pertinenciis Trefile", Ialim, Tarbuca, Terbasta, Suru, Beaueer, Camessrea, Tertramme, Fenes, Tercia, Gianot, Get, Cabbera, gastina Camelie, Iunite, Blutun, gastina Hamelie de pertinentiis Gianot, Castellum Regis. Testes: Balianus, dominus Sydonis; Odo de Monte Beliardo, comestabulus regni Ierosolimitani; Iohannes de Ybelino; Thomas, comes Acerranus, balivus regni Ierosolimitani; Ricardus Filangerius, „marescalcus noster"; Garnerius Alamannus.

I, 16 n. 25. E codice nostro ed. Huillard-Bréholles III, 117.

---

66. *1229 aprili apud Accon. Fridericus II imp. Hermanno magistro et fratribus d. s. M. Th. i. I. restituit Maronum, Quabrinquen*[1]*, Belide*[1]*, Cades, Lahare, Mees, duo Megeras, 7000 bisantiorum sarracenatorum annuatim de reditibus catenae et fundae Acconensium percipiendos, quae omnia quondam Henfrido iuveni cambio pro Turone et Castro novo dederant. Magister enim, quum ex Isabellae imperatricis et ipsius imperatoris concessione Iozcelini quondam comitis omnem haereditatem vel manibus Sarracenorum detentam possessurus terram Turonis restitutam a Sarracenis repetivisset, aliunde vero Alysa, quondam Henfridi iuvenis neptis, suam esse probaret, protulit tandem Guidonis Ierosolimitani regis et Sibillae uxoris privilegium (supra p. 19 n. 21) Ioscelino et haeredibus Turonum et Castrum novum confirmans, aut si ista ex iure vel ex Balduini regis VI et Henfridi pactionibus omittere deberet, Maronum, Quabrinquen caetera. Testes: Boemundus*[2]*, princeps Anthiochiae et comes Tripolitanus; Odo de Montebeliardo, comestabulus regni Ierusalem; Balianus, dominus Sydonis; Iohannes de Ybelino; Gualterus de Cesarea; Guarnerius Alemannus; Aymo nepos eiusdem; Daniel de Talremunde; Helyas de Nazareth; Adam Costa senex; Adam Costa iuvenis.*

I, 17 n. 26. E codice nostro edidit Huillard-Bréholles III, 123. In arch. Regim. R. 176 cum testificatione Estergi (i. e. Eustorgii 1211 ? † 1239), Nicosiensis archiepiscopi, in Thuringia.
1. p. 19 unum videbantur nomen. 2. sic pro Raimundus B corrigit H. B.

---

67. *1229 aprili apud Accon. Idem confirmat commutationem inter Hermannum magistrum domus s. Mariae Theutonicorum in Ierusalem et Iacobum de Amigdala factam, ex qua domus Iacobo dedit casale Mebelie, accipiens*

ab eo ex haereditate matris suis, Iozcelini quondam comitis filiae, provenientia casale Trefile, castrum novum Montfort a domo firmatum, iardinum et molendinum de pertinentiis Trefile. Testes: Balianus, dominus Sydonis; Odo de Montebeliardo, conestabulus regni Ierusalem; Iohannes de Ybelino; Guarnerius Alemannus; Aymo, nepos eiusdem Guarnerii[1]*; Aymarus, nepos fratris Aymari de domo hospitali s. Iohannis.*

I, 17 v. n. 27. E codice nostro ed. Huillard-Bréholles III, 120. 1. Gualterii B.

---

68. *1229 aprili apud Accon. Idem Hermanno magistro et domui hospitalis s. Mariae Theutonicorum in Ierusalem a praedecessoribus suis Romanorum imperatoribus felicibus inchoatae principiis, per progenitores suos divos augustos inclitae recordationis auctae et beneficiis ampliatae concedit 6400 bisancios sarracenatos annuatim de reditibus catenae et fundae Acconensium recipiendos. Testes: Odo de Montebeliardo, comestabulus regni Ierusalem; Balianus, dominus Sidonis; Iohannes de Ybelino; Guarnerius Alemannus; Aymo, nepos eiusdem; Aymarus, nepos fratris Aymari.*

I, 18 n. 28. E codice nostro ed. Huillard-Bréholles III, 122.

---

69. *1229 aprili apud Accon. Idem concedit iisdem in civitate sua Ierusalem domum quondam Balduini regis sitam in ruga Armeniorum prope ecclesiam s. Thomae, cum omni perprisio et pertinenciis et horto coniuncto, sex carrucatas terrae „sive de excadenciis sive demanio nostro civitatis eiusdem, si de excadenciis tantum non poterit inveniri, ubi per territorium civitatis ipsius conveniencius sit eis accipere et habere"; concedit de superabundanti gratia domum, quam olim Theutonici ante amissionem terrae sanctae in civitate Ierusalemitana tenebant, cum omnibus pertinenciis suis, iuribus et possessionibus et pertinentiis eius; omnia haec ab omni servitio exempta. Testes: Balianus, dominus Sydonis; Odo de Montebeliardo, conestabilis regni Ierosolimitani; Iohannes de Ibelino; Guarnerus Alemannus; Aymo, nepos eius; Aymarus*[1]*, nepos fratris Aymari de domo hospitalis sancti Iohannis.*

I, 19 n. 31 et 48 v. E codice nostro ed. Huillard-Bréholles III, 126. 1. Aymo, Haymo B.

---

70. *1229 aprili apud [Accon]. Idem concedit et confirmat iisdem domum emtam a Iohanne de Chonchi pro 620 marcis argenti et pro alia domo sitam iuxta ecclesiam s. Sepulcri, dans eis licentiam voltae construendae inde ad domum iam prius possessam, salva platea publica; et barbacanam a Iohanne rege concessam et totam terram inter murum civitatis Acconensis et mare, videlicet a porta, quae dicitur Gaufridi Torti, usque ad*

locum, ubi finit barbacana praedictae domus, cum licentia aedificandi ibi cuiuslibet aedificii, salva via publica. Testes: Balianus, dominus Sydonis; Odo de Montebeliardo, conestabilis regni Ierusalem; Iohannes de Ybelino; Guarnerius Alemannus; Aymo, nepos eius; Aymarus iuvenis, nepos fratris Aymari de domo hospitalis sancti Iohannis.

I, 20 n. 33 et 47 v. E codice nostro ed. Huillard-Bréholles III, 128.

---

71. *1229 iunio. Heinricus Cypri rex domui s. Mariae hospitalis Alamannorum donat casale de Clavodie et domum quandam Nicosiae sitam.*

Notum sit omnibus tam futuris quam presentibus, quod ego Henricus dei gracia rex Cipri casale de Clavodie cum omnibus pertinenciis suis, sicut dominus Iohannes de Milmars eum in integrum possidebat, in villanis, agris cultis et incultis, in arboribus, in chevagiis, aquis et in omnibus dricturis eidem casali pertinenciis[1] et domum, que fuit Druonis de Bedort, cum ambitu suo in Nichosia dono et concedo vobis, fratri Hermanno, venerabili magistro sancte domus beate Marie hospitalis Alamannorum in Ierusalem et conventui eiusdem domus presenti atque futuro libere et quiete et absolute in perpetuam elemosinam possidendum. Vos autem, venerabilis magister et conventus dicte domus, mihi domos, quas bone memorie Haymericus, quondam rex Cipri, avus meus, vobis in Nichosia per privilegium dederat, aquitatis, ab omnibus iniuriis et querimoniis me et heredes meos penitus absolventes. Ut autem ista donacio vobis et successoribus vestris stabilis permaneat et inconcussa, presens privilegium sigillo meo sigillari precepi et subscriptis testibus roborari, quorum hec sunt nomina: Guillelmus de Riveto; Aymericus Barlays; Amalricus de Bessano; Gauvanus; Hugo de Gibeleto. Actum apud Nicossiam anno ab incarnacione domini m° cc° xx° ix° secunde indictionis mense iunii.

I, 37 n. 84. 1. B.

---

72. *1230 iulii 10 Laterani. Gregorius papa IX omnes christianos monet, ut fratribus h. s. M. Th. i. I. succurrant ad aedificandum castrum Montis fortis in territorii Acconensis loco a duce Austriae donato.*

Gregorius episcopus servus servorum dei universis Christi fidelibus, ad quos littere iste pervenerint, salutem et apostolicam benedictionem. Dilecti filii fratres hospitalis sancte Marie Theutonicorum in Ierusalem, novi sub tempore gracie Machabei, abnegantes secularia desideria et propria relinquentes, tollentes crucem suam dominum sunt secuti. Ipsi sunt, qui orientalem ecclesiam a paganorum spurcitia liberare et christiani nominis inimicos expugnare nituntur; ipsi pro fratribus animos ponere non formidant et peregrinos ad sancta loca proficiscentes tam eundo quam redeundo ab incursibus paganorum defensare conantur. Sane, sicut dilectus filius Hermannus, magister hospitalis ipsius, in nostra proposuit presentia constitutus, ad tam sanctum et pium opus laudabiliter prosequendum in terra, quam nobilis vir dux Austrie predictis fratribus emit intuitu pietatis, castrum Montfort iuxta territorium Acconense edificare ceperunt, positum in confinio paganorum, per quod christianis in partibus illis immensa dinoscitur utilitas provenire, cum quasi quoddam frenum Sarracenos compescens ab insultibus consuetis fidelibus circumquaque securam tribuat libertatem; quia vero pre multitudine continua expensarum, que ipsis pro terre sancte subsidio et precipue pro refectione pauperum et necessitatibus infirmorum imminent faciende, ad perficiendum et regendum castrum predictum proprie ipsis non suppetunt facultates, sed, ut perfecte firmetur et potenti manu regatur, ipsis est fidelium suffragium oportunum, presertim cum sit a mari remotum, cui sicut ceteris civitatibus et munitionibus regni Ierosolimitani per mare non potest de succursu necessario provideri; universitatem vestram monemus et hortamur in domino in remissionem peccaminum vobis[1] iniungentes, quatenus eisdem fratribus vel eorum nuntiis, cum ad vos accesserint, ad opus huiusmodi grata pietatis subsidia impendatis, ut per subventionem vestram perfici et conservari valeat castrum prefatum, ac[2] vos per hec et alia bona, que domino inspirante feceritis, ad eterne possitis felicitatis gaudia pervenire. Nos autem[3] de omnipotentis dei misericordia et beatorum Petri et Pauli apostolorum eius auctoritate confisi, omnibus, qui de bonis sibi collatis a deo in hoc subvenerint fratribus memoratis eisque beneficia persolverint, annuatim septimam partem iniuncte penitentie relaxamus, presentibus post decennium minime valituris. Datum Laterani vi° idus iulii pontificatus nostri anno quarto.

Inveni apographum in Heinrici Guilelmi Schulz Dresdensis schedis cum nota: 'Carta sciolta n. 53 Baldanus'; videtur ex Neapolitano archivo depromtum. — In copiario Regimontano A. 16 p. 46 inter papalia, quae Baruli in domo Theutonica inveniebantur; contulit v. cl. Meckelburg.
1. vobis peccaminum Sch. 2. castrum ipsum et A. 16. 3. enim Sch.

---

73. *1230 octobri apud Accon. Radulfus abbas s. Mariae de valle Iosaphat consentit, quod Iohannes de Canay domui hospitalis Alamannorum vendidit casale Keisereth et gastinam Mahus.*

Noscant universi presentes et futuri, quod nos Radulfus abbas sancte Marie de valle Iosaphat de assensu et voluntate capituli nostri consensimus et ratam habuimus vendicionem casalis nostri nomine Keissereth et gastine nomine Mahus cum eorum appendiciis factam per Iohannem de Canay militem domui et fratribus hospitalis Alamannorum, pro quo casali idem Iohannes tenebatur reddere nobis annis singulis et nostris successoribus xxx^a^ bisantios sarracenatos censuales, renunciantes omni iuri, quod in eodem casali vel pro ipso casali et suis pertinenciis habebamus vel habere debebamus. Pro concessione vero venditionis eiusdem casalis et pertinenciarum suarum et quitatione[1] xxx^a^ bisanciorum censualium et renunciatione iuris, quod habebamus in predicto casali frater Haymo, vices gerens magni magistri citra mare, scilicet fratris Hermanni, et comune capitulum eiusdem hospitalis nobis nostrisque successoribus dare et assignare promiserunt l^{a} bisancios sarracenatos censuales annuatim recipiendos in perpetuum in festo sancti Martini, qui in commutationem et pagam predictorum l^{a} bisanciorum nobis nostrisque successoribus assignaverunt domum, quam tenebat ab ipsis Rollandus de Tercenal, pro xxiiii^{or} bisanciis censualibus, et omne ius, quod ipsi in ea habebant vel habere debebant, et gastinam unam cum domunculis et logiis, que sunt in illa, pro xxvi bisanciis censualibus. Que videlicet domus sita est in platea, qua itur ad cathenam, in vico inferiori prope mare. Gastina vero ab oriente contigua est gastine domini Haymonis militis Alamanni; ab occidente est via publica, que ducit ad albergam hospitalis sancti Iohannis; a meridie est viculus quidam; a septemtrione est contigua curie domini archiepiscopi Nazareni. Nos vero dicti abbas et capitulum nostrique successores pro commutatione[1] predicta nostre domui facta tenemur dictis fratribus, scilicet fratri Haymoni[2] et capitulo domus hospitalis Alamannorum, predictum casale Keissereth et gastinam Mahus cum eorum appendiciis defendere, garentizare et manutenere contra omnes homines, qui mori possunt et vivere et super hoc fratres predicti hospitalis vellent impetere et in iudicio convenire. Ad maiorem siquidem certitudinem et securitatem predictorum rogavimus venerabilem patrem G(eroldum) patriarchum Ierosolimitanum apostolice sedis legatum, ut presenti scripto sigillum suum duceret apponendum. Nos vero dictus G(eroldus) patriarcha Ierosolimitanus humilis et indignus apostolice sedis legatus ad preces et peticiones dicti abbatis eiusdemque conventus presenti scripto sigillum nostrum in testimonium duximus apponendum. Nos autem sepedictus abbas de Iosaphat presentem paginam sigilli nostri munimine duximus roborandam. Huius rei testes sunt dominus P(etrus) Cesariensis ecclesie archiepiscopus, et Thomas eiusdem ecclesie archidiaconus, et Guillelmus canonicus; frater Stephanus; frater Iohannes; frater Mel; frater Hugo et frater Petrus, monachi prenominate ecclesie de Iosaphat. Actum est hoc apud Accon anno dominice incarnationis m° cc° xxx° mense octobris.

I, 33 n. 76. 1. quitationē B. 2. Haymono B.

---

74. *1230 octobri. Haymo, Hermanni magistri domus hospitalis Alamannorum vices gerens, paciscitur cum Radulfo abbate et monasterio S. Mariae de Iosaphat „de domo Rolandi de Tercionario et gastina cum domunculis, quas assignavit domus abbati de Iosaphat pro l bisantiis censualibus“.*

Noscant universi presentes et futuri, quod nos, ego frater Haymo vices gerens fratris Hermanni magistri domus hospitalis Alamannorum ac capitulum eiusdem domus, confitemur et testamur nos debuisse abbati et conventui sancte Marie de Iosaphat quinquaginta bisancios sarracenatos censuales annuatim in perpetuum reddendos in festo sancti Martini dicto abbati et domui sancte Marie de Iosaphat pro concessione venditionis casalis Kassareth et gastine eiusdem nomine Mahus cum eorum appendiciis, quod nobis vendidit Iohannes de Chanay miles, et pro quittatione xxx^{a} bisanciorum sarracenatorum, quos habebant annuatim censuales in eodem casali, et pro remissione et quitatione tocius iuris, quod in eodem casali et suis pertinenciis habebant vel habere debebant. Nos autem, dictus frater Haymo et capitulum hospitalis Alemannorum, pro utilitate domus nostre pari assensu et una voluntate nostri capituli in commutacionem et pagam quinquaginta predictorum bisanciorum in perpetuum damus et assignamus tibi Radulfo, abbati monasterii sancte Marie de Iosaphat, et capitulo eiusdem loci vestrisque successoribus domum, quam tenebat a nobis Rollandus de Tercenal, pro xx^{ti} iiii^{or} bisanciis sarracenatis censualibus et omne ius, quod in ea habemus vel habere debemus, et gastinam unam cum domunculis et logiis, que sunt in illa, pro xx^{ti} sex bisanciis sarracenatis residuis; que domus sita est in platea, qua itur ad cathenam, in vico inferiori prope mare. Gastina vero ab oriente est contigua gastine domini Haymonis militis Alemanni; ab occidente est via publica, que ducit ad albergam hospitalis sancti Iohannis; a septemtrione est contigúa curie archiepiscopi Nazareni; a meridie viculus quidam. Predictam vero domum et gastinam et omne ius, quod in eis habemus vel habere debemus, tibi prenominato R(adulfo) abbati et conventui sancte Marie de Iosaphat tuisque successoribus tenemur defendere, garentizare et manutenere contra omnes, qui mori possunt et vivere, ita quod dictam domum et gastinam cum domibus et logiis suis libere et quiete sine drictura et sine taillia, sine omni exactione et angaria teneatis, possideatis, detis et vendatis et quicquid de eis et in eis volueritis faciatis. Si vero aliquo casu interveniente nos predictum capitulum hospitalis Alemannorum dictam domum vel gastinam vobis abbati et conventui predictis defendere non possemus, in recompensationem eiusdem domus, si a nobis evinceretur, vel gastine, tantum in domibus vel in terris vel aliis possessionibus domui nostre pertinentibus vobis et domui vestre conferre tenemur ad arbitrium et estimationem domini patriarche Ierosolimitani et aliorum virorum proborum, quantum supradictam domum et gastinam vobis et domui vestre a nostro capitulo extitit assignatum. Insuper prescriptas commutationes et concessiones a magistro nostro, cum venerit, vel ab eius successore facere teneri promittimus et sue bulle munimine confirmari. Ad maiorem siquidem certitudinem et securitatem predictorum rogavimus venerabilem patrem Geroldum patriarcham Ierosolimitanum apostolice sedis legatum, ut presenti scripto sigillum suum in testimonium duceret apponendum. Nos vero dictus G(eroldus), patriarcha Ierosolimitanus humilis et indignus apostolice sedis legatus, ad preces et peticiones dicti fratris Haymonis vices magistri gerentis tociusque conventus eiusdem domus presenti scripto sigillum nostrum in testimonium duximus apponendum. Nos autem sepe dictus frater Haymo assensu et voluntate capituli nostri presens scriptum fieri fecimus et sigilli capituli nostri munimine roborari. Huius rei testes sunt dominus P(etrus) ecclesie Cesariensis archiepiscopus, et Thomas eiusdem ecclesie archidiachonus; frater Luttolfus, preceptor dicte domus; frater Gonterus, marescalcus; frater Conradus Dessohen, castellanus; frater Henricus de Pluiose; frater Bruno, minor preceptor. Actum est hoc anno ab incarnatione domini m° cc° xxx° mense octobris.

I, 34 n. 78.

---

75. *1231 (?) 11 septbr. Accon. Castellana, Arnulfi Aurificis uxor, confirmante patriarcha Hierosolymitano, donat domui hospitalis Theutonicorum duas carrucatas terrae et unam voltam in casali Saphet.*

Notum sit omnibus tam presentibus quam futuris, quod ego Castellana, uxor Arnulfi Aurificis filiaque quondam Raimundi Barlerii, bona fide causaque devocionis cum voluntate atque assensu predicti Arnulfi, mariti mei, dono et concedo mea spontanea voluntate ad honorem dei et beate virginis Marie domui hospitalis Theutonicorum duas pecias terre, que sunt due carrucate, et unam voutam, quas et quam habeo vel habere debeo in casali dicti hospitalis, quod vocatur Saphet, que omnia mihi spectant ex parte predicti Raimundi patris mei; unde nos dicti iugales, scilicet Castellana et Arnulfus, eius maritus, promittimus et super sacrosancta dei evangelia iuramus hanc prenominatam donationem firmam et inconcussam et irrevocabiliter observare et nunquam contra venire per nos vel interpositam personam aliqua iuris vel facti subtilitate, ullo loco vel tempore, dictis vel factis, in iure vel extra ius. Ad maiorem igitur huius rei firmitatem nos G(eroldus) miseratione divina Ierosolimitanus patriarcha atque sedis sancte et apostolice legatus hanc nominatam donacionem in presencia nostra factam laudamus et confirmamus et rogati ab utraque parte presentem paginam sigillo nostro fecimus roborari. Datum Accon anno ab incarnatione domini m° cc° xx° ii°[1] tercio ydus septembris.

I, 29 n. 64. Quum Radulfo 1225 successerit Geroldus, apostolicae sedis legatus, annus 1222 verus esse nequit; nec tamen 1227 nec 1232. 1227 sept. 11 non fuit Accone; legatione eum 1232 ante iulii 26 Gregorius IX privavit (cf. Winckelmann Friedrich II. I, 278. 497). 1. m° cc° xx° ii° B pro quo coniccimus 1231. Hoc anno iuli 19 et oct. 27 in Accon moratus est; Mas Latrie Histoire de l'île de Chypre III, 631; Pauli Codice I, 120. CXII.

---

76. *1231 decembri Ravennae. Fridericus II imperator donat domui hospitalis s. M. Th. i. I. terram quandam incultam in Acconensis civitatis territorio.*

Fredericus dei gracia Romanorum imperator[1] semper augustus, Ierusalem et Sicilie rex. Gratum offertur altissimo nostre liberalitatis obsequium et in retributionis eterne merito[2] digna nobis recompensatione servatur, cum munificenciam nostram ad loca divino cultui deputata porrigimus et ipsorum commoditatibus providemus. Inde est igitur[3], quod, cum frater Hermannus magister hospitalis sancte Marie Theotonicorum[4] in Iherusalem, fidelis noster, celsitudini nostre humiliter supplicarit, quatinus quandam terram incultam curie in territorio civitatis nostre Acconis, de qua nulla curie proveniebat utilitas, subscriptis circumadiacentem[5] finibus de orto videlicet Acconensis episcopi usque ad[6] [terminos terre Ianuensium] turrim sancti spiritus et alio latere de via, que ducit ad Saphet[7], usque ad fluvium eidem hospitali sancte Marie Theotonicorum[4] concedere et donare de nostra gratia dignaremur; nos attendentes grata et devota servitia dicti magistri et[8] qualiter ipse et ceteri fratres predicti hospitalis in personis et bonis eorum sint[9] ad nostra servicia expositi et parati, quia[10] potenter et viriliter ad honorem crucis in partibus Syrie inimicis fidei se opponunt[11]; considerantes insuper, quod alie terre curie nostre inculte predicte terre contigue simili exemplo poterunt laborari et fieri nostre curie fructuose[12], ad supplicacionem eiusdem magistri predictam terram prenotatis finibus designatam memorato hospitali sancte Marie Theotonicorum[4] in Ierusalem de munificencie nostre gracia perpetuo concedimus et donamus. Ut autem hec nostra concessio eidem hospitali conservetur omni tempore inconcussa, presens privilegium fieri fecimus et bulla aurea typario nostre maiestatis impressa iussimus insigniri. Huius autem rei testes sunt: Balianus dominus Sydonis; Oddo de Montebeliardo, regni Ierosolimitani conestabulus; Warnerus Theotonicus; frater Terrisius, preceptor domorum hospitalis sancti Iohannis in Apulia; Zacharias senescalcus Antiochenus; Thomas comes Acerranus; Manfridus marchio Lanza; Berardus comes Loreti; Ricardus camerarius et alii quam plures. Acta sunt hec anno dominice incarnationis m° cc° xxx° i° mense decembris quinte indictionis, imperante domino nostro Frederico dei gratia invictissimo Romanorum imperatore semper augusto, Ierusalem et Sicilie rege, anno imperii xii°, regni Ierosolimitani vii°, regni vero Sicilie xxx° iiii° feliciter. Amen. Datum Ravenne anno, mense et indictione prescriptis.

I, 19 n. 30, et in Conradi regis confirmatione de 1243 decembri I, 47. Confirmationis Conradi IV de 1243 apographum saec. xv chartac. (R) mutilum in archivo Regimontano; contulit v. cl. Meckelburg. 1. imperator et B 2. 2. meritorio B 2. 3. deest R. 4. Theutonicorum B 2. 5. circumadiacentes B 1, circumiacentem R. 6. pro: terminos terre Ienuensium B 2 (Ianuensium R) turrim s. spiritus B 1. 7. Saphar R. 8. deest R. 9. B, R. 10. quam R. 11. opponant R. 12. et fieri fructuose curie nostre R. Excerptum sicut et confirmationis et diplomatis ipsius dedit Duellius hist. ord. Th. pars II, 7, quod Huillard-Bréholles IV, 278 repetiit.

---

77. *1234. Isabella de Betsan et Bertrandus Porcelet, coniuges, vendunt domui hospitalis s. Mariae Theutonicorum Hierosolymitani casale Arabiam.*

Ego Isabella de Betsan, filia quondam Philippi Rufi, et ego Bertrandus Porcelet, maritus eiusdem, notum facimus universis presentes litteras inspecturis, quod nos vendidimus et de bona et gratuita voluntate in perpetuum quitavimus fratri Luttolfo, tunc temporis preceptori domus hospitalis sancte Marie Theotonicorum Ierosolimitani, recipienti[1] loco et iure ipsius domus et magistri sui unum casale videlicet Arabiam cum omnibus pertinenciis et iusticiis eiusdem casalis et cum omnibus gastinis Berhenne, Mizera, Miscalim, cum omnibus terris laboratis et non laboratis, montibus, vallibus, planis, nemoribus, aquis et pascuis predicti casalis et gastinarum ipsarum et cum omnibus villanis et eorum uxoribus ac heredibus eorum, cum omnibus possessionibus et hereditatibus eorum supradictorum villanorum pro tribus milibus et sexcentis bisantiis sarracenatis, que tria milia bisantiorum et sexcentos nos recognoscimus recepisse ab eodem preceptore nomine dicte domus hospitalis ad habendum et possidendum idem casale cum omnibus gastinis et omnibus hominibus et tenimentis eorum pleno iure dominii et ad faciendum ex eis supra nominatis rebus, quicquid velint. In cuius rei testimonium ego Isabella de Betsan et ego Bertrandus Porcelet presentes litteras sigilli nostri plumbei munimine fecimus roborari. Actum est hoc in presencia Ricardi Filangerii marescalci imperialis et regni Ierosolimitani balivi et sacri imperii legati in partibus Syrie. Huius rei testes sunt Boemundus dominus Bothoronis; Thomas de Ham, conestabulus Tripolitanus; Henricus de Rufi et Radulfus nepos eius; Philippus de Maugastel, Ingeramus de Femium. Actum est hoc anno domini m° cc° xxx° iiii°.

I, 21 n. 35. 1. recipiente B.

---

78. *1234. Ricardus Filangerius, regni Hierosolymitani imperialis baiulus, confirmat, quod Isabella de Betsan et Bertrandus Porcelet domui h. s. M. Th. I. Arrabiam et Zechanim vendiderunt.*

Ego Ricardus Filangerius mariscalcus imperialis, regni Ierosolimitani baiulus et sacri imperii legatus in partibus Syrie, notum facio universis presentes litteras inspecturis, quod Isabella de Betsan, filia quondam Philippi Ruffi et Bertrandus Porcelet maritus suus in presencia mea et aliorum nobilium et curie regni Ierosolimitaui de bona et gratuita voluntate ipsorum dederunt in elemosinam et vendiderunt fratri Lutolfo, tunc temporis preceptori[1] domus hospitalis sancte Marie Theotonicorum Ierosolimitani, recipienti loco et iure ipsius domus et magistri sui duo casalia videlicet Arrabiam et Zechanim cum omnibus pertinenciis et iusticiis eorundem et gastinis[2] Berhenne, Mezera, Miskalym, cum villanis predictorum casalium et gastinarum ipsarum et eorum uxoribus ac filiis, terris laboratis et non laboratis, montibus, vallibus, planis, nemoribus, aquis et pascuis, receptis inde ab eodem preceptore nomine dicte domus hospitalis tribus milibus et sexcentis bisantiis sarracenatis ad habendum et possidendum eadem casalia cum gastinis et omnibus hominibus ac tenimentis ipsorum pleno iure dominii et ad faciendum ex eisdem casalibus quicquid velint; propter quod mihi dictus preceptor supplicavit, ut donationem et vendicionem ipsam sibi et domui dicte factam, prout superius continetur, sigillo meo roborarem. Ego igitur attendens grata et accepta dicte domus servicia, que domino imperatori dudum exibuit et exibet incessanter, suis precibus inclinatus donationem et venditionem sibi et domui sue factam ab eisdem Isabella et Bertrando Porcelet de casalibus supradictis, sicut superius est expressa, presenti pagina sigillo meo roboravi et subscriptis testibus confirmavi. Huius rei testes sunt: Boemundus dominus Botoronis; Thomas de Ham, conestabulus Tripolianus; Henricus de Rufi et Radulfus nepos eius; Philippus de Maugastel; Ingerrannus de Femium. Actum est hoc anno dominice incarnationis m° cc° xxx° iiii°.

I, 21 v. n. 37. 1. littolfo tunc temporis preceptoris B. 2. gastinis et B.

---

79. *1235 novembri Augustae. Fridericus II imperator confirmat Hermanno magistro hospitalis s. M. Th. in I. in sua praesentia constituto scriptum publicum, secundum quod Bertrandus de Porcelet et Isabella de Besan coram Ricardo Filangerio, imperiali marescalco, regni Ierosolimitani baiulo et legato imperii in partibus Syriae, vendiderunt Ludolfo praeceptori dictae domus casalia Arabiam et Zechanim cum gastinis Berhenne, Mezera, Miskelim.*

I, 21 v. n. 38 et 45. Apographum authenticum confirmationis de 1243 dec. in archivo Stuttgartensi. Edd. de Stillfried Mon. Zollerana. Halis Saxonum 1843. I, 46 n. 29 et Huillard-Bréholles IV, 792.

---

80. *1235 Accon. Robertus S. Mariae de Latina in Ierusalem abbas approbat, quod Iohannes Griffus hospitali s. Mariae Theutonicorum in Ierusalem quandam peciam terrae apud Accon sibi censualem vendidit.*

Rei geste servat memoriam et valoris confert perpetui fulcimentum scripture series, quia plerumque defectu testium aut per longi decursum temporis potest contrahere levitatem. Ea propter notum sit omnibus presentibus et futuris, quod nos Robertus ecclesie sancte Marie de Latina in Iherusalem humilis abbas de voluntate et consensu capituli nostri laudamus, volumus et approbamus vendicionem, quam nobilis vir Iohannes Griffus fecit de voluntate et beneplacito uxoris sue Marie in curia Acconensi fratri Lutolfo preceptori et locum magistri tenenti et conventui hospitalis sancte Marie Theutonicorum in Ierusalem de quadam pecia terre sita[1] prope Accon, quam idem Iohannes Griffus et uxor eius predicta a nobis et ecclesia nostra sub censuali titulo v^{e} bisanciorum auri sarracenatorum nobis et ecclesie iam dicte annuatim solvendorum tenebant. Eadem vero terra hiis correnciis terminatur: ex parte quidem orientali contigua est vinee Michaelis de Ierusalem, et ex parte occidentali iardino Pandolfi, ab australi vero parte contermina est partim iardino Templi et partim iardino Andree de Wienna; et a septentrione iardino domino Rollandi; et ingressum habet per viam publicam ante iardinum hospitalis sancti Iohannis. Preterea investivimus predictum L(udolfum) preceptorem nomine conventus et fratrum eiusdem hospitalis de pecia terre memorata[2] salvis v^{e} bisanciis auri sarracenatis nobis et sepe dicte ecclesie de Latina a dicto hospitali singulis annis pacifice et sine contradictione in festo omnium sanctorum census nomine persolvendis secundum usus et consuetudinem regni Ierosolimitani, sicut a dicto nobili et eius uxore antea reddebantur. Ut igitur hec nostra aprobatio et investiture concessio rata semper permaneat et illesa neve possit super hoc scrupulus dubitationis oriri, presentem paginam sigillo plumbeo nostri capituli fecimus roborari in testimonii firmitatem. Testes autem huius rei sunt: venerabilis pater Hugo, archiepiscopus Nazarenus; Hugo, Templi domini abbas; Hugo de Sabilone, sacerdos. Actum Accon anno incarnati verbi m° cc° xxx° v° indictionis viii°.

I, 30 v. n. 68. 1. site B. 2. memorate B.

---

81. *1236 ianuario Tripoli. Iohannes Barlaiz confirmat domui hospitalis s. Mariae Theutonicorum casalia Arabie et Zachani.*

El nom deu pere e deu fiz e deu saint espirit. Amen. Ge Johan Barlaiz, fiz Heimeri Barlaiz qui fu, fais a saver a tous ciaus qui sunt e qui avenir sunt, que je ai loe et otroie l'amoisne et la vente, que madamme Hisabiau de Bethsant, mere de mon pere, et mesires Bertrain Porcelet cez mariz firent et donerent pardurablement au maistre et a freires de la maison de l'ospital de sainte Marie des Alamans de Jerusalem, ce est a saver deus caseaus Araybe et Zecanin, o totes les gastines de Berhenne, Mesera, Mischalim, o totes les pertenences e o touz leis dreiz e o touz les homes des caseaus et des gastines, qui sunt nomez ci desus; e ai quite touz les dreiz, que je avoie o devoie aver a es devant dites choses, au maistre et aus freres de la devant dite maison, que eil les teignent quitament et franchement a touz jorz. E por cey, que cest los e cest otroi e ceste quitance seit remenbree a touz jorz mais, ce fo feit en la presence de Boemont per la grace de deu prince d'Anthioche et comte de Triple. De ceste chose sunt garenz Hue de Gibelet; Johan de Montenac; Renaut de Gibelet; Renaut Porcelet; Huge de Tabore. En tesmoingnage de ceste chose fis seelier cest present escrit de mon seel de plump, e fu fet a Triple l'an de l'encarnation nostre seingneor Jhesu Crist m et cc et xxxvi deu mes de genier.

I, 21 n. 36.

---

82. *1236 ianuario Tripoli. Boemundus IV, Antiochiae princeps, Tripolitanus comes, testatur Iohannem Barlaiz confirmasse domui hospitalis Alamannorum ab Isabella de Besan et Bertrando Porcelet donatum casale Arabia.*

Je Biemon per la grace de deu prince d'Anthioche et coms de Triple, filz de B(iemon) prince d'Anthioche et comte de Triple de bone memorie, faiz a saver a toz ceus qui sont, que Johan Barlaiz, fiz de Aimeri Barlaiz qui fu, vient en ma presence e en la presence de partie de mes homes, ce est a saver Henri mon frere, Th(omas)[1] de Han conestable de Triple, Guillelme le vesconte de Triple, Bertran Porcelet, Pierre de Scandalion, Johan de Farabel sire del Poi, Johan Harra, Guillelme del Moinetre, Guace de Ranis[2], Huge Fermin, en la presence de frere Lutol e de freire Lowiz e de freire Johan de l'hospital des Alamans et otrea la vente e le don d'aumoine, que dame Isabel de Besan e sire Bertran Porcelet firent a la maison de l'hospital de saincte Marie des Alamans parduraplement, ce est a saver deu casal Arabe et de toiz soz droiz e ses apartinences ensement, quita toz les droiz, qu'il y avoit ou devit aver pardurablement a l'avan dite maison. E por ce que cest ottrei e ceste quitance soit remembree a toz jornz mais en la manere, quele fo feite en[3] ma presence[4] desus nomoiz, je, a la priere de l'avan dit frere Lutol, ai fait garnir e efforcer cest present escrit de mon seel de plum. Guarens de ceste chose sunt: Huc de Gibelet; Jhoan de Monteignach; Reinaut de Gibeleth; Reinaut Porcelet; Huge de Tabore. Ce est fait en mon palaiz a Triple l'an de la incarnation Jhesu Crist m° cc° xxx° vi° el mois de genver en iii an de mon principe e de mon comte, par la man de Guillelme mon clers.

I, 22v. n. 29. Quum mortuo Balduino IV 1233 successerit Balduinus V, in huius tertium annum incidit ianuarius anni 1236. 1. C. H. B. 2. rāis B. 3. e B. 4. videtur deesse: e la presence des.

---

83. *1236 ianuarii 22. Eython, Armeniae rex, cum Elisabeth uxore donant domui hospitalis Alemannorum civitatem Haroniam cum annexis.*

Voluntate beneficii dei patris et gracia domini nostri Ihesu Christi et beneplacito sancti spiritus ego Eython Christi dei fidelis rex Armenie, filius Constantini stirpis regie, et Ehelisabeth regina eiusdem, filia quiescentis in Christo Leonis regis, notum facimus vobis, qui nunc estis et qui post futuri estis, quod dedimus ut peciit dei habitaculo domui hospitalis Alemannorum per manus sancti et religiosi magistri fratris Hermanni et dilecti dei comendatoris fratris Littoldi nominatam et speciosam civitatem Haroniam cum sui dispositione confinii, sicut est contiguum et separatum, secundum quod dominus Goufridus habebat, quando Haronie dominus erat, quod nominamus singillatim cum abbaciis, casalibus, gastinis, terra, aqua, molendinis, prediis, montibus, collibus et fructiferis, planis et omnibus fructibus et pertinenciis et possessionibus, quia vidimus sanctam et religiosam domum hospitalis Alemannorum impletam et refertam[1] omni bonitate in omnibus et per omnia cruce signatam et militantem contra inimicos crucis Christi et per ipsum vincentem in[2] adversarios in preliis, et ornatam et confortatam in servicio infirmorum, et semper sibi provident in dona pauperum et receperunt nostrum negocium in veram fraternitatem et sororitatem. Modo autem amplius coniuncti sumus non ficto amore, set verissimo vinculo, sicut confitentur nobis servare et tueri regnum nostrum ab omni parte sicut veri fratres et inseparabiles amici secundum mandatum Christi[3] dei nostri, quod est diligere invicem et in hoc discipulos eius fieri, sicut sancte domus Alemannorum fratres perficiunt omnem legem scriptam et christianam et pro transitoria vita voluerunt et emerunt immortalem et eternum regnum dei, sicut scriptum est: „Ubi ego sum, illic et minister meus erit“[4]; et iterum „Ubi duo vel tres congregati fuerint in nomine meo, ibi ego sum in medio eorum“. Propter hoc sanctam domum istam dei habitaculum appellamus et volumus ipsorum participes fieri in omnibus hiis bonis. Et dedimus eisdem supranominatam civitatem Haroniam cum terra sibi contigua et separata, cum suo confinio, sicut dispositum est et nunc recordamur per partes singillatim: civitatem Haroniam cum molendinis, abaciam Ovide, abbaciam sancti Mammas, abbaciam Saugre, casale Lalyan, casale Costinos, casale Gausquigne, casale Cherrare, casale Chacorim cum suo molendino, casale Cainchequice, Aguechemom, Castine, sanctum Danielem, Davenim, Saargague, sanctum Thoros, Cievaverac, Pirt, Quiang, Telagre, Mautrigue, Port, Guenecch, Hachoudagre, in quo sunt regis rustici, et unus rusticus domini Michaelis d'Andraple et alii regis legiorum hominum rustici et domini Baudin Emerance. Illos rusticos si volunt fratres dimittere, in sua terra dabunt, sicut ante erat constitutum, ut darent medietatem reddituum, qui dicuntur Armenice engague Haronie et cetera dominis suis. Sin autem accipiet unusquisque suos rusticos et exibit de loco, et remanebunt illa loca cum suis rebus integre et erit terra in mandato fratrum, secundum quod est intra eorum confinium. Igitur predictam civitatem et terram pretaxatam, quam nominatim recoluimus[5] et per confinia distincximus, dedimus angelice legionis fraternitati hospitalis Alamanorum in perpetuam et permansuram hereditatem, qui nunc sunt et qui post futuri sunt. Non ergo habeat aliquis potestatem in tota regione Armenie de subditis nostris neque magnus neque parvus sancte domui et spirituali fraternitati iniuriam[6] vel molestiam facere neque de confinio neque de pertinencia minuere, sed sit hospitalis Alemannorum supranominate et distincte terre auctoritas ex nostro magnifico mandato. Propter hoc ergo dedimus nostrum gratuitum privilegium et, ut maiorem habeat firmitatem, manu regia subscripsimus et sigillavimus aureo sigillo nostro. Datum ianuario mense xxii[a] die anno Armenorum dc [et quadragesimo] octogesimo v° indictione ix[a], per manum Manuelis cancellarii.

I, 36 v. n. 83. Datum corruptum est; abundat enim „et quadragesimo“. Secundum aeram Armenorum, cuius primus dies erat anni Christi 551 iulii 9, 685[us] annus incidit in vulgaris aerae 1235 et 1236, cuius ianuario indictio ix cucurrit. Hermannus de Salza 1236 ianuario in Italia fuit. 1. refectam B. 2. sic B. 3. Ev. Ioh. 15, 12 et 8. 4. Ev. Ioh. 12, 26. 5. recolimus B. 6. in B.

---

84. *1236 aug. 10 Accon. Beatrix, filia Galteri Ledur, vendit domui hospitalis b. Mariae Theutonicorum casale Sapheth lo Cathemon in terra de Torono.*

Notum sit omnibus tam presentibus quam futuris, quod ego domina Beatrix filia Galteri Ledur vendo et dono casale unum, quod vocatur Sapheth lo Cathemon et est in terra de Torono, cum omnibus suis pertinenciis et iurisdictionibus libere et quiete omnibusque suis terris laboratis et non laboratis, plenis, vacuis, forestis, bosquis, domesticis et salvaticis, introitibus et exitibus, omnibusque suis iuribus et dericturis et aquis ac pertinentibus tibi fratri Lutolfo, magno preceptori nomine[1] et vice et loco magni magistri sancte domus hospitalis beate Marie Theotonicorum de Ierusalem et fratribus eiusdem domus precio bisanciorum sarracenatorum mille auri, quos accepi et de quibus me quietam et solutam voco, ita quod xl bisantii sarracenati auri nomine census nostra comuni voluntate debeo habere in festo sancte crucis, quod est in medio mense septembris[2], annuatim de thesauro vestro Accon. Quod si habere non possem ibi, ego et heres meus debemus ipsum habere, ubicunque domus vestra habere posset, sine aliqua contradictione. Et quicquid contingeret de dicto casali vel aliquo impedimento, nichilominus debeo habere vel heres meus dictum censum omni tempore sine ulla contradictione. Possessionem et dominium de dicto casali et pertinenciis et omnibus supradictis tibi fratri Lutolfo recipienti pro dicta domo dedimus et tradidimus eo modo salvo censu, ut dictum est supra. Hec omnia dicta domina Beatrix fecit et autriavit consensu et voluntate sue filie Margarite et Philippi Malgastel mariti eiusdem. Et nos dicta Margarita filia dicte Beatricis insimul cum marito meo, Philippo de Malgastel, nostra bona voluntate autriavimus predictam vendicionem cum censu statuto, ut dictum est. Et hec omnia facta fuerunt iussu domine Alis princesse et domine de Torono et in eius presencia et sue curie et hominum suorum videlicet: Goffridus[3], dominus Cayphe; Balduinus de Florito; Hugo de Tabaria; Gervasius de Malgastel; et de hominibus imperatoris: Balduinus de Pinkeingin; Nicolaus Antelmus; Iohannes Apertus. Ad huius rei perpetuam firmitatem et noticiam presens scriptum nos dicta Beatrix et Philippus de Malgastel predictus sigilli nostri munimine roboravimus. Actum in civitate Accon anno dominice incarnationis m° cc° xxx° vi° die x° intrante mense augusti.

I, 29 v. n. 65. 1. nc pro ne B. 2. Exaltatio s. crucis sept. 14. 3. sic nomina sequuntur in nominativo.

---

85. *1239 ianuarii 24 Tyri. Riccardus Filangerius, imperialis marescalcus et legatus, regni Hierosolymitani baiulus, testatur Sitalmelech Surianam cum filiis domui hospitalis s. Mariae Theutonicorum quartam partem casalis Cabesie vendidisse.*

Die vicesimo quarto mensis ianuarii duodecime indictionis nos Riccardus Filangerius, imperialis marescalcus sacri imperii legatus in partibus cismarinis et regni Ierusalem baiulus, notum facimus presentibus et futuris, quod venientes ante presenciam nostram Sitalmelech, filia quondam Abdelmesie Suriani, et filii eius Munsur et Siliman in presencia nostra et hominum liciorum subscriptorum, scilicet domini Philippi de Malgastel, domini Guarnerii[1] Theutonici, vendiderunt domui hospitalis sancte Marie Theutonicorum quartam partem casalis eorum, quod dicitur Cabesie, pro bisanciis sarracenatis ducentis et sex.

Et destituerunt se de quarta parte predicti casalis et dederunt sasinam ipsius quarte partis fratri Deustisalvi de ipsa domo pro eadem domo. A quo fratre et[2] predicta domo precium prefate vendicionis receperunt et tam predicta Sitalmelech, quam et filii eius predicti debent et tenentur defendere dictam venditionem hinc ad annum et diem ab omnibus personis volentibus prefatam vendicionem molestare vel calumpniare secundum usum et consuetudinem regni Ierusalem. Unde ad futuram memoriam huius rei et prefate domus securitatem presens scriptum inde fieri fecimus nostra bulla cerea pendente munitum. Actum Tyri anno ab incarnatione domini m° cc° xxx° ix° die et mense inde pretitulatis.

I, 28 n. 60. 1. Gitarn'is B. 2. supplevi.

---

86. *1239 febr. Accon. Girardus, ecclesiae Montis Syon abbas, concedit domui s. Mariae Alamannorum quandam petiam terrae in Monte suspensorum territorii Acconensis sub annuo censu.*

Notum sit universis tam presentibus quam futuris, ad quos presens privilegium pervenerit, quod nos Girardus, sacrosancte ac primitive ecclesie montis Syon abbas humilis, totusque eiusdem loci conventus desiderantes utilitatem et comodum ecclesie nostre dedimus et tradidimus seu concessimus domui et fratribus sancte Marie Alamannorum quandam peciam terre sitam in territorio Accon in loco, qui dicitur Mons suspensorum, sub annuo censu habendam et tenendam in perpetuum et possidendam iure proprietario cum omnibus introitibus, exitibus et iuribus suis. Cuius confines sunt tales: ex parte orientis terra Templi, et ex parte occidentis rursum iardinum Templi, quod situm est prope cimiterium sancti Nicholay secundum indicationem signi nostri; et ex parte septemtrionis terra sancti Lazari de Bethania, et ex parte australi strata publica, ita tamen quod dicta domus hospitalis et[1] magister et fratres ibidem pro tempore existentes tenentur dare et solvere per singulos annos in kalendis marcii pro censu eiusdem pecie terre supradicte ecclesie montis Syon abbati et conventui, qui pro tempore fuerint, de thesauro ipsius domus bisancios xx sarracenatos ad pondus Accon bene ponderatos et numeratos, tali videlicet conditione, quod, si magister et fratres dicte domus hospitalis aliquo tempore voluerint dare et assignare ecclesie nostre aliquem certum locum in Accon, de quo ecclesia nostra possit percipere et habere libere et quiete in perpetuum sine laboribus et expensis per unumquemque annum xx bisancios sarracenatos, nomine permutacionis pro dicta pecia terre ipsum accipere promittimus, et viginti bisantios, quos pro censu ipsius terre ecclesie nostre annuatim tenentur de thesauro suo solvere, post contractum permutationis penitus remittere; permutatione autem facta et satisfacto nobis de loco competenti, in quo libere et quiete sine laboribus et expensis annuatim in perpetuum xx bisancios sarracenatos ad pondus Accon recipere valeamus, nobis tenentur dicti magister et fratres litteras patentes sui capituli sigillo roboratas dare, in quibus dicta assignatio et concessio dicti loci plenius contineatur, sicut superius est expressum et nos a simili dicta permutatione facta eisdem promittimus litteras nostri capituli patentes dare, in quibus plenius continebitur, quod nos dictam peciam terre, prout superius est expressum, eisdem dedimus et concessimus in perpetuum possidendam; et eisdem tenemur dictam terram garantizare, deffendere bona fide ad usus et consuetudines patrie seu civitatis Accon. Sane quod futura providenda sunt, si dicti fratres hospitalis requisiti nobis defficerent in persolutione dictorum xx bisantiorum in termino supradicto, dictam terram non obstante aliquo contractu cum omnibus hedificiis et seminatis et plantatis tanquam nostram reciperemus. Ut autem presens privilegium ratum et inconcussum in perpetuum permaneat, appositione sigilli plumbei capituli nostri necnon et testium subscriptione fecimus roborari, quorum vero nomina hec sunt: Bertrandus, dei gracia Cesariensis archiepiscopus; Radulfus, Acconensis episcopus; Iohannes, abbas sancti Samuelis; Guido, prior sancte Katerine, et alii quam plures. Actum Accon anno domini m° cc° xxx° ix° mense februarii.

I, 31 n. 70. Forsan anno 1240 adnumerandum. 1. supplevi.

---

87. *1239 aprili. Bertran de Comps, magister hospitalis S. Iohannis de Ierusalem, cedit domui hospitalis S. Mariae Theutonicorum casale Lanahie.*

Ge frere Bertran de Comps, maestre de la sainte maison de l'hospital de sen Johan de Jerusalem e garde des poures de Crist, fais a saveir a toz ceus, qui ceste present privilege verront, que je par l'otroi e per l'asentement deu chapitre e des freres de la maison d'avant dite e aquite a frere Lutol, venerable grant comandaor e en loc de maestre de la maison de l'hospital de nostre dame des Alamans de Jerusalem e as freres de cela mesme maison totes las raisons e les dretures, que nos porriems demander sur lo casal de Lanoye par aucune achaison, fur solement dos quintals de zucre, que nos i devoms recevir e aver des ore en avant chascun an en la festa de pascha a ous des malaudes de nostre mayson. E a ce que ceste chose seit ferme e estable, ge per l'otrei e par la volente de mes freres lur en ai feit faire ceste present privilege selle deu seel de plum deu chapitre de nostre mayson. De ceste chose sunt garens frere Perre de Vielle Bride, grant comandaur de l'ospital de san Johan; frere Robert, l'ospitaler; frare Raimon Motet; frare Sais, lo tresorier; frere Fortuner; frere Durant de Soreis; frere Johan l'aubergere e frere Guillelme d'Anthioche. Ce fu feit en l'an de la encarnacion nostre seigneur Jhesu Crist m° e cc° xxx° ix° en lo meis d'abril.

I, 32 n. 72.

---

88. *1239. Guiccardus, s. Mariae de Latina in Ierusalem abbas, confirmat hospitali s. Mariae Theutonicorum vineam sibi censualem venditam per filios Michaelis de Ierusalem.*

Notum sit omnibus tam presentibus quam futuris, quod Guiccardus humilis abbas ecclesie sancte Marie de Latina in Ierusalem una cum capitulo nostro confirmamus et corroboramus vendicionem vinee, quam fecerunt Giot et Iohan, filii Michaelis de Ierusalem, vobis fratri Lutolfo et conventui hospitalis sancte Marie Theutonicorum pro bisantiis sarracenatis vii^{c}, quam idem Iohannes tenebat a nobis sub annuo censu bisanciorum sarracenatorum xiii in festivitate omnium sanctorum persolvendorum. Nos vero Guicardus predictus abbas una cum capitulo nostro concedimus vobis fratri Lutoldo et conventui hospitalis sancte Marie Theutonicorum predictam vineam possidendam, ut liceat eam vobis vendere et alienare cuicunque volueritis preter militibus et filiis militum et domibus religionum et hominibus communium. Vos quoque tenemini nobis censum predictum solvere in festivitate omnium sanctorum. Cuius vinee hii sunt termini: ab oriente est vinea, que fuit Iohannis de Conche; ab occidente est iardinus domini Rollandi militis; a meridie est iardinus eiusdem domus Theutonicorum; a septentrione est via publica. Si vero predictam vineam aliquo tempore volueritis vendere, nobis vel successoribus nostris primum insinuare debetis et, si eam emere voluerimus, pro una marcha minus precio, quam ab aliis habere poteritis, nobis eam dare debetis. Si eam nos emere noluerimus, solvetis nobis de venditione bisantios iii sarracenatos Syrie. Vendere eam poteritis, cuicunque volueritis preterquam supra dictis personis, salvo per omnia iure ecclesie sancte Marie de Latina. Ut autem presens scriptum robur optineat firmitatis, presens scriptum vobis fieri fecimus subscriptorum[1] fratrum testimonio et sigilli nostri plumbei munimine roboratum. Anno incarnationis m° cc° xxx° ix°.

I, 31 n. 69. 1. nihil horum invenitur in B.

---

89. *1240 in domo hospitalis s. Iohannis. Petrus de Veteri Privata, s. domus hospitalis Ierusalem magister, convenit cum domo Theutonicorum de quarta parte reddituum casalis Arabiae domui suae reservanda, donec 5000 bisanciorum receperit.*

Nos frater Petrus de Veteri Privata dei gracia sancte domus hospitalis Ierusalem magister[1] humilis et pauperum Christi custos et conventus eiusdem domus, notum facimus tam presentibus quam futuris, quod talis convencio sive paccio intervenit inter nos ex una parte et fratrem Gerardum de Malberch, mariscalcum domus Theutonicorum, locum magistri tenentem, et conventum eiusdem domus ex altera, videlicet quod ipsi annuatim tenentur nobis dare redditus sive proventus quarte partis casalis, quod dicitur Arabia, cum pertinenciis suis; et ipsi fratres Theutonicorum ponent ibi baiulum aliquem de fratribus suis, cui coram preceptore hospitalis sancti Iohannis iniungetur et districte precipietur a magistro Theutonicorum sive ab alio, qui fuerit loco sui, quod idem baiulus bona fide et sine fraude et vicio aliquo debeat reddere redditus sive proventus quarte partis casalis Arabie cum pertinenciis suis magistro et fratribus hospitalis sancti Iohannis. Et idem baiulus de comunibus redditibus casalis et pertinenciis predictis retinebit sibi expensas moderatas et necessarias; et tam diu magister et fratres hospitalis sancti Iohannis percipient redditus quarte partis casalis Arabie cum pertinenciis suis, donec satisfactum fuerit hospitali sancti Iohannis de quinque milibus bisantiorum, pro quibus ipsum casale cum pertinenciis suis est penes magistrum et fratres hospitalis sancti Iohannis pignori obligatum. Et si aliqua sive secularis sive ecclesiastica persona vel quicumque alius fuerit, qui moveret questionem contra fratres domus Teutonicorum vel violenciam inferret eisdem de casali predicto et eius pertinenciis, magister et fratres hospitalis sancti Iohannis quantum de iure poterunt assistent fratribus Theutonicis et exibebunt eis secundum iusticiam eorum suffragium et iuvamen sicuti de sua gaggeria, quousque sibi fuerit satisfactum. Et cum magister et fratres predicti hospitalis sancti Iohannis perceperint quinque milia bisantiorum de redditibus supradictis, nullum ius ulterius pro dictis v milibus bisanciorum in dicto casali vendicabunt et dimittent ipsum quiete et pacifice fratribus Theutonicis possidere, et privilegium sive rationes, quod sive quas habent de predictis bisanciis, cum fuerit eis integre satisfactum, restituent fratribus Theutonicorum. Et si casu contingeret, quod dictum privilegium amitteretur infra tempus predictum, talem fratribus Theutonicorum facient caucionem, quod illud privilegium sive aliud, quodcunque repperietur de bisanciis antedictis, sint cassa, inutilia et inania et nullas vires in iudicio sive extra iudicium habebunt. Et, si evenerit, quod absit, quod dictum casale occupatum esset a Sarracenis, fratres Theutonicorum in nullo tenebuntur fratribus hospitalis sancti Iohannis, quamdiu a Sarracenis detinebitur occupatum. Et, si contingeret idem casale post longum vel breve tempus vel quandocunque redire ad manus fratrum Theutonicorum, dicta paccio seu convencio in suo vigore debeat remanere. Et, si contingeret, quod magistro et fratribus hospitalis sancti Iohannis infra tempus predictum esset de predictis bisanciis satisfactum sive in parte sive in toto, fratres Theutonicorum super predictis ulterius non molestabunt. Et ad maioris roboris firmitatem presentes litteras sigilli nostri munimine fecimus roborari. Acta sunt hec in domo hospitalis sancti Iohannis anno domini m° cc° xl° indictione xii^a[2] coram talibus[3]: fratre Guillelmo Silvanectensi, magno preceptore domus hospitalis sancti Iohannis; fratre Arnaldo de Monte Bruno; fratre Geraudo, preceptore domus hospitalis in Ioppen; fratre Guillelmo de Correllis; fratre Gaufrido Baucitensi; fratre Odone de Ermene. De fratribus Theutonicorum interfuerunt isti: frater Everardus, sacerdos; frater Conradus, castellanus Montisfortis; frater Petrus, drapperius; frater Evrardus, thesaurarius.

I, 31 v. n. 71. 1. Hunc (Petrum de Villebrida) Seb. Pauli I, 342. 1241 demum electum esse contendit. Diploma forsan pertinet ad 1241 ineuntem annum. 2. pro xiii. 3. l. testibus?

90. *1241 decembri Tyri. Philippus de Maugastel donat domui Theutonicorum casale Corsy in dominio Thabariae.*

Coneuse chose seit a toz ceaus, qui sunt e a qui avenir sunt, que je Philippes de Maugastel per l'otrei et per la plene volente de mon fil Thomas et de ma feme Margarite done, confirme e outroi pardurablement a la sainta maison des Alamans en tems de freire Lutolf, grant comandaur, de mon patrimone, qui est de ma escheete, que est en la terra e en la seignoria de Tabarie, un casal, que om apela Corsy, e totes ses partinences e toz ses vilanz e totes ces dreitures e totes ses pastures e totes ces aiques per l'arme de moi et per les armes de toz mes antecessors, e que nos armes soient parcevables[1] de lur orazonz e de lur benfaitz. E ceste don, ensi com il est desus meti, je vueill, que la devant dite maison la tenga quittament et franchement sen servize pardurablement. Et per ce que je vuoill, que cest don seit ferm e estable a toz jorns, je ai fait faire cest present escrit e seeler de mon seel de cera. E de ce sunt garenz: misire Luther[2] Filangier, marescalc deu reigname de Jerusalem; sire Perre, segnor de Scandalion; sire Garner l'Alaman; sire Raul l'Alaman; sire Aimarriz de Fenion, et sire Munreal. Escrit fu a Sur el mois de decembre l'an de la encarnation de Jhesu Crist m° cc° xli° quinta decima indictione.

I, 34 v. n. 79. 1. ? parconables B partim supra rasuram. 2. l. Richer.

---

91. *1242 aprilis 30 Accon. Radulfus Acconensis episcopus concedit domui hospitalis Alamanorum duos hortos censuales supra ripam fluminis Acconensis.*

Notum sit universis presens privilegium inspecturis, quod nos Radulfus miseratione divina Acconensis ecclesie minister humilis de consensu et voluntate capituli nostri pensata utilitate ecclesie nostre ad preces fratris Lutolfi magni preceptoris et tenentis locum magistri domus hospitalis Alamanorum in Accon et tocius conventus eiusdem domus dedimus et concessimus eidem fratri Lutolfo recipienti pro dicta domo duos iardinos ecclesie Acconensis sitos in territorio Acconensi supra rippam fluminis Acconensis sub annuo censu lxx^a^ v^e^ bisanciorum sarracenatorum[1] habendos et tenendos in perpetuum et possidendos iure proprietario cum omnibus introitibus, exitibus et iuribus suis, quorum fines sunt tales: ex parte orientis est molendinum regis, ex parte occidentis terra domus hospitalis Alamanorum, ex parte austri flumen Acconense, ex parte aquilonis via publica; tali conditione, quod magister, qui pro tempore fuerit, et domus dicti hospitalis tenentur dare et solvere sine dilatione et contradictione per singulos annos in festo exaltationis sancte crucis pro censu dictorum iardinorum nobis et successoribus nostris vel capitulo sede vaccante de thesauro domus iam dicte predictos lxx^a^ v^e^ bisancios sarracenatos ad pondus Acconense bene ponderatos et numeratos. Si autem in solutione dictorum bisanciorum per annum cessatum fuerit, postquam requisiti fuerint a nobis vel successoribus nostris vel capitulo sede vaccante, nos vel successores nostri vel capitulum sede vaccante sine contradictione aliqua non obstante privilegio aliquo vel contractu propria auctoritate sine lesione iuris alterius cum omnibus hedificatis, seminatis et plantatis iardinos supradictos habebimus et ad ius et ad proprietatem ecclesie Acconensis sine difficultate qualibet revertentur iardini superius nominati. Nos vero tenemur fratribus dicte domus deffensare et garentare secundum consuetudinem civitatis Acconensis iardinos superius memoratos, dicti autem fratres tenentur procurare et facere, quod magister domus, qui absens erat tempore contractus, hiis omnibus suum prebebit assensum et quod inter nos ex una parte et fratrem Lutolfum et conventum dicti hospitalis actum est, ratum habebit et firmum. Si vero predictus magister suum noluerit adhibere vel presentes litteras suo sigillo munire, dicti iardini ad ius et proprietatem Acconensis ecclesie libere revertentur, sicut superius expressum est. Ut autem presens privilegium ratum et inconcussum in perpetuum permaneat, appositione sigilli nostri plumbei et sigilli capituli necnon et canonicorum nostrorum et aliorum testium subscriptione fecimus roborari. Testes: Nicholaus, dechanus; Galterus, archidiachonus; Gaufridus, cantor; et Iohannes Yspanus, canonicus Acconensis; iudex Sanctorus et magister Matheus phisicus. Actum Accon anno domini m° cc° xl° ii° pridie kal. maii.

I, 33v. n. 77. 1. bisancios sarr. B.

---

92. *1242 aug. 18 apud Accon. Giraldus Magnus Alemannus donat domui hospitalis s. Mariae Theutonicorum duas domos Accone*[1] *in ruga caldariorum.*

In nomine domini amen. Cum optima mensura sit rerum donatarum ecclesie immensitas, ideo ego Geraldus Alemannus miles dictus Magnus, prosperitate corporis gaudens et sanitate, intuitu religionis et fidei et pro salute anime mee et parentum meorum dono et concedo domui hospitalis sancte Marie Theutonicorum et venerabilibus fratribus eiusdem domus duas domos meas coniunctas, que sunt apud Monmusart in ruga, que dicitur calderariorum, quarum ab uno latere est domus curie regalis, ab alio latere est domus Hugonis de Calderaria, et ab introitu ipsarum domorum est platea iuxta fossatum civitatis. Item dono et concedo prefate domui et fratribus supradictis totum meum harnesium militare tam in equitaturis et armis quam robis et aliis rebus; et, si qua bona habeo vel in vita mea me habere contingerit[2], ut amodo inantea sint in proprietate et dominio dicte domus et fratrum, reservato tamen mihi, donec vixero, usufructu ipsarum rerum. Post mortem vero meam usufructus[3] ipsorum bonorum redeat ad proprietatem et dominium dicte domus et fratrum. Ipsi vero fratres in meo obitu me tractabunt velut unum ex fratribus in exequiis et sepultura. Ut autem hec mea predicta donatio firma permaneat et inconcussa, ad prefate domus maiorem cautelam et perpetuam firmitatem ego prefatus Gerardus presentem paginam sibi inde fieri feci et sigilli venerabilis patris domini Radulfi Acconensis episcopi, quem ad hoc rogavi, et mei munimine roboratam. Actum apud Accon presentibus domino Radulfo, Acconensi episcopo; ..[3] archidiachono Acconensi; Ludulfo, preposito Monasteriensi[4]; domino Balduino de Pinkenie et domino Bertoldo militibus et fratre Iohanne priore dicte domus Alamanorum anno dominice incarnationis m° cc° xl° ii° indictione i[a] xv° kal. septembris.

I, 32 v. n. 74. 1. ita titulus. 2. sic B. 3. nulla lacuna; deest nomen (Gualterii). 4. 1241 febr. 18 Ludolfus S. Mauritii Monasteriensis praepositus Monasterii versatus est; cf. Wilmans Westfälisches Urkundenbuch. Münster 1859. III, 207 n. 382.

---

93. *1243 decembri ind. II apud Norinberc. Conradus, Friderici imp. filius, in Romanorum regem electus, heres regni Ierosolimitani, confirmat fratribus hospitalis s. Mariae domus Theutonicorum in Ierusalem patris sui privilegium de d. 1229 aprili apud Accon (supra n. 69).*

E copiariis duobus nostro I, 48 et altero archivi Regimontani edidit Huillard-Bréholles Hist. Fr. II dipl. VI, 853. cf. Böhmer n. 651. — N. 69 etiam ap. Hennes II, 39 n. 34.

---

94. *1243 decembri ind. II apud Noremberc. Idem iisdem confirmat eiusdem privilegium de eodem dato (supra n. 70).*

I, 47 v. Indidem edidit idem 851. Böhmer n. 650.

---

95. *1243 decembri ind. II apud Norimberch. Idem iisdem confirmat eiusdem privilegium d. d. 1235 novembri apud Augustam (supra n. 79).*

I, 45. Edd. Stillfried Monum. Zollerana I, 46 coll. cum copia authentica in archivo Stuttgartensi. Huillard-Bréholles VI, 849. Böhmer n. 820 et n. 30.

---

96. *1243 decembri ind. II apud Noremberc. Idem iisdem confirmat eiusdem privilegium d. d. 1231 decembri ap. Ravennam (supra n. 76).*

I, 46 v. Edd. Duellius Hist. ord. Theutonici app. p. 7. Huillard-Bréholles VI, 854. cf. Böhmer n. 697 et n. 61.

---

97. *1243 decembri ind. II apud Norimberc. Idem iisdem confirmat Isabellae privilegium d. d. 1226 ianuario (supra n. 59).*

I, 46. E codice nostro edidit Huillard-Bréholles l. c. VI, 850. cf. Böhmer n. 63. Isabellae privilegium etiam extat ap. Hennes Codex dipl. ord. s. M. Th. Mainz 1861. II, 24 n. 23.

---

98. *1244 iulii 7 Accon. Conventio inter domum hospitalis s. Mariae Theutonicorum et Iacobum de Amigdala de relictis a Iozelino comite terra Maronis et reditibus 7000 bisanciorum de funda Acconensi percipiendis.*

In nomine sancte et individue trinitatis, patris et filii et spiritus sancti. Amen. Ut rerum gestarum memoria vigeat, solent scripture testimonio commendari. Ideo per presens scriptum notum sit tam presentibus quam futuris, quod, cum discordia verteretur inter domum hospitalis sancte Marie Theotonicorum ex una parte et dominum Iacobum de Amigdalia ex altera super quibusdam privilegiis, que fuerunt quondam comitis Iozolini, que erant penes ipsam domum, continentibus terram Maronis cum pertinenciis suis et super septem milibus bisanciis, quos dictus comes habere debebat in funda et cathena Accon et super aliis iuribus et racionibus, quas idem comes habere debebat in regno Ierosolimitano, de quibus omnibus idem dominus Iacobus dicebat medietatem ad se pertinere ex ratione domine Agnetis, matris sue, filie dicti comitis Iozolini; et eciam medietatem fructuum perceptorum de Maron et pertinentiarum earum et medietatem septem milium bisantiorum perceptorum in funda et catnena Accon dicebat ad se pertinere. Ex altera parte frater Henricus de Honloch magister ipsius domus et alii fratres pro ipsa domo dicebant predicta omnia tenuisse bona fide et percepisse auctoritate privilegiorum suorum et aliorum iurium. Tandem interventu communium amicorum volentes parcere laboribus et expensis ad hanc concordiam insimul devenerunt, videlicet quod dictus frater Henricus de Honloch, magister dicte domus, de consensu et voluntate fratrum suorum et tocius conventus recognovit ipsum dominum Iacobum legitimum heredem de medietate Maronis cum pertinenciis suis et medietate predictorum septem milium bisantiorum et de medietate omnium aliorum iurium et rationum, quas idem comes Iozolinus habuit vel habere debebat in toto regno Ierosolimitano, et investivit eum de ipsa medietate Maronis cum pertinentiis suis et medietate vii^{tem} milium bisantiorum predictorum et de medietate omnium aliorum iurium et rationum, que fuerunt dicti comitis Iozolini, ut superius continetur. Et dictus dominus Iacobus de Amigdalia pro se et heredibus suis proinde dimisit et remisit dicto fratri Henrico magistro et fratribus pro domo ipsorum et eorum successoribus omne ius et omnem questionem seu querimoniam, quod vel quam modo quolibet habere posset super altera medietate Maronis cum pertinenciis suis et super altera medietate predictorum septem milium bisantiorum et super altera medietate omnium aliorum iurium et rationum dicti comitis Iozolini in regno Ierosolimitano; et voluit dictus dominus Iacobus et promisit pro se et heredibus suis, ut dicta domus hospitalis Theotonicorum teneat et custodiat dicta privilegia, que fuerunt dicti comitis Iozolini, utpote ea, quibus[1] contingit integra medietas bonorum omnium, que fuerunt dicti comitis Iozelini, ratione venditionis, quam domui fecit olim domina Beatrix primogenita filia dicti comitis Iozolini tam illorum, que sunt in manibus christianorum, quam illorum, que sunt in manibus paganorum, cum ad manus christianorum reddiderit ea deus. Et idem magister et fratres sui pro ipsa domo convenerunt et promiserunt dicto domino Iacobo et suis heredibus, ut, quociens opus erit eis, ipsa privilegia dabunt et exhibebunt, prestita prius securitate de ipsis privilegiis domui restituendis. Convenit etiam insuper dictus dominus Iacobus et promisit se vel heredes suos nullam de cetero controversiam seu querimoniam moturos ipsi domui de fructibus et accessionibus perceptis de ipsa medietate Maronis cum pertinentiis suis et de medietate vii^tem^ milium bisantiorum hactenus perceptorum ab ipsa domo in cathena et funda Accon usque ad diem, quo[2] facta fuit hec compositio. Et insuper convenit et promisit dictus dominus Iacobus, quod permutationem sive concambium factum ab eo de medietate Castri Regis cum pertinentiis suis pro sex milibus et quadringentis bisantiis per se et heredes suos omni tempore ratum et firmum habebit iuxta tenorem privilegiorum exinde confectorum, nec aliqua occasione per se vel alium seu heredes suos contravenire temptabit. Simili modo promisit ratam et firmam habere locationem sive concambium de medietate Maronis cum pertinentiis suis pro duobus milibus et quingentis bisantiis, prout in privilegio exinde facto inter eos plenius continetur. Et si aliquo tempore de bonis olim comitis Iozolini, que hodie tenentur a Sarracenis, contingerit[3] dante domino adipisci seu aliquo modo recuperari et devenire ad manus suas vel heredum suorum, promisit et convenit idem dominus Iacobus pro se et suis heredibus, quod ea non vendent nec pignori dabunt nec appaltabunt nec permutabunt in aliquam personam, si predicta bona ipsa domus habere voluerit equo precio ad arbitrium communium amicorum inter eos statuto. Promisit etiam, quod nec dabit vel recommandabit alicui persone vel loco in preiudicium et gravamen ipsius domus Theotonicorum. Predicta itaque omnia et singula utraque pars pro se et heredibus seu successoribus suis bona fide attendere et observare promisit, nec contra aliquo modo vel ingenio seu aliqua occasione venire, renunciantes omni iuri et beneficio, quod eis super hoc competere posset sub pena duorum[4] milium marcharum argenti ad invicem inter se promissa et conventa solvenda parti, que pactum et conventionem servaverit, et nihilominus ea soluta predicta omnia et singula perpetuam optineant firmitatem. Ad cuius rei memoriam duo consimilia privilegia de voluntate parcium exinde sunt confecta sigillis plumbeis pendentibus, capituli videlicet dicte domus et dicti domini Iacobi, sigillata. Huius autem rei testes sunt frater Conradus de Nasso, preceptor magnus; Guarnerus de Mereberc, marescalcus; Gunterus, commendator Apulie; Iohannes de Niflanda, castellanus Montis fortis; Conradus hospitalarius; Ludowicus, drapperius; Henricus de Diling et Symon[3] de Huasi, fratres de dicta domo hospitalis Theutonicorum; dominus Balduinus de Pinkin; dominus Stephanus de Sauvani; dominus Raulus Alemannus et Philippus Balduinus. Actum apud Accon in palatio dicti magistri anno dominice incarnationis m° cc° xliiii° indictione secunda nonas iulii.

III, 166v. Ubi titulus legitur „Rescriptum privilegii de casale Maronis". 1. cui B. 2. q̄, i. e. que B. 3. B. 4. duarum B.

99. *1244 iulii 7 Accon. Iacobus de Amigdalia locat domui hospitalis S. Mariae Theutonicorum medietatem Maronis.*

In nomine patris et filii et spiritus sancti. Amen. Notum sit omnibus tam presentibus quam futuris, quod ego Iacobus de Amigdalia pro me et meis heredibus de bona et gratuita voluntate dono et concedo fratri Henrico de Honloch venerabili magistro domus hospitalis sancte Marie Theotonicorum et fratribus eiusdem domus et eorum successoribus pro domo eorum predicta partem meam videlicet medietatem Maronis et omnium pertinentiarum suarum in excambium seu perpetuam locationem pro duobus milibus et quingentis bisantiis sarracenatis, quos debemus recipere ego et heredes mei libere et absque ullo servicio in Accon vel in castro, quod dicitur Montfort, annuatim de thesauro domus predicte, de tribus scilicet in tres menses secentos et viginti quinque bisantios Sarracenatos ad pondus Accon tali conditione, quod, si predicta domus differret per sex menses et viginti dies solvere mihi et heredibus meis predictos bisantios, ipsa domus tenetur mihi et meis heredibus dare mille bisantios pro pena ultra bisantios illis sex mensibus mihi et meis heredibus persolvendos. Si autem per annum integrum et viginti dies differret dicta domus solvere mihi et meis heredibus bisantios antedictos et mille bisantios pene supradicte, ego et heredes mei poterimus licite intrare in possessionem medietatis Maronis et omnium pertinenciarum suarum tanquam in hereditatem meam absque omni impedimento et contradictione supradicto excambio seu perpetua locatione[1] penitus anichilata; et alia medietas Maronis cum omnibus pertinentiis suis erit mihi et meis heredibus obligata iure pignoris pro bisanciis, quos per annum predictum debuimus recipere ego et heredes mei a dicta domo ratione excambii seu locationis perpetue antedicte, et pro mille bisantiis pene superius memorate, quam debemus tenere ego et heredes mei, donec percepimus de proventibus ipsius medietatis supradictos bisantios excambii scilicet pene vel aliter nobis a dicta domo de ipsis bisanciis fuerit satisfactum; quibus habitis vel perceptis dicta medietas ad dictam domum revertetur, et, si aliquis vellet nos impedire, quod non possemus supradicta facere, curia regia debet nos iuvare ad faciendum supradicta et omnem vim ammovere. Si autem medietas mea Maronis ad me et ad heredes meos revenerit, ego et heredes mei debemus facere dicte domui medietatem servicii, quod debetur pro Marone et pertinenciis suis. Si vero dicta domus per guerram sive alio modo absque culpa sua amiserit terram Maronis vel in parte vel in toto, fiet diminutio duorum milium et quingentorum bisantiorum supradictorum iuxta quantitatem medietatis[2] terre amisse, iudicio et arbitrio communi amicorum tota terra Maronis et pertinentiarum suarum ad valorem quinque milium bisantiorum extimata. Ad cuius rei memoriam ego predictus Iacobus presens scriptum inde eis fieri feci sigillo meo plumbeo pendenti et testimonio infra scriptorum virorum munimine roboratum. Huius autem rei testes sunt Conradus de Nasso, magnus preceptor; Guernerius de Mereberch, mareschalcus; Gunterius, commendator Apulie; Iohannes de Nifland, castellanus Montis fortis; Conradus,

hospitalarius; Ludowicus drapperius; Henricus de Diling, et Symon de Huasi, fratres de dicta domo hospitali Theotonicorum; Balduinus de Pinkin, Stephanus de Sawani, Raulus Alemannus, milites, et Philippus de Baduin. Actum apud Accon in palatio dicti magistri anno dominice incarnationis m° cc° xliiii° indictione ii^a nonas iulii.

III, 167. „Item aliud privilegium rescriptum super emptionem Maronis". 1. locatio B. 2. medietatem B.

---

100. *1249 aprilis 30. Iohannes Alemannus, dominus Caesareae, vendit domui hospitalis S. Mariae Theutonicorum bona sua Beitegen, Seifor, Nef, Haseinie, Mergecolon, Gelon, prope Acconem civitatem sita.*

Coneue chose seit a toz ceaus, qui sunt et qui avenir sunt, que je Johan l'Aleman, sire de Cesaire, ai apaute et apaute perpetuaument de ma terre, que je ai devant Acre, ce est a saveir Beitegen et Seisor et Nef et la Haseinie et Mergecolon et Gelon et toz ses devanz diz casaus o tot luer terroir et luer devises tex com il ont ne aveir deivent, seit en terre gaaignee ou non gaaignee, en bois, en aigues, en pastures, en gastines, en plains e en montaingnes apaute a l'ennorable frere Everart de Saine, grant comandeor au jor de l'ospitau de nostre dame des Alemans et en leu de maistre, et as freres de cele memes maison et por le grant profit d'eaus et de luer maison et par ce, que ma terre luer est bien seant et que, se ele fust venue en mains d'autres gens, que il fust torne a grant damage d'eaus et de luer maison, et par ce l'apauterent il de mei et par en tel maniere, que les devans nomez casaus furent adonc prisies chascun par sei et toz ensemble et par la bone volente et par l'otrei de mei devant nome Johan et des freres de la devant dite maison, ce est de luer covent; et tot avant fu prisie Beitegen quatre cens besanz sarracenaz de totes rentes; et Seisor set cens besanz et Nef sis cens bezans et la Haseinie cent bezans et Mergecolon deus mile bezans et Gelon deus cens bezans, don la some fu de tot encemble quatre mile bezans sarrazenaz; et tan furent il prisies ne au plus chier ne au plus vil et a reinables annees, et de ce pris Nabatige mil et sis cens bez. sarraz. a toz jors en eschange de sese mile bez. sarraz., que les freres de la devant dite maison me baillerent adonc; et le remanant qui demore, ce est a entendre deus mile et quatre cens bez. sarraz. au peis d'Acre, si me sunt tenuz ou a mes airs ou a mes comandemenz, et nos ont en covenant de baillier les nos en luer tresor de luer maison d'Acre ou en luer chastiau de Monfort, ce est assaveir la, ou je devant dit Johan ou mes airs ou nos comandemenz le amerons miaus a receveir, de ses deus lues franchement et quitement sans servise et sans reconoissance, que mei ne mes airs en seient tenuz de faire as freres de la devant dite maison de l'ospitau des Alemanz de cest apaut et par quatre termes de l'an, ce est a saveir chascun treis meis sis cens bez. sarraz. au peis d'Acre et sans nul autre delaiement et en peine de mil bez. sarraz. Por la quel peine il m'ont obligue a mei devant dit Johan et mis en gagiere par l'otrei et par la bone volente de luer covent et de luer chapistre un luer casau, que il ont es apartenances d'Acre, et marchist a Casal l'Inbert et a non La Bace, ce est a entendre en tel manierre, que, se le terme de quatre meis passast et il ne m'eussent paie enterinement les devanz dis sis cens bez. por la paie des treis mes, que il fussent encoru tot tronc envers mei ou envers mes airs ou envers nos comandemenz de la devant dite paine de mil bez. sarraz. sur tos les biens dou devant nome casau de La Bace, et que les freres de la devant dite maison de l'ospitau des Alemans ne nul home por ceaus ne nos en peust aler a l'encontre de nule chose jusques a ce, que nos devant nome Johan ou mes airs ou nos comandemenz eusiens reseu les devanz diz mil bez. de la peine, et apres ce que le casal reveigne arieres en luer mains et en tel maniere com il estet devant. Et se il passeit le terme de sis meis et que les freres de la devant nomee maison ne nos eussent paie ausi des dues paies enterinement, que l'apaut, qui est desus dit, de nos et d'eaus fust failli a toz jors mais et que mei ou mes airs devons aveir tote la terre et les devanz diz casaus enterinement sans contredit des freres de la devant nomee maison ne de home por eaus rendant luer les seze mile bez. desus diz suir toz nos biens, ce est assaveir dedens l'an apres ce que nos raurons eu tote la terre enterinement et les casaus desus nomes seront en nostre pooir; et les freres de la devant nomee maison des Alemans me sunt tenuz leiaument et en bone fei de partenir le devant dit apaut tot ensi com il est desus moti, et se devant nome apaut me sunt il tenus et m'ont en covenant leiaument et sur luer ames et par luer abit de faire a toz tens mais et en sunt hors totes pestilenses et totes forces de gens que que il seient, fors tant, que se force de Sarrazins venissient en la terre ou force dou seingnor dou reiaume de Jerusalem ou de celui qui sereit son bail ou reaume et en lue de lui; et por le fait de cest apaut nomeement et par ensi que les freres de la devant nomee maison de l'ospitau des Alemans ne pussent aveir ne tenir enterinement la terre que tant conse durereit, ne nos fussent rien tenuz de doner le devant dit apaut et se les Sarrazins ou le seingnor dou reaume ou celui, qui sereit son bail en lue de lui, ne feissent force que de partie de la terre et que les freres de la devant dite maison ou home por eaus tenissient l'autre partie de la terre, eaus nos sunt tenus et nos ont en covenant, ce est a mei ou a mes airs, de maintenir l'apaut selonc ce que aus tenreient de la terre par la forme dou pris des casaus desus diz et tot ensi com il est desus moti, ce est assaveir de paier nos ou nos airs ou nos comandementz chascun treis meis et nomeement selonc la quantite de ce que il tenreient de la terre et par la manierre, qui est desus dite, et de la peine ausi; et si me sunt tenuz et m'on en covenant les freres de la devant nomee maison de deffendre la terre et les casaus desus diz a luer pooir et en bone fei sans nul engin contre toz ceaus, qui la tenreient ne qui force i fereient, fussent crestiens ou Sarrazins, et je luer en sui tenuz d'aider les ent ausi a mon pooir en bone fei dedens cort et dehors cort contre toz ceaus, qui forse ou tort luer fereient; et quant eaus eussent arier la terre, il nos sont tenus et nos ont en covenant de paier le devant dit apaut de tot ensemble tot ensi com il est desus moti, et nos en somes tenuz de faire ent le servise a la seingnorie dou reiaume de Jerusalem et tel com ma terre le det de tot ensemble, ce est a saveir de treis chrs.[1] et tierce, et si luer sui tenuz ausi, que se dreit seingnor venist en la terre, ce est ou reiaume de Jerusalem, et aus pussent tant faire vers lui, que il vosist otroie se devant dit apaut en maniere devete perpetuaument as freres de la devant nomee maison de l'ospitau des Alemans de faire le sans aler a l'encontre de nule riens et de confermer luer au plus estable que je porrai par les covenans desus diz; et se il aveneit, que la seignorie de la terre ne vosist otroier la vente ne soffrir cest apaut, ainz en alast a l'encontre et en tel maniere, que les freres de la devant dite maison ne peussient tenir la terre ne les casaus desus nomez et que la tere et les casaus enterinement revenissient et fussent en mon pooir ou de mes airs, que nos lor somes tenuz de rendre luer les desus diz seze mile bez. dedens un an et sur toz nos biens ou que il seient. Et que tot, ce qui est desus moti de l'apaut, fust tot tronc failli de nos et d'eaus jusques a tant, que aus peussent aveir l'otrei de la seignorie dou devant dit reiaume et proprement de ce fait fust en apaut ou en vente par les covenans desus motis et totes ses devanz dites choses tot ensi, com eles sunt desus moties, luer ai ge faites et jurees et partenir les en bone fei et par l'otrei de ma leal espouse Marguerite dame de Cesaire et de ma suer Heilehuis ausi, qui l'ont ausi jure por mon profit et por le luer meemes. Et nos Marguerite dame de Cesaire et nos Heilehuis suer dou devant nome sire de Cesaire reconoissons an dues ensemble et chascune par sei, que nos l'avons jure et otroie a tenir tot ensi com il est desus dit, et quitons toz les drois, que nos i avons ne aveir jamais i devons[1], as freres de la devant dite maison de l'ospitau de nostre dame des Alemans, ce est assaveir sauf les covenans desus motis. Et por ce que ce seit ferm et estable pardurablement as freres de la devant dite maison de l'ospitau des Alemans et que je et mes airs en somes tenus tot ensi com il est desus dit et par en tel maniere, que le devant nome comandor et en lue de maistre por lui et por le covent de la devant dite maison de l'ospitau des Alemans nos a promis par son abit et sur s'ame, que tot piestant com luer maistre qui ore est ou autre maistre qui fust apres lui, venist en la terre de faire son pooir lui et tot son covent en bone fei et au plus enterinement que il porroit coment il otreiast et confermast enterinement por lui et por sa maison totes ses choses en la forme et tot en la maniere com eles sunt desus moties; et a greignor seurte dou fait et de la devant dite maison ai je fait faire se present previlege et confermer de mon seel de plomb et a la garentie de mes homes, ce est assaveir Hayme l'Aleman mon cozin et Jaque Vidau et Michel le fiz sire Raou de Bazele, et des homes de la seignorie mon cozin mesire Garnier l'Aleman. Ce fut fait en l'an de l'incarnation nostre seignor Jhesu Crist m et cc et xlix le derain jor dou meis d'avril.

III, 158. 1. bis.

---

101. *1252 ian. 11 Perusii. Innocentius papa IV Liddensem episcopum et Bethleemitanum electum iubet Ebronensi ecclesiae ablata in ius eius revocare.*

Innocentius episcopus servus servorum dei venerabili fratri episcopo Liddensi et dilecto filio electo Bethlemitano salutem et apostolicam benedictionem[1]. Cum ecclesiarum dampnis nequeamus passim occurrere precavendo, quin earum bona quamquam minus licite distrahantur, convenit, ut dampnificationi congruo remedio succurramus. Cum igitur, sicut ex parte venerabilis fratris nostri episcopi et capituli Ebronensis fuit propositum coram nobis, multa de bonis Ebronensis ecclesie alienata sint illicite et distracta, discrecioni vestre per apostolica scripta mandamus, quatenus alienata seu distracta huiusmodi ad ius et proprietatem ipsius ecclesie legitime revocetis, non obstantibus aliquibus possessionibus instrumentis seu litteris quibuscunque personis concessis vel penis adiectis aut interpositis iuramentis et confirmationibus ab apostolica sede in communi forma obtentis et constitutione de duabus dietis edita in concilio generali, dummodo ultra tertiam vel quartam extra suam diocesim altera pars ad iudicium non trahatur, contradictores per censuram ecclesiasticam appellatione postposita compescendo. Quodsi non ambo hiis exequendis potueritis interesse, alter vestrum ea nichilominus exequatur. Datum Perusii iii° idus ianuarii pontificatus nostri anno ix°.

Continetur in n. 104. 1. etc. pro et a. b., quod est in n. 102.

---

102. *1253 martii 8 Ioppe. Arnoldus Liddensis episcopus et G. Bethleemitanus electus Matthaeo canonico et praeceptori Dominici Sepulcri notum faciunt se recepisse Innocentii papae IV bullam supra n. 101, quam exequendam ei committunt.*

Arnoldus dei gratia sancti Georgii Liddensis episcopus et G.[1] eadem gratia Bethlemitanus electus discreto et venerabili viro Matheo canonico et preceptori Dominici Sepulchri in vero salutari salutem. Noveritis nos mandatum apostolicum recepisse in hac forma: „Innocentius episcopus servus servorum dei venerabili fratri episcopo Liddensi et dilecto filio electo Bethlemitano salutem et apostolicam benedictionem. Cum ecclesiarum dampnis nequeamus passim occurrere precavendo, quin earum bona" etc. sicut in papali littera superius continetur[2]. Verum cum nos apud Ioppen morari oporteat in exercitu christiano, quare de questionibus et querelis prefati episcopi et eius capituli personaliter ad presens cognoscere non valeamus, discretioni vestre vices nostras committendas duximus in hac parte, diffinitiva nobis sentencia reservata. Quocirca vobis auctoritate qua fungimur precipiendo mandamus, quatenus vocatis[3] qui fuerint evocandi, deum habentes pre oculis de questionibus memoratis cognoscatis causasque sufficienter instructas cum vestrarum testimonio literarum et actorum serie nobis transmittere procuretis. Datum ioppen anno domini m° cc° quinquagesimo tercio octavo die mensis marcii.

Continetur in n. 104. 1. Secundum Le Quien Or. Christ. III videtur Godefridi nomen habuisse. 2. cf. n. 101. 3. vocatur A. 16 l. evocatis.

---

103. *1253 martii 21. Iulianus dominus Saidae donat Petro de Avalon plateam in civitate Saidae contiguam domui hospitalis Theutonicorum.*

Coneue chose seit a touz ceaus qui sunt et qui avenir sunt, que ge Juliein par la grace nostre seignor sire de Saite doins et autrei et conferme a tei, Pierre d'Avalon, conestable de Tabarie et seignor d'Adelon, a tei et a tes hoirs paradurablement une place en ma cite de Saite, la quele place set sur la rive de la mer et devers levant se tent a la[1] maison de l'ospital des Alemans et devers migdi envers la maison des freres menors et d'occident dure jusque a la[1] mer, et devers orient dure jusque au chemin, qui vait a la[1] marine et passe entre la tue maison et la maison de madame Margarite ma mere, qui ja fu dite dame de Saite; la quele place te doins ge par tous tens mais quitement et franchement sens nul service ne sens nul homage ne sens nule redevance, ensi que tu la puisses laborrer et atefier et haucer a tote ta volente et la puisses vendre et doner et engaier et aliener a qui que tu vorras quitement et franchement sens nul contredit salve a eglise o a relegion. Et por ce que ceste chose soit ferme et estable a tous jors mais et que ge ne nui de mes hoirs ne autre por moi non puissons aler a l'encontre, ge ai fait faire ces present privilege et soeler de mes coigns de plomb a la[1] garentie de mes homes: sir Johan de la Tor, conestable de Saite; et sir Joufroi de Vilers; et sir Simon de Chevile; et sir Ralos d'Aachif; et sir Hoede de Cresel. Ce fu fait en l'an de l'incarnacion nostre seignor Jhesu Crist mil et doucenz et cinquante trois, lundi a vint et un jor de mois de mars.

III, 161 v. Forsan anno 1254 adnumerandum. Sed martii 21 dies 1253 in sextam feriam incidit, 1254 in sabbatum. 1. le B.

---

104. *1253 sept. 26 Accon. Coram magistro Matthaeo, canonico et praeceptore Dominici Sepulcri, Bartholomaeus Ebronensis episcopus et Poppo magister d. s. M. Th. de Montis Musardi proprietate conveniunt.*

Ad rei geste memoriam. Provide constat deliberatione statutum, ut ea, que inter mortales aguntur, ne processu temporis incommodum oblivionis incurrant, scripture testimonio commendentur in memoriam posteris relinquende. Hinc est, quod, cum venerabilis pater episcopus Ebronensis, frater Bartholomeus de Fossa nova, traxisset in causam religiosum virum fratrem Popum magistrum sancte Marie Theuthonicorum et eius conventum coram magistro Matheo canonico et preceptore Sepulchri Dominici, subdelegato a venerabilibus patribus dominis Liddensi episcopo et Bethlemitano electo, auctoritate literarum domini pape iudicibus delegatis pro iam dicto episcopo, quarum literarum domini pape et subdelegationis prefato magistro Matheo suscepte[1] a predictis iudicibus tenor talis est: „Innocentius“ *(n. 101)* et „Arnoldus“ *(n. 102)*. Super quibusdam vero rebus in libello contentis porrecto procuratori magistri et conventus, cuius forma talis est: „Coram vobis, domine Mathee, venerabilis canonice et preceptor[2] Dominici Sepulchri, subdelegate a venerabilibus patribus domino Liddensi episcopo et domino Bethlemitano electo auctoritate literarum domini pape iudicibus delegatis, proponit frater B(artholomeus) episcopus Ebronensis pro se et capitulo eius et ecclesia sua Ebronensi contra venerabilem dominum magistrum et conventum sancte Marie Theuthonicorum, quod ipsi detinent iniuste in dampnum et gravamen ecclesie Ebronensis quasdam domos in burgo Montis Musardi in Tauaria sitas in territorio ecclesie Ebronensis prope ecclesiam sancte Trinitatis et iuxta domum Philippi Tanaor, et unam aliam vultam parvam, que est in ruga sancte Katherine, quam dedit nobis dominus Turricus de Oufholt miles, que sita est in domibus, que fuerunt predicti militis, infra terminos in suo privilegio comprehensos, que omnia pertinent ad ius et proprietatem ecclesie Ebronensis iure dominii vel quasi, et paratus est dictus episcopus eis ostendere iudicis arbitrio. Quare petit dictus episcopus domos predictas per vos, domine iudex, sententialiter adiudicari sibi et ecclesie Ebronensi cum omni causa et iuribus suis, et dictos magistrum et conventum compelli ad restitucionem predictarum domorum cum pensionibus inde perceptis a viginti annis retro[3], quas estimat tria milia bisantiorum sarracenatorum, et hec proponit salvo iure addendi vel minuendi, et petit expensas, factas protestatur et faciendas.“ Magister vero et conventus in defensione iuris domus predicte excipiendo proposuerunt sub hac forma: „Frater Gualterius procurator domus sancte Marie Theuthonicorum excipiendo proponit procuratorio nomine, quod vos magister M(atheus), Iherosolimitanus canonicus, non habetis aliquam iurisdictionem nec habere potestis auctoritate literarum ad vos obtentarum per venerabilem patrem dominum episcopum Ebronensem et eius capitulum in magistrum et fratres predicte domus, cum ipsis magistro et fratribus a sede apostolica sit indultum, ne possint conveniri auctoritate literarum domini pape, nisi in ipsis literis fiat mentio de eorum ordine; et producta fuerunt privilegia ex parte Theuthonicorum ad probandas exceptiones predictas: „Gregorius episcopus servus servorum dei dilectis filiis Hermanno magistro hospitalis sancte Marie Theuthonicorum Iherosolimitani salutem et apostolicam benedictionem. Vestra religio, cuius bonus odor longe lateque diffunditur, specialem apostolice sedis favorem et graciam promeretur“ etc.“ Item: „Innocentius episcopus servus servorum dei magistro et fratribus Theuthonicorum. Quieti vestre providere volentes auctoritate vobis presencium indulgemus etc.“ — Tandem pro bono pacis et concordie, et quia erat honerosum et sumptuosum utrique parti iudicio litigare, nomine transactionis ad talem concordiam devenerunt, videlicet quod magister et conventus prefati convenerunt et promiserunt dare et solvere seu dari et solvi facere predicto episcopo et eius capitulo vel eorum certo nuncio pro domibus in libello petitis septem bysantios sarracenatos singulis annis in festo assumpcionis beate Marie virginis de mense augusti, promittentes sibi ad invicem habere predicta firma et rata et contra non venire aliquo modo vel iure; et super hiis omnibus renunciant omnibus iuribus, rationibus et actionibus, quibus contra predicta venire possent, et ad predicta firma habenda et tenenda se obligaverunt et suos successores et bona omnia suarum domorum et ecclesiarum sub pena quingentarum marcarum; et pena soluta vel[4] non[4] nichilominus presens scriptum suam obtineat firmitatem. In futuram rei memoriam et maiorem firmitatem presentem scripturam transactionis seu compositionis inter predictos ordinate et composite duxerunt suis bullis plumbeis roborandum. Datum Accon anno domini m° cc° liii° sexto kalendas octobris.

E copiario A. 16 archivi Regimontani p. 28—30 mecum communicavit v. cl. A. Meckelburg, qui notat titulum: Hec est quedam composicio facta inter dominum episcopum Ebronensem et magistrum hospitalis sancte Marie Theutonicorum super domibus in burgo Montis Musardi in Tauaria sitis in territorio eclesie Ebronensis, cuius tenor talis. 1. ? expectaveris: commisse. 2. preceptori A. 16. 3. citro A. 16. 4. deest in copiario.

---

105. *1253 octobr. Nicosiae. Heinricus Cypri rex et dominus regni Hierosolymitani Iohanni de Ibelino, domino de Baruth, confert feoda quondam patri eius collata.*

Coneue chose seit a toz ciaus qui sunt et seront, que je Henri, par la grace de deu rei de Cypre et segnor dou reaume de Jerusalem, otrei et conferm en pardurable fie a tei Johan d'Ibelin, segnor de Baruth, et a tes heirs en creissement de ton fie de Baruth le don et le fie, que je donai a Balian d'Ybelin, ton pere, segnor de Baruth jadis, et a ses heirs en creissiment dou fie de Baruth, ce est assaveir: Casal Ymbert, le Fierge, le Quiebre, la Sebeque, Jasson, la Guille, Quafrenēbit, la Meserefe, Douheyrap, Bene, Samah, la Gabasie, soient casaus ou prestries ou totes lor apartenances et ou totes lor devises et ou totes lor possessions et lor teneures et ou totes lor raisons et lor droitures et lor usages en terres laborees et non laborees, en plains, en montagnes, en aigues, en rivieres, en pasturages, en bois, en jardins, en molins, en maisons, en chemins, en fors, en vileins et en vileines, eaus et lor femes et lor anfanz qu'il ont et auront, et totes lor droitures et lor usages et en totes les autres choses et les droitures qui as devant diz leues apartienent. E por cestui fie et creissance tu es devenu mon home et tu et tes heirs apres tei en deves et feres a mei et a ceaus, qui la seignorie dou reaume de Jerusalem tendront apres mei, tel homage et tel servise, com vos devez de vostre fie de Baruth. E por ce que ce seit ferm et estable pardurablement, je ai cestui prevelige fait faire et garnir ou mon seel de plomb de mes coins dou reaume de Jerusalem par la garentie de mes homes de cellui meismes reaume, des quels ces sunt les noms: Bertheleme dou Morf, Phelippe de Nouaire[1],

Galter Quelbe Arab e Gautier Lanne. Ce fu fait a Nicossie en l'an de l'incarnacion de nostre segnor mcc et liii el mois de huitovre.

III, 154. 1. 1252 ap. Las Mattrie II, 67 Phelipe de Navaire.

---

106. *1254 febr. 19 Romae. Ottobonus cardinalis litem fratrum ordinis h. d. Th. I. et Aymerici Barlays de casalibus Arabie et Zachanim dirimit.*

In nomine domini. Amen. Causam, que vertitur inter magistrum et fratres domus sancte Marie Theuthonicorum Accone ex parte una et nobilem virum Aymericum Barlays ex altera super casalibus Arabie et Zachanim, dominus noster summus pontifex nobis Ottobono, miseracione divina sancti Adriani diacono cardinali, audiendam commisit. Constitutis igitur coram nobis fratre Conrado procuratore predictorum magistri et fratrum pro ipsis et Perino, dicto Yspano, procuratore predicti nobilis pro eodem, dictus frater Conradus libellum obtulit sub hac forma: „Coram vobis, venerabili patre domino Ottobono, sancti Adriani diacono cardinali, presentibus auditore concesso, proponit frater Conradus procurator etc., contra Perinum Yspaniolum, procuratorem domini Aymerici Barlays, nomine ipsius, quod, cum ipse magister et fratres essent in possessione casalium Arabie et Zachanim et predicta casalia cum iuribus et pertinentiis suis longo tempore possedissent, pacifice ac quiete et legitime possiderent, dictus Aymericus eosdem magistrum et fratres contra iustitiam spoliari procurans dictis casalibus et possessionibus eorundem ea indebite occupavit et detinet occupata in grave dampnum predictorum magistri et fratrum et in periculum anime sue et scandalum plurimorum. Unde petit nomine magistri et fratrum possessionem predictorum casalium cum pertinenciis eorundem sibi restitui cum fructibus perceptis medio tempore et percipiendis, quos estimat decem millia marcarum, de quibus omnibus petit ipsum dominum Aymericum et procuratorem eius pro eo sententialiter condempnari et ad predictorum satisfactionem compelli, et hoc petit cum dampnis et expensis factis, que et quas dicti magister et fratres sustinuerunt seu incurrerunt propter occupationem seu spoliacionem predictam, que omnia estimat mille marcas, et expensas faciendas protestatur, salvo iure etc." Lite itaque super predicto libello inter ipsos procuratores legitime contestata[1], prestitoque ab ipsis calumpnie iuramento, factis hinc inde positionibus et responsionibus ad easdem iuramentisque productis, datis eciam quibusdam articulis a procuratore nobilis memorati, supradictus frater Conradus intencionem suam fundatam asserens per confessionem maxime procuratoris eiusdem, per quam inter cetera constare dicebat, quod predictis fratribus possidentibus casalia memorata, dictus Aymericus, veniens ad ipsa casalia cum armatis, eorundem casalium possessione fratres spoliavit eosdem, diffinitivam sentenciam petiit pro se ferri. Verum predicti nobilis procurator respondit ex adverso, quod idem nobilis non propria auctoritate eorundem casalium possessionem invaserat, sed eam habuerat per executores illustris regis Cypri, domini ut dicebat regni Iherosolymitani, et per decretum regis eiusdem, ad hoc probandum quandam scripturam exhibens ipsius regis sigillo munitam, in qua quidem scriptura continetur expresse, quod idem rex, predicti nobilis conquestione recepta, quod supradicti fratres violenter et iniuste detinebant casalia supradicta, que idem nobilis ad se spectare dicebat, predictis fratribus legitime citatis nec coram eo curantibus comparere, ymmo se per contumaciam absentantibus, eundem nobilem in eorundem casalium possessionem ut rerum sui iuris induxit. Ceterum memoratus frater allegatum decretum supradicti regis, etiamsi esset dominus regni Iherosolimitani, utpote a non competenti iudice interpositum ad excusandam violentam seu iniustam oblationem possessionis dicebat invalidum sive nullum, cum ipsi fratres utpote persone religiose non sub seculari sed sub ecclesiastico debuerant iudice conveniri. Sed ad hoc fuit ex adverso responsum, quod, cum predicta casalia de feodo regni Iherosolimitani existant, coram ipso rege tanquam feodi domino iidem fratres conveniri poterant super ipsis, quin ymmo, etiam si non[2] feodalia existerent; cum tamen idem nobilis super ipsis casalibus querelam deposuerit ut de feodo, debuerant iidem fratres citati citatoris se conspectui presentare, ut saltem de hoc ipso cognosceretur, an ad ipsum regem iurisdictio pertineret; quod cum non fecerint, iure potuit et debuit idem rex propter contumaciam eorundem fratrum in possessionem rerum, de quibus agebatur, inducere causa custodie[3] petitorem. Sane allegationem istam predictus frater Conradus multis rationibus excludere nitebatur asserens, quod idem nobilis de violentia ipsorum fratrum et iniusta detentatione predictorum casalium conquestus fuerat, non de feodo, ut ex predicta scriptura dicebat colligi evidenter, dicens nichilominus, quod iidem[4] fratres ab eodem rege citati proponi fecerant coram eo, quod, cum ipsi essent persone religiose et casalia ipsa res ecclesiastice censerentur, utpote que erant eorum propria et eis in elemosynam assignata, non tenebantur coram eo super eisdem casalibus respondere, quod solum ad excusandam ipsorum fratrum absentiam fecisse dicebat, cum dici non possit, quod iidem[4] fratres, qui se feudatarios dicti regis non esse dicebant, cognitionem ipsius regis super hoc subire deberent, cui ex amissione vel victoria ipsius nobilis videbatur dampnum vel commodum eminere. Quod autem dicitur questionem feodalem coram domino feodi esse tractandam, tunc demum locum habere dicebat, cum vertitur inter duos, qui feodum ab eodem domino recognoscunt, ne alias videatur in causa propria iudicare. Adiecit preterea idem frater, quod scriptura, quam sepe memorati nobilis procurator ad probandum regis decretum produxit in medium interlocutoriam, se[5] diffinitivam potius demonstrabat, que quidem diffinitiva censeri debebat irrita et inanis, cum et per ipsam scripturam appareat et per confessionem procuratoris eiusdem, quod in ipso negotio nec libellus datus nec lis exstitit contestata[6]. Nos igitur auditis et intellectis hiis et aliis, que partes voluerunt dicere coram nobis, et fideliter domino pape relatis, de ipsius domini pape mandato dictum Perinum procuratorem dicti nobilis procuratorio nomine pro eo, et ipsum nobilem per eum ad restitucionem predictorum casalium et fructuum perceptorum ex ipsis casalibus per quoscunque annos, videlicet in tribus milibus bisanciis pro quolibet anno, predicto fratri Conrado procuratori dictorum magistri et fratrum procuratorio nomine pro eis, et eidem domui sententialiter condempnamus in scriptis, pro expensis autem factis in lite taxacione prehabita et iuramento ab eodem fratre Conrado prestito iam dictum Perinum pro ipso nobili et eundem nobilem per ipsum condempnamus in centum libris Proveniensibus predicto fratri Conrado nomine dictorum magistri et fratrum et ipsi magistro et fratribus persolvendis. Actum Rome in hospitio nostro apud ecclesiam sancti Clementis, presentibus venerabili patre domino Fulgerio episcopo Perusino, Alberto Azarii advocato curie, Iohanne Leccatorno canonico Placentino, magistro Garsia Yspano canonico Ilerdensi, Philippo de Pixano canonico Nymociensi, Raimondino clerico episcopi et Gifredino de Vezano notario nostro. In cuius rei testimonium et memorie future cautelam has literas inde scribi et publicari fecimus per eundem Gifredinum notarium et sigilli nostri munimine roborari, anno a nativitate domini m° cc° liiii° indiccione xii^a^ xi° kalendas marcii, pontificatus Innocentii pape quarti anno undecimo. — Lecta et recitata fuit predicta sentencia in scriptis per eundem dominum cardinalem coram predictis testibus et me predicto Gifredino de Vezano imperiali auctoritate notario, qui predicta omnia de mandato ipsius domini cardinalis scripsi et in publicam formam redegi meo signo et nomine confirmando.

Continetur in n. 107; v. cl. Meckelburg legit: Zacharum. 1. protestata A. 16. 2. supplevi. 3. custodire A. 16. 4. idem A. 16. 5. sed A. 16. 6. lex exstitit contesta A. 16.

---

107. *1254 febr. 27 Laterani. Innocentius IV confirmat Ottoboni cardinalis sententiam definitivam inter ordinem h. s. M. Th. et Aimericum Barlays de casalibus Arabie et Zachanim d. d. 1254 febr. 19 (n. 106).*

Innocentius episcopus servus servorum dei dilectis filiis magistro et fratribus hospitalis sancte Marie Theuthonicorum Iherosolymitani in Accon salutem et apostolicam benedictionem. Ea, que iudicio vel concordia terminantur, firma debent et illibata persistere, et, ne in recidive contentionis scrupulum relabantur, apostolico convenit presidio communiri. Sane in causa, que inter vos ex una parte et nobilem virum Aymericum Barlays Acconensis diocesis super casalibus Arabie et Zachanim ad vos spectantibus, quibus idem nobilis vos contra iusticiam spoliari procurans ea detinebat in vestrum preiudicium occupata, et rebus aliis ex altera vertebatur, dilectum filium nostrum O(ttobonum), sancti Adriani diaconum cardinalem, dedimus auditorem, qui cognitis eiusdem cause meritis et relatis fideliter coram nobis, ac procuratoribus utriusque partis presentibus dictum nobilem ad restitucionem dictorum casalium et fructuum exinde perceptorum vobis per diffinitivam sentenciam ac pro expensis in lite factis taxacione prehabita et iuramento a procuratore vestro prestito in certa summa pecunie condempnavit, prout in patentibus litteris cardinalis eiusdem confectis exinde ac[1] suo sigillo signatis plenius continetur. Nos itaque vestris supplicationibus inclinati sentenciam ipsam proinde latam ratam et firmam habentes eam, non obstante partis adverse ad nos ab eadem sentencia interiecta appellatione[2], quam velud frivolam non duximus admittendam, auctoritate apostolica confirmamus et presentis scripti patrocinio communimus. Tenorem autem litterarum ipsarum de verbo ad verbum presentibus fecimus annotari, qui talis est: *(sequitur n. 106).* Nulli ergo omnino hominum liceat hanc paginam nostre confirmacionis infringere vel ei ausu temerario contraire. Si quis autem hoc attemptare presumpserit, indignationem omnipotentis dei et beatorum Petri et Pauli apostolorum eius se noverit incursurum. Datum Laterani iii° kalendas marcii, pontificatus nostri anno ut supra.

E copiario A. 16 Regimontani archivi p. 30 sq. inter Veneta mecum communicavit v. cl. A. Meckelburg. 1. a A. 16. 2. suppletum.

---

108. *1257 („1256") ianuarii 4 Saidae. Iulianus dominus Saidae et Bellifortis donat Annoni magistro et fratribus hospitalis s. M. Theutoniorum terram suam Souf.*

Je Julien, seignior de Saiete et de Beaufort, faz a savoir a toz ceaus qui sunt et qui avenir sunt, que je doing et otroi et conferme a frere Anne honorable maistre de l'hospital de nostre dame des Alemans en Jerusalem et as freres de cele meisme maison, qui sunt et seront, en aumone perpetuel quitement et franchement por l'arme de moi et de mon pere et de ma mere et de mes ancestres et por le bon servise, que le devant dit maistre et les freres m'ont fait, toute ma terre dou Souf, que je au jor tenoie et devoie tenir, et toute la seigniorie et toute la justise et toutes les raisons et totes les droitures, que je et mez heirs avons et avoir devons en cele meisme terre, ce est a savoir Bullel, Mahasser le grant, Delbon, Bethlon, le Barouc, le Foraidis, Queffra, la Zembacquie, Haynzehalta[1], Haynhamer, Hainouzeih, la Orhanie, Bemmorhei, le Haddis, Ebbrih, Boussaih, la Fornie, Bahaclin, le Doeyir, Bossonnaih le haut, Caffar, Hommeledmith, Dardorith, Bessetfin, la Messeytie, Sarsorith, Tesfahta, la Homaira, la Loaize, la Fessaiteca, Kaffarhammie, Daircossa, la Bakha, la Kanzirie, Benemssin, Bessemharrir, la Mougarie, la Corratye, Bessonnaih le bais, Hommelmeguithe, Bahnayl, la Cuneyesce, et touz les cazaus et gastines nomees ou non nomees de cele meisme terre et totes lor apartenances et totes lor raisons et toutes lor dreitures quels que elles soient et ou quelles soient, en homes et en femes, en enfans, en bois, en aigues, en rivieres, en molins, en montaignies, en plains[2], en terres laborees et non laborees et en toutes les autres raisons, que la devant dite terre et casaus et lor apartenances ont et doivent avoir. Et por ce que je vueill, que ceste miene aumone desus dite et cestui mien don soient fermes et estables a toz jors mais al devant dit maistre et a ses freres en la maniere que il est desus devise et que je ne mes heirs ne autre por nos ne nul de nos successors en aucuns tens ne puissons aler a l'encontre de aucune chose fut en tout ou en partie, ai je fait cest present privilege seeller de mon seel de plomb empraint en mes droiz coinz de ma seigniorie de Saiete avec la garentie de mes homes, des quels ces sunt les nons: Johan de la Tor, conestable; Johan Harneis, mareschal; Felipe de Beaufort; Jofroi de Viliers; Hue de Viliers; Berteleme Monge; Felipe Hardel; Ote; Johan Genevois; Pierre d'Ancone; Johan de Nibar; Johan Pisan le vieill. Ce fu fait a Saiete en l'an de l'incarnasion[3] nostre seignior Jesu Crist m cc et lvi au quatorsime jor del mois de jenvier.

III, 160. Subtus in margine alia manu scriptum est fol. 160: ce sont le(s) gastines, de qui la question est dou Temple et de nous, qui sont sur le damer, des quels ce sont les nons: la Delhemie; la Lehedie; la Mechaiera; Margekeneiroh. 1. hayn7ehalta B. 2. plais B. 3. B.

---

109. *1257 („1256") ianuarii 4 Saidae. Iulianus dominus Saidae et Bellifortis vendit domui hospitalis S. Mariae Theutonicorum pro 23,500 bisantiorum sarracenatorum terram Souf cum pertinentiis, quam praecedenti alias quidem consono diplomate eidem videtur donare. A quo differunt quae sequuntur verba.*

Sayete. — que je ai vendu et otroie — perpetuaument a — henorable — serunt quitement et franchement por xxiiij mile besanz sarrasinas au poiz de Acre, les quels besanz je ai euz et receuz enterinement bien contes et bien pesez et despendus au profit de ma terre, toute ma terre — tote — tote — totes — toutes — mes heirs — Bulbel, Mahascer le grant — Haynzehalta — Haynoreih, la Carhanie — Bossaih — le Doeir — Cafarhommel Edmith — la Messeitie — la Fossaiteca Cafarhamme — Bennemssin, Bessemharir, la Mougairie, la Conrathie — Hummelmegunthe — toz les casaus — luer apartenances — et totez luer droitures quelz que eles soient et ou que eles — enfanz — montaignes — totez — luer — avoir. Et ce je l'ai fait por mon profit et por payer mes dettes, et por ce que je vueil, que ceste vente desus dite tot en la maniere que il est desus devise, soit ferme et estable a toz jors mais au — freres et que je ne — aucun — tot — sceller — ceel — seignorie — noms Jahan — Otte — vieil — incarnation — jenvier (in fine non valente scriptura lusum est: meis).

III, 160v.

---

110. *1257 ianuarii 4 Saidae. Iulianus dominus Saidae et Bellifortis donat hospitali s. Mariae Theutonicorum fortalicium dictum Cavam Tyronis.*

Je Julien, seignor de Saiete et de Beaufort, faz a savoir a toz ceaus qui sunt et qui avenir sunt, que je doing et otroi et conferme a frere Anne henorable maistre de l'hospital de nostre dame des Alemans en Jerusalem et as freres de cele meisme maison, qui sunt et serunt, en aumone perpetuel quitement et franchement por l'arme de moi et de mon pere et de ma mere et de mes ancestres et por le bon servise, que le devant dit maistre et les freres m'ont fait, ma forteresse, la quele est apelee Cave de Tyron, et totes ses raisons, que je et mes heirs avons et avoir devons en cele desus dite cave. Et por ce que je vueil, que ceste miene aumone desus dite et cestui mien don soient fermes et estables a toz jors mais au devant dit maistre et a ses freres en la maniere que il est desus devise et que je ne mes heirs ne autre por nous ne nul de nos sucsessors en aucun tens ne puissons aler a l'encontre, ai je fait cest present privilege sceller de mon seel de plomb empraint en mez droiz coinz de ma seigniorie de Saiete avec la garentie de mes homes, des quels ces sunt les noms: Johan de la Tor, conestable; Jofroi de Viliers; Hue de Viliers; Berteleme Monge. Ce fu fait en Saiete en l'an de l'incarnation nostre seignior Jesu Crist m cc et lvi au quatorsime jor del mois de jenvier.

III, 161. Cf. Scriptores rerum Prussicarum I, 633.

---

111. *1257 ianuarii 10 Saidae. Iulianus dominus Saidae et Bellifortis donat domui hospitalis s. Theutonicorum in Ierusalem a Iohanne de Schouf quondam possessa feoda Schuf et Gezin.*

Je Julien, seignor de Sayete et de Biaufort, faz a savoir a toz ceaus qui sont et qui avenir sunt, que je ai done et done a frere Anne honorable meistre de l'hospital des Alemans en Jerusalem et as freres de cele meisme maison, qui sunt et seront, en aumohne perpetuel quitement et franchement por l'arme de moi et de mon pere et de ma mere et de mes ancestres et por le bon servise, que le devant dit maistr et les freres m'ont fait, toute la seignorie et totes les raisons et totes les droitures, que je et mes heirs avons et avoir devons as fiefs dou Sschůf et de Gezin et totez lor apartenances, que sire Johan dou Sschůf au jor tenoit et devoit tenir de moi, c'est a savoir: Gezin, Esfif, la Judede, Haddris, Hazibe, Batun, Tyrun, Bikicin, Bennuefe, Elgabetye, Kaytule, Eschemacha, Elcolea, Toura, Elmizraa, Elhozaein, Niha, Elmecheirfe, Bether, Gebbach, Moreste, Elmunzura, Baadran, Elchoreibe, Elmohtara, Butine, Elmuchetne, Sarsurit, Ethchit, Beddei, Cafernebrach, Deir Zekarim, Mechacerbenni, Be'lhun, Deir Elchamar, Deir Bebe, Elbegelie, Boocosta, Ezsaronie, Elkardie, le jardin de Besel et totes lor gastines et totes lor apartenances et totes lor raisons et totes lor droitures, quelez que elles soient et ou que elles soient, en homes et en femes, en enfanz, en bois, en agues, en rivieres, et en molins, en montaignes, en plains, en terres laborees et non laborees et en totes les autres raisons, que les devant diz deus fiefs et lor apartenances ont et doivent avoir. Et por ce que je vueill, que ceste miene aumohne desus dite et cestui mien don soient fermes et estables a toz jors mais au devant dit maistre et a ses freres en la maniere, que il est desus devise, ai je jure sur les saintes evangiles por moi et por mes heirs et por mes successors de tenir et de faire tenir et de garder perpetuelment sanz aler a l'encontre de aucune chose en tot ou en partie totez les choses desus devisees. Et a greignior seurte de cestui fait ai je fait faire cest present escrit et seeller de ma boulle de plomb empreint de mes droiz coinz de ma seignorie de Seyete. Ce fu fait a Sayete en ma cort en la presence et en la garentie de mes homes liges, des quelz ce sunt les nomes: Johan de la Tor, conestable; Johan Harneis, mareschal; Phelippe de Biaufort, mon frere; Joffroi de Viliers; Eude de Creel; Maquaire; Raul de Hachif; Hue de Vilieres; Berteleme Monge; Phelippe Hardel. Ce fu fait en l'an de l'incarnation nostre seignor m cc et lvi au disime jor del meis de jenvier.

III, 164. Cf. l. c.

---

112. *1257 septbr. Accon. Florentii Acconensis episcopi compositio cum Annone magistro domus hospitalis S. Mariae Theutonicorum inita.*

Universis presentes litteras inspecturis Florentius miseratione divina episcopus et capitulum Acconenses salutem in domino sempiternam. Noverit universitas vestra, quod, cum inter nos pro nobis et ecclesia nostra Acconensi ex parte una et religiosos viros fratrem Annonem magistrum et conventum domus hospitalis sancte Marie Theutonicorum Ierosolimitani nunc commorantes in Accon pro se et domo sua ex altera super decimis et rebus aliis et peticionibus hinc inde questio verteretur, que petitiones tales erant: Petebamus namque nos episcopus prephatus pro nobis et ecclesia nostra a magistro et conventu dicte domus Theutonicorum marcham unam argenti pro ecclesia sua ratione cuiusdam compositionis dudum inter predecessores eorum et nostros facte et habite annuatim in festo purificationis Acconensi ecclesie persolvendam. Item petebamus manualem obediencium nobis exhiberi a capellano, qui ad serviendum eidem ecclesie pro tempore assumeretur, et quod idem capellanus ad vocationem nostram veniret et nostra successorumque nostrorum interdicta servaret et ea exequeretur, in quorum possessionem vel quasi restitui petebamus. Item petebamus de terris, arboribus et vineis sitis in diocesi Acconensi, quas iidem magister et fratres propriis sumptibus et laboribus excolebant et excolunt, decimas integras nobis solvi, in quarum possessione[1] vel quasi iuris percipiendi ipsas decimas dicebamus Acconensem ecclesiam extitisse. Item petebamus decimas integras de omnibus terre nascentibus quorundam casalium videlicet de Bassa et de Massob. Item de terris et proventibus casalium, que vocantur Cafriasim et Busenen et Saphet, integras decimas petebamus. Item petebamus restitui ad possessionem vel quasi iuris percipiendi decimas de casali, quod vocatur Noye; a quo iure per dictos fratres dicebamus spoliatam fuisse Acconensem ecclesiam. Item petebamus, quod dicti magister et fratres compellerent suos villanos et rusticos, quibus possessiones et terras suas sitas in diocesi Acconensi excolendas committunt, solvere integras decimas nobis et successoribus nostris nomine ecclesie Acconensis de illa portione fructuum, quam habent et retinent dicti rustici et villani pro agricultura seu quacunque alia ratione. Item petebamus integram decimam de proventibus molendinorum suorum, appaltis et aliis redditibus nobis et ecclesie Acconensi persolvi. Item petebamus restitui ad possessionem vel quasi iuris percipiendi decimas in domo episcopali, que est in Castro Regis, fructuum et proventuum ex omnibus pertinenciis dicti Castri Regis sitis in diocesi Acconensi; item et fetuum et fructuum, animalium et avium, que omnia dicebamus dictos magistrum et fratres solvere debere in domo predicta, ad quorum omnium vecturam usque ad locum predictum petebamus dictos magistrum et fratres condempnari debere. Item petebamus dictos magistrum et fratres condempnari ad solutionem quadraginta bisantiorum annuatim pro faciendo annuali Benencase, burgensis Castri Regis, qui legaverat in ultima voluntate sua eosdem bisantios recipiendos super possessionibus suis, quas dicebamus eosdem magistrum et fratres postmodum acquisivisse. Item petebamus, ut magister et fratres predicti nullatenus molestarent nos aut successores nostros exigendo a nobis vel successoribus nostris aliquam dricturam, exactionem vel tributa pro rebus et victualibus emptis ad usum nostrum et familie nostre in terra eorum. Quas quidem decimas et marcham petebamus tam pro preterito tempore quam etiam pro futuro.

Ex adverso vero petebant magister et fratres predicti pro se et domo sua a nobis episcopo et capitulo Acconensibus pro nobis et ecclesia nostra sibi restitui et solvi viginti iiii^or milia bisantiorum sarracenatorum pro decimis, quas dicebant se solvisse ecclesie Acconensi indebite et ignoranter de terris et possessionibus, quas ipsi propriis laboribus et sumptibus excolebant, et de novalibus et nutrimentis animalium et virgultis tam in pecunia quam aliis rebus. Item petebant domos, vineas, ortos et agros sitos in Castro Regis cum pertinentiis eorum, quos tenemur ad eos et domum suam iure dominii vel quasi pertinentes et nos ad restituendum sibi res ipsas condempnari et compelli cum fructibus inde perceptis et qui percipi potuerunt, quos extimabant triginta milia bisantiorum sarracenatorum. Item petebant nos condempnari sibi pro quadam contumacia in mille bisantiis sarracenatis.

Tandem mediantibus amicis communibus super omnibus predictis et aliis quibuscunque peticionibus, que ex quacunque causa tam nobis episcopo et capitulo pro nobis et ecclesia nostra contra predictos magistrum et fratres et domum eorum, quam eis pro se et domo sua contra nos et ecclesiam nostram inter nos vicissim competunt et competere possunt usque in hodiernum diem quantum ad ea, que ipsi perpetuo possident, pro bono pacis amicabilis compositio intervenit, prout inferius continetur, videlicet quod dicti magister et fratres et successores eorum dabunt et solvent nobis episcopo pro nobis et ecclesia nostra et successoribus nostris quintam decimam partem nomine decimarum de omnibus laboribus suis, sive ipsimet laborent sive per alios faciant laborari, de terris et de vineis et de omnibus illis rebus, quas ipsi recipiunt de suis villanis, scilicet de frumento, ordeo, ciceribus, lenticulis, fabis, avena, meliqua, coctono, milio, mais, pisaus, gerbains, et de omnibus, que plantantur et seminantur in terra, salvis dricturis, que sunt tales: portagium herbarum ad areas, scribanagium, mensuragium, gardagium, scenequie, que libere levabuntur, item et dricture Ysembardi et Lamberti in casalibus, in quibus recipi consueverunt tempore huius compositionis. Et hee res capientur ex parte dicte domus, antequam dicta quinta decima recipiatur; et de toto residuo, quod ipsi recipient pro recta portione sive partison, solverit dictam quintam decimam nobis episcopo vel ecclesie Acconensi. Et debent solvere dictam quintam decimam de vino suarum vinearum et de charagiis et de oleo suorum villanorum de tanto quantum inde recipiunt et de suomet oleo, de computagio caprarum, de apibus et de exeniis villanorum suorum per tres anni terminos stabilitis, scilicet in natali, carnisprivio et pasca; de gallinis, ovis et de caseo, pro quibus denarii in aliquibus locis recipiuntur et in aliquibus non recipiuntur, et de omnibus arboribus exceptis arboribus iardinorum exceptorum, et de arboribus villanorum suorum in tantum, quantum ipsi inde recipient, et de omnibus aliis rebus, que de terra nascuntur exceptis nemoribus sue montane, quam modo tenent, reservato nobis, episcopo et successoribus nostris, usu in dictis nemoribus ad ardendum et paxillos faciendum. Et ipsi et successores sui debent facere portari dictam quintam decimam de omnibus suis casalibus, que sunt ultra caveam, suis sumptibus ad domum episcopalem in Castro Regis. Et nos episcopus, si placuerit nobis, dabimus unum panem cuilibet villano, qui dictam quintam decimam[2] portabit. Etiam, si aliquo modo contingeret, quod dicti magister et fratres plantarent vel plantari facerent canamellas vel salinas facerent aut fieri facerent in aliquo casalium suorum et pertinentiis eorundem, ipsi et successores sui de tanta terra, quantam dicte canamelle et saline tenuerint vel occupaverint, dictam quintam decimam[2] solvent, medietatem videlicet in frumento et medietatem in ordeo iuxta extimationem virorum bonorum, acsi dicte terre essent frumento vel ordeo seminate. De omnibus vero molendinis suis, ubicunque sunt et erunt, de iardinis quoque, de molendinis et arboribus tocius cavee in tantum, quantum cavea protenditur in longum ab ortu magni fontis usque ad territorium Manuetti et in latitudine tantum, quantum unus homo, qui esset in fundo cavee, super ripam aque posset videre in altum ex utraque parte, nihil debent nobis et successoribus nostris solvere nomine decimarum. Et, si contingeret, quid intra fines predictos vinee plantarentur aut aliquid de seminibus superius nominatis seminaretur, ipsi et successores sui dictam quintam decimam de eis solvent nobis episcopo et ecclesie Acconensibus. Et iidem magister et fratres et successores eorum nihil solvent de suis iardinis irriguis vel abeveraiz, que ipsi inpresentiarum habent vel etiam fecerint et habuerint in futurum in terra, quam nunc tenent, nec ipsi et successores eorum exigent vel petent aliquam dricturam nec consuetudinem vel exactionem de rebus, quas nos episcopus vel alius pro nobis ememus vel emi fecerimus in terra eorum pro victu nostro. Et ipsi et successores eorum tenentur nos et successores nostros super burgesiis et tenimentis et una pecia terre, quam tenemus ab eis perpetuo ad censum unius bisantii sarracenati pro quolibet anno, que nunc habemus et tenemus in Castro Regis, nullatenus molestare. Et de omnibus istis rebus, sicut superius describuntur, ipsi et successores sui tenentur solvere et reddere, sicut superius est expressum, videlicet de omnibus terris tam de novalibus quam de aliis conquestibus, que nunc habent et habebunt perpetuo in tota diocesi Acconensi sive acquirantur per donum vel per emptionem vel per censum perpetuum seu per concambium aut per appaltum perpetuum, et specialiter de casalibus, que vocantur Labassa, Massob, Noye, Sapheth, Caffriasy et Busenen et de omnibus aliis casalibus et eorum pertinenciis ubicunque fuerint in episcopatu Acconensi, salvis rebus que superius eximuntur et excipiuntur. Insuper dicti magister et fratres et successores eorum tenentur solvere annuatim nobis, episcopo et capitulo, unam marcham argenti in die purificationis beate virginis in thesauro suo Acconensi, et renuntiant pro se et successoribus suis omnibus rationibus et exceptionibus, privilegiis obtentis et obtinendis, impetratis et impetrandis, concessis quocunque modo et concedendis et iuribus et aliis omnibus rebus, per quas predicte res et sepe dicta pax poterunt impediri vel turbari in toto vel in parte hoc salvo, quod ipsi et successores eorum suis privilegiis contra omnes alios possint uti, tamen contra nos et ecclesiam nostram, quantum ad dictam compositionem et pacem, privilegiis non utentur. Item ipsi magister et fratres pro se et successoribus suis et domo sua et nos episcopus et capitulum pro nobis et ecclesia nostra et successoribus nostris omnibus litibus, querelis et controversiis motis et habitis inter nos quantum ad ea, que perpetuo possident, renuntiamus expresse. Dictam autem compositionem et omnia et singula supra scripta nos episcopus et capitulum Acconenses pro nobis et ecclesia nostra et successoribus nostris promittimus prephatis magistro et conventui pro se et domo sua et eorum successoribus per stipulationem sollempnem perpetuo bona fide inviolabiliter servare et non contravenire per nos vel per alium seu alios aliquo ingenio, machinatione vel arte sub pena trium milium marcharum argenti. Quam penam nos episcopus et capitulum pro nobis et ecclesia nostra et successoribus nostris, si contra predicta vel aliquid predictorum faceremus vel veniremus per nos vel per alium seu alios aliquo modo promittimus et tenemur dictis magistro et conventui eorumque successoribus observantibus supra scripta persolvere, obligantes pro dicta pena omnia bona nostra et ecclesie nostre. Qua pena soluta vel non dicta compositio et singula contenta in ea nihilominus firma permaneant et in suo robore perseverent. Et nos episcopus sepe dictus pro nobis et capitulo nostro omnia et singula superius annotata promisimus firmiter observare et promittimus super hiis omnibus et singulis pro nobis et successoribus nostris a nobis corporali prestito iuramento in anima nostra et capituli antedicti. Quam compositionem placuit nobis episcopo et capitulo et dictis magistro et conventui etiam per summum pontificem confirmari. In cuius et quorum omnium testimonium et munimen presentem cartam plumbeis bullis nostris fecimus communiri. Actum fuit Accon anno domini millesimo ducentesimo quinquagesimo septimo mense septembri presentibus magistro Guillelmo, decano; dominis Adam, archidiacono; Bernardo, cantore; Iohanne, thesaurario; Gerardo, canonicis[3]; fratribus Evrardo, magno preceptore; Arnoldo, thesaurario; Ulrico, Winando et Frederico, fratribus domus Theutonicorum predicte.

III, 165 v. 1. possessionem B. 2. quintadecimam B. 3. canonibus.

113. *1257 nov. 1 Accon. Canonici Montis Sion vendunt domui hospitalis s. Mariae Theutonicorum in Accon domos suas cum solo et plateis et aedificiis hac in urbe.*

Noverint universi presentes pariter et futuri, quod nos Terricus divina permissione humilis abbas et conventus ecclesie Montis Syon de consensu et voluntate reverendi patris et domini nostri Iacobi, dei gracia sancte Ierosolimitane ecclesie patriarche, apostolice sedis legati, auctoritatem prestantis vendimus imperpetuum, tradimus, damus et concedimus religiosis viris fratri Annoni magistro et conventui domus hospitalis sancte Marie Theotonicorum in Accon domos cum solo, plateis et hedificiis, que habemus et tenemus nomine dicte ecclesie nostre ante domum ipsorum in Accon, que infra hos terminos continentur: ab oriente est via regalis et domus hospitalis sancti Iohannis Ierosolimitani, que fuerunt quondam Montis Thabor, contigue cum predictis domibus; ab occidente est domus predictorum magistri et conventus; a septentrione est similiter via regalis; a meridie est barbacana eorundem. Item vendimus, tradimus et concedimus[1] eisdem magistro et conventui quandam aliam domum parvam, que habet tales confines: ab oriente et meridie est via regalis; ab occidente est domus ipsorum magistri et conventus, que fuit quondam comitis Ioscelini; a septentrione est domus Albrici Botterii. Que omnia nomine ecclesie nostre vendimus, tradimus, damus et concedimus predicto magistro et conventui et successoribus eorum nomine domus eorum cum omni iure, commodo et utilitate et cum omnibus ad ipsas domos, plateas et solum pertinentibus liberas et absolutas ab omni honere servitutis, pro trecentis et novem bisanciis sarracenatis ad pondus Accon nobis et successoribus nostris annuatim in perpetuum integre et sine diminutione aliqua persolvendis et percipiendis in thesauro predictorum magistri et conventus Accon in tribus terminis inferius nominatis, videlicet per totum mensem februarii centum et tres bisantios et per totum mensem iunii centum et tres bisantios et per totum mensem octubris centum tres bisantios. Nos autem abbas et conventus predicti promittimus et tenemur predictis magistro et conventui eorum successoribus pro nobis et successoribus nostris nomine prephate ecclesie nostre predictas domos, plateas et solum cum hedificiis suis ab omni persona et universitate in iure defendere et garentire et eos in ipsis seu de ipsis non impedire sub pena sexcentorum bisantiorum sarracenatorum, concedentes predictis magistro et conventui, ut in predictis domibus, plateis et solo possint intrare et illa possidere et in eis edificare ac de ipsis facere sicut in suis et de suis, quando voluerint et viderint expedire, promittentes quoque ipsis firmiter et expresse, quod contra predicta vel aliquid de predictis nunquam veniemus nec per nos nec per alium, nec procurabimus, ut contractus huiusmodi rescindatur, sub pena predicta; qua soluta vel non omnia et singula superius annotata semper in suo robore perseverent. In quorum omnium testimonium et perpetuam firmitatem presentes litteras plumbea bulla nostra fecimus communiri, ac reverendus pater dominus patriarcha superius nominatus, qui auctoritatem suam huic contractui prestitit atque dedit, in testimonium fecit apponi presentibus plumbeam bullam suam. Actum et datum fuit Accon anno domini m° ducentesimo quinquagesimo septimo in kalendis novenbris.

III, 167 v. 1. cocedimus B.

---

114. *1258 martii 20. Iulianus dominus Saidae et Bellifortis confirmat domui hospitalis s. Mariae Theutonicorum casale Cafar-facouh a Iohanne de Turre, comestabulo Saidensi, et Isabella uxore emtum.*

Je Julien, seignor de Seete et de Biaufort, faz a saveir a toz ceaus qui sont et seront, que vindrent en ma presence et de ma cort Johan de la Tor, conestable de Seete, et Ysabeau, sa loyal espouse, conestablesce de Seete, et por les biensfaiz et les bontes, que il ount receu de la sainte maison de l'hospital de nostre dame des Alamans de Jerusalem, donerent et otroyerent par lor bone volente en perpetuel aumohne franchement et quitement sainz servise et sains aucune maniere de redevance a frere Anne honorable maistre de la dite maison et as freres de cele meisme maison qui sont et seront et a luer successors totes les raisons et les droitures, que il et lor heirs ont et avoir devont au casal, qui a nom Cafar-facouh, qui est en la terre dou Sschůff, o totes ses apartenances et o[1] tot son terroir et o totes ses divises et o totes ses possessions et ses teneures et ses raisons et ses droitures quelque elles seent et en quelque leuc que elles soient en homes, en femes, en enfanz, en terres laborees et non laborees, en plains, en montaignies, en montees, en valees, en bois, en rivieres, en pasturages, en aigues, en molins, en arbres, en vignies, en cortilz, en jardins, en chemins et hors chemins et en totes autres choses, que ici sunt moties et non moties. Por le quel devant dit don et aumohne le devant dit conestable et sa devant dite espouse reconurent devant mei et devant ma dite cort, que il dou devant dit maistre de la dite maison des Alemans et des freres de cele meesme mayson ont receu quatre mile besanz sarracinas au pois d'Acre, les quelex besanz il reconurent et confesserent que il les avoient euz et receuz enterinement bien pesez et bien nombrez et renoncierent por auz et por loı heirs a toutes ecceptions, que il ne lor heirs ne puissent dire ne se defendre, que il n'en ayent euz et receuz les besanz devant diz enterinement. Por la quel chose le devant nome conestable et sa dite espouse por aus et por lor heirs promirent et sont tenuz al devant dit maistre et as freres de la dite maison, qui sont et qui seront, que il et lor heirs garentiront et defenderont et maintendront le devant dit casal a la mayson devant dite ou toutes ses apartenances ensi com il est dessus devise de toz contensons, de toz chalonges, de toutez requestes, de toz travailes a lor propre despens contre toutez genz cristienees, qui por achason de l'aumohne et dou don, que il lor ont done dou dit casal, les travaillieroient ou vorroient travaillier. Et por ce que cest devant dit don et aumohne furent faiz en ma presence et de ma cort, je por la priere dou dit conestable et s'espouse devant dite et por l'amor, que je ai a la devant dite mayson, l'ay otroie et vueil, que il soit estable a toz jors mais ensi com il est dit dessus et le conferme par cest privilege pardurablement ensi, que je ne nul de mes heirs ne nule autre persone ne puissons aler a l'encontre en tout ou en partie, ai je fait faire cest present privilege et seeller de ma boule de plomb empreint de mes drois coinz de ma seignorie de Seete. Ce fu fait en l'an de l'incarnation nostre seignor Jhesu Crist m et cc et lvii mercredi a xx jors del mois de mars. Et ce sont les garens: Phelippe de Biaufort; Jofroi de Viliers; Macayre Gile; Berteleme Meinebuef; Eude de Creel; Andre Taillevent; Johan de Fenjon; Gui de Renay; Hue de Viliers.

III, 163 v. Cf. Scr. rer. Pruss. I, 633. Anno 1258 martii 20 dies feria quarta fuit; 1257 tertia. 1. a B.

---

115. *1258 iunii 11. Iulianus dominus Saidae et Bellifortis confirmat domui hospitalis s. Mariae Theutonicorum duo a Iohanne de Schouf emta feoda in terra Schuf.*

Je Juliens, seignor de Seete et de Biafort, faiz a savoir a toz ces, qui cest present escrit verront et oront, que an l'an de l'incarnation de nostre seignor Jhesu Christ m et cc et lvi ou mois de novembre vint a la presence de mon bailli Bartholomeu Monge et de ma cort frier Gautier le commandeor des freres des Alemans de Seete par le commandemant dou maistre et dou convent de la dite maison et sire Jehan dou Schuf, fiz de sire Andre de Schuf, et finerent ansamble por lor bone volunte et par la moie des deus fies, que le devant dit Jehan tenoit et devoit tenir de moi an tel maniere, que les freres de Alemans doivent tenir perpetuament le fie, que il tenoit de moy an la terre de Schuf an caseaus et an gastines et an autres droitures et an raisons et gesin et totes apartenances an caseaus et an gastines et totes lor raisons et totes lor droitures, queque part que elles soient et ou que elles soient, franchement et quitemant sanz servise par ansi que ansi que se devant dit Johan et ses heires apres li doivent recevoir de la dite maison chascun an au tens de trieve m bisans sarazinas au peis d'Acre a paier de trois an trois mois cc et l besanz et au tens de guerre v^{c} besanz a paier as devant diz termes c et xxv besanz franchement et quitemant senz servise a li et a ses heirs. Et sor tot ce le devant dit Jehan et ses heirs doivent retenir a lor ous dez devanz diz Schuf trois gastines, qui sunt pres de la ville de Seete, c'est a savoir la Sauraanie et la Begelie et Bescote, et le jardin et la terre, qui est au plain devant Seete, et les maison, qui sunt dedanz la ville de Seete. Et le devant dit Jehan jurai sor les sainz evangiles de tenir totes les covenances devant dites anterinement senz mal angin. Et de ce sunt garant sire Jofrei de Vilers et Hue sonz fiz et Gui de Mimars et plusors autres. Et por ce que cest fin fui faite par ma volunte et par mon otroi et par la volunte des parties desus nomes et que le devant dit bail avoit eu special commandement sor ce fait de moi, vul je, que elle soit tot jorx ferme et estauble et que nul[1] puise aler a l'ancontre an tot ou am partie et por ce ai je fait faire cest presant escrit seeler de ma bulle de plumb amepraint de mes drois coinz de ma seignorie de Seete. Et cest escrit fui fait an l'an de l'incarnation de nostre seignor Jhesu Christ m et cc et lviii a l'unceisme[2] jor de juing.

III, 162. In margine legitur: „Non valet, quia postmodum fuit factus alius contractus". 1. nus B. 2. unceume B.

---

116. *1258 octobris 9 Accon. Domorum Templi, hospitalis s. Iohannis, s. Mariae Theutonicorum concordia.*

In nomine patris et filii et spiritus sancti. Amen. Notum sit omnibus tam presentibus quam futuris, quod nos frater Thomas Berardi, domus milicie Templi magister humilis, et frater Hugo de Revel, domus hospitalis sancti Iohannis Ierosolimitani magister et pauperum Christi custos, et frater Anno de Sangerhusen, domus hospitalis sancte Marie Theotonicorum magister, de assensu et voluntate fratrum nostrorum ad laudem et gloriam et honorem domini nostri Ihesu Christi ac universalis ecclesie necnon summi pontificis sanctissimi patris nostri Alexandri quarti, cui soli post deum obedire tenemur, et ob salutem et prosperum statum tocius christianitatis, firmam pacem et gratam concordiam facimus et statuimus ac firmiter ordinamus, videlicet de omnibus et singulis questionibus et querelis, que inter nos et fratres nostros in regnis Ierosolimitano, Cypri et Armenie, principatu Antiocheno et comitatu Tripolitano mote sunt et que de cetero movebuntur, exceptis castris, castellaniis, villis et casalibus, que in compositione presenti non intelligantur inclusa, sed alibi per nos vel procuratores nostros in iudicio ecclesiastico vel seculari super eisdem possimus movere questiones, prout nobis et fratribus nostris melius videbitur expedire. Est igitur statutum et ordinatum inter nos et fratres nostros, quod magni preceptores nostrarum domorum regnorum Ierosolimitani, Cypri et Armenie ac etiam terre Antiochene et Tripolitane et castellani Grati et Margati et preceptor Tripolitanus, inter quas aliqua contentio mota erit, super ea vicissim loquantur et tractent ac pro posse nitantur bona fide et diligenti studio ipsam ad concordiam revocare infra mensem proximum, postquam unus predictorum a preceptore denuntiante ipsi preceptori illam controversiam esse motam fuerit requisitus. Si vero non possit concordare de illa discordia sopienda, debent infra unum alium mensem proximum subsequentem eligere de fratribus sue domus in dictis regionibus existentibus unum vel duos prout viderint expedire, ita tamen quod preceptor, qui controversiam motam notificaverit alteri preceptori, super qua concordia est tractanda, primo eligat et nominet arbitros unum vel duos et alter preceptor, cui denuntiatum fuerit, teneatur eligere subsequenter infra tercium diem unum vel duos; qui arbitri iurare debeant tactis sacrosanctis ewangeliis, se super questionibus, controversiis, querelis bona fide et sine strepitu iudicii processuros, ita tamen quod si super controversiis et querelis nequierint concordare, prephati preceptores debent eligere unum ex fratribus tercie domus illius controversie non participis in eisdem regionibus morantem, qui cum aliis arbitris intersit medius et communis ad illam discordiam sopiendam, qui similiter iuret ut alii duo arbitri; et totum et quicquid dicti arbitri vel maior pars eorum pronuntiaverint, statuerint, laudaverint vel dixerint eorum voluntate seu arbitrati fuerint in scriptis vel sine scriptis die feriato vel non feriato, exceptis diebus feriatis ob divinam reverentiam inductis partibus presentibus vel absentibus iuris ordine servato vel non servato, debet a nobis inviolabiliter observari. Arbitri vero communiter electi debent infra mensem unum proximum, ex quo electi fuerint, tractare et inquirere super controversia mota prout viderint expedire, et infra octo dies alios proximo subsequentes debent pronuntiare et statuere id, quod eis vel eorum maiori parti visum fuerit ordinandum. Sed si magni preceptores non concordarent de communi fratre et medio eligendo, debent infra mensem unum subsequentem per se vel alios benigne et humiliter requirere et supplicare magistro vel locum eius tenenti tercie domus, ut dignetur eis concedere unum fratrem pro mota discordia concordanda. Qui teneatur in continenti ex suis fratribus unum eis concedere, quem utrique parti magis viderit et cognoverit esse utilem et communem. In arbitros autem electi si arbitrium recipere recusarent, debeant secundum eorum religionem a suis superioribus recipere arbitrium coherceri nec alibi mittantur, nec etiam aliqua eisdem interim a suis superioribus iniungantur, quorum occasione arbitrium retardetur, donec discordia fuerit terminata; nec possint alia occasione suscipere arbitrium quam infirmitatis evidentissime excusari. Sed si arbitrorum aliquis infirmitate apertissima teneatur, ab illo, qui eum elegerat, alius eligatur, qui sit de religione fratris taliter excusati, ita tamen, quod, si aliquis magistrorum habet necesse aliquem de arbitris supradictis sue domus et magnis negociis sue religionis mittere ultra mare, eidem liceat in passagio, dummodo aliquem ydoneum et utilem ipsi negocio terminando in continenti in locum ipsius missi ultra mare teneatur subrogare. Arbitri vero sic electi possint, dummodo eis videatur expedire, exigere iuramentum de veritate dicenda a preceptoribus et castellanis, fratribus et aliis quibuscunque personis, quos super ipsa controversia scire crediderint veritatem. Sed si contingeret aliquem preceptorum non facere electionem arbitrorum superius annotatam vel non compellere arbitros sibi subditos, ut superius est expressum, per suum superiorem eligere et electos cogere compellatur in continenti omni occasione postposita, et ut intersit tractatui et inquisitioni ac concordie iniende. Verumtamen si aliquis frater de domo Theutonicorum in tercium vel quintum eligatur et propter hoc eum ire oporteat in terram Tripolitanam, Antiochenam vel regnum Cypri, eidem a partibus necessaria ministrentur, dum tamen sit in tercium vel quintum electus, ire teneatur et debeat de voluntate sui magistri vel locum eius tenentis vel alius eque ydoneus. Fratres vero domorum ipsarum debent sibi bona fide ubique consulere, manutenere et iuvare ac sine malo ingenio defensare expensis suarum domorum contra inimicos fidei ortodoxe, ita videlicet, quod in regno Ierosolimitano et in terra Tripolitana et Antiochena et in regno Armenie debet una domus alteram, cum requisita fuerit specialiter, adiuvare bona fide, salva evidenti necessitate regni Ierosolimitani et munitionibus castrorum domus, que taliter fuerit requisita. Attamen si fratres domus Theotonicorum irent in servicium aliarum domorum seu alterius earum in terram Tripolitanam vel Antiochenam, in eo casu providebitur eis de omnibus expensis victualium tam pro fratribus, quam etiam equitaturis ab illis, in quorum servicium eos contigerit accessuros. Si autem per regnum Ierosolimitanum citra flumen Iordanis ad earum alterius requisitionem ire contigerit fratres dicte domus Theutonicorum, sibi per mensem expensis propriis providebunt. Mense vero transacto domus, a qua fuerint requisiti, eisdem in necessariis victualium tam pro fratribus quam equitaturis tenebitur providere et eos per tres menses subsequentes tenere vel amplius ad eorum Theotonicorum beneplacita voluntatis. Utraque autem domus Templi et hospitalis sancti Iohannis cum expensis propriis dictam domum Theotonicorum ubique citra mare defensare tenebitur ac iuvare contra inimicos fidei ortodoxe. Si vero contingat, quod deus avertat, quod aliquis frater alterius domorum iniecerit manus violentas in aliquem fratrem alterius domus, ad peticionem preceptoris, cuius frater passus iniuriam fuerit, procedatur ad emendam iuxta statuta religionis domus illius, cuius frater manus violentas iniecerit, et nichilominus frater, qui iniuriam fecerit, mittatur ad partes alias, ubi domus habeant, ad voluntatem preceptoris fratris illius, qui fuerit passus iniuriam. Statuimus etiam et firmiter ordinamus, quod, si aliquis predictarum domorum preceptor voluerit emere in terra cismarina et Cypro aliquam rem immobilem, cuius precium non excedat quantitatem mille bisantiorum sarracenatorum, preceptor ille, qui talem facere voluerit emptionem, notificet superioribus aliarum[1] domorum existentium in civitate vel loco, ubi fuerit illa res, et post talem denuntiationem preceptores sive[2] superiores, quibus hoc fuerit denuntiatum, non intromittent se de illa re emenda nec prestet preceptori denuntianti aliquod nocumentum. Verumtamen si aliquis preceptor domorum voluerit emere in terra cismarina et Cypri rem aliquam immobilem, cuius precium excedat quantitatem mille bisantiorum sarracenatorum, fiat denuntiatio supradicta et talis emptio sit communis inter ipsas domus, si hoc voluerit domus, que super hoc fuerit taliter requisita, exceptis feudalibus et censivis et dominio sue domus, in quibus alie domus nihil habere possint nec requirere. Si vero dicta emptio rerum immobilium immediate iungeretur alteri domorum, in qua fratres morarentur, illi domui, cui fuerit vicinior dicta emptio, pro ipso precio debeat remanere. Hoc autem expressim ordinamus, quod, si preceptor alterius ipsarum domorum voluerit emere aliqua mobilia in civitate Acconensi sue domui necessaria, preceptores aliarum domorum, postquam eis fuerit nunciatum, non se intromittant nec illam emptionem impediant; verumtamen emptione completa preceptor, qui emerit, preceptoribus aliarum domorum de illa re empta, quotam partem habere voluerit, usque ad terciam pro quolibet preceptore reddere teneatur, soluto sibi precio pro rata, quo constat; exceptis mulis, equis, camelis et asinis et omnibus aliis animalibus vivis, de quibus liceat cuilibet preceptorum emere pro sue beneplacito voluntatis. Insuper statuimus et ordinamus, quod, si contingat aliquam elemosinam vel donationem fieri alicui de tribus domibus super censivis, burgesiis vel signoria aliarum domorum et aliis bonis descendentibus ab eisdem, preceptor domus, cui elemosina seu donatio facta fuerit, teneatur vendere infra annum seculari persone de dominio domus, a qua descendunt predicta, ita quod domus, cui servicium debetur, non possit de hoc servicio sibi debito defraudari. Ac eciam duximus statuendum, quod, si aliquis nostrum habeat in custodia bona alicuius, quicunque sit confrater vel alius et alter nostrum predicta bona capiat vel capi faciat seu preceptorum aliarum domorum, debeat preceptor illius domus, cui bona erant recommendata, petere emendam vel satisfactionem a preceptore alterius domus, qui taliter forefecit, et ipse facere emendam teneatur preceptori petenti secundum ordinacionem et dispositionem superius annotatam, videlicet ut fratres, sicut superius dictum est, cognoscant et diffiniant de plano et sine strepitu iudicii super offensa predicta, dum tamen hoc procedat de voluntate illius, cuius bona fuerint. Quodsi ille, cuius fuerint bona, noluerit hoc, domus illa, que dicta bona habuerit in custodia, non debeat se de hoc intromittere. Si vero contingat aliquos homines, qui sint de tribus domibus, habere discordias inter se super rebus mobilibus vel alia qualibet occasione, preceptores domorum teneantur predictas discordias ac etiam querelantes sedare et pacare secundum dispositionem et ordinationem superius annotatam, salvis hominibus legiis et feudatis, quorum questiones secundum assisias et consuetudines locorum, ubi degunt, debeant terminari. Quodsi homines unius domus ad terram alterius causa morandi venerint, bailivus, in cuius bailiva dicti homines devenerint, bailivo alterius domus significare tenetur infra octo dies post adventum ipsorum a tempore sue sciencie. Qui si probati fuerint homines esse alterius domus, per obedienciam fratris et scribe iuramentum fiat secundum usum regni Ierosolimitani. In terra vero Antiochena et Armenie et Cypri fiat, prout ibi de approbata consuetudine observatur. Postquam probatum fuerit, ut superius est expressum, in terra Tripolitana taliter observetur, quod, si homines alterius domus, qui causa morandi ad terram alterius devenerint, ad requisitionem cuius fuerint homines, arrestentur. Et si aliquo debito fuerint obligati illi domui, congregatis utriusque domus bailivis infra octo dies, quod probatum fuerit per religionis promissionem fratris et iuramentum scribere et servientis infra mensem sequentem illa domus, ad cuius terram devenerint, dictum debitum solvere teneatur, si in terra sua voluerint dicti homines remanere et dictus bailivus ipsos voluerit retinere. Quos quidem si retinere recusaverit, debet eosdem arrestare, donec de dicto debito illi domui, de cuius terra venerint, fuerit satisfactum. Si vero solvere recusaverint homines cum familia et rebus suis bailivo alterius domus, de cuius terra venerint, reddere teneatur. Ac eciam pro bono tocius christianitatis duximus statuendum, quod fratres alterius domus et eorum homines contra reliquam vel reliquas non possint nec debeant arma sumere vel portare. Si vero contingat, quod aliquis nostrum absentet se de partibus cismarinis vel regno Ierosolimitano, se absentans ante suum recessum roget aliarum domorum magistros, ut domus sua sit eisdem specialiter commendata et magistri domus absentantis se teneantur iuxta posse manutenere et defensare atque fratribus eiusdem domus, cum requisiti fuerint, bona fide super petitis suum consilium impertiri, et magister, qui se absentaverit in illis partibus, in quibus moram trahet, alias domos habeat commendatas et eas teneatur defensare et earundem fratribus bona fide consilium exhibere. Duximus etiam ordinandum, quod, si magister et conventus hospitalis sancti Iohannis moveret questionem de obediencia contra magistrum et fratres hospitalis sancte Marie Theotonicorum, neutra predictarum domorum in questione predicta teneatur servare formam compositionis presentis. Duximus etiam statuendum, quod non possit unus nostrum in dominio alterius domus de cetero emere, appaltare, scambire, nec alio modo acquirere rem quamcumque nec rationem seu ius ipsius domus retinere vel habere quoquo modo nec in custodia recipere, nisi de ipsius, cuius fuerit dominium, processerit voluntate. Insuper statuimus et ordinamus, quod, si contingat aliquem magistrum in aliqua domorum de novo creari, magister noviter creatus teneatur bona fide predictam compositionem servare et custodire et custodiri facere, donec vixerit, et hanc compositionem teneatur in suo capitulo generali coram duodecim fratribus de aliis duabus domibus facere recitari et iurare observare hanc compositionem et observari facere. Et nos quolibet anno debemus facere legi et recitari et successores nostri in capitulis nostris generalibus hanc compositionem et precipere et mandare fratribus, ut ab omnibus inviolabiliter observetur. Preceptores autem et castellani cismarini et Cypri domorum nostrarum, quociescunque creati fuerint, simile iuramentum facere teneantur et alios preceptores et castellanos et alios bailivos sibi subditos hanc compositionem et concordiam iurare faciant ipsos inviolabiliter et fideliter observare. Que omnia et singula supradicta de consensu et voluntate fratrum omnium domorum nostrarum convenimus et promittimus invicem per stipulationem sollempnem firmiter attendere, observare et non contravenire. Quod si contra predicta vel aliquid predictorum venerimus et compositionem predictam in partem vel in totum servare recusaverimus, obligamus nos invicem sollempni stipulatione ad penam mille marcharum argenti solvendarum parti servanti predicta. Que pena tociens committatur et solvatur parti servanti predicta, quociens ventum fuerit contra predicta vel aliquid predictorum, et pena predicta commissa soluta vel non, rata maneant nihilominus omnia et singula supradicta; obligantes nobis invicem pro omnibus et singulis supradictis nos et domos nostras et omnia bona domorum nostrarum habita et habenda, immobilia et mobilia ubicunque melius apparentia. Et ad maiorem firmitatem compositionis presentis prepositis et tactis sacrosanctis ewangeliis iuravimus ad sacrosancta dei ewangelia predicta omnia et singula firmiter attendere et observare et non contravenire, hoc acto expressim inter nos, quod illa domus, que in penam inciderit, compellatur predictam penam solvere per alias duas domos, et magistri et conventus predictarum duarum domorum sub obligatione et promissione predicti iuramenti prestiti teneantur cum toto eorum posse compellere domum, que in penam inciderit, penam solvere et predicta servare; renuntiantes invicem omnibus privilegiis et immunitatibus nobis concessis et concedendis, quibus contra predicta vel aliquid predictorum nos et domos nostras tueri aut iuvare possemus. Ut autem de predictis omnibus et singulis haberi valeat in posterum plena fides, presens scriptum exinde fieri fecimus bullis domorum nostrarum plumbeis roboratum. Actum Accon in domo Sepulcri Dominici anno domini millesimo ducentesimo quinquagesimo octavo die nona mensis octobris presentibus venerabili[3] patre domino Iacobo dei gratia patriarcha Ierosolimitano, apostolice sedis legato; nobilibus viris domino Iohanne de Ybellino, domino Azoti, conestabulo et baiulo regni Ierosolimitani; domino Gaufrido de Sarginis, senescalco eiusdem regni; domino Iohanne de Valentinis, domino Cayfe; domino Stephano de Savignino; magistro Guillelmo decano Acconensi et archidiacono Tyrensi et aliis quam pluribus.

III, 168. Addit rubricator: Amen. Notamus hic, quod inter testes Henrici Nazareni archiepiscopi 1259 oct. 24 apud Accon occurrit: „Frater Henricus Theotonicus magnus praeceptor hospitalis in Accon“ sine dubio ordinis s. Iohannis; Pauli I, 163. 1. aliorum B. 2. siues B. 3. supplevi.

---

117. *1261 martio. Iulianus dominus Saidae et Bellifortis donat domui hospitalis s. Mariae Theutonicorum complures possessiones (ut habet argumentum: „cest sie la confirmation de le terre de Sscuff“).*

Sachent tuit cil qui sont et seront, que je Julien, seignor de Seete et de Biaufort, doing et otrei et conferm en aumosne perpetuel a vos, frere Anne, honorable maistre de la maison de l'hospitau de nostre dame des Alemans de Jerusalem, et a vostre covent et a voz successors franchement et quitement sans servise et sans aucune maniere de redevance por l'ame de mei et de mon pere et de ma mere et de mes ancestres por le bon servise que vos le devant dit maistre et les freres de vostre maison avez fait a mei et a mes ancestres, c'est assaveir le Schuf, Henihati, le casau de Niha et ses gastines, Tyron, Achif, le Hossaim, Amellebene, Sarsouris, Elmesetye et le casau Besser et ses gastines, la Meissereyfe, la Gezeyre et le casau la Mensora et le casau Mouresthe et le casau Jebha et sa gastine Geisshou et le casau Baderen et ses gastines, Ouzelle, Houreybe, et la gastine de Beninemre, et Meisquir et la gastine de la Houreibe et le casau la Mohuthara et sa gastine Bede et le casau Bouthme et le Ssouff dou Ssoueizeni et le casau Cafrenebrach et ses gastines, le Doureip et une autre gastine, qui est en la devise de Maassar Beni Elhon et le casau Deir Zecaron et le casau Maassar Beni Elhon et le casau Befedin et le casau Deir Bebe et le casau Deir Elcamar et ses gastines, la gastine de Beni Belmene et la gastine de Beni Nemre et la gastine dou fiz de Negeme et le Sscůff de Medenes et de Beni Eleczem et le casau Gezin et ses gastines, la Couleya, la gastine de Beni Rages et Thora, Bergoiss, la Gabatie, la Ssemeha, Baraquedes, et la gastine de Beni Ougih et le casau Queitoule et sa gastine et le casau Bequicin et sa gastine Delgane et le casau Bennouthe et le casau Eissif et le casau la Gederde et le casau Bathon et le casau Hazibe et le casau Hadous et le casau Elhoussem et la gastine le Ssoucayef o totes luer appartenances et o totes luer gastines et o totes luer possessions et lor teneures[1] et lor raisons et lor dreitures quex qu'eles soient et ou qu'eles soient, en homes, en femes, en enfans, en terres laborees et non laborees, en plains, en montaignes, en montees, en valees, en arbres, en vignes, en jardins, en cortillages, en aigues corrans et non corrans, en fors, en bains, en molins, en bois, en rivieres, en pasturages, en justises, en chemins et hors chemins et en toutes autres choses, qui en ce presente privelige sont moties et non moties, qui a devant diz lues apartienent et doivent apartenir. Et je le devant nome Julien seignor de Seete et de Biaufort por mei et por mes heirs et por mes successors desorendreit otrei et promet et sui tenuz a vos le devant nome maistre et a vostre covent et a voz successors, que mei et mes heirs et mes successors vos garinterons et maintendrons et deffendrons les choses dessus dites totes ensemble et chascun par sei de toz contens, de totes chalonges et de totes requestes contre totes maniers de genz cristienes, qui a l'encontre vos enniroient ou voroient[2] aler par quelque maniere que ce fust. Et por ce que je voil, que les choses dessus dites totes ensemble et chascun par sei soient tenues et maintenues a toz tens fermes et estables, si que mei ne mes heirs ne mes successors ne autre por nos en aucun tens n'en puissons aler a l'encontre en tout ou en partie, l'ai ge jure sur les saintes evangiles de deu de tenir et maintenir totes les choses dessus dites et de non aler ent a l'encontre et de non soffrir, que autre en voise a l'encontre en aucune maniere, et a greignor seurte de vos, le dessus dit maistre, et de vos freres et de voz successors j'ai fait faire[3] ce present privelige buller de plumb empreint en mes drois coins de ma seignorie de Seete o la garentie de mes homes, de quex ce sont les nons: Johan de la Tor, conestable de ma dite seignorie de Seete; Johan Harneis, mareschal; Phelippe de Biaufort, mon frere; Joffroi de Villiers; Phelippe Hardel; Ode de Creel; Guy de Renay et de plusors autres. Ce fu fait en l'an de l'incarnation nostre seignor Jhesu Crist m cc lx ou meis de mars.

III, 163. 1. teneutes B. 2. supplevi: ou voroient. 3. fait fait faire B.

118. *1261 martio. Iulianus dominus Saidae et Bellifortis confirmat domui hospitalis s. Mariae Theutonicorum ab Andrea de Scuf emtum feodum Scuf.*

Je Julien, seignor de Seete et de Biaufort, fas assaveir a touz ceaus qui sont et seront, que André[3] de Schuf vint en la presence de me et de ma cort de ma dite seignorie de Seete et par[1] mon assent et par mon otrei et par ma volente dona et otrea perpetuaument por lui et por ses heirs a vos, frere Anne, honorable maistre de la maison de l'hospitau de nostre dame des Alemans et a vostre covent et a vos successors le fie, que il aveit dou Scuff et de ces appartenances, lequel est en ma dite seignorie de Seete, c'est assaveir le Schuff, de Miedenes et de Beni Eleczem, le casau Gezin et ses gastines, la Couleya, la gastine de Beni Raies et Thora, Bergoiss, la Gabatie, la Ssameha, Baraquedes et la gastine de Beni Ougih et le casau Queitoule et sa gastine et le casau Bequicin et sa gastine Delguane et le casau Bennouthe et le casau Eissif, et le casau la Gedeyde, et le casau Bathon, et le casau Hazibe et li casau Hadous et le casau Elhoussem et la gastine le Ssoucayef, les quex casaus o totes luer appartenances et o totes luer gastines et o totes luer possessions et luer teneures et luer raisons et luer dreitures, quex qu'eles soient e ou qu'eles soient, en homes, en femes, en enfans, en terres laborees et non laborees, en montaignes, en montes, en valees, en arbres, en vignes, en jardins, en cortillages, en aigues corrans et non corrans, en fors, en bains, en molins, en bois, en rivieres, en pasturages, en chemins et en justises et en totes autres choses, qui en ce present prevelige sont moties et non moties, qui a devant diz lues appartienent et doivent appartenir; et ce devant dit don tot en la maniere, com il est dessus devise, a fait le devant dit Andre por lui et por ses heirs a toz tens par mon otrei et par ma volente a vos le devant dit maistre et a vostre covent et a voz successors en eschange de sis mile besanz sarracinans, lex quex besanz il a eu et receu de vos enterinement en la presence de mei et de ma dite cort, et de treis cens besanz sarrazinas chaschun an franchement et quitement sans servise et sans aucune maniere de redevance, les quex vos avez done au devant nome Andre et a ses heirs assenez a receveir chascun an en nostre tresor d'Acre par quatre termines, c'est assaveir chascun treis meis sessante cinc besanz sarrazinas, et ce de la defailleit, sur totes vos autres rentes, que voz avez ou aures ou reaume de Jerusalem as miaus apparans. Et se il aveneit, que il ou ses heirs ne fussent parpaies enterinement des devant diz treis cens bezans par les termes dessus devises vos, le devant dit maistre, et vostre covent por vos et por voz successors dones a mei et a mes heirs desorendreit plain poeir un meis passant apres chascun terme, que il ne sereit paie, si com il est dessus dit, de prendre tant de voz biens, que vos avez en ma seignorie de Seete, que nos le puissons parpaier enterinement de ce, qui lor en defaudreit de lor dite paie; et le dit Andre por lui et por ses heirs vos otroie et promis, que il et ses heirs vos tendront et feront tenir et maintenir a toz tens ferme et estable ce devant dit don et eschange tot en le maniere com il est dessus devise, et se il ne le faiseent, ou il covenist, que par dreit les devant diz casaus tot ensi com il sont dessus devises, ce parteent de voz mains, les devant diz treis cens besanz doivent retorner sans eschampe et sans delai quites et delivres a vos et a voz successors et il et ses heirs sont tenuz de rendre, avant ce que les casaus dessus diz ce partent de vos mains, a vos ou a voz successors le devant nomez vi^{m} besanz sarrazinas, que le dit Andre a eu e receu de vos si com il est dessus dit, et toz les coustes et damanges et messions, que vos et voz freres et voz successors aures eu e receu por achason de ce; et de ce vos ai l'oblie por lui et por ses heirs desorendreit[2] toz luer biens, que il et ses heires ont et auront quex que il soient et ou que il soient as miaus apparans a la conoissance de vos ou de voz successors ou de voz commandemenz et en tel manier, que vos ou voz successors ou voz commandemenz en puissiez prendre et user et tenir et vendre tot a voz voluntez jusques a cele ore, que vos en soies parpaies enterinement de sis m besanz devant diz et de toz les coust et damages et messions, que vos auries eu e receu por achaison de ce devant dit fait si com il est dessus moti, renontiant desorendreit por lui et por ses heirs a totes manieres d'indulgenses et de preveliges, que il ou ses heirs avroient ou avoir porroient quex que il fussent et de costitutions veilles et noveles et leis et decres et decretales et d'usages et d'assises et de totes manieres de deffensions ques qu'eles fussent, por lesquex le dit Andre et ses heirs ce peussent et deussent deffendre ou aler a l'encontre des choses dessus dites ou d'aucunes d'eles en corte laye ou d'yglise; et par dessus tot ce ce sont obligies desorendreit[2] d'estre en la jurediction dou patriarche de Jerusalem ou de celui qui sereit en leu de lui, c'est assaveir en tel manier, que, ce le dit Andre ou ses heirs ou autre por eaus aloient a l'encontre des choses dessus dites, fust en tot ou en partie, que le dit patriarche ou celui qui sereit en leu de lui, les peust et deust escomenier sans assodre les en jusques a ce qu'il eussent enterinement acomplies totes les devant dites choses si com eles sont dessus devisees; et o tot ce a juré[3] le dit Andre sur les saintes evangiles de deu de tenir et maintenir totes les choses dessus dites tot ensi com eles sont devant devisees. Et por ce que ce soit ferm et estable pardurablement, je, le devant nome Julien seignor de Seete et de Biaufort, a la proiere et a la requeste dou dessus nome Andre otrei et conferm les choses devant dites si com eles sont dessus devisees totes ensemble et chascun par sei et vos promet et sui tenuz por mei et por mes heirs et por mes successors, que mei et mes heirs et mes successors vos garentirons et maintenrons et deffendrons totes les choses devant dites en tout et en partie de touz contens, de tous chalonges, de totes requestes contre totes manieres de genz cristiens, qui a l'encontre vos enniroient ou voroient aler par quel que maniere que ce fust. Et a greignor seurte de tote les dessus dites choses ai je fait faire ce present prevelige buller de plumb empreint en mes drois coins de ma seignorie de Seete o la garentie de mes homes, de quex ce sont les noms: Johan de la Tor, conestable de ma dite seignorie de Seete; Johan Harneis, mareschal; Phelippe de Biaufort, mon frere; Joffroi de Villiers; Phelippe Hardel; Odde de Creel; Guy de Renay; et de plusors autres. Ce fu fait en l'an de l'incarnation nostre seignor Jhesu Crist mil et deus cens et lx ou meis de mars.

III, 162. 1. supplevi. 2. tres orendreit B. 3. B.

---

119. *1261 ineunte novembri. Iohannes de Ibelino, dominus de Baruth, vendit domui hospitalis s. Mariae Theutonicorum casalia sua Casalimbert et le Fierge et le Quiebre in territorio Acconensi certis sub conditionibus.*

Sachent tuit cil qui sunt et serunt, que je Johan d'Ibelin seignor de Barut por mei et por mes heirs de mon bon gre et de ma bone volente et por le profit de mei et de mes heirs doing et otrei et conferm a vos frere Herteman de Helderongo, grant comandor de la sainte maison de l'hospital de nostre dame des Alemans ou reiaume de Jerusalem et tenant leuc de maistre, et a vos le covent de cele meimes maison resevant por le maistre de vostre devant dite maison et por vos et por vos suscessors en eschange et en non d'eschange perpetuel tote ma terre, que je ai ou terroer d'Acre, c'est a saver Casalimbert et le Fierge et le Quiebre o totes lor apartenances[1] et o totes lor devises et lor possessions et lor teneures et lor reisons et lor dreitures et lor franchises en casaus, en gastines nomees et non nomees ou que il soient et quels que il soient, qui as desus nomez casaus et a lor partenances apartienent ou apartenir doivent en aucune maniere, franchemant et quitemant sanz servise e sanz aucune meniere de redevance soient en homes, en fames, en enfans, en casaus, en gastines, en terres laborees et non laborees, en plains, en montaignes, en montees, en valees, en bois, en aigues, en riviers, en pasturages, en arbres, en vignes, en cortillez, en jardins, en fours, en molins, en bainz, en fluns, en pecheries, en justises, en dreitures, en chemins, en horschemins, et en totes autres choses et franchises qui sont ci moties et non moties, qui as devant diz casaus et a lor partenances apartienent et doivent apartenir, si com je et autres por mei les avions et tenions et posseions dedenz Acre ou dehors Acre, sauves ii charruees Francoises de terre, que je ai donees en aumosne perpetuel a la maison de l'ospital de saint Johan de Jerusalem, les quels sont mesurees selonc l'ousage dou reiaume de Jerusalem et bonees, des quels je les ai mis en saisine et en teneure, et sont jognant devers ponent a la terre de Manuet, por xi^{m} bezans sarracenas, que vos, le devant dit commandor et tenant luec de maistre, et vos le devant dit covent de la desus dite maison des Alemanz por le devant dit maistre et por vos et por voz successors m'avez done et devez doner a mei et a mes heirs en eschange et en nom d'eschange por les devant dit casaus et apartenances, si com il est desus devise, chascun au perpetuelement de rente franchement et quitement sanz servise et sanz aucune meniere de redevance a faire en totes noz voulentez, sauf ce que totes les asises et les dons, que mon pere et je paions ou faisions paier quels que il soient et a qui que il soient et que je ou mes heirs donrons ou asenerons sus les casaus desus motiz, doivent estre paiez de la some des xi^{m} bezans devant diz, les quels xi^{m} bezans sarracenas vos aves asene desorendreit mei et mes heirs ou noz commandemanz a receveir en vostre tresor d'Acre par tres termines de l'an, c'est a saveir chascun iiii mais iii^{m} vi^{c} lxvi bezans sarracenas et xvi karobles et par cels covenances, que por pestilences ne por faute ne por domage, que Saracins ne autres genz facent es casaus et en la terre devant dite ne es autres leus dou reiaume de Jerusalem ne por rien qui aveigne, ne deit demorer que vos et voz successors ne paiez a mei et a mes heirs les xi^{m} besanz devant diz si com il est desus devise, sauf ce que les devant diz casaus o totes lor apartenances, si com il sont desus devisez, je le devant dit J(ohan) d'Ybelin seignor de Barut por mei et por mes hers otrei et promet et sui tenuz a vos le devant dit commandeor et tenant leuc de maistre et a vos le covent de la devant dite maison des Alemans recevant por le desus nome maistre et por vos et por voz successors de deffendre et garentir de toz domages, qui avenir vos porroient par le seignor dou reiaume de Jerusalem et de touz ceaus et de totes celes, qui tendront la seignorie dou devant dit reiaume, qui cristien soient ou qui seront en luec dou seignor crestien, sauf ce que se dreit seignor venist ou reiaume de Jerusalem, qui par reison de reinast et conqueist les casaus desus diz si com il sunt desus devisez de moi ou de mes heirs ou les preist a force, que di qui en avant vos ne voz successors ne nos estes tenuz de rien paier des xi^{m} bisanz devant diz a mei ne a mes heirs ne aus autres, qui sont ou seront asenez sor les rentes des desus diz casaus ne de lor apartenances, ne je ne mes heirs ne somes tenuz a vos ne a voz successors de garentire ne de defendre ne de garder vos de domage, qui vos avenist ou peust avenir par achaison de ce que dreit seignor par raison de rainast et conqueist les casaus desus diz si com il est desus devise de mei ou de mes heirs ou les preist a force. Et encor je le devant dit J(ohan) d'Ybelin seignor de Barut por mei et por mes heirs vos otrei et promet et sui tenuz de defendre et garentir les casaus devant diz si com il est desus devise et de garder vos de toz damages dou fait dou disme, que l'evesque d'Acre requiert a aveir des rentes des devant diz casaus et de lor apartenances, et se il avenist, que la crestiente perdist la cite d'Accre, dont deu nos garde et defende, de tant de tens, com Acre sereit en la main et ou poer des mescreanz, vos ne voz successors n'estes tenuz de rien paier a mei ne a mes heirs ne as autres, qui asenez sont ou seront par mon pere ou par mei ou par mes heirs de la some des xi^{m} bezans devant diz; et se deu rendist Acre as crestiens, vos et voz successors estes tenuz a mei et a mes heirs ou a noz commendamenz de paier chascun an les xi^{m} bezans devant diz perpetuelment en la maniere com il est devant devise por les casaus devant diz et por lor apartenances, des quels devant diz casaus o totes lor apartenances et lor reisons et lor dreitures si com il est devant devise, je le devant dit J(ohan) d'Ybelin seignor de Barut, por mei et por mes heirs dessessisant mei de totes reisons et dreitures et possessions et teneures et seignories, que je ou mes heirs ou atres por nos y aveions et tenions et posseions ou aveir devions ou aveir puessiens, et sessant vos ent por le devant dit maistre et por vos et por voz successors en ai mis et met desorendreit vos le devant dit commandeor et le covant de vostre dite maison, recevant por le desus nome maistre et por vos et por voz successors, en corporau saisine et teneure en non d'eschange et por l'eschange devant dit, si com il est desus devise et vos en ai done et doins plain poer por mei et por mes heirs a vos le devant dit commandeor et au covent de vostre dite maison, recevant por le devant dit maistre et por vos et por voz successors, de tenir et posseir les devant diz casaus o totes lor apartenances si com il est desus devise et de prendre et receveir et aver les fruiz et les rentes et les reisons et les dreitures devant moties des devant diz casaus et de totes lor apartenances si com il est desus dit, et hedifier et faire de aus et en aus totes voz volentes et voz comandemanz si com des autres propres choses de vostre devant dite maison sanz contredit et debat et chalonge, que je ou mes heirs ou autre por nos y meissiens ou peussiens metre, et promet et sui tenuz por mei et por mes heirs a vos le desus nome comandeor et au covent de vostre dite maison recevant por le dit meistre et por vos et por voz successors de maintenir et tenir le devant dit eschange des casaus desus nomez et de lor apartenances o totes lor reisons et lor dreitures toutes ensemble et chascun per sei si com il est desus dit et toz les covenanz desus motiz et de non aler a l'encontre fust en tot ou en partie, et se il aveneit, que je ou mes heirs ou autres por nos alesiens en aucun tens en quel que meniere que ce fust a l'encontre dou devant dit eschange et dez devant diz covenanz fust en tot ou en partie, ou y meissiens chalonge ou contredit en court ou hors de court, en plait ou hors de plait, je, l'avant nome sire de Barut, por mei et por mes heirs sui tenuz a vos le desus nome comandeor tenant luec de meistre et recevant por le maistre et por vos et por vostre covent et por voz successors d'amander et restorer vos toz les domages, que vos y auriez, et de ce vos oblige mei et mes heirs et vos oblige et abandone toz les biens de mei et de mes heirs meubles et estables ou que il soient et quels que il soient et vos doing plain poer por mei et por mes heirs, que vos de vostre autorite et par la force et par l'autorite de toz ceaus, qui vos i porront ou voudront aidier a vostre requeste et a vostre porfit, o vos ou por vos puissies et doies et les autres por vos puissent et doivent nos constraindre et prendre sanz mesprendre nos biens et vendre ou faire vendre jusques a la parfaite paie dou restor dou damage, que vos de ce auriez eu par nos ou par noz heirs ou par autre por nos. Et outre tot ce l'eschange desus moti deit estre et parmeneir ferm et estable si com il est desus escrit et por ce que je veill, que totes les choses desus devisees totes ensemble et chascun par sei soient a toz jors tenues et maintenues fermes et estables, si que je ou mes heirs ou noz successors ou autre por nos par aucune maniere n'en puissons en aucun tens aler a l'encontre d'aucune chose fust en tot ou en partie, ai je fait faire ce present previlege bolle de plomb enpreint en mes dreiz coins generaus o la garentie de mes homes, des quels ce sont les nons: Balian de Mimars, Amauri Hardel, Johan de Gibelin, Phelipe de Retel, Johan Poilevilain, Gautier Mainebuef et plussors autres. Ce fu fait en l'an de l'incarnation nostre seignor Jhesu Christ m cc lxi a l'entree dou mais de novambre.

III, 154. 1. incipit alia manus.

---

120. *1261 novembri ineunte. Iohannes de Ybelino, dominus de Baruth, donat domui hospitalis s. Mariae Theutonicorum in regno Ierosolimitano toronum Ahmud in montibus Baruthensibus.*

Sachent tuit cil qui sont et qui seront, que je[1] Johan d'Ybelin, seignor de Baruth, doing et otrei et conferm a toz jors en aumosne perpetuel franchemant et quitemant sans servis et sans aucune meniere de redevance a vos, frere Herteman de Helderunge, grant commandeor de la sainte mayson de l'hospital de nostre dame des Alemanz ou reiaume de Jerusalem et tenant leuc de maistre, et a vos, le covent de cele meimes mayson, recevant por le religions et honeste frere Anne, honorable meistre de vostre desus nomee mayson, et por vos et por voz successors por le salu et la remission de l'arme de mon pere et de ma mere et de mei et de mes ancessors por les granz bontez et servises, que vos et vostre devant dite mayson m'avez faites en plusors choses, un toron, qui est en la montaigne de Baruth, qui est nome Ahmud, et toz les casaus et toutes les gastines et tote la[2] terre et tot ce, qui est entre le flum del Damor et le ruisel ou flum, qui est devers la terre de Baruth, qui ist et sort des fontaines, qui sont en la devant dite montaigne de Baruth, et au chief de son cors vient et chiet ou flum del Damor meimes. Et outre celui ruisel devers l'autre terre de Baruth vos doins et otrei ausi en aumosne perpetuel franchemant et quitemant ii charuees francoises de terre mesurees a la mesure selon l'usage dou reiaume de Jerusalem et par einsi, que dedens ces ii dites charuees, qui sunt outre le ruisel, ne deit aveir casau ne gastine, et se les apartenances dou desus dit toron et des casaus et des gastines, qui sont entre le flum del Damor et le ruisel devant dit, s'estendent de la, ou le devant dit ruisel neist et sort en amont vers orient, vos le desus nome commandeor et vos le dit covent et voz successors deves aveir enterignemant celes apartenances desus dites, c'est a savoir de la en amont, ou le dit ruisel neist et sort, et les fontaines meimes, dont il nest et sort, o totes les reisons et les dreitures, qui a ceaus casaus et gastines, qui sont entre le flum et le ruisel, apartienent, c'est a savoir dedenz le flum et le ruisel et de la ou le ruisel sor en amont vers orient, en homes, en fames, en enfanz, en terres[3] laborees et non laborees, en plains, en montaignes, en montees, en valees, en bois, en riveres, en aigues, en pasturages, en arbres, en vignes, en cortilz, en jardins, en fors, en molins, en bainz, en fluns, en rinsiaus, en pescheries, en justises, en dreitures, en chemins et hors chemins, et en totes autres choses, qui ci sont moties et non moties, qui au devant dit toron et casaus et gastines apartienent or doivent apartenir dedens les devises desus moties; des quex devant diz toron et casaus et gastines o les apartenances desus moties et les ii charruees francoises et le ruisel si come il sont desus devisez je, le devant dit J(ohan) d'Ybelin, seignor de Baruth, por mei et por mes heirs dessessisant mei de totes reisons et dreitures et seignories, que je ou mes heirs y avons ou aveir porrions ou toron et es casaus et en lor apartenances si come il est desus moti et es charrues et ou ruisel devant dit en ai mis et met desorendreit vos le desus nome commandeor et vos le devant dit covent recevant por le devant dit maistre et por vos et por voz successors en aumosne et en non d'aumosne perpetuel en saisine et en teneure et vos ai done et doing desorendreit por mei et por mes heirs a vos et a voz successors plain poer de tenir et posseir le toron et les casaus et les charrues et le ruisel devant dit o totes les apartenances desus moties et lor reisons et lor dreitures si come il est desus devise et de recevoir en les fruiz et les rentes et de tenir et user et de faire de aus et en aus fortereces et toz voz grez et voz volentez et vostre profit en totes choses si come en vostre aumosne et en voz autres propres choses sanz chalogne et contredit et debat, que je ou mes heirs ou autre por nos y meissiens ou feissiens ou peussiens metre. Le quel don et aumosne devant dit, que je vos ai fait si come il est desus devise, je le devant nome J(ohan) d'Ybelin, seignor de Baruth, por mei et por mes heirs otroi et promet et sui tenuz a vos le devant dit commandeor et tenant leuc de maistre et a vos le devant dit covent recevant por le devant dit meistre et por vos et por voz successors de tenir et maintenir a toz jors mais ferm et estable et de non aler a l'encontre fust en tot ou en partie. Et por ce que je veill, que totes les choses desus devisees totes ensemble et chascune par sei soient tenues et maintenues a toz jors fermes et estables, si que je ou mes heirs ou noz successors ou autre por nos par aucune meniere n'en puissiens en aucun tens aler a l'encontre d'aucune chose ffust en tot ou en partie, ai je fait faire ce present previlege bolle de plomb enpreint en mes dreiz coins generaus o la garentie de mes homes, dont ce sont les nons: Balian de Mimars; Amauri Hardel; Johan de Gibelin; Phelippe de Retel; Johan Poilvilain; Gautier Mainebuef et de plussors autres. Ce fu fait en l'an de l'incarnation nostre seignor Jhesu Crist mcclxi a l'entre dou mois de novembre.

III, 156 v. 1. supplevi. 2. le B. 3. terre B.

---

121. *1261 ineunte novembri. Hartmannus de Helderungen, magnus commendator domus hospitalis s. Mariae Theutonicorum, locum generalis magistri tenens, emit a Iohanne de Hibelino, Baruti domino, Casalimbert et Le Fierge et Le Quiebre in territorio Acconensi, certis sub conditionibus.*

Coneue chose seit a toz ceaus qui sont et seront, que nos frere Harteman de Helderunge, grant comandeor de la sainte maison de l'hospital de nostre dame des Alemanz, tenant luec de maistre, et por le maistre et tot nostre convent, por nos et por toz noz successors avons receu en eschange et en non d'eschange a toz jors pardurablement de vos, monseignor Johan d'Ebelin, seignor de Baruth, por vos et por voz heirs Casal Ymbert et le Fierge et le Quiebre o totes lor apartenances et devises et reisons et dreitures en casaus, en gastines nomees et en totes autres reisons et dreitures et franchises et justises et usages, qui as devant diz casaus apartienent ou apartenir doivent, si com il se contient ou previlege, que nos avons de vos de cestui eschange sauves les ii charruees francoises de terre que vos aves donees a l'ospital de saint Johan. Et por l'eschange desus moti nos vos avons done et devons doner et paier en eschange et en non d'eschange a toz jors pardurablement xi^m^ bezans sarracenaz chascun an bien nombrez et pesez au juste pois d'Acre franchement et quitemant sanz aucune meniere de redevance asenez a recevoir les vos et voz heires et vostre commandemant en nostre tresor d'Acre par iii termines de l'an, c'est a savoir chascun iiii mais iii^{m} vi^{c} lxvi et xvi karubles, les quels besanz le maistre qui est et toz ceaus qui apres lui seront maistres et nos et tot nostre convent et toz noz successors prometons et otroions et somes tenuz a vos le desus nome seignor de Baruht et a voz heirs et a vostre commandemant de rendre et paier les vos enteringnement par les termines desus establiz. Et se il avenist en aucune meniere, que aucuns des termines devant diz passast, que vos ne fussies parpaiez tant que l'autre termine prochien venant fust parfaiz, nos somes tenuz a vos et a voz heirs et a vostre commendement de vos parfaire la paie de deus termines ensemble et de vos doner m besanz saracenaz outre la paie a chascune foiz que ce avendreit. Et se il avenist, que nos tenissiens vostre paie tot enterignemant i[1] an parfaitement, nos vous donons plain poer de prendre et recovrer les leus desus motiz o toz les amendemanz, que nos y auriens faiz, se il vos plaist, et aveir et tenir les leus di qui en avant a toz jors come la vostre chose demaine, et ce poez et devez faire de vostre autorite se volens sanz contredit et sanz deffense, que nos et noz successors y puissons ne doions metre en aucune meniere; et outre tot ce nos somes tenuz de vos parfaire la paie dou tens, qui a celui jor sereit passe. Et se il avenist, que le maistre qui est ou sera ou nos o nostre covent qui somes ou serons, ou aucun ou plussors de noz successors alesiens a l'encontre de ce, qui est desus escrit en tot ou en partie, nos somes tenus a vos et a voz heirs et a vostre commandemant d'amander et restorer vos toz les domages, que vos y auries, et de ce nos obliions nos et vos obliions et abandonons toz les biens de nos et de nostre maison meubles et estables ou que il soient et quels que il soient, et vos donons plain poer por nos et por noz successors, que vos de vostre autorite et par la force et par la autorite de toz ceaus, qui vos i porront ou voudront aidier a vostre requiest et a vostre profit, o vos ou por vos puissiez et doiez et les autres por vos puissent et doivent nos constraindre a vostre profit et prendre sanz mesprendre noz biens et vendre ou faire vendre jusque a vostre parfaite paie et au restor dou damange, que vos de ce auriez eu par nos ou par noz successors ou par autre por nos, et toz les asenemanz et totes les paies, qui sont sus les leus desus motiz desdons dou tens passe, si come vos les solies paier ou faisiez paier, et ce meimes, que vos donries ou aseneriez de ci en avant, toz doivent estre contez et paiez en la soume et de la some des xi^{m} besanz devant diz en tel meniere, que por pestilence ne por faute ne por force ne por domage, que Sarasins ne autres gens faissent es casaus ne en la terre devant dite ne en lor rentes n'en autre leu dou reiaume de Jerusalem ne por rien qui aveigne ne avenir puisse, ne deit demorer, que nos et noz successors ne paions a vos et a voz heirs et a ceaus qui sunt ou seront asenez si come il est dit desus les xi^{m} besanz devant diz par les termines devises, sauf ce que vos le desus nome seignor de Baruht et voz heirs estes tenuz a nos le devant dit commandeor recevant en leu de maistre et a nostre convent et a noz sucessors de garentir et de deffendre les casaus desus nomes et lor reisons et lor dritures dou seignor dou reiaume de Jerusalem et de toz ceaus et de totes celes, qui tendront la seignorie dou reiaume de Jerusalem, qui cristien soient ou qui seront en leu de seignor cristien, et de ce nos devez vos garder de touz domages sauf ce que se dreit seignor venist ou reiaume de Jerusalem, qui par reyson de reinast[2] et conquest les casaus desus diz de vos ou de voz heirs ou les preist a force, que di qui en avant nos ne noz successors ne somes tenuz de rien paier des xi^{m} besanz desus motiz a vos ne a voz heirs ne a ceaus, qui sont ou seront asenez es leus devant diz, ne vos ne voz heirs n'estes tenuz a nos ne a noz successors de garentir ne de deffendre ne de garder nos de domage, qui nos avenist ou peust avenir par achaison de ce, que dreit seignor par reison de reinast et conquest les casaus desus diz si come il est desus devise ou les preist a force, et vos le dit seignor de Baruth et voz heirs nos devez garentir et deffendre encontre l'iglise de la disme, que l'avesque d'Accre requiert des rentes des casaus et des les devant diz et nos en devez garder de toz domages, et se il avenist, que la crestiente perdist la cite d'Accre, dont dex nos gart et deffende, de tant de tens come Accre sereit en le main et ou poer des mescreans, nos, noz successors ne somes tenuz de rien paier a vos ne a voz heirs ne as asis de la some des xi^{m} besanz devant diz, et se dex rendist Acre as crestiens, nos et noz successors somes tenus a vos et a voz heirs et a voz commandemanz de paier chacun an les xi^{m} besanz devant diz perpetuelment ensi com il est desus devise et nos et nostre covent et nos successors somes tenuz a vos le devant nome seignor de Barut et a voz heirs que dedanz demi an apres ce que nostre maistre sera venu ou reiaume de Jerusalem ou qu'il i aura autre meistre, que il a la requeste de vos ou de voz heirs ou de vostre commandemant otreiera et confermera toz les covenanz desus escriz et vos en feira previlege de la tenor de cestui saele de plomb, et se ce demorast en la defaute de nos ou de nostre meistre, nos volons et otroions, que toz les covenanz desus escriz soient nuls. Et por ce que nos volons, que totes les choses toutes ensemble et chascune par sei soient a toz jors tenues et maintenues, fermes et estables, si que nos ne nostre covent ne noz successors ou atre por nos en aucune meniere n'en puissens ne doiens en aucun tens aler a l'encontre d'aucune chose fust en tot ou en partie, avons nos fait faire ce present previlege bolle de plomb et enpraint es dreiz coinz generaus de nostre devant dite maison o la garentie de noz freres, dont ce sont les nons: frere Rapol, l'ospitalier; frere Gontier, le drapier; frere Friderich de Wida; frere Pierre de Covelence; frere Aymon, commandeor de Saiete; frere Conrat, le tresorier; frere Tierri Deste et plussors autres. Ce fu fait en l'an de l'incarnation nostre seignor Jhesu Christ mcclxi a l'entre dou mois de novambre.

III, 155v. 1. i. e. = 1. 2. minast B.

---

122. *1261 ineunte novembri. Iohannes de Ybelino, dominus de Baruth, vendit domui hospitalis s. Mariae Theutonicorum toronum Ahmit in montibus Baruthensibus cum annexis.*

Je Johan d'Ybelin, seignor de Baruth, faz a saveir a toz ceaus qui sont et seront, que je ai eu et[1] receu de vos, frere Harteman de Helderungen, grant commandeor de la maison de l'ospital de nostre dame des Alemans ou reiaume de Jerusalem et tenant leuc de maistre, et de vos, le covent de cele meimes maison, v^{m} bezans sarracenas au pois d'Accre bien nombres et bien peses por lo toron, qui est nome Ahmit, qui est en la montaigne de Baruth, et por les casaus et les gastines et la terre et tot ce qui est entre le flum del Damor et le ruisel ou flum devers la terre de Baruth, qui sort des fontaines, qui sont en montaigne de Baruth, et au chief de son cors vient et chiet ou flum meimes del Damor et por les ii charuees francoises de terre, qui sont outre le ruisel o le ruisel et les fontaines meimes o totes tels apartenances et reisons et dreitures come il se contient ou previlege, que vos avez de mon don, les quels je ai done por mei et por mes heirs a vos et a vostre dite maison et a voz successors en aumosne perpetuel si come il se contient ou previlege, que vos avez de mei, qui fait mancion dou don et aumosne perpetuel, que je vos ai fait des choses desus dites. Et por ce que je veill, que chascun sache, que je ai eu et receu de vos, le devant dit grant commandeor, et de vos, le covent de la desus dite maison, les v^{m} bezans desus diz por le don et aumosne, que je vos ai fait des choses desus dites si com il est desus devise, ai ge fait faire ce present previlege boller de plumb enpraint en mes dreiz coinz generaus o la garentie des mes homes, des quels ce sont les nons: Balian de Mimars, Amauri Hardel, Johan de Gibelin, Phelippe de Retel, Johan Poilvilain, Gautier Mainebuef, et de plussors autres. Ce fu fait en l'an de l'incarnation nostre seignor Jhesu Crist mcclxi a l'entree dou mois de novambre.

III, 157. 1. supplevi.

---

123. *1262 dec. 19 Accon. Thomas Bethlehemitanus episcopus, apostolicae sedis legatus, Hartmannus de Helderungen, magnus commendator domus s. Mariae Theutonicorum in regno Ierusalem et locum tenens magistri, caeteri arbitri dirimunt litem inter Templarios et Hospitalarios super molendinis de Doc et de Ricordane.*

En nom dou pere e dou filz et dou saint esperit. Amen. Nos frere Thomas, par la grace de deu evesque de Betlehem et legat de l'apostolial siege, et frere Hartyman de Helderongue, grant comandeor de la maison de nostre dame des Alemans ou reiaume de Jerusalem et tenant leu de maistre, et Gefrei de Gergines, seneschau et bail dou reyaume de Jerusalem, et Guillelme, seignor dou Botron et conestable dou dit reyaume, arbitres, arbitreors, arbitrians et amiables compositors sur les contenz et les descordes et questions, que sunt entre les maisons dou Temple et de l'Ospital, si cum il apert es istrumens, que sunt fait dou compromis, que sunt bolees de plomb des dues devant dites maisons, voillant acomplir nostre dite sur aucuns articles, des quels nos non aviens encores dit; por ce que nos ne volons que le terme de nostre poeir passast en vuit et que l'on ne nos peust charger, que par nos fust aucun defaut, nos d'un assent et d'une volonte concordablement sivant la composicion, que est faite entre la maison dou Temple et de l'Ospital des moulins de Doc et de Ricordane, que est bolee des boles les maisons et de plusors autres henorables persones, disons, prononcions, arbitrons, ordenons, establissons, que *(et sic usque ad:)* Ce fu fait a Acre l'an de l'incarnation nostre seignor Jhesu Crist mil et dues cens et sissante dues le disenovesme jor dou meis de decembre en la sixte indiccion etc.

Totum edidit ex archivo ordinis sui Hospitalis s. Iohannis Sebastianus Pauli Codice diplomatico del sacro militare ordine Ierosolimitano oggi di Malta. Lucca 1733. fol. I, 177 sq. n. CXLII. — Huic diplomati, quamvis non dicat expresse Pauli, affixa videtur esse capituli bulla, cuius utrumque exemplum exhibet tabula V n. 54. In qua legitur 1: S'. hospitalis sancte Marie; 2: domus Teutonicorum Irl'm. Meliores exhibet effigies Voſsberg Geschichte der Preuſsischen Münzen und Siegel von frühester Zeit bis zum Ende der Herrschaft des Deutschen Ordens. Berl. 1843. 4. tab. I n. 4, qui p. 53 antiquissimum ordinis vel ipso ex Terra Sancta oriundum monumentum hanc bullam fuisse recte coniecit. Etiam ap. Raimundum Duellium in Historia ordinis equitum Teutonicorum hospitalis s. Mariae V. Hierosolymitani. Viennae Austriae. fol. 1727, p. 128 n. 91, visuntur pessima exempla de carta anno 1451 scripta.

---

124. *(1263) aprilis 4 Accon. ind. vi. Thomas de ordine praedicatorum, Bethleemitanus episcopus, apostolicae sedis legatus, Hugo Revel, magister domus hospitalis sancti Iohannis Ierosolimitani, frater Thomas Berardus, humilis magister domus militiae Templi, frater Hartmannus („Mortymannus“), praeceptor domus hospitalis s. Mariae Theotonicorum et magistri eiusdem domus in regno Syriae vicem gerens, Henrico Angliae regi de miserrimo Terrae Sanctae statu scribunt utque promissam opem praestet implorant.*

Ex libro, qui inscribitur Antiquae constitutiones regni Angliae. Londini 1671. fol. p. 132 citant Echard et Quétif Scriptores ordinis praedicatorum. fol. I, 360.

---

125. *1263 exeunte iunio. Guilelmus de Amigdala, dominus Scandalionis cum uxore Agnete donant domui hospitalis s. Mariae Theutonicorum annuos redditus 400 bisantiorum. („Cest est le rescripte dou privelige en quale maniere misire Guillhelme lu seignor de Schandelion et sa feme damma Agnes donarunt a la maison des Alamans cccc[to] bisante sarracenas perpetualement en aumosne“.)*

Je Guillaume de la Mandelee, seignor de Schandelion, et je Agnes, dame de Schandelion, espouse dou dit Guillaume, fasons assaveir a toz ceaus qui sont et seront, que nos remembrant et conoissant les grans bontes et servises, que vos le religious et honestes frere Herteman de Helderunge, grant comandor de la sainte maison de l'hospital de nostre dame des Alemans et tenant luec de maistre ou reaume de Jerusalem, et les freres de la dite maison nos avez fait a nos granz besoignes et especiaument en aveir nostre seignorie de Scandelion, de nostre bon gre et de nostre bone volente donons et otreons en aumosne perpetuel a toz jors mais por nos et por noz heirs et por nos successors franchement et quitement a vos les devant diz comandor et freres de la dessus dite maison des Alemans receivant por le relegious et honeste frere Anne honorable maistre de la dite maison des Alemans et por vos et por voz successors quatre cens basanz saracenas au peis d'Acre de rente chascun an et asenons por nos et por noz heirs et por noz successors vos et voz successors a recever les devant diz quatre cens besanz de la feste de la toz-sains premier venant en avant chaschun an perpetuament par tout le meis de huitovre sur toutes les rentes, que nos avons et aurons quex queles soient et ou qu'eles soient as miaus aparans par tel maniere, que, se il aveneit, que nostre seignor feist son comandement de monseignor mon pere, mesire Jaque de la Mandelee, avant que de mei, le dessus nome Guillaume, je le devant nome Guillaume por mei et por mes heirs et por mes successors asene vos et voz successors a receveir chascun an les quatre cens besanz saracenas dessus diz sur l'escheete, qui escharoit a mei ou a mes heirs de par mon dit pere, et faisant vos prevelige valable et estable de l'asenement des quatre cens besanz devant diz sur la dite escheete vos m'estes tenuz a mei et a mes heirs et a mes successors por vos et por voz successors de quiter mei a toz jors ce devant dit asenement, que nos vos avons fait sur totes noz rentes por les dessus motis quatre cens besanz, que nos vos avons done chascun an de rente en aumone perpetuel, si com il est dessus devise, et de rendre mei ce present prevelige, le quel sera casce et nul. Et por ce que[1] nos volons que les choses dessus dites soient tenues et maintenues fermes et estables, si que nos ne noz heirs ne autre por nos n'en puissons aler a l'encontre d'aucune chose en tout ou en partie, avons nos fait faire ce present prevelige buller de plumb empreint en noz dreis coins de nostre seignorie de Schandelion ou la garentie de noz homes, de quex ce sont les nom: Aufrei de Schandelion; Jaque Vidau; Auberi Antiaume; Jaque de la Colee, prior de Proeis. Ce fu fait en l'an de l'incarnation nostre seignor Jhesu Crist m cc lxiii a l'issue dou meis de juin.

III, 168. 1. supplevi.

---

126. *1273 august. 11 Accon. Arnolfo decano Nicosiensi electo mediante coram Thoma Hierosolymitano patriarcha fratres domus s. M. Th. et Godofredus Ebronensis episcopus de domo, quae vocatur Mons Musardi Accone sita, conveniunt.*

In nomine domini. Amen. Cum questio quedam verteretur inter sindicum et procuratorem domus sancte Marie Theutonicorum Iherosolimitane pro ipsa domo ex una parte et venerabilem patrem fratrem Godofredum de ordine predicatorum dei gracia episcopum Ebronensem et ecclesiam ipsius ex altera occasione unius domus cum suis pertinentiis posite in civitate Accon in loco, qui dicitur Mons Musardus, cuius confines sunt hii: ab oriente est domus Bernhardi olivarii, ab occidente est domus predicti patris Ebronensis, a meridie est via publica, et sic alii sunt confines; quam domum petebat dictus syndicus Alemannorum a dicto domino episcopo et ecclesia Ebronensi; que quidem questio vertebatur in curia reverendi patris fratris Thome de ordine predicatorum, dei gracia patriarche Iherosolimitani, Acconensis ecclesie ministri humilis, apostolice sedis legati, ad talem concordiam, finem et pacem devenerunt, mediante discreto viro domino Arnolfo decano Nicossiensi electo, amico communi, assumpto ab utraque parte de communi voluntate; qui decanus electus Nicossiensis constitutus in presencia dicti domini patriarche Iherosolimitani, presentibus religioso viro fratre Conrado, magno preceptore dicte domus Alemannorum, cum dicto syndico eiusdem domus et predicto domino episcopo Ebronensi, et in presencia mei notarii publici infrascripti et testium infrascriptorum, de voluntate utriusque partis determinavit in hunc modum, videlicet quod dictus dominus episcopus Ebronensis reddat et restituat prefatam domum cum suis pertinenciis predicto fratri Conrado magno preceptori[2] dicte domus Alemannorum pro ipsa domo et conventu, et quod omnia iura, raciones et actiones, que et quas habet dictus episcopus et ecclesia Ebronensis in dicta domo, posita in Monte Musardo, cedat[3] et mandet ex causa finis, transactionis et pacis domino preceptori, recipienti pro dicta domo Alemannorum, et dictam domum dimittat in pace et quiete ipsi domui Alemannorum, salvo et reservato censu bisanciorum duorum sarracenatorum annuatim solvendorum in festo assumptionis beate Marie eidem episcopo et successoribus eius per ipsam domum Alemannorum eodem modo, prout alie censure tenentur eidem episcopo et successoribus suis, et quod dictus frater Conradus preceptor Alemannorum tradat et solvat in continente quinquaginta bisancios sarracenatos eidem episcopo, et quod predictos duos bisancios pro censu annuatim solvendos nomine census pro ipsa domo eidem episcopo solvet et successoribus eius in termino supradicto. Et hoc precepit dictus decanus electus ambabus partibus sic observari et teneri, ut laudatum est per eum, a dictis partibus sub pena centum bisanciorum sarracenatorum a parte non parente arbitrio alteri parti parenti et servanti et in fide stanti[4]. Quam compositionem et arbitrium, pacem et concordiam, finem et transactionem approbaverunt predicte partes expresse et promiserunt sollempni stipulatione interveniente sibi adinvicem prefatus episcopus Ebronensis pro se et successoribus suis et pro ecclesia sua cum auctoritate et consensu predicti domini patriarche ibidem presentis, et sepedictus preceptor et sindicus dicte domus pro ipsa domo Alemannorum dictam compositionem et omnia alia et singula supradicta omni tempore habere et tenere rata et firma et adimplere et contra non venire per se vel alium, sub pena centum bisantiorum solvendorum, prout superius est expressum, cum refectione dampnorum et expensarum, et pena soluta vel non, nichilominus omnia et singula supradicta in sua permaneant firmitate. Pro quibus omnibus et singulis observandis et adinplendis obligaverunt predicte partes sibi adinvicem omnia bona ecclesiarum suarum seu domorum, renunciando omnibus beneficiis sibi contra predicta vel aliquod predictorum patrocinantibus presentibus et futuris, et specialiter condicioni sine causa vel iniusta causa doli vel instituti privilegio fori. Qui dictus eciam episcopus Ebronensis, receptis predictis quinquaginta bisantiis a predicto preceptore, donavit eidem preceptori recipienti pro dicta domo Alemannorum possessionem dicte domus et cessit et mandavit omnia iura et actiones, que et quas ipse episcopus et ecclesia Ebronensis habebant in dicta domo. Et ad maiorem cautelam premissorum rogaverunt partes predicte dictum dominum patriarcham Iherosolimitanum, quod huic contractui suam apponeret auctoritatem et decretum, et voluerunt eciam, ut dictus dominus patriarcha suum sigillum duceret apponendum in testimonium premissorum. Et hunc contractum voluerunt dicte partes suorum sigillorum munimine roborari. Qui dominus patriarcha exaudito tenore dicti contractus suam interposuit auctoritatem et decretum et suum sigillum duxit similiter apponendum. Actum Accon in camera episcopali Acconitana anno domini m° cclxx tercio[5] indictione prima die Veneris undecima mensis augusti, presentibus domino Guilielmo de Caneta, mareschalco regni Iherosolimitani; domino Guilielmo de Flore, milite de Accon; magistro Accurso advocato; fratre Florencio; fratre Henrico de domo Alemannorum testibus ad hoc specialiter vocatis et rogatis. -- Ego Iohannes clericus Acconensis[6], assisinas ecclesie sancte crucis Acconis, sacrosancte Romane ecclesie auctoritate notarius publicus, predictis interfui et rogatus scripsi et in hanc publicam formam redegi.

E copiario archivi Regimontani A. 16, p. 27 sq. inter Veneta mecum communicavit v. cl. A. Meckelburg cum dato: mccxx tercio. Sed fuit patriarcha Hierosolymitanus Thomas inde a 1272 martio usque ad a 1277; Gaufridus de ordine praedicatorum Ebronensis episcopus 1268 ap. Le Quien Oriens Christianus III p. 1270. „Messire Guillem de Canet, marechau", occurrit 1269 Accon ap. Pauli I, 190; idem dominus Guillelmus de Canneto, marescalcus regni Hierosolymitani, secundum cursum Pisanum 1271, secundum vero morem patriarchatus Hierosolimitani 1270, ind. xiv martii 11, ubi et dominus Accursus de Arisio iuris peritus, Pauli I, 194. L'estoire de Eracles empereur XXXIV, cap. 16. Recueil des historiens des croisades. Paris 1859. II, 463 ad annum 1272 habet: „Et fu fait ... du roiaume de Jherusalem ... marechaus Guillaume de Canet". 1273 ind. i cucurrit. 1. fratre A. 2. preceptorem A. 3. cedet A. 4. desideratur: solvenda. 5. m° ccxx tercio A. 6. Acconis A.

---

127. *1275 martii 13 Lugduni. Gregorius papa X confirmat Hospitalariorum, Templariorum, fratrum domus hospitalis s. Mariae Theutonicorum concordiam de dirimendis inter ipsos exorturis litibus.*

Gregorius episcopus servus servorum dei dilectis filiis magistro et fratribus hospitalis Ierosolimitani salutem et apostolicam benedictionem. Cum a nobis petitur, quod iustum est et honestum, tam vigor equitatis quam ordo exigit rationis, ut id per sollicitudinem officii nostri ad debitum perducatur effectum. Exhibita siquidem nobis vestra petitio continebat, quod vestre et militie Templi ac hospitalis sancte Marie Theutonicorum Ierosolimitanorum[1] domorum magistri, preceptores et conventus earum considerantes attente, quod pretextu bonorum et iurium in Ierosolimitano, Cypri et Armenie regnis necnon principatu Antiocheno et comitatu Tripolitano ad domos ipsas spectantium frequenter inter partes suscitabatur materia questionum, et quod propter hoc dehonestabatur religionis integritas, caritatis inter eos vinculum solvebatur et non modicum deperibat[2] negotio Terre Sancte, ac provide his occurrere cupientes, diligenti deliberatione prehabita de proborum virorum consilio unanimiter et concorditer ordinarunt, ut, quotiescumque super huiusmodi bonis et iuribus suscitaretur inter eos ad invicem huiusmodi materia questionum, unus de vestra et qualibet domorum ipsarum singuli a preceptore suo fratres eligerentur ydonei pro questionibus ipsis amicabiliter dirimendis; ita quod quicquam huiusmodi fratres electi a vestro et preceptoribus ipsis ad hoc specialiter nominati[3] vel duobus ipsorum super questionibus ipsis ordinaretur, diffiniretur et amicabiliter terminaretur, inviolabiliter a partibus servaretur et inde observandis hiis a vobis ac dictis magistris, preceptoribus et conventibus, apposita certa pena et prestito corporaliter iuramento, prout in literis inde confectis plenius dicitur contineri. Nos itaque vestris supplicationibus inclinati ordinationem huiusmodi, sicut rite, sine pravitate ac ....[4] facta est et a partibus sponte recepta et in alicuius preiudicium non redundat, ratam et firmam habentes ipsam auctoritate apostolica confirmamus et presentis scripti patrocinio communimus. Nulli ergo omnino hominum liceat hanc paginam nostre confirmationis infringere vel ei ausu temerario contraire. Si quis autem hoc attemptare praesumpserit, indignationem omnipotentis dei et beatorum Petri et Pauli apostolorum eius se noverit incursurum. Datum Lugduni tertio idus martii pontificatus nostri anno tertio.

Ex originali archivi Melitensis ordinis hosp. s. Iohannis Baptistae edidit Sebastianus Pauli, Codice diplomatico del sacro militare ordine Gerosolimitano oggi di Malta. Lucca 1733. fol. I, 279, bolla XIV, unde mutuavimus. — Subiungimus hic notitiam de ultimo forsan ordinis Theutonici diplomate in Terra Sancta edito 1289 (aug. 14) Accon in domo nostra in vigilia assumpcionis virginis preelecte „frater Wirichus de Homberch, humilis preceptor hospitalis sancte Marie Theutonicorum de Ierusalem, vices gerens magistri generalis in terra sancta, totumque capitulum domus hospitalis eiusdem“ Lubicensem civitatem monet, ut pro redemtione Heinrici de Mekelenburg apud ipsam deposita mm marcarum argenti Anastasiae eius uxori et filiis reddat, „cum proch dolor non sit spes, quod istis temporibus nobilis dominus Henricus de Mekelenburch a Sarracenorum vinculis redimatur, donec deus viam aliam et modum redempcionis dignetur per suam misericordiam aperire“. Ex originali, cui appendet duplex sigillum (cf. supra n. 123) habens inscriptiones a) † s'. hospitalis sancte Marie, b) domus Teutonicorum Irl'm., in thesauro Lubicensi asservato ut taceam alia ed. in Urkundenbuch der Stadt Lübeck. Lübeck 1843. 4. I, 489 n. DXXXVIII. Mecklenburgisches Urkundenbuch. Schwerin 1865. 4. III, 354 n. 2030. 1. sic P. 2. deperebat P. 3. legendum videtur: quicquid ab huiusmodi fratribus electis a vestro et preceptoribus aliis ad hoc specialiter nominatis. 4. supplendum videtur: rationabiliter.

128. *Registrum, quod codicis prima folia 1—3 occupat, quum maximam partem Terram Sanctam respiciat, hic potissimum inserendum videbatur. Quod et complura in codice non contenta comprehendere nec tamen omnia in eo contenta facile patet.*

Hee sunt elemosine, empciones, confirmationes, commutationes atque privilegia domus sancte Marie Theutonicorum in Iherusalem.

Aput Castrum Regis vineam domini Iacobi Tripolitani, que sita est iuxta vineam domini Boonecase antiqui contra viam de Buchel, que empta est pro c bisantiis.

Item de domina de Amerun emit duo frusta terre[1], quorum unum situm est super vineam domini Andree in via de Tertille; aliud vero situm est iuxta vineam de novo plantatam domini Bernardi Divitis super cavam. Item emimus a domina predicta unam domum sitam prope domum domini archiepiscopi de Nazareth. Hec domus et predicta frusta terre constiterunt xxx[a] v[e] bisantiis.

Item de uxore domini Odonis de Furhun emit unum frustum terre, quod situm est iuxta terram domini Guidonis de Renay in terra Alba et unum propugnaculum, quod alio modo appellatur barbacana, quod contiguum est barbacane domini Guidonis de Renay, et unam cisternam aque, que est ante domum Ferrei-brachei, et unam domum cum cisterna, que in domo est, que sita est iuxta domum domini Symonis Galiothe. Hec predicta empta sunt pro ccc et xxx[a] bisantiis.

Item a Simone Galiothe totam hereditatem suam ccl bisantiis[2].

Item emit domus aput uxorem[3] domini Wernerii de Paris tres pecias terre, quarum una sita est infra terram domini Rauli militis et domini Ioseph; alia sita est apud fontem ville, que dicitur Terschia, et eciam est contigua terre sancti Sepulcri; tercia vero sita est in divisa ville, que dicitur Sivenete super viam de Acchon iuxta terram domini Guidonis de Renay. Item emit apud eandem unum ortum et intus unam cisternam, situm supra ortum Brachs-de-ferre et unam domum sitam iuxta veterem curiam. Hec constiterunt ccc et x bisantiis.

Item emit de domina Dulcia unam vineam sitam inter vineas episcopi et cuiusdam balistarii et duo frusta terre, quorum unum situm est super terram domini Petri Markise in via ville de Fenes; aliud situm est super vineam rufam domini Bernardi Divitis.

Item duas domos, quarum una destructa est, in qua est una cisterna aque; secunda sita est inter domum archiepiscopi et domum domini Henrici. Predicta vero domus destructa sita est ante domum prefati Henrici. Hec predicta constiterunt c bisantiis.

Item emit apud filiam Hugonis Merlin unam vineam inter vineam balistarii et inter vineam Petri de Schalun et duo frusta terre, quorum unum situm est sub vinea Martini; aliud situm est super vineam rufam domini Bernardi divitis, et unam domum, que est retro domum Galterii contra domum Stephani. Hec constant c bisantiis.

Item emit apud dominum Abraam Furnir unam domum, que est inter domum Martini et inter ortum Guillelmi Malinger et retro domum eandem unum ortum parvum et in eo duas cisternas. Hec constant c et x bisantiis.

Item emit de domina Guncelina unum ortum, quod est situm ultra ortum domini Petri Marchise; quod constat xi bisantiis.

Item emit apud Iohannem filium Marini de Iader unum frustum terre, quod situm est ultra vineam Iacobi de Triple; quod constat c et l bisantiis.

Item emit apud dominum Henricum dispensatorem episcopi unam vineam sitam in via Suphie, et est contigua vinee Galterii, et unam domum sitam contra domum archiepiscopi et retro[3*] domum eandem unum ortum et unam cisternam sitam prope ortum Rogerii et tres petias terre; una sita est apud ecclesiam sancte Marie Magdalene; alia iacet super vineam uxoris domini Martini; tercia sub vinea archiepiscopi. Hec constant d bisantiis.

Item emit de domina Iuliana unam domum sitam prope domum leprosorum, que constitit viii[4] bisantiis.

Item de domina Margarita duo frusta terre et iii domos et unum ortum pro lxxx et v bisantiis.

Item emit a Guillelmo Tabach duas vineas[5] et unum ortum apud Therum et unum alium apud turonum suspensorum et unam domum pro c et lx bisantiis.

Item a Robelino filio Guillelmi sutoris unam vineam pro c et xxv bisantiis.

Item a pueris domini Bernardi Divitis et Reinaldo sororio eorum medietatem unius molendini pro xxx[a] bisantiis.

Item a Iohanne Rosa domum unam pro xv bisantiis.

Item a Poncio, filio magistri Roberti de Ianie, unam vineam et ortum et unam domum et unam cisternam et totam hereditatem suam pro cc et xl[a] bisantiis.

Item a domino Rodulfo milite Theutonico unum ortum ante ortum puerorum fratris Franci prope villam pro l bisantiis.

Item emimus hereditatem Bonicasi pro uxore sua et domino Andrea Burguino et uxore sua et Henrico filio eorum pro cccc bisantiis.

De Kyssereth et Mahus. Item a domino Iohanne de Chanay emimus Kissereth et Mahus pro mmm et dccc bisantiis. [Cf. 1230 oct. p. 57 n. 73.]

De Saphet Cadamor. Item emit domus a domina Beatrice filia Galterii et a marito eius Saphet Cadamor pro m bisantiis. [1236 aug. 10 p. 66 n. 84.]

De Caffersyn. Item comes Henricus dedit nobis unum casale, quod vocatur Caphersin. [1193 febr. p. 25 n. 29.]

Item inter illud casale et casale Album unam peciam terre, quam dedit domui Guillelmus de Amigdala et uxor sua, filia comitis Ioscelini. [1200 oct. p. 31 n. 39.]

De iii carrucis in Saphet. Item comes Otto de Hennimberch dedit domui tres carrucatas terre et unam domum in Saphet. [1208 sept. p. 34 n. 43.]

Item in eodem casali dedit nobis Castellana uxor Harnulfi aurificis duas carrucatas terre consenciente marito eius. [1231? sept. 11 p. 60 n. 76.]

De Ioppen. Item comes Henricus dedit nobis in Ioppen quandam gastinam ad domos faciendas et quasdam vineas. [1196 mart. p. 27 n. 32.]

Item in Ioppen emimus unam peciam terre apud fornacem, que est prope curiam nostram, quam emimus a quadam domina nomine ... pro xxx^{a} bisantiis.

Item emimus per manum fratris Roberti unam peciam terre, que est sita extra villam Ioppen, pro xl^{a} bisantiis.

Ista sunt in Achon. Item comes Henricus dedit nobis unam voltam prope turrem sancti Nicholay. [1193 febr. p. 25 n. 29.]

Item rex Guido dedit nobis veterem curiam prope portam sancti Nicholay. [1192 febr. 10 p. 23 n. 27.]

De Agulla. Item rex Aymericus vendidit nobis casale Aguilla pro mmm bisantiorum. [1198 febr. 8 p. 27 n. 34.]

De Phergia. Item dedit nobis in Phergia quolibet die laborando in mazaro unam rotulam zuchari. [Ibidem p. 28.]

De casali Umberto. Item idem dedit nobis in pertinenciis casalis Umberti unam clincham frumenti et unam ordei et de singulis c capris, que yhemabunt in terra predicta, v^{e} carrublas et de singulis aliis x capris ii carrublas et de qualibet carruca iii carrublas et francisiam per totum regnum Cipri. [Ibidem p. 28.]

De venditione comitis Ottonis. Item a comite Ottone de Henninberch et ab uxore sua Beatrice, filia quondam comitis Ioscelini, et ab Ottone filio eorundem, omnem hereditatem, quam ex progenitorum suorum successione predicta Beatrix et Otto filius eius in regno Iherosolimitano possedit et possidere debuit, diminutione qualibet remota pro septem milibus marcharum argenti et pro v^{e} milibus bisantiorum et cc et l^{a} bisantiis, quam emit domui dux Lupoldus Austrie. [1220 maii 30 p. 42 n. 52.]

De Neapoli. Item rex Amalricus dedit domui cccc bisantios in funda Neapolis et duo casalia in pertinenciis sancti Abrahe, scilicet Deldol et Serie. [1173 mart. 26 p. 7 n. 6.]

De Ierusalem. Item idem in pertinenciis Iherusalem dedit domui de qualibet carruca rustici unam robbam frumenti et unam ordei et, si predictos cccc bisantios et frumentum domus in locis predictis recipere non posset, recipiat in funda Acchon. [1198 febr. 8 p. 28 n. 35.]

De porta David. Item predictus rex Amalricus dat domui nostre in porta David ccc bisantios et xxiiii^{or} modios frumenti et tantumdem ordei et vi modios leguminum et duo casalia in terra Neapolis scilicet Saphir et Caphirhune, et de qualibet mazera ii rotulas zuchari et de unaquaque pertica in qualibet ebdomada unam chudariam zuchari et iii vineas in montanea, que vocatur de Abel; dat eciam domui libertatem omnimodam eundi et exeundi, vendendi et emendi per totum regnum Iherosolimitanum, et si domus nostra hec predicta in locis predictis non posset recipere, recipiat in Iherusalem vel Acchon in funda. [1177 oct. 17 p. 9 n. 8.]

De domo regis B(alduini) in Ierusalem. Item imperator Fridericus dat domui domum quandam regis quondam Balduini in Iherusalem et sex carrucatas terre in territorio eiusdem civitatis et domum, quam habuerunt fratres Theutonici ante amissionem terre, cum omnibus pertinenciis, iuribus et possessionibus suis. [1229 april. p. 55 n. 69.]

De Arabia. Item emimus Arabiam cum omnibus pertinentiis suis, scilicet Berhenne, Mizera, Miscalyn a domina Ysabella de Bethsan et a marito eius pro mmm et dc bisantiis et eadem domina dedit nobis in helemosinam quoddam casale, quod vocatur Zachanin cum pertinenciis suis. [1234 p. 61 n. 77.]

De Cesarea. Item domina Iuliana de Cesarea dedit domui domos, que fuerunt Georgii Lorrinnive, et woltam Bernardi Falcille cum omnibus pertinenciis suis et gastinam, que est inter ipsas domos et turrim Mallart, cum platea et aliam parvam turrem, que est opposita in cantone civitatis a porta orientali. [1206 febr. p. 32 n. 40.]

De Noyam et Soffia. Item domus emit Nohyam et Soffiam a .... pro septem milibus et c bisantiis. [ante 1239; cf. p. 69 n. 87.]

De terra iuxta flumen Accon. Item imperator Fridericus dedit nobis terram iuxta fluvium Acchon subtus turonum de orto domini episcopi usque ad turrim sancti spiritus. [1231 dec. p. 60 n. 76.]

De ortis episcopi in Accon. Item episcopus Acchonensis dedit domui duos iardinos super rippam fluminis Acchonensis pro septuaginta v^e^ bisantiis quolibet anno solvendis de thesauro domus in exaltacione sancte crucis, et postquam requisiti fuerimus, si predictos bisantios non solverimus, dicti iardini revertentur ad ecclesiam Acchonensem. [1242 april. 30 p. 72 n. 91.]

De terra Montis Syon in turono in Accon. Item abbas et conventus Montis Syon dederunt sub annuo censu domui nostre quandam peciam terre in loco, qui dicitur Mons suspensorum, pro xx bisantiis in kalendis marciis persolvendis, et, si non solverent fratres hos bisantios annuatim, predicta terra ad predictam ecclesiam revertetur. [1239 febr. p. 68 n. 86.]

De vinea Guiot, que (est in)[6] novo orto in Accon. Item Guiot et Iohannes, filii Michaelis de Ierusalem, vendiderunt domui quandam vineam, que est in novo orto iuxta viam de Capharsin, pro dcc bisantiis consentiente abbate et conventu de Latina, de qua ipsi recipere debent xiii bisantios annuatim in festo omnium sanctorum. [1239 p. 70 n. 88.]

De terra Iohannis Griffi in ...[6] Item emimus a domino Iohanne Griffo quandam peciam terre in eodem orto pro m et dc (bisantiis) consenciente abbate et conventu de Latina, de qua ipsi recipere debent v^e^ bisantios annuatim. [1235 p. 63 n. 80.]

De Tyro. Item emimus a Guiot et Alberto et Rudulfo et uxore sua domum unam extra portam civitatis pro cc et l^a bisantiis, et debent dari annuatim iiii^or bisantii pro censu eiusdem.

Item emimus a domina Hensalme, soceri[7] domini Menebof, v^e carrucatas terre in Saphet et unam woltam pro m et ccc bisantiis.

[6]Item emimus in Tyro unum ortum super arenam p(ro) cc bisantiis.

[6]Item emimus in Tyro peciam terre, que tenet v^e (car)rucatas terre (que cohe)ret terre nostre .... che in monte .... ti pro lx^a v...

Item confirmat rex Aymericus domum et iardinum, qui fuerunt Pauli et fratris sui, filiorum Theodori de Sarepta. [1200 aug. p. 29 n. 36.]

Item comes Henricus confirmat domui domum et iardinum, que fuerunt Theodori de Sarepta, et ii^as carrucatas terre apud Sedinum. [1195 april. p. 26 n. 31.]

Item Innorannus dominus Bore vendidit domui unam domum in Tyro in presencia regis Iohannis. [1222 april. p. 45 n. 56.]

Item rex Iohannes confirmat domui vendicionem domus predicte. [1222 april. p. 46 n. 57.]

Item Conradus marchionis Montis ferrati filius dedit Martino Rochia civi Ianuensi domum Theodori Suriani in Tyro. [1189 sept. p. 21 n. 24.]

Item predictus Martinus Rochia civis Ianuensis dedit domui in presentia patriarche domum ipsius Theodori Suriani in Tyro pro cc bisantiis. [1211 febr. 14 p. 36 n. 45.]

De Cabecia in ... Item vendidit domui Sitalmale quartam partem unius casalis, quod vocatur Cabecie, consentientibus filiis suis Monsur et Silman; confirmatio Rauili Tyrensis. [1239 ianuar. 24 p. 67 n. 85.]

De Corfie in Taba(ria). Item dominus Philippus de Malgastel et uxor sua dat domui casale unum in pertinenciis Tabarie, quod vocatur Corsie.

De Arabia et hospitalariis. Item magister et conventus hospitalis sancti Iohannis, postquam receperint v^e milia bisantiorum, nichil penitus habent petere in casali Arabie. [1240 p. 70 n. 89.]

De turri sancti Nicholay super portam. Item rex Aymericus dedit domui turrem super portam sancti Nicholay. [1198 aug. p. 28 n. 35.]

De hospitali Armeniorum. Item rex Guido dedit nobis domum, in qua solebant hospitari Armeni, aut plateam iuxta eandem domum. [1190 sept. p. 22 n. 25.]

De terra Galopini. Item magister hospitalis et conventus reliquerunt nobis hereditatem Galopini. [1192 febr. 2 p. 25 n. 26.]

De barbacana prope portam s. Nicholai. Item comes Henricus dedit domui barbacanam, turres quoque et fossatum a meta proprisie usque ad portam sancti Nicholai. [1193 p. 24 n. 28.]

De barbacana prope domum senescalci. Item rex Iohannes dat domui barbacanam, que extenditur de domo senescalci usque ad portam Gaufridi Torti. [1217 aug. p. 41 n. 50.]

De lucro, quod habent fratres in armis. Item rex ohannes confirmat domui lucrum, quod habebant homines sui eo absente in armis. [1221 mart. p. 45 n. 55.]

De terra Garnerii Alamanni. Item rex Iohannes confirmat domui terram, quam dedit Garnerius Alamannus, que fuit Iuliani de Falouse, et iardinum, qui coheret areis de tarsia. [1217 aug. p. 41 n. 49.]

De libertate fratrum vendendi et emendi. Item comes Henricus dat domui libertatem vendendi et emendi ad usus proprios. [1191 oct. p. 26 n. 30.]

De domibus G(erardi) Fortis. Item Gerardus Fortis dat domui domos suas in rua caldariorum Acchon. [1242 aug. 18 p. 73 n. 92.]

De c bisantiis in Accon. Item princeps Anthiochie dat domui in funda et in cathena Acchon c bisantios. [1228 iunio ineunte p. 53 n. 64.]

De septem milibus bisantiorum in Accon. Item habemus de concambio Maronis in cathena et funda Acchon septem milia bisantiorum. [1244 iul. 7 p. 75 n. 98.]

Confirmatio imperatoris Friderici et imperatricis per regnum Ierusalem. Item imperator Fridericus et uxor eius regina filia regis Iohannis confirmant domui omnimodam libertatem et omnia, que habemus et habituri sumus in toto regno Iherosolimitano, et confirmant nobis donationem regis Iohannis. [1226 ianuar. p. 47 n. 58.]

De investicione magistri et Iacobi de Amigdala. Item in presencia imperatoris magister noster investivit Iacobum de Amigdala de omnibus, que eum contingebant ex parte matris sue, et ipse Iacobus magistrum et fratres investivit de eisdem in regno Ihrosolimitano. [1226 iulio p. 49 n. 60.]

De concambio Iacobi de Amigdala et domus. Item Iacobus de Amigdala commutavit cum domo nostra totam terram suam, quam tenebat a domo nostra in feudo, pro sex milibus et cccc bisantiis. [1228 april. 20 p. 51 n. 63.]

Confirmacio imperatoris de predictis. Item confirmavit imperator Fridericus nobis eandem commutationem et in presencia sua facta fuit. [1229 april. p. 53 n. 65.]

De concambio Mebelie et Trefile. Item confirmatio imperatoris de concambio, quod fecit domus nostra cum domino Iacobo de Amigdala de Mebelye casale, quod dederunt fratres ei pro Treffile et castro novo, quod dicitur Monfort. [1229 april. p. 54 n. 67.]

De sex milibus et cccc bisantiis in Accon. Item imperator Fridericus dedit nobis in funda et cathena Acchon sex milia et cccc bisantios in elemosinam. [1229 april. p. 55 n. 68.]

De concambio domus Margariti. Item domus dedit imperatori castrum Musani et domum Margariti in excambium pro sex milibus et cccc bisantiis recipiendis annuatim in cathena et in funda Acchon, et, si hos bisantios habere non possemus, illud excambium ad domum revertetur. [1229 aprili.]

Confirmacio regis Conradi Ierosolimitani. Item confirmat nobis rex Conradus filius imperatoris Friderici omnia, que dederunt et concesserunt et consentiverunt[8] nobis pater et mater eius, et omnia, que habemus et habebamus in regno Iherosolimitano sive a parentibus suis sive ab aliis. [1243 dec. p. 73 n. 93—97.]

De vendicione Iohannis Torti in Accon. Item Iohannes Tortus vendidit nobis domum suam, quam habebat in Acchon, pro sexcentis marchis argenti et dcc bisantiis consencientibus in hoc omnibus sibi attinentibus, confirmante eciam venditione hanc domino Iohanne[9] de Ybelyno.

De vendicione Iohannis de Conchis in Accon. Item emimus a domino Iohanne de Conchis unam domum in Acchon pro dcxx[ti] marchis argenti, consenciente et concedente imperatore hoc et confirmante nobis barbacanam, quam rex Iohannes dedit domui, et licenciante unam woltam fieri de predicta domo ad aliam. [1229 april. p. 55 n. 70.]

De vendicione Iohannis Strakei in Accon. Item emimus a Iohanne Strakei et de Guilion, hominibus Templi, unam curiam retro seleriam pro dc et l[a] bisantiis.

De domo retro palmanteriam in Acon. Item dedimus pro una domo retro palmanteriam cc et lxxx[a] bisantiis in Acchon.

De curia retro infirmaria in Accon. Item emimus curiam unam a monialibus de Tyro iuxta infirmariam nostram pro m bisantiis in Acchon.

De domo prope infirmariam in Accon. Item de archiepiscopo Iacobinorum emimus unam domum, que est prope curiam nostram et prope domum, quam emimus a monialibus Tyri, pro ccc et l[a] bisantiis.

De curia, que dicitur Chisseria, in Acon. Item emimus unam curiam retro palacium nostrum Acchon, que vocatur Chisseria, que fuit Nicholay et fratris sui scriptorum, pro mm et xxiiii bisantiis.

De domo Raimundi in Acon. Item emimus a Raimundo scriptore unam domum, que iacet retro curiam magistri, pro m et xii bisantiis.

De domo Petri Corvisarii in Acon. Item emimus a Petro Corvisario unam domum in rua domus dicti Raimundi pro c et lxx[a] v bisantiis.

De pecia terre ante barciam dicti Aymonis in Acon. Item emimus unam peciam terre, que est ante barriam domini Aymonis, pro xviii bisantiis et pro censu eiusdem debet solvi dimidius bisantius annuatim[10].

De Sydone. Item Balianus dominus Sydonis dedit domui mahumeriam magnam, que est inter duas portas Sydonis, et iardinum, qui dicitur iardinus comitisse, ante portam Sydonis et quandam terram, que dicitur terra coci, et aratrum unum ante Sydonem, vineam eciam quandam, que ibi est. [1228 febr. 11 p. 50 n. 62.]

Item emimus in eadem villa a rustico uno unam peciam terre, que est in vinea nostra pro xl[a] bisantiis.

De Tripoli. Item princeps Anthiochie dedit domui quandam peciam terre cum tribus turribus in Tripoli. [1209 sept. 4 p. 35 n. 44.]

De Anthiochia. Item idem princeps dedit domui unum molendinum et vineam quandam iuxta ipsum molendinum cum omnibus suis attinenciis in Anthiochia. [1228 ianuar. p. 50 n. 61.]

De Armenia. Item rex Leo dedit domui castrum Amodan et hec casalia: Cespin et Buquequia et Haaiym cum pertinenciis suis, et libertatem omnimodam tam in mari quam in terra in toto dominio suo in Armenia. [1212 apr. p. 37 n. 46.]

De Herenia. Item rex Eython, rex Herrenie, dat domui civitatem Aroniam cum pertinenciis suis. [1236 ianuar. 22 p. 65 n. 83.]

De Cypro. Item Henricus rex Cipri dat domui casale nominatum Clavodie et domum, que fuit Bruonis de Bedort in Nicossia. [1229 iun. p. 56 n. 71.]

Lacuna duarum linearum.

De Ungaria. Item rex A(ndreas) Ungarie dat domui terram Borcha ultra silvas et libertatem fororum et tributorum. [1211.]

Item Andreas rex Ungarie dat domui terram, que vocatur Bursiam, et omnimodam libertatem in eadem terra. [1222.]

De libertate numulariorum. Item idem rex dat domui libertatem, quod nullus numulariorum intret terram predictam. [1212.]

De hospitali sancti Iacobi in Andrevilla. Item G(aufridus) princeps Achaye et Romanie senescalcus dat domui hospitale sancti Iacobi cum omnibus pertinenciis suis in Andrevilla et domum unam in castro Clari montis. [1237 iul.]

Consensus prioris et capituli de Andrevilla. Item prior et capitulum sancti Iacobi rogant[u] dominum papam Gregorium, ut det eis licenciam intrandi ad ordinem nostrum cum omnibus bonis suis. [1237 iun.]

Concessio pape prior(i et) capitulo transeuntes[8] (ad) ordinem nostrum. Item concessit papa Gregorius eisdem licenciam intrandi ordinem nostrum cum omnibus bonis ipsius hospitalis. [1237 sept. 16.]

De estagiis de Villagort. Item dominus Robertus de Insula dat nobis duas estagias terre, que sunt in contrata de Vileguort et in pertinentiis de Chimenro. [1239 mart. ex.]

De hospitali in Barulo. Item Henricus imperator Romanorum vi[us] dat domui hospitale sancti Thome in Barulo et in Canato terras laboratas ad x paricla et ecclesiam sancti Nicholai cum omnibus pertinenciis suis in Rigula. [1197 maii 20.]

Confirmatio F(riderici) imperatoris hospitalis in Barulo. Item imperator Fridericus confirmat domui hospitale sancti Thome cum omnibus pertinenciis suis, sicut imperator H(enricus) nobis dedit, et dat eidem ecclesie vineas et ortum, que fuerunt Bertrandi medici, cum pertinenciis suis. [1204 sept.]

De hospitali sancti Martini in Montepessulano. Item consules Montispessulani et communitas civitatis dederunt nobis hospitale sancti Martini, quod est prope ecclesiam sancti Thome in suburbio Montispessulani extra portale Salinarie, cum universis domibus, ortis, vineis, campis et aliis possessionibus, iuribus et rationibus eidem hospitali pertinentibus. [1228 mart. 15.]

De casali Tuscano. Item imperator Fridericus dat domui casale, quod vocatur Tuscanum, cum omnibus hominibus et tenimentis et pertinentiis suis et omnimodam libertatem in mari et in terra in toto regno suo. [1206 ian.]

De domo Margariti in Brundusio. Item Fridericus imperator dat domui domum Margariti in Brundusio cum balneo et omnibus pertinentiis suis exceptis theloneis in moneta. [1215 oct. 20.]

De cc unciis auri apud Messanam. Item imperator Fridericus dat nobis aput Messanam pro mantellis et pellibus agninis cc[as] uncias auri annuatim. [1217 maii 25.]

Item de cc unciis in Brundusio. Item papa Honorius dedit domui ad peticionem imperatoris omnem libertatem, quam habent Templarii et Hospitalarii, et imperator dat nobis cc uncias auri pro mantellis privilegio imperatoris. [1221 dec.]

De usufructibus[12] ecclesiarum per annum. Item imperator Fridericus confirmat domui omnia, que dederunt nobis antecessores sui, et dat nobis omnem ecclesiam vaccantem in dominio suo per annum recipiendo ibi omnes usufructus, nec nobis preiudicetur, si infra annum prelatus in eis fuerit constitutus. [1223 mart.]

Donatio Lanfranci in Brundusio. Item Lanfrancus filius Milonis de Bogossa in Brundusio dedit nobis unum mansum et duas domos, que sunt in ipso manso, et vineam, que vocatur clausoria dulcis et est prope sanctum Laurencium iuxta terram domini Iohannelli de Verona, et unam aliam domum, que est ad portum Brundusii. [1218 aug.]

De libertate et cl unciis auri in Brundusio. Item imperator Fridericus accipit fratres et confratres ac servientes et bona domus tam presencia quam futura in protectione sua et confirmat omnia privilegia sua et antecessorum suorum et beneficia eorundem et dat domui cl[a] uncias auri et omnimodam libertatem tam in mari quam in terra in toto dominio suo, confirmante hoc uxore sua Constancia et filio eorum rege Henrico, sicut in privilegio plenius continetur. [1221 apr.]

Confirmatio Livonie. Item imperator Fridericus confirmat V(olquino) magistro domus milicie Christi et fratribus suis omnes possessiones et iura in partibus Livonie iuste possidentes[13] aut in futurum iusto titulo poterunt adipisci et metallum, quod super terram vel sub terra poterunt invenire. [1226 maio.]

1. terra B. 2. Haec nota in margine. 3. antea: filiam B. 3*. recto B. 4. correctum, antea: vii. 5. antea: unam vineam B. 6. in margine B praecisa caetera. 7. soceri B. 8. B. 9. dominus Iohannes B. 10. Abhinc dimidia columna vacat. 11. rogant B. 12. sufrufructibus B. 13. B.

ROMANIA.

129. *1214 febr. 4 Constantinopoli. Pelagius Albanensis cardinalis episcopus, ap. sed. legatus, hospitali s. Iacobi de Andrevilla in apostolicam protectionem suscepto enumerata bona et privilegia confirmat augetque.*

Pelagius, miseratione divina Albanensis episcopus, apostolice sedis legatus, dilectis filiis Bernardo magistro et fratribus hospitalis sancti Iacobi de Andrevilla tam presentibus quam futuris in perpetuum. Cum universis ecclesie filiis debitores[1] ex iniuncto nobis officio existamus, illis tamen locis atque personis propensiori nobis convenit karitatis studio imminere, qui secularibus vanitatibus derelictis post Ihesu Christi unguentorum odorem laudabili intencione festinant pietatis opera exercendo. Eapropter, dilecti in domino filii, cum elegeritis magis abiecti esse in domo domini, quam habitare in tabernaculis peccatorum[2], ne forte, quod absit, cuiuslibet temeritatis incursus aut vos a proposito revocet aut robur vestre sacre religionis infringat, prefatum locum, hospitale sancti Iacobi Andrevillensis[3], in quo divino estis obsequio mancipati, cum omnibus hospitalibus subiacentibus eidem in imperio Romanie et aliis pertinenciis suis a iurisdictione cuiuslibet ecclesiastice secularisve persone eximimus et ipsum ad ius et proprietatem beati Petri et sedis apostolice reservantes personas vestras et locum prefatum sub beati Petri et sedis apostolice protectione suscipimus et presentis scripti privilegio communimus, in primis siquidem statuentes, ut ordo vobis concessus a vobis perpetuis ibidem temporibus inviolabiliter observetur; preterea, quascunque possessiones, quecunque bona idem hospitale iuste vel canonice possidet aut in futurum concessione pontificum, largicione regum vel principum, oblatione fidelium seu aliis iustis modis prestante domino poterit adipisci, firma vobis vestrisque successoribus et illibata permaneant. In quibus hec propriis duximus exprimenda vocabulis: locum ipsum, in quo prefatum hospitale situm est, cum omnibus pertinenciis suis; hospitale sancti Iacobi de Macra Atteniensis diocesis; hospitale sancti Iacobi Spicacenensis et alie domus, possessiones cum pratis, vineis, erbis, nemoribus, usuagiis, pascuis, in bosco et plano, in aquis et molendinis, in viis et semitis, et omnibus aliis libertatibus et immunitatibus suis. Sane laborum vestrorum, quos propriis manibus aut sumptibus colitis, tam de terris cultis quam incultis sive de ortis et virgultis et piscationibus vestris vel de nutrimentis animalium vestrorum nullus a vobis decimas exigere vel extorquere presumat. Liceat quoque vobis clericos vel laicos liberos et absolutos et mulieres eciam e seculo fugientes ad conversionem recipere et eos absque contradictione aliqua retinere; illud districtius inhibentes, ne terras aut quodlibet beneficium ecclesie vestre collatum liceat alicui personaliter dare sive alio modo alienare absque consensu omnium fratrum vel maioris aut sanioris partis ipsorum. Si que vero donaciones aut alienationes aliter quam dictum est facte fuerint, eas irritas esse censemus. Crisma vero, oleum sanctum, consecrationes altarium seu basilicarum, ordinationes clericorum, qui ad sacros ordines fuerint promovendi, a diocesano suscipiatis episcopo, siquidem catholicus fuerit et communionem sacrosancte Romane sedis habuerit et ea vobis voluerit sine pravitate aliqua exhibere; alioquin liceat vobis quemcunque malueritis catholicum adire antistitem gratiam et communionem apostolice sedis habentem, qui nostra fretus auctoritate vobis quod postulatur impendat. Porro si episcopi vel alii ecclesiarum rectores in hospitale vestrum vel in personas ibi constitutas suspensionis, excommunicacionis vel interdicti sententias promulgaverint sive eciam in mercenarios vestros pro eo, quod decimas non solvitis, sive aliqua occasione eorum, que a nobis de benignitate et misericordia vobis indulta sunt, seu benefactores vestros pro eo, quod aliqua vobis beneficia vel obsequia ex caritate prestiterint vel ad laborandum adiuverint in illis diebus, in quibus vos laboratis et alii feriantur, eandem sententiam pertulerint, ipsam tanquam iniustam prolatam decernimus non tenere. Preterea, cum commune interdictum terre fuerit, liceat vobis in vestro hospitali nichilominus exclusis excommunicatis et interdictis divina officia celebrare et eos maxime confratres eidem hospitali annua beneficia exhibentes, qui in iam dicto hospitali elegerint sepulturam, nisi pro suis excessibus fuerint excommunicati et nominatim vel specialiter interdicti, libere et sine contradictione aliqua tumuletis. Paci quoque et tranquillitati vestre paterna in posterum sollicitudine providere volentes, legatione qua fungimur inhibemus, ut infra clausuras locorum seu grangiarum vestrarum nullus rapinam seu[4] furtum facere, ignem apponere, sanguinem fundere, hominem temere capere seu interficere seu violenciam audeat exercere. Decernimus ergo, ut nulli omnino hominum liceat prefatum hospitale temere perturbare aut eius possessiones auferre aut ablatas retinere, minuere seu quibuslibet vexationibus fatigare, sed omnia integra conserventur eorum, pro quorum gubernatione ac sustentatione concessa sunt, usibus omnimodis profutura. Si qua igitur in futurum ecclesiastica secularisve persona hanc nostre constitucionis paginam sciens contra eam temere venire temptaverit, secundo terciove commonita nisi reatum suum congrua satisfactione correxerit, potestatis honorisque sui dignitate careat reamque se divino iudicio existere de perpetrata iniquitate cognoscat et a sacratissimo corpore et sanguine dei et domini nostri Ihesu

Christi aliena fiat atque in extremo examine districte ultioni subiaceat. Cunctis autem eidem loco sua iura servantibus sit pax domini nostri Ihesu Christi, quatinus et hic fructum bone actionis percipiant et apud districtum iudicem premia eterne pacis inveniant. Amen. Amen. Amen. Datum Constantinopoli ii nonas februarii pontificatus domini Innocencii pape tercii anno septimo decimo.

I, 56v. n. 110. 1. bis B. 2. Ps. 83, 11. 3. Andrevill' i. e. de Andravida. Caeterum de historia ordinis Theutonici ballivae Romaniae cf. Caroli Hopf Veneto-byzantinische Analecten in Sitzungsberichte der k. k. Akademie zu Wien. 1859. Nov. p. 367 sq. (5 sq.) sub titulo: Der deutsche Orden in Griechenland, et eiusdem: Geschichte Griechenlands vom Beginne des Mittelalters bis auf unsere Zeit in Ersch et Gruber encyclopaedia A. 85. Lipsiae 1867. 4. seu B.

---

130. .... *Robertus de Insula donat hospitali S. Iacobi de Andrevilla duo estagia prope Vilegourt in pertinencia de Chimeron.*

Sachent tuit cil qui sont et qui cestes presentes letres veront, que mesire Robert de l'Isle[1] chavaliers a done a la maison de mon seignour sant Jaque d'Andrevile por deu et en aumoisne et par sa arme et par l'arme ma dame Peronele sa femma et par l'arme de son pere Johan et de Mehant sa mere et de feu Comes son frere dos estacges, qui sont ens el contorn de Vilegourt de la pertinence deu Chimeron de son propri fieu et de sa droite conqueste ab tota la terra et ab totas las vignes, qui apartinent als ii estacges devant nomes, sans ce que il en a retenu una pece de terra de iiii muis de forment de semeure. E avec les ii estaies devant nomes a done li davant dis Robers a la maison davant dite Johan Lagor et ses dos freres et lor meismes et Johan Catomerite et Vasile son frere et Curiache et Johanni Gonople et les meismes de tos ces homes nomes. E ceste aumosne a receu da frere Guillelmes maestre de la davant dite maison par la volente et par consel des freres de cele meisme maison par tel convenent, que li freres de la davant dite maison saint Jaque[2] d'Andrevile devent tenir pardurablement vii prestres Latin messe chantant sur cele meisme aumosne, qui davant est nommee. Et si il avenoit, que li frere de la davant dite maison defalissent al novre fois[3] del prestres tenir en la davant dite aumosne le termine de ii mois, li davant ditz Robert de l'Isle ou seu erez reprendoient et auroient l'aumosne davant nomee et en faroient com de lour chose sans home raimbre ne femme jusque aitant que li prestres Latins messe chantans i seront remis. Et quant li prestre i seront remis, li frere davant dite maison reprehendroient la lour chose et revendroit l'aumosne davant dite en lur mains por faire lo servise de Jhesu Crist et por tenir la covenence, si com davant es devisee. Et por ce[4], que ceste chose parmaigne ferme et estable pardurablement, je frere Guillelmes maestre de la davant dite maison par lo consel et par la volente des freires de cele meisme maison i ai mis le seel de la davant dite maison. Et je maestre Nicholes par la grace de deu avesques de Couronne i ai mis lo mien seel el non de tesmoignagne ceste.

I, 58 n. 112. 1. V. cl. Hopf docet e gente Carpiniorum de Vostitza oriundum fuisse. 2. Jaqe B. 3. a lour foi? 4. co B.

---

131. *1237 iunio ap. Andrevillam. Goffridus prior et fratres hospitalis s. Iacobi de Andrevilla Gregorium papam IX rogant, ut ipsos cum hospitali suo ordini s. Mariae Theutonicorum uniat.*

Sanctissimo et universali in Christo patri ac domino Gregorio dei gracia sacrosancte Romane ecclesie summo pontifici Goffridus prior hospitalis sancti Iacobi de Andrevilla una cum capitulo et universitate fratrum et sororum eiusdem hospitalis pedum oscula beatorum. Qualiter dominus Goffridus princeps Achaye bone memorie domum hospitalis sancti Iacobi de Andrevilla pro salute anime sue ad pauperum sustentamen fundaverit, vestram sanctitatem credimus bene scire. Et cum nos, qui sumus fratres dicti hospitalis licet indigni, non simus sufficientes ad distributiones dicti hospitalis elemosinarum pro pauperum sustentatione et regula nostri ordinis observanda, quoniam nullam inter nos possumus invenire personam ad hoc ydoneam et timemus, sicut apertissime cotidie[1] videmus, ne bona dicti hospitalis pro defectu gubernatoris pessime pertractentur, immo, quod deterius est, ad nichilum redigantur, ad vestram sanctitatem, sicut debemus et tenemur, recurrimus confidenter, quoniam post deum nullum scimus habere certum refugium nisi vestrum, vestre sanctitati cum lacrimarum effusione humiliter supplicantes, quatinus preces, quas vobis fundimus, dignemini exaudire. Et quoniam secundum dispositionem fundatoris hospitalitatem tenemur modis omnibus observare et, ut iam diximus, pro defectu pastoris regulam et elemosinarum officium congrue non possumus gubernare, petimus humiliter et devote, quatinus[2] nos ordini sancte Marie Theotonicorum vestra dignetur sanctitas submittere atque unanimiter sociare, ut eorum vestigia sequentes et regulam eorum observantes nos, qui deviare videmur, viam veritatis consequi valeamus. Nam, si eorum ordini suberimus tanquam eorum alii fratres tocius ordinis, terra domini principis propter residenciam armatorum, qui in eodem loco permanebunt, securior permanebit; secundo in eadem domo pauperes misericordiam miserisorditer consequentur; tercio nos, qui nullum extra Romaniam refugium habere videmur, quod deus avertat, si terra dominium amitteret Latinorum, ab eis nos fratres et sorores possemus congrue sustentari[3]. In cuius rei testimonium presentibus litteris sigilla nostra apposuimus. Et nos Benedictus Cephaloniensis et Iiacinctinus episcopus et Iohannes Andrensis episcopus et Gerardus decanus Thebanus ad peticionem prioris et capituli sancti Iacobi de Andrevilla sigilla nostra presentibus litteris apposuimus. Datum apud Andrevillam mense iunii anno domini m° cc° xxx° vii°.

I, 53 n. 100 mancum in fine; cum chronologia 55 v. n. 106. 1. c. a. 53 v. 2. ut 55 v. 3. caetera desunt 53 v.

---

132. *c. 1237. Fratrum hospitalis sancti Iacobi de Andrevilla querelae contra Iohannem praeceptorem suum.*

Fratres sancti Iacobi proponunt contra fratrem Iohannem et dicunt, quando ipsum fecerunt preceptorem, quod iuravit et promisit bona fide servare bonos usus et consuetudinem regule, et promisit, quod alius frater domus deberet portare bursam et expendere ea, que domui essent necessaria, et quod non debebat solus equitare sine uno fratre vel capellano boni nominis; quod omnino non servavit; unde fratres dicunt eum periurum. Proponunt eciam contra ipsum, quod sine eorum consilio vendidit equos, dextrarios, mulos, boves et bubalos, poledros, frumentum, vinum et oleum, et de thesauro domus extraxit aurum et argentum, omnemque istam peccuniam dedit ubi voluit et quibus voluit sine fratrum consilio et assensu, cum regula dicat, quod eorum summus magister non possit dare ultra dimidiam marcham absque fratrum consensu; unde fratres dicunt, quod propter hanc causam debet amittere domum. Dicunt eciam contra ipsum, quod vi habuit rem cum quadam sorore domus, sicut ipsa publice conquesta fuit capitulo et clericis ac laicis secularibus. Item proponunt fratres, quod habebat puellas, cum quibus ad libitum suum concumbebat et postea maritabat eas dando eis bona domus, que fratribus et pauperibus erogare debebat. Item dicunt, quod alienavit possessiones ecclesie, sicut apparet et manifestum est. Dicunt eciam, quod sine licencia et voluntate eorum recessit de domo et fuit apud Iacinctum ad domum predictorum fratrum, que dicitur sancti Leonis, et expulit inde fratrem et sororem, qui ipsam domum custodiebant, et detinuit eam vi et, quod peius est, bona ipsius domus dedit Templariis et, quamdiu ibi fuit, vixit luxuriose. Item, quod contra libertatem et privilegia domus fuit Patras et impetravit ab archiepiscopo et ab electo Olonensi sentenciam excommunicacionis et interdicti domus et fratrum, cum omnibus constet domum sancti Iacobi et personas ibi constitutas alium prelatum non habere nisi dominum papam. Item dicunt, quod sine consensu fratrem quendam violenter rapuit de domo et fugiebat in eo; postea fratres invenerunt ipsum in domo domini Thome et rogaverunt eum, ut rediret ad domum, cuius se dicit esse fratrem; et omnino recusavit dicens: „Nunquam evo vobiscum, quia vos estis ex parte Theutonicorum; et ideo nolo redire.“ Prior et fratres dixerunt: „Nos habemus habitum sancti Iacobi, quem tu portas, unde precipimus tibi per illam obedienciam, quam fecisti ecclesie sancti Iacobi, et per habitum, quem portas, ut venias nobiscum ad domum nostram!“; quod omnino facere recusavit. Item privilegia domus furtive abstulit et in tali loco deposuit, quod fratres ea rehabere nequaquam possunt, nec ipse reddere vult. Item sine conscientia fratrum navigio fecit asportari frumentum de quadam domo eorum, que dicitur Rotumni, et nesciunt, quid de ipso frumento fecerit. Hec et alia plura perpetravit contra regulam ordinemque[1] domus destruendo et dissipando bona ecclesie, que sibi per comune fratrum capitulum sunt comprobata. Tandem ipsum secundo furtive fugientem fratres ceperunt et posuerunt in custodia. Nos autem Benedictus

Cephaloniensis et Iacinctinus episcopus, scientes, quod omnia vera sunt, que in presenti pagina continentur, que a fratribus sancti Iacobi et sororibus dicto Iohanni sunt probata secundum eorum regulam, rogati[2] a dictis fratribus et sororibus huic presenti pagine sigillum nostrum apposuimus rei veritatem testificando et confirmando. Et nos fratres et sorores sancti Iacobi, secundum quod omnia, que in presenti scripto continentur, fratri Iohanni supradicto in capitulo nostro probavimus secundum regulam nostram manifeste, huic presenti scripto sigillum capituli nostri apposuimus rei veritatem similiter confirmando.

I, 55 in n. 105. 1. et ordinemque B. 2. rogatus B.

---

133. *1237 iulio. Gaufridus de Villaharduini Achaiae princeps confert domum hospitalis sancti Iacobi in Andrevilla cum pertinentiis et domo in castello Clarimontis hospitali b. Mariae Theutonicorum.*

Nos Gaufr(idus) de Villahar(duini), Achaye princeps et Romanie senescalcus, notum facimus universis tam modernis quam posteris presentes litteras inspecturis, quod, cum domum hospitalis sancti Iacobi sitam in Andrevilla, quam genitor noster pie recordationis fundavit ad honorem divini nominis et pauperum sustentamen, defectu rectoris dedecenter procurari liquide nosceremus, propter quod res domus a fratribus iam distrahi ceperant et hospitalitas pauperum deperire, nec ad reservanda hec omnia in eadem domo personas ydoneas videremus, iure patronatus, quod ad nos pertinet in illa, cupientes sepedicte domui commodius providere, ideo dedimus et concessimus eam hospitali beate Marie Theotonicorum Ierosolimitano cum pertinenciis et omnibus bonis suis habendam, sibi tenendam et possidendam perpetim sine nostra nostrorumque heredum seu successorum controversia vel requisitione, ita tamen, quod ipsum hospitale Theutonicorum in supradicta domo sancti Iacobi teneat hospitalitatem, sicut a fundationis primordio statutum fuit, et habeat ibidem perhenniter suis sumptibus iiii^{or} capellanos, qui pro aminabus parentum nostrorum ibi debeant celebrare. Similiter sepedictum hospitale Theutonicorum habeat caput conventus sui in partibus Romanie in predicta domo sancti Iacobi et habeat domum unam in castello nostro Clarimontis, quod, si expedierit pro defensione ipsius castri, totus conventus residenciam faciat in eodem. In cuius rei testimonium presens scriptum sigillo proprio communivi. Actum anno domini m° cc° xxx° vii° mense iulio.

I, 58v. n. 113.

---

134. *1237 sept. 16 Viterbii. Gregorius papa IX concedit fratribus hospitalis S. Iacobi de Andrevilla, ut ordini hospitalis s. Mariae Theutonicorum uniantur.*

Gregorius episcopus servus servorum dei dilectis filiis .. preceptori et fratribus hospitalis sancti Iacobi de Andrevilla Olenensis[1] diocesis salutem et apostolicam benedictionem. De locis divino cultui deputatis in desiderio nostro geritur, ut, que ipsorum statum prosperitatis obtinent, augmentum in illa suscipiant et iam collapsa repparacionis oportune remedium assequantur. Ex parte siquidem dilecti filii nobilis viri G(aufridi) principis Achaye fuit propositum coram nobis, quod clare memorie pater suus ad honorem beati Iacobi auctoritate bone memorie ..[2] Albanensis episcopi tunc in partibus illis apostolice sedis legati hospitale cum ecclesia eterne retributionis obtentu fundavit, que idem legatus exempcionis privilegio confirmato per sedem apostolicam communivit. Et quamquam ibidem iuxta fundatoris votum religio et hospitalitas vise fuerint aliquamdiu reflorere, tamen dictum hospitale refrigescente caritate habitancium in eodem in spiritualibus et temporalibus adeo collapsum esse dinoscitur, ut per se ipsum posse reformari facile non credatur. Cupiens igitur memoratus princeps, ut in eodem loco per divine laudis frequenciam et opera debite caritatis predicti fundatoris anime perhennis, quam vivens optavit, felicitas impetretur, nobis humiliter supplicavit, ut vobis, quorum ad hoc voluntas accedere dicitur et assensus, licenciam transeundi cum omnibus bonis vestris ad ordinem hospitalis sancte Marie Theotonicorum de Romania de benignitate solita largiremur, presertim cum, sicut asserit, per unionem huiusmodi Romanie[3] imperio ac terre sancte profectibus utilitatis multe materia procuretur. Nos igitur eiusdem principis supplicationibus inclinati dilectis filiis .. electo Coronensi, .. abbati et .. priori de Saracaz Corinthiensis diocesis[4] dedimus nostris litteris in mandatis, ut vobis, si, quod de hospitalis vestri exemptione proponitur, veritate fulcitur et nulli alteri ordini est subiectum, auctoritate nostra concedant licenciam postulatam. Datum Viterbii xvi° kal. octobris pontificatus nostri anno xi°.

I, 53 n. 101 et 55 v. n. 107. Abraham Bzovius Ann. eccles. XIII, Coloniae 1621, contendit 1239 Gregorium IX Achaiae principi praecepisse, ut Theutonicis militibus ex hospitali Andrevillae exclusis illud fratribus S. Iohannis Hierosolymitani restituat. 1. Olen̄ B. 53. 2. sc. Pelagii, v. p. 129. 3. Romano B. 53 v. 4. diachon̄ B.

---

135. *1237 sept. 16 Viterbii. Gregorius papa IX idem praeceptori et fratribus hospitalis s. Mariae Theutonicorum in Romania notum facit.*

Gregorius episcopus servus servorum dei dilectis filiis preceptori et fratribus hospitalis sancte Marie Theotonicorum in Romania salutem et apostolicam benedictionem. De locis divino cultui deputatis in desiderio nostro geritur, ut, que ipsorum statum prosperitatis obtinent, augmentum in illa suscipiant et iam collapsa repparationis oportune remedium assequantur. Ex parte siquidem dilecti filii nobilis viri G(aufridi) principis Achaye fuit propositum coram nobis consonat praecedenti bullae usque supplicavit, ut dilectis filiis .. preceptori et fratribus hospitalis eiusdem, quorum ad hoc voluntas accedere dicitur et assensus, licenciam transeundi ad ordinem vestrum cum bonis omnibus eorundem de benignitate solita largiremur, presertim cetera ut l. c. usque Romanie imperio usque ut eisdem preceptori et fratribus sancti Iacobi, si, quod de ipsius exempcione proponitur, veritate fulcitur et nulli alteri ordini est subiectum, auctoritate nostra concedant licenciam postulatam. Datum Viterbii xvi° kal. octobris pontificatus nostri anno xi°.

I, 53 n. 102 et 56 n. 108.

136. *1237 sept. 16 Viterbii. Gregorius papa IX executoribus de eadem re.*

Gregorius episcopus servus servorum dei dilectis filiis .. electo Coronensi, .. abbati et .. priori de Saracaz Corintiensis diocesis salutem et apostolicam benedictionem. De locis ut supra; pro clare: bone, pro bone pie — ad ordinem hospitalis sancte Marie Theotonicorum de Romania — Romanie imperio — inclinati, discretioni vestre per apostolica scripta mandamus, quatinus predictis preceptori et fratribus hospitalis sancti Iacobi, si, quod de ipsius exemptione proponitur, veritate fulcitur et nulli alteri ordini est subiectum, auctoritate vestra postulatam licentiam concedatis. Quodsi non omnes hiis exequendis poteritis interesse, duo vestrum ea nichilominus exequantur. Datum Viterbii xvi° kal. octobris pontificatus nostri anno undecimo.

I, 54 n. 103 et 56v. n. 109.

137. *1239 exeunte mart. Robertus de Insula donat domui s. Mariae Theutonicorum duo estagia in territorio de Vilegort in pertinentiis de Chimeron et 80 mansos.*

Sachent tuit cil qui sunt e qui avenir sunt, ge je Robers de l'Isle chevaliers ai done por dieu et en almosne por l'arme de moi et de Peronele ma feme et de mon pere et de ma mere et de sueu quenon[1] mon frere a la maison de nostre dame des Alamans dous estages de terre, qui sunt ens el terrier de Vilegort de la partenence de Chimeron e de ma propre[2] conqueste[3], sans ce que li davan dit Robers a retenu de cele terre meisme une piece de terre de quatre muis de semense, et avec ce il i a done Johan Lagot et ses dous freres et Johan Cathemerite et ses deus freres et Johannin Geunople. Et la davant dita maison de nostre dame des Alamans doit tenir vii prestres messe chantanz et vii clers et faire le service deu en cele propre aumoine devant nomee en cel propre leu et pardurablement. Et si il avenoit, que la davant dite maison defausist de sis mois, li devant dit Robert ou seu oir porront prendre[4] le davant dit leu et fere comme de la leur chose de ci aitant que li prestres i soit remis por faire le service dieu et por acomplir la covenense aisint come davant est dite. Et encor croist li davant dit Robers l'aumoisne de iiii^vins muis de terre de semeure, et gist a la close de lonc le flum. Ceste chose est reubeue par lo conseil des freres des Alamans; et il i ant mis lo seel de la maison en nom de testimoniage. Ce fu fait en l'an de l'incarnation de nostre seingnor Jhesu Crist m° cc° xxx° ix° el mois de mars et es kal. de april.

I, 58v. n. 114. 1. ? e in que epunctum videtur. Supra p. 131: de feu Comes. 2. prope B. 3. conqeste B. 4. pendre B.

138. *1240 maio. Executorum processus de uniendo hospitali S. Iacobi de Andrevilla ordini Theutonico. In fine transsumtoria formula de 1240 octobri.*

Universis presentes litteras inspecturis Petrus dechanus, Guido archidiaconus Monovasiensis salutem in domino. Noverint universi, quod venerabilis pater P. bone memorie quondam Coroniensis episcopus, .. abbas et prior de Saracaz litteras domini pape sub hac forma receperunt:

Gregorius episcopus etc. *(sequitur electo Coroniensi, abbati et priori de Saracaz missa bulla de 1237 sept. 16 Viterbii supra p. 136 n. 136).* Verum quia predicti episcopus et eius college legitime impediti mandatum domini pape exequi minime potuerunt, ut debebant, vices suas nobis totaliter delegaverunt. Volentes igitur eorundum obedire mandatis, ad dictam domum beati Iacobi anno domini m° cc° xxx° viii° mense septembri cum viris providis et discretis accessimus personaliter diligentissime inquirentes, utrum domus ipsa esset exempta vel alteri ordini subiecta. Unde, cum nobis veraciter constitisset dictam domum esse exemptam et alteri ordini non subiectam, sicut fratres, qui presentes erant, oretenus confitebantur, fratribus predicte domus ad ordinem Theutonicorum licenciam iuxta domini pape mandatum concessimus transeundi. Quedam vero pars dictorum fratrum sancti Iacobi habitum Theotonicorum pacifice susceperunt. Datum anno domini m° cc° xl° mense maio.

Universis Christi fidelibus, ad quos littere presentes pervenerint, Iohannes dei gracia episcopus et Albricus decanus Lacedemonenses salutem et prosperos ad vota successus. Noverit universitas vestra, quod nos vidimus omnes litteras sigillatas, quarum superius transscripta in presenti sedula[1] continentur et eadem de verbo ad verbum transscribi fecimus. In cuius rei testimonium sigilla nostra presenti cartule apposuimus. Actum anno domini m° cc° xl° mense octobri.

I, 54 n. 104 et 57 v. n. 111. 1. i. e. scedula. Agi videtur de n. 131. 134. 135. 136. 138, quae praecedunt.

---

139. *ante 1241 apr. 26. Gaufridus de Villaharduini, Achaiae princeps, supplicat Gregorio papae IX, ut S. Iacobi de Andrevilla hospitale ordini Theutonico confirmet. In fine formula transsumtoria de 1241 aprilis 26.*

Sanctissimo patri ac domino suo Gregorio dei gracia sacrosancte Romane ecclesie summo et universali pontifici devotus eius filius Gaufridus de Villeard(uini), Achaye princeps et Romanie senescalcus, ad sanctorum pedum oscula se devotum. Cum, sicut sanctitati vestre sepius innotuit, hospitale sancti Iacobi de Andrevilla a pie recordationis genitore nostro ad honorem divini nominis et pauperum sustentamen fundatum fuerit et ibidem aliquamdiu hospitalitas visa fuerit reflorere, tandem in eodem frigescente karitate pro defectu rectoris non solum hospitalitas deperiret, verum dicti hospitalis bona a fratribus distraherentur nec ad ipsius regimen in ipso persone sufficientes et idonee haberentur, nos prudencium virorum usi consilio, iure patronatus, qui ad nos pertinet, cupientes eidem commodius providere, ipsum cum omnibus pertinenciis suis, quantum ad nos pertinet, ad peticionem fratrum eiusdem hospitali sancte Marie Theotonicorum Ierusalem dedimus et concessimus libere ac pacifice sine contradictione aliqua in perpetuum possidendum. Vos vero de solita sedis apostolice benivolencia ad nostram et fratrum dicti hospitalis sancti Iacobi supplicationem ipsis fratribus ad ordinem Theutonicorum concessistis licenciam transeundi et ipsorum habitum assumendi dato vestris litteris in mandatis venerabili patri episcopo Coroniensi, abbati et priori de Zarcaz, quod, si de ipsius hospitalis exempcione sibi constaret et nulli alteri ordini subiaceret, fratribus eiusdem licenciam concederent postulatam. Qui facta diligenter et subtiliter inquisicione, cum de dicta exempcione plenius essent cerciorati et quod nulli alteri ordini esset subiectum, memoratis fratribus auctoritate vestra transeundi ad ordinem Theutonicorum et ipsorum habitum assumendi postulatam licenciam concesserunt. Fratres vero, qui soli digni fuerunt benedictione, fere omnes ipsorum habitum devote et humiliter susceperunt. Postmodum autem Iohannes Mancus et Iulianus, filii iniquitatis et mendacii, qui de communi fratrum sancti Iacobi iudicio pro excessibus et insolenciis suis habitum amiserant nec pro fratribus habebantur, ad vestram accedentes presenciam, verum tacentes et falsum suggerentes contra dictos fratres Theutonicos a vobis ad magistrum Bernardum subdiaconum vestrum spoliacionem mencientes litteras impetrarunt, quarum auctoritate ipsos vexantes dictam domum contra vestram et nostram concessionem reclamando, quod indigne ferimus, eisdem contra iusticiam dampnum inferunt et gravamen, unde memorati Theutonici iusticiam et innocenciam suam deffendentes bona domus adversus infirmorum et pauperum deputata inutiliter expendere compelluntur. Preterea, quod amplius indignamur, dicti apostate iniquitatem super iniquitatem apponentes, volentes venerabilis patris Patracensis archiepiscopi et electi Olonensis in causa sua pessima habere patrocinium et favorem, dicto electo obedienciam facientes spoponderunt, quod, si in dicta causa, quod, quoadusque vixerimus, fieri non potest, poterunt prevalere, ita quod Theutonicis expulsis dictum hospitale optineant contra privilegia exempcionis, quibus constat domum esse exemptam et nulli prelatorum nisi Romano pontifici subiacere, ipsam dicti electi subiacere dicioni, quod nullatenus vellemus tolerare. Unde, cum dominus Patracensis archiepiscopus inter omnes prelatos Romanie reverencior habeatur, fere omnes alii prelati ipsius favorem prosequentes dictis Theutonicis fratribus cum ipso se opponunt, partem adversam minus iuste sustinendo. Inde est, quod sanctitati paternitatis vestre supplicamus humiliter deprecantes, quatinus sepius nominatum hospitale secundum concessionem vestram et nostram confirmationis vestre privilegium precum nostrarum interventu dignetur vestra paternitas communire perpetuum dictis malignatoribus silencium imponendo, ut, quod tanti patris et nostra auctoritas actum esse ad honorem dei iuste et misericorditer dinoscitur, perhennitatis robore fulciatur et inviolabile conservetur nec in posterum alicui hominum confirmationi vestre ausu temerario liceat contraire, quia nullo modo volumus sustinere, quod tante karitatis plantatio, in qua felicis memorie pater et mater nostra sibi sepulturam elegerunt, pristine infamie subiaceret, quoniam testante sapiente[1],

non bene celestes impia dextra colit.

Domus enim, que per fratrum luxum et infamiam corruerat et fere ad nichilum redacta fuerat, unde et viri catholici et matrone, qui caritative suas pro pauperibus sustentandis helemosinas largiri consueverant, manus penitus ab eadem retraxerant, per dei graciam per Theutonicorum honestatem et providenciam respiravit, unde et dicti viri et matrone largas helemosinas largiendo manum aperiunt largitatis, et ibidem infirmi visitantur, pauperes colliguntur et alia omnia karitatis opera exercentur et fratres omnes oracionibus devotis et vigiliis intenti deo iugiter famulantur. Alii vero

desidie torpore graves luxuque soluti

omnia sancte domus diverticula incontinencie sue sordibus macularant.

Nos autem miseratione divina L(andus) Messanensis archiepiscopus et R(ainerius) sancte Marie in Cosmedin diaconus cardinalis notum facimus universis presentem paginam inspecturis, nos vidisse et perlegisse litteram non viciatam non cancellatam, nichil additum vel diminutum, sigillo nobilis viri G(aufridi) principis Achaye et Romanie senescalci sigillatam, cuius rescriptum de verbo ad verbum in superiori pagina continetur. In cuius rei testimonium presens scriptum sigillorum nostrorum munimine duximus roborandum. Datum Rome aput sanctum Clementem vi° kalendas madii pontificatus domini Gregorii pape noni anno quintodecimo.

I, 52 n. 99. 1. sc. Ovidio Heroid. VII, 130.

---

140. *1241 iulii 19 Romae. Duo cardinales transsumunt complura documenta hospitale S. Iacobi de Andrevilla spectantia.*

Nos divina miseratione Guiffredus Sabinensis[1] episcopus et Rainerius sancte Marie in Cosmedin diaconus cardinales notum facimus universis nos vidisse et perlegisse de verbo ad verbum litteras non cancellatas, non viciatas nec abolitas, nullo addito vel diminuto, sigillis debitis et integris sigillatas, quarum rescripta in presenti pagina subsecuntur in hunc modum:

(*Inserta sunt:* 1. Fratrum hospitalis sancti Iacobi de Andrevilla querelae contra Iohannem praeceptorem; supra p. 133 n. 132;

2. 1237 iunio apud Andrevillam. Goffridi prioris et capituli hospitalis s. Iacobi preces ad Gregorium papam IX missae, ut uniantur ordini Theutonico; supra p. 132 n. 131;

3. 1237 sept. 16 Viterbii. Gregorius papa IX concedit petentibus fratribus hospitalis s. Iacobi, ut uniantur ordini Theutonico; supra p. 134 n. 134;

4. 1237 sept. 16 Viterbii. Gregorius papa IX idem notum facit praeceptori et fratribus hospitalis s. Mariae Theutonicorum in Romania; supra p. 135 n. 135;

5. 1237 sept. 16 Viterbii. Gregorius papa IX electum Coroniensem, abbatem et priorem de Saracaz Corinthiensis diocesis executores constituit; supra p. 136 n. 136;

6. 1214 febr. 4 Constantinopoli. Pelagius Albanensis cardinalis legatus s. Iacobi de Andrevilla hospitale exemptum esse iubet et confirmat bona eius et libertates; supra p. 129 n. 129;

7. 1240 maio. Executorum apostolicae iussionis relatio de processu licentiae fratribus s. Iacobi ad ordinem Theutonicum transeundi datae (cf. supra p. 137 n. 138) cui insertum n. 5 p. 136 n. 136.)

In cuius rei testimonium sigilla nostra presenti pagine duximus apponenda. Datum Rome anno domini m° cc° xl° i° xiiii° kal. augusti.

I, 55—58. 1. sabbinensis B.

APULIA. ROMA. FRANCIA.

---

141. *1197 maii 20 Panormi (xiii kal. iunii ind. xv). Heinricus VI Romanorum imperator confirmat fratribus hospitalis Theutonicorum apud Ierusalem in honore b. Mariae constructi hospitale s. Thomae de ordine ipsorum apud Barolum inceptum et fundatum, in tenimento Cannarum prope Barolum terras laboratorias ad decem paricla, ecclesiam s. Nicolai de Rigula.*

I, 37 v. n. 85. A. Boehmero communicatum edidit I. H. Hennes Codex diplomaticus ordinis s. Mariae Theutonicorum. Urkundenbuch des Deutschen Ordens. Mainz 1845. 8. p. 1. Cf. infra 1204 septbr. — Pauca quaedam de aliis ordinis Theutonici conventibus praeter Barolitanum Hermanni de Salza funere clarum in Apulia quondam constitutis deposui in H. W. Schulz Denkmäler der Kunst des Mittelalters in Unteritalien. Dresden 1860. 4.; scilicet de Ostunensi ad s. Mariam de Ierusalem 1226 fundato I, 90 sq. nota 2; Andriensi (c. 1230) ad s. Leonhardum, s. Leonhardi (de la Marina) Sipontinae diocesis, Terlitiensi ad s. Mariam de Suberito, s. Leonhardi inter Asculum et Cerinolam I, 152 sq. 63 sq.

---

142. *1204 septembri in urbe felici Panormi. Fridericus Siciliae rex ecclesiam S. Thomae de Barolo in protectionem suam suscipit et donat ei domum et vineas quondam Berterami medici.*

Fredericus divina favente clemencia rex Sicilie, ducatus Apulie et principatus Capue. Prociens munificencie principalis salus et honor multimodis preconiis augmentatur et thesauros immarcessibiles curia regalis comparat in futurum, quociens largiciones sue munificencie locis venerandis[1] et divinis obsequiis dedicatis gratanter impendit et studet largis possessionibus ea cotidie sublimare. Attendentes itaque nos, qualiter gloriosissimi reges et triumphatores augusti divi progenitores nostri digne memorie pie consueverunt sacrosanctas ecclesias dicare et immensis ampliare tenimentis illorumque proponentes firmiter de bono in melius immutare vestigia et facta inviolabiliter conservare venerandam[1] ecclesiam sancti Thome de Barolo, tempore[3] quondam domini Henrici incliti patris nostri, magnifici Romanorum imperatoris, constructam, sub nostri culminis protectione manu tenere et augmentare cupimus, et pro redemptione animarum parentum nostrorum bone memorie ac pro salute nostra de innata nobis benivolencia concedimus atque donamus eidem ecclesie et presentis auctoritatis nostre munimine in perpetuum confirmamus vineas et ortum integrum, sicut quondam Berteramus medicus Baroli, dum vixerit, in demanio nostro, palude Baruli, tenuit et possedit, cum omnibus pertinenciis orti et vinearum ipsarum, statuentes et precipientes firmiter, ut amodo et in perpetuum prenominata ecclesia ac procuratores sui dictum ortum in integrum et vineas, sicut dictus Berteramus usque ad ultimum vite sue tenuit et possedit, quiete et sine alicuius contradictione hereditario iure teneant et possideant liberas et absolutas ab omni datione seu calumpnia. Et nulli sit licitum sub pena rerum suarum et nostre gracie indignatione de predictis possessionibus ipsam ecclesiam seu fratres eius et homines ratione vel occasione qualibet impedire, molestare seu fatigare. Ad huius autem concessionis, donationis et confirmationis nostre memoriam et firmitatem perpetuo valituram presens privilegium ei scribi et maiestatis nostre sigillo iussimus communiri anno, mense et indictione subscriptis. Datum in urbe felici Panormi anno dominice incarnationis m° cc° iiii° mense septembris indictionis viii° regni vero domini nostri Frederici dei gratia illustrissimi regis Sicilie[3], ducatus Apulie et principatus Capue, anno vii° feliciter. Amen.

I, 37 v. n. 86. Nota, quod Huillard-Bréholles I, 110 ex originali archivi Neapolitani s. Severini edidit eiusdem diploma de 1204 octbr. in urbe felici Panormi, quo Heinrici VI patris diploma de 1197 mai. 20 (supra p. 141 n. 141) confirmat et auget. 1. venerunt B. 2. temporum B. 3. scilicet B.

---

143. *1206 ianuario in urbe felici Panormi. Fridericus Siciliae rex donat ecclesiae s. Mariae et fratribus hospitalis Theutonicorum apud Ierusalem casale Tuscanum inter Salernum et Ebolum situm et statuit, ut porro omnia bona in regno libera possideant ab omni tributo et requisitione. Si quis fratrum vel servientium extraneorum vel hominum illorum praedicti casalis de aliquo conveniatur, non cogatur nisi in foro ecclesiae respondere, dummodo non fuerit de criminalibus appellatus, de quibus confessus vel comprobatus poenam corporis vel membrorum mutilitatem subire debeat.*

I, 39 n. 88. Ex apographo difficiliori lectu inter Neapolitani archivi membrana vol. VI, 1203—1212 asservato ed. Huillard-Bréholles I, 911; ubi lacunae e codice B sic suppleantur: regia largitione subsidia dignum maxime; — presertim cum non uni; — extraneis vel de hominibus predicti casalis.

---

144. *1214 aprilis 22 Romae ap. S. Petrum. Innocentius papa III confirmat fratribus hospitalis Theutonicorum de Accon a Friderico Siciliae rege donatum casale Tussanum.*

Innocentius episcopus servus servorum dei dilectis filiis magistro et fratribus hospitalis Theutonicorum de Accon salutem et apostolicam benedictionem. Iustis petencium desideriis dignum est nos facilem prebere consensum et vota, que a rationis tramite non discordant, effectu prosequente complere. Eapropter, dilecti in domino filii, vestris iustis postulationibus grato concurrentes assensu casale, quod dicitur Tussanum, situm inter Salernum et Ebolum[1], cum omnibus[2] possessionibus, tenimentis et omnibus pertinenciis suis a carissimo in Christo filio nostro F(riderico), Sicilie rege illustri, hospitali vestro pia liberalitate[3] collatum, sicut ea omnia iuste ac pacifice possidetis, vobis et per vos eidem hospitali auctoritate apostolica confirmamus et presentis scripti patrocinio communimus. Nulli ergo omnino hominum liceat hanc paginam nostre confirmationis infringere vel ei ausu temerario contraire. Si quis autem hoc attemptare presumpserit, indignationem omnipotentis dei et beatorum Petri et Pauli apostolorum eius se noverit incursurum. Datum Rome apud sanctum Petrum x kalendas maii pontificatus nostri anno xvii°.

I, 60. In copiario Regimontano A. 16 p. 37 exstat inter „papalia que inveniuntur in Barulo" referente v. cl. Meckelburg. 1. Ebirlum A. 16. 2. hominibus A. 16. 3. libertate B.

---

145. *1215 oct. 20 Hagenowie. Fridericus, Romanorum et Siciliae rex, attenta honestate domus hospitalis Theutonicorum in civitate Acchon terrae promissionis ad laudem dei et virginis Mariae ex donationibus regum et aliorum principum et nobilium constructae donat domum suam dictam Margariti in civitate Brundusina cum balneo; theloneum vero et monetam usque in moderna tempora in domo ista exercita sibi reservat.*

I, 39 n. 89, unde Boehmer communicavit cum v. cl. Hennes, qui ed. cod. ord. Theut. I, 17 n. 18. Huillard-Bréholles I, 428.

---

146. *1217 („1216") maii 25 Augustae. Fridericus, Romanorum et Siciliae rex, hospitali s. M. et domui Th. in I. donat de sicla et de ceteris proventibus regiis apud Messanum primo solvendis ducentas uncias auri bonorum tarenorum ad pondus Baroli singulis annis ad usus hiemales pro mantellis et agninis pellibus („pennis" B) usui fratrum et caeterorum pauperum transmarinorum mancipandis.*

I, 40 n. 90, unde Boehmer communicavit cum Hennes Cod. ord. Th. I, 31 n. 28; monet ille apographum de 1521 Stuttgarti adservatum praebere: viii kal. iulii. Huillard-Bréholles I, 510.

---

147. *1218 augusto. Brundusinorum iudicum testimonium de testamento a Lanfranco de Bogossa in favorem domus hospitalis Theutonicorum edito.*

Anno dominice incarnationis m° cc° x° viii° regnante domino nostro Frederico, dei gracia serenissimo Romanorum rege semper augusto et rege Sicilie, anno xx° mense augusti indictione sexta, nos Benedictus, Stephanus, Peregrinus et Ricardus, regales Brundusii iudices, declaramus, quod, cum Lamfrancus de Bogossa, filius Milonis de Bogossa, in Brundusio infirmitate detentus de rebus suis ultimam voluntatem ordinasset in presencia Iacobi de Potenciano, Alberici Parriciole, Nicolay Crassi, Bartholomei de Salerno et Garnerii filii Nauclerii[1] Ihohannotarii[2] de Berterando et eius dispositio per dictum Guarnerium et non per publicum[3] notarium in scriptis redacta fuisset, frater Gunterius, magister domus hospitalis Theotonicorum Brundusii, eo ibi ex ipsa infirmitate defuncto rogavit nos, ut predictos testes, qui dispositioni predicte Lamfranci de Bogossa interfuerunt, receperimus et disposicionem ipsius secundum testimonium ipsorum ad perpetuam memoriam, firmitatem et securitatem predicte domus hospitalis Brundusii Theutonicorum in scriptis per publicum notarium redigi faceremus. Nos autem iustam peticionem eius admittentes predictos homines, qui dicebantur ordinacioni predicti Lanfranci interfuisse, ante nos venire fecimus et in nostra presencia et aliorum proborum hominum testium subscriptorum eos, ut dicerent veritatem nobis de ultima voluntate predicti Lamfranci, iurare fecimus; et prestito ab eis iuramento dixerunt se interfuisse apud hospitale Theutonicorum Brundusii, ubi dictus Lanfrancus taliter disposuit, sicuti in litteris scriptis a predicto Guarnerio continetur, quarum tenor hic est:

„Ego Lanfrancus de Bogossa, iacens in lectulo meo gravi infirmitate detentus, considerans casum et transitum universe carnis, timens, ne ab hoc fragili seculo intestatus decederem et res mee inordinate remanerent, dum integer sensus et lingua recta mihi remanerent inlesi, probos homines testes subscriptos coram me venire rogavi, in quorum presencia de rebus meis sic dispono: In primis relinquo et iudico domui hospitalis sancte Marie Teotonicorum mansum unum de terra ad laborandum et duas domus, que sunt intus in ipso manso, et vineam cum arboribus fructiferis et infructiferis, que vinea vocatur Clausoria dulcis et est prope sanctum Laurentium iuxta terram domini Iohannelli de Verona. Relinquo eciam eidem domui hospitalis Theotonicorum unam alteram domum, que est ad portum et reddit in unoquoque anno libras denariorum novem de illa moneta et xii capones et ecclesie sancti Laurentii baccdam unam de oleo, et terra ipsius domus est longa xx et sex campi; et est prope domum domini Spera-in-deo. Volo eciam et statuo, ut post mortem meam omnes servi et serve mee sint liberi in perpetuum“.

Unde ad securitatem et perpetuam memoriam prefati hospitalis sancte Marie Theotonicorum disposicionem prefati Lamfranci de Bogossa in presencia prescriptorum proborum virorum scriptam et eorum sacramento approbatam, ut superius continetur in scriptis, redigi fecimus, quam scribere iussimus Angelum Brundusii regium notarium, qui una nobiscum in examinatione testium et iuramento interfuit et audivit anno, mense et indictione pretitulatis.

(Locus signi.)

+ Peregrinus iudex.

+ Benedictus iudex.

+ Signum manus proprie Bartolomei de Salerno.

+ Ego Nicholaus Gonso testis sum.

+ Ego Garnerius filius Nauclerii Iohannotarii[4] testis sum.

+ Ego Iacobus de Potenciano testis sum.
+ Ego Albericus Paruzola testis sum.
+ Stephanus iudex.

I, 42 n. 93. 1. nauclii B. 2. ihohannoccarii B l. Iohannis notarii? 3. plublicum B. 4. 7 auclerii Iohan notarii B.

---

148. *1220 iunii 15 apud Urbem Veterem. Honorius papa III hospitale extra portam Fogiae sub sua protectione suscipit.*

Honorius cet. dilectis filiis magistro et fratribus hospitalis extra portam Fogie in suburbio de Vassano salutem et apostolicam benedictionem. Cum a nobis petitur, quod iustum est et honestum, tam vigor equitatis quam ordo exigit rationis, ut id per sollicitudinem officii nostri ad debitum perducatur effectum. Eapropter, dilecti in domino filii, vestris iustis precibus inclinati, personas et hospitale vestrum cum omnibus bonis, que inpresentiarum rationabiliter possidetis aut in futurum prestante domino iustis modis poteritis adipisci, sub beati Petri et nostra protectione suscipimus et presentis scripti patrocinio communimus. Nulli ergo omnino hominum liceat hanc paginam nostre protectionis infringere vel cet. Si quis autem cet. Datum apud Urbem veterem xvii cal. iulii pontificatus nostri anno quarto.

Cum dato A. 16 p. 38 „Baruli". In margine: Honorius III°. Cum inscriptione „magistro et fr. h. S. M. Th. Ihr." et dato Laterani 17 cal. augusti p. n. a. 5 (1220 iul. 16) A. 16 p. 41 „Baruli" confirmatio donationis castri Mezani, ubi communis forma repetitur et loco verborum „personas et hospitale vestrum" dicitur „personas vestras et locum, in quo divino estis obsequio mancipati". Communicavit nobiscum v. cl. Meckelburg.

---

149. *1221 aprili Tarenti. Fridericus II imperator domum h. s. M. Th. i. I. cum omnibus bonis sub protectione sua recipit et bona eius omnia in regno Siciliae confirmat.*

Fredericus divina favente clemencia Romanorum imperator semper augustus et rex Sicilie. Etsi caduca sunt omnia et temporis diuturnitate labantur, sunt tamen ex omnibus aliqua perpetue stabilitati connexa, illa videlicet, que divinis addita cultibus hereditatis dei funiculum applicant[1], tunc precipue, cum loca venerabilia, in quibus placens[2] domino milicia militat, muniuntur munimine imperatorie maiestatis et eis[3] monimenta, que temporum vetustas non diluit, consideratione provida largiuntur. Eapropter notum facimus universis nostris fidelibus presentibus et futuris, quod nos meditatione piissima attendentes, qualiter sacra domus hospitalis sancte Marie Theutonicorum in Ierusalem a divo quondam augusto domino Frederico, avo nostro[4], pietatis intuitu propagata in multiplices fructus prodiit laude dignos et a domino quondam imperatore Henrico, recolende memorie patre nostro[4], rebus ac libertatibus premunita et incrementum suscepit spiritualiter et temporaliter domino famulando et fratrum ibidem militancium Ihesu Christo erga nostram magnificenciam cum fide devocio semper crevit; considerantes eciam celebrem vitam et honeste religionis cultum, quibus dilectus nobis in domino frater Hermannus magister hospitalis eiusdem et fratres ipsius clarere noscuntur, labores quoque ac sudores assiduos, quos pro fide christianorum et gloria sustinent incessanter, eterne retributionis obtentu ac pro remedio animarum progenitorum nostrorum recordationis inclite, necnon pro salutis nostre ac victorie incremento ipsorum favori ac profectui intendentes eandem sacram domum et ab ipsa quaslibet derivatas, fratres et confratres ipsarum cum omnibus bonis stabilibus et mobilibus, que per totum regnum nostrum rationabiliter possident in presenti et que inantea iustis modis poterunt adipisci, necnon subditos eorum eiusdem domus legacionem atque negocia exercentes, sub speciali protectione et defensione maiestatis nostre recepimus et eidem domui perpetuo confirmamus omnia privilegia et scripta quelibet tam a parentibus nostris quam a nobis sibi pia liberalitate[5] concessa, necnon casalia, homines et possessiones, que donatione regum vel principum, oblatione fidelium sive quolibet alio iusto titulo per totum regnum nostrum est adepta et que in futurum poterit adipisci, de quibus hec propriis vocabulis duximus exprimenda: in primis domum et hospitale sancti Thome, quod de ordine eorum aput Barolum est constructum, et in tenimento Cannarum prope Barolum terras laboratorias ad x paricla, et ecclesiam sancti Nicolay in Regula cum omnibus domibus, possessionibus ac pertinenciis suis et cum omni iure ac libertate earum, sicut olim largitione memorati domini patris nostri idem hospitale habuit et possedit, vineas eciam et ortum integrum, sicut quondam Bertannus medicus Bariolensis in demanio nostro, palude videlicet Baroli, tenuit et possedit, cum omnibus pertinenciis suis, sicut in instrumentis et privilegiis exinde ei indultis plenius continetur. Insuper confirmamus eisdem in perpetuum totum demanium nostrum, quod habemus in casali Tuscianensi, quod est inter Salernum et Ebolum, cum castellucio a comite Marcoardo ibidem constructo et cum omnibus hominibus, tenimentis et pertinentiis suis tam in mari quam in terra, sicut in privilegio maiestatis nostre eisdem domui et fratribus indulto expressius continetur. Necnon confirmamus eidem hospitali et fratribus in perpetuum cum consensu et voluntate Constancie, illustris Romanorum imperatricis et regine Sicilie, dilecte consortis nostre, et karissimi filii nostri regis Henrici domum quandam Margariti in civitate nostra Brundusii cum balneo et omnibus pertinenciis suis et cum omnibus aliis iusticiis et rationibus tam in mari quam in terra eidem domui pertinentibus, sicut ipsam prefatus Margaritus unquam melius dinoscitur tenuisse. De habundanciori quoque gracia nostra concedimus et confirmamus eidem hospitali in perpetuum castrum Mesanei[6] in terra Idronti, quod est inter Brundusium et Horiam, cum omnibus iustis tenimentis et pertinenciis suis, prout in privilegiis donationis ipsius domus et castri eidem hospitali a nostra maiestate indultis seriatim continetur. Quod castrum, prout novimus manifeste, eidem hospitali pia[7] liberalitate donaverat et concesserat dictus dominus pater noster, cuius concessionis privilegium casu fortuito[8] fuit amissum, quando Brundusini videlicet hospitale ipsum aggressi in ipsum et bona sua hostiliter ac rapaciter irruerunt. Concedimus predicta et confirmamus eidem sacre domui in perpetuum cum consensu et voluntate predicte consortis nostre c et quinquaginta uncias aureorum bonorum tarenorum scilicet ad pondus Baroli[9] de primis proventibus sicle, duane et aliorum reddituum civitatis nostre Brundusii annis singulis percipiendas, quas uncias eidem hospitali concessimus pro excambio cuiusdam tenimenti, quod ab eodem hospitali in Alamania recepimus, sicut in alio privilegio celsitudinis nostre eidem hospitali inde facto plenius continetur. Denique concedimus et confirmamus eidem hospitali et fratribus suis in perpetuum omnes libertates et immunitates per privilegia divorum augustorum parentum nostrorum et nostra eidem concessas, et ut specialiter ab omni plateatico, portulagio, palangio, tholonio et ab omni exactione et requisitione cuiuslibet iuris doanorum et portuum cum omnibus bonis suis per totum regnum nostrum in mari et in terra sint perpetuo liberi et immunes, et ut de passagio Fari a Sicilia in Calabriam et a Calabria in Siciliam cum omnibus rebus suis sint similiter perpetuo absoluti. Mandamus igitur auctoritate presentis privilegii firmiter statuentes, ne ulla unquam persona alta vel humilis, ecclesiastica vel secularis, prefatam sacram domum, fratres et omnia bona sua super predictis omnibus molestare presumat vel huic concessionis et confirmationis nostre pagine ausu temerario obviare; quod qui presumpserit, indignationem nostri[10] culminis et penam ducentarum librarum auri se noverit incursurum, medietatem camere nostre et reliquam medietatem passis iniuriam persolvendo. Ad huius autem concessionis, confirmationis et constitutionis nostre memoriam et robur perpetuo valiturum presens privilegium per manus Iohannis de Lauro notarii et fidelis nostri scribi et bulla aurea typario nostre maiestatis impressa duximus communiri, anno, mense et indictione subscriptis. Datum Tarenti anno dominice incarnationis m° cc° xx° i° mense aprilis indictione ix[a] imperii domini nostri Frederici dei gracia invictissimi Romanorum imperatoris semper augusti et regis Sicilie anno primi, regni vero Sicilie xx° iii° feliciter. Amen.

I, 42 v. n. 94. 1. ap'pliant B. 2. placere B. 3. eius B. 4. auuo meo B. 5. libertate B. 6. „hodie Misagna seu Mesagne" B. Speciale de hac confirmatione diploma et ipsum d. d. 1221 aprili Tarenti ex originali partim obliterato Neapolitani archivi edidit idem II, 163. 7. quia B. 8. fortuitu B. 9. boroli B. 10. nostre B.

---

150. *1221 decembri Cataniae. Fridericus II imperator (Imperium et regnum) declarat, se in coronatione sua imperiali Honorium papam flagitasse, ut domum s. M. Th. I., „quae divorum augustorum Friderici avi et Henrici patris nostri inclite recordationis structura fuit specialis", totum et integrum ordinem domorum Hospitalis s. Iohannis in pauperibus et infirmis et domus militiae Templi in clericis, militibus, aliis fratribus, atque immunitates utriusque concederet; papam vero concessisse petita. Ut vero magister et fratres in conservandis imperiali interventu obtentis suam munificentiam probarent, donat eis de redditibus sive baiulationis*

sive siclae Brundusinarum annuatim cc auri uncias ad emenda pallia alba, recipiendas, donec in regno cambio eis terrae laboratoriae assignarentur.

I, 40v. n. 91, unde edidit Huillard-Bréholles II, 224.

---

151. *1222 april. 19 Verulis. Honorius papa III confirmat domui h. s. M. Th. Friderici II imperatoris privilegium (n. 150) de redditibus annuis cc unciis auri Brundusii percipiendis.*

Honorius etc. magistro et fratribus etc. Iustis petencium desideriis dignum est, nos facilem prebere consensum et vota, que a rationis tramite non discordant, effectu prosequente complere. Cum igitur karissimus in Christo filius noster[1], Romanorum imperator semper augustus et rex Sicilie, in civitate Brundusii de redditibus suis sive de baiulatione sive de sicla specialiter pro emendis albis mantellis ad usum fratrum vestrorum militum annuatim cc uncias auri ad pondus Baruli vobis imperiali liberalitate donarit, tam diu vobis annis singulis exsolvendas[2] de redditibus supradictis, donec in terris laboratoriis seu aliis possessionibus regni competens vobis excambium imperialis munificencia largiatur, sicut in eius privilegio aurea bulla munito perspeximus contineri; nos ipsius imperatoris et vestris precibus inclinati donationem ipsam, sicut pie ac provide facta est et in ipso privilegio plenius continetur, auctoritate apostolica confirmamus et presentis scripti patrocinio co̅mmunimus. Nulli ergo etc. Si quis autem etc. Datum Verulis xiii kal. maii pontificatus nostri anno vi°.

I, 76v. n. 92. In Regimontano copiario A. 16 p. 14 inter papalia, quae inveniuntur Baruli. 1. videtur deesse F. 2. exsolvendis B.

---

152. *1228 mart. 15. Montis Pessulani consules assignant domui hospitalis Theutonicorum hospitale s. Martini in suburbio Montis Pessuli.*

Quia humane nature fragilitate hominis memoria labilis est et inbecillis et eius vita velut umbre transitus transit et deficit, utilitate hominum pensata est moribus et legibus introductum, ut res geste publicis monumentis fideliter comendentur. Hinc est, quod huius publici scripti testimonio universis expedit fieri manifestum, quod nos Petrus Ebrardi, Bernardus Carbonelli, Petrus de Perolis, Petrus Iaufridi, Iohannes Bondroe, Bertrandus de Ueurannis, Stephanus de Terviano, Petrus de Sumena, consules Montis P(essuli), per nos et consocios et successores nostros consules cum communi consilio nostro ad sonum campane publice congregato hoc approbante, attendentes, quod de virtute in virtutem oportet ascendere pietatis et misericordie opera exercendo, considerantes eciam honorem et utilitatem publicam huius universitatis et ville tocius Montis P(essuli), quam nos fovere ac promovere ex debito nostri officii compellimur et tenemur, spectantes[1] eciam firmiter ex hoc celestis favoris graciam captare et incrementum universorum et singulorum hominum velle in spiritualibus et temporalibus procurare, ex parte publica et pro iure et potestate, quod vel quam consules et ceteri probi homines Montis P(essuli) et habere et exercere consueverunt in ordinatione, provisione et assysmatione hospitalium in dicta villa et eius suburbiis constitutorum, damus, inperpetuum concedimus et irrevocabiliter assignamus pleno iure ad honorem et servicium dei et gloriose et beatissime virginis Marie et omnium sanctorum fratri Harmanno, magistro maiori domus hospitalis Theutonicorum in partibus ultramarinis, et successoribus eius et hospitali prefato et fratribus et pauperibus ipsius hospitalis et vobis, Iohanni de Gordone et Guillelmo de Mutels, confratribus et familiaribus dicti hospitalis, procuratoribus a dicto magistro ad hoc specialiter constitutis et pro ipso magistro et fratribus et pauperibus predicti hospitalis presens donum recipientibus, hospitale sancti Martini, quod est prope ecclesiam sancti Thome in suburbio Montis P(essuli) extra portale salnarie, cum universis domibus, ortis, vineis, campis et aliis possessionibus et omnibus et singulis bonis, iuribus et rationibus et pertinenciis dicti hospitalis sancti Martini vel ad ipsum hospitale quocunque modo seu racione spectantibus seu pertinentibus ad omnes utilitates et voluntates dicti magistri Harmanni et successorum suorum in posterum et fratrum et pauperum dicti hospitalis Theutonicorum plenarie faciendas, hoc tamen retento, quod volumus et sub hac conditione predicta facimus, ut in memorato hospitali sancti Martini semper pauperum hospitalitas, secundum quod aliis hospitalibus hospitalitati pauperum deputatis fit et consuetum est et fieri debet, per dictum magistrum Armannum et successores eius vel per alios fratres seu comendatores in dicto hospitali sancti Martini existentes devote fiat et humiliter exerceatur. Et, quia semiplenum bonum videtur, quod sine adiectione relinquitur, idcirco nos consules prefati per nos et socios et successores nostros consules dictum[2] hospitale sancti Martini et res ad ipsum in presenti et in futurum pertinentes et fratres et pauperes universos hospitalis et domus Theutonicorum et specialiter dicti hospitalis sancti Martini in toto nostro districtu et amicorum nostrorum in protectione et defensione nostra suscipimus. Verum, si forte, quod absit, iure vel potencia super predictis totalis vel particularis contingeret vel fieret evictio, nolumus ad interesse de evictione teneri; dabimus tamen sollicite operam et consilium et iuvamen, ut presens donum perpetua ac inviolabili gaudeat firmitate. Et ad maiorem firmitatem omnium predictorum habendam et ut predicta nemini in dubium veniant, nos dicti consules presentem cartam sigilli nostri munimine fecimus roborari. Acta sunt hec anno dominice incarnationis m° cc° xx° viii° ydus marcii in presencia[3] et testimonio Girardi de Regdidara, Petri de Fisce, Iohannis de Lates, Bernardi Dorna, iuris peritorum, Salvatoris de Antonitis, Petri de Furno, Bernardi Boreti, Petri Gintardi, Bertrandi Varlen nomnorum[4], Bernardi de Camarada, Bernardi Catalani, Guillelmi Iohanni[5], Berengarii de Lissax et Guillelmi Iordani, notarii dictorum consulum, qui mandato ipsorum consulum et rogatus a partibus hec scripsit et hoc signum suum apposuit. *(Locus signi.)*

I, 38 n. 87. [1]. i. q. exspectantes 2. domum B. 3. presencio B. 4. ? domnorum? 5. B.

---

153. *1229 aprili apud Accon. Fridericus II imperator a domo hosp. S. M. Th. emit castrum Mesanii inter civitatem Brundusii et castrum Horyae situm et domum quondam Margariti sitam prope portum civitatis illius pro 6400 bisantiis sarracenatis annuatim de redditibus catenae et fundae Acconensium solvendis. Testes: Balianus dominus Sidonis; Odo de Montebeliardo, comestabulus regni Ierosolimitani; Iohannes de Ibelino; Guarnerius Alemannus; Aymo, nepos eius; Aymarus, nepos fratris Aymari.*

I, 18v. n. 29, unde edidit Huillard-Bréholles III, 129, qui memorat originale adesse in archivo Neapolitano apud S. Severinum.

---

154. *(1239?). Clausula vidimationis Friderici II imperatoris diplomati de 1221 aprili (supra n. 149) affixa.*

Quod autenticum privilegium exemplavi ego Ionathas, publicus notarius Baroli, die Mercurii xx° vii° mensis ianuarii xiii^{a} indictione de mandato Angeli Bonelli et Sebastiani, imperialium iudicum Baroli, qui una mecum cum subscriptis testibus dictum autenticum privilegium sigillo aureo pendenti sigillatum viderunt et legerunt, ad peticionem fratris Conraudi, preceptoris domus[1] hospitalis sancte Marie domus[1] Theotonicorum in Barolo, et pro eo, quod dictus preceptor et alii fratres eiusdem hospitalis dictum privilegium secum deferre timebant, ne forte casu aliquo posset destrui vel deperdi.

+ Angelus Bonelli quasi imperialis Baroli iudex.

+ Sebastianus quasi imperialis iudex Baroli.

+ Umfredus filius Gurmundi militis testatur.

+ Nicolaus filius Gualterii de Porfido testatur. *(Locus signi.)*

I, 43v. n. 94. Indictio xiii quadrat in annos 1225 et 1240; 1239 xii cucurrit. Subiungimus hic notitiam diplomatum fortuito nobis praesertim in H. W. Schulz Dresdensis excerptis obviorum: 1269 iul. 21 in obsidione Luceriae. Karolus I Siciliae rex concedit ordini s. Mariae Theutonicorum, ut ex masseriis propriis per Apuliae portus Accon exportet 1500 salmos frumenti et 500 salmos hordei, quum antea Apuliae secretus quicquam exportari vetuerit. Archiv. Neapol. regest. Kar. I 1269 B. p. 145. — 1275 sept. 10. Regii praefecti salinis Cannarum et Baroli, ut exsequantur mandatum regium denuntiatum per litteras Peregrini de Meraldo, procuratoris salis Apuliae, sinunt religiosos Theutonicos asportare sal e quadam salina eorum ad massarias. Citatur in Syllabo membranarum ad regiae siclae archivum pertinentium. Neapoli 1824. 4. I, 107. — 1316 nov. 19 ind. xv r. n. 8. Robertus rex „pro parte religiosorum virorum preceptoris et fratrum sacre domus hospitalis s. Marie Theutonicorum in regno Sicilia devotorum“ suorum rogatus concedit, ut exportent 300 salmos frumenti et totidem hordei. Reg. Rob. 1316 B. 159v. — 1327 oct. 31 ind. xi r. a. 19. Idem fratres sacrae domus s. Mariae Theutonicorum, omnes domos eorum, grangias, bona sub caritatis suae clypeo recipit, monetque omnes officiales, ut tanquam regias possessiones ea protegant. Reg. Rob. 1327/8 B. 4v. — 1334. In eodem archivo 5 E. f. 80 occurrit „religiosus vir frater Valranus de Hornberg sacre domus hospitalis s. Marie Theutonice Ierosol. magnus preceptor in Apulia“.

1. domorum B.

155. *1278 martii 23 Romae. Nicolaus papa III repetit Honorii III privilegium, de quo cf. supra notam ad 148 de 1220 iulii 16.*

Nicolaus[1] dilectis filiis magistro et fratribus hospitalis s. Marie Theutonicorum Iherosolimitani salutem et apostolicam benedictionem. Cum a nobis — personas vestras et locum, in quo divino estis obsequio mancipati — specialiter autem decimas, domos, terras, prata, pascua, nemora, vineas, possessiones et alia bona vestra, sicut ea iuste ac pacifice possidetis, vobis et per vos eidem hospitali autoritate apostolica confirmamus et — communimus. Datum Rome apud s. Petrum x° kal. aprilis pontificatus nostri anno i°.

Cum dato „Baruli" A. 16 p. 50. 1. in margine iii°.

156. *1524 dec. 3 Onoltzpach. Albertus ordinis Theutonici magister generalis constituit procuratores ad supplicandum pontifici maximo, ut confirmet donationem de ordinis curia Romae sita fratribus suis factam.*

In nomine domini amen. Anno a nativitate eiusdem millesimo quinquagesimo vicesimo quarto indictione duodecima die tertia mensis decembris hora vesperarum vel quasi pontificatus sanctissimi in Christo patris et domini nostri domini Clementis, divina providencia pape septimi, anno secundo in arce oppidi Onoltzpach in mei notarii publici testiumque infra scriptorum ad hoc specialiter vocatorum et rogatorum presencia personaliter constitutus illustrissimus princeps et dominus, domiuus Albertus, ordinis Theutonici magnus magister, marchio Brandenburgensis, Stetinensis, Pomeranie, Cassuborum et Sclavorum rex, burggravius Nurmbergensis ac Rugie princeps, Herbipolensis diocesis, dicens et proponens, cum alias illustrissima dominatio sua superioribus diebus reverendissimis et illustrissimis principibus et dominis Ioanni Alberto, metropolitane Magdeburgensis et cathedralis Halberstadensis ecclesiarum coadiutori, et Gumperto, maioris ecclesie Bambergensis canonico, germanis fratribus suis charissimis, coniunctim et divisim et quibusvis eorum legittimis heredibus masculini sexus, precipue autem ab illustrissimo principe domino et genitore eorundem, videlicet domino Friderico marchione Brandenburgensi natis et ex iisdem natis adhuc legittime nascituris titulo mere liberalitatis et irrevocabilis donationis inter vivos pro se et quibuscunque ordinis et status sui successoribus curiam eiusdem ordinis sui in urbe Romana sitam cum omnibus et singulis eiusdem edibus, edificiis, privilegiis, libertatibus, emunitatibus, redditibus, censibus, accessibus, ingressibus et egressibus, pertinentiis, adiacentiis, coherentiis et servitutibus suis usque in vias publicas et cum omnibus, que infra predictos continentur fines, perpetuo iure possidendas dederit et concesserit ac omne ius et actiones pro eisdem competentibus in eos transtulerit, quemadmodum in litteris et inscriptionibus desuper confectis et emanatis plenius continetur, idque beneficentie et liberalitatis sue munus idem ipse illustrissimus dominus magnus magister Prussie etc. pro innata sua in predictos suos fratres germanos et eorundem heredes natos et nascituros benevolentia et observantia cupiat pro honore et commodis eorum perpetua firmitate et robore subsistere atque adeo predictam donationem per sanctissimum in Christo patrem et dominum nostrum dominum Clementem septimum, divina providentia sacrosancte Romane ac universalis ecclesie summum pontificem, de specialis dono gratie auctoritate apostolica fulciri, ideoque predictus magnus magister principalis principaliter pro se ipso, citra tamen quorumcunque procuratorum suorum per eum hactenus quomodolibet constitutorum revocationem, omnibus melioribus modo, via, iure, causa et forma, quibus melius et efficacius de iure potuit et debuit ac potest et debet, fecit, constituit, creavit et solenniter ordinavit suos veros, certos et legittimos et indubitatos procuratores, actores, factores negotiorumque infrascriptorum gestores et nunctios speciales et generales, ita tamen quod specialitas generalitati non deroget nec econtra, videlicet venerabiles, validos et circumspectos viros dominos magistrum Andream Puel, prepositum in Oringen, Theodericum de Redenn, Ioseph(um) Feyerabent, scolasticum et canonicum ecclesie divi Gumperti in Olnotzpach, et Ioannem Semelich, vicarium eiusdem ecclesie, absentes tanquam presentes et eorum quemlibet in solidum, ita tamen quod non sit melior conditio primitus occupantis nec deterior subsequentis, sed, quod unus eorum inceperit, alter eorundem id prosequi valeat, mediare pariter et finire, ad ipsius domini constituentis nomine humili qua poterit devotione predicto sanctissimo domino nostro supplicandum et apud eundem et eius apostolicam sedem ac celeberrimum sedis eiusdem cetum reverendissimorum dominorum cardinalium ipsosque dominos cardinales sigillatim instandum, quo predicta irrevocabilis donatio antedictis fratribus et eorum heredibus ut prefertur facta plenissima apostolice dignitatis auctoritate corroboretur et confirmetur, ut eadem sanctitas apostolica de sue apostolice potestatis plenitudine ac certa eiusdem scientia omnes et singulos defectus et solemnitates, si qui vel que in eadem donatione de iure vel de facto existunt, misericorditer et gratiose suppleat atque ut eadem sanctitas apostolica etiam de sue potestatis plenitudine similiter omnibus et singulis predicti Theutonici ordinis privilegiis, libertatibus, emunitatibus, constitutionibus etiam iuratis et consuetudinibus ceterisque quibuscunque in contrarium facientibus ad pleniorem effectum consequendum omnimode in hiis derogare dignetur, et generaliter omnia et singula in hiis faciundum, dicendum, gerendum et exercendum, que in premissis necessaria fuerint seu quomodolibet oportuna et que ipsemet dominus constituens faceret seu facere posset, si premissis presens et personaliter interesset, etiam si talia forent, que mandatum exigerent magis speciale, quam presentibus est expressum, unum quoque vel plures procuratorem seu procuratores loco sui substituendum eumque vel eos revocandum et eius procurationem in se reassumendum totiens, suis[1] procuratoribus predictis seu eorum alteri placuerit seu visum fuerit expedire, relevans nihilominus et relevare volens dictus illustrissimus dominus constituens prefatos suos constitutos ac substituendos ab eisdem seu eorum alteri ac ipsorum quemlibet ab omni onere satis dandi, iudicio sisti et iudicatum solvi sub ypotheca et obligatione omnium et singulorum bonorum suorum mobilium et immobilium presentium et futurorum ac omnium iuris et facti renunctiationum ad hec pariter et cautela, de et super quibus omnibus et singulis premissis prefatus dominus constituens sibi a me notario publico infrascripto unum vel plura publicum seu publica fieri confici petiit instrumentum vel instrumenta. Acta sunt hec anno, in-*(dictione)*[2], die, mense, hora, pontificatu et loco, quibus supra, presentibus ibidem nobilibus et honestis viris Melchiore de Rabenstein Bambergensis, Georgio Clingenbeck Pataviensis et Cristofero Gallenhoffer Herbipolensis diocesium testibus ad hoc specialiter rogatis atque requisitis.

(Signum notarii.)

Et ego Georgius Bonemilch clericus Moguntine diocesis, publicus sacra apostolica auctoritate notarius, quia dictis procurationi, constitucioni, potestatis dationi, ratihabitioni, relevationi omnibusque aliis et singulis premissis, dum sicut premittitur fierent et agerentur, unacum presentibus testibus presens interfui eaque omnia et singula sic fieri vidi et audivi, ideoque in notam recepi et quia hoc presens publicum instrumentum in fidem omnium et singulorum manu propria fideliter conscriptum exinde confeci, subscripsi, publicavi et in hanc publicam formam redegi signoque et nomine meis solitis et consuetis signavi.

Ex originali, quod asservatur in archivo secretiori Berolinensi. 1. Or., l. quotiens? 2. dictione scriba scribere oblitus est in initio lineae.

---

157. *1524 dec. 7. Albertus, ordinis Theutonici magister generalis, Iohanni Alberto et Gumperto fratribus suis curiam ordinis Romae sitam confert.*

Wir Albrecht von gottes gnaden Teutschordenns hohemaister, marggrafe zu Branndenburg, zu Stettin, Pommern, der Cassuben und Wennden hertzog, burggraf zu Nuremberg und furst zu Rugen, bekennen und thun kunth offennlich mit disem briefe gen allermenigclich, den dieser unnser briefe furkompt, angezaigt und gelesen wirdet, fur unns und alle unnser nachkommen, das wir mit wolbedachtem muet, rechter wissen und zeittigem vorrat, den wir mit den wirdigen unnsers Teutschen ordenns comenthurn, vogt, pflegern und gemainen conventsbrudern der lannde zu Preufsen derhalben mermals gehabt, und mit derselben sonderlichem mitgehellen und bewilligung in crafft einer rechtmefsigen freyen donacion und unwiderrufflichen ubergab unnder den lebenndigen aus vil redlichen beweglichen ursachen umb unnsers und unnsers ordens bessern nutz und frommen willen und von wegen der angebornnen lieb, trew und freuntschafft, damit unns die erwirdigen und hochgebornnen fursten, unnser freuntlliche liebe bruder, herr Johann Albrecht[1], coadjutor der beder stifft Magdenburg und Halberstatt, und her Gumbrecht[2], bede marggrafen zu Branndenburg, zu Stettin, Pommern, der Cassuben und Wennden hertzogen, burggrafen zu Nuremberg und fursten zu Rugen, verwant und zugethan sind, denselben beden und allen andern unnsern lieben brudern samptlich und ir yedem innsonderheit, die unns auch itzund, dieweyl wir in unnsers ordenns wichtigen henndeln und gescheffften personlich im heyligen Romischen reich gewesen, mit unnderhalltung und darstreckung ainer tapffern summa gelts und annderm bruderlichem und freuntlichem willen begegent, auch ir yedes manlichen eelichen erben, aber zuvorderst denjhenen, so von dem hochgebornnen fursten, unnserm lieben herrn und vatter, herrn Friderichen, marggrafen zu Branndenburg etc., eelich geborn und herkommen sind und hinfuro in ewigkait von denselben eelich erzeugt und geborn werden, unnsern und unnsers Teutschen ordenns hofe zu Rom in der statt gelegen, mit allen und yeden desselben zugehorungen, hewsern, anhengen, herrlicheiten, freyhaiten, nutzungen, gullten, zinssen, dinstbarkaiten, zuegenngen und auszgenngen, rechten, gerechtigkaiten und allen desselben zue- und eingehorungen, ganntz nichts davon auszgenomen, zugestellt und ubergeben haben; unnd wir thun auch solichs hiemit und inn crafft dits brieffs in der aller pessten form und weyſs, wie das in beden gaistlichen und weltlichen rechten am aller bestenndigsten und crefftigsten beschehen soll, kan oder mag, also das dieselben unnser lieb gebruedere gemaingclich und insonnderhait und ir mänlich eelich erben unnsers namens und stammens der marggrafen zu Branndenburg etc., aber zuvorderst unnser linien, wie obsteet, nu hinfuro in ewigkait solichen obvermelten hofe zu Rom mit allem seinem begriff, freyhaitten, herrlicheiten, zu- und eingehorungen inhaben, besitzen, nutzen, nieſsen, gebrauchen, besetzen, entsetzen und damit gar und gentzlich thon und laſsen solln und mogen, als mit andern iren aigen haben und gutern von uns allen, unsern nachkomen, unsers ordens comenthurn, vogten, pflegern, gemainen conventsbrudern und menigclich ungeirrt und unverhindert, dann wir unns desselben mit aller zue- und eingehörung auf solich ubergab fur unns und alle unnser nachkommen hiemit und in crafft dits brieffs genntzlich ennteuſsert und verzigen haben wellen. Wir geben inen auch freyen gewalt und macht, den beseſs vermelts hofs und seiner zugehorung aus ir aigen selbst gewalt und one erlaubnus und erkanntnus ainichs richters antzunemen und hinfuro zu behalten. Ferner aus ursach obbestimpter donacion und ubergab haben wir unnsern brudern und iren erben obgenannt auch zugestellt, ubergeben und befolhen alle und yegcliche unnser clag, spruch und forderung heblich und personnlich und alle andere clag, welicher gestallt die sein und unns, so wir solichen hofe noch innen hetten, von desselben hofs wegen gepuren möchten. Wir begeben und verzeyhen unns auch hiemit wissenntlich fur unns und alle unnser nachkommen aller rechten, freyhaiten, begnadungen, statuten, satzung, durch die babstlich heyligkait, kayserliche mayestatt oder anndere auffgesetzt und gegeben, die unns und unnsern nachkommen und orden an diser unnser ubergab in ainich weisz zuwider verstannden sein oder werden möchten, unnd sonnderlich dem rechten, das da spricht, das kain ubergab, die ubertreff die summa des rechten, nemlich funffhundert gulden, crefftig soll sein, die dem ordenlichen richter nit insinuirt oder verkunt werde, (so doch unnser meynung ist, das dise donacion bebstlicher heyligkait, als dises fals unnserm ordennlichen richter insinuirt werden soll), auch des rechten, das die gemainschafft nit furtreff die sunderhait, mitsampt allen anndern rechten, freyheiten, gesetzen, indulten von recht oder gewonheit herbracht und auffgesetzt, die wider dise unnser ubergab sein oder erdacht werden möcht, der aller wir unnser nachkomen unns kains wegs dawider gebrauchen sollen noch wöllen, sonndern wir gereden und versprechen solich ubergab genntzlich, steet, vest und unverbrochenlich zu halten one eintrag irrung, widerred, aufzzug und behelff, alle geverde und arglist hierinn ausgeslossen. Des zu warem urkund, stetter und vesster halltung haben wir Albrecht, Teutschordens hohemaister, marggraf zu Branndenburg etc., fur unns, unnsere comenthur, vögt, pfleger, convents- und gemaine bruder und glidmaſsen des Teutschen ordenns der lannde Preuſsen mit ir aller wissen und bewilligung von unnser und ir aller wegen unnsers ordenns groſz innsigel wissenntlich an disen brief thon hengen, weliche bewilligung und donacion wir gemelte comenthur, voyt, pfleger, convents- unnd gemaine bruder und glydmaſsen des Teutschen ordenns der lannd Preuſsen bekennen, bewilligen und versprechen hiemit und in crafft dits briefs, bey unnsern rechten, gueten, waren trewen fur unns und unnser nachkomen, das wir alle samptlich und ein yeder besonnder bemelte donacion steet, vest und unverbrochenlich hallten, auch nymmermer dawider thun sollen noch wellen gar und genntzlich in kain weiſz noch wege. Der geben ist am mitwochen nach Nicolai episcopi nach Cristi unnsers lieben herrn gepurt funffzehenhundert und im vierundzwaintzigisten jar.

Von gottes gnaden Albrecht T. o. hochmeister
marggraff zu Brandenburgk etc. manu propria
subscripsit.

Ex originali, quod asservatur Berolini in archivo secretiori. Appendet sigillum, cuius effigiem exhibet Voſsberg tab. XI. 1. Iohannes Albertus natus 1499 sept. 21, 1545 archiepiscopus Magdeburgensis, † 1550 martii 20. 2. Gumpertus natus 1503 iulii 16, canonicus Wirziburgensis et Babenbergensis, Leonis X pontificis maximi camerarius, † 1528 iunii 24 Neapoli.

B U R Z A.

158. *1211 (regni nostri anno 7). Andreas, Ungariae rex, cruciferis „de hospitali s. Marie, quod quandoque fuit Ierusalem, sed modo peccatis exigentibus situm est in Accaron“, confert terram desertam et inhabitatam Borza nomine ultra Silvas versus Cumanos sitam intra certos limites et cum certis libertatibus.*

I, 44 n. 96. Cf. etiam II, 125 v. Cf. supra p. 127. — In transsumto Philippi Firmani episcopi sedis apostolicae legati d. d. Wienne a. ab inc. dom. millesimo ducentesimo septuagesimo nono quinto kal. ian., id est 1278 dec. 28, in archivo Regim., nunc sine sigillo, primum cum titulo: „Hoc est privilegium donacionis terre de Borza“. Ediderunt Teutsch et Firnhaber, Urkundenbuch zur Geschichte Siebenbürgens. Wien 1857, in Fontibus rerum Austriacarum II, XV 1, p. 8 n. X et qui citantur ibi: I. K. Schuller Archiv für die Kenntnifs von Siebenbürgens Vorzeit und Gegenwart I, 214 ex transsumto de 1279 in Regimontano archivo asservato. Seivert Ung. Magaz. 10 p. 218. Bethlen Geschichtliche Darstellung des deutschen Ordens in Siebenbürgen p. 70. Fejér Codex diplomaticus Hungariae III, 1, 106; cf. etiam Schuller l. c. 227, Fejér III, 1, 370; III, 2, 246. Leguntur in codice ex Fejero additi sed uncinis inclusi testes ap. T. et F. 10. De caeteris nota: Gurieusi — Poht — regine, Marcello Reweviensem (corrige l. c. dativos caeteros in accusativos) et curiali comite Nicholao Posoniensem comitatus tenentibus.

---

159. *1212 (regni nostri anno 8). Andreas, Ungariae rex, petenti Theoderico, „crucifero hospitalis S. Marie de Accaron, quae (l. quod) quondam fuit in Ierusalem“, et fratribus eius in Transsilvania constitutis concedit, ut monetarii terram eorum non intrent, sed pro argento populo ibi sufficientem nummorum vim novae monetae ipsis dent, quum regno sint contra Cumanos firmum propugnaculum.*

I, 51 n. 97. Cf. II, 126. — In transsumto de 1278 dec. 28 in archivo Regimontano. — Ediderunt partim melioribus lectionibus Teutsch et Firnhaber Urkundenbuch zur Geschichte Siebenbürgens I, 10 n. XII (Fontes rerum Austriacarum II, XV. I. Wien 1857. 8.) et qui citantur ibi p. XX: Seivert Ung. Magaz. IV, 222. Fejér Cod. Ung. dipl. III, 1, 116. Graf Alexis Bethlen Geschichte des Deutschen Ordens in Siebenbürgen p. 74. Schlözer Kritische Sammlungen für Geschichte der Deutschen in Siebenbürgen p. 313. Schuller Archiv I, 217. — Titulus in codice: „De libertate, quam dedit domui rex Hungarie, quod nullus nummulariorum intret terram domus in Bursia“. Cf. etiam supra p. 127.

---

160. *1212. Andreas Ungariae rex donat „cruciferis de Bozza ab ipsis constructum castrum Cru(z)purg cum pratis adiacentibus“.*

I, 126 v. s. a. in confirmatione de 1231 apr. 26. Edd. Teutsch et Firnhaber XX n. 48, qui citant Schuller Archiv I, 220. Seivert Ungar. Magazin IV, 223. Graf Alexis Bethlen Geschichte des D. O. in Siebenbürgen p. 76. Fejér III, 1, 118.

---

161. *1213. Wilhelmus, Transsilvanus episcopus, fratribus hospitalis s. Mariae in Ierusalem de domo Teutonicorum in terra Borza decimarum exceptis de Hungaris et Siculis provenientibus perceptionem donat et institutiones sacerdotum reservatis sibi horum ordinatione, procuratione decenti, causarum criminalium, maxime ad sacerdotum depositionem pertinentium, iurisdictione.*

Continetur in n. 162 infra de 1218 april. 19. Ediderunt ultimo Teutsch et Firnhaber I, 11 n. XIII, antea, qui citantur ibi p. XXI.

---

162. *1218 aprilis 19 Laterani. Honorius papa III (Cum a nobis) confirmat ordini Theutonico n. 161 supra.*

Originale in archivo Regimontano. Edd. Teutsch et Firnhaber I, 12. XIV.

---

163. *1222 s. d. et l. regni nostri anno 17. Andreas, Ungariae rex, Hermanno, magistro religiosae fraternitatis hospitalis s. Mariae Theutonicorum Ierosolimitani, eiusque fratribus confert terram Burzam ultra Silvas versus Cumanos sitam desertam et inhabitatam cum multiplice libertate.*

I, 51 n. 98. Cf. supra 127. In Regimontano archivo, ubi originale non exstat (errant igitur Teutsch et Firnhaber reg. 77), tria habentur transsumta: 1. 1260—1270. L. guardiani fr. min. et L. supprioris fr. praedic Wiennensium, male m° cc° xxvii°; 2. 1280 martii 15. Rudolfi Romanorum regis; 3. 1317 sept. 29. Thomae, Strigoniensis archiepiscopi. Ediderunt satis male: Teutsch et Firnhaber Urkundenbuch zur Geschichte Siebenbürgens. Wien 1857. I, 17 n. XVIII et, qui citantur ibi: Schuller Archiv I, 224; Fejér Cod. Ung. III, 1, 370. Cf. Voigt G. P. II, 127. Adest Regim. etiam Honorii III orig. confirmatio d. d. Laterani 1222 dec. 19; male edd. T. et F. XIX.

---

164. *1224 april. 30 Laterani. Honorius papa III (Grata deo) terram Boze et ultra montes nivium petentibus magistro et fratribus hospitalis s. Mariae Theutonicorum Ierusalem in ius et proprietatem apostolicae sedis suscipit vetatque quemquam archiepiscopum vel episcopum ibi iurisdictionem exercere, archipresbytero terrae reservatam, quem per Strigoniensem archiepiscopum, tunc Agriensem episcopum, praeficiendum curaverat.*

II, 124 v. sine dato. Datum supplevi e Teutsch et Firnhaber l. c. I, 26 n. XXVI; qui etiam citant editores: Katona V, 260. Schlözer 321. Fejér III, 1, 459. Bardosy suppl. ann. Scep. p. 413. Bethlen D. O. p. 91. Schuller Archiv I, 226.

---

165. *(Inter 1223 iulii 24 et 1224 iulii 24) s. d. Laterani. Honorius papa III (Dilectorum filiorum) archiepiscopis et episcopis per Ungariam constitutis notum facit, se fratribus hospitalis s. Mariae Theutonicorum Ierosolomitani ab Andrea Ungariae rege donatam terram Borzae et ultra montes nivium tanquam exemtam immediate in apostolicae sedis protectionem et proprietatem suscepisse.*

II, 136v. ubi in fine legitur: „Ita invenitur de verbo ad verbum in registro domini Honorii papa III anno VIII. Martinus". — In transsumto de 1278 dec. 28 in archivo Regimontano cum introitu: „Item quod dominus papa recipit terram de Borza sub protectione sua". Edd. Schuller Archiv I, 238; Teutsch et Firnhaber I, 27 n. 27.

---

166. *1225 oct. 27 Reate. Honorius papa III (Iam meminisse) (Andream) Hungariae regem commonet de restituenda domui hospitalis s. Mariae Theutonicorum terra Borzae et ultra montes nivium.*

II, 127v. sine dato; in fine legitur: „Ita invenitur de verbo ad verbum in registro domini Honorii pape III anno X. Martinus". — In transsumto de 1278 dec. 28 in archivo Regimontano, cum introitu: „Post ablatam nobis terram Borze scribit dominus papa sepedictus regi Ungarie"; et clausula: „Ita invenitur caet." ut supra. Datum supplevi ex Teutsch et Firnhaber I, 37 n. 36, qui citant: Schuller Archiv I, 248; Fejér III, 2, 58.

---

167. *1231 apr. 26 Laterani. Gregorius papa IX (Ne super privilegiis) confirmat domui hospitalis s. Mariae Theutonicorum inserta privilegia de terra „Bozze":*

1. (1211) Andreas, Hungariae caet. rex (Inter regalis) (supr. n. 158);

2. (1212) Andreas, Hungariae caet. rex (Amplioris beneficium) (supra n. 159);

3. (1212) Andreas, Hungariae caet. rex, donat cruciferis de Bozza ab ipsis constructum castrum Cruzpurg cum pratis adiacentibus (supra n. 160).

II, 125v. sine dato cum clausula: „Ita invenitur de verbo ad verbum in registro domini Gregorii pape anno V capitulo LVIIII". Eadem in fine excerptae confirmationis in transsumto Regimontano de 1278 dec. 28. Tota confirmatio in archivi Regimontani codice A. 18 fol. 135. Edd. cum dato: Teutsch et Firnhaber l. c. 46 n. 44, ubi tamen de medio confirmato diplomate siletur, et qui ibi citantur p. XXXI: Fejér III, 2, 245. Schuller Archiv I, 255. Ungar. Magaz. IV, 218. Schlözer 326.

---

168. *1232 aug. 31 Anagniae. Gregorius papa IX (Dilecti filii) electum Penestrinensem, apostolicae sedis legatum, iubet Andream Ungariae regem et Belam filium eius ad restituendum domui hospitalis s. Mariae Theutonicorum ablatam terram ecclesiastica censura coercere.*

II, 128v. et in transsumto de 1278 dec. 28 („Item littere apostolice ad electum Penestrinensem ap. s. leg. super terra de Borza") in archivo Regimontano, utrobique cum clausula: „Ita invenitur de verbo ad verbum in registro domini Gregorii pape VIIII anno VI capitulo CCLXXXXII. Martinus". Datum praebent Teutsch et Firnhaber 51 n. LI, qui citant Schuller Archiv I, 258. Katona Historia regum Hungariae V, 604. Bethlen D. O. 101. Fejér III, 2, 303. Schlözer 550.

---

169. *(1260—1270) s. a. L. guardianus fratrum minorum et L. supprior fratrum praedicatorum in Wienna transsumunt petente B(ela IV) Ungariae rege († 1270) privilegium de 1222 (supra n. 163).*

Or. cum duobus sigillis in archivo Regimontano 29 n. 4.

---

170. *1278 („1279") dec. 28 (v kal. ianuar.) Wienne. Philippus Firmanus episcopus, ap. sed. legatus, exemplificat suo sub sigillo, quod nunc deest, quaternum sequentia privilegia descripta continentem:*

1. 1211. „Hoc est privilegium donacionis terre de Borza" Andreas caet. (supra n. 158);

2. 1212. „Aliud privilegium de libertate caet. terre de Borza" Andreas caet. (supra n. 159);

3. 1212. Excerptum supra ad n. 160.

4. 1231 apr. 26. Gregorius papa IX caet. Ne super privilegiis caet. (supra n. 167);

5. (Inter 1223 iunii 24 et 1224 iunii 24). Honorius papa III caet. Dilectorum filiorum (supra n. 165);

6. 1225 oct. 27. Honorius papa III; Iam meminisse (supra n. 166);

7. 1232 aug. 31. Gregorius papa IX; Dilecti filii (supra n. 168).

Or., cui nunc deest Philippi legati sigillum, in archivò Regimontano 29 n. 2. Communicavit nobiscum v. cl. Meckelburg.

---

171. *1280 martii 15 Wienne. Rudolfus Romanorum rex transsumit privilegium de 1222 (supra n. 163).*

Or. cum sigillo maiestatis in archivo Regimontano 29 n. 1. — Ed. Teutsch et Firnhaber l. c. n. CXXII.

---

172. *1317 (septbr. 29) in festo s. Michaelis archangeli datum prope Camarinum. Thomas, Strigoniensis archiepiscopus, petente fratre Bernhardo commendatore Viennensi transsumit privilegium de 1222 (supra n. 163).*

Or. cum sigillo in archivo Regimontano 29 n. 3; cf. Voigt Gesch. Pr. II, 127.

ALEMANNIA. BOHEMIA.

---

173. *1219 iunii 22 Reate (cf. 1219 iunii 25). Honorius III confirmat oi. Theo. Friderici II constitutionem (1214 septbr. 5) de acquirendis feodis imperii.*

Honorius episcopus, servus servorum dei, dilectis filiis magistro et fratribus hospitalis sancte Marie Theutonicorum Ierosolimitani salutem et apostolicam benedictionem. Iustis petentium desideriis dignum est nos facilem prebere consensum et vota, que a rationis tramite non discordant, effectu prosequente complere. Cum igitur carissimus in Christo filius noster Fridericus, illustris rex Sicilie, in Romanorum imperatorem electus, regia liberalitate concesserit, ut, quicunque aliqua de bonis imperii possidet nomine feudi, libere et licenter quantum voluerit ex eisdem tamquam de propriis valeat[1] domui vestre conferre, nos concessionem ipsam pie ac provide factam, sicut in ipsius regis privilegio continetur, auctoritate apostolica confirmamus et presentis scripti patrocinio communimus. Nulli ergo omnino hominum liceat hanc paginam nostre confirmationis infringere vel ei ausu temerario contraire. Si quis autem hoc attemptare presumpserit, indignationem omnipotentis dei et beatorum Petri et Pauli apostolorum eius se noverit incursurum. Datum Reate decimo kal. iulii pontificatus nostri anno tertio.

Sine dato: A. 20 n. LXXX Latine et Germanice. A. 16 p. 113 „Treviris". Cum dato „Reate x kal. iulii p. n. a. 3" in apographo transsumti e domo Ellingensi R. 49 n. 38, et iterum R. 73 inter Mergenthemensia. Cum dato „Reate vii kal. iulii p. n. a. 3": IV, 174v.; et copiarium saec. xv, unde edidit Hennes I, 41 n. 38.   1. valeret H.

---

174. *1219 iunii 25 Reate. Honorius papa III repetit n. 173 de 1219 iunii 22.*

Honorius etc. Iustis petentium etc. Datum Reate vii kal. iulii p. n. a. iii°.

---

175. *1222 aug. 26 ind. x. s. l. Ottakerus, Bohemiae rex, fratres h. s. M. d. Th. I. cum possessionibus et familia per Bohemiam et Moraviam protectione sua et immunitate donat.*

In nomine sancte trinitatis et individue unitatis. Ego Odoacer rex Boemorum tercius Hermanno magistro hospitalis sancte Marie Theotonicorum Ierosolimitani eiusque fratribus tam presentibus quam futuris in perpetuum. Cum regie magnificencie et munificentie beneficia etc. *usque* Robertus Olomucensis episcopus, abbas Gradicensis — Benarus — Prozimus castellanus Znoimensis, Echardus et frater Arthleybus castellani Znoimenses — Actum Olomuconi anno incarnationis m° cc° xxii° vii° kal. septembris indictione x data per manum Hermanni magistri regis notarii.

II, 123 v. in confirmatione Honorii III de 1222 dec. 19 (infra n. 176). — Cum confirmatione Wenceslai Bohemiae regis d. d. 1236 (sept. 28) iv kal. octbr. ind. ix Prage ex huius archetypo membranaceo in archivo Staniątcensi asservato ed. in compluribus melius Bartoszewicz in Rzyszczewski et Muczkowski Cod. diplom. Poloniae. Varsaviae 1858. 4. III, 19 sq. — Confirmatio Wenceslai confirmata a Przemislao, regis Wenceslai filio, 1251 (apr. 5) non. aprilis in Gradec; quod diploma ex originali duplici sigillo munito arch. Regim. ed. I. Voigt Die Ballei Böhmen. Wien 1863. app. II, ubi p. 57 l. 14 male pro xxx° est xxv° impressum. — Confirmatio Przemislai confirmata pro fratre Dytoldo praeceptore Bohemiae et Moraviae per Wenceslaum regem 1287 (i. e. 1286) (dec. 27) vi kal. ianuarii Prage; ex originali sigillato archivi Regimontani edidit I. Voigt l. c. app. III. — Confirmatio ipsius privilegii de 1222 aug. 26 a Karolo IV imperatore. a. 1348 ind. I. V id. iulii (iulii 11) Prage regnor. 2. Stiborio praeceptori concessa repetitur in huius confirmatione per Wenceslaum Rom. regem edita pro Iohanne Mulheim praeceptore d. d. 1387 nov. 6 regn. Bohem. a. 22. Roman. vero 12, cuius originale maiestatis sigillo munitum in Regimontano archivo adservatur.

---

176. *1222 dec. 19 Laterani. Honorius papa III confirmat fratribus h. s. M. d. Th. I. Ottakari Bohemiae regis diploma de 1222 aug. 26 (supra n. 175).*

Honorius episcopus servus servorum dei magistro et fratribus etc. Cum a nobis petitur *etc. usque* perducatur effectum. Eapropter, dilecti in domino filii, vestris iustis postulationibus grato concurrentes assensu libertates et immunitates[1] vobis ac domui vestre a karissimo in Christo filio nostro O. rege Boemorum illustri pia liberalitate concessas, sicut eas iuste ac pacifice obtinetis et in ipsius regis privilegio super hoc confecto plenius continetur, vobis et ipsi domui auctoritate apostolica confirmamus et presentis scripti patrocinio communimus. Ad rei autem evidentiam pleniorem tenorem ipsius privilegii presentibus de verbo ad verbum fecimus annotari, qui talis est.

> I. n. s. t. et i. u. Ego Odoacer *(supra n. 175 usque ad)* m° cc° xxii° vii° kal. septembris indictione x. Data per manum Hermanni magistri regis notarii.

Nulli ergo etc. nostre confirmationis infringere etc. Si quis autem etc. Datum etc.

II, 123 v. sine dato cum clausula: „Ita invenitur de verbo ad verbum in registro domini Honorii III anno septimo. Martinus“. Diem et locum supplevimus ex Erben, Regesta diplomatica necnon epistolaria Bohemiae et Moraviae. Pragae 1855. 4. I, 310 n. 667, quocum ex Honorii III registro communicavit Palacky. Boczek II, 144. 1. munitates B.

---

177. *1225 iuli. 13 Reate. Honorius papa III confirmat fratribus domus hospitalis s. Mariae Mergentheimensem decimam.*

Honorius etc. magistro et fratribus etc. Iustis petentium etc. *usque* compelli. Littere siquidem bone memorie Theoderici Herbipolensis episcopi suo et

Herbipolensis capituli ac nobilium virorum Gotfridi et Conradi[1] de Honloch fratrum communite sigillis nobis exhibite inter cetera contiuebant, quod, cum[2] iidem nobiles[3] decimam in Mergentem, quam tunc[4] in feudum ab ecclesia Herbipolensi tenebant, vobis dare fide interposita promisissent, prephatis episcopo et capitulo supplicarunt, ut vobis conferrent decimam memoratam, promittentes, quod pro illa competens vobis excambium assignarent. Prephata igitur decima tam a viris prudentibus de predicto capitulo quam a quibusdam fidelibus eiusdem ecclesie triginta et sex talentorum precio extimata, predicti nobiles proprietates suas triginta iiii^or talenta et amplius annis singulis exsolventes ipsi ecclesie contulerunt, ab ea in feudum recipientes easdem, vosque quandam proprietatem vestram annuatim solventem duo talenta, que deerant extimationi predicte, ipsi ecclesie contulistis. Idem ergo episcopus securitate recepta de restauratione facienda ipsi ecclesie, si aliquam partem prephati excambii contingerit evinci legitime, ab eadem prephatam decimam vobis de consensu tocius capituli sui contulit perpetuo libere obtinendam. Nos igitur vestris iustis precibus inclinati collationem ipsam, sicut provide facta est et in prephatis litteris plenius continetur, auctoritate apostolica confirmamus et presentis scripti patrocinio communimus. Nulli ergo etc. Si quis autem etc. Datum Reate iii idus iulii pontificatus nostri anno nono.

II, 128 sine dato; in fine additum: „Ita invenitur de verbo ad verbum in registro domini Honorii pape III. Martinus“. Cum dato in codice Regimontano R. 77 inter Mergentheimensia n. 31. 1. et Conradi B deest; supplevi. 1224 dec. 14. Theodericus Herbipolensis episcopus († 1225 febr. 20) concessit Godefrido et Conrado de Hohenlohe, ut decimam Mergentheimensem ab episcopo eis infeodatam tanquam liberam possessionem pro aliis feodis episcopi futuris bonis ordini Theutonico traderent; cf. Schönhuth Chronik der vormaligen Deutschordensstadt Mergentheim. Mergentheim 1857. 12mo. p. 13 sq. 2. supplevi. 3. idem nobilis B. 4. nunc B.

---

178. *1233 oct. 28 Erpurch. Fridericus, Austriae dux, confert fratribus hospitalis s. M. Th. in I. s. Cunigundis ecclesiam in colle prope Pairisch Graetz cum redditibus, villas Makau, Vlechingen, Wulfingerdorf, partim Mezendorf, alia bona, emendam sanguinis per omnia bona eorum suae ditionis, alias libertates.*

In nomine sancte et individue trinitatis. Amen. Fridericus dux Austrie et Styrie — cum sacram domum sancte Marie Theutonicorum in Ierusalem tamquam progenitorum nostrorum opus favorabili complectamur affectu et ubique per terras nostras protectione nostra gaudeant et favore — *usque* Acta sunt hec in Erpurch anno virginei partus m° cc° xxx° iii° indicione vi^a quinto kalendas novembris anno pontificatus domini Gregorii pape noni vii°, imperante gloriosissimo Romanorum imperatore Friderico feliciter. Amen.

VII, 368 v. v. Meiller Regesten zur Geschichte der Markgrafen und Herzoge Oesterreichs aus dem Hause Babenberg. Wien 1850. 152 sq., citat: Duellius Histor. ordin. Theut. III, 88 n. 1 im Auszug. — Pusch et Fröhlich Diplomataria sacra ducatus Styriae. Viennae, Pragae et Tergesti 1756. II, 177 n. 1 vollständig. — Caesar Annal. ducatus Stiriae II, 500 n. 64.

---

179. *1239 („1240“) dec. 25 ind. xiii in nativitate domini post composicionem et concordiam inter dominum nostrum imperatorem et nos sollempniter celebratam Wiennae. Fridericus, Austriae dux, fratribus h. s. M. Theutonicorum in Ierusalem renovat, confirmat, auget a patre Leopoldo duce concessa privilegia.*

VI, 356. Cf. v. Meiller Regesten zur Geschichte der Markgrafen und Herzoge Oesterreichs aus dem Hause Babenberg. Wien 1850. 4. p. 159; et quos ille citat: Duellius II. o. Th. II, 6 n. 6 (excerpt.); Caesar Annales ducatus Stiriae. Gratii 1768 sq. fol. II, 508 n. 78 (excerpt.); Hormayr Wien, seine Geschichte und seine Merkwürdigkeiten. Wien 1823—25. II. ii, Urk. 60 n. 222; Hennes Cod. dipl. ord. Th. 109 n. 100 excerpt. — Pusch et Froelich Diplomataria sacra ducatus Styriae. Viennae, Pragae et Tergesti 1756. II, 183 excerpt.

---

180. *(1256—1269). Ulricus, Carinthiae dux, fratribus domus Theutonicae ab ipso Laibaci constitutis confert libertates, quibus alias fruuntur, et iurisdictionem circumscribit.*

Wir Ulreich, von gots gnaden herczog in Kernden und ze Krain, tun kundt, das wir den brudern des Tewtschen haws, den wir haben wanung gegeben ze Laybach, alle recht und freyung, die sy in andern stetten oder anderswo habent, an minnrung wellen behalten, und gepietten gemainchleich unsern lanntrichtern, marchtrichtern, schaffern und schergen, das chainer von irem gesind oder ir lewt, die in zugehorent, umb chainerlay sache, die di rache des todes nicht angent, sullen richten; ausgenomen, ob yeman irs gesinde oder ir lawt yemant laidiget oder gelten solt, so sol unser richter oder schaffer mit im nemen den gelaydtigten oder den, dem man des gelts schuldig wirt, als die sache ist, und in der bruder haws gen ainem und dem andern das gerichte und die gerechtichait ze vordern; dem sol der schaffer oder des haws comentewr, uber das furgelegt oder das furzelegen wirt, ein zimleich pessrung und recht tun. Ob aber yemant der vorgenanten brueder lewt oder gesind tief tut oder ander unfug als grofse, dadurch der dyeb oder ubeltetter wirt ze verdampnen, so sol sein gut alles beleiben dem haws und sol man in plos unserm lantrichter oder marchtrichter geantwurten; uber den sol dann der richter nach der urtail des rechten richten. Ob auch unser richter auf iren guttern ettleich dieb vindet, die sol er chainen wais nemen nur zegegen irm sundern poten, das die andern gut um solich dief dem haws nicht werden entfueret.

VI, 358 v. Versio. Continetur in diplomate Alberti Austriae ducis de 1350 iulii 13 n. 186.

---

181. *(1256—1269). Ulricus, Carinthiae dux, fratres ordinis Theutonici per Carinthiam, Carniolam, Marchiam cum bonis et hominibus eorum eximit a iurisdictione ordinaria praeterquam in rebus capitalibus.*

Wir Ulreich, von gots gnaden herczog ze Kernden und her ze Krain, tun kunt, das wir die Tawtschen herren in unser herschaft ze Kernden und auf der Marich also in unser sunder gnad genomen haben, das sy von chainen unsern lawtten, wie sy genant sein, chain beswerung leyden sullent, wann in durich die erberchait irs lebens pillich wirdigkait ist zw erbietten, daruber all ir lewtt, holden oder aigen lewtt, die si habent oder gewinnent[1], die in zu recht zugehorent, sullen von unsern richtern, urtailern, schergen und amptlewtten frey und unbekümert sein, und wellen, was widermut, mishellung oder annder sach und chlag under iren läwtten aufderstett, daz das des haws commentewr oder der, dem er sein stat empholhen hat, pilleich straffe und pesser, und sullen unsern richtern nichts uber sölich sach chainen weis antwurtten. Wir wellen auch, wer ab dem lannde hincz irn lewtten mit rechter beschaidenhait ze chlagen hat, das der gee zw unsern richtern und vorder das recht und die, die von denselben werdent geladen, die sullen mit irs hawscommentewr poten erscheinen und vor unsern richtern antwurtten umb das man im zwspricht; noch zw anndern taidigen oder gerichten sol man sy furbas nicht vordern. Darüber das alle pöse ansuchung unser richter gänczlich absey, wellen wir, das alle wandel der vorgenanten brüder läwt, die uns oder unser richter angehent[2] sein, des commentewr noch das unser richter pey unsern gnaden das getürren widersprechen. Von der gnad sind ausgenomen, die mit gericht zw dem tod sind ze verdampmen, also das alles ir gut und ir erbe den brudern beleibe, aber den schuldigen sullen sy mit iren schergen ploz als in die gurttel begriffen hat, ze richten unsern richtern antwurten. Darzu zw ainer überflüzzigen gnad wellen wir, welicherlay ding oder tyer man denselben brüderen durich unser marcht und unser mawtstetten fürt zw irem nuez und choste, das man das die bruder oder ir poten in unser herschaft frey lasse durchfürn oder gen an mwt und an zol. Wir wellen auch, das chainer, der durch sicherhait in der vorgenanten brüder haws flewcht, von niemant werde gelaidigt. Ob auch das wär, das er ain todslag begangen hat oder ein so grofse missetat, die des leibes verdampnusse zubringt, darüber durich des ordens erberchait alle unczucht oder ubergeng, so ir hawsgesind tuet oder beget, emphelhen wir dem commentewr und den brüdern nach ir beschaidenhait ze pessern.

VI, 359. Versio. Continetur in n. 187. 1. gewinnet B. 2. angehernt B.

---

182. *1277 martii 1 Wienne. Rudolfus Romanorum rex universis imperii fidelibus per Austriam, Styriam, Karinthiam, Marchiam et Carniolam mandat, ut fratres h. s. M. de d. Theutonica in libertatibus et iuribus eorum manuteneant.*

Rudolfus, dei gracia Romanorum rex semper augustus, universis imperii Romani fidelibus per Austriam, Styriam, Karinthiam, Marchiam et Carniolam constitutis presentes litteras inspecturis graciam suam et omne bonum. Volentes honorabiles et in Christo dilectos fratres hospitalis sancte Marie de domo Theutonica in singulis et universis graciis, libertatibus et iuribus suis, quibus per veros dictarum terrarum principes sunt dotati, illesos perpetuo conservari, universis et singulis vobis sub obtentu gracie nostre districte precipiendo mandamus, quatenus eosdem in prefatis graciis, libertatibus et iuribus favorabiliter confoventes nullis ipsos in illis perturbacionum incommodis affici permittatis. Si quis autem hoc nostre maiestatis edicto temere vilipenso eorundem fratrum iuribus fuerit iniurius aut honoribus inhonorius[1], gravem nostre maiestatis offensam se noverit incursurum. In cuius rei testimonium presens scriptum maiestatis nostre sigillo duximus roborandum. Datum Wienne kal. martii indictione vi^{a} anno m^{o} cc^{o} lxx^{o} vii^{o} regni vero nostri anno quinto.

VI, 357 v., unde citat Boehmer reg. Rud. n. 337. Titulus: Sequitur tenor litere domini Rudolfi regis Romanorum sigillo suo regio in pressula pergameni appendente sigillato super conservacione libertatum fratrum Theutonicorum. 1. inhonoriis B.

---

183. *1298 febr. 20 Wiennae. Albertus, Austriae dux, fratribus o. Th. Wiennensibus confirmat privilegium insertum supra n. 179.*

Nos Albertus, dei gracia dux Austrie et Styrie, dominus Carniole, Marchie ac Portusnaonis, universis tam pressentibus quam futuris, ad quos presentes pervenerint, declaramus, quod in nostra constituti presencia viri devoti commendator et fratres domus Wiennensis ordinis fratrum hospitalis sancte Marie Theutonicorum in Ierusalem privilegium quoddam integrum, salvum, non cancellatum, non abolitum nec in ulla sui parte viciatum, ipsis fratribus et ordini ab illustri quondam principe domino Friderico, duce Austrie et Styrie, antecessore nostro recordacionis preclare, concessum liberaliter et indultum, exhibuerunt nobis ex parte ordinis humiliter supplicantes, quatenus idem privilegium ipsis innovare, approbare et confirmare dignaremur de gracia speciali. Cuius quidem privilegii tenor per omnia talis est:

I. n. s. e. i. t. a. Fridericus *(cet. supra n. 179)* anno incarnacionis dominice m^{o} cc^{o} xl^{o} indictione xiii^{a} coram *(cet. usque)* fide dignis.

Nos itaque gestientes operibus pietatis votis sinceris applaudere et ordinis prelibati, quem spirituali caritate prosequimur, ampliare comoda et profectus, pro reverencia summi regis et nichilominus ad deprecativam predictorum fratrum instanciam prenotatum privilegium, sicut de verbo ad verbum expressum est, favorabiliter approbamus, innovamus et scripti huius patrocinio confirmamus. In cuius rei testimonium et robur perpetuo duraturum hanc exinde paginam conscribi fecimus et sigilli nostri appensione muniri. Datum Wienne x^{o} kalendas marcii anno domini millesimo ducentesimo nonagesimo viii^{a} indictione undecima.

VI, 356. Continetur in documento infra n. 184 de 1299 nov. 4.

---

184. *1299 nov. 4 Wiennae. Wernhardus, Pataviensis episcopus, transsumit documentum supra n. 183.*

Nos Wernhardus, dei gracia ecclesie Pataviensis episcopus, presentibus confitemur, quod devoti viri commendator et fratres domus Wiennensis ordinis fratrum hospitalis sancte Marie Theutonicorum in Ierusalem nobis privilegium illustris principis domini Alberti quondam ducis Austrie et Styrie, nunc serenissimi regis Romanorum, exhibuerunt integrum et in omni parte sui salvum sine reprehensione qualibet, prout infra de verbo ad verbum presentibus est insertum, petentes, quatenus ipsum in formam publicam redigere et exemplari sub nostro sigillo mandaremus. Cuius privilegii est per omnia tenor talis:

Nos Albertus (v. supra n. 183). Datum Wienne x° kalendas marcii anno domini millesimo ducentesimo nonagesimo viii° indictione undecima.

Nos itaque predictorum fratrum iustis peticionibus annuentes premissum privilegium mandavimus exemplari et in formam publicam redegimus in hiis scriptis. In cuius rei testimonium presentes dedimus litteras nostro sigillo munitas. Datum Wienne anno domini m° cc° nonagesimo nono pridie nonas novembris presentibus magistro Ottone, domino Bernhardo de Prampach, ecclesie nostre canonicis, et Ulrico capellano nostro, Ottone[1], Ludwico, notariis nostris, Minhalmo de Watzmanstorf, Pilgrimo Pincerna, militibus nostris, et aliis pluribus fide dignis.

VI, 356. 1. Otttone B.

---

185. *1329 febr. 4 Tyrolis. Heinricus, Bohemiae et Poloniae rex, Karinthiae dux, confirmat ordini fratrum Theutonicorum omnes gratias, libertates, exemptiones in Karinthia, Carniola, Marchia a praedecessore Ulrico Karinthiae duce concessas.*

Nos Heinricus, dei gracia Bohemie et Polonie rex, Karinthie dux, Tyrolis et Goricie comes, Aquilegiensis, Tridentine et Brixnensis ecclesiarum advocatus, ad noticiam universorum tenore presencium volumus pervenire, quod nos predecessorum nostrorum vestigiis inherere cupientes, illorum precipue, qui sacras religiones et pia loca suis favoribus et beneficiis extulerunt, omnes gracias, libertates et exempciones, quas clare memorie illustris quondam dominus Ulricus, dux Karinthie, predecessor noster, donavit et concessit suo privilegio ordini fratrum Theutonicorum in dominio nostro Karinthie, Carniole et Marchie, sicut provide, rite ac racionabiliter facte et concesse sunt, approbamus, ratificamus easque auctoritate presencium confirmamus, dantes presentes litteras nostro sigillo munitas in testimonium super eo. Datum Tyrolis anno domini millesimo trecentesimo vicesimo nono die iii° februarii indiccione duodecima.

VI, 357 v.

---

186. *1350 iulii 13 Krain. Albertus, Austriae dux, Iohanni Laibacensi o. Th. commendatori confirmat privilegium (supra n. 180).*

Wir Albrecht, von gots gnaden herczog ze Osterreich, ze Steyr und ze Kernden, her ze Chrain, auf der Marich und ze Portenaw, graf ze Habspurch und ze Kyburch, lanntgraf in Oberen Elsassen und her ze Phirt, tun kunt offenleich an disem brief, das fur uns chom der erber man pruder Johanns, comentewr von Tewtschen[1] haws ze Laybach, und zaigt uns ain hanntvest in Latein geschriben, die herczog Ulreich sälig von Kernden dem Tewtschen haws daselbs ze Laybach geben hat, und pat uns der selb pruder Johanns, das wier im die vorgeschriben hanntvest durch got vernewten, bestetten und von Latein in Tewtsche brechten. Das haben wir getan, als von wart ze wart hernach geschriben stet:

Wir Ulreich (etc. supra n. 180).

Und wann wir gern unsern vordern an allen gutten dingen nachvolgten und begirlicher an den sachen, die geistleich ordnung angent, davon haben wir den prüdern des Tewtschen haws in der vorgenanten unser stat ze Laybach durich got und durich unser frawn sand Marein willen und unser vordern[2] und unsern selen ze hilf und ze trost vernewtt und bestätt alle die recht, gnad und freyung, die da oben an disem brif geschriben stent, und vernewen und bestetten auch die mit disem brief und wellen auch, das weder unser hawptlawt, richter noch annder niemant wider die selben gnad, recht und freyung tue oder in die in chainen weg zerbrech pey unsern hulden. Des geben wir ze urckund disen brief besigilten mit unserm insigel, der geben ist ze Krain an erichtag nach sannd Margretentag nach Crists gepurd dreuczehenhundert jar darnach in dem funfczigisten jar.

VI, 358. 1. Tewchsen B. 2. supplevi.

---

187. *1350 iulii 13 Laybach. Albertus, Austriae dux, confirmat Ulrici Carinthiae ducis privilegium (supra n. 181).*

Wir Albrecht, von gots gnaden herczog ze Osterreich, ze Steir, ze Kernden, her zu Chrain, uf der Marich und ze Portenaw, graf ze Habspurch und ze Kyburch, lanntgraf in Obern Elsassen und her ze Phirt, tun chunt offenlich an disem brief, das für uns chom der erber man bruder Johanns, comentewr vom Teutschen haws ze Laybach, und zaigt uns ain hanntvest in Latein geschriben, die herczog Ulreich salig von Kernden den Tewtschen herren gemainchleich ze Kernden, ze Krain und auf der Marich geben hat, und bat uns derselb pruder Johanns, das wir in die vorgeschriben hanntvesten durich got vernewten bestetten und von Latein in Täwtsch prechten. Das haben wir getan, als von wart zu wart hernach geschriben stet:

Wir Ulreich (supra n. 181).

Und wann wir gern unsern vordern an allen gutten dingen nachvolgen und begirlicher an den sachen, die geistleich orden angent, davon haben wir den Tewtschen herren in den vorgenanten unsern herschaften durich got und durich unser frawen sannd Marien willen und unser und unser vordern zelen ze hilf und ze trost vernewt und bestett all die recht, gnad und freyung, die da oben an disem brief geschriben stentt, und vernewen und bestatten auch die mit disem brief und wellen auch, das weder unser hawptlewt noch annder niemant wider dy selben gnad, recht vnd freyung tue oder in die in chainen weg zeprech pey unsern hulden. Des geben wir ze urkund disen brief versigilten mit unserm insigel. Geben ze Laybach in Krain an eritag nach sannd Margreten tag nach Christs gepurde drewczehenhundert jar darnach in dem funfczigisten jar.

VI, 359.

---

188. *1355 apr. 28 zu der Hoensein. Karolus IV imperator prohibet, ne quis balivae Franconiae ordinis Theutonici usum ab imperatoribus ordini concessorum privilegiorum impediat.*

Wir Karl, von gots gnaden Römischer keyser, zu allen zyten merer des reichs und kung zu Beheim, enbieten allen fursten, geistlichen und werntlichen, graven, fryen, banriczen, herren, rittern, knechten, stetten, merckten, lantgeriechten, dörffern und gemeynden und allen unsern und des reichs lieben getruwen und sunderlich zu Francken unser gnad und alles gut. Wann wir angesehen haben getruwen, steten, unverdrossenen dinste, den uns und dem heiligen reich die geistlichen bruder des ordens des spitales sente Marien des Dutschen huses von Jherusalem, unser lieben andechtigen, mit ganczem fleifze getan und vollenkomliche bewyst haben und ouch tun söllen und mögen in kunftigen zyten, darumb wir dem vorgenant orden und allen den balyen, husern und gelidern zu dem selben orden gehörig mit wolbedachtem mute, mit rade unser fursten, graven, herren und andern unsern und des reichs getruwen, mit rechter wissen und mit unser keyserlicher macht vollenkomliche bestetiget und confirmieret haben alle ire hantvesten, brieve und freyheit, die sie von uns oder seliger gedechtnusze von unsern vorfaren in dem riche Römischen keysern oder kunigen vormals erworben oder behalden habent uber ire lande, bürge, geriechte, herscheffte, wiltpenne, recht, gulde, nucze, renthe, gute und besiczunge, wie man die genennen möchte mit sunderlichen worten in allen artickeln, puncten, meynungen und worten, wie oder in welicher wyse die hantvesten, brieve und friheit begriffen sint und wir nu verstanden haben, das die geistlichen bruder desselben Tütschen ordens und die huser der balyen zu Francken gelegen an iren hantvesten, brieven und freyheiten beschediget, gehindert und grobbeliche geirret werden, sunderlich an wassern, weyden, hulczeren, czöllen und geleitgelde uff wassern und off lande, der man der egenant balyen und huser darinne nicht gebruchen noch geniefsen lesset, als ire hantvesten und brieve haltent, die sie von dem riche habent und von uns bestetiget; davon gebieten wir uch und iglichen besunder bey unsern keyserlichen hulden und wollen das ernstliche, das niemant die obgenant balien zu Francken noch kein hus darin gehörig wider unser keyserliche bestedunge beschedigen, hindern oder irren sullen in keyne wyse, und wer darwider dete freventlichen, der sal als dicke das geschiet, hundert punt lödiges goldes vervallen sein, und die selben sullen halb in unser und des heiligen richs camern und das ander halbteil der egenant balyen zu Francken und den husern darinne, die also beschediget, gehindert oder geirret wurden, genczliche werden und gevallen. Mit urkunde ditz brieves versigelt mit unserm keyserlichen insigel, der geben ist zu der Hoensein nach Cristus geburte druczenhundert jar darnach in dem funff und funffczigstem jar an dem nehesten dinstag vor sant Walpurgen tag in dem nunden jare unser riche und des keysertums in dem ersten.

IV, 297.

---

189. *1360 februarii 10 Grecz. Rudolfus IV Austriae archidux confirmat privilegium supra n. 178.*

In nomine sancte et individue trinitatis. Rudolfus quartus, dei gracia palatinus archidux Austrie, Stirie et Karinthie, princeps Swevie atque Alsacie, dominus Carniole, Marchie ac Portusnaonis, necnon sacri Romani imperii supremus magister venatorum, omnibus in perpetuum. Tociens ducalis serenitatis magnificencia extollitur alcius et ipsius status a domino, a quo datur omnis potestas, felicius gubernatur, quociens loca divino cultui[1] dedicata benigna consideracione reguntur et ad ipsorum gracias, donaciones et libertates servandas et facultates augendas graciosa proteccio principis invenitur. Cum igitur omnis gloria sive potencia principatus in subditorum consistat solidata fortunis, expediens arbitramur et condecens, ut simus subiectis et in iusticia faciles et in gracia liberales. Noverit igitur presens etas et futuri temporis successiva posteritas, quod constitutus in presencia nostra honorabilis et religiosus vir Bernhardus, comendator domus Theutunicorum in colle iuxta civitatem Payrisch Grecz site pro se et suo conventu nobis devote et humiliter supplicavit, quatinus privilegium sibi et suo conventui[2] a dive recordacionis quondam Friderico duce Austrie et Styrie pie traditum et concessum innovare, approbare et confirmare de speciali gracia dignaremur. Cuius quidem[3] privilegii tenor sequitur in hec verba:

I. n. s. e. i. t. A. Fridericus (supra n. 178).

Licet igitur ex indita nobis mansuetudine omnem religionis professionem favore prosequamur benivolo, ad dicti tamen ordinis quietem et comodum eo inclinamur propensius, quo ipsum, quem recolenda nostra dotavit prioritas, tamquam facturam propriam, in qua omnis animalis congnacio delectatur naturaliter, contemplamur. Idcirco dictorum commendatoris et conventus precibus inclinati dictum privilegium quoad singula sua capitula presentibus innovamus, approbamus et confirmamus de gracia speciali, excepta venacione indulta eis, ut predicitur, quam tollimus eisque ipsius usum inhibemus et interdicimus per presentes, declarantes nichilominus prenotatas viginti octo areas exemptas ab exaccione tributaria, quas eciam nos consimiliter eximimus, sitas in Gendorff a domo C. dicti Grawschof se protendentes per ordinem usque ad ipsarum tabernam in acie viculi sumptis eisdem extremis domibus inclusive. Nulli ergo omnino hominum liceat hanc paginam nostre innovacionis et confirmacionis infringere vel eidem in aliquo ausu temerario contraire. Quod qui forsitan attemptare presumpserit, se gracie nostre indignacionis offensam et ad hoc centum libras auri puri se noverit incursurum quarum quinquaginta libre nostre camere et quinquaginta libre passis iniuriam assignari debent et pro emenda. In cuius rei testimonium presentes fieri et nostri sigilli appressione iussimus communiri. Huius rei testes sunt illustres princeps Meinhardus marchio Brandenburgensis, superioris Bavarie dux, necnon comes Tyrolensis, consobrinus noster carissimus, et reverendi in Christo patres et domini, amici nostri carissimi, dominus Ludwicus, sancte sedis Aquilegensis patriarcha; dominus Ortolfus, archiepiscopus Salczburgensis apostolice sedis legatus; Paulus, episcopus Frisingensis; Gotfridus, episcopus Pataviensis; Iohannes, confirmatus Gurcensis, nostre curie cancellarius; Ulricus, episcopus Secoviensis; Ludwicus, episcopus Chymensis, et Petrus, episcopus Laventinus. Item nobiles viri, avunculi nostri dilecti, Albertus, palatinus comes Karinthie; Meinhardus et Hainricus, comites de Goricia, necnon comes Otto de Ortenburg. Item fideles nostri dilecti Ulricus et Hermannus fratres, comites de Cilia; comes Iohannes de Phannberg, capitaneus noster Karinthie[4]; Eberhardus de Walsse de Lincza, capitaneus noster supra Anasum; Eberhardus de Walsse, capitaneus noster[5] Styrie; Leutoldus de Stadekk, capitaneus noster Carniole; Stheffanus de Meissow, marschalcus; Albertus de Puchaim, dapifer; Haidenricus de Meissow, pincerna; Petrus de Eberstorff, camerarius; Fridericus de Chrevspach, magister venatorum Austrie. Item Fridericus de Walsse de Grecz, pincerna; Rud(olfus) Otto[6] de Liechtenstain, camerarius; Fridericus de Pettovia, marschalcus; Fridericus de Stubenberg, dapifer Styrie; Fridericus de Aufenstain, marschalcus; Hertnidus Chreiger, dapifer; Hermannus de Ostrawicz, pincerna Carinthie. Item Iohannes Turso de Rauhennekk; Ulricus et Otto de Stubenberg; Gotschalcus de Neytperg; Hermannus de Chranichperg; Hertnidus de Pettovia; Hainricus Wilthauser. Item Hermannus de Landenberg, noster provincialis marschalcus Austrie; Hainricus de Hakenberg, noster magister curie; Iohannes de Prunn, noster magister camere; Pilgrimus Strewno, nostre curie marschalcus; Hainricus de Prunn, pincerna; Albertus Ottenstainer, magister coquine; Albertus Pincerna, magister cellariorum; Wilhalmus Pincerna de Libenberg, dispensator panis nostre curie; et plures alii fide digni. Datum in Grecz in die sancte Scolastice virginis anno domini millesimo trecentesimo sexagesimo, etatis nostre anno vicesimo primo, regiminis vero nostri secundo.

+ Nos vero Rudolfus dux predictus hanc literam hac subscriptione manus proprie roboramus.

+ Et nos Iohannes dei gracie episcopus Gurcensis, prefati domini nostr ducis Austrie primus cancellarius, recognovimus omnia prenotata.

VII, 368. Froelich II, 197 praebet excerptum; ubi desunt quidam inter testes. Testes ed. ap. Duellium II, 22 n. 41. Cf. Lichnowsky Geschichte des Hauses Habsburg. Wien 1839. IV. Regestorum DXCI n. 144. 1. cultu B. 2. conventu B. 3. quidam B. 4. usque a deest F. 5. I. d. Ph. c. n. s. A. E. d. W. c. n. St. D. 6. Rudolf Otto F.

190. *1360 martii 27 Laybach. Rudolfus, Austriae archidux, O. Th. domui Laibacensi confirmat privilegia Alberti (n. 186 et 187).*

Wir Rudolf der vierd, von gots gnaden erczherczog ze Osterreich, ze Steyr und ze Kernden, furst ze Swaben und Elsazzen, her ze Chrain, auf der Marich und ze Portenaw und des heiligen Romischen reich obrister jägermaister, tun kund, das für uns köm der erber und geistlich man pruder Uczman, commentewr des Tewschen hawses ze Laybach, und zaigt uns zwo hanntfest, die in herczog Ulreich sälig in Kernden umb ir gnad, recht und freyung getan und gegeben hat, und die in darnach unser lieber her und vatter herczog Albrecht, dem got genad, hat bestetet, und pat uns der selb prueder Uczman diemütichleich, das wir im dieselben zwo hanntvest durich got auch gerüchten ze vernewen und ze bestetten. Das haben wir getan in der weis, als hienach geschriben stet. Die erst hanntvest hebt sich an also:

Wir Albrecht (cet. supra n. 186).

Der anndern hanntvest ordnung ist also:

Wir Albrecht (cet. supra n. 187).

Und wann wir vorgenant herczog Rudolf anhangund sein den fuzpan unser vorvordern und sunderleich unsers vorgenannten lieben herren und vatter herczog Albrecht salig, davon haben wir dem egenanten Tewtschen haws ze Laybach durich got und auch durich vleifsiger pete willen des vorgenanten comentewrs desselben hawses dieselben zwo hanntvest mit allen punten und artiklen darinne begriffen vernewt, bewert und bestett, und vernewn, bewern und bestetten auch in aller der weis, als da oben von wart ze wart geschriben stet. Darumb sol niemant erlaubt sein dieselben unser vernewng, bewarung und bestettung uberfarn oder ir mit chainer frevels geturstichait widersein. Wer es aber darüber tett, der sol wissen in unser ungnad und darczu hundert pfundt goldes ze wanndel vervallen sein, der fumfczig pfunndt in unser kamer und fumczig pfund den, die davon beswert sind, werden und gevallen sullen. Und das dise bestettung und vernewung fürbas gancz und unczebrochen beleibe und auch ewigkleich volfurt werde, so geben wir disen brief zw ainem offen urkunde versigelten mit unserm grofsen anhangunden insigel. Der sach sind zewgen, die hernach geschriben stent, die erwirdigen unser lieben frewnt her Ludweig, patriarch ze Aglay; her Orttolf, erczbischoffe ze Salczburg, legate des stuls ze Rom; her Pawl, bischof ze Freysing; her Gotfrid, bischof ze Passaw; her Johanns, bestetter bischof ze Gurgk, unser kanczler; bischof Ulreich von Seccow; bischof Ludweig von Kyemse; bischof Peter von Lavent, und der hochgeborne furst margraf Meinhart ze Brandenburg, herczog in Obern Payrn und graff ze Tyrol, unser lieber swager, und die edlen unser lieb ohaim graf Albrecht, phallenczgraff in Kernden; graf Meinhart und graf Hainreich von Gorcz und graf Otte von Orttenburg, und unser getrewen, lieben graf Ulreich und graf Herman, pruder von Cilii; graf Johanns von Phannberg, unser hawptman in Kernden; Fridreich der Auffenstainer, marsalkch daselbs in Kernden, und Kunrad sein bruder; Fridreich von Walsee auf der Steyrmarch, Eberhardt von Walsee, unser hawptman ob der Ens; Eberhardt von Walsee, unser hawptman in Steyr; Rudolf Ott von Lichtenstain, kamrer daselbs in Steir; Fridreich, Ulreich und Ott von Stubenberg; Leutold von Stadekk, unser hawptman in Krain, und Rudolf, sein pruder; Jans der Turs von Rauhennekk; Herman von Lanndenberg, unser lanntmarsalkch in Osterreich; Hainreich von Hakkenberg, unser hofmaister; Jans von Prunn, unser kamrmaister; Pilgrein der Strewn, unser hofmarsalkch; Hainreich von Prunn, unser schenk; Albrecht der Ottenstainer, unser kuchenmaister; Albrecht der Schenk, der kellermaister, und Wilhalm der Schenk, unser speismaister, und annder erber lewt genug. Der brief ist geben ze Laybach in Krain an freytag vor dem palmtag nach Christs gepurde trewczehenhundert jar darnach in dem sechczigisten jare unsers alters in dem ains und czwainczigisten und unsers gewalts in dem andern jar.

[1]Wir der vorgenant herczog Rudolf sterken disen brief mit dir underschrift uns selbs handt.

[2]Et nos Iohannes, dei gracia episcopus Gurcensis, prenotati domini nostri ducis Austrie primus cancellarius, recognovimus omnia prenotata.

VI, 358. 1. „Inferius vero scripta erant de alterius manus littera videlicet hec verba" B. 2. „Circa finem vero eiusdem littere scriptum erant de alia manu videlicet hec verba" B.

---

191. *1396 oct. 21 Grecz. Wilhelmus, Austriae dux, domui Theutonicae Gracensis confirmat, tanquam inserta essent, Rudolfi et Friderici ducum privilegia.*

Wir Wilhalm, von gottes gnaden herczog ze Osterreich, ze Steyr, ze Kernden und ze Krain, grave ze Tyrol etc. bechennen, daz fur uns kom der erber und geistlich unser getrewr andächtiger Michel, hauscomendewr des Tewtschen haufs hie ze Grecz, und zaigt uns ain Lateynischs privilegi, daz dem selben goczhaufs weilent der hochgeporen furst, unser lieber vetter herczog Rudolff seliger gedechtnufs hat gegeben, darinn geschriben stet ain ander hantvest, die demselben Teutschen haufs von weilent herczog Fridreichen, herczog ze Osterreich, auch unserm vettern, dem got gnad, geben ist und der da laut uber desselben goczhaufs leutt, nucz, gült, gütter, gnad, recht und freyhait, die er im verlihen hat, und pat uns diemutiklich, daz wir dem egenanten haus dieselben hantvest geruchten zu vernewn und ze pestetten. Haben wir angesehen die lautter pegird, die uns vordern seligen habent gehabt zu dem egenanten orden, der wir auch williklich nachvolgend sein, und haben demselben haufs Teutsches ordens die vorgenante hantvesten und brieff vernewt und pestett, vernewn und pestetten auch wissentlich mit kraft dicz brieff mit allen den punden und artikeln, die darinn sind begriffen, und maynen und wellen, das dasselb goczhaus und ain yglicher hauscommendewr und auch die geistlichen bruder, die got in demselben haus dienent, nu furbazzer ewikleich dabey an meniklichs irrung genczlich beleiben in aller der mafs, als die obgenanten ir czwo hantvesten lautent. Davon gebieten wir unsern lieben getrewn unserm hauptman in Steyr und auch allen andern herren, rittern und knechten, pflegern, burggraven, richtern und allen unsern undertanen gegenwurtigen und kunftigen und sunderlich unser stat hie ze Grecz und maynen ernstlich, daz si die egenanten Teutschen herren und ir goczhaus dabey genczlich lazzen beleiben und in dawider kain irrung noch beswerung tun, noch yemant andern tun lazzen in dhainen weg; mit urkund dicz briefs. Geben zu Grecz an der ainleftausent magden tag nach Christi gepurd drewczehenhundert jar darnach in dem sechs und newnczigistem jare.

VII, 369 v.

---

192. *1421 aug. 12 Laybach. Ernestus Austriae archidux domui O. Th. Laibacensi confirmat privilegia.*

Wir Ernst, von gots gnaden erczherczog ze Osterreich, ze Steyr, ze Kernden und ze Krain, grave ze Tyrol etc. bekennen, das für uns kom der erber und geistlich man bruder Caspar, comentewr des Dewtschen haws hie ze Laybach, und rufft uns an diemutichleich, das wir demselben haws durch got geruchten ze vernewen und ze bestätten zwo hantvesten, die weilent herczog Ulreich von Kernden saliger demselben haws und auch allen hawsern Tawtschs ordens in Kernden, in Krain und auf der Marich umb ir recht, gnad und freyhait hat gegeben. Dieselben hantvesten auch die hochgeborn fursten unser her und enee herczog Albrecht, herczog Rudolf, unser vetter, und herczog Wilhalm, unser bruder, säliger gedachtnisse, den got genedig sey, mit iren briefen habent bekreftigt, haben wir angesehen des egenanten comentewrs vleifsig und diemutig pitt und das wir unser egenanten vordern säligen fuzzphaden in allen gutten sachen pilleich sein nachvolgend und sunderlich in den sachen, die geistlichen ordnung antreffent, und haben dem selben Tewtschen haws hie ze Laybach durich got und der hochgelobten junkfrawn, seiner gepererin, unser frawen sannd Marein und unser vordern, unser und unser nachkomen seelen ze hilf und ze trost die egenanten zwo hanntveste von herczog Ulreichen und auch die drey bestettbrief unsers enen, vetter und bruder mit allen iren puntten und artikelen, so darinne sind begriffen, von newen dinge bekrefftigt, vernewt und bestett, vernewen, bewaren und bestetten auch die wissentlich von furstlicher macht in aller der mafs, als ob die von wart zu wart hieinne geschriben weren an geverde. Davon gebietten wir unsern lieben getrewn, allen unsern hauptläwtten, herren, rittern und knechten, phlegern, purkgrafen, vicztumben, richtern, burgern und allen anndern unsern amptlewtten gegenwurtigen und kunftigen, den der brief geczaigt wirt, und wellen ernstleich, das sy dy egenanten Tewtschen herren und ir haws hie ze Laybach bey den rechten gnaden und freyheiten, so der obgenant ir brief von herczog Ulreichen innhat, genczlich lassen beleiben und in dawider chain irrung noch invall nicht tun noch das andern gestatten ze tuen in chainen weg, sunder sy dabey von unsern wegen schirmen und halten. Wer aber dawider tett, der wifs swärlich wider unser huld und gnad haben getan und auch genczlich vervallen sein der peen, die in des obgenanten unsers vettern herczog Rudolfs brief geschriben stett, mit urkund des briefs. Geben zu Laybach an eritag nach sannd Laurenczen tag nach Krists gepurde vierczehenhundert jar darnach im ains und zwainczigisten jare.

VI, 360 v.

---

193. *1424 aug. 12 in castro nostro Horneck Herbipolensis diocesis. Eberhardus de Saunsheim, hospitalis b. M. Th. Hierosolymitani per Alemanniam et Italiam magister, fratrem Iohannem de Hoffenheym, ord. Theut., capellanum suum, procuratorem constituit.*

In nomine domini. Amen. Nos frater Eberhardus de Sawnsheym, hospitalis beate Marie Theutonicorum Ierosolimitani per Alamanniam et Italiam magister et preceptor, presentis instrumenti serie notum facimus universis, quod nos omnibus melioribus modo, via, iure, causa, stilo, ordine atque forma, quibus melius et efficacius possumus et debemus, facimus, constituimus, creamus et solempniter ordinamus in nostrum verum, indubitatum et legittimum sindicum, procuratorem, actorem, factorem, negociorum, gestorem et nuncium specialem atque generalem, ita[1] quod specialitas generalitati non deroget nec econtra, religiosum virum fratrem Iohannem de Hoffenheym, capellanum nostrum ac dicti hospitalis et ordinis professum, presentem et huiusmodi procuracionis onus in se sponte suscipientem, ad procurandum, tractandum, expediendum et complendum singula negocia, causas quascunque spiritualem aut generalem, iurisdictionem recipientem et requirentem, cum quibuscunque personis, cuiuscunque status, gradus, condicionis, eminencie aut dignitatis fuerint et esse censeantur, eciamsi regalis, cardinalatus, pontificalis aut quavis alia prefulgeant dignitate, coram quibuscunque iudicibus, legatis, auditoribus vel commissariis ordinariis vel extraordinariis, delegatis vel subdelegatis seu locumtenentibus eorundem ecclesiasticis vel secularibus, datis seu dandis, impetratis seu impetrandis, necnon ad agendum et comparendum pro nobis et dicto nostro ordine, nosque et iura nostra defendendum, libellum seu libellos et quascumque peticiones alias dandum, reddendum verbotenus vel in scriptis et contra nos editis et oblatis recipiendum, excusaciones dilatorias et peremptorias et quascunque alias ante litis contestacionem vel post, necnon quascunque protestaciones seu requisiciones proponendas et prosequendas et contra nos propositas recipiendum et ad easdem respondendum, satisdandum et quamcunque satisdationem vel caucionem, si necesse fuerit, in qualibet parte litis prestandum et sibi prestitas recipiendum, litem seu lites contestandum necnon de calumpnia vitanda et veritate dicenda ac quodlibet aliud licitum iuramentum in animam nostram prestandum, ponendum et articulandum, posicionibus et articulis respondendum, testes, litteras et instrumenta et quevis alia probacionum genera producendum et productis ex adverso respondendum et obiciendum, testes contra nos productos iurare videndum et contra ipsos et eorum dicta dicendum, crimina et defectus opponendum, replicandum, duplicandum, triplicandum, quadruplicandum, attestationes testium publicari videndum, in causa seu causis renunciandum et concludendum, iudicis officium implorandum, beneficium restitucionis in integrum et absolucionis simpliciter vel ad cautelam petendum et obtinendum, ius, sentenciam et sentencias tam interlocutorias arbitrales quam diffinitivas ferri petendum et audiendum et ab ipsis et quolibet alio gravamine nobis illato vel inferendo, si opus fuerit, provocandum, appellandum, reclamandum et supplicandum, apostolos petendum et recipiendum, expensas taxari petendum et recipiendum, litteras quascunque et mandata tam de gracia, quam de iusticia impetrandum et eis utendum, loca et iudices eligendum et recusandum et de eis conveniendum et super premissis omnibus et singulis transigendum, componendum, paciscendum et concordandum et generaliter omnia alia et singula faciendum, procurandum, gerendum et exercendum, que veri procuratores facere possent et deberent et que in premissis et circa premissa seu quodlibet premissorum et dependencium, emergencium et connexorum ex eis necessaria fuerint seu oportuna et que nosmet dicere, facere et exercere possemus, si premissis omnibus et singulis personaliter interessemus, eciam si que sint, que mandatum exigant magis speciale et maiora essent, quam in presenti procuratorio sint expressa, ac eciam si causa talis nature existat, quod presenciam nostram requirat, dantes et concedentes dicto nostro procuratori plenam et liberam potestatem et speciale mandatum predicta omnia et singula nomine nostro faciendum, gerendum et exercendum, necnon unum vel plures procuratorem vel procuratores in premissis omnibus et singulis seu eorum quolibet subsituendum ante vel post litis contestacionem ac substitutum vel substitutos revocandum et onus procuracionis in se reassumendum tociens, quociens sibi videbitur expedire, relevantes dictum nostrum procuratorem et substitutum vel substituendos ab omni onere satisdandi promittentesque notario nostro publico infra scripto legittime stipulantes et recipientes habere velle ratum et gratum, quidquid per dictum nostrum procuratorem ac substitutos vel substituendos ab eo actum, factum, gestum sive procuratum fuerit in premissis sive aliquo premissorum, iudicio sisti et iudicatum solvi sub omni nostrorum et magisterii[2] seu preceptorie nostre bonorum obligacione et ypotheca cum omnibus et singulis suis clausulis necessariis et oportunis. In quorum omnium fidem, robur et testimonium presentes litteras sive presens publicum instrumentum huiusmodi procuracionis mandatum in se continens exinde fieri et per notarium publicum infrascriptum subscribi et publicari mandavimus nostrique sigilli iussimus appensione communiri. Datum et actum in castro nostro Horneck Herbipolensis diocesis anno a nativitate domini millesimo quadringentesimo vigesimo quarto indicione secunda mensis augusti die duodecima hora terciarum vel quasi, pontificatus sanctissimi in Christo patris et domini nostri domini Martini divina providencia pape quinti anno septimo, presentibus discretis viris Godehardo de Brachel, armigere Coloniensis et Iohanne de Biebelnheym, clerico Maguntine diocesis, testibus ad premissa vocatis pariter et rogatis.

Et ego Theodricus Coci de Gressen clericus Treverensis diocesis, publicus imperiali auctoritate notarius, quia huiusmodi procuratoris constitucioni, ratihabicioni, promissioni omnibusque aliis et singulis, dum, sicut premittitur fierent et agerentur, unacum prenominatis testibus presens fui eaque sic fieri vidi et audivi. Ideo hoc presens publicum instrumentum exinde confeci, conscripsi et in hanc publicam formam redegi signoque et nomine meis solitis et consuetis signavi unacum appensione sigilli domini mei magistri et preceptoris antedicti in fidem et testimonium premissorum requisitus.

IV, 172. Editum ap. Caorsinum et ap. Wolfgangum Senner Privilegia et immunitates ordinis s. Iohannis. Lipsiae 1520. fol. D. IIII v. 1. itaque B. 2. magistry B.

---

194. *1428 martii 21 Heidelberg. Ludowicus palatinus comes Rheni ordini Theutonico complura privilegia transsumit.*

Ludowicus, dei gracia comes palatinus Reni, sacri Romani imperii archidapifer et Bavarie dux, universis et singulis presentes visuris et audituris modernis et futuris votivorum successuum ubertatem cum noticia subscriptorum in perpetuam rei memoriam. Litteras serenissimi ac invictissimi principis et domini nostri domini Sigismundi, Romanorum regis semper augusti necnon Hungarie, Bohemie, Dalmacie, Croacie et cetera regis, maiestatis sue regie sigilli appensione munitas, sanas, integras et illesas ac omni prorsus vicio et suspicione carentes nos cum illa, qua convenit, decencia noveritis recepisse, quarum tenor de verbo ad verbum est talis:

Sigismundus etc. (infra de 1427 martii 12).

Post quarum quidem litterarum recepcionem crustitutus coram nobis venerabilis et religiosus dominus Eberhardus de Sawnszheim, hospitalis beate Marie Theotonicorum Ierosolimitani per Alamaniam et Italiam magister et preceptor generalis, nos cum instancia requisivit, quatenus ad dictarum literarum execucionem procedere atque nonnullas litteras et munimenta certorum privilegiorum, concessionum, donacionum ac indultorum per divos Romanorum imperatores et reges magistris et fratribus prefati hospitalis presentibus et eorum predecessoribus ac memorato ordini dudum et successive factorum et concessorum, quarum in originali forma quedam sub bullis, typariis aureis impressis, alique sub imperialis et relique regalis maiestatis impendentibus sigillis cere rubee et albe, ut in ipsis litteris clare apparuit, exstiterunt sigillate, coram nobis in notariorum publicorum ac testium infrascriptorum presencia exhibuit et produxit, devote supplicans et instanter, ut earum transsumptum fieri, prout nobis in dictis literis regiis commissum exstat, decernere dignaremur. Iustis igitur suis supplicacionibus benignius annuentes atque regium nobis factum mandatum et commissum diligencius ut tenemur exequi volentes predictarum litterarum et munimentorum concessiones, donaciones, privilegia seu indulta continencium coram nobis ut premittitur productarum et exhibitarum, quas maturius perspicientes et examinantes easdem sanas integras et illesas vidimus, reperimus et invenimus, earum transsumptum fieri et in presenti volumine transsumi et transscribi de commissa nobis auctoritate regia decrevimus et mandavimus, quarum tenores sequuntur in hec verba:

Fridericus etc.	1214 ianuar. 23 ap. Hagenowe.
„	1214 sept. 5 in castris prope Iuliacum.
„	1221 aprili Tarenti.
„	1222 decembr. ap. Precinam.
„	1223 ianuar. Capue.
„	1223 martio ap. Ferentinum.
„	1223 aprili „
Heinricus VII	1227 martii 27 Aquisgrani.
Conradus	1242 iunio Hagenowie.
	Intus Fridericus 1223 ianuar. Capue.
Ricardus	1257 nov. 28 Nussie.
Rudolfus	(1274) febr. 21 Hagenowe.
„	1273 nov. 14 Colonie.
Adolfus	1293 maii 23 in Bopardia.
Albertus	1298 sept. 22 in Gebesedeln ap. Rotemburg.
Heinricus	1309 martii 6 Spire.
Ludowicus	1330 maii 5 in Monaco.
	Intus Otto IV 1213 maii 10 ap. Nuremberg.
„	1330 maii 5 in Monaco.
	Intus Fridericus 1221 april. 10 Tarenti.
„	1323 april. 17 ap. Nuremberg.
	Intus Albertus 1298 sept. 22 in Gebsed. ap. Rotemb.
„	1331 dec. 20 Franchenfurt.
	Intus Fridericus 1221 april. Tarenti.
Karolus	1347 nov. 18 Nuremberch.
	Intus Fridericus 1221 april. Tarenti.
„	1347 dec. 1 Nurnberg.
„	1355 dec. 17 Nuremberg.
	Intus Fridericus 1221 april. Tarenti.
„	1355 dec. 17 Nurenberg.
„	1355 dec. 13 Nuremberg.
„	1376 sept. 1 Nuremberg.
„	1378 aug. 19 Nuremberg.
„	1355 april. 28 zu der Hoensein.
„	1365 april. 19 Heilprunn.
Wenceslaus	1383 oct. 17 Nuremberg.
	Intus Karolus 1355 dec. 17 Nuremberg.
	Intus Fridericus 1221 april. Tarenti.

Wenceslaus	1383 oct. 17 Nurenberg.
„	1389 maii 7 zum Ellebogen.
„	1398 ianuar. 9 Frankenfurt.
Rupertus	1402 nov. 3 Nuremberg.
„	1403 aug. 19 Heidelberg.
„	1404 febr. 25 Heidelberg.
	Intus Fridericus 1221 april. Tarenti.
Sigismundus	1414 nov. 19 Bunne.
„	1415 febr. 27 Costencz.
„	1415 iunii 19 Costentz.

Et quia prefatas litteras imperiales pariter et regales, munimenta, concessiones, donaciones, privilegia et indulta et eorum seu earum sigilla in notariorum publicorum infrascriptorum et plurimorum nostrorum fidelium nobis assistencium nobilium, militarium et armigerorum, testium ad hoc vocatorum specialiter et rogatorum presencia attente consideravimus et vidimus ac, sicut premittitur, ipsas sanas, integras et illesas, non abolitas, non abrasas nec in aliqua sui parte viciatas vel suspectas invenimus atque de verbo ad verbum simul cum presenti transumpto mandavimus et fecimus legi et auscultari diligenter, et quia examinatum et inventum est presens transumptum suprascriptarum litterarum originalium tenores de verbo ad verbum absque addicione seu detrimento omnimode continere, nos de regia nobis in hac parte commissa potestate presenti decreto perpetue valituro statuentes firmiter statuimus et decernimus, quatenus presenti transsumptarum literarum volumini[1] plena et omnimoda fides adhibeatur et adhiberi debeat in imperiali seu regali et aliis quibuscunque curiis et iudiciis et extra sicut litteris ipsis originalibus supradictis atque, ut eandem vim et vigorem habeat et iuris effectum sortiatur et sortiri debeat ceu littere originales predicte, tribuimus et impertimur auctoritatem, ita videlicet ut, ubicunque locorum presens transumptum tam in iudiciis quam extra visum, exhibitum vel productum fuerit, eandem vim, fidem et robur firmitatis, credulitatis ac probacionis habeat et teneat, ac si ipse littere, munimenta originalia et indulta omnia aut ex ipsis aliquod seu aliqua ostensa et exhibita in specie forent vel producta, fraude et dolo semotis quibuscunque. Acta sunt hec in castro nostro Heydelberg presentibus illustri principe domino Ottone, comite palatino Reni, duce Bavarie, germano nostro, necnon nobilibus Georio Pincerna, domino in Limpurg, Heinrico, domino de Plawen et strenuis Iohanne de Veningen, magistro curie nostre; Iohanne Stormfeder seniore; Iohanne de Wingarten; Conrado de Capelle, magistro curie castri nostri Heidelberg, et Michaele Mospach, pincerna nostro, testibus ad premissa vocatis specialiter et rogatis. In quorum omnium fidem robur et testimonium presentes magni nostri appensione sigilli fecimus communiri. Datum Heidelberg vicesima prima die mensis martii anno domini millesimo quadrincentesimo vicesimo octavo indicione sexta, invictissimi principis domini Sigismundi Romanorum regis semper augusti Romanorum regni anno decimo octavo.

Et ego Iohannes Erbschad de Wonneck, clericus Moguntinensis diocesis, publicus imperiali auctoritate notarius, quia predictarum litterarum, munimentorum, concessionum, donacionum, privilegiorum seu indultorum presentacioni, requisicioni, visioni, consideracioni, transumpcionis mandato et decreto una cum suprascriptis testibus et Heinrico notario subscripto presens interfui ac de mandato illustris principis et[2] domini, domini Ludwici, comitis palatini Reni, sacri Romani imperii archidapiferi et Bavarie ducis, simul cum eodem Heinrico notario publico subscripto infrascriptas litteras, munimenta, concessiones, donaciones, privilegia seu indulta personaliter cum presenti transumpto perlegi diligenter et auscultavi ac inveni in omnibus concordare eaque sicut premittitur fieri vidi et audivi; idcirco presenti transumpto per alium, me aliis impedito negociis, fideliter scripto hic me manu propria subscripsi signoque et nomine meis solitis et consuetis unacum appensione sigilli magni prefati domini ducis Ludwici signavi rogatus et requisitus in fidem et testimonium omnium et singulorum premissorum.

Et ego Henricus Trost, clericus Moguntinensis diocesis, publicus imperiali auctoritate notarius, quia predictarum litterarum, munimentorum, concessionum, donacionum, privilegiorum seu indultorum presentacioni, requisicioni, visioni, consideracioni, transumptionis mandato et decreto una cum suprascriptis testibus et Iohanne notario publico presens interfui necnon de mandato illustris principis et domini, domini Ludovici, comitis palatini Reni, sacri Romani imperii archidapiferi et Bavarie ducis, simul cum eodem Iohanne publico notario suprascriptas litteras, munimenta, concessiones, donaciones, privilegia seu indulta personaliter cum presenti transumpto perlegi diligenter et auscultavi ac inveni in omnibus concordare eaque sicut premittitur fieri vidi et audivi, idcirco presenti transumpto per alium, me aliis impedito negociis, fideliter scripto hic me manu propria subscripsi signoque et nomine meis solitis et consuetis unacum appensione sigilli magni prefati domini ducis Ludovici signavi rogatus et requisitus in fidem et testimonium omnium et singulorum premissorum.

IV, 263—317 v. 1. volumen B. 2. supplevi.

---

195. *1430 iulii 20 Romae apud sanctos apostolos. Martinus papa V executores constituit sententiae contra Alexandrum Tridentinum episcopum ob ordinem Theutonicum exactione gravatum latae.*

Martinus episcopus servus servorum dei venerabilibus fratribus Electensi et Curiensi episcopis ac dilecto filio decano ecclesie Brixinensis salutem et apostolicam benedictionem. Exhibita nobis pro parte dilectorum filiorum Gotfridi Niederhawsen, balie Athesis, Nicolai in Bolsano, Leopoldi in Longemosz, Tridentinensis diocesis, et Eckardi Mulock, Tridentinensis, hospitalis beate Marie Theotonicorum Ierosolomitani domorum commendatorum, peticio continebat, quod, licet olim magistro et fratribus dicti hospitalis a sede apostolica fuisset indultum, ut sub imposicionibus decimarum seu caritativorum vel aliorum quorumlibet subsidiorum, quibuscumque nominibus nuncuparentur, in quibusvis eciam citra — vel ultramontanis partibus quacumque auctoritate ex quavis causa, quomodocumque aut qualitercumque tunc factis vel imposterum forsitan faciendis magister et fratres ac hospitale predicti ipsiusque hospitalis preceptorie, ecclesie, capelle, oratoria et alia eorum ac dicti hospitalis loca et bona, que tunc ubilibet obtinebant vel infuturum licite obtinerent, tam mobilia quam immobilia necnon persone in illis degentes nullatenus includi seu comprehendi deberent, sed magister, fratres, hospitale, preceptorie, ecclesie, capelle, oratoria ac degentes tunc presentes et futuri huiusmodi a solucione ac prestatione decimarum et aliorum onerum predictorum forent et esse deberent perpetuis futuris temporibus prorsus exempti et immunes; tamen venerabilis frater noster Alexander, episcopus Tridentinensis, indulto huiusmodi contra iusticiam se opponens ac prefatos commendatores super illo multipliciter molestans, vexans, perturbans et impediens asserensque, se de consilio dilectorum filiorum capituli ecclesie Tridentinensis causis tunc subsistentibus legitimis omnibus et singulis prelatis, clericis et beneficiatis civitatis Tridentinensis et sue diocesis iuxta quotam sive taxam fructuum, reddituum et proventuum beneficiorum suorum ecclesiasticorum, que inibi obtinebant, certam collectam sive caritativum subsidium sibi per eorum quemlibet persolvendum imposuisse, commendatores prefatos per suas certi tenoris litteras sub ecclesiasticis sentenciis, censuris aliisque tunc expressis monuit ac mandavit eisdem, ut infra certum terminum peremptorium eciam tunc expressum sibi certam collectam similiter tunc expressam, quam ipsis, ut dicebat, imposuerat, solvere et assignare curarent. A quibus quidem monitione et mandato commendatores predicti, quamprimum ad eorum noticiam pervenerant, sencientes exinde indebite se gravari ad sedem appellarunt eandem. Nos causam appellacionis huiusmodi et negocii principalis dilecto filio magistro Hartungo de Capell, capellano nostro et causarum palacii apostolici auditori, ad instanciam dictorum commendatorum audiendam commisimus et fine debito terminandam, qui cognitis ipsius cause meritis de consilio et assensu coauditorum suorum causarum dicti palatii, quibus super hiis relacionem fecit fidelem, per suam diffinitivam sententiam pronunciavit, decrevit et declaravit, prout hec omnia in libello pro parte dictorum commendatorum in huiusmodi causa exhibito petita fuerant, opposiciones, molestaciones, perturbaciones, vexaciones et impedimenta predicta fuisse et esse temeraria, illicita, iniqua, iniusta et de facto presumpta ipsique episcopo super hiis perpetuum silencium imponendum fore et imposuit, dictosque commendatores ab impeticione ipsius episcopi absolvendos fore et absolvit, necnon prefatum episcopum in expensis coram eo in dicta causa legitime factis condempnandum fore et condempnavit, illarum taxatione sibi imposterum reservata. A qua quidem sententia dicti auditoris fuit pro parte episcopi ad prefatam sedem appellatum nosque causam appellacionis a sententia auditoris interposite huiusmodi dilecto filio magistro Iohanni de Mella, eciam capellano nostro et causarum eiusdem palacii auditori, audiendam commisimus et fine debito terminandam; qui cognitis huiusmodi cause meritis de consilio et assensu coauditorum suorum causarum dicti palacii, quibus super hiis relacionem fecit fidelem, per suam diffinitivam sentenciam pronunciavit, decrevit et declaravit, per prefatum Hartungum auditorem in causa huiusmodi bene fuisse et esse processum, sententiatum et diffinitum, eiusque sententiam predictam confirmandam fore et confirmavit, ac ab illa pro parte ipsius episcopi male fuisse et esse appellatum, necnon prefatum episcopum in expensis coram eo in dicta causa legitime factis condempnandum fore et condempnavit, illarum taxatione sibi imposterum reservata. Cnmque a sentencia Iohannis auditoris huiusmodi fuisset pro parte dicti episcopi ad prefatam sedem appellatum, nos causam ipsius ultime appellacionis dilecto filio magistro Iohanni de Thomariis, capellano nostro et causarum eiusdem palacii auditori, audiendam commisimus et fine debito terminandam, qui cognitis ipsius cause meritis de consilio et assensu coauditorum suorum causarum dicti palacii, quibus super hiis relacionem fecit fidelem, per suam diffinitivam sententiam pronuncciavit, decrevit et declaravit, per prefatum Iohannem de Mella, auditorem in causa huiusmodi bene fuisse et esse processum, sententiatum et diffinitum eiusque sententiam predictam confirmandam fore et confirmavit ac ab illa pro parte ipsius episcopi male fuisse et esse appellatum, necnon predictum episcopum in expensis coram eo in causa huiusmodi legitime factis condempnandum fore et condempnavit, illarum taxacione sibi imposterum reservata. Et subsequenter dilectus filius, magister Iohannes Walling, eciam capellanus noster et causarum eiusdem palacii auditor, cui ex certis causis commisimus, ut expensas coram dicto Hartungo in huiusmodi causa factas taxaret et instrumentum super sententia Hartungi auditoris huiusmodi sigillaret, coram ipso Hartungo in quadraginta, Iohannes de Mella in triginta ac Iohannes de Thomariis auditores predicti in sedecim florenis auri de camera boni et iusti ponderis coram eis factas expensas huiusmodi providis moderacionibus taxarunt, procuratoris ipsorum commendatorum super eisdem iuramentis secutis, prout in instrumentis publicis inde confectis Iohannis de Mella, Iohannis de Thomariis et pro dicto Hartungo auditore Iohannis Walling auditorum prefatorum sigillis munitis dicitur plenius contineri. Cum autem, sicut eadem peticio subiungebat, prefati commendatores dubitent, quod ipse episcopus sententiis auditorum huiusmodi et presencium vigore habendis processibus reverenter parere non velit quodque processus ipsi episcopo predicto propter eius potenciam et aliis, quos concernunt, tute nequeant publicari, pro parte dictorum commendatorum nobis fuit humiliter supplicatum, ut super hiis eis de oportuno remedio providere dignaremur. Nos itaque huiusmodi supplicacionibus inclinati discrecioni vestre per apostolica scripta mandamus, quatenus vos vel duo aut unus vestrum per vos vel alium seu alios auditorum sententias huiusmodi, ubi et quando expedire videritis, auctoritate nostra sollempniter publicantes non permittatis dictos commendatores vel eorum aliquem occasione imposicionis ac literarum episcopi huiusmodi impeti indebite seu quomodolibet molestari, facientes eis de dictis florenorum summis pro expensis eisdem iuxta prefatorum instrumentorum earundem condempnacionum et taxacionum tenores plenam et debitam satisfactionem impendi, et insuper legitimis super hiis per vos habendis servatis processibus eos, quociens expedierit, aggravare curetis, contradictores per censuram ecclesiasticam appellacione postposita compescendo, invocato ad hoc, si opus fuerit, auxilio brachii secularis. Ceterum, si per summariam informacionem super hiis per vos recipiendam vobis constiterit, quod ipsorum episcopi et aliorum, quos huiusmodi processus concerneret, presencia pro monicionibus eis et citationibus de ipsis faciendis comode nequeat haberi, nos vobis processus, moniciones et citaciones huiusmodi per edicta publica locis affigenda publicis partibus illis vicinis, de quibus sit verisimilis coniectura, quod ad noticiam monitorum et citatorum huiusmodi pervenire valeant, faciendi plenam concedimus tenore presencium facultatem ac volumus, quod ipsi processus perinde eosdem monitos et citatos artent, ac si eis intimati et insinuati personaliter et presencialiter legitime extitissent, non obstantibus constitucionibus apostolicis et aliis contrariis quibuscumque seu, si episcopo prefato vel quibusvis aliis communiter vel divisim ab eadem sede indultum existat, quod interdici, suspendi vel excommunicari non possint per litteras apostolicas non facientes plenam et expressam ac de verbo ad verbum de indulto huiusmodi mencionem. Datum Rome apud sanctos apostolos xiii kalendas augusti pontificatus nostri terciodecimo.

IV, 252 v.

---

196. *1434 sept. 9 Basileae. Iulianus s. R. e. s. Angeli cardinalis, s. ap. per Germaniam legatus, petente Eberhardi de Saunsheim, magistri per Alemanniam, procuratore transsumit quaedam privilegia apostolica.*

Iulianus miseratione divina sancti Angeli sancte Romane ecclesie diaconus cardinalis, in Germania apostolice sedis legatus, universis et singulis presentes visuris vel audituris modernis et futuris salutem in domino et presentibus fidem indubiam adhibere. Notum facimus per presentes, quod pridem honorabilis et religiosus frater Iohannes de Hoffenheym, hospitalis beate Marie Theotonicorum Ierosolomitani professus, procurator et procuratorio nomine venerabilis et religiosi viri domini Eberhardi de Sawnsheym, magistri et preceptoris dicti hospitalis per Alamanniam et Italiam generalis, prout de sue procuracionis mandato per publicum desuper confectum instrumentum per eum tunc facto productum, cuius tenor de verbo ad verbum infra sequitur, plenam fecit fidem in nostri presencia personaliter constitutus, certas litteras apostolicas, munimenta, concessiones, privilegia et indulta diversorum summorum pontificum infrascriptorum necnon sanctissimi domini Eugenii pape quarti ac sacri concilii Constantiensis litteras more Romane curie bullatas in cordulis sericis et canapinis impendentibus bullatas salvas, sanas et integras, non viciatas, non cancellatas nec in aliqua sui parte suspectas, sed prorsus omni vicio et suspicione carentes coram nobis exhibuit et produxit, petens humiliter et instanter a nobis, ut huiusmodi litteras apostolicas, privilegia et indulta transsumi et exemplari ac in transsumptum et exemplar publicum ex auctotoritate legacionis nostre ita videlicet, quod ubilibet tam in iudiciis quam extra dictis transsumptis et exemplis publicis staretur ac plena et indubitata fides adhiberetur, sicut dictis litteris originalibus, si in medium producerentur, mandare dignaremur. Nos vero Iulianus cardinalis et legatus prefatus huiusmodi peticioni tamquam racioni consone favorabiliter annuentes volentesque in huiusmodi negocio rite et legittime procedere quasdam litteras citatorias tunc emisimus et fulminavimus et illas per audienciam publicam litterarum contradictarum sacrosancte generalis Basiliensis synodi legi, exequi et publicari mandavimus, per quas citari fecimus et citavimus omnes et singulos sua interesse putantes eorumque procuratores, si qui tunc essent in dicta synodo pro eisdem, quatenus certo peremptorio termino competenti in dictis citatoriis litteris expresso comparerent coram nobis in iudicio et iudicialiter ad videndum et audiendum predictas litteras apostolicas, privilegia et indulta cum decreti nostri interposicione transsumi et exemplari mandare ad perpetuam rei memoriam vel ad dicendum causam, si quam haberent racionabilem, quare premissa minime fieri deberent, allegandum et ostendendum; alioquin, prout iuris et iustum foret, circa predicta procederemus dictorum citatorum contumacia in aliquo non obstante. Cumque in huiusmodi citacionis termino non compareret quisquam pro parte dictorum citatorum, qui causam aliquam, propter quam huiusmodi littere apostolice privilegia, munimenta, concessiones et indulta transsumi et exemplari non debebant, allegarent, nos Iulianus cardinalis et legatus prefatus tunc ad iura reddendum in domo habitacionis nostre et loco nostro solito et consueto pro tribunali sedentes et prefati fratris Iohannis procuratoris coram nobis dicto nomine in iudicio comparentis et dictas litteras citatorias in audiencia publica litterarum contradictarum dicte sacre synodi, ut moris est, executas reproducentis instanciam in eorundem citatorum contumaciam ipsas litteras ad nos recepimus diligenter et inspeximus, vidimus et examinavimus. Et quia ipsas litteras apostolicas privilegia et indulta post diligentem visionem salvas, sanas et integras, non viciatas, non cancellatas nec in aliqua sui parte suspectas, sed omni prorsus vicio et suspicione carentes comperimus et invenimus, idcirco ipsas litteras apostolicas, privilegia, munimenta, concessiones et indulta per discretos viros Bartholomeum imperiali et Wilhelmum apostolica et imperiali auctoritatibus notarios nostros infrascriptos transscribi, publicari ac in formam publicam et exemplar redigi decrevimus et mandavimus. Tenor vero mandati predicti, de quo supra, sequitur et est talis:

In nomine domini amen. Nos frater Eberhardus de Sawnsheym etc. de 1424 aug. 12 (supra n. 193).

Tenores vero prefatarum literarum apostolicarum et primo felicis recordacionis domini Honorii pape tercii sequuntur et sunt tales:

Honorius etc. Cum dilectis (de 1216 dec. 19).
" Iustis petencium (de 1218 iunii 25).
" Etsi neque (de 1220 dec. 15).
" Vestra religio (de 1221 ian. 9).
" Non absque (de 1221 ian. 16).*
" Cum dilectis (de 1221 ian. 16).*
" Milites hospitalis (de 1221 ian. 16).*
" Iustis petencium (de 1221 ian. 16).
" Dilecti filii (de 1221 ian. 16).
" Cum dilecti (de 1221 ian. 16).*
" Quanto dilecti (de 1221 ian. 18).
" Quia plerumque (de 1221 ian. 18).*
" Dilecti filii (de 1221 ian. 20).
" Dilecti filii (de 1221 ian. 20).
" Militum domus (de 1221 ian. 20).
" Pervenit ad nos (de 1221 ian. 21).
" Decet pastoralis (de 1221 ian. 21).
" Attendentes quam (de 1221 febr. 5).*
" Quam laudabiliter (de 1221 febr. 5).
" Etsi universorum (de 1221 febr. 5).*
" Sicut evangelica (de 1221 febr. 5).*
" Significantibus vobis (de 1221 febr. 8).
" Cum dilecti (de 1221 febr. 8).
" Quam amabilis (de 1221 febr. 9).*
" Querela dilectorum (de 1223 ian. 16).*
" Graviter oculos (de 1223 febr. 1).

Secuntur littere domini Gregorii pape noni.

Gregorius etc. Dilecti filii (de 1228 febr. 3).*
" Pervenit ad nos (de 1228 febr. 3).*
" Si diligenter (de 1228 febr. 4).
" Dilecti filii (de 1228 febr. 6).*
" Etsi neque (de 1227 iulii 28).
" Religiosos viros (de 1227 aug. 5).
" Graviter oculos (de 1227 aug. 13).
" Paci et quieti (de 1231 sept. 15).*
" Dilectorum filiorum (de 1227 aug. 31).
" Non absque (de 1231 martii 29).
" Cum dilectis (de 1231 oct. 10).*
" Quieti vestre (de 1235 nov. 28).
" Signorum evidencia (de 1237 mai. 22).

Sequuntur littere domini Innocencii pape quarti.

Innocencius etc. Cum dilecti (de 1246 april. 21).
" Cum dilectis (de 1245 sept. 5).*

Innocencius etc. Quieti vestre (de 1247 iunii 13).
" Cum de viris (de 1247 iulii 20).
" Cum olim (de 1254 febr. 9).
" Devocionis vestre (de 1254 mai. 18).

Sequuntur littere domini Alexandri pape quarti.

Alexander etc. Vestre meritis (de 1257 april. 8).
" Vestra religio (de 1257 iunii 11).
" Cum vos tamquam (de 1257 iunii 16).*
" Pro consequenda (de 1257 iulii 28).
" Canonica constitucione (de 1257 aug. 8).
" Sincerissime devocionis (de 1257 aug. 8).
" Inducunt nos (de 1257 aug. 9).
" Dilectorum filiorum (de 1257 aug. 20).
" Cum dilectis (de 1257 sept. 9).*
" Hospitalitatis piissime (de 1257 nov. 5).*
" Affectu benivolencie (de 1258 iunii 11).
" Religiosos viros (de 1258 nov. 9?).
" Devocionis vestre (de 1258 nov. 9).*
" Quieti vestre (de 1258 nov. 12).
" Ex parte dilectorum (de 1258 nov. 22).*

Sequuntur littere domini Clementis pape quarti.

Clemens etc. Cum dilectis (de 1267 ian. 8).*

Sequuntur littere domini Urbani pape quarti.

Urbanus etc. Devocionis vestre (de 1261 nov. 25).
" Vestre meritis (de 1264 aug. 23).
" Dilectorum filiorum (de 1263 oct. 11).
" Ex parte dilectorum (de 1263 oct. 2).

Sequuntur littere domini Nicolai pape quarti.

Nicolaus etc. Signorum evidencia (de 1289 april. 1).
" Quanto dilecti (de 1289 april. 2).

Sequuntur littere domini Bonifacii pape noni.

Bonifacius etc. Quanto dilecti (de 1396 mai. 12).
" Sedis apostolice (de 1396 mai. 12).
" Affectione et (de 1397 april. 7).
" Sincere devocionis (de 1399 febr. 25).*
" Hiis que (de 1400 april. 13).*
" Etsi quibuslibet (de 1402 dec. 10).

Sequuntur littere a generali synodo Constantiensi concesse.

Sacrosancta et generalis synodus Constanciensis etc. Meruit vestre (de 1417 aug. 12).*

Sacrosancta et generalis synodus Constanciensis etc. Ad compescendos (de 1417 sept. 4).*

Sequuntur littere domini Martini pape quinti.

Martinus etc. Romani pontificis (de 1419 april. 10).
„ Disposicione divina (de 1419 mai. 17).*
„ Laudibus et honore (de 1419 mai. 17).*
„ Humilibus et honestis (de 1423 mart. 11).
„ Provisionis nostre (de 1419 aug. 24).
„ Regnum presidentes (de 1420 sept. 24).
„ Religionis zelus (de 1423 febr. 11).
„ Pro singulorum (de 1423 mart. 4).*
„ Paterne consideracionis (de 1429 nov. 6).
Intus Sigismundus (de 1415 iunii 19).
„ Exhibita nobis (de 1430 iulii 20).

Sequuntur littere domini Eugenii pape quarti.

Eugenius etc. Dudum felicis (de 1431 dec. 15).
„ Dudum felicis (de 1431 febr. 18).
Intus Martinus. Paterne considerat. (de 1429 nov. 6).
Intus Sigismundus (de 1415 iunii 19).

Et quia prefatas litteras apostolicas, munimenta, concessiones, privilegia et indulta ac eorundem bullas in notariorum nostrorum publicorum supra et infra nominatorum et plurimorum aliorum fide dignorum testium ad hoc vocatorum specialiter et rogatorum presencia productas et producta attente consideravimus et vidimus ac sicut premittitur ipsas sanas, integras et illesas, non abolitas, non viciatas, non cancellatas, non abrasas vel suspectas invenimus atque de verbo ad verbum simul cum presenti transsumpto mandavimus et fecimus legi et auscultari diligenter; et quia examinatum et inventum est presens transsumptum suprascriptarum litterarum originalium tenores de verbo ad verbum absque addicione seu detrimento omnimode continere, nos Iulianus cardinalis et legatus prefatus auctoritate nostre legacionis presenti decreto perpetue valituro statuentes firmiter statuimus et decernimus, quatenus presenti transsumptarum litterarum volumini plena et omnimoda fides adhibeatur et adhiberi debeat in quibuscumque iudiciis ecclesiasticis et secularibus et extra, sicut litteris ipsis originalibus suprascriptis, atque, ut eandem vim et vigorem habeat et iuris sorciatur effectum ac sortiri debeat ceu littere originales predicte, tribuimus et impertimur auctoritatem, ita videlicet ut, ubicumque locorum presens transsumptum tam in iudiciis quam extra visum, exhibitum vel productum fuerit, eandem vim, fidem et robur firmitatis, credulitatis ac probacionis habeat et teneat, ac si ipse littere, privilegia originalia et indulta omnia aut ex ipsis aliquod seu aliqua ostensa et exhibita in specie forent vel producta, fraude et dolo semotis quibuscumque. In quorum omnium et singulorum fidem, robur et testimonium premissorum presentes nostras litteras sive presens publicum instrumentum exinde fieri et per supra et infra nominatos notarios nostros publicos Wilhelmum et Bartholomeum subscribi et publicari mandavimus sigillique nostri oblongi, quo utimur, fecimus appensione communiri. Datum et actum Basilee et ibidem in domo habitacionis nostre apud sanctum Leonardum anno a nativitate domini millesimo quadringentesimo tricesimo quarto indictione duodecima pontificatus sanctissimi in Christo patris et domini, domini Eugenii divina providencia pape quarti, anno eius quarto die Iovis nona septembris hora vesperarum vel quasi, presentibus honorabilibus viris dominis Henrico Holland, preposito sancti Petri Imbriacensis Constantiensis diocesis, Iohanne Suszeler, canonico ecclesie Constantiensis, Wernero, clerico Monasteriensi, et Michaele de Wertheym, clerico Herbipolensis diocesium, notariis eciam publicis et pluribus aliis fide dignis testibus ad premissa vocatis specialiter et rogatis[1].

Et ego Wilhellmus Corten de Blisia, clericus Leodiensis diocesis, publicus apostolica et imperiali auctoritatibus notarius, quia preinsertarum litterarum exhibicioni, transumpcionis peticioni earumque transumpcioni omnibusque aliis premissis, dum sicut premittitur per reverendissimum patrem dominum Iulianum legatum fierent et coram eo agerentur, una cum Bartholomeo supra et infrascripto notario et dictis testibus presens fui, ideo presentis voluminis seu transumpti copias ex ipsis originalibus litteris fideliter exemplari et hic inseri procuravi et cum ipsis originalibus per diligentem auscultacionem in omnibus concordare inveni, nihil addendo vel minuendo nisi forsan litteram vel sillabam ex ignorancia vel errore et non vicio additam vel omissam, sensum seu facti materiam minime variando, et de mandato prefati domini Iuliani legati in hanc publicam formam redegi, subscripsi et publicavi signoque et nomine meis solitis una cum prefati domini Iuliani legati sigilli appensione et dicti Bartholomei notarii manus subscripcione et signi soliti signacione signavi rogatus in fidem omnium premissorum, rasuram per me supra approbatam, manu propria prout ibi et approbo non vicio, sed errore factam; ultra illam nullam rasuram suspectam approbo nec affirmo.

Et ego Bartholomeus de Batiferris Lunensis diocesis, publicus imperiali auctoritate notarius, premissis omnibus et singulis, dum sicut premittitur fierent et agerentur, una cum predicto Wilhelmo Corten notario et prenotatis testibus presens interfui et ea omnia sic fieri vidi et audivi et presentis voluminis seu transumpti instrumentum manu aliena fideliter scriptum una cum dicto Wilhelmo subscripsi et publicavi signoque et nomine meis solitis et consuetis una cum appensione sigilli prefati reverendissimi domini legati signavi in fidem et testimonium omnium premissorum vocatus et rogatus.

IV, 171—261 v. In transsumto de 1495 iunii 26 inter documenta ordinis hospitalis s. Iohannis Berolini in archivo secretiori fol. 25—55. Impressum ap. Caorsinum. Ap. Wolfgangum Sennerum D. IIII. Tamen his tribus locis tantum pars privilegiorum supra citatorum exhibita est, supra asterisco notata. 1. Sequitur subscripcio notariorum B.

---

197. *1444 aut 1445. Laurentius Aquileiensis patriarcha transsumit quaedam ordinis Theutonici privilegia.*

Laurentius dei gracia sancte sedis Aquilegiensis patriarcha, administrator ecclesie Laventine, universis et singulis Christi fidelibus tam presentibus quam futuris, ad quos presentes pervenerint, salutem in domino sempiternam. Quoniam[1] libertates, gracie aliaque[2] pro sustentamento religionum et ordinum ac ecclesiasticarum personarum in privilegiis a summis pontificibus necnon imperatoribus et sacri Romani imperii regibus concessis videntur contineri, dignum est et racioni consonum, ut privilegia huiusmodi, libertates, gracie et alia, quibus ecclesiastice persone in religione et extra constitute gaudere debeant, continentes summa debeant diligencia reservari et custodia debita premuniri. Hinc est, quod nobilis et religiosus vir, frater Iohannes de Pomersheym, laycus professus ordinis fratrum Theotonicorum hospitalis sancte Marie Ierosolimitani, commendator seu preceptor generalis balive Austrie eiusdem ordinis, certas litteras apostolicas libertates, gracias, exempciones, confirmaciones dicto ordini a summis pontificibus concessas in se continentes ipsorum veris bullis plumbeis in filis sericeis rubei et glauci coloris more Romane curie appendentibus bullatas, et alia privilegia regalia et ducalia cum ipsorum veris sigillis appendentibus simili modo libertates et comoda dicti ordinis et fratrum eiusdem continencia, sanas et sana, non suspectas neque suspecta, sed omni prorsus vicio et suspicione carentes et carencia nobis in presencia notarii publici et testium infrascriptorum presentavit, quas et que nos cum ea, qua decuit, reverencia noveritis recepisse, allegans dictus frater Iohannes et exponens, quod privilegia et originalia huiusmodi de loco ducere ad locum videretur periculosum et incautum propter discrimina maris, hostiles incursus, aquarum inundaciones et alios varios eventus, qui casu possent oriri, ut huiusmodi privilegia perderentur seu in aquis vel alio modo annullarentur, unde fratres et domus ordinis predicti incomoda gravia reportarent atque damna; quare nobis humiliter supplicavit omnia et singula privilegia papalia, regalia et ducalia ac alia nobis per ipsum sicut premittitur presentata sibi per nos transsumi, transscribi et exemplari et in perpetuam rei memoriam vallari, ita ut in iudicio et, ubicunque locorum huiusmodi transsumpta producta forent, ipsis tamquam originalibus litteris plenaria fides esset adhibenda. Quarum litterarum tenor sequitur secundum ordinem de verbo ad verbum et primo bulle domini Urbani pape quarti, cuius tenor est talis:

Urbanus etc. Cum dilecti etc. de 1263 oct. 1 apud Urbem veterem.

Sequitur transsumptum sive transscriptum privilegii domini Gregorii pape noni super libertate exaccionum pedagii et aliarum consuetudinum, ne a fratribus dicti ordinis vel eorum hominibus de rebus eorundem fratrum usibus deputatis extorqueantur[3]:

Gregorius etc. Religiosos viros etc. de 1227 iulii 31 Anagnie.

Sequitur tenor privilegii domini Nicolai pape quarti:

Nicolaus etc. Solet annuere etc. de 1288 maii 27 Reate.

Sequitur tenor privilegii domini Alexandri pape quarti:

Alexander etc. Vestra religio etc. de 1257 iunii 27 Viterbii.

Alexander etc. Sincerissime devocionis etc. de 1257 aug. 8 Viterbii.

Sequitur tenor et forma transsumpti litterarum et privilegiorum ducalium domini Bernhardi episcopi Pataviensis de et super libertatibus fratrum Theutonicorum sigillo suo oblongo in filis sericeis[4] appendente muniti, cuius tenor sequitur in hunc modum:

Nos Wernhardus etc. de 1299 nov. 4 v. supra n. 184.

Intus: Albertus etc. de 1298 febr. 20 v. supra n. 183.

Intus: Fridericus etc. de 1239 v. supra n. 179.

Sequitur tenor littere domini Rudolfi regis Romanorum sigillo suo regio in pressula pergameni appendente sigillate, super conservacione libertatum fratrum Theutonicorum:

Rudolfus etc. Volentes honorabiles etc. de 1277 martii 1 (s. n. 182).

Sequitur tenor privilegii domini Heinrici regis Bohemie etc.:

Nos Heinricus etc. de 1329 febr. 4 (supra n. 185).

Sequitur privilegium domini Rudolfi quarti ducis Austrie etc. transsumpta litterarum ducalium dominorum Alberti Austrie et Udalrici Karinthie ducum in se continens, sigillo suo ducali maiori rotundo in zona sericea appendente, cuius tenor talis est:

Wir Rudolf etc. de 1360 martii 27 (supra n. 190).

Intus: Wir Albrecht de 1350 iulii 13 (supra n. 186).

Intus: Wir Ulreich (supra n. 180).

Intus: Wir Albrecht de 1350 iulii 13 (supra n. 187).

Intus: Wir Ulreich (supra n. 181).

Sequitur tenor confirmacionis domini Ernesti ducis Austrie:

Wir Ernst etc. de 1421 aug. 12 (supra n. 192).

Et ego Iohannes Schawr de Weissenburg, clericus coniugatus Eystetensis diocesis, publicus imperiali auctoritate notarius, quia dictorum privilegiorum presentacioni, recepcioni, supplicacioni omnibusque aliis et singulis, dum sicut premittitur agerentur, et coram prelibato reverendissimo in Christo patre et domino, domino patriarcha fierent, una cum venerabilibus viris, magistris Nicolao Speyser, canonico ecclesie sancti Bartholomei Frisaci et Wilhelmo Polcz, plebano Wippaci Salczburgensis et Aquilegiensis diocesium presens interfui eaque sic fieri vidi et audivi; sed, quia suprascriptis transumptis completis prenonimatus dominus patriarcha presens non extiterat et propter huiusmodi sui absenciam et festinum recessum domini Iohannis de Pomersheim preceptoris balive Austrie ordinis fratrum Theutonicorum prescripta transumpta non poterant sigillari, quare transumpta huiusmodi per me inchoata et per alium fidelem, me aliis certis prepedito negociis, conscripta conspexi et cum alio fideli debite collacionavi, nichil inveniens cum originalibus discordare, quod sensum mutaret seu viciaret; ideo de mandato dicti domini Iohannis de Pomersheim me propria manu subscripsi et signo meo solito presentes signavi rogatus et requisitus in fidem et testimonium omnium et singulorum premissorum.

Signum notarii.

VI, 354 — 361 v. In pagina 353 legitur: Die privilegia hy um verschriben vindt man in dem haws ze Fryesach und zu Laybach. 1. Cum enim B. 2. et alia que B. 3. extorquentur B. 4. oblonge in silis sinceris B.

198. *1445 ianuarii 2 Constantiae. Notarius transsumit transsumta Iuliani cardinalis de 1434 septbr. 9 (supra n. 196) et Ludowici palatini comitis Rheni de 1428 martii 1 (supra n. 194).*

In nomine domini amen. Noverint universi et singuli, quos nosse fuerit oportunum, quod anno domini millesimo quadringentesimo quadragesimo quinto indiccione octava pontificatus sanctissimi in Christo patris et domini nostri domini Eugenii divina providencia pape quarti, anno eius quartodecimo die vero secunda mensis ianuarii comparuit coram me[1] notario publico infrascripto Constancie provincie Maguntinensis in domo solite habitacionis mee providus vir Caspar Lingg, curie causarum Constanciensis iuratus necnon venerabilis ac strenui viri domini Burckardi de Schellemberg, commendatoris provincialis per Sueviam et Ylsaciam fratrum hospitalis beate Marie Theutonicorum Iherosolimitani legitimus procurator, et nomine procuratorio eiusdem strenui domini Burckardi de Schellemberg idem Caspar Lingg duo, — unum videlicet litterarum apostolicarum, munimentorum, concessionum, privilegiorum et ipsis indultorum, videlicet hospitali seu ordini ac fratribus per diversos summos pontifices ac dictum sanctissimum dominum nostrum, dominum Eugenium papam quartum, et sacrosanctum generale concilium factarum et concessarum, factorum et concessorum, alias per reverendissimum in Christo patrem et dominum, dominum Iulianum miseracione divina sancti Angeli sancte Romane ecclesie diaconum cardinalem, in Germania apostolice sedis legatum, previa citacione legitima transsumptarum et transscriptarum transsumptorumque et transscriptorum in formam instrumenti publicam per notarios publicos in eisdem registris seu voluminibus nominatos de speciali eius mandato redactum ac sigillo dicti reverendissimi patris domini Iuliani cardinalis et legati [necnon illustris principis et domini, domini Ludowici comitis palatini Reni, sacri Romani imperii archidapiferi et Bavarie ducis,][a] singulis eiusdem registri seu voluminis, prout supra in ipsis voluminibus dinoscitur specificari, foliis transfixis; aliud vero litterarum, munimentorum, privilegiorum, concessionum, donacionum et indultorum predictis hospitali seu ordini et fratribus per divos Romanorum imperatores et reges factarum concessarumque et factorum, alias per prelibatum illustrem principem et dominum, dominum Ludovicum dei gracia comitem palatinum Reni, sacri Romani imperii dapiferum et Bavarie ducem, ex speciali sibi per inclite memorie Sigismundum Romanorum regem super hoc litteratorie facta commissione transsumptarum et transscriptarum transsumptorumque et transscriptorum, sigillo eiusdem domini Ludovici atque ducis et commissarii ut prefertur supra sigillatum et eciam ut premittitur singulis foliis transfixis *sive transfixo*, — volumina sive registra in pergameno conscripta sana et illesa, non rasa neque abolita, sed omni prorsus suspicione ut prima facie apparebat carentia in mei notarii publici infrascripti presencia exhibuit et in medium produxit, affirmans et proponens, quod dictus suus dominus pro defensione et tuicione bonorum, iurium et emunitatum ordinis et fratrum predictorum huiusmodi registris et voluminibus quoad litteras, concessiones, donaciones, munimenta, indulta et privilegia in eisdem contentas et descriptas contentaque et descripta in diversis et a se longe distantibus mundi partibus ac coram variis tam spiritualibus quam secularibus iudicibus uti necessario habeat atque frui, ubi et ad quos ac quociens expedierit dicta registra seu volumina transsumptorum tam propter gwerrarum pericula quam viarum discrimina et alios diffortunii multiplices casus transmittere seu deferre libere et secure[3] non valeat seu speret, ymo pocius de earundem laceracione, devastacione et totali ammissione formidare oporteat. Petiit propterea dictus Caspar Lingg quo supra nomine procuratorio a me notario publico infrascripto, quatenus registra seu volumina transsumptorum predicta cum singulis in eis contentis fideliter transscriberem et excopiarem ac in publicam formam redigerem. Visis igitur per me notarium publicum subscriptum registris seu voluminibus transsumptorum predictorum eadem sana et illesa, non abrasa neque in aliqua sui parte suspecta inveni; idcirco eadem, ut proxime supra precedenti folio premittitur, de verbo ad verbum nil penitus, quod sillabam immutet seu variet intellectum mutato seu variato transscripsi et excopiavi ac diligenti prehabita collacione reperi omnimode transscripcionem et excopiacionem huiusmodi cum originalibus registris seu voluminibus pretactis concordare. Subsequenter vero anno et indicione premencionatis die vero vicesima octava mensis aprilis pontificatus prelibati sanctissimi domini nostri, domini Eugenii pape quarti, anno eius quintodecimo, mencionatus venerabilis dominus Burckardus de Schellenberg, provincialis personaliter unacum prenominato Caspare Lingg, eiusdem procuratore, in pretacta civitate Constanciensi et ibidem in curia seu domo prelibati domini Burckardi ac in mei notarii publici subscripti necnon[4] discretorum testium, videlicet domini Conradi Weber, cappellani ecclesie sancti Iohannis Constanciensis, Friderici Ysenmann et Conradi Has, scribarum sive procuratorum prefate curie Constanciensis ad premissa vocatorum pariterque et requisitorum presencia constitutus idem venerabilis dominus Burkardus provincialis per organum predicti Casparis Lingg, ut prefertur procuratoris, prescripta volumina seu registra per me notarium subnotatum in eorundem testium presencia in formam publicam redigi[5] et subscribi petivit egoque notarius subscriptus ad requisicionem sepefati venerabilis domini provincialis huiusmodi volumina in formam publicam subnotatam redegi etc.

(Signum notarii.)

Et ego Ulricus Mollitoris, publicus imperiali auctoritate ac curie episcopalis Constanciensis notarius iuratus, quia dictorum registrorum sive voluminum exhibicioni et produccioni, affirmacioni, proposicioni, visioni et perspeccioni omnibusque et singulis aliis, dum sicut prefertur fierent et agerentur, unacum prescriptis testibus presens fui eaque sic fieri vidi et audivi ac volumina sive registra predicta unacum subscripcione notariorum in eisdem nominatorum de verbo ad verbum nil addito vel omisso, quod facti sillabam immutet seu variet intellectum, manu mea propria fideliter transscripsi et excopiavi et tandem cum ipsis originalibus hec transscripta et excopiata fideliter collacionavi et auscultavi repertaque omnimoda eorundem registrorum seu voluminum cum ipsis meis transscriptis et excopiatis concordancia eadem in hanc publicam formam me hic manu propria subscribendo duxi redigenda et redegi signoque et nomine meis solitis et consuetis signavi in fidem et testimonium omnium et singulorum premissorum rogatus pariter et requisitus.

IV, 317 v. 1. Constañ B. 2. Pro [* — *] l. sigillatum. 3. succure B. 4. nec B. 5. redegi B. Praeterea quaedam leviora mutavimus.

---

199. *1445 aprilis 21 Grecz. Notarius transsumit quaedam ordinis Theutonici privilegia.*

In nomine domini amen. Anno nativitatis eiusdem millesimo quadringentesimo quadragesimo quinto indictione octava die vero Mercurii mensis aprilis vicesima prima, serenissimo principe et domino nostro domino Friderico Romanorum rege etc. inclitissimo feliciter regnante anno sexto, in mei notarii publici testiumque infrascriptorum ad hoc vocatorum specialiter et rogatorum presencia constitutus personaliter venerabilis vir dominus Iohannes Magencz, commendator domus in Grecz ordinis beate Marie fratrum Theutunicorum, habens et tenens in suis manibus quasdam patentes litteras apostolicas et ducales dominorum ducum Austrie bullis plumbeis cordulis canapis ducalibus et sericiis impendentibus more Romane curie et ducali dominorum ducum Austrie bullatas, quas quidem litteras mihi notario infrascripto exhibuit et presentavit meque debita cum instantia peciit et requisivit, ut easdem tanquam publica et autentica persona transumi, exemplari et excopiari curarem, volens, ut asseruit, dictas litteras sicut premittitur transsumptas suis superioribus destinare. Ego vero considerans peticionem et requisicionem huiusmodi fore iustas et consonas racioni presentes litteras debite vidi, perlegi et inspexi; sed quia litteras huiusmodi sanas, salvas, integras, non viciatas, non cancellatas, non abrasas, sed omni prorsus vicio et suspicione carentes reperi, ideo easdem post diligentem collacionem factam transumi, exemplari et excopiari curavi. Quarum quidem litterarum apostolicarum et ducalium tenores de verbo ad verbum secuntur et sunt tales. Et prime:

Honorius etc. 1221. Non sine gravi etc. de 1221 ian. 20 Laterani.

Item secunde:

Honorius etc. Cum dilectis etc. de 1223 ian. 13 Laterani.

Item tercie:

Innocencius etc. Cum dilectis etc. de 1245 iunii 23 Lugduni.

Item quarte:

Gregorius etc. Paci et quieti etc. de 1227 aug. 11 Anagnie.

Item quinte:

Alexander etc. Canonica constitucione etc. de 1261 mart. 28 Laterani.

Item sexte:

I. n. s. e. i. t. a. Rudolfus quartus dei gracia palatinus archidux Austrie cet. de 1360 febr. 10 Grecz (supra n. 189).

Intus: Fridericus dux Austrie de 1233 oct. 28 Erpurch (s. n. 178).

Item septime:

Wir Wilhalm etc. herczog ze Osterreich etc. 1396 oct. 21 Grecz (supra n. 191).

Acta sunt hec in domo fratrum Theutunicorum supradictorum in Grecz anno indicione, die, mense, quibus supra, presentibus ibidem honorabilibus et[1] discretis viris dominis Wenczeslao capellano in Grecz, presbitero, Thoma Hewtel et Petro Scheplini, clericis Pragensis, Salczburgensis et Misnensis diocesium[2], testibus ad premissa vocatis specialiter et rogatis.

(Signum notarii Andreae de F.)

Et ego Andreas quondam Martini de Furstenberg, clericus Misnensis diocesis, publicus imperiali auctoritate notarius, quia predictarum litterarum apostolicarum et ducalium exhibicioni, presentacioni, leccioni et collacioni presens interfui easque salvas, sanas, integras et non viciatas reperi; ideo hoc presens publicum transsumptum per alium fideliter scriptum me aliis negotiis prepedito exinde confeci publicum et in hanc publicam formam redegi signoque et nomine meis solitis et consuetis presentibus testibus supradictis consignavi rogatus et debite requisitus in fidem et testimonium evidens omnium et singulorum premissorum.

VII, 367--369 v. 1. honorabili B. 2. diocesum B.

PRUSSIA. NOVA MARCHIA.

200. *1228 octbr. 28 Perusii. Gregorius papa IX (Solet annuere) confirmat a bonae memoriae [Christiano] primo episcopo Prutenorum ad exemplar militiae Christi de Livonia institutam militiam Christi contra Prutenos in Mazovia.*

II, 131 v. sine die e reg. Greg. E copiario archivi Regimontani n. 30 cum dato Perusii v kal. nov. p. a. 2 ed. I. Voigt cod. dipl. Pruss. I, 19 n. 20.

201. *1228 octbr. 28 Perusii. Gregorius papa IX (Sacrosancta Romana) magistri et fratrum militiae Christi contra Prutenos in Mazovia constitutorum cum enumeratis bonis et libertatibus protectionem suscipit.*

II, 131 v. sine die e reg. Greg. E copiario citato n. 29 ed. I. Voigt cod. dipl. Pr. I, 20 n. 21. E reg. Greg. IX. Theiner Vet. monum. Pol. et Lithuaniae. Romae 1860. fol. I, 17 n. 36.

202. *1230 iunio Cruszwitz ante pontes ind. iii. Conradus, dux Masoviae et Cuiaviae, confert hospitali s. Mariae domus Teutonicae totum Culmense territorium proprie possidendum; similiter quaecunque de paganis acquirere possint, fratribus auxilium ei contra Prutenos et alios paganos, quamdiu fidei hostes fuerint, promittentibus.*

II, 132. Incipit: „Super concessione privilegii ducis Maczovie et Cuiavie domui sancte Marie Theotonicorum Iherosolimitane". Explicit: „Ita invenitur de verbo ad verbum in registro domini Gregorii pape VIIII anno octavo capitulum CCLXXXVIIII. Martinus". — Saepius editum cf. Voigt reg. cod. dipl. Pruss. I p. V: Dreger I p. 138 n. 80. Duellius IV, 7 n. 10. Leibnitz Prodrom. ad cod. iur. gent. I. — Luenig Teutsches Reichsarchiv VII pars spec. p. 4. Acta Borussica I, 66. v. Baczko I, 237. Gustermann Gesch. Preufsens 143. — Theiner Monumenta Poloniae I, 19 n. 40 e reg. orig. Gregorii IX tom. IV ep. 289 fol. 223.

203. *1236 febr. 23 Viterbii. Gregorius papa IX fratres praedicatores per Poloniam constitutos monet, ut crucem praedicent contra Prutenos.*

Gregorius episcopus servus servorum dei dilectis filiis ... priori et fratribus ordinis predicatorum in Polonia consitutis predicantibus contra perfidiam

Prutenorum salutem et apostolicam benediccionem. Suavis dominus universis, qui nihil odivit eorum, que fecit[1], sed omnes salvos fieri et neminem vult perire, exurgens propter miseriam inopum et gemitum pauperum, per fidem in sanguine ipsius propiciatorem proposuit Iesum Christum ad ostensionem iusticie sue propter remissionem precedencium delictorum, ut iustificati gracia ipsius secundum spem vite eterne efficeremur heredes. Sed princeps mundi huius quorundam infidelium mentes adeo excecavit, ut non agnoscerent verum lumen nec in eos claritas evangelii radiaret, quin potius infidelitatis tenebris obvoluti non invocarent dominum, qui prope est omnibus invocantibus[2] eum in veritate, quia omnis, quicunque invocaverit nomen domini, salvus erit. Igitur, quum Prutenorum impietas visibilia deo et celorum virtutibus preferencium aëreas[3] potestates, quorum plurimi perceptam baptismatis graciam reliquerunt, illa fidelibus in Pruscie confinio constitutis inferret iacula tormentorum, que stupori audientibus et referentibus sunt horrori, providit pietas redemptoris, quod contra ipsos, qui et divini sermonis dulcedinem efficaciter non admittunt et exquisitis fraudibus sepe fallunt et perimunt tam precones domini quam alios sui nominis laudibus deputatos; dilecti filii .. magister et fratres hospitalis sancte Marie Theutonicorum Ierosolimitani pro reverencia omnium conditoris, cuius se obsequio devoverunt, in predictis partibus fidei negocium assumpserunt ex animo prosequendum, laboribus et expensis ac proprii effusioni sanguinis non parcentes, cum quibus deus, sicut relatu fide dignorum exultantes accepimus, misericorditer operatur, reprimendo per eos impetum barbare feritatis. Set tamen, quia ad tam arduum negocium sufficere per se nequeunt et egent fidelium subsidiis adiuvari, presertim quum civitates et castra, que in eisdem partibus fundaverunt, nequeant absque festino et grandi subsidio retineri, devocionem vestram monemus et obsecramus in domino in remissionem vobis peccaminum iniungentes, quatinus commisse vobis super huiusmodi negocio ab apostolica sede sancte predicacionis officium eo prompcius et efficacius prosequentes, quo prefatis fratribus peregrinorum presencia destitutis hoc in presenti potissime fore dinoscitur opportunum et spes quasi certa tribuitur, quod per desiderati iuvaminis interventum illic infra breve temporis spacium gloria christiane fidei plurimum auctore domino amplietur pauperum cruce signatorum in Polonia, cum quibus duximus dispensandum, vota peregrinacionis in succursum predictorum fidelium commutetis, et tam eos quam alios fideles in ipsa Polonia constitutos ad nimiam caritatem, qua Christus nos dilexit et diligit, respectum habere et ei retribuere aliquid pro omnibus, que retribuit ipse illis, monitis et exhortacionibus vestris secundum datam vobis a deo prudenciam informetis, diligenter et sollicite postulantes, ut ipsi redempti precio glorioso, in quos tanquam viros christianos et catholicos cadere obprobria exprobrancium Christo debent, se viriliter et potenter accingant tanquam zelum dei habentes ad ampliandam gloriam crucifixi et liberandum proximos de manibus paganornm, profecturi et acturi secundum fratrum consilia predictorum, ita quod et ipsis premium debeatur eternum et infideles non possint, quod impune Christi nomen impugnaverint, gloriari. Quum autem multa necessitas exigat, ut illuc fidelium subsidium transmittatur, et dignum sit, ut in tanto negocio laborantes debita pro labore stipendia consequantur, quatenus libencius, securi de retribucione, procedant; nos, de omnipotentis dei misericordia et beatorum Petri et Pauli apostolorum eius auctoritate confisi tam eis quam aliis eiusdem Polonie, qui laborem istum in propriis personis subierunt vel expensis, et eis, qui in alienis expensis illuc accesserunt ibidem ad minus per unius anni spacium servituri, seu illis, qui ad subvencionem fidelium de propriis facultatibus ministrabunt, iuxta quantitatem subsidii et devocionis affectum peccatorum suorum veniam sicut euntibus Ierosolimam indulgemus. Datum Viterbii viii kalendas martii pontificatus nostri anno nono.

Originale cum bulla plumbea possidet v. cl. praepositus Gnesnensis dr. Zienkiewicz; mecum communicavit v. cl. Grünhagen praefectus archivo regio quod est Wratislaviae. Bullam eiusdem tenoris codem die ad priorem et fratres ordinis praedicatorum in Bohemia constitutos exhibet Bullarium Dominicanum I, 83 CXLV ex apographo in archivo ordinis asservato; ubi etiam legitur originale Brunnae in Moravia esse. 1. Sap. 11, 25. 2. Ps. 144 (145), 18. 3. ereas.

---

204. *1237 martii 8 Gambin. Conradus, Masoviae dux, magistro et fratribus ordinis quondam Dobrinensis donat castrum Drohiczin.*

Cum secundum apostolum debeamus diem messionis extreme misericordie operibus prevenire, ut pro transsitoriis heredes fieri mereamur patrie permanentis, innotescat presentibus et futuris, quod ego C(onradus) miseratione divina dux Mazovie et Cuiavie cum communi consensu et unanimi voluntate filiorum meorum, videlicet B(oleslai) ducis Mazovie, K(asimiri) ducis Quyavie necnon aliorum duorum S(emowiti) et Z(emomisli) iuniorum pro nostrarum remedio animarum conferimus et donamus magistro B(runoni)[1] et fratribus suis ordinis militum Christi domus quondam Dobrinensis castrum Drochicin et totum territorium, quod ex eadem parte castri continetur a medietate fluminum Bug et Nur usque ad metas Ruthenorum salvo iure ecclesie Mazoviensis et nobilium, si quid in predictis fluminibus hactenus habuerunt, cum omni districtu et honore, castoribus, fluminibus, lacubus, saltubus, theloneo in ipso Drochicin de navibus sive de curribus et cum omni iure, quod supradictum castrum noscitur hactenus habuisse, iure hereditario perpetuo possidendum, ut Christo sub ordinis sui debito militantes ab instantia paganorum defendant populum christianum. Idem vero B(runo), videlicet magister ordinis antedicti, cum fratribus nobis et nostris filiis promiserunt precipue duci Mazovie ius patronatus fideliter observare, prefatam quoque terram, scilicet Mazoviam, una nobiscum defendere suorum auxilio subditorum contra quoslibet invasores, exceptis hereticis et Pruthenis seu cuiuslibet christiane fidei inimicis, quos tenentur personaliter impugnare. Nos etiam vice versa prenominatam terram scilicet Drochicin contra invasores promisimus fideliter defensare. Promiserunt insuper prelibati fratres neminem potentium in nostrum preiudicium ei gravamen in Drochicensi territorio collocare neque super eiusdem translatione vel vendicione, commutatione vel donatione seu cuiuslibet alienationis specie tractare sine nostro consilio et consensu. Ad hec etiam promiserunt homines nostros populares servilis seu libere conditionis nec per se nec per alios aliquatenus avocare, etiam, si ad ipsos sponte transierint, nullatenus retinere. Nos quoque promittimus fratribus antedictis, ut ipsorum cives et omnes habitatores territorii sepefati necnon ad ipsos, ut cum eis maneant, transeuntes per terras nostras et nostrorum filiorum ab omni exactione thelonei et aliorum iurium sint inmunes, et nisi iusto inpedimento prohibente magister ordinis vel ipsius loco alius constitutus per nos pro communi terre nostre vel ipsorum consilio evocatus accedere personaliter non recuset. Quicumque igitur principum seu potentium aliorum huic donationi nostre facto vel consilio voluerit contraire, indignacionem dei et beate virginis Marie necnon omnium electorum eius habiturus cum Dathan et Abiron accipiat porcionem. Actum anno gratie m° cc° xxx vii viii idus marcii littera dominicali D in Gambin.

Originale in charta pergamena, ex qua nunc tantum pendent secundum et tertium sigilla, ex Berolinensi archivo secretior Regimontum in archivum regium venit 1865. Partem edidit Voigt Geschichte Preufsens II, 277. 1. H. V. Cf. Lisch Der preufsische Orden der Ritter von Dobrin in Mecklenburg in Jahrbücher des Vereins für mecklenburgische Geschichte und Alterthumskunde. Schwerin 1849. XIV, 17. Quamvis Gregorius IX 1235 april. 19 (v. bullam Iustis petentium, Perusii xiii kal. maii p. n. a. 9 ap. Voigt in Beiträge zur Kunde Preufsens. Königsberg 1822. V, 495) unionem Dobrinensis et Theutonici ordinum confirmaverit, tamen non omnes illius equites hunc intraverunt. 1240 iunii 28 in Magnopoli Iohannes dominus Magnopolensis confirmat monasterio Campo Solis a „militibus Christi Prucie“ emtam curiam Tscelin. Praesentes nominantur inter testes: „frater Rauen, Wedeghe, Conradus de Sture, Fredericus de Lubowe, Reinhardus de Lu, Olricus de Lu, Iohannes, Heidenricus, Hermannus, Heinricus de Lu, milites Christi“. Quarum plurimos Megalopolitanos esse Lisch probat l. c. 18.

---

205. *1243 iulii 28 vel 29 (iiii° die stantis iulii) Anagniae. Guilelmus, episcopus Mutinensis, apostolicae sedis legatus, limitat quatuor Prussiae dioeceses.*

II, 134 v. In confirmatione Innocentii IV d. 1243 oct. 8. — Or. in archivo Regimontano; saepius impressum: Hartknoch ad Dusburg. Ienae 1679. p. 477. Acta Borussica. Regimonti et Lipsiae 1731. II, 612. Dreger cod. dipl. Pomeraniae p. 242 n. 158. Gebser Geschichte der Domkirche in Königsberg. Königsberg 1835. p. 10. Watterich Gründung des Deutschen Ordensstaates. Leipzig 1857. p. 258 n. 29. Monumenta Warmiae edd. Woelky et Saage. Moguntiae 1860. I, 5 n. 5. — De dato cf. scr. rer. Pruss. III, 464.

---

206. *1243 sept. 23 Anagniae. Innocentius papa IV mandat provinciali praedicatorum in Alamannia et caeteris qui enumerantur praelatis, ut pro subsidio fratrum hospitalis s. Mariae Theutonicorum in Livonia ac Prussia crucem praedicandam curent.*

Innocentius etc. priori provinciali fratrum ordinis predicatorum in Alamannia etc. Qui iustis causis hominum promovendis promptum favorem impendimus, tanto libentius vigilanti cura prosequi pia debemus negocia Ihesu

Christi, quanto deus homini preferendus esse dinoscitur et omnis sibi deberi reverentia comprobatur. Igitur cum, sicut relatu fide dignorum percepimus exultantes, conditor omnium in Livonie ac Pruscie partibus, dilectorum filiorum fratrum hospitalis sancte Marie Theutonicorum Ierosolimitani ac aliorum fidelium triumphanti dextera faciente, sit multipliciter exaltatus et spes sit, quod ibidem magis ac magis sui nominis gloria protendatur[1], si plantationi sue partium earundem favorem, quem in ipso possimus[2], impendentes oportunum illi per devotos ecclesie subsidium procuremus; devotionem tuam rogamus et hortamur in domino, per apostolica tibi scripta mandantes ac in remissionem peccaminum iniungentes, quatinus priores et fratres tui ordinis constitutos in Magdeburgensi et Bremensi provinciis, Ratisponensi, Pataviensi, Alberstatensi, Ildesemensi et Verdensi diocesibus negocio quaque preposita facultate[2*] deputare studeas et eosdem attentius exhortari, quod assumpto sancte predicationis officio propter deum fideles dictarum provinciarum et diocesium ad nimiam caritatem, qua Christus nos dilexit et diligit, respectum habere et ei retribuere aliquid pro omnibus, que tribuit ipse illis, piis exhortacionibus secundum datam sibi a deo prudentiam studeant informare, diligenter et sollicite petituri, ut ipsi redempti precio glorioso, in quos tanquam viros christianos et catholicos cadere[3] obprobria exprobrantium Christo debent, se viriliter et potenter accingant tamquam dei zelum habentes, ad ampliandum gloriam crucifixi et liberandum proximos de manibus paganorum, profecturi[4] et acturi secundum fratrum consilia predictorum, ita quod et ipsis premium debeatur eternum et[5] infideles non possint, quod impune Christi nomen impugnaverint, gloriari; illos vero de provinciis et diocesibus memoratis, qui crucis signaculo in Livonie sive Pruscie subsidium insigniti propter paupertatem seu debilitatem illuc nequeunt personaliter proficisci, a voto crucis absolvant[6], dummodo de bonis suis iuxta proprias facultates congruam subventionem exhibeant per manus eorundem fratrum in idem subsidium convertendam. Nos enim, ut, quod pro nomine redemptoris tam digne deposcitur, effectu facili compleatur, omnes dictarum provinciarum et diocesium in succursum[7] eorundem fidelium suscepto propter hoc crucis signaculo processuros necnon eorum familiam et bona omnia, donec de ipsorum reditu vel obitu certissime cognoscatur, sub protectione ac defensione sedis apostolice admittentes illis ac aliis, qui iuxta facultatem et qualitatem suam illuc bellatores ydoneos in expensis propriis duxerint destinandos necnon, qui ad subventionem dictarum Livonie vel Pruscie de bonis propriis congrue ministrarint vel qui in alienis expensis illuc accesserint ibidem ad minus per unius anni spacium servituri, iuxta quantitatem subsidii et devotionis affectum, illam indulgentiam idemque privilegium elargimur, que transeuntibus et subvenientibus in[8] terre sancte subsidium conceduntur. Preterea ut[9] prephatum negocium, quo pluribus contigit[10] iuvari remediis, prosperitatis optate suscipiat incrementum, prioribus et fratribus per te supradicto negocio deputandis presentium auctoritate concedimus, quod illis earundem provinciarum et diocesium, qui ad eorum sollempnem predicationem accesserint[2], xx dies de iniuncta penitentia relaxare ac eorum singulis illuc sumpto propter hoc crucis caractere processuris, qui pro incendiis et iniectione manuum in clericos vel alias religiosas personas excommunicationis laqueum incurrerunt, absolutionis beneficium iuxta formam ecclesie valeant impertiri, proviso[11], ut passis dampna et iniurias satisfaciant competenter, illis dumtaxat exceptis, quorum excessus adeo sunt difficiles et enormes, quod merito sint ad sedem apostolicam destinandi. Data Anagnie viiii kalendas octubris anno primo.

In eundem modum priori provinciali fratrum ordinis praedicatorum in Polonia, per regnum Boemie, Polonie et Pomeraniam.

In eundem modum p. p. f. o. p. in Dacia, per regna Dacie, Suecie et Norwecie.

Innocentius etc. priori et fratribus ordinis predicatorum Magdeburgensibus etc. Qui iustis *etc. usque* iniungentes, quod in Magdeburgensi, Brandeburgensi, Avelbergensi civitatibus ac diocesibus, Alberstatensi et Verdensi diocesibus, assumpto sancte predicationis officio propter deum fideles constitutos in illis *etc. usque* incrementum presencium vobis auctoritate concedimus, quod illis earundem civitatum et diocesium, qui ad sollempnem *etc. ut in alia verbis competenter mutatis.*

In eundem modum eisdem Ildesemensibus, per Ildesemenses civitatem et diocesim.

In eundem modum eisdem Bremensibus, per Bremenses et Verdenses civitates et dioceses.

In eundem modum eisdem Viennensibus per Patavienses civitatem et diocesim.

In eundem modum eisdem Alberstatensibus, per Alberstatenses civitatem et diocesim.

In eundem modum eisdem Lipicensibus Mersburgensis diocesis per Mersburgenses et Numburgenses civitates et dioceses, Magdeburgensem, Alberstatensem et Misnensem dioceses.

In eundem modum eisdem Amburgensibus Bremensis diocesis per Bremensem, Razeburgensem et Verdensem dioceses.

In eundem modum eisdem Ratisponensibus per Ratisponenses civitatem et diocesim.

In eundem modum eisdem Lubicensibus per Lubicenses, Razeburgenses et Zwerinenses civitates et dioceses et Verdensem diocesim.

In eundem modum eisdem Olomucensibus et Brunnensibus Olomucensis diocesis, per Olomucenses diocesim et civitatem.

In eundem modum eisdem Pragensibus per Pragenses civitatem et diocesim.

In eundem modum eisdem Friburgensibus per Misnenses civitatem et diocesim et Numburgensem diocesim.

In eundem modum eisdem Cracoviensibus per Cracovienses civitatem et diocesim.

In eundem modum eisdem Wratislaviensibus per Wratislavienses civitatem et diocesim.

In eundem modum eisdem de Wisbu Lingacopensis diocesis per Gotlandiam.

II, 138 mendose, cum clausula: „Ita invenitur de verbo ad verbum in registro domini Innocentii pape IIII anno primo Martinus capitulo CLXIII". 1. Semel scriptor scripsit „in ē. m." i. e. in eundem modum; duodecies: inest in eisdem. 2. Ed. ap. Liljegren diplomatarium Suecanum I, 297 n. 307 et Livl. U.-B. I, 228 n. 174 ex exemplari ad priorem et fratres ordinis praedicatorum de Wisbu Lingacopensis dioecesis per Gotlandiam misso. Ed. Theiner Vetera mon. Pol. I, 37 n. 77 ex reg. orig. I, ep. 162 et 163, fol. 28. 1. protenditur B. 2. B. 2*. postposita difficultate. 3. eadem B. 4. p'facturi B. 5. etiam B. 6. absolvent B. 7. secursum B. 8. supplevi. 9. in B. 10. B. 11. provisis B.

---

207. *1243 octbr. 8 Anagniae. Innocentius papa IV (Iustis petencium) confirmat petentibus magistro et fratribus hospitalis s. Marie Theutonicorum Irlmit. insertas litteras, quibus*

1243 iiii° die stantis iulii (i. e. 28 vel 29 iulii). Guilelmus episcopus quondam Mutinensis, ap. sed. legatus, limitat quatuor Prussiae episcopatus (supra n. 205).

II, 134 v. Ex apographis Regimontanis saec. xiv et xv ediderunt Hartknoch l. c. 476. Acta Boruss. II, 611. Iura reverendi capituli Warmiensis n. I B. — Cf. Raynaldus 1243 n. 33 Monum. Warm. I, 10 n. 7. — In codice 135 v. legitur: „Ita invenitur de verbo ad verbum in registro domini Innocentii pape IIII anno primo capitulo CXXI°. Martinus".

---

208. *1251 martii 9 vii id. martii Lugduni p. n. a. 8. Innocentius papa IV (Sua nobis) Olomucensi episcopo mandat, ut compositionem inter magistrum et fratres h. s. M. Th. in Prussia et archiepiscopum Livoniae Prussiaeque factam, ab ipso confirmatam, observandam curet.*

II, 137 v. sine dato. Ex originali archivi Regimontani ed. Livl. Mitth. VI, 234. Livl. U.-B. I, 280 CCXXI. — E regestis Vatic. Theiner Vet. mon. Pol. I, 48 n. 100.

---

209. *1261 ian. 11 (cf. 21) Laterani. Alexander papa IV Olomucensem episcopum iubet coercere fidei negotium in Livonia et Prussia promovendum inhibentes.*

Alexander cet. Pro fidei negotio cet.

Mancum in fine II, 139 v. Cum dato Laterani 3 id. ianuarii p. n. a. 7 ad episcopum Warmiensem ex originali Regimontano, ubi etiam transsumtum de 1387 maii 28, ap. Voigt Cod. dipl. I, 136 n. 134. Livl. U.-B. I, 455 n. 358. Mon. Warm. I, 77 n. 40. — Cum dato Laterani 12 kal. febr. p. n. a. 7 ad archiepiscopos et episcopos per Alemanniam constitutos R. 99 inter Alsatica n. 18.

---

210. *1337 nov. 15 Monaci. Ludowicus imperator Theoderico de Aldenburg, ordinis Theutonici generali magistro, et ipsi ordini Lituaniam terram donat.*

Ludowicus quartus dei gracia Romanorum imperator semper augustus universis Christi fidelibus presentibus et posteris graciam suam et omne bonum. Multifariam multisque modis variis christianus populus, quem orthodoxe fidei wlgor[1] illuminat, diversarum virtutum iubare irradians et preclarus sacrum ac felix Romanum imperium cunctis mundi presertim principatibus quibuslibet barbaris prepollere nationibus fecit in preterito, verum etiam disponente omnium domino efficiet in futuro. Nempe publice rei tuicio de stirpe gemina pullulans vimque suam exinde muniens celibi videlicet milicia solidat et confirmat sicque eminencia extollitur et perversorum, presertim crucis Christi inimicorum infidelium, malicia extra mundi terminos profugatur. Eapropter non tantum in nostris armatis militibus seu bellorum ducibus, quantum in religiosorum assidue deo militantium devotis intercessionibus et aliis piis operibus nostre spei anchoram fingentes[2] coruscantis glorie nostre solium sublimius et solidius in speculo[3] sublevatur. Religiosam itaque vitam ducentibus serenitatem nostram convenit prospicere, ipsorum utilitatibus intendere, ut felicis status recipiat incrementum et eorum facultates augendas graciosa largicio principis excitatur[4]. Inter ceteros autem illi precipue nostram graciam, beneficia et benevolenciam promerentur, quibus hospitalitatis piissime et defensionis reipublice necnon alia pietatis opera suffragantur, qui abiectis rebus suis, propriis voluntatibus abdicatis spretoque suorum corporum cruciatu ascendentes in adverso pro Romano imperio et domo Ierusalem[5] se murum non formidant exponere et in proprio sangwine pro fide catholica et paternis legibus animarum suarum pallia rubricare; veluti venerabiles in Christo frater Theodericus de Aldenburg, magister generalis, princeps noster et Romani imperii karissimus, ceterique fratres ordinis hospitalis beate Marie domus Theutonicorum Ierosolimitani, quorum sancta religio ab imperialibus beneficium[6] sumpsit initium ac imperialis ortus floridus, imperatorum plantula et factura a nullo principe tantum, quantum ab imperatoribus in rebus temporalibus incrementum. Sane quia venerabiles magister et fratres prelibati et totus illibatus ordo grata et laboriosa ad divini nominis laudem et gloriam et catholicam fidem ampliandam servicia, in quibus agendis incessanter et strennue se inmiscent, se nobis valde graciosos et placidos[7] representant, non inmerito ad tam pii negocii subsidium fervidis desideriis anhelamus ipsos ad benivolos applausive dulcedinis admittentes amplexus. Nam novissimis istis temporibus illustris princeps patruelis noster dilectus, Heinricus, dux Bawarie, egregias edificiorum iuncturas in infidelium Lytwinorum regionibus primogenitas indissolubiliter imperpetuum ad totius orthodoxe fidei machinam supportandam, annuente altissimo veluti columnarum prestancia permansuras, utpote castrum capitale tocius terre Lythowie provide construxit cooperante ad hoc venerabilium generalis magistri et suorum fratrum consilio et auxilio, ob eiusdem patruelis nostri interventum et strennua merita predictorum fratrum ipsis et beato ordini memorato ad laudem et gloriam omnipotentis dei et beatissime virginis Marie matris sue gloriose, terram Lythwinorum cum omnibus pertinenciis suis et partibus, cuiuscumque ydiomatis sive Samayten, Karsow vel Rusye seu alterius cuiuscumque existant, prout nunc sunt, vel ad quamcunque fidem declinaverint, de imperiali auctoritate donamus pure et irrevocabiliter, iure proprio in perpetuum pro se et suis successoribus recipientibus dictam terram, dictumque fratrem Theodericum, felicem[8] nostrum et imperii principem, nomine dicti sacri ordinis investimus de eisdem cum administracione temporalium et iurisdictione eiusdem plenaria principatus. Cui quidem castro principali idem noster patruelis dilectus nomen et insignia armorum et vexilli terre Bawarie, que Beyern dicitur, appropriavit, ita quod insignia sui vexilli ea debent honoris et dignitatis prerogativa pollere, ut pre omnibus vexillis aliis in expedicionibus contra Lythwinos sint anteriora in agressu et ultima in recessu et nichilominus predicte regionis incole, quos opitulante omnium conditore in eadem terra felici succedente tempore inhabitare contigerit, in prefato castro capitali debebunt requirere sua iura. Dictus etiam patruelis noster dilectus glorie et laudis dei matrisque sue gloriose non inmemor, sed iuste et religiose cogitans, deliberavit una cum prefato magistro generali maturo prehabito consilio instituendam et construendam fore in predicta terra, quam primum eam omnipotens deus fide catholica ampliaverit, ecclesiam kathedralem, in qua tamquam in ecclesia metropolitana archyepiscopus sit[9] metropolitanus una cum canonicis ibidem instituendis perpetuo permanebit et, si qui suffraganei opitulante domino imposterum creabuntur, illi eidem archyepiscopo tanquam suo metropolitano suberunt et sibi exhibebunt in omnibus obedienciam, reverenciam debitam et honorem, que quidem ecclesia et archiepiscopatus Beyern appellabitur in eternum. In cuius rei testimonium presentes conscribi et nostra bulla aurea signoque nostro consueto iussimus communiri. Datum Monaci xvii° nonas[10] decembris anno domini millesimo trecentesimo tricesimo septimo indiccione quinta regni nostri anno vicesimo tercio imperii vero decimo.

Signum domini Ludowici Romanorum imperatoris invictissimi.

(L. monogrammatis.)

Originale in archivo secreto Berolinensi adservatur pulchre quidem sed mirum in modum incorrecte scriptum. Appendet filis sericeis viridi et rubro bulla aurea. 1. Imperator in solio residens LVDOVICVS QVARTVS DEI GRACIA ROMANORVM IMPERATOR SEMPER AVGVSTVS. 2. Effigies urbis Romae: ROMA CAPVT MVNDI REGIT ORBIS FRENA ROTVNDI. In dorso: recognita per Pot. — In dorso: Ludowicus der vierde gipt und bestetigit der Littowen land mit alle sinen czuegehorungen, welcherley geczunge sy sin, alze Samaythen, Karschowen und Russen, welches anders geczunges sye sin alczo alsyge nue sin ader czue welchem gelouben sye sich neygin. Manu s. xv: Lodowicus imperator IIII donavit terras scilicet Samagitarum, Karsow etcetera. — Litteram initialem L valde ornatam edidit F. A. Vofsberg in Neue Preufsische Provinzialblätter. Königsberg 1850. I, 107: „Ueber die Verleihung der Baierfahne und des baierischen Wappens an die Baierburg", ubi variae lectiones transsumtorum. — Cum dato VI non. decembr. edidit Ludewig in reliquiis manuscriptorum. Francofurti et Lipsiae 1720. I, 336 n. 239 (bulla aurea). — Cum dato 17 dec. edidit Luenig Teutsches Reichsarchiv

VII (i. e. pars specialis continuationis I continuatio 3) p. 6 (bulla aurea) in transsumto notariali de d. 1412 nov. 27 die solis in castro Marienburg in stubella consilii domini magistri generalis, a notario ad preces Henrici de Plauen, magistri generalis, ipsum diploma in manibus tenentis perfecto. Describitur „bulla aurea“ in filis sericeis rubei ac viridis coloris appensa. „In cuius quidem litere bulla aurea, ut premittitur, subappensa ab una parte imago caesaris inter duos leones residens, in manu dextra sceptrum et in sinistra pomum cruce supraposita habens apparuit. Literae vero circumferentiales talis erant tenoris et primo crux: L. etc. v. supra. Ab alia vero parte figura cuiusdam civitatis Romae cum turribus et diversis moeniis videbantur, et in circumferentia tales literae legebantur et primo crux deinde: ROMA etc. v. supra. In initio vero literae imago cuiusdam caesaris coronata stans sub diversis picturis, in sinistra manu pomum cruce superposita, in dextra vero manipulare et sceptrum regale, ante quam imago cuiusdam fratris ordinis supradicti genu flexa in manibus cuspidem banderio appenso tenentem apparebant“. — In Regimontano archivo asservantur teste autore in N. P. P. B. 109 complura apographa XX, 1 in pergameno d. d. Ienti xvii non. dec., ut ipso ex male relato loco patet, pessimum; XX, 3 transsumtum in pergameno d. d. 1393 aprilis 28 Marienburg; XX, 4 et ipsum transsumtum in pergameno d. d. 1421 nov. 5 Schoenberg, quorum lectiones varias invenies ad calcem textus originalis N. P. P. B. Hic eas omittendas duximus. At nusquam in apographis legi id quod vult Voigt G. P. IV, 559 not. 1, pro dato: „Monaci xvii non. decembr. vel feria sexta ante Lucie virginis“ affirmatur ibidem. 1. sic pro: fulgor. 2. sic pro: figentes. 3. l. specula? 4. l. et ad e. f. a. g. l. p. excitetur. 5. sic pro: Israel. 6. sic pro: beneficiis. 7. l. placitos. 8. l. fidelem. 9. l. sicut. 10. error pro kalendas; nam nov. 15 in 23 regni annum usque ad nov. 25 currentem incidit.

---

211. *1337 dec. 7 Monaci. Ludowicus imperator iterum investit Theodericum de Aldenburg, ordinis Theutonici generalem magistrum de Lituania.*

Ludowicus etc. *(concordat fere cum praecedenti usque)* amplexus. Ipsis, videlicet predicto Theoderico, burgrafio de Aldenburg, magistro generali et suis successoribus ac fratribus necnon toti ordini domus Theutonice prefato in perpetuum ad laudem et gloriam omnipotentis dei et beatissime virginis Marie matris sue gloriose terram infidelium Litwinorum, crucis Christi inimicorum, videlicet Ouchsteten, Samayten, Karsow, Ruezzen ceterasque partes prenominatis terris adiacentes[1] cum omnibus suis pertinenciis et partibus cuiuscunque ydiomatis[2], prout nunc sunt vel ad quamcumque formam seu statum fidei declinaverint, de imperiali libertate damus, donamus pure et irrevocabiliter iure proprio in perpetuum pro se et suis successoribus recipientibus dictam terram dictumque fratrem Theodericum, burgrafium de Aldenburg, felicem nostrum et imperii principem, nomine dicti sacri ordinis investimus de eisdem cum aministracione temporalium et iurisdictione eiusdem plenaria principatus. In cuius rei testimonium presentes conscribi et nostre maiestatis sigillo iussimus communiri. Datum Monaci feria sexta ante Lucie virginis proxima anno domini millesimo trecentesimo tricesimo septimo regni nostri anno vicesimo quarto imperii vero decimo.

Tria transsumta in Regimontano archivo asservata citantur N. P. P. B. l. c. 110. XX, 2. 5. 6 d. d. 1393 april. 28 Marienburg et d. d. 1508 febr. 28 Nürnberg. Nihil hic de Bavariae duce vel de castro Bavariae. Refertur in N. P. P. B. l. c. 110 annotatione nullum transsumtorum chronologicam notam habere, qualem praebet Voigt G. Pr. IV 359 not. 1. „Monaci xvii non. decembr. vel feria sexta ante Lucie virginis“. Textum e l. c. 112 mutavimus. 1. sic legendum pro: adiacentibus. 2. ydoneitatis l. c.

---

212. *1338 nov. 26 Welen. Instrumenti treugarum fragmentum.*

.... cunque[1] ...... mus intercludi nolentes ipsis ...... spolia ...... aut incolis marchionis et principum predictorum de .... quantum proh...... s.... vio prohiberi poterint inferri aliqualiter consentire. Que vero si, quod absit, illata fuerint clam vel palam, extunc illatores dampnorum ipsorum iudicio stare procurabimus iudicatumque integraliter solvere, si se super innocencia sua duorum idoneorum sibi parium non poterunt testimonio expurgare. Si autem eos ad parendum iuri aut iudicio movere et ad solvendum iudicata compellere nequiremus, extunc ipsos et eorum quemlibet divisim, suffulti tamen presidio marchionis antedicti amici nostri karissimi, viis et modis, quibus compecierit, sine prohibicione qualibet prosequemur. Prohibemus eciam omnibus nostris fidelibus et subditis, cuiuscunque condicionis extiterint, nostre gracie sub optentu, ne amico nostro prenotato, terris, hominibus aut subditis suis quibuscumque ipsis treugis durantibus dampna inferant aliqualiter et ne persone extere terminos nostros aut ipsorum, nisi via peregrinacionis contra Lythwanos intenderent proficisci, in ipsius amici nostri prenotati dispendium pertranseant aut iacturam. Promittimus eciam pro domino Ottone et Barnim filio suo, ducibus prenotatis, ut premissa singula dictis treugis pendentibus servent et teneant inconvulsa. In cuius rei testimonium nostrum sigillum presentibus est appensum. Datum in Welen anno domini m° ccc° xxx° octavo in crastino festi beate Katherine virginis et martiris gloriose.

Fragmentum originalis quondam sigillati e codicis cuiusdam ligatura promtum in archivo regio sanctiori quod est Berolini asservatur. 1. cum pro?

---

213. *1429 sept. 7 Preszburg. Sigismundus, Romanorum et Ungariae rex, ordini Theutonico novam Marchiam Brandenburgensem appropriat.*

Wir Sigmund, von gotes gnaden romischer kunig, zu allen zeiten merer des reichs und zu Hungern, zu Behem, Dalmacien, Croacien etc. kunig, bekennen und tun kunt zu ewiger gedechnufs offenlich allen den, die disen brief sehen oder hören lezen. Under andern werken der gutigen barmherczikeyt, durch die man komet zu freuden des obersten kunigs, so kunnen wir der sele selikeit nit grofsern frommen und heile zucziehen, dann so wir geistlichen und geordenten personen, die dem almechtigen got in loblichem wezen dienen, solich gnad mitteilen, damit sy sich in fruchtlich merung breiten mogen, und sunderlich den, die gesaczt sind zu einem schild der kristenheit und den heiligen glauben mit vergiefsung ires plutes steticlich meren; und als wir vor etwevil jaren den erwirdigen .. hoemeistern, .. brudern und dem ganczen orden des Deutschen hawses unserr lieben frawen von Jherusalem, unsern lieben andechtigen, unser land der Newen Mark zu Brandemburg, das unser recht vaterlich erb ist, für ettlich summ geldes verschriben und verpfendet haben, nach lautt der brief, die sy doruber haben, also haben wir angesehen die loblich und wirdig stifftung desselben ordens und derselben bruder, die von anfang von einer eychen zu Alden Thorun in kleiner czal ritterlich und mennlich die heidenisch undyet hinder sich gedrungen, und dornach sich von sunderlichen gnaden des almechtigen gotes also gemeret haben, daz die heilig kristenheit durch ir mue, arbeyt und sorgveltikeit hinder in, als hinder einem vesten schild, bifz uff dise czit in gutem frid gesefsen und als in eynem garten der rue erquicket ist. Es sind ouch die ende derselben heiligen kristenheit durch sy gepraitet worden, die heidenisch undyet getempfet, vil vertriben, vil durch ir swert zu der tauf geladen und vil in den heiligen glouben gekrezemt, des alle kristenheit heutt difz tags trost und freud hat; und wann menniclich wol versteet, daz sy das mit unmefzlicher kost, mue und arbeit haben zu weg bringen mussen, wir geswigen der grofsen blutvergiefsung, dorinne sy ire leib in den namen unsers herrn Jhesu cristi geduldiclich gepurpert und gecziret haben, und sunderlich so haben wir fur augen genomen solich grofse ordnung, loblich leben und selige andechtikeit, dorynn sy sich in gotes dienst teglich uben, und daz der heiligen kristenheit noch in kumfftigen zeiten durch sy gros nucz, beschirmung und beschuczung entspriefsen mag, als wir in dann yeczund, dem almechtigen got und unser lieben frawen zu eren und zu lob und der kristenheit zu trost, durch unser sel selikeit willen ein grofsen teil in unserm lande zu Hungern ynngegeben und sy doselbs gestiftet haben, daz sy als ein new geseczte pflancz ouch furbafs wachsen zu vertilgung der Turken und anderr barbarn und heidenischer undyet. Wir haben ouch angesehen solich woltat und gutikeit, die unsere vorfaren Romische keyser und kunige, ander kristenkunig, fursten und hern demselben orden manigfeldiclich bewiset haben, in zu hilffe mit iren eygen person rittern und knechten geriten, slofser und vesten in dem land gepawet, in ire ampt und panyr bevolhen, der eren tafel daselbs wirdiclich beseczt, und sunderlich das unsere vordern, kunige zu Behem, bischofe, hern und ritterschafft desselben kunigrichs dem oftgenanten orden vil gnaden und furdrung bewiset haben, als man das alles clerlicher von den gnaden des almechtigen gotes vor augen sihet, wer das beschawet, dann man das mit schrifften uszgedruken mag oder kan. Wir haben ouch gar eygentlich betrachtet, das derselb orden die bruder und das land zu Preufsen von ettwevil jaren bifzher durch streitt, krieg und ander beswerung manigfalticlich geswechet worden sind, und wol ergeczung, hilf und steure bedorffen derworten, ob sy ymmer, da gott vor sey, angefochten wurden, daz sy dann dester kreftiger macht hetten solichen gewelten zu widersteen; ouch angesehen und vor andern sachen eygentlich und besunder besunnen, daz derselb orden an dem vorgenanten land der Newen Mark ein pforten und offen strafse hat, dadurch im fursten, hern, ritter und knechte ufz Deutschen und andern landen, wenn sy angefochten werden, wol mögen zu hilf reitten und komen, und ouch keinen andern bequemlichen weg haben, damit in zu statten mag komen und geholffen werden, als sich das in irem krieg, den sy mit iren widersachen langczit fürten, wol und scheinperlich bewiset hat, was hilff, zuschub, rates und furdrung sy durch das vorgenante land und von nyndert anders gehabt haben, und, wo sy desselben landes nicht gehabt hetten, so wer, als wir furchten, derselb orden zu solichem schaden und gedrang komen, die im zu ewigen zeiten unverwintlichen gewezt weren, und mocht ouch damit getempfet und vertriben worden sein; und, wo das gescheen were oder noch geschee, do got vor sey, so versteet menniclich wol, das zuvoraus die gancz kristenheit, und sunderlich Deutsche land also angefochten und gedrungen wurden, das man nit ufzgeschriben mag. Und dorumb solich unrat furczukomen, und durch der obgeschriben aller sache und ouch ander bewegung willen, und sunderlich daz uns der almechtig got von sinen heiligen gnaden und nicht durch unser verdienen zu dem heiligen Romischen rich erwelet und geruffen, und vil andere mechtige und prayte kunigreich, furstentum, land und leutt zu verwezen beuolhen hat, das wir des billich danknem sein und das gen seinen gotlichen gnaden mit demutikeit erkennen sollen; so haben wir mit wolbedachtem mute, gutem rat unserr und des heiligen reichs und unserr kunigrich fursten, graven und hern rechter wissen und eigner bewegnufz, dem almechtigen got unserm scheppfer, Jhesu Cristo, siner lieben mutter Marien der himelischen kunigynn und allen heiligen zu lob und zu eren, der heiligen kristenheit zu trost, dem kristenglouben und der heiligen Romischen kirchen zu praytung, und zu selikeit und heile unserr vordern und unserr sele, und zu ufnemen desselben ordens, ouch durch sunderlicher lieb und zuneygung willen, die wir zu in haben und durch solicher dienst willen, die sy der heiligen cristenheit tun sollen und mogen in kumfftigen czeiten, dem erwirdigen .. hoemeister, der itzund ist, und den, die nach im kunfftig sind, den brudern und dem ganczen orden unser land der Newen-Mark zu Brandemburg, das wir in vormals verseczet und verpfendet hetten, nu in dem namen gotes und durch vergebung willen unserr sund zu rechter goczgab gnediclich gegeben, und geben in das ouch von Romischer kuniglicher mact in krafft difz briefs, also, daz dieselben bruder und der orden dasselb land der Newen Mark mit allen dingen, die ob und under der erden sind, besucht und unbesucht, und mit allen gemerken und greniczen, die von alders her zu dem land gehoret haben, mit steten, slofsen, vesten, merkten, dorffern, vorwerken, velden, eckern gepawten und ungepawten, wisen, gerten, pergen, tälern, eben, welden, puschen, wustnussen, strafsen, wassern, stromen, wasserleuffen, zeen, teychen, wassermulen und wintmulen, geyegden, vogelweyden, vischereyen, gebieten, diensten, munczen, czollen, geleiten, kirchlehen und sufzt geistlichen und werltlichen lehen, ritterschafft, manscheffnten, czinsleuten, pawleuten, dienern, gerichten, pussen, fellen, nuczen, berkwerken, es sey golt, silber, kupfer, czin, bley, oder welicherley manyr das were, cristen, juden und allen andern zugehorungen, wie man die mit sunderlichen worten benennen mocht, nichts ufzgenomen zu ewigen ziten gleich anderm irem gut, landen und leuten, die sy ynne haben, und in solicher freyheit haben, halden und besiczen, und damit tun und lassen sollen und und mögen, wass sy wollen, von uns, unsern erben und nachkomen, und sunderlich dem hochgeborn Fridrichen, marggrafen zu Brandemburg, des heiligen rychs erczcammrer und burggraven zu Nuremberg, unserm lieben oheim und kurfursten, dem wir die Alden Mark gegeben vnd verschriben uff einen widerkouff und doch die Newen Mark dorynn nit begriffen haben, seinen erben und nachkomen und sufzt allermenniclich ungehindert. Wir behalden ouch uns und unsern erben und nachkomen an demselben land hinfur kein zuspruch, eigentschafft, herschafft oder erbschafft, sunder verczíehen uns der genczlich in crafft difz briefs, das nymmerme zu widerruffen zu ewigen zeiten. Wir verczíehen uns ouch aller stewer und hilf, die uns oder unsern nachkomen in geistlichen oder werntlichen rechten und geseczen, babstlichen oder keyserlichen brieven an demselben land zu hilf, und dem vorgenanten orden zu schaden komen mochten, von der vorgenanten Romischen kunglichen mact wegen, und gebieten dorumb allen und yglichen prelaten, graven, fryenhern, rittern, knechten, mannen, purggraven, vogten, amptluten, lantrichtern, richtern, burgermeistern, schepfen, ratleuten, burgern und inwonern aller und yglicher stete, merkt und dorffere, und allen andern zu der vorgenanten Newen Mark gehorenden und dorynne wonenden ernstlich und vesticlich mit disem briefe, daz sy sich alle an die vorgenanten hoemeister, bruder und den orden als ire rechte hern furbasz mer halden, und in also gewonlich gelubd und huldung tun, und in allen sachen gehorsam und gewertig sein one alle irrung, verczíehung und widersprechen. Und wir sagen ouch die vorgenanten inwoner desselben landes alle und ygliche, sie sein edel oder unedel, aller und yglicher irer huldung, gelubd und eyde uns als irem rechten erbherren getan ledig und loze mit disem briefe. Mit urkund difz briefs versigelt mit unserm kuniglichen majestat insigel. Geben zu Prespurg nach Crists geburt vierczehenhundert jar und dornach in dem newnundczweinczigisten jare, an unserr frawen abend nativitatis, unserr riche des Ungrischen etc. im drey und fierczigisten, des Romischen im newnczehenden, und des Behemischen im czehenden jaren. Dabey sind gewezen die erwirdigen Ludewig patriarch zu Agley, unser furst; Jorig erczbischoff zu Gran; Johann, bischoff zu Agram, unser canczler und lieben andechtigen; der hochgeboren Conrat genant Kentner, hertzog in der Slesien und herre zur Olsen und zur Kozel, unser lieber oheim und furst; die wolgeboren Herman graf zu Cili und im Seger, ban in Windischen Landen, unser sweher, Brunorius von der Leitter, unser und des reichs zu Bern und zu Viczencz gemeyner vicari, graf Hanns von Lupfen, lantgraff zu Stulingen und herre zu Hohennack, Johans graf zu Schawmburg; die edeln Conrat herre zu Winsperg, unser und des reichs erbcammrer; Erkinger von Saunfzheim, herre zu Swarczenberg, und die strengen Hartung von Clux und Conrat Nempcz rittere, unsere liebe getruen, und vil ander herrn, ritter und knecht, die wir zu diser unserr gab zu uns rufften zu warer geczeugnufz der vorgeschriben sache.

Ad mandatum domini regis Caspar Sligk.

V, 321 v. Originale cum sigillo in archivo Berolinensi in dorso: Quarta V. l. Item bestetigunge in Dewtsch Sigismundi des Romischen koniges obir die Nuwemark cum sigillo maiestatis, edd. Gercken Codex Brandenburgensis V, 254 omissis nonnullis. Riedel B. IV, 103 n. MDXXVII, qui etiam textum Latinum dedit p. 106 MDXXVIII ex copiario Regimontani archivi.

214. *1429 septbr. 8 an unser frauwen tag nativitatis Preszburg. Sigismundus, Romanorum et Ungariae rex, Gunthero Magdeburgensi archiepiscopo mandat, ut fratres ordinis Theutonici in possessionem Novae Marchiae intromittat populumque eis tanquam veris dominis iuramentum praestare iubeat.*

V, 323 v. E copiario Regimontano ed. Riedel Bd. IV, 108 MDXXIX.

---

215. *1443 febr. 19 czu der Newnstad. Fridericus III imperator iubet Franciscum Warmiensem episcopum, quotiens a magistro ordinis Theutonici requiratur, privilegia eius transsumere.*

Wir Friderich, von gotes gnaden Romischer kunig, zu allen czeiten merer des reichs, herczog zu Osterreich, zu Steir, zu Kernden und zu Krain, grave zu Tiroll etc. embieten[1] dem erwirdigen bischoven zu Hailsperg unserem fursten und lieben andechtigen unser gnad und alles gut. Erwirdiger furst und lieber andechtiger! Uns hat vorbringen lazzen der erwirdig Conrad von Erlichshausen, homeister Deutsches ordens, wie im und seynem orden bekumberlich und vast sorglich sey sein und des selben ordens hanntvesten, privilegia und brieve zu zeiten obir lande zu furen und der zu irer notdurft allenthalben zu gebrauchen, und hat uns dorauf diemuticlich lassen bieten, das wir in und den orden dorynne czu vorsehen genediclich geruchten und, nu uns solh bete zimlich bedaucht haben, so empfelhen wir dir und geben dir ganczen und vollen gewald von Romischer kuniglicher macht in craft diczs briefs, das du dem benanten homeister und seinem orden aller und yeglicher irr vorberurten hanntvesten, privilegia und brieve in von Romischen kaysern und kunigen, unsern vorfarn, uns unde allen andern cristgloubigen gegeben, wenn du dorumbe durch sie irsucht wirdest, mit deinen brieven bewarte vidimus und transsumpta, als oft in des not beschehen und sie begeern werden, geben sullest und magest. Wir mainen, setczen und ordenen auch van egemelter kunglicher macht, das solh dein vidimus und transsumpta an allen enden in den rechten und uszwendig des rechtens, wo die vorbracht[2] wurden, kraft und macht haben und also aufgenomen werden sullen, als die hoaptbrieve selber on geverde. Mit orkund dis briefs versigelt mit unserm kuniglichem anhangendem insigel. Geben zu der Newnstad an eritag vor sannd Peters tag ad cathedram nach Crists geburt vierczenhundert und dornach in dem drew unde vierczigisten jare, unsirs reichs im dritten jare.

Ad mandatum domini regis Wilhelmus Tatz canonicus Frisingensis.

V, 320. Continetur in Francisci Warmiensis episcopi transsumto s. a., ubi legitur descriptio appendentis sigilli: In cuius quidem sigilli medio figura aquile, supra cuius caput hee quinque vocales a e i o v, quam duodecim semicirculi in extremitatibus se attingentes circu(eunt) et quilibet eorum clipeum in se continentes. In quibus quidem clipeis diversa arma et clenodia et hee litere in circumferencia: „S. Friderici Romanorum reg.“ Deinde clipeus parvus, post quem hee littere: „is semper augusti ducis Austrie, Stirie, Karinthie et“; iterum clipeus parvus et post illum littere continuate in hiis verbis: „Carniole comitis Tirol et.“ A tergo vero eiusdem sigilli secretum parvum de cera rubea impressam, in quo figure quatuor capitum quasi hominum invicem in occipitibus coniunctorum facies suas ad quatuor mundi angulos dirigencium, prout prima facie videbatur, apparebant. — Deest apud Chmel. 1. embietem B. 2. vorbraucht B.

---

216. *1443 oct. 16 zu Frankenforde. Fridericus senior, Iohannes, Albertus, Fridericus iunior, marchiones Brandenburgenses, pacti cum Conrado de Erlichshusen, ordinis Theutonici magistro generali, a Sigismundo rege ordini factam Novae Marchiae cessionem ratam habent.*

Wir Friderich der elter etc. — gegeben — zu Frankenforde nach gotes geburt vierczehenhundert jar und dornach im drey und vierczigsten jare an der mittwoch sent Gallen tage — — —

V, 325. 328v. 333. 337. 341. 345v. 349v., unde edidit Riedel B. IV, 289 MDCLII collatis confirmationibus, quae infra citantur. Quum vero originale nobis non sit ad manus, repetere hic diploma supersedimus.

---

217. *1444 sept. 14 Nurenberg. Fridericus III rex confirmat n. 216 supra de 1443 oct. 16.*

Wir Fridreich, von gotes gnaden Romischer kunig, zu allen ziten merer des reichs, herczog zu Osterreich, zu Steyr, zu Kernden und Krain, herr auf der Windischen march und zu Portnaw, graf zu Habspurg, zu Tyrol, zu Phirt und zu Kyburg, marggraf zu Burgaw und lantgraff zu Ellsass, bekennen und tun kunt offembar mit disem brief allen den, die in sehen oder hören lesen. Als vormals nicht kleine stöſse, zwitracht und furdrung ufferstanden waren zwischen dem hochgeboren Fridrichen, marggraven zu Brandemburg, des heiligen Romischen reichs erczkamrer und burggraven zu Nuremberg, unserm lieben oheim und kurfursten, an einem und dem erwirdigen Conradten von Elrichshusen, des ordens der bruder des hospitals sant Marie des Deutschen hauses von Jerusalem hoemeister, seinen gebietigern, brudern und dem ganczen orden, unsern lieben andechtigen, am andern teil, als von der Marckh, etwan die Lanndsbergsche marckh und dornach und nu die Newmarckh uber Oder genant wegen, dieselb markh denn der allerdurchleuchtigste furst keiser Sigmund, unser vorfarn am reiche loblicher gedechtnuſse, do er noch in kuniglichem stande was, als uns furkomen ist, demselben orden zum ersten als sein warhaftig veterlich erbe umb eyne merkliche summe geldes uff einen widerkouff verkauf, yngegeben und geantwurt, und dornach dieselben markh gote zu lobe, unser lieben frawen zu eren, umb seiner selen heil und seligheit, dem genanten orden zu besserm bestant und merung, als sein warhaftig vaterlich erbe ewiglich und lediglich zugeeygent und gegeben hat, als denn seiner maiestat und ander brieve das clerlichen ausweisen, und aber unser egnanter oheim marggraf Fridrich und seine brudere, ouch marggrafen zu Brandemburg und burggraven zu Nuremberg, unser lieben oheimen und fursten, daentgegen meinten, keiser Sigmund hette des nicht macht gehabt zu vergeben nach zu verschreiben, nachdem und keiser Sigmund irem vater, marggrafen Fridrichen seligen, die markh zu Brandemburg mit allen zugehorungen erblich gegeben hette, ee die ewig verschreibunge dem orden ye gescheen were, sunderlich auch dieweil die guldein bulle und ire gesetcze clerlichen lauten und begreiffen, das kein kurfurstentumb des heiligen reichs sol noch möge geteilet nach zergledert werden zu ewigen zeiten, und wer das daruber tete, so sol es doch craftlos und unmechtig sein, als dann dieselben gesetcze mit mer worten ynnehalden. Und als nu der egenant unser oheim marggraf Fridrich und der orden von solcher vordrung und anspruch wegen mancherley tage besuchet und geleistet, daselbs ouch irer beider furnemung, rede und widerrede geynenander ercleret haben und doch one ende abegescheiden sind; also hat der egenant unser oheim marggraf Fridrich unser kuniglichen maiestat furbringen lassen, wie er sich mit dem obgenanten erwirdigen Conrad von Erlichshusen, Deutsches ordens homeister, und seinem orden yeczund uff dem leczsten tage zu Franckfurt uff der Oder solcher anspruch und zweitrechte gutlich und fruntlich vereynt habe, also das sich unser oheim marggraf Fridrich und seine brudere fur sich, ire erben, nachkomen, mannen, ire getruwen und alle ire nachkomen der egemeldten Newmarckh genczlich verczeigen, und die dem orden on furder anspruch gerulich nachgelassen haben. Und der obgenante marggraf Fridrich hat uns als einen Romischen kunig, seinen rechten herren, demuticlich bitten lassen, das wir von des heiligen Reichs wegen zu solcher richtung, vertragnifs, verczeigung und zueygung unsern gunst und willen zu geben, und die brieve, die daruber gemachet sind, zu bestetigen und zu confirmiren gnediglich geruchten. Dieselben brieve von wort zu worte hienach geschriben steen und also lauten: — Wir Fridrich der elder etc. *(s. n. 216)*. Des haben wir angesehen des egenanten unsers oheims marggraf Fridrichs demutige und fleifsige bete, sunderlich betrachtet das lobliche herkommen des wirdigen ordens, der denn zu breitung und merung cristlichs gloubens, mit grofser blutvergifsung der seinen, lange jar der cristenheit vyl genutczt hat, und auch das die Newmarckh ein pforten ist, dadurch dem orden hulff und beystandt zukomen mag, wo die ungeloubigen wider ubirhannd nemen, da got fur sey, und das ouch derselb orden uns und dem reiche insunderheit zugehöret und mit demselben lannde der Newmarckh und auch andern seinen lannden dem reich alczeit willig gewesen und nach ist, ouch das der egenante unser oheim marggraf Fridrich mit der vergnugung und erstatung, die im von dem orden gescheen ist, seine lannd, die des reichs lehen sind, wol bessern mag, also das dem heiligen reich solch richtung und vereygung allenthalben wol zu fromen komet; und darumb dem almechtigen gote zu lobe, seiner lieben muter Marien der hymelkunigin, der der orden ist, zu eeren, ouch das manichfeltig kryge, die zwusschen den partyen ufferstanden mochten sein, zu schaden dem heiligen Romischen reich und seinen lannden und leutten, dadurch gedemphet und hingelegt sind; so haben wir mit wolbedachtem mute, gutem rate, gunst und willen unser und des heiligen reichs kurfursten, anderer fursten, edeln und getruen und mit rechter wissen zu solcher richtung, vereygung, verczeigung und zueygung, alsdann hie oben vermeldet ist, unsern kuniglichen willen und gunst gnediclich gegeben, und den obengeschriben unser oheimen der marggraven, brief ouch die gabe und ewig verschreibung keyser Sigmunds uber die

Newmarckh, die gegeben ist zu Prespurg nach Crists gepurd vierczehenhundert jar und dornach in dem newn und czwenczigisten jare an unszer frawen abend nativitatis, und ouch alle ander brieve von dem gnanten keyser Sigmunden und andern dem orden uber dieselb Newmarkh gegeben, genczlich bestetiget, bevestent und confirmiret, bestetigen, bevestnen, confirmiren und geben ouch von newens die egenante Newmarkh dem egenanten orden ewiglich zu haben und zu besitczen in aller weiſz und form, als der obgemelde keyser Sigmundes gabebrief daruber gegeben von worte zu worte ynne helt, one alle unser und unserer nachkomen am reiche und meniclichs anspruch und irrung, daran ouch die gesetcze der guldein bullen, darinne nemlich begriffen ist, das die kurfurstentumb nicht sollen geteilet werden, den egenanten marggraven keinen fromen und dem orden und allen iren nachkomen kein verkurtzung ader schaden brengen sollen, wenn wir alle sulche gesetcze der guldein bullen und alle ander aussetczungen, recht und gewonheit, von wem ader wie die gemachet wern ader noch gemachet möchten werden, gemeinlich oder sunderlich von der egenanten Romischen kuniglichen machtvolkomenheit und mit willigem rate unsers und des richs kurfursten und anderer, als oben gemelt ist, gantcz binden, und als vil sy diser unser bestettung und ordnung wider weren ader gesein mochten in klein ader gros, verstricken und uncreftig machen, also das sy den egenanten marggraven ane fromen und dem orden und iren nachkomen ewiglichen one allen schaden sein sollen ynnerhalb und auſserhalb gerichts und an allen enden. Wir erfullen ouch von der egenanten Romischen kuniglichen macht alle gebrechen, die in den obgemeldten artikeln allen oder yeglichem besundern mochten erfunden werden, es were in zweivel etlicher worte ader unczimlicher bedewtung und auslegung unser meinung, in vergessung der czyrheit, ab sich einiche in disem unserm briefe heischet ader geburt, die sollen alle diser unsrer bestetung und verneuung unschedlich sein, und ab in den sachen allen wider den orden in kunpftigen zeiten icht gesucht wurde, es were mit gerichte ader sust, das tun wir abe und vernichten das genczlich yetz als dann und dann als yetcz, von der egenanten Romischen kuniglichen macht in kraft diss briefs, gebietende ernstlich und vesticlich bey unsern und des reichs hulden allen des reichs undertanen, in welichen wirden, adel ader wesen die sind, und sunst allermeniclich, das sy den egenanten homeister, gebietiger, bruder und orden bey solicher richtung und keiser Sigmunds ewiger verschreibung und unser bestetung uber die offtgenante Newmarckh gegeben gerulich, unangesprochen und ungehindert bleiben lassen, und sy dorane zu ewigen zeiten nymmer mer hindern nach irren, bey unsern und des reichs sweren ungnaden, und bey verlisung hundert pfund lottiges goldes, die ein iglicher, der dawider tete, verfallen sein sol, halb in des reichs camern und halb dem orden obgenant, als offt das geschehe, unleslich zu beczalen. Mit urkund diſs briefs versigelt mit unserr kuniglichen maiestat insigel. Geben zu Nuremberg nach Crists gepurd vierczehenhundert jar und dornach in dem vier und vierczigistem jare an des heiligen creucs tag exaltacionis unsers reichs im funfften jare. (*in plica*): Ad mandatum domini regis d. Gaspar cancellar. referen. (*in dorso*): R^ta Jacobus Widezl.

V, 328. 332 v. 336 v. 340 v. 344 v. 348 v. Ex or., cui modo deest sigillum, in archivo Berolinensi ed. Riedel Bd. IV, 340 sq. MDCLIX e B et originali; e regestis Chmel Regesta chronologico-diplomatica Friderici III Romanorum imperatoris. Wien 1840. LXIV.

---

218. *1444 sept. 21 Nuremberg. Theodericus, Moguntinus archiepiscopus, elector, consentit diplomati Friderici III regis de 1444 sept. 14 supra n. 217.*

Wir Dittrich, von gots gnaden der heiligen kirchen zu Mencz erczbischoff und des heiligen Romischen reichs durch Deutschelant erczkenczler und kurfurst, bekennen offinlich und thun kunt allen, die dise schriffte sehen, horen ader lesen; als der hochgeborne furst, herr Fridrich marggraff zu Brandenburg, des heiligen reichs erczkamrer und burggraff zu Nuremberg, unser besunder frunt und mitkurfurst, und der erwirdige herre Conrad von Erlichshusen, des ordens der bruder des hospitals sent Marie des Deutschen hauses von Jerusalem homeister, sein gebietiger und gantz orden sich yczunt vereynt und verrichtet haben von solcher annsproch wegen, die denn der egenante herre marggraf zu dem orden gehabt hat, als von der Marckhh etwann die Landsbergsche Markh, und darnach und nu die Newmarkh ubir Oder gnant, wegen sulch richtunge denn der allerdurchluchtigste furst und herr, herr Fridrich Romischer konig, zu allen zeiten merer des reichs, herczog zu Osterreich, zu Kernden, zu Krayn und grof zu Tyrol etc., unser allergnedigster herr, vergunnet und gnediklich bestetigt hat nach laute seiner koniglichen briefe daruber gegeben, die von wort zu wort hirinne begriffen sint und also lauten: — Wir Friderich von gotes gnaden Rom. Konig (n. 217). Also haben wir durch begerung seiner koniglichen gnaden und durch merklicher ursach in denselben briefen eigentlich begriffen, auch durch des vachgnanten marggraf Fridrichs willen, der uns demutiglich mit fleifse bitten hat lassen, zu solcher richtung und zueygung der Newmarkh dem egnanten orden und auch zu bestetung seiner koniglichen gnaden, wie die von worte zu worte hie uben begriffen ist, unsern gunst, verhengnufs und willen gutlich und williglich gegeben, und geben auch mit wolbedachtem mute und rechten wissen in krafft diss briefs als ein erczbischoff[1] zu Mentz und kurfurst des heiligen reichs fur uns und unser nachkomen zu ewigen zeiten, und des zu urkund haben wir unser gewonlich ingesigel angehangen dissem brief, der gegeben ist zu Nuremberg nach Christi geburt vierczen hundert jar und darnach im vier und vierczigsten jare an sint Matheus tag des heiligen zwelfboten und ewangelisten.

V, 332 v. Or. cum sigillo laeso in archivo Berolinensi. Editum ap. Riedel B. IV, 343 MDCLX. 1. or. eczbischoff.

---

219. *1444 sept. 21 Nüremberg. Iacobus, Trevirensis archiepiscopus, elector, similiter consentit n. 217.*

Wir Jacob von gots gnaden der heiligen kirchen zu Trier erczbischoff und des heiligen Römischen reichs durch Franckreich und das künigreich zu Arlat erczkanczler etc. *concordat cum n. 218[1]; intus:*

Wir Fridrich etc. n. 217 de 1444 sept. 14, *intus:*

Wir Fridrich etc. n. 216 de 1443 oct. 16.

— — — als ein erczpischoff zu Trier — — unser secret ingesigel — gegeben — czu Nüremberg nach Cristi geburt vierczehenhundert jar und darnach im vierundvierczigstem jare an sant Matheus tag des heiligen czwelfpoten und ewangelisten.

V, 340. Or. cum sigillo in archivo Berolinensi. 1. denn deest; additur: zu Steir.

220. *1444 sept. 21 Nuremberg. Fridericus, Saxoniae dux, elector, consentit similiter n. 217.*

Wir Fridrich von gotes genaden herczog zu Sachsen, des heiligen Romischen reichs erczmarschalk und kurfurst, landgraff zu Doringen und marggraff zu Meissen etc. etc. *concordat cum n. 218, intus:*

Wir Fridrich etc. n. 217 de 1444 sept. 14, *intus:*

Wir Fridrich etc. n. 216 de 1443 oct. 16.

— — — als ein herczog zu Sachsen — unser gewonlich ingesigel — gegeben — zu Nuremberg nach Cristi geburt vierczenhundert jar und darnach im vier und vierczigsten jare an sint Matheus tag des heiligen zwelfpoten und ewangelisten.

V, 348 v. Or. cum sigillo in archivo Berolinensi.

221. *1444 sept. 29 Nüremberg. Theodericus, Coloniensis archiepiscopus, elector, similiter consentit n. 217.*

Wir Dietrich von gots gnaden der heiligen kirchen zu Cöln erczbischoff, des heiligen Römischen reichs durch Welschen landen erczkanczler unde kurfürst, herczog czu Westvalen und Engers etc. etc. *concordat cum n. 218, intus:*

Wir Fridrich etc. n. 217 de 1444 sept. 14, *intus:*

Wir Fridrich etc. n. 216 de 1443 oct. 16.

— — — als ein erczbischoff zu Cöln — unser secret ingesigel — gegeben ist zu Nüremberg nach Cristi geburt vierczehenhundert jar und darnach im vier und vierczigsten jare an sant Michels tage des heiligen erczengels.

V, 336 v. Or. cum sigillo in archivo Berolinensi.

222. *1444 oct. 11 Heidelberg. Ludowicus, comes palatinus Rheni, elector, consentit n. 217.*

Wir Ludwig von gots gnaden pfalczgraff bey Reyn, des heiligen Römischen reichs ercztruchsesz und kurfurst und herczog czu Beyrn etc. *concordat cum n. 218, intus:*

Wir Fridrich etc. n. 217 de 1444 sept. 14, *intus:*

Wir Fridrich etc. n. 216 de 1443 oct. 16.

— — — als ein pfalczgraff bey Reyn — unser gewönlich ingesigel — gegeben — zu Heidelberg nach gots geburt vierczehenhundert jar und darnach im vier und vie(r)czigsten jare am suntage nach sant Dyonisii tag.

V, 344 v. Or. cum sigillo in archivo Berolinensi.

---

223. *(1448). Franciscus Warmiensis episcopus transsumit diplomata de Nova Marchia, sc. n. 217 regis confirmationem et n. 218—222 electorum ratihabitiones.*

In nomine domini Amen. Nos Franciscus dei et apostolice sedis gracia episcopus Warmiensis de Heilsberg communiter appellatus, commissarius a serenissimo principe et domino domino Friderico Romanorum rege semper augusto ad exemplandum, transsumendum et in publicam ac autenticam formam redigendum omnia et singula privilegia, litteras et indulta a divis Romanorum imperatoribus et regibus ac principibus sacri imperii electoribus ac aliis quibuscumque magnifico principi et domino domino magistro generali ordinis beate Marie domus Theotunicorum Ierosolimitani totique ordini eidem graciose facta et concessa specialiter deputatus, notum facimus per hoc presens publicum transsumpti instrumentum universis et singulis, quorum interest, intererit aut quomodolibet interesse poterit in futurum, quod nos pridem quasdam litteras commissionis prefati serenissimi principis et domini Friderici Romanorum regis eius vero sigillo rotundo de cera rubea in capsa de cera communi glauci coloris impresso in cordula sericea viridis brunaticique coloris impendente sigillatas, non viciatas, non cancellatas, non abrasas, nec in aliqua sui parte suspectas, sed omni prorsus vicio et suspitione carentes, in cuius quidem sigilli medio figura aquile, supra cuius caput hee quinque vocales a e i o v, quam duodecim semicirculi in extremitatibus se attingentes circuire et quilibet eorum clipeum in se continere, in quibus quidem clipeis diversa arma et clenodia et hee littere in circumferencia: S. Friderici Romanorum reg; deinde clipeus parvus, post quem hee littere: is semper augusti ducis Austrie, Stirie, Karinthie, et iterum clipeus parvus et post illum littere continuate in hiis verbis: Carniole comitis Tirolis e; a tergo vero eiusdem sigilli secretum parvum de cera rubea impressum, in quo figure quatuor capitum quasi hominum invicem in occipitibus coniunctorum facies suas ad quatuor mundi angulos dirigencium, prout prima facie videbatur, apparebant, nobis pro parte magnifici principis et domini, domini Conradi de Erlichshwsen, dicti ordinis magistri generalis, ac eiusdem ordinis sui presentatas cum ea, qua decuit reverencia recepimus. Quarum tenor sequitur de verbo ad verbum et est talis:

Wir Friderich etc. (Newnstad 1443 febr. 19). (v. supra n. 215).

Cuius quidem commissionis pretextu in nostra constitutus presencia personaliter venerabilis vir dominus Wichardus Heilsperg, officialis curie ac canonicus ecclesie nostre Warmiensis, prefati domini Conradi magistri generalis et ordinis sui procurator et sindicus, prout de sui procuracionis et sindicatus mandato nobis per patentes litteras prefati domini Conradi magistri generalis vero sigillo sigillatas plenam fecit fidem, nonnullas litteras, privilegia et indulta a divis Romanorum imperatoribus et regibus ac sacri imperii electoribus et aliis principibus presertim concessionis terre Nove Marchie Brandenburgensis trans Oderam vulgariter nunccupate ac mandati investiture ad eandem a domino quondam Sigismundo dive memorie Romanorum rege necnon renuncciationum eiusdem Nove Marchie illustrissimorum principum et dominorum, dominorum Friderici senioris, sacri Romani imperii archicamerarii, Iohannis, Alberti et Friderici iunioris, germanorum marchionum Brandenburgensium etc., ac eciam ratihabicionum et confirmacionum omnium predictorum dicti serenissimi et invictissimi principis et domini Friderici Romanorum regis semper augusti, Austrie, Stirie, Karinthie, Carniole ducis comitisque Tirolis etc., consensumque predictarum concessionum, renuncciacionum et confirmacionum reverendissimorum in Christo patrum et dominorum, dominorum Theoderici Maguntinensis, Theoderici Coloniensis et Iacobi Treverensis archiepiscoporum, ac illustrissimorum principum et dominorum, dominorum Ludovici comitis palatini Reni et Friderici ducis Saxonie etc., sacri Romani imperii electorum, prelibato domino magistro generali et ordini suo datas et concessas veris predictorum dominorum sigillis sigillatas, salvas, sanas et integras, non cancellatas, non viciatas nec in aliqua sui parte suspectas, sed omni prorsus vicio et suspicione carentes nobis exhibuit et produxit, allegans dictum dominum magistrum generalem ac ordinem suum eisdem litteris, privilegiis et indultis in diversis locis eciam longinquis quam plurimum indigere, timens tum propter viarum discrimina, que inopinabilia sunt, tum eciam propter vetustatem huiusmodi litteras privilegia et indulta lacerari aut in totum deperdi seu anichilari posse. Unde nobis humiliter supplicavit, quatenus predicta privilegia, litteras et indulta originalia transsumi, exemplari ac in debitam et autenticam formam redigi mandare ac decretum nostrum interponere auctoritate regia prefata dignaremur. Nos igitur Franciscus episcopus et commissarius prefatus attendentes supplicacionem huiusmodi fore iustam et consonam rationi, volentesque mandatum regium nobis factum et commissum diligenter exequi, ut tenemur, nolentes tamen in preiudicium cuiusvis in huiusmodi negocio precipitari seu viam cuiquam precludere defensionis, sed rite et legitime procedere, omnes et singulos sua communiter vel divisim interesse putantes eorumque procuratores, si qui essent in dyocesi Warmiensi seu alibi, pro eisdem per nostras certi tenoris litteras citatorum, quas in valvis maioris ecclesie nostre Warmiensis affigi volumus, fecimus et mandavimus ad instar edictorum publicorum, quatenus peremptorio termino in eisdem litteris expresso comparerent in iudicio et iudicialiter coram nobis in castro nostro Heilsperg, ad videndum et audiendum huiusmodi litteras, privilegia et indulta exemplari et transsumi, transsumptumque huiusmodi in publicam et autenticam formam redigi mandare ac decretum nostrum dicta auctoritate regia nobis commissa interponere ad perpetuam rei memoriam testesque de et super recognitione sigillorum eisdem litteris, privilegiis et indultis appensorum produci, recipi et ad iurandum admitti singulaque sigilla recognosci vel ad dicendum et causam, si quam haberent rationabilem, quare premissa fieri non deberent, allegandum et ostendendum, alioquin prout iustum et iuris foret circa predicta procederemus dictorum citatorum contumacia in aliquo non obstante, citavimus citarique mandavimus et fecimus ad certum peremptorium terminum competentem, videlicet ad diem et horam inferius annotatos. Cumque in huiusmodi citationis termino non compareret quisquam pro parte citatorum dictorum, qui causam aliquam, propter quam huiusmodi littere, privilegia et indulta, transsumi et exemplari non debebant, allegaret, comparuit coram nobis iudicialiter in dicto castro nostro Heilsberg et loco nostro solito et consueto ad iura reddendum pro tribunali sedentibus, dominus Wichardus Heilsberg, procurator predictus et nomine procuratorio, quo supra, litteras huiusmodi nostras citatorias in valvis dicte ecclesie nostre Warmiensis affixas ac debite executioni demandatas reproduxit, citatorumque in eisdem contentorum non comparencium contumaciam accusavit ipsosque contumaces reputari et in ipsorum contumaciam privilegia, litteras et indulta predicta transsumi, testes ibidem per eum super recognitione sigillorum privilegiis eisdem litteris ac indultis appensorum productos recipi, ad iurandum admitti et examinari sigillaque huiusmodi pro recognitis haberi transsumptumque per nos cum nostra decreti interpositione auctoritate regia nobis in hac parte commissa autenticari et publicari adeoque eidem transsumpto ubique locorum tam in iudicio quam extra ac quibuscumque curiis tam spiritualibus quam secularibus merito valeat fides plenaria adhiberi, debita cum instancia peciit et postulavit. Nos tunc Franciscus episcopus Warmiensis et commissarius prefatus dictos citatos non comparentes neque termino huiusmodi in aliquo satisfacere curantes sufficienter tamen expectatos reputavimus merito prout erant exigente iusticia contumaces, et in eorum contumacia predictas litteras, privilegia et indulta ad nos recepimus, vidimus, conspeximus, palpavimus et examinavimus diligenter, testesque super recognicione sigillorum eisdem litteris, privilegiis et indultis appensorum coram nobis productos rite recepimus ac in forma iuris ad iurandum admisimus iuratosque diligenter examinavimus ac post ipsorum diligentem examinationem omnia et singula sigilla eisdem litteris, privilegiis et indultis appensa pro sufficienter recognitis habuimus, habemus ac haberi volumus. Et quia ipsas litteras, privilegia et indulta post diligentem huiusmodi visionem, inspectionem, contrectationem et examinationem sanas, integras, non viciatas, non cancellatas, non abrasas nec in aliqua sui parte suspectas, sed omni prorsus vicio et suspicione carentes ac veris sigillis supradictorum dominorum regum et principum electorum sigillatas fore comperimus et invenimus; idcirco ipsas litteras, privilegia et indulta ad futurum rei memoriam et propter causas supradictas per discretum virum Wernerum de Putten, clericum Culmensis dyocesis, publicum imperiali auctoritate notarium nostrumque ac curie nostre scribam iuratum ac ceteros notarios publicos infrascriptos transscribi, publicari et in formam publicam et autenticam ac exemplar seu presens volumen redigi de commissa nobis auctoritate regia decrevimus et mandavimus, quarum tenores sequuntur et sunt tales. Et primo tenor prime videlicet donationis sive concessionis Nove Marchie domini quondam Sigismundi Romanorum regis sigillo rotundo de cera glauca et communi in filis sericis nigri croceique colorum impendente sigillate, in cuius superficie a lateribus ciboriata, desuper decorata sedes, in cuius medio regis imago vestibus regalibus circumiuncta, corona regia coronata, in dextra manu sceptrum regale, in sinistra vero pomum cum cruce desuper deferens, circa cuius dextrum pedem clipeus parvus, in cuius superficie leonis figura, secus sinistrum autem iterum clipeus parvus, in quo forme trium capitum leonum apertorum et in dextro latere iterum duo clipei, in superiori figura aquile extensis alis, in sub eo leonis forma, in sinistro vero latere eciam duo clipei; in superiori crux dupplicata, in sub eo quatuor tractus plani per transversum, et hee littere in circumferencia circulari: Sigismundus dei gracia Romanorum rex semper augustus ac Hungarie, Dalmacie, Croacie, Rame, Servie, Galicie, Lodomirie, Comanie Bulgarieque rex, marchio Brandenburgensis necnon Bohemie et Lucemburgensis heres, ut prima facie videbatur, apparebant, sequitur de verbo ad verbum et est talis:

(p. 321 v.) I. n. s. et i. t. feliciter amen. Sigismundus etc. d. d. Posonii 1429 sept. 7 (supra n. 213).

Tenor secunde littere eiusdem Sigismundi videlicet mandati investiendi dictum ordinem ad dictam Novam Marchiam consimili sigillo supra descripto sigillate in pressula pergamenea appenso sequitur de verbo ad verbum et est talis:

(p. 323 v.) Wir Sigmund etc. d. d. Preszburg 1429 sept. 8 (s. n. 214).

Tenor vero tercie littere videlicet venundationis eiusdem terre Nove Marchie illustrissimorum principum dominorum Friderici senioris, Iohannis, Alberti et Friderici iunioris germanorum marchionum Brandenburgensium etc., quatuor sigillis eorundem dominorum marchionum de cera rubea in capsulis de cera communi glauci coloris impressis in pressulis pergameneis impendentibus sigillate; in quorum quidem sigillorum primi superficie tres clipei, quorum unus quasi in medio aliis maior in quo figura aquile extensis alis, super quem galea coronata tectura seu ligatura galeali circumcincta, a dextris et a sinistris per eandem, acsi vento continue propelleretur, duabusque alis desuper extensis et erectis redimita. Sub quo quidem clipeo alii duo parvi clipei, unus a dextris, in quo leonis forma coronata, alius a sinistris, in quo in superiori medietate due quadrature, una videlicet a dextris modicum elevata et alia a sinistris depressa, in inferiori vero medietate eiusdem clipei duo anguli obtusi, unus a dextris eque quadrature superiori depressus, alius a sinistris quadrature superiori a dextris equaliter elevatus; in sinistro autem latere forma leonis ad cursum velocem figurata cum dextro pede anteriori clipeum superiorem attingens, cum sinistro vero clipeum inferiorem a sinistris, pedem autem dextrum posteriorem sub eodem clipeo, sinistrum vero ad circumferenciam cum cauda protendens, in dextro autem latere leopardi forma cum sinistro pede anteriore superiorem clipeum, cum dextro vero inferiore versus dextrum attingens, pedem autem sinistrum posteriorem sub eodem clipeo et dextrum ad circumferenciam eciam cum cauda girata protendens; de ore enim eiusdem leopardi cedula usque ad circumferenciam et ulterius circumferencialiter circuiens, in qua hee littere: „sigillum Friderici dei gracia marchionis Brandeburgensis et burggravii Nurembergensis“, ut videbatur, apparebant. In secundi autem sigilli superficie tres clipei quasi equalis latitudinis, unus in superiori parte, in quo figura aquile extensis alis, duo sub eo, unus a dextris, in quo figura leonis erecti, alius a sinistris, in quo in superiori medietate similiter due quadrature, una a dexteris modicum elevata et alia a sinistris depressa, in inferiori vero medietate eiusdem clipei duo anguli obtusi, unus a dextris eque angulo superiori a sinistris posito depressus; alius vero a sinistris inferioris medietatis quadrature superiori a dextris posite equaliter elevatus; a dextris eciam figura angeli clipeum superiorem et sub eo a dextris inferiorem connectentis, a sinistris autem similiter figura angeli clipeum superiorem et a sinistris inferiorem similiter connectentis; hee vero littere circumferenciales: S. Iohannis d. g. marchionis Brandenburgensis burggravii Nurembergensis, ut videbatur, apparebant; in tercii vero sigilli superficie structura ciboriata, in cuius ciborii dextro latere effigies humana, a sinistro vero latere eiusdem ciborii similiter effigies humana; in structura autem clipeus, in quo figura aquile extensis alis, supra quem galea corona, tectura seu ligatura galeali a dextris et a sinistris ornate circumcincta duabusque alis desuper extensis et erectis decorata; sub quo quidem clipeo duo alii clipei minores superiore, unus a dextris, in quo figura leonis, alius a sinistris, in quo in superiori medietate eciam due quadrature, una a dextris modicum elevata, alia vero a sinistris depressa, in inferiori autem medietate eiusdem clipei duo anguli obtusi, unus a dextris anguli superiori a sinistris posito eque depressus, alius vero a sinistris inferioris medietatis quadrature superiori a dextris posite equaliter elevatus, et hee littere circumferenciales: S. Alberti d. g. marchionis Brandeburgensis et burgravii Nurembergensis, ut videbatur apparebant; in quarti vero sigilli superficie quatuor semicirculi in extremitatibus eorum in medio florum se contingentes, in quorum medio clipeus magnus in quatuor partes divisus, in prima quadratura versus dextrum figura aquile extensis alis, in secunda versus sinistrum leonis figura in medietate inferiori et in angulo obtuso versus dextrum iterum leonis forma et in angulo obtuso versus sinistrum iterum aquile figura extensis alis; in semicirculo superiori quedam florisature, sub quibus hee littere: iunior; in semicirculo inferiori quedam florisature, sed in semicirculo a dextris figura angeli tenentis clipeum versus eandem partem; in semicirculo autem sinistri lateris iterum figura angeli versus idem latus clipeum tenens et hee littere in circumferencia circulari: S. Friderici marchio' Brandeburgñ ac burggra' Nurembergñ o, ut videbatur apparebant, sequitur et est talis:

(p. 325.) Wir Friderich der alter etc. d. d. 1443 oct. 16 (supra n. 216).

Tenor vero quarte littere videlicet ratihabicionis et confirmacionis predictorum dicti serenissimi principis domini Friderici Romanorum regis, vero eius maiestatis sigillo de cera communi glauci coloris in filis sericeis brunatici viridisque coloris impendente sigillate, in cuius superficie ab una parte sedes regalis ciboriata a lateribus et sursum multipliciter redimita; in cuius medio imago regis corona regali, supra quam crux parva coronata, indumentis regalibus induta, in dextra manu sceptrum, in sinistra vero pomum cum cruce desuper deferens, et in dextro latere extra ciborium duo clipei, unus superius, in quo quinque aquilarum figure extensis alis, supra quem cedula, has quinque continens vocales a e i o v; sub eo vero due leonum figura, una quasi dorso suo, alia vero erecta pedibus suis anterioribus clipeum eundem sustentantes; alius clipeus inferius dyametraliter in duas partes divisus, in una versus regis imaginem tres leonum figure, alia versus circumferenciam plana, in cuius medio quadratura elevata; sub hoc clipeo figura leonis, eundem clipeum quasi capite sustentantis, ab eadem eciam parte ymagini regis magis propinque et in ciboriata sede iterum duo clipei, unus sursum, alius vero deorsum, in quorum quolibet figura aquile extensis alis, in latere autem sinistro extra sedem ciboriatam iterum duo clipei, unus superius, in quo forma leonis, supra quem figura cedule sine literis; sub clipeo vero due leonum forme quasi clipeum deferentes; sub illis autem alter clipeus, in quo figura aquile extensis alis, sub quo figura leonis eundem in ore deferens; in eodem eciam latere ymagini regis magis propinque et in sede ciboriata iterum duo clipei, unus superius planus, quem planus tractus per transversum equaliter elevatus dividit, in sub eo figura leonis; sub ymagine vero regis et quasi inter pedes eius signetum de cera rubea impressum, in quo figure quatuor capitum quasi hominum in occipitibus coniunctorum facies suas ad quatuor mundi angulos dirigencium; sub pede vero ipsius sedis et dicto secreto cedula cum hiis litteris: qui natus est in die Mathei sub anno domini m cccc xv; in circumferencia duo circuli cum hiis literis: sigillum maiestat. Friderici dei gracia Romanorum regis semper augusti ducis Austrie Stirie Karinthie et Carniole comitisque Tirolis etc. In alia vero parte dicti maiestatis sigilli septem semicirculi, quorum extremitates in globulo lilium deferente se contingunt; in quorum medio figura aquile extensis alis, supra cuius caput semicirculus unus, in quo clipeus, in quo pluvialis cappellus ad instar cappellorum prelatorum zona et toldis redimitus, supra quem clipeum galea coronata tectura galee circumornata, et supra illam galeale signum quasi rotale dicti capelli figuram in superficie habens; in semicirculo immediate sub eo et secundo a dextris iterum clipeus in duas partes equales, videlicet ab angulo acuto sinistro ad angulum obtusum a dextris per tractum planum divisus, in cuius superiori parte tres corone et inferiore similiter tres; supra quem galea tectura redimita pro signo galeali sex similes coronas, tres in uno ordine supra et tres in alio ordine infra per tractum planum divisus deferens; in semiquidem circulo sub eo immediate et tercio iterum clipeus in superficie figuram valve aperte, duabus tabulis unam a dextris et aliam a sinistris continens; supra quem galea tectura soliti decoris ornata similem supra se valve figuram pro signo deferens galeali, in semicirculo autem sub illo immediate et quarto iterum clipeus ab angulo acuto sinistro ad angulum obtusum dextrum per tractum planum equaliter divisus, in cuius qualibet parte figura leonis caudam supra dorsum suum baiulantis, supra clipeum autem galea coronata solitis ligaturis circumcincta erectam supra se figuram leonis in capite suo opus decoris quasi ex pennis strutionum factum habentem deferens pro signo galeali; in quinto semicirculo iterum clipeus equaliter per tractum elevatum dyametraliter divisus, quem tres tractus plani similiter elevati unus citra medium versus angulum acutum dextralem per indirectum eundem tractum dyametralem contingens usque ad extremitatem lateris sinistri, alter ab angulo acuto ad angulum obtusum eundem tractum dyametralem intersecans, tercius a parte dextra in angulo obtuso iterum eundem tractum dyametralem contingens parum ultra se extendens, supra quem clipeum galea coronata consueta tectura decorata, desuper ala extensa et erecta, in qua iterum planus tractus desuper per alios tres indirecte intersecatus redimita; in semicirculo autem sexto iterum clipeus, in quo due piscium figure dorsa sibi mutuo vertentes, oribus suis angulos acutos, caudis vero angulos obtusos clipei, una a dextris et alia a sinistris incurvatim attingentes; supra clipeum autem galea coronata ac solitis tecturis decorata, supra quam due similes piscium figure ventribus adinvicem versis caudis sursum protensis, oribus vero coronam galee quasi contingentes, in quarum medio figura mulieris erecta; in septimo semicirculo iterum clipeus in duas partes equaliter dyametraliter divisus, in cuius una parte, videlicet ad dextrum, figura aquile extensis alis, in alia autem parte, scilicet ad sinistrum, duo tractus equales modicum elevati dyametraliter protensi, supra quem galea coronata tecturali ornamento solite decorata, supra quam figura aquile coronate extensis alis erecta, in cuius collo immediate supra humeros eius tractus planus per transversum, in angulis vero quasi acutis a contingencia semicirculorum supra descriptorum ab extra causalis infra scripte figure, videlicet in angulo primo causato a semicirculo supra caput aquile posito et immediate a dextris sequente ymago angeli alas dilatantis; in secundo vero angulo forma volucris unam alam, videlicet dextram quasi ante se extendentis, cum sinistra vero se contegentis; in tercio autem angulo forma quasi draconis alas habentis unam, videlicet sinistram, alam ante se extendentis, cum alia vero, scilicet dextra, se contegentis; in quarto angulo forma draconis quasi reptantis et flosculum in ore gestantis; in quinto autem angulo figura draconis quasi similis; in sexto vero opus quasi simile; in septimo autem angulo iterum angeli figura alis dilatatis et in circumferencia circulus has continens litteras: aquila Ezechielis sponse missa est de celis, volat ipsa sine meta, quo nec vates nec propheta evolavit alcius a e i o v, ut videbatur, apparebant, sequitur et est talis:

(p. 328.) Wir Friderich von gotes gnaden Romischer kunigk etc., d. d. Nuremberg 1444 sept. 14 (supra n. 217).

Intus: Wir Fridrich der elter etc. Frankenforde 1443 oct. 16 (supra n. 216).

Tenor autem quinte littere eciam ratihabicionis predictorum reverendissimi in Christo patris domini Theoderici archiepiscopi Maguntinensis, sacri imperii electoris etc., vero eius sigillo de cera viridi in capsa rotunda de cera glauca et communi in zona sericea rubei coloris impendente impresso sigillate; in cuius superficie quatuor semicirculi in extremitatibus se contingentes, in medio quorum ymago presulis ornamentis pontificalibus induta, in sinistra manu formam libri clausi, in dextra vero crucem deferens, in dextro autem latere ipsius ymaginis clipeus, in quo figura rote cum octo specubus, in sinistro latere iterum clipeus in duo equalia per transversum divisus, in superiori due figure stellarum, in inferiori una, et hee littere circumferenciales: „Sigillum † Theodrici † archiepiscopi † Maguntini“ ut videbatur apparebant, sequitur de verbo ad verbum et est talis:

(p. 332 v.) Wir Dietrich von gotes gnaden der heiligen kirchen czu Mentz ertzbischoff etc. d. d. Nuremberg 1444 sept. 21 (supra n. 218).

Intus: Wir Fridrich von gotes gnaden Romischer kunig etc. d. d. Norenberg 1444 sept. 14 (supra n. 217).

Intus: Wir Frederich der elter d. d. 1443 oct. 16 (supra n. 216).

Tenor sexte littere eciam ratihabitionis predictorum dicti reverendissimi in Christo patris et domini, domini Theoderici archiepiscopi Coloniensis et sacri imperii electoris, eius vero sigillo de cera viridi in capsula rotunda de cera glauca et communi in sona serica rubei coloris impendente impresso sigillate, in cuius superficie crux lata in extremitatibus modicum elevata, in qua clipeus per tractum planum modicum elevatum in equalia per transversum divisus, et hee littere in circumferencia circulari: „Secretum Theoderici archiepiscopi ecclesie Coloniensis“, ut videbatur apparebant, sequitur de verbo ad verbum et est talis:

(p. 336 v.) Wir Dietrich von gots gnaden der heiligen kirchen zcu Collen erczbisschoff etc. d. d. Nuremberg 1444 sept. 29 (supra n. 219).

Intus: Wir Fridrich von gotes gnaden Romischer kunig etc. d. d. Norenberg 1444 sept. 14 (supra n. 217).

Intus: Wir Frederich der elter d. d. 1443 oct. 16 (supra n. 216).

Tenor vero septime littere eciam ratihabitionis predictorum dicti reverendissimi in Christo patris domini Iacobi archiepiscopi Treverensis, sacri imperii electoris, eius vero sigillo de cera viridi in capsula rotunda de cera communi glauci coloris in zona sericea rubei coloris impendente impressa sigillate, in cuius superficie crux lata, in qua clipeus et in illo tractus latus ab angulo acuto dextro ad angulum obtusum sinistrum protractus, in quo figure tres testarum concharum in Theotunico vulgari mosschelen, et hee littere in circumferencia circulari: „Secretum Iacobi dei gracia archiepiscopi Treverensis“ ut videbatur apparebant, sequitur de verbo ad verbum et est talis:

(p. 340.) Wir Jacob von gots gnaden der heiligen kirchen zcu Trier ertzbisschoff etc. de 1444 sept. 21 (supra n. 221).

Intus: Wir Fridrich von gotes gnaden Romischer konigk etc. de 1444 sept. 14 (supra n. 217).

Intus: Wir Frederich der elter etc. de 1443 oct. 16 (supra n. 216).

Tenor autem octave littere eciam ratihabicionis predictorum dicti illustrissimi principis et domini Ludovici ducis Bavarie, comitis palatini Reni ac sacri imperii electoris, eius vero sigillo de cera rubea in capsula rotunda de cera communi in filis sericeis flavei albique colorum impendente impresso sigillate, in cuius sigilli superficie tres clipei, unus a dextris, in quo leonis figura, alter a sinistris, in quo figure cuneorum seu rutarum, quorum aliqui equaliter elevati et alii equaliter depressi per indirectum protensi, inter quos clipeos tercius angulo acuto sinistro elevatus et cum angulo dextro circumferenciam attingens planus, in cuius medio quedam concavitas et angulus obtusus parum elevatus, supra predictos clipeos galea tectura redimita, supra quam pro galeali signo figura leonis erecta et coronata pedibus galeam tenens et caudam in dorso deferens, et hee littere in cedula ab acie dextra clipei dextralis incipiente usque ad circumferenciam circumferencialiter circuiente et eundem circulum intersecante et protendente quasi ad angulum acutum sinistrum clipei sinistralis: S. Ludovici dei gracia comitis palatini Reni sacri Romani imperii archidapiferi et Bavarie ducis 4 2 d c" 2 ut videbatur apparebant, sequitur de verbo ad verbum et est talis:

Wir Lodwig von gotes gnaden pfaltzgraff bei Rein etc. d. d. Heidelberg 1444 oct. 13 (supra n. 222).

Intus: Wir Fridrich von gotes gnaden Romischer koning etc. de 1444 sept. 14 (supra n. 217).

Intus: Wir Frederich der alter etc. de 1443 oct. 16 (supra n. 216).

Tenor vero none littere eciam ratihabicionis predictorum dicti illustrissimi principis et domini, domini Friderici ducis Saxonie ac sacri imperii electoris, eius vero sigillo de cera rubea in capsula rotunda de cera communi glauci coloris in zona rubea sericea impendente impresso sigillate, in cuius sigilli superficie quatuor semicirculi in extremitatibus se contingentes, in quorum medio quinque clipei, unus in semicirculo superiori, in quo forme duorum gladiorum manubria versus angulos obtusos et acucies versus angulos acutos habentes per modum crucis se intersecantes, in semicirculo vero versus dextrum iterum clipeus, in quo leonis forma pedes sursum et dorsum deorsum vertentis, in semicirculo tercio inferiori iterum clipeus, in quo figura aquile extensis alis, in semicirculo autem quarto et versus sinistrum iterum clipeus, in quo figura leonis pedes deorsum et dorsum sursum vertens, in medio autem predictorum clipeorum et semicirculorum clipeus magnus, in quo quinque plani tractus modicum elevati per transversum protensi, super quos figura serti ab angulo acuto dextro ad angulum obtusum sinistrum protensa, et hee littere in circumferencia circulari: „S. Friderici ducis Saxonie, Thuringie lantgravii et marchionis Misnensis“, ut videbatur, apparebant, sequitur de verbo ad verbum et est talis:

Wir Fridrich von gotes gnaden herczog czu Sachsen d. d. 1444 sept. 21 (supra n. 220).

Intus: Wir Fridrich von gotes gnaden Romischer kunig etc. d. d. 1444 sept. 14 (supra n. 217).

Intus: Wir Frederich der alter etc. d. d. 1443 oct. 16 (supra n. 216).

Et quia prefatas imperiales pariter et regales ac dicti sacri imperii electorum litteras donacionum scilicet, investiture, renunciationum, ratihabitionum et confirmationum predictarum nobis in notariorum publicorum supra et infra nominatorum et plurimorum aliorum fidedignorum testium ad hoc vocatorum specialiter et rogatorum presencia exhibitas et productas earundemque sigilla attente consideravimus et vidimus ac, sicut premittitur, ipsas sanas, integras et illesas, non abolitas, non viciatas, non cancellatas, non abrasas vel suspectas sed omni prorsus vicio et suspicione carentes, ac recognitis veris sigillis supradictorum dominorum sigillatas invenimus atque de verbo ad verbum simul cum presenti transsumpti volumine mandavimus et fecimus legi et auscultari diligenter in nostra presencia; et tandem post diligentem examinationem, auscultationem et collationem presentis transsumpti cum litteris originalibus predictis reperimus et invenimus huiusmodi transsumptum seu exemplum de verbo ad verbum absque addicione seu detrimento cum ipsis originalibus totaliter concordare et in nullo penitus discrepare, nos Franciscus episcopus Warmiensis et commissarius prefatus auctoritate regia nobis in hac parte concessa pro tribunali sedentes decreto perpetue valituro statuentes firmiter statuimus et decernimus, quatenus presenti transsumptarum litterarum volumini plena et omnimoda fides adhibeatur et adhiberi debeat in quibuscumque locis et curiis, iudiciis et extra sicut ipsis litteris originalibus supra descriptis et insertis, atque ut eandem vim et vigorem habeat et iuris sorciatur effectum et sortiri debeat ceu littere originales predicte, tribuimus et impartimur auctoritatem, ita videlicet ut, ubicumque locorum presens transsumptum tam in iudiciis quam extra visum, exhibitum vel productum fuerit, eandem vim et robur firmitatis, credulitatis et probationis habeat et teneat, acsi ipse littere originales supra descripte omnes aut ex ipsis aliqua seu alique ostense et exhibite coniunctim seu divisim forent vel producte[1].

V, 319—352 v. 1. Hic textus desinit nec sigillatum fuit transsumtum. Originale transsumtum Francisci episcopi, quod est in Regimontano archivo, citat Voigt Die Erwerbung der Neumark. Berlin 1863. 277 n. 1 ad annum 1448. Quatuor appensa sigilla praeter illius episcoporum testium sunt.

224. *1517 martii 10 Moscoviae. Basilius, totius Russiae imperator, cum Alberto, ordinis Theutonici magistro generali, foedus init contra Sigismundum, Poloniae regem.*

Per dei voluntatem et per magni domini graciam nos magnus dominus Basilius, dei gracia imperator ac dominator tocius Russie et magnus dux Volodimerie, Moscovie, Novogradie, Plescovie, Smolenski, Tferie, Iugorie, Permie, Wetchie, Bolgarie etc. dominator ac magnus dux, Novogradie inferioris terre et Tzernigovie, Rezanie, Volotskii et Sevie, Belevie, Rostovie, Iaroslavie, Belozerie, Udorie, Obdorie Condonieque etc., dedimus hanc nostram litteram Alberto, ordinis Theotonicorum generali magistro Pruscie, marchgrabio Brandenborgiensi, Statiniensi, Pomeriensi, Cassubiensi et Vendeniensi duci, burggravio Nurbergiensi principique Rugenensi, super hoc, quia misit ad nos suos nuncios nos rogare propterea, quatinus nos vellemus sibi graciam prestare et fovere ac contra nostrum inimicum, regem Polonie, in unitate ipsum nobiscum facere atque tuere[1] eum et ipsius terras a nostro inimico, rege Polonie ac magno duce Litwanie. Nos autem magnus dominus Basilius, dei gracia imperator ac dominator tocius Russie, et magnus dux Alberto, ordinis Theotonicorum generali magistro, graciam nostram fecimus contra istum nostrum inimicum Sigismundum, regem Polonie, in unitate ipsum nobiscum ordinavimus, pro eo et pro terra ipsius volumus stare et defendere eum et terras eius volumus ab inimico nostro, rege Polonie et magno duce Litwanie, ac iuvare sibi contra istum suum inimicum, quantum nobis deus iuvabit[2]. Quando autem nos, magnus dominus Basilius, dei gracia imperator ac dominator tocius Russie et magnus dux, personaliter equum ascendemus et ibimus contra inimicum nostrum, regem Polonie et magnum ducem Litwanie, aut principes ac duces nostros cum potencia nostra in ipsius terram mitteremus, Alberto autem, ordinis Theotonicorum generali magistro, nunciabimus; tunc ipse cum suis amicis ac cum tota sua potencia in nostri inimici, regis Polonie ac magni ducis Litwanie, terram, quam possidet, etiam debetis ire et agere illum nostrum actum cum isto nostro inimico, rege Polonie, una cum nostris principibus et ducibus in illa expedicione. Et, si esset aliqua causa vobis Alberto, ordinis Theotonicorum generali magistro, cum illo nostro inimico, Sigismundo, rege Polonie et magno duce Litwanie, ibitisque contra ipsum personaliter cum vestris amicis ac cum tota vestra potencia et mitteretis ad nos magnum dominum nos rogando, tunc nos magnus dominus Basilius, dei gracia imperator ac dominator tocius Russie et magnus dux, vobis, generali magistro, contra illum nostrum inimicum, Sigismundum, regem Polonie et magnum ducem Litwanie, volumus iuvare vos et terram vestram defendere, quantum nobis deus adiuvabit, principes et duces nostros in ipsius terram mitteremus et inimiciciam nostram regi Polonie mandaremus facere, quantum nobis deus adiuvabit. Vos autem Albertus, ordinis Theotonicorum generalis magister, contra istum nostrum inimicum, regem Polonie, debetis stare firmiter et constanter et debetis esse contra istum nostrum inimicum in illa expedicione una nobiscum. Quos autem nostros oratores mitteremus, nos magnus dux Basilius, dei gracia imperator ac dominator tocius Russie et magnus dux, ad fratrem nostrum Maximilianum, electum imperatorem Romanorum ac supremum regem, etiam ad alios dominos per vestras terras, aut si ad nos a fratre nostro Maximiliano, electo imperatore Romanorum ac supremo rege, transibunt nostri oratores et ipsius oratores, etiam ex aliis dominis si ibunt ad nos oratores per vestram terram, tunc nostris oratoribus, etiam fratris nostri Maximiliani, electi imperatoris Romanorum et supremi regis, atque aliorum dominorum oratoribus per vestram terram et aquam via munda sine omni impedimento, simili modo etiam ad vos nostris oratoribus venire atque redire per terram et aquam via munda absque omni impedimento; etiam nostris mercatoribus. Quos autem ad nos magnum dominum mitteretis vos Albertus, ordinis Theotonicorum generalis magister, vestros nuncios, tunc vestris nunciis per nostra dominia, per terram et aquam via munda sine omni impedimento et venire ipsis ad nos atque redire libere absque omni impedimento, etiam vestris mercatoribus. Ad maiorem autem confirmationem nos magnus dominus Basilius, dei gracia imperator ac dominator tocius Russie et magnus dux, ad nostram firmam litteram, quam dedimus Alberto, Theotonicorum ordinis generali magistro, sigillum nostrum mandavimus ad eam appendi et conciliariis[3] nostris mandavimus super hanc litteram crucem osculare[3], conciliario nostro duci Dimitreo Wlodimerowitzu, eciam conciliario nostro Gregorio Theodorowitzu, atque tezaurario nostro Georgio Dimitreewitzu. Scriptum in nostro doimio[3] in nostra civitate in Moscovia anno septimo millessimo vicessimo quinto menciis[3] marcii decima die.

Ex originali membranaceo cum originali et ipso membranaceo Russice scripto bullae aureae duplicibus filis aureis et purpureis colligato, quod asservatur in archivo secreto Berolinensi. Visitur in bullae aureae una facie s. Georgius eques draconem lancea perforans et inscriptio, in altera facie aquila biceps coronata et ipsa inscriptione circumdata. — Textum Russicum publicabimus alio loco. Caeterum de hoc foedere cf. Voigt Geschichte Preufsens IX, 535 sq. 1. et defendere cum et terras supra rasuram. 2. istum — iuvabit supra rasuram. 3. sic.

LIVONIA.

225. *1210 oct. 20 (xiii kal. novembr. p. n. a. 13) Laterani. Innocentius papa III (Cum super sorte) Wolcuino magistro et fratribus militiae Christi in Livonia constitutis confirmat compositionem cum Alberto Rigensi episcopo initam, ex qua inter alia ipsi tertiam partem Lettiae et Livoniae teneant, ob hoc nullum inde temporale servitium praestituri praeter perpetuam defensionem contra paganos; caetera.*

II, 147 v. sine dato. Edd. Baluze Epp. Innoc. III lib. XIII ep. 142 (II, 479), caeteri, qui citantur in Livl. U.-B., ubi est I, 23 XVII.

---

226. *1224 iulii 23 (x kal. aug.) in Riga. Hermannus, Lealensis episcopus, fratribus militiae Christi tradit dimidiam fere partem episcopatus sui, terram scilicet Sackele, Normigunde, Mocke, (Alenpois p. 149), dimidiam partem terrae Waigele salvo sibi iure spirituali.*

In confirmatione Honorii III de 1226: II, 132. 142 v. 144 v. 148 v. E coaevo apographo Petropolitanae bibliothecae ed. in Livl. Mitth. IV, 37. Scr. rer. Liv. I, 414 sq. n. LXVI c. Livl. U.-B. I, 66 n. LXII, ubi reg. p. 16 n. 71 etiam citantur transsumta Iohannis Lubecensis episcopi d. a. 1519 mai. 3 ap. Dogiel V, 6 n. XII. Gadebusch I, 176 sq. ann. a. et Wilhelmi legati de 1225 aug. in Hiärn Collect. p. 285 sq. Brotze Sylloge I, 187. Arnd II, 16 k. Brandis 143 n. 5.

---

227. *1224 iulii 24 (ix kal. augusti p. n. a. 25) in Riga. Albertus, Livoniensis episcopus, consensu Hermanni Estoniae episcopi (Lealensis), fratrum militiae Christi caet. innovat ordinationem Estoniae.*

II, 144 v. 148. 150 v. Or. et coaevum transsumtum in bibliotheca Petropolitana, Livl. Mittheil. IV, 34. Scr. rer. Liv. I, 413 LXVI a. Livl. U.-B. I, 67 LXIII. E transsumto Iohannis Lubecensis episcopi de 1519 mai. 3. Dogiel V, 6 XII. Gadebusch 179 ann. d., caet.

---

228. *1225 aug. Rigae. Wilhelmus, Mutinensis episcopus, apostolicae sedis legatus, dirimit litem inter Hermannum Lealensem episcopum et Volqui-*

num magistrum militiae Christi de iurisdictione. Inserta sunt documenta de

1224 iulii 23. Hermanni Lealensis episcopi (supra n. 226) et
1224 iulii 24. Alberti Livoniensis episcopi (supra n. 227).

Coram nobis Willelmo, miseratione divina Mutinensi episcopo, apostolice sedis legato, inter Hermannum, episcopum Lealensem sive Iohannem, prepositum Rigensem, procuratorem dicti episcopi, secundum quod per patentes litteras eiusdem episcopi apparebat, ex una parte, et V(olcwinum), magistrum militie Christi ex altera, questio huiuscemodi vertebatur. Petebat namque dictus magister quandam concordiam, factam inter se et dominum episcopum super divisione regionum Estonie, que sunt in episcopatu suo, confirmari secundum formam litterarum ipsius episcopi, quarum tenor talis erat: I. n. s. e. i. t. Herimannus etc. (cf. supra n. 226). Ex adverso respondebat prepositus, procurator eiusdem episcopi, quod dicta concordia debebat confirmari non secundum formam litterarum predictarum, sed secundum formam litterarum Alberti Rigensis episcopi, quarum tenor talis erat Albertus etc. (cf. supra n. 227). Dubitationem facere videbatur diversitas litterarum, et quia in primis non fuerat appositum, quod in secundis videbatur expressum, item quia littere, que dicebantur et ex ipsa verborum serie videbantur ultime, inspecta litterarum data prime potius videbantur, unde allegabatur intervenisse scriptoris errorem. Movebat etiam, quod in litteris episcopi Hermanni de quodam autentico mentio habebatur, sed dubitabatur, de quo autentico diceretur. Super hiis interrogatus procurator episcopi, respondebat, quod littere vere essent, sed verbum quoddam iurisdictionis ibi expressum non debuisset litteris taliter insertum fuisse. Magister vero super verbo iurisdictionis interrogatus respondit, quod, si de persona sua vel alterius magistri pro tempore existentis querimonia fieret, ipse magister teneretur sub episcopo respondere. Clerici vero magistri, sive eiusdem religionis fuerint sive non, debent sub episcopo in spiritualibus tantum respondere. Cause vero spirituales debent sub episcopo diffiniri. Fratres autem tenentur respondere solummodo sub magistro. Homines etiam habitantes in parte magistri debent sub magistro similiter respondere, ita tamen, quod, si sentirent in diffinitiva sententia se gravatos, possint ad dominum episcopum, si voluerint, appellare. Super quibus procurator interrogatus respondit, in omnibus ita esse. Visis igitur et auditis utriusque partis instrumentis, attestationibus et rationibus, habito etiam sapientum consilio, firmam et ratam predictam concordiam iudicamus, et ipsam insuper auctoritate, qua fungimur, confirmamus. Super verbo autem iurisdictionis iudicamus et pronunciamus ut supra, videlicet, quod magister tantum teneatur sub episcopo respondere, clerici magistri, cuiuscunque ordinis vel religionis sint, debeant episcopo tantum in spiritualibus respondere et omnes cause spirituales debeant sub episcopo cognosci; fratres autem sub magistro respondeant, et homines de parte ipsius magistri debeant sub ipso magistro in omnibus temporalibus respondere, ita quod possint a diffinitiva sententia ad episcopum appellare. Lata est hec sententia in Riga, in ecclesia sancti Iacobi, anno domini m° cc° xxv°, mense augusto, xiii° indictionis. Testes interfuerunt[1] Albertus, Rigensis episcopus, Lambertus, episcopus Semigallie, magister Ludolphus, canonicus Lubicensis, Sigfridus, canonicus Ildesemensis, Arnoldus, capellanus episcopi Alberti et multi alii.

II, 150. Ex apographo in Hiärnii Collectaneis editum in Livl. U.-B. I, 79 LXXIV. Dein non in omnibus melius e codice B per v. cl. de Goetze in Mittheilungen a. d. Geb. d. Gesch. Liv-, Esth- und Kurlands. Riga 1855. 8. VIII, 123 I, unde repetitum in Livl. U.-B. III, 8 n. 74. 1. Caetera desunt.

---

229. *1225 aug. in Riga in ecclesia b. Iacobi. Wilhelmus, Mutinensis episcopus, apostolicae sedis legatus, litem inter Hermannum Lealensem episcopum et Volcwinum magistrum militiae Christi de iurisdictione utriusque dirimit.*

II, 144. Est idem ac praecedens diploma et ipsum mancum in fine.

---

230. *1225 mense augusti ind. 13 in Riga in ecclesia s. Iacobi. Wilhelmus, Mutinensis episcopus, ap. sed. legatus, dirimit litem de iurisdictione in tertia parte Livoniae et Lettiae ab Alberto Livoniensi episcopo magistro et fratribus militiae Christi donata inter episcopum et hunc ordinem.*

II, 129 sine anno et 141, unde cum Honorii III confirmatione ed. v. Goetze l. c. VIII, 126 n. 2, unde Livl. U.-B. III, 7 n. 73 b.

---

231. *1225 decbr. ind. 13 Riga. Wilhelmus, Mutinensis episcopus, ap. sed. legatus, dirimit litem inter Albertum Livoniensem episcopum, Iohannem Rigensem praepositum, Volcwinum magistrum militiae Christi in Livonia ex una parte et Albertum syndicum civitatis Rigensis nomine huius ex altera de iurisdictione, moneta, Gothici iuris vi, caeteris.*

II, 130. Ex or. perg. archivi Rigensis ed. Livl. U.-B. I, 81 n. LXXV, ubi etiam citantur editiones Gadebusch I. I, 187 sq. nota o. Bunge Beiträge p. 50 ann. 150; cum transsumto de 1226 Turgenew Hist. Russ. mon. I, 18 n. 18; cum Alexandri IV de 1257 april. 19 confirmatione Livl. Mitth. VI, 238 n. 6.

---

232. *1226 april. 10 (iiii idus aprilis) in Riga. Wilhelmus, Mutinensis episcopus, ap. sed. leg., dirimit quaestionem inter I(ohannem) Rigensem praepositum et V(olquinum) magistrum militiae Christi de sacris apud mercatores et peregrinos hyemantes Rigae aut annum vel amplius ibi commorantes agendis.*

II, 146, unde ed. de Goetze l. c. 127 III, unde Livl. U.-B. III, 11 n. 82 a.

---

233. *1226 april. 28 (iiii kal. maii) in Dunemunde. Wilhelmus, Mutinensis episcopus, ap. sed. leg., decernit magistrum et fratres militiae Christi a Rigensi praeposito excommunicari non posse.*

II, 146 v., unde ed. de Goetze l. c. 128 IV, unde Livl. U.-B. III, 12 n. 85 a.

---

234. *1226 maii 7 (nonas maii) Dunemunde. Wilhelmus, Mutinensis episcopus, ap. sed. leg., dirimit litem inter Hermannum, Lealensem episcopum, et ordinem militiae Christi de terminis inter Sackalam et Huganiam.*

II, 147, unde ed. de Goetze l. c. 129 v, unde Livl. U.-B. III, 13 n. 87 a.

---

235. *1226 maio apud Parmam. Fridericus II imperator V(olquino) magistro et fratribus domus militiae Christi in Livonia per Iohannem filium Vollardi, canonicum Lubecensem, Wilhelmum, filium Bertholdi, Iohannem dictum de Brema, burgenses et nuntios Lubecenses, petentibus confirmat omnes possessiones et iura, quae a Livoniensi et Lealensi episcopis possident, et omne genus metalli, quod in illis possit inveniri. Inter testes: Hermannus, venerabilis magister domus h. s. M. Th. i. I.*

I, 43 v., unde edidit Huillard-Bréholles II, 583. Ex Hiärnii Collectaneis p. 134—136 in Livl. Mitth. IV, 426 n. 38, ed. in Livl. U.-B. I, 107 n. XC.

---

236. *1226 novbr. 19 (xiii kal. decembr.) p. n. a. 11. Honorius papa III (Ea que) confirmat Wilhelmi Mutinensis episcopi, ap. sed. leg., diffinitivam sententiam de 1225 decbr. (cf. supra n. 231).*

II, 130 sine dato. In fine: „Ita invenitur de verbo ad verbum in registro domini Honorii pape III. Martinus". — E registro Honorii III ed. Turgenew Hist. Russ. mon. I, 18 n. 18. Transsumtum de 1287 mart. 29 archivi Rigensis citant Livl. Mittheil. IV, 422 n. 35. Livl. U.-B. I reg. 25 n. 102.

---

237. *1226 dec. 10 (iiii id. decembr.) Laterani p. n. a. 11. Honorius papa III (Ea que) confirmat ordinationem Hermanni Lealensis episcopi de a. 1224 iulii 23 (cf. supra n. 226).*

II, 130 v. In fine: „Ita invenitur de verbo ad verbum in registro domini Honorii pape III anno XI. Martinus".

---

238. *1226 dec. 10 (iiii id. decembr.) p. n. a. 11 Laterani. Honorius papa III (Ea que) confirmat petentibus magistro et fratribus militiae Christi in Livonia diffinitivam sententiam de 1225 aug. Riga. Wilhelmi Mutinensis episcopi (v. supra n. 230).*

II, 129 sine dato. In fine legitur: „Ita invenitur de verbo ad verbum in registro domini Honorii pape III anno XI. Martinus". Unde edidit v. Goetze Livl. Mitth. VIII, 126 II, unde memorat Livl. U.-B. III, 15 n. 92 a, ubi notae chronologicae supplentur e Porthan Accessio ad Celsii recensionem bullarii Romano-Sveogothici. Abo 1797. 4. n. 48.

---

239. *1226 dec. 10. Honorius papa III (Ea que) confirmat insertam diffinitivam sententiam de*

1225 aug. in Riga in ecclesia s. Iacobi. Wilhelmi, Mutinensis episcopi, ap. sed. leg., qui inter Albertum Livoniensem episcopum et magistrum fratresque militiae Christi de iurisdictione litem dirimit (n. 230).

II, 141; est idem ac praecedens. Ad calcem legitur: In registro est.

---

240. *1226 dec. 10 Laterani. Honorius papa III Rigensi episcopo permittit, quod sententias a Semigallensi episcopo in magistrum et fratres militiae Christi latas requisitus relaxet.*

Honorius etc. episcopo Rigensi etc. Magister et fratres militie Christi in Livonia nobis humiliter supplicarunt, ut, cum possessiones habeant in Simigallia et contingat interdum, quod in questionibus emergentibus in eos seu in eorum aliquos a venerabili fratre nostro episcopo Semigallie excommunicationis sententia proferatur et propter locorum distantiam eis difficile sit apostolicam sedem adire, quociens id contingit, super hec eis paterna providere sollicitudine dignaremur[1]. Volentes igitur eosdem magistrum et fratres sub religionis obtentu in hoc et in aliis quantum secundum deum possumus exaudire, fraternitati tue per apostolica scripta mandamus, quatenus requisitus ab eis excommunicationis seu interdicti sententias, quas in eos vel eorum loca predictum episcopum contingerit[2] promulgare, relaxes iuxta formam ecclesie consuetam, nisi idem episcopus a te commonitus eos relaxare curaverit infra terminum, quem ei tua providentia duxerit prefigendum, auditurus postmodum, si quid remanserit questionis, et fine debito decisurus. Si autem te causa predicandi ad loca remotiora ire contingerit[2], alicui viro prudenti committas interim vices tuas. Datum Laterani iv idus decembris pontificatus nostri anno vii.

II, 129v. Cum clausula: „Ita invenitur de verbo ad verbum in registro domini Honorii pape III anno XI. Martinus". Datum praebet Livl. U.-B. III reg. p. 6 n. 104 a ex: Porthan Accessio ad Celsii recensionem bullarii Romano-Sveogothici. Abo 1797. 4. p. 20 n. 49. 1. dignaremini B. 2. B.

---

241. *1228 iunii 29 (iii kal. iulii) s. l. Godefridus, Osiliensis episcopus, concedit fratribus militiae Christi terciam partem Osiliae, Monae, aliarum episcopatus insularum iure temporali.*

II, 142, unde ed. de Goetze l. c. 131 VII, unde Livl. U.-B. III, 19 n. 99a.

---

242. *1234 s. d. in Tarbato. Hermannus, Tarbatensis episcopus, notum facit se pro loco Leale de consilio Wilhelmi quondam Mutinensis episcopi, tunc ap. sed. leg., sedem elegisse Tarbatum renovatque pro novo hoc suo insertam suam sub titulo tanquam Lealensis episcopi de 1224 iulii 23 cum fratribus militiae Christi de territoriis Sackele, Norme-*

gunde, Mocke, Alenpois, dimidio Waigele, illis concessis (cf. supra n. 226) pactam conventionem.

II, 148 v. cum falso anno 1224, ed. Livl. U.-B. I, 179 n. 140; e codice B ed. de Goetze l. c. 135 x, unde annotationem dat Livl. U.-B. III reg. p. 10 n. 156.

---

243. *1235 mart. 24 (nono kal. april.) Rige. Henricus, Osiliensis episcopus, confirmat fratribus militiae Christi a Godefrido praedecessore concessam tertiam Osiliae partem et addit Morne, Horele, trecentos uncos in Kylegunde.*

II, 143, unde edidit de Goetze l. c. 137, unde Livl. U.-B. III, 23 n. 141 a.

---

244. *1237 maii 12 (iiii idus maii p. a. 11). Gregorius papa IX (Grato dilectorum) praeceptori et fratribus militiae Christi in Livonia notum facit, se secundum preces eorum ipsos fratribus hospitalis s. Mariae Theutonicorum Ierusal. univisse.*

II, 140, unde ed. de Goetze l. c. 139; cf. Livl. U.-B. III reg. 11 n. 168.

Eodem tenore legato episcopo Mutinensi mutato exitu.

II, 140 v. Cum dato iiii id. maii, Turgenew I, 47 n. 51; 50 n. 54 e registris Vaticanis. Livl. U.-B. I, regest. n. 168 p. 42.

Eodem tenore episcopis Rigensi, Tharbatensi, Osiliensi, mutato exitu.

II, 140 v. In fine legitur: „Tria predicta privilegia sunt dompni Gregorii pape VIIII; sunt registrata". Ed. Raynald. 1237 cap. 64. Gruber orig. Liv. 274 n. 54. Script. rer. Livon. I, 402 n. 54. Livl. U.-B. I, 191 n. 149. E registris ipsis Gregorii IX Turgenew I, 49 n. 53.

---

245. *1251 febr. 24 (vi kal. martii) p. d. Inn. p. IV a. 8 Lugduni. Petrus, Albanensis et Guillelmus, Sabinensis episcopi et Iohannes tit. s. Laurentii in Lucina presbyter cardinales amicabilem compositionem faciunt inter Albertum, Livoniae et Prussiae archiepiscopum, ac Th(eodericum) magistrum et fratres hospitalis s. Mariae Theutonicorum in Prussia et Curonia.*

II, 137 et 143 v. Ex or. in archivo Regimontano (ubi etiam transsumtum perg. de 1393 mai. 29), ed. Livl. U.-B. I, 275 n. 218. v. Kotzebue Preufs. Gesch. I, 429.

---

246. *1251 mart. 3 Lugduni. Petrus, Albanensis et Guillelmus, Sabinensis episcopi ac Iohannes tituli s. Laurentii in Lucina presbyter cardinales Semigalliensem diocesim incorporant Rigensi.*

Petrus, miseratione divina Albanensis, et Guillelmus eadem miseratione Sabinensis episcopi, ac Iohannes, dei gratia tituli sancti Laurentii in Lucina presbiter cardinalis, omnibus Christi fidelibus, ad quos presens scriptum pervenerit, salutem in nomine Iesu Christi. Vestra noverit universitas evidenter, quod, cum dominus papa, diligenter attendens, quod quedam ordinationes, que Rigensem, Semigalliensem et Curoniensem tangebant ecclesias, reformationem et correctionem in quibusdam non immerito requirebant, correctionem et reformationem ordinationum huiusmodi nobis viva voce duxerit committendum; nos, attendentes, quod Rigensis ecclesia, que in dilatatione fidei christiane, utpote primitiva et precipua pre universis ecclesiis in partibus Livonie et Estonie, laboravit, adeo in suis iam fuerat diminuta limitibus, quod, nisi eiusdem ecclesie ampliarentur termini, paganorum incursibus, quibus frequentius conquassatur, resistere non valeret, nec divinus cultus, sicut ab eadem cepit ecclesia, debitum susciperet incrementum, ut eiusdem ecclesie sollicitudini condigno respondeatur affectu, terram, que Semigallia dicitur, auctoritate nobis in hac parte commissa diocesi eiusdem Rigensis ecclesie decrevimus uniendam, ita quod Rigensis episcopus ipsam Semigalliam cum omni iurisdictione et iure temporali et spirituali possideat, excepta tertia parte eiusdem Semigallie, quam fratres domus sancte Marie Theutonicorum cum decimis et omni iure et iurisdictione temporali possident et hactenus possederunt, et sic nullus de cetero in eadem Semigallia preficiatur episcopus, quia cum quedam pars[1] sit Rigensis diocesis, que tante latitudinis non existit, quod, si tota etiam conversa foret ad fidem, proprium non posset episcopum sustinere. Verum cum bone memorie S(ifridus) Maguntinus archiepiscopus discretum virum, fratrem Henricum dictum de Luccelburg de ordine fratrum minorum, facti illarum partium prorsus ignarus, in Semigalliensem episcopum auctoritate apostolica duxerit promovendum, nos eundem fratrem ad totam Curoniensem diocesim, nunc pastore vacantem, duximus transferendum, quam totam Curoniam sive Curlandiam pro sue diocesis terminis tam idem frater Henricus quam successores eius pacifice possideant et quiete, ita tamen, quod magister et fratres domus sancte Marie Theutonicorum in eadem Curonia duas partes eiusdem terre cum decimis et omni iure et iurisdictione temporali possideant, et eodem modo prefatus Curoniensis episcopus tertiam partem residuam eiusdem terre cum omni iure et iurisdictione temporali et spirituali pacifice possideat et quiete. Quia vero capitulo Rigensi ab eodem Rigensi episcopo ante presentem ordinationem nostram ducentorum uncorum in Donedange et Thargele in eadem Curoniensi diocesi redditus fuerant assignati, redditus ipsos prefatos capitulum exnunc in perpetuum cum decimis et omni temporali iurisdictione et iure retinere volumus et mandamus; quos tamen iidem capitulum a diocesano loci suscipient et etiam possidebunt, prout superius est expressum, tam in portione fratrum et capituli predictorum, quam in tota diocesi Curoniensi, episcopo diocesano omnibus iuribus reservatis, que non possunt nisi per episcopum exerceri. Et quoniam propter paganorum frequentes incursus et alia emergentia negotia peragenda Curoniensem episcopum in civitate Rigensi contingit sepius commorari, domum et aream, quam bone memorie Semigalliensis episcopus habuerat in eadem civitate Rigensi, eidem Curoniensi episcopo decernimus et volumus assignari, cum idem Curoniensis pretium, pro quo eedem domus et area redempte fuerunt, paratus Rigensi episcopo fuerit exhibere. Et, ne sedes metropolitica, que ab eodem domino papa de novo in illis partibus est creata, debito careat fundamento, ex sue titulo dignitatis decrevimus ordinandum, ut archiepiscopus, qui ad illam metropolim est assumptus, in civitate Rigensi predicta, que nobilior ex multis causis et habilior aliis ecclesiis illarum partium esse videtur, sedem archiepiscopalem constituat, secundum quod ei per litteras apostolicas est indultum. Si autem idem Rigensis episcopus cedere episcopatui Rigensi vel ad alium episcopatum se transferre voluerit, id ei auctoritate presentium indulgemus, et sic memoratus archiepiscopus nominatam Rigensem ecclesiam pro metropoli libere valeat adipisci; alioquin dictus Rigensis, quoad vixerit, pacifice in statu presenti tam in civitate quam diocesi Rigensi permaneat, eodem archiepiscopo tam in civitate Rigensi, quam per totam suam provinciam iurisdictionem metropoliticam exercente. Ut autem huiusmodi ordinatio, facta de consensu eiusdem archiepiscopi et fratris Theoderici dicti de Grueningen, magistri eiusdem domus sancte Marie Theutonicorum in Pruscia et Livonia, et discreti viri Alexandri sacriste, et Lamberti, canonici Rigensis, procuratorum episcopi et capituli Rigensis predictorum, et Ezelini, canonici sancti Theobaldi Metensis, procuratoris eiusdem fratris Henrici, quondam Semigalliensis episcopi, nunc vero episcopi Curoniensis, rata permaneat et inviolabiliter observetur, sigillorum nostrorum munimine, una cum sigillis predicti archiepiscopi ac memorati magistri, ipsam duximus roborandam. Datum Lugduni, v nonas martii, pontificatus domini Innocentii pape IV anno octavo.

II, 135v. mendose in confirmatione Innocentii IV de 1251 (v. infra). Ed. locis ibi citatis et ap. Nettelbladt Fasciculus rerum Curlandicarum I, 150 ad 1245, quem secuti editores scriptorum rerum Livonicarum I, 403 LV p. a. 3. Gruber Origines Livonicae 274 LV ad 1245.
1. quia que cum dampno pars B. „quia cum" abundat.

---

247. *1251 mart. 9 vii idus mart. p. n. a. 8 Lugduni. Innocentius papa IV (Ea que) confirmat trium cardinalium diffinitivam sententiam de 1251 febr. 24 (cf. supra n. 245).*

II, 137 in fine additur: CCCCLXXXVI. Ex transsumto de 1415 dec. 14 in archivo Regimontano ed. Livl. U.-B. I, 279 n. 220.

---

248. *1251 mart. 14 Lugduni. Innocentius papa IV confirmat reformationem Rigensis Semigallensis Curoniensis ecclesiarum.*

Innocentius episcopus servus servorum dei venerabilibus fratribus .. archiepiscopo Lyvonie et Pruscie ac .. Rigensi et .. Curoniensi episcopis et dilectis filiis capitulo Rigensi ac fratri Thetrico magistro et fratribus hospitalis sancte Marie Theutonicorum in Lyvonia et Curonia salutem et apostolicam benedictionem. Que de speciali mandato nostro sunt instituta provide ac salubriter ordinata, decet apostolica communire presidio, ut inconcusse robur firmitatis habeant et illabata persistant. Sane cum ordinationes, que Rigensem, Semigalliensem et Curoniensem tangebant ecclesias, reformatione et correctione indigere in aliquibus viderentur, nos ordinationes ipsas corrigendas et reformandas venerabilibus fratribus P(etro) Albanensi et Guillelmo Sabinensi episcopis ac dilecto filio nostris I(ohanni) tituli sancti Laurentii in Lucina presbitero cardinali duximus committendas, qui diligenter naturam huiusmodi negotii attendentes certam super hiis ordinationem vobis, frater archiepiscope ac fili magister, necnon procuratoribus vestris, fratres episcopi et filii capitulum, presentibus et consentientibus fecisse noscuntur, prout in patentibus litteris inde confectis et signatis sigillis episcoporum et cardinalis predictorum ac etiam vestris, iam dicti archiepiscope et magister, plenius continetur. Nos itaque vestris supplicationibus inclinati ordinationem huiusmodi per Albanensem ac Sabinensem episcopos et cardinalem prefatos super premissis provide factam ratam et firmam habentes eam auctoritate apostolica confirmamus et presentis scripti patrocinio communimus, tenorem autem litterarum ipsarum de verbo ad verbum presentibus fecimus annotari, qui talis est:

Petrus etc. de 1251 martii 3 Lugduni (supra n. 246).

Nulli ergo omnino hominum liceat hanc paginam nostre confirmationis infringere vel ei ausu temerario contraire. Si quis autem hoc attemptare presumpserit, indignationem omnipotentis dei et beatorum Petri et Pauli apostolorum eius se noverit incursurum. Datum Lugduni ii idus marcii pontificatus nostri anno octavo.

II, 135 v. sine dato, cum clausula: „Ita invenitur de verbo ad verbum in registro domini Innocentii pape IIII anno VIII cap. CCCCLXXXXII“. Editum hic ex originali optime conservato, cui appendent fila sericea rubra et flava, a possessore b. m. Daniele Friedlaender quondam Prussiae regi a secretis iustitiae consiliis nobiscum communicato. Signum archivi cuiusdam III c. In dorsi parte antrorsum subtus inverso legitur veterrima manu scriptum ad sinistram S, ad dextram: Scribe aliam Stephane. In dorso: Sancta Maria. R(script(. — littere de terra Curonie. Manu s. xiv ex.: Innocencius de IIII idus marcii anno eius octavo hevet bestediget de orderinge der prelaten Albanensis, Sabinensis und des cardinales sente Laurencius, dat dat bisschopdom van Semigallen sall hebben de (erasum: ercz) bisschop van Rige, uppe dat he sik desde beth moghe berghen, beholden deme orden sine gudere darinne, und do wort de bisschopt van Rige gemaket en erczebisschop, alze hirinne steit. Ok sande do de erczebisschop van Mens enen mynrebroder geheiten Hinrik Lutcelborch bestediget to Semigallen vor enen bisschop, den de vorbenonten prelaten do satten to Cwrlande, wonte dar do nyn bisscop en was, beholden den borderen ere twe part des landes mit aller rechti heit. Dein: ave Maria. Ediderunt ante Dogiel cod. dipl. Pol. V, 17 n. XXIV. Nettelbladt Fascic. rer. Curland. 150 (male ad 1245). Livl. U.-B. I, 281 n. 222, ubi etiam citantur copia in archivo Regimontano asservata et editio ap. Turgenew I, 70 n. LXXX. Gruber Origg. Livon. 274 LV. Scr. rer. Liv. I, 403 LV.

249. *1254 (sept. 13) in vigilia exaltationis sancte crucis Bohem. P(oppo) de Osternach, hospitalis s. Mariae Theutonicorum Ierusalem magister generalis, Livoniensi archiepiscopo eiusque suffraganeis notum facit se ad concordandum cum istis de lite contra fratres O. Th. Livoniae Theoderico de Gruninge, Alemanniae commendatori, plenam dedisse facultatem.*

Reverendis in Christo patribus ac dominis, .. dei gracia archiepiscopo Lyvonie, ac eiusdem suffraganeis, frater P(oppo) de Osternach, hospitalis sancte Marie Theotonicorum Ierosolimitani magister, devotam in domino reverentiam cum promptitudine famulandi. Paternitatem vestram scire volumus, quod fratri Th(eoderico) de Grunyngen, Alamannie commendatori, vobiscum conveniendi, ordinandi seu disponendi supra contentione, que inter vos ex una parte et fratres nostros Lyvonie ex parte altera vertitur, prout sibi expedire videbitur, liberam seu plenariam concedimus facultatem, ratum et gratum habentes, quicquid idem frater Th(eodericus) fecerit in premissis. Datum Bohem(ie), anno domini m cc l iiii, in vigilia exaltacionis sancte crucis.

II, 141 v. E transsumto de 1254 dec. 12 (cf. infra) ed. mendose Dogiel V, 20 n. 28, unde repetiit Livl. U.-B. I, 356 n. 274.

---

250. *1254 decbr. 12 in civitate Senonensi. Albertus, archiepiscopus Livoniae, Estoniae, Prussiae ac Rigensis ecclesiae, Henricus Osiliensis et Henricus Curoniensis episcopi, simul nomine Tharbatensis episcopi cum Theodorico de Groninge, praeceptore ordinis hospitalis s. Mariae Theutonicorum in Alemannia, cuius commissio (supra n. 249) de 1254 sept. 13 inseritur, nomine fratrum ordinis eius in Livonia conveniunt de obedientia per ordinem in Livonia episcopis facienda.*

Albertus, dei gracia archiepiscopus Lyvonie, Estonie, Pruscie ac Rigensis ecclesie, et eadem gracia Henricus Osiliensis et Henricus Curoniensis episcopi, omnibus Christi[1] fidelibus presentes inspecturis, salutem in nomine Iesu Christi[1]. Universitati vestre notum facimus et presentibus protestamur, quod, cum inter nos et dominum Tharbatensem episcopum ex una parte, et magistrum et fratres hospitalis sancte Marie Theutonicorum in Lyvonia ex altera super diversis articulis questio verteretur; convenientibus nobis archiepiscopo et Osiliensi et Curoniensi episcopis ante dictis apud civitatem Senonensem in crastino s. Nicolai confessoris, comparuit[2] ibidem magister Theodericus, dictus de Grunyngen, preceptor dicti ordinis hospitalis s. Marie Theutonicorum in Alemannia, vices agens magistri generalis in hac causa, qui litteras dicti magistri generalis exhibuit sub hac forma: Reverendis etc. frater P(oppo) etc. (cf. supra n. 249 de 1254 sept. 13). Habito igitur diligenti tractatu hinc et inde, in talem formam concorditer est conventum, quod dictus frater Theodericus nobis, archiepiscopo Rigensi et Osiliensi episcopo presentibus, et Tharbatensi episcopo, licet absenti, cuilibet nostrum, pro suo episcopatu obedientiam, quam magister de Lyvonia nobis iuxta continentiam litterarum super ea hincinde confectarum facere debet et tenetur, et quam ipse olim in dictis partibus magister existens ac post eum sui successores dominis Rigensi, Osiliensi ac Tharbatensi episcopis eo tempore presidentibus fecerant publice, in capitulo fratrum predicatorum dicti loci Senonensis fecit et dictos magistrum et fratres de Lyvonia taliter iurisdictioni ipsorum dominorum archiepiscopi et episcoporum subesse, qualiter in privilegiis super hiis hincinde confectis continetur[3], recognovit, insuper, quod dicti magister et fratres nobis, archiepiscopo et episcopis antedictis, de spiritualibus et temporalibus facient, secundum quod in privilegiis super hiis hincinde confectis plenius continetur. Et hec omnia fecit dictus preceptor sub protestatione sufficienti, quod ex huiusmodi interruptione consuetudinis, que talis est, quod dicta obedientia a magistro Lyvonie et infra terminos Lyvonie fieri consuevit, ordini ipsorum preiudicium nequaquam generetur, sed potius eadem consuetudo de cetero debet inviolabiliter observari. Postquam vero magister Anno vel eius successor obedienciam predictam fecerit nobis archiepiscopo et episcopis antedictis, prefatus preceptor Th(eodericus) erit a iam prestita obedientia absolutus. De ordinatione vero facta inter dominum Curoniensem et fratres in Curonia commorantes in speciali littera plenius continetur. Promisit etiam supradictus magister[4] Th(eodericus), quod per litteras et nuncium magistro et fratribus in Lyvonia constitutis auctoritate magistri generalis sibi in hac parte commissa districtius iniunget et mandabit, quod ipsi omnia supradicta faciant et observent, et quod de singulis querelis episcoporum eis[4] satisfaciant, ut tenentur. In omnium igitur premissorum testimonium[5] et munimen sigilla nostra cum predicti magistri Theoderici et predicatorum et minorum fratrum Senonensium sigillis presentibus sunt appensa. Datum in civitate Senonensi anno domini millesimo ducentesimo quinquagesimo quarto, in vigilia beate virginis Lucie.

II, 141 v. sine dato. Ex originali archivi tunc Varsoviensis ed. Dogiel Cod. Pol. dipl. V, 20 XXVIII, unde repetiit Livl. U.-B. I, 358 n. 277. 1. Christi — Christi deest B. 2. apparuit B. 3. continetur — confectis deest in B. 4. deest B. 5. cetera desunt B.

---

251. *1419 aug. 25 Florentiae. Martinus papa V revocat provisionem Wigando Grabow de Curoniensi praepositura factam declaratque privilegia oi. Thco. concessa, quod invitus non teneatur respondere provisionibus apostolicis seu legatorum, in vigore permanere.*

Martinus episcopus servus servorum dei ad futuram rei memoriam. Provisionis nostre debet provenire subsidio, ut dubia, que ex concessionibus per nos factis oriri posse arbitrantur, ne litis, anfractuum seu scandalorum parturiant fomentum, nostro moderamine declarentur. Dudum siquidem per nos accepto, quod dilectus filius Wygandus Grabow, clericus Curoniensis, cupiebat una cum dilectis filiis magistro et fratribus hospitalis beate Marie Theotonicorum Ierosolimitani in hospitali ipso, in quo certus fratrum numerus non existit, sub regulari habitu virtutum domino famulari quodque prepositura ecclesie Curoniensis per predictos fratres regi consueta, quam quondam Andreas de Cur, ipsius ecclesie prepositus, dum viveret, obtinebat, per eiusdem Andree obitum, qui extra Romanam curiam diem clausit extremum, vacaverat et vacabat, tunc nos certis iudicibus per quasdam, ut prefatum Wygandum, si foret ydoneus et aliud canonicum non obsisteret, auctoritate nostra in eodem hospitali, dummodo ex hoc nimium non gravaretur, facerent recipi in fratrem sibique iuxta ipsius hospitalis consuetudinem regularem habitum exhiberi ac de communibus ipsius hospitalis proventibus sicut uni ex aliis prefati hospitalis fratribus integre responderi ipsumque ibidem sincera in domino caritate tractari et nichilominus regularem professionem per eosdem fratres emitti solitam ab ipso Wygando, si eam in illorum manibus sponte emittere vellet, eadem auctoritate reciperent et admitterent, ac per alias nostras litteras dedimus in mandatis, ut preposituram predictam, que curata et dignitas maior post pontificalem in dicta ecclesia existit, sive ut premittitur, sive alias quovis modo aut ex alterius cuiuscumque persona vacaret, dummodo tunc non esset in ea alicui specialiter ius quesitum, cum omnibus iuribus et pertinenciis suis eidem Wygando, postquam in fratrem, ut premittitur, ipsius hospitalis receptus et sibi habitus ipse exhibitus foret et professionem emisisset, eandem conferre et assignare curarent, prout in eisdem litteris plenius continetur. Postmodum vero, sicut exhibita nobis nuper pro parte dictorum magistri et fratrum peticio continebat, orta inter dilectum filium Theodericum Tanken, fratrem dicti hospitalis, cui de prefata prepositura sic vacante ordinaria fuit auctoritate provisum quique illam assecutus extitit, ac eundem Wygandum super dicta prepositura et eius occasione materia questionis et causa huiusmodi per appellacionem dicti Theoderici ad sedem apostolicam legitime introducta, nos causam ipsam dilecto filio magistro Geminiano de Prato, capellano nostro et causarum palatii apostolici auditori, ad instanciam prefati Wygandi audiendam commisimus et fine[1] debito terminandam; ac successive, postquam idem auditor in ea ad nonnullos actus citra tamen conclusionem inter partes ipsas processerat, pro parte dicti Wygandi nobis exposito, quod a nonnullis assereretur, neutri ipsorum Wigandi et Theoderici in dicta prepositura seu ad eam ius competere; nos denuo prefato Wygando de ipsa prepositura sub certis modo et forma graciose concessimus provideri. Cum autem, sicut eadem peticio subiungebat, licet iuxta privilegia et indulta apostolica necnon consuetudines legitimas hospitalis eiusdem ipsi magister et fratres de quacunque prelatura seu dignitate vel baliva aut etiam quovis officio dicti hospitalis per quascumque dicte sedis aut legatorum eiusdem litteras providere alicui minime teneantur inviti sive earum pretextu ad illam vel illud admittere aut in dicti hospitalis fratrem recipere quemquam soliti non existant, an tamen per literas nostras necnon concessionem predictas ipsis privilegiis indultis et consuetudinibus derogari voluerimus, ab aliquibus hesitetur; nos ad huiusmodi ambiguitatis tollendum dubium per literas nostras et concessionem predictas, eciam sub quavis verborum forma concepte reperiantur, premissis privilegiis, indultis et consuetudinibus aut alicui ex illis minime derogari voluisse sive velle, sed illa nichilominus in suo vigore plenarie permansisse et remanere debere presentium serie declaramus, decernentes literas nostros et concessionem predictas ac quecumque inde secuta, in quantum eisdem privilegiis, statutis et consuetudinibus aut ipsorum alicui adversari sive detrahere videantur, nullius subsistere robore firmitatis, non obstantibus premissis ceterisque contrariis quibuscumque. Nulli ergo omnino hominum liceat hanc paginam nostre declaracionis et constitucionis infringere vel ei ausu temerario contraire. Si quis autem hoc attemptare presumpserit, indignacionem omnipotentis dei et beatorum Petri et Pauli apostolorum eius se noverit incursurum. Datum Florencie viii kalendus septembris pontificatus nostri anno secundo.

Garisendes. Pro Arpino

Io. Leonis 777.

IV, 246 v. Originale cum bulla plumbea in filis sericeis rubris et luteis pendente in archivo Regimontano citat Napiersky Index I, 208 n. 911, unde subscriptiones mutuavimus. 1. sine B.

IMPERATORUM ET REGUM ROMANORUM PRIVILEGIA GENERALIA.

252. *1212 („1213") mai. 10 ap. Nuremberg (vi id. mai. in l. xiv). Otto IV, Romanorum rex, hospitale Theutonicorum cum omnibus bonis in imperio sitis sub protectione sua suscipit.*

IV, 282. Boehmer reg. n. 169 ad 1212 annum revocandum edocet. Edd. Duellius Hist. ord. Theut. 11. Scheid Orig. Guelf. III, 819. (Feder) Hist. diplom. Unterricht von des .. T. R. O. Ballei Hessen. 1751. fol. n. 1. Hennes Cod. dipl. ord. Theut. 11.

253. *1214 sept. 5 in castris prope Iuliacum (ind. ii non. sept.). Fridericus II, Romanorum et Siciliae rex, concedit hospitali s. M. Th. i. I., ut, quicunque aliquid de bonis imperii possideat nomine feudi, licenter ac libere, quantum voluerit ex iisdem tanquam proprium illi conferre valeat.*

IV, 265. Edd. (Feder) Unterricht n. 3. Duellius Hist. ord. Theut. app. 13. Hennes Cod. ord. Theut. I, 14 n. 15. Huillard-Bréholles I, 313. Cf. Boehmer n. 92.

254. *1216 („1214") ianuar. 23 apud Hagenowiam (x kal. febr. ind. iiii). Fridericus II, Romanorum et Siciliae rex, attenta honestate religionis in domo hospitali s. M., quae est Theutonicorum in Ierusalem, et honestate personarum illic sub domino militantium concedit, ut fratres domus semper in curia imperii locum familiaritatis obtineant, et, ut melius apud imperium negotia sua promovere possint, pro feudo concedit, ut, quotiescunque magister bonis eorum in partibus Alemaniae praefectus ad curiam imperii accesserit, familiae curiae imperialis sit adscriptus et ipsi cum uno socio, fratre domus, et cum sex equitaturis tanquam alii familiae in omnibus necessariis abundanter provideatur. Item concedit domui, ut ad procurandam eleemosynam imperialem continue duos domus fratres curia imperii habeat vicissim venientes et recedentes, quorum alter semper in curia remaneat; pro utroque tres equitaturae cum omnibus aliis necessariis habeantur et ipsis de curia abundanter provideatur.*

IV, 264. Edd. Duellius Hist. ord. Theut. app. 12 XIII. (Feder) Unterricht n. 2 ex originali. — Brandenburgische Usurpationsgeschichte 87, mendose Hennes I, 20 n. 20. Huillard-Bréholles I, 438. Cf. Boehmer n. 158.

255. *1221 april. 10 Tarenti (iiii idus april.). Fridericus II imperator (Excellentia imperialis) attendens, qualiter domus h. s. M. Th. in I. ab avo suo Friderico imperatore propagata in multiplices fructus prodierit laude dignos et a patre suo Henrico imperatore rebus ac libertatibus premunita incrementum susceperit, praeterea ob celebrem vitam et labores assiduos Hermanni magistri et fratrum concedit, ut, quicunque aliquid de bonis imperii nomine feodi possideat, licenter ac libere quantum voluerit tanquam proprium eidem hospitale conferre valeat.*

IV, 283. Editum in Brandenburgische Usurpationsgesch. 92; unde apud Hennes Cod. dipl. I, 59 n. 56. Huillard-Bréholles II, 159. Cf. Karoli IV confirmationem de 1354 ianuarii 2 in Livl. U.-B. regesta n. 951. Cf. Boehmer n. 442.

---

256. *1221 april. 10 Tarenti (iiii id. april.). Fridericus II imperator (Per presens) hospitale s. M. Th. in Ierusalem „tanquam locum illum, qui a felicibus augustis progenitoribus nostris recolende memorie principium habuit“, et domos omnes inde derivatas, fratres et confratres, sub speciali sua protectione recipit; privilegia omnia et concessiones confirmat, statuitque, ne per totum imperium quidquam pro plateatico, passagio, theloneo, portagio, ripatico, falangatico vel quolibet alio iure terra marique, in fluminibus vel in aquis solvere teneantur, neve glandaticum, herbaticum vel aquaticum tribuant pro animalibus suis.*

Ex originali Vindobonensi ed. Hennes Cod. dipl. I, 57 n. 54; unde Huillard-Bréholles II, 156. Cf. Boehmer n. 443. Memoratur hic ob verba de principio ordinis.

---

257. *1221 aprili Tarenti. Fridericus II imperator (Inter alia) domum h. s. M. Th. in Ierusalem a praedecessoribus suis propagatam et ab Henrico (VI) patre rebus ac libertatibus praemunitam ob fidelitatem honestamque vitam Hermanni magistri et fratrum, dein ob labores eorum assiduos fidei christianae impensos cum derivatis ab ipsa domibus, fratres et confratres cum bonis eorum per totum imperium, subditos eorum velut etiam legationem ac negotia exercentes sub speciali protectione recipit et domui omnia privilegia et possessiones confirmat, eximens ab omni onere et exactione, et concedens libertatem aquarum, herbarum, lignorum ubique per proprias imperii terras ad domorum usus. Eximit ipsos a portatico, plateatico, falangatico, ripatico, aliis exactionibus terra marique et in omnibus fluminibus vetatque fratres de possessionibus hospitalis sine iudicio et iustitia „dissasiri“. Confirmat fratribus, ut quicunque aliquid de bonis imperii nomine feudi teneat, licenter et libere tanquam proprium conferre valeat hospitali.*

IV, 266. 286. 288. 291. 299 v.; versio Germanica: 310 v. R. 133 inter Marburgensia. — Transsumtum Casparis Pomesaniensis episcopi de 1441 in Regimontano archivo. Edd. Luenig Reichsarchiv VII, 3. Duellius Hist. ord. Theut. append. p. 14 n. 15. Ludewig Rel. Ms. VI, 44. Schurzfleisch Hist. Ensiferorum 11. (Feder) Unterricht n. 5. Brandenburg. Usurpationsgesch. 90. Hennes cod. ord. Theut. I, 60 n. 57. Huillard-Bréholles II, 160. Ed. Germ. Schannat Sammlung alter histor. Schrifften u. Documenten. Franckfurt a. M. 1727. 4. I, 70. Cf. Boehmer n. 441. Or. c. bulla aurea Vindobonae. Transsumtum Casparis Pomes. ep. de 1441 Regimonti.

---

258. *1222 dec. ap. Precinam. Fridericus II imperator sancit, ne quis, postquam domus s. M. Th., quae avi et patris suorum et sua structura sit specialis, religionem assumpserit et habitum gestaverit, super debitis ante hunc susceptum contractis, requiratur aut ea solvere compellatur, sed illi pro ipsis debitis teneantur, ad quorum dominium haereditatis et bonorum successio devoluta sit, etiamsi ipsi fratres, quum ordinem assumpserint, partem bonorum suorum domui contulerint.*

IV, 267 v. Edd. Duellius Histor. ord. Theut. app. n. 15. Hennes Cod. ord. Theut. I, 67 n. 62. Huillard-Bréholles II, 282. Cf. Boehmer n. 488.

---

259. *1223 ian. Capuae. Fridericus II imperator Hermanno magistro hospitalis s. M. Th. in I. petente confirmat huic concessionem a se ante susceptum imperium (scilicet 1214 sept. 5 in castris apud Iuliacum supra n. 253) factam, ex qua, quicunque aliquid de bonis imperii possideat nomine feudi, quantum voluerit inde hospitali libere tanquam proprium conferre possit.*

IV, 268 v. 274 v. R. 109 e domo Buckheim. Edd. Duellius Hist. ord. Theut. app. n. 15. (Feder) Unterricht n. 4. — Brandenburgische Usurpationsgeschichte 94 n. 44. Huillard-Bréholles II, 294. Cf. Boehmer n. 496.

---

260. *1223 mart. ap. Ferentinum. Fridericus II imperator considerans, quod Henricus imperator domum h. s. M. Th. I. fundaverit et dotaverit, in qua divini servitii cultus et religio conserventur, pauperum et infirmorum procuretur necessitas, dum contra paganos fratres se offerant victimas, quum coronationis suae die ad preces suas Romana ecclesia domui contulerit, ut ecclesiarum ad sustentationem fratrum commorantium in servitio terrae sanctae concessarum, assignato vicariis satis magno proventu pro victu honesto et iuribus episcopalibus, caeteros proventus usibus suis habeant deputatos; et ipse sancit, ut prorsus domus eadem in omnibus ecclesiis tam imperii quam patrimonii imperatoris, in quibus ius patronatus et repraesentationis imperator habet, hanc habeat potestatem, ut vacantibus ecclesiis portionem mobilium rerum ad opus imperii recipi solitum ad usus suos retineant et vacantium ecclesiarum proventus per annum a die vacationis percipiant, clericis honesto sumptu proviso. Pergit:*

— — res et bona ecclesiastica fideliter interim et efficaciter procurantes, nec eis preiudicet, si infra annum prelatus in eis fuerit constitutus, quin omnia supradicta percipiant, prout superius est expressum. Post completum vero annum procuracionem et percepcionem proventuum et usufructuum earundem ecclesiarum sequentis scilicet temporis manibus et custodie illius vel illorum, qui in eis rite fuerint instituti, debeant resignare, nec se inde ulterius intromittant, nisi ecclesiam vacare contigerit, ut iurisdictionem exerceant constitutam, quam non nisi uno anno, quociens aliqua vel alique ecclesie vacaverint in percipiendis proventibus et usufructibus vacancium ecclesiarum, sicut superius continetur, decernimus valituram, prohibentes firmiter et mandantes, ut nulla persona ecclesiastica vel mundana, alta vel humilis, scultetus („seculi heres"!), advocatus, ministerialis vel officialis eandem domum contra presentis constitutionis et concessionis paginam inquietare vel molestare presumat. Quod qui presumpserit, indignacionem nostram se noverit incursurum, insuper in penam temeritatis sue c libras auri componat, medietatem videlicet nostro erario applicandam et reliquam medietatem predicte domui iniuriam pacienti. Ad huius autem constitutionis et concessionis nostre paginam et robur valiturum perpetuo presens privilegium fieri et aurea bulla, typario nostre maiestatis, impressa iussimus communiri. Huius autem rei testes sunt (*etc. fere ut ap. H.-B. II, 338 f. sed paucis transpositis, aliis depravatis nominibus, inter Eberardum de Wintersteten et Willelmum de Aquisgrano inseritur „Arnoldus de Geminihe" [„Gemenec"]*).

I, 41. IV, 270. Edd. Duellius Hist. ord. Theut. app. p. 16 n. 18. (Feder) Unterricht n. 6. Brand. Usurpationsgesch. 96 n. 45. Huillard-Bréholles II, 336 diploma fere concinens cum nostro usque p. 338 „prelegitur deputatos"; inde a quo loco duo apographa in B. I, 41 et IV, 270 paulo fusius quam diploma de aprili ap. Brandenburg. Usurpationsgesch. 98. Hennes I, 68 n. 64. Huillard-Bréholles II, 339, in archivo Stuttgartensi bis originaliter exsistens, pergunt modo citato. Cf. Boehmer n. 509.

---

261. *1223 april. (pro martio) ap. Ferentinum. Friderici II imperatoris modo citato diplomati de ecclesiis vacantibus domui h. s. M. Th. i. I. competentibus simillimum.*

IV, 272. Or. c. s. Vindobonae. Duo originalia, alterum etiamnunc cum sigillo cereo pendente, in archivo Stuttgartensi. R. 106 e domo Buckheim. R. 177 inter Thuringica. Edd. Brandenburg. Usurpationsgesch. 98. Hennes Cod. ord. Theut. I, 68 n. 64. Huillard-Bréholles II, 339. Cf. Boehmer n. 513.

---

262. *1227 mart. 27 Aquisgrani in curia solempni (vi kal. april. ind. xv). Heinricus VII, Romanorum rex, fratribus domus Theut. s. M. i. I. concedit, ut privilegia et confirmationes e curia regali vel imperiali sine ulla exactione obtineant, et ad imitationem Friderici imperatoris patris confirmat veterem iustitiam, ut praeceptori Alemanniae in curia imperiali praesenti tanquam familiae ascripto septem personarum et equorum sumptus et expensae ministrentur et trium equorum eleemosynario fratri, scilicet eleemosynas pauperibus eroganti.*

IV, 273 v. Editum in Brandenburg. Usurpationsgesch. ex originali archivi quondam Mergenthemensis p. 100 n. 47; apud Duellium Hist. ord. Theut. app. p. 18 n. 19 ad martii 29 paulo breviori forma tantum de familiaritate in curia generaliter agens; coll. cum copia authentica in archivo Stuttgartensi, Huillard-Bréholles III, 309.

---

263. *1242 iunio Hagenowiae (ind. xv). Conradus, Friderici filius, in Romanorum regem electus, heres regni Ierusalem, transsumit et ratum habet*

privilegium a Friderico II patre 1223 ian. Capuae hospitali s. Mariae de domo Theutonicorum concessum (supra n. 259).

IV, 274 v. Ed. in Brandenburg. Usurpationsgesch. 102, unde collatum cum copia authentica in archivo Stuttgartensi, Huillard-Bréholles VI, 838. Cf. Boehmer n. 50.

---

264. *1257 nov. 28 Nussiae. Ricardus, Romanorum rex, fratribus domus s. M. Th. privilegia, immunitates, libertates, iura, exemtiones a praedecessoribus concessa confirmat.*

IV, 276 v. Cf. Boehmer Reg. 35, qui citat (Feder) Unterr. n. 9; Brandenb. Usurpationsgesch. 103 ex or.; Gercken Cod. dipl. Brand. VII, 106 XXXVI; Gebauer Leben König Richards 362.

---

265. *1273 nov. 14 Coloniae (xviii kal. dec. r. n. a. l.). Rudolfus rex magistrum et fratres h. s. M. d. Th. I., subditos et bona eorum in protectionem suam suscipit.*

IV, 277 v. Edd. (Feder) Unterricht n. 10. Duellius Hist. ord. Theut. app. 18 n. 20. Brandenburg. Usurpationsgesch. 103 ex or. Gerbert Cod. epistolaris Rudolfi regis 16 sine dato. Cf. Boehmer n. 21.

---

266. *1274 febr. 21 Hagenowiae. Rudolfus, Romanorum rex, vetat ordinem Theutonicum turbari ob generalem commissionem de imperii bonis revocandis usque ad speciale mandatum.*

Rudolfus, dei gracia Romanorum rex semper augustus, omnibus advocatis, officialibus ac procuratoribus dilectis fidelibus suis graciam suam et omne bonum. Ad noxam vergere nonnumquam cernitur, quod salubriter ad remedium providetur. Proclivis enim est cursus ad malum ac imitatricem natura se indicat vitiorum, dum sub pietatis specie committitur inpietas ac veritati commoditas racionique prerogat se voluntas. Cupientes itaque sic bona et iura sacri imperii iam multis dimembrata temporibus ad debite integritatis formam reducere, quod alias non oporteat iniurias, iacturam et dispendia tollerare, presertim autem viros religiosos, quibus mundane conversacionis homines plerumque infesti sunt opido et nacta materia malignandi ac exercenda in ipsos malicia gratulantur, presentibus duximus declarandum, quod occasione generalis commissionis vobis facte de bonis imperialibus et quibuscumque detentis hactenus ad nostre dicionis dominium revocandis dilectis in Christo fratribus hospitalis sancte Marie domus Theutonicorum Iherusalem nullam volumus turbacionis materiam generari, sed bona, que possident, licet sint vel asserantur imperialia, in ipsorum placitum nobis est potestate resistere, donec personaliter per speciale mandatum aliud duxerimus disponendum. In mente etenim revolvimus ac revolvendo cognovimus, quod racione bonorum imperialium iidem fratres in bonis propriis possent recipere detrimentum. Eapropter revocacionem eorum, que imperialia detinent, nobis specialiter providimus reservandam. Datum Hagen(ovie) nono kalendas martii regni nostri anno primo.

IV, 277. Cf. Boehmer n. 58.

---

267. *1293 mai. 23 in Bopardia (x kal. iun.). Adolfus rex magistri et fratrum h. s. M. d. Theutonicae Ierusalem protectionem suscipit eisque privilegia praedecessorum et aliorum confirmat.*

IV, 278 v. Edd. (Feder) Unterricht von der Ballei Hessen n. 11. Brandenb. Usurpationsgesch. 105 ex or. Citat Boehmer Reg. 125.

---

268. *1298 sept. 22 in Gebesedeln ap. Rotenburg (x kal. oct.). Albertus, Romanorum rex, imitatur Rudolfi regis protectorias litteras de 1273 nov. 14 (supra n. 265).*

IV, 279 v. et 284 v. Ed. Brandenburg. Usurpationsgesch. 106 ex or. Citat Boehmer 52.

---

269. *1309 mart. 6 Spirae (ii non. mart.). Heinricus VII, Romanorum rex, imitatur Rudolfi regis protectorias litteras de 1273 nov. 14 (supra n. 265).*

IV, 280 v. Edd. Brandenburg. Usurpationsgesch. 107 ex or. (Feder) Unterricht von der Ballei Hessen n. 13. Cf. Boehmer n. 40.

---

270. *1323 april. 17 apud Nuremberg (xv kal. mai.). Ludowicus imperator magistro et fratribus h. s. M. d. Th. I. confirmat insertum privilegium de 1298 sept. 22 in Gebesedeln apud Rotenburg. Alberti regis (supra n. 268).*

IV, 284. Ed. Brandenburg. Usurpationsgesch. 109 n. 55 ex or.

---

271. *1330 mai. 5 in Monaco. Ludowicus, Romanorum imperator, confirmat domui Theutonicae insertum Ottonis IV privilegium de 1212 mai. 10 Norinbergae (supra n. 252).*

Ludowicus, dei gracia Romanorum imperator semper augustus, honorabilibus et religiosis viris preceptori generali, commendatoribus ceterisque singularibus fratribus hospitalis sancte Marie de domo Theotonica, fidelibus suis devotis, gratiam suam et omne bonum. Celsitudinis nostre celsa sublimitas ad hoc precipuum sue debet consideracionis aciem inclinare, qualiter devotis imperii et precipue personis divinis dedicatis obsequiis ob sue probitatis et devocionis merita augmentet commoda et honores. Per hoc enim imperium principantis gloria ineffabili a subditis sublimatur, subditi quoque ad obsequendum alliciuntur prompcius et ad bene merendum fervencius inducuntur. Ex parte itaque vestra nostre celsitudini extitit humiliter supplicatum, quatenus privilegium vobis concessum per dive memorie Ottonem quartum, imperatorem Romanum, predecessorem nostrum, imperiali benivolencia confirmare dignaremur. Cuius quidem privilegii tenor sequitur in hec verba:

Otto quartus etc. de 1213 (sc. 1212) maii 10 Nuremberg (supra n. 252).

Nos itaque intacte fidei puritatem ac sincere devocionis fervorem, quem ad nos et sacrum habetis imperium, piis considerantes oculis[1], cupientes vos speciali beneficiorum munificencia graciosius decorari, vestris peticionibus ostium augustalis clemencie reserantes privilegium prescriptum cum toto suo tenore gratum et ratum habentes presentis scripti patrocinio perpetuo valituro ex certa sciencia ratificamus, approbamus, confirmamus ac eciam de novo concedimus et innovamus. Nulli ergo omnino hominum liceat hanc nostre rectificacionis, approbacionis et confirmacionis paginam infringere aut ei ausu temerario contraire. Si quis autem contravenire presumpserit, preter indignacionem nostram, quam ipsum[2] incurrere volumus ipso facto, penam centum librarum auri puri, quarum medietatem fisco, id est nostre imperiali camere, reliquam vero iniuriam passis applicari volumus, se noverit incurrisse[3]. In cuius rei testimonium presentes conscribi et nostre maiestatis sigillo iussimus communiri. Datum in Monaco die sabbati post invencionem sancte crucis anno domini millesimo tricentesimo tricesimo regni nostri anno sexto decimo imperii vero tercio.

IV, 281 v. Orig. Stuttgart. citat Boehmer n. 1123. 1. ex uotis B. 2. deest B. 3. B.

---

272. *1330 mai. 5 in Monaco. Ludowicus imperator domui Theutonicae confirmat privilegium de 1221 april. 10 Tarenti. Friderici II imperatoris (supra n. 255).*

Ludowicus, dei gracia Romanorum imperator semper augustus, honorabilibus et religiosis preceptori generali, commendatoribus ceterisque singularibus fratribus hospitalis sancte Marie de domo Theotonica, fidelibus suis devotis, graciam suam et omne bonum. Celsitudinis nostre celsa sublimitas ad hoc precipuum sue debet consideracionis aciem inclinare, qualiter devotis imperii et precipue personis divinis dedicatis obsequiis ob sue probitatis et devocionis merita augmentet commoda et honores. Per hoc enim imperium principantis gloria ineffabili a subditis sublimatur, subditi quoque ad obsequendum alliciuntur prompcius et ad bene merendum fervencius inducuntur. Ex parte itaque vestra nostre celsitudini extitit humiliter supplicatum, quatenus privilegium vobis concessum per dive memorie Fridericum secundum, imperatorem Romanum, predecessorem nostrum, imperiali benivolencia confirmare dignaremur. Cuius quidem privilegii tenor sequitur in hec verba:

In nomine sancte et individue trinitatis. Fridericus secundus etc. de 1221 aprilis 10 Tarenti (supra n. 255).

Nos itaque intacte fidei puritatem ac sincere devocionis fervorem, quem ad nos et sacrum habetis imperium piis considerantes oculis[1], cupientes vos speciali beneficiorum munificencia graciosius decorari, vestris peticionibus ostium augustalis clemencie reserantes privilegium prescriptum cum toto suo tenore gratum et ratum habentes presentis scripti patrocinio perpetuo valituro ex certa sciencia ratificamus, approbamus, confirmamus ac eciam de novo concedimus et innovamus. Nulli ergo omnino hominum liceat hanc nostre ratificacionis, approbacionis et confirmacionis paginam infringere aut ei ausu temerario contraire. Si quis autem contravenire presumpserit, preter indignacionem nostram, quam ipsum incurrere volumus ipso facto, penam centum librarum auri puri, quarum medietatem fisco, id est nostre imperiali camere, reliquam vero iniuriam passis applicari volumus, se noverit incursurum. In cuius rei testimonium presentes conscribi et nostre maiestatis sigillo iussimus communiri. Datum in Monaco die sabbati post invencionem sancte crucis sub anno domini millesimo tricentesimo tricesimo regni nostri anno sexto decimo imperii vero tercio.

IV, 283. Originale Stuttgartense citat Boehmer n. 1124. 1. exuotis B.

---

273. *1331 dec. 20 in vigilia Thome apostoli Franckenfurt. Ludowicus imperator confirmat magistro et fratribus h. s. M. Hierosolymitani domus Theutonicae privilegium de 1221 april. Tarenti. Friderici II imperatoris (supra n. 257).*

IV, 285 v. Edd. (Feder) Hist. dipl. Unterricht n. 14. Brandenburg. Usurpationsgesch. 110 ex or. Cf. Boehmer n. 1392.

---

274. *1347 nov. 18 in Nuremberch (xiiii kal. dec.). Karolus IV, Romanorum rex, supplicantibus Wolframo de Nellenburg, praeceptore Alamanniae, et Bertholdo, burggravio de Nuremberch, provinciali Franconiae, confirmat fratribus h. s. M. Hierosolymitani d. Theutonicae privilegium de 1221 april. Tarenti. Friderici II imperatoris (supra n. 257).*

IV, 288 et 299. Edd. (Feder) Hist. dipl. Unterricht n. 15. de Ludewig Reliquiae Mss. Francofurti et Lipsiae 1724. VI, 43. Lünig Teutsches Reichsarchiv XVI, 9. Brandenburg. Usurpationsgesch. 115 n. 59 ex or.

---

275. *1347 dec. 1 (am sampcztag nach sant Andres tag) Nurnberg. Karoli IV regis protectoria pro ordinis Theutonici hominibus in imperii bonis sedentibus et vice versa.*

IV, 290 et 296 v. E copiario Regimontano R. e domo Norinbergensi n. 24 p. 14 ed. I. Voigt Cod. dipl. Pruss. III, 78 n. 55.

---

276. *1355 dec. 13 Nuremberg (an sant Lucien tag). Karolus IV imperator confirmat magistro et toti universitati domus Theutonicae s. M. h. Hierosolymitani omnia privilegia a praedecessoribus concessa.*

IV, 294 v. et 303 sine testibus. Germanice ed. Schannat Sammlung alter historischer Schrifften und Documenten. Franckfurt am Mayn 1727. 4. I, 26.

---

277. *1355 dec. 17 Nurenberg. Karolus IV imperator Theutonico ordini confirmat omnia privilegia a praedecessoribus suis concessa.*

In nomine sancte et individue trinitatis feliciter amen. Karolus quartus, divina favente clemencia Romanorum imperator semper augustus et Boemie rex, ad perpetuam rei memoriam. Etsi imperatorie maiestatis circumspecta benignitas universorum saluti dignatur intendere et publica commoda frequenti sollicitudine promovere, laborat plus de subditorum quiete contenta, quam si proprii thesauri tumulos adaugeat; ad illos tamen quadam singulari gracia benigne dirigitur, qui sub honorande professione virtutis grata religione militant et divinis laudibus insistentes gratum reddunt obsequium altissimo creatori. Sane pro parte religiosorum magistri generalis et tocius universitatis fratrum et Cristi militum domus Theutonice ordinis sancte Marie hospitalis Ierosolimitani, devotorum imperii et dilectorum nobis fidelium, cesario culmini nostro nuper oblata supplicacio continebat, quatenus ordini et universitati ipsorum tam in capite quam in membris universa et singula privilegia, litteras, libertates, gracias et indulta, que et quas a recolende memorie divis Romanorum imperatoribus et regibus predecessoribus nostris super quibuscumque possessionibus, rebus, iuribus aut honoribus obtinuisse noscuntur, approbare, ratificare et confirmare de imperialis celsitudinis gracia dignaremur. Nos, consideracione dei omnipotentis ad honorem gloriosissime virginis, beatissime genitricis ipsius, cuius preciose vocabulo decoratur tytulus ordinis supradicti, habito respectu ad multiplicia merita probitatis et indefesse virtutis constanciam, quibus ordo predictus et clari professores ipsius nos et ipsum sacrum imperium sollicitis animis et pervigili studio frequencius honorarunt, presertim cum supplicatio predicta de fonte racionis emanet et iuste petentibus non sit denegandus assensus, animo deliberato, sano principum, baronum et procerum nostrorum et sacri imperii accedente consilio ordini supradicto tam in capite quam in membris universa et singula privilegia sive litteras, que et quas super bonis antedicti ordinis in genere et singularium locorum, domorum seu habitacionum in specie, in quibuscumque eciam regnis, principatibus, comitatibus, dominiis sive terris aut insulis consistant, quibuscumque iuribus, possessionibus, proprietatibus, castris, civitatibus, terris, provinciis, territoriis, vasallis, vasallagiis, feodis, feodatariis, iudiciis, theoloneis, vectigalibus, daciis, monetis, gabellis, libertatibus, emunitatibus, honoribus, obvencionibus, proventibus, redditibus et singulis quibuscumque rebus, utilitatibus sive emolumentis, quibuscumque eciam specialibus designentur vocabulis, a divis Romanorum imperatoribus et regibus, predecessoribus nostris, obtinuerunt hactenus, in omnibus suis tenoribus, sentenciis, punctis et clausulis de verbo ad verbum, prout scripta seu scripte sunt, acsi tenores omnium forent inserti presentibus, eciamsi de hiis iure vel consuetudine deberet fieri mencio specialis, auctoritate imperiali et ex certa nostra sciencia approbamus, ratificamus et de singulari benignitatis gracia confirmamus. Nulli ergo omnino hominum liceat hanc nostre approbacionis, ratificacionis et confirmacionis paginam infringere vel ei ausu temerario contraire.

Si quis autem contrarium attemptare presumpserit, penam centum librarum auri puri se noverit irremissibiliter incurrisse, quarum medietatem imperiali fisco[1] nostro sive erario, reliquam vero partem ipsis fratribus et eorum ordini volumus applicari.

Signum serenissimi principis et domini *(Locus monogrammatis.)* domini Karoli quarti, Romanorum imperatoris invictissimi et gloriosissimi Boemie regis.

Testes huius rei sunt venerabilis Gerlacus, sancte sedis Maguntine archiepiscopus, sacri Romani imperii per Germaniam archicancellarius; et magnificus Rupertus senior, comes palatinus Reni, archidapifer et dux Bavarie; Rudolphus, dux Saxonie, archimarescallus sacri Romani imperii; necnon illustres Bolko Falkembergensis, Bolko[2] Opuliensis, Iohannes Oppavie et Przimislaus[3] Teschinensis duces; et spectabiles Iohannes Nurembergensis, Burghardus Magdeburgensis burgravii et alii quam plures presencium sub bulla aurea typario nostre maiestatis impressa testimonio litterarum. Datum Nurenberg anno domini millesimo tricentesimo quinquagesimo quinto indiccione octava xvi kalendas ianuarii, regnorum vero nostrorum anno decimo imperii autem primo.

IV, 293. 1. fistcho B. 2. Balko B. 3. przmislaus B.

---

278. *1355 dec. 17 Nuremberg (xvi kal. ian.). Karolus IV imperator petentibus Wolframo de Nellenburg, praeceptore Alemanniae, et Rudolfo de Houmborch, provinciali Bohemiae et Moraviae, fratribus h. s. M. Hierosolymitanae domus Theutonicae confirmat privilegium de 1221 april. Tarenti. Friderici II imperatoris (supra n. 257).*

IV, 290 v. Ed. Duellius Hist. ord. Theut. app. 19 n. 21 ad xv kal. ianuarii. (Feder) Hist. dipl. Unterricht n. 5.

---

279. *1365 april. 19 Heilprunn (an dem nehesten sunabende nach dem heiligen ostertage regnorum 19 i. 11). Karolus IV imperator omnes imperii fideles iubet, si frater ordinis Theutonici in Alemannia Philippo de Bickenbach, magistro ordinis per Alemanniam, vel successoribus non obedierit et statuta violaverit, monentem magistrum adiuvare, ut ad obedientiam reducat.*

IV, 298. Ed. Schannat Sammlung alter historischer Schrifften und Documenten. Franckfurt am Mayn 1727. 4. I, 5, ubi male in margine: 1363.

---

280. *1376 sept. 1 zu Nuremberg (an sente Egidien tage r. 31 i. 22). Karolus IV imperator petente Iohanne de Heyn, magistro d. Theutonicae s. M. ordinis hospitalis Hierosolymitani per Alemanniam et Italiam, omnibus imperii fidelibus mandat, ut ordinis fratres, homines, domus, bona privilegiis imperialibus uti patiantur neve exactionibus quibuslibet aggravent.*

IV, 295 v. Ed. Schannat Sammlung I, 18 n. V.

---

281. *1378 aug. 19 Nuremberg (an dem nehisten donirstage noch unser frauwen tag assumptionis r. R. 33, B. 32, imp. 24). Karolus IV imperator repristinat regales suas litteras:*

1347 dec. 1 (am sampcztage nach sant Andres tag) Karoli IV regis etc. (supra n. 275).

IV, 296. Ed. (Feder) Hist. dipl. Unterricht n. 17.

---

282. *1383 oct. 17 Nurenberg (an nehesten sunabende nach sant Gallen tag B. 21, R. 8). Wenceslaus, Romanorum et Bohemiae rex, petente Seyfrido de Venyngen magistro ordinis s. M. hospitalis Hierosolymitani domus Theutonicae per Alemanniam, confirmat privilegium de 1355 dec. 13 Nurenberg Karoli IV (v. supra n. 276).*

IV, 302 v. Ed. Schannat Sammlung I, 26.

---

283. *1383 oct. 17 (xvi kal. nov.) Nuremberg. Wenceslaus, Romanorum et Boemiae rex, petente Seyfrido de Veningen, ordinis s. M. h. Hierosolymitani domus Theutonicae praeceptore per Alemanniam generali, confirmat privilegium*

1355 dec. 17 Nuremberg. Karoli IV (supra n. 278), confirmans privilegium.

1221 april. Tarenti. Friderici II imperatoris (supra n. 257).

IV, 299. Ediderunt Duellius app. n. 19. (Feder) Hist. dipl. Unterricht n. 18.

---

284. *1389 mai. 7 Ellebogen. Wenceslaus, Romanorum et Bohemiae rex, ordinem Theutonicum ob Seyfridi de Venygen, magistri ord. Th. per Alemanniam, merita ab omni hospitalitatis onere et aliis exactionibus eximit.*

Wir Wenczlaw, von gots gnaden Romischer kunig, zu allen zyten merer des reichs und kunig zu Beheim, enbieten allen und iglichen fursten, geistlichen und werntlichen, graven, freyen herren, dinstluten, rittern, knechten, amptluten, pflegern, hauptleuten, reten und gemeinden der stetten und allen anderen unsern und des reichs undertanen und getrewen, in welicherley adel, wirden ader wesen die sein, den dieser brieff geczeiget wirdet, unser gnad und alles gute. Lieben getruwen, als wir vormals an vergangen zyten die geistlichen meister und brüder des Dütschen ordens in Deutschen landen, unsere lieben andechtigen, ire heuser, lute und güter in unser und des reichs sunderliche schucze und schirme genomen und empfangen haben, und sie auch in unser camer gehoren und uns und dem reiche und niemanden anders sten zu versprechen; also haben wir durch redlicher und annemer dienste willen, die uns und dem reiche der ersame Seyfrid von Venygen, meister Dutsches ordens in Deutschen landen, unser rate und lieber andechtiger, offt und dicke getan hat, teglichen tut und furbas tun sol und mag in kunftigen czeiten, denselben Deutschen orden alle und ygliche seine heusere, lute und guter, wie die genant und wo die gelegen sein, von allerley gastungen, wagenferten, diensten und allen andern beswerungen, welicherley die weren, gnediclichen gefryet und fryen sie von Römischer kuniglicher machte in crafft dicz brieffs und meynen, seczen und wollen, das sie sulicher gastungen, wagenferten, dinsten und allen andern beswerungen furbas mer ledig und genczlich uberhaben sein und damit uns und dem reiche und niemanden anders gewarten sollen. Darumb gebieten wir euch allen und ewer yglichem besunder ernstlichen und vestiglichen bey unsern und des reichs hulden, das ir die obgenant meister seiner und seins ordens huser, guter und lute mit sulichen gastungen, wagenferten, dinsten und anderen sachen furbasz mer nicht besweret noch dringet in dheine weis, sunder sie bey solicher unser freyheit und gnaden geruchlichen und ungedrungen bleiben lasset, und, wie wol das sey, das ewer etliche desselben ordens und seiner huser an ettlichen stetten von unsern und des reichs wegen verweser und versprecher seit, iedoch so meinen und wollen wir, das sie sulicher obgeschribener[1] beswerungen von euch und den eweren genczlichen entladen sein sollen. Und were es sache, das ir oder ewer yemand die obgenanten den meister, brüder und ire hüser, lute und güter wider dise gegenwertige unser freyheit und gnade mit sulichen beswerungen dringen wölte, wie wol der oder die ire versprecher weren, als vor geschriben stet; so haben wir von Romischer küniglicher mechte widerruffet und abgetan, widderruffen und abetun mit disem brive suliche versprechunge, die euch von uns und dem reiche empfolhen und gegeben were, also das sie furbaſs mer keinerley crafft oder macht haben solle. Mit urkund dicz brives versigelt mit unserm kuniglichen maiestat insigel. Geben zum Ellebogen nach Crists geburte dreiczehenhundert jar und darnach in dem newn und achczigsten jare, des freytags nach sant Johans tage ante portam, unser reiche der Behemischen in dem sechsundczwenczisten und des Römischen in dem dreyczehenden jaren.

IV, 305. 1. obgeschriber B.

---

285. *1398 ianuar. 9 Frankenfurt. Wenceslaus, Romanorum et Bohemiae rex, ordini Theutonico concedit, ne, quicunque servilis conditionis homo intra eius civitatem per annum et diem consederit, a quoquam repeti possit.*

Wir Wentzlaw, von gots gnaden Römischer kunig, zu allen czeitten merer des reichs und kunig zu Beheim, bekennen und tun kunt offenlichen mit diesem brieff allen den, die in sehen oder hören lesen; wann uns von Römischer küniglicher werdikeit und gewalt zugehoret und auch von angeborner miltekeit und tugent sullen und wollen, das wir allen unsern und des reichs getrewen vorsyn mit allem flisze und sie mancherley flisze und sie mancherley bekummernis von bedrangs uberheben, die in unczeitlichen und wieder bescheidenheit dicke widerfarent; des ist fur uns kommen von dem ersamen Conrade von Egloffstein, meister Dütsches ordens in Dutschen und Welischen landen, unserm lieben rate und andechtigen, das er und sin orden zu Tutschen landen in vergangen zyten vil ansprache und bekummernis gehabt haben von wegen eygener lute, die zu yme und in des ordens stette vom lande ziehen und wonhafft by in werden, von den, die dan meynent ire herren zu sin und in dienstpflichtig sint. Des haben wir angesehen und betrachten suliche gneme und unverdrossene dinste und truwe, die uns und dem riche der vorgenant Conrat vom Egloffstein und derselbe orden getan und erzeiget haben, teglich tun und furbas tun sollen und mogen in kunfftigen zyten, und haben in darumb durch sunderlichs gemachs und frides willen der bruder gemeinlich und besserunge willen ires ordens mit wolbedachtem mute und gutem rate unser und des reichs fursten und von rechter wissen diese besunder gnade getan und tun in die mit crafft ditz brieves und Römischer küniglicher machte volkomenheit, also was eigener lute in ire stat Mergentheim und auch andere ire und ires ordens stette, wie die genennet syn, in dem riche gelegen, ziehen werden in kunfftigen zyten oder yczunt geczogen sin, die darinne jar und tag siczen werden oder gesessen sin, das in die furbasser nyemandes, in welichem namen, wirden oder wesen der were, abefordern oder abeheischen sulle oder muge in dheine weis noch kein recht oder eygenschafft zu in haben oder fordern sulle, und sullen noch durffen nyemands darumb deheines rechten pflichtig sin oder antworten an keiner stat, dafur wir sie auch von egenant kunglicher macht genczlich gefryet haben und fryen mit crafft dicz brieffs und gebieten darumb allen und iglichen fursten geistlichen und weltlichen, graven, fryen, dinstluten, rittern, knechten, lantrichtern[1], richtern, burgermeistern, reten und gemeynden der stette, merchte und dörffer und sust allen andern unsern und des reichs undertanen und getruwen ernstlich und vesticlich mit diesem brieve, das sie den egenant meister, sine nachkomen und den orden gemeinlich an sulichen iren freyheiten nicht hindern noch irren in dheine weys, sunder sie dabey geruchlichen bleyben lassen und ouch hanthaben, schuczen und schirmen, als lieb yn sey unser und des reichs swer ungnade zu vermiden und darzu ein pene sechtzig march lötiges goldes, die ein yderman, der hierwider dete, als offte das geschee, genczlich verfallen sein sol, die halb in unser und des reichs camer, und das ander halbteil den vorgenanten meister und orden unleczlich gevallen sollen. Mit urkunt dicz brifs versigelt mit unser kuniglicher maiestat insigel. Geben zu Frankenfurt nach Christes geburt dreiczenhuudert jar und darnach in dem achte und neunczigsten jaren des mitwochen nach dem obersten tage unser reiche des Behemischen in dem funffundtrissigstem und des Bemischen in dem czwey und czwenzigisten jaren.

IV, 306. 1. lantrichern B.

286. *1402 nov. 3 Nuremberg (off den nehesten fritag nach aller heiligen tage R. 3). Rupertus, Romanorum rex, ob servitia a Conrado Egloffsteyn, magistro ordinis Theutonici per Alemanniam et Italiam, citra et ultra montes praestita annullat, si quid ipse sive Wenceslaus praedecessor contra ordinis privilegia et libertates statuerit.*

IV, 307 v. Edid. (Feder) Hist. dipl. Unterricht n. 19. Lünig VII, 18. Cf. Chmel Regesta Ruperti n. 1341.

---

287. *1403 aug. 19 Heidelberg (uff den sontag nach unser frauwen tag als sie zu hiemel fure R. 3). Rupertus, Romanorum rex, petente Conrado de Egloffstein, magistro ordinis Theutonici per Alemanniam et Italiam, confirmat omnia ordini a praedecessoribus concessa privilegia omniaque bona; concedit insuper, ne quis personas vel bona ad domos confugientium vi ibi capiat, ut liceat fratribus villas suas firmare, ut exemti sint ab hospitalitate et a iudiciis curiae et terrestribus, sed ius de eis a magistro et commendatoribus petatur.*

IV, 308 v. Edd. (Feder) Hist. dipl. Unterricht n. 20. Lünig VII, 18. Cf. Chmel Regesta Ruperti n. 1532.

---

288. *1404 febr. 25 Heidelberg (off den nehesten montag nach dem sontag als man singet in der heiligen kirchen Reminiscere in der vasten R. 4). Rupertus, Romanorum rex, petente Conrado de Egloffstein, magistro ordinis s. Mariae hospitalis Hierosolymitani domus Theutonicae per Alemanniam et Italiam, confirmat privilegium*

1221 april. Tarenti. Friderici II imp. (supra n. 257).

IV, 310. Germanice. — Cf. Chmel n. 1682. Edidit Schannat Sammlung alter historischer Schrifften I, 70 n. 21.

---

289. *1410 februario ineunte Pragae. Wenceslai Romanorum regis arbitrium inter Polonos ordinemque Theutonicum.*

Wenceslaus Romanorum et Bohemie rex etc. Notum facimus etc., quia serenissimus princeps dominus Wladislaus rex Polonie etc., frater noster carissimus, pro se et toto regno suo, adiutoribus et adherentibus suis ab una, et venerabilis Ulricus de Iungingen, magister generalis ordinis cruciferorum de domo Theutonica, devotus noster dilectus, pro se et toto suo ordine, adiutoribus et adherentibus suis parte ab altera, in, de et super omnibus et singulis litibus, guerris, rixis, dissensionibus, disturbiis, rancoribus et displicenciis inter ipsos utrimque subortis ad nos tamquam ipsorum verum et legitimum arbitrum de alto et basso potencialiter devenerunt, sic videlicet, quod ipsi pronunciacionem et arbitracionem nostram regalem inter ipsos utrimque racione premissorum faciendam ab utraque parte tenere ac[1] prosequi volunt et debent et eandem firmam, integram et inviolabilem observare, prout ad ipsam[2] in literis, quas utreque partes sub earum sigillis[3] pendentibus serenitati[4] nostre desuper dedisse noscuntur, plenius continetur. Nos itaque visis et auditis utriusque partis impeticionibus, querelis, allegacionibus, responsionibus, literis et munimentis agnovimus ex eisdem, multas causas et particulas, quas ipse partes in ipsarum allegacionibus et responsionibus posuerunt de presenti, a longis transactis temporibus concordatas, compositas et ante presentem litem sive guerram fore decisas et integraliter complanatas et literas sibi invicem datas desuper et roboratas; ideo animo deliberato et de certa nostra sciencia primo pro vero iure pronunciamus et dicimus, quod omnes cause et querele[5] inter predictas partes utrimque prius iuxta cuiuslibet partis literarum tenorem concordate, decise, composite et complanate a nulla parte moveantur, sed quod concordia, composicio et complanacio pretextu predictarum causarum facta firma, integra et, prout literis roboratum est, inviolabilis teneatur[6] et observetur, nec ab aliqua parte contra eandem quidquid de cetero amputetur, fraude et dolo quibuslibet penitus procul motis.

Item pronunciamus pro vero iure et dicimus, quod quelibet pars circa terras et homines cum ipsorum pertinenciis pacifice permanere et easdem iuxta literarum tenorem, quas a sede apostolica necnon a dive memorie[7] serenissimis quondam predecessoribus nostris Romanorum imperatoribus et regibus, ac eciam aliarum literarum, quas ipse partes inter se super hoc habere noscuntur, eo modo et forma, quemadmodum easdem quelibet pars, antequam presens et novissima lis et guerra inchoata et incepta fuit, habuit, tenuit et possedit[8], possidere debeat et una pars alteram in eisdem quomodolibet[9] temporibus perpetuis nullatenus impedire.

Item dicimus et pronunciamus pro vero iure, predicto fratri nostro domino Wladislao regi Polonie terram Dobrinensem, quatenus in et de eadem terra magister et sui una cum omnibus aliis castris, civitatibus, opidis, villis et bonis aliis, quibuscumque nominibus censeantur, cum ipsorum pertinenciis eidem fratri nostro regi Polonie et suis in presente guerra tam spiritualibus quam secularibus expugnaverunt et occupaverunt, integraliter restitui et ad plenum, sic quod prefatus magister suo et ordinis sui nomine de predicta Dobrinensi[10] terra cum omnibus aliis civitatibus, opidis et villis, sicud prescribitur, ac eciam hominibus in ipsis degentibus et morantibus illi, quem ad eum abinde cum literis nostris regalibus duxerimus transmittendum, confestim, cum desuper fuerit requisitus, loco et nomine nostris ad manus nostras sine omni contradiccione et dilacione condescendat[11] eadem demum predicto fratri nostro regi Polonie nostro nomine reddenda pariter et tradenda.

Item pro parte Samagittarum dicimus et pro vero iure pronunciamus, quod prefati magister et ordo circa terram Samagitarum iuxta continenciam literarum, quas a Romanis pontificibus et sacro Romanorum[12] imperio ceterisque regibus et principibus et presertim fratre nostro domino Wladislao rege Polonie et[13] illustri principe Withowdo prefato duce Lithwanie desuper obtinere noscuntur, remanere debent, sic quod ipsi se de eadem terra Samagittarum intromittere ac in possessionem ipsius redire possint, et valeant eandem terram, quemadmodum ipsam prius cum obsidibus, antequam presens guerra originem cepit[14] et mota fuit, in possessione habuerunt et tenuerunt, possidendam, et quod ipsi in eadem perpetuis temporibus non impediantur quovis modo; et in casu[15], quo quispiam, cuiuscumque condicionis existat, se de predicta Samagitarum terra intromittere et predictum magistrum et ordinem in ipsa impedire conaretur, extunc prefatus frater noster Wladislaus rex Polonie cum suo toto regno ceterisque suis principatibus et terris, qualitercumque nuncupentur, ac aliis suis et eorundem suorum principatuum subditis tam spiritualibus quam secularibus illos, qui magistrum et ordinem in terra Samagittarum impedirent, contra et adversus ipsum magistrum et ordinem suum et eorum terras et homines nullo modo adiuvent seu auxilium prestent dolo et fraude penitus procul motis, sed ipse magister et ordo ipsius debent[16] circa predictam terram Samagittarum iuxta tenorem literarum, quas ipse magister et ordo et notanter a predicto fratre nostro domino Wladislao rege Polonie et duce Witholdo desuper obtinent, perpetuo permanere; predictus etiam frater noster rex Polonie hiis contraire non debet seu[17] per quempiam admittere contrairi, sic quod ipse dominus rex et dux Withowdus seu hii, qui eandem terram Samagittarum possident cum omnibus suis pertinentiis necnon cum aliis castris, civitatibus[18], opidis, villis sive bonis, quibuscumque censeantur nominibus, cum ipsorum pertinentiis ad magistrum et ordinem spectantibus per prefatum dominum Wladislaum regem Polonie, fratrem nostrum karissimum, et suos in presenti guerra expugnatis, acquisitis, occupatis et optentis una cum predictis hominibus in predicta terra Samagittarum et aliis castris et bonis, sicut prefertur, degentibus et morantibus illi, quem abinde ad ipsos cum literis nostris regalibus transmittendum confestim duxerimus[19], dum desuper requisiti fuerint, vice et nomine nostris ad manus nostras sine omni contradiccione et dilacione condescendat eandem terram Samagittarum cum aliis bonis, sicud prescribitur, demum predicto magistro generali et ordini suo nomine nostro reddendam pariter et tradendam.

Item pro iure dicimus et pronunciamus, quod prefatus frater noster dominus Wladislaus et singuli sui successores reges Polonie incredulis et infidelibus contra et adversus magistrum et ordinem predictos et singulos ipsorum successores et totam christianitatem nullum amminiculum[20], consilium[21] et auxilium prestare, nec eosdem armis et aliis rebus fortificare seu ipsis contra christianitatem in succursum venire debeant quovis modo.

Item modo consimili magister et ordo predicti et singuli ipsorum successores infidelibus contra et adversus predictum dominum Wladislaum et singulos suos successores reges Polonie et ipsorum terras christianas auxilium et consilium[22] prestare non debeant aut iuvamen.

Item dicimus pro iure et pronunciamus, quod universi et singuli captivi de utraque parte liberi dimitti[23] debeant, et quilibet ipsorum ad bona et hereditates reverti pacifice et quiete debeat[24]; eciam omnes captivi in[25] terra Samagittarum captivati ad magistrum supremum et ordinem suum spectantes[26] liberi dimitti penitus et soluti. In casu vero, quo ille vel illi, qui eosdem captivos in captivitate detinent, id ipsum facere non curarent, extunc prefatus dominus Wladislaus rex Polonie, frater noster, cum suis terris et earum gentibus ac hominibus eisdem nullum prestare debebit, ut prescribitur, auxilium vel iuvamen.

Item, quemadmodum predictus serenissimus dominus Wladislaus rex Polonie, frater noster, magistrum et ordinem inculparet pretextu pacis perpetue, quam inter se ab utraque parte habuerunt, quod ipsi eandem violasse et infregisse debuissent, et idem magister et ordo eundem dominum Wladislaum regem Polonie, fratrem nostrum, per ipsum et suos eandem pacem fore inculpant violatam, eundem articulum una cum dampnis, homicidiis, incendiis, stupris, vituperiis et pacis fractionibus utriusque partis maiestati nostre reservamus, volentes consiliarios et amicos nostros ad hoc transmittere easdem causas perscrutandi causa[27]; et, si de eisdem edocti fuerimus, extunc super eisdem ante festum sancti Iohannis Baptiste pronunciare volumus et utrisque partibus ad nostre maiestatis presenciam super die[28] octava post festum sancti Urbani proxime venturum terminum statuimus revertendi, sic quod quelibet pars super eodem die consiliarios[29] suos cum potestate sua premissis ex causis ad nostre maiestatis presenciam, ubi protunc constituti fuerimus, transmittere debebit pronunciacionem et arbitracionem nostram audituros[30] acceptandam[31] et hanc prosequendam[32]. Et quidquid inter serenissimum principem dominum Wladislaum regem Polonie, fratrem nostrum, et magistrum et ordinem suum predictos et alios principes et dominos tam spirituales quam seculares utrarumque partium pro omnibus huiusmodi dampnis, homicidiis, spoliis, incendiis, stupris, vituperiis et pacis fractionibus, prout superius expressum est, pronunciaverimus, in hoc celsitudini nostre quelibet pars parere debebit et integraliter obedire, et una pars partem alteram, sive sint spirituales sive seculares, pretextu premissorum inantea et de cetero impetere seu causam movere non debeat foro ecclesiastico seu seculari, sed de pronunciacione nostra plenarie integraliter contentari.

Item, quidquid illustrem fratrem Iohannem ducem Mazovie[33], principem consanguineum nostrum, pretextu questionum et querelarum maiestati nostre pro parte ipsius contra et adversus magistrum et ordinem prefatos porrectarum concernit, apud nos reservamus volentes super hiis plenius perscrutari et super dicta die octava post festum sancti Urbani proxime venturum in eadem materia similiter pronunciare.

Item pretextu castri Dresno et aliorum castrorum eciam nil dicimus seu pronunciamus ex eo, quod hoc negocium ad serenissimum principem dominum Sigismundum regem Ungarie etc., fratrem nostrum carissimum, dinoscitur pertinere etc.

Item pronunciamus et dicimus, quod illustris Conradus, dux Slesie et Olsnicensis[34], et filius ipsius dictus Senior, consangwinei nostri carissimi, et omnes alii nobiles et honorabiles prudentes consiliarii[35] et nuncii nostri, cuiuscumque dignitatis aut condicionis existant, fideles nostri dilecti, quos alias[36] ad pacificandam guerram ad[37] prefatum fratrem nostrum, dominum Wladislaum regem Polonie, et predictum magistrum generalem ordinis Theutonicorum transmisimus, ab utraque parte sine omni oblocucione et suspicione mala esse debeant nec eis id ipsum in malum verti seu imputari debeat quoquomodo, ex eo presertim, quia ipsi predictum negocium pro utraque parte, prout plenius sumus informati, fideliter et sine omni dolo quolibet nostro nomine tractaverunt.

Item pronunciamus pro vero iure et dicimus, quod prefatus frater noster, dominus Wladislaus rex Polonie, et omnes sui principes, barones, milites et clientes, cives et subditi spirituales et seculares prefati magistri generalis, ordinis sui, ipsius preceptorum[38], prelatorum, militum, clientulorum, civium et subditorum spiritualium et secularium et ipsorum adiutorum et omnium aliorum, qui in hac causa suspecti habentur, boni et sinceri amici esse debent, et similiter prefatus magister cum ordine suo et omnibus suis preceptoribus et subditis prefati fratris nostri domini Wladislai, regis Polonie, suorum principum, baronum, militum et subditorum et eorum adiutorum et illorum, qui in hac causa suspecti habentur, boni et sinceri amici esse debeant, et omnis inimicicia et rancor inter ipsos ex utraque parte prorsus tollatur sine dolo; et super hoc prefatus frater noster, rex Polonie, cum suis principibus, prelatis et baronibus necnon magister et ordo[39] cum suis episcopis, prelatis et preceptoribus antiquam[40] perpetuam pacem serenissimi principis quondam domini Kazimiri regis Polonie et eciam perpetuam pacem inter ipsos utrimque per prefatum dominum Wladislaum regem Polonie modernum, fratrem nostrum carissimum, conceptam, stabilitam, factam et firmatam innovare, ratificare, approbare et confirmare debebunt et eciam sigillis[41] roborare, sic quod eadem pax per dominum apostolicum sub excommunicacionis pena et per nos tamquam Romanorum regem sub penis necessariis confirmetur, et ad hoc consiliarios[42] et ambassiatores nostros solempnes per festum penthecostes venturum proxime in civitatem nostram Wratislaviensem volumus destinare, in quam eciam civitatem prefati dominus Wladislaus rex Polonie frater noster[43] suo et regni sui nomine et magister suo et ordinis sui nomine ipsorum consiliarios[44] cum potestate plenaria transmittere et destinare debebunt ad innovandam[45], ratificandam, approbandam et confirmandam ac inter ipsas partes utrimque dictam pacem perpetuam sigillandam; et, postquam prefata pax coram consiliariis[46] nostris sic innovata, approbata et per utramque partem confirmata et sigillis roborata fuerit, extunc cuilibet parti de terra sua cum pertinentiis suis ac eciam hominibus ibidem degentibus et morantibus, sicud prescribitur, condescendi debebitur et sibi eadem tradi in suam vice versa omnimodam potestatem[47].

Item dicimus et pro iure pronunciamus, quod huiusmodi pacis treuge, que inter prefatum fratrem nostrum regem Polonie et regnum suum ac subditos ipsorum ab una et predictum magistrum generalem et ordinem suum ac subditos eorum parte ex altera sunt alias stabilite et usque ad festum sancti Iohannis Baptiste proxime venturum durature, in omnimoda et solida sua iuxta tenorem literarum desuper hinc inde confectarum permanere debeant firmitate[48], quodque nulla partium premissarum per se vel suos partem alteram dicto durante termino impedire seu molestare debeat quovis modo sub penis in literis prefate pacis inter ipsos ut prefertur stabilite contentis et expressis.

Acta coaeva comitiorum electoralium in Francofurtensi arch. vol. I, 85 v.—88, comm. v. cl. Menzel. E transsumto de anno 1412, quod in arch. Regim. asservatur, Germanice ed. Lucas David Preufs. Chronik VIII, 189, unde repetiit partem Baczko Preufs. Gesch. II, 400. Citat Voigt VIII, 60 etiam copiarium magnum Regimontani archivi p. 179. Cf. Aschbach König Sigmund I, 245 not. 4. Titulus: „Sequitur arbitrium super premissis latum per dominum Wenceslaum regem Bohemorum tamquam regem Romanorum inter partes antedictas, quod magister et fratres dicti hospitalis approbarunt, rex vero Polonie prefatus in illo non consensit, ut hic fama laborat".

1. supplevi. 2. ? ipm̄ F. 3. eorum singulis F. 4. serenitate F. 5. querele? frele F. 6. teneat F. 7. dive memorie a F. 8. possidit F. 9. qūolibet F. 10. dobronensi F. 11. conscendat F. 12. supplevi. 13. supplevi. 14. cepisset F. 15. casum F. 16. dicunt F. 17. sed F. 18. civibꝰ F. 19. supplevi. 20. am̄iculū F. 21. concilium F. 22. concilium F. 23. demitti F. 24. debēt F. 25. et F. 26. spectantē F. 27. supplevi. 28. de F. 29. conciliarios F. 30. auditur F. 31. acceptant F. 32. psequēd F. 33. Mazonie F. 34. Olsnicens. F. 35. conciliarii F. 36. ats F. 37. et F. 38. p̄ceptos F. 39. magistro et ordine F. 40. antequam F. 41. sigillum F. 42. conciliarios F. 43. fratri nostro F. 44. conciliarios F. 45. mouand, F. 46. conciliariis F. 47. potestate F. 48. debeat F.

---

290. *1414 nov. 19 zu Bunne (an sant Elszbethen tag r. U. 28, R. el. 5 cor. 1). Sigismundus, Romanorum et Ungariae rex, petente Conrado de Egloffstein, magistro O. Th. per Alemanniam et Italiam, confirmat ordini Theutonico omnia privilegia et bona, quorum specialem protectionem suscipit.*

IV, 312 v. Ed. (Feder) Hist. dipl. Unterricht n. 21.

---

291. *1415 febr. 27 Constantiae. Sigismundus, Romanorum et Ungariae rex, liberat ordinem Theutonicum ab omni impetitione sua sponte in Prussiam militatum profectorum.*

Wir Sigmund, von gots gnaden Romischer kunig, zu allen zyten merer des richs, und zu Ungern, Dalmatien, Croatien etc. kunig, bekennen und tun kunt offenbar mit diesem brieff allen den, die in sehen oder horen lesen, das fur uns komen ist der erwirdige Conrat von Eggloffstein, meister Tutsches ordens in Tutschen und Welschen landen, unser rat und lieber andechtiger, und hat uns furgelegt, wie das er und sines ordens bruder, huser, stette, vesten, lute und guter vaste beswäret werden von manichen unsern und des richs undertanen, graven, herren, rittern, knechten und andern von vorderung wegen irer scheden, die sie meynen genomen haben an den czugen[1] und inreyten gen Prewfsen dem selben irem orden zu hilffe, der eyn teil durch ritterschafft sich annemen dahin zu reyten, ettliche umb solt, die doch nit gebetten, bestellet oder gerufft werden von dem meister oder sinen undertanen. Wann nu der vorgenant meister und orden mit allen sinen brudern, festen, stetten, husern, luten und gutern mit allen iren zuegehorungen besunder vor andern geistlichen luten in unsern und des heiligen richs schutze und schirme herkomen sind und wir auch von göttlichen gnaden darzu gesatzt sin einem iglichen frid und gemach zu fugen, sunderlich den, die da gots dienst uben; darumb mit wolbedachtem mute, gutem rate und rechter wissen tun wir dem selben meister und orden diese besunder gnade, welich die sein, die umb ritterschafft oder umb solt gein Prewssen geritten weren oder furbasz in kunfftigen zyten dahin riten werdent, die von dem vorgenant meister, seinen gebietigern oder iren nachkomen muntlich oder mit iren brieffen zu ryten nit bestellet werden, sunder das von in selbst teten, das sie denselben darumb nichcz schuldig weren zu tun oder zu geben in dhein wys. Darumb gebieten wir allen und iglichen fursten, greven, freyen herren, rittern, knechten und andern unsern und des richs undertanen und getruwen, das sie die vorgenant meister und orden mit sölichen unbillichen forderungen und beswerungen fürbasz mer unbekummert und unbeschediget lassen, als lieb in sy unsere sware ungnade zu vermiden. Mit urkunt difz brieffs versigelt mit unser kuniglichen maiestat insigel. Geben zu Costencz nach Cristi geburt viertzehenhundert jar und darnach in dem funffczehendisten jare des nechsten mitwochen nach dem sontag Reminiscere, unser riche des Ungrischen in dem acht und czwenczigsten und des Romischen in dem funfften jaren.

IV, 314. 1. ezugen B.

---

292. *1415 iun. 19 Constantiae. Sigismundus, Romanorum et Ungariae rex, concedit ordini Theutonico, ne eius homines profugi quamvis intra annum repetiti a civitatibus tanquam burgenses retineantur.*

Wir Sigmunt, von gots gnaden Römischer kunig, zu allen zyten merer des reichs und zu Ungern, Dalmatien, Croatien etc. kunig, bekennen und tun kunt offenbar mit diesem brieff allen den, die in sehen oder hören lesen, das fur uns komen ist der erwirdig Conrat von Egloffstein, meister Tutsches[1] ordens in Tutschen und Welischen landen, unser rat und lieber andechtiger, und hat uns furgelegt, wie das ettliche herren, stette und gemeinde in dem heiligen Römischen riche gesessen und gelegen im und dem orden ire eygen lute, die von in fluchtig werden, zu burgern offnemen und empfahen und, wie wol sie die von in widerfordern inner jars frist nach uszwysunge der guldin bullen, ydoch halten sie yn vor die obgenant ire eigen lute, und das dieselben herren, stette und gemeinde desselben meister und orden hindersessen, knechte, dienere und amptlute, die von in an urlaub unverrechent und fluchticlich cziehen noch rechtfertig worden sint, zu burger uffnemen und emphahen und wollen, habe der selb meister oder orden zu in zu sprechen, das sy das vor den selben herren, stetten und gemeinden suchen mit dem rechten, und auch, das ettliche lute in dem riche erwerben fryheit ire dörffer zu bevesten mit mauren, graben und andere vestunge und das sie marckrecht da mögen gehaben, was dann der meister und der orden eygener lute darinne habent, meynen da, das sie furbafs fry sin sollen, und, ob yemand in ire gutere vergrube oder sust ruren wurde in zu schaden, an derselben merckte baw meinen sie in auch nichts furzetun noch abzulegen, das in doch alles mit gewalt an recht oder wider iren willen beschicht; und hat uns als einen Römischen kunig angerufft, das wir in daruber zu versehen gnediglich geruchten. Wann nu die vorgenant meister und der orden zu uns und dem riche gehören und wir in auch alle ire rechte, freyheite, gnade, gute gewonheite und hantvesten, die sie von Römischen keysern und kungen, unsern vorfarn an dem riche, erworben und herbracht haben, vernewet und bestetigt haben, und meynen sie auch dabey zu schirmen, zu halten und ze beleiben lassen; darumb mit wolbedachtem mute, gutem rate und rechter wissen setzen und orden wir von Römischer kuniglicher macht in crafft diesz brieffs, daz der selbig meister und seine nachkomen alle seine und des ordens eygene lute, die von in fluchtig sin oder wurden, an welicher statt das beschicht, inner jars frist wider fordern söllen und mögen, und das man in die folgen lassen sol unverzogenlich und an widerrede. Was aber desselben orden hindersessen knechte, dienere oder amptlute, die von in fluchtig sind oder sy verhandelt oder verunrecht hetten oder wurden, oder ander, die in iren gerichten frevelten oder verhandelten, das sol gerechtvertigt werden an den stetten, da die selbe verhandelung oder unrecht beschehen ist. Wo dann desselben orden gut oder eigen lute verbawen oder vergraben werden oder sind, von wellicherley gnade, freiheit und verleyhnusse das beschehen were oder wurde, das sol dem vorgenanten orden an sinen rechten, fryheiten, gnaden und alten herkommen dheinen schaden noch intrag brengen noch dieselben eigen lute dafur freyen oder erledigen in dhein wys. Davon gebieten wir allen und iglichen fursten, geistlichen und werntlichen, graven, freyen herren, ritteren, knechten, lantvögten, vogten, pflegern, lantrichtern, richtern, amptluten, schultheizen, burgermeystern, reten und gemeynden aller und iglicher stette, merckte und dörffere und sust allen anderen unsern und des reichs undertanen und getruwen ernstlich und vesticlich mit diesem brieff, das sie die vorgenant meister und den orden Tutsches ordens in Tutschen und Welischen landen by sölichen unsern geseczen und ordnungen hanthaben und schuczen und sie daran nit irren noch hindern in dhein wyse, sunder sie der gerulich gebruchen lassen, als lieb yn sy unser und des richs sware ungnade zu vermiden, und by einer pene funffczig marck lötiges goldes, der ein yglicher, der dawider frevenlichen tut, halb in unser und des reichs camer und halb dem vorgenant meister und dem orden unleslich zu beczalen verfallen sin sol. Mit urkund diesz brieffs versigellt mit unserer Römischen kuniglichen maiestat insigel. Geben zu Costentz nach Cristi geburt vierczehenhundert jar und darnach in dem funffczehendisten jare des nechsten mittwochen vor sant Johanns tag baptiste, unserer riche des Ungerischen etc. in dem newnundczwenczigsten und des Römischen in dem funfften jaren.

IV, 315. Ed. Schannat Sammlung alter historischer Schrifften und Documenten. Franckfurt am Mayn 1727. 4. I, 127 n. XXXVII. 1. Tüsches B.

---

293. *1415 iun. 19 Constancie. Sigismundus, Romanorum et Ungariae rex, praecedens diploma Latine redditum.*

Nos Sigismundus, dei gracia Romanorum rex semper augustus et Ungarie, Dalmacie, Croacie etc. rex, recognoscimus et notum facimus litteras per presentes cunctis illas visuris et audituris, quod constitutus coram nobis venerabilis Conradus de Egloffsteyn, magister religionis Theotonicorum in Alamanie et Italie partibus, noster consiliarius dilectus et devotus, nobis proposuit, quod quidam domini, civitates et communitates in sacro imperio commorantes et constituti suos et dicte religionis proprietarios ab eis fugitivos in burgenses recipiunt et assumunt, et, quamvis illos ex ipsis repetant infra anni spacium iuxta tenorem auree bulle, ipsi nichilominus eosdem detinere presumunt, quodque iidem domini, civitates et communitates eorundem magistri et religionis subditos, ascripticios, familiares, servitores et officiales, qui ab eis sine legitima causa, nulla facta de administratis racione et alias fugitive recedunt nec super hiis se expurgant, in burgenses assumunt et recipiunt volentes, quod, si magister et religio predicti contra eos querulare habeant, super hiis coram eisdem dominis, civitatibus et communitatibus de iure debeant experiri[1]; nonnulle eciam persone dicti imperii impetrant privilegia villas suas fortificandi muris, fossatis et aliis municionibus et, ut immunitatem liberam habere valeant ibidem pretendentes, quod proprii homines magistri et religionis predictorum in illis commorantes ab eis inantea debeant esse liberi sique[2] quisquam ipsis in eorum bonis fossata faciendo aut alias invadendo[3] immunitatem eandem dampna inferat, illis ad refusionem aliquam minime teneri, que tamen omnia cum violencia contra iusticiam et eorum voluntatem inferuntur eisdem. Quare a nobis imploravit, quatenus eis super hoc providere graciose dignaremur. Cum igitur magistro et religioni prefatis, prout ad nos et dictum imperium pertinent[4], etiam omnia eorum iura, privilegia, gratias, consuetudines et immunitates, que ipsi a Romanorum imperatoribus et regibus nostris predecessoribus in imperio predicto hactenus impetrarunt et obtinuerunt, innovaverimus et confirmaverimus, intendentes eos iuxta illa defendere, conservare et permanere debere; idcirco deliberato animo, sano consilio et ex certa sciencia auctoritate regia tenore presencium statuimus et ordinamus, quod prefatus magister et sui successores omnes suos et dicte religionis proprios homines, qui ab eis fugierunt aut fugient, in quocunque id eveniet, infra anni spacium repetere debeant et possint illique ipsis restitui debeant sine mora et contradictione quacumque, quodque religionis eiusdem subditi, ascripticii, familiares, servitores vel officiales ab eis pro tempore fugientes delinquentes aut alias inhoneste se gerentes seu alii, qui infra eorum iurisdictiones temere excesserunt aut deliquerunt, super hiis de iure respondere debeant in eo loco, ubi excessus et delicta huiusmodi fuerunt perpetrata, necnon ubicunque eiusdem religionis bona seu proprietarii ex fossatis seu municionibus huiusmodi fuerint gravata, ex quacumque gracia, privilegio et concessione hoc factum foret seu fieret, id predicto magistro in suis iuribus, privilegiis, graciis et antiquis observanciis nullum dampnum seu preiudicium debet afferre nec dictos proprios homines liberare aut eximere quoquo modo, mandantes propterea omnibus et singulis principibus, comitibus, baronibus, militibus, clientibus, advocatis, provisoribus provinciarum et aliis iudicibus, officialibus, scultetis, burgimagistris, consiliis et communitatibus omnium et singulorum civitatum, opidorum et villarum necnon omnibus aliis nostris et dicti imperii subditis et fidelibus seriosius et districtius per presentes, quod prenominatos magistrum et religionem Theotonicorum in Alamanie et Italie partibus in talibus nostris statutis et ordinacionibus manuteneant et defendant et eos in hoc nullatenus impediant seu molestent, sed eos illis pacifice gaudere permittant, sicut ipsi nostram et dicti imperii gravem indignacionem cupiunt evitare, et sub pena quinquaginta marcharum puri auri, quam quilibet contra hoc veniens temere pro una nostre et camere dicti imperii et alia medietatibus prefato magistro irremissibiliter persolvendam incidat. Cum testimonio presencium litterarum nostre Romanorum regie maiestatis sigillo signatarum. Datum Constancie anno a nativitate domini millesimo quadringentesimo quinto decimo die proxima Mercurii ante festum sancti Iohannis baptiste regnorum nostrorum Ungarie vicesimo nono et Romanorum quinto.

IV, 258. Continetur in confirmacione Eugenii IV de 1431 febr. 18. 1. experire B. 2. seque B. 3. faciendi a. a. invadendi B. 4. pertinet B.

---

294. *1427 mart. 12 Marienburg Strigoniensis diocesis. Sigismundus, Romanorum, Ungariae, Bohemiae rex, Ludowico palatino Rheni committit, ut petenti ordinis Theutonici magistro privilegia imperatorum et regum transsumat.*

Sigismundus, dei gracia Romanorum rex semper augustus ac Hungarie, Boemie, Dalmacie, Croacie etc. rex, illustri Ludovico, comiti palatino Reni, sacri Romani imperii archidapifero ac duci Bavarie, principi electori et avunculo nostro carissimo graciam regiam et omne bonum. Expositum est nobis pro parte venerabilis et religiosi viri fratris Eberhardi de Sawnszheim, hospitalis beate Marie Theotonicorum Iherosolimitani per Alamaniam et Italiam magistri et preceptoris generalis, consiliarii nostri fidelis dilecti, quomodo ipse et dictum hospitale certa habeant privilegia ac munimenta ipsis a divis imperatoribus Romanorum et regibus predecessoribus nostris a nobisque gratiosius concessa et indulta, que pro defensione domorum et iurium dicti hospitalis necesse habeant coram diversis iudicibus terrarumque rectoribus transducere, ostendere et exhibere, que propter viarum discrimina, locorum distanciam, ammissionis et lesionis eorundem pericula timent per dicta loca transferre, transducere et portare. Quare nobis humiliter ac instanter supplicari fecit, quatenus sibi et dicto hospitali super hiis de oportuno remedio providere dignaremur. Nos igitur attendentes dictum hospitale cum suis membris per divos Romanorum imperatores et reges salubriter et feliciter institutum et fundatum ac per eosdem et nos diversis privilegiis et immunitatibus pro sui status conservacione felici munitum et dotatum, que ut dignum iudicamus eidem hospitali illesa et illibata conservare, volentes tue dileccioni presentibus committimus et mandamus, quatenus eadem privilegia, munimenta et indulta, que pro parte magistri et hospitalis prefatorum coram te necnon certis notariis et tabellionibus publicis per te assumendis producta et exhibita fuerint, diligenter videas et examines et, si eadem illesa, sana et integra per te reperta fuerint ac inventa, eadem transscribi, exemplari facias et transsumi, sigillo tuo munias et robores, auctoritate nostra regali decreto tuo interposito decernas eisdemque talem ac tantam fidem et auctoritatem tribuas et impertiaris[1], quam et quas ipsa originalia habere noscuntur, ita videlicet ut, ubicumque locorum dicta transsumpta tam in iudiciis quam extra visa, exhibita vel producta fuerint, eandem vim, fidem et robur firmitatis, credulitatis ac probacionis habeant et teneant, acsi ipsa privilegia originalia et indulta ostensa et exhibita in specie forent vel producta, presencium sub nostri regalis sigilli appensione testimonio literarum. Datum in Marienburg dyocesis Strigoniensis anno domini millesimo quadringentesimo vigesimo septimo duodecima die marcii regnorum nostrorum anno Hungarie etc. quadragesimo Romanorum decimo septimo et Boemie septimo.

IV, 263. 1. impartiaris B.

PONTIFICUM ROMANORUM PRIVILEGIA GENERALIA.

295. *1191 febr. 6 Laterani. Clemens III fratrum Theutonicorum ecclesiae s. Mariae Hierosolymitanae protectionem suscipit.*

Clemens episcopus servus servorum dei dilectis filiis fratribus Theotonicis ecclesie sancte Marie Ierosolimitane salutem et apostolicam benedictionem. Quotiens postulatur a nobis, quod religioni et honestati convenire dinoscitur, animo nos decet libenti concedere et iuxta petentium voluntatem consentaneam rationi effectu prosequente complere. Eapropter, dilecti in domino filii, devotionem, quam erga nos et Romanam ecclesiam geritis, attendentes, ecclesiam ipsam et personas vestras cum omnibus bonis, que inpresentiarum racionabiliter possidetis vel in futurum iustis modis prestante domino poteritis adipisci, sub beati Petri et nostra protectione suscipimus et presentis scripti patrocinio communimus, statuentes, ut nulli omnino hominum fas sit personas vestras vel bona temere perturbare seu hanc paginam nostre protectionis infringere vel ei ausu temerario contraire. Si quis autem contra hoc venire presumpserit, indignationem omnipotentis dei et beatorum Petri et Pauli apostolorum eius se noverit incursurum. Datum Laterani viii idus februarii pontificatus nostri anno quarto.

I, 59, primum inter papalia generalia in toto codice B. Titulus rubricatoris sonat: „Clemens papa confirmat domui" (hic verbum est abstersum), „ea que habemus et habituri sumus et recipit domum, fratres et bona domus in sua protectione". Jaffé Regesta Pontificum Romanorum. Berolini 1851. n. 10,290. Originale, quondam in archivo ordinis Theutonici asservatum sive post Thorunensem pacem a. 1466, sive post Cracoviensia pacta a. 1525 cum plurimis aliis privilegiis Poloniae regi extraditum, in regni huius archivo diu latuit, ubi inter Prussiae diplomatis erat antiquissimum. Citatur in: „Inventario omnium et singulorum privilegiorum, litterarum, diplomatum, scripturarum et monumentorum, quaecunque in archivo regni in arce Cracoviensi continentur; confecto 1682. Lutetiae Parisiorum, Berolini et Posnaniae 1862". 8. p. 61 cum nota: „Data atramento inducta, ita ut agnosci non possit". Polonia dilacerata Berolinum delatum usque 1865 anni iulium mensem in archivo secretiori regio ibi fuit, quo tempore Regimontano archivo restitutum est. — Ex originalis meo apographo edidit R. liber baro de Toll: „Zur Chronologie der Gründung des Ritterordens vom St. Marienhospitale des Hauses der Deutschen in Jerusalem" in Mittheilungen aus dem Gebiete der Geschichte Liv-, Esth- und Kurlands. Riga 1865. p. 118. Ex transsumto d. d. 1441 dec. 22 per Casparum Link, Pomesaniensem episcopum, tempore ante maculam illam conceptam facto ed. E. Hennig ad Lucae Davidis Preufsische Chronik IV Vorrede IV.

Königsb. 1813, unde etiam nos quasdam notae chronologicae syllabas (sc.: ..us et p. n. a. quarto) atramento in originali obtectas supplevimus. Edidit etiam Hennes Cod. ord. Theutonici I, in praefatione p. III. Vidimatam copiam d. d. 1302 ian. 31 ex archivo ordinis Theutonici Vindobonensi citat B. Dudik Des hohen Deutschen Ritterordens Münzsammlung in Wien. Wien 1858. 4. p. 45.

---

296. *1196 dec. 21 Laterani. Coelestinus III fratrum hospitalis s. Mariae Alemannorum protectionem suscipit.*

Celestinus episcopus servus servorum dei dilectis filiis fratribus hospitalis sancte Marie Alemanorum[1] Ierosolimitani tam presentibus quam futuris regulariter substituendis[2] in perpetuum. Effectum iusta[3] postulantibus indulgere et vigor equitatis et ordo exigit rationis, presertim quando petencium voluntatem et pietas adiuvat et veritas non relinquit. Eapropter, dilecti in domino filii, vestris iustis postulationibus clementer annuimus et prefatum hospitale sancte Marie Alemannorum Ierosolimitanum, in quo divino mancipati estis[4] obsequio, sub beati Petri et nostri protectione suscipimus et presentis scripti privilegio communimus, statuentes, ut, quascunque possessiones, quecunque bona idem hospitale inpresenciarum iuste et canonice possidet, aut in futurum concessione pontificum, largicione regum vel principum, oblatione fidelium seu aliis iustis modis prestante domino poterit adipisci, firma vobis vestrisque successoribus et illabata permaneant. In quibus hec[5] propriis duximus exprimenda vocabulis: locum ipsum, in quo prefatum hospitale situm est, cum omnibus pertinentiis suis; domum, quam habetis Scalone, cum vineis et omnibus pertinenciis suis; Zamzi cum omnibus pertinenciis suis et domos, quas habetis apud Ramas, cum omnibus pertinenciis suis; domum[6] et vineas et possessiones, quas habetis apud Iaffam[7] cum omnibus pertinenciis suis et domum, quam habetis apud Accon civitatem cum omnibus pertinenciis suis et casale de Capharsin et vultam prope portam sancti Nicholay cum omnibus pertinenciis suis et domum, quam habetis in Tyro cum omnibus pertinenciis suis. Sane novalium vestrorum, que propriis manibus aut sumptibus colitis, sive de nutrimentis animalium vestrorum nullus a vobis decimas exigere aut extorquere presumat. Crisma vero, oleum sanctum, consecrationes altarium seu basilicarum vestrarum, ordinaciones clericorum vestrorum, qui ad sacros ordines fuerint promovendi, et alia ecclesiastica sacramenta a diocesano episcopo, siquidem catholicus fuerit et gratiam atque communionem apostolice sedis habuerit, vobis gratis et sine pravitate aliqua precipimus exhiberi. Sepulturam preterea eiusdem loci liberam esse omnino decernimus, ut eorum devocionis extreme voluntati, qui se illic seppeliri deliberaverint, nisi forte excommunicati vel interdicti sint, nullus obsistat[8]; salva tamen iusticia illarum ecclesiarum, a quibus mortuorum corpora assumuntur. Paci quoque et tranquillitati vestre paterna in posterum sollicitudine providere volentes, auctoritate apostolica districtius inhibemus, ne infra clausuras domus vestre ullus[9] rapinam seu furtum facere, ignem apponere, sanguinem fundere, hominem temere capere vel interficere seu molestiam audeat exercere. Preterea libertates et immunitates eidem hospitali vestro concessas necnon racionabiles consuetudines actenus observatas ratas habemus et eas futuris temporibus illibatas manere sancimus. Auctoritate insuper apostolica vobis concedimus, ut eligendi magistrum, qui vobis et domui vestre presit, habeatis plenam potestatem, et obeunte illo, qui pro tempore vobis et ipsi domui vestre preerit, nullus ibi qualibet subreptionis[10] astucia seu violencia preponatur, nisi quem fratres eiusdem loci vel fratrum maior et sanior pars secundum deum providerit[11] eligendum. Decernimus ergo, ut nulli omnino hominum liceat prefatum hospitale temere perturbare aut eius possessiones auferre vel ablatas retinere, minuere seu quibuslibet vexationibus fatigare, set omnia integra conserventur eorum, pro quorum gubernacione ac sustentacione concessa sunt, usibus omnimodis profutura, salva sedis apostolice auctoritate et diocesani episcopi canonica iusticia. Si qua igitur in futurum ecclesiastica secularisve persona hanc nostre constitutionis paginam sciens contra eam temere venire presumpserit, secundo terciove commonita, nisi reatum suum congrua satisfactione correxerit, potestatis honorisque sui careat dignitate reamque se divino iudicio existere de perpetrata iniquitate cognoscat, et a sacratissimo corpore et sanguine dei et domini redemptoris nostri Ihesu Christi aliena fiat, atque in extremo examine divine ulcioni subiaceat. Cunctis autem eidem loco sua iura servantibus fiat pax domini nostri Ihesu Christi, quatinus et hic fructum bone accionis percipiant et apud districtum iudicem premium eterne pacis inveniant[12]. Amen. Amen[13]. Amen.

Datum Laterani per manus Cencii sancte Lucie in Orchea diachoni cardinalis domini pape camerarii xii kal. ianuarii indictione xv^a^ incarnacionis dominice anno m° c° xc° vi° pontificatus vero domini Celestini pape III[14] anno sexto.

I, 59. Ed. in Scriptoribus rerum Prussicarum. Lipsiae 1861. I, 225. 1. elemanorum B. 2. subtituendis B. 3. iuxta B. 4. estis mancipati estis B. 5. hoc B. 6. domos B. 7. B. 8. correctum in B pro existat. 9. nullus B. 10. subiectionis B. 11. p̄viderit B. 12. inveniat B. 13. Tironice B. 14. III° B. Deest ap. Jaffé. Impudenter fictum tanquam Coelestini III privilegium de 1191 febr. 12, quod iam novit Lucas David II, 203, edidit Leo in Historia Prussiae. Amstelodami 1726. fol. p. 62, unde valde de fide dubitans repetiit de Wal Histoire de l'ordre Teutonique. Paris et Rheims 1784. 8. I, 44. Hinc nos pro comparatione cum genuino repetimus. Versionem Germanicam exhibent: I. C. Venator Historischer Bericht vom Marianisch Teutschen Ritterorden desz Hospitals unser lieben Frauen zu Jerusalem. Nürnberg 1680. 4. p. 8. Lünig Teutsches Reichsarchiv, Spicilegium ecclesiasticum pars I cont. (vol. XVI) p. 78 LXX, et Notice historique sur l'ancienne grande commanderie des chevaliers de l'ordre Teutonique dite des Vieux-Jones dans la province actuelle de Limbourg. Gand. 1849. 8. p. 41. — Episcopus Coelestinus servus servorum dei dilecto filio nostro Henrico Valpach, magistro hospitalis sanctae Mariae in Ierusalem et consociis eius in charitate dei et fraterna fide congregatis, praesentibus et futuris apostolicam benedictionem et unitatem sanctae Romanae ecclesiae, cuius nos indigni caput sumus, filiis nostris in domino charissimis, qui nunc in terra sancta contra inimicos crucis Christi pugnant. Cum intellexerimus, qualiter spiritualem statum iuxta sanctum evangelium inceperitis, nempe, ut curam aegrorum habeatis et tempore necessitatis contra gentes pugnetis, in quo etiam hactenus constantes permansistis; ad multorum preces confirmavimus eum, vos collocantes sub regula et omnium statutorum sancti Augustini, quae cum tempore ad perfectionem reducetis, cum titulo „fratres domus Teutonicae hospitalis sanctae Mariae in Ierusalem", in nomine patris et filii et spiritus sancti, amen; optimam spem habentes, quod vos cum successoribus vestris dei et Romanae ecclesiae laudem et honorem semper aucturi sitis. Datum Romae apud sanctum Ioannem de Laterano duodecimo die februarii pontificatus nostri anno primo, et post natum Christum 1191. — Annotare hic libet Baronii verba Ann. eccles. ad 1198 n. 2, quae tamen minime diplomatis niti videntur, sed chronico nescio quo. „Fuere eiusdem Coelestini digna alia factorum monimenta, quae certis eius pontificatus annis non sunt affixa, et inter alia confirmatio religiosae militiae ordinis Teutonicorum. Rogatus enim ab Henrico imperatore donavit eosdem idem pontifex veste alba et cruce nigra, subiecit vero regulae s. Augustini".

---

297. *1199 febr. 19 Laterani. Innocentius III hospitalis Theutonici protectionem suscipit, cui ordinationem secundum Templariorum et Hospitalariorum regulas compositam confirmat.*

Innocentius etc. magistro et fratribus hospitalis, quod Theutonicum appellatur etc. Sacrosancta Romana ecclesia[1] etc. *usque ad verbum* suscipimus. Specialiter autem ordinationem factam in ecclesia vestra iuxta modum Templariorum in clericis et militibus, et ad exemplum Hospitalariorum in pauperibus et infirmis, sicut provide facta est et a vobis recepta et hactenus observata, devotioni vestre auctoritate apostolica confirmamus et presentis scripti pagina communimus. Nulli ergo etc. nostre protectionis et confirmationis etc. Datum Laterani xi kal. martii (pont. a. 1).

E registro Innocentii III ed. Baluze in Epistolis Innocentii. 1682. fol. lib. I ep. 570; vol. I, 327; unde repetiit Hennes I, 5 n. 4 ad 1198 remittens. Sed de chronologia Innocentii cf. Boehmeri regesta 290. Baluzio etiam nos debemus. In epistola de 1199 febr. 8 idem papa tantum loquitur omisso hospitalis titulo de „Theutonicis" monasterio s. Trinitatis Panormitano eiiciendis; Baluze l. c. 324; Hennes I, 4 n. 3, quum Heinricus VI imperator diplomate de 1197 iul. 18 id concesserit „ecclesiae sanctae Mariae et hospitali" ipsorum ad preces „fratrum hospitalis Theutonicorum apud Hierusalem constructi in honorem b. M. v." Cf. Antonium Mongitore Monumenta historica sacrae domus mansionis s. Trinitatis militaris ordinis Theutonicorum urbis Panormi et magni eius praeceptoris. Panormi 1721. fol. p. 13. Hennes I, 2 n. 2. 1. Formulae specimen praebet infra Innocentii IV privilegium de 1247 aprilis 25.

---

298. *1209 iun. 27 Viterbii (cf. 1215 febr. 18). Innocentius III fratrum hospitalis s. Mariae Alemannorum Hierosolymitani ad instar Coelestini III protectionem suscipit eique omnia bona confirmat.*

Innocentius episcopus servus servorum dei dilectis filiis fratribus hospitalis sancte Marie Alemannorum Ierosolimitani tam presentibus, quam futuris regulariter substituendis[1] in perpetuum. Effectum[2] iusta postulantibus indulgere et vigor equitatis et ordo exigit rationis, presertim quando petentium voluntatem et pietas adiuvat et veritas non relinquit. Eapropter, dilecti in domino filii, vestris iustis postulationibus clementer annuimus, et prefatum[3] hospitale sancte Marie Alemannorum Ierosolimitanum[4], in quo divino mancipati estis obsequio, ad exemplar felicis recordationis Celestini pape predecessoris nostri sub beati Petri et nostra protectione suscipimus, et presentis scripti privilegio communimus, statuentes, ut, quascumque possessiones, quecumque bona idem hospitale inpresentiarum iuste et canonice possidet aut in futurum concessione pontificum, largitione regum vel principum, oblatione fidelium seu aliis iustis modis prestante domino poterit adipisci, firma vobis vestrisque successoribus et illibata permaneant. In quibus hec propriis duximus vocabulis exprimenda[5]: locum ipsum, in quo prefatum hospitale situm est, cum omnibus pertinentiis suis; domum, quam habetis Scalone, cum vineis et omnibus pertinentiis suis, et Zanzi cum omnibus pertinentiis suis, et domos, quas habetis apud Ramas, cum omnibus pertinentiis suis; domum, vineas et possessiones, quas habetis apud Iaphaz cum omnibus pertinentiis suis; domum, quam habetis apud Accon civitatem, cum omnibus pertinentiis suis, et casale de Cafirsin et voltam prope portam sancti Nicholai cum omnibus pertinentiis suis; domum, quam habetis in Tyro, cum omnibus pertinentiis suis; domum, quam habetis apud Cesaream, cum omnibus pertinentiis suis; casale, quod dicitur Bezal[6]; curiam, quam habetis in Cipro[7], que dicitur sancti Georgii cum omnibus pertinentiis suis; duas villas, quas habetis in Armenia, videlicet Combedefort[8] et Heion, cum omnibus pertinentiis suis. Sane novalium vestrorum, que propriis manibus aut sumptibus colitis, sive de nutrimentis animalium vestrorum nullus a vobis decimas exigere aut extorquere presumat. Crisma vero, oleum sanctum, consecrationes altarium seu basilicarum vestrarum[9], ordinationes clericorum vestrorum, qui ad sacros ordines fuerint promovendi, et alia ecclesiastica sacramenta a diocesano episcopo, siquidem catholicus fuerit et gratiam atque communionem apostolice sedis habuerit, vobis gratis et sine pravitate aliqua precipimus exhiberi. Sepulturam preterea ipsius loci liberam esse decernimus, ut eorum devotioni et extreme voluntati, qui se illic sepeliri deliberaverint, nisi forsan excommunicati vel interdicti sint, nullus obsistat, salva tamen iustitia illarum ecclesiarum, a quibus mortuorum corpora assumuntur. Ad hec ordinationem factam in ecclesia vestra iuxta modum Templariorum in clericis et militibus, et ad exemplum Hospitalariorum in pauperibus et infirmis, sicut provide facta est et a vobis recepta et hactenus observata, devotioni vestre auctoritate apostolica confirmamus. Paci quoque et tranquillitati vestre paterna in posterum sollicitudine providere volentes auctoritate apostolica districtius inhibemus, ne infra clausuras domus vestre ullus rapinam seu furtum facere, ignem apponere, sanguinem fundere, hominem temere capere vel interficere seu violentiam audeat exercere. Preterea libertates et immunitates hospitali vestro concessas necnon rationabiles consuetudines hactenus observatas ratas habemus et eas futuris temporibus illibatas manere sanccimus. Auctoritate insuper apostolica vobis concedimus, ut eligendi magistrum, qui vobis et domui vestre presit, habeatis plenariam potestatem et obeunte illo, qui pro tempore vobis et ipsi domui vestre preerit, nullus ibi qualibet surreptionis astutia seu violentia preponatur, nisi quem fratres eiusdem loci vel fratrum maior et sanior pars secundum deum providerit eligendum. Decernimus ergo, ut nulli omnino hominum liceat prefatum hospitale temere perturbare aut eius possessiones auferre vel ablatas retinere, minuere seu quibuslibet vexationibus fatigare, sed omnia integra conserventur eorum, pro quorum gubernatione ac sustentatione concessa sunt, usibus omnimodis profutura, salva sedis apostolice auctoritate et diocesani episcopi canonica iusticia. Si qua igitur in futurum ecclesiastica secularisve persona hanc nostre constitutionis paginam sciens contra eam temere venire temptaverit, secundo tertiove commonita, nisi reatum suum congrua satisfactione correxerit, potestatis honorisque sui careat dignitate, reamque se divino iudicio existere de perpetrata iniquitate cognoscat, et a sacratissimo corpore ac sanguine dei et domini redemptoris nostri Ihesu Christi aliena fiat atque in extremo examine divine subiaceat ultioni. Cunctis autem eidem loco sua iura servantibus sit pax domini nostri Iesu Christi, quatinus et hic fructum bone actionis percipiant et apud districtum iudicem premia eterne pacis inveniant. Amen. Amen. Amen.

(*Locus emblematis:* Scs. Petrus. Scs. Paulus. Innocentius papa III. † Fac mecum domine signum in bonum.)

(*Locus:* Bene valete.)

Ego Innocentius katholice ecclesie episcopus subscribo.

+ Ego Iohannes Albanensis episcopus subscribo.

+ Ego Iohannes Sabinensis episcopus subscribo.

+ Ego Nicholaus Tusculanensis episcopus subscribo.

+ Ego Cencius sanctorum Iohannis et Pauli presbiter cardinalis tituli Pamachii subscribo.

+ Ego Petrus tituli sancti Marcelli presbiter cardinalis subscribo.

+ Ego Benedictus tituli sancte Susanae presbiter cardinalis subscribo.

+ Ego Rogerius tituli sancte Anastasie presbiter cardinalis subscribo.

+ Ego Gregorius sancti Georgii ad velum aureum diaconus cardinalis subscribo.

+ Ego Gwido sancti Nycholai in carcere Tulliano diaconus cardinalis subscribo.

+ Ego Iohannes sancte Marie in via lata diaconus cardinalis subscribo.

+ Ego Octavianus sanctorum Sergii et Bachi diaconus cardinalis subscribo.

+ Ego Iohannes sanctorum Cosme et Damiani diaconus cardinalis subscribo.

+ Ego Pelagius sancte Lucie ad septa solis diaconus cardinalis subscribo.

Datum Viterbii per manum Iohannis sancte Marie in Cosmidin diaconi cardinalis, sancte Romane ecclesie cancellarii v kalendas iulii indictione xii incarnationis dominice anno m° cc° viiii°, pontificatus vero domini Innocentii pape tercii anno duodecimo.

A. Transscriptum papyraceum ineuntis xiv saeculi (non post annum 1330 ut videtur) confectum in archivo Regimontano Voigtio G. Pr. II, 65 nota 1 saeculi xiii esse visum est. Sed iniuria vel tunc iam periisse ipsum originale conclusit ex schedula, in qua manu saec. xv inscriptum legitur: „Ista copia indulti Innocentii tercii concordat in tenore per omnia cum illa laniata, que est in camera literarum penes fenestram; attamen in datis et loco datis (!) et in annis pontificis discordant, quum laniata data est Avinione anno pontificatus xviii, hec autem Viterbii anno xii". — Ex Alberti Ierosolimitani patriarchae (1204—1214) transsumto cum bulla eius in filis sericeis purpureis appendente, ex facie verba ALBERTVS IEROSOLIMITANVS PATRIARCHA ex altera parte liberationem patrum ex limbo repraesentante (HANACTACIC), a. 1805 in archivo ordinis Mergenthemensi, nunc Vindobonensi, asservato ed. de Wal Recherches sur l'ancienne constitution de l'ordre Teutonique. A Mergentheim 1807. I, 369; cf. Dudik Des hohen Deutschen Ritterordens Münzsammlung. Wien 1858. 4. p. 44 not. 4. — Eximia liberalitate celsissimus princeps Guilelmus, Austriae archidux, ordinis Theutonici generalis magister, nobis, ut eo utamur, transmitti iussit. Imitatur transsumptum originalis formam; super dati lineam scripta est alia manu linea: „Ego Albertus indignus Ierosolimitan(e) ecclesie patriarcha huic exemplo, quod ex autentico scriptum est, in quo nec plus nec minus quam in ipso autentico continetur, ad maiorem veritatis noticiam bullam meam apponi feci". — In superiori parte carta aliquantum humore maculata. In dorso scripsit vetusta manus: „Innocencius"; manus s. xv exeuntis extractum et n. XX; etiam posteri alia. — In designatione Livoniensis archivi ordinis Theutonici, quondam per Gothardum de Ketteler Mitoviam, inde 1621 Holmiam delati, „Förteckningh uppå dhe skriffter och documenter som bleffwe tagne uthi Mitow åhr 1621" apud C. Schirren Verzeichnifs livländischer Geschichts-Quellen in schwed. Archiven und Bibliotheken. Dorpat 1861—1868, p. 127 citatur: 1209 P. Innocentius III recipit in protectionem ordinem Theutonicum et eius bona. — Sine dato A. 20 n. CVI Latine et Germanice cum nota: „In ultramarinis partibus". 1. instituendis Hennig ad 1215. 2. in perpetuam memoriam W. 3. deest H. 4. Allemannorum Ierusalemitanum H, Ierosolimitanorum W. 5. exprimenda vocabulis H. 6. Besal H. 7. Cypro H. 8. Combedefor Transs. Vindob., Cambedefor H, Cambedeford' A. 9. deest H. De exemplari alio cf. 1215 febr. 18.

299. *1210 aug. 27 Laterani. Innocentius III vetat fratres hospitalis Theutonicorum Acconensis alba pallia deferre.*

Innocentius etc. magistro et fratribus hospitalis Theutonicorum Acconensis[1] etc. Suam nobis dilecti filii fratres militie Templi querimoniam obtulerunt, quod, cum in primordio institutionis ordinis sui eis fuerit ab apostolica sede concessum, ut in religionis signum milites militie Templi albis palliis uterentur ad differentiam aliorum; vos, in confusionem ordinis supradicti nuper alba pallia portare cepistis. Nolentes igitur, ut ex hoc inter vos et ipsos emulationis seu discordie materia suscitetur, presentium vobis auctoritate precipiendo mandamus, quatinus vestro contenti habitu existentes huiusmodi alba pallia, que, sicut premissum est, in signum religionis concessa fuerunt Templariis antedictis, nullatenus deferatis. Alioquin venerabili fratri nostro patriarche Ierosolymitano, apostolice sedis legato, nostris damus litteris in mandatis, ut inquisita plenius et cognita veritate id appellatione remota super hoc statuat, quod religioni pariter et saluti viderit expedire. Datum Laterani vi kal. septembris pontificatus nostri anno tertiodecimo.

E registro Innocentii III lib. XIII ep. 125 ed. Baluze II, 471. 1. Acconensi Bal.

300. *1210 aug. 27 Laterani. Innocentius III rescribit Hierosolymitano patriarchae de eadem re.*

Innocentius etc. Ierosolymitano patriarche, apostolice sedis legato etc. Suam nobis dilecti filii fratres militie Templi querimoniam obtulerunt, quod, cum in primordio institutionis ordinis sui eis fuerit ab apostolica sede concessum, ut in religionis signum milites militie Templi albis palliis uterentur ad differentiam aliorum, dilecti filii magister et fratres hospitalis Theutonicorum Acconensis in confusionem ordinis supradicti nuper alba pallia portare coeperunt. Nolentes igitur, ut ex hoc inter predictos fratres emulationis seu discordie materia suscitetur, eisdem magistro et fratribus hospitalis dedimus in preceptis, ut suo contenti habitu existentes huiusmodi alba pallia nullatenus deferant, que, sicut premissum est, in religionis signum concessa fuerunt Templariis antedictis. Quocirca fraternitati tue per apostolica scripta mandamus, quatinus inquisita plenius et cognita veritate id super hoc statuas appellatione remota, quod religioni pariter et saluti videris expedire, faciens, quod statueris, per censuram ecclesiasticam firmiter observari. Datum Laterani vi kal. septembris pontificatus nostri anno tertio decimo.

E registro Innocentii III lib. XIII ep. 126 ed. Baluze II, 472.

---

301. *1211 iul. 28 Laterani. Innocentius III fratribus hospitalis s. M. Th. in Accon confirmat Alberti patriarchae statutum de ferendis palliis de stanforti.*

Innocentius servus servorum dei dilectis filiis fratribus hospitalis sancte Marie Theutonicorum[1] in Accon salutem et apostolicam benedictionem. Cum a nobis petitur, quod iustum est et honestum, tam vigor equitatis quam ordo exigit rationis, ut id per sollicitudinem nostri officii ad debitum perducatur effectum. Eapropter, dilecti in domino filii, vestris iustis precibus inclinati statutum, quod de mantellorum depositione[2] alborum, super quibus dilectos filios magistrum et fratres milicie Templi senciebatis infestos, licet ipsorum mantellorum usus a quibusdam nostris predecessoribus Romanis pontificibus vobis extiterit confirmatus, et deferendis palliis tam a vobis quam a vestris successoribus amodo de stanforti a venerabili[3] fratre nostro Al(berto), Ierosolimitano patriarcha, apostolice sedis legato, inter vos et Templarios supradictos pro bono pacis firmatum est[4], auctoritate vobis apostolica confirmamus et presentis scripti patrocinio communimus. Nulli ergo omnino hominum liceat hanc paginam nostre confirmationis infringere vel ei ausu temerario contraire. Si quis autem hoc attemptare presumpserit, indignationem omnipotentis dei et beatorum Petri et Pauli apostolorum eius se noverit incursurum. Datum Laterani v° kalendas augusti pontificatus nostri anno xiiii°.

I, 60. — A. 16 p. 25, unde partem edidit Voigt Gesch. Preufsens II, 66. 1. thetonicorum B. 2. dispositione A. 16. 3. uenerabile B. 4. supplevi.

---

302. *1215 febr. 18 Laterani. Innocentii III repetit bullam sub n. 298 supra 1209 iun. 27.*

Innocentius etc. Effectum iusta etc. (*concordat cum* n. 298 de 1209 iunii 17). Amen. Amen. Amen.

(*Locus emblematis:* Sanctus Petrus. Sanctus Paulus. Innocentius papa III. † Fac mecum domine signum in bonum.)

(*Locus:* Bene valete.)

Ego Innocentius catholice ecclesie episcopus subscribo.

Ego Nicholaus Tusculanensis episcopus subscribo.

Ego Guido Prenestinus episcopus subscribo.

Ego Hug(olinus) Ostiensis et Velletrensis episcopus subscribo.

Ego Benedictus Portuensis et Fardusine episcopus subscribo.

Ego Pelagius Albanensis episcopus subscribo.

Ego Cinthius tituli sancti Laurentii in Lucina presbiter cardinalis subscribo.

Ego Cencius sanctorum Iohannis et Pauli presbiter cardinalis tituli Pamachii subscribo.

Ego Leo tituli sancte crucis in Iherosolyma presbiter cardinalis subscribo.

Ego Petrus sancte Pudentiane tituli Pastoris presbiter cardinalis subscribo.

Ego Guila sancti Martini presbiter cardinalis tituli Equicii subscribo.

Ego Robertus tituli sancti Stephani in Celio monte presbiter cardinalis subscribo.

Ego Stephanus basilice duodecim apostolorum presbiter cardinalis subscribo.

Ego Guido sancti Nicolai in carcere Tulliano diaconus cardinalis subscribo.

Ego Gregorius sancti Theodori diaconus cardinalis subscribo.

Ego Octavianus sanctorum Sergii et Bachi diaconus cardinalis subscribo.

Ego Petrus sancte Marie in Aquiro diaconus cardinalis subscribo.

Ego Gregorius sancti Georgii ad velum aureum diaconus cardinalis subscribo.

Datum Laterani per manum Thome sancte Romane ecclesie subdiaconi et notarii, Neapolitani electi, xii kal. martii indiccione iiii, incarnationis dominice anno m° cc° xv°, pontificatus vero domini Innocentii pape III anno octavo decimo.

Transsumtum, ad cuius calcem legitur: „Ego Radulfus patriarcha Ierusalem vidi et tenui autenticum" (fuit Radulfus de Merencort patriarcha post 1214 mortuum praedecessorem, ipse defunctus 1225) adservatur in archivo Regimontano, unde edidit Hennig ad Lucam Davidem II, 204 sq. Fila cannabina, e quibus olim pendebat bulla patriarchae, supersunt etiam nunc. Verborum: „Decernimus ergo" usque „Amen. Amen. Amen" transsumptum sub dato 1413 aug. 27 Mariaeburgi petente Heinrico de Plauen magistro generali per Iohannem Pomesaniensem episcopum et Nicolaum Polplinensem abbatem (sed talis tunc non fuit abbas, et in ipso sigillo legitur: s. fr. Petri abbatis de Polpelyn, unde spurium videtur transsumtum) confectum, ubi legitur magistrum obtulisse quasdam litteras apostolicas videlicet Innocentii pape III, eius vera bulla plumbea cum filis rubei et glauci coloris more curie Romane bullatas cum subscriptione omnium protunc s. R. e. cardinalium, non abolitas, non abrasas nec in aliqua sui parte suspectas. Initium et datum Laterani xii cal. mart. concordant. Omnino depravatum datum praebet inventarium archivi Cracov. p. 61: „Subscriptum privilegium ab ipso papa et 17 cardinalibus. Datum Rome anno 1215 15 calend. martii p. a. 17".

303. *1216 dec. 8 Romae ap. s. Petrum. Honorius III confirmat ordinis Theutonici bona privilegia, constitutiones.*

Honorius episcopus servus servorum dei dilectis filiis Hermanno magistro hospitalis sancte Marie Alemannorum Ierosolimitani eiusque fratribus tam presentibus quam futuris regulariter substituendis in perpetuum. Effectum iusta postulantibus indulgere et vigor equitatis et ordo exigit rationis, presertim quando petentium voluntatem et pietas adiuvat et veritas non relinquit. Eapropter, dilecti in domino filii, vestris iustis postulationibus clementer annuimus et prefatum hospitale sancte Marie Alemannorum Ierosolimitanum, in quo divino mancipati estis obsequio, ad exemplar felicis recordationis Celestini et Innocentii, predecessorum nostrorum, Romanorum pontificum, sub beati Petri et nostra protectione suscipimus et presentis scripti privilegio communimus, statuentes, ut quascunque possessiones, quecunque bona idem hospitale inpresentiarum iuste et canonice possidet aut in futurum concessione pontificum, largitione regum vel principum, oblatione fidelium seu aliis iustis modis prestante domino poterit adipisci, firma vobis vestrisque successoribus et illibata permaneant. In quibus hec propriis duximus exprimenda vocabulis: locum ipsum, in quo prefatum hospitale situm est, cum omnibus pertinentiis suis; domum, quam habetis Scalone, cum vineis et omnibus pertinentiis suis; et Zanzi[1] cum omnibus pertinentiis suis; et domos, quas habetis apud Ramas cum omnibus pertinentiis suis; domum, vineas et possessiones, quas habetis apud Iaphaz[2], cum omnibus pertinentiis suis; domum, quam habetis apud Accon civitatem, cum omnibus pertinentiis suis; et casale de Cafirsin[3]; et voltam prope portam sancti Nicholai cum omnibus pertinentiis suis; domum, quam habetis in Tyro, cum omnibus pertinentiis suis; domum, quam habetis apud Cesaream, cum omnibus pertinentiis suis; casale, quod dicitur Bezal[4]; curiam, quam habetis in Cypro, que dicitur sancti Georgii, cum omnibus pertinentiis suis; duas villas, quas habetis in Armenia, videlicet Combedefor et Heyon, cum omnibus pertinentiis suis. Sane novalium vestrorum, que propriis manibus aut sumptibus colitis, sive de nutrimentis animalium vestrorum nullus a vobis decimas exigere aut extorquere presumat. Crisma vero, oleum sanctum, consecrationes altarium seu basilicarum vestrarum, ordinationes clericorum vestrorum, qui ad sacros ordines fuerint promovendi, et alia ecclesiastica sacramenta a diocesano episcopo, siquidem catholicus fuerit et gratiam atque communionem apostolice sedis habuerit, vobis gratis et sine pravitate aliqua precipimus exhiberi. Sepulturam preterea ipsius loci liberam esse decernimus, ut eorum devotioni et extreme voluntati, qui se illic sepeliri deliberaverint, nisi forsan excommunicati vel interdicti sint, nullus obsistat, salva tamen iusticia illarum ecclesiarum, a quibus mortuorum corpora assumuntur. Ad hec ordinationem factam in ecclesia vestra iuxta modum Templariorum in clericis et militibus et aliis fratribus, et ad exemplum Hospitalariorum in pauperibus et infirmis, sicut provide facta est et a vobis recepta et hactenus observata, devotioni vestre auctoritate apostolica confirmamus. Paci quoque et tranquillitati vestre paterna in posterum sollicitudine providere volentes auctoritate apostolica districtius inhibemus, ne infra clausuras domus vestre ullus rapinam seu furtum facere, ignem apponere, sanguinem fundere, hominem temere capere vel interficere, seu violentiam audeat exercere. Preterea libertates et immunitates hospitali vestro concessas ratas habemus, et eas futuris temporibus illibatas manere sanccimus. Adicimus insuper, ut, quemadmodum domus vestra huiusce vestre institutionis et ordinis fons et origo esse promeruit, ita nichilominus omnium locorum ad eam pertinentium caput et magistra in perpetuum habeatur. Precipimus etiam, ut, obeunte te, dilecte in domino fili magister, vel tuorum quolibet successorum, nullus eiusdem domus fratribus preponatur nisi militaris et religiosa persona, que vestre religionis habitum sit professa; nec ab aliis nisi ab omnibus fratribus insimul vel a saniori eorum parte, qui preponendus fuerit, eligatur. Porro nulli ecclesiastice secularive persone infringere vel minuere liceat rationabiles consuetudines ad vestre religionis et officii observantias a magistro et fratribus communiter institutas. Easdem quoque consuetudines a vobis aliquanto tempore observatas et scripto firmatas, nisi a magistro, consentiente tamen saniori parte capituli, non liceat immutari. Prohibemus preterea et omnimodis interdicimus, ne ulla ecclesiastica secularisve persona a magistro et fratribus eiusdem domus exigere indebite audeat fidelitates, hominia seu iuramenta vel reliquas securitates, que a secularibus frequentantur. Si quando vero loca deserta fuerint eidem domui pia devotione collata, liceat vobis ibidem edificare villas et ecclesias et cimiteria ad opus hominum ibidem manentium fabricare, ita tamen, ut in vicinia illa abbatia vel religiosorum virorum collegium non existat, qui ob hoc valeant perturbari. Cum autem terre culte vobis quolibet iusto titulo conferentur, facultatem et licentiam habeatis, ibidem ad opus transeuntium et eorum tantum, qui de mensa vestra fuerint, construendi oratoria et cimiteria faciendi, sine iuris preiudicio alieni. Est enim indecens et periculo proximum animarum, religiosos fratres occasione adeunde ecclesie se virorum turbis et mulierum frequentie immiscere. Decernimus ergo, ut nulli omnino hominum liceat prefatum hospitale temere perturbare, aut eius possessiones auferre vel ablatas retinere, minuere seu quibuslicet vexationibus fatigare; sed omnia integra conserventur eorum, pro quorum gubernatione ac sustentatione concessa sunt, usibus omnimodis profutura, salva sedis apostolice auctoritate et diocesani episcopi canonica iusticia. Si qua igitur in futurum ecclesiastica secularisve persona hanc nostre constitutionis paginam sciens contra eam temere venire temptaverit, secundo terciove commonita, nisi reatum suum congrua satisfactione correxerit, potestatis honorisque sui careat dignitate reamque se divino iudicio existere de perpetrata iniquitate cognoscat, et a sacratissimo[5] corpore ac sanguine dei et domini redemptoris nostri Ihesu Christi aliena fiat atque in extremo examine divine ultioni subiaceat. Cunctis autem eidem loco sua iura servantibus sit pax domini nostri Ihesu Christi, quatinus et hic fructum bone actionis percipiant et apud districtum iudicem premia eterna pacis inveniant. Amen. Amen. Amen.

(In forma sigilli): Sanctus Petrus. Sanctus Paulus. — Honorius papa III. — Perfice gressus meos in semitis tuis.

(Bene valete.)

Ego Honorius catholice ecclesie episcopus.
Ego Nicholaus Tusculanus episcopus.
Ego Guido Prenestinus episcopus.
Ego Hugo Hostiensis et Velletrensis episcopus.
Ego Pelagius Albanensis episcopus.
Ego Centhius[6] tituli sancti Laurentii in Lucina presbiter cardinalis.
Ego Leo tituli sancte crucis in Ierusalem presbiter cardinalis.
Ego Robertus tituli sancti Stephani in Celio monte presbiter cardinalis.
Ego Stephanus basilice duodecim apostolorum presbiter cardinalis.
Ego Gregorius tituli sancte Anastasie presbiter cardinalis.
Ego Petrus tituli sancti Laurentii in Damaso presbiter cardinalis.
Ego Thomas tituli sancte Sabine presbiter cardinalis.
Ego Guido sancti Nicholai in carcere Tulliano diaconus cardinalis.
Ego Octavianus sanctorum Sergii et Bachi diaconus cardinalis.
Ego Iohannes sanctorum Cosme et Damiani diaconus cardinalis.
Ego Gregorius sancti Theodori diaconus cardinalis.
Ego Rainerius sancte Marie in Cosmidin diaconus cardinalis.
Ego Romanus sancti Angeli diaconus cardinalis.
Ego Stephanus sancti Adriani diaconus cardinalis.

Datum Rome apud sanctum Petrum, per manum Ranerii prioris sancti Fridiani Lucani, sancte Romane ecclesie vicecancellarii, sexto idus decembris, incarnationis dominice anno m° cc° xvi°, indictione v, pontificatus vero domini Honorii pape III anno primo.

I, 77. Ex originali bullato archivi ordinis Theutonici, quod est Vindobonae, edidit Hennes in Codice diplomatico ordinis s. Mariae Theutonicorum. Moguntiae 1845. I, 26 n. 25. In archivo Regimontano exstat transsumtum d. d. Romae 1318 aug. 1 scriptum „per manum Augustini Luce, s. R. e. p. auctoritate notarii, prout inveni in ipso privilegio papali“, per quatuor alios notarios et „rectorem“ auscultatum; apographum minus bonum in A. 16 p. 5—7 inter bullas Venetiae servatas; A. 16 p. 42 inter Baruli servatas; sine dato R. 158 „in Iuncis“ et A. 16 p. 97 sq. — 1. Canci H. 2. Iaphac H. 3. Cafusin H. 4. Becal H. 5. sanctissimo H. 6. Cinthius R. In supscriptionibus supple: subscribo.

---

304. *1216 decembris 19 Romae ap. S. Petrum. Honorius III ordinis Theutonici desertores eorumque fautores censura ecclesiastica coerceri iubet.*

Honorius episcopus servus servorum dei venerabilibus fratribus archiepiscopis et episcopis, et dilectis filiis aliis ecclesiarum prelatis, ad quos littere iste pervenerint, salutem et apostolicam benedictionem. Cum dilectis filiis, fratribus hospitalis sancte Marie Theotonicorum Ierosolimitani, a sede apostolica sit indultum, ut eorum fratribus post factam in eorum domo professionem sine ipsorum licencia non liceat discedere ab eadem; per apostolica vobis scripta mandamus, quatenus eorundem fratres, quos ab ipsorum domo discedere contigerit licencia non obtenta, ut revertantur ad ipsam, ac illos, ad quorum consorcia se transtulerint, ut eos contra ipsorum fratrum non teneant voluntatem, singuli per suas dioceses monicione premissa per censuram ecclesiasticam appellatione postposita compellatis. Datum Rome apud sanctum Petrum xiiii kal. ianuarii pontificatus nostri anno primo.

IV, 174. Originale quondam in domo Treverensi asservatum nunc Vindobonae in archivo ordinis Theutonici exstat. R. 140 inter Treverensia; — „a. 1 Treviris" A. 16 p. 113.

---

305. *1218 oct. 1 ap. Urbem Veterem (cf. 1221 ianuar. 16 Laterani et 1226 iunii 27 Laterani). Honorius III sancit, ne ab aliquo in fratres ois. Thci. sententia excommunicationis vel interdicti promulgetur.*

Honorius episcopus servus servorum dei venerabilibus fratribus archiepiscopis et episcopis, et dilectis filiis abbatibus, prepositis[1], prioribus, archidiaconis, decanis et aliis ecclesiarum prelatis, ad quos littere iste pervenerint, salutem et apostolicam benedictionem. Cum dilecti filii fratres hospitalis sancte Marie Theutonicorum Ierosolimitani nullum habeant episcopum vel prelatum preter Romanum pontificem et speciali prerogativa gaudeant libertatis; non decet vos in eos vel clericos aut ecclesias eorum, in quibus potestatem[2] ecclesiasticam non habetis, absque mandato nostro excommunicationis vel interdicti sententiam[3] promulgare, sed, si quando vos vel subditos vestros iidem fratres iniuste gravaverint, per vos aut nuntios vestros id Romano pontifici significare debetis ac per ipsum de memoratis fratribus iusticiam obtinere. Inde est, quod universitati vestre per apostolica scripta precipiendo mandamus, quatinus in predictos fratres sive[4] clericos[4] aut ecclesias eorum, in quibus auctoritatem nequaquam habetis, excommunicationis vel interdicti sententiam promulgare nullatenus presumatis, nec eos alias[5] indebita vexatione gravetis, sed erga ipsos[6] vos taliter habeatis, quod non habeant adversum[7] vos materiam querelandi, scituri, quod, si mandatum nostrum neglexeritis in hac parte, dimittere non poterimus, quin eisdem fratribus in sua iusticia, si apud nos querelam iterum deposuerint, efficaciter providere curemus. Datum apud Urbem Veterem kal. octobris pontificatus nostri anno iii.

II, 90v. sine dato. — Cum dato: ap. Urb. Vet. kal. oct. p. a. 3: A. 20 n. 3 Latine et Germanice, ubi legitur: „Est in Confluentia; et Innocencius in Colonia; Gregorius in Nurenberg et Alexander et cetera". — Cum dato: Laterani xvii kal. febr. p. a. 5: IV, 183. — A. 16 p. 61 „in Marpurg.". — R. 129 inter Marburgensia. — Ioh. 30. — Edd. Caorsinus p. C et Senner p. D 6v. — Cum dato: Laterani 5 kal. iulii a. 10 „Colonie" A. 16 p. 75. — Or. cum bulla in filis sericeis appendente, quondam Veteribus-Iuncis (Confluentiae?), nunc Vindobonae in archivo ois. Thci. 1. deest IV. 2. partem IV, R. 3. sententias IV. 4. deest IV, R, A. 20. 5. alias eos IV. 6. ipsos sive clericos A. 20. 7. adversus IV.

---

306. *1220 dec. 15 Laterani (cf. 1227 iulii 28 Anagniae). Honorius III confirmat et auget ordinis Theutonici privilegia.*

Honorius episcopus servus servorum dei dilectis filiis Hermanno, magistro religiose fraternitatis hospitalis sancte Marie Theotonicorum Ierosolimitani eiusque fratribus tam presentibus quam futuris in perpetuum. Etsi neque qui plantat neque qui rigat sit aliquid, sed qui incrementum dat, deus[1], humana tamen diligentia impensioris cure sollicitudinem debet impendere circa plantas, que adhuc novelle fructus uberes offerunt et uberiores suo tempore repromittunt. Cum igitur vestre religionis novella plantatio flores et fructus odoris et honestatis tempestiva fecunditate produxerit et deo incrementum dante sic inceperit expandere ramos suos, ut uberrimam fructuum copiam promittere videatur; nos, qui custodes in dominica vinea positi et cultores circa virtutum plantaria debemus diligentioris culture ac cure studium adhibere, novellam plantationem vestram rore apostolice gratie irrigare proponimus et fecunditatem bonorum operum, qua viget ad presens et vigebit divina favente gratia in futurum, vigilantis cure impendio adiuvare. Eapropter, dilecti in domino filii, vestris iustis postulationibus clementer annuimus et domum vestram seu hospitale, in quo estis ad dei laudem et gloriam atque defensionem suorum fidelium et liberandam Christi ecclesiam congregati, cum omnibus possessionibus et bonis suis, que inpresentiarum legitime habere cognoscitur aut in futurum concessione pontificum, liberalitate regum vel principum, oblatione fidelium seu aliis iustis modis prestante domino poterit adipisci, sub beati Petri et nostra protectione suscipimus et presentis scripti privilegio communimus statuentes, ut perpetuis futurisque temporibus sub apostolice sedis tutela et defensione consistant. Statuimus etiam, ut ordo fratrum Hospitalis Ierosolimitani circa pauperes et infirmos, ordo vero fratrum militie Templi circa clericos et milites ac alios fratres iuxta institutionem domus vestre perpetuis ibidem temporibus observetur. Ad hec statuimus, ut, cum pro tuenda catholica ecclesia et ea, que est sub paganorum tyrannide, de ipsorum spurcitia eruenda intrepide laboretis, liceat vobis libere in usus vestros convertere ea, que de spoliis ipsorum ceperitis paganorum; et, ne de hiis contra velle vestrum portionem alicui dare cogamini, prohibemus. Presenti quoque decreto sancimus, ut fratres in domo vestra deo servientes caste et sine proprio vivant et professionem suam dictis et moribus comprobantes magistro suo aut quibus ipse preceperit subiecti et obedientes existant. Preterea, quemadmodum domus ipsa vestre sancte institutionis et ordinis fons et origo esse promeruit, ita omnium locorum ad eam pertinentium caput et magistra in perpetuum habeatur. Ad hec adicientes precipimus, ut, obeunte te in domino, fili Hermanne, domus iam dicte magister, vel tuorum quolibet successorum, nullus eiusdem domus fratribus preponatur nisi militaris et religiosa persona, que vestram religionem et habitum sit professa, nec ab aliis nisi ab omnibus fratribus insimul vel a maiori et saniori eorum parte, qui preponendus fuerit, eligatur. Porro nulli ecclesiastice secularive persone infringere vel minuere liceat consuetudines ad vestre religionis et officii observantiam a magistro et fratribus salubriter institutas. Easdem quoque consuetudines a vobis aliquanto tempore observatas et scripto firmatas, nisi ab eo, qui magister extiterit, consentiente tamen saniori parte capituli, non liceat immutari. Prohibemus insuper et omnimodis interdicimus, ne ulla ecclesiastica secularisve persona a magistro et fratribus eiusdem domus exigere audeat fidelitates, hominia, iuramenta seu securitates reliquas, que a secularibus frequentantur. Fratribus quoque vestris post factam in domo vestra professionem et habitum religionis assumptum revertendi ad seculum omnem interdicimus facultatem nec alicui eorum fas sit post factam professionem et semel assumptam crucem habitum vestre professionis abicere vel ad alium locum maioris sive minoris religionis obtentu invitis sive inconsultis fratribus aut eo qui magister extiterit migrare; nullique ecclesiastice secularive persone ipsos suscipere liceat vel tenere. Sane laborum vestrorum, quos propriis manibus aut sumptibus colitis, de possessionibus habitis ante concilium generale, seu de vestrorum animalium nutrimentis nullus a vobis decimas exigere vel extorquere presumat. Ad hec decimas, quas consilio et assensu episcoporum de manu clericorum vel laicorum habere poteritis, quasve consentientibus episcopis et eorum clericis acquiretis, auctoritate vobis apostolica confirmamus. Ut autem vobis ad curam animarum vestrarum et salutis plenitudinem nihil desit atque sacramenta ecclesiastica et divina officia vestro sacro collegio commodius valeant exhiberi, sancimus, ut liceat vobis honestos clericos et sacerdotes secundum deum quantum ad vestram scientiam ordinatos undecumque ad vos venientes suscipere et tam in principali domo vestra quam etiam in obedientiis et locis subditis vobiscum habere, dummodo, si e vicino sint, eos a propriis episcopis expetatis, iidemque nulli alii professioni vel ordini obnoxii teneantur. Quodsi episcopi eos vobis concedere forte noluerint, nihilominus tamen eosdem suscipiendi vel retinendi auctoritate sancte Romane ecclesie licentiam habeatis. Si vero aliqui horum post factam professionem turbatores vestre religionis aut domus fuerint fortassis inventi, liceat vobis eos cum saniori parte capituli amovere ipsisque transeundi ad alium ordinem, ubi secundum deum vivere velint et valeant, dare licentiam, et loco ipsorum alios idoneos surrogare, qui etiam unius anni spatio in vestra societate probentur, eoque peracto[2], si eorum exegerint mores et utiles fuerint ad servitium domus vestre inventi, tunc demum professionem faciant regularem, promittentes se regulariter vivere ac magistro proprio obedire, ita tamen quod eundem vobiscum victum habeant et vestitum necnon lectisternia, hoc excepto quod clausa vestimenta portabunt. Sed nec ipsis liceat de capitulo vel cura domus vestre se temere intromittere, nisi quantum fuerit eis a vobis iniunctum. Preterea nulli persone extra vestrum capitulum sint subiecti, tibique, dilecte in domino fili magister, tuisque successoribus tanquam magistro ac prelato suo deferant secundum vestri ordinis instituta. Consecrationes vero altarium seu basilicarum, ordinationes clericorum, qui ad sacros ordines fuerint promovendi, et cetera ecclesiastica sacramenta a diocesanis suscipietis episcopis, siquidem catholici fuerint et gratiam atque communionem sedis apostolice habuerint et ea gratis et absque pravitate aliqua vobis voluerint exhibere; alioquin liceat vobis catholicum quemcumque malueritis adire antistitem, qui nostra fultus auctoritate quod postulatur impendat. Si quando vero loca deserta fuerint eidem venerabili domui ab aliquo pia devotione collata, liceat vobis ibidem edificare villas, ecclesias et cimiteria ad opus hominum ibidem manentium fabricare, ita tamen ut in illa vicinia abbatia vel religiosorum virorum collegium non existat, que ob hoc valeat perturbari. Cum autem terre culte vobis quolibet iusto titulo conferentur, facultatem et licentiam habeatis ibidem ad opus transeuntium et eorum tantum, qui de mensa vestra fuerint, construendi oratoria et cimiteria faciendi; est enim indecens et periculo proximum animarum, religiosos fratres occasione adeunde ecclesie se virorum turbis et mulierum frequentie immiscere. Quicumque sane[3] in vestro collegio suscipientur, stabilitatem loci, conversionem morum seque militaturos domino diebus vite sue sub obedientia magistri vestri, posito scripto super altare, in quo contineantur ista, promittant. Decernimus ergo, ut receptores vestrarum fraternitatum sive collectarum salvo iure dominorum suorum in beati Petri et nostra protectione consistant et pace in terris, quibus fuerint, potiantur. Simili quoque modo sancimus, ut hiis, qui fuerint in vestra fraternitate recepti ita, quod ordini vestro adhuc manentes in seculo sint oblati mutato habitu seculari vel vobis inter vivos dederint bona sua retento sibi quamdiu in seculo vixerint usufructu, si forsan ecclesie ad quas pertinent a divino fuerint officio interdicte ipsosque mori contigerit, sepultura ecclesiastica non negetur apud vestras vel aliorum non interdictas ecclesias, quibus elegerint sepeliri, nisi excommunicati vel nominatim fuerint interdicti; tales quoque confratres, si eos ecclesiarum prelati non permiserint apud suas ecclesias sepeliri, apud vestras ecclesias deferre possitis tumulandos. Preterea, si qui[4] fratrum vestrorum ad recipiendum easdem fraternitates vel collectas a vobis missi fuerint in quamlibet civitatem, castrum vel villam, in eadem civitate, castro vel villa una tantum ecclesia ipsius ordinis fratribus in eorum iocundo adventu semel aperiatur in anno, ut exclusis excommunicatis et nominatim interdictis divina ibidem officia celebrentur. Statuimus etiam, ut nulli episcopo in ecclesiis vobis utroque iure subiectis interdicti vel excommunicationis sententiam liceat promulgare; verumtamen, si generale interdictum terre fuerit in locis illis prolatum, exclusis excommunicatis et nominatim interdictis clausis ianuis absque signorum pulsatione plene divina officia celebretis. Decernimus insuper auctoritate apostolica, ut, apud quemcunque locorum vos venire contigerit, ab honestis atque catholicis sacerdotibus postremam unctionem seu quelibet alia ecclesiastica sacramenta vobis suscipere liceat, ne forte ad perceptionem spiritualium bonorum aliquid vobis desit. Quia vera omnes unum sumus in Christo et non est personarum differentia apud deum, tam remissionis peccatorum quam alterius beneficentie atque apostolice benedictionis, que vobis indulta est, tam familiam vestram quam vestros participes esse volumus servientes. Nulli ergo omnino hominum liceat predictum locum temere perturbare aut eius possessiones auferre vel ablatas retinere, imminuere[5] seu quibuslibet vexationibus fatigare, sed omnia integra conserventur vestris atque aliorum dei fidelium usibus omnimodis profutura, salva in omnibus apostolice sedis auctoritate. Si quis igitur huius nostre constitutionis paginam sciens contra eam temere venire temptaverit, secundo tertiove commonitus nisi reatum suum congrua satisfactione correxerit, potestatis honorisque sui careat dignitate reumque se divino iudicio existere de perpetrata iniquitate cognoscat et a sacratissimo corpore ac sanguine dei et domini redemptoris nostri Iesu Christi alienus fiat atque in extremo examine districte subiaceat ultioni. Conservantes autem hec omnipotentis dei et beatorum Petri et Pauli apostolorum eius benedictionem et gratiam consequantur. Amen, amen, amen.

Ego Honorius catholice ecclesie episcopus subscripsi[6].
Ego Guido Prenestinus episcopus subscripsi.
Ego Hugo Hostiensis et Veletrensis episcopus subscripsi.
Ego frater Nicolaus Tusculanus episcopus subscripsi.
Ego Leo tituli sancte crucis in Hierusalem presbiter cardinalis subscripsi.
Ego Guala sancti Martini presbiter cardinalis tituli Equitii subscripsi.
Ego Gregorius tituli sancte Anastasie presbiter cardinalis subscripsi.
Ego Thomas tituli sancte Sabine presbiter cardinalis subscripsi.
Ego Guido s. Nicolai in carcere Tulliano diaconus cardinalis subscripsi.
Ego Otto sanctorum Sergii et Bachi diaconus cardinalis subscripsi.
Ego Gregorius sancti Theodori diaconus cardinalis subscripsi.
Ego Rainerus sancte Marie in Cosmedin diaconus cardinalis subscripsi.
Ego Stephanus sancti Adriani diaconus cardinalis subscripsi.
Ego Petrus s. Georgii ad velum aureum diaconus cardinalis subscripsi.

Datum Laterani per manum Wilhelmi sancte Romane ecclesie vicecancelarii, xviii kal. ianuarii, indictione ix, incarnationis dominice anno m° cc° xx°, pontificatus domini Honorii pape tertii anno quinto.

Cum dato: 1220 xviii kal. ianuarii indict. ix: ex originali ed. (Feder) Historisch-diplomat. Unterr. n. 35. — IV, 231 v.; Ioh. 44. — E copiario saec. xv cum subscriptionibus, quae in B. et R. desunt, ed. Hennes Cod. ord. Theut. I, 50 n. 49. Ante ediderunt Caorsinus C. 7 v.; Senner F. iii; Duellius Hist. ord. Theut. dipl. app. 1 n. I; male ex or. Kotzebue Gesch. Preufsens I, 351. — In Regimontano archivo asservantur tria transsumta: 1. Confirmationis de 1417 aug. 12 auctoritate et sub sigillo Gerhardi Pomesaniensis episcopi ad instanciam Nicolai Schouemberg, procuratoris magistri, per duos notarios confectum d. d. 1426 dec. 20 in castro nostro Marienwerder. — 2. Eiusdem confirmationis auctoritate et sub sigillo Iohannis Pomesaniensis episcopi ad instanciam Casparis Linke, capellani et syndici magistri, per notarium Martinum Alwer de Dirsaw d. d. 1438 sept. 26 in castro nostro Resemburg. — 3. Transsumti sine dato, quod sigillatum erat per Nicolaum tituli sancti Eusebii et Vitalem tituli s. Martini in montibus presbyteros cardinales, subscriptum per notarios Iohannem Petri Gualterii de Aquamundula, Petrum Iohannis de Verulis, Michaelem Ludovici de Summervelt, sigillatum per Henricum Wladislaviensem et Iohannem Revaliensem episcopos ac Iohannem abbatem Polpelinensem petente Wennemaro de Bruggenoye magistro per Livoniam, scriptum per Nicolaum de Pantelitz Roskildensis diocesis notarium d. d. 1393 maii 29 in suburbio castri Marienborch. — Cum dato: 1227 v kal. augusti ind. xv Anagnie. Latine et Germanice A. 20 n. 79 cum nota „Gregorii simile in Mergentheym". Sed facile patet, scribam duo similis tenoris privilegia alterum Honorii III alterum Gregorii IX in unum conferruminasse. — In designatione Mitoviensis archivi Holmiae asservati ap. Schirren l. c. 127 citatur: „1220. Transsumptum bullae Honorii III, in qua continetur prima fundatio et confirmatio ordinis Teutonici, cum beneficiis et gratiis tempore Hermanni primi magistri ipsis concessis". 1. 1 Cor. 3, 7. 2. K. pacto F, H, Du. 3. s. q. F. 4. K. quis F, H. 5. K. minuere F. 6. F. potius: subscribo.

307. *1220 dec. 16 Laterani (cf. 1221 ianuar. 21). Honorius III iubet violatores ad domos ois. Thci. pro salute confugientium censura ecclesiastica coerceri.*

Honorius episcopus servus servorum dei venerabilibus fratribus archiepiscopis et episcopis, et dilectis filiis abbatibus, prioribus, archidiaconis[1], decanis et aliis ecclesiarum prelatis, ad quos littere iste pervenerint, salutem et apostolicam benedictionem. Pervenit ad nos ex conquestione religiosorum virorum[2], fratrum hospitalis sancte Marie Theutonicorum Ierosolimitani[3], quod, cum aliqui ad domos eorum[4] pro salute sua[5] se transferunt aut res suas[6] deponunt[7], hostes eorum infra ambitum[8] domorum ipsarum eos et res suas, dei reverencia et timore postposito, capiunt et captos incarcerant et ad redemptionem compellunt. Quoniam[9] igitur id[10] indignum est penitus et absurdum et fidelium saluti prorsus contrarium, universitati vestre per apostolica scripta precipiendo mandamus[11], quatinus universis[12] generaliter sub excommunicationis interminatione prohibere curetis, ne qui in illos, qui ad domos predictorum fratrum pro salute sua confugiunt, vel in res eorum infra ambitum domorum ipsarum manus iniciant violentas. Si qui autem nostre prohibitionis fuerint transgressores, ipsos contradictione et appellatione cessante vinculo anathematis astringatis[13] et faciatis usque ad satisfaccionem[14] condignam sicut excommunicatos ab omnibus arcius[15] evitari. Provideant tamen fratres, ut homicidis et pestilentibus hominibus ad dispendium pacis atque iusticie sub hac indulgentia nisi forte intercedendo presidium non impendant[16]. Datum Laterani xvii kal. ianuarii pontificatus nostri anno v.

Sine dato I, 70 v.; II, 106 v. n. LVI. — A. 20 n. 54 Latine et Germanice cum nota: „In Akon invenietur privilegium istud". D. 57. — Cum dato: xvii kal. ianuar. Laterani p. n. a. 5: R. 56 inter Ratisponensia n. ŏ. — In Regimontano archivo transsumta duo ad instantiam et preces fratris Iohannis, magni praeceptoris d. h. s. M. Th. I., per Bonacursum, Tyrensem archiepiscopum, vicarium patriarchatus Ierosolimitani et episcopatus Acconensis, et Gailardum, Bethlehemitanum episcopum, d. d. in domo episcopali Acconensi 1277 oct. 19; cf. Napiersky Index I, 3 n. 11. Legitur in sigillis rubris cereis: 1. quod tantum in altero exstat: „S. fris. Bonacursi ord. p̄dic. dei grā. archiep̄i. Tyrensis"; ex aversa parte „Secretum † Tyrus metropolis Syrie"; 2. „S. fr̄is. Gailardi dei grā. Bethleemitan̄. ep̄i."; ex aversa parte super pastoribus et angelo: „† gloria in excelsis deo". Tertium huiusmodi transsumtum de eodem die in archivo Vindobonensi ordinis Theutonici asservatur, unde edidit Hennes I, 225 n. 258. — Cum dato: Laterani xii kal. februarii p. n. a. 5: IV, 186 v. — Originale cum bulla in filis sericeis appendente, quondam Mergenthemi, nunc Vindobonae in archivo ois. Thci. asservatur. 1. d. a. I. 2. virorum religiosorum T, R. 3. Ierosolimitanorum T. 4. eorum domos II, domus eorum I. 5. deest T, p. s. se t. animarum R. 6. sua IV. 7. aut — deponunt TT deest, pro quibus: animarum. 8. abitum IV. 9. Quia I. 10. deest II. 11. mandamus atque precipimus R. 12. deest I. 13. constringatis R. 14. dignam satisfactionem IV. 15. deest I, IV. 16. Provideant — impendant deest T, II, R.

---

308. *1221 ianuarii 9 Laterani. Honorius III confirmat oi. Thco. usum mantellorum et aliarum vestium secundum statutum.*

Honorius episcopus servus servorum dei dilectis filiis Hermanno[1] magistro et fratribus etc. salutem et apostolicam benedictionem. Ea, que statuta sunt provide et apostolice sedis munimine roborata, inconcussa decet et[1] illibata servari et gaudere perpetua firmitate. Cum igitur ordinem fratrum Hospitalis Ierosolimitani circa pauperes et infirmos, fratrum vero milicie Templi circa clericos et milites ac alios fratres in domo vestra statueritis observandum, idque sit sedis apostolice privilegio[3] confirmatum; auctoritate vobis presencium indulgemus, ut nullius contradictione obstante libere utamini mantellis et aliis vestibus secundum statutum ordinis vestri nostro privilegio confirmatum, districtius inhibentes, ne quis id aliquatenus prohibere vel impedire presumat. Nulli ergo omnino hominum liceat hanc paginam nostre concessionis et inhibitionis infringere vel ei ausu temerario contraire. Si quis autem hoc attemptare presumpserit, indignationem omnipotentis dei et beatorum Petri et Pauli apostolorum eius se noverit incursurum. Datum Laterani v idus ianuarii pontificatus nostri anno quinto.

Sine dato: I, 70v.; II, 92. A. 20 n. 8 Latine et Germanice, ubi Hermanni nomen deest. D. Cum dato: Laterani v id. ianuar. p. a. 5. R. 66 inter Mergenthemensia 6. — A. 16 p. 4 „Venetiis". Partem ed. Hennes I, 55 nota 1. 1. deest II, A. 20. 2. deest II. 3. Cf. bullam n. 309. „Vestra religio". d. d. 1221 ianuarii 9.

---

309. *1221 ianuarii 9 Laterani (cf. 1223 ianuarii 12, 1226 iulii 1). Honorius III ordini Theutonico concedit immunitates Hospitalis et Templi.*

Honorius episcopus servus servorum dei dilectis filiis Hermanno magistro et fratribus hospitalis sancte Marie Theutonicorum Ierosolimitani salutem et apostolicam benedictionem. Vestra religio, cuius bonus odor longe lateque diffunditur, specialem[1] apostolice sedis favorem et gratiam promeretur. Cum igitur ordinem fratrum Hospitalis Ierosolimitani circa pauperes et infirmos, fratrum vero milicie Templi circa clericos et milites ac alios fratres in domo vestra provide institutum laudabiliter observetis, nos volentes, ut sitis pares in assecucione apostolici beneficii, quibus in operatione virtutum pio studetis proposito adequari, omnes libertates, immunitates ac indulgencias venerandis domibus predictorum Hospitalis et Templi ab apostolica sede concessas domui vestre concedimus; et, ut eis utamini libere sicut illi, vobis auctoritate presencium indulgemus. Nulli ergo omnino hominum liceat hanc paginam nostre concessionis infringere vel ei ausu temerario contraire. Si quis autem hoc attemptare presumpserit, indignationem omnipotentis dei et beatorum Petri et Pauli apostolorum eius se noverit incursurum. Datum Laterani v idus ianuarii pontificatus nostri anno quinto.

Hoc privilegium ut papa ordini Theutonico daret, Fridericus II in coronatione sua imperiali Romae 1220 nov. 22 ab Honorio III sese impetrasse dicit; v. supra p. 147. — Sine dato: R. 143 inter Treverensia; R. 11 ex domo Nurenbergensi n. 20 in apographo transsumti per Ottonem Herbipolensem episcopum confecti. A. 20 n. 1 cum nota: „Et est in Confluencia vel Treveri; Gregorius eiusdem tenoris in Marcburg et Allexander in Wysenburg". — Cum dato: Laterani v idus ianuar. p. n. a. 5. I, 63v.; II, 90; IV, 178. R. 53 inter Ratisponensia n. 2. A. 16 p. 112 „Treviris". Or. quondam Mergenthemense cum bulla plumbea in filis sericeis appendente nunc Vindobonae est. E copiario saec. xv ed. Hennes I, 54 n. 50. — Cum dato: Laterani ii id. ianuar. p. n. a. 7 „Venetiis" A. 16 p. 22; „Hoc privilegium invenitur eciam in Mechelinia" p. 67 in margine. — Cum dato: Laterani kal. iulii p. a. 10. Or. iam dudum domus Vindobonensis cum bulla in filis sericeis appensa in archivo ois. Thci. Vindobonensi. 1. spūalem I, sedis apostolice A. 20.

---

310. *1221 ianuarii 15 Laterani. Honorius III interpretatur constitutionem apostolicam, ut ordinis Theutonici novalia et aliae terrae, quos fratres propriis manibus aut sumptibus excolant, seu animalium eius nutrimenta minime decimis onerentur. Iubet violatores fratrum excommunicari.*

Honorius episcopus servus servorum dei venerabilibus fratribus archiepiscopis et epicopis et dilectis filiis abbatibus, prioribus, archidiaconis, decanis et aliis ecclesiarum prelatis, ad quos littere iste pervenerint, salutem et apostolicam benedictionem. Audivimus et audientes mirati sumus, quod, cum dilectis filiis fratribus hospitalis sancte Marie Theotonicorum Ierosolimitani duxerimus indulgendum, ut de laboribus, quos propriis manibus aut sumptibus excolunt, nemini decimas solvere teneantur, quidam ab eis nichilominus contra concessionem nostram decimas exigere ac extorquere presumunt[1] et prava ac[2] sinistra interpretatione privilegiorum nostrorum capitulum pervertentes asserunt de novalibus debere intelligi, ubi de laboribus noscitur esse scriptum. Quoniam igitur manifestum est omnibus, qui recte sapiunt, interpretationem huiusmodi perversam esse et intellectui sano contrariam, cum secundum capitulum illud a solutione decimarum tam de terris illis, quas duxerint[3] vel deducunt ad cultum, quam de terris etiam cultis, quas propriis manibus vel sumptibus excolunt, liberi sint penitus et immunes, ne[4] ullus contra eos materiam habeat malignandi, universitati vestre per apostolica scripta mandamus atque precipimus, quatenus omnibus parrochianis vestris auctoritate apostolica prohibere curetis, ne a memoratis fratribus de novalibus vel de aliis terris, quas propriis manibus aut sumptibus excolunt, seu de nutrimentis animalium ullatenus[5] decimas exigere vel quomodolibet[6] extorquere presumant. Quia vero[7] non est conveniens vel honestum, ut contra sedis apostolice indulgentias temere veniatur, que inviolabilem firmitatem obtinere deberent, mandamus vobis firmiterque precipimus, ut, si qui monachi, canonici, clerici vel laici contra privilegia sedis apostolice memoratos fratres super decimarum exactione gravaverint, laicos excommunicationis sententia percellentes, monachos, canonicos sive clericos contradictione, dilatione et appellatione cessantibus ab officio suspendatis, et tam excommunicationis quam suspensionis sententias faciatis usque ad dignam satisfactionem inviolabiliter observari, salva semper in omnibus moderatione concilii generalis. Ad hec presentium vobis auctoritate apostolica precipimus, quatenus, si quis[8] eorundem parrochianorum vestrorum in sepe dictos fratres violentas manus iniecerit[9], eum accensis candelis excommunicatum publice nuntietis et tamquam[10] excommunicatum[11] faciatis ab omnibus cautius evitari, donec eisdem fratribus congrue satisfaciat et cum litteris diocesani episcopi veritatem[12] continentibus[12] apostolico se conspectui representet. Datum Laterani xviii kal. februarii pontificatus nostri anno quinto.

Sine dato: II, 99 n. 33; A. 20 n. 33 Latine et Germanice; D. 32 Germanice. — Cum dato: A. 16 p. 38 sq. „Baruli". 1. presumant A. 16. 2. et II. 3. duxerint II, A. 20. 4. nec A. 16. 5. nullatenus A. 16, A. 20. 6. quamlibet II. 7. vero A. 16. 8. quatenus si quis II, si quis deest A. 16. 9. iniacientes A. 16, iniecerint eum II. 10. et tam diu A. 16. 11. II. 12. deest II.

---

311. *1221 ianuarii 15 Laterani (cf. 1225 maii 31 Tybure). Honorius III concedit ordini Theutonico, quod, si contra privilegia eius quid a sede apostolica fuerit decretum, non teneatur respondere.*

Honorius episcopus servus servorum dei dilectis filiis magistro et fratribus hospitalis sancte Marie Theotonicorum Ierosolimitani salutem et apostolicam benedictionem. Cum vos tanquam speciales ecclesie Romane filios religionis intuitu et consideratione obsequii, quod in ultramarinis partibus in defensione nominis christiani deo ferventer impenditis, semper apostolica sedes sincera caritate dilexerit et specialia curaverit privilegia indulgere; nostro imminet officio providendum, ut, si per falsam suggestionem aut tacendi fraudem littere a nobis contra ipsa privilegia emanaverint, nullum ex eis libertas vestra sustineat detrimentum. Eapropter auctoritate vobis apostolica indulgemus, ut, si contra privilegia vestra littere a quoquam per subrepcionem contra privilegiorum ipsorum tenorem obtente nisi ex certa conscientia nostra procedant, in iudicio alicuius non teneamini disceptare, salva moderatione concilii generalis. Nulli ergo omnino hominum liceat hanc paginam nostre concessionis infringere vel ei ausu temerario contraire. Si quis autem hoc attemptare presumpserit, indignationem omnipotentis dei et beatorum Petri et Pauli apostolorum eius se noverit incursurum. Datum Laterani xviii kal. februarii pontificatus nostri anno quinto.

Sine dato: I, 74; II, 96 n. 21; A. 16 p. 94 „Iuncis", p. 112 „Treviris"; R. 153 „Iuncis". A. 20 n. 21 Latine et Germanice cum nota: in Bysen. — Cum dato: Laterani xviii kal. februar. p. n. a. 5. 142 inter Treverensia. — Citat catalogus archivi ois. Thci. Vindobonensis privilegium eiusdem dati et tenoris cum bulla plumbea in filis sericeis appensa, quondam Treveris asservatum, quod tamen incipiat: „Vestra religio". — Cum dato: Tybure ii kal. iunii p. n. a. 9. R. 77 inter Mergenthemensia n. 30. Or. cum bulla in filis sericeis appendente quondam Veteribus Iuncis, nunc in archivo ordinis Theutonici Vindobonensi.

---

312. *1221 ianuarii 15 Laterani. Honorius III vetat praelatos ordinem Theutonicum de eleemosynis vexare.*

Honorius episcopus servus servorum dei venerabilibus fratribus archiepiscopis et episcopis etc. salutem et apostolicam benedictionem. Quanto dilecti filii, fratres domus hospitalis sancte Marie Theotonicorum Ierosolimitani, maiori religione et honestate preminent et contra christiani nominis inimicos graviori iugiter labore decertant; tanto et universis christianam professionem tenentibus fervenciori caritate debent diligi et eorum iura ipsis propensiori sollicitudine conservari, ut, qui pro universorum salute extrema non dubitant experiri pericula, ab omnibus grata senciant incrementa. Inde est, quod universitatem vestram monemus ac per apostolica vobis scripta mandamus atque precipimus, quatinus predictos fratres super elemosinis, que ipsis a dei fidelibus conferuntur, a nemine permittatis indebita presumpcione vexari, sed, si aliqui eos super hiis absque ordine iudiciario gravare presumpserint, ipsos, nisi[1] commoniti infra triginta dies post commonicionem vestram destiterint, usque ad satisfaccionem condignam sublato appellationis remedio ecclesiastica sentencia feriatis. Datum Laterani xviii kal. februarii pontificatus nostri anno quinto.

Sine dato: I, 74; II, 108v. n. 62; A. 20 n. 60 Latine et Germanice cum nota: „Et est in Mergentheym"; D. 61. — Cum dato: R. 43 inter Ellingensia 29, transsumtum per Iringum Herbipolensem episcopum (r. 1254—1266); R. 76 inter Mergenthemensia n. 28. Originale quondam Mergenthemense, a quo appendens quondam bulla avulsa est, asservatur Vindobonae in archivo ordinis Theutonici. 1. nō I.

---

313. *1221 ianuarii 16 Laterani. Honorius III repetit n. 305 de 1218 oct. 1.*

Honorius cet. Cum dilecti cet. Datum Laterani xvii kal. febr. p. n. a. v°.

---

314. *1221 ianuarii 16 Laterani (cf. 1223 ianuarii 13, 1226 iulii 2). Honorius III praelatis ordinem Theutonicum commendat ob eleemosynarum collectionem, cet.*

Honorius episcopus servus servorum dei venerabilibus fratribus archiepiscopis et episcopis et dilectis filiis abbatibus, prioribus, archidiaconis, decanis et aliis ecclesiarum praelatis, ad quos littere iste pervenerint, salutem et apostolicam benedictionem. Cum dilectis filiis, fratribus hospitalis sancte Marie Theotonicorum Ierosolimitani, duxerimus indulgendum, ut semel in anno recipiantur in ecclesiis ad elemosinas colligendas, quidam vestrum avaricie ardore succensi confratrias suas confratriis illorum eadem die in ipsorum adventu preponunt, et sic fratres ipsi confusi aut nihil exinde aut modicum consequuntur. Quia igitur hoc indecens est et in contemptum dei et ecclesie Romane redundat, universitati vestre per apostolica scripta precipiendo mandamus, quatinus, cum fratres ipsi ad loca vestra pro eleemosinis accesserint colligendis, benigne recipientes eosdem et honeste tractantes ipsos in ecclesiis vestris ammonere populum et elemosinas libere querere permittatis, confratrias vestras, quas facere potestis cottidie, ipsorum confratriis, que semel in anno fiunt, nullatenus preponentes, ne occasione illarum elemosine Christi pauperum depereant et impediantur opera pietatis. Statuimus etiam, ut nemo excommunicet fratres ipsos vel eorum oratoria interdicat sine mandato sedis apostolice speciali, presentium vobis auctoritate mandantes, ut ipsos excommunicare aut eorum ecclesias interdicere nullatenus presumatis; de parrochianis autem vestris, qui domos illorum invadunt per violentiam vel infringunt aut indebitis molestiis opprimunt fratres ipsos et tam deposita quam res diripiunt eorundem, cum exinde querimoniam deposuerint coram vobis, tam districtam eis faciatis iustitiam et ita iura eorum defendere et manutenere curetis, quod ipsi ad nos pro defectu iustitie sepe recurrere non cogantur, sed nos sollicitudinem et obedientiam vestram debeamus merito commendare, vosque beneficiorum, que in sancta domo eorum fiunt, participes existatis. Preterea liberas et absolutas personas, que se domui eorum in sanitate vel infirmitate reddiderunt, libere ac sine molestia recipi permittatis ab eis, nec ipsos super hoc temptetis aliquatenus impedire. Illud autem non mediocriter movet nos nec modicum ecclesiastice derogat honestati, quod quidam vestrum contra institutionem sanctorum patrum in Turonensi concilio editam fratrum ipsorum corpora, cum decedunt, nolunt sine pretio sepelire; unde, quia tam prava exactio et iniqua non est aliquatenus tolleranda, in obedientie vobis virtute precipimus, ut nullo modo a fratribus ipsis vel aliis pro sepultura quidquam exigere vel accipere, nisi quod spontanea decedentium liberalitas vel parentum devotio vobis contulerit, attemptetis, sed absque ullo pretio sepeliatis corpora mortuorum, et, si quis hoc ulterius attemptaverit, taliter animadvertatis in eum, quod amplius similia non presumat. Ad hec presentium vobis auctoritate precipimus, ne ab eis contra ea, que fratribus ipsis indulsimus, de nutrimentis animalium suorum, sive de ipsis animalibus decimas exigere presumatis. Cum autem oratoria vel cimiteria secundum quod eis concessimus duxerint construenda, vos, fratres archiepiscopi et episcopi, eis pro se ac familia sua tantum oratoria dedicare ac cimiteria benedicere procuretis nec aliquis vestrum contra concessionem nostram id impedire audeat aliquatenus vel turbare. De cetero fratres hospitalis s. Marie Theotonicorum in vestris episcopatibus constitutos, qui crucem et suum habitum deponentes per illecebras seculi et vitiorum abrupta vagantur, et illos etiam, qui prioribus suis contumaces et rebelles existunt, et balivas detinent contra voluntates ipsorum, moneatis instanter et pro vestri officii debito compellatis, ut habitum depositum resumentes in obedientia prelatorum suorum devote ac humiliter perseverent et balivas sive alia officia per violentiam detinere nullo modo presumant. Quicumque autem mandatorum nostrorum extiterint contemptores, excommunicationis eos sententia percellatis, quam faciatis usque ad satisfactionem condignam inviolabiliter observari. Preterea, quicumque de facultatibus sibi collatis a deo fratribus subvenerit sepe dictis et in eorum sancta fraternitate statuerit se collegam eisque beneficia persolverit annuatim, ei de beatorum apostolorum Petri et Pauli auctoritate confisi septimam partem iniuncte penitentie relaxamus. Apostolica quoque auctoritate ob reverentiam ipsius venerabilis domus statuimus, ut iis, qui eorum fraternitatem assumpserint, si forsan ecclesie, ad quas pertinent, a divinis fuerint officiis interdicte ipsosque mori contigerit, sepultura ecclesiastica non negetur, nisi excommunicati vel nominatim fuerint interdicti. Volumus autem, ut liceat eis confratres suos, quos ecclesiarum prelati apud ecclesias suas malitiose non permiserint sepeliri, nisi excommunicati vel nominatim fuerint interdicti aut etiam publici usurarii, tumulandos deferre ad ecclesias suas et oblaciones tam pro eis quam pro aliis, qui in eorum cimiteriis requiescunt, exhibitis sine alieni iuris preiudicio retinere; hoc etiam addito, ut receptores fraternitatis eiusdem seu etiam collectarum salvo iure dominorum suorum sub beati Petri et nostra protectione consistant. Adicimus insuper, ut, si qui eorundem fratrum, qui ad easdem fraternitates missi fuerint vel collectas, in quamlibet civitatem, castellum vel vicum advenerint, si forte locus ipse a divinis fuerit officiis interdictus, in eorum iocundo adventu semel aperiantur ecclesie annuatim et excommunicatis eiectis divina ibidem officia celebrentur, salva in omnibus supradictis declaratione concilii generalis. Ad maiorem quoque vestre mercedis cumulum nichilominus vobis mandando precipimus, quatinus hanc nostram constitutionem per parrochias vestras nuntiari propriis litteris faciatis. Mandamus etiam, ut, si qui de clericis ecclesiarum vestrarum prefati hospitalis Theotonicorum fratribus cum licentia prelati sui sponte ac gratis per annum vel biennium decreverint deservire, nequaquam impediantur, et interim sua beneficia et ecclesiasticos redditus non amittant. Datum Laterani xvii kal. februarii pontificatus nostri anno v.

Sine dato: I, 80; II, 94 n. 18. A. 20 n. 18 Latine et Germanice cum nota: In Leodio; Innocencius in Mergintheym; Allexander in Colonia simile vel in Martpurg vel in Praga etc. — Cum dato: Laterani xvii kal. febr. p. n. a. 5. IV, 179v.; Ioh. 28. Edd. Caorsinus p. B. 8. Senner p. D. 5v. Duellius Hist. ord. Theuton. app. 4 n. II; cf. II, 12 not. de or. Vindobon. — R. 132 memoratur inter Marburgensia. — Cum dato: Laterani idus ianuarii p. n. a. 7. A. 16 p. 30 sq. ex transsumto Venetiis asservato, quod (sine dato) frater Bartholomaeus minister fratrum minorum in Austria et frater Henricus subprior fratrum praedicatorum in Wienna exemplificaverunt. — Or., quod iam dudum in Vindobonensi domo Theutonica fuit, etiam hodie ibi exstat cum bulla in filis sericeis rubris et luteis pendente. — Cum dato: Laterani 6 nonas iulii p. a. 10. Transsumtum quondam Mergenthemense A. abbatis et M. decani s. Mariae in Lucenburch d. d. 1247 feria VI in hebdomada pasche (april. 5) Lucenborch in eodem archivo.

---

315. *1221 ianuarii 16 Laterani. Honorius III vetat fratres ordinis Theutonici molestari de sepeliendis confratribus, de malefactoribus persequendis, de eleemosynis quaerendis in aliorum ecclesiis.*

Honorius episcopus servus servorum dei venerabilibus fratribus archiepiscopis et episcopis et dilectis filiis abbatibus, prioribus, archidiaconis, decanis et aliis ecclesiarum prelatis, ad quos littere iste pervenerint, salutem et apostolicam benedictionem. Dilecti filii, fratres hospitalis sancte Marie Theotonicorum Ierosolimitani, nobis graviter sunt conquesti, quod vos confratres suos et eligentes in eorum cimiteriis sepulturam ab ipsis non permittitis fratribus sepeliri et eisdem exhibere iusticiam de suis malefactoribus negligentes in vestris non patimini ecclesiis fratres ipsos elemosinas querere, nec ad largiendum eis pias elemosinas populum exhortari[1]. Quocirca universitati vestre per apostolica scripta in virtute obediencie districte precipiendo mandamus, quatinus vos ipsi ab impedimentis huiusmodi penitus desistatis et vestros subditos taliter per censuram ecclesiasticam appellacione remota cogatis desistere ab eisdem, quod dicti fratres super hiis non possint de cetero querelari. Datum Laterani xvii kal. februarii pontificatus nostri anno v.

Sine dato: I, 73 n. 40; II, 98 n. 29; A. 20 n. 29 Latine et Germanice cum nota: „Et est in Marpurg" etc. D. 28. — Cum dato: Laterani xvii kal. febr. p. n. a. 5. A. 16 p. 63 „in Marpurg". 1. exortari I.

---

316. *1221 ianuarii 16 Laterani (cf. 1223 febr. 1). Honorius III vetat praelatos partem tertiam ordini Theutonico legatorum petere.*

Honorius episcopus servus servorum dei venerabilibus fratribus archiepiscopis et episcopis, et dilectis filiis abbatibus, prioribus, archidiaconis, decanis et aliis ecclesiarum prelatis, ad quos littere iste pervenerint, salutem et apostolicam benedictionem. Dilecti filii nostri, fratres hospitalis sancte Marie Theotonicorum Ierosolimitani, gravem contra[1] vos in auditorio nostro[2] deposuere querelam, quod vos[3] terciam partem eorum, que illis in testamento legantur, extorquetis pro[4] vestre voluntatis arbitrio ab eisdem[5] et alia ipsis gravamina multimoda irrogantes pro litteris nostris nullam eis curatis iustitiam exhibere. Quoniam igitur sic vobis adesse volumus, quod memoratis fratribus deesse in iusticia minime videamur; universitati vestre per apostolica scripta[6] mandamus atque precipimus, quatinus de hiis, que memoratis fratribus dantur ab aliquibus in sanitate vel in[7] infirmitate, sive[8] postea convaluerint aut apud alios[9] fuerint tumulati, partem[10] aliquam non queratis; de aliis vero parrochianis vestris, qui laborantes in extremis apud predictos fratres eligunt sepeliri, quarta[11] sitis testamenti parte contenti nec aliquid ab eis amplius exigatis. Sed nec sepulturam, quam per indulgenciam apostolice sedis habere noscuntur, occasione ista quisquam[12] vestrum impedire presumat[13]. Taliter autem ab ipsorum[14] molestiis et vos abstinere et parrochianos vestros compescere studeatis, quod[15] nec ipsi pro defectu iusticie ad presenciam nostram laborent nec vos de negligencia[16] vel contemptu mandati apostolici possitis[17] merito reprehendi. Nos enim, cum universis Christi[18] fidelibus simus[19] ex iniuncto nobis officio[20] debitores, predictis fratribus tanto forcius tenemur adesse, quanto ea, que ipsis beneficia[21] conferuntur[22], ad maiorem orientalis ecclesie[23] defensionem non est[24] dubium provenire; nec parum potest divinum formidare iudicium, quisquis eos, imo Christum in eis, fuerit persecutus[25], cum dicturus dominus in fine legatur: „Quod uni ex minimis meis fecistis, michi fecistis". Datum Laterani xvii kal. februarii pontificatus nostri anno quinto.

Sine dato: I, 71 v. n. 35; II, 97 v. n. 28; A. 20 n. 28 Latine et Germanice cum nota: Et est in Treveri etc. Germanice D. 27. — Cum dato: Laterani xvii kal. febr. p. a. 5. IV, 182 v. n. 9; R. 66 e domo Mergenthemensi n. 5. — Mergenthemense originale nunc Vindobonae est in archivo ordinis cum bulla plumbea in filis sericeis appendente. — Cum dato: Laterani kal. febr. p. n. a. 7. R. 141 inter Treverensia. A. 16 p. 113 „Treviris". 1. in II. 2. i. a. n. deest I.

3. deest A. 16. 4. pro⁹ I. 5. legantur p. v. v. a. a. e. extorquetis A. 16. 6. u. v. p. a. s. deest IV. 7. deest IV, A. 16. 8. si A. 16. 9. eos I. 10. porcionem A. 16. 11. q. tantum A. 20. 12. quisque A. 16. 13. contendat A. 16, IV. 14. iniuriis et molestiis abstinere A. 16. 15. ut A. 16. 16. neglieucia IV. 17. r. p.; merito deest I, IV. 18. Christi deest I, IV. 19. sumus IV, deest A. 16, A. 20. 20. n. sumus o. A. 16, n. o. d. sumus A. 20. 21. beneficio I. 22. conferimur IV. 23. terre A. 16. 24. deest I. 25. eis persequatur I.

---

317. *1221 ianuarii 16 Laterani. Honorius III vetat praelatos ab ordine Theutonico hospitationes exigere.*

Honorius episcopus servus servorum dei venerabilibus fratribus archiepiscopis et episcopis, et dilectis filiis abbatibus, prioribus, archidiaconis, decanis et aliis ecclesiarum prelatis, ad quos littere iste pervenerint, salutem et apostolicam benedictionem. Evangelice doctrine, que prohibet alterum alteri facere, quod sibi fieri[1] nollet, et honestati ecclesiastice contradicit aliquam religiosam domum in inmensa multitudine visitare et lautas[2] epulas querere illum, qui in domo propria procurationes sobrias vix interdum aliis sine scandalo exhiberet[3]. Accepimus autem, quod quidam vestrum domos dilectorum filiorum, fratrum hospitalis sancte Marie Theotonicorum[4] Ierosolimitani, in magna multitudine equorum et hominum adeuntes, in eis fratribus contradicentibus hospitantur et expensis gravissimis inquietant, quos debebant ad reverentiam nostram, ad cuius defensionem specialiter pertinent, et consideracione[5] obsequii, quod defensioni[6] christianitatis exhibent in partibus transmarinis, contra alios sollicite adiuvare. Quia igitur tolerare in paciencia[7] non debemus, ut in diebus nostris honera predictis fratribus imponantur, que antea non portarunt; universitati vestre auctoritate apostolica districtius inhibemus, ne in domibus eorum ipsis queratis renitentibus hospitari, nisi forte in concessione ipsarum domorum vobis vestrisque successoribus manifeste apparuerit reservatum, sed ea pocius reverencia et obsequiis sitis contenti, quod per scriptum autenticum declaratur. Datum[8] Laterani[9] xvii kal. februarii pontificatus nostri anno v.

Sine dato: I, 67; II, 101 n. 38; D. 37; A. 20 n. 36 Latine et Germanice cum nota: „In Akon vel in Mergintheim", „Das ist zcu Akon adir zcu Mergentheym". — Cum dato citatur R. 77 inter Mergenthemensia n. 29. 1. fieri sibi II. 2. latas I. 3. i. s. s. a. e. II. 4. Theut- II. 5. considerationem II. 6. defensione II. 7. in patientia tollerare II. 8. caetera desunt II. 9. caetera desunt I.

---

318. *1221 ianuarii 16 Laterani (cf. 1223 febr. 26). Honorius III vetat praelatos vicariorum ab ordine Theutonico ad ecclesias eius vel fratrum eius a patronis ad alias praesentatorum institutionem denegare.*

Honorius episcopus servus servorum dei venerabilibus fratribus archiepiscopis et episcopis et dilectis filiis abbatibus, prioribus, archidiaconis, decanis et aliis ecclesiarum prelatis, ad quos littere iste pervenerint, salutem et apostolicam benedictionem. Ex insinuacione dilectorum filiorum, fratrum domus hospitalis sancte Marie Theotonicorum Ierosolimitani, ad apostolatus nostri audienciam est delatum, quod, cum in ecclesiis vacantibus, que in terris ipsorum fundate sunt, vel in aliis, quarum ad ipsos advocacio dinoscitur pertinere, pro ipsis volunt vicarios instituere vel cum ipsi fratres ad ecclesias alias vacantes a patronis legitimis diocesanis episcopis aut prelatis aliis, ad quos earundem pertinet institutio, presentantur, ipsi vicarios, quos iidem fratres pro se presentant, recipere vel ipsos fratres ab aliquibus presentatos instituere contradicunt, et sic fratres ipsos impediunt et perturbant, ut ecclesias illas, secundum quod eis indulsimus pro subvencione terre sancte, non valeant in proprios usus convertere seu aliam professionem canonicam adipisci, in quo fratres ipsi se asserunt incurrisse non modicum detrimentum. Cum igitur ipsis fratribus hoc presertim tempore, cum laborant efficaciter in servicio crucifixi[1], debeamus specialius apostolicum presidium impertiri et ad dilectionem ipsorum aliorum animos invitare, discretionem vestram rogamus, monemus et per apostolica vobis[2] scripta precipiendo mandamus, quatinus eos in suis racionibus efficacius confoventes sic permittatis eis[3] in obtinendis et possidendis ecclesiis concessa ipsis a sede apostolica libertate gaudere, quod iustam de vobis non possint habere materiam murmurandi[4] et nos pro ipsis super hoc vobis[2] scripta non cogamur dirigere duriora. Datum Laterani, xvii kal. februarii pontificatus nostri anno quinto.

Sine dato: I, 72; II, 102 n. 43; R. 153 memoratur inter Iuncensia; cum nota: „et habetur prius in Marpurg, similiter et Treveris" A. 20 n. 41 Latine et Germanice cum nota: In Bysen vel in Buken vel in Mergintheym. — Cum dato: p. a. 5 xvii kal. febr. A. 16 p. 42 „Baruli". — Cum dato: p. a. 7 iv kal. febr. Or. cum bulla in filis sericeis rubris et luteis appendente, quondam Veteribus Iuncis asservatum, nunc est archivi ordinis Theutonici Vindobonensis. Ibidem etiam transsumtum d. d. Basileae vii kal. maii fratris Achillis prioris ord. praedic. Basiliensis, Henrici praepositi, Henrici decani ecclesiae Basileensis cum tribus sigillis: 1. S. prioris fratrum predicatorum Basilee (Christus ad columnam alligatus flagellatur). 2. S. Henrici prepositi eccl. Basil. et domini pp. cappellani. 3. S. Henrici decani ecclesie Basileensis. 1. Ihesu Christi II, A. 20. 2. deest II, A. 20. 3. eos II, A. 20. 4. querelandi II, A. 20.

---

319. *1221 ianuarii 16 Laterani. Honorius III decimas ab ordine Theutonico exigi vetat.*

Honorius episcopus servus servorum dei etc. Ex parte dilectorum filiorum, fratrum hospitalis sancte Marie Theotonicorum Ierosolimitani, nobis est oblata querela, quod quidam vestrum occasione concilii generalis pro sue voluntatis arbitrio decimas laborum de possessionibus habitis ante concilium memoratum, quos ipsi propriis manibus aut sumptibus excolunt, et nutrimentis suorum animalium ab eis contra ea, que a nobis indulta sunt, non metuunt extorquere. Quocirca universitati vestre per apostolica scripta in virtute obediencie districte precipiendo mandamus, quatinus non obstante longa violentia super dictis exactionibus eisdem fratribus irrogata et vos ipsi ab extorsione huiusmodi penitus desistatis et vestros subditos taliter per censuram ecclesiasticam appellatione remota cogatis desistere ab eisdem, quod dicti fratres super hiis non possint de cetero querelari. Datum Laterani xvii kal. februarii pontificatus nostri anno v.

Sine dato: I, 72; II, 102 n. 44; A. 20 n. 42 Latine et Germanice; D. 42. — Cum dato: xvii kal. febr. Laterani p. a. 5. Or. cum bulla plumbea in filis sericeis appendente quondam Mergenthemi, nunc Vindobonae in archivo ordinis Theutonici exstat. R. 69 inter Mergenthemensia n. 14 forsan per lapsum calami xviii.

---

320. *1221 ianuarii 16 Laterani (cf. 1223 ianuarii 13). Honorius III concedit ordini Theutonico, ut quemvis cruce signatum, dummodo non obstet impedimentum canonicum, inter fratres recipere ei liceat.*

Honorius episcopus servus servorum dei dilectis filiis magistro et fratribus hospitalis sancte Marie Theotonicorum Ierosolimitani salutem et apostolicam benedictionem. Iustis petencium desideriis dignum est nos facilem prebere consensum et vota, que a rationis tramite non discordant, effectu prosequente complere. Eapropter, dilecti in domino filii, vestris iustis postulationibus grato concurrentes assensu presentis scripti pagina vobis duximus indulgendum, ut liceat vobis quemlibet sancte crucis signaculo[1] signatum in fratrem recipere, si impedimentum aliquod canonicum[2] non obsistat[3]. Nulli ergo omnino hominum liceat hanc paginam nostre concessionis infringere, vel ei ausu temerario contraire. Si quis autem hoc attemptare presumpserit, indignacionem omnipotentis dei et beatorum Petri et Pauli apostolorum eius se noverit incursurum. Datum Laterani xvii kalendas februarii pontificatus nostri anno quinto[4].

Sine dato: A. 20 n. 46 Latine et Germanice cum nota: Et est in Mergentheym; I, 67v. et II, 103v. n. 48. — Cum dato: Laterani xvii kal. febr. p. n. a. 5. IV, 182 et R. 67 inter Mergenthemensia n. 8. Or. cum bulla in filis sericeis appendente Vindobonae in archivo ordinis Theutonici. — Cum dato: Laterani ydus ianuarii p. n. a. 7. R. 68 inter Mergenthemensia n. 11. — 1. deest I. 2. aliquod impedimentum can. IV, impedimentum canonicum aliquod II. 3. obsistit. Nulli ergo etc. Si quis autem etc. Datum etc. II. 4. Lat. etc. I (caetera desunt).

---

321. *1221 ianuarii 16 Laterani. Honorius III ordinis Theutonici benefactoribus concedit indulgentiam ipsique facultatem, ut in fratrum adventu semel in anno ecclesiae interdicto subiectae aperiantur.*

Honorius episcopus servus servorum dei venerabilibus fratribus archiepiscopis et episcopis et dilectis filiis abbatibus, prioribus, archidiaconis, decanis et aliis ecclesiarum prelatis, ad quos littere iste pervenerint, salutem et apostolicam benedictionem. Milites hospitalis sancte Marie Theutonicorum Ierosolimitani novi sub tempore gratie Machabei, abnegantes secularia desideria et propria relinquentes, tollentes crucem suam, dominum sunt secuti; ipsi sunt, per quos deus orientalem ecclesiam a paganorum spurcitiis liberat, et christiani nominis inimicos expungnat; ipsi pro fratribus animas ponere non formidant et peregrinos ad sancta loca proficiscentes tam in eundo quam[1] redeundo defensant ab incursibus paganorum. Et, quoniam ad tam sanctum et pium opus explendum eis proprie non suppetunt facultates, universitatem vestram presentibus litteris exhortamur, quatinus populum vobis a deo commissum collectas facere commoneatis, ex quibus eorum inopia suppleatur. Quicumque vero de facultatibus sibi a deo collatis ipsis subvenerit et in eorum sancta fraternitate statuerit se collegam eisque beneficia persolverit, annuatim, septimam ei partem iniuncte sibi poenitentie confisi de beatorum Petri et Pauli apostolorum meritis indulgemus. Cui etiam, cum eum mori contigerit, si tamen nec excommunicatus nec nominatim fuerit interdictus aut publice usurarius, sepultura ecclesiastica non negetur. Cum autem fratres ipsius hospitalis Theutonicorum, qui ad collectam suscipiendam destinati fuerint, in civitatem, castellum vel vicum advenerint, si forte locus ille interdictus sit, in eorum iocundo adventu pro ipsius hospitalis honore et eorundem militum reverentia semel in anno aperiantur ecclesie et excommunicatis et nominatim interdictis exclusis divina officia celebrentur. Que vero de non excommunicatis et nominatim interdictis eorundem militum fratribus ecclesiastice sepulture tradendis et ecclesiis in eorum adventu excommunicatis et nominatim interdictis exclusis semel aperiendis a nobis statuta sunt, vobis archiepiscopis et episcopis mandando precipimus, ut per vestras parrochias faciatis irrefragabiliter observari, salva in omnibus moderatione concilii generalis. Preterea fraternitati vestre rogando mandamus, quatinus personas et bona eorum pro reverentia beati Petri et nostra manuteneatis et nullam eis irrogare lesionem vel iniuriam permittatis. Datum Laterani xvii kal. februarii pontificatus nostri anno v.

Sine dato: I, 74 v.; II, 104 v. n. 52; A. 20 n. 50 Latine et Germanice cum nota: In Marpurg etc. R. 1 n. 2 e domo Norimbergensi. D. 51. — Cum dato: Laterani xvii kal. febr. p. n. a. 5. Ioh. 29. — Or. cum bulla in filis sericeis appensa, quondam Mergenthemense, nunc Vindobonae in archivo ois. Thci. — Ediderunt Caorsinus B. 8; Senner p. D. 6 v.; Duellius Hist. ord. Theut. in appendice 5 n. III. 1. q. in A. 20.

---

322. *1221 ianuarii 16 Laterani (cf. 1225 maii 31 Tiburc). Honorius III iubet ordinis Theutonici molestatores ecclesiasticis sententiis coerceri.*

Honorius episcopus servus servorum dei venerabilibus fratribus archiepiscopis et epicopis et dilectis filiis abbatibus, prioribus, archidiaconis, decanis et aliis ecclesiarum prelatis, ad quos littere iste pervenerint, salutem et apostolicam benedictionem. Non absque dolore cordis et plurima turbacione didicimus, quod ita in plerisque partibus ecclesiastica censura dissolvitur et canonice sententie severitas enervatur, ut viri religiosi et hii maxime, qui per sedis apostolice privilegia maiori donati sunt libertate[1], passim a malefactoribus suis iniurias sustinent et rapinas, dum vix invenitur, qui congrua illis protectione subveniat et pro fovenda pauperum innocencia se murum defensionis opponat. Specialiter autem dilecti filii fratres hospitalis sancte Marie Theotonicorum Ierosolimitani tam de frequentibus iniuriis quam de ipso cotidiano defectu iustitie conquerentes universitatem vestram literis petierunt apostolicis excitari, ut ita videlicet eis in tribulacionibus suis contra malefactores suos prompta debeatis magnanimitate consurgere, quod ab angustiis, quas sustinent, et pressuris vestro possint presidio respirare; ideoque universitati vestre per apostolica scripta mandamus atque precipimus, quatinus illos, qui possessiones vel res seu domos predictorum fratrum vel hominum suorum irreverenter invaserint vel ea iniuste detinuerint, que predictis fratribus ex testamento decedentium relinquuntur, seu in ipsos fratres contra apostolice sedis indulta sentenciam excommunicacionis aut interdicti presumpserint promulgare vel decimas laborum de possessionibus habitis ante concilium generale seu nutrimentis ipsorum spretis privilegiis apostolice sedis extorquere, monicione premissa, si laici fuerint, publice candelis accensis excommunicationis sentencia percellatis; si vero clerici vel canonici regulares seu monachi fuerint, eos appellacione remota ab officio e' beneficio suspendatis, neutram relaxaturi sentenciam, donec predictis fratribus plenarie satisfaciant, et tam laici quam clerici seculares, qui pro violenta manuum inieccione anathematis vinculo fuerint innodati, cum diocesani episcopi litteris ad sedem apostolicam venientes ab eodem vinculo mereantur absolvi[2]. Villas autem, in quibus bona predictorum fratrum vel hominum suorum detenta fuerint, quamdiu ibi sunt, interdicti sententie supponatis. Datum Laterani xvii kal. februarii pontificatus nostri anno quinto.

Sine dato: I, 71; II, 105 n. 53; A. 20. 51 Latine et Germanice cum nota: in Traiecto inferiori. Dis privilegium is zcum nedirsten Utrecht. R. 126 inter Marburgensia, cf. 196. — Cum dato: Laterani xvii kal. febr. p. a. 5. IV, 178v.; Ioh. 27; A. 16 p. 62 „in Marpurg". „Hoc etiam invenitur in Mechelinia". Edd. Caorsinus B. 7; Senner D. 5v. — Cum dato: Tibure ii kal. iunii a. 9. „Traiecti" A. 16 p. 106. 1. II. libertati caeteri. 2. Caetera desunt II.

---

323. *1221 ianuarii 17 Laterani (cf. 1223 ian. 12 et 31, febr. 3 et 4 Laterani). Honorius III iubet parochianos cogi ecclesiastica disciplina, ut ordini Theutonico iustitiam praestent.*

Honorius episcopus servus servorum dei archiepiscopis et episcopis et[1] dilectis filiis abbatibus, prioribus, archidiaconis, decanis et aliis ecclesiarum prelatis, ad quos littere iste pervenerint, salutem et apostolicam benedictionem. Cum a religiosorum virorum pressuris et molestiis illi, quorum pedes sunt veloces ad malum, severitate debeant ecclesiastica cohiberi et inferiorum culpe merito ad prelatos desides referantur, quia facientis culpam habet, qui, quod potest corrigere, negligit emendare; miramur, sicut possumus de ratione mirari, quod, sicut dilectis filiis fratribus hospitalis sancte Marie Theutonicorum Ierosolimitani significantibus accepimus, parrochianos vestros, de quibus apud vos querelam deponunt, non compellitis ad iusticiam exhibendam; si vero aliquos excommunicationi interdum vel interdicto supponitis, sentenciam vestram remittitis fratribus inconsultis et satisfactione congrua pretermissa. Quia igitur sustinere nolumus incorreptum[2], quod in nostrum[3] et subiectorum nostrorum[4] periculum attemptatur, universitati vestre per apostolica scripta mandamus atque precipimus, quatenus, cum a iam dictis fratribus acceperitis de vestris parrochianis querelam, eos ad exhibendam iusticiam omni gracia et timore postposito, contradictione quoque et appellatione remota ecclesiastica districtione cogatis attentius provisuri, ne sententiam, quam tuleritis, fratribus ignorantibus[5] absque satisfactione congrua relaxetis, scituri a vobis[6] dampna ipsorum districtius requirenda, si preceptum neglexeritis, quod non credimus, adimplere[7]. Datum Laterani xvi kal. februarii pontificatus nostri anno quinto.

Sine dato: II, 95 v.; A. 20 n. 19 Latine et Germanice cum nota: in Trevere vel in Martpurg; memoratur: R. 147 inter Treverensia; R. 153 inter Iuncensia; necnon A. 16 p. 94 et 95. — Cum dato: xvi kal. febr. p. a. 5 Laterani. R. 75 inter Mergenthemensia n. 25. — Cum dato: ii id. ian. p. a. 7 Laterani; originale cum bulla in filis sericeis rubris et luteis pendente Vindobonae in archivo ois. Thci., quondam Iuncis. — Cum dato: ii kal. febr. p. a. 7 Laterani; or. cum bulla in filis sericeis rubris et luteis pendente Vindobonae in archivo ois. Thci., quondam Iuncis. — Cum dato: iii non. febr. p. a. 7 Laterani. R. 128 et A. 16 p. 61 utrobique inter Marburgensia n. 7. „Treviris" A. 16 p. 117. — Cum dato: ii non. febr. p. a. 7 Laterani. A. 16 p. 37 „Baruli". 1. hinc usque benedictionem supplevi sec. R. 128. 2. incorrectum R. 75, A. 16 bis. 3. vestrum R. 41. Inn. IV. 4. vestrorum R. 41. 5. ingratantibus A. 16 p. 62. 6. nobis II. A. 20. 7. adimpleri I.

---

324. *1221 ianuarii 17 Laterani. Honorius III vetat liberam sepulturam in ordinis Theutonici coemeterio impediri benefactoresque molestari.*

Honorius episcopus servus servorum dei venerabilibus fratribus archiepiscopis et episcopis et dilectis filiis abbatibus, prioribus, decanis, archidiaconis et aliis ecclesiarum prelatis, ad quos littere iste pervenerint, salutem et apostolicam benedictionem. Gravem ex parte dilectorum filiorum fratrum hospitalis sancte Marie Theotonicorum Ierosolimitani querelam accepimus, quod, cum ipsi ex indulgencia sedis apostolice liberam habeant in suo cimiterio sepulturam, parrochianis vestris, ne ibidem debeant sepeliri, presumitis inhibere, omnes illos, qui in eorum ecclesia officiis divinis intersunt aut elemosinas offerunt, asserentes excommunicacionis sententie subiacere. Quia igitur nulla ratione sustinere possemus, ut eis tantam iniuriam inferretis, per apostolica vobis scripta precipiendo mandamus, quatinus ab huiusmodi presumpcionibus desistentes omnino super dampnis et iniuriis irrogatis omni contradictione et excusatione cessantibus[1] congrue satisfacere non tardetis. Datum Laterani xvi kal. februarii pontificatus nostri anno v.

Sine dato: I, 69; A. 20 n. 6 Latine et Germanice cum nota: „Est in Trevere etc." A. 16 p. 112 „Treviris". — Cum dato: xvi kal. febr. p. a. 5. R. 148 inter Treverensia. — Or. cum bulla plumbea in filis sericeis rubris et luteis appendente in archivo ordinis Theutonici Vindobonae; unde mihi venit etiam notitia quondam Veteribus Iuncis illud fuisse. 1. cessante A. 16. A. 20. possumus .. inferatis A. 20.

---

325. *1221 ianuarii 17. Honorius III concedit ordini Theutonico, ut iura sua fratrum testimonio probare et tueri possit.*

Honorius episcopus servus servorum dei dilectis filiis .. magistro et fratribus hospitalis sancte Marie Theotonicorum Ierosolimitani salutem et apostolicam benedictionem. Quociens postulatur a nobis, quod rationi conveniat et canonice consonet sanctioni, petencium desideriis facilem debemus prebere consensum, ne in eo difficiles videamur, quod convenit celeriter indulgeri. Eapropter vestris postulationibus inclinati, ut iura vestra testimonio vestrorum fratrum probare et tueri possitis, liberam vobis concedimus facultatem. Nulli ergo omnino hominum liceat hanc paginam nostre concessionis infringere vel ei ausu temerario contraire. Si quis autem hoc attemptare presumpserit, indignationem omnipotentis dei et beatorum Petri et Pauli apostolorum eius se noverit incursurum. Datum Laterani xvi kal. februarii pontificatus nostri anno quinto.

Sine dato: I, 67v.; II, 110v. n. 66; A. 20 n. 64 Latine et Germanice; D. 66. — Cum dato: Laterani xvi kal. febr. p. n. a. 5. Originale in archivo Regimontano; R. 57 inter Ratisponensia n. 10. In archivo Regimontano (cf. Napiersky I, 4 n. 13) transsumtum d. d. Accone 1277 oct. 19 per Bonacursum Tyrensem archiepiscopum, Ierosolimitani patriarchatus et Acconensis episcopatus vicarium, cuius adest sigillum, et Gailardum, Bethlehemitanum episcopum, Iohanne Acconensi clerico, notario Romano, subscribente confectum. Cuius transsumti apographum e domo Ellingensi in R. 40 n. 24. Alterum transsumti originale est in archivo ordinis Theutonici Vindobonensi, unde edidit Hennes I, 226 n. 259.

---

326. *1221 ianuarii 18 Laterani. Honorius III concedit fratribus ordinis Theutonici, ut ob excessus in ipsos vel alios religiosos aut clericos commissos etiam ante susceptum habitum a diocesanis episcopis absolutionem adipisci possint.*

Honorius episcopus servus servorum dei dilectis filiis magistro et fratribus hospitalis sancte Marie Theotonicorum Ierosolimitani salutem et apostolicam benedictionem. Ea, que pro defensione nominis christiani sustinetis, discrimina, nos inducunt, ut vos et ordinem vestrum favore continuo prosequentes quieti vestre propensius intendamus et studeamus vobis auferre materiam gravaminis et laboris. Hinc est, quod vobis auctoritate presencium indulgemus, ut, si qui e fratribus vestris in[1] se invicem sive in alios religiosos quoslibet seu eciam in clericos seculares manus iniecerint violentas, per diocesanos episcopos absolutionis beneficium assequantur, eciamsi[2] eorum aliqui, priusquam habitum vestrum susciperent, tale aliquid commiserunt, propter quod ipso actu excommunicationis sentenciam incurrissent, nisi excessus eorum[3] esset difficilis et enormis, utpote si esset ad mutilationem membri vel sanguinis effusionem processum aut violenta manus in episcopum vel[4] in abbatem iniecta, cum excessus tales et similes sine scandalo nequeant preteriri. Nulli ergo omnino hominum liceat hanc paginam nostre concessionis infringere vel ei ausu temerario contraire. Si quis autem hoc attemptare presumpserit, indignationem omnipotentis dei et beatorum Petri et Pauli apostolorum eius se noverit incursurum. Datum Laterani xv kal. februarii pontificatus nostri anno v.

Sine dato: I, 68 („Lat.") et I, 75 v.; II, 101 n. 39; A. 20 n. 37 Latine et Germanice cum nota: „In Mergintheim, et Allexander huic simile in Buken". — Cum dato: Laterani xv kal. febr. p. a. 5. R. 65 e domo Mergenthemensi n. 2. — A. 16 p. 39 „Baruli". 1. deest I p. 68, A. 16. 2. si A. 16. 3. ipsorum I, 75 v. 4. deest I, 68. II. A. 20.

---

327. *1221 ianuarii 18 Laterani. Honorius III iubet praelatos ab ordine Theutonico ad ecclesias suas praesentatos vicarios, dummodo sufficientes redditus pro sustentatione et episcopi iusticia assignentur, recipere.*

Honorius episcopus servus servorum dei venerabilibus fratribus archiepiscopis et episcopis et dilectis filiis abbatibus, prioribus, archidiaconis, decanis, et aliis ecclesiarum prelatis, ad quos littere iste pervenerint, salutem et apostolicam benedictionem. Quanto dilecti filii, .. magister et fratres domus hospitalis sancte Marie Theotonicorum Ierosolimitani, propriis derelictis ferventius pro christianitatis commodo iugiter elaborant nec ponere pro fratribus animas reformidant, tanto ipsis in suis manutenendis iustitiis diligencius adesse nos convenit, et eorum incommoditatibus paterna sollicitudine providere, ne, si fuerimus, quod absit, in eorum manutenenda iustitia negligentes, a Sarracenorum impungnatione, qui christianum nomen insufflant et fidelium effundere sanguinem moliuntur, desistere conpellantur et amplius adversus christianos eorum insolentia convalescat. Cum autem prenominatis fratribus de indulgentia sedis apostolice misericorditer duxerimus indulgendum[1], ut fructus ecclesiarum, que ad eorum donationem pertinent, assignato vicariis unde congrue valeant sustentari et diocesano episcopo eiusque officialibus de suis possint iustitiis respondere, debeant in subventionem terre Ierosolimitane convertere; quidam episcopi, archidiaconi et decani, ad quos illarum ecclesiarum investitura pertinet, clericos, quos iidem fratres idoneos representant, recipere pro sua voluntate contempnunt, nisi easdem ecclesias clericis, qui de eorum mensa fuerint, seu aliis, licet minus existant idonei, largiantur, si vero iidem fratres, easdem ecclesias, prout desiderant, non assignant, ut libere possint redditus earum percipere, illos per longa tempora faciunt a divinorum celebratione cessare, ut sic fratres ipsi voluntates eorum exequi compellantur. Nos igitur tante predictorum fratrum incommoditati prospicere cupientes, ne tantam iacturam malitiose cogantur de cetero sustinere, universitati vestre[2] per apostolica scripta mandamus atque precipimus, quatinus clericos idoneos, quos iidem fratres ad ecclesias suas vobis duxerint presentandos, ammodo benignius admittatis; alioquin noveritis, quod ipsis auctoritate apostolica liberam indulsimus facultatem, ut fructus earundem ecclesiarum, donec predicta occasione vacaverint, in subventionem[3] Ierosolimitane terre convertere et illos valeant libere detinere. Preterea, quia quidam vestrum fratres ipsorum et eorum clericos contra privilegium sedis apostolice ipsis indultum, sicut dicitur, interdicere et excommunicare presumunt, districtius inhibemus, ne ipsos fratres vel eorum clericos de cetero taliter interdicere et excommunicare aliquatenus attemptetis. Quod si ammodo, quod non credimus, fuerit attemptatum, eandem volumus sententiam non tenere. Datum Laterani xv kal. februarii pontificatus nostri anno v.

Sine dato: I, 66 v.; II, 91; A. 20 n. 5 Latine et Germanice cum nota: Est in Goslaria vel Alsacia etc. — Cum dato: Laterani xv kal. febr. p. n. a. 5. IV, 183 v.; R. 1 e domo Nurembergensi. — Or. cum bulla filis sericeis appendente quondam Mergenthemi, nunc Vindobonae in archivo ordinis Theutonici. — Transsumtum de 1418 dec. 2 petente Iohanne de Hofheym, ordinis Theutonici syndico et procuratore, per Wernherum canonicum et officialem Herbipolensem factum in archivo Regimontano. Ed., sed male, Duellius in appendice p. 6 n. IV. 1. sedis apostolice sit misericorditer indultum A. 20. 2. vobis A. 20. 3. subvencione A. 20.

---

328. *1221 ianuarii 18 Laterani (cf. 1221 iunii 2, 1224 iunii 22 Laterani). Honorius III vetat ab ordinis Theutonici novalibus vel terris post concilium acquisitis, quas fratres propriis aut manibus aut sumptibus colant, decimas exigi.*

Honorius episcopus servus servorum dei venerabilibus fratribus [patriarchis,][1] archiepiscopis et episcopis, et dilectis filiis abbatibus, prioribus, archidiaconis, decanis et aliis ecclesiarum prelatis, ad quos littere iste pervenerint, salutem et apostolicam benedictionem. Quia plerumque veritatis integritas per minorem intelligentiam aut malitiam hominum depravatur, non videtur incongruum, si ea, que non manifesta dicta videntur, ad omnem ambiguitatis scrupulum amovendum evidentius exponantur et turbatoribus veritatis omnis auferatur contradictionis occasio, quatenus ea, que dicta sunt, nulla valeant obumbratione fuscari. Accepimus autem, quod, cum dilectis filiis .. magistro et fratribus domus hospitalis sancte Marie Theutonicorum Ierosolimitani duxerimus concedendum, ut de laboribus, quos propriis manibus vel sumptibus excolunt, de possessionibus habitis ante concilium generale nemini decimas solvere teneantur, quidam ab eis nihilominus post celebrationem generalis concilii contra indulgentiam sedis apostolice decimas de predictis possessionibus exigere ac extorquere presumunt, ac prava et sinistra interpretatione apostolici privilegii capitulum pervertentes asserunt de novalibus debere intelligi, ubi noscitur de laboribus esse scriptum. Quoniam igitur manifestum est omnibus, qui recte sapiunt, interpretationem huiusmodi perversam esse et intellectui sano contrariam, cum secundum capitulum illud a solutione decimarum tam de terris illis, quas deduxerunt vel deducunt ad cultum, quam de terris etiam cultis, quas propriis manibus vel sumptibus excolunt, liberi penitus sint et immunes, ne ullus contra eos materiam habeat malignandi vel quomodolibet ipsos contra iustitiam molestandi, vobis per apostolica scripta mandamus et districte precipimus, quatenus omnibus parrochianis vestris auctoritate apostolica prohibere curetis, ne a memoratis fratribus de novalibus vel aliis terris post dictum concilium acquisitis,* quas propriis manibus vel sumptibus excolunt, seu de nutrimentis animalium suorum nullatenus decimas exigere vel extorquere presumant. Nam si de novalibus tantum vellemus intelligi, ubi ponimus de laboribus, de novalibus poneremus. Quia vero non est conveniens vel honestum, ut contra statuta sedis apostolice veniatur, que obtinere debent immobilem firmitatem, mandamus vobis firmiterque precipimus, ut, si qui canonici, clerici, monachi vel laici contra privilegia sedis apostolice predictos decimarum de novalibus vel terris predictis exaccione gravaverint, canonicos, clericos sive monachos contradictione et appellacione cessante, sicut iustum fuerit, monicione premissa ab officio suspendatis, laicos excommunicationis sententia percellatis et tam excommunicationis quam suspensionis sententiam faciatis usque ad dignam satisfactionem inviolabiliter observari, salva moderatione concilii generalis. Ad hec vobis presentium auctoritate mandamus atque precipimus, quatenus, si quis in predictos fratres manus violentas iniecerit, eum accensis candelis tam diu sicut excommunicatum publice nuncietis et faciatis ab omnibus caucius evitari, donec congrue satisfaciat predictis fratribus et cum litteris diocesani episcopi rei veritatem continentibus apostolico se conspectui representet. Datum Laterani xv kal. februarii pontificatus nostri anno quinto.

Sine dato: I, 76; II, 109 v. n. 65; R. 143 inter Treverensia. — Cum dato: Laterani xv kal. febr. p. n. a. 5. IV, 184 v. n. 12. Ioh. 30. Originale, quod quondam Veteribus Iuncis fuisse perhibetur, cum bulla plumbea in filis sericeis rubris et luteis appendente in archivo ordinis Theutonici asservatur. — Alterum originale, cui deest modo bulla, in archivo Regimontano, ubi etiam tria asservantur transsumta: 1. confectum Accon 1277 aug. 30 requirente Iohanne magno praeceptore auspiciis Thomae ord. praedic., Ierosolimitani patriarchae et ministri Acconensis ecclesiae, ap. sed. legati, per Iohannem clericum Acconensem, ecclesiae s. crucis Acconensis assisium; quod memoratur in R. 10 in domo Nurenbergensi n. 18; 2. confectum Accon 1281 sept. 12 requirente religioso fratre Iohanne de Saxonia, procuratore, syndico domus Alamannorum, sub auspiciis Gaufridi, Ebronensis episcopi, Eliae Ierosolimitani patriarchae, ministri Acconensis ecclesiae et apostolici legati (cuius appendet sigillum), Rampnulphi Nicossiensis archiepiscopi, per Iohannem clericum Acconensem, assisium, notarium apostolicum. — Ediderunt Caorsinus B. 8 v., Senner p. E., Duellius II, 5 n. V et e transsumto de 1281 sept. 12, Livl. U.-B. I, 63 n. 60. — Cum dato: Tibure 4 nonas iunii p. n. a. 5, simplex copia in archivo ordinis Theutonici Vindobonae asservatur, quae iam dudum fuit domus Vindobonensis. — Cum dato: Laterani x kal. iulii p. n. a. 8. I, 76. 1. Duellius.

---

329. *1221 ianuarii 18 Laterani. Honorius III ordinem Theutonicum sub apostolicae sedis protectione iubet esse conceditque, ut undique clericos suscipiat et liberae sepulturae privilegio fruatur.*

Honorius episcopus servus servorum dei magistro et fratribus hospitalis sancte Marie Theutonicorum Ierosolimitani salutem et apostolicam benedictionem. Quociens a nobis petitur, quod religioni et honestati convenire dinoscitur, animo nos decet libenti concedere et petencium desideriis congruum suffragium impertiri. Eapropter, dilecti in domino filii, vestris iustis postulationibus clementer annuimus et domum vestram, in qua estis ad dei laudem et gloriam et defensionem suorum fidelium et liberandam dei ecclesiam congregati, cum omnibus possessionibus et bonis suis, que inpresenciarum legitime habere cognoscitur aut in futurum concessione pontificum, liberalitate regum vel principum, oblatione fidelium seu aliis iustis modis prestante domino poterit adipisci tam trans mare quam cis mare, vobis auctoritate apostolica confirmamus et[1] perpetuis futuris temporibus sub apostolice sedis tutela et protectione consistant. Ut autem vobis ad curam animarum vestrarum et salutis plenitudinem nichil desit atque ecclesiastica sacramenta et divina officia vestro sacro collegio exhibeantur commodius, statuimus, ut liceat vobis honestos clericos et sacerdotes secundum deum quantum ad vestram conscientiam ordinatos undecumque ad vos venientes suscipere et tam in principali domo vestra quam eciam in obedienciis et locis sibi subdictis vobiscum habere, dummodo, si e vicino sint, eos a propriis episcopis expetatis iidemque nulli alii professioni vel ordini teneantur obnoxii. Preterea nulli persone extra vestrum capitulum sint subiecti tibique, dilecte in domino fili magister, tuisque successoribus tanquam magistro et prelato suo deferant secundum vestri ordinis instituta. Quicunque vero in cimiterio vestro elegerint sepeliri, ad sepulturam recipiendi, educendi et sepeliendi, nisi forte excommunicati vel nominatim fuerint interdicti aut eciam publice[2] usurarii, facultatem liberam habeatis, salva tamen iusticia illarum ecclesiarum, a quibus mortuorum corpora assumuntur. Decernimus ergo, ut nulli omnino hominum liceat hanc paginam nostre confirmationis et constitutionis infringere vel ei ausu temerario contraire. Si quis autem hoc attemptare presumpserit, indignationem omnipotentis dei et beatorum Petri et Pauli apostolorum eius se noverit incursurum. Datum Laterani xv kal. februarii pontificatus nostri anno v.

Sine dato: I, 71 v.; II, 107 n. 59; A. 20 n. 57 Latine et Germanice. — Cum dato: Laterani xv kal. febr. p. n. a. 5. Originale cum bulla in archivo Regimontano; cf. Napiersky I, 4 n. 14. Apographum vidimationis factae per Bonacursum de ordine cet. et Gailardum cet. d. d. Accon 1277 oct. 19 e domo Ellingensi: R. 39. — Protectionis clausulam transsumsit Nicolaus Pomesaniensis episcopus 1371 iunii 7 petente Swedero de Pelland o. T. thesaurario, Iohanne quondam Sonchen de Rosinberg et Iohanne Muench de Elbingo, notariis, subscribentibus. Originale cum episcopi sigillo in archivo Regimontano. 1. I. R. ut II. A. 20. 2. sic. Originale; alii: publici.

---

330. *1221 ianuarii 18 Laterani. Honorius III vetat de ordinis Theutonici rebus caucagium caetera exigi; iubet clericos interdictum ob violatos fratres emissum despernentes compesci.*

Honorius episcopus servus servorum dei venerabilibus fratribus archiepiscopis et episcopis et dilectis filiis abbatibus, prioribus, decanis, archidiaconis et aliis ecclesiarum prelatis, ad quos littere iste pervenerint, salutem et apostolicam benedictionem. Religiosos viros, fratres hospitalis domus sancte Marie Theutonicorum Ierosolimitani, pro religione et honestate sua tanto propensius a malignorum incursibus protegere volumus et tueri, quanto puriorem devocionem circa nos et Romanam ecclesiam exhibere noscuntur. Inde est, quod vobis per apostolica scripta precipiendo mandamus, quatinus universis parrochianis vestris sub interminatione anathematis prohibere curetis, ne a prefatis fratribus vel eorum hominibus de victualibus, vestimentis, pecudibus seu de aliis rebus eorundem fratrum usibus deputatis caucagium seu aliquamlibet consuetudinem exigere vel extorquere presumant. Si qui autem contra prohibitionem nostram venire presumpserint, eos a presumptione sua non differatis per excommunicationis sententiam cohercere, et in terris eorum, si quas habent, omnia divina preter baptisma parvulorum et penitentias morientium prohibeatis officia celebrari. Ad hec, quia, sicut predicti fratres asserunt, quidam presbiteri et alii clerici vestre iurisdictionis in ecclesiis illis, que pro excessibus in domum predictorum fratrum commissis sub interdicto tenentur, divina celebrare presumunt, eos, si res ita se habet, a sue presumptionis audacia per suspensionis et excommunicationis sententiam compescatis. Datum Laterani xv kal. februarii pontificatus nostri anno quinto.

Sine dato: I, 75; II, 112 n. 71; D. 71; A. 20 n. 69 Latine et Germanice cum nota: „Gregorius in Mergintheym; Allexander in Maguncia et Confluentia“ (versio exit: „zcu Mentz und Colne“). — Cum dato: Laterani xv kal. febr. p. n. a. 5 ex originali archivi quondam Confluentinae domus nunc ordinis Theutonici Vindobonensis, cui filis sericeis appendet bulla, ed. Hennes I, 55 n. 51. A. 16 p. 74 „Colonie“.

---

331. *1221 ianuarii 19 Laterani. Honorius III confirmat ordini Theutonico liberas confratrum sepulturam eleemosynarumque quaestionem.*

Honorius episcopus servus servorum dei venerabilibus fratribus archiepiscopis et episcopis et dilectis filiis abbatibus, prioribus, decanis, archidiaconis, prepositis, archipresbiteris et aliis ecclesiarum prelatis, ad quos littere iste pervenerint, salutem et apostolicam benedictionem. Cum apostolica sedes dilectis filiis fratribus domus hospitalis sancte Marie Theotonicorum Ierosolimitani indulserit, ut corpora fratrum[1] suorum ecclesiastice possint tradere sepultura, dignum est, ut super hoc apostolica statuta serventur. Mandamus itaque vobis atque precipimus, quatinus memoratis fratribus nullam molestiam inferatis vel a subditis vestris permittatis inferri, quominus confratres suos, nisi excommunicati vel nominatim interdicti decesserint, libere more aliorum fidelium, quandocunque ipsos mori contigerit, valeant sepelire. Eosdem quoque fratres ad querendas elemosinas pauperum iuxta indulgenciam nostram in ecclesiis vestris recipi faciatis et, si qui subditorum vestrorum eis super hoc impedimentum prestiterint, sublato appellationis obstaculo censura canonica compescatis. Datum Laterani xiiii kal. februarii pontificatus nostri anno v.

Sine dato: I. 70; II, 93; A. 20 n. 14 Latine et Germanice. — Cum dato: Laterani xiiii kal. febr. p. n. a. 5 bis in R.: 1. 61 n. 19 privilegiorum in Ratisponensi domo asservatorum; 2. 38 inter Ellingensia 22, tanquam apographum transsumti Accon 1277 oct. 19 per Bonacursum Tyrensem archiepiscopum et Gailardum Bethleemitanum episcopum confecti. A. 16 p. 5 „Venetiis“. 1. addit serior manus: con I. confratrum A. 20.

---

332. *1221 ianuarii 19 Laterani. Honorius III vetat praelatos de bonis ordini Theutonico collatis pro expeditionibus et excubiis faciendis vicesimam vel alias exactiones extorquere.*

Honorius episcopus servus servorum dei venerabilibus fratribus archiepiscopis et episcopis et dilectis filiis abbatibus, prioribus, decanis, archidiaconis, prepositis, archipresbiteris et aliis ecclesiarum prelatis, ad quos littere iste pervenerint, salutem et apstolicam benedictionem. Cum de viris ecclesiasticis, quibus plurimum expedire dinoscitur, ut in cunctis actibus[1] suis modum ordinemque conservent, nobis aliqua referuntur, que illos reprehensibiles reddant, paterno dolemus affectu et de ipsorum emendatione curam volumus gerere pastoralem. Significantibus sane dilectis filiis, fratribus domus hospitalis sancte Marie Theotonicorum Ierosolimitani, accepimus, quod de possessionibus, que ipsis a vivis sive defunctis racionabiliter conferuntur, pro vestris expedicionibus et excubiis faciendis vicesimam questam et exacciones ab ipsis indebitas[2] presumitis extorquere. Quocirca universitati vestre[3] per apostolica scripta mandamus et districte precipimus, quatinus ab huiusmodi exaccionibus penitus desistentes iura predictorum fratrum in aliquo ledere nullatenus presumatis, sed ita ipsos sua permittatis libertate gaudere, quod nec ipsi de vobis habeant iustam materiam conquerendi[4] nec nos ea districcius requirere conpellamur. Datum Laterani xiiii kal. februarii pontificatus nostri anno quinto.

Sine dato: I, 68; A. 20 n. 12 Latine et Germanice, ubi in titulis legitur: Innocencius in Leodio etc. et: „Dis privilegium Innocencius und is zcu Leodik dem glich. — Cum dato: A. 16 p. 38 „Baruli" cum annotatione „verte folium et invenies de verbo ad verbum in privilegio domni Innocentii IV". 1. deest I. 2. indebitis I. 3. vobis universis A. 20. 4. quod ipsi de vobis nullam habeant materiam querelandi nec A. 16.

---

333. *1221 ianuarii 19 Laterani. Honorius III vetat quemquam fratrum ordinis Theutonici praeter magistri licentiam specialem observantiam facere.*

Honorius episcopus servus servorum dei dilectis filiis magistro et[1] fratribus domus hospitalis sancte Marie Theotonicorum Ierosolimitani salutem et apostolicam benedictionem. Cum vobis secundum apostolum cor unum et anima una debeat esse, nolentes, ut ex diversitate votorum vestre religionis idemptitas[2] pati valeat sectionem, auctoritate vobis presencium inhibemus, ne aliquis fratrum vestrorum absque sui magistri licencia speciali abstinenciam vel observanciam faciat preter illam, que a capitulo vestre domus regulariter observatur. Nulli ergo omnino hominum liceat hanc paginam nostre inhibitionis infringere vel ei ausu temerario contraire. Si quis autem hoc attemptare presumpserit, indignationem omnipotentis dei et beatorum Petri et Pauli apostolorum eius se noverit incursurum. Datum Laterani xiiii kal. februarii pontificatus nostri anno quinto.

Sine dato: I, 75 v.; II, 93 n. 13; A. 20 n. 13 Latine et Germanice. D. 12. — Cum dato: or. cum bulla in archivo Regimontano. 1. II. et I. 2. idemptitas Or.

---

334. *1221 ianuarii 19 Laterani. Honorius III vetat de ordinis Theutonici possessionibus vicesimam aut alias exactiones extorqueri.*

Honorius episcopus servus servorum dei venerabilibus fratribus archiepiscopis et episcopis et dilectis filiis abbatibus, prioribus, prepositis, decanis, archidiaconis, archipresbiteris et aliis ecclesiarum prelatis, ad quos littere iste pervenerint, salutem et apostolicam benedictionem. Dilecti filii .. magister et fratres domus hospitalis sancte Marie Theotonicorum Ierosolimitani nostro apostolatui sunt[1] conquesti, quod quidam magnates, comites et alii nobiles in vestris diocesibus constituti de possessionibus, que ipsis a vivis sive defunctis racionabiliter conferuntur, pro suis expedicionibus et excubiis faciendis vicesimam questam et exacciones ab ipsis indebitas extorquere presumunt. Quocirca universitati vestre per apostolica scripta mandamus atque precipimus, quatinus iam dictos molestatores, ut ab huiusmodi molestatione[2] omnino desistant et iura predictorum fratrum in aliquo ledere non presumant, monicione premissa per censuram ecclesiasticam appellatione postposita conpellatis. Datum Laterani xiiii kal. februarii pontificatus nostri anno quinto.

Sine dato: I, 69 v.; II, 97 v. n. 26; A. 20 n. 26 Latine et Germanice; D. 25 Germanice. — Cum dato: A. 16 p. 41 „Baruli". 1. conquesti fuerunt II. 2. exaccionibus II. A. 20.

---

335. *1221 ianuarii 19 Laterani. Honorius III vetat praelatos de haereditate hominum ordinis Theutonici partem sibi vindicare.*

Honorius episcopus servus servorum dei venerabilibus fratribus archiepiscopis et episcopis et dilectis filiis abbatibus, prioribus, prepositis, decanis, archidiaconis, archipresbiteris et aliis ecclesiarum prelatis, ad quos littere iste pervenerint, salutem et apostolicam benedictionem. Ex parte dilectorum filiorum, fratrum domus hospitalis sancte Marie Theotonicorum Ierosolimitani, fuit propositum coram nobis, quod, cum ipsi terciam partem omnium bonorum suorum hominum, qui post se relinquunt heredes, soliti sint percipere ac medietatem illorum, qui absque heredibus vel uxore decedunt, eciam homines ipsi ad hoc fide interposita teneantur; presbiteri et clerici terciam partem porcionis, que ipsos fratres de iure contingit, sibi presumunt contra iusticiam vendicare, predictos fratres super ea molestatione indebita fatigantes. Cum igitur eisdem fratribus, qui presertim hoc tempore pro servitio Ihesu Christi exponunt se multis laboribus et expensis, indebita nolumus inferre gravamina, sed grata subsidia ministrare; universitati vestre per apostolica scripta mandamus atque precipimus, quatenus presbiteros et clericos antedictos, ut ab indebita molestatione nominatorum fratrum super porcione iam dicta penitus desistentes eam permittant ipsis fratribus pacifice possidere, monitione premissa per censuram ecclesiasticam sublato appellationis obstaculo compellatis, mandatum apostolicum taliter impleturi, quod non possitis de inobediencia reprehendi, immo pocius de obediencia commendari. Datum Laterani xiiii kal. februarii pontificatus nostri anno v.

Sine dato: I, 67; II, 100 v. n. 37. D. 36. — Cum dato: R. 76 n. 27 inter Mergenthemensia. A. 20 n. 35 Latine et Germanice, cum notis 1. Dis is zcu Akon adir zcu Mergintheym. 2. Is zcu Akon und zcu Mergintheym.

---

336. *1221 ianuarii 19 Laterani. Honorius III concedit ordini Theutonico, ut undique presbyteros ad servitium suum assumere possit et in locis sibi collatis oratoria et coemeteria pro usu proprio construere.*

Honorius episcopus servus servorum dei venerabilibus fratribus patriarchis[1], archiepiscopis et episcopis, et dilectis filiis abbatibus, ad quos littere iste pervenerint, salutem et apostolicam benedictionem. Milicia dei, que dicitur domus fratrum hospitalis sancte Marie Theutonicorum Ierosolimitani, quam sit orientali ecclesie commoda, digna[2] meritis, deo grata, universitatem vestram credimus non latere. Fraterna igitur caritas nos hortatur, ut, in quantum possumus, necessaria eis subsidia ministremus. Et, quoniam religiose viventes devote student divinis officiis interesse, liberam eis concedimus facultatem idoneos[3] presbiteros ad suum servitium assumere undecunque, qui tamen rite sint in presbiteros ordinati et a propriis episcopis licentiam impetrarint. Ad hec eisdem fratribus cupientes commodius providere, minuere tamen nullius vestrum ius parrochiale volentes vel decimas sive oblationes aut sepulturas auferre, in locis sibi collatis, ubi familia videlicet habitat, eorundem construendi eis oratoria licentiam dedimus, in quibus celebrationi divinorum intersint, et, si quis de ipsis fratribus aut eorum servientibus mortuus fuerit, tumuletur. Est enim indecens et parit interdum periculum animarum, si viri religiosi occasione ecclesie adeunde[3] se virorum turbis et frequentationibus immisceant mulierum. Quapropter universitati vestre per apostolica scripta mandamus atque precipimus, quatenus, cum vos, fratres patriarche, archiepiscopi vel episcopi, ab eisdem fratribus fueritis requisiti, oratoria eorumdem dedicetis absque aliqua pravitate ac pro sepelienda eorum familia in prefatis locis cimiteria benedicere procuretis[4], sine iuris preiudicio alieni. Presbiteros quoque manere sinatis in pace, quos ipsi pro exhibendo sibi divino servitio sociarunt. Ad hoc ergo complendum vestra fraternitas opem consilium prebeat et assensum, nec eos in oratoriis construendis impediat aut impediri permittat. Datum Laterani xiiii kal. februarii pontificatus nostri anno v.

Sine dato: II, 103 v. n. 50; A. 20 n. 48 Latine et Germanice cum nota: In Marpurk. — Cum dato: Laterani xiv kal. februarii p. n. a. 5. Originale cum bulla et subscriptione cancellarii Zachariae in archivo Regimontana. 1. deest II. A. 20. 2. dignā II. 3. ad eundē II. 4. sine iuris preiudicio alieni II eddit. A. 20.

---

337. *1221 ianuarii 19 Laterani (cf. 1223 ianuarii 16 Laterani). Honorius III vetat ordinis Theutonici homines pecuniaria poena puniri et ecclesiis aut presbyteris exactiones indebitas imponi.*

Honorius episcopus servus servorum dei venerabilibus fratribus archiepiscopis et episcopis et dilectis filiis abbatibus, prioribus, decanis, archidiaconis, prepositis, archipresbiteris et aliis ecclesiarum prelatis[1], ad quos littere iste pervenerint, salutem et apostolicam benedictionem. Querela dilectorum filiorum fratrum domus hospitalis sancte Marie Theotonicorum Ierosolimitani ad nos transmissa pervenit, quod homines eorundem, quos adulterio vel alio crimine deprehenditis irretitos, contra libertates a regibus et aliis principibus ipsis indultas pecuniaria pena punitis, presbiteros eciam ecclesiarum suarum et omnes alias, quas tenent, non dubitatis ut dicitur indebitis[2] exactionibus aggravare. Quia igitur gravamen predictorum fratrum dissimulare non possumus nec debemus, quos propter pauperes Christi, quorum sunt obsequiis mancipati, in suis volumus iusticiis confovere, universitati vestre auctoritate apostolica inhibemus, quatinus homines ipsorum contra libertatem eis indultam pena pecuniaria non multetis nec ecclesiis eorum aut presbiteris exactiones indebitas imponatis, sed ab eorum molestiis desistentes contra iniurias malignancium vestrum curetis patrocinium exhibere, ita quod querela super hoc ad audienciam nostram iterata venire non debeat, nec vos possitis de avaricia merito vel contemptu sedis apostolice reprehendi. Datum Laterani xiiii kal. februarii pontificatus nostri anno v.

Sine dato: I, 69 v.; II, 110 v. n. 67; A. 20 n. 65 Latine et Germanice cum nota: in Mergintheym. D. 67. — Cum dato: Laterani xiiii kal. febr. p. n. a. 5; R. 70 inter Mergenthemensia n. 17. — Cum dato: Laterani xvii kal. febr. p. n. a. 7; IV, 191 n. 25; Or. quondam Mergenthemense cum bulla in filis sericeis appensa in archivo ordinis Theutonici Vindobonensi. Transsumtum de 1418 dec. 2 in archivo Regimontano. Ioh. 32. Ediderunt Caorsinus fol. C. 2. Senner fol. E. 2. Lünig, Teutsches Reichsarchiv XVI, 80 n. 77. 1. episcopis, prioribus, archidiaconis, decanis et a. e. p. IV. Ioh. etc. 2. deest I. R. 70.

---

338. *1221 ianuarii 20 Laterani. Honorius III iubet vicarios ad servitium in ordinis Theutonici ecclesiis obligatos in propriis personis id praestare.*

Honorius episcopus servus servorum dei venerabilibus fratribus archiepiscopis et episcopis et dilectis filiis abbatibus, prioribus, archidiaconis, decanis, prepositis, archipresbiteris et aliis ecclesiarum prelatis, ad quos littere iste pervenerint, salutem et apostolicam benedictionem. Dilecti filii, fratres domus hospitalis sancte Marie Theotonicorum Ierosolimitani, gravem ad nos querimoniam destinarunt, quod quidam eorum vicarii, qui tenentur in suis ecclesiis personaliter deservire, contra voluntatem ipsorum et inhibicionem sedis apostolice vicarios alios in eisdem ecclesiis instituere non formidant, bona illa, que de suis percipiunt vicariis, in usus extraordinarios expendentes. Quia vero, sicut temporalia metimus, ita et spiritualia[1] serere nos oportet, discrecioni vestre per apostolica scripta mandamus atque precipimus, quatinus dictos vicarios, ut in ecclesiis eorundem fratrum vicarios alios instituere minime presumant, immo personaliter, ut tenentur, deserviant[2] in eisdem, monicione premissa per ipsorum beneficiorum subtractionem appellatione remota cogatis. Datum Laterani xiii kal. februarii pontificatus nostri anno v.

Sine dato: I, 69 v. n. 26; II, 97 v. n. 27; A. 20 n. 27 Latine et Germanice cum nota: In Bysen etc.; R. 154 inter Iuncensia. A. 16 p. 94 „Iuncis". D. 26. — Cum dato: Laterani xiii kal. februarii p. n. a. 5. IV, 185 v. n. 13. Originale quondam Iuncense cum bulla in filis rubris et luteis appendente nunc Vindobonae in archivo ordinis Theutonici asservatur. 1. superflua I. 2. ymmo — deserviant deest I deserviant II.

---

339. *1221 ianuarii 20 Laterani. Honorius III vetat homines ordinis Theutonici pecuniaria poena puniri.*

Honorius episcopus servus servorum dei venerabilibus fratribus archiepiscopis et episcopis et dilectis filiis abbatibus, prioribus, decanis, archidiaconis et aliis ecclesiarum prelatis, ad quos littere iste pervenerint, salutem et apostolicam benedictionem. Dilecti filii, fratres domus hospitalis sancte Marie Theotonicorum Ierosolimitani, transmissa[1] nobis insinuacione monstrarunt, quod archidiaconi et decani in vestris partibus constituti tam per se quam per officiales suos homines predictorum fratrum pro excessibus suis ad iudicium ecclesiasticum pertrahunt, ut eorum pocius pecuniam tollant, quam ut dignam eis penitenciam pro peccatis iniungant, cum[2] indignum sit, ut[3] predicti fratres, qui ad defensionem orientalis ecclesie pias ab[4] aliis[5] helemosinas[6] querunt, dispendium aliquod vel gravamen in rebus, que ad eos pertinent, paciantur; ideoque fraternitati vestre per apostolica scripta mandamus atque precipimus, quatinus predictos archidiaconos et decanos seu quoslibet[7] officiales[8] eorum[9] appellatione et excusatione cessantibus per censuram ecclesiasticam compescatis, ne homines predictorum fratrum pro excessibus suis pena pecuniaria puniant, sed alia eis imposita penitencia[10] bona eorum ad usus predictorum fratrum in pace ac quiete dimittant[11]. Datum Laterani xiii kal. februarii pontificatus nostri anno quinto.

Sine dato: I, 68; II, 97 n. 24; A. 20 n. 24 Latine et Germanice cum nota: „Gregorius huic simile in Marpurg etc." D. 23. — Cum dato: Laterani xiii kal. febr. p. a. 5. R. 68 inter Mergenthemensia n. 10. Originale cum bulla in filis sericeis appendente, quod quondam fuit Mergenthemi, nunc asservatur Vindobonae in ordinis Theutonici archivo. 1. sua I. 2. Cum itaque A. 20. 3. quod I. 4. deest I. 5. sic II. 6. ab eis A. 20. petunt I. 7. quoscunque A. 20. 8. pro officiales eorum I habet alios. 9. deest I. 10. pena I. 11. permittant A. 20.

---

*340. *1221 ianuarii 20 Laterani. Honorius III vetat ordinis Theutonici apostatas ad aliam religionem transituros recipi.*

Honorius episcopus servus servorum dei venerabilibus fratribus archiepiscopis et episcopis, et dilectis filiis abbatibus, prioribus, decanis, archidiaconis, prepositis, archipresbiteris et aliis ecclesiarum prelatis, ad quos littere iste pervenerint, salutem et apostolicam benedictionem. Militum domus hospitalis sancte Marie Theotonicorum Ierosolimitani professio, sicut in scriptis eorum et privilegiis continetur, est talis, ut ne cui post factam professionem semel assumptam crucem dominicam et habitum ipsius abicere vel alium locum seu eciam monasterium maioris sive minoris religionis obtentu invitis sive inconsultis fratribus aut eo, qui magister extiterit, liceat transmigrare nullique ecclesiastice secularive persone ipsos suscipere liceat vel tenere. Cum enim ad defendendam orientalem ecclesiam et paganorum seviciam reprimendam relictis pompis secularibus dei sint servicio mancipati, si transeundi ad alia loca et sumptum habitum relinquendi daretur eis licentia, magnum ecclesie dei posset exinde contingere detrimentum, ideoque universitati vestre per apostolica scripta mandamus, atque precipimus, quatinus[1], si, quis ex ipsis in parrochiis vestris vel locis vobis commissis id attemptare presumpserit, tam ipsum quam qui eum ausu temerario retinere temptaverit, omni occasione remota excommunicationis vinculo innodetis. Datum Laterani xiii kal. februarii pontificatus nostri anno v.

Sine dato: I, 69; II, 104 n. 51; A. 20 n. 49 Latine et Germanice cum nota: „in Marpurg; item Gregorius in Leodio et Alexander in Marburg. — Cum dato: IV, 186 n. 15 et A. 16 p. 62 „in Marpurg". 1. mandamus ut IV precipiendo mandamus ut II. A. 20.

---

341. *1221 ianuarii 20 Laterani (cf. 1221 ianuarii 25). Honorius III vetat praelatos ordinem Theutonicum ratione generalis concilii molestare.*

Honorius episcopus servus servorum dei venerabilibus fratribus archiepiscopis et episcopis, et dilectis filiis abbatibus, prioribus, decanis, archidiaconis, prepositis, archipresbiteris et aliis ecclesiarum prelatis, ad quos littere iste pervenerint, salutem et apostolicam benedictionem. Non sine gravi apostolice sedis iniuria et grandi contumelia creatoris quidam, qui ponunt lucem tenebras et tenebras lucem, dilectos filios fratres hospitalis sancte Marie Theutonicorum Ierosolimitani ab ecclesia Romana specialis privilegii prerogativa donatos et deputatos specialiter servicio Ihesu Christi occasione concilii generalis plus debito et amplius solito gravare presumunt, novis et inexquisitis eos molestiis affligentes, propter quod elemosina, que solebat proficere pauperibus Christi et subsidio terre sancte, sic est per iniquitatis dispendium angustata, quod eadem est ex parte maxima[1] diminuta. Preterea libertates et indulgencias eis ab apostolica sede concessas per malitiose interpretacionis calumpniam pervertentes ipsis temere se opponunt nec confratres eorum et eligentes in eorum ecclesiis[2] sepulturas, qui nec excommunicati sunt nec eciam[3] nominatim interdicti, permittunt apud se libere sepeliri. Exhortationem quoque ad populum pro recipiendis elemosinis consuetis[4], confratrias[5] eciam ipsorum[6], que precipue nullis aliis interpositis esse debent, impediunt pro sue arbitrio voluntatis[7], propter hoc tantum eorum profectibus invidentes, quia vident eos causam[8] pauperum, ymmo eius, qui simul in unum voluit esse dives et pauper, relictis mundi vanitatibus procurare. Cum igitur prefati fratres post deum nullum habeant preter Romanum pontificem defensorem; universitati vestre per apostolica scripta districte precipiendo mandamus[9], quatinus eos, immo Christum in eis, cuius sunt servicio deputati, recipientes honorifice et benigna caritate tractantes ipsos[10] occasione concilii[11] nec gravetis indebite nec paciamini ab aliquibus temere molestari. Et, cum ipsius sit interpretari iura[12], qui condere ipsa potest, a supersticiosa interpretatione concilii curetis vos ipsos et alios cohibere ac confratres iporum et alios eligentes ex pietate in eorum ecclesiis sepulturas, dummodo non sint excommunicati vel nominatim interdicti aut publice[13] usurarii, dimittatis apud eos libere[14] sepeliri, salva iusticia illarum[15] ecclesiarum, a quibus mortuorum corpora assumuntur. Et, si dicti fratres vel[16] eorum nuncii semel in anno ad vos vel ad ecclesias venerint vestre iurisdictioni subiectas, elemosinas in pace querere ac exhortari populum permittatis, nullis confratriis aliis interpositis ea die; populum nichilominus vestrum moneatis et efficaciter inducatis, ut eorum fraternitates[17] assumere ac legata eis in ultima voluntate relicta et alia illis[18] beneficia sine difficultate studeant exhibere. Nos vero eis, qui dictis fratribus manum porrexerint pietatis, si vere fuerint penitentes, iuxta devocionis[19] affectum et subsidii quantitatem suorum peccaminum veniam pollicemur, presentium vobis auctoritate mandantes, ut presentes literas, quociens a dictis fratribus fueritis[20] requisiti, per vestras faciatis dioceses et parrochias publicari et subditos vestros, qui super premissis eis impedimentum prestiterint vel gravamen, censura canonica secundum officii vestri debitum compescatis. Datum Laterani xiii kal. februarii pontificatus nostri anno quinto.

Sine dato: II, 105 v.; A. 20 n. 52 Latine et Germanice; D. 55. — Cum dato: xiii kal. febr. p. n. a. 5: ex originali Gracensi VII, 367, quod sequimur. Originale, quod iam antiquitus in domo Theutonico Vindobonensi fuisse perhibetur, cum bulla in filis rubris et luteis appendente ibidem vel nunc est. — Cum dato: viii kal. febr. p. n. a. 5, ed. Duellius Hist. ord. Theut. II, 4 n. 3. (errore?) 1. deest II. 2. ecclesiis eorum II. 3. deest A. 20 nominatim eciam II. 4. conswetis et A. 20. 5. confraternitates A. 20. 6. eorum A. 20. 7. v. a. A. 20. 8. causas A. 20. 9. sc. p. m. A. 20. 10. eos A. 20. 11. generalis A. 20. 12. cura A. 20. 13. publici A. 20. 14. publice VII. 15. aliarum II. 16. aut A. 20. 17. confraternitates A. 20. 18. aliis illa VII. 19. defensionis II. 20. fuerint II.

---

342. *1221 ianuarii 21 Laterani (cf. 1222 ianuarii 21 Laterani). Honorius III iubet false, ut eleemosynas colligerent, nigris ordinis Theutonici crucibus ornatos, ecclesiastica disciplina coërceri.*

Honorius episcopus servus servorum dei venerabilibus fratribus archiepiscopis et episcopis et dilectis filiis abbatibus, prioribus, archidiaconis, decanis, et aliis ecclesiarum prelatis, ad quos littere iste pervenerint, salutem et apostolicam benedictionem. Decet pastoralis sollicitudinem dignitatis, pravas et enormes iniquitates evellere et vicia, que periculum pariunt animarum, radicitus amputare. Detestandum siquidem facinus et plurimum abhorrendum per diversas mundi partes accepimus pullulare, quod quidam avaricie amore cecati pocius quam zelo religionis accensi nigras cruces, quas fratres hospitalis sancte Marie Theotonicorum Ierosolimitani deferunt, sibi imponere et eas portare minime verentur, ut sic possint sub tali velamento elemosinas pauperibus deputatas colligere et sibi animarum perniciem generare. Quocirca universitati vestre[1] per apostolica scripta mandamus, quatenus eos, qui crucem nigram portandam assumunt aut signum, quod dictorum fratrum homines deferunt et oblati, cum non sint de professione ac collegio ipsorum fratrum, omni cum districtione compellere studeatis, ut a tanta stulticia et errore desistant et crucem aut dictum signum nulla racione ulterius deferre presumant. Si quis vero a vobis commonitus a sua noluerit temeritate cessare, in eum ecclesiastice animadversionis gladium auctoritate nostra, omni occasione et appellatione postpositis, exeratis. Datum Laterani xii kal. februarii pontificatus nostri anno quinto.

Sine dato: II, 96 v. n. 23; A. 20 n. 23 Latine et Germanice cum nota in Mergentheim etc. D. 22. — Cum dato: Laterani xii kal. febr. p. n. a. 5. I, 66; IV, 187 n. 17; R. 68 inter Mergenthemensia n. 12. Or. cum bulla in filis sericeis appendente, quod quondam Mergenthemi fuit, nunc Vindobonae in archivo ordini Theutonici asservatur. — Cum dato: Laterani xii kal. febr. p. n. a. 6 (num error sit, dubitari potest) edidit Duellius in appendice 7 n. 5. 1. vobis A. 20.

343. *1221 ianuarii 21 Laterani. Honorius III repetit n. 307 de 1220 dec. 16.*

Honorius etc. Pervenit ad nos etc. Datum Laterani xii kal. februarii pontificatus nostri anno v.

344. *1221 ianuarii 25 Laterani. Honorius III repetit n. 341 de 1221 ian. 20.*

Honorius etc. Non sine gravi etc. Datum Laterani viii kal. februarii pontificatus nostri anno v.

Ed. ap. Duellium II, 4 n. 3. Forsan errore viii pro xiii positum.

345. *1221 februarii 4 Laterani. Honorius III vetat ab ordine Theutonico ad munitiones erigendas vicesimam extorqueri.*

Honorius episcopus servus servorum dei venerabilibus fratribus archiepiscopis et episcopis et dilectis filiis abbatibus, prioribus, archidiaconis, decanis et aliis ecclesiarum prelatis, ad quos littere iste pervenerint, salutem et apostolicam benedictionem. Cum bona fratribus hospitalis sancte Marie Theutonicorum Ierosolimitani fidelium devotione collata defensioni terre orientalis et pauperum receptioni ac sustentationi proficiant, providere quantum possumus nos oportet, ne ab aliis minus necessariis presumptione aliqua usurpentur. Pervenit autem ad nos, quod quidam ab eis et hominibus eorum ad claudendas villas atque castella et erigendas munitiones vicesimam extorquere presumunt et, si non dederint, auferunt violenter et ecclesiam orientalem et pauperes sepulchrum domini visitantes indebite pro magna parte sustentatione defraudant, quam fratres hospitalis ipsius multo studio et labore acquirere moliuntur. Unde, quia per vos ista convenit emendari, universitati vestre per apostolica scripta mandamus, quatinus, ne predicte super eos ulterius et eorum homines fiant exactiones, districtius inhibere curetis. Si quis autem contra inhibitionem nostram venire presumpserit, per excommunicationis et interdicti sententias a tanto eum revocetis excessu et taliter ad emendationem eorum suscepte amministrationis exerceatis officium, ut sepe dicti fratres non cogantur longius proferre querelam et vos de tuitione pauperum Christi retributionem eternam in extremo examine recipere valeatis. Datum Laterani ii non. februarii pontificatus nostri anno quinto.

Sine dato: II, 94 n. 17; A. 20 n. 17 Latine et Germanice cum nota: In Confluentia. D. — Cum dato: Laterani ii non. febr. p. n. a. 5. Ex originali archivi ordinis Theutonici Vindobonensis, quod quondam Confluentiae fuit, cum bulla in filis sericeis appendente, edidit Hennes I, 56 n. 52. A. 16 p. 74 „Colonie". In archivo Vindobonensi etiam transsumtum per Baldum not. imp. d. d. Tridenti in palatio episcopali 1244 aug. 2 factum.

---

346. *1221 februarii 5 Laterani Honorius III mandat praelatis, ut ordinis Theutonici privilegia diligenter perlecta accurate observanda curent.*

Honorius episcopus servus servorum dei venerabilibus fratribus archiepiscopis et episcopis et dilectis filiis abbatibus et aliis ecclesiarum prelatis, ad quos littere iste pervenerint, salutem et apostolicam benedictionem[1]. Attendentes, quam devote dilecti filii fratres hospitalis sancte Marie Theotonicorum Ierosolimitani domino inspirante intendant operibus pietatis et quam ferventer se et sua infirmorum[2] pauperum susceptioni et sustentationi exponant, paterna eos affectione diligimus et peticiones, in quibus cum iusticia possumus, clementer admittimus et profectibus ipsorum et commodis per vos et per alios efficaciter debemus et volumus imminere. Eapropter universitati vestre per apostolica scripta mandamus atque precipimus, quatenus privilegia, que fratribus ipsis intuitu pietatis indulsimus, cum vobis exhibita fuerint, diligenter legatis, fideliter exponatis et inviolabiliter remoto appellationis diffugio faciatis ab omnibus, quantum in vobis fuerit, observari, ita quod iidem fratres de acceptis privilegiis fructum obtineant et vos pauperum necessitatibus compati videamini et eorum velle utilitatibus propter deum utiliter subvenire. Datum Laterani non. februarii pontificatus nostri anno v.

Sine dato: II, 100 n. 35; A. 20 n. 82 Latine et Germanice cum nota: In Bysen. D. 34 Germanice. A. 16 p. 94 „Iuncis". — Cum dato: Originale, quod quondam fuit Iuncis, nunc Vindobonae est in archivo ordinis Theutonici cum bulla in filis sericeis appendente. 1. et dilectis — benedictionem deest A. 16. 2. i. et p. A. 16.

347. *1221 februarii 5 Laterani. Honorius III concedit ordini Theutonico vacantium ecclesiarum per viginti dies retentionem.*

Honorius episcopus servus servorum dei dilectis filiis magistro et fratribus hospitalis sancte Marie Theotonicorum Ierosolimitani salutem et apostolicam benedictionem. Attendentes, quam devote et laudabiliter pietatis operibus et defensioni christiani nominis in transmarinis partibus insistatis, iustis petitionibus vestris libenter annuimus vobisque contra indebitas molestias, quantum cum deo possumus, providemus. Unde, quia ad audienciam apostolatus nostri pervenit, quod decedentibus ecclesiarum vestrarum rectoribus episcopi et officiales eorum ipsarum nonnunquam ordinacionem differunt et fructus in usus proprios pro sua voluntate convertunt; auctoritate vobis presencium indulgemus, ut, cum ecclesie vestre vacaverint, liceat vobis eas per viginti dies in manibus vestris sine contradictione aliqua retinere, ita quod infra eundem terminum a vobis rector ydoneus diocesano episcopo presentetur. Nulli ergo omnino homini liceat hanc paginam nostre concessionis infringere vel ei ausu temerario contraire. Si quis autem hoc attemptare presumpserit, indignationem omnipotentis dei et beatorum Petri et Pauli apostolorum eius se noverit incursurum. Datum Laterani non. februarii pontificatus nostri anno v.

Sine dato: II, 100 v. n. 36; A. 20 n. 34 Latine et Germanice cum nota: in Mergintheym. D. 35. — Cum dato: IV, 187 v. n. 18; R. 66 e domo Mergenthemensi n. 4. Ioh. 31. Ediderunt Caorsinus fol. C. Senner fol. E. v.

---

348. *1221 februarii 5 Laterani. Honorius III vetat ordinem Theutonicum impediri, quominus confratribus suis in coemeteriis suis sepulturam praebeat.*

Honorius episcopus servus servorum dei venerabilibus fratribus archiepiscopis et episcopis et dilectis filiis abbatibus, prioribus, prepositis, decanis, archidiaconis, archipresbiteris et aliis ecclesiarum prelatis, ad quos littere iste pervenerint, salutem et apostolicam benedictionem. Cum dilectis filiis, fratribus hospitalis sancte Marie Theotonicorum Ierosolimitani, duxerimus indulgendum, ut hiis, qui eorum confratriam assumpserint, si forte locus, in quo decedunt, interdictus fuerit[1], nisi vinculo excommunicationis teneantur astricti aut nominatim sint interdicti, sepultura ecclesiastica non debeat denegari; nimis graviter excederetis, si, quod fratribus eisdem concessimus, presumeretis infringere, qui alios ad observanda ecclesie Romane statuta verbo et exemplo debetis propensius informare. Infringi namque sustinere nolentes, quod fratribus indulsimus antedictis, universitati vestre per apostolica scripta mandamus atque precipimus, quatenus nullo tempore quisquam vestrum impedire presumat, quominus corpora ipsorum, qui confratriam predictorum fratrum assumpserint vel assument in posterum, nisi excommunicati vel nominatim fuerint interdicti aut eciam[2] publice usurarii, in eorum valeant cimiteriis sepeliri, si eciam locus, in quo decedunt, fuerit interdictus, sed ita in hoc et in aliis statuta sedis apostolice integra et illibata servetis, quod devotio vestra possit et debeat non immerito commendari nec nos inveniamus in vobis in hac parte, quod merito corrigere debeamus. Datum Laterani non. februarii pontificatus nostri anno v.

Sine dato: II, 96 v. n. 22; A. 20 n. 22 Latine et Germanice cum nota: In Traiecto inferiori invenitur etc. D. 21. — Cum dato: Laterani non. febr. p. n. a. 5. R. 195 incerti loci. A. 16 p. 107 „Traiecti". 1. sit A. 16. 2. addit A. 16.

---

349. *1221 februarii 5 Laterani. Honorius III concedit ordini Theutonico, ut confratrum corpora per praelatos ab ecclesiis eorum prohibita apud suas sepelire liceat.*

Honorius episcopus servus servorum dei dilectis filiis magistro et fratribus hospitalis sancte Marie Theotonicorum Ierosolimitani salutem et apostolicam benedictionem. Ea, que vobis[1] superni conditoris intuitu ad prosequenda opera pietatis, quibus intenditis, duximus indulgenda, in sua convenit firmitate persistere, et, ne ipsorum evacuetur auctoritas, contra quorumlibet calumpniancium pravitatem presidium vobis debet apostolicum non deesse. Quoniam igitur quidam de prelatis ecclesiarum vobis contra indultum privilegium contradicunt, ne confratres vestros libere possitis tradere sepulture, presenti vobis pagina duximus concedendum, ut liceat vobis confratrum vestrorum corpora, que prelati ecclesiarum apud ecclesias suas malitiose[2] non permiserint sepeliri, nisi excommunicati vel nominatim fuerint interdicti aut eciam publice usurarii, ad ecclesias vestras auctoritate nostra tumulanda deferre et sine contradictione aliqua in vestris cimiteriis sepelire et in ecclesiis vestris pro eorum animabus missarum sollempnia celebrare. Nulli ergo omnino hominum liceat hanc paginam nostre concessionis infringere vel ei ausu temerario contraire. Si quis autem hoc attemptare presumpserit, indignationem omnipotentis dei et beatorum Petri et Pauli apostolorum eius se noverit incursurum. Datum Laterani nonis februarii pontificatus nostri anno v.

Sine dato: II, 101 v. n. 42; A. 20 n. 40 Latine et Germanice cum nota: Innocencius eiusdem tenoris in Marpurg; D. 41 Germanice. — Cum dato: A. 16 p. 75 „Colonie". 1. bonis A. 20. 2. addit A. 16 p. 75.

---

350. *1221 februarii 5 Laterani (cf. 1222 febr. 5, 1223 ian. 13). Honorius III concedit ordinis Theutonici fratribus, ut ad ianuas suas expositos vel natos pueros in pelvi vel alio vase modico baptizent.*

Honorius episcopus servus servorum dei dilectis filiis magistro et fratribus hospitalis sancte Marie Theutonicorum Ierosolimitani salutem et apostolicam benedictionem. Etsi universorum iustas preces admittere debeamus, eos tamen volumus et debemus facilius exaudire, qui sub religionis observantia caritatis sunt et hospitalitatis obsequio deputati. Cum igitur pueros, qui ad ianuam vestram alendi[1] sepius deportantur vel in vestra domo[2] nascuntur, contingat pluries[3] sine baptismatis sacramento decedere, nos vestris iustis postulationibus inclinati ac tante incommoditati misericorditer[4] providere volentes presentium vobis auctoritate concedimus, ut liceat vobis pueros, qui ad ianuas domus vestre proiiciuntur alendi seu ibidem nascuntur, causa necessitatis, sine alicuius preiudicio, in pelvi vel alio vase modico baptizare. Nulli ergo omnino hominum liceat hanc paginam nostre concessionis infringere vel ei ausu temerario contraire. Si quis autem hoc attemptare presumpserit, indignationem omnipotentis dei et beatorum Petri et Pauli apostolorum eius se noverit incursurum. Datum Laterani non. februarii pontificatus nostri anno v.

Sine dato: II, 101 v. n. 40; A. 20 n. 38 Latine et Germanice. D. 39; R. 75 inter Mergenthemensia n. 26 (male. Etsi diversorum). — Cum dato: Laterani non. febr. p. a. 5. IV, 188 v. n. 20. Ioh. 31 Or. quondam Mergenthemense cum bulla in filis sericeis appendente in archivo ordinis Theutonici. Edd. Caorsinus C.; Senner E. v. — Cum dato: Laterani non. febr. p. a. 6 (forsan per errorem typographi?) ed. Duellius app. 7 n. 6. — Cum dato: Laterani id. ianuarii p. n. a. 7 A. 16 p. 39 „Baruli". 1. alendi causa A. 16. 2. d. v. A. 16. 3. plures A. 16. 4. deest A. 16.

---

351. *1221 februarii 5 Laterani. Honorius III vetat ordini Theutonico exactiones pro murorum, pontium, vallorum reparatione, caeteris, imponi.*

Honorius episcopus servus servorum dei dilectis filiis .. magistro et fratribus hospitalis sancte Marie Theutonicorum Ierosolimitani salutem et apostolicam benedictionem. Iustis petentium desideriis dignum est nos facilem prebere consensum et vota, que a rationis tramite non discordant, effectu prosequente complere. Eapropter, dilecti in domino filii, vestris iustis postulationibus grato concurrentes assensu auctoritate vobis presencium duximus indulgendum, ne quis vobis aut ecclesiis vestris pro reparatione murorum, pontium vel vallorum seu pro quibuslibet publicis functionibus aliquas exactiones imponat. Nulli igitur liceat vim et libertatem eorum[1], que vobis et domui vestre indulsimus per litteras aliquas auferre vel temeritate aliqua vacuare. Nulli ergo omnino etc. Si quis autem etc. Datum Laterani non. februarii, pontificatus nostri anno quinto.

Sine dato: II, 103 v. n. 49; A. 20 n. 47 Latine et Germanice. — Cum dato. Originale cum bulla in filis sericeis appendente, quod quondam fuit Confluentiae, in archivo ordinis Vindobonensi adservatur, unde edidit Hennes I, 57 n. 53. A. 16 p. 85 „Confluentie". 1. l. ius et l. e. q. II, l. ius et l. q. A. 20.

---

352. *1221 februarii 5 Laterani. Honorius III concedit ordini Theutonico ius appellandi ad sedem apostolicam, dummodo et causa recipiat appellationem nec huiusmodi remedium iam commissione fuerit denegatum.*

Honorius episcopus servus servorum dei dilectis filiis magistro et fratribus hospitalis sancte Marie Theutonicorum Ierosolimitani salutem et apostolicam benedictionem. Pervenit ad nos, quod in causis, quas alii contra vos vel vos contra alios exercetis, vobis frequenter intercluditur appellationis auxilium, quamvis illud in commissionis litteris vobis minime denegetur. Cum itaque vobis non debeat subtrahi, quod communiter conceditur universis, presentibus vobis litteris duximus indulgendum, ut in quacumque causa vel a quocunque iudice libere vobis liceat a manifestis gravaminibus ad sedem apostolicam appellare, nisi forsan talis sit causa, que appellationem non recipiat vel in commissionis litteris appellationis remedium fuerit denegatum. Datum Laterani non. februarii pontificatus nostri anno v.

Sine dato: II, 106v. n. 57; A. 20 n. 55 Latine et Germanice; D. 57. — Cum dato: R. 65 inter Mergenthemensia. n. 3.

---

353. *1221 februarii 5 Laterani. Honorius III vetat ordinis Theutonici apostatas foveri.*

Honorius episcopus servus servorum dei venerabilibus fratribus archiepiscopis et episcopis et dilectis filiis abbatibus, prioribus, archidiaconis, decanis et aliis ecclesiarum prelatis, ad quos littere iste pervenerint, salutem et apostolicam benedictionem. Quam laudabiliter dilecti filii fratres hospitalis sancte Marie Theotonicorum Ierosolimitani per opera pietatis servicio conditoris immineant et quot de subventione ipsorum infirmi et pauperes sustententur, neminem, qui christiana lege censetur, utilitas, que de operibus ipsis provenit, patitur ignorare. Sane conquerentibus ipsis accepimus, quod quidam fratres ipsorum sepius de domibus propriis exeuntes contra magistros suos dampnabili rebellione ducuntur et in hoc frequenter a viris ecclesiasticis et secularibus roborantur; quidam eciam ab ipsis fratribus pecuniam recipiunt preter conscienciam aliorum eamque in preiudicium hospitalis detinent et reddere contradicunt depositores ipsius in sua malicia defendentes. Quia vero tam graves iniurias predictorum fratrum sustinere nec volumus nec debemus, universitati vestre per apostolica scripta mandamus atque precipimus, quatinus neminem predictorum fratrum quisquam vestrum presumat defendere vel eis in rebellione sua et contumacia favorem aliquem dampnabiliter exhibere, nec pecuniam a quoquam fratrum recipiat vel receptam retineat, nisi ei fuerit de communi fratrum consilio commendata. Si vero aliquis, quod non credimus, contra huius apostolice iussionis tenorem venire temptaverit, nisi commonitus infra viginti dies errorem suam debita satisfactione correxerit, eum usque ad satisfaccionem congruam excommunicationi decernimus subiacere. Datum Laterani non. februarii pontificatus nostri anno v.

Sine dato: II, 111 n. 69; A. 20 n. 67 Latine et Germanice; R. 55 inter Ratisponensia n. 7; D. 69. — Cum dato: IV, 187v. n. 19. Originale, cum bulla in filis sericeis pendente, quondam Mergenthemi nunc Vindobonae in archivo ordinis Theutonici.

---

354. *1221 februarii 5 Laterani. Honorius III concedit ordini Theutonico, quod ei legata duorum vel trium testium verbo probare possit.*

Honorius episcopus servus servorum dei dilectis filiis magistro et fratribus hospitalis sancte Marie Theotonicorum Ierosolimitani salutem et apostolicam benedictionem. Sicut ewangelica veritate attestante[1] didicimus, stat in ore duorum vel trium testium omne verbum. Quia ergo piis et deo dicatis locis ex amministracione suscepti regiminis benignum debemus conferre consultum, paci et humilitati vestre imposterum clementer providere volentes presenti decreto statuimus, ut ea, que in testamentis vel quolibet relicti genere a devotione fidelium vestro xenodochio racionabili providencia dimittuntur vel largiuntur in presencia duorum vel trium testium legittimorum, auctoritate nostra suscipiendi habeatis liberam facultatem. Nulli ergo omnino hominum liceat hanc paginam nostre concessionis infringere vel ei ausu temerario contraire. Si quis autem hoc attemptare presumpserit, indignacionem omnipotentis dei et beatorum Petri et Pauli apostolorum eius se noverit incursurum. Datum Laterani non. februarii pontificatus nostri anno v.

Sine dato: II, 113v. n. 67; A. 20 n. 75 Latine et Germanice cum nota: in Mergintheym; D. 76. — Cum dato: IV, 188v. n. 21; R. 67 inter Mergenthemensia 7. — Originale, cum bulla in filis sericeis appendente, quondam Mergenthemi, nunc Vindobonae in archivo ordinis Theutonici asservatur. Ioh. 31. Edd. Caorsinus fol. C. v.; Senner fol. E. v. 1. Matth. 18, 16.

---

355. *1221 februarii 8 Laterani. Honorius III commendat praelatis ordinis Theutonici confratrias, ecclesias, clericos tuendos.*

Honorius episcopus servus servorum dei venerabilibus fratribus archiepiscopis et epicopis et dilectis filiis abbatibus, prioribus, archidiaconis, decanis et aliis ecclesiarum prelatis, ad quos littere iste pervenerint, salutem et apostolicam benedictionem. Ad iniurias et molestias propulsandas, que religiosis hominibus inferuntur, nullos magis quam prelatos ecclesiarum convenit congruam sollicitudinem adhibere. Sicut autem dilecti filii fratres domus hospitalis sancte Marie Theotonicorum Ierosolimitani sua nobis insinuatione monstrarunt, quod vos de novo quasdam confratrias in vestris ecclesiis statuentes eorundem confratrias fieri prohibetis et contra ea, que ipsis indulsimus, tam ecclesias quam clericos eorundem occasione qualibet emergente subponitis interdicto, illos quoque, qui in dictos fratres manus iniciunt violentas, domos eorum diruunt vel invadunt, eis res alias auferentes vel ipsos quomodolibet aggravantes corrigere non curatis. Quoniam igitur officio nostro multum detrahitur, si viris religiosis gravamen aliquod inferatur nec eos ab eorum molestiis defensetis, universitati vestre per apostolica scripta mandamus atque precipimus, quatenus opera pietatis, que fiunt in illo[2] fratrum predictorum xenodochio, venerando, diligentius attendentes super confratriis eorum nullum dampnum eisdem fratribus per quaslibet alias confratrias seu preiudicium inferatis nec ab aliis permittatis inferri nec eorum ecclesias vel clericos contra privilegia, que ipsis apostolica sedes indulsit, aliquatenus aggravetis. Illos autem, quos vobis constiterit predictis fratribus detrimentum vel iniuriam irrogasse, satisfacere vel exhibere plenam iusticiam moneatis, et, si necesse fuerit, appellatione remota censura ecclesiastica compellatis. Datum Laterani vi idus februarii pontificatus nostri anno v.

Sine dato: II, 99 v. n. 34; D. 33; A. 20 n. 81 Latine et Germanice cum nota: Et est in Nurenberg. — Cum dato: R. 23 inter privilegia in Ellingensi domo asservata n. 1. 2. sūt nllo II.

---

356. *1221 februarii 8 Laterani. Honorius III vetat de ordinis Theutonici ante concilium possessis bonis, sive de eiusdem hortis, virgultis, piscationibus, animalium nutrimentis primitias vel decimas extorqueri.*

Honorius episcopus servus servorum dei venerabilibus fratribus archiepiscopis et episcopis et dilectis filiis abbatibus, prioribus, archidiaconis, decanis et aliis ecclesiarum prelatis, ad quos littere iste pervenerint, salutem et apostolicam benedictionem. Cum dilecti filii fratres hospitalis sancte Marie Theotonicorum Ierosolimitani pro sue religionis observancia et zelo fidei[1], quam defendunt, per sedem apostolicam magna sint libertatis prerogativa donati, quidam, qui aquam vino miscent et de scripturis falsum eligunt intellectum, privilegia ipsorum ultra quam deceat pro sua voluntate restringunt et querentes extraneum intellectum[2] ab ipsis primicias et decimas de possessionibus et novalibus habitis ante concilium generale sive de ortis, virgultis et piscacionibus eorum vel de suorum animalium nutrimentis extorquere presumunt. Volentes igitur dictorum fratrum indempnitatibus providere per apostolica vobis scripta mandamus, quatenus ab extorsione decimarum et primiciarum super premissis omnibus desistatis et vestros subditos appellatione remota ab eadem desistere compellatis. Datum Laterani vi idus februarii pontificatus nostri anno v.

Sine dato: II, 93 n. 15; A. 20 n. 15 Latine et Germanice; D. 14. — Cum dato: IV, 189 v. n. 23. Originale, cum bulla in filis sericeis appendente, quondam Mergenthemi, nunc Vindobonae in archivo ordinis Theutonici asservatur. 1. dei IV. 2. privilegia — intellectum deest II, A. 20.

---

357. *1221 februarii 8 Laterani. Honorius III monet praelatos, ut excitent populos ad subsidium de bonis eorum ordini Theutonico cito ferendum.*

Honorius episcopus s. s. d. venerabilibus fratribus archiepiscopis et episcopis etc. Gravis illa et nimis dolenda ruina, quam dilecti filii fratres hospitalis sancte Marie Theutonicorum Ierosolimitani pro defensione fidei christiane diebus novissimis pertulerunt, illum debet ipsis et suis domibus in oculis omnium impetrare favorem, ut ad eorum consolationem et remedium tam importabilis excidii detrimento pie compassionis adhibende obtentu singuli sponte currere debeant potius, quam aliorum expectent suggestionibus invitari. In hoc enim articulo per experimenti certitudinem evidentius apparebit, quis zelum dei habeat, quis iniuriam populi christiani et tam enorme orientalis populi detrimentum pro amore domini et fidei christiane constantia desideret propulsari. Cum igitur retributionem largitatis exoptare divine secura confidentia valeat, quisquis tam gravis necessitatis articulo predicte domui ad tanti reparationem exterminii subsidium de bonis temporalibus studuerit impertiri, universitatem vestram hortamur in domino, rogamus etiam attentius et mandamus, quatenus subiectos vestro regimini populos moneatis et per urgentissime pulsationis instantiam inducatis, sicut fieri posse celerius et commodius cognoscetis, ut ob peccatorum suorum remissionem non eis tantum, sed potius universitati catholice de bonis suis, que de manu divini beneficii perceperunt, subsidium non differant exhibere. Res enim tam urgentis et immensi discriminis moram non patitur, sed in ictu oculi, si posset fieri, remedium exigeret festinatum. Datum Laterani vi idus februarii pontificatus nostri anno quinto.

Sine dato: II, 102v. n. 46; A. 20 n. 44 Latine et Germanice. — Cum dato: In transsumto complurium bullarum, d. d. Wiennae 1396. aug. 18 in archivo Regimontano, cf. Napiersky I, 5 n. 16; edidit Duellius II, 5 n. 4. Originale, cum bulla in filis sericeis pendente, ut iam dudum etiamnunc Vindobonae in archivo ordinis Theutonici.

---

358. *1221 februarii 8 Laterani. Honorius III iubet ordinis Theutonici violatores censura ecclesiastica coerceri.*

Honorius episcopus servus servorum dei venerabilibus fratribus archiepiscopis et episcopis et dilectis filiis abbatibus, prioribus, archidiaconis, decanis et aliis ecclesiarum prelatis, ad quos littere pervenerint, salutem et apostolicam benedictionem. Quanto maior ab universis dei fidelibus apostolice sedi reverencia exhibetur et quanto ab eisdem sacrosancte Romane ecclesie et nobis ipsis honor et maius vinculum caritatis offertur, tanto amplius in eorum tuicione nos convenit esse sollicitos atque ex nostri auctoritate officii de eorundem utilitatibus attencius cogitare[1] et tam ipsos quam eorum bona protegere a[2] malignorum incursibus et rapinis. Illos autem summi pontificatus officium nos ammonet et hortatur in suo iure fovere specialiter atque a pravorum incursione defendere ac tueri, quos in caritate ferventes agnoscimus et in opere perpendimus efficaces. Qualiter autem dilecti filii fratres hospitalis sancte Marie Theotonicorum Ierosolimitani parentes, patriam et propinquos intuitu eternorum reliquerint et qualiter de terra sua et cognatione egressi ad terram viventium, terram videlicet promissionis, quam monstravit deus diligentibus se, ardenti desiderio et ferventi caritate aspirent, vobis non extat incognitum, cum universo orbi fere sit manifestum. Ipsi nimirum vivifice crucis signum ad ignitorum serpentum et malignorum spirituum expulsionem et defensionem anime et etiam corporis portantes in pectore salvatorem mundi sequuntur et elemosinas per diversas partes orbis colligere et illas ad terram, quam dominus corporaliter visitavit, ad opus pauperum, refectionem infirmorum ac illorum sustentationem, qui non habent, ubi caput reclinent, student diligentissime transportare. Inde est, quod tam fortes Christi athletas in suo sancto proposito volentes attentius confovere, ad defensionem eorundem sollicitudinem vestram duximus commendandam, ut magis ac magis possint ad promovendum propositum, quod sumpserunt, intendere, cum fuerint sollicitudine prelatorum ecclesie a malignantium inquietatione securi. Monemus itaque universitatem vestram, hortamur atque precipimus, quatenus, si quando parrochiani vestri in aliquem predictorum fratrum ipsum capiendo vel de suis equitaturis deiciendo vel alias inhoneste tractando violentas manus iniciunt, huiusmodi presumptores sublato appellationis remedio candelis accensis dilatione et occasione postpositis excommunicatos publice nuntietis et tam diu faciatis sicut excommunicatos artius evitari, donec passo iniuriam satisfaciant competenter et pro absolutionis beneficio impetrando apostolico se conspectui cum diocesani episcopi litteris representent. Eos vero, qui in dictos fratres manus iniciunt violentas et equitaturas aut alia bona eorum diripiunt violenter, si a vobis commoniti ablata eis noluerint restituere et de illatis iniuriis satisfactionem congruam exhibere, vinculo anathematis astringatis et ipsos usque ad satisfactionem condignam teneatis astrictos. Datum Laterani vi idus februarii pontificatus nostri anno v.

Sine dato: II, 111 n. 70; A. 20 n. 68 Latine et Germanice cum nota: in Mergintheym. — Cum dato: R. 64 e domo Mergenthemensi. 1. excogitare II, A. 20. 2. ab i. m. e. r.

---

359. *1221 februarii 8 Laterani. Honorius III confirmat ordini Theutonico ecclesias contra episcoporum quorundam se ab initio consensum non prestitisse asserentium oblocutionem.*

Honorius episcopus servus servorum dei dilectis filiis magistro et fratribus hospitalis sancte Marie Theotonicorum Ierosolimitani salutem et apostolicam benedictionem. Significantibus vobis ad audienciam apostolatus nostri pervenit, quod, cum nonnullas ecclesias habeatis, quibus archiepiscopi et episcopi crisma, oleum sanctum, ordinaciones clericorum[1], consecrationes altarium[1] et alia pontificalia sine questione ad postulationem vestram diucius contulerunt, quidam eorum movent vobis super ipsis ecclesiis questionem dicendo videlicet, quod ab inicio vobis super illis ecclesiis consensum suum minime prestiterint. Quia igitur occasiones huiusmodi frivolas reputamus, nos quieti vestre paterna sollicitudine providere volentes auctoritate vobis apostolica indulgemus, ut tali occasione nequaquam obstante, si aliud canonicum non obsistat, liceat vobis ecclesias taliter acquisitas auctoritate apostolica libere possidere. Nulli ergo omnino hominum liceat hanc paginam nostre concessionis infringere vel ei ausu temerario contraire. Si quis autem hoc attemptare presumpserit, indignationem omnipotentis dei et beatorum

Petri et Pauli apostolorum eius se noverit incursurum. Datum Laterani vi idus februarii pontificatus nostri anno v.

Sine dato: II, 113 v. n. 65; A. 16 p. 112 „Treviris"; A. 20 n. 73 Latine et Germanice; D. 75. — Cum dato: IV, 189 n. 22; R. 142 inter Treverensia. Originale, cum bulla in filis sericeis appendente, quondam Confluentiae, nunc Vindobonae in archivo ordinis Theutonici asservatur. Ibidem transsumtum ex domo E. (?) per Montanarium, Friderici imperatoris II notarium, Ottonem sacri palatii notarium, Aldricum Tridentinum episcopum de 1222. 1. clericorum, altarium deest IV, R. 142.

---

360. *1221 februarii 9 Laterani. Honorius III vetat ordinis Theutonici apostatas foveri.*

Honorius episcopus servus servorum dei venerabilibus fratribus archiepiscopis et episcopis et dilectis filiis abbatibus etc. salutem et apostolicam benedictionem. Cum nemo manum mittens ad aratrum et retro aspiciens[1] aptus sit regno dei, nec, qui supra tectum ascendit, descendere debeat in domum, ut resumat tunicam derelictam, grave nimis gerimus et indignum, quod quidam fratres domus hospitalis sancte Marie Theotonicorum Ierosolimitani sponte a sui propositi tramite discedentes habitu religionis abiecto ad nuptias transeunt seculares et ponentes in cordibus suis, quod non sit deus nec sit scientia in excelso, nec requirat ista, qui scrutator est cordium et etiam medullarum, deserta celestis regis milicia cingulum secularis milicie recipere non verentur, et frequenter quidam de ipsis fratribus exterioris religionis signo retento, cum intus se a tocius religionis observantia abdicarint, ad personas se transferunt ecclesiasticas vel mundanas, que ipsos non tam fovent in sue rebellionis contumacia[2] quam defendunt. Nonnunquam etiam iidem fratres ducti animi levitate potius[3] quam religionis ardore, ut evitent regularis observantie disciplinam, cum pocius velint religionem fugere quam mutare, ad aliam regulam simulant se transferre, ubi sic mentito religionis habitu fructu primi propositi careant[4] et secundi. Cum igitur plantationes huiusmodi pestilentes de agro domini sint extirpande, ne forte, quod absit, alios aspectu inficiant venenoso; universitatem vestram monemus et hortamur[5] attentius[6], per apostolica vobis scripta precipiendo[7] mandantes, quatinus, nisi tales ad monitionem vestram se correxerint et ad suum ordinem et viam redierint veritatis, ipsos excommunicationis vinculo publice innodetis, sub interminatione anathematis omnibus prohibentes, ne dictos apostatas recipere vel[8] retinere receptos aut in sua malicia confovere vel, quod absit, eis in suarum animarum periculum communicare presumant. Datum Laterani v idus februarias pontificatus nostri anno quinto.

Sine dato: II, 93 v. n. 16; A. 20 n. 16 Latine et Germanice cum nota: Est in Confluentia etc. — Cum dato: „Colonie A. 16 p. 75. Originale, quondam Confluentinum, de quo bulla avulsa, nunc Vindobonae in archivo ordinis Theutonici asservatur. 1. Luc. 9. 62. 2. audacia A. 16. 3. post II, A. 20. 4. l. carent? 5. exhortamur II. 6. attentius II. 7. deest A. 16. 8. deest II.

---

361. *1221 februarii 9 Laterani (cf. 1223 febr. 3). Honorius III iubet ordinis Theutonici violatores censura ecclesiastica compesci.*

Honorius episcopus servus servorum dei venerabilibus fratribus archiepiscopis et episcopis et dilectis filiis abbatibus, prioribus, archidiaconis, decanis et aliis ecclesiarum praelatis, ad quos littere iste pervenerint, salutem et apostolicam benedictionem. Etsi apostolice servitutis officium nos constituat omnibus in iusticia debitores, viris tamen religiosis et eis maxime, quos per sedis apostolice privilegia maiori donavimus libertate, specialiter adesse tenemur[1], ne iidem, quod absit, malignorum incursibus exponantur, si non fuerit, qui pro eis se murum defensionis opponat. Cum igitur dilecti filii magister et fratres hospitalis sancte Marie Theotonicorum Ierosolimitani ex eo nobis graviter sit conquesti, quod, cum ipsi a malefactoribus suis passim iniurias sustineant et rapinas, vix[2] invenitur, qui congrue illis protectione subveniat, universitati vestre per apostolica scripta mandamus et in obediencie virtute districte precipimus, quatenus illos, qui fratres predictos et eorum homines in personis vel rebus offenderint vel ipsorum domos violenter invaserint aut rapuerint bona sua, tam diu excommunicatos publice nuntietis et lcoa, in quibus eorundem bona detenta fuerint, supponatis ecclesiastico interdicto, donec malefactores ipsi ablata universa restituant et de illatis iniuriis satisfaciant competenter. Datum Laterani v idus februarii pontificatus nostri anno v.

Sine dato: II, 101 v. n. 41; A. 20 n. 39 Latine et Germanice; D. 40 Germanice. — Cum dato: Laterani 5 id. febr. p. n. a. 5. R. 27 e domo Ellingensi 10; R. 196 dubii loci. — Cum dato: Laterani 3 non. febr. p. a. 7 in transsumto C(onradi) archiepiscopi Coloniensis. dd. iunii 25 in crastino b. Ioh. bapt. (Colonie?), a quo sigillum avulsum, in archivo ordinis Theutonici Vindobonensi. 1. teneamur R. 27. 2. dum vix RR.

---

362. *1221 februarii 9 Laterani. Honorius III commendat praelatorum populorumque munificentiae ordinem Theutonicum propositis indulgentiis. Clericis concedit, ut retentis beneficiis per annum vel biennium ei serviant.*

Honorius episcopus servus servorum dei venerabilibus fratribus archiepiscopis et episcopis et dilectis filiis abbatibus, prioribus, archidiaconis, decanis et aliis ecclesiarum prelatis, ad quos littere iste pervenerint, salutem et apostolicam benedictionem. Quam amabilis deo et quam venerandus hominibus locus existat, quam eciam iocundum et utile receptaculum peregrinis et pauperibus prebeat xenodochium hospitalis sancte Marie Theotonicorum Ierosolimitani, hii, qui per diversa maris pericula pie devocionis intuitu sanctam civitatem Ierusalem et sepulchrum domini visitant, assidue recognoscunt. Ibi enim indigentes et pauperes reficiuntur, infirmis multimoda sanitatis obsequia adhibentur et diversis laboribus et periculis fatigati resumptis viribus recreantur atque, ut ipsi ad sacrosancta loca domini nostri Ihesu Christi corporali presencia dedicata securius valeant proficisci, servientes, quos fratres eiusdem domus ad hoc officium specialiter deputatos proprios sumptibus retinent, cum oportunitas exigat, devote ac diligenter efficiunt. Quia ergo eisdem fratribus ad tantorum sumptuum immensitatem proprie non sufficiunt facultates, caritatem vestram duximus rogandam et hortandam, quatenus de vestra habundancia eorum inopiam suppleatis et populum vobis commissum ipsorum fraternitatem assumere et ad peregrinorum sustentationem collectas facere in peccatorum suorum remissionem frequentibus exhortacionibus moneatis, hoc scientes, quoniam dictum hospitale Theotonicorum cum omnibus ad ipsum pertinentibus sub beati Petri tutela suscepimus et, quicunque de facultatibus sibi a deo collatis fratribus eisdem subvenerit et in tam sancta fraternitate statuerit se collegam eique beneficia persolverit annuatim, secundum quantitatem subsidii et devocionis effectum peccatorum suorum veniam confisi de beatorum Petri et Pauli apostolorum meritis pollicemur. Ob reverenciam quoque ipsius venerabilis domus auctoritate apostolica constituimus, ut hiis, qui eorum fraternitatem assumpserint, si forte ecclesie, ad quas pertinent a divinis fuerint officiis interdicte eosque mori contigerit, dummodo nec excommunicati nec nominatim fuerint interdicti aut eciam publice usurarii, sepultura ecclesiastica non negetur, hoc eciam addito, ut receptores fraternitatis eiusdem seu eciam collectarum salvo iure dominorum suorum sub beati Petri et nostra protectione consistant, adicientes insuper, ut, si qui eorundem fratrum, qui ad recipiendas easdem fraternitates missi fuerint vel collectas, in quamlibet civitatem, castellum vel vicum advenerint, si forte locus ipse a divinis fuerit officiis interdictus, in eorum adventu semel in anno aperiantur ecclesie et excommunicatis eiectis divina ibi officia celebrentur. Ad maiorem quoque vestre mercedis cumulum nichilominus vobis mandando precipimus, quatenus hanc nostram constitutionem per vestras parrochias nunciari propriis litteris faciatis. Mandamus eciam, ut, si qui de clericis ecclesiarum vestrarum prefati hospitalis fratribus cum licentia prelati sui sponte ac gratis per annum vel biennium servire decreverint, nequaquam impediantur et interim sua beneficia vel ecclesiasticcs redditus non amittant. Ad hec universitatem vestram literis presentibus exhortamur, ut ad subventionem eorundem fratrum debite caritatis affectibus intendatis et tam hiis quam aliis modis, quibus eisdem servis dei prodesse poteritis, ipsos iuvare et fovere curetis. Datum Laterani v idus februarii pontificatus nostri anno v.

Sine dato: II, 109 n. 64; A. 20 n. 62 Latine et Germanice cum nota: In Marpurg. D. 63.— Cum dato: IV, 190 n. 24; A. 16 p. 59 „in Marpurg". Ioh. 31. Edd. Caorsinus fol. C. v.; Senner fol. E. 2.

---

363. *1221 martii 13 Laterani. Honorius III vetat praelatos de haereditate hominum ordinis Theutonici parochianorum suorum plus exigere, quam testamento sit sancitum aut haeredes concesserint.*

Honorius episcopus servus servorum dei venerabilibus fratribus archiepiscopis et episcopis et dilectis filiis ecclesiarum prelatis, ad quos littere iste pervenerint, salutem et apostolicam benedictionem. Quanto sincerioris[1] caritatis affectu dilectos filios fratres hospitalis sancte Marie Theotonicorum Ierosolimitani pro sua honestate ac religione diligimus, tanto propensius ad ea extirpanda, que in eorum preiudicium attemptari dicuntur, intendere volumus omnimodis et debemus. Eorundem fratrum nobis est relatione suggestum, quod sacerdotes in vestris diocesibus constituti homines predictorum fratrum parrochianos suos nolunt in obitu ad sepulturam recipere, nisi eorum heredes de bonis defunctorum eisdem sacerdotibus velint iuxta eorum beneplacitum erogare; quod quam indignum sit et ecclesiastice dignitati contrarium, nos quidem plenius cognoscimus et discretionis vestre probitas non ignorat. Quocirca universitati vestre per apostolica scripta mandamus, quatenus sacerdotes per vestras dioceses constitutos monere diligenter et compellere studeatis, ut homines predictorum fratrum, qui in eorum parrochiis commorantur, cum eos mori contigerit, sine huiusmodi gravamine ad sepulturam recipiant non plus ab eis aliquatenus exacturi propter hoc, quam vel decedentium extrema voluntas vel heredum liberalitas eis sponte duxerit largiendum. Datum Laterani iii idus martii pontificatus nostri anno v.

Sine dato: II, 108 v. n. 63; A. 16 p. 112 „Treviris“; A. 20 n. 61 Latine et Germanice; D. 62 Germanice. — Cum dato: Originale, cum bulla in filis sericeis rubris et luteis appendente, in archivo ordinis Theutonici Vindobonensi. Innocentii IV memoratur inter Marpurgensia, Honorii IV inter Trevirensia R. 141. 1. sinceriores II, sinceriore A. 20.

---

364. *1221 iunii 2 Tibure. Honorius III repetit n. 328 de 1221 ianuarii 18.*

Honorius etc. Quia plerumque etc. Datum Tibure iv nonas iunii pontificatus nostri anno v.

---

365. *1222 ianuarii 21 Laterani. Honorius III repetit n. 342 de 1221 ian. 21.*

Honorius etc. Decet pastoralis etc. Datum Laterani xii kal. februarii pontificatus nostri anno vi.

---

366. *1222 februarii 5 Laterani. Honorius III repetit n. 350 de 1221 febr. 5.*

Honorius etc. Etsi universorum etc. Datum Laterani nonas februarii pontificatus nostri anno vi[1].

1. forsan ex errore typographi Duelliani pro V, velut etiam in n. 364.

---

367. *1222 februarii 20 Laterani (1223 ianuar. 13 Laterani). Honorius III iubet praelatos ordinem Theutonicum manu tenere in quaerendis per ecclesias eleemosynis et legatis plenarie recipiendis.*

Honorius episcopus servus servorum dei venerabilibus fratribus archiepiscopis et episcopis et dilectis filiis abbatibus, prioribus, archidiaconis, decanis et aliis ecclesiarum prelatis, ad quos littere iste pervenerint, salutem et apostolicam benedictionem. Querelam gravem recepimus dilectorum filiorum fratrum hospitalis sancte Marie Theotonicorum Ierosolimitani, quam pre magnitudine culpe ac pauperum dispendio dissimulare nec volumus nec debemus. Proposuerunt siquidem iam dicti fratres, quod, cum pro confratriis et elemosinis pauperum requirendis secundum quod eis indulsimus[1] ad ecclesias quorundam presbiterorum accedunt, eos recipere nolunt, sed, quod gravius est, ab ecclesiis ipsis predictos fratres eicere non verentur, cum deberent eos benigne ac pacienter audire et parrochianos suos ad conferendas pauperibus elemosinas attencius exhortari. Accedit ad hec, quod iidem presbiteri[2] quandam partem elemosinarum pauperum exigunt impudenter, et, ut possint extorquere quod querunt, parrochianis suis reclamantibus pauperum obsequium impedire pro sue voluntatis arbitrio non formidant[3]. Unde, quoniam tantum predictorum fratrum gravamen et pauperum dispendium clausis non debemus[4] oculis pertransire, quibus ex debito pastoralis officii patrocinium tenemur[5] contra omnium insolentiam impertiri, universitati vestre per apostolica scripta mandamus atque precipimus[6], quatinus universis presbiteris vestre potestati subiectis sub pena officii et beneficii iniungatis, ut predictos fratres in ecclesiis suis ad opus pauperum predicare et elemosinas libere[7] querere iuxta quod eis duximus indulgendum[8] sine qualibet contradiccione permittant, salva moderacione concilii generalis[9], nec ab eis aliquid exigere vel extorquere presumant. Si vero postmodum de iam dictis presbiteris ad audienciam vestram querela pervenerit, in transgressores precepti nostri iuxta modum culpe taliter vindicetis, quod eos sue temeritatis peniteat et fratres ipsi pro defectu iusticie non cogantur ad nostram presenciam laborare. Pervenit preterea ad audienciam nostram, quod, si quando parrochiani vestri prefatis fratribus de rebus suis quicquam in testamento relinquunt, heredes eorum vel illi, qui res ipsas penes se habent, ipsum legatum eis solvere contradicunt. Quia vero gravem culpe maculam contrahunt et non mediocriter oculos divine maiestatis offendunt, qui ea, que sacris dei ecclesiis et viris religioni et honestati deditis racionabiliter in testamento legantur, temeritate qualibet detinere presumunt; universitati vestre per apostolica scripta precipiendo[10] mandamus, quatinus, si quando predicti fratres apud vos exinde querimoniam deposuerint, illos, quos vobis nominaverint, si vobis ita esse constiterit, moneatis attencius et districtius compellatis, ut ea, que predictis fratribus sunt in testamento legata, remoto appellacionis obstaculo sine maliciosa dilatione absque diminucione persolvant vel in presencia vestra appellatione remota exhibeant iusticie complementum. Quodsi monitis vestris parere contempserint, eos appellatione cessante usque ad condignam satisfaccionem excommunicacionis vinculo astringatis. Datum Laterani x kalendas marcii pontificatus nostri anno sexto.

Sine dato: I, 72v. n. 39; II, 107v. n. 60 — Cum dato: Laterani 10 cal. marcii p. n. a. 6; A. 16 p. 59 „in Marpurg". — Cum dato: Laterani id. ian. p. n. a. 7; R. 44 inter Ellingensia n. 31.
1. iuxta consuetudinem suam auctoritate apostolica confirmatam R. 2. deest I, A. 16. 3. pre-

sumant I. 4. debetis I, A. 16. 5. debemus R. 6. deest I. 7. deest I. II. A. 16. 8. iuxta quod eis apostolica sedes indulget R. 9. salva — generalis deest I, A. 16. 10. deest I, A. 16.

368. *1222 aprilis 17 Verulis. Honorius III dehortatur Templarios, ne ob alba mantella a fratribus ordinis Theutonici ferri solita moveantur.*

Honorius episcopus servus servorum dei dilectis filiis .. magistro et fratribus domus militie Templi salutem et apostolicam benedictionem. Quanto vos ampliori caritate diligimus, tanto nobis amplius displiceret, si, quod absit, reprehensione seu etiam irrisione dignum aliquid faceretis. Siquidem privilegia fratribus domus sancte Marie Teutonicorum ab apostolica sede concessa manifeste demonstrant, quod ordo vester in clericis et militibus ac aliis fratribus, Hospitalis vero in pauperibus et infirmis in ipsa domo iam dudum extitit institutus et per sedem apostolicam confirmatus. Licet autem fratres ipsi tum propter negligentiam suam, dum essent pauci et pauperes, tum etiam propter scandali vestri metum tam in habitu deferendo quam in quibusdam aliis aliquando contra institutionem fecerint memoratam, nos tamen inclinati sue religionis merito et precibus carissimi in Christo filii nostri F(riderici), Romanorum imperatoris illustris semper augusti et regis Sicilie, qui in die coronationis sue id a nobis pro speciali munere postulavit[1], institutionem ipsam de communi consilio fratrum nostrorum nostro privilegio confirmavimus, domum ipsam aliis privilegiis, indulgentiis et libertatibus munientes. Accepimus autem, quod vos occasione alborum mantellorum, super quibus deferendis specialem a nobis indulgentiam impetrarunt[2], pro eo quod in hoc specialiter fecisse contra institutionem huiusmodi videbantur, moti estis aliquantulum contra eos, quod quantum sit vestra religione indignum, quisquis recogitare voluerit, facile recognoscet. Si enim vos ab huiusmodi motu nec apostolica nec imperialis reverentia cohibet, cohibere saltem omnium id audientium subsanatio vos deberet, quibus videtur sicut est revera ridiculum vos indigne ferre alios a vobis album portare mantellum presertim a vestro habitu sic distinctum signaculo speciali, ut timeri non possit, ne quis unius ordinis fratres ordinis esse alterius arbitretur. Ideoque circumspectionem vestram attente rogandam duximus et hortandam, quatinus omni rancore deposito, si quem forte contra dictos fratres occasione huiusmodi concepistis, ambuletis in caritatis spiritu et unitatis vinculo cum eisdem, eorum profectum, sicut decet viros religiosos, proprium reputantes, ita quod idem imperator, cum illuc deo dante pervenerit, fraternam inter vos inveniat unitatem, quia, si aliter faceretis[3], non solum apostolicam et imperialem incurreretis offensam, verum etiam in detractionem vestram ora quorumlibet audientium laxaretis. Datum Verul. xv kal. maii pontificatus nostri anno sexto.

Sine dato: A. 20 n. 78 Latine et Germanice cum nota: Dis privilegium is zcu Mergintheym. D. 80; R. 73 Mergenthemensium 23. — Cum dato: I, 76 v.; II, 114 n. 70. Originale cum bulla in filis cannabinis pendente in archivo ordinis Theutonici Vindobonensi, ediderunt de Wal Recherches I, 375 et Hennes I, 64 n. 60. 1. cf. ad n. 309. 2. 1221 ianuar. 9. n. 308. 3. faceritis W. H.

369. *1223 ianuarii 4 (cf. ianuar. 12) Laterani. Honorius III vetat parochianos prohiberi, quominus ordinis Theutonici ecclesias frequentent, ei subsidia erogent, in coemeteriis eius sepulturam quaerant.*

Honorius episcopus servus servorum dei venerabilibus fratribus archiepiscopis, episcopis, et dilectis filiis abbatibus, prioribus etc. Gravem dilectorum filiorum fratrum hospitalis sancte Marie Theotonicorum Ierosolimitani recepimus questionem, quod quidam vestrum parrochianos suos ad ecclesias et capellas fratrum ipsorum causa orationis accedere ac eis pia elargiri beneficia non permittunt, quin immo, quod gravius est, eligentes in eorum cimiteriis sepulturas et caritatis eis subsidia exhibentes interdicere ac excommunicare presumunt in dictorum fratrum non modicum detrimentum. Quia igitur predictorum fratrum iniuriam tanto minus dissimulare possumus, quanto amplius Christi pauperibus, quorum iidem ministri existunt, et terre sancte succursui est dampnosa; universitati vestre per apostolica scripta mandamus precipiendo, quatinus et vos ipsi penitus ab huiusmodi desistentes iniuriis et vestros subditos a similibus compescentes fratres predictos non impediatis nec paciamini, quantum in vobis fuerit, ab aliis impediri, quominus Christi fideles causa orationis, cum voluerint, eorum adeant ecclesias et capellas grata eis subsidia et pias elemosinas erogando et eligendo in cimiteriis iuxta indulta sedis apostolice sepulturam. Datum Laterani ii nonas ianuarii pontificatus nostri anno septimo.

Sine dato: I, 73v; R. 6 inter Norimbergensia; A. 20 n. 7 Latine et Germanice cum nota: In Trevere vel Nurenberg; D. Germanice. — Cum dato: 2 nonas ianuarii p. a. 7. Originale cum bulla in filis sericeis rubris et luteis appendente in archivo ordinis Theutonici Vindobonensi, quondam Iunecense; ibidem alterum Mergenthemense. — Cum dato: 2 id. ianuarii p. a. 7. Orig. cum bulla in filis sericeis appendente quondam Mergenthemense ibidem. Ubi etiam Montanarii, imperatoris Friderici II et Iacobi Heinrici regis Romanorum notariorum publicorum transscriptum, quondam in domo E(llingensi?)

---

370. *1223 ianuarii 5 Laterani (cf. 1223 ianuarii 13, febr. 4, 1225 maii 31). Honorius III commendat ordinem Theutonicum in recuperanda terra sancta laborantem munificentiae Christi fidelium, proposita indulgentia.*

Honorius episcopus servus servorum dei universis Christi fidelibus, ad quos littere iste pervenerint, salutem et apostolicam benedictionem. Ad eripiendam de paganorum manibus terram illam, quam dominus Ihesus Christus proprio sanguine consecravit, tanto forcius et libencius debent intendere christiani, quanto propius et cercius, ut speramus, eiusdem terre liberatio appropinquat. Quisquis enim[1] in adventu summi regis desiderat esse tutus, ut ab eo eterne felicitatis premia consequatur, in instantis necessitatis articulo sue debet devocionis indicia demonstrare, securus utique, quod, si ipse oportuno bonorum omnium servierit largitori, nunquam sibi deesse poterit merces magna, cum sit omnipotens dominus largissimus retributor, qui pro terrenis celestia et[1] pro transitoriis dat eterna. Ut igitur vos possitis huius retributionis premia promereri, ad mittendum vestre subventionis subsidium terre sancte hilares vos ostendere debetis, et, qui ad eiusdem terre succursum laborare personaliter non potestis, eius saltem defensoribus et propugnatoribus manus vestri auxilii porrigatis. Universitatem vestram itaque rogandam duximus et monendam, per apostolica scripta vobis mandantes et in remissionem peccaminum iniungentes, quatinus dilectis filiis fratribus domus sancte Marie Theotonicorum, qui ad recuperandam et defendendam terram predictam laborare totis viribus non desistunt, in eorum confratriis assumendis, legatis et aliis beneficiis exhibendis habeatis pro dei et nostra reverencia pietate solita commendatos, diligentius attendentes, quod dicti fratres tanquam fideles animarum vestrarum ministri non querunt, que sua sunt, sed que Ihesu Christi, non sibi tantummodo thesaurizant, sed facultates vestras fideliter Christi pauperibus subministrant, quorum manus in thesauris celestibus eas condunt, ubi nec erugo exterminat nec tinea demolitur. Nos enim de beatorum apostolorum Petri et Pauli auctoritate confisi omnibus, qui de facultatibus sibi collatis a deo fratribus subvenerint antedictis et in tam sancta fraternitate statuerint se collegas eisque beneficia persolverint annuatim, septimam partem iniuncte penitencie relaxamus. Datum Laterani non. ianuarii pontificatus nostri anno septimo.

Sine dato: R. 5 e domo Norimbergensi; sed missa: „archiepiscopis etc." II, 98 v. n. 32 et A. 20 n. 32 Latine et Germanice cum nota: Et est in Marpurg etc.; D. 31 Germanice. — Cum dato: Laterani non. ianuar. p. n. a. 7; A. 16 p. 61 „in Marpurg". — Cum dato: Laterani id. ianuar. p. n. a. 7; R. 197 dubii loci; A. 16 p. 106 „Traiecti". — Cum dato: Laterani 2 nonas febr. p. n. a. 7. I, 71. — Cum dato: Tibure 2 cal. iunii p. n. a. 9 A. 16 p. 93 „Mechilinia". Originale, de quo bulla avulsa, quondam Veteribus Iuncis, nunc in archivo ordinis Theutonici Vindobonae. 1. autem II. 2. deest II.

---

371. *1223 ianuar. 12 Laterani. Honorius III repetit n. 323 de 1221 ianuar. 17.*

Honorius etc. Cum a religiosorum etc. Datum Laterani ii idus ianuarii pontificatus nostri anno septimo.

---

372. *1223 ianuar. 12 Laterani. Honorius III repetit n. 369 de 1223 ianuar. 4.*

Honorius etc. Gravem dilectorum etc. Datum Laterani ii idus ianuarii pontificatus nostri anno septimo.

---

373. *1223 ianuar. 12 Laterani. Honorius III repetit n. 309 de 1221 ianuar. 9.*

Honorius etc. Vestra religio etc. Datum Laterani ii id. ianuarii pontificatus nostri anno septimo.

---

374. *1223 ianuar. 13 Laterani. Honorius III repetit n. 370 de 1223 ianuar. 5.*

Honorius etc. Ad eripiendam etc. Datum Laterani idus ianuarii pontificatus nostri anno septimo.

---

375. *1223 ianuar. 13 Laterani. Honorius III repetit n. 314 de 1221 ianuar. 16.*

Honorius etc. Cum dilectis cet. Datum Laterani idus ianuarii pontificatus nostri anno septimo.

---

376. *1223 ianuar. 13 Laterani. Honorius III repetit n. 350 de 1221 febr. 5.*

Honorius etc. Etsi universorum etc. Datum Laterani idus ianuarii pontificatus nostri anno septimo.

---

377. *1223 ianuar. 13 Laterani. Honorius III repetit n. 320 de 1221 ianuar. 16.*

Honorius etc. Iustis petentium cet. Datum Laterani idus ianuarii pontificatus nostri anno septimo.

---

378. *1223 ianuar. 13 Laterani. Honorius III repetit n. 367 de 1222 febr. 5.*

Honorius etc. Querelam gravem etc. Datum Laterani idus ianuarii pontificatus nostri anno septimo.

---

379. *1223 ianuarii 16 Laterani (cf. 1223 aprilis 7, iulii 31). Honorius III excommunicari iubet, quicunque fratres ordinis Theutonici capiendo, de equitaturis deiiciendo, alias inhoneste tractando violaverint.*

Honorius episcopus servus servorum dei venerabilibus fratribus archiepiscopis et episcopis et dilectis filiis abbatibus, prioribus, archidiaconis, decanis et aliis ecclesiarum prelatis, ad quos littere iste pervenerint, salutem et apostolicam benedictionem. Paci et quieti religiosorum virorum fratrum hospitalis sancte Marie Theutonicorum Ierosolimitani apostolica nos convenit sollicitudine providere et tam ipsos quam eorum bona tanto sollicitius a malignorum incursibus et rapinis tenemur protegere, quanto pro fide christiani nominis se diuturnioribus exponunt periculis et adversus pravas et exteras nationes labores subeunt graviores. Inde est, quod tam fortes Christi athletas in suo sancto proposito volentes attentius confovere, ad defensionem sui sollicitudinem vestram duximus commonendam, ut magis ac magis possint ad promovendum propositum, quod sumpserunt, intendere, cum fuerint sollicitudine prelatorum ecclesie a malignorum inquietatione securi. Monemus itaque universitatem vestram atque precipimus, quatinus, si quando clerici vel laici parrochiani vestri in aliquem predictorum fratrum capiendo vel de suis equitaturis deiciendo aut alias inhoneste tractando violentas manus iniciunt, huiusmodi presumptores sublato appellationis obstaculo accensis candelis dilatione et occasione postposita excommunicatos publice nuntietis et tam diu faciatis sicut excommunicatos artius evitari, donec passo iniuriam congrue satisfaciant et pro absolutionis beneficio impetrando apostolico se conspectui representent. Eos vero, qui in predictos fratres manus non iniciunt violentas, sed eos verbis contumeliosis afficiunt et equitaturas aut alia eorum bona violenter diripiunt, si a vobis commoniti ablata eis restituere noluerint et de illatis iniuriis satisfactionem congruam exhibere, vinculo anathematis astringatis, quo ipsos usque ad condignam satisfactionem teneatis astrictos. Datum Laterani xvii kal. februarii pontificatus nostri anno septimo.

Sine dato: I, 74v.; II, 106v. n. 58; A. 20 n. 56 Latine et Germanice cum nota: Et est in Marpurg. Germanice D. 57. — Cum dato: Laterani xvii kal. febr. p. n. a. 7 ex originali quondam Confluentino nunc archivi ordinis Theutonici Vindobonensis cum bulla in filis sericeis appensa ed. Hennes Cod. ord. Theut. I, 68 n. 63. — Cum eodem dato: A. 16 p. 85 „Confluentie; eciam invenitur in Iuncis sub eodem papa". — In eodem archivo Vindobonensi specialiter haec epistola ad Moguntinum archiepiscopum, suffraganeos eius aliosque provinciae istius praelatos sub dato (1223 april. 7) Laterani vii id. aprilis p. n. a. 7 directa. Cum eodem dato: Laterani vii id. aprilis p. n. a. 7 ad Moguntinum archiepiscopum caeteros R. 71 inter Mergenthemensia n. 10. — Cum dato: Signie ii kal. aug. p. n. a. 8 ad Remensem archiepiscopum caeteros R. 127 inter Marburgensia, ubi additur: Item Gregorius papa IX de eodem de verbo ad verbum; R. 154 memoratur initium inter Iuncensia cum nota: „habetur prius in Marpurg de verbo ad verbum sicut est per eundem Honorium III et Treveren. per Innocencium IV. A. 16 p. 60 „in Marpurg".

---

380. *1223 ianuar. 16 Laterani. Honorius III repetit n. 337 de 1221 ianuar. 19.*

Honorius etc. Querela dilectorum etc. Datum Laterani xvii kal. februarii pontificatus nostri anno vii.

---

381. *1223 ianuar. 29 Laterani. Honorius III repetit n. 318 de 1221 ianuar. 16.*

Honorius etc. Ex insinuatione etc. Datum Laterani iiii kal. februarii pontificatus nostri anno septimo.

---

382. *1223 ianuar. 31 Laterani. Honorius III repetit n. 323 de 1221 ianuar. 17.*

Honorius etc. Cum a religiosorum etc. Datum Laterani ii kal. februarii pontificatus nostri anno vii.

---

383. *1223 ianuarii 31 Laterani. Honorius III iubet praelatos ordinis Theutonici privilegia apostolica legere, observare, observanda curare.*

Honorius episcopus servus servorum dei venerabilibus fratribus archiepiscopis et episcopis etc. salutem et apostolicam benedictionem. Si discrimina, que dilecti filii fratres hospitalis sancte Marie Theotonicorum Ierosolimitani pro defensione christianitatis cotidie sustinent in partibus transmarinis, et beneficia, que pauperibus subministrant, consideracione sollicita pensaretis, non solum ab eorum molestiis cessaretis, sed alios studeretis districtius cohibere. Ceterum audivimus et audientes nequivimus[1] non mirari, quod eos quidam vestrum durius solito persequentes non solum querelas eorum dissimulant, sed ipsos gravibus iniuriis vexaverunt et in dampnabili proposito adhuc perseverant, litteras nostras generales et quandoque speciales legere contempnentes, quas si interdum legerint vilipendunt. Unde clerici et laici sumentes audaciam adversus eos securius[2] insolescunt, elemosinas et beneficia subtrahunt consueta; invasores quoque bonorum ipsorum fratrum non arguunt, sed in familiaritate sua[3] recipiunt, fratres ipsos intolerabiliter[4] deprimentes, quos pro sue religionis honestate deberent attencius confovere[5]. Unde, quoniam gravamen eorum tanto minus volumus in paciencia sustinere, quanto gravius iusto dei iudicio permittente iugiter ipsos inimici[6] christiani nominis persequuntur, universitati vestre per apostolica scripta mandamus et in obediencie virtute precipimus, quatinus litteras, quas pro eis dirigimus, sive generales fuerint sive[7] eciam speciales, recipiatis humiliter et fideliter exponatis, subiectos vestros ad elemosinas et beneficia solita sollicitis[8] monitis et exhortacionibus diligencius[9] inducentes[10], fratres autem benigne recipiatis et honeste tractetis attencius provisuri, ut de parrochianis vestris vel de subditis aliis, si querelam detulerint, ipsos ad exhibendam iusticiam omni gracia et timore postpositis canonica severitate cogatis, ita quod fratres ipsi ex negligencia vestra ad sedem apostolicam non laborent[11]; scituri quod, si precepto nostro presumpseritis contraire, in vos sicut inobedientes animadvertere severius conpellemur. Datum Laterani ii kal. februarii pontificatus nostri anno vii.

Sine dato: I, 75; II, 113 n. 74; A. 20 n. 72 Latine et Germanice cum nota: In Traiecto inferiori (czu Utrecht); D. 74 Germanice. — Cum dato: A. 16 p. 107 „Traiecti". 1. nequimus I. 2. severius I, A. 16. 3. s. f. II. A. 20. 4. inviolabiliter I. 5. sustentare II, A. 20. 6. inimicos A. 20. 7. seu II, A. 16. 8. e. solitas et b. sollicitis II, A. 20. 9. deest II, A. 20. 10. indulgentes I. 11. scituri usque compellemur deest A. 16. scituri usque ad finem deest I.

---

384. *1223 febr. 1 Laterani. Honorius III repetit n. 316 de 1221 ianuar. 16.*

Honorius etc. Dilecti filii etc. Datum Laterani kalendas februarii pontificatus nostri anno septimo.

---

385. *1223 februarii 1 Laterani (cf. 1223 febr. 3). Honorius III vetat fratres Theutonicos ordinem sine magistri licentia relinquere.*

Honorius episcopus servus servorum dei dilectis filiis magistro et fratribus hospitalis sancte Marie Theutonicorum Ierosolimitani salutem et apostolicam benedictionem. Graviter oculos divine maiestatis offendunt et thesaurizant sibi iram in die iudicii iusti dei, qui religionis habitum assumentes et incipientes domino famulari ad Egipti delicias derelictas inhiant et pepones, abiectoque iugo domini secularibus negociis se inmiscent et illicita mercimonia, ymmo detestanda contubernia contrahere non formidant[1]. Plerique etiam, qui deo in fictis operibus menciuntur obtentu false religionis, quam pocius volunt fugere quam mutare, non petita magistri sui licencia vel obtenta se ad alium religionis locum transferunt, non advertentes, quod deus non fallitur nec altissimus irridetur. Nos igitur super hiis volentes speciali quadam sollicitudine providere, auctoritate presencium inhibemus, ne quis post professionem ordinis vestri vobis regulariter factam habitumque receptum ad seculum vel mundi miliciam aut seculares nupcias licenciam habeat transeundi. Nullus quoque maioris vel minoris religionis obtentu sine magistri sui licentia presumat ad alium ordinem transvolare. Nulli ergo omnino hominum liceat hanc paginam nostre inhibicionis infringere vel ei ausu temerario contraire. Si quis autem hoc attemptare presumpserit, indignacionem omnipotentis dei et beatorum Petri et Pauli apostolorum eius se noverit incursurum. Datum Laterani kal. februarii pontificatus nostri anno septimo.

Sine dato: II, 106 n. 55; A. 20 n. 53 Latine et Germanice; R. 194. — Cum dato: Laterani kal. febr. p. n. a. 7 I, 76 v.; IV, 191 v. n. 26; R. 55 inter Ratisponensia 6; A. 16 p. 38 „Baruli". Originale quondam Mergenthemense cum bulla in filis sericeis appensa asservatur in archivo ordinis Theutonici Vindobonensi. — Cum dato: Laterani iii nonas febr. p. n. a. 7 originale, quod Freudenthalii asservabatur; unde excerpta edidit Boczek in Codice diplomatico et epistolari Moraviae Olomucii 1839. 4°. II, 145 n. 142. Originale nunc sine bulla in archivo ordinis Theutonici Vindobonensi asservatur. 1. verentur I. II, A. 20.

---

386. *1223 febr. 3 Laterani. Honorius III repetit n. 323 de 1221 ianuar. 17.*

Honorius etc. Cum a religiosorum etc. Datum Laterani iii non. februarii pontificatus nostri anno septimo.

---

387. *1223 febr. 3 Laterani. Honorius III repetit n. 361 de 1221 febr. 9.*

Honorius etc. Etsi apostolice etc. Datum Laterani iii non. februarii pontificatus nostri anno septimo.

---

388. *1223 febr. 3 Laterani. Honorius III repetit n. 384 de 1223 febr. 1.*

Honorius etc. Graviter oculos etc. Datum Laterani iii non. februarii pontificatus nostri anno septimo.

---

389. *1223 februarii 3 Laterani. Honorius III universos Christi fideles proposita indulgentia hortatur ad succurrendum ordini Theutonico eleemosynis.*

Honorius episcopus servus servorum dei universis Christi fidelibus, ad quos litere iste pervenerint, salutem et apostolicam benedictionem. Inter cetera, que inducunt miseracionis pacienciam ad parcendum, sola est elemosina, que operiens multitudinem peccatorum offensam divinam mitigat, dat in presenti graciam et adicit gloriam in futuro. Ipsa enim dispersa multiplicatur et crescit et reposita in manus pauperum celestes congeritur in thesauros, quin potius, quod uni ex minimis factum fuerit de operibus caritatis, ipsi domino factum secundum veritatis eloquium perhibetur. Non est autem alicui, sicut arbitramur, incognitum, quod dilecti filii, fratres hospitalis sancte Marie Theotonicorum Ierosolimitani, qui sua omnia, immo et se ipsos superimpendunt servitio Ihesu Christi, sic intenti sunt circa opera caritatis, specialiter ad defensionem fidei christiane, emulantes quodammodo zelum Mathathie, cum videret sancta domini ab exteris nationibus prophanari, qui vitam in patientia tollerant et in desiderio mortem habent, bonis tamen celestibus inhiantes. Cum igitur dicti fratres[1], qui effundunt opes et tradunt corpora pro zelo fidei christiane, ad elemosinas non sufficiant consuetas, nisi fidelium suffragiis adiuventur; universitatem vestram rogandam duximus et monendam in remissionem vobis peccaminum iniungentes, quatinus, cum iidem fratres vel eorum nuntii ad vos venerint elemosinas petitum pro sustentatione pauperum ac terre sancte succursu, grata eis subsidia conferatis, ita quod per hec et alia pietatis opera, que domino inspirante feceritis, proficiatis bonis temporalibus et donis non destituamini sempiternis. Nos vero[2] eis, qui dictis fratribus manum porrexerint pietatis, si vere fuerint penitentes, secundum quantitatem subsidii et devotionis affectum suorum veniam peccaminum pollicemur. Datum Laterani iii non. februarii pontificatus nostri anno vii.

Sine dato: Missa archiepiscopis et episcopis etc. II, 103 n. 47; A. 20 n. 45 Latine et Germanice. — Cum dato: R. 70 inter Ratisponensia n. 16. 1. A. 20 dilecti filii fratres R. dilecti fratres et filii II. 2. enim R.

---

390. *1223 febr. 4 Laterani. Honorius III repetit n. 370 de 1223 ianuar. 5.*

Honorius etc. Ad eripiendam etc. D. Laterani ii non. febr. p. n. a. vii.

Bullam p. 288 tanquam de 1223 febr. 26 citatam v. ianuar. 29 n. 381.

---

391. *1223 aprilis 7 Laterani. Honorius III repetit n. 379 de 1223 ianuar. 16.*

Honorius episcopus servus servorum dei venerabilibus fratribus archiepiscopo Maguntino et suffraganeis eius et dilectis filiis abbatibus, prioribus, archidiaconis, decanis et aliis ecclesiarum prelatis per Maguntinam provinciam constitutis salutem et apostolicam benedictionem. Paci et quieti etc. Datum Laterani vii ydus aprilis pontificatus nostri anno vii.

---

392. *1223 iulii 31 Signie. Honorius III repetit n. 379 de 1223 ianuar. 16.*

Honorius episcopus servus servorum dei venerabilibus fratribus archiepiscopo Remensi et eius suffraganeis et dilectis filiis abbatibus, prioribus, prepositis, decanis, archipresbiteris, archidiaconis et aliis ecclesiarum prelatis in Remensi provincia constitutis salutem et apostolicam benedictionem. Paci et quieti etc. Datum Signie ii kalendas augusti pontificatus nostri anno viii.

---

393. *1221 iunii 22 Laterani. Honorius III vetat ab ordinis Theutonici novalibus vel aliis terris post concilium acquisitis, quas fratres propriis aut manibus aut sumptibus colant, decimas exigi. (cf. n. 328.)*

Honorius episcopus servus servorum dei venerabilibus fratribus patriarchis, archiepiscopis et episcopis et dilectis filiis abbatibus, prioribus, archidiaconis, decanis et aliis ecclesiarum prelatis, ad quos littere iste pervenerint, salutem et apostolicam benedictionem. Quia plerumque veritatis integritas per minorem intelligentiam aut malitiam hominum depravatur, non videtur incongruum, si ea, que non manifesta dicta videntur, ad omnem ambiguitatis scrupulum amovendum evidentius exponantur et turbatoribus veritatis omnis auferatur contradictionis occasio, quatinus ea, que dicta sunt, nulla valeant obumbratione fuscari. Accepimus autem, quod, cum dilectis filiis magistro et fratribus domus hospitalis s. Marie Theutonicorum Ierosolimitani duxerimus concedendum, ut de laboribus, quos propriis manibus vel sumptibus excolunt, nemini decimas solvere teneantur, quidam ab eis nihilominus post celebrationem concilii Lateranensis contra indulgentiam sedis apostolice decimas exigere et extorquere presumunt ac prava et sinistra interpretatione apostolici privilegii capitulum pervertentes asserunt de novalibus debere intelligi, ubi noscitur de laboribus esse scriptum. Quoniam igitur manifestum est omnibus, qui recte sapiunt, interpretationem huiusmodi perversam esse et intellectui sano contrariam, cum secundum capitulum illud a solutione decimarum tam de terris illis, quas deduxerunt vel deducunt ad cultum, quam de terris etiam cultis, quas propriis manibus vel sumptibus excolunt, liberi sint penitus et immunes, ne ullus contra eos materiam habeat malignandi vel quomodolibet ipsos contra iustitiam molestandi, vobis per apostolica scripta mandamus et districte precipimus, quatenus omnibus parrochianis vestris auctoritate apostolica prohibere curetis, ne a memoratis fratribus de novalibus vel aliis terris, quas propriis manibus vel sumptibus excolunt, seu de nutrimentis animalium suorum ullatenus decimas exigere vel extorquere presumant. Nam si de novalibus tantum vellemus intelligi, ubi ponimus de laboribus, de novalibus poneremus. Quia vero non est conveniens vel honestum, ut contra statuta sedis apostolice veniatur, que obtinere debent immobilem firmitatem, mandamus vobis firmiterque precipimus, ut, si qui canonici, clerici, monachi vel laici contra privilegia sedis apostolice predictos fratres decimarum exactione gravaverint, canonicos, clericos sive monachos contradictione et appellatione cessante, sicut iustum fuerit, monitione premissa, ab officio suspendatis, laicos excommunicationis sententia percellatis, et tam excommunicationis quam suspensionis sententiam faciatis usque ad dignam satisfactionem inviolabiliter observari, salva moderatione concilii generalis. Ad hec vobis presentium auctoritate mandamus atque precipimus, quatinus, si quis in predictos fratres manus violentas iniecerit, eum accensis candelis tamdiu sicut excommunicatum publice nuncietis et faciatis ab omnibus cautius evitari, donec congrue satisfaciat predictis fratribus et cum litteris diocesani episcopi rei veritatem continentibus apostolico se conspectui representet. Datum Laterani x kal. iulii pontificatus nostri anno octavo.

Quum pluribus locis abhorreat hic textus a n. 328, utimur occasione repetiti privilegii, ut etiam hunc sistamus secuti II, 109 v. cf. Caorsinum et Sennerum etc. Vacillat inter utrumque A. 20 n. 63. Nunc nobis refertur, id quod addimus ad p. 297 relata, Regimonti esse originale cum dato: Laterani x kal. iulii p. n. a. 8. Cum dato: Laterani xi (errore?) kal. iulii p. n. a. octavo in A. 16 p. 25 sq. ex transsumpto Venetiis asservato, sub auctoritate Henrici, archiepiscopi Nazareni, et archiepiscopi Liddensis facto. Formulam conclusionis, diem, annum scriptor omisit. — Cum dato: (Tibure iii kal. iun. a. 9?) „Colonie" A. 16 p. 74 sq. Originale quondam Veteribus Iuncis cum bulla in filis sericeis rubris et luteis nunc in archivo ordinis Theutonici Vindobonensi. cf. p. 296 sq. Concordat illud per alia textui n. 328 „patriarchis" etc.; multum praecisum et infractum modo bulla caret, quod sequuntur omnia archivi eiusdem transsumta. In dorso 2. 1281 facti legitur: Rescriptum privilegii de decimis non dandis; et: Qualiter privilegium de non dandis decimis sit interpretandum, et quid papa intelligit (!) per novale in privilegiis ordinis. Transsumtum 3. de 1426 pars actorum in causa decimae per Pomeraniam solvendae, huius est tenoris: Bernhardus, abbas Olivensis, executor litterarum compulsoriarum subdeputatus a commissariis apostolicis, Cnuczone praeposito Olomucensi et Iohanne Gundissalvi canonico Hispalensi, decretorum doctoribus et sacri palatii auditoribus, iudicibus causarum inter Iohannem episcopum Wladislaviensem (decimam, quae vulgo Bischoffsscheffel dicitur, de agris ordinis in Pomerania exigentem) et magistrum ordinis, partem dicta die non comparentem in se contumacem proclamans, ad instantiam Andreae Sloman, rectoris parochialis ecclesie St. Mariae in Gdanzk, a procuratore ordinis substituti, litteras Honorii III papae datas Laterani x kal. iulii a. viii° de originali sibi producto mandat transsumi et sigilli appensione muniri iubet. Valentinus de Reddin, clericus Culmensis diocesis, publicus s. imperiali auctoritate notarius, subscripsit pro se et collega suo Iohanne. Datum Gedani 1426. 13 marcii.

---

394. *1225 maii 31 Tibure. Honorius III repetit n. 370 de 1223 ianuar. 5.*

Honorius etc. Ad eripiendam etc. Datum Tibure ii kal. iunii pontificatus nostri anno viiii.

---

395. *1225 maii 31 Tibure. Honorius III repetit n. 311 de 1221 ianuar. 15.*

Honorius etc. Cum vos tanquam etc. Datum Tibure ii kal. iunii pontificatus nostri anno nono.

---

396. *1225 maii 31 Tibure. Honorius III repetit n. 322 de 1221 ianuar. 16.*

Honorius etc. Non absque etc. Datum Tibure ii kalendas iunii pontificatus nostri anno nono.

---

397. *1226 iunii 27 Laterani. Honorius III repetit n. 305 de 1218 oct. 1.*

Honorius etc. Cum dilecti etc. Datum Laterani v kal. iulii pontificatus nostri anno x.

---

398. *1226 iulii 1 Laterani. Honorius III repetit n. 309 de 1221 ianuar. 9.*

Honorius etc. Vestra religio etc. Datum Laterani kal. iulii pontificatus nostri anno x.

---

399. *1226 iulii 2 Laterani. Honorius III repetit n. 313 de 1221 ianuar. 16.*

Honorius etc. Cum dilectis etc. Datum Laterani vi non. iulii pontificatus nostri anno x.

---

400. *(Inter 1216 iulii 24 et 1227 martii 18). Honorius III ordini Theutonico concedit, quod fratres eius ob minora delicta ante susceptum habitum commissa intra ipsum ordinem absolutionem possint adipisci.*

Honorius episcopus servus servorum dei dilectis filiis .. magistro et fratribus hospitalis sancte Marie Theotonicorum Ierosolimitani salutem et apostolicam benedictionem. A sede apostolica nec petitur improbe nec iniuste conceditur, per quod sic unius votum admittitur, quod iuri alterius iniuria non infertur. Ex parte siquidem vestra fuit propositum coram nobis, quod, cum plerumque contingat fratres vestros illa confiteri delicta, que ante habitum religionis assumpte se recolunt commisisse, vos eis penitenciam iniungere dubitatis. Volentes igitur vestre ac fratrum vestrorum saluti paterna sollicitudine providere, auctoritate vobis presencium indulgemus, quatinus eisdem fratribus super delictis huiusmodi domus ordine non relicto secundum deum libere penitencias iniungatis, nisi excessus eorum esset difficilis et enormis, utpote si esset ad mutilacionem membri vel sanguinis effusionem processum aut violenta manus in episcopum vel abbatem iniecta, cum excessus tales et similes sine scandalo nequeant preteriri. Nulli ergo omnino hominum liceat hanc paginam nostre concessionis infringere vel ei ausu temerario contraire. Si quis autem hoc attemptare presumpserit, indignationem omnipotentis dei et beatorum Petri et Pauli apostolorum eius se noverit incursurum. Datum etc.

Sine dato: I, 68 v.; II, 98 v. n. 31; A. 20 n. 31 Latine et Germanice.

---

401. *(Inter 1216 iulii 24 et 1227 martii 18.) Honorius III vetat ordinis Theutonici homines compelli, ut contra christianos praelientur.*

Honorius episcopus servus servorum dei venerabilibus fratribus archiepiscopis et episcopis et dilectis filiis abbatibus etc. Cum de viris ecclesiasticis, quibus plurimum expedire dinoscitur, ut in cunctis actibus suis modum ordinemque conservent, nobis aliqua referuntur, que illos reprehensibiles reddant, paterno dolemus affectu et de ipsorum emendacione curam volumus gerere specialem. Significantibus sane dilectis filiis fratribus domus hospitalis sancte Marie Theotonicorum Ierosolimitani accepimus, quod pro communitatibus, que in partibus quorundam vestrum fiunt, magna domibus ipsorum per vos inferuntur incommoda, cum homines illorum contra iuramentum prestitum super christianos preliaturos ire compellitis, unde et ipsi periurium incurrunt et iidem fratres ea, que pro defensione christianitatis in transmarinis partibus expendere consueverant, pro redempcione ipsorum, cum capiuntur in prelio, tradere compelluntur. Quod quam indignum et sacerdotali officio sit contrarium, vestra discrecio recte sapiens non ignorat. Volentes igitur in tanto dispendio prenominatis fratribus, sicut debemus, paterna sollicitudine providere discrecioni vestre per apostolica scripta mandamus et districte precipimus, quatinus homines eorundem fratrum ad certamina communia ire de cetero non cogatis nec ab eis propter hoc aliquid exigere presumatis, sed ita ipsos sua permittatis libertate gaudere, quod nec ipsi de vobis iustam habeant materiam conquerendi nec nos ea requirere districcius compellamur. Datum etc.

Sine dato: II, 92 v.; A. 20 n. 10 Latine et Germanice; tantum cum loco Laterani „universis Christi fidelibus, ad quos littere iste pervenerint, inscripta I, 66 v.

---

402. *(Inter 1216 iulii 24 et 1227 martii 18.) Honorius III vetat praelatos ordinem Theutonicum procurationibus vel exactionibus aggravare.*

Honorius episcopus servus servorum dei venerabilibus fratribus archiepiscopis et episcopis etc. Cum ex suscepte amministracionis officio debeatis viros religiosos a pravorum malignitate defendere et ipsos a gravaminibus relevare, nequaquam eis graves esse debetis nec exacciones novas imponere aut aliquas iniurias erogare. Pervenit autem ad nos, quod quidam ex vobis dilectos filios fratres domus hospitalis sancte Marie Theotonicorum Ierosolimitani crebris procurationibus et aliis exaccionibus graviter inquietant et bona eorum, que ad defensionem orientalis ecclesie necessaria plurimum esse noscuntur, pro sue voluntatis arbitrio minuere non formidant. Quapropter universitatem vestram attencius duximus ammonendum per apostolica vobis scripta precipiendo mandantes, quatinus fratres ipsos super premissis nullatenus aggravetis, verum ipsos pocius a presumpcione malignancium et in eorum bona presumencium debachari, quociens ad vos querela pervenerit, taliter defendatis et suam faciatis iusticiam obtinere, quod ex hoc vobis a deo premium augeatur et ipsi liberi valeant inimicis crucis Christi resistere et illis resistentibus grata subsidia ministrare. Datum etc.

Sine dato: I, 73 v.; II, 96 n. 20; A. 20 n. 20 Latine et Germanice cum nota: in Buken etc.

---

403. *(Inter 1216 iulii 24 et 1227 martii 18.) Honorius III monet praelatos, ut parochianos ab iniuriis ordinis Theutonici possessionibus inferendis arceant.*

Honorius episcopus servus servorum dei venerabilibus fratribus archiepiscopis et episcopis et dilectis filiis abbatibus, prioribus, decanis, archidiaconis, prepositis, archipresbiteris et aliis ecclesiarum prelatis, ad quos littere iste pervenerint, salutem et apostolicam benedictionem. Cum fratres domus hospitalis sancte Marie Theotonicorum Ierosolimitani tanquam veri Machabei crucem dominicam in proprio corpore baiulantes sese pro defensione christianitatis extremis exponant periculis et carnalia desideria negligentes discipulos sese constituerint Ihesu Christi, dignum est et racioni consentaneum, ut eosdem fratres intuitu religionis et honestatis sue sincerius in domino diligamus et famam ipsorum, que per graciam dei ubique terrarum noscitur redolere, modis omnibus satagamus conservare illesam et ita eos apostolice proteccionis clipeo muniamus, quod ab inpugnancium persecutionibus quieti esse valeant et securi. Quocirca universitati vestre per apostolica scripta mandamus atque precipimus, quatinus parrochianis vestris sub interminatione anathematis prohibeatis, ne predictis fratribus in domibus, animalibus aut aliis possessionibus suis aliquam iniuriam inferant vel gravamen. Si qui[1] autem parrochianorum vestrorum bona eorundem fratrum perturbaverint, nisi moniti eis plenarie satisfecerint, ipsos publice accensis candelis excommunicetis et faciatis tanquam excommunicatos ab omnibus evitari. Datum etc.

Sine dato: I, 70 n. 30; II, 98 n. 30; A. 20 n. 30 Latine et Germanice; D. 29 Germanice.
1. quis I.

---

404. *(Inter 1216 iulii 24 et 1227 martii 18.) Honorius III concedit ordini Theutonico, ut de decimis caet. non sit astrictus respondere apostolicis litteris, si non ordinis expressam faciant mentionem.*

Honorius episcopus servus servorum dei dilectis filiis magistro et fratribus etc. Cum inter vos et ecclesiasticas et seculares personas super decimis et pluribus aliis questio sit suborta, ipsi litteras a sede apostolica impetrantes domos vestras litigiis, sicut significantibus vobis accepimus[1], expensis difficilibus inquietant. Volentes igitur sollicite providere, ne super hiis possitis qualibet temeritate vexari, auctoritate vobis apostolica indulgemus, ut, si contra vos super decimis et aliis non facta mentione fratrum hospitalis eiusdem littere fuerint a sede apostolica impetrate, eis minime teneamini respondere. Datum etc.

Sine dato: II, 92 v.; A. 20 n. 11 Latine et Germanice; D. Germanice. 1. deest et?

---

405. *(Inter 1216 iulii 24 et 1227 martii 18.) Honorius III mandat, ne cui sine speciali apostolicae sedis iussu liceat in ordinem Theutonicum vel servientes eius excommunicationis vel interdicti sententiam promulgare.*

Honorius episcopus servus servorum dei dilectis filiis magistro et fratribus domus hospitalis sancte Marie Theotonicorum Ierosolimitani salutem et apostolicam benedictionem. Cum vos tamquam speciales Romane ecclesie filios vestre religionis intuitu et consideracionis obsequii, quod deo ferventer impenditis in ultramarinis partibus in defensione christiani nominis, diligamus, vestris precibus inclinati auctoritate presencium vobis indulgemus, ut nemini liceat sine mandato Romani pontificis speciali in vos, presbiteros et laicos vestros, quorum vobis aliqui gratis, alii vero ad solidos serviunt, excommunicacionis vel interdicti sentenciam promulgare, et, si quando in vos vel in eos ab aliquo huiusmodi sentencia lata fuerit, non obmittatis ecclesias frequentare aut servicio domus vestre vel[1] divinis officiis interesse, cum huiusmodi sententia sit irrita penitus et inanis. Nulli ergo hominum liceat hanc nostre concessionis infringere vel ei ausu temerario contraire. Si quis autem hoc attemptare presumpserit, indignacionem omnipotentis dei et beatorum Petri et Pauli apostolorum eius se noverit incursurum. Datum etc.

Sine dato: II, 90; A. 20 n. 2 Latine et Germanice cum nota: „Est in Martpurg; Urbanus huic simile in Treveri et Alexander in Frankinford et cetera". D. Germanice. 1. in A. 20.

---

406. *(Inter 1216 iulii 24 et 1227 martii 18.) Honorius III vetat praelatos a capellanis ecclesiarum ordini Theutonico pleno iure concessarum fidelitatem aut obedientiam exigere; iubet aliorum obedientia esse contentos.*

Honorius episcopus servus servorum dei venerabilibus fratribus archiepiscopis et episcopis et dilectis filiis abbatibus, prioribus, archidiaconis, decanis et aliis ecclesiarum prelatis, ad quos littere iste pervenerint, salutem et apostolicam benedictionem. Dilecti filii[1] .. magister et fratres domus hospitalis sancte Marie Theotonicorum Ierosolimitani post concilium multipliciter fatigati, ut asserunt, graves querimonias coguntur in nostro auditorio replicare. A capellanis quidem illorum fidelitatem et obedienciam preter solitum queritis, et, quia vestre nolunt satisfacere voluntati, eos pro vestre voluntatis arbitrio molestatis non attendentes, quantum sit iam dictis fratribus consideracione obsequii, quod christianitati in partibus transmarinis exhibent, deferendum[2]. Quia igitur gravamen eorum sustinere in paciencia non debemus, quibus, quantum cum deo possumus, prescripti obsequii et sue devocionis intuitu in sua tenemur iusticia providere, universitati vestre per apostolica scripta mandamus atque precipimus, quatinus a capellanis ecclesiarum, que pleno iure iam dictis fratribus sunt concesse, nec fidelitatem nec obedienciam exigatis, quia tantum Romano pontifici sunt subiecti, ab aliis vero iuramentum fidelitatis non queratis, sed obediencie sitis promissione contenti, scituri, quod, si eos post inhibicionem nostram indebite gravaveritis, non sine rubore vestro[3] ipsis curabimus auctore domino providere. Privilegium enim[4] meretur ammittere, qui commissa[5] sibi abutitur potestate. Datum etc.

Sine dato: I, 68 v.; II, 97 n. 25; A. 20 n. 25 Latine et Germanice cum nota: Allexander eiusdem tenoris in Methi; D. 24 Germanice. 1. Dilectis filiis A. 20. 2. defendendum I. 3. rubore vestro ipsorum curabimus. ib. Trspt. de 1277. 19. octbr. repetitionis Innoc. IV. d. Lugd. 1246. maii 6 habet. 4. quidem ib. 5. permissa ib.

---

407. *(Inter 1216 iulii 24 et 1227 martii 18.) Honorius III decimas ab ordine Theutonico exigi vetat. (Simillimum cf. 1221 ianuar. 15 n. 319.)*

Honorius etc. archiepiscopis et episcopis etc. Ex parte dilectorum filiorum fratrum hospitalis sancte Marie Theutonicorum Ierosolimitani nobis est oblata querela, quod quidam vestrum pro sue voluntatis arbitrio occasione Lateranensis concilii decimas et primicias laborum, quos ipsi propriis manibus et sumptibus excolunt, de possessionibus habitis ante concilium memoratum et suorum animalium nutrimentis, arboribus fructiferis, feno et rebus aliis contra tenorem privilegiorum nostrorum ab eis non metuunt extorquere. Quocirca universitati vestre per apostolica scripta districte precipiendo mandamus, quatenus et vos ipsi ab extorsione huiusmodi penitus desistatis et vestros subditos taliter per censuram ecclesiasticam appellatione remota cogatis desistere ab eadem, quod dicti fratres super hiis non possint de cetero querelari. Datum etc.

Sine dato: II, 102 v. n. 45; A. 20 n. 43 Latine et Germanice; D. 43.

---

408. *(Inter 1216 iulii 24 et 1227 martii 18.) Honorius III concedit ordini Theutonico, ut ecclesiarum suarum redditibus, assignato tantum vicariis, unde honeste vivant et debita praestent, alias utantur.*

Honorius episcopus servus servorum dei dilectis filiis magistro et fratribus hospitalis etc. salutem et apostolicam benedictionem. Iustis petencium desideriis dignum est nos facilem prebere consensum et vota, que a rationis tramite non discordant, effectu prosequente complere. Eapropter, dilecti in domino filii, vestris iustis postulationibus grato concurrentes assensu, apostolica vobis auctoritate concedimus, ut in ecclesiis, que vobis ad sustentationem eorum, qui in transmarinis partibus pro defensione christianitatis animas suas ponere non formidant, sunt concesse, assignato vicariis, unde honeste vivant et in spiritualibus et sinodalibus possint episcopis et eorum officialibus[1] respondere, liceat vobis cetera ad usus vestros, quibus deputata sunt, retinere salva moderatione concilii generalis[2]. Nulli ergo omnino hominum liceat hanc paginam nostre concessionis infringere vel ei ausu temerario contraire. Si quis autem hoc attemptare presumpserit, indignationem omnipotentis dei et beatorum Petri et Pauli apostolorum eius se noverit incursurum. Datum etc.

Sine dato: I, 73 v. n. 43; II, 90 v.; A. 20 n. 4 Latine et Germanice; D. Germanice. 1. possint — officialibus deest I. 2. salva — generalis deest I.

---

409. *(Inter 1216 iulii 24 et 1227 martii 18.) Honorius III iubet praelatos ordinis Theutonici bona et iura tueri, iustitiam quaerenti non denegare, parochianorum apud fratres sepulturam non impedire.*

Honorius episcopus servus servorum dei venerabilibus fratribus archiepiscopis et episcopis et dilectis filiis abbatibus, prioribus etc., ad quos littere iste pervenerint, salutem et apostolicam benedictionem. Licet omnibus dei fidelibus in suis simus iusticiis debitores, religiosis tamen fratribus hospitalis sancte Marie Theotonicorum Ierosolimitani propensius in suo iure convenit nos adesse. Inde est, quod universitati vestre per apostolica scripta precipiendo mandamus, quatenus predictorum fratrum possessiones et iura integra, quantum in vobis fuerit, et illibata servetis et, cum de aliquibus malefactoribus suis, parrochianis vestris, querelas a fratribus receperitis memoratis, de ipsis eis ita districtam iustitiam faciatis, quod bona eorum per sollicitudinem vestram a pravorum sint vexatione quieta. Ad hec presentium vobis auctoritate iniungimus, ut parrochianos vestros, qui in ultima voluntate apud ecclesias predictorum fratrum elegerint sepeliri, nisi excommunicati vel nominatim fuerint interdicti aut etiam publice usurarii, apud ecclesias ipsas sepulturam habere libere permittatis, salva tamen iusticia illarum ecclesiarum, a quibus mortuorum corpora assumuntur. Datum etc.

Sine dato: II, 114 n. 69; A. 20 n. 77 Latine et Germanice; D. 78 Germanice.

---

410. *(Inter 1216 iulii 24 et 1227 martii 18.) Honorius III concedit ordini Theutonico, ut in locis de Saracenorum manibus ereptis ecclesias soli summo pontifici subiiciendas construant.*

Honorius episcopus servus servorum dei dilectis filiis .. magistro et fratribus hospitalis sancte Marie Theotonicorum Ierosolimitani salutem et apostolicam benedictionem. Quanto maiora pro defensione christianitatis discrimina sustinetis, tanto benigniori vos debemus oculo intueri et libencius, ubi cum iusticia possumus, vestris vestrorumque commodis providere. Eapropter, dilecti[1] in domino filii, vestris postulationibus annuentes presentibus vobis litteris indulgemus, ut in locis, que de Sarracenorum manibus poteritis cum auxilio celestis gracie liberare, si non fuerint sedes episcopales in eis, ecclesias construatis, que soli Romane ecclesie debeant subiacere, ita ut a nullo prelatorum ecclesie post Romanum pontificem aliquid iuris in eis valeat[2] vendicari. Nulli ergo omnino hominum liceat hanc paginam nostre concessionis infringere vel ei ausu temerario contraire. Si quis autem hoc attemptare presumpserit, indignationem omnipotentis dei et beatorum Petri et Pauli apostolorum eius se noverit incursurum. Datum etc.

Sine dato: I, 70; II, 110v. n. 68; A. 20 n. 66 Latine et Germanice; D. 67 Germanice.
1. deest I. 2. valeant I.

---

411. *(Inter 1216 iulii 24 et 1227 martii 18.) Honorius III bonorum ab ordine Theutonico possessorum protectionem suscipit.*

Honorius episcopus servus servorum dei dilectis filiis .. magistro et fratribus hospitalis sancte Marie Theotonicorum Ierosolimitani salutem et apostolicam benedictionem. Quociens a sede apostolica postulatur, quod ad pacem religiosorum locorum respicit et profectum, iuxta petentium voluntatem consentaneum racioni libenter apostolicum impertimur assensum et effectu prosequente complemus. Eapropter vestris iustis postulationibus annuentes domos vestros et omnes alias vestras possessiones seu quecunque bona tam in decimationibus quam in aliis rebus ecclesiasticis racionibus possidetis aut in futurum prestante domino iustis modis poteritis adipisci, sub beati Petri et nostra proteccione suscipimus et presentis scripti patrocinio communimus, statuentes, ut nulli omnino hominum liceat hanc paginam nostre protectionis infringere vel ei ausu temerario contraire. Si quis autem hoc attemptare presumpserit, indignationem omnipotentis dei et beatorum Petri et Pauli apostolorum eius se noverit incursurum. Datum etc.

Sine dato: I, 74; II, 108 n. 60; A. 20 n. 59 Latine et Germanice; D. 60 Germanice.

---

412. *(Inter 1216 iulii 24 et 1227 martii 18.) Honorius III apostatarum ordinis Theutonici fautores censura ecclesiastica cohiberi iubet.*

Honorius episcopus servus servorum dei venerabilibus fratribus archiepiscopis et episcopis etc. salutem et apostolicam benedictionem. Res quidem ad nos omnino detestabilis et regulari discipline inimica pervenit, quod, cum quidam de fratribus vel professis hospitalis sancte Marie Theotonicorum Ierosolimitani diabolo instigante a voto et proposito ordinis sui resilientes relicto religionis habitu de milicia Christi ad miliciam mundi redire nullatenus erubescant, quidam etiam[1] animi levitate potius ducti quam zelo religionis accensi sine licentia magistri sui ad alium ordinem transire presumant; quidam vestrum de presumptione huiusmodi vigiles et studiosi existere et excessus corrigere negligunt eorundem, sed quosdam ipsorum ad miliciam secularem et nuptias transire et iuxta sue voluntatis arbitrium in seculari vita manere permittunt, propter quod prefato ordini multa scandala et detrimenta sepius provenire noscuntur, in quo utique et vos ipsi animarum vestrarum potestis periculum non modicum formidare. Nos igitur statum predicti ordinis integrum et illesum conservare volentes et tanti scandali materiam non valentes aliquatenus sustinere, universitati vestre per apostolica scripta mandamus atque precipimus, quatenus, si quos huius inveneritis vie viros, in synodis et conventibus vestris excommunicatos publice nuntietis, eis, inter quos illorum conversatio esse dinoscitur, sub interminatione anathematis prohibentes, ut illos apud se retinere et eisdem communicare nulla ratione presumant, et hoc tam diu faciatis inviolabiliter observari, donec prefati viri ad se redeuntes reverti ad suum ordinem compellantur et votum, quod violaverunt, omnimodis observare. Datum etc.

Sine dato: II, 112 n. 72; A. 20 n. 70 Latine et Germanice cum nota: in Buken. 1. enim II, A. 20.

---

413. *(Inter 1216 iulii 24 et 1227 martii 18.) Honorius III iubet praelatos favere ordini Theutonico nec de donatis ei sibi quicquam vindicare, quarta parte testamenti parochianorum apud illum sepeliri cupientium esse contentos, exceptis armis et equis. Fratribus sacerdotibus licere confessionem recipere apud ordinem sepeliri eligentium.*

Honorius episcopus servus servorum dei venerabilibus fratribus archiepiscopis et episcopis etc. salutem et apostolicam benedictionem. Si diligenter attenditis, quanta dilectis filiis fratribus hospitalis sancte Marie Theotonicorum Ierosolimitani reverencia debeatur, numquam hiis inveniemini[1] graves existere aut molesti, qui sustentacioni et refrigerio pauperum pia noscuntur sollicitudine mancipati[2]. Quoniam igitur iidem fratres ad hoc principaliter elaborant, ut se pariter et omnia, que acquirunt, devotis obsequiis pauperum undique confluencium diligenter impendant; universitatem vestram monemus attencius et per apostolica vobis scripta precipiendo mandamus, quatinus ab ipsorum[3] gravaminibus abstinentes[4] ad solacia, que pro pauperum consolacione requirunt, vestram pocius curam et sollicitudinem convertatis, et in hiis, que domui eorum ab aliquibus fidelibus sanis vel egrotantibus conferuntur, sive convalescant[5] sive apud alios recipiant sepulturam, nichil vobis in eorum domus preiudicium vendicetis; pro[6] parrochianis autem vestris, qui videlicet ad extrema deducti in cimiteriis hospitalis Theotonicorum elegerint sepeliri, quarta tantum sitis testamenti porcione contenti nec aliud pro ipsis a iam dictis fratribus exigatis non impedientes occasione qualibet sepulturam, quam eis misericorditer duximus indulgendam, ex quo pretaxatam partem pro illis ecclesiis, a quibus mortuorum corpora assumuntur, fideliter resignarint. In hiis autem elemosinis, que pietatis intuitu predictorum fratrum domui a sanis et bene valentibus conferuntur, nemo vestrum presumat aliquam sibi exigere porcionem. Ex illa vero quarta, quae vobis conceditur exigenda arma et equos excipi volumus et mandamus, que predicte domui ad defensionem terre[7] Ierosolimitane a quibuslibet decedentibus dimittuntur. Liceat autem fratribus supradictis eos, qui apud ipsos elegerint sepeliri, ad confessionem de occultis peccatis recipere per sacerdotes suos et per eosdem illis viaticum ministrare atque cum cruce et processione ad cimiterium suum corpora eorum libere et sine impedimento tumulanda deferre. Datum etc.

Sine dato: I, 72 v.; II, 112 v. n. 63; A. 20 n. 71 Latine et Germanice cum nota: In Mergentheym; D. 72 Germanice. 1. inveniremini A. 20. 2. mancipati III. A. 20. 3. eorum II. A. 20. 4. abstineatis et A. 20. 5. reconvalescant A. 20. 6. deest II, A. 20. 7. t. sancte Ierosolimitane II.

---

414. *(Inter 1216 iulii 24 et 1227 martii 18.) Honorius III iubet praelatos, ne fratres ordinis Theutonici violati prorsus testimonio destituantur de violentia a suspectis parochianis censura ecclesiastica proposita purgatorium exigere iuramentum.*

Honorius episcopus servus servorum dei venerabilibus fratribus archiepiscopis et episcopis etc. salutem et apostolicam benedictionem. Significarunt nobis dilecti filii fratres hospitalis sancte Marie Theotonicorum Ierosolimitani, quod quidam eorum verberati aliquando et vulnerati interdum destituuntur testibus et probare violenciam non valentes nullam de malefactoribus iusticiam consequuntur. Volentes igitur super hoc eisdem fratribus paterna sollicitudine providere, universitati vestre per apostolica scripta mandamus atque precipimus, quatenus quisque vestrum parrochianum suum, qui de hoc suspectus habetur et fama vexabitur, si convinci[1] nequiverit[2], ut se purget per proprium iuramentum, districte compellat. Quod si facere noluerit, sicut excommunicatum faciatis[3] ab omnibus evitari. Datum etc.

Sine dato: II, 113 v. n. 66: A. 20 n. 74 Latine et Germanice cum nota: In Mergintheym; D. 75 Germanice. 1. converti II. 2. nequiret A. 20. 3. faciat II.

---

415. *(Inter 1216 iulii 24 et 1227 martii 18.) Honorius III ordini Theutonico concedit, ut in terris de Saracenorum manibus aut per ipsum ereptis aut ipsi donatis liceat villas, castra, oratoria, coemeteria construere.*

Honorius episcopus servus servorum dei dilectis filiis .. magistro et fratribus domus hospitalis sancte Marie Theutonicorum Ierosolimitani salutem et apostolicam benedictionem. Vestris piis postulationibus inclinati auctoritate vobis presencium indulgemus, ut in terris, quas dante[1] domino populus christianus a Sarracenorum eripuerit[2] manibus, si ad vos postmodum iusto titulo fuerint devolute, ac eis eciam, quas vos ipsi eisdem auferre poteritis Sarracenis, villas et castra vobis edificare liceat, ecclesias, oratoria et cimiteria fabricare ad opus hominum morancium[3] in eisdem; statuentes insuper, ut predicta omnia sub apostolice sedis et nostra protectione consistant. Nulli ergo omnino hominum liceat hanc paginam nostre concessionis, constitutionis et protectionis infringere vel ei ausu temerario contraire. Si quis autem hoc attemptare presumpserit, indignationem omnipotentis dei et beatorum Petri et Pauli apostolorum eius se noverit incursurum. Datum etc.

Sine dato: I, 69; II, 114 n. 68; A. 20 n. 76 Latine et Germanice. D. 77 Germanice. 1. concedente II. 2. eripiunt I. II. 3. morientium II.

---

416. *1227 iunii 12 Anagniae. Gregorius IX repetit Honorii III n. 309 de 1221 ianuarii 9.*

Gregorius episcopus servus servorum dei dilectis filiis Hermanno magistro et fratribus hospitalis sancte Marie Theutonicorum Ierosolimitani salutem et apostolicam benedictionem. Vestra religio — concessas ad exemplar felicis memorie Honorii pape predecessoris nostri domui etc. incursurum. Datum Anagnie ii idus iunii pontificatus nostri anno primo.

Cum dato: ii id. iunii p. a. 1 Anagnie or., cui nunc deest plumbum, in archivo Regimontano; I, 80 v.; R. 132 inter Marburgensia. Citatur 1253 sept. 26 supra p. 83. Ex or. Regim. ed. ap. O. Kienitz, Vierundzwanzig Bücher livländischer Geschichte. Dorpat 1847. 8°. I, 313; Scr. rer. Livon. Rigae et Lipsiae 1853. I, 366. not. 1. — Or. cum bulla in filis sericeis appensa, quondam Mergenthemi, nunc in archivo ordinis Theutonici Vindobonensi asservatur. — A. 16 p. 49 „Baruli"; p. 67 „in Marpurg". Citatur in R. 143: „Et istud privilegium confirmavit iterato Gregorius papa nonus, et habetur de verbo ad verbum, sicut est in privilegiis prescriptis in Marpurg". Monemus hic apud Schirren p. 154 n. 938 in designatione Mitoviensis archivi citari duo bullarum transsumta, secundum quae ordo Theutonicus immediate papae est subiectus, et aliae libertates ordini confirmantur. Sed cuius fuerint papae, non potest colligi, ita ut etiam n. 937 transsumtum bullae prohibentis, quominus fratres in colligendis eleemosynis impediantur.

---

417. *1227 iulii 2 Anagniae. Gregorius IX repetit Honorii III n. 308 de 1221 ianuarii 9.*

Gregorius episcopus servus servorum dei dilectis filiis .. magistro et fratribus hospitalis sancte Marie Theotonicorum Ierosolimitani salutem et apostolicam benedictionem. Ea, que statuta etc. Datum Anagnie vi nonas iulii pontificatus nostri anno primo.

Cum dato: Or. in archivo Regimontano cum bulla et nota primiceriae P. B. Concinit per omnia textui Honoriano.

---

418. *1227 iulii 3 Anagniae (cf. 1228 febr. 1, 1230 iulii 10 et 1233 iulii 1). Gregorius IX confirmat Honorii III n. 305 de 1218 octobris 1.*

Gregorius episcopus servus servorum dei venerabilibus fratribus archiepiscopis et episcopis et dilectis filiis abbatibus, prioribus, archidiaconis, decanis et aliis ecclesiarum prelatis, ad quos littere iste pervenerint, salutem et apostolicam benedictionem. Cum dilecti filii etc. — eorum ecclesias — curemus. Datum Anagnie v nonas iulii pontificatus nostri anni primo.

Sine dato: citatur inter Norimbergensia n. 11 R. 7 tanquam concinens Innocentii IV privilegio. — Cum dato: Anagnie v nonas iulii p. n. a. 1: I, 81; et alia manu s. xiii. I, 84 v.; R. 48 inter Ellingensia 36 transsumtum per Conradum Eystentensem episcopum (II, 1297 - 1305). — Cum dato: Laterani kal. febr. p. n. a. 1. Originale cum bulla in filis sericeis appensa quondam Mergenthemi, nunc Vindobonae in archivo ordinis Theutonici asservatur. Ibidem transsumtum Iringi Herbipolensis episcopi d. d. Herbipoli xi kal. aug. 1260 quondam in domo Ellingensi. Transsumtum ad instantiam Rudigeri de Dulken, hospitalis in Brotselden magistri, factum per Iohannem de Herpfe, clericum Herbipolensis diocesis, publ. auct. imp. notarium, datum in domo ordinis Theutonici in oppido Mergentheim 1406, sept. 9; nunc in archivo Regimontano. Subtus in margine: Gregorius papa nonus. — Cum dato: Laterani vi idus iulii p. n. a. 4. or. cum bulla in filis sericeis appensa in archivo ordinis Theutonici Vindobonensi, quondam Mergenthemense; citatur R. 84 inter Mergenthemensia 40. Transsumtum d. d. Wirzburgi 1418 dec. 2 in archivo Regimontano. — Cum dato: Laterani kal. iulii p. n. a. 7 in transsumto d. d. Marienburg 1393 maii 29 ad instantiam magistri Livoniae facto et altero transsumto d. d. Revaliae 1415 dec. 14 in archivo Regimontano. — In designatione Mitoviensis archivi Holmiae asservati ap. Schirren p. 137 n. 321 citantur transsumta, quae ad hoc privilegium videntur referenda: 1. de 1390 duarum bullarum papalium, ex quibus nullus episcopus habeat potestatem ordinis excommunicandi. 2. p. 139 n. 397 episcopi Curoniae de 1434, quod ordo sine papae consensu excommunicari non debeat. 3. n. 398 eiusdem tenoris. Ibidem p. 128 n. 34 citatur bulla, qua Gregorius IX eximit ex speciali gratia magistrum et fratres hospitalis s. Mariae a decimarum solutione de ipsorum proventibus.

---

419. *1227 iulii 3 Anagniae (cf. 1228 februarii 3). Gregorius IX repetit Honorii III n. 406.*

Gregorius episcopus etc. Dilecti filii etc. providere ad exemplar felicis recordacionis Honorii pape predecessoris nostri universitati etc. Datum Anagnie v nonas iulii pontificatus nostri anno primo.

Sine dato: R. 8 inter Norimbergensia 14; deest in fine: Privilegium — potestate. — Cum dato: Anagnie 5 non. iulii p. n. a. 1. A. 16 p. 47 „Baruli“. — Cum dato: Laterani 3 non. febr.

p. n. a. 1. originale cum bulla in filis sericeis appensa quondam Mergenthemense nunc in archivo ordinis Theutonici Vindobonensi; IV, 192 n. 1; Ioh. p. 32. Edd. Caorsinus fol. C. 2 et Senner fol. E. 2 v. uterque per errorem typographi anno septimo pro primo.

---

420. *1227 iulii 14 Anagniae (cf. 1228 febr. 5, 1231 martii 29 et sept. 17). Gregorius IX repetit Honorii III n. 322 de 1221 ianuarii 16.*

Gregorius episcopus servus servorum dei venerabilibus fratribus archiepiscopis et episcopis ac dilectis filiis abbatibus, prioribus, decanis, archidiaconis et aliis ecclesiarum prelatis, ad quos littere iste pervenerint, salutem et apostolicam benedictionem. Non absque dolore etc. Datum Anagnie ii idus iulii pontificatus nostri anno primo.

Sine dato citatur R. 145 inter Trevirensia. — Cum dato: Anagnie ii idus iulii p. n. a. 1. A. 16 p. 2 „Venetiis". A. 16 p. 26 ex transsumto Venetiis asservato sub auctoritate Ildebrandini episcopi Paduani 1328 oct. 29 facto. R. 34 inter Ellingensia n. 17 in transsumto auctoritate fratris Bonacursi de ordine praedicatorum, Tyrensis archiepiscopi et vicarii patriarchatus Ierosolimitani atque episcopatus Acconensis, et fratris Gailardi eiusdem ordinis, Bethleemitani episcopi, petente fratre Iohanne, magno praeceptore domus hospitalis sanctae Mariae Theutonicorum Ierosolimitani, per Iohannem clericum Acconensem notarium publicum confecto; sine dato. Cuius originale d. d. 1277 oct. 19 Accone asservatur Regimonti; cf. Napiersky I, n. 32. — Cum dato: Laterani non. febr. p. n. a. 1 R. 53 inter Ratisponensia 1. — Cum dato: Laterani 4 kal. aprilis p. n. a. 5. or. quondam Mergenthemense cum bulla in filis sericeis appensa in archivo ordinis Theutonici Vindobonensi; IV, 199 v. n. 12; R. 43 inter Ellingensia 30 (male: Nos non absque); utrobique tantum usque „mereantur absolvi"; omissa clausula finali „villas — supponatis". Tanquam concinens Ellingensi citatur sine dato R. 84 Mergenthemensium 39; A. 5 „Treviris"; A. 16 p. 118. — Cum dato: Reate 15 kal. octobr. p. n. a. 5 „Venetiis" in transsumto d. d. Tarvisii 1267 ind. X facto sub sigillo Alberti episcopi Tarvisini et signis fr. Patavini prioris s. Salvatoris de Fonte, fr. Bonaventurae, mansionarii ecclesiae Tarvisinae, Ottonis de Nigrosia, not. palat., qui exemplavit, exscripto in A. 16 p. 16 sq. Or. ex domo E(llingensi?) in archivo ordinis Theutonici Vindobonensi. — Cum dato: A. 5 „Treviris" A. 16 p. 118 Gregorio VIII adscriptum. — Una cum privilegio de 1231 sept. 25 (Paci et quieti) in transsumto requirente Theodorico de Treveris, commendatore Bozensi, Tridenti 1318 april. 13, autoritate Heinrici Tridentini episcopi, cuius adest sigillum, confecto per Ottonellum et Bonumjohannem, ap. et imp. ant. notarios, confecto et subscripto, in archivo Regimontano.

---

421. *1227 iulii 20 Anagniae. Gregorius IX repetit Honorii III n. 337 de 1221 ianuar. 19.*

Gregorius episcopus servus servorum dei venerabilibus fratribus archiepiscopis et episcopis et dilectis filiis abbatibus, prioribus etc. Querela dilectorum filiorum etc. Datum Anagnie xiii kal. augusti pontificatus nostri anno primo.

A. 16 p. 474 „Baruli".

---

422. *1227 iulii 21 Anagniae (cf. 1227 novbr. 25, 1228 februar. 4 et 1231 martii 29). Gregorius IX repetit Honorii III n. 413.*

Gregorius episcopus servus servorum dei venerabilibus fratribus archiepiscopis et episcopis, et dilectis filiis abbatibus, prioribus, decanis, archidiaconis ac aliis ecclesiarum prelatis, ad quos littere iste pervenerint, salutem et apostolicam benedictionem. Si diligenter etc. inveniremini — mancipati — ab eorum ducti, quam eis a sede apostolica misericorditer constat esse indultam, ex — dimittantur — deferre. Datum Anagnie xii° kal. augusti pontificatus nostri anno primo.

Cum dato: Anagnie xii kal. aug. p. n. a. 1; I, 81. — Cum dato: Laterani vii kal. decbr. p. n. a. 1 „Baruli" A. 16 p. 49. — Cum dato: Laterani 2 non. febr. p. n. a. 1. IV, 193; R. 12 inter Norimbergensia n. 21 in apographo transsumti 1260 xi kal. aug. (iulii 22) Herbipoli p. n. a. 6 per Yringum Herbipolensem episcopum confecti; cui tanquam consonum citatur R. 84 inter Mergenthemensia n. 38. — Or. quondam Mergenthemense cum bulla in filis sericeis appensa in archivo ordinis Theutonici Vindobonensi; ubi etiam et ipsum quondam Mergenthemense transsumtum Iringi episcopi. — Cum dato: Laterani 4 kal. april. p. n. a. 5, quoad cetera concinens Norimbergensi citatur R. 61 inter Ratisponensia n. 20; A. 16 p. 3 „Venetiis". Transsumtum Tyrensis archiepiscopi et Bethlehemitani episcopi, cuius superest sigillum, d. d. Accon 1277 oct. 19 in archivo Regimontano; cf. Napiersky I, 11 n. 38.

---

423. *1227 iulii 21 Anagniae. Gregorius IX repetit Honorii III n. 383 de 1223 ianuar. 31.*

Gregorius episcopus servus servorum dei venerabilibus fratribus archiepiscopis et episcopis et dilectis filiis abbatibus, prioribus, decanis, archidiaconis et aliis ecclesiarum prelatis, ad quos littere iste pervenerint, salutem et apostolicam benedictionem. Si discrimina etc. ab ipsorum — sustentare — solitas — ulterius contraire. Datum Anagnie xii kal. augusti pontificatus nostri anno primo.

Originale in archivo Regimontano; subscripsit primiceriae regens P. B., quae nota, etsi nunc deest plumbum, satis Gregorium papam nonum accusat auctorem, non decimum, cui perperam attribuunt Hennig apud Napiersky I. n. 206 et Livl. Urk. I, 535 n. 424.

---

424. *1227 iulii 28 Anagniae. Gregorius IX repetit Honorii III n. 306 de 1220 dec. 15.*

Gregorius episcopus servus servorum dei dilectis filiis Hermanno magistro religiose fraternitatis hospitalis sancte Marie Theotonicorum Ierosolimitani eiusque fratribus tam presentibus quam futuris in perpetuum. Etsi neque etc. ac cure — largicione regum — adipisci ad exemplar felicis memorie Honorii pape predecessoris nostri sub beati Petri — perpetuis futuris — alios fratres observetur. Ad — transmigrare — locis sibi subditis — suscipiendi et retinendi — peracto, si mores eorum exegerint — apostolice sedis — edificare villas — in vicinia illa — consequantur. Amen.

✠ Ego Gregorius, catholice ecclesie episcopus.
✠ Ego Conradus, Portuensis et sancte Rufine episcopus.
✠ Ego Guido, Prenestinus episcopus.
✠ Ego Stephanus, basilice duodecim apostolorum presbiter cardinalis.
✠ Ego Thomas, tituli sancte Sabine presbiter cardinalis.
✠ Ego Iohannes, tituli sancte Praxedis presbiter cardinalis.

+ Ego Otto, sanctorum Sergii et Bachi diaconus cardinalis.
+ Ego Rainerius, sancte Marie in Cosmedin diaconus cardinalis.
+ Ego Stephanus, sancti Adriani diaconus cardinalis.
+ Ego Petrus, sancti Georgii ad velum aureum diaconus cardinalis.

Datum Anagnie per manum magistri Sinibaldi sancte Romane ecclesie vicecancellarii v kalendas augusti indictione xv incarnacionis dominice anno millesimo ducentesimo vicesimo septimo, pontificatus vero domini Gregorii pape noni anno primo.

Sine dato: R. 161 et A. 16 p. 100, utrobique inter Iuncensia. D. 82 Germanice. — Cum dato: 1227 5 kal. aug. ind. 15 p. n. a. 1. Anagnie I, 82 v.; II, 115 n. 71; IV, 194 n. 5; Latine et Germanice A. 20 n. 79 tanquam Honorii III, cum dato Gregoriano. Titulus in IV: „Bulla fundamentum ordinis continens, quomodo presbiteri subsunt magistro“. Or. in archivo ordinis Theutonici Vindobonensi.

---

425. *1227 iulii 30 Anagniae. Gregorius IX repetit Honorii III n. 332 de 1221 ianuarii 19.*

Gregorius etc. Cum de viris ecclesiasticis — compellamur. Datum Anagnie iii kal. augusti pontificatus nostri anno primo.

A. 16 p. 47 „Baruli“.

---

426. *1227 iulii 30 Anagniae (cf. 1227 aug. 11, 1230 aug. 6, 1231 sept. 15 et 25). Gregorius IX repetit Honorii III n. 379 de 1223 ianuar. 16.*

Gregorius episcopus servus servorum dei venerabilibus fratribus archiepiscopis et episcopis et dilectis filiis abbatibus, prioribus, decanis, archidiaconis et aliis ecclesiarum prelatis, ad quos litere iste pervenerint, salutem et apostolicam benedictionem. Paci et quieti etc. Datum Anagnie iii kalendas augusti pontificatus nostri anno primo.

Sine dato citatur R. 128 inter Marburgensia; R. 155 inter Iuncensia; R. 48 transsumtum per Hermannum Augustanum episcopum (1249—1286); Germanice D. 57. — Cum dato: Anagnie 3 kal. aug. p. n. a. 1. R. 7 inter Norimbergensia 12. — Cum dato: Anagnie 3 id. aug. p. n. a. 1 ex originali Gracensi VII, 368. — Cum dato: Anagnie 8 id. aug. p. n. a. 4 ex archivo ordinis Theutonici Vindobonensi or. cum bulla in filis sericeis rubris et luteis appensa etiamnunc ibi asservatum citat Duellius Hist. ord. Th. II, 10 ad XIII. — Cum dato: Reate 17 kal. octbr. p. n. a. 5. IV, 198 v. n. 10; citatur R. 84 inter Mergenthemensia 37 et A. 16 p. 66 „in Marpurg“. Ioh. 33. Originale cum bulla in filis sericeis appensa in archivo ordinis Theutonici Vindobonensi, quondam Mergenthemi. Edd. Caorsinus fol. C. 2 v. Senner fol. E. 3. — Cum dato: Reate 7 kal. octbr. p. n. a. 5 in transsumto archivi Regimontani de 1318 april. 13, cf. ad n. 420 de 1227 iulii 14. „Non absque“ de n. 455 1231 sept. 17. Legitur ibi „manus non iniecerint violentas, sed eos contumeliosis verbis afficiunt“.

---

427. *1227 iulii 31 Anagniae (cf. 1227 augusti 4 et 5). Gregorius IX repetit Honorii III n. 330 de 1221 ianuarii 18.*

Gregorius episcopus servus servorum dei venerabilibus fratribus archiepiscopis et episcopis ac dilectis filiis abbatibus, prioribus, decanis, archidiaconis et aliis ecclesiarum prelatis, ad quos littere iste pervenerint, salutem et apostolicam benedictionem. Religiosos viros — deputatis pedagium, vendam, passagium, caucagium seu aliam quamlibet — presumpcione sua moni cione premissa non — baptismata — prohibeatis appellatione remota officia — sententias appellacione postposita[1] compescatis. Datum Anagnie secundo kalendas augusti pontificatus nostri anno primo.

Cum dato: 2 kal. aug. p. n. a. 1. Anagnie VI, 354 inter Frisacensia et Laibacensia. A. 16 p. 21 „Venetiis". — Cum dato: 2 non. aug. p. n. a. 1 Anagnie or. cum bulla in archivo Regimontano; cf. Napiersky I, 10 n. 33. Or. cum bulla in filis sericeis appensa in archivo ordinis Theutonici Vindobonensi. — Cum dato: nonas augusti p. n. a. 1 Anagnie IV, 197 v. n. 6; R. 83 inter Mergenthemensia 36. 1. sic originale Regimontanum; sententias sublato appellacionis obstaculo IV. VI. R.

---

428. *1227 augusti 2 Anagniae. Gregorius IX iubet desertores ordinis Theutonici censura ecclesiastica coerceri.*

Gregorius episcopus servus servorum dei venerabilibus fratribus archiepiscopis et episcopis et dilectis filiis abbatibus, prioribus, decanis, archidiaconis et aliis ecclesiarum prelatis, ad quos littere iste pervenerint, salutem et apostolicam benedictionem. Fratrum hospitalis sancte Marie Theutonicorum professio, sicut in scriptis eorum et privilegiis continetur, est talis, ut ne cui post factam professionem semel assumptam crucem dominicam[1] et habitum ipsius abicere vel ad alium locum seu eciam monasterium maioris sive minoris religionis obtentu invitis sive inconsultis fratribus aut eo, qui magister extiterit, liceat transmigrare nullique ecclesiastice secularive persone ipsos suscipere liceat vel tenere. Cum enim ipsi ad defendendam orientalem ecclesiam et paganorum seviciam reprimendam relictis pompis secularibus dei sint servicio mancipati, si transeundi ad alia loca et sumptum habitum relinquendi daretur eis licencia, magnum ecclesie dei posset exinde contingere detrimentum; ideoque universitati vestre per apostolica scripta precipiendo mandamus, ut, si quis ex ipsis in parrochiis vestris vel locis vobis commissis id attemptare presumpserit, tam ipsum quam qui eum ausu temerario retinere temptaverit omni occasione remota excommunicacionis vinculo innodetis. Datum Anagnie iiii nonas augusti pontificatus nostri anno primo.

I, 81 n. 61. Or. ex domo E(llingensi?) in archivo ordinis Theutonici Vindobonensi. Cf. n. 439. 1. supplevi.

---

429. *1227 augusti 4 Anagniae (cf. 1231 sept. 18). Gregorius IX repetit Honorii III n. 367 de 1222 febr. 20.*

Gregorius episcopus servus servorum dei venerabilibus fratribus archiepiscopis et episcopis et dilectis filiis abbatibus etc. Querelam gravem etc. Datum Anagnie ii non. augusti pontificatus nostri anno primo.

Cum dato: 2 non. aug. p. a. 1 Anagniae. A. 16 p. 48 „Baruli". — Cum dato: Laterani 14 kal. octbr. p. a. 5. originale quondam E(llingense?) in archivo ordinis Theutonici Vindobonensi.

---

430. *1227 augusti 4 Anagniae. Gregorius IX repetit n. 427 de 1227 iulii 31.*

Gregorius etc. Religiosos viros etc. Datum Anagnie ii nonas augusti pontificatus nostri anno primo.

---

431. *1227 augusti 5 Anagniae. Gregorius IX repetit n. 427 de 1227 iulii 31.*

Gregorius etc. Religiosos viros etc. Datum Anagnie nonas augusti pontificatus nostri anno primo.

---

432. *1227 aug. 7 Anagniae (cf. 1227 aug. 12). Gregorius IX repetit Honorii III n. 410.*

Gregorius etc. Quanto maiora etc. Datum Anagnie vii idus augusti pontificatus nostri anno primo.

Cum dato: Anagnie 7 id. aug. p. n. a. 1. or., cui modo deest plumbum, in archivo Regimontano. Deest in originali: vestrorumque. — Cum dato: Anagnie 2 id. aug. p. n. a. 1. or. cum bulla et signo cancellariae P. B. ibidem.

---

433. *1227 aug. 11 Anagniae. Gregorius IX repetit n. 426 de 1227 iulii 30.*

Gregorius etc. Paci et quieti etc. Datum iii idus augusti pontificatus nostri anno primo.

---

434. *1227 aug. 12 Anagniae. Gregorius IX repetit n. 432 de 1227 aug. 7.*

Gregorius etc. Quanto maiora etc. Datum Anagnie ii idus augusti pontificatus nostri anno primo.

---

435. *1227 aug. 13 Anagniae. Gregorius IX repetit Honorii III n. 385 de 1223 febr. 1.*

Gregorius etc. Graviter oculos etc. Datum Anagnie idus augusti pontificatus nostri anno primo.

Cum dato: Anagnie id. aug. p. n. a. 1. or. cum bulla in archivo Regimontano; I, 81 v. n. 65; IV, 198.

---

436. *1227 aug. 18 Anagniae (cf. 1235 nov. 28). Gregorius IX concedit, quod fratres ordinis Theutonici ad epistolas apostolicas de privilegiis eius apostolicis non respondeant nisi de ordine speciali facta mentione.*

Gregorius episcopus servus servorum dei dilectis filiis magistro et fratribus hospitalis sancte Marie Theotonicorum Ierosolimitani salutem et apostolicam benedictionem. Quieti vestre providere volentes auctoritate vobis presencium indulgemus, ut, si contra vos super hiis, que ordini vestro a sede apostolica sunt indulta, contra tenorem privilegiorum vestrorum apostolicas litteras impetrari[1] contigerit, que de ordine vestro non fecerint mencionem, per eas non teneamini respondere. Nulli ergo omnino hominum liceat hanc paginam nostre concessionis infringere vel ei ausu temerario contraire. Si quis autem hoc attemptare presumpserit, indignacionem omnipotentis dei et beatorum Petri et Pauli apostolorum eius se noverit incursurum. Datum Anagnie xv kalendas septembris pontificatus nostri anno primo.

Sine dato: A. 20 n. 83 Latine et Germanice cum nota: In Leodio, in Praga. Citatur R. 155 inter Iuncensia. — Cum dato: Anagnie 15 kal. septbr. p. n. a. 1. originale cum bulla in archivo Regimontano. — Cum dato: Viterbii 4 kal. decbr. p. n. a. 9. IV, 202 v. n. 14. originale quondam Vetero-Iuncense cum bulla in filis sericeis rubris et luteis appensa in archivo ordinis Theutonici Vindobonensi. 1. impetrare IV.

---

437. *1227 aug. 21 Anagniae. Gregorius IX concedit ordini Theutonico, ut in causis suis fratres testes producere possit.*

Gregorius episcopus servus servorum dei dilectis filiis magistro et fratribus hospitalis sancte Marie Theutonicorum Ierosolimitani salutem et apostolicam benedictionem. Iustis petentium desideriis dignum est nos facilem prebere consensum et vota, que a racionis tramite non discordant, effectu prosequente complere. Eapropter, dilecti in domino filii, vestris iustis postulacionibus grato concurrentes assensu, auctoritate vobis apostolica duximus indulgendum, ut in causis vestris fratres vestros possitis ad testimonium ferendum producere nec pro eo, quod fratres vestri sunt, si alia causa racionabilis et manifesta non obstat, a ferendo testimonio repellantur, dummodo, sicut censura canonum et legum sentit auctoritas, velint testimonium perhibere. Nulli ergo omnino hominum liceat hanc paginam[1] nostre constitucionis infringere vel ei ausu temerario contraire. Si quis autem hoc attemptare presumpserit, indignacionem omnipotentis dei et beatorum Petri et Pauli apostolorum eius se noverit incursurum. Datum Anagnie xii kal. septembris pontificatus nostri anno primo.

Cum dato: Anagnie 12 kal. sept. p. n. a. 1. R. 95 inter privilegia reposita in baliva Alsatiae. 1. supplevi.

---

438. *1227 aug. 31 Anagniae. Gregorius IX repetit Honorii III n. 323 de 1221 ian. 17.*

Gregorius etc. Cum a religiosorum etc. Datum Anagnie ii kal. septembris pontificatus nostri anno primo.

Cum dato: Anagnie 2 kal. septbr. p. n. a. 1. R. 95 n. 2 citatur inter Alsatica.

---

439. *1227 aug. 31 Anagniae. Gregorius IX iubet ordinis Theutonici apostatas et eorum fautores censura ecclesiastica coerceri.*

Gregorius episcopus servus servorum dei venerabilibus fratribus archiepiscopis et episcopis et dilectis filiis abbatibus, prioribus, decanis, archidiaconis et aliis ecclesiarum prelatis, ad quos littere iste pervenerint, salutem et apostolicam benedictionem. Dilectorum filiorum fratrum hospitalis sancte Marie Theotonicorum Ierosolimitani professio, sicut in scriptis eorum et privilegiis continetur, est talis, ut ne cui post factam professionem semel assumptam crucem dominicam et habitum ipsius abicere vel ad alium locum seu eciam monasterium maioris sive minoris religionis obtentu invitis sive inconsultis fratribus aut eo, qui magister extiterit, liceat transmigrare nullique ecclesiastice secularive persone ipsos suscipere liceat vel tenere. Cum enim ipsi ad defendendum orientalem ecclesiam et paganorum seviciam reprimendam relictis pompis secularibus dei sint servicio mancipati, si transeundi ad alia loca et sumptum habitum relinquendi daretur eis licentia, magnum ecclesie dei posset exinde contingere detrimentum; ideoque universitati vestre per apostolica scripta precipiendo mandamus, quatinus, si quis ex ipsis in parrochiis vestris vel locis vobis commissis id attemptare presumpserit, tam ipsum quam qui eum ausu temerario retinere temptaverit, omni occasione remota excommunicacionis vinculo astringatis. Datum Anagnie ii kalendas septembris pontificatus nostri anno primo.

Cum dato: Anagnie 2 kal. septbr. p. n. a. 1. IV, 199 n. 11. originale cum bulla in filis sericeis appensa quondam Mergenthemense in archivo ordinis Theutonici Vindobonensi. Transsumtum sub Iohannis, decani ecclesiae ss. Mariae et Georgii Francofurtanae ad Moenum, auctoritate et sigillo per Hermannum Manegolt de Cassel, clericum Moguntinae diocesis, publicum imperiali auctoritate notarium, scriptum et subscriptum; datum in Sassinhusen, 1385. febr. 17. in archivo Regimontano. Ed. Lünig Teutsches Reichsarchiv XVI, 82 n. 80. Cf. supra n. 428.

---

440. *1227 nov. 25 Laterani. Gregorius IX repetit n. 422 de 1227 iulii 21.*

Gregorius etc. Si diligenter etc. Datum Laterani vii kal. decembris pontificatus nostri anno primo.

---

441. *1228 februarii 1 Laterani. Gregorius IX repetit n. 418 de 1227 iulii 3.*

Gregorius etc. Cum dilecti filii magister et fratres etc. Datum Laterani kal. februarii pontificatus nostri anno primo.

---

442. *1228 februarii 3 Laterani. Gregorius IX repetit n. 419 de 1227 iulii 3.*

Gregorius etc. Dilecti filii etc. Datum Laterani iii nonas februarii pontificatus nostri anno primo.

---

443. *1228 februarii 3 Laterani. Gregorius IX repetit Honorii III n. 307 de 1220 dec. 16.*

Gregorius etc. Pervenit ad nos etc. Datum Laterani iii nonas februarii pontificatus nostri anno primo.

Cum dato: IV, 192 v. n. 2, ubi etiam legitur: Hoc privilegium habetur in Mergetheim in rotulo desuper confecto. Originale quondam Mergenthemense cum bulla in filis sericeis appensa in archivo ordinis Theutonici Vindobonensi. Ioh. 35. Edd. Caorsinus fol. C. 2; Senner fol. E. 2 v.

---

444. *1228 februarii 4 Laterani. Gregorius IX repetit n. 422 de 1227 iulii 21.*

Gregorius etc. Si diligenter etc. Datum Laterani ii nonas februarii pontificatus nostri anno primo.

---

445. *1228 februarii 5 Laterani. Gregorius IX repetit n. 420 de 1227 iulii 14.*

Gregorius etc. Non absque etc. Datum Laterani nonas februarii pontificatus nostri anno primo.

---

446. *1228 februarii 6 Laterani (cf. 1231 martii 29). Gregorius IX repetit Honorii III n. 338 de 1221 ianuarii 20.*

Gregorius etc. Dilecti filii — fraternitati vestre ad exemplar felicis recordacionis Honorii pape predecessoris nostri per apostolica — dimittant. Datum Laterani viii idus februarii pontificatus nostri anno primo.

Sine dato: „Iuncis" A. 16 p. 100, ubi verba „ad exemplar f. r. Honorii p. pred. nostri" omissa. — Cum dato: Laterani 8 id. febr. p. n. a. 1. IV, 193 v. n. 4. Or. quondam Vetero-Iuncense cum bulla in filis rubris et luteis appensa in archivo ordinis Theutonici Vindobonensi. Ioh. 33. Edd. Caorsinus fol. C. 2 v.; Senner fol. E. 3. — Cum dato: Laterani 4 kal. aprilis p. n. a. 5. R. 129 et A. 16 p. 67 utrobique inter Marburgensia; cui de verbo ad verbum concinens, sed sine dato et tanquam Gregorii VIII citatur R. 153.

---

447. *1230 iulii 10 Laterani. Gregorius IX repetit n. 418 de 1227 iulii 3.*

Gregorius etc. Cum dilecti etc. Datum Laterani vi idus iulii pontificatus nostri anno quarto.

---

448. *1230 aug. 6 Anagniae. Gregorius IX repetit n. 426 de 1227 iulii 30.*

Gregorius etc. Paci et quieti etc. Datum Anagnie viii idus augusti pontificatus nostri anno quarto.

---

449. *1230 septbr. 15 Anagniae. Gregorius IX vetat Templarios ordinem Theutonicum de mantellorum alborum usu molestare.*

Gregorius episcopus servus servorum dei dilectis filiis .. magistro et fratribus domus milicie Templi salutem et apostolicam benedictionem. Cum ordinem vestrum dextera divina plantatum speciali prerogativa dileccionis et gracie in Christi visceribus amplexantes delectemur in eo tanquam in odore agri pleni, cui dominus benedixit, et ad profectus vestros intimis aspirantes affectibus, que vobis profutura cognoscimus, nullis preventi precibus eo[1] libencius procuremus, quo votis vestris accedit conspectius quicquid vobis grati provenit incrementi, nequaquam egre ferre vos decet, sed debetis pocius acceptare, si vobis in eo deferendum non ducimus, in quo et nobis et vobis posset apud deum et homines iustissime derogari. Sane, cum abnegantes salubriter vosmetipsos illi vos dicaveritis voto sollempni, qui celsitudinem divinitatis humilians et formam servi suscipiens exaltat humiles in salutem, nimis vos redderetis notabiles nosque graviter turbaretis, si, quod absit, aliquo spiritu elationis abducti humilitatis Christi negligeretis vel in modico disciplinam, vel, quod avertat dominus, emulationis livore percussi erga illos vestram remitti pateremini caritatem, quos vobiscum uni domino famulantes ardenti debetis amore complecti, ut diligentes servi conservos famulatum vestrum reddatis domino graciorem. Ceterum intellecto iam dudum, quod aliqui vestrum scandalizari videbantur utcunque, quin eciam questione suborta pro eo, quod . . magister et fratres domus hospitalis sancte Marie Theotonicorum mantellis albis utantur, quasi esset eis in hoc similitudo vestri habitus interdicta, nos cupientes de regno ecclesie colligere scandala venerabili fratri nostro patriarche Ierosolimitano, apostolice sedis legato, sicut nostis[2], pluries super hoc direximus[3] scripta nostra, quorum tenores vos non credimus ignorare. Cumque dictus patriarcha processus per eum habitos suis nobis litteris intimans tandem totum negocium ad nostram presenciam destinarit, quia idem magister predicte domus sancte Marie Theotonicorum apud sedem apostolicam constitutus privilegium[4], per quod statuitur, ut ordo domus vestre circa clericos et milites et alios fratres in domo sua perpetuis temporibus observetur et indulgenciam, per quam omnes libertates, immunitates et indulgencie domui vestre ab apostolica sede concesse sue domui conceduntur, necnon et specialem indulgenciam de mantellis ordini suo a pie memorie Honorio predecessore nostro clementer indultas[5] et innovatas a nobis[6], ac confirmationem ab eodem predecessore nostro sibi concessam[7] super cc unciis auri, quas karissimus in Christo filius noster F(ridericus), Romanorum imperator[8] illustris semper augustus et rex Sicilie, pro albis mantellis emendis ad usum fratrum militum sue domus sibi et fratribus suis pia liberalitate donavit exsolvendas annis singulis, nobis exhibuit intuendas, nequaquam vobis vidimus expedire, ut in negocio procederetur eodem, ne forsitan notaremini, si eveniret exinde aliquid, quod nolletis. Cum autem iam multi remurmurent admirantes, quod super huiusmodi articulo scandalum vel questio potuerit suboriri, prout potestis plenius intelligere, quam nos deceat, ne videretur asperum explicare; universitatem vestram rogamus, monemus et hortamur in domino per apostolica scripta mandantes, quatinus provide attendentes, quod, si huiusmodi zelus et contentio ultra procederent, facile vobis posset apostolica auctoritate concludi, quod adhuc secundum hominem ambulatis, qui spiritu credimini ambulare, eo quod caritas non emulatur nec que sua sunt expetit sed que Christi, a questione tali spontanei desistatis, que nec debuerat inchoari, cum, si forsitan obtineretis in ea, nil inde vobis nisi nota quedam accresceret, que vix posset de facili aboleri; sed eosdem magistrum et fratres sincera in domino caritate tractetis ita, quod ex hoc deo et hominibus placeatis nosque devocionem vestram possimus merito commendare. Ad hec, quia venerabilibus fratribus nostris patriarche Ierosolimitano[9] et Acchonensi episcopo[10] nostris damus litteris in mandatis, ut vos ad premissa moneant et inducant, volumus, ut eorum monitis attencius intendatis ipsorum consilium ad effectus graciam deducentes. Datum Anagnie xvii° kalendas octobris pontificatus nostri anno quarto.

I, 82. Templi magister tunc erat Petrus de Monteacuto. 1. et I. 2. nostris I. 3. direxerimus I. 4. Est constitutio: „Vestra religio". 5. v. n. 308 de 1221 ianuar. 9. 6. v. n. 417 de 1227 iulii 2. 7. 1222 april. 19 v. n. 151. 8. tunc nondum imperator; v. n. 146 de 1217 maii 25. 9. Geraldus. 10. Iohannes.

---

450. *1231 martii 29 Laterani. Gregorius IX repetit n. 416 de 1228 febr. 6.*

Gregorius etc. Dilecti filii etc. Datum Laterani iiii kal. aprilis pontificatus nostri anno quinto.

---

451. *1231 martii 29 Laterani. Gregorius IX repetit n. 420 de 1227 iulii 14.*

Gregorius etc. Non absque etc. Datum Laterani iiii kalendas aprilis pontificatus nostri anno quinto.

---

452. *1231 martii 29 Laterani. Gregorius IX repetit n. 422 de 1227 iulii 21.*

Gregorius etc. Si diligenter — inveniemini — mancipati — quatinus ab eorum gravaminibus abstinentes — et in hiis, que hospitali eorum — in cimiteriis hospitalis iam dicti elegerint s. — nec aliud pro ipsis a predictis fratribus exigatis, nec impediatis occasione — quam eis a sede apostolica misericorditer constat esse indultam, ex quo — a quibus assumuntur corpora mortuorum fideliter — intuitu hospitali dictorum fratrum a sanis — equos et arma — que hospitali predicto ad defensionem terre Ierosolimitane a quibuslibet decedentibus[1] — per proprios sacerdotes etc. Datum Laterani iiii kalendas aprilis pontificatus nostri anno quinto.

1. decendentibus A. 16; ubi etiam caetera varietas hic producta invenitur.

---

453. *1231 april. 9 (cf. oct. 10, 1235 febr. 10, april. 27, 1238 aug. 26). Gregorius IX repetit Honorii III n. 314 de 1221 ianuarii 16.*

Gregorius episcopus servus servorum dei venerabilibus fratribus archiepiscopis et episcopis et dilectis filiis abbatibus, prepositis, prioribus, decanis, archidiaconis, archipresbyteris et aliis ecclesiarum prelatis, ad quos littere iste pervenerint, salutem et apostolicam benedictionem. Cum dilectis filiis — fuerit a bone memorie H(onorio) papa predecessore nostro indultum et a nobis postmodum confirmatum, ut semel — confratrias suas confratrie illorum — redundat, prefati predecessoris nostri vestigiis inherentes, universitati — pietatis. Sane quoniam est ab eodem predecessore nostro statutum et innovatum a nobis, ut nemo — presentium vobis auctoritate precipimus, ut — que in sancta domo illa fiunt — personas, que se — reddiderint, libere — ne ab eis contra tenorem privilegiorum apostolice sedis de nutrimentis animalium — secundum quod eis est beneficio privilegiorum ecclesie Romane concessum, duxerint construenda — ne aliquis vestrum contra tenorem privilegiorum ipsorum id impedire — fratres hospitalis eiusdem in — voluntates ipsorum. — Preterea quicumque — subvenerint antedictis et in tam sancta fraternitate statuerint se collegas — persolverint annuatim eis de beatorum — ut hiis qui eorum — interdicti. Volumus autem, ut liceat eis confratres suos, quos ecclesiarum prelati apud ecclesias suas malitiose non permiserint sepeliri, nisi excommunicati vel nominatim fuerint interdicti aut eciam publice usurarii, ad ecclesias suas tumulandos deferre, et oblationes tam pro eis quam pro aliis, qui in eorum cimiteriis requiescunt, exhibitas sine alieni iuris preiudicio retinere, hoc eciam addito — semel aperiantur ecclesie annuatim et excommunicatis et nominatim interdictis eiectis — beneficia vel ecclesiasticos redditus non amittant. Datum Laterani v idus aprilis pontificatus nostri anno quinto.

Cum dato: Laterani 5 id. aprilis p. a. 5 originale Vindobonense, etiamnunc ibi asservatum, citat Duellius II., 12 ann. — Cum dato: Reate 6 id. octobris p. a. 5. IV, 200 n. 13. Ioh. 34. Edd. Caorsinus fol. C. 2v. Senner fol. E. 3v. Liljegren Diplomatarium Suecanum I, 261 n. 261. — Cum dato: Perusii 4 id. febr. p. a. 8 originale cum bulla in archivo Regimontano, cuius exhibemus supra varietatem. Cf. Napiersky n. 49. — Cum dato: Perusii 5 kal. maii p. a. 9. R. 96 inter Alsatica. — Cum dato: Anagnie 7 kal. sept. p. a. 12 in transsumto sub sigillo Iohannis Caminensis episcopi facto d. d. Corlin 1356. feria III post miser. dom. (maii 10), cui sigillum semifractum appendet, in archivo Regimontano.

---

454. *1231 septembr. 15 Reate. Gregorius IX repetit n. 426 de 1227 iulii 30.*

Gregorius etc. Paci et quieti etc. Datum Reate xvii kalendas octobris pontificatus nostri anno quinto.

---

455. *1231 sept. 17 Laterani. Gregorius IX repetit n. 420 de 1227 iulii 14.*

Gregorius etc. Non absque etc. Datum Reate xv kal. octobris pontificatus nostri anno quinto.

---

456. *1231 sept. 18 Laterani. Gregorius IX repetit n. 429 de 1227 aug. 4.*

Gregorius etc. Querelam gravem recepimus etc. Datum Laterani xiiii kal. octobris pontificatus nostri anno quinto.

---

457. *1231 sept. 25 Reate. Gregorius IX repetit n. 426 de 1227 iulii 30.*

Gregorius etc. Paci et quieti etc. Datum Reate vii kal. octobris pontificatus nostri anno quinto.

---

458. *1231 octobr. 10 Reate. Gregorius IX repetit n. 453 de 1231 aprilis 9.*

Gregorius etc. Cum dilectis etc. Datum Reate vi idus octobris pontificatus nostri anno quinto.

---

459. *1232 februarii 13 Reate. Gregorius IX repetit Honorii III n. 342 de 1221 ianuarii 21.*

Gregorius etc. Decet pastoralis etc. Datum Reate idus februarii pontificatus nostri anno quinto.

Originale cum bulla et nota primiceriae P. B. in archivo Regimontano. Addimus hic ad calcem ultimi privilegii de anno pontificatus quinto, quod apud Schirren in designatione Mitoviensis archivi p. 128 n. 40 citatur documentum, quo Gregorius IX vetat omnes episcopos et praelatos, dummodo papa non iubeat ipse, familiarem ordinis Theutonici excommunicare, quum ordo non habeat episcopum nisi papam; anno v. Sapit hoc bullam initii „Cum dilecti".

---

460. *1233 iunii 28 Laterani (cf. 1235 april. 28). Gregorii IX repetit Honorii III n. 329 de 1221 ianuarii 18.*

Gregorius etc. Quociens a nobis etc. Datum Perusii iiii kalendas iulii pontificatus nostri anno septimo.

Cum dato: Laterani 4 kal. iulii a. 7 „Baruli". A. 16 p. 48. — Cum dato: Perusii 4 kal. maii a. 9 inter Alsatica 6 citatur R. 96 tanquam simile Alexandri Ratisponensium n. 15.

---

461. *1233 iulii 1 Laterani. Gregorius IX repetit n. 418 de 1227 iulii 3.*

Gregorius etc. Cum dilecti etc. Datum Laterani kal. iulii pontificatus nostri anno septimo.

---

462. *1235 februarii 10 Perusii. Gregorius IX repetit n. 453 de 1231 april. 9.*

Gregorius etc. Cum dilectis etc. Datum Perusii iiii idus februarii pontificatus nostri anno octavo.

---

463. *1235 apr. 27 Perusii. Gregorius IX repetit n. 453 de 1231 april. 9.*

Gregorius etc. Cum dilectis etc. Datum Perusii v kalendas maii pontificatus nostri anno nono.

---

464. *1235 april. 28 Perusii. Gregorius IX repetit n. 460 de 1233 iunii 28.*

Gregorius etc. Quociens a etc. Datum Perusii iiii kal. maii pontificatus nostri anno nono.

---

465. *1235 novbr. 28 Viterbii. Gregorius IX repetit n. 436 de 1227 aug. 18.*

Gregorius etc. Quieti vestre etc. Datum Viterbii iiii kal. decembris pontificatus nostri anno nono.

---

466. *1237 maii 22 Viterbii. Gregorius IX concedit ordini Theutonico, ut clericos suos ad ecclesias patronatus sui praesentet.*

Gregorius episcopus servus servorum dei dilectis filiis .. magistro et fratribus hospitalis sancte Marie Theutonicorum Ierosolimitani salutem et apostolicam benedictionem. Signorum evidencia declarante, quod studio caritatis intenditis et sedem apostolicam benignam vobis reddere cultu gratitudinis vigilatis, digne ad concedendum vobis inducimur, per quod universitati vestre prosperitas augeatur. Eapropter, dilecti in domino filii, vestris devotis precibus inclinati presencium vobis auctoritate concedimus, ut fratres clericos ordinis vestri ad ecclesias, in quibus ius patronatus habetis, diocesanis episcopis presentare possitis, sibi de spiritualibus et vobis de temporalibus responsuros. Nulli ergo omnino hominum liceat hanc paginam nostre concessionis infringere vel ei ausu temerario contraire. Si quis autem hoc attemptare presumpserit, indignacionem omnipotentis dei et beatorum Petri et Pauli apostolorum eius se noverit incursurum. Datum Viterbii xi kalendas iunii pontificatus nostri anno undecimo.

Sine dato: R. 155 inter Iuncensia „Datum Viterbii". A. 16 p. 103 inter Iuncensia; A. 20 n. 84 Latine et Germanice cum nota „in Confluentia". — Cum dato: Viterbii 11 kal. iulii p. n. a. 11. IV, 202 v. n. 15 „Colonie" A. 16 p. 76. Originale quondam Confluentinum cum bulla in filis sericeis appensa in archivo ordinis Theutonici Vindobonensi; edidit Hennes I, 107 n. 97. Originale quondam Iuncense cum bulla in filis sericeis rubris et luteis appensa, ut etiam transsumtum fratris Hugonis tituli s. Sabinae presbyteri cardinalis, apost. sed. legati, d. d. Colonie xiv kal. octobr. p. Innocentii IV anno nono, cum sigillo cereo albo appenso laeso: (S. H)UG. TT. SCE. SABINE. PBR. CARD., quondam Mergenthemense in archivo ordinis Theutonici Vindobonensi.

---

467. *1238 augusti 26 Anagniae. Gregorius IX repetit n. 453 de 1231 apr. 9.*

Gregorius etc. Cum dilectis etc. — amittant. Datum Anagnie vii kalendas septembris pontificatus nostri anno duodecimo.

---

468. *1240 ianuarii 12 Laterani. Gregorius IX fratres hospitalis s. Mariae Theutonicorum in Accon citat usque ad festum s. Michaelis proximum, ut de subtractione ab hospitalis s. Iohannis obedientia respondeant.*

Gregorius episcopus servus servorum dei dilectis filiis fratribus hospitalis sancte Marie Theutonicorum in Accon salutem et apostolicam benedictionem. Dilecti filii magister et fratres Hospitalis Ierosolimitani nobis exponere curaverunt, quod, cum felicis recordationis Celestinus papa, predecessor noster, volens ipsorum et vestre quieti ac paci paterna sollicitudine providere, duxerit statuendum, ut domus vestra cum reliquis sibi subiectis sub obedientia et dispositione prioris sive magistri Hospitalis eiusdem, qui pro tempore foret, omnino maneret, ita tamen, quod de gente Theutonicorum priorem et servientes idoneos constitueret in eis, qui Christi pauperibus in lingua sua responderent ac eis necessaria ministrarent et prefato priori sive magistro sicut alii fratres eius humiliter obedirent, prout in eiusdem Celestini privilegio a bone memorie Adriano papa postea roborato plenius asserunt contineri; vos tamen postmodum proponentes domum eamdem auctoritate apostolice sedis[1] exemptam et penitus a subiectione ipsorum immunem conati estis privilegium infringere antedictum, ab eorumdem obedientia et aliis, in quibus ipsis tenemini, vos subtrahere indebite satagendo, in magnum Hospitalis predicti preiudicium et gravamen. Unde petierunt instanter, ut sibi super hiis exhiberi iustitiam, in qua tenemur singulis, faceremus. Volentes igitur unicuique sua iura servari per apostolica vobis scripta mandamus, quatenus usque ad festum dedicationis beati Michaelis proximo venturum, quod pro peremptorio termino vobis prefigimus, per responsalem sufficientem et idoneum coram nobis comparere curetis prefatis magistro et fratribus super predictis, secundum quod iustitie ordo dictaverit, responsuri. Datum Laterani ii idus ianuarii pontificatus nostri anno tertio decimo.

Ex bullario originali archivi Melitensis n. 10 edidit Sebastianus Pauli I, 272 n. 6, unde repetiit Hennes I in praefatione p. 5. Nec Coelestini II (1143 sept. 26 — 1144 martii 8) nec Hadriani IV (1154 decbr. 5 — 1159 sept. 1) pro hospitali quodam Theutonicorum Acconensi innotuit privilegium; ipsum tale hospitale tunc extitisse aliunde probari non potest, ita ut dubitari debeat, num hoc sit genuinum. Neque enim carent alias hospitalis s. Iohannis bullaria supposititiis privilegiis, ut hoc utar (Caorsinus D. 5, Senner G. 3), quod falsarius male historicus magnae litis futuram causam Gregorio VIII („Religionis vestre") ascripsit. Caeterum ne 1258 quidem anno hospitalis s. Iohannis praetensionem de obedientia ab hospitali s. Mariae sibi debita omnino fuisse sopitam edocet diploma de 1258 oct. 9 supra n. 116 p. 102. Cf. etiam L'estoire de Eracles empereur et la conqueste de la terre d'outremer. XXV cap. 3 in Recueil des historiens des croisades II, 141 sq.

1. sedis apostolice H.

469. .... *apud Urbem Veterem. Gregorius IX ordinis Theutonici libertates et privilegia confirmat.*

Gregorius episcopus servus servorum dei dilectis filiis etc. Cum a nobis petitur, quod iustum est et honestum, tam vigor equitatis quam ordo exigit racionis, ut id per sollicitudinem officii nostri ad debitum perducatur effectum. Eapropter, dilecti in domino filii, vestris iustis postulacionibus grato concurrentes assensu omnes libertates et immunitates a predecessoribus nostris Romanis pontificibus sive per privilegia vel alias indulgencias vobis vel hospitali vestro concessas necnon libertates et exempciones secularium exaccionum a regibus et principibus vel aliis Christi fidelibus racionabiliter vobis seu hospitali predicto indultas, sicut iuste et pacifice obtinetis, vobis per nos eidem hospitali auctoritate apostolica confirmamus et presentis scripti patrocinio communimus. Nulli ergo omnino hominum etc. Si quis autem etc. Datum apud Urbem Veterem ...

A. 16 p. 103 „Iuncis". R. 156 habet inter Iuuccnsia tanquam Gregorii X.

---

470. *1244 februarii 9 Lateran. Innocentius IV fratribus ordinis Theutonici concedit, quod quosdam regulae articulos ipsi immutent.*

Innocentius episcopus servus servorum dei dilectis filiis magistro et fratribus hospitalis sancte Marie Theutonicorum Ierosolimitani salutem et apostolicam benedictionem. Pro reverentia gloriose Marie virginis, cuius laudibus pie devotionis studio desudatis, affectum libenter ad illa dirigimus, que vobis statum quiete mentis afferant et conscientie scrupulum titubantis excludant. Sane in vestra, sicut audivimus, regula continetur, quod hii, qui volunt in vestra fraternitate recipi, debent locorum episcopis presentari et tandem partes transmarinas adire, ut, si eorum vita tali sit digna collegio, a magistro et fratribus admittantur. Dicitur etiam in eadem, quod in quarta feria debetis vesci carnibus, si precedenti die illas pro alicuius sollempnitatis vigilia dimittatis, et quod tribus diebus in ebdomada duo vel tria vobis in leguminibus aut pulmentis fercula ministrentur, necnon quod generaliter duo ac duo fratres pro parapsidum penuria comedant, et nullum in eorum lanceis tegimen habeatur. Pro hiis enim et quibusdam aliis articulis predicte regule conscientia vestra sepe dubia et multotiens redditur inquieta, maxime cum quidam ex eis olim postpositi sint a vobis et, si observare velletis eosdem, perplexitas inde vobis multa incumberet et importabile dispendium immineret. Quare supplicatione humili postulastis, ut apostolica benignitas super hoc vobis et pie consulere et providere salubriter dignaretur. Nos itaque paterno considerantes affectu, quod in hiis tranquillitatem mentium et profectum vestrum queritis animarum, ut libere cum conventu vestro vel maiori et saniori parte ipsius predictos et alios articulos vestre regule, in quorum observantia nec spiritualis utilitas nec salubris continetur honestas, deum habendo pre oculis immutare possitis, ita quod nullum ex hoc alicui preiudicium generetur, vobis auctoritate presentium concedimus facultatem. Ceterum ut veniam, quam queritis, ex apostolice provisionis obtinere gratia valeatis, fratri sacerdoti presidenti clericis conventus vestri concedimus, ut super eo, quod olim aliquos de ipsius articulis regule non servastis, iniuncta salutari penitentia vos absolvat. Nulli ergo omnino hominum liceat hanc paginam nostre concessionis infringere vel ei ausu temerario contraire. Si quis autem hoc attemptare presumpserit, indignationem omnipotentis dei et beatorum Petri et Pauli apostolorum eius se noverit incursurum. Datum Laterani v idus februarii pontificatus nostri anno primo.

Cum dato: Laterani 5 id. febr. p. n. a. 1 ex originali tunc Mergenthemensi nunc Vindobonensi edd. de Wal Recherches I, 377 n. 4. Hennes I, 118 n. 113. Duo originalia cum plumbis in archivo Regimontano; cf. Napiersky Ind. I, 17 n. 64; R. 122 inter Marburgensia. Vocem „lanccae" mensae speciem sine dubio significantem non novit Du Cange. Napiersky coniicit forsan e lanceis fuisse compositam; quod vix intelligi potest. Perperam idem articulos in privilegio citatos etiam ipsa in regula 1442 immutata (ed. Hennig. Königsberg 1806. p. 54) esse retentos refert; quum iam in redactione saec. xiii med. ed. Schönhuth. Heilbronn 1847. Regele § 15 mutati sint praeter: „in ir huseren ezzen ouch die brudere zwene unt zwene miteinander ane muse unt trinken sunderliche".

---

471. *1244 februarii 13 Laterani. Innocentius IV concedit ordini Theutonico, ut eius clerici super alias vestes camisias albas deferant, deinde, ut pro officio ordinis sancti sepulcri porro officio secundum ordinem fratrum praedicatorum utatur.*

Innocentius episcopus servus servorum dei dilectis filiis magistro et fratribus hospitalis sancte Marie Theutonicorum Ierosolimitani salutem et apostolicam benedictionem. Augmentum honoris et commodi vestre religioni producitur, si clerus eiusdem sub illo habitu videatur, qui et divinis sit aptus officiis et decori clericalis conveniat honestatis. Hinc est, quod nos digne volentes, ut universi fratres clerici vestri ordinis discernantur ab aliis vestis differentia congruentis, quod iidem super vestes alias libere camisiis albis utantur, vobis auctoritate presentium indulgemus. Caeterum, quia divinum officium secundum ordinem sancti sepulchri pro eo, quod a pluribus ex iisdem fratribus clericis ignoratur, vix absque scandalo, sicut accepimus, in vestro potest ordine observari, quod illud secundum ordinem fratrum predicatorum amodo in vestris ubique domibus celebretur, vobis concedimus facultatem. Nulli ergo omnino hominum liceat hanc paginam nostre concessionis infringere vel ei ausu temerario contraire. Si quis autem hoc attemptare praesumserit, indignationem omnipotentis dei et beatorum Petri et Pauli apostolorum eius se noverit incursurum. Datum Laterani idibus februarii pontificatus nostri anno primo.

Originale quondam Mergenthemense cum bulla in filis sericeis appensa, nunc in archivo ordinis Theutonici Vindobonensi. R. 89 inter Mergenthemensia n. 50. Ex originali tunc Mergenthemensi ed. de Wal Recherches II, 351 n. 5. Originale cum bulla in archivo Regimontano; cf. Napiersky in Indice I, 17 n. 65; A. 16 p. 36 „Baruli"; p. 68 „in Marpurg".

---

472. *1244 martii 31 Laterani. Innocentius IV repetit Gregorii IX n. 469.*

Innocentius etc. Cum a nobis — communimus. Datum Laterani ii kal. aprilis pontificatus nostri anno primo.

Transsumtum sub autoritate et sigillo Iohannis Rigensis archiepiscopi ad instantiam magistri H(enrici) de Plawen factum, d. Marienburg 1412 dec. 22, valde corrosum sigillique expers, in archivo Regimontano.

---

473. *1244 aprilis 20 Laterani (cf. 1247 iulii 20, 1248 ianuarii 19). Innocentius IV repetit Honorii III n. 332 de 1221 ianuarii 19.*

Innocentius etc. Cum de viris — compellamur. Datum Laterani xii kal. maii pontificatus nostri anno primo.

Sine dato: A. 16 p. 98 „Iuncis". — Cum dato: Laterani 12 kal. maii p. n. a. 1. originale in archivo ordinis Theutonici Vindobonensi. — Cum dato: Lugduni 13 kal. aug. p. n. a. 5. originale in archivo Regimontano; cf. Napiersky Ind. I, 21 n. 79. Originale cum bulla in filis sericeis rubris et luteis appensa, quondam (Confluentibus?) Iuncis, nunc in archivo ordini Theutonici Vindobonensi. — Cum dato: Laterani 14 kal. febr. p. n. a. 5. A. 16 p. 36 „Baruli".

474. *1244 aprilis 20 Laterani (cf. maii 15, 1245 martii 2, 1246 april. 21, aug. 28, 1247 mart. 12). Innocentius IV repetit Gregorii IX n. 418 de 1227 iulii 3.*

Innocentius etc. Cum dilecti — curemus. Datum Laterani xii kal. maii pontificatus nostri anno primo.

Sine dato: R. 6 inter Norimbergensia n. 8. Citatur R. 53 inter Ratisponensia n. 4; R. 89 inter Mergenthemensia n. 51; R. 171 inter Thuringica. — Cum dato: Laterani 12 kal. maii p. n. a. 1 ex transsumto, quod Venetiis asservabatur, exemplato et subscripto a quatuor notariis imperialis aulae de anno 1244 ind. II exscriptum in A. 16 p. 19. Transsumtum per Tuscum Geri, imperialis aulae notarium 1247 Bononiae ind. V mens. ianuar., iterum confirmatum per Marchisinum Egizi, s. pal. publ. not., d. d. Venetiis 1258 I ind. febr. ex domo E(llingensi?) in archivo ordinis Theutonici Vindobonensi. — Cum dato: Laterani id. maii p. n. a. 1. transsumtum Vindobonae 1278. 10 kal. ianuar. per Philippum Firmanum episcopum legatum apostolicum, cuius sigillum iam deest, in archivo Regimontano. — Cum dato: Lugduni 6 idus martii p. n. a. 2 transsumtum d. d. Wirziburgi 1418 dec. 2 sub sigillo curiae et autoritate Werneri de Hayn officialis factum ad instantiam fratris Iohannis de Hoffheim et subscriptum manu Henrici Vischer notarii in archivo Regimontano. — Cum dato: Lugduni 11 kal. maii p. n. a. 3. originale cum bulla in filis sericeis appensa quondam Mergenthemi nunc Vindobonae in archivo ordinis Theutonici. IV, 203 n. 1. Transsumtum per Tyrensem archiepiscopum (cum sig.) et Bethlehemitanum episcopum d. d. 1277 oct. 19 Accon in archivo Regimontano ex sinistra parte adeo laesum, ut papae nomen cum dimidia scriptura deperierit. Alterum huius transsumti originale asservatur in archivo ordinis Theutonici Vindobonensi, unde ed. Hennes I, 227 n. 260. — Cum dato: Lugduni 5 kal. septbr. p. n. a. 4 transsumtum sub sigillis nunc deficientibus fratris Iohannis, prioris ordinis s. Augustini ecclesiae in Stargard Caminensis diocesis, et Th., vicepraepositi dicti de Slotenis, d. d. 1292 8 kal. novbr. (oct. 25) Stargard, in archivo Regimontano. — Cum dato: Lugduni 4 id. martii p. n. a. 4. originale, de quo plumbum quondam in filis sericeis appensum avulsum, iam dudum domus Theutonicae Vindobonensis, etiamnunc ibi in archivo ordinis Theutonici asservatur. Transsumtum d. d. 1396 aug. 18 Vindobonae in archivo Regimontano cf. Napiersky I, 5 n. 16 p. 5. Edd. Duellius II, 9 n. 11; (Feder) Historisch-diplomatischer Unterricht n. 36.

475. *1244 aprilis 20 Laterani. Innocentius IV repetit Honorii III n. 322 de 1221 ianuarii 16.*

Innocentius etc. Non absque dolore etc. Datum Laterani xii kal. maii pontificatus nostri anno primo.

Transsumtum d. d. Vindobonae 1396 aug. 18 Regimontani archivi citat Napiersky I, 5. n. 16 n. 4.

476. *1244 aprilis 22 Laterani. Innocentius IV repetit Honorii III n. 323 de 1221 ianuarii 17.*

Innocentius etc. Cum a religiosorum — adimplere. Datum Laterani x kal. maii pontificatus nostri anno primo.

Or. valde laesum cum bulla in archivo Regimontano. R. 62 inter Ratisponensia n. 22. R. 41 inter Ellingensia n. 27 in apographo transsumti, cuius initium est: „In nomine domini. Amen. Per hoc transscriptum publicum pateat universis tam presentibus quam futuris, quod in presencia mei, Bartholomei de Firmo, notarii publici infrascripti, reverendus in Christo pater dominus frater Thomas de ordine predicatorum, dei gracia patriarcha Ierosolimitanus (scriptum est: „infirmus"), minister ecclesie Acconensis, apostolice sedis legatus, vidit et diligenter inspexit quasdam litteras domini pape Innocencii quarti sanas etc., quarum tenor per omnia talis est": (sequitur). Clausula finalis sonat: „Et ego Bartholomeus de Paganellis de Firmo, imperiali auctoritate notarius publicus et nunc notarius curie predicti domini patriarche legati, rogatus a religioso viro fratre Iohanne magno preceptore domus hospitalis predicti predictas papales litteras bullatas bulla pendenti plumbea, prout in autentico reperi ac de mandato prefati domini patriarche legati mihi facto per eum vive vocis oraculo in domo episcopali in camera, scilicet ubi ipse iacebat, fideliter exemplavi, auscultavi et in hanc publicam formam redegi nil addens, minuens vel mutans, preter punctum vel sillabam, que veritatis substantiam non inmutant, sub anno domini a nativitate 1277 indictione sexta die tercio decimo septembris. Et idem dominus patriarcha legatus ad preces preceptoris predicti huic transscripto publico sigillum suum appendi fecit in testimonium omnium premissorum". Transsumtum originale sub eiusdem Thomae autoritate per Iohannem clericum Acconensem 1277 aug. 30 in domo episcopali Accon confectum, quod est in archivo ordinis Theutonici Vindobonensi, ed. Hennes I, 224 n. 257.

---

477. *1244 aprilis 22 Laterani (cf. 1247 martii 12). Innocentius IV repetit Honorii III n. 342 de 1221 ianuarii 21 Laterani.*

Innocentius etc. Decet pastoralis — exeratis. Datum Laterani x kal. maii pontificatus nostri anno primo.

Cum dato: 10 kal. maii p. a. 1 Laterani. Originale dudum et nunc Vindobonensis archivi ordinis Theutonici cum bulla in filis sericeis rubris et luteis appendente. Ed. Duellius Hist. ordinis Theutonici II, 6 n. 7. Transsumtum de 1396 aug. 18 in archivo Regimontano, cf. Napiersky Index I, 5 n. 16. 2). — Cum dato: Lugduni 4 idus marcii p. n. a. 4 „Venetiis". A. 16 p. 14.

---

478. *1244 maii 3 Laterani (cf. octobr. 19, 1245 ianuar. 17. 18, iunii 21. 23, sept. 5, 1246 martii 11, maii 11). Innocentius IV repetit Honorii III n. 314 de 1221 ianuarii 16.*

Innocentius episcopus servus servorum dei venerabilibus fratribus archiepiscopis et episcopis et dilectis filiis abbatibus, prioribus, decanis, archidiaconis et aliis ecclesiarum prelatis, ad quos littere iste pervenerint, salutem et apostolicam benedictionem. Cum dilectis etc. fuerit a predecessoribus nostris indultum et a nobis postmodum confirmatum — predecessorum nostrorum vestigiis inherentes universitati vestre per — sane quoniam ab eisdem nostris predecessoribus est statutum et innovatum a nobis — amittant. Datum Laterani v nonas maii pontificatus nostri anno primo.

Sine dato citatur R. 195 inter bullas incerti loci; R. 42 citatur Hildebrandi Eystetensis episcopi, Moguntinae sedis cancellarii, transsumtum inter Ellingensia n. 28. — Cum dato: Laterani 5 nonas maii p. n. a. 1 transsumtum sub sigillo Ulrici scholastici Pragensis, administratoris Pragensis episcopatus, d. d. Pragensis 1325 8 id. maii, cui nunc sigillum deest, in archivo Regimontano. — Cum dato: ap. castrum Stelle 14 kal. novbr. p. n. a. 2. ed. Liljegren Diplomatarium Suecanum I, 306 n. 319 „a. c. Selle"; R. 130 inter Marburgensia. — Cum dato: Lugduni 16 kal. febr. a. 2 „Colonie" A. 16 p. 77 sq. — Cum dato: Lugduni 15 kal. febr. p. n. a. 2. originale cum bulla in filis appensa in archivo ordinis Theutonici Vindobonensi. — Cum dato: Lugduni 11 kal. iulii p. n. a. 2. originale, de quo quondam filis sericeis appensa avulsa nunc deest, quondam Mergenthemi modo in Vindobonensi ordinis Theutonici archivo asservatur. — Cum dato: Lugduni 9 kal. iulii p. n. a. 2. originale cum bulla in filis sericeis rubris et luteis appensa iam dudum domus Vindobonensis, in archivo ordinis Theutonici Vindobonensis. Citat Duellius II, 12 not. Ex originali Gracensi VII, 367 v. — Cum dato: Lugduni non. sept. p. n. a. 3. IV, 203 v. Ioh. 35. Ediderunt Caorsinus fol. C. 3 v. Senner fol. E. 4. — Cum dato: Lugduni 5 idus marcii p. n. a. 4. A. 16 p. 106 „Traiecti". — Cum dato: Lugduni 5 id. maii p. n. a. 3. originale cum bulla in archivo Regimontano. In apographo transsumti R. 28. Ellingensia n. 12: Noverint universi presens publicum instrumentum inspecturi, quod nos frater Bonacursus de ordine predicatorum dei gracia Tyrensis archiepiscopus et vicarius patriarchatus Ierosolimitani ac episcopatus Acconensis et nos Matheus eadem gracia Cesariensis archiepiscopus et nos frater Geirhardus (!) ordinis predicatorum et eadem gracia Bethleemitanus episcopus vidimus, legimus et de verbo ad verbum diligenter inspeximus quasdam literas domini Innocencii pape IIII sanas et integras, non abolitas, non cancellatas, non rasas nec in aliqua sui parte viciatas, quarum tenor per omnia talis est (qui sequitur). Quas quidem litteras transscribi et publicari fecimus per Iohannem clericum Acconensem notarium publicum ad instanciam et preces religiosi viri fratris Hermanni magistri hospitalis sancte Marie Theutonicorum Ierosolimitani. In cuius rei testimonium presenti instrumento sigilla nostra duximus apponenda. (Signum notarii.) Ego Iohannes clericus Acconensis, assisius ecclesie sancte crucis Acconensis, sacrosancte Romane ecclesie auctoritate notarius publicus, predictas literas vidi et diligenter inspexi et eas de mandato prefatorum dominorum Tyrensis et Cesariensis archiepiscoporum et domini episcopi Bethleemitani transscripsi et in hanc publicam formam redegi nichil addito vel mutato, quod sentenciam mutet. Quod mandatum fecerunt mihi dominus archiepiscopus Tyrensis et dominus episcopus Bethleemitanus predicti in domo episcopali Acconensi anno domini 1277 indictione 6 die 19 mensis octobris, presentibus discretis viris domino Nycolao archidyacono, domino Michaele thesaurario Acconensi, domino Petro thesaurario Cesariensi, fratre Iohanne predicatore, domino Augustino canonico Bethleemitano, testibus ad hoc specialiter vocatis et rogatis".

---

479. *1244 maii 3 Laterani (cf. 1247 martii 11). Innocentius IV repetit Honorii III n. 317 de 1221 ianuarii 16.*

Innocentius etc. Evangelice doctrine — declaratur. Datum Laterani nonas maii pontificatus nostri anno primo.

Cum dato: Laterani 5 nonas maii p. n. a. 1 citatur R. 97 inter Alsatica n. 8 tanquam concinens Ratisponensi; R. 77 ad calcem n. 31 Honoriani privilegii citatur simile (sine dato) Innocentii tanquam Ratisponae exstans. — Cum dato: Lugduni 5 id. martii p. n. a. 4. R. 54 inter Ratisponensia 3, duo transsumta iubentibus fratre Bonacurso de ordine praedicatorum Tyrensi archiepiscopo et fratre Gailardo eiusdem ordinis Bethlehemitano episcopo per Iohannem Acconensem notarium confectum Accone 1277 oct. 19, in archivo Regimontano (cf. Napiersky Index I, 21 n. 78). In utroque tantum episcopi sigillum nunc exstat. Apographum transsumti in R. 37 inter Ellingensia n. 21. Edidit Lünig Teutsches Reichsarchiv XVI, 82 n. 81.

---

480. *1244 maii 15 Laterani. Innocentius IV repetit n. 474 de 1244 aprilis 20.*

Innocentius etc. Cum dilecti etc. Datum Laterani idus marcii pontificatus nostri anno primo.

---

481. *1244 maii 17 Laterani (cf. 1246 maii 6, 1247 iulii 25). Innocentius IV repetit Honorii III n. 406.*

Innocentius etc. Dilecti filii — post concilium — potestate. Datum Laterani XVI kalendas iunii pontificatus nostri anno primo.

Cum dato: Laterani 16 kal. iunii p. n. a. 1 „Baruli; A. 16 p. 14 sq. — Cum dato: Lugduni 2 non. maii p. n. a. 3. A. 16 p. 14 sq. „Venetiis"; Transsumtum R. 58 inter Ratisponensia 15; R. 9 apographum transsumti inter Nurembergensia 15 citatur: „Noverint universi presens publicum instrumentum inspecturi, quod nos frater Bonacursus de ordine predicatorum, Tyrensis archiepiscopus et vicarius patriarchatus Ierosolimitani ac episcopatus Acconensis, et nos Gailardus, eiusdem ordinis et eadem gracia Bethleemitanus episcopus, vidimus, legimus et de verbo ad verbum diligenter inspeximus quasdam literas domini Innocentii pape IIII sanas et integras, non abolitas, non cancellatas, non rasas nec in aliqua sui parte viciatas, quarum tenor per omnia talis est" ... „Quas quidem literas transscribi et publicari fecimus per Iohannem clericum Acconensem, notarium publicum, ad instanciam et preces religiosi viri fratris Iohannis dei gracia magni preceptoris domus hospitalis sancte Marie Theutonicorum Ierosolimitani. In cuius rei testimonium presenti instrumento sigillo nostra duximus apponenda et tunc ... Ego Iohannes clericus Acconensis, assisius ecclesie sancte crucis Acconensis, sacrosancte Romane ecclesie auctoritate notarius publicus, predictas literas etc. anno domini 1277 indictione 6 die 19 mensis octobris cum testibus" etc. Cuius transsumti originale unum valde situ laesum, tantum cum Gailardi sigillo, asservatur in archivo Regimontano; alterum in archivo ordinis Theutonici Vindobonensi, unde edidit cum bulla inserta Hennes I, 229 n. 262. — Cum dato: Lugduni 8 kal. augusti a. 5 „Colonie". A. 16 p. 79.

---

482. *1244 octobris 19 apud castrum Stelle. Innocentius IV repetit n. 478 de 1244 maii 3.*

Innocentius etc. Cum dilectis etc. Datum apud castrum Stelle xiiii kalendas novembris pontificatus nostri anno secundo.

---

483. *1245 ianuarii 16 Lugduni. Innocentius IV notum facit ordini Theutonico se Gerardo de Malberch quondam magistro eius transitum ad Templarios concessisse.*

Innocentius episcopus servus servorum dei dilectis filiis .. magistro et fratribus hospitalis sancte Marie Theutonicorum Ierosolimitani salutem et apostolicam benedictionem. Innocentia vestre pie congregationis audita, cui de religiose vite studio ac impugnatione solicita hostium crucifixi clarum testimonium perhibetur, dignum fore providimus, ut ordini vestro quietis et pacis procurare materiam studeremus. Hinc est, quod nos pensato solicite, quod frater Gerardus de Malberch, quondam magister vester, sine vestro gravi scandalo non poterat in ordine remanere, sustinendum duximus, quod transiret ad Templarios ipsorum habitum recepturus. Vos itaque de huiusmodi duri casus angustia feliciter expediti, ut indissolubile inter vos caritatis vinculum habeatur et odor bone fame de vestra semper operatione procedat, omne, quod poteritis, studium habeatis, secura de nobis concepta fiducia, quod ordinem vestrum in deo sincere diligimus et vos libenter per gratie nostre subsidium in statu prospero conservamus. Datum Lugduni xvii kal. februarii pontificatus nostri anno secundo.

N. 485 — 488 e regestis archivi Vaticani edd. de Wal Recherches II, 365. Hennes I, 119 n. 114.

---

484. *1245 ianuarii 16 Lugduni. Innocentius IV similiter.*

Innocentius episcopus servus servorum dei dilectis filiis preceptoribus et fratribus universis hospitalis sancte Marie Theotonicorum salutem et apostolicam benedictionem. Audita innocentia dilectorum filiorum .. magistri et fratrum vestrorum de partibus transmarinis, quibus et vobis omnibus de religiose vite studio ac impugnatione etc.[1] Datum Lugduni xvii kal. februarii pontificatus nostri anno secundo.

Edd. de Wal Recherches II, 366. Hennes I, 120 n. 115. 1. ut in praecedenti n. 4.

---

485. *1245 ianuarii 16 Lugduni. Innocentius IV similiter ad universos praelatos et omnes Christi fideles.*

Innocentius episcopus servus servorum dei venerabilibus fratribus archiepiscopis et episcopis ac aliis ecclesiarum prelatis et universis Christi fidelibus presentes litteras inspecturis salutem et apostolicam benedictionem. Audita innocentia dilectorum filiorum .. magistri et fratrum hospitalis sancte Marie Theutonicorum, quibus de religiose conversationis et vite studio ac de impugnatione sollicita hostium crucifixi clarum testimonium perhibetur, dignum fore providimus, ut ordini eorum quietis et pacis procurare materiam studeremus. Hinc est etc.[1] Vos itaque contrarium non credentes, si forte illud vobis olim suggestum fuerit vel imposterum suggeratur, dictis magistro et fratribus dignis gratia et honore pro divini honore nominis benigni et benevoli iugiter existatis. Datum Lugduni xvii kal. februarii pontificatus nostri anno secundo.

Edd. de Wal Recherches II, 367. Hennes I, 120 n. 116. 1. ut in n. 483.

---

486. *1245 ianuarii 16 Lugduni. Innocentius IV ordinem Theutonicum non teneri declarat de debitis a Gerardo quondam magistro post resignationem illegitimo sub magisterii sigillo contractis.*

Innocentius episcopus servus servorum dei dilectis filiis .. magistro et fratribus hospitalis sancte Marie Theotonicorum Ierosolimitani salutem et apostolicam benedictionem. Exposuistis humiliter coram nobis, quod frater Gerardus, quondam magister vester, postquam vobis in castro vestro Monteforti suum magisterium resignavit, autentico et perpetuo sigillo magistri, quod habuerat, iuxta morem super altari dimisso, ad domum militie Templi de vestra domo confugiens sibi de novo temere fecit fabricari sigillum. Verum, cum vos, sicut asseritis, non modicum timeatis, quod ipse sub eodem novo sigillo domum vestram aliquibus debitis obligarit, nos vestre paci et eiusdem indempnitati domus providere volentes presentium vobis auctoritate concedimus, ut, si post predictam resignationem magisterii et sigilli aliqua debita ipse contraxit, nulli de ipsis teneamini respondere, presertim cum tu, fili magister, sibi apud sedem apostolicam quadringentas marcas argenti dederis pro suis debitis persolvendis. Datum Lugduni xvii kal. februarii pontificatus nostri anno secundo.

Edd. de Wal Recherches II, 367. Hennes I, 121 n. 117.

---

487. *1245 ianuarii 17 Lugduni. Innocentius IV repetit n. 478 de 1244 maii 3.*

Innocentius etc. Cum dilectis etc. Datum Lugduni xvi kal. februarii pontificatus nostri anno secundo.

---

488. *1245 ianuarii 17 Lugduni. Innocentius IV inhibet, quominus ex Gerhardi de Malberch, quondam magistri ordinis Theutonici, ad Templarios transitu huic praeiudicium generetur confirmatque constitutionem, ne quis relicto Theutonico Templariorum intret ordinem.*

Innocentius epicopus servus servorum dei dilectis filiis .. magistro et fratribus hospitalis sancte Marie Theutonicorum Ierosolimitani salutem et apostolicam benedictionem. In venerandis domibus militie Templi et Hospitalis ac in vestra etiam semper, sicut audivimus, observatur, quod nullus ex fratribus ipsarum domorum ob aliquam causam in alterius fratrem recipitur, immo, si aliquis ex eisdem de sua domo recedens ad aliam quandoque confugiat et nullatenus redire velit ad suam, resignato habitu fratribus, quos reliquit, domum, ad quam confugit, egreditur religionem aliam intraturus. Verum, licet nos pro pace et quiete vestri ordinis, que per fratrem Gerardum de Malberch, quondam magistrum vestrum, si remansisset in illo, graviter poterat perturbari, duxerimus sustinendum, quod transiret ad Templarios ipsorum habitum recepturus, tamen, ne propter hoc ordini vestro aliquod in posterum possit preiudicium generari, auctoritate presentium districtius inhibemus, quod nullus fratrum vestrorum ad Templarios ipsos de cetero transire presumat nec aliquis etiam ex eisdem cum fratre transeat memorato, eis dumtaxat exceptis, qui sibi, postquam vobis suum resignavit magisterium, adheserunt, et nostras de transeundi licentia litteras presentabunt. Nulli ergo omnino hominum liceat hanc paginam nostre inhibitionis infringere vel ei ausu temerario contraire. Si quis autem hoc attemptare presumpserit, indignationem omnipotentis dei et beatorum Petri et Pauli apostolorum eius se noverit incursurum. Datum Lugduni xvi kalendas februarii pontificatus nostri anno secundo.

Sine dato: R. 94 Ottingense unicum; R. 156 inter Iuncensia „Datum Luduen". — Cum dato: Duo originalia quorum, alterum Mergenthemense, cum bulla in filis sericeis appensis in archivo ordinis Theutonici Vindobonensi; R. 88 inter Mergenthemensia n. 47. Edd. Ludovicus a Baczko

Gerhard von Malbergh, Hochmeister des deutschen Ordens. Königsberg 1806. 8°. p. 23 n. 3. de Wal II, 368. Hennes I, 121 n. 119 Huc confer, quod in A. 20 n. 90 legitur excerptum Latine et Germanice, cum nota: „In Leodio et Mergetheym", huius tenoris" Innocentius: indulget magistro et fratribus indulgenciam, quod nullus fratrum de domo Theutonica ad Templarios vel Hospitalarios sine speciali licentia sedis apostolice valeat se transferre".

---

489. *1245 ianuarii 18 Lugduni. Innocentius IV repetit n. 478 de 1244 maii 3.*

Innocentius etc. Cum dilectis etc. Datum Lugduni xv kal. februarii pontificatus nostri anno secundo.

---

490. *1245 martii 2 Lugduni. Innocentius IV repetit n. 474 de 1244 aprilis 20.*

Innocentius etc. Cum dilecti etc. Datum Lugduni vi idus martii pontificatus nostri anno secundo.

---

491. *1245 iunii 21 Lugduni. Innocentius IV repetit n. 478 de 1244 maii 3.*

Innocentius etc. Cum dilectis etc. Datum Lugduni xi kalendas iulii pontificatus nostri anno secundo.

---

492. *1245 iunii 23 Lugduni. Innocentius IV repetit n. 478 de 1244 maii 3.*

Innocentius etc. Cum dilectis etc. Datum Lugduni ix kalendas iulii pontificatus nostri anno secundo.

---

493. *1245 sept. 5 Lugduni. Innocentius IV repetit n. 478 de 1244 maii 3.*

Innocentius etc. Cum dilectis etc. Datum Lugduni nonas septembris pontificatus nostri anno tercio.

---

494. *1245 septembris 5 Lugduni (cf. 1247 martii 14). Innocentius IV repetit Honorii III n. 322 de 1221 ianuarii 16.*

Innocentius etc. Non absque dolore etc. Datum Lugduni nonas septembris pontificatus nostri anno tercio.

Sine dato: citatur R. 169 inter Thuringica, tanquam simile Honoriani Marburgensis. — Cum dato: Lugduni non. sept. a. 3 citatur R. 97 inter Alsatica 9. — Cum dato: Lugduni 2 id. martii p. a. 4, transsumtum, ut in dorso legitur, non satis autenticum, Andreae Magni, notar. imp., d. d. Marienburgi 1413 april. 14 in archivo Regimontano, ubi etiam duo transsumta d. d. Marienburgi 1413 aug. 27 per Iohannem Pomesaniensem episcopum et Nicolaum abbatem Polplinensem (de hoc cf. supra p. 271) edita. Ex transsumpto Venetiis asservato sub sigillo Pagan episcopi Paduani d. d. Padua 1306 iulii 28, per manus Berofini de Giraldis s. palat. notarii exemplato, descriptum in A. 16 p. 15.

---

495. *1245 septembris 12 Lugduni (cf. decembris 18). Innocentius IV repetit Honorii III n. 367 de 1222 februarii 20.*

Innocentius etc. Querelam gravem — astringatis. Datum Lugduni ii idus septembris pontificatus nostri anno tercio.

Sine dato citatur R. 157 inter „Iuncensia" tanquam simile Alexandri IV Treverensi et A. 16 p. 98. — Cum dato: 2 id. septbr. Lugduni p. a. 3 or. cum bulla in filis sericeis rubris et luteis appensa in archivo ordinis Theutonici Vindobonensi. — Cum dato: 15 kal. ianuar. Lugduni p. a. 3 in transsumto de 1396 aug. 18 archivi Regimontani; cf. Napiersky Index I, 5 n. 16. 4. Or. domus Vindobonensis cum bulla in filis sericeis rubris et luteis appensa in archivo ordinis Theutonici Vindobonae. Ed. Duellius II, 8 n. 10.

---

496. *1245 decembris 18 Lugduni. Innocentius IV repetit n. 495 de 1245 septembris 12.*

Innocentius etc. Querelam gravem etc. Datum Lugduni xv kal. ianuarii pontificatus nostri anno tercio.

---

497. *1246 ianuarii 4 Lugduni. Innocentius IV concedit ordini Theutonico, quod, quum fratres eius se invicem percusserint, a priore suo absolutionem possint adipisci.*

Innocentius episcopus servus servorum dei dilectis filiis magistro et fratribus hospitalis sancte Marie Theutonicorum Ierosolimitani salutem et apostolicam benedictionem. Canonica constitutione cavetur, quod monachi et canonici regulares, quocumque modo se percusserint, non sunt ad apostolicam sedem mittendi, sed secundum discrecionem et providentiam sui abbatis discipline subdantur. Quodsi abbatis discretio ad eorum correctionem non sufficit, providentia est diocesani episcopi adhibenda, nisi excessus difficilis fuerit et enormis, propter quem merito sit ad Romanam ecclesiam recursus habendus. Nos ergo ad vos statutum huiusmodi duximus extendendum, auctoritate presentium statuentes, ut in tali casu, nisi maioris sit providentia requirenda, per priorem vestrum, qui, sicut audivimus, presbiter esse debet, fratribus vestris absolutionis beneficium impendatur. Datum Lugduni ii nonas ianuarii pontificatus nostri anno tercio.

Sine dato: „preceptori et fratribus hospitalis sancte Marie Theutonicorum in Alemannia" inscripta citatur R. 88 inter Mergenthemensia n. 48; „preceptori et fratribus hospitalis sancte Marie Theutonicorum in Marpurg Moguntine diocesis" citatur R. 123 inter Marburgensia. Or. praeceptori et fratribus hospitalis sanctae Mariae Theutonicorum in Alemannia missum cum bulla in filis cannabinis appensa in archivo ordini Theutonici Vindobonensi. Germanice D. n. 81. — Cum dato: I, 85.

---

498. *1246 martii 11 Lugduni. Innocentius IV repetit n. 478 de 1244 maii 3.*

Innocentius etc. Cum dilectis etc. Datum Lugduni v idus martii pontificatus nostri anno quarto.

---

499. *1246 aprilis 21 Lugduni. Innocentius IV repetit n. 474 de 1244 april. 20.*

Innocentius etc. Cum dilecti etc. Datum Lugduni xi kal. maii pontificatus nostri anno tercio.

---

500. *1246 maii 4 Lugduni. Innocentius IV repetit Honorii III n. 383 de 1223 ianuarii 31.*

Innocentius etc. Si discrimina etc. Datum iiii nonas maii pontificatus nostri anno tercio.

In R. 33 e domo Ellingensi n. 16 apographum transsumti per fr. Thomam ord. praed., patriarcham Ierosolimitanum, Acconensis ecclesiae ministrum, apostolicae sedis legatum, ad instantiam Iohannis magni praeceptoris d. h. s. M. Th. I. in domo episcopali Acconensi 1277 ind. V 30 aug. praesentibus fratre Symone de ordine praedicatorum, socio patriarchae, et Bartholomaeo camerario confecti per Iohannem clericum Acconensem, assisium ecclesiae s. crucis Acconensis, s. R. e. auctoritate not. publ. Originale transsumti asservatur in archivo ordinis Theutonici Vindobonensi, unde edidit Hennes I, 227 n. 261. In R. 57 citatur inter Ratisponensia 12.

---

501. *1246 maii 6 Lugduni. Innocentius IV repetit n. 481 de 1244 maii 17.*

Innocentius etc. Dilecti filii etc. Datum Lugduni ii nonas maii pontificatus nostri ann tercio.

---

502. *1246 maii 11 Lugduni. Innocentius IV repetit n. 478 de 1244 maii 3.*

Innocentius etc. Cum dilectis etc. Datum Lugduni v idus maii pontificatus nostri anno tercio.

---

503. *(Inter 1245 iunii 24 et 1246 iunii 23) (cf. 1247 martii 11). Innocentius IV repetit Honorii III n. 379 de 1223 ianuarii 16.*

Innocentius etc. Paci et quieti etc. Datum etc. pontificatus nostri anno tercio.

Sine dato: partim R. 147 inter Treverensia. — Cum dato: a. 3 „Treviris". A. 16 p. 119. — Cum dato: Lugduni 5 idus martii p. n. a. 4 transsumtum sub auspiciis Iohannis Pomesaniensis episcopi et Nicolai Polplinensis abbatis d. d. Marienburg (1413 aug. 27) in archivo Regimontano. Cum sigillis Iohannis episcopi et Petri abbatis; cf. supra ad n. 302 et 494.

---

504. *1246 aug. 28 Lugduni. Innocentius IV repetit n. 474 de 1244 april. 20.*

Innocentius etc. Cum dilecti etc. Datum Lugduni v kal. septembris pontificatus nostri anno quarto.

---

505. *1247 martii 11 Lugduni. Innocentius IV repetit n. 479 de 1244 maii 3.*

Innocentius etc. Evangelice doctrine — declaratur. Datum Lugduni v idus marcii pontificatus nostri anno quarto.

---

506. *1247 martii 11 Lugduni. Innocentius IV repetit n. 503 de 1245 aut 1246.*

Innocentius etc. Paci et quieti etc. Datum Lugduni v idus marcii pontificatus nostri anno quarto.

---

507. *1247 martii 12 Lugduni. Innocentius IV repetit n. 474 de 1244 april. 20.*

Innocentius etc. Cum dilecti etc. Datum Lugduni iiii idus martii pontificatus nostri anno quarto.

---

508. *1247 martii 13 Lugduni. Innocentius IV repetit n. 500 de 1246 maii 4.*

Innocentius episcopus servus servorum dei venerabilibus fratribus archiepiscopis et episcopis et dilectis filiis abbatibus, prioribus, decanis, prepositis, archidiaconis et aliis ecclesiarum prelatis, ad quos littere iste pervenerint, salutem et apostolicam benedictionem. Si discrimina etc. — scituri ...... Datum Lugduni iii idus martii pontificatus nostri anno quarto.

Or. in archivo Regimontano valde corrosum et ex laeva parte laniatum, ita ut bulla et margo plane deficiant.

---

509. *1247 martii 14 Lugduni. Innocentius IV repetit n. 494 de 1245 sept. 5.*

Innocentius etc. Non absque dolore etc. Datum Lugduni ii idus martii pontificatus nostri anno quarto.

---

510. *1247 aprilis 17 Lugduni. Innocentius IV concedit fratribus ordinis Theutonici, quod de iis, quae ad forum ecclesiae spectant, coram saeculari iudice respondere non sint coacti.*

Innocentius episcopus servus servorum dei dilectis filiis magistro et fratribus etc. Iustis petentium desideriis dignum est nos facilem prebere consensum et vota, que a rationis tramite non discordant, effectu prosequente complere. Eapropter, dilecti in domino filii, vestris iustis postulationibus grato concurrentes assensu, ne super hiis, que spectant ad forum ecclesie, teneamini coram seculari iudice respondere, vobis auctoritate presentium indulgemus, districtius inhibentes, ut nullus super hoc vos de cetero turbare audeat vel molestare presumat. Nulli ergo etc. paginam nostre concessionis et inhibitionis infringere etc. Si quis autem etc. Datum Lugduni xv kal. iunii pontificatus nostri anno quarto.

A. 16 p. 109 inter privilegia papalia Traiecti asservata. In margine adscriptum: „In Welhen“, sic ut altera vox post haec deleta esse videatur.

---

511. *1247 aprilis 25 Lugduni. Innocentius IV confirmat ordini Theutonico bona acquisita et acquirenda, et eius protectionem suscipit.*

Innocentius episcopus servus servorum dei dilectis filiis .. preceptori et fratribus hospitalis sancte Marie Theutonicorum Ierosolimitani salutem et apostolicam benedictionem. Sacrosancta Romana ecclesia devotos et humiles filios ex assuete pietatis officio propensius diligere consuevit et, ne pravorum hominum molestiis agitentur, eos tamquam pia mater sue protectionis munimine confovere. Eapropter, dilecti in domino filii, vestris iustis postulacionibus grato concurrentes assensu personas vestras et locum, in quo divino estis obsequio mancipati, cum omnibus bonis, que impresentiarum rationabiliter possidetis aut in futurum iustis modis prestante domino poteritis adipisci, sub beati Petri et nostra protectione suscipimus. Specialiter autem libertates et immunitates a Romanis pontificibus predecessoribus nostris hospitali vestro concessas, necnon libertates et exemptiones secularium exactionum a regibus et principibus aliisque Christi fidelibus rationabiliter vobis indultas, necnon terras, possessiones, domos, vineas et alia bona vestra, sicut ea omnia iuste ac pacifice possidetis, vobis et per vos hospitali vestro auctoritate apostolica confirmamus et presentis scripti patrocinio communimus. Nulli ergo omnino liceat hanc nostre confirmationis paginam infringere vel ei ausu temerario contravenire. Si quis autem hoc attemptare presumpserit, indignationem omnipotentis dei et beatorum Petri et Pauli apostolorum eius se noverit incursurum. Datum Lugduni vii kalendas maii pontificatus nostri anno quarto.

Originale, cui modo plumbum deest, quondam (1466 aut 1525) ab ordine Theutonico Polonis exhibitum in archivo regni Polonici asservabatur. Citatur in Inventario archivi Cracoviensis p. 65: Innocentius papa IV bona eorundem cruciferorum sub protectionem b. Petri et sedis apostolicae suscipit, libertates a Romanis pontificibus indultas approbat. Lugduni p. a. 4. Cracovia Varsoviam, inde in regium Prussicum Berolinense devectum est, hinc a. 1865 iulio Regimontano archivo restitutum, ubi etiam servatur transsumtum Iohannis Progk, imperialis notarii, d. d. Marienburgi 1389 maii 20.

---

512. *1247 iunii 13 Lugduni. Innocentius IV magistro et fratribus ordinis Theutonici indulget, quod, si contra eis a sede apostolica concessa privilegia apostolicas litteras impetrari contigerit, quae de ordine non faciant specialem mentionem, respondere ad eas non teneantur.*

Innocentius etc. Cum dilecti filii etc. Datum Lugduni idibus iunii pontificatus nostri anno quarto.

Originale cum bulla in filis sericeis rubris et luteis appensa quondam Confluentibus et Veteribus Iuncis nunc in archivo ordinis Theutonici Vindobonensi. Textum non habuimus ante oculos.

---

513. *1247 iunii 13 Lugduni. Innocentius IV repetit Gregorii IX n. 465 de 1235 novbr. 28.*

Innocentius etc. Quieti vestre etc. Datum Lugduni idus iunii pontificatus nostri anno quarto.

Sine dato (tantum Ludon̄) citatur R. 157 inter „Iuncensia“ et A. 16 p. 99. Citatur iam anno 1253 sept. 26 supra 83. — Cum dato: IV, 205 v. n. 3; exemplum transsumti per Cunradum decanum Basileensis maioris ecclesiae, Erkenfridum cantorem, Heinricum scolasticum et magistrum Ruedegerum praepositum de Columbaria confectum R. 103 inter Alsatica n. 17; A. 16 p. 108 „Traiecto“.

---

514. *1247 iulii 20 Lugduni. Innocentius IV repetit n. 4[illegible]3 de 1244 apr. 20.*

Innocentius etc. Cum de viris — compellamur. Datum Lugduni xiii kalendas augusti pontificatus nostri anno quinto.

Legitur etiam IV, 205 v.

---

515. *1247 iulii 23 Lugduni. Innocentius IV repetit Gregorii IX n. 436 de 1227 aug. 18.*

Innocentius etc. Quieti vestre etc. Datum Lugduni x kal. augusti pontificatus nostri anno quinto.

Duo originalia cum bullis et nota G. Ar., sibi simillima, quorum in altero pontificatus annus humore absumtus, asservantur in archivo Regimontano.

---

516. *1247 iulii 25 Lugduni. Innocentius IV repetit n. 481 de 1244 maii 17.*

Innocentius etc. Dilecti filii etc. Datum Lugduni viii kal. augusti pontificatus nostri anno quinto.

---

517. *1247 sept. 13 Lugduni. Innocentius IV repetit Honorii III n. 337 de 1221 ianuar. 19.*

Innocentius etc. venerabilibus etc. Querela dilectorum filiorum — reprehendi. Datum Lugduni idus septembris pontificatus nostri anno quinto.

Transsumtum in archivo Regimontano extans, ad instantiam Rudolfi de Dulchen comm. Spir. per iudices curiae episcopalis Spirensis confectum Spirae 1390 febr. 17 citat Napiersky I, 22 n. 81.

---

518. *1247 sept. 13 Lugduni. Innocentius IV repetit Honorii III n. 337 de 1221 ianuar. 19.*

Innocentius etc. Querela dilectorum etc. Datum Lugduni idus septembris pontificatus nostri anno quinto.

R. 146 inter Treverensia. Tantum a. 5 „Treviris“ A. 16 p. 116.

---

519. *1248 ianuarii 19 Laterani. Innocentius IV repetit n. 473 de 1241 apr. 20.*

Innocentius etc. Cum de viris etc. Datum Laterani xiiii kalendas februarii pontificatus nostri anno quinto.

---

520. *(Inter 1247 iunii 24 et 1248 iunii 23.) Innocentius IV repetit Honorii III n. 339 de 1221 ianuarii 20.*

Innocentius episcopus servus servorum dei etc. Dilecti filii, fratres hospitalis — fraternitati vestre per apostolica scripta — dimittant. Datum etc. anno quinto.

Cum dato: a. 5 „Treviris" sine inscriptione A. 16 p. 120.

---

521. *1251 ianuarii 18 Lugduni. Innocentius IV concedit praeceptori et fratribus ordinis Theutonici in Iuncis Leodiensis dioecesis, quod decimas in parochiis alienis de manibus laicorum redimere possint, rectorum ecclesiarum, in quarum parochiis decimae ipsae consistunt, et dioecesanorum earum accedente consensu.*

Or. quondam (Confluentinum?) Iuncense cum bulla in filis sericeis rubris et luteis appensa in archivo ordinis Theutonici Vindobonensi. Sed etiam generale eiusmodi emanasse colligere forsan licet inde, quod ad calcem Alexandri IV privilegii (Affectu sunt) de 1260 nov. 16 in A. 20 n. 103 legitur „Innocencius eiusdem tenoris in Leodio".

---

522. *1251 ianuarii 20 Lugduni. Innocentius IV liberum declarat ordinem Theutonicum in Alemannia ab exactionibus per praelatos in subsidium ecclesiae Romanae solvendis.*

Innocentius episcopus servus servorum dei dilectis filiis preceptori et fratribus hospitalis sancte Marie Theutonicorum in Alemannia salutem et apostolicam benedictionem. Ex tenore vestre petitionis accepimus, quod nonnulli ecclesiarum prelati ac nuncii et legati sedis apostolice pretextu subsidii ecclesie Romane aliquando quartam, quandoque quintam, interdum vero decimam seu vicesimam partem vestrorum proventuum a vobis exigere ac extorquere presumunt. Cum itaque vestra ferventer ad hoc desudet intentio, ut bona vobis provenientia refundatis in terre sancte subsidium et convertatis assidue in auxilium egenorum, et ex hoc dignum sit vobis in necessitatis continue constitutis articulo subveniri potius, quam de proventibus ipsis subsidium postulari; nos vestris supplicationibus annuentes, ut ad predictam quartam vel quintam aut decimam vel vicesimam solvendas minime teneamini, vobis auctoritate presentium concedimus de gratia speciali. Nulli ergo omnino hominum liceat hanc nostre concessionis paginam infringere vel ei ausu temerario contraire. Si quis autem hoc attemptare presumpserit, indignationem omnipotentis dei et beatorum Petri et Pauli apostolorum eius se noverit incursurum. Datum Lugduni xiii kal. februarii pontificatus nostri anno octavo.

Sine dato: A. 20 n. 88 Latine et Germanice, cum nota: In Colonia vel Methi. — Cum dato: Lugduni 13 kal. febr. p. n. a. 8 ed. Duellius II, 10 n. 12. — Cum dato: Lugduni 12 kal. febr. p. n. a. 8 ad praeceptorem et fratres hospitalis sancte Mariae Theutonicorum in Moravia, Boemia, Polonia missa R. 97 inter Alsatica n. 10.

---

523. *1252 martii 6 Perusii (cf. 1254 febr. 10). Innocentius IV eximit ordinem Theutonicum a constitutione nova, quod vel ipsi exemti de quibusdam apud ordinarios possint conveniri.*

Innocentius servus servorum dei dilectis filiis .. magistro et fratribus hospitalis sancte Marie Theutonicorum Ierosolimitani salutem et apostolicam benedictionem. Cum nuper duxerimus statuendum, ut exempti, quantacumque gaudeant libertate, nichilominus tamen racione delicti seu contractus aut rei, de qua contra ipsos agitur, iure possint coram locorum ordinariis conveniri et illi quoad hec suam in ipsos iurisdictionem, prout ius exegerit, exercere, vos dubitantes, ne per constitucionem huiusmodi libertatibus et immunitatibus vobis et ordini vestro per privilegia et indulgentias ab apostolica sede concessis preiudicari valeat, nobis humiliter supplicastis, ut providere super hoc indempnitati vestre paterna sollicitudine curaremus. Quia vero eiusdem ordinis sacra religio sic vos apud nos dignos favore constituit, ut nobis votivum existat vos ab omnibus, per que vobis possent provenire dispendia, immunes libenti animo preservare, auctoritate vobis presentium indulgemus, ut occasione constitutionis[1] huiusmodi nullum eisdem libertatibus et immunitatibus inposterum preiudicium generetur. Nulli ergo omnino hominum liceat hanc paginam nostre concessionis infringere vel ei ausu temerario contraire. Si quis autem hoc attemptare presumpserit, indignationem omnipotentis dei et beatorum Petri et Pauli apostolorum eius se noverit incursurum. Datum Perusii ii nonas marcii pontificatus nostri anno nono.

I, 85. Concordat n. 526 excepto initio. 1. consitutione I.

---

524. *1253 ianuarii 5 Perusii (cf. 1253 martii 17). Innocentius IV confirmat ordini Theutonico privilegia a praedecessoribus et quibusvis aliis collata.*

Innocentius episcopus servus servorum dei dilectis filiis magistro et fratribus hospitalis sancte Marie Theutonicorum Ierosolimitani salutem et apostolicam benedictionem. Solet annuere sedes apostolica piis votis et honestis petencium precibus favorem benivolum impertiri. Eapropter, dilecti in domino filii, vestris iustis postulacionibus grato concurrentes assensu omnes libertates et inmunitates a predecessoribus nostris Romanis pontificibus ac etiam archiepiscopis, episcopis, abbatibus et aliis ecclesiarum prelatis sive per privilegia seu alias indulgencias vobis et hospitali vestro concessas, necnon libertates et exempciones secularium exaccionum ab imperatoribus, regibus, principibus, ducibus, marchionibus, comitibus vel aliis Christi fidelibus racionabiliter vobis indultas, sicut eas iuste ac pacifice obtinetis, vobis et per vos eidem hospitali auctoritate apostolica confirmamus et presentis scripti patrocinio communimus. Nulli ergo omnino hominum liceat hanc nostre confirmationis paginam infringere vel ei ausu temerario contraire. Si quis vero hoc attemptare presumserit, indignacionem omnipotentis dei et beatorum Petri et Pauli apostolorum eius se noverit incursurum. Datum Perusii nonas ianuarii pontificatus nostri anno decimo.

Cum dato: Perusii non. ianuarii p. n. a. 10 citatur R. 97 inter Alsatica 11. Cum iisdem die et loco s. a. citatur R. 48 transsumtum Berchtoldi Basiliensis episcopi (sc. 1249 — 1262). — Cum dato: Perusii 16 kal. aprilis p. n. a. 10. originale cum bulla, ex veteri archivo ordinis Theutonici in Polonicum, inde in regium Prussicum Berolinense, hinc a. 1865 n Regimontanum devenit; ibidem transsumta 1. d. d. 1335 iulii 28 ad instantiam magistri a tribus notariis subscriptum et „in maiorem evidentiam" sigillis xxxiii praelatorum et personarum ecclesiasticorum communitum et 2. Iohannis Rigensis archiepiscopi d. d. 1412 decbr. 22. Mariaeburgi. Notandum hic est, in inventario Cracoviensis archivi p. 65 post Innocentii IV quasdam litteras datas Perusii quinto idus martii anno 1252 citari alias huius tenoris: „Idem omnes immunitates a Romanis pontificibus, ab archiepiscopis, episcopis, abbatibus ordini cruciferorum concessas libertatesque exactionum ab imperatoribus, regibus, principibus confirmat. Datum die et anno ut supra". Vix dubito, quin revera originale nunc Regimontanum spectetur; quum, quam pusilla fides inventarii illius compositorum sollertiae sit habenda, satis superque demonstraverimus; cf. N. P. P. B. 1861. 8, 284 sq. et v. Sybel Histor. Zeitschrift. 1864. 12, 249.

---

525. *1253 martii 17 Perusii. Innocentius IV repetit n. 524 de 1253 ian. 5.*

Innocentius etc. Solet annuere etc. Datum Perusii xvi kalendas aprilis pontificatus nostri anno decimo.

---

526. *1254 februarii 10 Laterani (cf. 1252 martii 6). Innocentius IV declarat constitutionem de exemtis coram ordinariis ob certas res conveniendis non derogare ordinis Theutonici libertatibus.*

Innocencius episcopus servus servorum dei dilectis filiis magistro et fratribus hospitalis sancte Marie Theotonicorum Ierosolimitani salutem et apostolicam benedictionem. Cum olim duxerimus statuendum, ut exempti, quantacunque gaudeant libertate, nichilominus tamen ratione delicti seu contractus aut rei, de qua contra ipsos agitur, rite possint coram locorum ordinariis conveniri et illi quoad hec suam in ipsos iurisdictionem, prout ius exigit, exercere; vos dubitantes, ne per constitucionem huiusmodi libertatibus et immunitatibus vobis et ordini vestro per privilegia et indulgencias ab apostolica sede concessas preiudicari valeat, nobis humiliter supplicastis, ut providere super hoc indempnitati vestre paterna sollicitudine curaremus. Quia vero eiusdem ordinis sacra religio sic vos apud nos dignos favore constituit, ut nobis votivum existat vos ab omnibus, per que vobis possent provenire dispendia, immunes libenti animo preservare, vobis auctoritate presencium indulgemus, ut occasione constitucionis huiusmodi nullum eisdem libertatibus et immunitatibus imposterum preiudicium generetur. Nulli ergo omnino hominum liceat, hanc paginam nostre concessionis infringere vel ei ausu temerario contraire. Si quis autem hoc attemptare presumpserit, indignacionem omnipotentis dei et beatorum Petri et Pauli apostolorum eius se noverit incursurum. Datum Laterani iiii idus februarii pontificatus nostri anno undecimo.

Sine dato: A. 20 n. 87 Latine et Germanice cum nota: „In Marpurg est privilegium". Ao. 11 „Treviris" A. 16 p. 117; IV, 20υ; R. 148 inter Treverensia. — Cum dato: Laterani 4 id. febr. p. n. a. 11. originale cum bulla in filis sericeis rubris et luteis appensa in archivo ordinis Theutonici Vindobonensi, quondam (Confl.) Vetero-Iuncense. Transsumtum abbatis s. Martini Treverensis, de quo sigillum avulsum, de 1268 2 kal. febr. in eodem archivo. In archivo Regimontano extat transsumti per officialem curie Treverensis 1292 apr. 5 in vigilia paschae editi transsumtum per officialem curiae Treverensis 1328 iunii 4 sabbato post festum sancti sacramenti confectum, a Iacobo quodam subscriptum et duplici sigillo munitum.

---

527. *1254 februarii 11 Laterani. Innocentius IV vetat a fratribus ordinis Theutonici exigi pecuniarium subsidium ad erigendas munitiones.*

Innocentius episcopus servus servorum dei venerabilibus fratribus archiepiscopis et episcopis ac dilectis filiis abbatibus etc. Ex parte dilectorum filiorum magistri et fratrum hospitalis sancte Marie Theutonicorum Ierosolimitani nobis gravis est oblata querela, quod nonnulli nobiles, milites et laici ab eis pro claudendis villis et castris ac erigendis[1] munitionibus subsidium pecuniarium contra iusticiam exigunt, quod si non dederint, illud ab eis auferunt violenter. Cum autem bona dictorum magistri et fratrum sint per totum deputata redemptoris obsequiis, pro cuius attollendo nomine ipsi nec rerum sustinere dispendium nec subire metuunt pericula personarum, discrecioni vestre per apostolica scripta mandamus, quatenus nobiles et alios supradictos, quod ab indebita illorum super premissis molestatione desistant, monere attentius et inducere procuretis, eos ad id, si necesse fuerit, per censuram ecclesiasticam, appellatione postposita, compescendo, non obstante, si aliquibus a sede apostolica sit indultum, quod suspendi vel interdici aut excommunicari non possint, nisi de indulto huiusmodi sibi concesso plena et expressa in nostris litteris mentio habeatur. Datum Laterani iii idus februarii pontificatus nostri anno undecimo.

Originale cum bulla in filis cannabinis appensa in archivo ordinis Theutonici Vindobonensi. A. 16 p. 78 sq. „Colonie". Ed. Hennes I, 143 n. 151 ex or. 1. irrigendis A. 16.

---

528. *1254 maii 18 Asisii. Innocentius IV ordini Theutonico in Alemannia reservat fratrum eius iura haereditaria exceptis feudalibus.*

Innocencius episcopus servus servorum dei dilectis filiis magistro et fratribus hospitalis sancte Marie Theotonicorum in Alamania salutem et apostolicam benedictionem. Devocionis vestre precibus inclinati, ut possessiones et alia bona mobilia et inmobilia, exceptis feudalibus, que liberas personas fratrum ad ordinem vestrum mundi relicta vanitate volancium et professionem facientium in eodem, si remansissent in seculo, racione successionis vel quocumque alio iusto titulo contigissent, petere, recipere ac retinere libere valeatis, vobis auctoritate presencium indulgemus. Nulli ergo omnino hominum liceat hanc paginam nostre concessionis infringere vel ei ausu temerario contraire. Si quis autem hoc attemptare presumpserit, indignacionem omnipotentis dei et beatorum Petri et Pauli apostolorum eius se noverit incursurum. Datum Asisii xv kal. iunii pontificatus nostri anno undecimo.

Sine dato: A. 20 n. 89 Latine et Germanice cum nota: „In Bysen et Alexander huic simile in Confluentia. Gregorius eiusdem tenoris". A. 16 p. 99 „Iuncis". — Cum dato: IV, 206 v. n. 6. Citatur „Asissii etc." R. 157 inter Iuncensia. Or. quondam Iuncense cum bulla in filis sericeis rubris et luteis appensa in archivo ordinis Theutonici Vindobonensi.

---

529. *(Inter 1243 iunii 28 et 1254 decbr. 7.) Innocentius IV ordini Theutonico concedit, ut in parochiis ecclesiarum suarum novalium quoque decimas percipiant.*

Innocentius episcopus servus servorum dei dilectis filiis etc. salutem et apostolicam benedictionem. Cum a nobis petitur, quod iustum est et honestum, tam vigor equitatis quam ordo exigit racionis, ut id per sollicitudinem officii nostri ad debitum perducatur effectum. Eapropter, dilecti in domino filii, vestris iustis postulacionibus grato concurrentes assensu, presencium vobis auctoritate concedimus, ut infra parrochias ecclesiarum vestrarum pro ea portione, quam ibidem habetis et percipitis maiores et veteres, novalium quoque decimas, de quibus aliquis hactenus non percepit, sine alieni iuris preiudicio percipere valeatis. Nulli ergo omnino hominum liceat hanc nostre concessionis paginam infringere vel ei ausu temerario contraire. Si quis autem hoc attemptare presumpserit, indignacionem omnipotentis dei et beatorum Petri et Pauli apostolorum eius se noverit incursurum. Datum etc.

Sine dato: R. 156 et A. 16 p. 99 utrobique inter Iuncensia.

---

530. *(Inter 1243 iunii 28 et 1254 decbr. 7.) Innocentius IV (Devotionis vestre) praeceptori et fratribus h. s. M. Th. de Nurenberg Babinbergensis dioecesis concedit, ut, quum generale terrae fuerit interdictum, liceat eis clausis ianuis non pulsatis campanis excommunicatis exclusis voce suppressa in capella propria divina officia celebrare.*

R. 7 inter Norimbergensia privilegia n. 9, ubi 33 memoratur, quod eiusdem transsumtum per Thomam ord. praed. patriarcham Ierusalemitanum Acconensis ecclesiae ministrum, ap. sed. legatum in praesentia Bartholomaei de Firmo notarii publici factum in Ellingensi domo sub n. 15 asservetur. Sine dubio hoc erat generale. Eadem concessio specialis de 1249 iunii 17

d. d. Lugduni xv kal. iulii p. a. 6 (Devotionis vestre) pro praeceptore et domo in Achingen Augustensis diocesis (Aichach in Bavaria); originale cum bulla in filis sericeis in archivo ordinis Theutonici Vindobonensi, quondam Mergenthemi. In designatione Mitowiensis archivi ap. Schirren 129 n. 66 citatur: Innocentius IV indulget magistro et fratribus Theutonicis in Livonia et Prussia clausis ianuis, non pulsatis campanis, voce suppressa sacra peragere exclusis tamen nominatim excommunicatis et interdictis.

---

531. *(Inter 1243 iunii 28 et 1254 decbr. 7.) Innocentius IV repetit Honorii III n. 329, de 1221 ianuar. 18 et Gregorii IX n. 464 de 1235 april. 28.*

Innocentius etc. Quociens a nobis etc.

Memoratur in Alexandri IV privilegio de 1257 aug. 16; vide infra ad hunc annum. Subiungimus hic fragmenta constitutionis Innocentianae, quae ordinem Theutonicum non tangit, sed novitiorum probationem apud Benedictinos videtur spectare. Quum tamen in codice B. I, 85 sq. quamvis plurimam partem erasa inveniatur, hic sistendum fuit. Num forsan alio loco diu prelo subiecta sit integra, notitiam non habui. „Innocentius episcopus servus servorum dei et cetera. Non solum in favorem conversi, sed eciam monasterii probationis tempus a sanctis patribus est indultum, ut ille asperitatem istius et istud mores illius valeat experiri. In regula quoque beati Benedicti legitur, ut ad conversionem noviter venienti non facilis sit ingressus, sed, sicut dicit apostolus, an sit a deo spiritus comprobetur et dura et aspera, per que itur ad dominum, exponantur. Preterea in eadem regula subiungitur, ut dicatur: „Ecce lex, sub qua militare desideras; si eam observare potes, ingredere; alioquin, liber venisti, liber discede!" Insuper felicis recordacionis papa Gregorius, predecessor noster, statuit, ut positi in probacione novicii ante susceptum religionis habitum, qui profitentibus dari consuevit, seu ante professionem emissam ad statum pristinum redire possint libere infra annum, et ad omnem ambiguitatem amovendam, cum in quibusdam locis religiosis habitus novitiorum non distinguatur[1] ab habitu professorum probationis tempore. . . a . tur vestes, que profitentibus conceduntur, ut novitiorum ac professorum habitus discernatur. Licet igitur zelum animarum habentes eas lucrari domino sollicite cupiamus, quia tamen decet et expedit, ut de ordine p . . . . non desit . . cium racionis, ne, unde spiritualis pro . . queratur, inde salutis dispendium subscipiatis, vobis de fratrum nostrorum consilio in virtute obedientie et sub pena excommunicacionis auctoritate presencium districtius inhibemus, ne ante annum probacionis elapsum, qui in . . . . in sub . . . um . . . humane fragilitatis regulariter ins . . . . . quequam ad pro . . . . . . vestri ordinis seu rerum rem seculi faciendam recipere presumatis nec constitutum in probacione novicium aliquatenus inpedire, quominus infra eundem annum probacionis ad aliam religionem quam maluerit transeat . . . . et sua . . . . non obstante . . . . a nobis . . . . quod . . . . in quibuslibet literis apostolicis inpetratis seu etiam inpetrandis, que de premissis expressam non faciant mentionem. Quodsi forte contra huiusmodi inhibicionem quemquam recipere presumpseritis . . . . receptum . . . . . . nullatenus vestro esse ordini alligatum vosque a receptione quorumlibet ac professione eorum fore ipso facto suspensos et insuper pene subiiciendos, que fratribus ipsius ordinis pro culpis iniungi gravioribus consuevit".

1. extinguatur B.

---

532. *1255 martii 15 Neapoli. Alexander IV concedit ordini Theutonico in Livonia et Prussia, quod fratres, qui in saeculo de rapinis vixerint, consilio fratrum confessorum suorum de absolucione acquiescant.*

Alexander episcopus servus servorum dei dilectis filiis magistro et preceptoribus universis hospitalis sancte Marie Theutonicorum in Livonia et Pruscia salutem et apostolicam benedictionem. Ex parte vestra fuit propositum coram nobis, quod aliqui ex fratribus vestre cure commissis super eo conscientie scrupulum patiuntur, quod de rapinis et incendiis, que adhuc manentes in seculo perpetrarunt, sive de debitis, quibus tenebantur astricti ante susceptum religionis habitum, satisfacere neglexerunt, unde contingit, quod, licet ipsi sub obediencie iugo in remotis vagent nec habeant bona, de quibus iniuriam et dampna passis valeat satisfactio provenire, tamen instanter a vobis petunt, ut eos ad propria remittatis veniam, que de ipso facto provenire non potest, saltem precibus obtenturos. Quia vero huiusmodi discursus posset in grave dispendium ordinis et etiam animarum periculum redundare, nos super hoc de circumspectione sedis apostolice salubriter providentes presentium vobis auctoritate concedimus, quod predicti fratres confessorum suorum in hac parte acquiescant consilio saniori et illo sint omnino contenti, maxime cum ipsi tamquam aliquod proprium non habentes a predicta satisfactione per inopiam excusentur et apud deum pro contritione spiritus ac voluntate bona maneant absoluti, cum etiam sit decentius, quod ipsi, qui relictis omnibus secuti sunt dominum, infra domos vestras obedientie virtuti humili devocione deserviant, quam quod tali pretextu labori dampnoso et redundanti vobis ac fratribus vestris in scandalum se committant. Datum Neapoli idus marcii pontificatus nostri anno primo.

Or. cum bulla in archivo Regimontano, in cuius dorso legitur: „privilegium fratris Hinrici de Rechteren comm. in Dantzik" (i. e. 1348—51).

---

533. *1255 martii 18 Neapoli. Alexander IV ordini Theutonico in Prussia concedit, quod presbyteri eorum in minoribus delictis a priore ordinis presbytero absolutionem adipiscantur.*

Alexander episcopus servus servorum dei dilectis filiis . . magistro et fratribus hospitalis sancte Marie Theutonicorum in Pruscia salutem et apostolicam benedictionem. Canonica constitutione cavetur, quod — se in claustro — non sunt ad apostolicam sedem mittendi, sed — merito sit ad Romanam ecclesiam recursus habendus. Nos ergo ad vos statutum huiusmodi duximus — requirenda per . . priorem ordinis vestri, qui sicut audivimus, presbyter esse dinoscitur, fratribus vestris absolucionis beneficium impendatur. Datum Neapoli xv kal. aprilis pontificatus nostri anno primo.

Cum dato: Neapoli 15 kal. apr. p. n. a. 1 originale cum bulla in archivo Regimontano. Hic adhibitum, ut conferatur cum privilegio de 1257 iulii 11, quod differentem habet finem.

---

534. *1256 aprilis 8 Laterani. Alexander IV concedit ordini Theutonico, ut praelatis de eius ecclesiis tantum vetera iura petere liceat.*

Alexander etc. magistro et fratribus etc. Ante oculos mentis nostre[1] habemus cotidie necessitatem maximam terre sancte. Non enim possumus nec debemus casus ipsius miserabiles oblivisci et ideo ad devotionis vestre fervorem, cum pro subventione terre predicte nec personis vestris parcatis nec rebus, sicut est hoc tempore oportunum, debitum respectum habentes dignis vos laudibus exinde commendamus. Quia vero, sicut eiusdem terre negocium maius subsidium exigit et vos[2] ei habundantius subvenire[3], sic ampliorem promeremini dilectionis[4] graciam et favorem, cum ita viscera pietatis et compassionis expandatis ad dictum negocium, ut a nobis et aliis vos oporteat ad tante caritatis opus liberaliter adiuvari, iura vestra[5], quantum nobis gracia divina concedit, integra et inconcussa servare proponimus et vobis benignitatis nostre habundantiam in benedictionibus dulcedinis exhibere. Quapropter, dilecti in domino filii, quieti et tranquillitati vestre providere volentes auctoritate vobis presentium vestris inclinati supplicationibus indulgemus, ut archiepiscopi et episcopi et alii ecclesiarum prelati in vestris, quas habetis et tenetis, ecclesiis salva procuratione, si qua debetur eisdem, eo tantummodo sint iure contenti, quod ipsi et predecessores eorum a vobis et predecessoribus vestris noscuntur hactenus habuisse. Quodsi amplius ex dictis ecclesiis petere vel extorquere contenderint, vobis id liceat auctoritate sedis apostolice denegare super hoc coram nobis exhibere paratis iusticie complementum. Nulli ergo etc. Si quis autem etc. Datum Laterani vi idus aprilis pontificatus nostri anno secundo.

Sine dato: II, 118 n. 74. — Cum dato: A. 16 p. 24 ex instrumento Venetiis asservato d. d. Padua 1349 mense ianuario facto et a tribus notariis subscripto. 1. pro mentis nostre: nostros A. 16. 2. exigit vos A. 16. 3. subvenitis A. 16. 4. dilectionem II. 5. vita nostra II.

535. *1256 iulii 11 Anagnie. Alexander IV domus ordinis Theutonici liberat ab impensis et sumtibus legatis vel nunciis s. Romanae ecclesiae praestandis.*

Alexander episcopus servus servorum dei dilectis filiis magistro et fratribus hospitalis sancte Marie domus Theutonicorum Iherosolimitani salutem et apostolicam benedictionem. Cum preter pauperem victum vestrum omnia bona vestra hospitalitati et aliis piis operibus officiosissime sint exposita, satis inhumane aliis auferri videtur egenis, quidquid[1] a vobis violencia vel ingenio extorquetur, nec, quia dominus manuum vestrarum operibus benedicens viaticum peregrinationis vestre, quanto magis illud fraterna caritate in usus pauperum distribuitis, tanto magis celesti alimonia multiplicat, vos[2] estis deterioris conditionis habendi, sed potius melioris, cum nonnisi vasis paratis[3] celestis gracie oleum infundatur, quod pauperis deficientibus vasis stetit. Licet igitur largiente domino domus vestre plus solito temporalium floreant ubertate, quia tamen exinde uberius pauperibus subvenitur, nos volentes eo vos de speciali gracia favorabilius confovere, quo exinde illi propensius complacere nos credimus, qui, quod uni ex minimis suis fit, sibi reputat esse factum, devocioni vestre auctoritate presentium indulgemus, ne apostolice sedis legati vel nuncii, cardinalibus ecclesie Romane duntaxat exceptis, procurationes pecuniarias a vobis et domibus vestris exigere vel extorquere presumant, sed, cum ad domos vestras accesserint, cibis regularibus sint contenti. Nulli ergo omnino hominum liceat hanc paginam nostre concessionis infringere etc. Si quis autem etc. Datum Anagnie v idus iulii pontificatus nostri anno secundo.

Ex transsumto de 1201 sc. 1301 (m° cc° primo!!) sub sigillis Philippi abbatis Scotorum et fratris Friderici gardiani fratrum minorum Wumam (i. e. Wiennae) commorantium, facto, quod Venetiis asservabatur, in A. 16 p. 23. — In designatione Mitowiensis archivi ap. Schirren p. 130 n. 101 Alexandri IV duplex ibi existens concessio citatur, ut, ubicunque ordini Theutonico placuerit, mercaturam facere ei liceat. Quod privilegium secundum Dudik Des hohen Deutschen Ritterordens Münzsammlung p. 85, transsumtum per Albertum Brunswicensem ducem, provincialem balivae ad Athesin (c. 1338), est in archivo ordinis Theutonici Vindobonae: (1256 aug. 13) Viterbii id. aug. p. a. 3 praeceptori et fratribus hospitalis s. Mariae Theutonicorum in Livonia. (Cum preter) concedit, quum absque mercimoniis laudabiliter iuxta votum negocium fidei non possent, in omnibus locis et terris, ubi viderint expedire, merces eorum vendere et emere per idoneas ordinis personas. 1. quidquam A. 16. 2. alimonie multiplicati non A. 16. 3. parattis A. 16.

---

536. *1257 februarii 27 Laterani. Alexander IV confirmat ordini Theutonico divinum officium secundum ordinem Praedicatorum redactum.*

Alexander episcopus servus servorum dei dilectis filiis magistro et conventui[1] hospitalis sancte Marie Theutonicorum Ierosolimitani salutem et apostolicam benedictionem. Pie conversationis et vite vestre merita nos inducunt, ut desideria vestra in hiis, que digne possumus, affectu benevolo compleamus. Sane divinum officium, quod secundum ordinem dilectorum filiorum fratrum Predicatorum in ordine vestro ex concessione sedis apostolice, prout accepimus, observatur, ad quamdam formam secundum deum religioni vestre congruam et salubrem per quosdam ex fratribus vestris clericis viros utique timoratos et providos ac in spiritualibus circumspectos cum magna diligentia et vigilante studio est redactum. Nos itaque vestris supplicationibus inclinati, quod in hac parte factum est, ratum habentes et firmum, id auctoritate apostolica de certa scientia confirmamus et presentis scripti patrocinio communimus, districtius inhibentes, ut de predicta forma ipsius officii, que ad presens in eodem ordine vestro servatur, nullus sine consensu maioris et sanioris partis vestrum aliquid de cetero innovare vel immutare presumat. Irritum etiam et inane decernimus, si contra huiusmodi confirmationem et inhibitionem nostram secus fuerit attemptatum. Nulli ergo omnino hominum liceat hanc paginam nostre confirmationis, inhibitionis et constitutionis infringere vel ei ausu temerario contraire. Si quis autem hoc attemptare presumpserit, indignationem omnipotentis dei et beatorum Petri et Pauli apostolorum eius se noverit incursurum. Datum Laterani iii kal. martii, pontificatus nostri anno tertio.

Sine dato: II, 133 v. magistro et conventui; A. 20 n. 104 Latine et Germanice cum nota: „est in Meguncia vel in Mergintheym, Frankinfort vel Erfordia vel Aldinburg“; „Is ist zcu Mencze item zcu Mergentheym adir Frankinfort, Erffort ader Aldenburg“. Apographum fere de anno 1423 valde corruptum et mutilum in fine e codice 4 n. 10 bibliothecae, quae dicitur Omnium Sanctorum, ad aedem Marianam Dantisci asservatae ed. Th. Hirsch Die Oberpfarrkirche von S. Marien in Danzig. Danzig 1843. 8°. I, 211, unde repetiit male Alexandro V (1409 — 1410) adscribens Krüger Der kirchliche Ritus in Preufsen während der Herrschaft des Deutschen Ordens in Zeitschrift für die Geschichte und Alterthumskunde Ermlands. Braunsberg 1866. III, 704. — Cum dato ex originali tunc Mergenthemensia archivi, quod nunc cum bulla in filis sericeis appensa in archivo ordinis Theutonici Vindobonensi asservatur, ed. de Wal Recherches II, 352; unde repetiit Hennes I, 152 n. 163. — Cum dato etiam A. 16 p. 4 sq. „Venetiis". 1. conventui II. 2. fratribus H.

---

537. *1257 martii 6 Laterani. Alexander IV ordini Theutonico confirmat privilegia.*

Alexander episcopus servus servorum dei dilectis filiis magistro et fratribus hospitalis sancte Marie Theutonicorum Ierosolimitani salutem et apostolicam benedictionem. Ad assiduum Christi servitium deputatos favore precipuo prosequi Romana debet ecclesia, ut in illos potissime gratiam sue benignitatis extendat, qui vacando divinis obsequiis noscuntur amplius promereri. Quia igitur eterni regis beneplacitis vos taliter mancipastis, cum acceptabile valde ipsius obsequium personarum periculis minime formidatis, intrepidis prosequamini animis et viribus indefessis pro terre Ierosolimitanae tutela Christi sanguine rubricate continue decertantes, decet profecto et expedit, ut copiosis vos corroboremus favoribus vestroque ordini apostolice gratie dexteram porrigamus. Cum igitur apostolica sedes nonnulla privilegia et quamplures indulgentias et gratias eidem ordini sub diversitate temporum duxerit concedenda, nos cupientes ea, que ipsi ordini et vobis a predicta sede concessa sunt, non solum integra et illesa servare, immo potius, quantum cum deo possumus, adaugere, vestris supplicationibus inclinati huiusmodi privilegia, indulgentias et gratias dicto ordini, non obstantibus quibuslibet constitutionibus, provisionibus, diffinitionibus, ordinationibus et declarationibus factis et promulgatis a sede predicta, per quas vestris privilegiis et indulgentiis, gratiis et libertatibus in nullo derogari volumus, auctoritate apostolica confirmamus et presentis scripti patrocinio communimus, decernentes omnes excommunicationis, interdicti et suspensionis sententias, si quas in vos vel vestrum aliquos, aut in ecclesias seu quelibet loca dicti ordinis pretextu predictarum constitutionum, provisionum, diffinitionum, declarationum necnon litterarum super hiis a sede obtentarum eadem promulgari contigerit, irritas et inanes. Declarationem tamen, constitutionem et ordinationem a predicta sede factam vel editam super decimis novalium et circa indultum apostolicum, quod plerisque conceditur, ut pro ea portione, qua veteres eos contingunt, novalium decimas percipere valeant, volumus et precipimus inviolabiliter observari. Nulli ergo omnino hominum liceat hanc nostre confirmacionis, constitucionis et precepti paginam infringere vel ei ausu temerario contraire. Si quis autem hoc attemptare presumpserit, indignacionem omnipotentis dei et beatorum Petri et Pauli apostolorum eius se noverit incursurum. Datum Laterani ii non. martii pontificatus nostri anno tertio.

E transsumto fr. Bonacursi, Tyrensis archiepiscopi de ord. praed., vicarii patriarchatus Ierosolimitani et episcopatus Acconensis, et fr. Gailardi, Bethleemitani episcopi, auctoritate ad instantiam fr. Iohannis magni praeceptoris domus hospitalis sancte Marie Theutonicorum Ierosolimitanae per Iohannem clericum Acconensem 1277 oct. 19 Accon confecto in archivo Regimontano ed. in Livl. Urkundenb. I, 382 n. 295. Apographum transsumti huius in R. 36 inter Ellingensia n. 19. In eodem archivo etiam tria transsumta exstant: 1. d. d. 1341 dec. 2. Rigae per fr. guardianum, cuius sigillum appendet, ceterosque fratres minores in Riga. 2. d. d. 1321 vigilia pentecostes (iunii 6) in castro Velin per Nicolaum Tarbatensem episcopum, cuius sigillum deest, Egbertum abbatem Padensem, Wezcelum priorem ord. praedic. Rigensem. 3. 1393 maii 29 in castro s. Mariae petente Wenemaro magistro Livoniae per Heinricum Wladislaviensem et Iohannem abbatem Polplinensem. Transsumtum Henrici Babenbergensis et Alberti Ratisponensis episcoporum d. d. ind. XV (1257?) mensis iulii die 8, „cum Viterbii in supradicti domini pape (sc. Alexandri IV) curia existeremus", in archivo ordinis Theutonici Vindobonensi; sigilla avulsa. Memoratur a Duellio II, 11 n. 15. — A. 20 n. 130 Latine et Germanice cum nota: „Est in Velin" „unde is zcu Velin Lyfflande".

538. *1257 martii 8 Laterani. Alexander IV ordini Theutonico concedit, quod ad provisionem alicuius per litteras apostolicas vel legatorum non teneatur, si non expressa indulgentiae huius ibi fiat mentio.*

Alexander episcopus servus servorum dei dilectis filiis magistro et fratribus hospitalis sancte Marie Theotonicorum Ierosolimitani salutem et apostolicam benedictionem. Vestre meritis devocionis inducimur, ut vos speciali gracia prosequamur. Hinc est, quod nos vestris supplicacionibus annuentes auctoritate vobis presencium indulgemus, ut ad provisionem alicuius impensionibus vel beneficiis ecclesiasticis per litteras apostolice sedis et legatorum eius impetratas, per quas non sit ius alicui acquisitum, aut eciam impetrandas minime teneamini nec ad id compelli possitis, nisi huiusmodi littere apostolice impetrande de indulgencia huiusmodi et toto tenore ipsius expressam fecerint mencionem. Nulli ergo omnino hominum liceat hanc paginam nostre concessionis infringere vel ei ausu temerario contraire. Si quis autem hoc attemptare presumpserit, indignacionem omnipotentis dei et beatorum Petri et Pauli apostolorum eius se noverit incursurum. Datum Laterani viii idus marcii pontificatus nostri anno tercio.

Sine dato: R. 154 inter Iuncensia; A. 20 n. 105 Latine et Germanice cum nota: „In Markburg vel in Bysin". „Dis is zcu Marcburg. Item zu Bisin". — Cum dato: IV, 207. Originale cum bulla in filis rubris et luteis appensa quondam Iuncense in archivo ordinis Theutonici Vindobonensi.

539. *1257 maii 3 Laterani (cf. iulii 11). Alexander IV ordinis Theutonici fratribus in terrae sanctae servitio occupatis indulgentiam transeuntibus in eiusdem subsidium concessam concedit.*

Alexander episcopus servus servorum dei dilectis filiis magistro et fratribus hospitalis sancte Marie Theutonicorum Ierosolimitani salutem et apostolicam benedictionem. De fervore sincerissime devotionis vestre inspirante divina gracia processisse dinoscitur, quod reliquistis omnia et sequuti estis dominum, ut de ipsius ineffabili pietate vobis proveniat gloria civium supernorum. Huiusmodi siquidem obtentu glorie vos cum omni diligentia desudatis obsequiis terre sancte ducentes pro deliciis, si pro Christi nomine bibatis calicem salutifere passionis. Verum, licet pro huiusmodi piis meritis acquiratur vobis premium perpetue claritatis, quia tamen decens et dignum esse dinoscitur, ut a benignitate sedis apostolice pretextu meritorum ipsorum specialem gaudeatis graciam recepisse, nos de omnipotentis dei misericordia et beatorum Petri et Pauli apostolorum eius auctoritate confisi vobis universis et singulis vere penitentibus et confessis, quamdiu manetis in predicte terre servitio, illam concedimus veniam peccatorum, que transeuntibus in eiusdem terre sancte subsidium a sede apostolica in generali concilio est concessa. Datum Laterani v non. maii pontificatus nostri anno iii.

Sine dato: II, 118v. n. 76 Praeceptori et fratribus hospitalis s. Mariae Theutonicorum in Livoniae partibus directa („quamdiu in Livoniae servitio maneant") A. 20 n. 133 Latine et Germanice. — Cum dato: Laterani 5 non. maii p. a. 3 „Baruli" A. 16 p. 46. — Cum dato: Viterbii 5 idus iulii p. n. a. tertio „preceptoribus et fratribus universis hospitalis s. Marie Theutonicorum in Pruscie partibus constitutis". Orig. cum bulla in archivo Regimontano. „Secuti — Huiusmodi siquidem obtentu glorie vos fidei negotium in Pruscie partibus studetis cum omni diligentia promouere, ducentes pro deliciis, — quamdiu manetis in eiusdem Pruscie seruitio, illam — transeuntibus in terre sancte" etc. — Cum dato: 5 id. aug. Viterbii p. n. a. 3 or. cum bulla in filis sericeis appensa in archivo ordinis Theutonici Vindobonensi. Ed. Hennes I, 154 n. 167.

---

540. *1257 maii 3 Laterani (cf. 1257 iunii 11, 1257 aug. (8) 9). Alexander IV ordini Theutonico concedit, ut Friderici quondam imperatoris aut filiorum eius asseclis aut ob aliam rem excommunicatis receptis in ordinem huius clerici absolutionem impertiri possint, in pristinam sententiam relapsuris, si forte ad saeculum redeant.*

Alexander episcopus servus servorum dei dilectis filiis magistro et fratribus hospitalis sancte Marie Theutonicorum Ierosolimitani salutem et apostolicam benedictionem. Qui ex apostolici cura tenemur officii circa religionis augmentum attenti et vigiles inveniri, super hiis digne votis vestris annuimus, in quibus honorem vestri ordinis et animarum profectum contineri sentimus. Hinc est, quod nos vestris supplicationibus inclinati vobis auctoritate presencium indulgemus, ut illis, qui pro favore impenso quondam Frederico Romanorum imperatori aut Conrado seu Manfredo, natis eius, vel pro quacunque alia causa suspensionis aut interdicti vel excommunicacionis sentenciis sunt ligati et vestro cupiunt aggregari collegio, fratres presbiteri vestri ordinis possint absolucionis beneficium iuxta formam ecclesie impertiri, dummodo ipsi habitum vestrum assumant et sub illo una vobiscum virtutum domino famulentur. Volumus tamen, quod, si aliqui ex eisdem propter debitum sentenciis huiusmodi sunt astricti, de ipso satisfaciant, ut tenentur; ac eciam, quod ipsi, si forte vestro habitu derelicto ad seculum redeant, in pristinam sentenciam relabantur. Nulli ergo omnino hominum liceat hanc paginam nostre concessionis infringere vel ei ausu temerario contraire. Si quis autem hoc attemptare presumpserit, indignacionem omnipotentis dei et beatorum Petri et Pauli apostolorum se noverit incursurum. Datum Viterbii v nonas maii pontificatus nostri anno tercio.

Sine dato: R. 98 inter Alsatica n. 13 citatur. In designatione Mitowiensis archivi ap. Schirren p. 130 n. 99. — Cum dato: Laterani 5 non. maii p. n. a. 3 inter Treverensia „Cū ex" R. 136; A. 16 p. 116 „Baruli" p. 44 sq. Or. cum bulla in filis rubris et luteis appensa quondam Iuncense (Confluentinum) in archivo ordinis Theutonici Vindobonensi. — Cum dato: Viterbii 3 idus iunii p. n. a. 3. originale (cum dato mutilo; numerus enim ante idus est corrosus) in archivo Regimontano; R. 87 inter Mergenthemensia n. 45; A. 20 n. 91 Latine et Germanice cum nota: In Buken, in Treveri, in Colonia et in Mergintheim. — Cum dato: Viterbii 5 id. aug. p. n. a. 3. originale cum bulla in archivo Regimontano. Originale cum bulla in filis sericeis appensa, quondam Confluentinum, in archivo Vindobonensi, unde ed. Hennes I, 154 n. 167. Sed in catalogo archivi lego 6 idus aug. A. 16 p. 69 „Colonie" in duplo.

---

541. *1257 maii 29 Viterbii (cf. maii 30, 1258 iunii 25 et nov. 1). Alexander IV repetit Gregorii IX n. 427 de 1227 iulii 31.*

Alexander etc. Religiosos viros — compescatis. Datum Viterbii iv kal. iunii p. n. a. iii.

Sine dato: II, 120 v. n. 82*b*; A. 16 p. 115 „Treviris". — Cum dato: Viterbii 4 kal. iunii p. n. a. 3 originale cum bulla in filis sericeis rubris et luteis appensa dudum in domo Theutonica Vindobonensi, etiamnunc in archivo ordinis ibidem. — Cum dato: Viterbii 3 kal. iunii p. n. a. 3 originale cum bulla in archivo Regimontano; cf. Napiersky Index I, 33 n. 133; in eodem archivo transsumtum d. d. Accon 1277 octbr. 19 auctoritate Bonacursi Tyrensis archiepiscopi et Gailardi Betlehemitani episcopi per Iohannem clericum Acconensem confectum; cuius transsumti apographum R. 40 inter Ellingensia n. 25; R. 58 inter Ratisponensia n. 14. Ed. Duellius II, 11 n. 16 (passagium, caucagium). — Cum eodem dato in A. 16 p. 26 ex transsumto Venetiis asservato, sub sigillis Angeli, Gradensis ecclesiae patriarchae Dalmatiaque primatis, et Alberti episcopi Tarvisini d. 1257 m. iulii die xiiii exeuntis (i. e. iulii 18), indic. XV per Marcum presbyterum. Originale huius transsumti ex domo E(llingensi?) devenit in archivum ordinis Theutonici Vindobonense, ubi vel hodie exstat. Cum dato: Viterbii 7 kal. iulii p. n. a. 4. or. iam dudum domus Vindobonensis, cum bulla in filis sericeis rubris et luteis appensa in archivo ordinis Theutonici Vindobonensi. Citatur ap. Duellium l. l. in nota. De eodem dato: A. 16 p. 13 „Venetiis". — Cum dato: Anagnie 5 (sic!) nonas novembris (passagium, pontenagium, thelonium, tantagium (= caucagium) IV, 213 v. n. 12; R. 139 inter Treverensia ed. Lünig Teutsches Reichsarchiv XVI, 79 n. 73 et Notice historique sur l'ancienne Grande Commanderie dite des Vieux-Joncs. Gand 1849. 8°. 45 n. 5. Or. cum bulla in filis sericeis rubris et luteis appensa, quondam Iuncense, in archivo ordinis Theutonici Vindobonensi.

---

542. *1257 maii 30 Viterbii (cf. iunii 16). Alexander IV negat ordinem Theutonicum absque speciali mandato apostolico excommunicatione seu interdicto posse feriri.*

Alexander quartus episcopus servus servorum dei dilectis filiis magistro et fratribus hospitalis sancte Marie Theutonicorum Ierosolomitani salutem et apostolicam benedictionem. Cum vos tanquam speciales ecclesie Romane filios vestre religionis intuitu et consideratione obsequii, quod deo ferventer impenditis in ultramarinis partibus in defensione christiani nominis, diligamus; vestris precibus inclinati auctoritate vobis presentium indulgemus, ut nemini liceat sine speciali mandato Romani pontificis in vos presbiteros et laicos vestros, quorum aliqui vobis gratis, alii vero ad solidos serviunt, excommunicationis vel interdicti sententiam promulgare et, si quando in vos vel in eos ab aliquo huiusmodi sententia lata fuerit, non obmittatis ecclesias frequentare aut servitio domus vestre vel divinis officiis interesse, cum huiusmodi sententia sit irrita penitus et inanis. Nulli ergo omnino hominum liceat hanc paginam nostre concessionis infringere vel ei ausu temerario contraire. Si quis autem hoc attemptare presumpserit, indignationem omnipotentis dei et beatorum Petri et Pauli apostolorum eius se noverit incursurum. Datum Viterbii iii kalendas iunii pontificatus nostri anno tertio.

Sine dato citatur R. 140 inter Trevirensia, necnon A. 16 p. 115. Citatur in designatione Mitowiensis archivi 1621 Holmiam delati apud Schirren p. 131 n. 109 Bernhardi Tarbatensis episcopi et cuiusdam abbatis transsumtum. — Cum dato: Viterbii 17 kal. iunii p. n. a. 3 habent Caorsinus C. 4 et Senner fol. E. 5 (male: Cum nos), sed procul dubio errore typographi pro 16 kal. iulii, quod ex eodem transsumto exhibent IV, 207 v. et Ioh. 37. — Cum dato: Viterbii 3 kal. iunii p. n. a. 3. or. cum bulla in filis sericeis rubris et luteis appensa Iuncense quondam, nunc in archivo ordinis Theutonici Vindobonensi. E transsumto per Michaelem archiepiscopum Rigae confectum 1495 aug. 17 in archivo Regimontano asservato ed. Livl. U. B. I, 391 n. 303. In eodem archivo etiam tria transsumta 1. d. d. 1335 febr. 25. Rigae per Iacobum Osilianum episcopum confecto. Citat ex Hiärnii Collectaneis ad historiam Livonicam Napiersky in Indice II, 277 n. 3305. A. 16 p. 72 „Colonie"; 2. d. d. 1393 maii 29 Marienburgi ad instantiam magistri Livoniae confectum; 3. d. d. 1406 sept. 6 Herbipoli, requirente Rudigero de Dulken, magistro hospitalis in Brotselden, ord. hosp. s. M. Th. professo, per Wernerum de Hayn, officialem curiae Wirciburgensis. — Cum dato: Viterbii 16 kal. iulii p. n. a. 3. originale cum bulla in archivo Regimontano. R. 57 inter Ratisponensia n. 11; IV, 207 v. n. 3; Joh. 37; R. 47 inter Ellingensia n. 34 et A. 16 p. 64 „Marpurg". „Invenitur etiam in Mechelinia" apographum transsumti Gwidonis etc. nempe eiusdem ac R. 9 inter Norimbergensia n. 16. Cuius introitus: „Noverint universi presens publicum instrumentum inspecturi, quod nos frater Gwido de ordine sancti Augustini, dei gracia sancte Gradensis ecclesie patriarcha et Veneciarum Dalmacieque primas, et nos frater Iohannes de ordine fratrum minorum, divina miseracione Barine et Canusine sedis archiepiscopus, vidimus et de verbo ad verbum inspeximus et ad instanciam religiosi viri fratris Hartmanni de Heldruingen magistri hospitalis sancte Marie Theutonicorum Ierosolimitani transscribi et publicari fecimus quasdam literas felicis recordacionis domini Allexandri pape IIII cum vera bulla plumbea et filo serico integro et sano, non abolitas, non rasas, non cancellatas nec in aliqua sui parte viciatas, nichil addito vel diminuto vel mutato, quod possit immutare sentenciam vel substanciam, quarum tenor per omnia talis est". Clausula vero finalis: „In cuius rei testimonium et evidenciam pleniorem nos patriarcha et primas ac archiepiscopus supradicti ad instanciam prefati magistri, ut predictum est, transscriptum huiusmodi de verbo ad verbum de predicto originali sumptum et publicatum fecimus nostrorum sigillorum munimine roborari. Datum Viterbii anno domini m°. cc° lxxviii° indictione (vii^a omissum) nona die intrantis mensis septembris pontificatus domini Nycolai pape III anno primo". In archivo Regimontano transsumtum Casparis Pomezaniensis episcopi d. d. 1453 febr. 12 Risenburgi. — Caeterum textus concordat Honoriano n. 405 p. 334.

---

543. *1257 maii 30 Viterbii. Alexander IV repetit n. 541 de 1257 maii 29.*

Alexander etc. Religiosos viros etc. Datum Viterbii iii kal. iunii pontificatus nostri anno tercio.

---

544. *1257 iunii 1 Viterbii (cf. 1257 iunii 27, septbr. 9, 1258 novbr. 29). Alexander IV repetit Innocentii IV n. 478 de 1244 maii 3.*

Alexander etc. Cum dilectis etc. universitati vestre ad instar felicis recordacionis Innocencii pape predecessoris nostri etc. amittant. Datum Viterbii kal. iunii pontificatus nostri anno tercio.

Sine dato: R. 149 inter Treverensia; A. 20 n. 129 Latine et Germanice, ubi alio loco innuitur: Nota: Allexander in Colonia simile vel in Martpurg vel in Praga etc. — Cum dato: Viterbii kal. iunii p. n. a. 3. R. 55 inter Ratisponensia 5 (initium); A. 16 p. 2 sq. „Venetiis". Or. cum bulla in filis sericeis rubris et luteis appensa in archivo ordinis Theutonici Vindobonensi, iam dudum in domo Theutonica Vindobonensi. Transsumtum fr. Hartberi ministri fratrum ord. minorum per Austriam et conventus fratrum eiusdem ordinis in Wienna et fr. Rogeri prioris ord. praedicatorum in Wienna d. d. in Wienna 1271 xvi kal. maii cum tribus sigillis in eodem archivo. — Cum dato: Viterbii 5 idus septembris p. n. a. 3. or. cum bulla in filis sericeis rubris et luteis appensa, quondam Iuncense, in archivo ordinis Theutonici Vindobonensi. IV, 210 v. Ioh. 37; edd. Caorsinus C. 4 et Senner E. 5. — Cum dato: Viterbii 5 kal. iulii p. n. a. 4. or. ex parte mutilum cum bulla in filis sericeis rubris et luteis appensa in archivo ordinis Theutonici Vindobonensi, iam dudum in domo Vindobonensi. — Cum dato: Anagnie 3 kal. decembr. p. n. a. 4. transsumtum abbatis de Claustro et Arnoldi abbatis b. M. v. in Lucelburg et H. decani eiusdem villae cum sigillis 1. sigillum abbatis de claustro, 2. s. Arnoldi dei gra. abbat. scc. Marie de Lucelburg, 3. s. decani de Lucelbuch; in archivo ordinis Theutonici Vindobonensi d. d. 1258 in quadragesima Lutzelburg (i. e. 1259 ob aliud anni initium).

---

545. *1257 iunii 3 (cf. 15. 18. 27., iulii 1. 5.) Viterbii. Alexander IV repetit Honorii III n. 309 de 1221 ianuarii 9.*

Alexander etc. Vestra religio — indulgemus — incursurum. Datum Viterbii iii nonas iunii pontificatus nostri anno tercio.

Sine dato: „Treviris" A. 16 p. 116. — Cum dato: Viterbii 3 non. iunii p. n. a. 3. originale cum bulla in filis sericeis appensa quondam Mergenthemense in archivo ordinis Theutonici Vindobonensi. Aliud originale, cui deest bulla, ex ordinis Theutonici archivo in Polonicum, inde in regium Prussicum Berolinense, inde in Regimontanum venit. Citatur in Inventario archivi Cracoviensis p. 66: „Alexander IV cruciferis ordinis Theutonici eorumque terris, templis, omnes immunitates et indulgentias Templariis concessas communicat. Viterbii tertio non. iunii 1258". R. 41 inter Ellingensia n. 26 e transsumto: „Noverint universi etc., quod nos Matheus, dei gracia Cesariensis archiepiscopus, et nos frater Gaufridus de ordine predicatorum, eadem gracia episcopus Ebronensis, vidimus, legimus et de verbo ad verbum diligenter inspeximus quasdam litteras domini pape Alexandri IIII sanas et integras etc., quarum tenor per omnia talis est": ... „Quas quidem litteras scribi et publicari fecimus per Iohannem clericum Acconensem etc. anno domini m° cc° lxxvii° indictione vi^a die ultima mensis augusti, presentibus Petro de Maro, Petro de Castro regis, Nycolao clerico Acconensi"; Regimonti extat transsumtum d. d. Accon 1277 oct. 19 per Tyrensem archiepiscopum et Bethleemitanum episcopum confectum. IV, 207 n. 9. Edd. Duellius II, 11 n. 14. Lünig Teutsches Reichsarchiv XVI, 78. — Cum dato: Viterbii 17 kal. iulii p. n. a. 3. originale cum bulla in filis sericeis appensa in archivo ordinis Theutonici Vindobonensi, dudum domus Vindobonensis. E transsumto Regimontani archivi d. d. 1396 aug. 18 Vindobonae. ed. in Livl. U. B. I, 392. CCCIV. — Cum dato: Viterbii 14 kal. iulii p. n. a. 3. originale nunc sine plumbo in archivo Regimontano; A. 16 p. 46 „Baruli". — Cum dato: Viterbii 5 kal. iulii p. n. a. 3. VI, 355. — Cum dato: kal. iulii (p. n. a. 3) originale cum bulla in archivo ordinis Theutonici Vindobonensi. — Cum dato: Viterbii 3 non. iulii p. n. a. 3. ed. in Notice historique sur l'ancienne grande commanderie des chevaliers de l'ordre Teutonique dite des Vieux-Jones. Gand 1849. 8°. 44 n. 4.

---

546. *1257 iunii 5 (cf. 15.) Viterbii. Alexander IV repetit Honorii III n. 410.*

Alexander etc. Quanto maiora etc. Datum Viterbii nonas iunii pontificatus nostri anno tercio.

Cum dato: Viterbii non. iunii p. n. a. 3. originale cum bulla in archivo Regimontano. — Cum dato: Viterbii 17 kal. iulii p. n. a. 3. originale, cui modo deest bulla, in archivo Regimontano, ubi etiam transsumta 1. Engelberti Tarbatensis episcopi d. d. 1324 oct. 25 Segewolde; 2. per Rogerium de Barolo, archidiaconum, vicarium Bartholomaei, Tranensis archiepiscopi, vicecancellarii regni Siciliae, et Nicolaum Bertonum, Barolitanum iudicem Baroli 1336 maii 31 confectum; 3. d. d. Marienburgi 1393 maii 29. — A. 16 p. 46 „Baruli".

547. *1257 iunii 9 Viterbii. Alexander IV repetit Innocentii IV n. 497 de 1246 ianuarii 4.*

Alexander etc. Canonica constitutione etc. Datum Viterbii v id. iunii pontificatus nostri anno tercio.

Cf. infra 1257 iulii 11; quum non videatur nisi error iunii pro iulii. cf. n. 558.

548. *1257 iunii 11 Viterbii. Alexander IV repetit n. 540 de 1257 maii 3.*

Alexander etc. Quoniam ex etc. Datum Viterbii iii idus iunii pontificatus nostri anno tercio.

Hoc originale initium „Quoniam ex" habere diserte perhibetur.

549. *1257 iunii 13 Viterbii. Alexander IV repetit Innocentii IV n. 503 de 1245/46.*

Alexander etc. Paci et quieti — astrictos. Datum Viterbii id. iunii pontificatus nostri anno tercio.

Originale, de quo bulla avulsa deest, iam dudum domus Vindobonensis, etiamnunc in archivo ordinis Theutonici Vindobonensi, ed. Duellius II, 10 n. 13.

550. *1257 iunii 15 Viterbii. Alexander IV repetit n. 546 de 1257 iunii 5.*

Alexander etc. Quanto maiora etc. Datum Viterbii xvii kalendas iulii pontificatus nostri anno tercio.

551. *1257 iunii 15 Viterbii. Alexander repetit n. 545 de 1257 iunii 3.*

Alexander etc. Vestra religio etc. Datum Viterbii xvii kalendas iulii pontificatus nostri anno tercio.

552. *1257 iunii 16 Viterbii. Alexander IV repetit n. 542 de 1257 maii 30.*

Alexander etc. Cum vos tamquam etc. Datum Viterbii xvi kalendas iulii pontificatus nostri anno tercio.

553. *1257 iunii 18 Viterbii. Alexander IV repetit n. 545 de 1257 iunii 3.*

Alexander etc. Vestra religio etc. Datum Viterbii xiiii kalendas iulii pontificatus nostri anno tercio.

---

554. *1257 iunii 22 Viterbii. Alexander IV repetit Honorii III n. 339 de 1221 ianuarii 20.*

Alexander etc. Dilecti filii etc. Datum Viterbii x kal. iulii pontificatus nostri anno tercio.

Ex orig. bullato arch. Regim. ed. Voigt C. d. P. I, 105 n. 107; Livl. U. B. I, 393 n. 306.

---

555. *1257 iunii 27 Viterbii. Alexander IV repetit n. 545 de 1257 iunii 3.*

Alexander etc. Vestra religio etc. Datum Viterbii v kalendas iulii pontificatus nostri anno tercio.

---

556. *1257 iulii 1 (Viterbii). Alexander repetit n. 545 de 1257 iunii 3.*

Alexander etc. Vestra religio etc. Datum (Viterbii) kal. iulii pontificatus nostri anno tercio.

---

557. *1257 iulii 5 Viterbii. Alexander IV repetit n. 545 de 1257 iunii 3.*

Alexander etc. Vestra religio etc. Datum Viterbii iii nonas iulii pontificatus nostri anno tercio.

---

558. *1257 iulii 11 Viterbii (cf. 1257 aug. 8, 1261 martii 28, aprilis 5). Alexander IV repetit Innocentii IV n. 497 de 1246 ianuarii 4.*

Alexander etc. Canonica constitutione — se in claustro percusserint — sedem apostolicam — recursus ad Romanam ecclesiam sit — Nos igitur statutum huiusmodi ad vos duximus extendendum apostolica auctoritate statuentes — requirenda et excessus, ut predictum est, adeo gravis existat, quod super eo apostolice provisionis auxilium debeat implorari, fratribus vestris absolutionis beneficium per fratres presbiteros vestri ordinis impendatur. Datum Viterbii v idus iulii pontificatus nostri anno tercio.

Sine dato: magistro et fratribus etc. inscripta A. 20 n. 93 Latine et Germanice cum nota: „Et est in Colonia. Item Innocencius eiusdem tenoris in Marpurg". Specialiter inscriptum: praeceptori et fratribus in Alemannia R. 85 inter Mergenthemensia 42. — Cum dato: Neapoli 15 kal. aprilis p. n. a. 1 (i. e. 1255 martii 18) inscriptum „magistro et fratribus h. s. M. Th. in Prusia" originale in archivo Regimontano. In designatione Holmiensi Mitowiensis archivi ap. Schirren p. 131 n. 103 citatur: 1255 aut 1257 Alexandri papae IV constitutio de absolutione fratrum ordinis. Ibidem etiam p. 130 n. 98: Papa Alexander IV facultatem dat presbyteris ordinis absolvendi futuros fratres a rapinis, incendiis aliisque ante commissis delictis, cum poenitentiae salutaris impositione. — Cum dato: Viterbii 5 id. iulii p. n. a. 3 duo originalia cum bullis in archivo Regimontano; ibidem duo transsumta Bonacursi Tyrensis archiepiscopi, vicarii patriarchatus

Ierosolimitani et episcopatus Acconensis, et Gailardi Bethlehemitani episcopi per Iohannem clericum Acconensem d. d. Accon 1277 oct. 19 cum sigillis; apographum transsumti R. 35 inter Ellingensia n. 18. R. 56 inter Ratisponensia 9; A. 16 p. 71 „Colonie". Ex originali Vindobonensi quondam Confluentino, cum bulla in filis cannabinis appensa ed. Hennes I, 154 n. 166 (Canonica institutione). — Cum dato: Viterbii 5 id. iunii p. n. a. 3. A. 16 p. 44 „Baruli"; cf. n. 547; ita ut erroris praesumptio non sit exclusa. — Cum dato: Viterbii 6 idus augusti p. n. a. 3. originale cum bulla in filis cannabinis appensa in archivo ordinis Theutonici Vindobonensi inscriptum „preceptoribus et fratribus h. s. M. Th." IV, 209 n. 6; A. 16 p. 66 et R. 123 inter Marburgensia „preceptoribus et fratribus h. s. M. Th. presentes litteras inspecturis". — „Colonie" „preceptori et fratribus" A. 16 p. 73. „Praeceptoribus et fratribus ordinis Theutonici in Alemannia" originale cum bulla in filis cannabinis appensa quondam Mergenthemi, nunc in archivo ordinis Theutonici Vindobonensi exstat. — Cum dato: Laterani 5 kal. aprilis p. n. a. 7. ex originali Gracensi VII, 368. — Cum dato: Laterani non. aprilis p. n. a. 7. A. 16 p. 24 sq.

---

559. *1257 iulii 11 Viterbii. Alexander IV repetit n. 539 de 1257 maii 3.*

Alexander etc. preceptoribus et fratribus universis hospitalis s. Marie Theutonicorum in Pruscie partibus constitutis etc. De fervore etc. Datum Viterbii v idus iulii pontificatus nostri anno tertio.

---

560. *1257 iulii 28 Viterbii (cf. aug. 2. 9.). Alexander IV concedit ordini Theutonico, ut clericos et laicos statim pro fratribus recipiant; receptos invitum deserere vetat.*

Alexander episcopus servus servorum dei dilectis filiis preceptoribus et fratribus universis hospitalis s. Marie Theutonicorum presentes litteras inspecturis salutem et apostolicam benedictionem. Pro consequenda gloria celestis patrie, que fidelibus universis vacantibus innocentis vite studio a divina provenit pietate, nos toto cordis affectu ad hoc semper intendimus, ut animarum salutem in omnibus et per omnia procuremus. Sane nonnulli ex fratribus vestri ordinis in terra sancta et Livonie ac Pruscie partibus pro defensione catholice fidei manibus infidelium, prout accepimus, crudeliter sunt occisi, unde fit, quod idem ordo plurimum indigere dinoscitur, ut de novellis fratribus restauretur et per consequens in obsequio crucifixi sit eo robustior, quo plures habuerit ad pugnam idoneos et ad triumphale bravium expeditos. Pro tanta siquidem necessitatis ac utilitatis evidentia et obtentu etiam dilecti filii magistri Ioannis de Capua, notarii nostri, qui devotis frequenter implorat precibus, ut ordinem ipsum apostolice benignitatis gratia iugiter perfundamus, universitati vestre auctoritate presentium de speciali gratia indulgemus, ut clericos seu laicos liberos et absolutos, qui relicta vanitate seculi vestro sacro collegio desiderant aggregari et propter devotionis sue fervorem petunt humiliter ac instanter a vobis statim recipi et sine dilatione vestrum habitum sibi dari, libere, prout in eodem ordine vestro fuit hactenus observatum, in fratres recipere valeatis. Statuimus etiam, quod illi, qui post factam in ordine ipso professionem assumpserunt vestre religionis habitum vel assumpserint in futurum, revertendi ad seculum pretextu alicuius constitutionis contrarie nullam habeant facultatem nec ipsorum alicui licitum sit post factam professionem et semel assumptam crucem habitum vestre professionis abiicere vel ad alium locum maioris seu minoris religionis obtentu invitis sive inconsultis fratribus aut eo, qui magister exstiterit, transmigrare, nullique ecclesiastice secularive persone ipsos suscipere liceat vel tenere. Si vero, quod absit, aliquis fratrum ipsorum contra huiusmodi constitutionem nostram ad seculum redire presumpserit vestro habitu derelicto, volumus, quod in eum per fratres presbyteros sepedicti ordinis vestri excommunicationis sententia proferatur nullatenus relaxanda, donec ad ordinem ipsum humiliter redeat et restitutionem vestri habitus salva disciplina ordinis mereatur. Nulli ergo omnino hominum liceat hanc paginam nostre concessionis et constitutionis infringere, vel ei ausu temerario contraire. Si quis etc. Datum Viterbii v kal. augusti pontificatus nostri anno tercio.

Sine dato: magistro et fratribus etc. II, 122 v. n. 90; A. 20 n. 98 Latine et Germanice cum nota: In Marburg. — Cum dato: Viterbii 5 kal. aug. p. n. a. 3. originale cum bulla in archivo Regimontano, cf. Napiersky Index I, 34 n. 137. Quondam Mergenthemense originale in archivo ordinis Theutonici Vindobonensis, de quo bulla avulsa. IV, 208 n. 4. Ed. Livl. U. B. I, 395 n. 309. Duellius App. 8 n. 7. — „Praeceptoribus et fratribus universis h. s. M. Th. presentes literas inspecturis". R. 125 inter Marburgensia, necnon A. 16 p. 64; „Colonie" p. 71. „Preceptori et fratribus hospitalis s. Marie Theutonicorum in Alemannia" A. 16 p. 43 in Barulo. — Cum dato: Viterbii an. 3 citatur originale in designatione Mitowiensis archivi Holmiam 1621 delati ap. Schirren p. 131 n. 110. — Cum dato: Viterbii [4] non. aug. p. n. a. 3. „preceptori et fratribus h. s. M. Th. in Pruscia". Originale cum bulla in archivo Regimontano, valde corrosum in laeva parte. Cum eodem dato A. 16 p. 45 preceptori et fratribus in Alemannia „Baruli". „Magistro et fratribus h. s. M. Th." transsumtum ad instantiam mgri. Annonis sub bulla plumbea Iacobi Ierosolimitani patriarchae, legati apostolici, d. d. Accon 1257 mense octobris, quod et ipsum Regimonti citatur Livl. U. B. Regesta p. 88 n. 355 tanquam originalis de 1257 iulii 28. — Cum dato: Viterbii 5 idus augusti p. n. a. 3 „preceptoribus et fratribus etc." originale cum bulla in filis sericeis appensa in archivo ordinis Theutonici Vindobonae, quondam Mergenthemi. Alterum originale cum bulla in archivo Regimontano; et duo transsumta ibidem 1. d. d. 1418 dec. 2. Werneri de Hayn, canonici et officialis Wirciburgensis; 2. d. d. 1421 nov. 5 Schonbergi episcoporum Iohannis Culmensis et Gerhardi Pomesaniensis. R. 85 inter Mergenthemensia n. 43; cui simile s. d. R. 103 inter Alsatica 18 transsumtum s. d. citatur Cunradi decani maioris ecclesiae Basileensis, Erkenfridi cantoris, Heinrici scolastici, Ruedegeri praepositi de Columbaria. Hic notandum, quod in designatione Mitowiensis archivi ap. Schirren p. 130 n. 100 citatur: Adhortatio Alexandri IV pontificis ad universos Christi fideles, ut pro virili fratribus hospitalis s. Mariae auxiliares manus ferant, quo illi in suscepto amplificandae christianitatis munere alacriter et feliciter pergere valeant.

---

561. *1257 augusti 2 Viterbii. Alexander IV repetit n. 560 de 1257 iulii 28.*

Alexander etc. Pro consequenda etc. Datum Viterbii [iiii] non. kal. augusti pontificatus nostri anno tercio.

---

562. *1257 augusti 8 Viterbii. Alexander IV repetit n. 558 de 1257 iulii 11.*

Alexander etc. dilectis filiis preceptoribus et fratribus hospitalis sancte Marie Theutonicorum presentes litteras inspecturis etc. Canonica constitutione etc. Datum Viterbii vi idus augusti pontificatus nostri anno tercio.

---

563. *1257 augusti 8 Viterbii. Alexander IV negat ordinem Theutonicum invitum per literas apostolicas seu legatorum ut provideat cuiquam teneri.*

Alexander episcopus servus servorum dei dilectis filiis preceptoribus et fratribus universis hospitalis s. Marie Theutonicorum presentes literas inspecturis salutem et apostolicam benedictionem. Sincerissime devotionis obsequium, quod deo et redemptori nostro domino Ihesu Christo ferventer impenditis, ut apud ipsius clementiam vobis celestis patrie gloriam acquiratis, benignitatem sedis apostolice promptam et facilem reddit ad omnia, que cordibus vestris affectionis sancte proferant incrementa. Sane vestri honestas ordinis dilecta deo et grata fidelibus universis multum, prout accepimus, ex eo clara redditur et in domino roboratur, quod nullus de ordine ipso procuret aut petat aliquam sibi provisionem fieri specialem, sed hiis contentus, que in regula et statutis eiusdem ordinis continentur, humiliter et simpliciter vivat ut alii, qui sunt ad obediendum in omnibus et per omnia expediti. Ob hanc siquidem causam laudabilem et salubrem ac etiam, quia vos in Christo sincera caritate diligimus, universitati vestre de speciali gratia indulgemus, quod alicui preceptori vel fratri predicti ordinis vestri de prelatura seu dignitate aut officio vel baliva seu domo aut de quibuscunque bonis eiusdem ordinis per literas sedis apostolice aut legatorum eius impetratas vel de cetero impetrandas inviti non teneamini providere. Irritum etiam et inane decernimus, si quid contra tenorem ipsius indulgentie fuerit attentatum. Nulli ergo etc. concessionis et constitutionis etc. Si quis etc. Datum Viterbii vi id. augusti pontificatus nostri anno tertio.

Sine dato: magistro et fratribus etc. A. 20 n. 94 Latine et Germanice cum nota: In Colonia, in Marpurg, item in Mergentheym; II, 122v.; preceptori et fratribus h. s. M. Th. in Appullia. R. 97 inter Alsatica n. 12. — Cum dato: Viterbii 6 id. aug. p. n. a. 3. VI, 355v. ed. Duellius II, 14 n. 18; „preceptori et fratribus in Prussia" A. 16 p. 44 „Baruli"; p. 65 „in Marpurg". Inscripta „preceptori et fratribus h. s. M. Th." in Alemannia IV, 209 n. 6; R. 85 inter Mergenthemensia n. 41. Mergenthemense quondam originale cum bulla in filis sericeis appensa hodie in archivo ordinis Theutonici Vindobonensi. „Preceptori et fratribus h. s. M. Th. in Pruscia" R. 124 inter Marburgensia et in apographo trium bullarum, quod ad mandatum magistri generalis d. d. Marienburgi 1336 ianuarii 6 in publicam formam redegit Bando Stenionis imp. aut. not. publicus, asservato in archivo Regimontano; ed. Livl. U. B. I, 400 n. 313. Cum inscriptione: „preceptori et fratribus h. s. M. Th. in Livonia" in transsumto Iohannis Culmensis et Gerhardi Pomesaniensis episcoporum d. 1421 nov. 4 Schönbergi. In designatione Mitowiensis archivi Holmiensi citatur ap. Schirren p. 131 n. 111: „Constitutio Alexandri papae IV, qua continetur, ut fratres de Livonia ulli praeceptori aut fratri non teneantur inviti providere per literas apostolicae sedis aut legatorum eius impetrandas vel impetratas. Data 6 id. aug. pontificatus a. 3. Cum inscriptione: „preceptoribus et fratribus h. s. Marie Th. Ihr." et eodem dato Viterbii 6 id. aug. p. n. a. 3 „Colonie" A. 16 p. 70. — Praeceptoribus et fratribus ordinis Theutonici (in rubro legitur: pro Boemia, Moravia, Austria) cum bulla in filis sericeis rubris et luteis in archivo ordinis Theutonici Vindobonensi; dudum domus Vindobonensis.

---

563 a. *1257 augusti 8 (9?) Viterbii. Alexander IV repetit n. 540 de 1257 maii 3.*

Alexander etc. Qui ex etc. Datum Viterbii vi (v?) id. aug. pontificatus nostri anno tertio.

---

564. *1257 aug. 9 Viterbii. Alexander IV concedit ordini Theutonico, quod de male acquisitis et de redemtionibus votorum usque ad m marcas sterlingorum ad opus magistri et fratrum suorum in partibus transmarinis recipere ei liceat.*

Alexander episcopus servus servorum dei dilectis filiis preceptori et fratribus hospitalis sancte Marie Theotonicorum in Alamannia salutem et apostolicam benedictionem. Inducunt nos merita dilectorum filiorum magistri et fratrum vestri ordinis manencium in partibus transmarinis, ut eos prosequamur gracia, que ipsorum necessitatibus esse dinoscitur oportuna. Hinc est, quod nos inclinati precibus eorundem, ut de usuris, rapinis et aliis male acquisitis, dummodo hii, quibus ipsorum restitucio fieri debeat, omnino sciri et inveniri non possint, necnon de redempcionibus votorum, que fuerint auctoritate diocesanorum pontificum commutata, Ierosolimitano dumtaxat excepto, usque ad summam mille marcharum sterlingorum ad opus dictorum magistri et fratrum recipere valeatis, auctoritate vobis presencium duximus concedendum, si tamen ipsi pro similium recepcione alias non sint a nobis huiusmodi graciam consecuti, ita tamen, quod, si aliquid de ipsis mille marcis dimiseritis vel restitueritis aut dederitis illis, a quibus ea receperitis, huiusmodi dimissum, restitutum seu datum nil ad liberacionem eorum prosit nec quantum ad illud habeantur aliquatenus absoluti. Nulli ergo omnino hominum liceat, hanc paginam nostre concessionis infringere vel ei ausu temerario contraire. Si quis autem hoc attemptare presumpserit, indignacionem omnipotentis dei et beatorum Petri et Pauli apostolorum eius se noverit incursurum. Datum Viterbii v idus augusti pontificatus nostri anno tercio.

Sine dato: A. 16 p. 106 „Iuncis". — Sine dato citatur R. 154 inter Iuncensia; „et habetur privilegium prius Trevere de verbo ad verbum, sicut est per eundem Alexandrum IIIItum et exprimitur hic plane usque ad summam mille marcarum, et alibi nisi usque ad summam centum marcarum". — Cum dato: IV, 209 v. n. 7. — Ex transsumto Robini de Millen, decani ecclesiae s. Servatii Traiectensis Leodiensis diocesis, cuius datum omisit scriptor, A. 16 p. 108 „Traiecto". Transsumtum C. decani et M. archidiaconi Leodiensium, nunc sine sigillis in archivo ordinis Theutonici Vindobonensi, quondam Confluentino-Iuncense.

---

565. *1257 aug. 9 Viterbii. Alexander IV n. 560 de 1257 iulii 28.*

Alexander etc. Pro consequenda etc. Datum Viterbii v idus augusti pontificatus nostri anno tercio.

---

566. *1257 augusti 9 Viterbii. Alexander IV declarat constitutionem suam de exemtorum privilegiis locorum ordinariis producendis ordinem Theutonicum non tangere.*

Alexander etc. magistro et fratribus hospitalis beate Marie Theutonicorum Ierosolimitani salutem et apostolicam benedictionem. Quandam constitucionem nos edidisse meminimus, ut, si[1] hii, qui se asserunt per privilegia seu indulgencias apostolice sedis[2] exemptos, de quorum scilicet exempcione seu libertate non[3] constat vel qui videlicet in exempcionis seu[4] libertatis possessione per longa tempora non fuerint a locorum ordinariis requisiti, huiusmodi privilegia vel indulgencias, quibus dicunt se[5] fore munitos saltem quoad illos[6] articulos, super quibus questio vel[7] controversia fuerit, ipsis ordinariis in loco congruo et securo vel aliquibus prudentibus viris omni suspicione carentibus ad hoc per dictos[8] ordinarios deputatis non exhibuerint vel ostenderint et iidem ordinarii sua iurisdiccione usi fuerint contra eos, nequaquam tunc ipsi ordinarii hac[9] occasione per conservatores a sede apostolica illis deputatos eadem molestari valeant aut aliquatenus inpediri; quinimo sentencie vel[10] processus conservatorum ipsorum, que vel qui prolate vel habiti fuerint contra eosdem ordinarios, in hoc casu omnino non teneant nullumque robur habeant vel vigorem. Cum autem nota sit plene vestra exempcio et libertas, scire vos volumus, quod huiusmodi constitucio tangit illos, de quorum exempcione seu[10] libertate non constat vel qui[11] videlicet in exempcionis seu[10] libertatis possessione per longa tempora non fuerint, nisi forte diceretis a sede predicta super aliquibus capitulis vel articulis exempcionis privilegia vos habere, de qua liquido non constaret. Datum Viterbii v idus augusti pontificatus nostri anno tercio.

Sine dato: A. 20 n. 95 Latine et Germanice cum nota: „In Colonia; et vidimus unum in curia Romana sub sigillo audiencie cum publico instrumento. Bulla est in Confluencia". — Cum dato: Viterbii 5 id. augusti a. 3 „Confluentie" A. 16 p. 84. Transsumtum Conradi Coloniensis archiepiscopi d. d. Boloniae 1258 decbr. 8 cum sigillo cereo albo maculato in plumbea capsula appenso et secreto in dorso in archivo ordinis Theutonici Vindobonensi. 1. deest A. 20. 2. s. a. A. 20. 3. nichil A. 20. 4. vel A. 20. 5. se dicunt A. 20. 6. deest A. 20. 7. seu A. 20. 8. hoc predictos A. 20. 9. ac A. 16. 10. et A. 20. 11. deest A. 20.

---

567. *1257 augusti 9 Viterbii. Alexander IV concedit ordini Theutonico, quod ad litteras apostolicas aut legatorum nec Popponi quondam magistro nec cuiquam alii de dignitate providere sit coactus.*

Alexander episcopus servus servorum dei dilectis filiis magistro et fratribus hospitalis sancte Marie Theutonicorum Ierosolimitani salutem et apostolicam benedictionem. Sincerissime devotionis obsequium, quod deo redemptori nostro domino Ihesu Christo ferventer impenditis, ut apud ipsius clementiam vobis celestis patrie gloriam acquiratis, benignitatem sedis apostolice promptam et facilem reddit ad omnia, que cordibus vestris affectionis sancte proferant incrementa. Cum itaque, fili .. magister, ad generale tui ordinis regimen secundum instituta ipsius de novo, prout accepimus, sis assumptus[1], nos dignis laudibus id in domino commendantes universitati vestre firmam de vobis volumus adesse fiduciam, quod vos in Christo paterna caritate complectamur, et gratioso favore prosequi assidue delectamur. In cuius rei signum vobis de speciali gracia indulgemus, quod fratri Popponi quondam magistro vestro seu cuicumque preceptori vel fratri ordinis vestri de prelatura seu dignitate aut officio vel baliva seu domo aut de quibuscumque bonis eiusdem ordinis per litteras sedis apostolice seu legatorum eius impetratas vel de cetero impetrandas inviti non teneamini providere. Irritum etiam et inane decernimus, si quid contra tenorem ipsius indulgentie fuerit attemptatum. Nulli ergo omnino hominum liceat hanc nostre concessionis paginam infringere vel ei ausu temeario contraire. Si quis autem hoc attemptare presumpserit, indignacionem omnipotentis dei et beatorum Petri et Pauli apostolorum se noverit incursurum. Datum Viterbii v idus augusti pontificatus nostri anno iii.

Sine dato: II, 117v. n. 73. — Cum dato: A. 16 p. 45 „Baruli"; p. 11 „Venetiis" in transsumto 1346 Venetiis facto.

---

568. *1257 augusti 12 Viterbii (cf. 1257 aug. 20). Alexander IV repetit Gregorii IX n. 439 de 1227 aug. 31.*

Alexander etc. Dilectorum filiorum etc. — vinculo innodetis. Datum Viterbii ii idus augusti pontificatus nostri anno tercio.

Sine dato: II, 122v. n. 88. — Cum dato: Viterbii 2 idus augusti p. n. a. 3 „in Marpurg" A. 16 p. 64. — Cum dato: Viterbii 13 kal. septbr. p. n. a. 3 „Colonie" A. 16 p. 70; IV, 210 n. 8. Originale cum bulla in archivo Regimontano, ubi etiam tria eius transsumpta d. d. Marienburgi 1416 april. 10 auctoritate Iohannis Pomesaniensis episcopi per Iohannem Sternchen ap. et imp. ant. not. publ. confecta. Originale Mergenthemense cum bulla in filis sericeis appensa in archivo ordinis Theutonici Vindobonensi.

---

569. *1257 augusti 16 (cf. septbr. 13) Viterbii. Alexander IV repetit Innocentii IV n. 531.*

Alexander etc. Quociens a nobis — quam cis mare felicis recordacionis Honorii, Gregorii, Innocencii, predecessorum nostrorum, Romanorum pontificum vestigiis inherentes vobis etc. Datum Viterbii xvii kal. septembris pontificatus nostri anno tercio.

Cum dato: Viterbii 17 kal. septbr. p. n. a. 3. R. 59 inter Ratisponensia 15. Transsumtum s. d. ab Heinrico Ratisponensi episcopo ad instantiam fr. Gotfridi, commendatoris ordinis Theutonici per Austriam et Styriam, editum in archivo ordinis Theutonici Vindobonensi iam dudum domus Vindobonensis. — Cum dato: Viterbii idus septbr. p. n. a. 3. R. 138 inter Treverensia; A. 16 p. 43 „Baruli". Originale cum bulla et transsumptum d. d. Revaliae 1415 decbr. 24 sub sigillis Iohannis ep. Revaliensis et capituli eius necnon abbatis de Padis, auctoritate dicti episcopi confectum in archivo Regimontano. Originale quondam Iuncense (Confl.?) in archivo Vindobonensi, cum bulla in filis sericeis rubris et iuteis appensa, unde edidit Hennes I, 156 n. 69; A. 16 p. 73 „Colonie".

---

570. *1257 augusti 20 Viterbii. Alexander IV repetit n. 568 de 1257 aug. 12.*

Alexander etc. Dilectorum filiorum etc. Datum Viterbii xiii kalendas septembris pontificatus nostri anno tercio.

---

571. *1257 septbr. 7 Viterbii (cf. decbr. 7, 1258 decbr. 11). Alexander IV repetit Innocentii IV n. 474 de 1244 aprilis 20.*

Alexander etc. Cum dilecti etc. Datum Viterbii vii idus septembris pontificatus nostri anno tercio.

Cum dato: Viterbii 7 id. septbr. ex originali Vindobonensi, quondam Iuncensi, cum bulla in filis sericeis rubris et luteis appensa ed. Hennes I, 155 n. 168. 7 (?) septbr. p. n. a. 3. A. 16 p. 114 „Treviris". — Cum dato: Viterbii 7 idus decembris p. n. a. 3. A. 16 p. 72 „Colonie". Anagnie 3 idus decembris p. n. a. 4. A. 16 p. 4 „Venetiis".

572. *1257 septbr. 9 Viterbii. Alexander IV repetit n. 544 de 1257 iunii 1.*

Alexander etc. Cum dilectis etc. Datum Viterbii v idus septembris pontificatus nostri anno tercio.

573. *1257 septbr. 13 Viterbii. Alexander IV repetit n. 569 1257 aug. 16.*

Alexander etc. Quociens a nobis etc. Datum Viterbii idus septembris pontificatus nostri anno tercio.

574. *1257 novbr. 5 Viterbii. Alexander IV concedit ordini Theutonico, quod non teneatur per literas papales vel legatorum in personis vel rebus subvenire cuiquam nisi plenam huiusmodi indulgentiae facientes mentionem.*

Alexander episcopus servus servorum dei dilectis filiis magistro et fratribus hospitalis sancte Marie Theotonicorum Ierosolimitani salutem et apostolicam benedictionem. Hospitalitatis piissime ac defensionis terre sancte studium, cui ferventer intenditis, vos apud sedem apostolicam dignos constituit favoris gracia specialis. Hinc est, quod nos vestris supplicacionibus annuentes auctoritate vobis presencium indulgemus, ut[1] per litteras apostolice sedis et legatorum eius inpetratas vel de cetero inpetrandas in personis vel[2] rebus non teneamini alicui[3] subvenire, nisi dicte littere apostolice impetrande plenam et expressam de hac indulgencia fecerint mencionem. Nos enim nichilominus processum aut sentenciam, si secus in vos aut ecclesias seu domos vestras haberi contigerit, decernimus[4] nullius existere firmitatis. Nulli ergo omnino hominum liceat hanc paginam nostre concessionis et constitucionis infringere vel ei ausu temerario contraire. Si quis autem hoc attemptare presumpserit, indignacionem omnipotentis dei et beatorum Petri et Pauli apostolorum eius se noverit incursurum. Datum Viterbii nonas novembris pontificatus nostri anno tercio.

Sine dato: II, 122 v. n. 89; R. 7 inter Norimbergensia 10; citatur R. 140 inter Trevirensia; A. 20 n. 107 Latine et Germanice cum nota: In Treveri; in Nurenburg; item in Marpurg habetur privilegium. — Cum dato: IV, 212 v. n. 10; originale cum bulla in filis sericeis appensa in archivo ordinis Theutonici Vindobonensi, ubi etiam secundum originale domus Vindobonensis cum bulla in filis sericeis rubris et luteis appensa; R. 60 inter Ratisponensia n. 17; R. 125 et A. 16 p. 65

inter Marburgensia. Transsumtum iudicii episcopalis Spirensis d. d. 1390 febr. 17. Spire in domo Theutonica extat in archivo Regimontano, ubi etiam transsumptum officialis Herbipolensis d. d. 1418 decbr. 2; Ioh. 38. Edd. Caorsinus fol. C. 4 v. et Senner E. 5. v. Duo transsumta 1258 aug. 8 ind. I de mandato et auctoritate Iohannis Patavini et fr. Bartholomaei Vicentini episcoporum per Aicardinum filium quondam Oliveri de Boccka, sacri palati. notarium, et Conradum, imperialis aulae notarium, in archivo ordinis Theutonici Vindobonensi. 1. ut T. 1390, T. 1418 Senner, ne II. 2. et II. 3. alicui deest II. 4. decernimus T. 1390, T. 1415, decrevimus II.

---

575. *1257 novbr. 17 Viterbii. Alexander IV repetit Honorii III n. 338 de 1221 ianuarii 20.*

Alexander etc. Dilecti filii .. magister et fratres hospitalis etc. ita spiritualia — vicarios alios contra formam inhibitionis dudum a predecessoribus nostris facte instituere non presumant — per ipsius beneficii subtractionem[1] appellatione remota cogatis nullis litteris obstantibus veritati et iusticie preiudicantibus a sede apostolica impetratis. Datum Viterbii xv kalendas decembris pontificatus nostri anno tercio.

II, 117 v. n. 72. 1. pro ipsius beneficii subtractione II.

---

576. *1257 decbr. 7 Viterbii. Alexander IV repetit n. 571 de 1257 septbr. 7.*

Alexander etc. Cum dilecti etc. Datum Viterbii vii idus decembris pontificatus nostri anno iii.

---

577. *1258 februarii 9 Viterbii. Alexander IV concedit ordini Theutonico, ut castra sua ubique non solum contra paganos verum etiam contra alios auferre molientes defendere ei possit.*

Alexander etc. dilectis filiis .. magistro et fratribus hospitalis sancte Marie Theutonicorum Ierosolimitani salutem et apostolicam benedictionem. Favoris nostri provenire decet auxilio, ut, que digne seu iuste cupitis, libere ac sine trepidatione aliqua perficere valeatis. Sane munitiones et castra quedam ad honorem dei et sancte Romane ecclesie, sicut accepimus, tenetis in transmarinis et cismarinis partibus, que non solum pagani sed etiam alii quamplures homines reprobi et perversi auferre vobis per violentiam moliuntur. Quia vero de ammissione munitionum et castrorum ipsorum vobis et negotio fidei, quod per vos in terra sancta necnon in Livonia et Pruscia seu quibuscumque aliis locis per dei gratiam utiliter et potenter agitur, grave dispendium immineret, nos devotionis vestre precibus inclinati, ut munitiones et castra predicta defendere vim vi repellendo cum inculpate tutele moderamine valeatis, vobis auctoritate presentium concedimus facultatem. Nulli ergo etc. nostre concessionis etc. Si quis autem etc. Datum Viterbii v id. febr. pontificatus nostri anno quarto.

Sine dato: II, 119 n. 77; A. 20 n. 96 Latine et Germanice cum nota: In Colonia. Sub falso anno 1256 citatur in designatione Mitowiensis archivi 1621 Holmiam delati ap. Schirren p. 131 n. 118. — Cum dato: ex originali bullato in archivo Regimontano edd. Voigt Cod. dipl. Prussiae I, 111 n. 113. Livl. U. B. I, 407 n. 319; ex originali musei antiquitatum Holmiensis ed. Liljegren Dipl. Suec. I, 387 n. 446; R. 169 inter Thuringica; A. 16 p. 71 „Colonie". Tria transsumta in archivo Regimontano 1. d. d. Baroli 1336 maii 31 per Rogerium archidiaconum Barolitanum, Bartholomaei, Tranensis archiepiscopi, regni Siciliae vicecancellarii, vicarium et Nicolaum Bertonum iudicem Barolitanum; 2. de 1393 maii 29 in castro S. Mariae; 3. de 1412 decbr. 22 Marienburgi per Iohannem archiepiscopnm Rigensem. Ex originali Vindobonensi cum bulla in filis sericeis appensa ed. Hennes I, 160 n. 173.

---

578. *1258 maii 18 Viterbii (cf. 1259 aprilis 24). Alexander IV concedit ordini Theutonico, quod presbyteri eius fratribus ob certa delicta ante susceptum habitum commissa absolutionem dare possint.*

Alexander episcopus servus servorum dei dilectis filiis .. magistro et fratribus hospitalis sancte Marie Theutonicorum salutem et apostolicam benedictionem. Ex parte vestra fuit propositum coram nobis, quod nonnulli ex fratribus ordinis vestri, dum adhuc manerent in seculo, rapinas, incendia et depopulaciones[1] rerum quamplurium commiserunt, propter quod humiliter petivistis, ut eorum in hac parte providere saluti misericorditer curaremus. Nos itaque vestris devotis precibus inclinati presencium vobis auctoritate concedimus, quod fratres vestri presbiteri providi et discreti confessionem predictorum fratrum, qui talia commiserunt, cum super hoc ab eis fuerint requisiti, audiant et ipsis iuxta formam ecclesie absolucionis beneficium largiantur ac iniungant eciam penitenciam salutarem, ita tamen, quod predicti fratres, qui se reputant fuisse culpabiles in premissis, sine ipsorum discursu seu vagacione, quam fieri penitus inhibemus, devotis mentibus iuxta consilium vestrum ordinent et procurent, ut de bonis suis, que in seculo dimiserunt, vel de bonis consanguineorum et amicorum suorum si possint[2] passis dampnis huiusmodi congrua satisfaccio impendatur. Datum Viterbii xv kalendas iunii pontificatus nostri anno quarto.

Sine dato: II, 121 v. n. 85. — Cum dato: „anno 4°." A. 16 p. 116 „Treviris". In designatione Mitowiensis archivi ap. Schirren p. 131 n. 122 legitur (1258) „Alexander indulget, ut fratres presbyteri possint absolvere omnes illos excommunicatos, qui volunt fieri fratres" Viterbii a. 4°." — Cum dato: Viterbii 15 kal. iunii p. n. a. 4. R. 139 inter Treverensia; A. 20 n. 109 Latine et Germanice cum nota: In Colonia habetur hoc; zcu Tervis A. 16 p. 71 et p. 73 „Colonie". Originale cum bulla in filis cannabinis appensa in archivo ordinis Theutonici Vindobonensi; ed. Hennes I, 162 n. 177. — Cum dato: Anagnie 8 kal. maii p. n. a. 5 R. 99 inter Alsatica n. 17.
1. depredaciones A. 20. 2. A. 16 possunt II. H.

---

579. *1258 maii 18 Viterbii (cf. 1259 april. 24). Alexander IV concedit ordini Theutonico, ut satisfactionem fratrum ob incendia, rapinas, usuras in saeculo commissa, dummodo laesi nequeant inveniri, in subsidium terrae sanctae, Livoniae, Prussiae convertat.*

Alexander episcopus servus servorum dei dilectis filiis magistro et preceptoribus et fratribus universis[1] hospitalis sancte Marie Theutonicorum salutem et apostolicam benedictionem. Ex parte vestra fuit propositum coram nobis, quod nonnulli ex fratribus ordinis vestri, dum adhuc manerent in seculo, multis modis, sed precipue per incendia, rapinas et usuras personis quam pluribus dampna gravia intulerunt; propter quod humiliter petivistis, ut super hoc providere salubriter curaremus. Nos itaque devocionis vestre precibus annuentes presencium vobis auctoritate concedimus, ut satisfaccionem pro huiusmodi dampnis et usuris debitam illis dumtaxat personis, que omnino sciri et inveniri non possunt, in subsidium terre sancte ac eciam Lyvonice et Pruscie, ubi fidei negocium per vos ad dei gloriam magnanimiter et potenter agitur, prout melius expedire videritis, convertatis. Datum Viterbii xv kalendas iunii pontificatus nostri anno quarto.

Sine dato: A. 20 n. 108 Latine et Germanice. — Cum dato: Viterbii 15 kal. iunii a. 4 „Colonie" A. 16 p. 73. In volumine archivi Regimontani fol. A. 186. Ex originali quondam Confluentino, nunc Vindobonensi, cui appendet in funiculo cannabino bulla, edidit Hennes I, 162 n. 178. — Cum dato: Anagnie 8 kal. maii p. n. a. 5 „Baruli". A. 16 p. 43. Transsumtum Conradi Coloniensis archiepiscopi cum sigillo duplice d. d. 1258 dec. Colonie in archivo ordinis Theutonici Vindobonensi. 1. deest A. 16.

580. *1258 maii 24 Viterbii (cf. iunii 24). Alexander IV praelatos iubet in ordinis Theutonici ecclesiis a praedecessoribus recepto iure esse contentos.*

Alexander episcopus servus servorum dei dilectis filiis magistro et fratribus hospitalis sancte Marie Theutonicorum salutem et apostolicam benedictionem. Plenitudine favoris et gracie vos apud sedem apostolicam illa de causa dignos[1] vos potissime reputamus, quia pie conversacionis ac vite studio ferventer intenditis et pro subsidio terre sancte ac pro fidei negocio in Livonie et Pruscie partibus magnifice promovendo labores multos et infinitas angustias ac eciam mortis periculum ad honorem divini nominis corde intrepido frequentissime sustinetis[2]. Inde fit, quod nos quieti et tranquillitati vestre[3] paterna diligencia providere volentes vestris inclinati precibus auctoritate vobis presencium indulgemus, ut archiepiscopi et episcopi et alii ecclesiarum prelati in vestris, quas habetis et tenetis, ecclesiis salva procuracione, si qua debetur eisdem, eo tantummodo sint iure contenti, quod ipsi et predecessores eorum a vobis et predecessoribus vestris noscuntur hactenus habuisse. Quodsi amplius ex predictis ecclesiis petere vel extorquere contenderint, vobis id liceat auctoritate sedis apostolice denegare super hoc coram nobis exhibere paratis iusticie conplementum. Nulli ergo hominum liceat hanc paginam nostre concessionis infringere vel ei ausu temerario contraire. Si quis autem hoc attemptare presumpserit, indignacionem omnipotentis dei et beatorum Petri et Pauli apostolorum eius se noverit incursurum. Datum Viterbii viiii kalendas iunii pontificatus nostri anno quarto.

Sine dato: A. 20 n. 100 Latine et Germanice cum nota: In Confluencia et Langele. — Cum dato: Viterbii 9 kal. iunii a. 4 „Colonie" A. 16 p. 69. — Cum dato: Viterbii 8 kal. iulii p. a. 4 R. 137 inter Treverensia. — „A. 4 Treviris" A. 16 p. 114 et 117. 1. deest R. 2. sustinentes R. 3. vestra R.

581. *1258 iunii 8 (cf. iunii 9; inter 1258 decbr. 12 et 1259 decbr. 11) Viterbii. Alexander IV concedit ordini Theutonico, ut ad ecclesias suas diocesanis clericos saeculares idoneos praesentent.*

Alexander episcopus servus servorum dei dilectis filiis .. magistro et fratribus hospitalis sancte Marie Theutonicorum Ierosolimitani salutem et apostolicam benedictionem. Iustis petentium desideriis dignum est nos facilem prebere assensum et vota, que a rationis tramite non discordant, effectu prosequente complere. Ex parte siquidem vestra fuit propositum coram nobis, quod, cum vos ad ecclesias ad vos spectantes, cum eas vacare contingit, interdum fratres vestri ordinis, plerumque vero idoneos clericos seculares, qui vobiscum in vestris domibus commorantes in mensa vestra comedant et dormiant in vestro dormitorio, diocesanis episcopis, prout ad vos pertinet, presentetis; quidam ipsorum eos admittere pro sue voluntatis arbitrio contradicunt, nisi tantum eis de ipsorum proventibus assignetis[1], quod sibi et suis extra domus vestras morantibus plene sufficiat, hospitalitatem observent et de iuribus episcopalibus diocesanis episcopis integre studeant respondere; quanquam vos hospitalitatem servetis ac illis de ipsis iuribus sitis respondere parati. Quare pro vobis fuit nobis humiliter supplicatum, ut, cum propter hoc eedem ecclesie debitis obsequiis defraudentur et vobis magnum immineat detrimentum, providere super hiis misericorditer dignaremur. Vestris igitur supplicationibus benignum impertientes assensum presentium vobis auctoritate concedimus, ut huiusmodi personas idoneas prefatis diocesanis ad easdem ecclesias vobis liceat presentare, dummodo dicte ecclesie nullum defectum in divinis officiis patiantur et de premissis iuribus faciatis locorum episcopis plenarie responderi. Nulli ergo etc. Datum Viterbii v idus iunii pontificatus nostri anno quarto.

Sine dato: A. 20 n. 99 Latine et Germanice cum nota: In Confluentia et in Buken; memoratur R. 141 inter Treverensia; II, 118 v. n. 75. — Cum dato: Viterbii 6 idus iunii a. 4 „Colonie“ A. 16 p. 69. — Cum dato: Viterbii 5 idus iunii a. 4 originale cum bulla in archivo Regimontano; ubi etiam transsumtum saec. xiv; ed. Livl. U. B. I, 413 n. 327. Ex originali „in Antfeld“ exstante ed. Hennes II, 121 n. 128. Originale cum bulla in filis sericeis rubris et luteis appensa, quondam Confluentino-Iuncense, nunc Vindobonae in archivo ordinis Theutonici. — Cum dato: a. 5 Treviris A. 16 p. 114. 1. ipsarum p. assignetur L. U.

---

582. *1258 iunii 9 Viterbii. Alexander IV repetit n. 581 de 1258 iunii 8.*

Alexander etc. Iustis petentium etc. Datum Viterbii v idus iunii pontificatus nostri anno quarto.

---

583. *1258 iunii 11 (cf. 22) Viterbii. Alexander IV concedit ordini Theutonico, quod ad solvendas procurationes pecuniarias legatis et nuntiis invitus non cogatur.*

Alexander episcopus servus servorum dei dilectis filiis .. magistro et fratribus hospitalis sancte Marie Theutonicorum salutem et apostolicam benedictionem. Affectu benevolencie specialis illa de causa vos prosequi delectamur, qui vigilanter ac ferventer ad hoc intenditis, quod in conspectu dei et hominum per honeste conversacionis ac pie vite studium placeatis. Sane vos in exhibendis procuracionibus legatis et nunciis apostolice sedis, prout accepimus, ex eo gravamini, quod ipsi non contenti procurationibus, quas eisdem parati estis in victualibus ac aliis necessariis exhibere, a vobis et ecclesiis et domibus vestris occasione procuracionum huiusmodi frequenter non modicam pecunie summam exigunt et extorquent. Cum autem propter hoc vestrum pium quandoque impediatur propositum et terre sancte negocio derogetur; nos vestris supplicationibus inclinati, ut predictis legatis et nunciis, exceptis tamen fratribus nostris Romane ecclesie cardinalibus, ad solvendas procuraciones pecuniarias huiusmodi cogi aliquatenus non possitis, vobis auctoritate presencium indulgemus, dummodo predictos legatos et nuncios in victualibus et aliis necessariis procuretis. Sentencias vero, si que in vos vel aliquem de ordine vestro contra indultum huiusmodi de cetero fuerint promulgate, irritas exnunc esse decrevimus et inanes. Nulli ergo omnino hominum liceat hanc paginam nostre concessionis et constitucionis infringere vel ei ausu temerario contraire. Si quis autem hoc attemptare presumpserit, indignacionem omnipotentis dei et beatorum Petri et Pauli apostolorum eius se noverit incursurum. Datum Viterbii iii id. iunii pontificatus nostri anno quarto.

Sine dato: A. 20 n. 97 Latine et Germanice cum nota: In Colonia; II, 120 n. 81. Ed. J. N. Becker Versuch einer Geschichte der Hochmeister in Preufsen seit Winrichs (sic) von Kniprode bis auf die Gründung des Erbherzogthums. Berlin 1798. 8°. p. 109. — Cum dato: Viterbii 3 id. iunii p. n. a. 4 IV, 213 n. 11; R. 98 inter Alsatica n. 14; A. 16 p. 84 „Confluentibus". Originale cum bulla in filis sericeis rubris et luteis appensa quondam Confluentinum (Iunc. Trevir.) in archivo ordinis Theutonici Vindobonensi. — Cum dato: Viterbii 3 idus iunii (p. n. a. 4, ad 1258) magistro et praeceptoribus ac fratribus ordinis Theutonici, originale, quondam Confluentinum, Vindobonae in archivo ordinis Theutonici cum bulla appensa in filis sericeis. Ed. Duell. App. p. 9. n. 9. — Cum dato: Viterbii 10 kal. iulii p. n. a. 4. originale, iam dudum domus Vindobonensis, cum bulla in filis sericeis rubris et luteis in archivo ordinis Theutonici Vindobonensi, ed. Duellius II, 14 n. 19.

---

584. *1258 iunii 22 Viterbii. Alexander IV repetit n. 533 de 1258 iunii 11.*

Alexander etc. magistro et fratribus h. s. M. Th. etc. Affectu benevolencie etc. Datum Viterbii x kalendas iulii pontificatus nostri anno quarto.

---

585. *1258 iunii 24 Viterbii. Alexander IV repetit n. 580 de 1258 maii 24.*

Alexander etc. Plenitudine favoris etc. Datum Viterbii viii kal. iulii pontificatus nostri anno quarto.

---

586. *1258 iunii 25 Viterbii. Alexander IV repetit n. 541 1257 maii 29.*

Alexander etc. Religiosos viros etc. Datum Viterbii vii kal. iulii pontificatus nostri anno quarto.

---

587. *1258 iunii 27 Viterbii. Alexander IV repetit n. 544 de 1257 iunii 1.*

Alexander etc. Cum dilectis filiis etc. Datum v kal. iulii pontificatus nostri anno quarto.

Supra ad n. 544 p. 384 legendum est: 1257 sept. 9, 1258 iunii 27, nov. 29.

---

588. *1258 novbr. 1 Anagniae. Alexander IV repetit n. 541 de 1257 maii 29.*

Alexander etc. Religiosos viros — pedagium, vendam, passagium, pontenagium, theolonium, caucagium seu aliam — compescatis. Datum Anagnie v nonas novembris pontificatus nostri anno quarto.

---

589. *1258 novbr. 5 Anagniae. Alexander IV iubet decanum s. Germani Spirensis invigilare, ne hospitale ordinis Theutonici eique subiecta hospitalia et domus in Alemannia aut personae in eis degentes contra indulta eis a sede apostolica privilegia a quoquam indebite molestentur.*

Alexander etc. Ad hospitalem etc. Datum Anagnie non. novembris pontificatus nostri anno quarto.

In transsumto facto c. 1258 per Wernherum praepositum et decanum maioris ecclesiae Spirensis cum duobus sigillis in archivo ordinis Theutonici Vindobonensi.

---

590. *1258 novbr. 9 Anagniae. Alexander IV repetit Innocentii IV n. 528 de 1254 maii 18 paucis mutatis.*

Alexander episcopus servus servorum dei dilectis filiis magistro et fratribus hospitalis sancte Marie Theotonicorum Ierosolimitani salutem et apostolicam benedictionem. Devocionis vestre precibus inclinati presencium vobis auctoritate concedimus, ut possessiones et alia bona mobilia et immobilia, que liberas personas fratrum vestrorum mundi relicta vanitate ad vestrum ordinem convolancium et professionem faciencium in eodem ure successionis vel alio iusto titulo, si remansissent in seculo, contigissent et ipsi potuissent libere aliis erogare, rebus feudalibus dumtaxat exceptis, possitis petere, recipere ac eciam retinere. Nulli ergo etc. Datum Anagnie v idus novembris pontificatus nostri anno quarto.

Originale cum bulla in filis sericeis appensa quondam Mergenthemense in archivo ordinis Theutonici Vindobonensi. IV, 214 v. n. 13; Ioh. 39. Copia saec. xiv in archivo Regimontano extat. Edd. Caorsinus C. 5 Senner E. 6. — Cum dato (1258 iunii 1) Viterbii kal. iunii p. n. a. 4 preceptori et fratribus h. s. M. Th. in Confluentia Trev. dioc. inscripta ex originali nunc Vindobonensi bullato ed. Hennes I, 163 n. 179; ubi praesertim pro „ordinem" legitur „hospitale". „Colonie" A. 16 p. 72; „Confl." p. 84.

---

591. *1258 novbr. 11 Anagniae. Alexander IV repetit Honorii III n. 406.*

Alexander etc. Dilecti filii etc. archiepiscopis et episcopis, ad — fatigati multipliciter — vestro ipsorum auctore domino iustitie providere — quidem -- permissa — potestate. Datum Anagnie iii idus novembris pontificatus nostri anno quarto.

Ex transsumto archivi Regimontani d. d. Revaliae 1415 dec. 14 male ed. in Livl. U. B. I, 422 n. 333. In eodem archivo aliud transsumtum d. d. Marienburgi 1393 maii 29.

---

592. *1258 novbr. 12 Anagniae. Alexander IV repetit Innocentii IV n. 515 de 1247 iulii 23.*

Alexander etc. Quieti vestre etc. — respondere. Datum Anagnie ii idus novembris pontificatus nostri anno quarto.

IV, 214v. n. 14. „A. 4 Treviris" A. 16 p. 114. Originale quondam Treverense cum bulla in filis sericeis rubris et luteis appensa in archivo ordinis Theutonici Vindobonensi.

---

593. *1258 novbr. 22 Anagnie (cf. 1260 iulii 10). Alexander IV iubet episcopos ab ordine Theutonico praesentatos fratres clericos ad ecclesias patronatus eius investire.*

Alexander episcopus servus servorum dei venerabilibus fratribus archiepiscopis et episcopis ac dilectis filiis archidiaconis, ad quos littere iste pervenerint, salutem et apostolicam benedictionem. Ex parte dilectorum filiorum magistri et fratrum hospitalis sancte Marie Theutonicorum Ierosolimitani nobis est oblata querela, quod, licet eis a sede apostolica sit indultum, ut fratres clericos ordinis sui ad vacantes ecclesias, in quibus ius obtinent patronatus, diocesanis episcopis, responsuros eis de spiritualibus ac dictis magistro et fratribus de temporalibus, valeant presentare, aliqui tamen vestrum se illis super hoc molestos et graves sepius exhibentes predictos fratres clericos, quos dicti magister et fratres iuxta predictum indultum eis presentant ad ecclesias memoratas, instituere denegant in eis pro sue arbitrio voluntatis. Cum autem ipsi apostolice benignitatis auxilium super hoc duxerint humiliter inplorandum; universitatem vestram rogamus et hortamur attente per apostolica vobis scripta precipiendo mandantes, quatenus provide attendentes, quod iidem magister et fratres pro sue religionis meritis nullis molestiis affici, sed piis debent beneficiis confoveri, vos eis in premissis nullius difficultatis apponatis obstaculum, sed favorem benivolum ad id pocius impendatis, ita quod nec ipsi conquerendi de vobis materiam habeant nec eis super hoc per nos oporteat aliter provideri. Datum Anagnie x kalendas decembris pontificatus nostri anno quarto.

Cum dato: „anno 4" A. 16 p. 116 „Treviris". — Cum dato: Anagnie 10 kal. decbr. p. a. 4. A. 16 p. 72 „Colonie, invenitur etiam in Mechelinia sub eodem papa"; R. 138 inter Treverensia. Ex originali quondam Confluentino, nunc Vindobonensi cum bulla in funiculo cannabino ed. Hennes I, 165 n. 183. In eodem archivo ordinis Theutonici Vindobonensi alterum originale quondam Mergenthemense cum bulla in filis sericeis quondam annexa, nunc tamen avulsa. Transsumptum de 1418 decbr. 2 in archivo Regimontano. — Cum dato: Anagnie 6 id. iulii p. n. a. 6. originale quondam (Confl.) Iuncense cum bulla in filis sericeis rubris et luteis appensa in archivo ordinis Theutonici Vindobonensi.

594. *1258 novbr. 22 Anagniae. Alexander IV vetat de ordinis Theutonici victualibus, vestimentis, pecudibus, aliis rebus exactiones extorqueri.*

Alexander episcopus servus servorum dei venerabilibus fratribus archiepiscopis et episcopis et dilectis filiis abbatibus, prioribus, decanis, archidiaconis et aliis ecclesiarum prelatis, ad quos littere iste pervenerint, salutem et apostolicam benedictionem. Ex parte dilectorum filiorum .. magistri et fratrum hospitalis sancte Marie Theotonicorum Ierosolimitani nobis est oblata querela, quod, licet vobis per litteras nostras dederimus in mandatis[1], ut subiectos vestros, ne ab eisdem magistro et fratribus vel eorum hominibus de victualibus, vestimentis, pecudibus seu de aliis rebus eorundem fratrum usibus deputatis pedagium, passagium, caucagium seu theloneum aut aliam quamlibet consuetudinem exigere vel extorquere presumant, per excommunicacionis in personas et in terras eorum interdicti sententias, si necesse fuerit, compellatis; vos tamen non solum id efficere negligitis, verum eciam, quod est gravius, licet hoc de facili credere non possumus, ab eis premissa pro voluntate vestra facitis extorqueri. Cum autem ipsi apostolice benignitatis auxilium super hoc duxerint humiliter implorandum, universitatem vestram rogamus et hortamur attente per apostolica vobis scripta precipiendo mandantes, quatenus provide attendentes, quod iidem magister et fratres pro sue religionis meritis nullis molestiis affici, sed piis debent beneficiis confoveri, a predictis exactionibus et extorsionibus penitus desistatis et taliter ipsos iuxta litterarum nostrarum tenorem super hiis defendatis ab aliis, quod exinde apud nos possitis merito commendari nec super hoc dictis fratribus oporteat aliter provideri. Datum Anagnie x kalendas decembris pontificatus nostri quarto.

Sine dato: II, 120 v. n. 82 *a*; A. 20 n. 102 Latine et Germanice cum nota: In Confluentia. — Cum dato: IV, 215 n. 15 et in confirmatione Martini V de 1418 ianuar. 2; Ioh. 39. Edd. Caorsinus C. 5, et Senner fol. E. 6 cum depravato initio Quod pro parte. 1. cf. 1257 maii 29 etc. Religiosos viros.

595. *1258 novbr. 22 Anagniae. Alexander IV concedit ordini Theutonico, ut cum simonia irretitis fratribus eius presbyteri fratres possint dispensare.*

Alexander episcopus servus servorum dei dilectis filiis magistro et fratribus etc. Ex parte vestra fuit nobis humiliter supplicatum, ut, cum aliqui ex vobis in vestri ordinis ingressu, nonnulli vero in receptione aliorum ad ipsum incurrerint vitium simonie, vobiscum super hoc rigorem temperando concilii misericorditer agere curaremus. Nos igitur devotionis vestre precibus inclinati presentium vobis auctoritate concedimus, ut fratres vestri presbiteri, qui sunt providi et discreti, cum illis, quibus ad hoc laudabilis conversationis et vite merita noverint suffragari, tam super irregularitate, si quam exinde contraxerint, penitentia eis imposita salutari, quam etiam quod in suis locis remanere possint, si hoc animarum suarum saluti ac utilitati domorum, in quibus sic recepti esse noscuntur, expedire viderint auctoritate nostra valeant dispensare. Reliquos vero mittant ad alias domos eiusdem ordinis et cum ipsis super irregularitate dispensent, quam exinde contraxerunt. Quodsi forsan aliarum domorum difficilis eis reddatur ingressus, ipsos, ne tanquam oves errantes lupi rapacis morsibus pateant, in eisdem domibus tamquam de novo auctoritate predicta recipi faciant, eis in choro et refectorio locis ultimis deputatis. Datum Anagnie x kalendas decembris pontificatus nostri anno quarto.

Sine dato: A. 20 n. 92 „praeceptori et fratribus etc." Latine et Germanice cum nota: In Frankinford et in Buken. — Cum dato: Originale praeceptori et fratribus ordinis Theutonici Alemanniae missum cum bulla in funiculo cannabino appensa in archivo ordinis Theutonici Vindobonensi, quondam Mergenthemi. R. 98 inter Alsatica 15. Ex originali archivi Regimontani, cui modo deest bulla, edd. v. Kotzebue Geschichte Preufsens I, 466 et Livl. U. B. I, 423 n. 334; inscribitur praeceptori et fratribus h. s. M. Th. I. in Alemannia.

---

596. *1258 novbr. 22 Anagniae. Alexander IV vetat praelatos ordini Theutonico molestos esse ob patronatus ecclesiarum ab ipso obtentos aut ob decimas de manibus laicorum redemtas.*

Alexander episcopus servus servorum dei venerabilibus fratribus archiepiscopis et episcopis etc. salutem et apostolicam benedictionem[1]. Suam ad nos dilecti filii .. magister et fratres hospitalis sancte Marie Theutonicorum Ierosolimitani querimoniam destinarunt, quod, si contingat eosdem ius patronatus aliquarum ecclesiarum in vestris diocesibus aut decimas vel alios proventus ecclesiasticos ab illis, ad quos pertinent, legitime obtinere vel decimas redimere de manibus laicorum, vos, quantumcumque sitis ab eis humiliter requisiti, ad hoc vestrum assensum adhibere non vultis in grave ipsorum fratrum preiudicium et sui ordinis detrimentum, licet ipsi parati sint sufficientem caucionem prebere, quod decimas ipsas de manu[2] laicorum redemptas restituent ecclesiis, in quarum sunt parrochiis constitute, quociens eis fuerit de redempcionis precio satisfactum. Cum autem dicti magister et fratres et alii de ordine ipsorum illa de causa potissime digni sint favoris gracia specialis, quia hospitalitatis officio ac defensioni terre sancte necnon fidei katholice in Livonie ac Pruscie partibus magnanimiter promovende cum omni diligencia et attencione desudant; universitatem vestram attente rogandam duximus et monendam per apostolica scripta precipiendo mandantes, quatinus circa dictos magistrum et fratres pro divina et nostra reverencia benignum et benivolum dirigentes affectum eis super premissis consensum vestrum, quociens opus fuerit, liberaliter tribuatis preces nostras et preceptum taliter impleturi, quod exinde vobis gracie divine premium et favoris nostri proveniat incrementum. Datum Anagnie x kalendas decembris pontificatus nostri anno quarto.

Sine dato: A. 20 n. 101 Latine et Germanice cum nota: In Frankinfort; in Colonia, in Confluencia, in Treviris. — A. 16 p. 115. — Cum dato: R. 61 inter Ratisponensia n. 21. Ex originali quondam Confluentino, nunc Vindobonensi cum bulla in filis sericeis appensa ed. Hennes I, 116 n. 184. In eodem archivo Vindobonensi extat etiam aliud originale quondam Trevirense (Iuncense?) eiusdem dati cum bulla in filis sericeis rubris et luteis appensa. „Colonie" A. 16 p. 70. Eadem bulla sub eodem dato R. 136 inter Treverensia cum tali initio: Cum dilecti filii fratres h. s. M. Th. etc. 1. Cum dilecti filii fratres hospitalis sancte Marie Theutunicorum Ierosolomitani solum gaudeant de nostra paternali protectione, suam ad nos querimoniam destinarunt R. 136. 2. manibus R. 136. In sequentibus tantum pauca transposita verba.

---

597. *1258 novbr. 22 Anagniae. Alexander IV concedit ordini Theutonico, quod de male acquisitis, si laesis nequeant restitui, et de redemtionibus certorum votorum ad c marcas recipere possit.*

Alexander episcopus servus servorum dei dilectis filiis etc. salutem et apostolicam benedictionem. Vestre meritis religionis inducimur, ut vos prosequamur gracia, que vestris necessitatibus esse dinoscitur oportuna. Hinc est, quod nos vestris supplicationibus annuentes, ut de usuris[1], rapinis et alias male aquisitis, dummodo hii, quibus ipsorum restitucio fieri debeat, omnino inveniri et sciri non possunt, necnon de redempcionibus votorum, que fuerint auctoritate dyocesanorum pontificum commutata, Ierosolimitano duntaxat excepto, usque ad summam centum marcarum argenti recipere valeatis, auctoritate vobis presencium indulgemus[1] et duximus concedendum, si pro similium recepcione alias non sitis a nobis graciam huiusmodi consecuti, ita quod, si aliquid de ipsis centum marcis dimiseritis vel restitueritis aut dederitis illis, a quibus eas receperitis, huiusmodi dimissum[2] vel restitutum seu datum nichil ad liberacionem eorum prosit nec quantum ad illud habeantur aliquatenus absoluti. Nulli ergo hominum liceat hanc paginam nostre concessionis infringere vel ei ausu temerario contraire. Si quis autem hoc attemptare presumpserit, indignationem omnipotentis dei et beatorum Petri et Pauli apostolorum eius se noverit incursurum. Datum Anagnie x kalendas decembris pontificatus nostri anno quarto.

Sine dato: „Treviris" A. 16 p. 114. — Cum dato: originale cum bulla in filis sericeis appensa in archivo ordinis Theutonici Vindobonensi. R. 149 inter Treverensia. Cf. 1257 aug. 9. Inducunt nos. Speciale pro praeceptore et fratribus h. s. M. Th. in Luzelburc Trever. dioc. in archivo ordinis Theutonici Vindobonensi cum bulla in filis sericeis rubris et luteis appensa. 1. usura R. deest A. 16. 2. remissum A. 16.

---

598. *1258 novbr. 29 Anagniae. Alexander IV repetit n. 544 de 1257 iunii 1.*

Alexander etc. Cum dilectis filiis etc. Datum Anagnie iii kal. decembris pontificatus nostri anno quarto.

---

599. *1258 decbr. 11 Anagniae. Alexander IV repetit n. 571 de 1257 septbr. 7.*

Alexander etc. Cum dilecti etc. Datum Anagnie iii idus decembris pontificatus nostri anno quarto.

---

600. *1258 decbr. 11 Anagniae. Alexander IV repetit Innocentii IV n. 495 de 1245 sept. 12.*

Alexander etc. Querelam gravem etc. Datum Anagnie iii idus decembris pontificatus nostri anno quarto.

Sine dato: „Treviris" A. 16 p. 115. — Cum dato: R. 144 inter Trevirensia. Or. quondam Trevirense cum bulla in filis sericeis rubris et luteis appensa in archivo ordinis Theutonici Vindobonensi. — Sub dato: Viterbii p. a. 4 citatur in designatione Mitowiensis archivi 1621 Holmiam delati ap. Schirren p. 131 n. 119 „Alexander papa rescribit praeceptori et fratribus hospitalis Teutonici potestatem faciens discretis fratribus presbyteris, ut crucis signaculum in subsidium ordinis assumptum ab iis vicissim auferre queant, qui vel votum suum sancte sint executi vel illud pecunia data redimere cupiant". Sed velut privilegia eiusdem d. d. 1257 aug. 7 Viterbii L. U. I, 400 n. 312 et d. d. 1258 maii 10 Viterbii L. U. I, 411 n. 323 specialiter praeceptori Livoniensi vel Prussico videtur transmissum.

---

601. *1258 decbr. 17 Anagniae. Alexander IV magistro et fratribus ordinis Theutonici concedit, ut fratres eorum presbyteri fratribus et familiaribus ordinis ob iniectas in alios manus excommunicatis absolutionem impertiri possint.*

Alexander etc. Devotionis vestre etc. Datum Anagnie xvi kal. ianuarii pontificatus nostri anno quinto.

Or. in archivo ordinis Theutonici Vindobonensi.

---

602. *1259 febr. 22 Anagniae. Alexander IV repetit Honorii III n. 326 de 1221 ianuar. 18.*

Alexander etc. Ea, que pro etc. Datum Anagnie viii kalendas marcii pontificatus nostri anno quinto.

Citatur R. 99 inter Alsatica 16.

---

603. *1259 febr. 22 Anagnie. Alexander IV vetat homines molentes in ordinis Theutonici molendinis vel in furnis eius coquentes aut vendendo vel emendo cum eo communicantes excommunicari.*

Alexander episcopus servus servorum dei venerabilibus fratribus archiepiscopis et episcopis, in quorum diocesibus ecclesie ac domus hospitalis sancte Marie domus Theutonicorum Ierosolimitani consistunt, salutem et apostolicam benedictionem. Quanto amplius esse debetis iustitie zelatores, tanto magis vos dedecet facere fraudem legi et presertim in apostolice sedis iniuriam et contemptum. Sane dilecti filii .. magister et fratres hospitalis sancte Marie Theutonicorum Ierosolimitani gravem nobis querimoniam obtulerunt, quod quidam vestrum et eorum officiales, cum in eos non possint excommunicationis et interdicti proferre sententias eo, quod super hoc apostolice sedis privilegiis sunt muniti, in homines eorum et eos, qui molunt in molendinis vel coquunt in furnis eorum, quique vendendo seu emendo vel alias eis communicant, sententias proferunt memoratas, et sic apostolicorum privilegiorum non vim et potestatem, sed sola verba servantes, ordinis dicti fratres quodammodo excommunicant et cum eis alios communicare non sinunt, ex quo illud evenit inconveniens, ut ipsi fratres quantum ad hoc iudicentur iudicio Iudeorum, et qui eis communicant in predictis, maiorem excommunicationem incurrant, quam etiam excommunicatis communicando fuerant incursuri. Nolentes igitur hec crebris ad nos clamoribus iam perlata ulterius sub dissimulatione transire vobis universis et singulis per apostolica scripta mandamus, quatinus huiusmodi sententias in fraudem privilegiorum suorum de cetero non feratis, quia, si super hoc ad nos denuo[1] clamor ascenderit, non poterimus conniventibus oculis pertransire, quin promulgatores talium sententiarum severitate debita castigemus. Datum Anagnie viii kalendas marcii pontificatus nostri anno quinto.

Sine dato: II, 121 v. n. 86. — Cum dato: ex originali bullato in archivo Regimontano mendose ed. in Livl. U. B. I, 429 n. 339. 1. d. a. n. II.

---

604. *1259 febr. 22 Anagnie. Alexander IV vetat ordinem Theutonicum molestari ob damna a servientibus illata, ob quae a fratribus abiecti sint.*

Alexander episcopus servus servorum dei venerabilibus fratribus archiepiscopis et episcopis et dilectis filiis etc. salutem et apostolicam benedictionem. Querelam dilectorum filiorum .. magistri et fratrum hospitalis sancte Marie Theutonicorum Ierosolimitani recepimus continentem, quod, cum contingat[1] interdum servientes ipsorum[2] laycos aliquibus dampna[3] inferre ipsis fratribus inconsultis ac ipsi propter hoc eosdem abiciant servientes, offensi tamen nichilominus occasionem frivolam mendicantes eos sub tali pretextu contra iusticiam aggravant et molestant. Cum igitur fratres ipsi a nobis et predecessoribus nostris specialibus privilegiis sint donati[4] ac ipsorum molestiam non possimus gerere non molestam[5], discretioni[6] vestre per apostolica scripta precipiendo[7] mandamus[8], quatenus, si qui premissorum occasione molestare presumpserint fratres ipsos, eos[9], ut ab ipsorum super[10] hiis[10] molestatione indebita conquiescant[10], monitione premissa per censuram ecclesiasticam, sicut iustum fuerit[11], appellatione postposita compescatis. Datum Anagnie viii kal. marcii pontificatus nostri anno quinto.

Sine dato: II, 119 n. 78. — Cum dato: A. 16 p. 45 „Baruli". 1. contigerit II. 2. eorum II. 3. i. a. d. II. 4. dotati II. 5. i. n. possimus g. molestiam A. 16 possumus II. 6. universitati A. 16. 7. deest II. 8. mandantes II. 9. premissorum dictos fratres occasione huiusmodi molestare presumunt, eos A. 16. 10. deest II. 11. fuerit compellatis. Datum etc. II.

---

605. *1259 aprilis 24 Anagniae. Alexander IV repetit n. 579 de 1258 maii 18.*

Alexander etc. Ex parte vestra etc. Datum Anagnie viii kalendas maii pontificatus nostri anno quinto.

---

606. *1259 april. 30 Anagniae. Alexander IV repetit n. 544 de 1257 iunii 1.*

Alexander etc. Cum dilectis filiis etc. Datum Anagnie ii kal. maii pontificatus nostri anno quinto.

In transsumpto d. d. Paduae 1336 april. 3 facto per Bertolanum Çaçarinum, notarium sacri palatii Paduen., sub auctoritate Paduani de Buçacharinis, iudicis, Andrea notario teste, qui subscripserunt, exstat in archivo Regimontano.

607. *1259 iulii 23 Anagniae. Alexander IV repetit Gregorii IX n. 424 de 1227 iulii 28.*

Alexander episcopus servus servorum dei dilectis filiis magistro religiose fraternitatis hospitalis sancte Marie Theutonicorum Ierosolimitani eiusque fratribus tam presentibus quam futuris in perpetuam memoriam. Etsi neque etc. — ad exemplar felicis memorie Honorii et Gregorii predecessorum nostrorum Romanorum pontificum sub — consequantur. Amen.

Ego Alexander catholice ecclesie episcopus.
Ego Odo Tusculanus episcopus.
Ego Stephanus Prenestinus episcopus.
Ego frater Iohannes tituli sancti Laurentii in Lucina presbiter cardinalis.
Ego frater Hugo tituli sancte Sabine presbiter cardinalis.
Ego Riccardus sancti Angeli diaconus cardinalis.
Ego Octavianus sancte Marie in via lata diaconus cardinalis.
Ego Iohannes sancti Nicolai in carcere Tulliano diaconus cardinalis.

Datum Anagnie per manum magistri Iordani, sacre Romane ecclesie notarii et vicecancellarii, x kal. augusti, indictione ii incarnationis dominice m° cc° l° viiii° anno pontificatus domini Alexandri pape iiii anno quinto.

„Privilegium Alexandri Venetiis repertum sine aliqua bulla pendenti et sine data in eo scripta" A. 16 p. 8—10. — Cum dato: 1259 x kal. aug. Anagnie p. a. 5. originale, cui nunc deest plumbum, in archivo Regimontano; male ed. Livl. U. B. I, 431 n. 341, cuius tamen variam lectionem quippe non satis probatam apponere supersedimus. In eodem archivo tria transsumta: 1. Gerhardi, Pomesaniensis episcopi d. d. Resinburg 1419 aug. 9. c. sig. Editum etiam apud: Dzialynski Lites ac res gestae inter Polonos ordinemque cruciferorum. Posnaniae 1855. I, b. 84. 2. Iohannis Culmensis et Gerhardi Pomesaniensis episcoporum d. d. Schoenbergi 1421 nov. 5. 3. Iohannis Pomesaniensis episcopi d. d. Risenburgi 1438 sept. 26 cum sig.

608. *(Inter 1258 decbr. 12 et 1259 decbr. 11.) Alexander IV repetit n. 581 de 1258 iunii 8.*

Alexander etc. Iustis petentium etc. Datum etc. pontificatus nostri anno quinto.

609. *1260 ianuarii 25 Anagniae. Alexander IV iterato praelatos commonet, ne ordinis Theutonici homines pecuniaria poena puniant.*

Alexander episcopus servus servorum dei venerabilibus fratribus archiepiscopis et episcopis, ad quos littere iste pervenerint, salutem et apostolicam benedictionem. Dignos plenitudine apostolici favoris et gratie dilectos filios fratres hospitalis sancte Marie Theutonicorum illa de causa potissime reputamus, quia pie conversationis et vite studio sine intermissione desudant et pro subsidio terre sancte ac pro fidei negotio in Livonie et Pruscie partibus magnifice promovendo labores plurimos et infinitas angustias ac etiam mortis periculum ad honorem divini nominis corde intrepido frequentissime patiuntur. Inde fit, quod nos olim vobis nostras dicimur direxisse litteras continentes, ut vestros decanos et archidiaconos arceatis, ne homines dictorum fratrum pro suis excessibus pecuniaria pena puniant, sed, imposita illis penitentia competenti, bona eorum ad usus fratrum ipsorum in pace dimittant, maxime cum indignum sit, quod iidem fratres, qui ad defensionem fidei totis viribus elaborant, in rebus ad ipsos spectantibus aliquod sustineant detrimentum. Quia vero vos ipsi, prout mirantes audivimus, homines dictorum fratrum huiusmodi pecuniaria pena punitis, propter quod iidem fratres ad apostolice sedis clementiam recurrere sunt coacti, nos universitatem vestram attente rogandam duximus et monendam, per apostolica vobis scripta districte precipiendo mandantes, quatinus, circa fratres eosdem affectum benivolum pro divina et nostra reverentia dirigentes, prefatos ipsorum homines nullatenus de cetero taliter puniatis, sed eis prout hiis, in quibus excesserint, iuxta formam vobis traditam contra decanos et archidiaconos memoratos, iniuncta penitentia competenti bona illorum ad usus eorundem fratrum pacifice relinquatis, ita quod nos super hoc non aliud adhibere consilium, sed teneamur vobis ad actiones uberes gratiarum. Datum Anagnie viii kalendas februarii pontificatus nostri anno sexto.

Transsumta duo d. d. Romae 1427 iunii 6 iubente magistro Heinrico Gedde, ordinis procuratore generali, ad preces Iohannis Tirgarth, procuratoris, Curoniensis episcopi, per Iulianum de Cesarinis, i. u. d., papae capellanum ac sacri palacii apostolici causarum eiusque camerarii necnon curiae causarum camerae apostolicae generalem auditorem. Ed. in Livl. U. B. I, 443 n. 349.

---

610. *1260 ianuarii 25 Anagniae. Alexander IV ordini Theutonico loca de manibus paganorum erepta confirmat.*

Alexander episcopus servus servorum dei dilectis filiis magistro et fratribus hospitalis sancte Marie Theutonicorum Ierosolimitani salutem et apostolicam benedictionem. Operis evidentia declarante, quod vos ad hoc ferventer insistitis, ut cultum catholice fidei tam in orientis quam Pruscie et Livonie et in conterminis eis partibus ad dei gloriam amplietis, sedi apostolice delectabile redditur, ut vos gratiosi favoris affluentia prosequatur. Hinc est, quod nos vestris supplicationibus inclinati omnes terras, regiones, castra, villas seu oppida et quecunque loca, que vos adiuti subsidio exercitus christiani eripere poteritis de manibus paganorum, dummodo non pertineant ad aliquos christianos vel christiani ea non possederint a tempore, cuius memoria non existit, exnunc in ius et proprietatem beati Petri suscipimus et illa sub speciali protectione ac defensione apostolice sedis, postquam ad christianum cultum reducta fuerint, perpetuis temporibus permanere sancimus, ipsaque vobis et domui vestre cum omni iure et proprietatibus suis ac decimis exinde proventuris concedimus in perpetuum libere possidenda, ita quod terre, castra, ville aut oppida et loca ipsa per vos aut quoscumque alios nullius unquam subiiciantur dominio potestatis. Volumus tamen, quod, postquam illa deo propitio a vobis fuerint acquisita et possessa pacifice, vos omnium ipsorum et predictarum etiam decimarum certam partem ecclesiis earumque prelatis constituendis ibidem iuxta providentiam sedis apostolice teneamini assignare. Nulli ergo omnino liceat hanc paginam nostre protectionis et concessionis infringere vel ei ausu temerario contraire. Si quis autem hoc attemptare presumpserit, indignationem omnipotentis dei et beatorum Petri et Pauli apostolorum eius se noverit incursurum. Datum Anagnie viii kalendas februarii pontificatus nostri anno sexto.

Ex originali quondam Cracoviensis archivi ed. Dogiel Cod. dipl. Poloniae IV, 29 n. 33. In inventario archivi Cracoviensis p. 66 citatur: „Alexander IV terras per cruciferos subsidio christiani exercitus acquisitas in ius et proprietatem s. Petri accipit, dummodo loca illa christianorum non fuerint nec ad aliquos christianos pertineant a tempore, cuius memoria nunc (!) exstat, ditionesque eiusmodi ordini donat. Anagniae 7 kal. februarii pontificatus anno 6". E duobus transsumtis archivi Regimontani de 1324 oct. 25 et 1393 maii 29 ed. in Livl. U. B. I, 441 n. 346. Privilegium simillimi tenoris de locis in Ruscia vel de Tartaris acquirendis magistro et fratribus h. s. M. Th. I. missa de eodem dato ex originali archivi Regimontani, ubi extant etiam transsumta de 1393 maii 29; Casparis d. d. Riesenburgi 1445 nov. 20 et Iobi Pomesaniensium episcoporum d. d. Konigsbergi 1506 oct. 14, ed. Livl. U. B. I, 440 n. 345.

---

611. *1260 maii 15 Anagniae. Alexander IV confirmat ordini Theutonico immunitatem a praestatione decimarum.*

Alexander episcopus servus servorum dei venerabilibus fratribus archiepiscopis, episcopis etc. Cum abbates Cisterciensis ordinis tempore concilii generalis congregati, ut occasione privilegiorum suorum ecclesie ulterius minime gravarentur, ad commonicionem felicis recordacionis Innocencii pape predecessoris nostri statuerint[1], ut de cetero fratres ipsius ordinis nisi pro monasteriis de novo fundandis non emant possessiones, in quibus decime debentur ecclesiis, et, si pro monasteriis de novo fundatis tales possessiones pia fidelium devocione collate eis fuerint aut empte, committantur aliis colende, a quibus ecclesiis decime persolvantur; dictus predecessor noster statutum huiusmodi gratum habens et ratum decrevit, ut dicti fratres de alienis terris ab eo tempore acquirendis, eciamsi eas propriis manibus aut sumptibus excolant, decimas persolvant ecclesiis, quibus racione prediorum antea solvebantur, nisi cum ipsis ecclesiis aliter ducerent componendum; quod et ad alios regulares, qui gaudent similibus privilegiis, extendi voluit et mandavit, ut ecclesiarum prelati prompciores et efficaciores existerent ad exhibendum ipsis de suis malefactoribus iusticie complementum eorumque privilegia diligencius et perfeccius observarent. Sed, quod dolentes referimus, in contrarium res est conversa, quia, sicut ex gravi querela dilectorum filiorum magistri et fratrum hospitalis sancte[2] (Marie Theutonicorum)[3] Ierosolimitani frequenter audivimus, nonnulli ecclesiarum prelati et alii clerici eorum privilegia temere contempnentes et contendentes maliciose ipsorum pervertere intellectum eosdem multipliciter inquietant. Nam, cum sit ipsis indultum, ut de novalibus, que propriis manibus excolunt aut sumptibus sive de ortis, virgultis et piscacionibus suis vel de suorum animalium nutrimentis nullus ab eis decimam exigere aut extorquere presumat, quidam perverso intellectu conficte dicentes, quod hec non possunt nec debent intelligi nisi de hiis, que sunt ante concilium generale acquisita, ipsos super hiis multiplici vexacione fatigant. Nos igitur eorum quieti paterna sollicitudine providere volentes universitati vestre per apostolica scripta mandamus, quatenus dictos fratres a prestacione decimarum tam de possessionibus habitis ante concilium memoratum quam de novalibus sive ante sive post idem concilium acquisitis, que propriis manibus aut sumptibus excolunt, de quibus novalibus aliquis hactenus non percepit, necnon de ortis, virgultis et piscacionibus suis et de suorum arantium nutrimentis[1] singuli vestrum omnino servetis immunes contradictores per censuram ecclesiasticam appellacione postposita compescendo. Datum Anagnie idus maii pontificatus nostri anno sexto.

R. 105 inter Alsatica n. 19 in triplicis transsumti apographo: 1. Iudicum delegatorum Spirensium ad petitionem magistri et fratrum ordinis Theutonicorum domus asserentium ipsis periculosum esse presentem literam dnci de loco ad locum. 1276 in crastino Egidii (sept. 2) intus in 2. Iudicum Curiae Spirensis transsumto 1303 feria IV post dom. q. c. Oculi ad preces magistri et fratrum Th. intus in 3. officialis archidiacon. curiae Basileensis d. d. 1303 vi kal. maii Basileae. 1. statuerunt R. 2. sic R. 3. M. T. deest R. 4. nut'mentibus.

---

612. *1260 iulii 10 Anagnie. Alexander IV repetit n. 593 de 1258 novbr. 22.*

Alexander etc. Ex parte dilectorum etc. Datum Anagnie iv idus iulii pontificatus nostri anno sexto.

---

613. *1260 novbr. 16 Laterani. Alexander IV concedit ordini Theutonico in Alemannia, quod decimas in parochiis alienis de manibus laicorum redimere possit.*

Alexander episcopus servus servorum dei dilectis filiis preceptori et fratribus hospitalis sancte Marie Theutonicorum in Alamannia salutem et apostolicam benedictionem. Affectu sunt admittende benivolo preces devote petencium, cum sic eis gracia favoris inpenditur, quod alieno iuri nulla prorsus iniuria irrogatur. Hinc est, quod nos vestris supplicationibus annuentes redimendi decimas de manibus laycorum in parrochiis alienis, rectorum ecclesiarum, in quarum parrochiis decime ipse consistunt, et diocesanorum earum accedente consensu, auctoritate vobis presencium concedimus facultatem, sufficienti a vobis prius prestita cautione de restituendis decimis ipsis eisdem ecclesiis, quandocunque vobis ab illarum rectoribus fuerit de redemptionis precio satisfactum. Nulli ergo omnino hominum liceat hanc paginam nostre concessionis infringere vel ei ausu temerario contraire. Si quis autem hoc attemptare presumpserit, indignationem omnipotentis dei et beatorum Petri et Pauli apostolorum eius se noverit incursurum. Datum Laterani xvi kalendas decembris pontificatus nostri anno sexto.

R. 124 inter Marburgensia; etiam A. 16 p. 66. — Cum titulo magistro et fratribus etc. A. 20 n. 103 Latine et Germanice cum nota: In Marpurg. Innocencius eiusdem tenoris in Leodio.

---

614. *1261 martii 28 Laterani. Alexander IV repetit n. 558 de 1257 iulii 11.*

Alexander etc. Canonica constitutione etc. Datum Laterani v kalendas aprilis pontificatus nostri anno septimo.

---

615. *1261 aprilis 5 Laterani. Alexander IV repetit n. 558 de 1257 iulii 11.*

Alexander etc. Canonica constitutione etc. Datum Laterani nonas aprilis pontificatus nostri anno septimo.

---

616. *1261 aprilis 12 Laterani. Alexander IV repetit Gregorii IX n. 437 de 1227 aug. 21.*

Alexander etc. Iustis petentium etc. Datum Laterani ii idus aprilis pontificatus nostri anno septimo.

Or. cum bulla in archivo Regimontano. Alterum or. cum bulla in filis sericeis luteis et rubris appensa in archivo ordinis Theutonici Vindobonensi iam dudum domus Vindobonensis. Ed. Duellius II, 15 n. 21.

---

617. *(Inter 1254 decbr. 12 et 1261 maii 25). Alexander IV vetat episcopos ordinis Theutonici ecclesias post recessum vicariorum occupare, sed infra quadraginta dies ab ordine praesentatis conferre.*

Alexander etc. archiepiscopis et episcopis etc. Cum dilectos filios fratres hospitalis sancte Marie Theutonicorum Ierosolimitani consideratione laboris, quem ad christianitatem servandam tolerant in partibus transmarinis, speciali diligamus affectu et apud omnes cultores nominis christiani haberi conveniat specialiter commendatos, non est rationi conveniens ut a viris ecclesiasticis, qui debent laicos ad subveniendum eis inducere, aliquam iniuriam patiantur; ideoque universitati vestre auctoritate apostolica prohibemus, ne ecclesie illis concesse et a diocesanis episcopis confirmate post decessum vel recessum vicariorum vel personarum ab episcopis vel eorum officialibus occupentur, sed infra quadraginta dies post decessum vel recessum eorum ad presentationem fratrum instituantur in eisdem ecclesiis persone ydonee, que episcopis de spiritualibus respondeant et debitam subiectionem adhibeant, fratribus autem sua iura conservent et prebeant illibata. Data etc.

II, 121 n. 83.

---

618. *(Inter 1254 decbr. 12 et 1261 maii 25). Alexander IV concedit ordini Theutonico, quod nequeat conveniri per literas apostolica nisi specialem eius facientes mentionem.*

Alexander etc. magistro et fratribus etc. Cum ordinis vestri titulus per dei graciam adeo sit insignis, quod vix credatur ab hiis, qui contra vos litteras impetrant, sine malicia subticeri, nos et illorum fraudibus obviare et innocentiam vestram volentes favorabiliter confovere, auctoritate vobis presentium indulgemus, ut nequeatis per litteras apostolicas conveniri, que de ordine vestro non fecerint mentionem. Nulli ergo etc. Si quis autem etc. Data etc.

II, 121 v. n. 84.

---

619. *1261 novbr. 25 Viterbii. Urbanus IV repetit Alexandri IV n. 590 de 1258 novbr. 9.*

Urbanus episcopus servus servorum dei dilectis filiis .. magistro et fratribus hospitalis sancte Marie Theutonicorum in Alamannia salutem et apostolicam benedictionem. Devocionis vestre etc. Datum Viterbii vii kalendas decembris pontificatus nostri anno primo.

IV, 217 v. R. 100 inter Alsatica n. 11.

---

620. *1261 novbr. 26 Viterbii. Urbanus IV ordinis Theutonici parochialibus ecclesiis indulgentias quasdam confert, ad vitam Annonis magistri valituras.*

Urbanus episcopus etc. dilectis filiis Annoni magistro et fratribus hospitalis sancte Marie Thentonicorum Ierosolmitani salutem et apostolicam benedictionem. Innocentis vite studium et pietatis opera, quibus ferventer intenditis pro consequenda gloria perpetue claritatis, accendunt corda fidelium, quod ipsi, prout accepimus, libenter in ecclesiis vestri ordinis implorant a domino suorum peccatorum veniam et celestium munera gaudiorum. Ut autem et vos de vestris laudabilibus meritis a nobis condigna suscepisse premia gaudeatis et predicti fideles eo magis sint in caritate fervidi, quo pleniorem gratiam pro sue devotionis affectu fuerint a sede apostolica consecuti, nos de omnipotentis dei misericordia et beatorum Petri et Pauli apostolorum eius auctoritate confisi omnibus vere penitentibus et confessis, qui, postquam in ecclesiis, quarum parochiani existunt, sollemnia missarum audierint, ad predictas ecclesias vestri ordinis in nativitatis, resurrectionis dominice, pentecostes, assumptionis et purificationis gloriose virginis Marie ac omnium sanctorum festivitatibus et in cena domini causa devotionis accesserint, annuatim quadraginta dies de iniuncta sibi penitentia misericorditer relaxamus; presentibus, fili magister, post obitum tuum minime valituris. Datum Viterbii, vi kalendas decembris pontificatus nostri anno primo.

Ex originali, cui modo deest plumbum, in archivo Regimontano, ed. in Livl. U. B. I, 465 n. 364. Obiit Anno magister 1273 aut 1274 iulii 8.

---

621. *1261 decbr. 13 Viterbii. Urbanus IV repetit Alexandri IV n. 558 de 1257 iulii 11.*

Urbanus etc. dilectis filiis preceptoribus et fratribus etc. Canonica constitutione etc. Datum Viterbii idus decembris pontificatus nostri anno primo.

Citatur tanquam concinens Alexandri IV inter Ratisponensia n. 9; R. 100 inter Alsatica 12.

---

622. *1261 decbr. 15 Viterbii. Urbanus IV repetit Gregorii IX n. 466 de 1237 maii 22.*

Urbanus etc. dilectis filiis .. magistro et fratribus hospitalis sancte Marie Theutonicorum Ierosolimitani salutem et apostolicam benedictionem. Signorum evidentia declarante etc. Datum Viterbii xviii kal. ianuarii pontificatus nostri anno primo.

Originale cum bulla in archivo Regimontano. A. 16 p. 93 „Mechelinia". Citatur in confirmatione Nicolai IV de 1289 aprilis 1.

---

623. *1262 ianuarii 23 Viterbii (cf. 1264 ianuarii 30). Urbanus IV repetit Alexandri IV n. 607 de 1259 iulii 28.*

Urbanus etc. Etsi neque etc. Datum Viterbii per manus magistri Iohannis Iordani s. Romane ecclesie vicecancellarii et notarii x kal. februarii indiccione v anno ab incarnatione domini mcclxi[1] pontificatus vero domini Urbani pape iv anno primo.

Ego Urbanus catholice ecclesie episcopus[2].
Ego Odo Tusculanus episcopus.
Ego Stephanus Prenestinus episcopus.
Ego frater Hugo s. Sabine presbiter cardinalis.
Ego Ricardus s. Angeli diaconus cardinalis.
Ego Ottobonus s. Adriani diaconus cardinalis.
Ego Godofredus s. Georgii ad velum aureum diaconus cardinalis.
Ego frater Iohannes s. Laurentii in Lucina presbiter cardinalis.
Ego Ottomarus s. Marie in via lata diaconus cardinalis.
Ego Iohannes s. Nicolai in carcere Tulliano diaconus cardinalis.
Ego Iacobus s. Marie in Cosmedin diaconus cardinalis.
Ego Ubertus s. Eustachii diaconus cardinalis.

A. 16 p. 53 cf. 57 „Baruli". 1. sic; cf. n. 632. 2. hunc versum supplevi.

---

624. *1262 augusti 31 apud Montemflasconis. Urbanus IV repetit Alexandri IV n. 594 de 1258 novbr. 22.*

Urbanus etc. venerabilibus fratribus archiepiscopis et episcopis et dilectis filiis abbatibus, prioribus etc. Ex parte dilectorum filiorum — litteras apostolice sedis datum fuerit in mandatis — passagium, cauchagium seu theolonium — provideri. Datum apud Montemflasconis ii kal. septbr. pontificatus nostri anno primo.

A. 16 p. 55 „Baruli". Urbanus 1261 aug. 29 electus; consecratus est sept. 4; 31 ergo aug. p. a. 1 anno Christi 1262 adnumerandus est.

---

625. *1263 martii 22 apud Urbem Veterem. Urbanus IV repetit Alexandri IV n. 600 de 1258 decbr. 11.*

Urbanus etc. Querelam gravem etc. — requirendis iuxta consuetudinem suam auctoritate apostolica confirmatam ad ecclesias — recipere — sed — quod iidem presbyteri quandam — non formidant — non debemus — tenemur — atque precipimus — ut predictos fratres, dummodo ydonei et bone opinionis existant, in ecclesiis suis — predicare et elemosinas querere iuxta quod eis apostolica sedes indulsit, sine — salva moderatione concilii generalis nec aliquid ab eis — taliter veritate cognita vindicetis — predictis fratribus — presumunt, precipimus, ut, si quando predicti fratres —. Datum apud Urbem Veterem xi kal. aprilis pontificatus nostri anno secundo.

Originale cum bulla in archivo Regimontano.

---

626. *1263 martii 28 apud Urbem Veterem. Urbanus IV repetit Alexandri IV n. 544 de 1257 iunii 1.*

Urbanus etc. Cum dilectis filiis etc. Datum apud Urbem Veterem v kal. aprilis pontificatus nostri anno secundo.

A. 16 p. 1 „invenitur in Venetiis". A. 16 p. 55 „Baruli". Transsumtum, ut legitur in dorso, „non satis authenticum" d. d. Paduae 1336 april. 3 factum auctoritate et testibus, quibus transsumtum bullae Alexandri IV n. 606 de 1259 april. 30 in archivo Regimontano.

627. *(Ante 1263 maii 28). Urbanus IV eximit per triennium ordinem Theutonicum a procurationibus pecuniariis legatis solvendis.*

Citatur a Clemente IV 1266 maii 28 (Affectu benevolencie).

---

628. *1263 octbr. 1 apud Urbem Veterem. Urbanus IV repetit Honorii III n. 305 de 1218 octbr. 1.*

Urbanus episcopus servus servorum dei venerabilibus fratribus archiepiscopis et episcopis ac dilectis filiis abbatibus, prioribus, prepositis, archidiaconis, decanis et aliis ecclesiarum prelatis, ad quos littere iste pervenerint, salutem et apostolicam benedictionem. Cum dilecti — curemus. Datum apud Urbem Veterem kal. octobris pontificatus nostri anno tercio.

Originale, de quo bulla quondam filis sericeis appensa avulsa iam deest, in archivo ordinis Theutonici Vindobonensi iam dudum domus Vindobonensis. VI, 353 v. In apographo sine dato, quod signis confirmaverunt: frater Placidus dei gracia humilis Andrensis episcopus, dompnus Bartholomeus, rector ecclesie s. Bartholomei et vicarius Baroli, frater Symon humilis abbas s. Samuelis de Barolo, frater Godefridus humilis abbas s. Marie de Stirpeto Baroli, descriptum „Venetiis" A. 16 p. 15. 16; A. 16 p. 55 „Baruli". Etiam tria transsumta in archivo Regimontano asservantur: 1. d. d. Rige 1335 febr. 25. 2. d. d. Strafsburg 1336 iunii 14. 3. d. d. Marienburg 1393 maii 29.

---

629. *1263 octbr. 1 apud Urbem Veterem. Urbanus IV repetit Alexandri IV n. 542 de 1257 maii 30.*

Urbanus etc. Cum vos tanquam etc. inclinati ad instar felicis recordacionis Alexandri pape predecessoris nostri auctoritate vobis presentium etc. Datum apud Urbem Veterem kal. octobris pontificatus nostri anno tercio.

Cum dato: R. 148 inter Treverensia. — Cum dato: a. 3 „Treviris" A. 16 p. 114 et 120. Originale quondam E(llingense?) in archivo ordinis Theutonici Vindobonensi.

---

630. *1263 octbr. 3 apud Urbem Veterem. Urbanus IV repetit Alexandri IV n. 570 de 1257 aug. 20.*

Urbanus episcopus servus servorum dei venerabilibus fratribus archiepiscopis et episcopis et dilectis filiis abbatibus, prioribus, prepositis, archidiaconis, decanis et aliis ecclesiarum prelatis, ad quos littere iste pervenerint, salutem et apostolicam benedictionem. Dilectorum filiorum — ideoque universitati vestre ad instar felicis recordacionis Alexandri predecessoris nostri per — vinculo innodetis. Datum apud Urbem Veterem v nonas octobris pontificatus nostri anno tercio.

IV, 218 v.; R. 168 inter Thuringica.

---

631. *1263 octbr. 4 apud Urbem Veterem. Urbanus IV repetit Alexandri IV constitutionem n. 593 de 1258 novbr. 22, ex qua ordo Theutonicus ad ecclesias sui patronatus clericos ordinis sui praesentare possit.*

Urbanus episcopus servus servorum dei venerabilibus fratribus archiepiscopis et episcopis et dilectis filiis archidiaconis, ad quos littere iste pervenerint, salutem et apostolicam benedictionem. Ex parte dilectorum filiorum magistri et fratrum hospitalis sancte Marie Theotonicorum Ierosolimitani nobis est oblata querela, quod, licet eis a sede apostolica sit indultum, ut fratres clericos ordinis sui ad vacantes ecclesias, in quibus ius obtinent patronatus diocesanis episcopis, responsuros eis de spiritualibus, dictis magistro et fratribus de temporalibus, valeant presentare; aliqui tamen vestrum se illis super hoc molestos et graves sepius exhibentes predictos fratres clericos, quos dicti magister et fratres iuxta predictum indultum eis presentant ad ecclesias memoratas, instituere denegant in eis pro sue arbitrio voluntatis. Cum autem ipsi apostolice benignitatis auxilium super hoc duxerint humiliter implorandum, universitatem vestram rogamus et hortamur attente ad instar felicis recordacionis Alexandri pape predecessoris nostri per apostolica vobis scripta precipiendo mandantes, quatenus provide attendentes, quod idem magister et fratres pro sue religionis meritis nullis molestiis affici, sed piis debent beneficiis confoveri, vos eis in premissis nullius difficultatis opponatis obstaculum, sed favorem benivolum ad id potius impendatis, ita quod nec ipsi conquerendi de vobis materiam habeant, nec eis super hoc per nos oporteat aliter provideri[1]. Datum apud Urbem Veterem iiii nonas octobris pontificatus nostri anno tercio.

Sine dato: A. 20 n. 85 Latine et Germanice cum nota: Prage habetur. — Cum dato: IV, 219 A. 16 p. 117 „Treviris". Or. quondam Mergenthemense cum bulla in filis sericeis appensa in archivo ordinis Theutonici Vindobonensi. 1. providere IV.

---

632. *1264 ianuarii 30 apud Urbem Veterem. Urbanus IV repetit n. 623 de 1262 ianuarii 23.*

Urbanus etc. Etsi neque etc. Datum apud Urbem Veterem per manum magistri Michaelis de Tholosa sacre Romane ecclesie vicecancellarii iii kalendas februarii indictione vii incarnationis dominice anno mcclxiii°[1] pontificatus vero domini Urbani pape iv anno tercio.

Ego Urbanus catholice ecclesie episcopus.
Ego Odo Tusculanus episcopus.
Ego Stephanus Prenestinus episcopus.
Ego frater Iohannes Portuensis et s. Ruffine episcopus.
Ego Rudulphus Albanensis episcopus.
Ego Heinricus Ostiensis et Velletrensis episcopus.
Ego Guido Sabinensis episcopus[2].
Ego Symon tituli s. Martini presbyter cardinalis.
Ego Guillelmus tituli s. Laurentii presbyter cardinalis.
Ego Symon s. Cecilie presbyter cardinalis.
Ego Riccardus s. Angeli diaconus cardinalis.
Ego Iohannes s. Nicolai in carcere Tulliano diaconus cardinalis.
Ego Ottobonus s. Adriani diaconus cardinalis.
Ego Iacobus s. Marie in Cosmedin diaconus cardinalis.
Ego Ubertus s. Eustachii diaconus cardinalis.
Ego Iordanus ss. Cosme et Damiani diaconus cardinalis.
Ego Matheus s. Marie in porticu diaconus cardinalis.

Transsumtum Iohannis Pomesaniensis episcopi, cui subscripsit Martinus Alwer, de 1438 sept. 26 Risenburgi, cum sigillo in archivo Regimontano. 1. cf. n. 623. 2. Turbatum ordinem, quum episcopi cardinales caeteris praecedere debent, restitui; in transsumto episcopi ultimi esse perhibentur.

---

633. *1264 aug. 23 apud Urbem Veterem. Urbanus IV vetat pro constructionibus ordini Theutonico exactiones imponi.*

Urbanus episcopus servus servorum dei dilectis filiis magistro et fratribus hospitalis sancte Marie Theotonicorum Ierosolimitani salutem et apostolicam benedictionem. Vestre meritis devocionis inducimur, ut vos favore benivolo prosequamur et in hiis, que digne deposcitis, habeamus providencie[1] studium efficacis. Exhibita siquidem nobis vestra peticio continebat, quod felicis recordacionis Honorius papa predecessor noster per litteras suas vobis indulsit, ne quis vobis aut ecclesiis vestris pro reparacione murorum, poncium et vallorum seu pro quibuslibet publicis functionibus aliquas exactiones imponat nec alicui liceat vim et libertatem eorum, que predecessor ipse vobis et domui vestre indulsit, per litteras aliquas auferre vel temeritate aliqua vacuare. Nos itaque vestris supplicacionibus inclinati premissa, sicuti idem predecessor vobis per huiusmodi litteras suas indulsit, sic et nos devocioni vestre auctoritate presencium indulgemus. Nulli ergo omnino hominum liceat hanc paginam nostre concessionis infringere vel ei ausu temerario contraire. Si quis autem hoc attemptare presumpserit, indignacionem omnipotentis dei et beatorum Petri et Pauli apostolorum eius se noverit incursurum. Datum apud Urbem Veterem x kal. septembris pontificatus nostri anno tercio.

Cum dato: IV, 218. — Sine dato: „apud Urbem Veterem" R. 158 et A. 16 p. 103 inter Iuncensia. Originale quondam Iuncense cum bulla in filis sericeis rubris et luteis appensa in archivo ordinis Theutonici Vindobonensi. 1. providere IV.

---

634. *Inter 1261 septbr. 4 et 1264 octbr. 2. Urbanus IV repetit Honorii III n. 351 de 1221 febr. 5.*

Urbanus etc. magistro et fratribus etc. Iustis petentium — vacuare. Nulli ergo etc. Si quis etc. Datum etc.

Sine dato: A. 16 p. 103 „Iuncis".

---

635. *1265 maii 4 Perusii. Clemens IV repetit Alexandri IV n. 597 de 1258 novbr. 22.*

Clemens etc. dilectis filiis preceptori et fratribus in Apulia etc. Vestre meritis — usuris, rapinis et aliis male acquisitis, si hii — debeat edicto publice proposito in ecclesiis et aliis locis competentibus omnino — non possint in subsidium necessitatum vestrarum usque ad summam cc unciarum auri per provinciam Tranensem recipere valeatis, auctoritate apostolica vobis duximus concedendum. Si per — itaque si — cc unciis — laborationem — prosit, nec quantum — absoluti in presentibus post biennium minime valituris. Nulli — incursurum. Datum Perusii iiii non. maii pontificatus nostri anno primo.

Cum dato: Perusii 4 non. maii a. 1 „preceptori et fr. in Apulia" A. 16 p. 52 „Baruli". Quamvis sit speciale hoc privilegium super formulam etiam generaliter editam, tamen hic sistere libuit, quum remotiorem spectet ordinis provinciam, iam a nobis absolutam, quum transscriptum Regimonto nobis veniret.

---

636. *1265 maii 11 Perusii (cf. maii 20). Clemens IV repetit ordini Theutonico in Alemannia confirmationem Gregorii IX n. 469.*

Clemens episcopus servus servorum dei dilectis filiis preceptori et fratribus hospitalis sancte Marie Theutonicorum in Alemannia salutem et aposcolicam benedictionem. Cum a nobis etc. Datum Perusii v idus maii pontificatus nostri anno primo.

Cum dato: Perusii 5 id. maii p. n. a. 1 „Venetiis“ A. 16 p. 16. — Cum dato: Perusii 13 kal. iunii p. n. a. 1. praeceptori et fratribus h. s. M. Th. in Alemannia R. 91 inter Mergenthe-rensia 56. — Cum dato: a. 3 „Treviris“ A. 16 p. 118. — Nescio cuius Clementis tale privilegium Mecheliniae fuit; v. infra ad 1336 febr. 8.

---

637. *1265 maii 20 Perusii (cf. 1267/8). Clemens IV repetit n. 636 de 1265 maii 11.*

Clemens etc. preceptori et fratribus h. s. M. Th. in Alemannia etc. Cum a nobis etc. Datum Perusii xiii kal. iunii pontificatus nostri anno primo.

---

638. *1265 maii 31 Perusii (cf. iunii 2). Clemens IV ordini Theutonico indulget, quod fratres per litteras apostolicas in ius vocari non possint nisi expressam de hoc indulto facientes mentionem.*

Clemens episcopus servus servorum dei dilectis filiis magistro et fratribus domus hospitalis Iherosolimitani s. et a. b. Devocionis vestre promeretur effectus, ut, quod a[1] nobis suppliciter petitis, ad exaudicionis graciam, quantum cum deo possumus, favorabiliter admittamus. Eapropter, dilecti in domino filii, vestris supplicationibus inclinati, ut ab aliquibus in causam trahi per litteras apostolicas, nisi plenam et expressam de hac indulgentia et ordine vestro faciunt mencionem, minime valeatis, auctoritate vobis presentium indulgemus. Nulli ergo omnino hominum liceat hanc paginam nostre concessionis infringere etc. Si quis autem etc. Datum Perusii ii kal. iunii pontificatus nostri anno primo.

Cum dato: Perusii 2 kal. iunii p. a. 1; A. 16 p. 12 „Venetiis“. — Cum dato: Perusii 4 non. iunii a. 1 „Colonie“ A. 16 p. 76 sq. 1. supplevi.

---

639. *1265 maii 31 Perusii. Clemens IV repetit Alexandri IV n. 610 de 1260 ianuarii 25.*

Clemens etc. Operis evidentia etc. Datum Perusii ii kalendas iunii pontificatus nostri anno primo.

Originale cum bulla, cuius filis sericeis affixa scedula pergamenea, in qua legitur: „nota diligenter subscriptam clausulam“ (i. e. ut nullius unquam subiiciantur dominio), quondam Polonis extraditum, dein Cracoviae, Varsaviae, Berolini asservatum, 1865 Regimontano archivo restitutum, quod habet etiam alterum originale cum bulla et transsumta tria Pomesaniensium episcoporum Casparis d. d. Risenburgi 1445 novbr. 20 et 1453 maii 16, necnon Iobi d. d. Regimonti 1506 octbr. 14. Inventarium archivi Cracoviensis p. 66 citat: „Clemens papa IV confirmat cruciferis acquisita et acquirenda de paganis, pontificatus anno primo“.

---

640. *1265 iunii 2 Perusii. Clemens IV repetit Alexandri IV n. 600 de 1258 decembris 11.*

Clemens etc. Querelam gravem etc. Datum Perusii iiii nonas iunii pontificatus nostri anno primo.

Originale domus Vindobonensis, nunc ibidem in archivo ordinis, cum bulla in filis sericeis appensa. citat Duellius II, 8 ann. Transsumptum de 1396 aug. 18 Vindobonae in archivo Regimontano. — Sine dato citatur R. 195.

641. *1265 iunii 22 Perusii. Clemens IV repetit Honorii III n. 305 de 1218 octobris 1.*

Clemens etc. venerabilibus fratribus archiepiscopis et episcopis etc. Cum dilecti filii fratres Iherosolimitani hospitalis nullum habeant episcopum — curemus. Datum Perusii x kal. iulii pontificatus nostri anno primo.

Cum dato: A. 16 p. 12 „Venetiis". Quamvis Regimonto mecum sub titulo repetitionis citatae communicatum tamen ordinem s. Iohannis tangere videtur.

642. *1265 iunii 24 Perusii (cf. 1266 octobr. 26, 1267 ianuar. 8 [9]). Clemens IV repetit Urbani IV n. 626 de 1263 martii 28.*

Clemens etc. archiepiscopis et episcopis ac dilectis filiis abbatibus etc. Cum dilectis filiis fratribus hospitalis sancte Marie Theutonicorum Ierosolimitani fuerit a predecessoribus nostris indultum etc. amittant. Datum Perusii viii kal. iulii pontificatus nostri anno primo.

Sine dato: A. 16 p. 104 „Iuncis", partim R. 158 inter Iuncensia. — Cum dato: Perusii 8 kal. iulii a. 1 originale, cui bulla et fila sericea nunc desunt, in archivo Regimontano; cf. Napiersky in Indice I n. 194 ann. p. 49. Transsumtum d. d. Resinburg 1438 septbr. 26 autoritate Iohannis Pomesaniensis episcopi factum et a notario mag. Alwer subscriptum asservatur ibidem, ubi etiam duo exemplaria transsumpti primae clausulae, scilicet de eleemosynis semel per annum colligendis, nomine Iohannis, episcopi antedicti, et Nicolai abbatis Polplinensis facta d. Marienburg 1413 augusti 27 per notarios Ioh. Rosener et Balth. Weifs, qui subscripserunt. Sigilla sunt Iohannis episcopi et Petri abbatis Polplinensis. De hoc vide supra ad n. 302. 494. 503. — Cum dato: Viterbii 7 kal. novbr. a. 2 „Traiecti" A. 16 p. 106. — Cum dato: Viterbii 6 id. ianuarii p. a. 2. IV, 215 v. Originale quondam Mergenthemense cum bulla in filis sericeis appensa in archivo ordinis Theutonici Vindobonensi. C. d.: quinto idus ianuarii p. n. a. 2. Ioh. 39. Edd. Caorsinus C. 5. Senner E. 6 v.

643. *1266 maii 28 Viterbii. Clemens IV prorogat ordini Theutonico ab Urbano IV concessam exemtionem de procurationibus pecuniariis legatis praestandis in alterum triennium.*

Clemens etc. dilectis filiis .. magistro et preceptoribus ac fratribus universis hospitalis s. Marie Theutonicorum presentes litteras inspecturis salutem et apostolicam benedictionem. Affectu benivolentie specialis illa de causa vos prosequi delectamur, quia vigilanter et ferventer ad hoc intenditis, quod in conspectu dei et hominum per honeste conversationis et pie vite studium placeatis. Sane vos in exhibendis procurationibus legatis et nuntiis apostolice sedis, prout accepimus, ex eo gravamini, quod ipsi, non contenti procurationibus, quas eisdem parati estis in victualibus exhibere, a vobis et ecclesiis ac domibus vestris occasione procuracionum huiusmodi frequenter non modicam pecunie summam exigunt et extorquent. Quare felicis recordationis Urbanus papa, predecessor noster, intellecto, quod propter hoc quandoque vestrum impediretur propositum et derogaretur negotio terre sancte, vobis, ut predictis legatis et nuntiis ad solvendas procurationes pecuniarias cogi non possetis inviti, per suas litteras extunc post triennium minime valituras indulsit. Quia vero huiusmodi triennium est elapsum, nos vestris supplicationibus annuentes, ut eisdem legatis et nuntiis, exceptis tamen de latere nostro missis, ad solvendum pecuniarias procurationes compelli exnunc ad futurum triennium minime valeatis, vobis auctoritate apostolica indulgemus, dummodo predictos legatos et nuntios in victualibus procuretis. Sententias vero, si que in vos vel aliquem de ordine vestro contra indultum huiusmodi de cetero fuerint promulgate, irritas exnunc decernimus et inanes. Nulli ergo etc. Si quis etc. Datum Viterbii v kalendas iunii pontificatus nostri anno secundo.

Ex originali in archivo Regimontano asservato ed. in Livl. U. B. I, 501 n. 397.

---

644. *1266 octobris 18 Viterbii. Clemens IV repetit Innocentii IV n. 494 de 1245 septembris 5.*

Clemens etc. Non absque dolore — absolvi. Datum Viterbii xv kal. novembris pontificatus nostri anno secundo.

Cum dato: A. 16 p. 107 „Traiecti“.

---

645. *1266 octobris 26 Viterbii. Clemens IV repetit n. 642 de 1265 iunii 24.*

Clemens etc. Cum dilectis etc. Datum Viterbii vii kal. novembris pontificatus nostri anno secundo.

---

646. *1267 ianuarii 8 [9] Viterbii. Clemens IV repetit n. 642 de 1265 iunii 24.*

Clemens etc. Cum dilectis etc. Datum Viterbii vi [v] idus ianuarii pontificatus nostri anno secundo.

---

647. *1267 ianuarii 11 Viterbii. Clemens IV praedicantes crucem pro subsidio terrae sanctae auditores inducere iubet, ut ordinis Theutonici necessitatibus succurrant.*

Clemens episcopus servus servorum dei venerabilibus fratribus archiepiscopis et episcopis ac dilectis filiis abbatibus, prioribus, prepositis, decanis, archidiaconis et aliis ecclesiarum prelatis cunctisque personis ecclesiasticis tam religiosis quam secularibus predicantibus crucem pro subsidio terre sancte, ad quos litere iste pervenerint, salutem et apostolicam benedictionem. Plus lugendum quam legendum terre sancte statum vix absque lacrimis audire possumus, et de ipso loqui sine multe interventu tristitie non valemus, maxime, cum preter infinita discrimina, que in partibus illis olim frequentissime pertulit religio christiana, sit ibi de

27*

novo multitudo perempta fidelium et ipsorum residuo in personis et rebus quasi per dies singulos multiplex immineat detrimentum, prout illa mestissima nos in presenti edocet coniectura, quod dilecti filii ... magister et fratres hospitalis s. Marie Theutonicorum Ierosolimitani, devotissimi quidem Christi pugiles et predicte terre imperterriti defensores, licet in votis semper habeant, ut ad gloriam divini nominis bibant calicem salutifere passionis, nunc tamen ob illam causam afficiuntur vite tedio, quia per hostes crucis sublata est eis bonorum desiderabilium multitudo, ita ut nec solite hospitalitatis frequentare possint officium nec pia prestare subsidia necessitatibus egenorum, immo, quod est gravius et amarissime deplorandum, fratres ipsi, qui Saracenorum incursum olim in partibus illis triumphaliter refrenabant, iam infra civitatis Acconensis menia coguntur tabescendo persistere gravati nimia paupertate. Hec etenim fratrum ipsorum afflictio cor nostrum in anxietatis augmento posuit et sibi cuiusdam novi doloris acerbitatem induxit, presertim cum olim fuerit nobis multitudo fiducie, quod ab eisdem fratribus, aliorum fidelium favente subsidio, assidue conteri deberent christiani nominis inimici. Quia vero ad sedis apostolice pietatem spectare dinoscitur, ut ipsa personas pro exaltatione catholice fidei preliantes gratiosi favoris affluentia prosequatur, sed tunc potissime, quando persone huiusmodi sub egestatis multe sarcina lacrimosis coguntur suspiriis inundare; universitati vestre per apostolica scripta mandamus, quatinus pro reverentia regis eterni, cuius in hac parte causa geritur cuiusque honor principaliter promovetur, vos fratrum ipsorum angustiis et pressuris pio condolentes affectu et circa ipsos fructuose benivolentie promptitudinem exercentes in predicationibus, quas pro predicte terre subsidio facitis ad humilem requisitionem nuntiorum hospitalis eiusdem, Christi fideles ad predicationes huiusmodi concurrentes piis monitis efficaciter inducatis, quod ipsi obtentu perempnis glorie necessitati fratrum ipsorum de suis facultatibus studeant liberaliter subvenire, ita quod iidem fratres talibus adiuti remediis sepe dicte terre negotium magnanimiter promovere valeant iuxta votum nobisque per consequens exultationis producatur inde materia et vobis gratie divine premium ac nostri favoris proveniat incrementum. Datum Viterbii iii id. ianuarii pontificatus nostri anno secundo.

Originale quondam Confluentinum, cum bulla in funiculo cannabino appensa in archivo ordinis Theutonici Vindobonensi; ed. Hennes I, 182 n. 207. In eodem archivo etiam aliud originale cum bulla in funiculo cannabino appensa. A. 16 p. 77 „Colonie". Antea ed. Duellius II, 15 n. 23. 1. ven. fr. archiepiscopis et episcopis et dilectis filiis abbatibus, prioribus, decanis, archidiaconis et aliis ecclesiarum rectoribus A. 16 p. 77.

---

648. *(Inter 1267 februar. 22 et 1268 februar. 21.) Clemens IV repetit n. 636 de 1265 maii 11; n. 637 de 1265 maii 20.*

Clemens etc. Cum a nobis etc. Datum etc. pontificatus nostri anno tercio.

---

649. *1268 maii 15 Viterbii. Clemens IV repetit Urbani IV n. 629 de 1263 octobris 1.*

Clemens etc. Cum vos tanquam etc. Datum Viterbii idus maii pontificatus nostri anno quarto.

Transsumptum iudicis episcopalis Spirensis de 1350 iulii 6 in archivo Regimontano.

---

650. *1272 maii 30 Laterani. Gregorius X repetit Innocentii IV privilegium n. 650 de 1253 ianuarii 5.*

Gregorius etc. Solet annuere etc. Datum Laterani iii kalendas iunii pontificatus nostri anno primo.

Duo originalia, quorum alterum magistro, alterum praeceptori et fratribus inscriptum, cum bullis, successive Cracoviae, Varsaviae, Berolini asservata, inde ab a. 1865 Regimonti, quae citat Inventarium archivi Cracoviensis p. 67 „Gregorius papa X immunitates a Romanis pontificibus et libertates a regibus concessas cruciferis confirmat. Datum Laterani 3 kal. iunii pontificatus anno primo". Ibidem sub inscriptione praeceptoris et fratrum h. s. M. Th. I. in Prussia transsumtum per Thomam Wratislaviensem episcopum d. d. 1273 9 kal. octbr. Otmuchoviae. — P. ac f. h. s. M. Th. in Alemania Gregorius etc. R. 173 inter Thuringica cum nota: hoc prilegium continetur in Biezen per Gregorium papam X. A. 16 p. 50 „Baruli": A. 16 p. 109 „Monasterium" (Traiecti). De privilegio, quod in Livl. Urk. I, 535 n. 424 (Si discrimina) fertur Gregorii X 1271 (1272 erat scribendum) iulii 21 vide Gregorium IX 1227 iulii 21.

---

651. *1274 octobris 19 Lugduni (cf. 1274 novembris 2). Gregorius X eximit ordinem Theutonicum a praestatione decimae clero in concilio generali impositae.*

Gregorius episcopus servus servorum dei dilectis filiis magistro et fratribus hospitalis sancte Marie Theutonicorum Ierosolimitani salutem et apostolicam benedictionem. Ipsa nos cogit pietas honestis peticionibus vestris exaudicionis graciam non negare, quibus efficax ex eo patrocinium suffragatur, quod pro christiane fidei tutela, cui perpetuum religionis vestre obsequium dedicastis, in fervore caritatis intrepide ac prudenter exponitis contra infidelium impetus res et vitam. Sane peticio vestra nobis exhibita continebat, quod nos nuper in concilio generali[1] volentes terre sancte, que ab inimico nominis Christi detinetur miserabiliter occupata, remedia procurare, per que posset de ipsorum inimicorum manibus liberari, decimam omnium proventuum ecclesiasticorum, proventibus quorundam religiosorum duntaxat exceptis, pro ipsius terre subsidio duximus deputandum. Quare nobis humiliter supplicastis, ut, cum vos ad hoc principaliter laboretis, ut vos pariter et omnia, que habetis, pro ipsius terre sancte defensione ac christiane fidei exponatis, vos eximere a prestacione huiusmodi decime de benignitate apostolica curaremus. Nos igitur attendentes discrimina, que pro defensione predicte terre sancte continue sustinetis ac volentes vos propter hoc speciali gracia prosequi et favore vobis, quod de proventibus vestris decimam huiusmodi solvere minime teneamini nec ad id compelli possitis, auctoritate presentium indulgemus, nolentes, quod occasione ipsius decime aliquam excommunicacionis sentenciam iam latam vel proferendam de cetero incurratis et, si in vos vel in vestrum aliquem nominatim ferri contigerit, eam vires decernimus non habere. Nulli ergo omnino hominum etc. Si quis etc. Datum Lugduni xiiii kalendas novembris pontificatus nostri anno tercio.

Cum dato: Lugduni 14 kal. novbr. a. 3 originale cum bulla in archivo Regimontano, ubi etiam transsumta duo: 1. 1427 febr. 13 Regimonti Michaelis episcopi Sambiensis ad petitionem Pauli de Russdorf magistri generalis. 2. Transsumptum d. Frisaci 1488 octbr. 1 ex transsumpto iudicii Spirensis ibidem. R. 102 inter Alsatica n. 15; R. 146 inter Trevirensia. — Cum dato eodem: A. 16 p. 19 sq. ex transsumpto Venetiis asservato d. d. Marienburch 1347 ianuarii 24 sub sigillis episcoporum Culmensis et Sambiensis. A. 16 p. 49 „Baruli"; A. 16 p. 76 „Colonie". — Cum dato: Lugduni 4 non. novbr. p. n. a. 3 transsumtum d. d. Vindobonae 1396 aug. 18. 1. scilicet Lugdunensi 1274 maii 7 incepto.

---

652. *1274 novbr. 2 Lugduni. Gregorius X repetit n. 651 de 1274 octobr. 19.*

Gregorius etc. Ipsa nos etc. Datum iiii nonas novembris pontificatus nostri anno tercio.

---

653. *1275 februarii 1 Lugduni. Gregorius X repetit ordini Theutonico in Prussia Alexandri IV privilegium n. 590 de 1258 novembris 9.*

Gregorius episcopus servus servorum dei dilectis filiis preceptori et fratribus hospitalis sancte Marie Theutonicorum in Prusia salutem et apostolicam benedictionem. Devocionis vestre etc. — exceptis valeatis petere, recipere ac etiam retinere sine iuris preiudicio alieni. Nulli ergo etc. Datum Lugduni kalendas februarii pontificatus nostri anno tercio.

Speciale privilegium super formula generali. Originale cum bulla in archivo Regimontano; in dorso legitur: „Eiusdem tenoris littera est etiam in Bohemia". Ed. Duellius II, 18 n. 30.

---

654. *1276 martii 31 Laterani. Innocentius V repetit n. 636 de 1265 maii 11.*

Innocentius etc. Cum a nobis etc. Eapropter etc. — communimus. Datum Laterani ii kal. aprilis pontificatus nostri anno primo.

Cum dato: Laterani 3 kal. aprilis p. n. a. 1. A. 16 p. 37 „Baruli" et inscriptione: „dil. f. magistro et fr. h. s. M. Th. Iher. in regno Sicilie". — Cum dato: Laterani 2 kal. april. p. a. 1 originale cum bulla quondam Cracoviae, Varsaviae, Berolini, nunc Regimonti asservatum; generale.

---

655. *1276 novembris 17 Viterbii. Iohannes XXI repetit n. 654.*

Iohannes etc. Cum a nobis etc. Datum Viterbii xv kalendas decembris pontificatus nostri anno primo.

Cum dato: anno 1 „Treviris" etc. A. 16 p. 118. — Cum dato: Viterbii 15 kal. decbr. p. a. 1 originale cum bulla nunc ex filis soluta quondam Cracoviae, Varsaviae, Berolini, nunc Regimonti asservatur. Citatur in Inventario archivi Cracoviensis p. 67: „Ioannes papa XXI confirmat iura cruciferorum Teutonicorum. Datum Viterbii 15 kal. decbr. anno pontificatus I." A. 16 p. 52 „Baruli".

656. *1278 martii 23 Rome apud s. Petrum (cf. iulii 18). Nicolaus III repetit n. 655.*

Nicolaus etc. Cum a nobis etc. Datum Rome apud s. Petrum x kal. aprilis pontificatus nostri anno primo.

Cum dato: Rome ap. s. Petrum 10 kal. april. p. 1. A. 16 p. 64 „in Marpurg", p. 109 „Monasterium". — Cum dato: Viterbii 15 kal. aug. p. n. a. 1 originale cum bulla quondam Cracoviae, Varsaviae, Berolini, nunc Regimonti asservatum. Perperam in Inventario archivi Cracoviensis p. 67 tanquam Nicolai IV citatur, qui „iura et privilegia cruciferis concessa approbat eximitque eos a secularibus exactionibus regum et principum. Datum Viterbii 15 kal. aug. pontificatus anno primo". Eiusdem tenoris privilegium a Nicolao III datum tanquam Mecheliniae asservatum citatur ad Benedicti XII 1336 febr. 8.

---

657. *1278 iulii 18 Viterbii. Nicolaus III repetit n. 656 de 1278 martii 23.*

Nicolaus etc. Cum a nobis etc. Datum Viterbii xv kalendas augusti pontificatus nostri anno primo.

---

658. *1281 augusti 19 apud Urbem Veterem (cf. inter 1282 martii 23 et 1283 martii 22, 1283 iunii 1). Martinus IV repetit Innocentii IV privilegium n. 524 de 1253 ianuarii 5.*

Martinus etc. Solet annuere etc. Datum apud Urbem Veterem xiiii kalendas septembris pontificatus nostri anno primo.

Sine dato: A. 16 p. 104 „Iuncis". — Cum dato: ap. Urbem Veterem 14 kal. septbr. p. n. a. 1 duo originalia cum plumbis quondam Cracoviae etc., nunc Regimonti. Citatur in Inventario archivi Cracoviensis p. 67: „Martinus papa IV iura ordinis cruciferorum approbat. Datum apud Urbem Veterem 14 kal. septbr. anno 1282". A. 16 p. 30 „Colonie"; „Invenitur etiam in Mechelinia". — Cum dato: ap. Montemflasconem .... p. n. a. 2 originale paene corrosum in archivo Regimontano; cuius inferior pars cum bulla omnino desiderantur. — Cum dato: ap. Urbem Veterem kal. iunii a. 3. A. 16 p. 51 „Baruli".

---

659. *(Inter 1282 martii 23 et 1283 martii 22) apud Montemflasconem. Martinus IV repetit n. 658 de 1281 augusti 19.*

Martinus etc. Solet annuere etc. Datum apud Montemflasconem etc. pontificatus nostri anno secundo.

---

660. *1283 iunii 1 apud Urbem Veterem. Martinus IV repetit n. 658 de 1281 augusti 19.*

Martinus etc. Solet annuere etc. Datum apud Urbem Veterem kal. iunii pontificatus nostri anno tercio.

---

661. *1285 iulii 23 Tibure. Honorius IV repetit Martini IV n. 658 de 1281 augusti 19.*

Honorius etc. Solet annuere — incursurum. Datum Tybure x kalendas augusti pontificatus nostri anno primo.

Cum dato: Tybure 10 kal. aug. p. a. 1. R. 73 inter Mergenthemensia n. 22. A. 16 p. 13 inter privilegia Venetiis asservata; p. 87 „Confluentibus". — Cum dato: Rome ap. s. Sabinam 10 kal. novbr. a. 2 et cum inscriptione: „magistro et fratribus h. s. M. Th. I. in Tuscia"; originale cum bulla in archivo Regimontano. A. 16 p. 51 „Baruli".

---

662. *1288 maii 27 Reate. Nicolaus IV repetit Honorii IV n. 661 de 1285 iulii 23.*

Nicolaus etc. magistro et fratribus hospitalis s. Marie Theutonicorum Ierosolimitani salutem et apostolicam benedictionem. Solet annuere etc. Datum Reate vi kal. iunii pontificatus nostri anno primo.

Originale cum bulla quondam Cracoviae, Varsaviae, Berolini, nunc Regimonti, ubi etiam transsumtum d. d. in Strafspurgk 1336 iunii 14 sub sigillo Laurentii Gurcensis episcopi factum. A. 16 p. 50 „Baruli". Citatur in Inventario archivi Cracoviensis p. 67: „Nicolaus IV confirmat immunitates a Romanis pontificibus et a regibus ordini cruciferorum collatas, 6 kal. iunii anno 1288 pontificatus anno primo". Privilegium, quod ibidem a Nicolao IV Viterbii 15 kal. aug. p. a. 1 editum esse praetenditur, potius Nicolai III est; cf. supra n. 656. Inscriptum: „preceptori et fratribus (h. s. M. Th. I.) in Almania" sine dato citatur R. 164 inter Thuringica. Invenitur IV, 354 v.; R. 90 inter Mergenthemensia n. 52. Ed. apud Lünig Teutsches Reichsarchiv XVI, 81 n. 79.

---

663. *1289 aprilis 1 Romae apud s. Mariam maiorem. Nicolaus IV repetit Urbani IV n. 622 de 1261 decbr. 15.*

Nicolaus etc. Signorum evidencia etc. — inclinati ad instar felicis recordacionis Urbani pape quarti predecessoris nostri presencium — incursurum. Datum Rome apud sanctam Mariam maiorem kalendas aprilis pontificatus nostri anno secundo.

IV, 219 v. R. 103 inter Alsatica n. 16; R. 25 inter Ellingensia n. 7; A. 16 p. 80 „Colonie".

---

664. *1289 aprilis 2 Romae apud s. Mariam maiorem. Nicolaus IV extendit Honorii III n. 327 de 1221 ianuarii 18 super ecclesias, quarum patronatus inde ab isto tempore ordo Theutonicus acquisierit.*

Nicolaus episcopus servus servorum dei venerabilibus fratribus archiepiscopis et episcopis et dilectis filiis abbatibus, prioribus, archidiaconis, decanis et aliis ecclesiarum prelatis, ad quos littere iste pervenerint, salutem et apostolicam benedictionem. Quanto dilecti filii .. magister et fratres domus hospitalis sancte Marie Theotonicorum Ierosolimitani propriis derelictis fervencius pro christianitatis commodo iugiter elaborant nec ponere pro fratribus animas reformidant, tanto ipsis in suis manutenendis iusticiis diligencius adesse nos convenit et eorum incommoditatibus paterna sollicitudine providere, ne, si fuerimus, quod absit, in eorum manutenenda iusticia negligentes, a Saracenorum impugnacione, qui christianum nomen insufflant et fidelium effundere sanguinem moliuntur, desistere compellantur et amplius adversus christianos illorum insolencia convalescat. Cum autem felicis recordacionis Honorius papa tercius predecessor noster prenominatis fratribus misericorditer duxerit indulgendum, ut fructus ecclesiarum, que ad ipsorum fratrum donacionem spectabant, assignato vicariis, unde congrue sustentari possent et diocesano episcopo eiusque officialibus de suis posset iusticiis responderi, deberent in subvencionem terre Ierosolimitane convertere, prefatus predecessor intellecto postmodum, quod quidam episcopi, archidiaconi et decani, ad quos illarum ecclesiarum investitura spectabat, clericos, quos iidem fratres idoneos presentabant eisdem, recipere pro sue voluntatis libito contempnebant, nisi predicti fratres easdem ecclesias clericis, qui de episcoporum, archidiaconorum et decanorum predictorum mensa essent seu aliis eciam non ydoneis largirentur, ita quod, si iidem fratres easdem ecclesias, prout iidem episcopi, archidiaconi et decani cupiebant, minime assignabant, ut ipsi libere possent redditus earum percipere, illos per longa tempora faciebant a divinorum celebracione cessare, ut per hoc fratres ipsi voluntates eorum exequi cogerentur; ac tante predictorum fratrum incommoditati prospicere cupiens, ne maliciose tantam iacturam cogerentur sustinere, universis archiepiscopis, episcopis, abbatibus, prioribus, archidiaconis et aliis ecclesiarum prelatis sub ea forma suis dedit litteris in preceptis, ut clericos ydoneos, quos iidem fratres ad ecclesias suas presentarent, eisdem extunc benigne admittere procurarent, alioquin scirent, quod dictus predecessor nominatis fratribus auctoritate apostolica concesserat facultatem, ut fructus earundem ecclesiarum, donec predicta occasione vacarent, in subvencionem Ierosolimitane terre convertere et illos possent libere detinere. Preterea, quia quidam ex archiepiscopis et episcopis, abbatibus, prioribus, archidiaconis, decanis et aliis prelatis nominatis fratres ipsos et eorum clericos contra privilegium sedis apostolice fratribus ipsis indultum, ut dicebatur, excommunicare et interdicere presumebant, idem predecessor per litteras ipsas districte inhibuit, ne archiepiscopi et episcopi, abbates, priores, archidiaconi, decani et alii prelati predicti predictos fratres vel eorum clericos extunc taliter interdicere et excommunicare aliquatenus attemptarent. Quodsi secus existeret attemptatum, nominatus predecessor sententiam ferendam voluit non tenere. Verum, quia, sicut accepimus, post huiusmodi concessiones prefatis fratribus ius patronatus in pluribus aliis ecclesiis est concessum, in quibus, cum vacant, quidam ex vobis, qui institucionem seu investituram in illis ad se pertinere proponunt, presentaciones de personis idoneis per dictos fratres ad eas ipsis factas admittere nolunt, ut earundem ecclesiarum interim faciant fructus suos aut predicti fratres clericos de mensa dictorum prelatorum aut alias non idoneos ad nominatas ecclesias presentare ipsis iuxta eorum beneplacitum compellantur; nos tantis eorundem fratrum incommodis prospicere cupientes, ne tantam iacturam non absque ipsius terre maximo detrimento maliciose cogantur de cetero sustinere, universitati vestre per apostolica scripta districte precipiendo mandamus, quatenus clericos idoneos, quos iidem fratres ad ecclesias suas, in quibus eis ius huiusmodi taliter est quesitum, ad illas eciam, in quibus prenominatis fratribus imposterum ius simile prestante domino concedetur, vobis duxerint presentandos, de cetero benignius admittatis, ita quod preter boni meritum, quod vos commissum vobis officium iuste ac fideliter exequendo perceperitis, apud deum devocionem vestram possimus propter hoc in domino non immerito commendare. Datum Rome apud sanctam Mariam maiorem iiii nonas aprilis pontificatus nostri anno secundo.

Citatur p. a. 2 in designatione Mitoviensis archivi 1621 Holmiam delati ap. Schirren p. 132 n. 162. IV, 219 v. R. 121 et A. 16 p. 63 inter Marburgensia; A. 20 n. 118 Latine et Germanice. — Cum dato pleno: A. 16 p. 79 sq. „Colonie"; A. 16 p. 63 „Marpurg". Collatus est textus cum transsumto d. d. Wirzburgi 1418 decbr. 2 sub autoritate et sigillo Werneri de Hayn, officialis episcopalis, facto, quod asservatur in archivo Regimontano. Partim in apographo transsumti Wernheri Wiltzenburgensis abbatis d. d. Wissenburg 1317 iulii 7. R. 11 inter Nurembergensia.

---

665. *1290 martii 1 apud Urbem Veterem (cf. 1291 februarii 20). Nicolaus IV ordinis Theutonici domus eximit a decimae tertia parte solvenda, quam Siciliae regi in subsidium concesserat.*

Nicolaus etc. dilectis filiis magistro et fratribus hospitalis domus sancte Marie Theutonicorum Ierosolimitani salutem et apostolicam benedictionem. Reducentes ad sedule considerationis examen, quod vos tamquam athlete domini pugilesque intrepidi nostri redemptoris obsequia in transmarinis partibus votis ferventibus prosequentes non dubitatis contra infidelium impetus exponere vos et vestra, dignum duximus et rationi consonum arbitramur, ut petitionibus vestris reserata benignius apostolice gratie ianua, quantum cum deo possumus, favorabiliter annuamus. Cum itaque, sicut habet vestre devotionis assertio, ad minus tertia pars omnium fructuum, proventuum et reddituum domorum et locorum vestrorum quorumlibet consistentium citra mare ad partes terre sancte pro sustentatione fratrum vestrorum ibi degentium ac defensione terre predicte annis singulis destinetis, nos indignum et indecens reputantes, ut decimam per nos regni Sicilie subsidio deputatam de huiusmodi parte tertia persolvatis, vobis, ut de predicta tertia parte decimam solvere minime teneamini et ad eam solvendam compelli ab aliquibus non possitis, auctoritate presentium indulgemus. Nulli ergo omnino etc. Si quis autem etc. Datum apud Urbem veterem kal. marcii pontificatus nostri anno tertio.

Cum dato: apud Urbem Veterem kal. marcii p. n. a. 3. A. 16 p. 5 „Venetiis". — Cum dato: apud Urbem Veterem 10 kal. martii a. 3. A. 16 p. 50 „Baruli". — Transsumptum ad instantiam Henrici, praeceptoris dom. mansionis Panormitanae, facto manu Armanni de Munda, judicis per regnum Siciliae et notarii regii et archiepiscopalis, d. d. Panormi 1487 octobris 5, in archivo Regimontano.

---

666. *1291 februarii 20 apud Urbem Veterem. Nicolaus IV repetit n. 665 de 1290 martii 1.*

Nicolaus etc. Reducentes ad etc. Datum apud Urbem Veterem x kal. marcii pontificatus nostri anno tertio.

---

667. .... *Nicolaus IV repetit Gregorii IX n. 469.*

Nicolaus etc. Cum a nobis etc. — communimus. — Datum etc.

Sine dato: A. 20 n. 117 Latine et Germanice.

---

668. *1294 novembris 27 Neapoli. Coelestinus V ordinem Theutonicum iam omnibus ultramarinis possessionibus privatum negat ad procurationes apostolicis nuntiis praestandas obligatum esse nisi expressa exemtionis facta mentione.*

Celestinus episcopus servus servorum dei dilectis filiis .. magistro et fratribus domus hospitalis s. Marie Theutonicorum Ierosolimitani salutem et apostolicam benedictionem. Gerentes ad vos ex eo paterne compassionis effectum, quod per perfidos Sarracenos, inimicos nominis christiani, estis bonis omnibus, que habebatis in ultramarinis partibus, spoliati, ac volentes vobis alicuius subventionis remedium pro relevandis vestris necessitatibus exhibere, universitati vestre auctoritate presentium indulgemus, ut vos aut preceptores et fratres domorum subiectarum domui vestre ad prestandum procurationes pecuniarias legatis, nuntiis et cursoribus sedis apostolice, vel ad contribuendum in huiusmodi procurationibus cum prelatis et clericis aliquibus minime teneamini nec ad id compelli aliquatenus valeatis per litteras apostolicas iam concessas vel in posterum concedendas, nisi littere huiusmodi concedende plenam de verbo ad verbum de indulto huiusmodi ac de vobis et domibus vestris expressam faciant mentionem. Nos enim excommunicationis, suspensionis et interdicti sententias, si quas in vos vel vestrum aliquos aut domos predictas contra huiusmodi indulti tenorem promulgari contingerit vel promulgate fuerint temporibus[1] predecessoris nostri, exnunc decernimus irritas et inanes. Volumus autem, quod fratribus nostris sacre Romane ecclesie cardinalibus officio legationis fungentibus pecuniariam vel alias procurationes, prout acceptaverint, impendatis. Nulli ergo omnino hominum liceat hanc paginam nostre concessionis et constitutionis infringere vel etc. Si quis autem etc. Datum Neapoli x kal. decembris pontificatus nostri anno primo.

Transsumtum per iudicium Tranensis archiepiscopi Barolitanum apud Barolum 1336 maii 31, petente Iohanne Overstolz magno praeceptore Apuliae ex originali domus dicti hospitalis in „Barulo“ confectum in archivo Regimontano; cf. Napiersky indic. I, 62 n. 249. In eodem archivo alterum exstat transsumtum factum Panormi ad instantiam praeceptoris domus mansionis ibidem 1487 octbr. 5. Ex transsumpto d. d. Baroli 1346 iulii 8 facto, quod exhibet datum: Neapoli 10 kal. decbr. p. n. a. 1. A. 16 p. 10 „Venetiis“. 1. tempore T. de 1487.

---

669. *1296 ianuarii 16 Romae apud s. Petrum (cf. 1298 novembris 5). Bonifacius VIII repetit Nicolai IV n. 662 de 1288 maii 27.*

Bonifacius etc. Solet annuere etc. Datum Rome apud sanctum Petrum xvii kalendas februarii pontificatus nostri anno secundo.

Cum dato: Romae ap. s. Petrum 17 kal. febr. p. n. a. 2: originale cum bulla quondam Cracoviae, Varsaviae, Berolini asservatum, nunc Regimonti. Citatur in Inventario archivi Cracoviensis p. 67: „Bonifacius papa VIII omnia iura et privilegia cruciferorum confirmat Romae apud s. Petrum anno 1296". A. 16 p. 57 „Baruli". In transsumto 1346 facto A. 16 p. 11 „Venetiis". — Cum dato: Reate nonis novembris a. 4 „Colonie" A. 16 p. 76.

---

670. *1296 februarii 9 Romae apud s. Petrum. Bonifacius VIII ordinem Theutonicum eximit a decima praestanda per clerum pro negotio regni Siciliae per Carolum regem promovendo.*

Bonifacius episcopus servus servorum dei dilectis filiis magistro et fratribus domus hospitalis s. Marie Theutonicorum Ierosolimitani salutem et apostolicam benedictionem. Dum paterne considerationis indagine perlustramus gravia personarum discrimina, iacturas innumeras et multimoda damna rerum, que dudum in civitate Acconensi miserabili plenaque doloribus captione Christi prosequentes obsequia pertulistis, dum etiam recogitamus attentius, quod vos pro defensione ac exaltatione fidei orthodoxe in Livonie ac Pruscie partibus cum inimicis christiani nominis in partibus ipsis degentibus constantibus animis non sine multo personarum periculo et multiplici bonorum dispendio dimicantes, gravia proinde subire oportet onera expensarum; dignum duximus et rationi consonum arbitramur, ut vobis benignitatis et munificencie apostolice ianuam reserantes vos et domum vestram prerogativa specialis favoris et gratie prosequi studeamus. Volentes igitur vobis devotionis affectum, quem erga vos gerimus, ostendere per effectum et ad vestram dicteque domus relevationem benivolis studiis intendentes vos et domum ipsam ac hospitalia, domos, membra et loca sibi subiecta a prestatione decime ecclesiasticorum proventuum, quam carissimo in Christo filio nostro Carolo regi Sicilie illustri ad prosequendum negotium regni Sicilie duximus concedendam, de gratia eximimus speciali, vobis nichilominus indulgentes, ut nequaquam teneamini ad prestationem decime supradicte, non obstante, quod in litteris super decima ipsa concessis de ordine seu domibus vestris habetur mentio specialis. Universas quoque excommunicationis, suspensionis et interdicti sententias contra huius executionis et concessionis nostre tenorem in vos et domum ipsam prolatas et quas in posterum promulgari contigerit, irritas decernimus et inanes ac nullius prorsus existere firmitatis. Nulli ergo etc. Si quis etc. Datum Rome apud sanctum Petrum v idus februarii pontificatus nostri anno secundo.

E copiario A. 16, ubi p. 13 et 57 legitur, archivi Regimontani ed. in Livl. U. B. I, 703 n. 562. In eodem archivo extat etiam exemplar, d. d. Panormi, 1487 octbr. 5 ad instantiam Henrici, praeceptoris domus mansionis ibidem, per Armannum de Munda, iudicem regni et notarium regium et archiepiscopalem, factum et subscriptum.

---

671. *1298 novbr. 5 Reate. Bonifacius VIII repetit n. 669 de 1296 ianuar. 16.*

Bonifacius etc. Solet annuere etc. Datum Reate nonis novembris pontificatus nostri anno quarto.

---

672. *1300 februarii 15 Laterani. Bonifacius VIII repetit Gregorii IX n. 469*

Bonifacius etc. Cum a nobis etc. Datum Laterani xv kalendas martii pontificatus nostri anno sexto.

E transsumto de 1393 maii 29 in archivo Regimontano asservato editum in Livl. U. B. I, 756 n. 588. Aliud transsumtum d. d. Reval 1415 decbr. 24 sub sigillis episcopi Revaliensis et eius capituli, necnon abbatis de Padis, autoritate dicti episcopi factum in eodem archivo.

---

673. *1307 maii 22 Avinione (cf. 1308 martii 20, 1309/10, 1311 martii 15). Clemens V repetit n. 672.*

Clemens etc. dilectis filiis magistro et fratribus hospitalis beate Marie Theutonicorum Ierosolimitani salutem et apostolicam benedictionem. Cum a nobis petitur — communimus. Datum Avinione xi kal. iunii pontificatus nostri anno secundo.

Cum dato: Avinione 11 kal. iunii p. n. a. 2 „in Marpurg" A. 16 p. 68. — Cum dato: Pictavis 13 kal. aprilis p. n. a. 3 originale cum bulla ab ordine Polonis extraditum in Inventario archivi Cracoviensis p. 68 citatur: „Clemens papa V omnia iura, libertates et indulgentias magistro et ordini Teutonico concessas confirmat. Pictavii anno 1308. Cracovia Varsaviam, inde Berolinum translatum nunc est in archivo Regimontano. Ibidem instrumentum datum Marienburg 1389 iunii 20, petente Henrico Brunner, fratre ordinis Theutonici factum manu Iohannis Proyk clerici Warmiensis imperiali autoritate notarii. — Cum dato: a. 5 „Treviris" A. 16 p. 119. — (Cum dato: Avinione 7 idus marcii p. n. a. sexto et inscriptione: dilectis filiis preceptori et fratribus hospitalis beate Marie Theutonicorum Iherosolimitani in Apulia in transsumto anni 1346 iulii 8 scripto, quod Venetiis asservabatur A. 16 p. 11 „Cum a nobis — personas — communimus".) — Cum dato: Avinione idus marcii p. n. a. 6 „Baruli" A. 16 p. 52.

---

674. *1308 martii 20 Pictavis. Clemens V repetit n. 673 de 1307 maii 22.*

Clemens etc. Cum a nobis etc. Datum Pictavis xiii kal. aprilis pontificatus nostri anno tertio.

---

675. *(Inter 1309 novembris 14 et 1310 novembris 13.) Clemens V repetit n. 673 de 1307 maii 22.*

Clemens etc. Cum a nobis etc. Datum etc. pontificatus nostri anno quinto.

Annotare hic libet, quod Clemens V 1310 martii 9 Nicolai III privilegium supra n. 155 p. 151 de 1278 martii 28 confirmavit: Clemens etc. dilectis filiis preceptori et fratribus hospitalis b. Marie Theutonicorum Ierosolimitani in Apulia. Cum a nobis — personas — communimus. Datum Avinione vii idus marcii p. n. a. sexto. E transsumto de anno 1346 iulii 8, quod Venetiis asservabatur A. 16 p. 11.

---

676. *1311 martii 15 Avinione. Clemens V repetit n. 673 de 1307 maii 22.*

Clemens etc. Cum a nobis etc. Datum Avinione idus marcii pontificatus nostri anno sexto.

---

677. *1319 iulii 12 Avinione. Iohannes XXII quosdam delegat conservatores, qui iuris exceptionibus a Bonifacio VIII concessis postpositis ordini Theutonico subveniant contra vim atque iniuriam.*

Iohannes episcopus servus servorum dei venerabilibus fratribus Nsi. et Nsi. archiepiscopis ac episcopo Nsi. salutem et apostolicam benedictionem. Etsi quibuslibet religiosis personis et locis ex iniuncto nobis servitutis officio assistere defensionis presidio teneamur, illis tamen specialius et efficacius adesse nos convenit, qui sedi apostolice immediate subiecti non habent preter Romanum pontificem alium defensorem. Sane dilectorum filiorum .. magistri et fratrum hospitalis sancte Marie Theutonicorum Ierosolimitani ad Romanam ecclesiam nullo medio pertinentis conquestione percepimus, quod nonnulli archiepiscopi, episcopi, abbates et alii clerici ecclesiasticeque persone tam religiose quam seculares, necnon comites et barones, nobiles, milites, universitates et alii seculares civitatum et diocesium ac partium vicinarum, in quibus dictum hospitale necnon et alia loca et membra eidem hospitali pleno iure immediate subiecta ad eandem sedem duntaxat spectantia consistere dinoscuntur, occuparunt et occupari fecerunt ecclesias, grangias, obedientias, castra, casalia, terras, vineas, possessiones, census, redditus et proventus, iura, iurisdictiones et nonnulla alia bona mobilia et immobilia ad dictum hospitale et alia prelibata eius membra spectantia, seu eadem detinentibus prestant auxilium et favorem, nonnulli etiam civitatum et diocesium ac partium predictarum, qui nomen domini in vacuum recipere non formidant, dictis magistro et fratribus dicti hospitalis in ecclesiis, grangiis casalibus, castris, terris, iurisdictionibus, iuribus, bonis et rebus aliis ad hospitale predictum spectantibus multiplices molestias ac iniurias inferunt et iacturas. Quare dicti magister et fratres nobis humiliter supplicarunt, ut, cum valde difficile reddatur eisdem et aliis membris suis pro singulis querelis ad apostolicam sedem habere recursum, providere eis super hoc paterna diligentia curaremus. Nos igitur adversus occupatores, detentores, presumptores, molestatores et iniuriatores huiusmodi illo volentes eis remedio subvenire, per quod ipsorum compescatur temeritas et aliis aditus committendi similia precludatur, fraternitati vestre per apostolica scripta mandamus, quatenus vos vel duo aut unus vestrum per vos vel alium seu alios, etiamsi sint extra loca, in quibus deputati estis conservatores et iudices, magistro, fratribus et membris predictis efficacis defensionis presidio assistentes non permittatis, eosdem super his et quibuslibet aliis bonis iuribus ad ipsos spectantibus ab eisdem et quibuscunque aliis indebite molestari vel sibi gravamina seu dampna vel iniurias irrogari, facturi ipsis, cum ab eis vel eorum aliquo seu procuratore vel procuratoribus eorundem vel alicuius eorum fueritis requisiti, de predictis et aliis personis quibuslibet super restitutione ecclesiarum, grangiarum, castrorum, casalium, terrarum, possessionum, iurisdictionum, iurium et bonorum immobilium et mobilium, redditum quoque, proventuum et aliorum quorumcunque bonorum, necnon et quibuslibet iniuriis et molestiis atque dampnis presentibus et futuris, in illis videlicet, que iudicialem requirunt indaginem, de plano sine strepitu et figura iudicii, in aliis vero, prout qualitas ipsorum exegerit, iustitie complementum, occupatores seu detentores molestatores, presumtores et iniuriatores huiusmodi necnon contradictores quoslibet et rebelles, cuiuscunque status, ordinis vel conditionis, etiamsi archiepiscopalis vel episcopalis dignitatis extiterint, quandocunque et quotienscunque expedierit, auctoritate nostra appellatione postposita compescendo, invocato ad hoc, si opus fuerit, auxilio brachii secularis, non obstantibus felicis recordationis Bonifacii pape viii, predecessoris nostri, in quibus precavetur, ne aliquis extra suam civitatem et diocesim, nisi in certis exceptis casibus et in illis ultra unam dietam a fine sue diocesis ad iudicium evocetur, seu ne iudices et conservatores a sede deputati predicta extra civitatem et diocesim, in quibus deputati fuerint, contra quoscunque procedere, sive alii vel aliis vices suas committere aut aliquos ultra unam dietam a fine diocesis eorundem trahere presumant, seu quod de aliis quam de manifestis iniuriis et violentiis, que iudicialem indaginem exigunt, penis in eos, si secus egerint, et in id procurantes adiectis, conservatores se nullatenus intromittant et tam de duabus dietis in concilio generali, dummodo ultra tertiam vel quartam dietam aliquis extra suam civitatem et diocesim auctoritate presentium ad iudicium non trahatur quam aliis quibuscunque constitutionibus a predecessoribus nostris Romanis pontificibus, tam de iudicibus delegatis et conservatoribus, quam personis ultra certum numerum ad iudicium non vocandis aut aliis editis, que vestre possent in hac parte iurisdictioni aut potestati eiusque libero exercitio quomodolibet obviare, seu si aliquibus communiter vel divisim a predicta sit sede indultum, quod interdici, suspendi vel excommunicari seu extra vel ultra certa loca ad iudicium evocari non possint per litteras apostolicas non facientes plenam et expressam ac de verbo ad verbum de indulto huiusmodi et eorum personis, locis, ordinibus et nominibus propriis mentionem et qualibet alia dicte sedis indulgentia generali vel speciali cuiuscunque tenoris existat, per quam presentibus non expressam vel totaliter non insertam vestre iurisdictionis explicatio valeat quomodolibet impediri et de qua cuiusque toto tenore de verbo ad verbum in nostris litteris habenda sit mentio specialis. Ceterum volumus et apostolica auctoritate decernimus, quod quilibet vestrum prosequi valeat articulum etiam per alium inchoatum, quamvis idem inchoans nullo fuerit impedimento canonico impeditus, quodque a data presencium sit vobis et unicuique vestrum in premissis omnibus et eorum singulis ceptis et non ceptis presentibus et futuris perpetuata potestas et iurisdictio attributa, ut eo vigore eaque firmitate possitis in premissis omnibus ceptis et non ceptis presentibus et futuris et pro predictis procedere, acsi predicta omnia et singula coram vobis cepta fuissent et iurisdictio vestra et cuiuslibet vestrum in predictis omnibus et singulis per citationem vel modum alium legitimum perpetuata exstitisset, constitutione predicta super conservatoribus et alia qualibet in contrarium edita non obstante. Datum Avinione iiii idus iulii pontificatus nostri anno tertio.

Transsumptum litterarum archiepiscopis Coloniensi et Magdeburgensi atque episcopo Traiectensi inscriptarum datum Brule 1332 iulii 19 factum auctoritate et sigillo Walrami, archiepiscopi Coloniensis s. R. i. per Italiam archicancellarii ad instantiam fratris Iohannis de Kettwich ordinis Theutonici originale cum sigillo exstat in archivo Regimontano. Aliud de 1386 aug. 23 Holmiae in archivo regio; Livl. U. B. reg. p. 49 n. 782. cf. Schirren p. 9 n. 97. A. 16 p. 82 „Colonie". — Exemplar litterarum archiepiscopo Salzburgensi et episcopis Augustensi ac Tridentino inscriptarum, datum Bozani 1338 ianuar. 5, factum manu notarii coram testibus et a duobus collegis subscriptum orig. in archivo Regimontano. Ed. Livl. U.B. II, p. 117 n. 869. Transsumptum litterarum archiepiscopis Treverensi et Coloniensi atque episcopo Metensi inscriptarum, datum Constantie 1417 decbr. 22 factum autoritate et sigillo Conradi, episcopi Metensis, qui hoc instrumento, a notariis publicis subscripto, tres canonicos subdelegat conservatores et iudices, originale, cui nunc deest sigillum, ubi supra.

---

678. *(Inter 1320 septembris 5 et 1321 septembris 4.) Iohannes XXII*[1] *repetit n. 669 de 1296 ianuarii 16.*

Iohannes episcopus servus servorum dei dilectis filiis magistro et fratribus etc. Solet annuere — libertates et immunitates — communimus. Datum etc. anno quinto.

Cum dato: a. 5 „Treviris" A. 16 p. 117 In designatione Mitoviensis archivi Holmiam 1621 delati citatur apud Schirren p. 134 n. 212 cum falso anno 1310: Iohannis papae confirmatio omnium a prioribus papis ordini concessorum privilegiorum.

---

679. *1336 februarii 8 Avinione (cf. aprilis 22). Benedictus XII repetit n. 673 de 1307 maii 22.*

Benedictus etc. dilectis filiis magistro et fratribus hospitalis beate Marie Theutonicorum Ierosolimitani etc. Cum a nobis — communimus. Datum Avinione vi idus februarii pontificatus nostri anno secundo.

Cum dato: Avinione 6 idus februarii p. n. a. 2: duo originalia cum bullis in archivo Regimontano ex archivo Cracoviensi etc. tandem huc delata. Ibidem transsumptum autoritate episcopi Revaliensis d. d. 1415 decbr. 24 factum. In transsumpto 1346 facto A. 16 p. 12 „Venetiis"; A. 16 p. 51 „Baruli"; A. 16 p. 87 „Confl., invenitur eciam in Mechelinia sub Nicolao III et aliud sub Clemente". — Cum dato: Avinione 10 kal. maii p. n. a. 2 originale cum bulla in archivo Regimontano itidem Cracovia tandem huc delatum. Transsumtum d. d. Marienburgi 1393 maii 29 ad instantiam Wenemari, magistri per Livoniam, sub sigillis episcoporum Wladislaviensis et Revaliensis atque abbatis de Polplin. Ibidem exstat aliud transsumtum autoritate episcopi Revaliensis sub sigillis eiusdem, capituli eius et abbatis de Padis 1415 decbr. 24 factum.

---

680. *1336 aprilis 22 Avinione. Benedictus XII repetit n. 679 de 1336 febr. 8.*

Benedictus etc. dilectis filiis magistro et fratribus hospitalis beate Marie Theutonicorum Ierosolimitani etc. Cum a nobis — communimus. Datum Avinione x kal. maii pontificatus nostri anno secundo.

---

681. *1343 novembris 4 Avinione (cf. 1344 martii 23, 1348 maii 21). Clemens VI repetit n. 678 de 1320/21.*

Clemens etc. dilectis filiis magistro et fratribus hospitalis beate Marie Theutonicorum Ierosolimitani salutem et apostolicam benedictionem. Solet annuere etc. Datum Avinione ii nonas novembris pontificatus nostri anno secundo.

Cum dato: Avinione 2 non. novbr. a. 2 „Confluentibus" A. 16 p. 89 bis scriptum. — Cum dato: Avinione 10 kal. aprilis p. n. a. 2 originale cum bulla in archivo Regimontano, huc tandem Cracovia delatum. In Inventario archivi Cracoviensis non citatur. — Cum dato: Avinione 12 kal. iunii p. n. a. 6 „Venetiis" A. 16 p. 14.

---

682. *1344 martii 23 Avinione. Clemens VI repetit n. 681 de 1343 novbr. 4.*

Clemens etc. Solet annuere etc. Datum Avinione x kal. aprilis pontificatus nostri anno secundo.

---

683. *1347 maii 21 Avinione. Clemens VI repetit n. 681 de 1343 novbr. 4.*

Clemens etc. Solet annuere etc. Datum Avinione xii kal. iunii pontificatus nostri anno sexto.

---

684. *1355 octobris 14 Avinione. Innocentius VI ordini Hospitalis Theutonici ordinis laudes proponit.*

— — Pugnastis quidem in umbra deliciarum, et ecce! quod sequens religio, videlicet beate Marie Theutonicorum, que non longe lapsis temporibus erat absque comparatione in omnibus minor vestra, que laborare non destitit, vos dormientes eximiis meritis, devotionis abundantia, felicibus successibus ac gloriosis acquisitionibus antecedit; et, quanto ista illi cedunt ad gloriam, tanto vobis ad ignominiam et pudorem.

Annotare haec lubet Innocentii VI verba, quae facit in bulla „Dudum intellecti" (1355) octbr. 14 Avinione (p. n. a. 3; 2 id. octbr.) ad Petrum de Cordillano magistrum et ordinem hospitalis s. Iohannis Hierosolymitani cum ordine Theutonico eos comparans (ap. Seb. Pauli, Codice di Malta I, 61 n. 73.

---

685. *1376 iunii 16 Avinione. Gregorius XI ad instar Alexandri IV omnes libertates, immunitates etc. domibus fratrum hospitalis s. Iohannis Ierosolimitani a sede apostolica concessas concedit fratribus hospitalis beatae Mariae Theutonicorum Hierosolymitani.*

Gregorius etc. dilectis filiis magistro et fratribus hospitalis beate Marie Theutonicorum Iherosolimitani salutem et apostolicam benedictionem. Dum inter religiones alias, quas celestis agricola in agro plantavit ecclesie rigavitque voce sue benedictionis et gracie, ut fructus producerent ampliores, religionem hospitalis beate Marie Theutonicorum Iherosolimitani, cuius professores experiencie militari studentes contra hostes fidei orthodoxe tamquam bellatores fortes et intrepidi dimicare, ut de militia terrena, quam gerunt, exercitui celestis aggregentur milicie, non metuunt, interne considerationis oculis intuemur, dignum et rationi consonum arbitramur, ut religionem eandem inter nostra et apostolice sedis precordia recumbentem oportunis prosequi favoribus et graciis procuremus. Hinc est, quod nos vestris devotis supplicationibus grato concurrentes assensu, ad instar felicis recordationis Alexandri pape iiii, predecessoris nostri, omnes libertates, immunitates ac indulgentias domibus fratrum hospitalis sancte Iohannis Iherosolimitani ab apostolica sede concessas, dummodo sint racionabiles et a iure non fuerunt[1] revocate, domui vestre concedimus, et, ut eis utamini libere sicut illi, auctoritate presencium indulgemus. Nulli ergo omnino etc. Si quis autem etc. Datum Avinione xvi kal. iulii pontificatus nostri anno sexto.

Originale cum bulla in archivo Regimontano huc tandem e Cracoviensi, Varsoviensi, Berolinensi archivis delatum. Citatur in Inventario archivi Cracoviensis p. 72: „Gregorius papa XI instar Alexandri IV papae immunitates et indulgentias fratribus hospitalis s. Ioannis Hierosolimitani a sede apostolica concessas fratribus ordinis Teutonici b. v. Mariae communicat. Datum Avenione 16 kal. iunii pontificatus anno sexto". — Transsumtum datum 1380 tertia die intrantis m. aprilis per Nicolaum de Seligenstad, imp. aut. notarium, sub autoritate et sigillo iudicii episcopalis Spirensis, habetur in archivo Regimontano. Aliud transsumtum exemplar d. d. Danzig 1426 martii 13 sigillo Bernardi, abbatis Olivensis, confirmatum, a notariis Ioh. Rosener et Valentino de Reddin subscriptum, ibidem. Ibidem exemplar datum Panormi 1487 octbr. 5 per Armannum de Munda, notarium regni Siciliae etc. Editum in Livl. U. B. III, 316 n. 1117. 1. sic.

---

686. *1389 decembris 11 Romae apud s. Petrum. Bonifacius IX hospitali s. Iohannis concedit omnia hospitali s. Mariae Theutonicorum a sede apostolica concessa privilegia.*

Bonifacius etc. dilectis filiis magistro et fratribus hospitalis sancti Iohannis Hierosolymitani salutem et apostolicam benedictionem. Vestre devotionis sinceritas, quam ad nos et Romanam geritis ecclesiam, promeretur, ut votis vestris, quantum cum deo possumus, favorabiliter annuamus. Vestris igitur in hac parte supplicationibus inclinati omnes libertates, immunitates ac indulgentias et privilegia quecumque dilectis filiis magistro et fratribus hospitalis sancte Marie Theutonicorum Hierosolymitani et in eorum hospitali et domibus ab apostolica sede concessa vobis ac hospitali et domibus vestris auctoritate apostolica tenore presentium concedimus et, ut illis libere uti et fungi possitis, prout ipsi uti et fungi possunt, devotioni vestre auctoritate presentium de speciali gratia indulgemus, quibuscunque libertatibus, immunitatibus et indulgentiis aliis vobis et hospitali et domibus vestris predictis alias a predicta sede concessis in suo nihilominus robore duraturis. Nulli ergo etc. nostre concessionis infringere etc. Si quis etc. Datum Rome apud sanctum Petrum tercio idus decembris anno primo.

Ex privilegiorum pontificiorum Hospitali s. Iohannis concessorum transsumto de 1495 iunii 26, quod in archivo Berolinensi asservatur (Ioh.), p. 22. Edd. Caorsinus b. IIII v. (p. 205). Privilegia, immunitates et indulgentiae ordinis s. Iohannis. Lipsiae ed. Wolfgang Senner 1520. fol. D. III. Huius concessionis causa in istas collectiones ordinis Theutonici privilegia recepta sunt. Vice versa Hospitalariorum privilegia ordini Theutonico quondam cum Templariorum generaliter 1221 ianuarii 9, dein ab Alexandro IV (cf. n. 685) specialiter concessa et 1376 iunii 16 (n. 685) confirmata sunt.

---

687. *1394 martii 18 Rome. Bonifacius IX repetit usitatam confirmationem omnium ordini Theutonico concessarum libertatum etc.*

Bonifacius etc. dilectis filiis magistro et fratribus hospitalis beate Marie Theutonicorum Ierosolimitani etc. Solet annuere — communimus. Datum Rome apud s. Petrum xv kal. aprilis pontificatus nostri anno quinto.

Transsumtum d. d. Reval 1415 decbr. 24 autoritate episcopi Revaliensis et sub sigillis episcopi dicti eiusque capituli, necnon abbatis de Padis factum exstat in archivo Regimontano. Iam anno p. sui 4 idem Bonifacius eisdem ac magistrum generalem in Prussia privilegiis et indulgentiis frui magistrum et ordinem in Livonia iusserat; cf. designationem Mitoviensis archivi Holmiam 1621 delati ap. Schirren p. 137 n. 327. Cf. infra n. 690.

---

688. *1394 martii 20 (cf. martii 25) Romae apud s. Petrum. Bonifacius IX indulget presbyteris ordinis Theutonici facultatem absolvendorum familiarium a peccatis in casibus, in quibus fratres absolvere possint.*

Bonifacius episcopus servus servorum dei dilectis filiis magistro generali et universis fratribus hospitalis b. Marie Theutonicorum Ierosolimitani salutem et apostolicam benedictionem. Sincere devotionis affectus, quem ad nos et Romanam geritis ecclesiam, promeretur, ut votis vestris, illis presertim, per que animarum saluti consulitur, quantum cum deo possumus, favorabiliter annuamus. Hinc est, quod nos vestris devotis supplicationibus inclinati, ut quilibet vestrum in presbiteratus ordine constitutus quoscunque familiares vestros seu alicuius vestrum, quotiens ei confiteantur[1], ab eorum peccatis, que sibi confessi fuerint, in illis vel similibus casibus apostolica auctoritate absolvere ipsisque pro commissis salutarem penitentiam iniungere valeat, in quibus aliquis aliquem vestrum sibi confitentem vigore concessionis auctoritate predicta vobis et vestro hospitali facte posset absolvere, tenore presentium indulgemus. Nulli ergo etc. Datum Rome apud sanctum Petrum xiii calendas aprilis pontificatus nostri anno quinto.

C.
C.
C.

Mar. B. de Pistorio. P. de Bosco.
Ioh. de Ortega etc.

Ex originali archivi Holmiensis ed. in Livl. U. B. IV, 9 n. 1354. Citatur in designatione archivi Mitoviensis 1621 Holmiam delati ap. Schirren p. 137 n. 330. Transsumtum d. d. 1415 decbr. 15, ubi datum sonat: 8 kal. aprilis, in Regimontano archivo; cf. Livl. U. B. IV Regesta n. 1641.

1. confiteatur L. U.

---

689. *1394 martii 25 Romae apud s. Petrum. Bonifacius IX repetit n. 688 de 1394 martii 20.*

Bonifacius etc. Sincere devotionis etc. Datum Rome apud s. Petrum viii kalendas aprilis pontificatus nostri anno quinto.

---

690. *1395 aprilis 15 Romae. Bonifacius IX ordini Theutonico confirmat a praedecessoribus suis concessa privilegia.*

Videtur esse initii „Solet annuere". Citatur cum dato Rom. 1395 d. 15 april. in designatione archivi Mitoviensis 1621 Holmiam delati ap. Schirren p. 138 n. 335. Cf. supra 1394 martii 18, quocum forsan depravato dato idem est.

---

691. *1396 aprilis 7 Romae apud s. Petrum. Bonifacius IX hospitali s. Iohannis Hierosolymitano confirmat exemtionem a procuratione legatorum et a praestatione eorum, quae de beneficiis suis per duos primos annos eveniant, mentione etiam de ordine Theutonico facta.*

Bonifacius episcopus servus servorum dei ad perpetuam rei memoriam. Sedis apostolice providentia circumspectas personas sub religionis observantia vacantes assidue studio pie vite benigno favore prosequitur et, ut earum consulatur commoditatibus, ut quietius domino famulari valeant, libenter se propiciam exhibet et benignam. Exhibita siquidem nobis nuper pro parte dilectorum filiorum prioris et fratrum prioratus hospitalis sancti Iohannis Hierosolymitani in Alamannia petitio continebat, quod, licet priori dicti prioratus et preceptoribus pro tempore existentibus ac fratribus prefati hospitalis infra prioratum ipsum consistentium a sede apostolica per ipsius litteras indultum existat, quod ad solutionem, procurationem seu ad contributionem aliquam legatis aut nuntiis dicte sedis faciendam extra domos predictas vel cum aliquo ex ipsis, sancte Romane ecclesie cardinalibus dumtaxat exceptis, super huiusmodi procurationibus aut contributionibus concordare seu ad prestationem fructuum duorum primorum annorum ecclesiarum parrochialium et aliorum beneficiorum suorum vacantium aut aliquarum collectarum, subsidiorum vel aliarum exactionum quarumcunque imponendarum solutionem minime teneantur, tamen plerumque contingit, quod in litteris apostolicis, que legatis aut nunciis huiusmodi a dicta sede conceduntur, huiusmodi verba seu saltem in effectu similia apponuntur, videlicet: „Volumus autem, quod non solum vos prelati et persone ecclesiastice terrarum et locorum ipsorum, sed etiam vos patriarche, archiepiscopi, episcopi hospitalium sancti Iohannis Hierosolymitani ac beate Marie Theutonicorum magistri, priores, preceptores et fratres vicinorum locorum ac civitatum et diocesium circumpositarum in provisionibus et subventionibus contribuatis pro oneribus huiusmodi supportandis, non obstante, si vos aut vestrum alicui vel quibusvis aliis locis aut ordinibus vestris communiter vel divisim a dicta sit sede indultum, quod nunciis ipsius sedis procurationem aliquam exhibere vel in ea contribuere, nisi ad vos declinaverint, minime teneamini et ad id compelli aut quod interdici, suspendi vel excommunicari non possitis per litteras apostolicas non facientes plenam et expressam ac de verbo ad verbum de indulto huiusmodi mentionem et quibuslibet privilegiis, indulgentiis et litteris apostolicis generalibus vel specialibus quibuscunque locis, personis vel hominibus aut ordinibus sub quacunque forma vel expressione verborum ab eadem sede concessis, de quibus quorumque totis tenoribus de verbo ad verbum in nostris litteris plena et expressa mentio sit habenda et per que presentis nostri mandati effectus valeat impediri quomodolibet et differri," *sq. vetantur praelati molestare priorem et fratres hospitalis s. Iohannis procurationibus vel exactione beneficiorum duorum primorum annorum.* Datum Rome apud sanctum Petrum decimo quinto kalendas maii anno septimo.

In transsumto archivi Berolinensis de 1495 iunii 26 (Ioh.) p. 17. Edd. Caorsinus b. v.; Senner C. 6, qui addunt: „In fine vero dicti sumpti talis erat subscriptio: Sumptum ex registro literarum apostolicarum. Collationatum per me F. Ponzetum, eiusdem registri magistrum, et concordat".

---

692. *1396 maii 11 Romae apud s. Petrum. Bonifacius IX confirmat ordini Theutonico praesentationis ius ad ecclesias patronatui eius subiectas.*

Bonifacius episcopus servus servorum dei ad perpetuam rei memoriam. Quanto dilecti filii magister et fratres hospitalis beate Marie Theotonicorum Ierosolimitani pro defensione et propagacione catholice fidei fervencius ponunt iugiter se et sua, tanto per sedem[1] apostolicam in suis iuribus conservandis foveri merentur defensionis presidio fortiori. Sane peticio pro parte dictorum magistri et fratrum nobis nuper exhibita continebat, quod, licet ipsi ad parrochiales ecclesias et alia beneficia ecclesiastica, in quibus ius obtinent patronatus, cum illa vacare contigerit, personas idoneas locorum ordinariis observato iuris ordine presentare ipsique ordinarii personas easdem ad ecclesias et alia beneficia huiusmodi sic presentatas sine aliqua contradiccione seu exactione admittere et eas instituere consueverint in rectores ecclesiarum et beneficiorum aliorum huiusmodi eciam iuxta specialia privilegia magistro et fratribus prefatis a sede predicta concessa, tamen a non longo tempore cura quidam locorum ordinarii in Alamania novum et illicitum gravacionis et exactionis modum contra eosdem magistrum et fratres exquirentes huiusmodi personas per eos ad ecclesias et beneficia supradicta presentatos admittere et in illorum rectores instituere indebite recusant[2], nisi eedem persone medietatem seu aliam certam partem vel quottam fructuum primi anni ecclesiarum et beneficiorum ipsorum dictis ordinariis, ad quos institucio huiusmodi communiter vel divisim pertinet, persolvant in ipsorum magistri et fratrum non modicum preiudicium et gravamen. Quare pro parte dictorum magistri et fratrum nobis fuit humiliter supplicatum, ut super hoc eis de oportuno remedio providere de benignitate apostolica dignaremur. Nos igitur huiusmodi supplicacionibus inclinati huiusmodi locorum ordinariis ubicumque locorum constitutis, eciamsi archiepiscopali vel episcopali aut alia quavis prefulgeant dignitate, ad quos admissio personarum et institutio rectorum huiusmodi pertinet communiter vel divisim, tenore presencium auctoritate apostolica sub excommunicacionis pena, quam contrarium facientes eo ipso incurrant, districte precipiendo mandamus, quatenus ab illicitis exactionibus et gravaminibus huiusmodi penitus abstinentes et qualibet difficultate cessante personas idoneas, quas prefati magister et fratres ad ecclesias et beneficia supradicta, in quibus pacifice et quiete, ut prefertur, ius obtinent patronatus, vacantia et imposterum vacatura duxerint presentandas, prout ad eos communiter vel divisim pertinuerit, legittimo impedimento cessante pure et libere et absque aliqua exactione huiusmodi admittere et in eorundem, ad que sic presentate fuerint, ecclesiarum et beneficiorum rectores instituere procurent et nichilominus, si cum debita instancia requisiti id infra mensem a tempore requisicionis huiusmodi racionabili causa cessante facere recusaverint vel distulerint, extunc conservatores eisdem magistro et fratribus contra inferentes eis in bonis aut rebus vel personis ipsorum iniurias vel iacturas a sede predicta deputati vel deputandi aut unus eorum per se vel alios huiusmodi sic presentatas personas ea vice auctoritate presencium loco huiusmodi ordinariorum, si aliud canonicum non obsistat, admittant vel admittat ac instituant vel instituat. Quibus quidem conservatoribus et eorum cuilibet eciam presencium tenore precipimus et mandamus sub huiusmodi excommunicacionis pena, quam, ut premissum est, contrarium facientes incurrant ipso facto, ut ad requisicionem magistri et fratrum predictorum loco ordinariorum huiusmodi in rectores ecclesiarum et aliorum beneficiorum predictorum huiusmodi eis presentatas personas, ut prefertur, instituant nec unus conservatorum ipsorum super hoc requisitus per alium se excuset vel expectet, et alia, que circa hec necessaria fuerint, exequi non omittant, contradiccione qualibet et constitucionibus apostolicis necnon statutis et consuetudinibus et aliis contrariis non obstantibus quibuscunque. Nos enim exnunc irritum decernimus et inane, si secus super hiis a quoquam quavis auctoritate scienter vel ignoranter contigerit attemptari. Nulli ergo omnino hominum liceat hanc paginam nostre constitucionis infringere vel ei ausu temerario contraire. Si quis autem hoc attemptare presumpserit, indignacionem omnipotentis dei et beatorum Petri et Pauli apostolorum eius se noverit incursurum. Datum Rome apud sanctum Petrum v idus maii pontificatus nostri anno septimo.

IV, 221. 1. fidem IV. 2. recusauit IV.

---

693. *1396 maii 11 Romae apud s. Petrum. Bonifacius IX ordini Theutonico confirmat uniones parochialium ecclesiarum domibus eius factas.*

Bonifacius episcopus servus servorum dei ad perpetuam rei memoriam. Sedis apostolice providencia circumspecta personas sub religionis observancia vacantes assiduo studio pie vite benigno favore prosequitur et, que pro personarum ipsarum ac locorum et prelatorum suorum oneribus et necessitatibus supportandis provida deliberacione fiunt, consuevit apostolico munimine roborare. Exhibita siquidem nobis nuper pro parte dilectorum filiorum magistri et fratrum hospitalis beate Marie Theotonicorum Ierosolimitani peticio continebat, quod olim nonnulli dive memorie imperatores Romani ac reges et principes, duces, comites, barones et milites alieque laicales persone pia devocione ducti iura patronatus, que in certis parrochialibus ecclesiis tunc obtinebant, pro fundacione quarundam domorum in diversis diocesibus consistencium dicti hospitalis ac pro sustentacione fratrum dicti hospitalis in eisdem domibus degencium pro largicione donaverunt ac eciam concesserunt et insuper huiusmodi et nonnulli alii fratres in ipsis ac eciam in quibusdam aliis domibus dicti hospitalis commorantes nonnullas alias ecclesias parrochiales ac ius patronatus earum aliis iustis, ut creditur, titulis acquisiverunt, quarum aliquas ac ius patronatus huiusmodi et presentandi rectores ad illas habuerunt et possederunt pacifice et quiete a tanto tempore, cuius contrarii memoria non existit, et ex huiusmodi ecclesiis nonnulle dudum sunt erecte in domos conventuales et per modum conventuum a fratribus prefati hospitalis hactenus gubernate, ad quasdam vero ex ipsis, cum vacant, huiusmodi fratres soliti sunt, prout solent, locorum ordinariis presentari ac per illos in rectores earum institui, nonnulle etiam ex eisdem et aliis parrochialibus ecclesiis fuerunt prout sunt successivis vicibus diversis domibus prefati hospitalis per locorum diocesanos ex certis racionabilibus et legittimis causis auctoritate ordinaria unite, annexe et incorporate ac huiusmodi fratres in eisdem domibus pro tempore degentes ecclesias ipsas vigore unionum, annexionum et incorporacionum huiusmodi assecuti illas per quadraginta annos et ultra tenuerunt et possederunt, prout tenent et possident pacifice et quiete. Cum autem, sicut eadem peticio subiungebat, prefati magister et fratres dubitent in donacionibus, concessionibus, acquisicionibus, erectionibus, unionibus, annexionibus et incorporacionibus huiusmodi, quas cum earum tenoribus pro expressis et singulariter specificatis ac presentibus insertis ex certa sciencia haberi volumus, quoad aliquas ex ecclesiis antedictis, quas penitus ignorant, locorum diocesanorum et ipsorum capitulorum auctoritatem et consensum necnon tractatus et alias sollempnitates et formas ad hec oportunas non intervenisse seque propterea super ecclesiis ipsis aut ipsorum aliquibus posse imposterum molestari, pro parte ipsorum magistri et fratrum nobis fuit humiliter supplicatum, ut premissis non obstantibus donacionibus, concessionibus, acquisicionibus, erectionibus, unionibus, annexionibus et incorporacionibus ante dictis robur apostolice firmitatis adiicere de benignitate apostolica dignaremur. Nos igitur huiusmodi supplicacionibus inclinati ac ecclesias ipsas et earum necnon domorum predictarum, quibus ecclesie ipse, ut prefertur, unite, annexe et incorporate sunt, veros valores annuos secundum communem extimacionem presentibus pro expresso habere volentes donaciones, concessiones, acquisiciones, erectiones, uniones, annexiones et incorporaciones predictas et quecunque inde secuta rata et grata habentes illa auctoritate apostolica ex certa sciencia confirmamus et presentis scripti patrocinio communimus, supplentes nichilominus sollempnitates omissas et omnes defectus, si qui forsan intervenerint in eisdem, non obstantibus tam felicis recordacionis Urbani pape sexti predecessoris nostri, quibus cavetur, quod quicumque impetrantes confirmaciones unionum teneantur exprimere valorem tam beneficii uniti quam eciam ecclesie vel monasterii aut mense episcopalis vel abbatialis seu alterius beneficii, cui huiusmodi unio facta fuerit, alioquin confirmaciones ipse non valeant, quam aliis constitucionibus et ordinacionibus apostolicis contrariis quibuscumque. Nulli ergo omnino hominum liceat hanc paginam nostre confirmacionis, communicionis et suppletionis infringere vel ei ausu temerario contraire. Si quis autem hoc attemptare presumpserit, indignacionem omnipotentis dei et beatorum Petri et Pauli apostolorum eius se noverit incursurum. Datum Rome apud sanctum Petrum v idus maii pontificatus nostri anno septimo.

IV, 222 v.

---

694. *1397 aprilis 7 Rome apud s. Petrum. Bonifacius IX concedit magistro et fratribus ordinis Theutonici, ad ecclesias patronatus seu vicarias presentatos fratres nutu superioris revocari in domum vel conventum et alios loco illorum praesentari posse, quociens placeret.*

Bonifacius etc. ad perpetuam rei memoriam. Ad ea, que ecclesiarum et ecclesiasticorum beneficiorum statum prosperum respiciunt, libenter intendimus et, ut ecclesie et beneficia ipsa laudabiliter gubernentur, presertim cum a nobis requiritur, favorem apostolicum impertimur. Cum itaque, sicut exhibita nobis nuper pro parte dilectorum filiorum magistri et fratrum hospitalis beate Marie Theutonicorum Ierosolimitani petitio continebat, quod, cum sepe contingat fratres dicti hospitalis ad parochiales ecclesias vel earum perpetuas vicarias per magistrum eiusdem hospitalis pro tempore existentem ac ipsos fratres vel aliquem seu aliquos ex eis, prout ad eum vel eos presentatio huiusmodi pertinet, presentatos et per locorum ordinarios institutos se minus honeste regere ac male conversari; pro parte magistri et fratrum predictorum nobis fuit humiliter supplicatum, ut eis, quod ipsi aut ille vel illi ex eis, ad quem vel ad quos presentatio huiusmodi ut premittitur pertinet, presentatos hactenus et imposterum presentandos fratres huiusmodi ad ecclesias et vicarias predictas pro solo nutu magistri et fratrum prefatorum aut illius vel illorum ex eis, ad quem vel ad quos presentatio huiusmodi pertinet, ut prefertur, quotiens ei vel eis videbitur, ad domum seu claustrum dicti hospitalis revocare et loco revocatorum huiusmodi alios fratres ydoneos eiusdem hospitalis ad ecclesias et vicarias antedictas instituendos ordinariis ipsis presentari possint, concedere de benignitate apostolica dignaremur. Nos igitur huiusmodi supplicationibus inclinati eisdem magistro et fratribus, quod ipsi aut ille vel illi ex eis, ad quem vel ad quos presentatio huiusmodi pertinet, ut prefertur, presentatos hactenus et imposterum presentandos fratres huiusmodi ad ecclesias et vicarias predictas pro solo nutu magistri et fratrum prefatorum aut illius vel illorum ex eis, ad quem vel ad quos presentatio huiusmodi pertinet, ut prefertur, quociens ei vel eis videbitur, ad domum seu claustrum dicti hospitalis revocare et loco revocatorum huiusmodi alios fratres ydoneos eiusdem hospitalis ad ecclesias et vicarias predictas instituendos ordinariis ipsis presentare libere et licite valeant, auctoritate apostolica tenore presencium de speciali gratia indulgemus et volumus, quod huiusmodi presentationes loco revocatorum ipsorum, ut premittitur, faciende perinde valeant et sortiantur effectum, acsi ecclesie necnon vicarie predicte alias de iure et de facto vacavissent, constitutionibus apostolicis ac statutis et consuetudinibus dicti hospitalis contrariis non obstantibus quibuscunque. Nulli ergo omnino etc. Si quis autem etc. Datum Rome apud sanctum Petrum vii idus aprilis pontificatus nostri anno octavo.

Originale cum bulla „ad mandatum dom. pape gratis“ extraditum in archivo Regimontano. Textus prima pars videtur depravata.

---

695. *1397 aprilis 7 Romae apud s. Petrum. Bonifacius IX occasione capellanatus apostolici Iohanni de Colonia collati declarat clericos ordinis Theutonici in capellanorum apostolicorum consortium receptos non subtrahi ordinis obedientiae.*

Bonifacius episcopus servus servorum dei ad futuram rei memoriam. Affectione et devotione precipuis, quas ad dilectos filios magistrum et fratres hospitalis beate Marie Teutonicorum Ierosolimitani gerimus, merito inducimur, ut ea, per que fratres ipsi a regularibus observantiis retrahi possint, submovere sollicite studeamus. Nuper siquidem dilectum filium Iohannem de Colonia, fratrem dicti hospitalis, in nostrum et apostolice sedis capellanum gratiose recepimus ac nostrorum et aliorum sedis eiusdem capellanorum consortio favorabiliter aggregavimus, prout in nostris inde confectis litteris plenius continetur. Cum autem, sicut exhibita nobis nuper pro parte magistri et fratrum prefatorum petitio continebat, dictus Ioannes litteras huiusmodi ac etiam nonnullos processus per easdem ad hoc fieri procurasse credatur, ut ab obedientia magistri et hospitalis predictorum eximeretur, et, si per alios fratres dicti hospitalis similia attemptarentur, in magnam turbationem observantie regularis hospitalis cederet antedicti, pro parte ipsorum magistri et fratrum nobis fuit humiliter supplicatum, ut providere ipsis super hoc de benignitate apostolica dignaremur. Nos igitur huiusmodi supplicationibus inclinati, eisdem magistro et fratribus auctoritate apostolica tenore presentium concedimus, quod tam ipse Iohannes quam etiam quicunque alii fratres prefati hospitalis, qui forsan in capellanos dicte sedis hactenus sunt recepti vel inposterum recipientur, perinde suis ordinariis iudicibus ac superioribus subsint ac parere et intendere teneantur, acsi capellani dicte sedis minime forent et super hoc litteras apostolicas cum processibus huiusmodi vel sine illis minime impetrassent, huiusmodi impetratis ac impetrandis litteris et processibus necnon constitutionibus apostolicis ac statutis et consuetudinibus dicti hospitalis et aliis contrariis non obstantibus quibuscumque. Nulli ergo hominum liceat hanc paginam nostre concessionis infringere etc. Si quis etc. Datum Romae apud sanctum Petrum vii idus aprilis pontificatus nostri anno octavo.

Ed. Duellius in appendice 9 n. 10. Transsumtum autoritate et sigillo Werneri de Hayn, officialis Herbipolensis curiae, d. 1418 decbr. 2 factum in archivo Regimontano.

---

696. *1399 februarii 25 Romae apud s. Petrum. Bonifacius IX concedit ordini Theutonico, ut, quando placeat, in ecclesiis eius per ordinis sacerdotes et alios praedicacionem faciat, audientibusque indulgentiam proponit.*

Bonifacius episcopus servus servorum dei dilectis filiis magistro generali hospitalis beate Marie Theotonicorum Ierosolimitani ac universis commendatoribus, preceptoribus et fratribus domorum eiusdem hospitalis ubilibet consistencium salutem et apostolicam benedictionem. Sincere devocionis affectus, quem ad nos et Romanam geritis ecclesiam, non indigne meretur, ut peticionibus vestris, illis presertim, per quas divinus cultus et devocio populi in dei laudem feliciter augmentatur, favorabiliter annuamus. Hinc est, quod nos vestris in hac parte supplicationibus inclinati, ut quilibet ex vobis et fratribus hospitalis et domorum predictorum in sacerdocio constitutus[1] in capellis et ecclesiis eciam non parrochialibus ad vos et vestras domos pertinentibus verbum dei, quociens hoc vestrum alicui placuerit, publice ad populum predicare seu per alios sacerdotes facere predicari alicuius licentia super hoc minime requisita libere et licite possit, devocioni vestre auctoritate apostolica tenore presencium indulgemus, et nichilominus de omnipotentis dei misericordia et beatorum Petri et Pauli apostolorum eius auctoritate confisi omnibus vere penitentibus et confessis, qui huiusmodi predicaciones devote audierint, singulis videlicet vicibus, quibus predicaciones ipsas audierint, ut prefertur, unum annum et unam quadragenam de iniunctis eis penitenciis misericorditer relaxamus, universis et singulis auctoritate predicta districtius inhibentes, ne vos in huiusmodi predicacionibus quomodolibet impediant aut Christi fideles ab huiusmodi predicacionibus retrahant quoquomodo constitucionibus, privilegiis, indulgenciis et litteris apostolicis generalibus vel specialibus, quorumcunque tenorum existant, per que presentibus non expressa vel totaliter non inserta effectus earum impediri valeat quomodolibet vel differri et de quibus quorumque totis tenoribus habenda sit in nostris litteris mencio specialis et aliis contrariis non obstantibus quibuscunque. Nulli ergo omnino hominum liceat hanc paginam nostre concessionis et constitucionis infringere vel ei ausu temerario contraire. Si quis autem hoc attemptare presumpserit, indignacionem omnipotentis dei et beatorum Petri et Pauli apostolorum eius se noverit incursurum. Datum Rome apud Sanctum Petrum v kalendas marcii pontificatus nostri anno decimo.

IV, 224v. Ioh. 41. Edd. Caorsinus c. 6; Senner F.   1. constitutis B.

---

697. *1399 februarii 25 Romae apud s. Petrum. Bonifacius IX fratribus et oblatis ordinis Theutonici indulgentias quasdam concedit.*

Bonifacius episcopus servus servorum dei ad perpetuam rei memoriam. Ad ea ex apostolice servitutis officio libenter intendimus, per que Christi fidelium animarum saluti salubriter providetur. Dudum siquidem pro parte dilectorum filiorum, magistri generalis et fratrum hospitalis beate Marie Theotunicorum Ierosolimitani, nobis exposito, quod quilibet ipsorum fratrum, postquam regularem professionem dicti hospitalis emisisset, ex laudabili consuetudine septies in anno, videlicet in nativitatis domini nostri Iesu Christi et purificationis Marie virginis necnon in die Iovis sancta ac in resurrectionis domini nostri Iesu Christi ac in pentecostes necnon assumtionis dicte beate Marie festivitatibus et in celebritate omnium sanctorum enkaristie sacramentum sumere consueverit[1], nos cupientes ipsorum fratrum et etiam suorum familiarium animarum saluti providere omnibus ex dictis fratribus et familiaribus vere penitentibus et confessis, qui huiusmodi septem vicibus sacramentum predictum devote sumerent, annuatim singulis videlicet vicibus huiusmodi, quibus sacramentum ipsum, ut prefertur, sumerent, illam indulgentiam et remissionem peccatorum suorum concessimus, que devote visitantibus ecclesiam Warmiensem in octava dicte festivitatis assumtionis beate Marie auctoritate apostolica est concessa, prout in nostris inde confectis litteris plenius continetur. Cum autem, sicut[1] exhibita nobis nuper pro parte dictorum magistri et fratrum petitio continebat, plerumque contingat, nonnullas personas laicales causa devotionis fraternitatem dictorum fratrum assumere ac se et bona sua, usu tamen bonorum ipsorum sibi ad eorum vitam duntaxat reservato, ad diversas domus dicti hospitalis imperpętuum offerre et donare et sic in seculo remanentes virtutum domino famulari; nos pium talium personarum propositum plurimum in domino commendantes ac cupientes eas indulgentie seu remissionis memorate fieri participes, de omnipotentis dei misericordia et beatorum Petri et Pauli apostolorum eius auctoritate confisi omnibus ex eisdem personis vere penitentibus et confessis, qui sic fraternitatem dictorum fratrum actu assumserunt ac se et bona sua ad domus dicti hospitalis obtulerunt et donarunt seu inantea assumserint, obtulerint et donaverint, et qui iuxta prefatam consuetudinem huiusmodi septem vicibus predictum sacramentum devote sumpserint annuatim, singulis videlicet vicibus huiusmodi, quibus ipsum sacramentum sumpserint, ut prefertur, eandem indulgentiam et remissionem suorum peccatorum concedimus, que eisdem fratribus per nos, ut premittitur, est concessa, et nichilominus eisdem personis auctoritate apostolica tenore presentium indulgemus, ut omnibus et singulis aliis indulgentiis, privilegiis, immunitatibus, libertatibus et exemtionibus uti et gaudere possint, quibus prefati fratres gaudent seu quomodolibet potiuntur, constitutionibus, privilegiis, indulgentiis et litteris apostolicis generalibus vel specialibus, quorumcunque tenorum existant, per que presentibus non expressa vel totaliter non inserta effectus earum impediri valeat quomodolibet vel differri, et de quibus quorumque totis tenoribus de verbo ad verbum habenda sit in nostris litteris mentio specialis, et aliis contrariis non obstantibus quibuscunque. Nulli ergo etc. Datum Rome apud sanctum Petrum v kalendas martii pontificatus nostri anno decimo.

Ex transsumto de 1401 aprilis 16 in archivo Regimontano (cf. Napiersky in Indice n. 530) ed. in Livl. U. B. IV, 230 n. 1482. cf. n. 699. 1. supplevi.

698. *1399 martii 22 Rome. Bonifacius IX excommunicat, quicunque beneficia ecclesiastica ordini Theutonico incorporata a sede apostolica vel aliunde impetraverint, possessores re impedire aut molestare presumpserint.*

Bonifacius episcopus servus servorum dei ad perpetuam rei memoriam. Magne devotionis affectus, quem dilecti filii magister et fratres hospitalis s. Marie Theutonicorum Ierosolimitani ad nos et Romanam ecclesiam gerere comprobantur, merito nos inducit, ut ipsos specialibus favoribus et graciis prosequamur. Volentes igitur eosdem magistrum et fratres premissorum intuitu favoribus prosequi graciosis, motu proprio, non ad ipsorum magistri et fratrum aut alicuius alterius pro eis nobis super hoc oblate petitionis instantiam, sed de nostra mera liberalitate apostolica auctoritate irrefragabiliter statuimus et eciam ordinavimus, quod de cetero nulli, cuiuscunque status gradus aut conditionis fuerit, liceat sub excommunicacionis pena, quam post insinuacionem presentium ei factam, si non desistat, incurrat ipso facto, ecclesias eciam parrochiales, capellas, altaria aut alia beneficia ecclesiastica cum cura vel sine cura eisdem magistro et fratribus aut hospitali seu alicui vel aliquibus ex domibus eiusdem hospitalis ubicunque consistenti vel consistentibus apostolica vel alia quavis auctoritate incorporata a sede apostolica vel alias aliunde impetrare vel ea quovis quesito colore petere seu super ipsis magistrum et fratres predictos vel quoscunque commendatores vel preceptores domorum dicti hospitalis impedire seu quomodolibet molestare; decernentes eciam irritum et inane, quidquid in contrarium a quoquam quavis auctoritate scienter vel ignoranter contigerit attemptari. Nulli ergo etc. Si quis autem etc. Datum Rome apud s. Petrum xi kal. aprilis pontificatus nostri anno decimo.

Transsumtum d. d. 1402 decbr. 11 a duobus notariis Argentinensibus factum et subscriptum, quod asservatur in archivo Regimontano, ubi etiam apographum fere coaevum bullae, in charta papyracea scriptum ex originali, ut videtur.

---

699. *1400 aprilis 13 Romae ap. s. Petrum. Bonifacius IX confirmat complura ordinis Theutonici privilegia de dedicatione oratoriorum, indulgentiis, processionibus, caeteris.*

Bonifacius episcopus servus servorum dei dilectis filiis magistro et fratribus hospitalis sancte Marie Theutonicorum Ierosolimitani ac universis commendatoribus, preceptoribus et fratribus domorum[1] eiusdem hospitalis ubilibet consistentium salutem et apostolicam benedictionem. His, que fidelibus, presertim sub religionis habitu domino militantibus ex graciosa apostolice sedis benignitate provide facta sunt, ut illibata consistant, libenter adiicimus roboris firmitatem. Dudum siquidem, ut vobis et cuilibet vestrum in presbiteratus ordine constituto liceret totiens, quotiens expediret, capellas seu altaria in ecclesiis ad vos pertinentibus sita et alia pia loca de locis suis removere et removeri facere et ad alia loca ad hoc congrua et apta reponere et reponi facere, ac etiam in ipsis vestris ecclesiis capellas et altaria de novo erigere, dotare et fundare, ordinarii loci et cuiuscumque alterius licentia super hoc minime requisita, quodque, si ordinarius loci, ad hoc alias debite requisitus, capellas et altaria huiusmodi sic ad alia loca reposita seu de novo erecta consecrare seu consecrari facere differret et resusaret, liceret similiter vobis et cuilibet vestrum, etiam absque specialibus mandato et licentia ordinarii ipsius et cuiuscumque alterius, ipsas capellas et altaria ad huiusmodi alia loca, ut prefertur, reposita seu de novo erecta per alium catholicum antistitem gratiam et communionem dicte sedis habentem facere consecrari, vobis et cuilibet vestrum duximus indulgendum; et deinde pro parte vestra nobis exposito, quod quilibet vestrum, postquam regularem professionem dicti hospitalis emiseratis, ex laudabili consuetudine septies in anno, videlicet in nativitate domini nostri Iesu Christi et purificationis beate Marie virginis necnon in die Iovis sancta ac in resurrectionis domini nostri Iesu Christi ac in pentecostes necnon assumptionis dicte beate Marie festivitatibus ac celebritate omnium sanctorum eucharistie sacramentum sumere consueveratis, nos vobis et familiaribus vestris vere penitentibus et confessis, qui huiusmodi septem vicibus sacramentum predictum devote sumerent, ut prefertur, illam indulgentiam et remissionem peccatorum suorum concesseramus, quam devote visitantibus ecclesiam Warmiensem in octava dicte festivitatis assumptionis dicte beate Marie autoritate apostolica erat concessa. Et quod plerumque contingebat nonnullas personas laicales causa devotionis fraternitatem vestram assumere ac se et bona sua, usu tamen bonorum ipsorum sibi ad eorum vitam dumtaxat reservato, ad diversas domos hospitalis s. Marie Theutonicorum in perpetuum offerre et donare et sic in seculo remanentes virtutum domino famulari; nos omnibus ex eisdem personis similiter penitentibus et confessis, qui sic fraternitatem predictam assumpserant et bona sua ad domos dicti hospitalis contulerant et donaverant et inantea assumerent, offerrent, donarent, et qui iuxta prefatam consuetudinem huiusmodi septem vicibus predictum sacramentum devote sumerent annuatim[2], similes indulgentiam et remissionem peccatorum suorum concessimus, que vobis per nos, ut premittitur, erant concesse, ipsisque personis, ut[3] omnibus et singulis aliis indulgentiis, privilegiis, immunitatibus, libertatibus et exemptionibus uti et gaudere possent, quibus vos potiebamini seu quomodolibet gaudebatis, duximus indulgendum. Privilegia[3*], immunitates et gratias vobis et vestris hospitalibus ac domibus et preceptoriis a predecessoribus nostris Romanis pontificibus ac a quibuscunque prelatis et personis ecclesiasticis, etiam a regibus et principibus ac aliis dominis temporalibus et per nos eisdem hospitalibus et domibus ac preceptoriis predictis concessa confirmamus et litterarum nostrarum patrocinio communimus. Et quia, sicut pro parte vestra nobis significato vos nonnullos questuarios habebatis, declaravimus constitutionem felicis recordationis Clementis quinti predecessoris nostri in concilio Viennensi contra questuarios editam, que incipit ‚Abusionibus', ad vos vel hospitalia ac domus et loca seu privilegia vel indulgentias vestra et vobis concessa aliqualiter non extendi. Et[3*] deinde, ad dilectorum filiorum commendatoris et fratrum domus hospitalis beate Marie Theutonicorum Ierosolimitani in suburbio Argentinensi instantiam, ut in ecclesia beate Marie virginis dicte domus eucharistie domini nostri Iesu Christi venerabile sacramentum in cristallo vel vase perspicuo seu perlucido, ita quod quilibet volens huiusmodi sacramentum videre posset in nativitatis, epiphanie, resurrectionis et ascensionis prefati domini nostri Iesu Christi, pentecostes, necnon nativitatis, assumptionis, purificationis et annunciationis beate Marie virginis, ac inventionis et exaltacionis sancte crucis et[4] in beate Elisabethe vidue ac in ipsius ecclesie dedicationis festivitatibus necnon in celebritate omnium sanctorum a primis vesperis cuiuslibet festivitatum et celebritatis huiusmodi usque ad[5] secundas vesperas, donec completorium finiretur, in patenti teneri et in qualibet earundem festivitatum et celebritatis tempore missarum ad hoc congruo cum processione per ambitum dicte ecclesie solemniter et devote portari licite valeret, duximus similiter indulgendum, dummodo tamen dictus locus generali non subiaceat interdicto. Et nihilominus omnibus, ut premittitur, penitentibus et confessis, qui dictam ecclesiam in prefatis festivitatibus et celebritate devote visitarent et coram dicto sacramento orationem et salutationem huiusmodi dicerent, ut prefertur, illam videlicet indulgentiam et peccatorum suorum remissionem concessimus, que visitantibus ecclesiam sancti Petri iunioris Argentinensem bona feria quarta scilicet proxima post dominicam palmarum dicta erat auctoritate concessa. Et insuper, quia, sicut pro parte vestra nobis exposito, nonnullis archiepiscopis, episcopis et aliis locorum ordinariis a sede apostolica indultum seu alias eadem vel ordinaria auctoritatibus sub certis penis in diversis partibus mandatum fore dicebatur, quod in ipsorum archiepiscoporum, episcoporum et ordinariorum episcopatibus et diocesibus littere seu mandata apostolica publicari seu executioni demandari non possent nec ipsis litteris subditi archiepiscopi vel episcopi, in cuius civitate vel diocesi fieret, obedire tenerentur, nisi prius per eundem archiepiscopum vel episcopum, in cuius civitate vel diocesi fieret, seu per alium ab eo ad hoc deputatum ipse littere et mandata visa et examinata et in signum visionis et examinationis huiusmodi eiusmodi archiepiscopi, episcopi et ordinarii litere testimoniales, quas vulgariter vidimus appellant, existerent concesse; nos vobis, ut, quascunque literas et mandata, privilegia et indulgentias seu alias concessiones sive gratiam sive iusticiam continentes ab eadem sede vobis hactenus facta vel concessa seu in posterum concedenda ac processus eorum vigore habitos et habendos in quibuscunque civitatibus et diocesibus et alias ubicunque expediret publicari et executioni demandari facere libere et licite valeatis, ac executores, conservatores et alii iudices vobis ad hoc deputati et deputandi seu eorum subdelegati etiam ad publicationem huiusmodi et executionem procedere tenerentur et deberent, literis testimonialibus per vos a quocunque archiepiscopo, episcopo vel ordinario seu alias ad hoc deputato non petitis nec obtentis duximus eadem auctoritate similiter indulgendum, decernentes executores, conservatores, iudices et subdelegatos huiusmodi necnon notarios et testes, quos huiusmodi executioni et publicationi interesse contingeret, nullis propterea penis et sententiis posse laqueari, ac irritum et inane, si secus super his a quoquam quavis auctoritate scienter vel ignoranter contingeret attentari. Mandamus etiam executoribus, conservatoribus, iudicibus, subdelegatis et tabellionibus, notariis et testibus, necnon aliis clericis civitatum et diocesium quarumcunque, etiamsi exempti essent, super hoc pro parte vestra pro tempore requirendis sub excommunicationis pena, quam, si secus facerent, ipsam incurrere volumus ipso facto, quatinus ad publicationem et executionem huiusmodi diligenter et debite procederent ac etiam personis, quas litere et mandata apostolica a nobis impetrata seu impetranda concernerent, ut eis humiliter obedirent et intenderent, prout alias tenerentur et deberent. Et[6] deinde, ut quilibet ex vobis in sacerdotio constitutus in capellis et ecclesiis etiam non parochialibus ad vos et vestras domos pertinentibus verbum dei, quotiens hoc vestrum alicui placeret, publice ad populum predicare seu per alios sacerdotes facere predicari, alicuius licentia super hoc minime requisita, libere et licite possetis, vobis predicta auctoritate duximus indulgendum. Et nihilominus omnibus, ut premittitur, penitentibus et confessis, qui huiusmodi predicationes devote audirent, singulis videlicet vicibus, quibus huiusmodi predicationes audirent, ut prefertur, unum annum et unam quadragenam de iniunctis eis penitenciis misericorditer relaxamus, eadem auctoritate districtius inhibentes universis et singulis, ne vos in huiusmodi predicationibus quomodolibet impedirent aut Christi fideles ab huiusmodi predicationibus retraherent quoquo modo. Et insuper motu proprio, non ad vestram vel alicuius alterius pro vobis super hoc nobis oblate petitionis instantiam, sed de nostra mera liberalitate, eadem auctoritate irrefragabiliter statuimus et etiam ordinamus, quod de cetero nulli, cuiuscunque status, gradus aut conditionis esset, liceret sub excommunicationis pena, quam post insinuationem presentium ei factam, si non desisteret, incurreret ipso facto, ecclesias etiam parochiales, capellas, altaria aut alia beneficia ecclesiastica cum cura vel sine cura vobis aut hospitali seu alicui vel aliquibus ex domibus eiusdem hospitalis, ubicumque consistenti seu consistentibus dicta apostolica vel alia quavis[7] auctoritate incorporata, a sede predicta vel alias aliunde impetrare, vel ea quovis quesito colore petere vel super ipsis vos impedire seu quomodolibet molestare, prout in diversis nostris inde confectis litteris, quarum tenores alias presentibus haberi volumus pro sufficienter expressis, plenius continetur. Cum autem, sicut exhibita nobis nuper pro parte vestra petitio continebat, a nonnullis vertitur in dubium literas ipsas et alia inde secuta in aliquibus sui partibus iuribus non subsistere, vosque posse super ipsis in posterum molestari, pro parte vestra nobis fuit supplicatum, ut eisdem et inde secutis apostolice confirmationis robur adiicere et alias vobis providere super hoc de benignitate apostolica dignaremur; nos igitur vestris in hac parte supplicationibus inclinati prefatas literas et quecunque inde secuta et que in futurum proinde sequi poterunt rata habentes et grata ea auctoritate apostolica et certa scientia tenore presentium confirmamus et presentis scripti patrocinio communimus supplentes omnes defectus, si qui commissi fuerint in eisdem[8]. Nulli ergo omnino hominum liceat hanc paginam nostre confirmationis et supplementi infringere vel ausu temerario contraire. Si quis autem hoc attentare presumpserit, indignationem omnipotentis dei et beatorum Petri et Pauli apostolorum eius se noverit incursurum. Datum Rome apud sanctum Petrum idus aprilis pontificatus nostri anno undecimo.

Ioh. 41. Edd. Caorsinus c. 6; Senner F. v.; Duellius in appendice 10 n. 11 valde mutilum. Cf. n. 697. 1. dominorum D. 2. pro annuatim: ut prefertur S. 3. ac S. 3* Privilegia — Et deest D. 4. ac — et deest D. 5. post D. 6. dummodo — deberent. Et deest D. 7. vel alia quavis II deest. 8. Cum autem — in eisdem deest D.

---

700. *1400 iunii 16 Romae apud s. Petrum. Bonifacius IX indulget, quod prior domus ordinis Theutonici in Marienburg diebus solempnibus coram magistro divina celebrans uti possit pontificalibus insigniis.*

Bonifacius episcopus servorum dei dilecto filio priori domus hospitalis beate Marie Theutonicorum Ierosolimitani in Marienburg Pomezaniensis diocesis salutem et apostolicam benedictionem. Ad ecclesiastici decoris augmentum insignia reperta sunt dignitatum, que sancta Romana ecclesia congrua in singulos libertate distribuit et devotionis filiis, prout dignum iudicat, suscipienda et obtinenda concedit. Hinc est, quod nos dilecti filii Conradi de Iungingen, magistri generalis hospitalis beate Marie Theutonicorum Ierosolimitani, supplicacionibus inclinati, ut tu, fili prior et successores tui, priores domus dicti hospitalis in Marienburg Pomezaniensis diocesis, ubi prefatus magister residere consuevit, qui pro tempore fuerint, in solennibus festivitatibus, cum in eis missarum solennia et alia divina officia celebraveris, mitra, anulo, baculo pastorali et aliis pontificalibus insigniis uti libere et licite valeas, tibi et eisdem successoribus auctoritate apostolica tenore presentium de speciali gratia indulgemus. Nulli ergo etc. Si quis autem etc. Datum Rome apud sanctum Petrum xvi kal. iulii pontificatus nostri anno undecimo.

Originale cum bulla in archivo Regimontano.

---

701. *1402 decembris 10 Romae apud s. Petrum. Bonifacius IX eximit ordinem Theutonicum ut ab omnibus exactionibus episcoporum ita a Burkardi Augustensis.*

Bonifacius episcopus servus servorum dei ad perpetuam rei memoriam. Etsi quibuslibet personis et locis religiosis ex iniuncto nobis apostolice servitutis officio defensionis presidio assistere teneamur, magistro tamen et fratribus hospitalis beate Marie Theotonicorum Ierosolimitani tanto specialius et efficacius in eorum oportunitatibus adesse nos convenit, quanto frequencius pro conservacione et augmento fidei orthodoxe contra acerrimos nominis christiani inimicos se rerum et corporum periculis promptis animis exponere non formidant. Sane ad nostrum nuper pervenit auditum, quod, licet dictis magistro et fratribus a sede apostolica per specialia eiusdem sedis privilegia indultum existat, quod ad dandum aut solvendum collectas vel caritativa aut alia subsidia seu exactiones, quibuscumque nominibus censeantur, locorum ordinariis vel quibusvis aliis personis vel ad contribuendum in collectis subsidiis aut exactionibus huiusmodi minime teneantur nec ad id compelli possint inviti, nosque eciam, cum aliqui locorum ordinarii in partibus Alamanie constituti novum et illicitum gravaminis et exactionis modum contra eosdem magistrum et fratres exquirentes personas per ipsos ad parrochiales ecclesias et beneficia ecclesiastica, in quibus ius obtinent patronatus, presentatas admittere et in illorum rectores instituere indebite recusarent, nisi eedem persone medietatem vel aliam certam partem vel quottam primi anni ecclesiarum et beneficiorum ipsorum dictis ordinariis, ad quos huiusmodi institucio communiter vel divisim pertinebat, persolverent eisdem ordinariis ubilibet constitutis, eciamsi archiepiscopali vel episcopali aut alia quavis prefulgeant dignitate, ad quos admissio personarum et institucio rectorum huiusmodi pertineret, communiter vel divisim per nostras literas auctoritate apostolica sub excommunicacionis pena, quam contrarium facientes eo ipso incurrerent, districte precipiendo mandaverimus, quatenus ab illicitis exactionibus et gravaminibus huiusmodi penitus abstinentes et qualibet difficultate cessante personas ydoneas, quas prefati magister et fratres ad ecclesias et beneficia supradicta, in quibus pacifice et quiete, ut prefertur, ius obtinerent patronatus, tunc vacancia et in antea vacatura ducerent presentandas prout ad eos communiter vel divisim pertinent legittimo impedimento cessante pure et libere et absque aliqua exactione huiusmodi admittere et in eorundem, ad que sic presentate forent ecclesiarum et beneficiorum rectores instituere curarent et nichilominus, si cum debita instancia requisiti idem infra mensem a tempore requisicionis huiusmodi racionabili causa cessante facere recusarent vel differrent, extunc conservatores eisdem magistro et fratribus contra inferentes eis in bonis aut rebus vel personis ipsorum iniurias vel iacturas a sede deputati predicta vel deputandi aut unus eorum per se vel per alios huiusmodi sic presentatas personas ea vice auctoritate dictarum litterarum loco huiusmodi ordinariorum, si aliud canonicum non obstaret, admitterent vel admitteret ac instituerent seu institueret; ac decernimus irritum et inane, si secus super hiis a quoquam quavis auctoritate scienter vel ignoranter contingeret attemptari, prout in eisdem litteris plenius continetur. Tamen venerabilis frater noster Burckardus episcopus Augustensis, cui et successoribus suis episcopis Augustensibus qui essent pro tempore, iuxta consuetudines antiquas eciam a tempore, cuius contrarii memoria, ut ipse Burckardus episcopus asserebat, non extabat, collectam seu caritativum subsidium annuatim moderate tamen a quibuscumque personis ecclesiasticis secularibus et regularibus exemptis et non exemptis eciam in dignitatibus, personatibus et officiis constitutis in civitate et diocesi Augustensibus beneficia ecclesiastica obtinentibus ac eciam annatam seu medios fructus primi anni a beneficiis, que monasteriis necnon abbatibus et conventualibus mensis ac aliis locis et personis predictarum et aliarum civitatum et diocesium unita, annexa et incorporata seu alias appropriata forent petendi exigendi et recipiendi, contradictores quoque per censuram ecclesiasticam appellacione postposita compescendi auctoritate predicta plenam et liberam per diversas alias nostras litteras, quarum tenores presentibus haberi volumus pro sufficienter expressis, concessimus facultatem, consuetudines predictas per easdem litteras nichilominus confirmando, huiusmodi consuetudinis ac litterarum et facultatis pretextu collectam seu caritativum subsidium a fratribus dicti hospitalis in civitate et diocesi Augustensibus predictis preceptorias, commendatorias, domos seu beneficia obtinentibus ac eciam annatam seu medios fructus huiusmodi pro institucionibus rectorum ad parrochiales ecclesias et alia beneficia huiusmodi in dictis civitate et diocesi consistencia, in quibus iidem magister et fratres ius obtinent patronatus, nititur extorquere. Nos igitur equum reputantes et congruum, ut magister et fratres predicti ab oppressionibus et gravaminibus tueantur et in suis libertatibus conserventur ac privilegiis eis digne concessis libere pociantur, motu proprio non ad ipsorum vel alterius pro eis nobis super hoc oblate peticionis instanciam, sed de nostra mera liberalitate omnia et singula privilegia, exemptiones, libertates, litteras et immunitates per nos et predecessores nostros Romanos pontifices dictis magistro et fratribus contra huiusmodi subsidii et annate seu medietatis fructuum solucionem vel exactionem concessa et quecunque inde secuta rata habentes et grata, ea decernimus auctoritate apostolica predicta in sui roboris firmitate debuisse et debere irrefragibiliter perdurasse et perdurare; ipsaque eadem auctoritate motu simili ex certa sciencia confirmamus et presentis scripti patrocinio communimus et nichilominus auctoritate prefata similibus motu et sciencia declaramus predictas et quascumque alias litteras eisdem Burkardo episcopo et successoribus suis seu quibuscumque locorum ordinariis vel aliis super huiusmodi subsidii et annate seu medietatis solucione vel exactione hactenus concessas seu imposterum concedendas ad dictos magistrum et fratres vel eorum aliquem se minime extendisse aut extendere in futurum nostreque intencionis non fuisse nec esse, quod ipsi magister et fratres aut eorum aliquis huiusmodi litterarum Burckardo episcopo et successoribus suis prefatis seu quibuscumque aliis locorum ordinariis super huiusmodi subsidii et annate seu medietatis solucione vel exactione sub quacumque forma vel expressione verborum concessorum vel imposterum concedendarum pretextu aliquid solvere tenerentur seu ad id quoquam coartari possent inviti, decernimus, quoad ipsos magistrum et fratres quoscumque processus et sentencias dictarum litterarum pretextu contra presencium tenorem habitos et habendos, latas et ferendas et quidquid aliud in contrarium a quoquam quavis auctoritate scienter vel ignoranter attemptatum forsan est hactenus vel imposterum contigerit attemptari, irritos irratas et inanes ac irritum et inane, litteris predictis super huiusmodi subsidii et annate seu medietatis solucione vel exactione hactenus concessis et imposterum concedendis necnon constitutionibus apostolicis et aliis contrariis non obstantibus quibuscumque. Nulli ergo omnino hominum liceat hanc paginam nostre constitucionis, confirmacionis, communicionis et declaracionis infringere vel ei ausu temerario contraire. Si quis autem hoc attemptare presumpserit, indignacionem omnipotentis dei et beatorum Petri et Pauli apostolorum eius se noverit incursurum. Datum Rome apud sanctum Petrum iiii idus decembris pontificatus nostri anno quartodecimo.

IV, 229 cf. supra 1319 iulii 12.

---

702. *1412 novbr. 16 Romae apud s. Petrum. Iohannes XXIII confirmat ordinis Theutonici immunitates et privilegia.*

Iohannes etc. Cum a nobis etc. Datum Rome apud sanctum Petrum kalendas decembris pontificatus nostri anno tercio.

Citat Duellius II, 11 in nota. Transsumptum d. d. Marienburg 1413 aug. 27 in archivo Regimontano.

---

703. *1417 aug. 12 Constantiae. Synodus generalis ordini Theutonico confirmat Honorii III n. 306 de 1220 decbr. 15.*

Sacrosancta et generalis synodus Constantiensis dilectis ecclesie filiis magistro et fratribus hospitalis beate Marie Theotonicorum Ierosolimitani salutem et dei omnipotentis benedictionem. Meruit vestre devocionis sinceritas quam ad nos et universalem, quam in spiritu sancto legitime congregati representamus, geritis ecclesiam, ut vos, qui pro eiusdem ecclesie ac fidei orthodoxe defensione contra diversarum sectarum eas oppugnantes infideles athletas et pugiles vos exhibetis indefessos, vestrumque hospitale in hiis presertim, que vobis apostolicorum concessorum privilegiorum conservationem respiciunt, favoribus prosequamur oportunis. Sane pro parte vestra nobis nuper fuit humiliter supplicatum, ut litteras felicis recordacionis Honorii pape tercii vobis concessas, cum incipiant nimia vetustate consumi, innovare dignaremur. Quarum tenor sequitur in hec verba:

„Honorius cet. Etsi neque cet. (cf. n. 306). Datum Laterani per manum Wilhelmi sancte Romane ecclesie vicecancellarii, xviii kalendas ianuarii indictione viiii, incarnacionis dominice anni m.cc.xx pontificatus domini Honorii pape tercii anno quinto“.

Nos igitur huiusmodi supplicationibus inclinati litteras ipsas, quas in cancellaria apostolica diligenter inspici fecimus, tenore presencium innovamus et presentis scripti patrocinio communimus. Per hoc tamen constitucioni pie memorie Clementis pape quinti in concilio Viennensi super hoc edite, qua fratres milicie Templi Ierosolimitani supradictos eorumque statum habitum atque nomen substulit illosque et dictam miliciam perpetua prohibicione supposuit, nolumus in aliquo derogare; neque ullum ius de novo vobis vel aliis acquiri volumus, sed quod antiquum, si quod habetis, tantummodo conservari. Nulli ergo omnino hominum liceat hanc paginam nostre innovacionis communicionis et voluntatis infringere vel ei ausu temerario contraire. Si quis autem hoc attemptare presumpserit, indignacionem omnipotentis dei et beatorum Petri et Pauli apostolorum eius se noverit incursurum. Datum Constancie ii idus augusti anno a nativitate domini millesimo quadringentesimo decimo septimo, apostolica sede vacante.

IV, 231 v. De transsumtis huius confirmationis vide supra sub n. 306 p. 279. Ioh. 44. Edd. Caorsinus C. 7 v. Senner F. 3. 1220. Entdeckter Ungrund ex or. C. 3, ubi etiam effigies bullae appendentis *a*) S. PA. S. PE. *b*) S. SACRE · SINODI · CONSTANCIEN̄.

---

704. *1417 septbr. 4 Constantiae. Synodus generalis Moguntinum archiepiscopum et episcopos Argentinensem Herbipolensemque ordini Theutonico conservatores facit.*

Sacrosancta et generalis synodus Constanciensis venerabilibus fratribus archiepiscopo Maguntino et Argentinensi ac Herbipolensi episcopis salutem et dei omnipotentis benedictionem. Ad compescendos conatus nepharios perversorum, qui personas et loca ecclesiastica super bonis et iuribus suis offendere ac multiplicibus perturbare molestiis non verentur, tanto magis decet per sacrum generale concilium oportuno remedio providere, quanto per amplius turbaciones huiusmodi et molestie in divine maiestatis offensam necnon ecclesiastice libertatis redundare dispendium dinoscuntur. Dudum siquidem, cum in diversis mundi partibus consules civitatum et rectores necnon alii, qui potestatem habere videbantur, tot onera frequenter imponerent ecclesiis, ut deterioris conditionis factum sub eis sacerdocium videretur, quam sub Pharaone fuisset, qui legis divine noticiam non habebat quique omnibus aliis servituti subactis sacerdotes et possessiones eorum in pristina libertate dimisit et de publico eis alimoniam ministravit, in concilio Lateranensi ecclesie immunitati providendo sub anathematis districtione prohibitum extitit, ne consules, rectores aut alii predicti ecclesias et viros ecclesiasticos talliis seu collectis vel exactionibus aliis aggravare presumerent transgressores et fautores eorum precipiendo anathematis sententie subiacere, donec satisfactionem impenderent competentem et eciam deinde in generali concilio edictum fuerit, quod si episcopi forte simul cum clericis, eciamsi tantam necessitatem vel utilitatem inspicerent, ut absque ulla coactione ad relevandas communes utilitates vel necessitates, ubi laicorum non suppeterent facultates, subsidia per ecclesias laicis ducerent concedenda minime super hoc consulto Romano pontifice, concessiones et sentencie, que a talibus vel de ipsorum mandato forent promulgate, essent irrite et inanes nullo umquam tempore valiture, ac eciam in ipso generali concilio decretum extitit, illum, qui infra tempus sui regiminis propter fractionem, constitucionum vel sanctionum huiusmodi sustineret, anathema tamquam post illud non esset ad satisfactionis debitum compellendus necnon ipsius successorem, qui non satisfaceret infra mensem, monere ecclesiastica censura conclusum, donec satisfaceret competenter cum succederet in onere qui substitueretur in honore. Postmodum vero felicis recordacionis Honorius papa tercius attente considerans, quod quondam Fredericus secundus olim Romanorum imperator, tunc sub obediencia et devotione sancte Romane ecclesie persistens, ad laudem eiusdem ecclesie et sacri decus Romani imperii cupiens, ut expurgatis quorundam erroribus et iniquis statutis penitus destitutis de cetero ecclesie et ecclesiastice persone plena vigerent quiete et secura libertate gauderent, ac pie et iuste attendens, quod quorundam perversorum iniquitas adeo habundaverat, ut non dubitarent contra ecclesiasticam disciplinam et sacros canones statuta sua consurgere adversus ecclesiasticas personas et ecclesiasticam libertatem, edictali lege huiusmodi statuta iniqua irritaverat et preceperat irrita nunciari et omnia statuta et consuetudines, que civitates et loca, postestates vel consules aut quecumque persone contra libertatem ecclesie vel personas ecclesiasticas huiusmodi edere aut servare temptarent contra canonicas vel imperiales sanctiones de ipsorum capitularibus infra duos menses post ipsius legis publicationem penitus aboleri facerent et, si de cetero talia attemptarent, illa ipso iure decrevit esse nulla et eos sua iurisdictione privatos necnon locum, ubi deinceps talia presumpta fuissent, banno mille marcharum auri fisco imperiali preceperat subiacere, potestates vero, consules, statutarii et scriptores statutorum predictorum necnon consiliarii locorum ipsorum, qui secundum statuta et consuetudines memorata iudicarent, ex tunc essent ipso iure infames, quorum sententias et actus legittimos statuerat aliqualiter non tenere, quodque, si per annum prefatarum constitucionum inventi forent contemptores, bona eorum per totum suum imperium mandavit impune ab omnibus occupari, salvis nichilominus aliis penis contra tales in eisdem generalibus conciliis promulgatis. Et insuper voluit idem tunc imperator, quod nulla communitas vel persona publica seu privata collectas seu exactiones, angarias vel perangarias ecclesiis vel aliis piis locis aut ecclesiasticis personis huiusmodi imponere seu invadere ecclesiastica bona presumeret; quod si secus faceret et requisita ab ecclesia vel imperio huiusmodi emendare contempneret, tripliciter refunderet et nichilominus banno imperiali subiaceret, quod sine satisfactione debita nullatenus remitteretur. Statuerat insuper, quod, quecumque communitas vel persona per annum in excommunicacione propter libertatem ecclesie violatam persisteret, ipso iure similiter dicto banno imperiali subiaceret, a quo nullatenus extraheretur nisi prius ab ecclesia beneficio absolucionis obtento. Et insuper ordinaverat, ut nullus ecclesiasticam personam in criminali questione vel civili ad iudicium seculare trahere presumeret contra easdem canonicas sanctiones et constituciones imperiales; quod si secus faceret, actor a suo iure caderet et iudicatum non teneret et iudex foret extunc iudicandi auctoritate privatus, quodque iudices temporales, qui clericis et personis ecclesiasticis iusticiam denegare presumerent, tercio requisiti suam iurisdictionem amitterent. Constitucionem ipsam de consilio eciam fratrum suorum sancte Romane ecclesie cardinalium, qui tunc erant, auctoritate apostolica approbans et confirmans, ipsam mandavit inviolabiliter observari necnon statutarios et scriptores ac violatores predictos excommunicatos eadem auctoritate nunciari. Et deinde ad audienciam dive memorie Caroli quarti eciam Romanorum imperatoris semper augusti deducto, quod nonnulle seculares persone in potestatibus et officiis publicis constitute, videlicet duces, marchiones, comites, barones et alii domini temporales necnon consules civitatum, opidorum, villarum et locorum rectores in diversis provinciis eiusdem imperii dei timore postposito statuta singularia et iniquas ordinaciones motu proprio et de facto contra ipsas personas ecclesiasticas et ecclesiarum libertates ac eorum privilegia condiderant illisque de facto et publice utebantur contra canonicas et legittimas sanctiones, utpote quod nulla bona temporalia in potestatem ecclesiasticam transferrentur et, ne clerici in sacris ordinibus constituti ad agendum et testificandum in civilibus et maxime in piis causis aliquatenus admitterentur, quodque excommunicati laici et publice denunciati in civili foro minime repellerentur et insuper predicti domini temporales, consules et rectores per secularem potestatem res et bona clericorum occuparent, arrestarent et oblaciones Christi fidelium minuerent atque restringerent exactiones et tallias indebitas de bonis et redditibus ecclesiarum exigerent et extorquerent possessiones ecclesiarum et personarum earundem devastarent incendiis et rapinis contractus inter clericos et laicos factos legitime ad libros civitatum, villarum et locorum predictorum inscribere et sigillare recusarent donataque et legata ad fabricas et ecclesiarum structuras contra prelatorum voluntatem ac aliorum, quorum intererat temere usurpare presumerent ac in fraudem et odium clericorum de bonis etiam et rebus eorundem clericorum, que non causa negociacionum, sed pro eorum propriis usibus per eorum terras ducebant seu duci faciebant, theolonium exigere et recipere non verebantur et confugientes ad ecclesias et earum cimiteria inde extrahere contra canonicas et imperiales sanctiones huiusmodi presumpserant et presumebant. Idem Carolus imperator tamquam christianissimus princeps volens in premissis providere de remedio salutari, eciam de quorundam principum, ducum, comitum, baronum fideliumque aliorum sacri imperii sepedicti consilio et auctoritate imperiali quecumque statuta et consuetudines predicta tamquam per civiles et canonicas sanctiones expresse reprobata cassavit, irritavit et annulavit, ac cassa et irrita nulliusque esse voluit roboris vel momenti; precipiens sub imperialis banni pena universis et singulis principibus ac dominis temporalibus consulibus, potestatibus et aliis in officiis publicis in eodem imperio constitutis, quatenus extunc ipsorum statuta et ordinaciones, sicut in preiudicium ecclesiastice libertatis edita fuerant, omnino revocarent et de luce tollerent, quodque secundum ea non iudicarent amplius nec sententias dictarent aut de eisdem in iudicio vel extra iudicium quomodolibet pro se et contra eandem ecclesiasticam libertatem potirentur. Pronunciavit insuper et eadem decrevit auctoritate, quod, quicumque laicus, cuiuscumque status aut condicionis existeret, ausu sacrilego et proprie temeritatis audacia sacerdotem vel clericum secularem vel religiosum diffidaret, proscriberet, captivaret, spoliaret, occideret, mutilaret aut in carcere detineret vel huiusmodi maleficia perpetrantes scienter receptaret vel eis favorem prestaret, preter penas a sacris canonibus ac legalibus sanctionibus in tales inflictas eo ipso redderetur infamis ac omni honore privatus nec ad placita vel consilia nobilium admitteretur quovismodo; hortans insuper in domino et requirens ecclesiasticos prelatos in illis partibus, in quibus committerentur talia, constitutos, ut legem imperialem huiusmodi per eorum ecclesias et synodos publicarent, ne transgressores huiusmodi per simulatam ignoranciam suam valerent in hac parte maliciam excusare, prout in constitucionibus et sanctionibus conciliorum et Honorii predictorum ac Imperialibus prefatis plenius continetur. Cum autem, sicut lamentabili querela dilectorum ecclesie filiorum magistri et fratrum hospitalis beate Marie Theotonicorum Ierosolimitani nuper accepimus, nonnulli principes, duces, comites, barones ac alie seculares potestates earundem constitucionum et sanctionum canonicarum et legalium forsan ignari et contra ipsos a magistro et fratribus predictis communiter vel divisim tallias et gabellas et alias exactiones illicitas hactenus extorserint et adhuc extorquere nitantur ac eciam bona magistri et fratrum predictorum eciam communiter vel divisim invaserint, arrestaverint, occupaverint, detinuerint et suis usibus applicaverint, necnon occupare, invadere, arrestare, detinere et eisdem usibus suis applicare similiter de facto presumant in animarum suarum periculum necnon magistri et fratrum predictorum non modicum preiudicium atque dampnum; nos ipsis magistro et fratribus in premissis oportune providere volentes, fraternitati vestre per hec nostra scripta in virtute sancte obediencie districte precipiendo mandamus, quatenus vos vel duo aut unus vestrum per vos vel alium seu alios magistro et fratribus predictis communiter vel divisim contra quoscumque transgressores et violatores constitucionum et sanctionum earundem, cuiuscumque status, dignitatis et excellentie fuerint, efficacis defensionis auxilio assistentes, non permittatis eos contra canonicas et legales sanctiones et constituciones huiusmodi indebite molestari necnon easdem constituciones, ubi et quando expedire videritis, sollempniter publicantes faciatis transgressores et violatores huiusmodi, si et prout iustum fuerit ac ubi et quociens expedierit, tamdiu excommunicatos aut anathematizatos publice nunciari, donec ab earundem talliarum, collectarum, imposicionum et quarumlibet extorsionum necnon bonorum magistri et fratrum predictorum invasione, arrestacione, occupacione, detencione et appellacione omnino desistant, necnon eciam efficaciter restituant eisdem magistro et fratribus occasione premissorum per eos communiter vel divisim lesis seu gravatis tallias, gabellas et exactiones ipsas ac eciam bona magistri et fratrum predictorum arrestata, occupata, detenta et applicata communiter vel divisim ipsis aut, que per se vel alios illo pretextu quomodolibet receperunt, ymmo verius temere et illicite usurparunt, a se libere et omnino relaxent ac in manibus vestris iuraverint, quod de cetero talia non conmittant et ea committentibus non prestent auxilium, consilium vel favorem, contradictores per censuram ecclesiasticam et alia iuris oportuna remedia compescendo, invocato eciam ad hoc si opus fuerit auxilio brachii secularis. Ceterum, si forsan huiusmodi transgressorum et violatorum vel ea fieri mandancium ipsisque consenciencium seu dancium in illis per se vel alios directe vel indirecte, publice vel occulte auxilium, consilium vel favorem presencia pro monicionibus et requisicionibus per vos de ipsis faciendis tute, secure vel commode haberi nequiret nos vobis moniciones et requisiciones huiusmodi ac citaciones quaslibet per edicta publica et locis affigenda publicis, de quibus sit verisimilis coniectura, quod ad noticiam dictorum citatorum et monitorum huiusmodi pervenire valeant, faciendi plenam et liberam concedimus tenore presencium potestatem; volentes, quod moniciones, requisiciones et citaciones huiusmodi perinde ipsos citatos, requisitos et monitos, ut premittitur, arctent, ac si eis facte et insinuate presencialiter et personaliter extitissent; non obstantibus tam pie memorie Bonifacii VIII, quibus cavetur, ne aliquis extra suam civitatem vel diocesim nisi in certis exceptis casibus, et in illis ultra unam dietam a fine sue diocesis ad iudicium evocetur seu ne iudices extra civitatem et diocesim, in quibus deputati fuerint, contra quoscumque procedere aut alii vel aliis vices suas committere seu aliquos ultra unam dietam a fine diocesis eorundem trahere presumant, dummodo ultra duas dietas aliquis auctoritate presentium non trahatur ac de personis ultra certum numerum ad iudicium non vocandis quam aliis constitucionibus apostolicis contrariis quibuscumque aut, si aliquibus communiter vel divisim a sede apostolica indultum existat, quod interdici, suspendi vel excommunicari aut extra vel ultra certa loca ad iudicium evocari non possint per litteras apostolicas non facientes plenam et expressam ac de verbo ad verbum de indulto huiusmodi mencionem. Datum Constancie ii nonas septembris anno a nativitate domini millesimo quadringentesimo decimo septimo, apostolica sede vacante.

IV, 235 v. Ioh. 46. Edd. Caorsinus D. Senner F. 4 verso.

---

705. *1418 ianuarii 2 Constantiae. Martinus V ordini Theutonico confirmat litteras Alexandri IV n. 594 de 1258 novbr. 22 datas, nimia vetustate consumtas, nihil autem iuris inde concedens, nisi quod predecessor indulserat.*

Martinus etc. Meruit devocionis sinceritas etc. Datum iiii nonas ianuarii, pontificatus nostri anno primo.

Transsumtum d. d. Würzburg 1418 decbr. 2 factum autoritate Werneri de Hayn, curiae officialis in archivo Regimontano exstat.

---

706. *1418 maii 7 Constantie. Martinus V ad instar predecessorum ordini Theutonico omnia privilegia, immunitates etc. confirmat.*

Martinus etc. Dilectis filiis magistro et fratribus domus hospitalis beate Marie Theutonicorum Ierosolimitani Marienborg Pomezaniensis diocesis salutem et apostolicam benedictionem. Cum a nobis — communimus. Datum Constantie nonas maii, pontificatus nostri anno primo.

Originale cum bulla in archivo Regimontano, huc tandem Cracovia delatum. In Inventario archivi Cracoviensis ed. Parisiis 1862 p. 80 citatur: Martinus papa V iura et privilegia cruciferis concessa confirmat. Datum Constantiae nonis maii pontificatus anno primo. Ibidem transsumptum Caspari episcopi Pomesaniensis d. d. Riesenburgi 1445 novbr. 17 eius sigillo munitum.

---

707. *1419 april. 10 Florentiae. Martinus V declarat, ecclesias et alia loca domus hospitalis s. Mariae Theutonicorum exemta esse a praestatione decimae, quam de omnibus proventibus ecclesiasticis per unum annum Sigismundo Romanorum regi concesserat.*

Martinus episcopus servus servorum dei ad futuram rei memoriam. Romani pontificis circumspectio provida nonnunquam gesta per eam, ne sub ignorancia facti regulari presertim ascripti castimonie vexacionibus adigantur indebitis, dilucidat dirimitque liberaminis ope condecentis, sicut rerum et temporum qualitate pensata id conspicit in domino salubriter expedire. Dudum siquidem, videlicet vii kal. februarii pontificatus nostri anno primo carissimi in Christo filii nostri Sigismundi Romanorum regis illustris devocionis merita, quibus erga deum et universalem ecclesiam presertim circa unionem eiusdem non sine magnis eciam personalibus laboribus et expensis claruerat et clare dinoscebatur attenta meditacione, pensantes propterea et ex certis aliis causis nostrum ad id animum moventibus matura cum venerabilibus fratribus nostris sancte Romane ecclesie cardinalibus super hoc deliberacione prehabita ac de ipsorum consilio necnon venerabilium fratrum nostrorum archiepiscoporum, episcoporum et dilectorum filiorum electorum, administratorum necnon abbatum et aliorum de natione Germanica percepto beneplacito voluntatis ac eciam predecessorum nostrorum Romanorum pontificum et aliorum pro Romanis pontificibus habitorum circa hoc vestigiis inherentes decimam integram unius anni omnium reddituum et proventuum ecclesiasticorum in provinciis, civitatibus et diocesibus, terris et locis nacionis Germanice tocius provincie Treverensis necnon Basiliensis et Leodiensis civitatum et diocesium sub Romano imperio consistencium dictorum cardinalium necnon sancti Iohannis et beate Marie Theotonicorum Ierosolimitani hospitalium personis, bonis, redditibus et proventibus dumtaxat exceptis ab omnibus et singulis archiepiscopis, episcopis, electis, administratoribus, regularibus et secularibus ecclesiarum metropolitanarum et cathedralium exemptis et non exemptis in provinciis et civitatibus supra scriptis constitutis, prout eorum quemlibet concerneret, solvendam et auctoritate nostra per deputandos a nobis exigendam infra kal. novembris tunc proxime futuri in moneta in singulis partibus cursum habente et secundum constitucionem super talibus editam in concilio Wyeniensi ac in ipsius usus pro eius voluntatis libito convertendam imponentes serenitati sue de apostolice sedis munificencia per nostras litteras assignavimus, concessimus atque donavimus, non obstantibus exemptionibus, immunitatibus, privilegiis et aliis quibuscumque gratiis et concessionibus quibusvis archiepiscopis, episcopis, electis et administratoribus huiusmodi seu eorum ecclesiis communiter vel divisim cardinalibus, hospitalibus, personis et bonis prefatis dumtaxat exceptis per sedem apostolicam aut alias quovismodo concessis, eciamsi de illis eorumque toto tenore de verbo ad verbum in dictis litteris habenda foret mentio specialis, que ipsis quoad hoc nolumus in aliquo suffragari, prout in ipsis litteris plenius continetur. Cum autem, sicut exhibita nobis nuper pro parte dilectorum filiorum magistri et fratrum dicti hospitalis beate Marie peticio continebat, licet in litteris ipsis, que generali Constanciensi vigente concilio concesse fuerunt, eiusdem hospitalis beate Marie persone bona redditusque et proventus excepta fuerint, ut prefertur, an tamen ecclesie et alia loca ecclesiastica ipsi hospitali beate Marie canonice appropriata sive unita, ab illo quoque dependencia et ei subiecta sub predicta exceptione comprehendi et per consequens ab huiusmodi solucione decime libera et exempta censeri debeant ab aliquibus hesitetur; nos itaque in litteris eisdem, quod concessio ipsa huiusmodi ecclesias et alia loca includere debeat, minime contineri attentius recensentes, eorundem quoque magistri et fratrum, qui secularia abnegantes desideria pro fidei tuicione orthodoxe sanguinem proprium exponere non formidant, gravia quoque propterea dietim labores perferunt et onera statui et indempnitatibus in premissis oportune providere volentes ad omne super hiis ambiguitatis tollendum dubium ecclesias et loca huiusmodi ubicumque sita illorumque personas cum omnibus rebus et bonis necnon iuribus et pertinenciis eorundem, in quibuscumque consistant et undecumque proveniant, sub huiusmodi excepcione comprehendi debuisse, atque debere et ad solvendum sive prestandum quidquam racione imposicionis ac litterarum huiusmodi minime teneri nec ad id aliquem ex dictis magistro et fratribus et personis eciam racione ecclesiarum et locorum predictorum sive alicuius eorundem a quoquam quavis auctoritate compelli posse, omnes preterea processus necnon excommunicacionum, suspensionum et interdicti sententias, censuras ecclesiasticas atque penas, quos haberi vel promulgari necnon totum id et quicquid fieri contigerit pretextu litterarum earundem contra magistrum, fratres, personas, ecclesias et loca huiusmodi sive illorum aliquod nullius firmitatis vel momenti existere decernimus per presentes, non obstantibus premissis ac aliis contrariis quibuscumque. Nulli ergo omnino hominum liceat hanc paginam nostre constitucionis infringere vel ei ausu temerario contraire. Si quis autem hoc attemptare presumpserit, indignacionem omnipotentis dei et beatorum Petri et Pauli apostolorum eis se noverit incursurum. Datum Florencie iiii idus aprilis, pontificatus nostri anno secundo.

IV, 240.

---

708. *1419 maii 17 Florentiae. Martinus V confirmat ordini Theutonico libertatem a praestatione decimarum et omnium subsidiorum.*

Martinus episcopus servus servorum dei dilectis filiis magistro et fratribus hospitalis beate Marie Theotonicorum Ierosolomitani salutem et apostolicam benedictionem. Laudibus et honore dignissima religio vestra ab ipsius institucione felici per latitudinem orbis terre diversitate virtutum semper emicuit et vestrorum claritate meritorum oculis ecclesie sacrosancte frequenter infulxit pie memorie predecessoribus nostris Romanis pontificibus propter hec tanta iocunditate perfusis, ut eis votivum et delectabile fieret dictam religionem interno et efficaci amore in Christo diligere et sincerrima prosequi voluntate multis ipsam attollendo presidiis et fovendo beneficiis opulentis. Nos autem, postquam apostolici curam officii divina providencia disponente suscepimus, tantorum patrum pia vestigia piis imitantes affectibus corde concepimus, quod religionem ipsam nobis specialem et carissimam inter alias haberemus. Huiusmodi benivolencia postmodum sic per operacionis evidenciam elucescente, quod in professores religionis eiusdem dona multiplicia effunderemus[1] graciarum, quas in melius, si oportunum fuerit, ampliantes in pleno vigore conservare proponimus ac vobis et hospitali vestro fructum desideratum producere affectamus, cum sit nobis firma fiducia, quod, quanto plus dicta religio benignitatis apostolice favore reficitur, tanto in ipsa devocionis et reverencie studium circa predictam ecclesiam adaugetur. Hinc est, quod nos eorundem predecessorum vestigiis inherentes vobis auctoritate apostolica tenore presencium indulgemus, ut in imposicionibus decimarum seu caritativorum vel aliorum quorumlibet subsidiorum, quibuscumque nominibus nuncupentur, in quibusvis eciam citra vel ultra montanis partibus per nos aut nostra vel alia quacumque auctoritate concessis seu ex quavis causa hactenus quomodocumque aut qualitercumque factis vel forsitan imposterum faciendis vos ac huiusmodi hospitale illius preceptorie, ecclesie, capelle, oratoria et alia vestra et dicte religionis loca et bona, que nunc ubilibet obtinetis vel in futurum annuente domino licite obtinebitis tam mobilia quam immobilia necnon persone in illis degentes nullatenus includi[2] seu comprehendi debeatis sed vos ac huiusmodi hospitale necnon preceptorie, ecclesie, capelle, oratoria atque degentes in illis presentes et posteri pro tempore a solucione et[3] prestacione decimarum et aliorum onerum huiusmodi sitis et esse debeatis perpetuis futuris temporibus prorsus exempti et immunes, prout eciam preteritis temporibus et a tempore, cuius contrarii memoria non existit, predecessores vestri magistri et fratres necnon preceptores ac rectores hospitalis preceptoriarum, domorum, ecclesiarum et oratoriorum prefatorum, qui fuerunt pro tempore per specialia privilegia sedis apostolice, quibus non est prorsus in aliquo derogatum, liberi et immunes hactenus extiterunt; decernentes eciam irritos et inanes necnon pro infectis haberi volentes omnes processus necnon excommunicacionis, suspensionis et interdicti sentencias et quaslibet alias censuras sive penas spirituales aut temporales sedis predicte vel legatorum eius seu alia quavis auctoritate in vos necnon preceptores et rectores atque personas hospitale ecclesias, oratoria necnon eiusdem hospitalis loca huiusmodi occasione premissorum scilicet non solucionis decimarum aut subsidiorum predictorum sub quavis verborum forma forsitan hactenus promulgatas et si quas promulgari contigerit quomodolibet in futurum. Nulli ergo omnino hominum liceat hanc paginam nostre concessionis, constitucionis et voluntatis infringere vel ei ausu temerario contraire. Si quis autem hoc attemptare presumpserit, indignacionem omnipotentis dei et beatorum Petri et Pauli apostolorum eius se noverit incursurum. Datum Florencie xvi kal. iunii pontificatus nostri anno secundo.

IV, 243 v. in confirmatione Martini V de 1423 martii 11. IV, 245. Initium ex originali tunc Mergenthemensi edidit de Wal Recherches II, 350 n. 4. Citat Duellius II, 5. Transsumptum sub sigillo curiae apostolicae autoritate Dominici de S. Geminiano, D. D., cam. apost. auditoris gen., datum Rome 1422 martii 20, exstat in archivo Regimontano, ubi aliud transsumptum d. d. 1488 octbr. 1 ex transsumpto Spirensi f. Ioh. 51. Edd. Caorsinus D. 4. Senner F. 6 v. Entdeckter Ungrund n. 103 b. ex originali. 1. effuderimus B. 2. concludi T. 3. ac B.

---

709. *1419 maii 17 Florentiae. Martinus V ordini Theutonico Bonifacii IX constitutionem n. 692 de 1396 maii 11 de patronatus iure innovat, confirmat, extendit.*

Martinus episcopus servus servorum dei ad futuram rei memoriam. Dispositione divina gregi dominico quamvis immeriti presidentes dum preclara dilectorum filiorum magistri et fratrum hospitalis beate Marie Theotonicorum Ierosolimitani merita intra nostre mentis recensemus archana et ad conmendabiles, quibus operosis eorum ministeriis erga deum et homines indesinenter exuberant, fructus, digne nostros diffundimus cogitatus, votis illis gratum libenter efferimus auditum, per que ipsorum statui ac indempnitatibus consulitur et ea, que pro illorum commodo profectibusque exquisita comperimus, solidioris presidio muniminis apostolici iugiter perseverent. Sane pro parte dictorum magistri et fratrum nobis nuper exhibita peticio continebat, quod olim felicis recordacionis Honorius tercius, Alexander quartus et Nicolaus quartus Romani pontifices predecessores nostri recensentes attentius, quod ipsi magister et fratres veluti nominis christiani pugiles pro fidei tuicione catholice eorum personas et animas ponere nullatenus formidarent, unde nonnulli imperatores, reges, duces comitesque et alii seculares principes ac laicales persone pia devocione moti cupientesque ipsis magistro et fratribus in eorum necessitatibus subvenire ius patronatus diversarum ecclesiarum prout ad ipsos tunc spectabat pro fundacione domorum dicti hospitalis et eorundem fratrum sustentatione dictis magistro et fratribus pia largitione donarunt ad eosdem magistrum et fratres speciali destinato favore per quasdam indulserunt eisdem, ut, quocienscumque aliquam ex predictis ecclesiis, quarum ipsi ius patronatus pro tempore obtinerent, vacare contingerit, aliquos ydoneos ex eisdem fratribus vel alios clericos locorum ordinariis presentare possent, qui taliter presentatos in prefatis ecclesiis, ad quas presentati forent, instituere, ipsique clerici sic presentati de administracione per eos circa prefatas ecclesias in spiritualibus ordinariis et in temporalibus magistro et fratribus eisdem respondere tenerentur. Et subsequenter quondam Bonifacius in sua obediencia, de qua partes ille erant, tunc VIIII nuncupatus considerans sollicicius donaciones iuris patronatus ac indulta huiusmodi quodque nonnulli ex fratribus predictis tunc quasdam alias parrochiales ecclesias et earum ius patronatus ex aliis iustis, ut credebatur, titulis acquisiverant, quarum aliquas ac ius patronatus huiusmodi habuerant et possederant pacifice et quiete, eciam a tanto tempore, cuius contrarii memoria non extabat. Ex huiusmodi quoque ecclesiis nonnulle dudum fuerant erecte in domos conventuales et per modum conventuum a fratribus predicti hospitalis eatenus gubernate; ad quasdam vero ex ipsis, dum vacarent, huiusmodi fratres soliti erant ipsis ordinariis presentari et per illos in rectores institui earundem; nonnulle eciam ex predictis et aliis parrochialibus ecclesiis fuerant successivis vicibus diversis dicti hospitalis domibus per locorum diocesanos ex certis racionabilibus et legittimis causis auctoritate ordinaria unite et incorporate, quarum fratres in domibus pro tempore degentes huiusmodi earundem unionum et incorporationum vigore possessionem adepti illas per quadraginta annos tenuerant et possederant, prout tunc tenebant et possidebant pacifice et quiete, per alias suas litteras ecclesias predictas ac earum necnon dictarum domorum, quibus huiusmodi uniones et incorporaciones facte fuerant, ut prefertur, veros valores annuos secundum communem extimacionem habens pro sufficienter expressis donaciones, concessiones, acquisiciones, erectiones, uniones et incorporaciones predictas et quecumque inde secuta rata habens et grata illa ex certa sciencia confirmavit et sui scripti patrocinio communivit supplens nichilominus sollempnitates omissas et omnes defectus, si qui forsan intervenerant in eisdem, prout in predictis litteris dicitur plenius contineri. Cum autem, sicut eadem peticio subiungebat, eciam postea plerisque dicti hospitalis domibus et locis ius patronatus nonnullarum aliarum ecclesiarum parrochialium concessum atque donatum ac ipse ecclesie diversis auctoritatibus unite necnon annexe et incorporate fuerint, ad earum deductis effectum plurimis ex posterioribus unionibus necnon annexionibus et incorporacionibus antedictis, pro parte prefatorum magistri et fratrum nobis fuit humiliter supplicatum, ut indultis necnon donacionibus, concessionibus, acquisicionibus, erectionibus, unionibus, annexionibus et incorporacionibus predictis pro earum subsistencia firmiori robur apostolice confirmacionis adiicere de benignitate apostolica dignaremur. Nos igitur omnes ecclesias easdem ac ipsarum necnon domorum et locorum, quibus ille, ut prefertur, unite, annexe et incorporate fuerint, huiusmodi veros annuos valores fructus quoque redditus et proventus etiam secundum extimacionem predictam habentes literis presentibus pro sufficienter expressis, easdem quoque presentes litteras non minus, quam si in ipsis valores necnon fructus, redditus et proventus secundum dictam extimacionem exprimerentur, iidem validas et efficaces censeri et ubilibet reputari debere nec propterea aliquatenus impugnari posse, sed nichilominus et alias suis subsistere viribus auctoritate apostolica decernentes eisdem supplicacionibus inclinati indulta donaciones, concessiones, acquisiciones, erectiones necnon uniones, annexiones et incorporaciones predictas et quecumque inde secuta rata habentes et grata illa eadem auctoritate ex simili sciencia confirmamus et presentis scripti patrocinio communimus, supplentes omnes defectus, si qui forsan intervenerint in eisdem non obstantibus premissis necnon constitucionibus et ordinacionibus apostolicis eciam huiusmodi valores, fructus, redditus et proventus secundum dictam extimacionem exprimi debere disponentibus, statutis quoque et consuetudinibus hospitalis predicti iuramento confirmatione apostolica vel quavis alia firmitate vallatis ceterisque contrariis quibuscumque. Nulli ergo omnino hominum liceat hanc paginam nostre confirmacionis et communicionis infringere vel ei ausu temerario contraire. Si quis autem hoc attemptare presumpserit, indignacionem omnipotentis dei et beatorum Petri et Pauli apostolorum eius se noverit incursurum. Datum Florencie xvi kal. iunii pontificatus nostri anno secundo.

IV, 241 v. Transsumptum sub sigillo curie apostolice, autoritate Pantaleonis de Bredis de Utino, D. D. et cam. apost. auditoris generalis, dato. Florentiae 1419 novbr. 10. Exstant in archivo Regimontano duo exemplaria. Ioh. 50. Edd. Caorsinus D. 2. Senner F. 6. 1419 aug. 25 Florentiae Martinus V confirmat ordini Theutonico, quod invitus non teneatur respondere provisionibus apostolicis seu legatorum, occasione praelaturae cuiusdam Curoniensis. Vide supra n. 251 p. 236.

---

710. *1420 septbr. 24 Viterbii. Martinus V ordini Theutonico conservatores constituit privilegii, ex quo sine exactione liceat praesentare idoneos ad ecclesias sui patronatus.*

Martinus episcopus servus servorum dei dilectis filiis abbati monasterii sancti Egidii Nurenbergensis et sancti Spiritus Heidelbergensis Bambergensis et Warmaciensis diocesium ac sancti Gungolffi Maguntinae ecclesiarum decanis salutem et apostolicam benedictionem. Regnum presidentes universalis ecclesie pro fidelium presertim religiosorum ac piorum locorum et ecclesiarum quarumlibet statu salubriter dirigendo, prout ex debito nobis iniuncti pastoralis tenemur officii, sollicite consideracionis intuitum extendimus et ad ea, per que cuiusvis dispendii sublata materia illorum indempnitatibus consulitur, libenter adhibemus nostre sollicitudinis partes. Sane pro parte dilectorum filiorum magistri et fratrum hospitalis beate Marie Theotonicorum Ierosolimitani nobis nuper exhibita peticio continebat, quod, licet ipsi iuxta specialia eis a sede apostolica concessa privilegia, quibus in aliquo derogatum non existit, ad parrochiales ecclesias et alia beneficia ecclesiastica, in quibus ius obtinent patronatus sive presentandi, cum illa vacare contigerit, personas ydoneas locorum ordinariis iuris ordine observato presentare ipsique ordinarii personas easdem ad ecclesia et beneficia huiusmodi sic presentatas sine aliqua contradictione seu exactione admittere et eas in rectores ecclesiarum et beneficiorum instituere consueverint antedictorum, nonnulli tamen ex ordinariis ipsis contra magistrum et fratres predictos novum et illicitum gravacionis et exactionis modum exquirentes personas huiusmodi eis ad ecclesias et beneficia predicta per eosdem magistrum et fratres presentatas admittere et in eorum rectores instituere indebite recusant, nisi persone ipse medietatem seu certam aliam quotam fructuum et proventuum primi anni ecclesiarum et beneficiorum predictorum dictis ordinariis, ad quos huiusmodi institucio communiter vel divisim pertinet, persolverint in ipsorum magistri et fratrum ac personarum non modicum preiudicium et gravamen. Quare pro parte dictorum magistri et fratrum nobis fuit humiliter supplicatum, ut super premissis eis de oportuno remedio providere de benignitate apostolica dignaremur. Nos igitur, quorum desideriis insidet fratres ipsos ab oppressionibus quibuslibet tueri, huismodi supplicationibus inclinati discrecioni vestre per apostolica scripta mandamus, quatenus vos vel duo aut unus vestrum per vos vel alium seu alios omnes et singulos ordinarios predictos, eciamsi archiepiscopali, episcopali vel alia quavis prefulgeant dignitate, ad quos admissio personarum et institucio rectorum huiusmodi communiter vel divisim pertinet aut pro tempore pertinebit, ut a percepcione medietatis seu quote fructuum et proventuum ecclesiarum et beneficiorum huiusmodi necnon aliis exactionibus et gravaminibus penitus abstinentes omni difficultate cessante personas ydoneas, quas prefati magister et fratres ad ecclesias et beneficia supradicta, in quibus ut prefertur ius obtinent patronatus sive presentandi vacancia et imposterum vacatura duxerint presentandas, prout ad eos communiter vel divisim pertinuerit, impedimento cessante legittimo, pure libere et absque aliqua exactione admittere et in eorum, ad que sic presentate fuerint, ecclesiarum et beneficiorum rectores instituere non postponant, quocienscumque opus fuerit, auctoritate apostolica per censuram ecclesiasticam compellere et nichilominus si illi, ad quos huiusmodi instituciones pertinuerint debitis non contenti iuribus absque alterius vexationis sive exactionis onere personas huiusmodi in ecclesiis et beneficiis predictis ad que presentate fuerint pro tempore instituere recusaverint sive infra competentem eis super hoc per vos aut unum vestrum statuendum peremptorium terminum distulerint, extunc, ne occasione vacacionum earundem huiusmodi ecclesie et beneficia in spiritualibus et temporalibus detrimenta paciantur ad instituciones procedere antedictas omnes et singulas excommunicacionis, suspensionis et interdicti sententias, quas propter premissa in magistrum, fratres et personas presentandas necnon ecclesias et beneficia huiusmodi per ipsos ordinarios quomodolibet promulgari contigerit, irritas et inanes decernere et declarare curetis, non obstante, si eisdem ordinariis vel quibusvis aliis communiter vel divisim a sede apostolica sit indultum, quod interdici, suspendi vel excommunicari non possint per litteras apostolicas non facientes plenam et expressam ac de verbo ad verbum de indulto huiusmodi mentionem. Datum Viterbii viii kal. octobris pontificatus nostri anno tercio.

IV, 248.

---

711. *1423 febr. 11 Romae apud s. Petrum. Martinus V concedit fratribus ordinis Theutonici, quod in ecclesiis cet. suis in schismaticorum terris constitutis vel praesentibus familiaribus Graecis cet. sacra celebrare liceat.*

Martinus episcopus servus servorum dei dilectis filiis magistro generali, commendatoribus et fratribus hospitalis beate Marie Theotonicorum Ierosolimitani ubilibet constitutis presentibus et futuris salutem et apostolicam benedictionem. Religionis zelus et vestre devocionis sinceritas promerentur, ut votis vestris in hiis presertim que animarum vestrarum salutem respiciunt quantum cum deo possumus favorabiliter annuamus. Vestris itaque supplicacionibus inclinati, vobis et vestrum cuilibet, ut in ecclesiis, domibus et capellis, quas habetis in terris Grecorum et scismaticorum aberrancium a catholica ecclesia et veritate, quociens ad illa loca vos declinare vel in eisdem contigerit commorari, liceat vobis in illis missas et alia divina officia alta voce publice apertis ianuis eciam in presencia familiarium vestrorum Grecorum et aliorum habitatorum illarum parcium celebrare aut per vestros sacerdotes ydoneos facere celebrari auctoritate presentium indulgemus, constitucionibus apostolicis et aliis in contrarium facientibus non obstantibus quibuscumque. Nulli ergo omnino hominum liceat hanc paginam nostre concessionis infringere vel ei ausu temerario contraire. Si quis autem hoc attemptare presumpserit, indignationem omnipotentis dei et beatorum Petri et Pauli apostolorum eius se noverit incursurum. Datum Rome apud sanctum Petrum iii idus februarii pontificatus nostri anno sexto.

IV, 249.

---

712. *1423 martii 4 Romae apud s. Petrum. Martinus V concedit ordini Theutonico, ut ad ecclesias et alia beneficia ecclesiastica ipsi subiecta pro libitu aut personas ordinis aut saeculares clericos ordinariis possit praesentare.*

Martinus episcopus servus servorum dei ad futuram rei memoriam. Pro singulorum fidelium presertim religiosarum personarum statu salubriter dirigendo, prout ex debito nobis iniuncti pastoralis tenemur officii, solicite consideracionis intuitum extendentes ad ea, per que status religionis continuum suscipiat incrementum et religiosorum dispendiis occurratur, libenter adhibemus solicitudinis nostre partes, prout rerum et temporum qualitate pensata in domino conspicimus salubriter expedire. Sane peticio pro parte dilectorum filiorum magistri et fratrum hospitalis beate Marie Theotonicorum Ierosolimitani nobis nuper exhibita continebat, quod ipsi in diversis provinciis et locis ius patronatus et presentandi personas ydoneas ad parrochiales ecclesias et alia beneficia ecclesiastica per clericos seculares gubernari consueta habere dinoscuntur et, si ipsi magister et fratres ad ecclesias et beneficia huiusmodi aliquociens personas dicti hospitalis ordinariis locorum aut aliis, ad quos institucio earundem personarum spectat de consuetudine vel de iure presentare possent ac ecclesie et beneficia huiusmodi per personas dicti hospitalis regi et gubernari valerent, et hoc ipsi magister et fratres ab importunis instanciis plerumque petencium essent liberi et quieti pro parte magistri et fratrum predictorum nobis fuit humiliter supplicatum, ut ipsis ad ecclesias et beneficia huiusmodi personas dicti hospitalis aut alias ecclesiasticas ordinariis locorum aut aliis ut premittitur presentandi licenciam concedere et alias eis in premissis oportune providere de benignitate apostolica dignaremur. Nos igitur ipsorum magistri et fratrum in hac parte supplicacionibus inclinati ipsis, ut ad ecclesias et beneficia huiusmodi, que in quibusvis provinciis sive locis nunc obtinent et in futurum dante domino iuste obtinebunt, eciam per quoscumque regi consueta, quocienscumque illas et illa vacare contigerit, personas dicti hospitalis aut alias ecclesiasticas, prout ipsis melius visum fuerit, ordinariis locorum sive aliis, ad quos institucio earundem personarum quomodolibet ut premittitur spectabit, de consuetudine vel de iure presentare et ordinariis ipsis personas hospitalis huiusmodi aut alias ecclesiasticas instituere necnon personis predictis, postquam in illis institute fuerint, illa regere et gubernare libere et licite possint et valeant, licenciam elargimur, non obstantibus apostolicis et provincialibus et synodalibus editis constitucionibus et ordinacionibus, eciamsi de illis presentibus mencio esset facienda specialis et aliis contrariis quibuscumque, decernentes eciam irritum et inane si secus super hiis a quoquam quavis auctoritate scienter vel ignoranter contigerit attemptari. Nulli ergo omnino hominum liceat hanc paginam nostre concessionis et constitucionis infringere vel ei ausu temerario contraire. Si quis autem hoc attemptare presumpserit, indignacionem omnipotentis dei et beatorum Petri et Pauli apostolorum eius se noverit incursurum. Datum Rome apud sanctum Petrum iiii nonas marcii pontificatus nostri anno sexto.

IV, 249 v. et 255 v. Transsumtum sub sigillo curiae apostolicae autoritate Iohannis de Cesarinis, D. D. cam. apost. auditoris gen. dat. Rome 1424 decbr. 22. Exstat in archivo Regimontano. Ioh. 52. Edd. Caorsinus D. 4; Senner G.

---

713. *1423 martii 11 Romae ap. S. Petrum. Martinus V ordini Theutonico privilegii sui de 1419 maii 17 constituit conservatores.*

Martinus episcopus servus servorum dei dilectis filiis abbati monasterii sancti Egidii in Nurenberg et sancti spiritus in Heidelberg Bambergensis et Wormaciensis diocesium ac sancti Gungolffi Maguntinensis ecclesiarum decanis salutem et apostolicam benedictionem. Humilibus et honestis supplicum votis libenter annuimus eaque favoribus prosequimur oportunis. Dudum siquidem dilectis filiis magistro et fratribus hospitalis beate Marie Theotonicorum Ierosolimitani litteras nostras concessimus in hac verba:

„Martinus cet. Laudibus et honore cet. (*supra n. 708*). Datum Florencie xvi kal. iunii pontificatus nostri anno secundo". Cum autem, sicut exhibita nobis nuper pro parte magistri et fratrum predictorum peticio continebat, licet ipsi a prestacione et solucione decimarum et aliorum onerum huiusmodi hactenus ut prefertur liberi et immunes extiterint, timent tamen per aliquos de facto se super illis posse imposterum molestari, pro parte ipsorum magistri et fratrum nobis fuit humiliter supplicatum, ut eis oportune providere misericorditer dignaremur. Nos ita ipsis magistro et fratribus et eorum quieti in hac parte consulere cupientes, huiusmodi eorum supplicacionibus inclinati, discretioni vestre per apostolica scripta mandamus, quatenus vos vel duo aut unus vestrum per vos vel alium seu alios prefatis magistro et fratribus auctoritate nostra in premissis oportune defensionis auxilio assistentes non permittatis ipsos super prestacione et solucione aliquarum decimarum et subsidiorum per quoscumque indebite molestari, invocato ad hoc, si opus fuerit auxilio brachii secularis, contradictores per censuram ecclesiasticam appellacione postposita compescendo; non obstantibus si aliquibus communiter vel divisim a sede predicta indultum insistat, quod interdici, suspendi vel excommunicari non possint per litteras apostolicas non facientes plenam et expressam ac de verbo ad verbum de indulto huiusmodi mencionem. Datum Rome apud sanctum Petrum v idus marcii pontificatus nostri anno sexto.

IV, 244v. Transsumti d. d. Basilee 1441 iunii 14 auctoritate Andreae Hasselmann, archidiaconi in Adlevessen D. Dris, et Rudolfi de Rudisheim, locum tenentis auditoris cam. gen., D. Dris, quod fecit ad instantiam Anselmi Eichhorn, ordinis Theutonici, procuratoris magistri per Alemmanniam, Jac. Tyrner de Sobernheim, notarius a. e. i. a., exstat apographon in charta factum in archivo Regimontano.

---

714. *1423. Martinus V ordinem Theutonicum et bona eius in protectionem suam suscipit et privilegia eius confirmat.*

Citatur in designatione Mitoviensis archivi 1621 Holmiam delati ap. Schirren 139 p. 368. Sapit initium „Solet annuere“.

---

715. *1429 novbr. 6 Romae prope sanctos Apostolos. Martinus V ordini Theutonico confirmat Sigismundi Romanorum regis constitutionem de 1415 iunii 19 supra n. 293 p. 260.*

Martinus episcopus servus servorum dei ad futuram rei memoriam. Paterne consideracionis perscrutantes indagine multiplicia dilectorum filiorum magistri et fratrum hospitalis beate Marie Theotonicorum Ierosolimitani merita et eorum felicem laudibus et honore dignissime religionis successum sinceris contemplantes affectibus illa libenter apostolici roboris firmitate communire satagimus, que pro conservandis ipsorum magistri et fratrum iuribus et intendendis eorum comodis ac profectibus digesto processisse liberamine recensemus. Sane pro parte dictorum magistri et fratrum nobis nuper exhibita peticio continebat, quod olim carissimus in Christo filius noster Sigismundus Romanorum rex illustris eorundem magistri et fratrum statui et indempnitatibus providere gestiens inter alia auctoritate regali statuit et ordinavit, quod ipsi magister et fratres presentes ac futuri omnes et singulos eorum necnon dicti hospitalis proprios homines ab ipsis pro tempore in quibusvis locis reperiantur infra anni spacium repetere possint ac locis presidentes eisdem fugientes et repetitos huiusmodi magistro et fratribus prefatis omni mora et contradictione propulsis restituere debeant ac teneantur, quodque de excessibus et iniuriis, quos subditi et ascripticii necnon servitores familiares et officiales magistri ac fratrum predictorum pro tempore perpetraveriut in locis discuti debeat in quibus ipsi excessus et iniurie fuerint commissi necnon hospitale et fratres huiusmodi aut eorum homines de structuris, municionibus et fossatis, in quibusvis locis et ex quibuscumque graciis, privilegiis, concessionibus pro tempore faciendis nullum debeant in suis iuribus, libertatibus, privilegiis et observanciis dampnum vel preiudicium sustinere, mandans rex ipse omnibus et singulis sibi et imperio subditis ut huiusmodi statuta et ordinaciones manuteneant ac defendant nec contra illa dictos magistrum et fratres quomodolibet molestent sub quinquaginta marcharum auri puri pena pro una camere imperiali et alia medietatibus magistro et fratribus predictis irremissibiliter applicanda, prout in quibusdam auctenticis in vulgari patrie illius ydeomate desuper confectis litteris ipsius regis sigillo munitis quarumque substanciam et effectum nullo addito vel detracto, quod facti substanciam huiusmodi alteret vel immutet per nonnullos in talibus expertos fideliter elici et transferri ac post diligentem eorum in cancellaria apostolica de nostro mandato subsecutam examinacionem de verbo ad verbum presentibus inseri fecimus lacius extensiusque prospicitur contineri. Quare pro parte dictorum magistri et fratrum nobis fuit humiliter supplicatum, ut ipsis statutis et ordinacionibus pro illorum subsistencia firmiori robur apostolice confirmacionis adiicere de benignitate apostolica dignaremur. Nos igitur eisdem supplicacionibus inclinati statuta et ordinaciones huiusmodi ac quecumque inde secuta rata habentes et grata illa auctoritate apostolica ex certa sciencia confirmamus et approbamus presentisque scripti patrocinio communimus. Tenor vero effectus litterarum huiusmodi talis est:

„Nos Sigismundus cet. (*supra n. 293 p. 260*). Datum Constancie anno a nativitate domini millesimo quadringentesimo quinto decimo, die proxima Mercurii ante festum sancti Iohannis Baptiste, regnorum nostrorum Ungarie etc. vicesimo nono et Romanorum quinto".

Nulli ergo omnino hominum liceat hanc paginam nostre confirmacionis, approbacionis et communicionis infringere vel ei ausu temerario contraire. Si quis autem hoc attemptare presumpserit, indignacionem omnipotentis dei et beatorum Petri et Pauli apostolorum eius se noverit incursurum. Datum Rome prope sanctos apostolos viii idus novembris pontificatus nostri anno duodecimo.

IV, 250 et 257. Transsumtum de 1434 iulii 9 cf. n. 718 de 1431 febr. 18.

---

716. *1435 iunii 20. Basileensis synodus concedit ordini Theutonico, ut ad comprobandas causas suas legitima transsumta autographorum producere satis sit ipsi.*

Sacrosancta gen. synodus Basilienssis in spiritu sancto legittime congregata, universalem ecclesiam representans, venerabilibus Revaliensi, Pomezaniensi et Warmiensi episcopis salutem et omnipotentis dei benedictionem. Ad hoc singulis potissime ecclesiasticis personis — quibuscunque. Datum Basilee xii kal. iulii anno a nativitate domini m°cccc°xxx°v°.

Originale cum bulla in archivo Regimontano. Cuius privilegii exemplaria asservabantur quondam etiam in Livonia, quamvis minus accurate citentur tria diversae inscriptionis, quae sequuntur, 1435 iunii 20 Basileae (Napiersky Index 1376) Basileensis synodus Revaliensem episcopum iussit omnia ordinis privilegia transsumere; designatio Mitoviensis archivi ap. Schirren p. 140 n. 402; eodem die eadem eundem, Pomezaniensem, Warmiensem (male Pomeraniae et Wormatiensem) episcopos facere iussit; l. c. 403, eodem die Revaliensem et Pomesaniensem episcopos l. c. 404. — E transsumto Casparis Pomezaniensis episcopi d. d. 1452 in castro Resenburg praesentibus Ludovico de Erlichhausen magistro generali et Udalrico de Ysenhofen magno commendatore memorat Duellius II, 11 in nota. Praefixit enim ille episcopus hanc suam commissionem omnibus in synodo producendis etiam postea factis transsumtis, ut hoc utar bullae Pietati proximum de confirmatione terrae Culmensis 1234 aug. 3, d. d. Risenburg 18 novbr. 1448.

---

717. *1435. Synodus Basileensis hortatur occupatores et quoslibet detentores bonorum ordinis Theutonici.*

Citatur in designatione archivi Mitoviensis 1621 Holmiam delati ap. Schirren 140 n. 406.

---

718. *1431 febr. 18 Romae apud s. Petrum. Eugenius IV ordini Theutonico Martini V constitutionis n. 715 de 1429 novbr. 6 conservatores constituit.*

Eugenius episcopus servus servorum dei venerabili fratri episcopo Leodiensi et dilectis filiis Herbipolensi ac sancti spiritus Heidelbergensis Wormaciensis diocesium ecclesiarum decanis salutem et apostolicam benedictionem.

Dudum felicis recordacionis Martini pape V predecessoris nostri emanarunt littere tenoris subsequentis:

„Martinus etc. Paterne consideracionis etc. (supra n. 715). Datum Rome prope sanctos apostolos viii idus novembris pontificatus nostri anno duodecimo“.

Cupientes igitur, ut premisse littere irrefragibiliter observentur, discrecioni vestre per apostolica scripta mandamus, quatenus vos vel duo aut unus vestrum per vos vel alium seu alios litteras predecessoris huiusmodi ac omnia et singula in eis contenta, ubi et quando expedire videritis quociensve super hoc pro parte magistri et fratrum predictorum requisiti fueritis auctoritate nostra sollempniter publicantes dictisque magistro et fratribus super hiis oportune defensionis auxilio solercius assistentes non permittatis a quoquam, cuiuscumque eciam episcopalis dignitatis, status, gradus, ordinis vel condicionis fuerint, litterarum predecessorum huiusmodi effectum quovis quesito colore aliquatenus intercipi vel impediri aut eosdem magistrum et fratres vel illorum aliquem contra dictarum ipsius predecessoris litterarum continenciam sive formam quomodolibet vexari, impeti vel molestari, contradictores per censuram ecclesiasticam et quevis oportuna iuris remedia appellacione postposita, compescendo, invocato ad hoc, si opus fuerit, auxilio brachii secularis, non obstantibus pie memorie Bonifacii pape VIII eciam predecessoris nostri, quibus cavetur, ne quis extra suam civitatem vel diocesim nisi in certis exceptis casibus et in illis ultra unam dietam a fine sue diocesis ad iudicium evocetur, seu ne iudices a sede apostolica deputati ultra civitatem et diocesim, in quibus deputati fuerint contra quoscumque procedere sive alii vel aliis vices suas committere aut aliquos ultra unam dietam a fine diocesium earundem trahere presumant, dummodo ultra duas dietas aliquis auctoritate presencium non trahatur et aliis apostolicis constitucionibus contrariis quibuscumque seu si aliquibus communiter vel divisim ab eadem sede sit indultum, quod interdici, suspendi vel excommunicari aut extra vel ultra certa loca ad iudicium evocari non possint per litteras apostolicas non facientes plenam et expressam ac de verbo ad verbum de indulto huiusmodi mencionem. Datum Rome apud sanctum Petrum anno incarnacionis dominice millesimo quadringentesimo tricesimo primo xii kalendas marcii pontificatus nostri anno primo.

IV, 257. Exstat in archivo Regimontano exemplar earundem litterarum, quibus n. 712 de 1423 mart. 4 praecedunt. Hae litterae transsumtae sunt d. d. Florentie in ambitu monasterii b. Mariae Novellae 1434 iulii 9, auctoritate Bartholomei de Bonitis, D. D., cubicularii papae auditoris generalis locum tenentis, sub sigillo curiae apostolicae.

---

719. *1431 decbr. 15 Romae apud s. Petrum. Eugenius IV conservatores dat ordini Theutonico constitutionis Martini V n. 712 de 1423 martii 4.*

Eugenius episcopus servus servorum dei dilectis filiis sancti Cornelii et sancti Egidii in Nurenberg monasteriorum abbatibus ac decano ecclesie Sancti spiritus Heidelbergensis Leodiensis, Bambergensis et Wormaciensis diocesis salutem et apostolicam benedictionem. Dudum felicis recordacionis Martinus papa V predecessor noster dilectis filiis magistro et fratribus hospitalis beate Marie Theotonicorum Ierosolimitani suas concessit litteras tenoris subsequentis: „Martinus etc. Pro singulorum etc. (supra n. 712). Datum Rome apud sanctum Petrum quarto nonas marcii pontificatus nostri anno sexto“.

Cum autem, sicut exhibita nobis nuper pro parte dictorum magistri et fratrum peticio continebat, ipsi ordinarii et alii, ad quos institucio spectat huiusmodi, nulla legitima subsistente causa frequenter institucionem predictam facere renuant sive non curent, nos cupientes, quod dicte littere sorciantur effectum, discrecioni vestre per apostolica scripta mandamus, quatenus vos vel duo aut unus vestrum per vos vel alium aut alios si et quociens vobis legitime constiterit, quod ordinarii et alii predicti personas easdem, quas ipsi magister et fratres ad ecclesias et beneficia prefata pro tempore presentaverint in illis absque racionabili causa instituere recusaverint vel post huiusmodi presentacionem per mensem distulerint sive neglexerint et pro parte illorum, quorum intererit, desuper requisiti fueritis vos presentatas personas eciam hospitalis huiusmodi, dummodo alias ydonee sint in ipsis ecclesiis et beneficiis, ad que presentate fuerint eadem auctoritate apostolica instituatis inducentes per vos vel alium seu alios ipsas presentatas personas vel procuratores suos eorum nominibus in corporalem possessionem ecclesiarum et beneficiorum predictorum, ad que presentate, ut premittitur extiterint, iuriumque et pertinenciarum eorundem et defendentes inductas ac facientes ipsis personis prout illas contigerit de ecclesiarum et beneficiorum huiusmodi fructibus, redditibus, proventibus, iuribus et obvencionibus universis integre responderi; non obstantibus omnibus supradictis seu si prefatis ordinariis vel quibusvis aliis communiter vel divisim a dicta sit sede indultum, quod interdici suspendi vel excommunicari non possint per litteras apostolicas non facientes plenam et expressam ac de verbo ad verbum de indulto huiusmodi mencionem, contradictores auctoritate nostra appellacione postposita compescendo. Datum Rome apud sanctum Petrum anno incarnacionis dominice millesimo quadringentesimo tricesimo primo, decimo octavo kalendas ianuarii pontificatus nostri anno primo.

IV, 255 v. Cf. supra ad n. 718 de 1431 febr. 18.

---

720. *1442 iunii 9 Florentie. Eugenius IV repetit confirmationem omnium ordinis Theutonici libertatum, immunitatum etc. communi forma usitatam.*

Eugenius etc. dilectis filiis magistro et fratribus hospitalis beate Marie Theutonicorum Ierosolimitani et preceptoribus ac aliis fratribus hospitalium necnon domorum ab hospitali predicto dependentium eique subiectorum salutem et apostolicam benedictionem. Sedis apostolice graciosa benignitas — communimus. Datum Florencie anno incarnationis dominice millesimo quadringentesimo quadragesimo secundo, quinto idus iunii pontificatus nostri anno duodecimo.

Originale cum bulla in archivo Regimontano, huc tandem Cracovia etc. a. 1865 delatum. Citatur in Inventario archivi Cracoviensis p. 85: „Eugenius papa IV confirmat iura cruciferorum. Datum Florentiae, 5 idus iunii, anno 1442". Transsumtum d. d. Riesenburgi 1445 novbr. 17 auctoritate et sub sigillo Caspari episcopi Pomezaniensis factum exstat ibidem.

---

721. *1447 aprilis 27 Romae. Nicolaus V privilegia Martini V aliorumque confirmat, quibus ordo Theutonicus a decimis et subsidiis eximitur.*

Nicolaus etc. Etsi Romanus pontifex — censeri debere immunes. Datum Rome apud s. Petrum anno incarnationis millesimo quadringentesimo quadragesimo septimo, quinto kal. maii pontificatus nostri anno primo.

Originale cum bulla, quondam ex archivo Cracoviensi Varsoviam, inde Berolinum delatum, inde ab anno 1865 in Regimontano asservatur.

---

722. *1450 novbr. 21 Romae. Nicolaus V repetit privilegia ordinis.*

Nicolaus etc. Cum a nobis etc. Datum Rome a. i. d. millesimo quadringentesimo quinquagesimo undecimo kalendas decembris pontificatus nostri anno quarto.

Originale cum bulla, quondam Cracoviae, inde ab a. 1865 in archivo Regimontano servatum. Citatur in Inventario archivi Cracoviensis p. 86 sub dato secundo kal. decbr.: „Nicolaus papa V omnes indulgentias magistro et ordini cruciferorum libertatesque et exemptiones ab exactionibus secularium, a regibus, principibus et aliis Christi fidelibus tum a Romanis pontificibus rationabiliter datas et concessas, confirmat".

---

723. *1474 iulii 30 Romae apud s. Petrum. Sixtus IV confirmat privilegia et indulgentias ordinis Theutonici.*

Sixtus etc. Cum a nobis etc. Datum Rome apud s. Petrum anno incarnationis dominice millesimo quadringentesimo septuagesimo quarto pontificatus nostri anno tertio.

Citatur in Inventario archivi Cracoviensis p. 93 cum falso dato: „3 idus augusti". Originale cum bulla ex archivo Cracoviensi demum Regimontum delatum.

---

724. *1484 novbr. 3 Romae apud s. Petrum. Innocentius VIII privilegia ordinis Theutonici confirmat.*

Innocentius etc. Cum a nobis etc. Datum Rome apud s. Petrum anno incarnationis dominice millesimo quadringentesimo octuagesimo quarto, tertio nonas novembris pontificatus nostri anno primo.

Originale cum bulla ex Cracoviensi archivo tandem Regimontum delatum. Citatur in Inventario archivi Cracoviensis p. 96 sub falso titulo: „Sixtus papa IV omnia iura et privilegia cruciferorum confirmat. Datum Romae tertio nonas ..... anno 1484".

---

725. *1494 decembris 24 Romae. Alexander VI iura ordinis Theutonici confirmat.*

Alexander etc. Cum a nobis etc. Datum Romae apud s. Petrum anno incarnationis dominice millesimo quadringentesimo nonagesimo quarto, nono kalendas ianuarii pontificatus nostri anno tercio.

Originale cum bulla ex Cracoviensi archivo postremo 1865 in Regimontanum delatum. Citatur in Inventario archivi Cracoviensis p. 97 cum dato non completo „calendas ianuarii". Quomodo hoc privilegium impetratum sit, cf. Voigt Hist. Pruss. IX, 191 sq.

INDEX RERUM.

B.

F.

G.

H.

I. Y. cf. Hi.

K cf. C. Q.

L.

S.

Z.

CORRIGENDA.

p. 14. v. 37. *pro* Hierosolymitanis ... archiepiscopis *scribe* Hierosolymitanus ... archiepiscopo.
p. 19. v. 15. *pro* Quabriquembelide *scribe* Quabriquem, Belide.
p. 27. v. 21. *pro* testus *scribe* testes.
p. 57. v. 11. *pro* suppetunt *scribe* suppetant.
p. 58. v. 20. *pro* patriarchum *scribe* patriarcham.
p. 81. v. 9 *pro* dampnificationi *scribe* dampnificatis.
p. 83 v. 34. *ante* privilegia *adde* infrascripta.
p. 83. v. 35. *post* magistro *adde* et fratribus.
p. 85. v. 15. *pro* praesentibus *scribe* partibus.
p. 85. v. 21. *ante* possessionibus *adde* iuribus et.
p. 119. v. 16. *pro* ordinaretur *scribe* ordinarent.
p. 119. v. 21. *in lacuna adde* provide.
p. 151. v. 23. *pro* rex *scribe* dux.
p. 270. v. 38. *pro* Innocentii *scribe* Innocentius.
p. 273. v. 15. *pro* ad *scribe* ac.
p. 318. v. 13. *pro* sit *scribe* sint.
p. 365. v. 37. *pro* 1246 *scribe* 1247.

Berolini apud Weidmannos (J. Reimer).

Typis Gustavi Schade, Berolinensis.